CONTRACTS

ELEVENTH EDITION

STEVEN L. EMANUEL

Founder & Editor-in-Chief, *Emanuel Law Outlines* and
Emanuel Bar Review
Harvard Law School, J.D. 1976
Member, NY, CT, MD and VA bars

The *Emanuel® Law Outlines* Series

Printed in the United States of America.

1 2 3 4 5 6 7 8 9 0

ISBN 978-1-4548-7014-2

SUSTAINABLE FORESTRY INITIATIVE   Certified Sourcing   www.sfiprogram.org   SFI-00756

About Wolters Kluwer Law & Business

Wolters Kluwer Law & Business is a leading global provider of intelligent information and digital solutions for legal and business professionals in key specialty areas, and respected educational resources for professors and law students. Wolters Kluwer Law & Business connects legal and business professionals as well as those in the education market with timely, specialized authoritative content and information-enabled solutions to support success through productivity, accuracy and mobility.

Serving customers worldwide, Wolters Kluwer Law & Business products include those under the Aspen Publishers, CCH, Kluwer Law International, Loislaw, ftwilliam.com and MediRegs family of products.

CCH products have been a trusted resource since 1913, and are highly regarded resources for legal, securities, antitrust and trade regulation, government contracting, banking, pension, payroll, employment and labor, and healthcare reimbursement and compliance professionals.

Aspen Publishers products provide essential information to attorneys, business professionals and law students. Written by preeminent authorities, the product line offers analytical and practical information in a range of specialty practice areas from securities law and intellectual property to mergers and acquisitions and pension/benefits. Aspen's trusted legal education resources provide professors and students with high-quality, up-to-date and effective resources for successful instruction and study in all areas of the law.

Kluwer Law International products provide the global business community with reliable international legal information in English. Legal practitioners, corporate counsel and business executives around the world rely on Kluwer Law journals, looseleafs, books, and electronic products for comprehensive information in many areas of international legal practice.

Loislaw is a comprehensive online legal research product providing legal content to law firm practitioners of various specializations. Loislaw provides attorneys with the ability to quickly and efficiently find the necessary legal information they need, when and where they need it, by facilitating access to primary law as well as state-specific law, records, forms and treatises.

ftwilliam.com offers employee benefits professionals the highest quality plan documents (retirement, welfare and non-qualified) and government forms (5500/PBGC, 1099 and IRS) software at highly competitive prices.

MediRegs products provide integrated health care compliance content and software solutions for professionals in healthcare, higher education and life sciences, including professionals in accounting, law and consulting.

Wolters Kluwer Law & Business, a division of Wolters Kluwer, is headquartered in New York. Wolters Kluwer is a market-leading global information services company focused on professionals.

Dedication

To my son Michael,
who was conceived after this book was
and who was born before this book was

S.L.E.

Abbreviations Used in Text

CASEBOOKS

Barnett — Randy Barnett, *Contracts, Cases and Doctrine* (5th Ed. 2012 — Wolters Kluwer)

CPB&B — Calamari, Perillo, Bender & Brown, *Cases and Problems on Contracts* (6th Ed. 2011 — West / Thomson)

C&W — Crandall & Whaley, *Cases, Problems and Materials on Contracts* (6th Ed. 2012 — Wolters Kluwer)

D,H&H — Dawson, Harvey and Henderson, *Contracts, Cases and Comments* (7th Ed. 1998 — Foundation)

FSCB&G — Farnsworth, Sanger, Cohen, Brooks & Garvin, *Cases and Materials on Contracts* (8th Ed. 2013 — Foundation)

FYSC&B — Farnsworth, Young, Sanger, Cohen & Brooks, *Cases and Materials on Contracts* (7th Ed. 2008 — Foundation)

F&E — Fuller and Eisenberg, *Basic Contract Law* (6th Ed. 1996 — West Publishing)

KC&P — Knapp, Crystal & Prince, *Problems in Contract Law* (7th Ed. 2012 — Wolters Kluwer)

HORNBOOKS & TREATISES

C&P Hnbk — Calamari and Perillo, *The Law of Contracts* (6th Ed. 2009 — West Publishing)

Corbin — Arthur Corbin, *Corbin on Contracts* (One-Volume Ed., 1952 — West Publishing)

Farnsworth — E. Alan Farnsworth, *Contracts* (4th Ed. 2004 — Aspen)

Murray — John Murray, Jr., *Murray on Contracts* (3rd Ed. 1990 — Michie)

Simpson — Laurence Simpson, *Handbook of the Law of Contracts* (1965)

W&S — White and Summers, *Uniform Commercial Code* (4th Ed. 1995 — West Publishing)

Williston — Samuel Williston, *Williston on Contracts* (3rd. Ed. 1959 — Baker, Voorhis)

RESTATEMENTS AND CODES

Rest. 1st — *First Restatement of Contracts* (1932)

Rest. 2d — *Second Restatement of Contracts* (1981)

UCC — *Uniform Commercial Code* (2011)

OTHER

E — This volume. References of the form "E II(G)(1)(d)" refer to the paragraph with that numbering scheme within the *current* chapter. These references occur mostly in Tables and in Notes to Flow Charts.

SUMMARY OF CONTENTS

TABLE OF CONTENTS

Chapter 1
INTRODUCTION

Chapter 2
OFFER AND ACCEPTANCE

Chapter 3
CONSIDERATION

Chapter 4

PROMISES BINDING
WITHOUT CONSIDERATION

Chapter 5

MISTAKE

Chapter 6

PAROL EVIDENCE AND INTERPRETATION

Chapter 7

CONDITIONS, BREACH,
AND OTHER ASPECTS OF PERFORMANCE

Chapter 8
ANTICIPATORY REPUDIATION
AND OTHER ASPECTS OF BREACH

Chapter 9
STATUTE OF FRAUDS

Chapter 10
REMEDIES

Chapter 11
CONTRACTS INVOLVING
MORE THAN TWO PARTIES

Chapter 12

IMPOSSIBILITY, IMPRACTICABILITY, AND FRUSTRATION

Chapter 13

MISCELLANEOUS DEFENSES: ILLEGALITY, DURESS, MISREPRESENTATION, UNCONSCIONABILITY, AND LACK OF CAPACITY

Chapter 14
WARRANTIES

Chapter 15

DISCHARGE OF CONTRACTS

TABLE OF FLOW CHARTS, CHECKLISTS AND OTHER GRAPHIC AIDS

Preface

Thank you for buying this book.

It's a big book. But don't panic — the book has lots of special features that you can decide to use or not, depending on how much time you have.

I think the special features that are part of this edition will help you a lot. These include:

- **Capsule Summary** — I've boiled the black-letter law of Contracts down to 98 pages. I've designed this Capsule Summary to be read in the last week or so (maybe even the last night) before your exam. If you want to know more about a topic, cross-references in the Capsule point you to the pages in the main text that cover the topic more thoroughly.

- **Casebook Correlation Chart** — This chart, located just after this Preface, correlates each section of the Outline with the pages covering the same topic in the leading Contracts casebooks.

- **Exam Tips** — I've compiled these by reviewing dozens of actual past essay questions and hundreds of multiple-choice questions asked in past law-school and bar exams. The *Exam Tips* are at the end of each chapter.

- **Quiz Yourself** questions — I've adapted these short-answer questions from the *Law in a Flash* flash-card deck on Contracts. (I've re-written most answers, to better mesh with the outline's approach.) You'll find these distributed within each chapter, usually at the end of a roman-numeraled section. Each "pod" of Quiz Yourself questions can easily be located by using the Table of Contents.

- **Flow Charts, Issue Checklists and Tables** — I've distilled many of the legal principles in this book into special visual aids that help you see how the pieces fit together. These include Flow Charts, Issue Checklists, Recap Tables, and the like. You'll find them at various places in most chapters, usually after the full treatment of the material in question. There is a Table of these visual aids on p. xxxiii, after the Table of Contents.

I intend for you to use this book both throughout the semester and for exam preparation. Here are some suggestions about how to use it:[1]

1. During the semester, use the book in preparing each night for the next day's class. To do this, first read your casebook. Then, use the *Casebook Correlation Chart* at the front of the outline to get an idea of what part of the outline to read. Reading the outline will give you a sense of how the particular cases you've just read in your casebook fit into the overall structure of the subject. You may want to use a yellow highlighter to mark key portions of the *Emanuel*.

2. If you make your own outline for the course, use the *Emanuel* to give you a structure, and to supply black letter principles. You may want to rely especially on the *Capsule Summary* for this pur-

---

1. The suggestions below relate only to this book. I don't talk here about taking or reviewing class notes, using hornbooks or other study aids, joining a study group, or anything else. This doesn't mean I don't think these other steps are important — it's just that on this one page I've chosen to focus on how I think you can use the *Emanuel*.

pose. You are hereby authorized to copy small portions of the *Emanuel* into your own outline, provided that your outline will be used only by you or your study group, and provided that you are the owner of the *Emanuel*.

3. When you first start studying for exams, read the *Capsule Summary* to get an overview. Also, review the *Flow Charts, Issue Checklists* and *Tables*. These tasks will probably take you all or part of two days.

4. Either during exam study or earlier in the semester, do some or all of the *Quiz Yourself* short-answer questions. When you do these questions: (1) record your short "answer" in the book after the question, but also: (2) try to write out a "mini essay" on a separate piece of paper. Remember that the only way to get good at writing essays is to write essays.

5. A couple of days before the exam, review the *Exam Tips* that appear at the end of each chapter. You may want to combine this step with step (4), so that you use the *Tips* to help you spot the issues in the short-answer questions. You'll also probably want to follow up from many of the *Tips* to the main outline's discussion of the topic.

6. At some point during the week or so before the exam, do some or all of the full-scale essay exams at the back of the book. Write out a full essay answer under exam-like conditions (e.g., closed-book if your exam will be closed book). If you can, exchange papers with a classmate and critique each other's answer.

7. The night before the exam: (1) do some *Quiz Yourself* questions, just to get your writing juices flowing; and (2) re-read the various *Exam Tips* sections (you should be able to do this in 1-2 hours).

My deepest thanks go to my colleagues at Wolters Kluwer, Barbara Lasoff and Barbara Roth, who have helped greatly to assure the reliability and readability of this and my other books. Warm thanks also to Don Bushell, a recently-admitted member of the California Bar, who helped me decide what developments to highlight in this new edition.

Good luck in your Contracts course. If you'd like any other Wolters Kluwer publication, you can find it at your bookstore or at **www.WKLegaledu.com**. If you'd like to contact me, you can email me at **semanuel@westnet.com**.

Steve Emanuel

Larchmont, NY

August 2015

CASEBOOK CORRELATION CHART

(**Note:** general sections of the outline are omitted from this chart. **NC** = not directly covered by this casebook.)

Emanuel's Contracts Outline *(by chapter and section heading)*	Barnett **Contracts: Cases and Doctrine** (5th Ed. 2012)	Farnsworth, Sanger, Cohen, Brooks & Garvin **Cases and Materials on Contracts** (8th Ed. 2013)	Calamari, Perillo, Bender & Brown **Cases and Problems on Contracts** (6th Ed. 2011)	Crandall & Whaley **Cases, Problems, and Materials on Contracts** (6th Ed. 2012)	Knapp, Crystal & Prince **Problems in Contract Law** (7th Ed. 2012)
CHAPTER 2 **OFFER AND ACCEPTANCE**					
I. **Intent to Contract**	263-78, 293-302, 655-58, 674-92	125-39	1-16	1-17, 27-32	31-43
II. **Offer and Acceptance Generally**	279	139	NC	NC	43-44, 202-04
III. **Validity of Particular Kinds of Offers**	279-91, 330-36	140-56	22-38, 84-94	17-27	44-92, 142-202
IV. **The Acceptance**	316-30, 342-43	156-76	94-103	32-77	54-62
V. **Acceptance Varying from Offer**	309-13, 344-67, 430-60	170-75, 199-234	129-70	42-48, 111-32	159-88
VI. **Duration of the Power of Acceptance**	302-06, 336-42	177-94	103-29	77-103	44-71, 155-58
VII. **When Acceptance Becomes Effective**	313-16	194-99	122, 171-74	103-11	47-48, 125, 247
VIII. **Indefiniteness**	394-402	121, 256, 262-71, 364, 454	38-82	132-45	75, 141, 460-67, 1023
IX. **Misunderstanding**	370-82	465-67, 848-49, 864	290-93	527-31	391-402
CHAPTER 3 **CONSIDERATION**					
II. **The Bargain Element — Gift Promises**	592-612, 667-74	41-48, 59	82-84, 176-85	148-53	106-119
III. **The Bargain Element — "Past Consideration"**	612-30	48-58	232-242	182-97	131-132, 307
IV. **The "Detriment" Element Generally**	646-53	35-38, 243, 366	185-88	149-61	103-104, 109-110
V. **The Pre-Existing Duty Rule**	630-46	65-66, 359-74	188-206	161-69, 198-203	717, 723, 725-727
VI. **Mutuality of Consideration**	NC	51	212-14	180-82	141-142, 260
VII. **Illusory, Alternative and Implied Promises**	402-18	68, 73-90, 261, 632	214-31	169-82	141, 460, 466-467

CASEBOOK CORRELATION CHART (continued)

Emanuel's Contracts Outline *(by chapter and section heading)*	Barnett **Contracts: Cases and Doctrine** (5th Ed. 2012)	Farnsworth, Sanger, Cohen, Brooks & Garvin **Cases and Materials on Contracts** (8th Ed. 2013)	Calamari, Perillo, Bender & Brown **Cases and Problems on Contracts** (6th Ed. 2011)	Crandall & Whaley **Cases, Problems, and Materials on Contracts** (6th Ed. 2012)	Knapp, Crystal & Prince **Problems in Contract Law** (7th Ed. 2012)
CHAPTER 3 **CONSIDERATION (Cont.)**					
VIII. Requirements and Output Contracts	402-07, 418	80-86, 634	219-26	176-82	481-484
IX. Miscellaneous Consideration Problems	NC	72, 74	NC	NC	NC
CHAPTER 4 **PROMISES BINDING WITHOUT CONSIDERATION**					
II. Promises to Pay Past Debts	NC	52-54	236-67	203-09	311-12
III. Promise to Pay for Benefits Received	614-30	54-57	232-36, 238-42	188-97	276-322
IV. Other Contracts Binding Without Consideration	644-46, 658-67	184-45, 315-25	NC	NC	562-63, 733-34
V. Promissory Estoppel	693-793	92-112, 187-92, 237-41, 373	243-66	210-48	209-76, 507-08, 985-88
CHAPTER 5 **MISTAKE**					
III. Mutual Mistake	1053-74	365, 850-53	352-62	531-55	438, 675-78
IV. Unilateral Mistake	1076-84	151-55, 356, 854-65	363-68	556-62	53, 251, 686-88
V. Defenses and Remedies	1074-76	857, 915	NC	NC	677
VI. Reformation as Remedy for Error in Expression	480-83	416-18	369-72	563-70	677
CHAPTER 6 **PAROL EVIDENCE AND INTERPRETATION**					
II. Total and Partial Integration	461-80	410-20	267-78	467-81	410-413, 427
III. The Roles of the Judge and Jury	NC	439	NC	467, 480-81, 498-500	412-13, 704
IV. Situations in Which Parol Evidence Rule Does Not Apply	NC	411-15	278-80	461-93	414-16
V. Interpretation	389-94	421-459	280-93	493-504, 515-518	429-30, 374-405

CASEBOOK CORRELATION CHART (continued)

Emanuel's Contracts Outline *(by chapter and section heading)*	Barnett Contracts: Cases and Doctrine (5th Ed. 2012)	Farnsworth, Sanger, Cohen, Brooks & Garvin **Cases and Materials on Contracts** (8th Ed. 2013)	Calamari, Perillo, Bender & Brown **Cases and Problems on Contracts** (6th Ed. 2011)	Crandall & Whaley **Cases, Problems, and Materials on Contracts** (6th Ed. 2012)	Knapp, Crystal & Prince **Problems in Contract Law** (7th Ed. 2012)
CHAPTER 6 **PAROL EVIDENCE AND INTERPRETATION (Cont.)**					
VI. **Trade Usage, Course of Performance, and Course of Dealing**	385-94	447-48, 553-54	293-301	505-15	392-93, 450-52
VII. **Omitted Terms Supplied by Court**	401, 797-812	467-77, 487	NC	NC	384, 457-532
CHAPTER 7 **CONDITIONS, BREACH, & OTHER ASPECTS OF PERFORMANCE**					
II. **Classification of Conditions**	839-40	725-26	384-85	722-75	788-815
III. **Distinction Between Conditions and Promises**	839-40, 844-51	734	385-406	708-22	796
IV. **Express Conditions**	840-44	726-40	380-84, 498-508	725-42	789-809
V. **Constructive Conditions**	863-75	72, 725-79	406-39	742-50	788, 797, 815, 836
VI. **Substantial Performance**	889-912	756-59, 662-68	411-15	750-79	71, 815-16
VII. **Excuse of Conditions**	851-61	752-53, 808-89,	439-98	779-809	799-800
VIII. **Repudiation and Prospective Inability to Perform as Failures of Constructive Conditions**	885-89	799-823	516-20	814-23	828-46
CHAPTER 8 **ANTICIPATORY REPUDIATION & OTHER ASPECTS OF BREACH**					
I. **Total and Partial Breach**	NC	786-89	424	NC	937-41
II. **Anticipatory Repudiation Generally**	876-84	799-823	508-16	811-13	828-46
III. **Other Aspects of Repudiation**	884	809-18	NC	823-31	835-43

CASEBOOK CORRELATION CHART (continued)

Emanuel's Contracts Outline *(by chapter and section heading)*	Barnett **Contracts: Cases and Doctrine** (5th Ed. 2012)	Farnsworth, Sanger, Cohen, Brooks & Garvin **Cases and Materials on Contracts** (8th Ed. 2013)	Calamari, Perillo, Bender & Brown **Cases and Problems on Contracts** (6th Ed. 2011)	Crandall & Whaley **Cases, Problems, and Materials on Contracts** (6th Ed. 2012)	Knapp, Crystal & Prince **Problems in Contract Law** (7th Ed. 2012)
CHAPTER 9 **STATUTE OF FRAUDS**					
II. Suretyship Agreements	674	292-99	748-55	410-14	NC
III. The Marriage Provision	NC	271	755-57	414	NC
IV. The Land Contract Provision	485-88	290-95, 315-26	757-61	415	336-46
V. One-Year Provision	488	273-88	709-21	416-22	328-33
VI. Contract for the Sale of Goods	489-93	310-27, 420	732-48	423-27	359-71
VII. Satisfaction of Statute by Memorandum	494-500, 507-12	303-39	722-27	427-33	328-36
VIII. Effect of Non-Compliance	NC	317-19	NC	NC	NC
IX. Oral Rescission and Modification	NC	420	727-32	422-23	735-744
X. Restitution, Reliance, and Estoppel	488, 493	315-22	NC	433-57	354-356, 367
CHAPTER 10 **REMEDIES**					
II. Equitable Remedies	173-218	579-80, 617-42	635-52	384-405	1013-36
IV. Expectation Damages	60-69, 110-29, 912-31	16-18, 652-56, 677-78, 810-16	554-58, 596-604	253-71, 282-93	847-969
V. Reliance Damages	69-75, 123-29, 562-64	15-20, 99-100, 106-12, 239-40	564-68	272-81	971-88
VI. Restitution	225-40, 564-65	18-21, 640, 657	623-35	368-79	989-1011
VII. Substantial Performance as a Basis for Suit on the Contract	NC	756-59	NC	NC	NC
VIII. Suits in Quasi-Contract	241-46	112-19	630-35	357-68, 380-83	276-78, 286
IX. Foreseeability	91-110	687-701, 878, 956	558-61	294-307	874-890
X. Avoidable Damages	129-151	650-51, 682-83, 742-49	561-64, 581-95	307-21	905-09, 979-80
XI. Nominal and Punitive Damages	170, 246-60	11-12, 24-27	604-06	340-46	847, 937-41, 985-88

CASEBOOK CORRELATION CHART (continued)

Emanuel's Contracts Outline *(by chapter and section heading)*	Barnett **Contracts: Cases and Doctrine** (5th Ed. 2012)	Farnsworth, Sanger, Cohen, Brooks & Garvin **Cases and Materials on Contracts** (8th Ed. 2013)	Calamari, Perillo, Bender & Brown **Cases and Problems on Contracts** (6th Ed. 2011)	Crandall & Whaley **Cases, Problems, and Materials on Contracts** (6th Ed. 2012)	Knapp, Crystal & Prince **Problems in Contract Law** (7th Ed. 2012)
CHAPTER 10 **REMEDIES (Cont.)**					
XII. Liquidated Damages	157-72	709-24	609-623	322-40	1036-53
XIII. Damages in Sales Contracts	75-90, 152-57	647-56, 674-83	569-581	347-55	943-50
CHAPTER 11 **CONTRACTS INVOLVING MORE THAN TWO PARTIES**					
II. Assignment	515-26	962-1001	680-83, 694-708	874-901	767-75
III. Delegation of Duties	526-32	959-969	683-93	869-74, 901-08	767-69, 775-86
IV. Third Party Beneficiaries	544-56	925-60	653-79	833-68	745-66
CHAPTER 12 **IMPOSSIBILITY, IMPRACTICABILITY, AND FRUSTRATION**					
II. Impossibility of Performance	1085-93	870-902	521-46	680-83	667-717
III. Impracticability	1093-1101	862-902	521-46	683-701	667-717
IV. Frustration of Purpose	1101-11	899-915	546-53	701-06	667-717
V. Restitution and Reliance Where the Parties Have Been Discharged	1105-06	915-23	NC	NC	715
CHAPTER 13 **MISCELLANEOUS DEFENSES: ILLEGALITY, DURESS, MISREPRESENTATION, UNCONSCIONABILITY AND LACK OF CAPACITY**					
I. Illegality	579-88	574-88	770-92	620-40	414-415, 561
II. Duress	983-95	356-81	206-12, 315-24	593-620	547-53
III. Misrepresentation	965-82	395-402	333-52	570-93	571-99
IV. Unconscionability and Adhesion Contracts	418-30, 1008-49	489-550	372-79	649-79	395-97, 404-05, 599-637
V. Capacity	941-63	340-56	302-14	640-49	533-53

CASEBOOK CORRELATION CHART (continued)

Emanuel's Contracts Outline *(by chapter and section heading)*	Barnett **Contracts: Cases and Doctrine** (5th Ed. 2012)	Farnsworth, Sanger, Cohen, Brooks & Garvin **Cases and Materials on Contracts** (8th Ed. 2013)	Calamari, Perillo, Bender & Brown **Cases and Problems on Contracts** (6th Ed. 2011)	Crandall & Whaley **Cases, Problems, and Materials on Contracts** (6th Ed. 2012)	Knapp, Crystal & Prince **Problems in Contract Law** (7th Ed. 2012)
CHAPTER 14 **WARRANTIES**					
I. **Warranties Generally**	813-14	470	NC	553-55	515-17
II. **Express Warranties**	817-31	486-87	348-49	553-54	517-26
III. **Implied Warranty of Merchantability**	814-17	470-71	NC	554-55	517-32
IV. **Warranty of Fitness for a Particular Purpose**	814-17	470, 474	490-92	555	517-26
V. **Warranties of Title and Against Infringement**	NC	470	NC	553-54	NC
VI. **Privity**	NC	NC	NC	NC	523, 529-30
VII. **Disclaimers of Warranty**	831-37	478-486	NC	555	524-25
VIII. **Modifying Contract Remedies**	158-59	NC	NC	331-40	NC
CHAPTER 15 **DISCHARGE OF CONTRACTS**					
I. **Rescission**	NC	NC	NC	NC	NC
II. **Executory Accords, and "Accord and Satisfaction"**	NC	NC	762-66	203-09	740
III. **Substituted Agreement**	NC	NC	762	203-09	NC
IV. **Novation**	NC	293-94	766-69	838-39	NC
V. **Account Stated**	NC	NC	NC	NC	NC
VI. **Release and Covenant Not to Sue**	NC	NC	NC	542-49	NC

CAPSULE SUMMARY

This Capsule Summary is intended for review at the end of the semester. Reading it is not a substitute for mastering the material in the main outline. Numbers in brackets refer to the pages in the main outline where the topic is discussed. The order of topics is occasionally somewhat different from that in the main outline.

CHAPTER 1

INTRODUCTION

I. MEANING OF "CONTRACT"

A. Definition: A "contract" is an agreement that the law will enforce.

    1. Written v. oral contracts: Although the word "contract" often refers to a written document, a writing is not always necessary to create a contract. An agreement may be binding on both parties even though it is oral. Some contracts, however, must be in writing under the Statute of Frauds.

II. SOURCES OF CONTRACT LAW

A. The UCC: Contract law is essentially common law, i.e. judge-made, not statutory. However, in every state but Louisiana, sales of *goods* are governed by a statute, *Article 2* of the *Uniform Commercial Code*.

    1. State enactments: A national drafting body, the National Conference of Commissioners of Uniform State Laws (NCCUSL) proposes revisions to various UCC Articles from time to time. Each state legislature then makes its own decision about whether and when to adopt the proposed revision.

        a. 2003 Revision: The NCCUSL drafted a *revision* of Article 2 in *2003*. That revision made some significant changes, especially in the area of electronic commerce. However, *no state adopted it*. Therefore, the NCCUSL withdrew the 2003 revision in 2011. Consequently, the version of Article 2 in force virtually everywhere in the U.S. as of this writing (early 2015) is the *1990 text*.

        b. Our text: Therefore, when this book refers to an Article 2 provision, the reference is to the *1990 version* of Article 2, which is essentially unchanged since the original promulgation of Article 2 in 1957.

    2. Common law: If the UCC is silent on a particular question, the common law of the state will control. See UCC § 1-103.

CHAPTER 2

OFFER AND ACCEPTANCE

I. INTENT TO CONTRACT

A. Objective theory of contracts: Contract law follows the *objective theory of contracts*. That is, a party's intent is deemed to be what a ***reasonable person*** in the position of the other party would think that the first party's objective manifestation of intent meant. For instance, in deciding whether *A* intended to make an offer to *B*, the issue is whether *A*'s conduct reasonably indicated to one in *B*'s position that *A* was making an offer. [6-7]

> **Example:** *A* says to *B*, "I'll sell you my house for $1,000." If one in *B*'s position would reasonably have believed that *A* was serious, *A* will be held to have made an enforceable offer, even if subjectively *A* was only joking.

B. Legal enforceability: The parties' intention regarding whether a contract is to be ***legally enforceable*** will normally be effective. Thus if both parties intend and desire that their "agreement" not be legally enforceable, it will not be. Conversely, if both desire that it be legally enforceable, it will be even if the parties mistakenly believe that it is not. [7-8]

> **Example:** Both parties would like to be bound by their oral understanding, but mistakenly believe that an oral contract cannot be enforceable. This arrangement will be enforceable, assuming that it does not fall within the Statute of Frauds.

1. Presumptions: Where the evidence is ambiguous about whether the parties intended to be bound, the court will follow these rules: (1) In a ***"business"*** context, the court will presume that the parties intended their agreement to be legally enforceable; (2) but in a ***social*** or ***domestic*** situation, the presumption will be that legal relations were ***not*** intended.

> **Example:** Husband promises to pay a monthly allowance to Wife, with whom he is living amicably. In the absence of evidence otherwise, this agreement will be presumed not to be intended as legally binding, since it arises in a domestic situation.

C. Intent to put in writing later: If two parties agree (either orally or in a brief writing) on all points, but decide that they will subsequently put their entire agreement into a more formal written document later, the preliminary agreement may or may not be binding. In general, the parties' ***intention*** controls. (*Example*: If the parties intend to be bound right away based on their oral agreement, they will be bound even though they expressly provide for a later formal written document.) [8]

1. Where no intent manifested: Where the evidence of intent is ambiguous, the court will generally treat a contract as existing as soon as the mutual assent is reached, even if no formal document is ever drawn up later. But for very large deals (e.g., billion dollar acquisitions), the court will probably find no intent to be bound until the formal document is signed.

II. OFFER AND ACCEPTANCE GENERALLY

A. Definitions: [9]

1. "Offer" defined: An ***offer*** is "the manifestation of willingness to enter into a bargain," which justifies another person in understanding that his assent can conclude the bargain. In other words, an offer is something that creates a power of acceptance.

2. "Acceptance" defined: An ***acceptance*** of an offer is "a manifestation of assent to the terms thereof made by the offeree in a manner invited or required by the offer."

> **Example:** *A* says to *B*, "I'll sell you my house for $100,000, if you give me a check right now for $10,000 and promise to pay the rest within 30 days." This is an offer. If *B* says, "Here is my $10,000 check, and I'll have the balance to you next week," this is an acceptance. After the acceptance occurs, the parties have an enforceable contract (assuming that there is no requirement of a writing, as there probably would be in this situation).

B. Unilateral vs. bilateral contracts: An offer may propose either a bilateral or a unilateral contract. [9-10]

    1. Bilateral contract: A *bilateral* contract is a contract in which *both* sides make *promises*.

        Example: *A* says to *B*, "I promise to pay you $1,000 on April 15 if you promise now that you will walk across the Brooklyn Bridge on April 1." This is an offer for a bilateral contract, since *A* is proposing to exchange his promise for *B*'s promise.

    2. Unilateral contract: A *unilateral* contract is one which involves an exchange of the *offeror's promise* for the *offeree's act*. That is, in a unilateral contract *the offeree does not make a promise*, but instead simply acts.

        Example: *A* says to *B*, "If you walk across the Brooklyn Bridge, I promise to pay you $1,000 as soon as you finish." *A* has proposed to exchange his promise for *B*'s *act* of walking across the bridge. Therefore, *A* has proposed a unilateral contract.

III. VALIDITY OF PARTICULAR KINDS OF OFFERS

A. Offer made in jest: An offer which the offeree knows or should know is made *in jest* is not a valid offer. Thus even if it is "accepted," no contract is created. [20]

B. Offer must indicate that other party can seal the bargain: For an expression to be an "offer," the other person must be justified in thinking that the would-be offeror has intended to give the other person the ability to *"seal the deal" immediately, without further assent from the offeror.* [11]

    1. More details to work out: Therefore, if a statement by one party, call her *A*, to *B* indicates that *A* believes that *further details must be worked out* between *A* and *B* before a deal is completed — details that *A* must approve — *A*'s statement is almost certainly *not* an offer, but merely an invitation to continue discussions or negotiations.

    2. "Let's discuss": Thus if *A* and *B* have had discussions about a deal, and *A* then makes a statement or proposal accompanied by words like *"Let's discuss,"* those words probably put *B* on notice that *A* has not just made an offer, but has merely invited continuing negotiations. In that event, there is nothing for *B* to "accept," and *B* cannot unilaterally bind *A* to a contract by *B*'s response. [11]

C. Preliminary negotiations: If a party who desires to contract *solicits bids*, this solicitation is not an offer, and cannot be accepted. Instead, it merely serves as a basis for preliminary negotiations. [26]

    Example: *A* says, "I would like to sell my house if I can get at least $100,000." This is almost certainly a solicitation of bids, rather than an offer, so *B* cannot "accept" by saying, "Here's my check for $100,000."

D. Advertisements: Most *advertisements* appearing in newspapers, store windows, etc., are *not* offers to sell. This is because they do not contain sufficient words of commitment to sell. (*Example*: A circular stating, "Men's jackets, $26 each," would not be an offer to sell jackets at that price, because it is too vague regarding quantity, duration, etc.) [13]

    1. Specific terms: But if the advertisement contains specific words of commitment, especially a promise to sell a *particular number* of units, then it may be an offer. (*Example*: "100 men's jackets at $26 apiece, first come first served starting Saturday," is so specific that it probably is an offer.)

2. **Words of commitment:** Look for words of *commitment* — these suggest an offer. (*Example*: "Send three box tops plus $1.95 for your free cotton T-shirt," is an offer even though it is also an advertisement; this is because the advertiser is committing himself to take certain action in response to the consumer's action.)

E. **Auctions:** When an item is put up for *auction*, this is usually *not* an offer, but is rather a solicitation of offers (bids) from the audience. So unless the sale is expressly said to be "without reserve," the auctioneer may withdraw the goods from the sale even after the start of bidding. See UCC § 2-328(3). [14]

IV. THE ACCEPTANCE

A. **Who may accept:** An offer may be accepted *only by a person in whom the offeror intended to create a power of acceptance*. [18]

> **Example:** O says to *A*, "I offer to sell you my house for $100,000." *B* overhears, and says, "I accept." Assuming that O's offer was reasonably viewed as being limited to *A*, *B* cannot accept even though the consideration he is willing to give is what O said he wanted.

B. **Must be in response to an offer:** An acceptance must be *in response to an offer,* not in response to something other than an offer such as a *solicitation* of offers.

> **Example:** An uncle mails a letter to his adult nephew that says: "I am thinking of selling my pickup truck. I would consider taking $7,000 for it." The nephew writes back, "I will buy the truck for $7,000 cash." Because the uncle's letter is a solicitation of offers, not an offer, the nephew's response "I will buy" is *not an acceptance* (but is instead itself an offer). [19]

C. **Offeree must know of offer:** An acceptance is usually valid only if the offeree *knows of the offer* at the time of his alleged acceptance.

1. **Rewards:** Thus if a *reward* is offered for a particular act, a person who does the act without knowing about the reward cannot claim it.

D. **Method of acceptance:** The offeror is the *"master of his offer."* That is, the offeror may prescribe the *method* by which the offer may be accepted (e.g., by telegram, by letter, by mailing a check, etc.). [20-26]

1. **Can suspend mailbox rule:** The offeror's right to prescribe the method of acceptance means that the offeror can *suspend* the usual *"mailbox"* rule, under which an acceptance is effective upon dispatch. (See *infra*, C-12). The offeror can do this by saying, "No acceptance shall be effective until received by offeror" — such a provision will be *enforced*.

2. **Where method not specified:** If the offer does not specify the mode of acceptance, the acceptance may be given in *any reasonable* method. [20]

3. **Acceptance of unilateral contract:** An offer for a unilateral contract is accepted by *full performance* of the requested act. [20]

> **Example:** *A* says to *B*, "I'll pay you $1,000 if you cross the Brooklyn Bridge." This can only be accepted by *A*'s act of completely crossing the bridge. (However, the offer will be rendered temporarily irrevocable once *B* starts to perform, as discussed below.)

4. **Offer invites either promise or performance:** If the offer does not make clear whether acceptance is to occur through a promise or performance, the offeree may accept by *either* a promise or performance. [21]

a. **Shipment of goods:** For instance, if a buyer of goods places a "purchase order" that does not state how acceptance is to occur, the seller may accept by either promising to ship the goods, or by in fact shipping the goods. UCC § 2-206(1)(b).

b. Accommodation shipment: If the seller is "accommodating" the buyer by shipping what the seller knows and says are *non-conforming goods*, this does *not* act as an acceptance. In this *"accommodation shipment"* situation, the seller is making a counter-offer, which the buyer can then either accept or reject. If the buyer accepts, there is a contract for the quantity and type of goods actually sent by the seller, not for those originally ordered by the buyer. If the buyer rejects, he can send back the goods. In any event, seller will not be found to be in breach. UCC § 2-206(1)(b). [22]

> **Example:** Buyer sends Seller an order for "100 red gizmos, at $5.75 each, for immediate shipment." Seller sends 100 blue gizmos, with a note reading "I'm all out of red gizmos. I've taken the liberty of shipping you 100 blue ones instead, at the same price, hoping that they'll do for you."
>
> Seller's shipment of the blue gizmos is an accommodation shipment under § 2-206(1)(b). Therefore, Seller's shipment does not constitute an acceptance. Instead, it is a counter-offer of blue gizmos. Buyer can accept the counter-offer (by keeping them, in which case he owes the $5.75 for each with no discount for the non-conformity) or reject the counter-offer (by sending them back). If Buyer rejects the counter-offer by sending the blue gizmos back, Seller has not breached (because there was never any accepted order), so Seller does not owe Buyer any compensation.

5. Acceptance by silence: Generally, an offer cannot be accepted by *silence*. But there are a few *exceptions*: [23-25]

a. Reason to understand: Silence can constitute acceptance if the offeror has given the offeree *reason to understand* that silence will constitute acceptance, and the offeree subjectively intends to be bound.

b. Benefit of services: An offeree who silently receives the benefit of *services* (but not goods) will be held to have accepted a contract for them if he: (1) had a reasonable opportunity to reject them; and (2) knew or should have known that the provider of the services *expected to be compensated*.

c. Prior conduct: The *prior course of dealing* may make it reasonable for the offeree's silence to be construed as consent. (*Example*: Each time in the past, Seller responds to purchase orders from Buyer either by shipping, or by saying, "We don't have the item." If Seller now remains silent in the face of an order by Buyer for a particular item, Seller's silence will constitute an acceptance of the order.)

d. Acceptance by dominion: Where the offeree receives *goods*, and *keeps them*, this exercise of "dominion" is likely to be held to be an acceptance.

e. "Implied-in-fact" contracts: The above scenarios in which the parties do not expressly exchange an offer and acceptance, but in which they *indicate by their silence (or non-verbal conduct)* their understanding that a contract is being formed, are sometimes said to involve *"implied-in-fact"* contracts.

i. Distinction: Be sure to distinguish the true implied-in-fact contract situation (in which each party, by his conduct, knowingly leads the other to believe that they have an agreement) from a situation in which at least one party *fails to take any action* that would justify the other in believing that a contract is intended.

ii. Intra-familial transactions: For example, when one party performs small-scale services for another and the two are *close relatives*, if neither party expressly brings home to the other that payment is expected, the court is likely to conclude that the services were a *gift* rather than a commercial transaction.

6. **Notice of acceptance of unilateral contract:** Where an offer looks to a unilateral contract, most courts now hold that the offeree must give *notice* of his acceptance after he has done the requested act. If he does not, the contract that was formed by the act is discharged. [23]

> **Example:** *A* says to *B*, "I'll pay you $1,000 if you cross the Brooklyn Bridge by April 1." *B* crosses the bridge on time. As soon as *B* crosses, a contract is formed. But if *B* does not notify *A* within a reasonable time thereafter that he has done so, *A*'s obligation will be discharged.

V. ACCEPTANCE VARYING FROM OFFER

A. **Common law "mirror image" rule:** Under the common law, the offeree's response operates as an acceptance only if it is the *precise mirror image* of the offer. If the response conflicts at all with the terms of the offer, or adds new terms, the purported acceptance is in fact a rejection and counter-offer, not an acceptance. [28]

> **Example:** *A* writes to *B*, "I'll sell you my house for $100,000, closing to take place April." *B* writes back, "That's fine; let's close April, however." At common law, *B*'s response is not an acceptance because it diverges slightly from the offer, so there is no contract.

B. **UCC view:** The UCC *rejects the "mirror image" rule*, and will often lead to a contract being formed even though the acceptance diverges from the offer. Wherever possible, the UCC tries to find a contract, so as to keep the parties from weaseling out (as they often try to do when the market changes). This entire "battle of the forms" is dealt with in UCC § 2-207, probably the most important UCC provision for the Contracts student. [28-29]

1. **General:** At the most general level, § 2-207(1) provides that any *"expression of acceptance"* or *"written confirmation"* will *act as an acceptance* even though it states terms that are "additional to or different from" those contained in the offer.

> **Example:** Buyer sends a "purchase order" containing a warranty. Seller responds with an "acknowledgment," containing a disclaimer of warranty. There will be a contract under the UCC, even though there would not have been one at common law.

2. **Acceptance expressly conditional on assent to changes:** An "expression of acceptance" does *not* form a contact if it is *"expressly made conditional on assent to...additional or different terms."* § 2-207(1). So if the purported "acceptance" contains additional or different terms from the offer, and also states something like, "This acceptance of your offer is effective only if you agree to all of the terms listed on the reverse side of this acceptance form," *there is no contract* formed by the exchange of documents. [30-31]

a. **Limited:** Courts are reluctant to find that this section applies. Only if the second party's form makes it clear that that party is *unwilling to proceed with the transaction* unless the first party agrees to the second party's changes, will the clause be applied so as to prevent a contract from forming.

3. **"Additional" term in acceptance:** Where the offeree's response contains an *"additional"* term (i.e., a clause taking a certain position on an issue with which the offer does not deal at all), the consequences depend on whether both parties are merchants. [34]

a. **At least one party not merchant:** If at least one party is *not a merchant*, the additional term does not prevent the offeree's response from giving rise to a contract, but the additional term becomes part of the contract only if the offeror *explicitly* assents to it.

> **Example:** Consumer sends a purchase order to Seller, which does not mention how disputes are to be resolved. Seller sends an acknowledgment form back to Consumer, which correctly

recites the basic terms of the deal (price, quantity, etc.), and then says, "All disputes are to be arbitrated."

Even though the acknowledgment (the "acceptance") differed from the purchase order by introducing the arbitration term, the acknowledgment formed a contract. However, since at least one party (Consumer) was not a merchant, this additional term will only become part of the contract if Consumer explicitly assents to that term (e.g., by initialing the arbitration clause on the acknowledgment form).

b. **Both merchants:** But if *both parties* to the transaction are *"merchants,"* then the additional term *automatically becomes part of the contract*, as a general rule. (*Example:* On facts of prior example, if Buyer was a merchant, the arbitration clause would become part of the contract.) However, there are two important exceptions to this "additional term becomes part of the contract" rule:

    i. **Materiality:** The addition will not become part of the contract if it is one which *"materially alters"* the contract. For instance, a *disclaimer of warranty* will always be found to materially alter the contract, so if the seller includes such a disclaimer in his acknowledgment form after receiving the buyer's purchase order, the disclaimer will not become part of the contract.

    ii. **Objection:** If the offeror *objects* to having the additional term become part of the contract, it will not so become.

4. **Acceptance silent:** If an issue is handled in the first document (the offer), but *not in the second* (the acceptance), the acceptance will be treated as covering *all* terms of the offer, not just those on which the writings agree. [33]

    Example: Buyer's purchase order says that disputes will be arbitrated; Seller's acknowledgment is silent on the issue of arbitration. The Seller's form will be found to be an acceptance, and disputes will be arbitrated.

5. **Conflicting terms in documents:** If an issue is covered one way in the offering document and another (*conflicting*) way in the acceptance, most courts apply the *"knock out" rule*. That is, the conflicting clauses "knock each other out" of the contract, so that *neither enters the contract*. Instead, a UCC "gap-filler" provision is used if one is relevant; otherwise, the common law controls. [34-35]

    Example: Buyer's purchase order states that disputes will be litigated in New York state court. Seller's acknowledgment form states that disputes will be arbitrated. Most courts would apply the "knock out" rule, whereby neither the "New York courts" nor "arbitration" clauses would take effect. Instead, the common law — allowing an ordinary civil suit to be brought in any state that has jurisdiction — would apply.

6. **Response diverges too much to be acceptance:** If a purported acceptance *diverges greatly* from the terms of the offer, it will not serve as an acceptance at all, so *no contract is formed*. [36]

7. **Contract by parties' conduct:** If the divergence referred to in the prior paragraph occurs (so that the exchange of documents does not create a contract), the parties' *conduct* later on can still cause a contract to occur. Section 207(3) provides that "conduct by both parties which recognizes the existence of a contract is sufficient to establish a contract for sale although the writings of the parties do not otherwise establish a contract." [36-37]

    Example: Buyer's purchase order is for 100 widgets at $5 each. Seller's acknowledgment form is for 200 widgets at $7 each. Buyer does not say anything in response to the acknowledgment form. Seller ships the 200 widgets, and Buyer keeps them. Even though the exchange of documents did not create a contract, the parties' conduct gave rise to a contract by performance. [36]

    a. **Terms:** Where a contract by conduct is formed, the terms "consist of those terms in which the writings of the parties agree, together with any supplementary terms incorporated under any other provisions of this Act." § 2-207(3). For instance, the price term would be a "reasonable price at the time for delivery," as imposed by § 2-305's price "gap filler."

8. **Confirmation of oral contract:** If the parties initially reach an *oral agreement*, a document later sent by one of them memorializing the agreement is called a *"confirmation."* [37-44]

    a. **Additional terms in confirmation:** If the confirmation contains a term that is *additional* to the oral agreement, that additional term becomes part of the contract unless either: (1) the additional term *materially alters* the oral agreement; or (2) the party receiving the confirmation *objects* to the additional terms.

    b. **"Different" term in confirmation:** If a clause contained in the confirmation is *"different"* from a term on the same issue reached in the oral agreement, the new clause probably does *not* become part of the agreement.

    c. **Request that confirmation be signed:** Suppose that, after an oral agreement, one party sends a confirmation, and *requests that the other party sign and return that confirmation.* In this kind of scenario, there will be *no consequence* if the recipient doesn't sign or return the confirmation — the deal is complete when the confirmation is received. [38]

9. **"Terms to follow" contracts (a/k/a "rolling" contracts):** Goods are sometimes sold under what is sometimes called a *"terms to follow"* or *"rolling" contract.* In such a contract, the buyer, usually a consumer, orders and pays for the goods *without seeing most of the contract terms.* The detailed terms are then contained *on or in the box* containing the goods. The buyer is told that if she does not agree with the detailed terms, she has a certain time within which to return the goods for a full credit. Courts are split on how to analyze such rolling contracts. [38-42]

    a. **The "not formed until receipt" approach:** Some courts say that § 2-207 doesn't apply, and that *no contract is formed until the buyer has received the goods and has kept them* for beyond the prescribed return period. This approach tends to yield a contract that includes *all of the seller's terms,* on the theory that the action of the buyer in keeping the goods rather than returning them should be interpreted as an *acceptance by performance,* an acceptance that includes the buyer's assent to all of the seller's proposed terms.

    Example: P orders a personal computer from D (the manufacturer) by phone. No forms are exchanged at the time. The box arrives, containing the computer and a document of "Standard Terms," which include an arbitration clause. The Standard Terms say that P can return the computer for a full refund anytime within 30 days of receipt; thereafter, the computer is no longer returnable, and P will be deemed to have accepted the Standard Terms. P doesn't return, then sues, and D contends that the arbitration clause became part of the contract.

    Some courts would hold for D, on the theory that (1) § 2-207 doesn't apply because it's not a "battle of the forms" (only D has used a form); and (2) no contract was formed until P kept the computer for 30 days, at which point P was deemed to have accepted the Standard Terms, including the arbitration clause. Therefore, the arbitration clause would be held to have become part of the contract. Cf. *Hill v. Gateway 2000,* so holding. [38]

    b. **Contract formed under § 2-207 at time of order:** But other courts hold that § 2-207 *does* apply to the rolling-contract scenario, and that *a contract is therefore formed at the time of the order.* Under this approach, the buyer is usually considered to be the offeror, the seller is an offeree who is proposing additional or different terms, and at least where the buyer is a consumer those terms *never become part of the contract* unless the buyer expressly agrees to them (which she usually doesn't). This is probably the better approach.

Example: Same facts as above Example. Probably the better view is that § 2-207 applies (even though the only form ever used is D's Standard Terms document, which acts as a confirmation of the parties' earlier oral deal). P is an offeror, and D is an offeree who is proposing the arbitration clause as an additional term. Because P is a consumer, the arbitration clause doesn't become part of the contract under § 2-207(2) unless P agrees to it, which P didn't do. Therefore, there is no arbitration clause in the contract. Cf. *Klocek v. Gateway, Inc.*, so holding. [41]

VI. DURATION OF THE POWER OF ACCEPTANCE

A. General strategy: For an acceptance to be valid, it must become effective while the power of acceptance is still in effect. So where there is doubt about whether the acceptance is timely: (1) pinpoint the moment at which the "acceptance" became effective; and (2) ask whether the power of acceptance was still in effect at that moment. If the answer to part (2) is "yes," the acceptance was timely. [46]

B. Ways of terminating power of acceptance: The offeree's power of acceptance may be *terminated* in five main ways: (1) *rejection* by the offeree; (2) *counter-offer* by the offeree; (3) *lapse* of time; (4) *revocation* by the offeror; and (5) *death or incapacity* of the offeror or offeree. [47-52]

1. Rejection by offeree: Normally, if the offeree *rejects* the offer, this will terminate her power of acceptance. [47]

    a. Exceptions: But rejection will not terminate the power of acceptance if either: (1) the offeror indicates that the offer *still stands* despite the rejections; or (2) the offeree states that although she is not now accepting, she wishes to *consider the offer further* later.

2. Counter-offer: If the offeree makes a *counter-offer*, her power to accept the original offer is terminated just as if she had flatly rejected the offer. [47-48]

    Example: On July 1, A offers to sell B 100 widgets at $5 each, the offer to be left open indefinitely. On July 2, B responds, "I'll buy 50 at $4." A declines. On July 3, the market price of widgets skyrockets. On July 4, B tells A, "I'll accept your July offer." No contract is formed, because B's power of acceptance was terminated as soon as B made her counter-offer on July.

    a. Contrary statement: But as with a rejection, a counter-offer does not terminate the power of acceptance if either offeror or offeree *indicates otherwise*. (*Example*: On facts of above example, if B said on July 2, "I'll buy 50 from you right now for $4; otherwise, I'd like to keep considering your original offer," A's offer would have remained in force.)

    b. Distinguish counter-offer from exploration: Be careful to distinguish a counter-offer from a response by the offeree that is too *equivocal* or *uncertain* to be a counter-offer, and that instead merely *explores the possibility of some other arrangement* while keeping the original offer alive. Statements like *"Would you consider...?"* or "I might be interested instead in ..." will typically have this non-counter-offer effect (so that the original offer remains in place).

3. Lapse of time: The offeror, as "master of his offer," can set a *time limit* for acceptance. At the end of this time limit, the offeree's power of acceptance automatically terminates. [48-49]

a. End of reasonable time: If the offeror does not set a time limit for acceptance, the power of acceptance terminates at the end of a ***reasonable*** time period.

    i. Face-to-face conversation: If the parties are bargaining face-to-face or over the phone, the power of acceptance continues ***only during the conversation***, unless there is evidence of a contrary intent.

4. Revocation: The offeror is free to ***revoke*** his offer ***at any time*** before it is accepted (except in the case of option contracts). [49-50]

    a. Effective upon receipt: A revocation by the offeror does not become effective until it is ***received by the offeree***.

    Example: On June 15, *A* mails an offer to B. On July 1, *A* mails a revocation to B. On July 3, *B* has a letter of acceptance hand delivered to A. On July 5, *A*'s revocation is received by B. *B*'s acceptance is valid, because *A*'s revocation did not take effect until its receipt by *B*, which was later than the July 3 date on which *B*'s acceptance took effect.

    i. Lost revocation: If the letter or telegram revoking the offer is ***lost*** through misdelivery, the revocation ***never becomes effective***.

    b. Indirect communication of revocation: If the offeror behaves in a way ***inconsistent with an intention to enter the contract*** she has proposed and the offeree learns (even ***indirectly***) that the offeror has taken such an action, there is a revocation, even though the offeror never intended to communicate directly with the offeree. [50]

    Example: *A* offers to sell Blackacre to *B* at a stated price, and gives *B* a week in which to respond. Within the week, *A* contracts to sell the land to *C*, and *B* learns of this through a tenant of Blackacre. *B* nonetheless sends a formal acceptance, which is received by *A* within the week. There is no contract between *A* and *B*, because *A*'s offer to *B* was revoked at the time that *B* learned that *A* had made the contract with *C*. [50]

    i. Negotiations or offer not enough: But the mere fact that the offeror has entered into ***negotiations*** with a third person, or even that she has made an ***offer*** to a third person, is generally ***not*** sufficient to constitute a revocation when the original offeree learns of it.

5. Death or incapacity of offeror or offeree: If either the offeror or offeree ***dies*** or loses the ***legal capacity*** to enter into the contract, the power to accept is terminated. This is so even if the offeree does not learn of the offeror's death or incapacity until after he has dispatched the "acceptance." [50]

    Example: On July 1, *A* sends an offer. On July 2, *A* dies. On July 3, *B* telegraphs her "acceptance." On July 4, *B* learns of *A*'s death. There is no contract.

C. Irrevocable offers: The ordinary offer is ***revocable*** at the will of the offeror. (This is true even if it states something like, "This offer will remain open for two weeks.") However, there are some exceptions to this general rule of revocability: [52-55]

1. Standard option contract: First, the offeror may grant the offeree an ***"option"*** to enter into the contract. The offer itself is then referred to as an "option contract." [52]

    a. Common law requires consideration: The traditional common-law view is that an option contract can be formed only if the offeree gives the offeror ***consideration*** for the offer.

    b. Modern (Restatement) approach: But the modern approach, as shown in the Restatement, is that a ***signed*** option contract that ***recites*** the payment of consideration will be irrevocable, even if the consideration was never paid.

2. **"Firm offers" under the UCC:** The UCC is even more liberal in some cases: it allows formation of an irrevocable offer even if no recital of the payment of consideration is made. By § 2-205, an offer to buy or sell goods is irrevocable if it:

    [1] is by a *merchant* (i.e., one who "deals in goods of the kind or otherwise by his occupation holds himself out as having knowledge or skill peculiar to the practices or goods involved in the transaction");

    [2] is in a *signed writing*; and

    [3] gives *explicit assurance* that the offer will be *held open*.

Such an offer is irrevocable even though it is without consideration or even a recital of consideration. [53]

> **Example:** Jeweler gives Consumer a signed document stating, "For the next 120 days, I agree to buy your two-carat diamond antique engagement ring for $4,000." Even though Consumer has not paid consideration for the irrevocability, and even though there is no recital of consideration in the signed offer, Jeweler's offer is in fact irrevocable for 120 days, because it is by a merchant (Jeweler deals in goods of the kind involved in the transaction), is in a signed writing, and explicitly assures that the offer will be held open.

   a. **Three month limit:** No offer can be made irrevocable for any longer than *three months*, unless consideration is given. § 2-205. If the offer lists a period longer than three months, the offer *becomes revocable* after three months. [54]

> **Example:** On July 1, Dealer, a car dealer, sends a signed email to Consumer offering to sell Consumer a Model X car with certain specs for $20,000; the email says that the offer "will remain open until the end of the year." On Nov. 1, Dealer phones Consumer to say, "The offer is withdrawn." Consumer immediately purports to accept, citing the "open until the end of the year" language.
>
> No matter what the offer said, it was not irrevocable under § 2-205 past September 30 (three months). Therefore, Dealer's revocation was effective, and Consumer's acceptance was not effective. (But if Dealer had purported to revoke on *August 1* and Consumer purported to accept on August 2, then the revocation would have been ineffective and the acceptance would have been effective.)

      i. **Can still be a valid offer:** Even after an offer becomes revocable because the three months have passed, that doesn't mean it can't still be a valid, outstanding offer. Thus in the above Example, on Oct. 1, Consumer could still have accepted, since nothing had occurred by then to actually revoke the offer.

   b. **Forms supplied by offeree:** If the firm offer is on a form drafted by the *offeree*, it is irrevocable only if the particular "firm offer" clause is *separately signed* by the offeror.

   c. **Effect if not by a merchant:** Be on the lookout for a purported firm offer that relates to a sales contract, but that is *made by a non-merchant* (i.e., a consumer) — such an offer is *not firm*, and will therefore be *revocable*. [54]

> **Example:** Consumer sends a letter to Furniture Co. offering to sell it some used office shelving presently on the walls of Consumer's house. The letter says that the offer "will remain open for the next 60 days." After 40 days, Consumer sends another letter, saying "I sold the shelving to someone else."
>
> This revocation letter is effective, because Consumer is not a "merchant," and only "merchants" can make firm offers. (For purposes of firm offers, virtually any person who is making an offer during the course of her business is a "merchant," but Consumer does

not meet this definition.) Consequently, the offer was revocable even though it recited that it wasn't. [54]

3. **Part performance or detrimental reliance:** The offeree's part performance or detrimental reliance (e.g., preparations to perform) may transform an otherwise-revocable offer into a temporarily irrevocable one. [55-59]

    a. **Offer for unilateral contract:** Where the offer is for a *unilateral* contract, the *beginning of performance* by the offeree makes the offer *temporarily irrevocable*. As long as the offeree continues diligently to perform, the offer remains irrevocable until he has finished. [55]

    Example: *A* says to *B*, "I'll pay you $1,000 if you cross the Brooklyn Bridge anytime in the next three hours." Before *B* starts to cross the bridge, *A* may revoke. But once *B* starts to cross the bridge, *A*'s offer becomes temporarily irrevocable. If *B* crosses the bridge within three hours, a contract is formed and *A* owes *B* the money. If *B* starts to cross, then changes his mind, neither party will be bound.

      i. **Preparations:** This doctrine applies only to the beginning of *actual performance*, not the making of *preparations* to perform. (*Example*: On facts of above example, if *B* went out and bought expensive walking shoes in preparation for crossing, this act would not cause his offer to be irrevocable.)

    b. **Preparations by offeree:** If the offer is for a *bilateral* contract (i.e., a contract which is to be accepted by a return promise), the offeree's making of *preparations* will cause the offer to be *temporarily irrevocable* if justice requires. "An offer which the offeror should reasonably expect to induce action or forbearance of substantial character on the part of the offeree before acceptance and which does induce such action or forbearance is binding as an option contract *to the extent necessary to avoid injustice*." Rest.2d, § 87(2). [59]

      i. **Offers by sub-contractors:** Most importantly, an offer by a *sub-contractor* to a general contractor will often become temporarily irrevocable under this rule.

      Example: *A*, sub-contractor, offers to supply steel to *B* on a job where *B* is bidding to become the general contractor. *B* calculates his bid in reliance on the figure quoted by A. *B* gets the job. Before *B* can accept, *A* tries to revoke.

      If *B* can show that he bid a lower price because of *A*'s sub-bid, the court will probably hold *A* to the contract, or at least award *B* damages equal to the difference between *A*'s bid and the next-lowest available bid. But observe that *B*, the offeree, is *not* bound, so *B* could accept somebody else's sub-bid.

VII. WHEN ACCEPTANCE BECOMES EFFECTIVE

A. Mailbox rule: In most courts, the acceptance is *effective upon proper dispatch*. This is called the *"mailbox"* rule. [60-62]

    Example: On July 1, *A* offers to sell 100 widgets to *B* at $5 apiece. On July 2, *B* deposits a properly-addressed acceptance in the mail. On July 10, *A* finally receives the letter, several days later than would ordinarily be expected from first-class mail. A contract was formed on July 2. Any attempt at revocation by *A* on, say, July 5 would have been ineffective.

1. **Offer provides otherwise:** The "mailbox" rule does not apply if the offer provides otherwise (e.g., "This offer will be accepted when and if your letter of acceptance is personally received by me").

2. **Lost in transmission:** If the acceptance is *lost in transmission* or *delayed*, the applicability of the mailbox rule depends on whether the communication was properly addressed.

a. **Properly addressed:** If the acceptance is ***properly addressed***, it is effective at the time of dispatch even if it is lost and ***never received*** by the offeror at all. (But a court might "discharge" the offeror in this circumstance, for instance if he had sold the goods to someone else.)

b. **Not properly addressed:** If the acceptance is ***not*** properly addressed, or not properly dispatched (e.g., sent by an unreasonably slow means), it will be effective upon dispatch only if it is ***received within the time*** in which a properly dispatched acceptance would normally ***have arrived***. If it comes later than this "normal" time, it will not be effective until receipt.

Example: On July 1, *A* sends an offer letter to *B*, and says that *B* should "give me your answer in writing by July 10." On July 8, *B* mails an acceptance letter, but uses a slightly wrong address for *A*. Assume that a properly addressed letter would have been delivered on July 10. *B*'s letter arrives on July 11. Meanwhile, *A* revokes by phone on the evening of July 10.

B's letter is not effective upon dispatch, because it did not arrive within the same time in which a properly addressed letter would have arrived. (But if the misaddressed letter had arrived on July 10, at the same time as a properly-addressed letter, it would have been retroactively deemed effective upon dispatch, and a revocation by *A* on July 9 would have been too late.)

B. **Both acceptance and rejection sent by offeree:** If the offeree sends ***both*** an acceptance and rejection, the rule depends on which is dispatched first. [62-63]

1. **Rejection sent first:** If the ***rejection*** is sent first, then the acceptance will be effective if (and only if) the offeror receives it before he receives the rejection.

2. **Acceptance dispatched first:** If the acceptance is sent before the rejection, the acceptance is effective upon dispatch, and the subsequently-dispatched "rejection" (really a "revocation of acceptance") does not undo the acceptance, whether that rejection is received by the offeror before or after he receives the acceptance.

C. **Option contracts:** The acceptance of an ***option contract*** is effective upon ***receipt*** by the offeror, ***not upon dispatch***. [63]

VIII. INDEFINITENESS

A. **Generally:** No contract will be found if the terms of the parties' "agreement" are unduly ***indefinite***. (*Example*: *A* and *B* agree that *B* will buy widgets from *A* from time to time. The parties do not decide anything about quantity, price, delivery, etc. A court would probably find that even though *A* and *B* may have meant to conclude a binding agreement, the absence of terms makes their agreement void for indefiniteness.) [67]

1. **Court supplies missing term:** But if the court believes that the parties intended to contract, and the court believes that it can supply a *"reasonable"* value for the missing term, it will generally do so. [67]

a. **UCC:** The UCC expressly allows the court to fill in terms for price, place for delivery, time for shipment, time for payment, etc., as long as the parties have intended to make a contract. See § 2-204(3). [68-71]

b. **Non-UCC:** In non-UCC cases, most modern courts follow this "supply the missing term on a reasonable basis" approach, as long as the parties have shown an intent to create a binding contract. [71]

C
A
P
S
U
L
E

S
U
M
M
A
R
Y

   c. Too indefinite: But there may be situations where even though the parties intended to create a binding contract, they have fleshed out the terms of their deal so little that the court simply cannot meaningfully supply all of the missing terms. In that case, the court will find the agreement void for indefiniteness. (But this is rare.) [71]

  2. Implied obligation of good faith: In both UCC and non-UCC contracts, an important type of term the court will supply is an obligation of *good faith* and *fair dealing*. See, e.g., UCC § 1-304, which says that "every contract or duty within this Act imposes an obligation of good faith in its performance or enforcement." (§ 1-201(19) then defines good faith as "*honesty* in fact and the observance of *reasonable commercial standards of fair dealing*.") [69-70]

   a. Consistency with other party's expectations: An important aspect of this duty of good faith is that a party is required to behave in a way that is consistent with the other party's *reasonable expectations* about how the contract will work.

   Example: Insurer writes a homeowner's policy on Owner's home. The policy says that in the event Owner suffers a loss, Owner must report the loss "in detail" and in writing to Insurer within 30 days. 28 days after Owner's home is burglarized, he submits a one-sentence description of the loss to Insurer. Insurer says merely, "Your description is not specific enough," but refuses to tell Owner what type of detail must be added. (Assume that Insurer's evasiveness is an intentional attempt to prevent Owner from submitting a claim meeting the requirements of the policy.) The deadline passes without Owner's rewriting the description, and Insurer refuses to pay to the claim.

     A court would probably find that Insurer's intentionally evasive behavior violated its implied duty of good faith, because the behavior was an attempt to deprive Owner of his reasonable expectation that his loss would be covered by the policy.

  3. Agreement to agree: The court will generally supply a missing term if the parties intentionally leave that term to be *agreed upon later*, and they then don't agree. See, e.g., UCC § 2-305(1)(b), which allows the court to supply a reasonable *price* term if "the price is left to be agreed by the parties and they fail to agree…." [71]

  4. Part performance: Even if an agreement is too indefinite for enforcement at the time it is made, the *subsequent performance* of the parties may cure this indefiniteness. [73]

   Example: *A* contracts to make a suit for *B*, without specifying the type or color of material to be used. This is probably unenforceable for indefiniteness when made. But if *A* begins to make the suit with gray cotton cloth, and *B* knows this and raises no objection, the indefiniteness will be cured by this part performance.

IX. MISUNDERSTANDING

A. General rule: If the parties have a *misunderstanding* about what they are agreeing to, this may prevent them from having the required "meeting of the minds," and thus prevent a contract from existing. No contract will be formed if: (1) the parties each have a different subjective belief about a term of the contract; (2) that term is a material one; and (3) neither party knows or has reason to know of the misunderstanding. [73-75]

  Example: *A* offers to ship goods to *B* on the steamer "Peerless." *B* accepts. Unknown to both, there are in fact two steamships by this name. *A* intends to use the later one; *B* subjectively intends to get shipment on the earlier one. Because both are in subjective disagreement about the meaning of a material term, and neither has reason to know of the disagreement, there is no contract. [*Raffles v. Wichelhaus*]

1. **Fault:** Conversely, if one party *knows* or *should know* that he has a different understanding as to the meaning of an ambiguous term than the other, a contract will be formed on the term as understood by the other (innocent) party.

    Example: Same facts as above example. This time, *A* knows or should know that there are two Peerlesses, and knows or should know that *B* means the earlier one. *B* doesn't and shouldn't know know that there are two. *A* contract is formed for shipment on the earlier (the one understood by *B*, the "innocent" party).

B. **Offeree doesn't understand offer:** Where the offeree fails to *understand* or *read* the offer, a similar "fault" system applies: [74-75]

1. **Offeree is negligent:** If the offeree's failure to read or understand the offer is due to his own negligence, he is bound by the terms of the contract as stated in the offer.

2. **Misrepresentation:** But if the offeree's misunderstanding is due to the offeror's *misrepresentation* of the terms of the offer, and the offeror knows this, there is a contract on the terms as understood by the offeree.

CHAPTER 3

CONSIDERATION

I. INTRODUCTION

A. **Definition of consideration:** As a general rule, a contract will not be enforceable unless it is supported by "consideration." (The few exceptions are treated in "Promises binding without consideration" below.) A promise is supported by consideration if: [86]

1. **Detriment:** The promisee *gives up something of value*, or *circumscribes his liberty* in some way (i.e., he suffers a *"legal detriment"*); *and*

2. **Exchange:** The promise is given as part of a *"bargain"*; that is, the promisor makes his promise *in exchange* for the promisee's giving of value or circumscription of liberty.

B. **More about "legal detriment":** The *"legal detriment"* (the "something of value or circumscription of liberty") that the promisee must exchange for the promisor's promise, can consist of *any of the following* kinds of things:

❑ an *act* by the promisee.

   Example: Promisor promises to pay $100 if Promisee actually walks across the Brooklyn Bridge. Promisee does the walk. The act of walking is consideration for Promisor's promise to pay $100.

❑ a *forbearance* by the promisee.

   Example: Promisor promises to pay $100 if Promisee refrains from smoking for the next month. Promisee in fact refrains. Promisee's forbearance from smoking is consideration for Promisor's promise to pay $100.

❑ a *return promise* by the promisee.

   Example: Promisor promises to pay $100 if Promisee promises now to walk across the Brooklyn Bridge next Saturday. Promisee makes this promise. Promisee's making of the promise to walk is consideration for Promisor's promise to pay $100.

❑ an act, forbearance or return promise *by a third person* (someone other than the promisee).

Example: Promisor promises Promisee that if Promisee's sister Sue paints Promisor's house, Promisor will pay Promisee $100. Even though Sue is not the promisee, her act of painting will be consideration for Promisor's promise to pay Promisee the $100.

❏ a promise or act by the promisee, **delivered to a third person**, rather than to the promisor.

> **Example:** Promisor promises $100 to Merchant if Merchant delivers $100 in groceries to Promisor's son. Merchant delivers. The fact that the bargained-for performance is rendered to one other than Promisor does *not* prevent Merchant's delivery to the son from being consideration for Promisor's promise to pay $100.

See generally Rest. 2d, § 71. [87]

C. Uses of doctrine: The requirement of consideration renders unenforceable two main types of transactions: [86]

[1] Promises to **make gifts** (which are promises that do not satisfy the "**bargain**" element); and

[2] Business situations in which one party has **not really promised to do something** or given anything up, even though he may appear to have done so (scenarios that do not satisfy the "**detriment**" element). The main situations falling into this category are cases where the parties to an existing contract **modify** it to the sole benefit of one of the parties (the "pre-existing duty" scenario).

II. THE BARGAIN ELEMENT

A. Promises to make gifts: A **promise to make a gift** is generally **unenforceable**, because it lacks the "bargain" element of consideration. [87-92]

> **Example:** *A* says to *B*, his daughter, "When you turn 21 in four years, I will give you a car worth $10,000." The four years pass, *A* refuses to perform, and *B* sues for breach of contract. *B* will lose, because there was no consideration for *A*'s promise. In particular, *A*'s promise was not "bargained for."

1. Existence of condition: Even if the person promising to make a gift requires the promisee to meet certain **conditions** in order to receive the gift, there will still be no consideration (and the promise will thus be unenforceable) if the meeting of the conditions is not really "bargained for" by the promisor. [87-92]

> **Example:** *A* promises his widowed sister-in-law *B* a place to live "if you will come down and see me." In response, *B* travels to see *A*, thereby incurring expenses. Even though *B* has suffered a "detriment" (the expenses), the "bargain" element is lacking — *A* was not promising *B* a place to live because he wanted to see her, but was merely imposing a necessary pre-condition for her to get the gift. Therefore, his promise is unenforceable for lack of consideration. [*Kirksey v. Kirksey*]

a. Occurrence of condition is of benefit to promisor: But if the promisor imposes a condition, and the occurrence of this condition is of **benefit** to him, then the bargain element probably **will** be present.

> **Example:** *A* promises his nephew *B* $5,000 if *B* will refrain from smoking, drinking and gambling until age 21. *B* so abstains. Here, *A*'s promise was "bargained for" (and thus supported by consideration), because *A* was attempting to obtain something he regarded as desirable. [*Hamer v. Sidway*]

   i.   **Altruistic pleasure not sufficient:** But the fact that one who promises to make a gift expects to derive *altruistic pleasure*, or love and affection, from making the gift is *not* sufficient to constitute a "bargain."

  b.   **Mixture of bargain and gift:** Where a transaction is a *mixture of a bargain and a gift,* the consideration requirement is nonetheless *satisfied*. For instance, if one party promises to sell the other an item at a price that both parties recognize is a *large discount* to its market value, that promise is supported by consideration (in the form of the buyer's promise to pay, or actual payment of, the discounted price). [89]

       Example: *A* is a close friend of *B*. *B* has long admired *A*'s painting "Irises" by Picasso, which as both parties know has a market value of $200,000. *A* promises to sell "Irises" to *B* for $20,000, and *B* promises to buy it for that price. The contract is enforceable because each promise is supported by consideration, notwithstanding the presence of a significant "gift" element to the exchange. [89]

 2.   **Executed gifts:** It is only the *promise* to make a gift, not the actual making of a gift, that is unenforceable for lack of consideration. Once the promisor makes the gift, he cannot rescind it for lack of consideration. [92]

B. **Sham and nominal consideration:** Even though a deal looks on its face as if it is supported by consideration, the court may conclude that the purported consideration is *sham* or *nominal*, and is thus not consideration at all. [90]

 1.   **Nominal amount:** Thus where the "consideration" that has been paid is so small as to be *nominal*, the court may conclude as a factual matter that there is no real "bargain" present at all. If so, the promise will not be enforced, due to lack of consideration.

       Example: *A* says to *B*, his son, "In consideration for $1 paid and received, I promise to give you a car worth $10,000 four years from now." Even if the $1 is actually paid, the court will probably conclude that *A* did not "bargain" for the $1, and that there is thus no consideration; *A*'s promise will therefore be unenforceable.

  a.   **"Adequacy" irrelevant:** But if the consideration is big enough to suggest that there was a bargain, the fact that it is "inadequate" is irrelevant. (See *infra*.)

 2.   **Payment not in fact made:** If a non-trivial payment is recited, but the payment was *not in fact made*, most courts will take this as evidence that no bargain was present. Always, the question is whether there was in fact a bargain, and payment or non-payment is merely non-dispositive evidence of whether there was a bargain.

C. **Promisee unaware:** Generally, the promisee must be *aware* of the promise, for the act performed by him to be consideration for the promise. This means that if a *reward* is promised for a certain act, and the act is performed without the actor's being aware of the reward, he cannot recover. [91]

D. **Promise exchanged for previous detriment:** If the promise is made in return for detriment *previously* suffered by the promisee, there is no bargain, and thus no consideration.

 1.   **"Past consideration is no consideration":** As the idea is often put, *"past consideration is no consideration."* This statement is essentially correct.

 2.   **Illustrations:** Thus promises to *pay a pre-existing debt,* and promises to *pay for services already received,* usually lack the "bargain" element, so there is no consideration to support them. (But these two types of promises may be binding even without consideration, as discussed below.) [92-93]

III. THE "DETRIMENT" ELEMENT

A. Generally: For consideration to be present, the promisee must suffer a ***"detriment."*** That is, she must do something she does not have to do, or refrain from doing something that she has a right to do. (*Example*: After P has already retired from working for D, D promises P a lifetime pension, for which P need not do anything. At common law, this promise would probably be unenforceable, because P has not suffered any detriment in return for it.) [94]

    1. Non-economic detriment: Even a ***non-economic*** detriment will suffice. (*Example*: If *A* promises *B* $5,000 in return for *B*'s abstaining from alcohol and tobacco, *B*'s refraining will be a "detriment" that will serve as consideration for *A*'s promise. Thus *A*'s promise will be enforceable.) [94]

    2. Adequacy not considered: The court will ***not*** inquire into the ***"adequacy"*** of the consideration. As long as the promisee suffers ***some detriment, no matter how small,*** the court will not find consideration lacking merely because what the promisee gave up was of much less value than what he received. [95-97]

        Example: D is desperate for funds during WWII, and promises to pay P $2,000 after the war in return for $25 now. Held, there is consideration for D's promise, so P may collect. Mere "inadequacy of consideration" is no defense. [*Batsakis v. Demotsis*].

        a. Minor effort or other thing of non-monetary value: The principle that courts will not acquire into the adequacy of the consideration means that consideration can consist of the promisee's doing something that requires ***only a tiny bit of effort and has no financial value.*** For instance, the promisee's effort in ***clipping a coupon*** or ***filling out a contest entry form*** will typically be ***enough*** to constitute consideration for the other side's promise.

        Example: D, an auto manufacturer, runs an online contest that says, "Fill out this form, and if your entry is drawn, you'll get a brand new car." P spends 30 seconds filling out the form online, and is lucky enough to have his entry selected. D then refuses to deliver the car, raising a lack-of-consideration defense. P would almost certainly win — the court would hold that P's act of spending 30 seconds filling out the form constituted consideration sufficient to support D's promise of a car to the winner. [96]

        b. Lack of bargain: But remember that an ***extreme disparity*** in value between what the promisee gives up and receives may suggest that there is not in fact a "bargain," in which case there will be no consideration even though the detriment requirement is satisfied.

B. Pre-existing duty rule: If a party does or promises to do what he is ***already legally obligated*** to do, or if he forbears or promises to forbear from doing something which he is ***not legally entitled to do***, he has not incurred a "detriment" for purposes of consideration. This is the ***pre-existing duty*** rule. [98]

    1. Modification: This general rule means that if parties to an existing contract agree to ***modify*** the contract for the sole benefit for one of them, the modification will usually be unenforceable at common law, for lack of consideration. Be on the lookout for this scenario especially in ***construction*** cases. [98-100]

        Example: Contractor agrees to pave Owner's driveway for $5,000, the job to be completed by May 1. Halfway through the project, Contractor tells Owner, "I've gotten very busy. Increase the price to $6,000, or I'll have to finish 6 weeks late." Owner says, "OK, I agree to pay you $6,000, now just finish on time." Contractor finishes on time, but Owner refuses to pay more than $5,000. Contractor sues for the extra $1,000.

        Owner's promise to pay the extra $1,000 (a modification of the contract) will ***not be enforceable*** — the contract was modified to the sole benefit of Contractor, who was merely promising to do what he was already legally obligated to do. Therefore, he did not furnish consideration to support Owner's promise of the extra $1,000. [98]

    a. **Restatement:** The Second Restatement, and most modern courts, follow this general rule.

2. **Exception for unanticipated circumstances:** But modern courts (and the Restatement) make an *exception* to the pre-existing duty rule where the modification is "*fair and equitable* in view of circumstances *not anticipated* by the parties when the contract was made." [99]

    Example: Contractor makes a six-year contract, for $50,000 per year, to annually repaint a bridge owned by City, using specified paint to be furnished by Contractor. Before the fourth year, Contractor tells City (truthfully) that the cost of the particular paint specified in the contract has doubled in the last year, due to new safety legislation. City agrees to adjust the contract price to $55,000, which would restore Contractor to the same level of profit as both parties anticipated when the contract was originally signed. When the time comes for payment, City refuses to pay the extra $5,000, citing the pre-existing duty rule.

    Even though, in return for the promise of extra money, Contractor merely promised to do what he was always required to do (paint the bridge and supply the specified paint), the modification is "fair and equitable in view of circumstances not anticipated by the parties when the contract was made." So City's promise to modify will not be invalid for lack of consideration, and Contractor can require City to pay the extra $5,000.

3. **Extra duties:** Even under the traditional pre-existing duty rule, if the party who promises to do what he is already bound to do assumes the *slightest additional duties* (or even *different* duties), his undertaking of these new duties *does* constitute the required "detriment." [100]

    Example: Contractor agrees to build a house for Owner for $30,000. Midway through the job, Contractor realizes he's losing money, and threatens to walk off the job if Owner does not increase the price to $40,000. In return for this price increase, Contractor is willing to change the kind of fittings in the windows, as requested by Owner; this change will actually save Contractor money.

    Most courts would hold that the change of specifications, even though actually less burdensome to Contractor, constituted consideration for Owner's promise to pay more for the house.

    a. **Where change is mere pretense:** The "additional" or "different" duties promised by the person already legally bound must not, however, be merely a *pretense* for avoiding the pre-existing duty rule. [100]

4. **Rewards and bonuses:** Outside of the modification context, a promise to pay a *reward* or *bonus* will be unenforceable under the pre-existing duty rule, if the promisee is *already under a legal obligation* to perform the act being rewarded. [101]

    Example: Officer, employed by City, has the duty to investigate crimes and arrest the guilty. He learns of a reward offered by City for "information leading to the arrest and conviction of..." the person responsible for a particular robbery. Officer arrests a suspect, who is convicted. Officer won't be entitled to the reward, because there is no consideration for his act of making the arrest — he was only doing what his job already required him to do.

5. **UCC:** For contracts for the sale of goods, the UCC *abolishes the pre-existing duty rule*. Section § 2-209(1) provides that "an agreement modifying a contract...needs no consideration to be binding." But there must be good faith, and any no-oral-modification clause must be complied with. [100]

6. **Agreement to accept part payment of debt:** Some courts apply the pre-existing duty rule to render unenforceable a creditor's promise *not to require payment* by his debtor *of the full debt*. These courts also treat as unenforceable a creditor's promise to allow the debtor *extra time* to pay. These courts reason that the debtor already owes the money, and is therefore not promising to do something he was not already required to do. This is known as the *rule of Foakes v. Beer*. [101-104]

   a. **Modern trend:** But the modern trend is to *abolish or limit* the rule of *Foakes v. Beer*. For instance, the UCC, in § 2-209(1), says that "an agreement modifying a contract within this article needs no consideration to be binding...." This seems to overrule *Foakes v. Beer*, and to make a seller's promise to take partial payment in return for goods enforceable.

   b. **Disputed debt:** Also, the rule of *Foakes v. Beer* applies only to debts where the parties are in agreement about amount and liability, called *"liquidated"* debts. If the debtor in good faith and reasonably *disputes* his liability, or the *amount* of that liability, then a settlement by which the creditor agrees to take less than *he* thinks is due is *enforceable* (even in courts following the traditional *Foakes v. Beer* rule).

   c. **Cashing of check tendered as settlement:** Debtors sometimes send a check for less that the amount due, and mark it *"in full settlement."* Even if the creditor writes *"In protest"* on the check, but cashes it, the UCC holds that the cashing normally constitutes an acceptance by the creditor of the proposed settlement, and the creditor cannot sue for the balance. § 3-311. [102]

      i. **Requirements:** But § 3-311 allows the debtor to be discharged by the creditor's cashing of the check only if *three conditions* are met:

         ❑ the check or accompanying written communication contained a *"conspicuous statement* to the effect that the instrument was tendered as full satisfaction of the claim," and

         ❑ the claim was either *"unliquidated"* or was "subjected to a *bona fide dispute*," and

         ❑ the debtor acted in *good faith.*

      ii. **Right to return payment:** There's an important exception that can hurt the debtor, though: the creditor has the right, within 90 days after cashing the check, to reverse the transaction by *paying the debtor back* the amount of the check; the creditor is thereby restored to the rights it had before cashing the check. § 3-311(c)(2).

7. **Other settlements (e.g., tort suits):** Settlements of other kinds of suits (e.g., tort suits) may similarly raise consideration problems. If the plaintiff is surrendering a claim that is in fact invalid, has he given consideration to support the defendant's promise to pay a settlement? To facilitate settlements, courts today generally take a relaxed view of what's needed to constitute consideration by the plaintiff in return for the settlement promise:

   a. **Valid claim surrendered:** If a plaintiff promises to waive a *valid claim*, all courts are in agreement that this promise is a "detriment" to the plaintiff, and constitutes consideration for the defendant's promise to pay a settlement.

   b. **Surrender of invalid claim:** If, on the other hand, the claim that the plaintiff promises to forbear from suing on is *invalid* (or of uncertain validity), things are trickier. But even here, the modern view (represented by the Second Restatement) is that the forbearing plaintiff gives consideration if *either:*

      ❑ the plaintiff's forborne claim is one *whose validity is uncertain*, *or*

      ❑ the plaintiff *subjectively believes* that the forborne claim has possible merit (even if it doesn't in fact have any possible merit). [104]

i. **Execution of release:** Furthermore, even if the would-be plaintiff who is forbearing from asserting her claim *does not subjectively believe* that the claim is valid, if the plaintiff *executes a written instrument settling the claim,* and the prospective defendant *bargained* for that instrument, the instrument itself will be sufficient consideration for the defendant's counter-promise, in most states. [105]

IV. ILLUSORY, ALTERNATIVE AND IMPLIED PROMISES

A. **Illusory promises:** An *"illusory"* promise is not supported by consideration, and is therefore not enforceable. An illusory promise is a statement which appears to be promising something, but which in fact does not *commit* the promisor to do anything at all. [111-115]

Example: *A* says to *B*, "I'll sell you as many widgets at $4 apiece, up to 1,000, as you choose to order in the next 4 weeks." *B* answers, "Fine, we've got a deal." *B* then gives *A* an order for 100 widgets, and *A* refuses to sell at the stated price because the market has gone up. *B*'s promise is illusory, since she has not committed herself to do anything. Therefore, *A*'s promise is not supported by consideration, and is not binding on him.

1. **Right to terminate:** If the contract allows one or both parties to *terminate* the agreement at his option, this right of termination might make the promise illusory and the contract therefore unenforceable. [113]

   a. **Unfettered right:** If the agreement allows one party to terminate simply by giving *notice at any time*, the traditional common-law view is that the party with the termination right has not furnished consideration. But the modern trend is to hold that as long as the terminating party has the obligation to *give notice* (even if this obligation is an *implied* one), this duty of notice itself furnishes consideration.

B. **Implied promises:** Courts try to avoid striking down agreements for lack of consideration. One way they do this is by finding that the promisee has made an *implied promise* in return. [114-115]

Example: D, a fashion designer, gives P the exclusive right to sell products made from D's designs. P promises to pay royalties on any product sold, but the agreement does not expressly require P to make sales. D violates the agreement by letting someone else sell her designs. P sues D, who defends on the grounds that P did not really promise to do anything, and that there is thus no consideration for D's promise of exclusivity.

Held, for P — P can be impliedly found to have promised to use reasonable efforts to market D's designs, thus furnishing consideration for D's counter-promise. [*Wood v. Lucy, Lady Duff Gordon*].

V. REQUIREMENTS AND OUTPUT CONTRACTS

A. **Requirements and output contracts generally:** In a *requirements* contract, the parties agree that the seller will be the exclusive source of all the buyer's requirements for a particular type of item for a particular time. In an *output* contract, the buyer agrees to take all of the seller's output of a particular type of item. [115-117]

1. **Enforceable today:** Under traditional consideration rules, requirements and output contracts were sometimes found lacking in consideration. But today, requirements contracts are generally *enforced*, assuming (as is usually the case) that the buyer is found to have *implicitly promised to use his best efforts to generate a need for the goods.* Similarly, output contracts are generally enforced, as long as the seller has implicitly promised to attempt to maintain his production at a reasonable level.

2. **UCC approach:** The *UCC explicitly validates requirements and output contracts.* UCC § 2-306 provides that "a term which measures the quantity by the output of the seller or the requirements of the buyer means such actual output or requirements as may occur in *good faith*, except that no quantity *unreasonably disproportionate* to any stated estimate or in the absence of a stated estimate to any normal or otherwise comparable prior output or requirements may be tendered or demanded."

     a. **Best efforts imposed on buyers and sellers:** There is a special type of good-faith obligation imposed by § 2-306 on buyers and sellers under requirements contracts. § 2-306(2) says that "A lawful agreement by either the seller or the buyer for exclusive dealing in the kind of goods concerned *imposes* unless otherwise agreed an obligation by the *seller to use best efforts to supply the goods* and by the *buyer to use best efforts to promote their sale.*" [116]

         i. **Significance:** Therefore, under a requirements contract the buyer must make best efforts to promote the sale of the goods, and *cannot simply decide that the entire product line is not worth carrying*. Conversely, under an output contract the seller cannot simply decide to *stop selling or manufacturing* the item, and must instead make best efforts to supply the goods.

CHAPTER 4

PROMISES BINDING WITHOUT CONSIDERATION

I. PROMISES TO PAY PAST DEBTS

A. General rule: Most states enforce a *promise to pay a past debt*, even though no consideration for the promise is given. Thus promises to pay debts that have been discharged by bankruptcy, or that are no longer collectible because of the statute of limitations, are enforceable in most states. [127-128]

     1. **Writing required:** Most states require a *signed writing*, at least where the promise is to pay a debt barred by the statute of limitations.

II. PROMISE TO PAY FOR BENEFITS RECEIVED

A. Generally: A promise to pay for *benefits* or *services* one has previously received will generally be enforceable even without consideration. This is especially likely where the services were *requested*, or where the services were furnished without request in an *emergency*. [129-130]

III. OTHER CONTRACTS BINDING WITHOUT CONSIDERATION

A. Modification of sales contracts: Under the UCC, a *modification* of a contract for the sale of goods is binding without consideration. See § 2-209. [131] (*Example*: A contracts to supply 100 widgets to B at $4 a piece. Before shipment, A says, "My costs have gone up; I'll have to charge you $5." B agrees. Under UCC § 2-209, this modification is enforceable, even though B received no consideration for promising to pay the higher price.)

     1. **No-oral-modification clauses:** But a "no oral modifications" clause in a sales contract will normally be enforced. (*Example*: On the facts of the above example, if the original contract between A and B said that any modification must be in writing, B's promise to pay the higher price would be enforceable only if in writing.)

B. Option contracts: Recall that *option contracts* are sometimes enforceable without consideration. Thus an offer that purports to be enforceable, and that falsely recites that consideration was paid for the irrevocability, will be enforced in most courts. Also, remember that UCC § 2-205 renders enforceable "firm offers" under certain circumstances. [133]

C. **Guaranties:** In most states, a *guaranty* (that is, a promise to pay the debts of another) will be enforced without consideration. Generally, the guarantee must be in writing, and must state that consideration has been paid (though the consideration does not in fact have to have been paid). [134-135]

IV. PROMISSORY ESTOPPEL

A. **General approach:** Promises which foreseeably induce *reliance* on the part of the promisee will often be enforceable without consideration, under the doctrine of *promissory estoppel ("P.E.")*. Rest.2d, § 90's definition of the doctrine is as follows: "A promise which the promisor *should reasonably expect to induce action or forbearance* on the part of the promisee or a third person and which does induce such action or forbearance *is binding if injustice can be avoided only by enforcement of the promise*." [137]

> **Example:** *A* promises to pay for *B*'s college education if *B* will attend school full time. *A* intends this to be a gift. *B* gives up a good job and enrolls in college, incurring a liability of $5,000 for the first year. *A* then refuses to pay the bill. Under the doctrine of P.E., *B* would be able to recover at least the value of the lost job and first-year tuition from *A*, even though *A*'s promise was a promise to make a gift and was thus not supported by consideration.

1. **Actual reliance:** The promisee must *actually rely* on the promise. (*Example*: On the facts of the above example, *B* must show that without *A*'s promise, *B* would not have quit his job and attended college.) [138]

2. **Foreseeable reliance:** The promisee's reliance must also have been *reasonably foreseeable* to the promisor. [138]

B. **Possible applications:**

1. **Promise to make a gift:** The P.E. doctrine is most often applied to enforce promises to *make gifts*, where the promisee relies on the gift to his detriment. [138]

   a. **Intra-family promises:** The doctrine may be applied where the promise is made by one member of a *family* to another. (*Example*: Mother promises to pay for Son's college education, and Son quits his job. Probably the court will award just the damages Son suffers from losing the job, not the full cost of a college education.)

2. **Charitable subscriptions:** A written promise to make a *charitable contribution* will generally be binding without consideration, under the P.E. doctrine. Here, the doctrine is watered down: usually the charity does not need to show detrimental reliance. (But *oral* promises to make charitable contributions usually will not be enforceable unless the charity relies on the promise to its detriment.) [139]

3. **Gratuitous bailments and agencies:** If a person promises to *take care of* another's property (a "gratuitous bailment") or promises to carry out an act as another person's *agent* (gratuitous agency), the promisor may be held liable under P.E. if he does not perform at all. (However, courts are hesitant to apply P.E. to promises to *procure insurance* for another.) [140]

4. **Offers by sub-contractors:** Where a *sub-contractor* makes a *bid* to a general contractor, and the latter uses the bid in computing his own master bid on the job, the P.E. doctrine is often used to make the sub-bid temporarily irrevocable. [141]

   a. **Reliance by general contractor:** In the sub-contractor-bid scenario, be sure to *check for reliance by the general contractor (GC).* If there is no real (and justifiable) reliance by the GC on the sub-contractor's bid, the GC will *not be permitted to use P.E.* to make the sub-contractor's bid temporarily irrevocable. [141]

Example: Suppose the sub-contractor discovers its bid is too low and tells the GC about this *before* the GC's own bid has been opened by the owner. In this scenario, the GC might be able to avoid the problem by revising or withdrawing its master bid. If the GC has this opportunity and doesn't use it, then the GC has not reasonably relied, and will not qualify for promissory estoppel.

5. **Promise of job:** If an employer promises an **at-will job** to an employee, and then revokes the promise before the employee shows up for work, P.E. may apply. [143]

> **Example:** *A* offers a job to *B*, terminable by either at any time. *B* quits his established job. Before *B* shows up for work, *A* cancels the job offer. A court might hold that even though *B* could have been fired at any time once he showed up, *B* should be able to collect the value of the job he quit from *A*, under a P.E. theory.

6. **Negotiations in good faith:** A person who **negotiates** with another may be found to have a duty to **bargain in good faith**; if bad faith is found, the court may use P.E. to furnish a remedy. [143-147]

> **Example:** *A*, owner of a shopping mall, promises that it will negotiate a lease for particular space with *B*, a tenant. *B* rejects an offer of space from another landlord. *A* then leases the space to one of *B*'s competitors for a higher rent. A court might apply P.E., by holding that *A* implicitly promised to use good faith in the negotiations and breached that promise.

   a. **Promises of franchise:** The use of P.E. to protect negotiating parties is especially likely where the promise is a promise by a national corporation to award a **franchise** to the other party.

   > **Example:** P, a national company that runs a fast food chain, promises B a franchise. B quits his job and undergoes expensive training in the restaurant business. If A then refuses to award the franchise, a court might use P.E. to enforce the promise, at least to the extent of reimbursing B for his lost job and training expenses.

   b. **Unequal bargaining power:** Beyond the promise-of-a-franchise situation, the court may apply P.E. in any scenario like this: two parties (call them *A* and *B*) engage in a lengthy business negotiation, where *A* is a powerful company that seems to be *"stringing along"* the relatively powerless *B* by holding out the likelihood that if *B* does certain acts, *A* will likely enter into some sort of business arrangement with *B* to *B*'s benefit. If the court believes that *A* has acted in bad faith for the purpose of gaining the *"upper hand"* over *B*, the court may apply P.E. to protect at least *B*'s reliance interest, **even if there was no reasonably-definite "contract" that the parties were negotiating.** [146]

   > **Example:** Bank, a large money-center bank, holds a mortgage on a home owned by O. O loses her job. At a time when O has not yet fallen behind on her mortgage, O calls Bank to find out whether Bank would be willing to give her any relief. Bank responds, "We can and will negotiate with you to see if your mortgage can be modified to make it easier for you to pay. However, we can do that only if you first furnish certain financial information, and only if your mortgage is in default at the time you furnish the info." O, in response, stops paying the mortgage and immediately furnishes the required information. Bank refuses to enter into modification negotiations, and instead immediately starts a foreclosure proceeding.
   >
   > There is a respectable chance that the court will find that O can successfully assert the promissory estoppel defense. There is a large disparity of bargaining power between Bank and O, and there is evidence that Bank has "strung O along," by foreseeably causing O to fall into default, thereby enabling Bank to bring a foreclosure that it could not otherwise have brought. And the court might well apply P.E. even though Bank never promised to actually enter into a loan modification, merely to negotiate towards one. (That is, the court would in effect be

enforcing the *promise to negotiate*, not enforcing any actual modification.) [Cf. *Dixon v. Wells Fargo, N.A.*] [145]

C. Amount of recovery: Where P.E. is used, the damages awarded are generally limited to those necessary to *"prevent injustice."* Usually, this will mean that the plaintiff receives **reliance** damages, rather than the greater expectation measure. In other words, P is placed in the position he would have been in had the promise never been made. [148-149]

>   **Example 1:** If *A* promises *B* a franchise, and *B* quits his job in reliance, the court will probably award *B* the value of the lost job, not the greater sum equaling profits that *B* would have made from the franchise.

>   **Example 2:** On facts like the mortgage-modification example *supra*, the court will probably restore O's mortgage to its pre-default status, not impose an actual mortgage modification of the sort that Bank promised to negotiate towards. Then, if O can't resume making timely mortgage payments in the original amount, Bank would be permitted to resume the foreclosure.

CHAPTER 5

MISTAKE

I. MISTAKE GENERALLY

A. Definition: A "mistake" is a *"belief that is not in accord with the facts."* [155-156]

1. **Mutual mistake:** If both parties have the same mistaken belief, the mistake is said to be *"mutual."*

2. **Unilateral:** By contrast, if only one party has the mistaken belief, the mistake is *"unilateral."*

3. **Existing fact:** The doctrines applicable to mistake apply only to a mistaken belief about an *existing fact*, *not* an erroneous belief about *what will happen in the future*.

>   **Example:** If Buyer and Seller both think that a stone is an emerald when it is in fact a topaz, this is a mistake. But if Buyer and Seller both think that the price of oil will remain relatively stable over the next five years, and in fact it goes up by 50% per year, this is not a mistake, since it does not relate to existing fact.

4. **Mistake of law:** A mistake about a *legal principle*, according to most courts today, can be a mistake.

II. MUTUAL MISTAKE

A. Three requirements for avoidance: Three requirements must be satisfied before the adversely-affected party may *avoid the contract* on account of *mutual mistake*: [157]

1. **Basic assumption:** The mistake must concern a *basic assumption* on which the contract was made. (*Examples*: The belief that a violin is a Stradavarius when it is in fact a worthless 20th century imitation is a "basic" mistake. But the seller's belief that a buyer to whom he is selling on credit is credit-worthy is probably a "collateral" rather than a "basic" mistake.)

2. **Material effect:** The mistake must have a *material effect* on the "agreed exchange of performance." (*Example*: If both Buyer and Seller thinks that a violin is a Stradavarius, but it is in fact a Guarnarius worth almost the same amount, the mistake would not have a "material effect" on the agreed exchange.)

3. **Risk:** The adversely-affected party (the one seeking to avoid the contract) must not be the one on whom the contract has implicitly *imposed the risk* of the mistake. Often, the contract does not make it clear which party is to bear the risk of a certain type of mistake, so the court allocates this risk in the manner that it finds to be *"reasonable"* in the circumstances.

B. **Special contexts:** [157-162]

1. **Market conditions:** Mistakes as to *market conditions* will generally *not* be "basic" ones, so the mistaken party will not be able to avoid the contract. (*Example*: Seller agrees to sell Blackacre to Buyer. Both parties believe that comparable land is worth $5,000 per acre. Buyer can't avoid the contract if comparable land is really worth $2,000 per acre.) [158]

2. **Existence of subject matter:** The *existence* of the subject matter of the contract is usually a "basic" assumption. [158]

>   **Example:** Seller agrees to sell land containing timber to Buyer. Both parties believe that there are 100,000 board feet on the property. In fact, fire has destroyed much of the timber, so that only 20,000 feet remain. This will be a basic assumption, so Buyer can avoid the contract when the facts emerge, whether this is before or after closing.

3. **Quality of subject matter:** A major mistake as to the *quality* of the contract's subject matter is often a "basic" assumption, so the disadvantaged party can avoid the contract. (*Example*: If both parties believe a violin is a Stradavarius when in fact it is an almost worthless imitation, this will be a mistake on a basic assumption, and Buyer can avoid the contract.) [158-159]

4. **Minerals in land:** In land-sale contracts, the Seller will almost always bear the risk that valuable *oil and gas* deposits will be found on the land (i.e., Seller cannot avoid the contract when such a discovery is made). [161]

5. **Building conditions:** When a builder contracts to *construct a building* on land owned by the other party, the builder will almost always be found to bear the risk of a mistake about soil or other unexpected conditions, so he cannot avoid the contract if construction proves much more difficult than expected. [161]

6. **Used paintings and other collectibles:** Suppose the owner of a painting or other *used "collectible"* sells it in a private sale, and the object turns out to be of a fundamentally different — and more valuable — nature than either side believed. Courts generally have allocated this risk to the *owner/seller*, on the theory that seller had the opportunity to ascertain the true value and can't ride on the coattails of a buyer who does so. [161]

III. UNILATERAL MISTAKE

A. **Modern view:** Where the mistake is *unilateral*, it is more difficult for the mistaken party to avoid the contract than in the mutual mistake situation. The mistaken party must make the same three showings as for mutual mistake (basic assumption, material effect, and risk on the other party), *plus* must show *either* that: [164-166]

[1] **Unconscionability:** The mistake is such that enforcement of the contract would be *unconscionable*; *or*

[2] **Reason to know:** The other party had *reason to know* of the mistake, or the other party's *fault* caused the mistake.

1. **An offer too good to be true:** As indicated in [2] above, a person who wants to avoid a contract on account of unilateral mistake will often try to show that the *other party had reason to know of the mistake.* In the case of a mistake reflected in an *offer* that the offeree accepted, and that the offeror now wants to rescind for mistake, the offeror will try to show that the *offeree knew or*

should have known that the offer (with the mistake embedded in it) was *"too good to be true."* [164]

   a. **"Snapping up" the offer:** If the offeror can make this "too good to be true" showing, she will have a good chance of meeting all the elements for rescission on grounds of unilateral mistake. As the idea is usually put, "[a]n offeree *may not snap up an offer* that is on its face *manifestly too good to be true."* [*Lange v. U.S.*] [164]

   b. **Mechanical errors and "mental blunders":** Most often, what makes an offer "too good to be true" is that the circumstances would suggest to any reasonable offeree that the offer is probably the result of a *"mechanical error"* or a *"mental blunder."*

   > **Example:** Two parties, *A* and *B*, have been negotiating a contract under which *A* will pay *B* about $2 million for certain services by *B*; *A* indicates a willingness to pay up to $2.51 million, and *B* insists on receiving at least $2.53 million. Then, *A* emails *B*, "I'll meet you halfway — I hereby offer to pay $2.55 million." *B* emails back, "I accept — $2.55."
   >
   > In view of the prior discussions (where *B* indicated that he would take $2.53 million) and *A*'s current "meet you halfway" remark, *B* should know that *A*'s "$2.55 million" offer was likely a computational error or some other sort of basic blunder, not a thought-out concession. Therefore, *B* was not entitled to "snap up" the offer, and *A* will likely succeed in using the unilateral-mistake doctrine to have the contract either thrown out entirely, or reformed to $2.52 million (halfway between the $2.51 and $2.53 numbers previously discussed). [Cf. *Sumerel v. Goodyear Tire & Rubber Co.*] [164-165]

B. **Construction bids:** One common type of unilateral mistake occurs where a *contractor* or sub-contractor makes an error on a *bid* for a construction job. [165-166]

   1. **Unconscionability:** The mistaken contractor will succeed in showing *unconscionability* (one of the two alternate special showings needed for unilateral mistake) only if he shows that not only will he be *severely harmed* if forced to perform, but also that the other party *has not relied* on the bid.

   > **Example:** Sub-contractor gives contractor a bid of $50,000 for electrical work. Contractor relies on this bid to prepare her own master bid for the entire project. Contractor gets the contract, enters into a sub-contract with Sub-contractor, and Sub-contractor then discovers that his $50,000 bid should have been $75,000, due to a clerical error. The court would probably not find it unconscionable to hold Sub-contractor to the contract, because Contractor has relied on the $50,000 sub-bid.

   2. **"Snapping up" of offer:** Alternatively, the mistaken bidder can win on unilateral mistake if she can show that the other party either *knew* or had *reason to know* of the error, and *"snapped up"* this offer that was "too good to be true." (See Par. 1(a) and 1(b) above.)

   > **Example:** In the above example, if Sub-contractor can show that Contractor should have known that there probably was a mistake, because Sub-contractor's bid was 50% lower than all other sub-bids, the court is likely to let Sub-contractor avoid the contract based on unilateral mistake.

IV. DEFENSES AND REMEDIES

A. **Negligence:** Where a party seeks to avoid the contract because of his own (or both parties') mistake, the fact that the mistake was due to his *negligence* will ordinarily *not prevent relief*.

1. **Failure to read writing:** But if the mistake stems from a party's *failure to read the contract*, he will *not* normally be entitled to rescind. [168]

B. **Remedies:** There are two main *remedies* that may be appropriate for mistake: [168-169]

1. **Avoidance:** The most common remedy is *avoidance* of the contract (sometimes called *"rescission"*). Here, the court treats the contract as if it has never been made, and attempts to return each party to the position he was in just before the contract was signed. Generally, *restitution* will be ordered — each party will return the benefits he has received from the other.

> **Example:** Seller agrees to sell its interest in a particular parcel of vacant land to Buyer, under an installment contract. Buyer makes it clear to Seller that Buyer's only intended use for the property is to grow a particular shrub on it, something which requires adequate water supplies. After the purchase, wells drilled by Buyer show that there is no adequate water beneath the property. Buyer sues Seller for rescission on grounds of mutual mistake.
>
> A court would hold that Buyer is entitled to return of its down payment. However, the court would also probably require Buyer to pay Seller for the fair rental value of the property during the time Buyer had possession of it. Conversely, Seller would be required to compensate Buyer for any increase in the value of the property brought about by Buyer's drilling of test wells. (But Buyer wouldn't get the cost of the drilling of the test wells, except to the extent those wells increased the value of the property.) [169]

2. **Reliance:** Alternatively, the court may award *reliance* damages, especially where restitution/avoidance would not work because one party has suffered losses but the other has not received benefits.

V. REFORMATION AS REMEDY FOR ERROR IN EXPRESSION

A. **Generally:** If the parties orally agree on a deal, but mistakenly prepare and execute a document which *incorrectly reflects* the oral agreement, either party may obtain a court order for *reformation* (i.e., a re-writing of the document). [170]

> **Example:** Seller orally agrees to sell Blackacre to Buyer for $100,000. Their oral deal includes a provision that Buyer will also assume an existing mortgage of $50,000. The written agreement neglects the assumption provision. At either party's request, the court will reform the document so that it includes the assumption provision.

CHAPTER 6

PAROL EVIDENCE AND INTERPRETATION

I. PAROL EVIDENCE RULE GENERALLY

A. **What the rule does:** The parol evidence rule limits the extent to which a party may establish that discussions or writings prior to the signed written contract should be taken as part of the agreement. In some circumstances, the rule bars the fact-finder from considering any evidence of certain preliminary agreements that are not contained in the final writing, even though this evidence might show that the preliminary agreement did in fact take place and that the parties intended it to remain part of their deal despite its absence from the writing. [175-176]

II. TOTAL AND PARTIAL INTEGRATIONS

A. **Definitions:** [176]

1. **"Integration":** A document is said to be an *"integration"* of the parties' agreement if it is intended as the *final expression* of the agreement. (The parol evidence rule applies *only to documents which are "integrations,"* i.e., final expressions of agreement.)

2. **Partial integration:** A *"partial"* integration is a document that is intended to be final, but that is *not* intended to include *all details* of the parties' agreement.

3. **Total integration:** A *"total"* integration is a document that is not only a final expression of agreement, but that is also intended to include *all details* of the agreement.

B. **Statement of rule:** The "parol evidence rule" is in fact two sub-rules: [176-177]

1. **Partial integration:** When a writing is a *partial integration*, no evidence of prior or contemporaneous agreements or negotiations (oral or written) may be admitted if this evidence would *contradict* a term of the writing.

2. **Total integration:** When a document is a *total integration*, no evidence of prior or contemporaneous agreements or negotiations may be admitted which would *either contradict* or *add* to the writing.

3. **Summary:** Putting the two sub-parts together, the parol evidence rule provides that evidence of a prior agreement may never be admitted to *contradict an integrated writing*, and may furthermore not even *supplement* an integration which is intended to be *complete*.

4. **Prior writings and oral agreements:** The parol evidence rule applies to *oral agreements and discussions* that occur *prior* to a signing of an integration. It also applies to *writings* created prior to an integration (e.g., draft agreements that were not intended to be final expressions of agreement). [177]

5. **Contemporaneous writing:** If an *ancillary writing* is signed at the *same time* a formal document is signed, the ancillary document is treated as *part of the writing*, and will not be subject to the parol evidence rule.

6. **Subsequent agreements:** The parol evidence rule *never bars consideration of subsequent oral agreements*. That is, *a written contract may always be modified after its execution*, by an oral agreement.

   a. **"No oral modifications" clause:** However, if the written document contains a *"no oral modification"* clause, that clause will usually be enforced by the court, unless the court finds that the defendant *waived* the benefits of that clause.

C. **UCC:** Section-202 of the *UCC* essentially follows the common-law parol evidence rule as summarized above. [179-180]

III. ROLES OF JUDGE AND JURY

A. **Preliminary determinations made by judge:** Nearly all courts hold that the *judge*, not the jury, decides: (1) whether the writing was intended as an integration; (2) if so, whether the integration is "partial" or "total"; and (3) whether particular evidence would supplement the terms of a complete integration. [181]

1. **Conflicting views:** Courts disagree about how the judge should make these decisions. Two extreme positions are: (1) the *"four corners"* rule, by which the judge decides whether there is an integration, and whether it is total or partial, by looking *solely at the document*; and (2) the "Corbin" view, by which these questions are to be answered by looking at *all available evidence*, including testimony, to determine the *actual intention* of the parties. [181-183]

2. **Merger clause:** Most contracts contain a *"merger" clause*, i.e., a clause stating that the writing constitutes the sole agreement between the parties. The presence of such a clause makes it more likely that the court will find the writing to have been intended as a total integration (in which case not even consistent additional prior oral or written terms may be shown). [182]

IV. SITUATIONS WHERE PAROL EVIDENCE RULE DOES NOT APPLY

A. **Fraud, mistake or other voidability:** Even if a writing is a total integration, a party may always introduce evidence of earlier oral agreements to show *illegality, fraud, duress, mistake, lack of consideration*, or any other fact that would make the contract void or voidable. In other words, the parol evidence rule never prevents the introduction of evidence that would show that *no valid contract exists* or that the contract is voidable. [184]

Example: In order to induce Buyer to buy a rental property, Seller lies about the profitability of the property. The parties then sign a sale contract that contains a standard "merger" clause, reciting that the contract constitutes the sole agreement between the parties. The parol evidence rule will not prevent Buyer from showing that Seller made fraudulent misrepresentations to induce him to enter into the contract.

1. **Particular disclaimer:** But if the contract contains a very specific statement that no representations of a *particular sort* have been made, some courts prevent a party from showing that the disclaimer is false.

   Example: On the facts of the above example, suppose that the contract stated, "Seller has made no representations or warranties regarding the profitability of the property, and Buyer has relied solely on his own investigation as to profitability." Some courts — though probably a minority — would prohibit Buyer from showing that Seller in fact made fraudulent misrepresentations about profitability.

B. **Existence of a condition:** If the parties orally agree on a *condition* to the enforceability of the contract, or to the duty of one of them, but this condition is then not included in the writing, courts generally *allow proof* of this condition despite the parol evidence rule. [185-187]

   Example: *A* and *B* agree that *A* will sell a patent to *B* for $10,000 if C, an engineer advising *B*, approves. *A* and *B* sign a written agreement that seems to be complete, except that the contract does not mention C's approval. Nearly all courts would allow *B* to prove that the oral agreement regarding approval was in fact made.

C. **Collateral agreements:** An oral agreement that is supported by *separate consideration* may be demonstrated, even though it occurred prior to what seems to be a total integration. [185]

   Example: In a written agreement that seems to be a complete expression of the parties' intent, *A* promises to sell *B* a particular automobile. As part of the transaction, the parties orally agree that *B* may keep the car in *A*'s garage for one year for $15 per month. Because the alleged oral agreement is supported by separate consideration — the $15 per month — *B* may prove that the oral agreement occurred even though there is an integrated writing that does not include that agreement.

1. **Not inconsistent with total integration:** However, if the writing is a total integration, the separate agreement must not be *directly inconsistent* with the writing. [185]

   Example: Same facts as above example. Assume the writing has a merger clause, saying that there are no other agreements between the parties regarding the automobile transaction. Suppose further that the writing says, "*B* shall have no right to keep the car in *A*'s garage at any time." *B* will not be allowed to prove the alleged oral collateral agreement, since that agreement is directly inconsistent with the writing, and the writing is a total integration.

D. Subsequent transactions: Recall that the parol evidence rule never bars evidence that *after the signing of the writing*, the parties orally or in writing agreed to modify or rescind the writing. [187]

E. Interpretation: The parol evidence rule does not bar extrinsic evidence when offered to aid in the *interpretation* to be given to an *ambiguous term* of the contract. This rule is discussed extensively in the next section, "Interpretation," immediately below.

V. INTERPRETATION

A. Modern view: Most courts today allow parties to introduce extrinsic evidence to aid in the *interpretation* of a contract, even if the writing is an integration. However, courts vary on the details of how and when extrinsic evidence is allowed in connection with a question of interpretation.

   1. Extrinsic evidence in the case of ambiguous terms: *All courts agree* that if a term is found by the trial court to be *ambiguous* — capable of more than one meaning — *extrinsic evidence must be allowed*. [188]

      a. Evaluated by jury: Furthermore, courts are in near-universal agreement that this extrinsic evidence is to be *evaluated by the jury*, not by the judge.

      b. Evidence of parties' own pre-contract negotiations: Finally, courts are in unanimous agreement that the types of extrinsic evidence that are to be allowed to help resolve the meaning of the ambiguous term are *extremely broad*. In particular, courts agree that evidence about what the parties' own *pre-contract negotiations* indicated to be the meaning of the ambiguous term is to be *admitted*, and heard by the jury.

      Example: Seller sells a business to Buyer. Part of the purchase price is a delayed payment equal to 10% of the "Gross Profit" of the business in the first year after sale. The parties have a dispute about what "Gross Profit" means. If the trial court finds that the term is ambiguous, the judge will then let the jury hear testimony from each side about any statements either party made during the negotiations that might bear on what the term means.

   2. Unambiguous terms: Now, let's suppose that the trial judge decides that the term in question is completely *unambiguous*. Here, too, courts are in virtual unanimity about what happens next. Since the term is unambiguous, it is *for the judge*, not the jury, to *say what the term means*. Consequently, the jury will be instructed by the judge on the term's meaning, and the jury will never hear any sort of extrinsic evidence about what the term means. [189]

   3. How judge determines existence of ambiguity: The area of main disagreement among courts is *how the judge should decide whether the term is ambiguous*. There are three main approaches: (1) the *"four corners"* rule; (2) the *"plain meaning"* rule; and (3) the *"liberal"* rule.

      a. The "four corners" rule: The *"four corners"* rule is the most stringent of the three. Under this approach, when the judge decides whether the term is ambiguous, the judge *may not consult any extrinsic evidence whatsoever.* That is, the existence of ambiguity is to be determined *solely by looking within the "four corners" of the contract itself.* Thus not only will the court not consider evidence about the parties' negotiations, it will not even consider evidence about the context surrounding the making of the agreement. This hyper-strict rule is followed by relatively few courts. [189]

b. **The "plain meaning" rule:** The *"plain meaning"* rule is in the *middle* of the three approaches in terms of strictness. The most significant aspect of the plain meaning rule is that when the court goes to decide whether a term used in the agreement is ambiguous, the court *will not hear evidence about the parties' preliminary negotiations.* (However, the court *will* hear evidence about the circumstances, or *"context,"* surrounding the making of the agreement.) [189]

Example: On the facts of the above example, suppose the judge is deciding whether the term "Gross Profit" is ambiguous. A court following the "plain meaning" rule would probably hear testimony about what the term usually means in contracts of this sort (just to help the judge determine whether the term is or isn't ambiguous), but would *not* hear testimony about what the parties said during their negotiations (e.g., testimony by Seller that "Buyer told me that 'everybody knows that Gross Profit means [thus-and-such]' ").

c. **The "liberal" rule:** Finally, what might be called the *"liberal"* rule rejects — or at least significantly weakens — the plain meaning approach. Under the liberal view, *evidence of the parties' statements during their pre-contract negotiations* is *admissible* for the limited purpose of letting the trial judge determine whether the term is ambiguous. [189]

Example: On the facts of the above example, a court following the liberal approach would, when trying to decide whether the term Gross Profit is ambiguous, hear Seller's testimony about what Buyer told him during the pre-contract negotiations about the meaning of the term.

B. **Maxims of interpretation:** There are a number of "maxims" that courts use in deciding which of two conflicting interpretations of a clause should be followed: [191]

1. **Primary purpose:** If the *"primary purpose"* of the parties in making the contract can be ascertained, that purpose is given great weight.

2. **All terms made reasonable, lawful and effective:** All terms will be interpreted, where possible, so that they will have a *reasonable, lawful* and *effective* meaning.

3. **Construed against drafter:** An ambiguous term will be *construed against the person who drafted the contract.*

4. **Negotiated terms control standard terms:** A term that has been *negotiated* between the parties will control over one that is part of a standardized portion of the agreement (i.e., the fine print "boilerplate"). (*Example*: A clause that has been typewritten in as a "rider" to a pre-printed form contract, or a clause that has been handwritten onto a typewritten, agreement, will have priority.)

C. **One party knows or should know of the other's meaning:** Where the parties *attach different meanings to a particular term,* some special rules of interpretation apply:

❏ If one party *knows* (or has *reason to know*) that the two parties attach different meanings to the term, and the other *does not know or have reason to know* this, then the meaning given by the latter *("innocent") party controls*;

❏ If *neither* party *knows or should know* that the two parties attach different meanings to the term, then *neither party is bound* by the other's meaning. In that case, the court will *supply a reasonable value* for the unagreed-upon term. [191]

VI. TRADE USAGE, COURSE OF PERFORMANCE, AND COURSE OF DEALING

A. **Definitions:** There are three special sources which are used in interpreting the terms of a contract. These are especially important in sales contracts, since the UCC gives these sources specific treatment: [192-194]

1. **Course of performance:** A *"course of performance"* refers to the way the parties have previously conducted themselves in performing the *particular contract at hand*.

    Example: The contract calls for repeated deliveries of "highest grade oil." Evidence as to the quality of oil delivered and accepted in the first installments would be admissible as a course of performance to help determine whether oil delivered in a later installment met the contract standard.

2. **Course of dealing:** A *"course of dealing"* refers to how the parties have acted with respect to *past contracts*.

3. **Usage of trade:** A *"usage of trade"* is "any *practice* or method of dealing having such *regularity of observance* in a place, vocation or *trade* as to justify an expectation that it will be *observed with respect to the transaction in question*." UCC § 1-303(c). Thus the meaning attached to a particular term in a certain region, or in a certain industry, would be admissible.

B. **Used to interpret even a complete integration:** Course of dealing, course of performance, and usage of trade may be introduced to help interpret the meaning of a writing *even if the writing is a complete integration*. That is, these sources are *not affected by the parol evidence rule* — even though a writing is found to be the final and exclusive embodiment of the agreement, it may still be explained by evidence from these three sources. [193-194]

    Example: Customer orders 1,000 letterheads from Printer. Assume that it is a custom in the printing industry that where a particular quantity is ordered, any variation by the printer from that quantity is acceptable as long as it is not greater than 5% above or below it. Printer delivers 960 letterheads, and Customer rejects the shipment as non-conforming.

    Notwithstanding the parol evidence rule, Printer will likely be able to introduce this 5%-variation custom as a "trade usage." To do so, Printer will have to show that the custom is so regularly observed in the industry as to *"justify an expectation that it will be observed* with respect to the transaction in question" — § 1-303(c). But Printer doesn't have to show that Customer *actually* knew of the trade usage, merely that Customer *should* have known of it, due to its regular observation in the industry.

    1. **Contradiction of express terms:** But these customs may not be used to *contradict* the express terms of a contract. See UCC § 1-303(e). However, if these customs can reasonably be harmonized with the writing, then the customs may be shown and may become part of the contract.

C. **Priorities:** Where more than one of these types of customs is present, the *most specific pattern controls*. Thus an express contractual provision controls over a course of performance, which controls over a course of dealing, which controls over a trade usage. UCC § 1-303(e)(1)-(3). [194]

VII. OMITTED TERMS SUPPLIED BY COURT

A. **Generally:** Courts will generally *supply a missing term* (that is, a term as to which the contract documents are silent) if it is apparent that the parties wanted to bind themselves, and there is a reasonable way for the court to go about formulating the missing term. Here are some examples: [195]

1. **Good faith:** The court will normally supply a term imposing on each party a *"duty of good faith."* (*Example*: Where *A* agrees to have exclusive marketing rights to a design or invention produced by *B*, *A* will be found to have an implied duty to make good faith efforts to promote *B*'s product.) [195] See *supra*, p. C-14, for more about this obligation of good faith.

2. **Duty to continue business:** In requirement and output contracts, generally there will ***not*** be a duty to ***continue the business*** (assuming the owner acted in good faith when she closed it down.) [195-196]

3. **Termination of dealership or franchise:** Some but not all courts will supply a term to prevent one party from arbitrarily terminating a ***franchise*** or ***dealership*** arrangement. Sometimes, the court will refuse to allow termination except for cause. More commonly, courts will find an implied requirement of a ***reasonable notice*** prior to termination. [196]

4. **Termination of employment contract:** A strong minority of courts now find that an ***at-will employment contract*** contains an implied term prohibiting the employer from terminating the arrangement in ***bad faith***. In these courts, an employer may not terminate an at-will arrangement in order to deprive the employee of a pension, to retaliate for the employee's refusal to commit wrongdoing at the employer's urging, or for other bad faith reasons. [197-198]

CHAPTER 7

CONDITIONS, BREACH AND OTHER ASPECTS OF PERFORMANCE

C
A
P
S
U
L
E

S
U
M
M
A
R
Y

I. CONDITIONS GENERALLY

A. **Definition of "condition":** An event which must occur before a particular performance is due is called a ***"condition"*** of that performance. [203]

> **Example:** Seller promises to ship Buyer 100 widgets. Buyer promises to pay for the widgets within 30 days of receipt. The parties agree that if the widgets don't meet Buyer's specs, he may return them and he will not have to pay for them. It is a condition of Buyer's duty of payment that the widgets be shipped, and that they meet his specifications. Buyer's duty is said to be conditional on the shipment of satisfactory widgets.

1. **Concurrent:** A ***concurrent*** condition is a particular kind of condition precedent which exists only when the parties to a contract are to exchange performances at the ***same time***. (*Example*: *A* promises to deliver his car to *B* on a certain date, at which time *B* is to pay for the car. Delivery and payment are "concurrent conditions," since performance by both is to be rendered simultaneously.) Concurrent conditions are found most frequently in contracts for the sale of goods and contracts for the conveyance of land.

2. **Express and constructive conditions:** If the parties explicitly agree that a duty is conditional upon the happening of some event, that event is an ***"express"*** condition. If, instead, the happening of an event is made a condition of a duty because a court so determines, the condition is a ***"constructive"*** one (or a condition "implied in law"). [205-206]

> **Example of express condition:** *A* is to ship widgets to *B*, and *B* agrees to either return them if they don't satisfy her, or pay for them. The contract states, "*B*'s duty to pay for the widgets shall be conditional upon her being satisfied with them." This is an express condition.

> **Example of constructive condition:** Same facts as above example — *A* contracts to ship widgets to *B*, and *B* agrees to either return the widgets as unsatisfactory, or pay for them. No language of condition is used in the agreement. As a matter of common law (or the UCC), the court will impose a constructive condition: *B*'s duty to pay for the widgets will be constructively conditioned upon her receiving them and being satisfied with them.

 a. **Significance of distinction:** The reason we distinguish between express and constructive conditions is that *strict compliance* with express conditions is ordinarily necessary, but merely *substantial compliance* is usually required to satisfy a constructive condition.

B. **Distinction between conditions and promises:** The fact that an act is a condition does not by itself make it also a promise. If the act is a condition on the other party's duty, and the act fails to occur, the other party won't have to perform. If the act is a promise, and it doesn't occur, the other party can sue for damages. But the two don't automatically go together. [206-208]

 Example: Landlord promises Tenant that Landlord will make any necessary repairs on the leased premises, provided that Tenant gives him notice of the need for such repairs. Tenant's giving notice of the needed repairs is an express condition to Landlord's duty to perform the repairs. But such notice is not a promise by Tenant.

 Therefore, if Tenant does not give the notice, he has not committed any breach of contract, but a condition to Landlord's duty has failed to occur. Landlord is relieved from having to make the repairs, but cannot sue Tenant for breach.

 1. **Distinguishing:** To determine whether a particular act is a condition, a promise, or both, the main factor is the *intent of the parties*. Words like "upon condition that" indicate an intent that the act be a condition; words like "I promise" or "I warrant" indicate a promise (though as described below, failure to keep the promise will also generally constitute the failure of a constructive condition).

II. EXPRESS CONDITIONS

A. **Strict compliance:** *Strict compliance* with an express condition is ordinarily required. [209-212]

 Example: *A* contracts to sell his house to *B* for $100,000. The contract provides that *B*'s duty to consummate the purchase is "conditional upon *B*'s receiving a mortgage for at least $80,000 at an interest rate no higher than 9%." If the best mortgage *B* is able to obtain, after reasonable effort, is at 9.25%, the court will probably hold that *B* is not obligated to close, since the condition is an express one, and strict compliance with express conditions is ordinarily required.

 1. **Avoidance of forfeiture:** However, courts often avoid applying the "strict compliance" rule where a *forfeiture* would result. A forfeiture occurs when one party has *relied* on the bargain (e.g., by preparing to perform or by making part performance), and insistence on strict compliance with the condition would cause him to fail to receive the expected benefits from the deal.

  Example: *A* contracts to build a house for *B* on land owned by *B*, for a price of $100,000. The contract provides that "*B*'s duty to pay for the house is expressly conditional upon the finished house exactly matching the specifications of *B*'s architect." *A* builds the house in general accordance with the specifications, but the living room is six inches shorter than shown on the plans, a deviation which does not noticeably affect the market value of the house.

  Despite the rule that strict compliance with an express condition is ordinarily required, the court would probably hold that strict enforcement here would amount to a forfeiture, and would therefore hold that the condition was satisfied despite the trivial defect.

  a. **Excuse of condition:** Alternatively, a court may find that the fulfillment of the express condition is *"excused"* where extreme forfeiture would occur. This will only be done, however, if the damage to the other party's expectations from non-occurrence of the condition is relatively *minor*. (*Example*: On the facts of the above example, the damage to *B*'s expectations from the short living room is very small, so the court would probably excuse the non-occurrence of the condition.)

B. Satisfaction of a party: If a contract makes one party's duty to perform expressly conditional on that party's being **satisfied** with the other's performance, the court will usually presume that an **objective** standard of *"reasonable"* satisfaction was meant. [212-213]

　　1. Subjective: But it is the **intent** of the parties that controls here: If the parties clearly intend that one party's **subjective** satisfaction should control, the court will honor that intent. This is likely to be true, for instance, where the bargain clearly involves the **tastes** of a person. Here, dissatisfaction that is in good faith but unreasonable will still count as the non-occurrence of the condition.

C. Satisfaction of third person: If the duty of performance is expressly conditioned on the satisfaction of some **independent third party** (e.g., an architect or other professional), the third party's subjective judgment usually controls.

　　1. Good faith: But this third-party judgment must be made in **good faith**. [213]

　　　　a. Lack of careful consideration: If there is an indication that the third party did not even **give careful consideration** to the issue requiring satisfaction, this will be powerful evidence that the third party did not act in good faith. In that case, the court will treat the satisfaction condition as being waived.

　　　　Example: Owner's duty to make progress payments to Builder for construction of a house is made conditional upon approval of each phase of the work by Architect, Owner's architect, and the payments are due 5 days after such approval. Builder submits to Architect a description of the work done up to a particular point, and requests the progress payment. Architect goes out of town for two months, does not inspect the work, and sends an email from abroad saying "I don't approve the work." Builder waits a month, then cancels the contract and sues Owner.

　　　　A court would almost certainly hold that Architect's failure to inspect the work means that his lack of satisfaction was not determined in good faith, and that the non-occurrence of the condition of satisfaction should therefore be deemed waived by Owner. Consequently, when Owner didn't pay, that non-payment was itself a breach justifying Builder in canceling the contract.

III. CONSTRUCTIVE CONDITIONS

A. Use in bilateral conditions: Remember that a **constructive condition** is a condition which is not agreed upon by the parties, but which is supplied by the court for fairness. The principal use of constructive conditions is in bilateral contracts (where each party makes a promise to the other). [215-216]

　　1. General rule: Where each party makes one or more promises to the other, **each party's substantial performance of his promise is generally a constructive condition to the performance of any subsequent duties by the other party**.

　　　　Example: Contractor agrees to build a house for Owner for $100,000. The contract provides that Owner will pay $10,000 upon completion of the foundation, and provides a schedule on which the work is to proceed. No language of condition is used anywhere in the document. Contractor builds the foundation on schedule, but Owner without cause refuses to pay the $10,000 charge.

　　　　Owner's fulfillment of his promise — to pay $10,000 — is a constructive condition of Contractor's duty to continue with the work. Therefore, Contractor does not have to continue with the work until Owner pays the $10,000, even though the contract does not expressly make Contractor's duty of continuation conditional upon Owner's making the first payment. The court simply supplies this "constructive condition" for fairness, reasoning that Contractor shouldn't have to keep doing work if Owner hasn't been keeping his part of the bargain.

B. Order of performance: Be careful to interpret the contract to determine the *order* in which the parties' performances are to occur. [216-220]

   1. Intent: The parties' *intent* always controls. Where the intent is not clear, the court supplies certain presumptions, as discussed below.

   2. Periodic alternating: The parties may agree that their performances shall *alternate*. This is true of most *installment* contracts. Here, a series of alternating constructive conditions arises: each party's obligation to perform his duty is constructively conditioned on the other's having performed the prior duty. It's therefore important to decide who was the *first* to fail to substantially perform, since that failure of substantial performance is the non-occurrence of a constructive condition of the other party's subsequent duty. [216-217]

   3. No order of performance agreed upon: If the parties do not agree upon the order of performance, there are several general presumptions courts use: [218-219]

      a. Only one party's work requires time: Where the performance of one party requires a *period of time*, and the other's does not, the performance requiring time must ordinarily occur first, and its performance is a constructive condition to the other party's performance. This applies to contracts for *services* — a party who is to perform work must usually *substantially complete* the work before he may *receive payment* if the parties do not otherwise agree.

      b. Sales of goods and land: If each party's promised performance can occur at the *same time* as the other's, the court will normally require that the two occur *simultaneously*, in which case the two performances are "concurrent conditions." This applies to *sales of goods and land*.

         i. Tender of performance: Courts express this by saying that where the two performances are concurrent, each party must *"tender"* (i.e., *conditionally offer*) performance to the other. See UCC §§ 2-507(1) and 2-511(1).

         Example: Seller contracts to sell Blackacre to Buyer. The closing is to take place on July 1, at which time Seller will deliver a deed to the property free and clear of liens, and Buyer will deliver a certified check for $100,000. Since each performance can occur simultaneously, the court will presume that simultaneity is what the parties intended.

         Therefore, on July 1, Seller's duty to deliver the deed will be conditional upon Buyer's coming forward with the certified check, and Buyer's duty to come forward with the check will be conditional upon Seller's tendering the deed. If Seller fails to show up with a proper deed, Buyer will not be able to sue Seller for breach unless Buyer shows that he tendered the certified check, i.e., had the check in his possession and arrived at the place of closing with it.

C. Independent or dependent promises: In the normal bilateral contract, the court will presume that the promises are *in exchange for each other*. That is, the court will treat the promises as being *mutually dependent*, so that each party's duty is constructively conditional upon the other's substantial performance of all previous duties. [220-221]

   1. Independent promises: But in a few situations, circumstances may indicate that the promises are intended to be *independent* of each other. Here, the court will *not* apply the theory of constructive conditions.

      a. Real estate leases: For instance, promises in the typical *real estate lease* are generally construed as being *independent* of each other. Thus a tenant's promise to pay rent, and a landlord's return-promise to make repairs, are treated as independent, so if the landlord does not make the repairs, the tenant cannot refuse to pay the rent (though he can of course sue for damages). But a growing minority of courts have rejected this rule of independence.

D. Divisible contracts: A *divisible* contract is one in which both parties have divided up their performance into units or installments, in such a way that each part performance is roughly the compensation for a corresponding part performance by the other party. If a contract is found to be divisible, it will for purposes of constructive conditions be treated as a series of *separate contracts*. [221-225]

    1. Significance: If the contract is found to be divisible, here's the significance: if one party partly performs, the other will have to make *part payment*. If the contract is not divisible, then the non-breaching party won't have to pay anything at all (at least under the contract).

        Example: In a single document, Contractor agrees to build a deck for Owner and renovate Owner's kitchen. The contract lists a price of $30,000 for the renovation and $20,000 for the deck. Payment on the entire contract is due when all work is done. Contractor completes the deck but never even starts on the kitchen.

        If the contract is found to be divisible into two parts, Owner will be required to pay $20,000 for the deck even though he never gets the kitchen. If the contract is not divisible, Contractor will be found to not have substantially performed the whole, and he will not be able to recover on the contract for the work on the deck (though he will be able to recover the fair value of what he has done on a quasi-contract or restitution theory).

    2. Test for divisibility: A contract is divisible if it can be "apportioned into corresponding pairs of part performances so that the parts of each pair are properly regarded as *agreed equivalents*...." (*Example*: On the facts of the above example, a court would probably find that the parties implicitly agreed that $20,000 would be an agreed equivalent for the deck and $30,000 for the kitchen. Therefore, the court would probably find that the contract was divisible.) [222-225]

        a. Employment contracts: Most *employment* contracts are looked on as being divisible. Usually, the contract will be divided into lengths of time equal to the *time between payments*. Thus if the employee is paid by the week, the contract will be divided into one-week "sub-contracts"; payment for a particular week will be constructively conditioned only on the employee's having worked that week, not on his having fulfilled the entire contract.

        b. Fairness: The court will not find a contract to be divisible if this would be *unfair* to the non-breaching party. For instance, even though the contract recites separate prices for different part performances, requiring the non-breaching party to pay the full stated price for the part performance received may deprive him of fair value.

        Example: A construction contract requires Owner to pay one-tenth of the contract price for each of 10 weeks of estimated work. The first week, Contractor does everything scheduled for that week, but the scheduling is very light, consisting mainly of site preparation. If Contractor breaches after the first week, the court will probably not find the contract divisible, since a finding of divisibility would require Owner to pay one-tenth of the contract price for performance that represents less than one-tenth of the full job.

IV. SUBSTANTIAL PERFORMANCE

A. Doctrine generally: Recall that it is a constructive condition to a party's duty of performance that the other party have made a *"substantial performance"* of the latter's previous obligations. In other words, if one party fails to substantially perform, the other party's remaining duties do not fall due. [226]

B. Suspension followed by discharge: If a party fails to substantially perform, but the defects could be fairly easily cured, the other party's duty to give a return performance is merely *suspended*; the defaulter then has a chance to *cure* his defective performance. If, on the other hand, the defect is so substantial that it cannot be cured within a reasonable time, or if the defaulter fails to take advantage of a chance to cure, the other party is then completely *discharged*, and may also sue for breach. [227]

C. **Factors regarding materiality:** Here are some factors that help determine whether a breach is material (i.e., whether the breaching party has nonetheless substantially performed): [227-229]

1. **Deprivation of expected benefit:** The more the non-breaching party is deprived of the *benefit which he reasonably expected*, the more likely it is that the breach was material. [227]

2. **Part performance:** The *greater the part of the performance* which has been rendered, the less likely it is that a breach will be deemed material. Thus a breach occurring at the very *beginning* of the contract is more likely to be deemed material than the same "size" breach coming near the end. [228]

3. **Likeliness of cure:** If the breaching party seems likely to be able and willing to *cure*, the breach is less likely to be material than where cure seems impossible. [228]

4. **Willfulness:** A *willful* (i.e., *intentional*) breach is more likely to be regarded as material than a breach caused by negligence or other factors. [228]

5. **Delay:** A delay, even a substantial one, will not necessarily constitute a lack of substantial performance. The presumption is that *time* is *not "of the essence"* unless the contract so states, or other circumstances make the need for promptness apparent. (Even if the contract *does* contain a "time is of the essence" clause, a short delay will not be deemed "material" unless the circumstances show that the delay seriously damaged the other party.) [228]

D. **Material breach in contracts for the sale of goods:** The UCC imposes special rules governing what constitutes substantial performance by a seller of goods (and thus when a buyer can reject the goods). [229-234]

1. **"Perfect tender" rule:** UCC § 2-601 says that as long as the contract does not involve installments (i.e., multiple deliveries), "Unless otherwise agreed…if the goods or tender of delivery fail *in any respect* to conform to the contract, the buyer may (a) reject the whole; or (b) accept the whole; or (c) accept any commercial unit or units and reject the rest." On its face, this section seems to impose the *"perfect tender"* rule — that is, it seems to give the buyer the right to cancel the contract, and refuse to pay, if the goods deviate from the contract terms in any respect, no matter how slight. [229]

   a. **Not so strict:** But in reality, there are loopholes in this "perfect tender" rule. Courts usually only allow buyers to reject the seller's delivery if the defect is a substantial one. Also, the buyer must follow strict procedures for rejecting the delivery, and the seller generally has the right to "cure" the defect. See below.

2. **Mechanics of rejection:** The buyer may *"reject"* any non-conforming delivery from the seller. As noted, in theory this right exists if the goods deviate *in any respect* from what is required under the contract. But the buyer's right of rejection is subject to some fairly strict procedural rules: [231]

   a. **Time:** Rejection must occur within a *"reasonable time"* after the goods are delivered. The buyer must give prompt *notice* to the seller that buyer is rejecting. § 2-602(1).

   b. **Must not be preceded by acceptance:** The buyer can only reject if he has not previously "accepted" the goods. He will be deemed to have "accepted" them if either: (1) after a reasonable opportunity to *inspect*, buyer has indicated to the seller that the goods are conforming or that he will keep them despite non-conformity; or (2) buyer fails to make a timely rejection (though this cannot happen until buyer has had a reasonable inspection opportunity); or (3) buyer does "any act inconsistent with the seller's ownership" (e.g., using the goods as part of a manufacturing process). See § 2-606(1).

3. **Revocation of acceptance:** Even if the buyer has "accepted" the goods, if he then discovers a defect he may be able to *revoke* his acceptance. If he revokes, the result is the same as if he had never accepted — he can throw the goods back on the seller and refuse to pay. [232]

   a. **Revocation vs. rejection:** The buyer who wants to revoke an acceptance must make a *stronger showing of non-conformity* than the buyer who rejects — the revoker must show that the non-conformity "substantially impairs" the value of the goods, whereas the rejecter must merely show that the goods fail to conform "in any respect." On the other hand, a buyer probably gets more time to revoke than to reject.

4. **Cure:** Both the buyer's right to reject and his right to revoke an acceptance are subject to the seller's right to *cure* the non-conformity. See § 2-508(1). [233-233]

   a. **Beyond contract:** Even *after* the time for performance under the contract has passed, the seller has a limited right to cure: he gets additional time to cure once the time for delivery under the contract has passed, if he *reasonably thought* that either: (1) the goods, though non-conforming, would be *acceptable* to the buyer; or (2) the buyer would be satisfied with a *money allowance*. See UCC § 2-508(2).

5. **Installment contracts:** The Code is more lenient to sellers under *installment* contracts (i.e., contracts calling for several deliveries) than in single delivery contracts. In the case of an installment contract, "the buyer may reject any installment which is non-conforming if the non-conformity *substantially impairs the value* of that installment and *cannot be cured*...." § 2-612(2).

   a. **Slight non-conformity not enough:** So a *slight* non-conformity in one installment does not allow the buyer to reject it, as he could in a single-delivery contract. [230]

   Example: Cotton, Inc. contracts to deliver 100 blue towels each month to Hotel for one calendar year. This monthly delivery is intended to replenish Hotel's existing stock of towels as they wear out. In July, Cotton delivers only 97 blue towels, and indicates that it will make up for this shortage by delivering 103 towels in August. Assume that there's no reason to believe that Hotel can't simply keep 3 of its pre-July towels in service for one extra month.

   The non-conformity (the 3-towel shortage) hasn't "substantially impaired the value" of the July installment. Therefore, Hotel can't reject the 97 towels (as it could in a one-shot deal for 100 towels, assuming that the shortage was not curable).

   i. **Right to cure:** Even where the non-conformity is major, the buyer can't reject the installment without giving the seller a *chance to cure* if circumstances permit. (This rule is the same as in the non-installment "one-shot" scenario.)

   b. **Cancellation of whole:** The buyer has the right to cancel the *entire installment contract* if the defect is grave enough: cancellation of the whole is allowed if the defective installment "*substantially impairs* the value of the *whole contract*." § 2-612(3). [231]

   Example: Seller contracts to deliver a computer on May 1, as well as a printer on June 1 customized to work only with that computer. Buyer's application requires both parts to work successfully. Seller delivers a defective computer on May 1, fails in its first attempt to cure, and says that it won't make any further attempts to do so.

   Buyer can cancel the whole contract, since the defect in the computer substantially impairs the value to him of the whole contract, including the customized printer. [231]

i. Reasonable fears of later non-conformities: Another way the defective installment might impair the value of the whole contract is if the defect in the early installment gives the buyer **reasonable fears** that the seller will not adequately perform on the later installments, and the seller fails to give satisfactory assurances that this will not be the case. [231]

V. EXCUSE OF CONDITIONS

A. Introduction: In some instances, the non-occurrence of a condition is *"excused,"* so that the other party nonetheless must perform. [236]

B. Hindrance: Where one party's duty is conditional on an event, and that same party's wrongful conduct *prevents* the occurrence of the condition, the non-occurrence of the condition is excused, and the party must perform despite the non-occurrence. [236-238]

1. Implied promise of cooperation: Courts sometimes express this concept by saying that each party makes the other an "implied promise of cooperation." One consequence of a breach of this implied promise is that the non-occurrence of the condition to that party's duty is excused.

> **Example:** P agrees to live with D, his grandmother, and to care for her for the rest of her life, in return for D's promise to leave P $100,000 in D's will. P lives with D for seven years, at the end of which D unreasonably forces P to leave the house. Five years later, D dies. P will be able to recover the $100,000, even though he did not live with D for the rest of her life. The reason is that the non-occurrence of the condition — caring for D for the rest of her life — was excused by D's failure to cooperate.

a. Causality issue: But even if the beneficiary of a condition failed to use reasonable efforts to cause the condition to be satisfied, the condition won't be deemed excused unless the beneficiary's failure to make reasonable efforts *substantially contributed* to the non-occurrence of the condition. That is, if the condition *wouldn't have been satisfied even if the beneficiary had made all reasonable efforts to make it be satisfied*, no constructive waiver will be found. [237]

> **Example:** Seller contracts to sell Blackacre to Buyer. Buyer's duty to close is made conditional on Buyer's obtaining a mortgage of at least $200,000 at no more than 7% from First Bank. Buyer never submits any application to First Bank. However, in a breach action brought by Seller, Buyer shows that even if Buyer *had* submitted a complete and truthful application to First Bank, First Bank would not have given a loan of at least $200,000 at an interest rate of 7% or lower.
>
> In this scenario, Buyer's failure to make the reasonable efforts to satisfy the condition (i.e., failure to make an application) did not change the outcome — the condition wouldn't have been satisfied anyway — so Buyer will be entitled to rely on the non-occurrence of the condition.

C. Waiver: A party who owes a conditional duty may indicate that he will *not insist* upon the occurrence of the condition before performing. A court will often take the party at his word, and enforce that party's willingness to forego the benefit of the condition. In this event, the party is said to have *waived* the condition. [238-241]

1. Minor conditions: Generally, the court is much more likely to find that the condition is waived if it is a *minor* one, such as a procedural or technical one. [255]

2. **Continuation of performance:** If a promisor *continues his own performance* after learning that a condition of duty has failed to occur, his conduct is likely to be found to operate as a waiver of the condition. [239]

> **Example:** Insurer insures Owner's house for fire; Insurer's duty to pay a claim is expressly conditional upon notice by Owner within seven days of any fire. Owner gives notice three weeks after a fire. Insurer sends an adjuster, attempts to make a settlement, and otherwise behaves as if it is not insisting on strict compliance with the notice provision. This continuation of performance will probably be found to be a waiver of the timely-notice condition.

a. **Right to damages not lost:** When a party continues his own performance after breach, or otherwise waives a condition, he has *not* necessarily lost his right to recover *damages,* if the non-occurrence of the condition was also a *breach* of a promise. [240]

b. **Waiver of subsequent conditions:** If a contract contains a series of similar conditions, will waiver of one condition (e.g., by the acceptance of a defective performance) excuse the later conditions? Generally, the answer is "no." However, *if a party accepts several similarly defective performances without objecting, his conduct may lead the other party to justifiably conclude that all conditions were intended to be excused.* If so, these later conditions are *waived*. [240]

> **Example:** P contracts to build a movie theater for D. The contract price is to be paid in installments, and an architect's certificate is a condition to D's duty to make each installment. However, D makes six or seven payments without insisting on such a certificate. When P does not receive the final portion of the contract price, he sues. D defends on the grounds that no architect's certificate for the last payment was ever procured.
>
> *Held*, for P. D, by his continued failure to enforce the requirement of a certificate, has waived his right to assert that condition as to the final payment. [*McKenna v. Vernon*]. [240]

c. **Retraction of waiver:** If there has been no consideration given for the waiver, and the party receiving the benefit of the waiver *has not detrimentally relied* on it, the person who waived may at any time *retract* the waiver, thereby *reinstating* the condition. [241]

> **Example:** On February 1, Sehl agrees to sell his house to Bye. Bye makes a $5,000 deposit. The contract provides that closing will occur on April 1, with time to be of the essence, so that if Bye is not ready to close by exactly April 1, Sehl may retain the deposit. On February 15, Sehl tells Bye that Sehl will not insist on the April 1 date, and that Sehl will convey as long as Bye is ready to close by May 1. On February 20 (before Bye has relied in any way on the later closing date), Sehl tells Bye, "I've changed my mind. I'm insisting that you close by April 1, or I'll keep your deposit."
>
> Since Bye has not yet detrimentally relied on Sehl's waiver of the condition that Bye close by April 1, Sehl's reinstatement of the condition was proper. Therefore, if Bye isn't ready to close on April 1, and tries to close on April 9, Sehl can refuse to do so, and can keep Bye's deposit.
>
> But now suppose that Bye *relied* on the Feb. 15 waiver, by waiting until March 20 to apply for a mortgage (a date that would still have been enough in advance of the new May 1 closing date to allow Bye to get an appropriate mortgage). Suppose further that on March 28, Sehl attempted to reinstate the April 1 closing date. Bye's material change of position would make it unjust for Sehl to reinstate the condition, so Sehl will not be permitted to do so, and the waiver of closing until May 1 will stand. [242]

VI. REPUDIATION AND PROSPECTIVE INABILITY TO PERFORM

A. General effect of prospective breach: If a party indicates that he will *subsequently* be unable or unwilling to perform, this will act as the non-occurrence of a constructive condition, in the same way as a present material breach does. In other words, the other party has the right to *suspend his own performance*. [244]

    1. Distinction: Where the party indicates that he will *refuse* to perform, this is called an *"anticipatory repudiation"* of the contract. If he indicates that he would like to perform but will be unable to do so, this is an indication of *"prospective inability to perform"* but not repudiation; however, the consequence is still that the other party may suspend performance. [244]

B. Insolvency or financial inability: If a party is *insolvent* or otherwise financially incapable of performing, this will entitle the other party to stop performance.

    1. Cancellation: If the prospective inability or unwillingness to perform is *certain* or almost certain, the other party can not only suspend her performance, but can actually *cancel* the contract. But where it is not so clear whether the first party will be unable or unwilling to perform, the other party may only *suspend* performance.

C. Right to adequate assurance of performance: If a party's conduct or words don't constitute an outright repudiation, but merely suggest that that party may not perform, the other party may *demand assurances* that the first party will perform. If the first party fails to provide these assurances, this failure will itself be *considered a repudiation*, entitling the innocent party to cancel. [245-249]

    1. UCC § 2-609: Thus UCC § 2-609(1) provides that "when reasonable grounds for insecurity arise with respect to the performance of either party the other may *in writing demand adequate assurance of due performance* and *until he receives such assurance* may, if commercially reasonable, *suspend any performance* for which he has not already received the agreed return." [245]

        Example: Buyer places two orders (separate contracts) with Seller, one for shipment on July 1 and the other for shipment on September 1. Each shipment is to be paid for within 30 days. Seller ships the first order promptly, and by August 28 the bill is almost one month past due.

        Seller may in writing demand assurances that Buyer will pay for both the first order and the second order in a timely fashion. If Buyer fails to respond, Seller may cancel the second contract, and sue for breach of both. But if Buyer furnishes reasonable assurances — as by demonstrating that non-payment of the first invoice was a clerical omission, and immediately rectifying it — Seller must reinstate the second contract.

    2. Repudiation: Once the party who has reasonable grounds for insecurity makes a written demand for adequate assurance, the other party *must furnish the requested assurance within a reasonable time*. If the receiving party *doesn't* do this, the party who made the demand for assurance may *treat the failure to give it as a repudiation*, and may cancel the contract even though the time for performance has not yet arrived. See UCC § 2-609(4): "After receipt of a justified demand[,] failure to provide within a reasonable time not exceeding thirty days such assurance of due performance as is adequate under the circumstances of the particular case *is a repudiation of the contract.*" [246]

    3. What qualifies as "demand for assurance": Notice that the party who is worried that the other may default gets rights under § 2-609(1) only if the worrier "in writing *demand[s] adequate assurance* of due performance[.]" What words constitute a "demand for assurances"?

Courts are generally pretty *easy to satisfy* on this point: they usually hold that the writing *does not need to expressly use the words "demand" or "assurances."*

a. **A general insistence on performance suffices:** Rather, it's usually enough if the worried party (call her *A*) gets across in writing to the possibly-about-to-default party (*B*) the more general message that *A has reason to fear that B may default,* and that if *B* doesn't promptly show she intends to perform, *A intends to assert all her legal rights*. [252]

Example: Buyer writes (accurately) to Seller, "You've been consistently late on delivery under our other recent contracts with you. As to the present contract, if you don't satisfy us immediately that you will make next week's delivery on time, we will cancel the contract now, and pursue our legal remedies." This probably qualifies as a "demand for assurances" § 2-609, even though it doesn't use the words "demand" or "assurances." Therefore, if Seller doesn't furnish the requested assurance of timely delivery reasonably soon, Buyer will have the right to cancel the contract (and procure substitute goods) even before the contracted-for delivery date arrives. [Cf. *Rocheux Int'l of N.J. v. U.S. Merchants Fin. Group*] [250]

CHAPTER 8

ANTICIPATORY REPUDIATION AND OTHER ASPECTS OF BREACH

I. ANTICIPATORY REPUDIATION

A. **General rule:** If a party makes it clear, even before his performance is due, that he cannot or will not perform, he is said to have *anticipatorily repudiated* the contract. All states except Massachusetts allow the victim of such an anticipatory repudiation to *sue before the repudiator's time for performance has arrived*. This is sometimes called the rule of *Hochster v. De La Tour*. [262]

Example: Star promises Movie Co. that Star will act in Movie Co.'s movie, shooting for which is scheduled to commence in the U.S. on July 1. On June 1, Star announces to the press that he is going to live abroad for a year beginning the next day and will not do the movie. Under the rule of *Hochster v. De La Tour*, in force in nearly all states, Movie Co. can sue Star for breach as soon as he issues his press statement; Movie Co. need not wait until July 1, the time at which Star's performance is due.

B. **What constitutes repudiation:** An anticipatory repudiation occurs whenever a party clearly indicates that he cannot or will not perform his contractual duty. [263-264]

1. **Statement:** Sometimes, the repudiation takes the form of a *statement* by the promisor that he intends not to perform. (The above example illustrates this.)

a. **Vague doubts not enough:** But the fact that the promisor states *vague doubts* about his willingness or ability to perform is *not enough*. [263-264]

Example: On the basic facts of the above example, suppose Star says, "I'm feeling pretty exhausted, so I don't know if I'll be able to perform the role, but let's hope I'll feel well enough." This would probably not be an anticipatory repudiation, because it is equivocal.

Note: But even the expression of vague doubts may entitle the promisee to request *assurances of performance*, and the promisor's failure to give such assurances would be a repudiation. See *supra*, p. C-43.

b. **Grudging willingness to perform:** Similarly, if the promisor merely indicates *unhappiness* about the deal, or a feeling that it is "unfair," or a wish to get out of it, this will not be a repudiation as long as the promisor either (1) indicates that if legally obligated to do so, he will perform or (2) refrains from any clear indication that he intends *not* to perform. [263]

2. **Voluntary actions:** The repudiation may occur by means of an *act* by the promisor that makes his performance impossible. [264]

> **Example**: Seller contracts to convey Blackacre to Buyer, the closing to take place on July 1. On June 15, Seller conveys Blackacre to X. This is an anticipatory repudiation by action, and Buyer may sue immediately, rather than waiting until July 1.

3. **Prospective inability to perform:** Something analogous to anticipatory repudiation occurs when it becomes evident that the promisor will be *unable* to perform, even though he desires to do so. When this occurs, all courts agree that the promisee may *suspend her performance*. But courts are split on whether the promisee may bring an immediate suit for breach, as she is allowed to do where the repudiation is a statement or a voluntary act. [264]

   a. **Insolvency:** The promisor's *insolvency* usually is *not* considered to be the type of anticipatory repudiation that allows the other party to sue immediately for breach. But the promisee may request assurances of performance, and if the promisor can't give these (e.g., he can't show that he will become sufficiently solvent to perform), then an immediate suit for breach is allowed.

II. OTHER ASPECTS OF REPUDIATION

A. **Repudiation after performance is due:** Similar rules apply where a party's time for performance becomes due, and the party then repudiates (i.e., he indicates by word or deed that he cannot or will not perform). Here, even though the repudiation is not "anticipatory," the other party may cancel the contract and bring an immediate suit for breach, just as in the anticipatory situation. [266]

B. **Retraction of repudiation:** A repudiation (whether anticipatory or occurring after the time for performance) may normally be *retracted* until some event occurs to make the repudiation final.

1. **Final acts:** In most courts, the repudiator's time to retract *ends* as soon as the other party: (1) *sues* for breach; (2) *changes her position* materially in *reliance* on the repudiation; or (3) states that she *regards the repudiation as final*. See UCC § 2-611(1). [266]

2. **Cancellation and new contract with someone else:** These retraction rules mean that if the repudiatee cancels the contract and *makes an alternative contract* with someone else, the repudiation can no longer be retracted. [267]

   a. **UCC illustrations:** So, for instance, in a UCC context, the following events would *end* the repudiator's time to retract:

   ❏ The *buyer* repudiates, and the seller *sells the goods in question* to someone else (even if the repudiator didn't yet know of this sale);

   ❏ The *seller* repudiates, and the buyer instead *buys comparable goods* from someone else.

C. **Mitigation required:** After a repudiation occurs, the repudiatee may *not* simply ignore the repudiation and continue the contract, if this would aggravate her damages. That is, the repudiatee must *mitigate her damages* by securing an alternative contract, if one is reasonably available. If she does not do this, she cannot recover the damages that could have been avoided. [267-268]

1. **UCC:** The UCC, in § 2-610(a), expresses this mitigation requirement by saying that the repudiatee may "for a *commercially reasonable time* await performance by the repudiating party...." Comment 1 to this section then says that "If [the repudiatee] awaits performance

beyond a commercially reasonable time he cannot recover resulting damages which he *should have avoided*." [267]

D. Repudiation ignored, then sued on: Most courts hold that the repudiatee may *insist on performance*, at least for a while, rather than cancelling the contract. Then, if the repudiator fails to retract the repudiation, the repudiatee may sue without being held to have waived any rights. [268]

   1. UCC in accord: The UCC similarly takes the view that the repudiatee's insistence on performance *does not constitute a waiver of his right to sue* for breach. [268]

      a. Party has choice of remedies: Whether it is the buyer or seller who anticipatorily repudiates, UCC § 2-610 gives the repudiatee a choice of remedies if the lost performance "will *substantially impair the value of the contract*" to him.The repudiatee gets the choice between:

      ❑ "*await[ing] performance* by the repudiating party" for a "commercially reasonable time"; or

      ❑ "*resort[ing] to any remedy for breach* ..., even though [the repudiatee] has notified the repudiating party that he would await the latter's performance and has urged retraction."

      Example: On Oct. 1, Buyer orders a new Vista automobile from Seller, delivery to occur Dec. 1. On Nov. 1, Seller repudiates by saying that he won't be able to ship the car for a full year. A full-year delay would certainly "substantially impair the value of the contract" to Buyer.

      Therefore, on Nov. 1, Buyer can choose: (1) he can wait to see whether Seller changes his mind and performs (and, if Buyer wishes, Buyer can urge Seller to change his mind); or (2) he can immediately "resort to any remedy for breach." Choice (2) means that he can *cover* (i.e., buy the goods from a different seller) and immediately sue for the contract-cover differential, or alternatively *not cover* and sue for the contract-market differential. If Buyer elects course (1) (waiting and hoping), he can at any time switch to course (2). [268]

E. Repudiatee owes no remaining duties: If the repudiatee *does not owe any remaining performances* as of the time of the repudiation, he is generally *not* permitted to bring an immediate suit for anticipatory repudiation; instead, he must wait until the time for the other party's performance is due. The reason is that the ordinary rule allowing immediate suit is designed to give the innocent party a chance to avoid having to render his own performance; where the innocent party does not owe any performance, the rationale does not apply. [269-270]

   1. Payment of money: This exception means that an anticipatory repudiation of an unconditional unilateral obligation to *pay money* at a fixed time does not give rise to a claim for breach until that time has arrived.

      Example: The tycoon Donald Tramp contracts to repay to Bank a $100 million loan, repayment to occur July 1. On June 1, Tramp declares publicly, "I won't be paying Bank back on July 1. Let 'em sue me." Because Bank does not owe any further performance under the contract (it's already made the loan), Bank may *not* sue Tramp until July 1 arrives and the payment is not made.

   2. Installments: This also means that if a debtor fails to pay a particular *installment* of a debt, and says that he will not make later payments, the creditor cannot bring suit for those later installments until they fall due. But lenders ordinarily avoid this problem by inserting an *"acceleration clause"* into the loan agreement, by which failure to pay one installment in a timely manner causes all later installments to become immediately due; such acceleration clauses are enforceable.

F. UCC damages for repudiation: Pay special attention to damages suffered by a *buyer* under a contract for the sale of goods, where the seller has anticipatorily repudiated the contract. UCC § 2-713(1) says that "the measure of damages for...repudiation by the seller is the difference between the market price *at the time when the buyer learned of the breach* and the contract price, together with any incidental and consequential damages." [270-271]

1. **Meaning:** The phrase "time when the buyer learned of the breach" is ambiguous. Most courts hold that this phrase means "time when the buyer *learned of the repudiation.*"

CHAPTER 9
STATUTE OF FRAUDS

I. INTRODUCTION

A. **Nature of Statute of Frauds:** Most contracts are valid despite the fact that they are only oral. A few types of contracts, however, are *unenforceable* unless they are *in writing*. Contracts that are unenforceable unless in writing are said to fall "within the Statute of Frauds." The Statute of Frauds is pretty much identical from state to state. [275-276]

B. **Five categories:** There are five categories of contracts which, in almost every state, fall with the Statute of Frauds and must therefore be in writing: [276]

1. **Suretyship:** A contract to answer for the *debt* or duty of *another*.

2. **Marriage:** A contract made upon *consideration of marriage*.

3. **Land contract:** A contract for the *sale of an interest in land*.

4. **One year:** A contract that cannot be performed within *one year* from its making.

5. **UCC:** Under the UCC, a contract for the sale of *goods* for a price of *$500* or more.

II. SURETYSHIP

A. **General rule:** A promise to pay the *debt* or duty of *another* is within the Statute of Frauds, and is therefore unenforceable unless in writing. [276-277]

B. **Main purpose rule:** If the promisor's chief purpose in making his promise of suretyship is to further *his own interest*, his promise does *not* fall within the Statute of Frauds. This is called the *"main purpose"* rule. [277-278]

> **Example:** Contractor contracts to build a house for Owner. In order to obtain the necessary supplies, Contractor seeks to procure them on credit from Supplier. Supplier is unwilling to look solely to Contractor's credit. Owner, in order to get the house built, orally promises Supplier that if Contractor does not pay the bill, Owner will make good on it. Because Owner's main purpose in giving the guarantee is to further his own economic interest — getting the house built — his promise does *not* fall within the suretyship provision, and is therefore not required to meet the Statute of Frauds. So it is enforceable even though oral.

C. **Memorandum requirement:** A document signed by the surety will meet the requirement of a writing even if it is *not addressed to the obligee*, even if it is not created until *long after the oral promise* of guarantee, and even if it is *never seen* by the obligee. (See p. C-51 for more about what type of document satisfies the memorandum requirement.)

> **Example:** *A* orally promises *B* that if *B* will extend credit to *C*, *A* will guarantee repayment. *B* extends credit to *C*. Two months later, *A* writes a letter to *C*, saying "I'm not sure you knew this, but I guaranteed *B* that I would repay your debt if you do not." The promise by *A* falls within the suretyship provision: *C* is the primary obligor, and *A* is the surety. However, the letter to *C* satisfies the writing requirement — even though this writing was

not addressed to *B*, or ever sent to him, it is a sufficient memorandum. Therefore, *A*'s oral guarantee is enforceable against him.

III. THE MARRIAGE PROVISION

A. Contract made upon consideration of marriage: A promise for which the consideration is *marriage* or a promise of marriage is within the Statute. [279]

> **Example:** Tycoon says to Starlet, his girlfriend, "If you will promise to marry me, I'll transfer to you title to my Malibu beach home even before our marriage." Starlet replies, "It's a deal." No document is signed. If Tycoon changes his mind, Starlet cannot sue to enforce either the promise of marriage or the promise to convey the beach house, since the consideration for both of these promises was her return promise to marry Tycoon. Conversely, if Starlet changes her mind, Tycoon cannot sue for breach either.

1. Exception for mutual promises to marry: But if an oral contract consists *solely of mutual promises to marry* (with no ancillary promises regarding property transfers), the contract is *not* within the Statute of Frauds, and is enforceable even though oral. That is, *an ordinary oral engagement is an enforceable contract*.

IV. THE LAND CONTRACT PROVISION

A. Generally: A promise to transfer or buy *any interest in land* is within the Statute. The Statute does not apply to the conveyance itself (which is governed by separate statutes everywhere) but rather to a *contract providing for* the subsequent conveyance of land. [279-284]

> **Example:** O, the owner of Blackacre, orally promises to convey it to *A* in return for *A*'s payment of $100,000. If *A* fails to come up with the $100,000 by closing date, O cannot sue for breach. Conversely, if O refuses to make the conveyance even though *A* tenders the money, *A* cannot sue O for breach.

1. Interests in land: The Statute applies to promises to transfer not only a fee simple interest in land, but to transfer most other kinds of interests in land. [280]

    a. Leases: For instance, a *lease* is generally an "interest in land," so that a promise to make a lease will generally be unenforceable if not in writing.

        i. One year or less: But most states have statutes making oral leases enforceable if their duration is *one year or less*.

    b. Mortgages: A promise to give a *mortgage* on real property as security for a loan also usually comes within the Statute.

    c. Contracts incidentally related to land: But contracts that relate only *incidentally* to land are not within the Statute. Thus a contract to *build a building* is not within the Statute, nor is a promise to lend money with which the borrower will buy land.

B. Part performance: Even if an oral contract for the transfer of an interest in land is not enforceable at the time it is made, subsequent *acts* by either party may make it enforceable. [280-284]

1. Conveyance by vendor: First, if the vendor under an oral land contract makes the contracted-for conveyance, he may recover the contract price.

2. Part performance of the alleged contract: Second, the court will often grant specific performance of an oral land contract at the vendee's request if the vendee has *committed acts* (apart from payment to the vendor) that seem to have been made in reliance on the alleged contract. However, the acts must be of a sort that the vendee is *very unlikely to have committed* had the alleged oral contract not existed. Generally, the acts by the vendee that are most likely to be found to have been made in reliance on the contract consist of his having taken possession of the property and *making improvements on it.* [281]

> **Example:** O owns Whiteacre, a vacant 1/4 acre parcel. P buys a mobile home; then, with O's permission, P pays for the pouring of a concrete foundation on Whiteacre. P has the home installed on the foundation and moves into the home without objection by O. Soon after, P asserts that O orally promised P that O would sell P the property for its market value, and that P bought the home and built the foundation in what O knew was reliance on this promise. O asserts that he made no such promise, and merely let P buy the home and pay for the foundation in lieu of paying rent to O for the first year of occupancy.
>
> At least if the court believes that O really made the alleged promise of sale, the court would likely conclude that P's improvements constituted part performance of that oral contract of sale. If so, the part performance would be deemed to take the contract out of the Statute of Frauds, making it enforceable against O by specific performance.

a. **The "unequivocally referable to the contract" standard:** There's an obvious danger that a purported "vendee" will *falsely claim* that she made improvements or otherwise relied on the promise of a conveyance. To fight this danger, many courts apply a tough standard: the would-be vendee has to show that her actions were *"unequivocally referable"* to the asserted oral agreement of sale, and not explainable by some other motive that's plausible under the known circumstances. [281]

> **Example:** P claims that D orally promised to sell P Blackacre, which contains a house, for $100,000. The only acts that P points to as her conduct in reliance on D's oral promise of sale are that she moved onto Blackacre, and made four $2,000 payments to D, one in each of four consecutive months, after which D refused any further payments and tried to evict P. P says that these were initial payments under an oral installment-sale agreement, and that at the end of all agreed-upon payments D was to transfer title to P. D claims that these payments were made pursuant not to a sale agreement but rather, to an oral lease cancellable by either party on one month's notice. D also shows that $2,000 would be a reasonable monthly lease payment for Blackacre.
>
> A court applying the tough "unequivocally referable" standard is likely to hold that P has *not met* standard here. That's because the payments here are just as consistent with being *lease payments* as with being installment-purchase payments. Therefore, it can't be said that the payments were unequivocally referable to the alleged oral installment-sale contract. The Statute of Frauds will apply, and the court will deny P an order of specific performance. [281]

V. THE ONE-YEAR PROVISION

A. **General rule:** If a promise contained in a contract is *incapable of being fully performed within one year* after the making of the contract, the contract must be in writing. [285]

1. **Time runs from making:** The one-year period is measured from the *time of execution of the contract*, not the time it will take the parties to perform.

> **Example:** On July 1, 2011, Star promises Network that Star will appear on a one-hour show that will take place in September 2012. This contract will be unenforceable if oral,

because it cannot be performed within one year of the day it was made. The fact that actual performance will take only one hour is irrelevant.

B. Impossibility: The one-year provision applies only if complete performance is *impossible* within one year after the making of the contract. The fact that performance within one year is highly unlikely is not enough. [285-287]

1. Judge from time of contract's execution: The possibility of performing the contract within one year must be judged *as of the time the contract is made*, not by benefit of hindsight.

Example: O orally promises *A* that O will pay *A* $10,000 if and when *A*'s husband dies. *A*'s husband does not die until four years after the promise. The promise is nonetheless enforceable, because viewed as of the moment the promise was made, it was possible that it could be completed within one year — the fact that it ended up not being performed within one year is irrelevant.

C. Impossibility or other excuse: It is only the possibility of *"performance,"* not the possibility of *"discharge,"* that takes a contract out of the one-year provision. Thus the fact that the contract might be discharged by *impossibility, frustration,* or some other excuse for non-performance will not take the contract out of the Statute. [286-287]

1. Fulfillment of principal purpose: It will often be hard to tell whether a certain kind of possible termination is by performance or by discharge. The test is whether, if the termination in question occurs, the contract has *fulfilled its principal purpose*. If it has fulfilled this purpose, there has been performance; if it has not, there has not been performance. Using this rule gives these results:

a. Personal service contract for multiple years: A *personal services contract* for more than one year of employment falls within the one-year rule (and is thus unenforceable unless in writing) even though the contract would terminate if the employee died. The reason is that when the employee dies, the contract has merely been *"discharged,"* not performed. [286]

Example: Boss and Worker orally agree that Worker will work for Boss for 5 years. Even though the contract would end at the moment of Worker's death or disability (which might happen in the first year), that possibility doesn't prevent the one-year provision of the Statute from applying. (Such an event would be a discharge, not a "full performance.") Therefore, the agreement is unenforceable against either party, because it's not in writing.

b. Lifetime employment: By contrast, a promise to employ someone for his *lifetime* is probably *not* within the one-year provision, since if the employee dies, the essential purpose of guaranteeing him a job forever has been satisfied. So an oral promise of a lifetime job is probably enforceable.

c. Non-compete: A promise by a seller of a business *not to compete* with the buyer for a period longer than a year is *not* within the one-year provision, since if the seller dies within a year, the buyer has received the equivalent of full performance (he knows the seller won't be competing with him).

D. Termination: Courts are *split* about whether the existence of a *termination clause* that permits termination in less than a year will remove a more-than-one-year contract from the one-year provision. [287]

Example: Boss orally hires Worker to work for three years. Their oral agreement allows either party to cancel on 60 days notice. Courts are split on whether this contract is within the one-year agreement and must therefore be in writing. The Second Restatement seems to say that the giving of 60 days notice would be a form of "performance," so that this contract will be enforceable even

CONTRACTS FOR THE SALE OF GOODS

though oral — Worker might give notice after one month on the job, in which case the contract would have been "performed" within three months of its making, less than one year.

E. Full performance on one side: Most courts hold that *full performance* by *one party* removes the contract from the one-year provision. This is true even if it actually takes that party more than one year to perform. [287]

> **Example:** On Jan. 1, 2011, Producer and Star orally agree that Star will perform in Producer's Broadway show 6 nights a week for 18 months, beginning on July 1, 2012. Star's fee for the entire run is set at a total of $200,000. Because Star develops cash needs, Producer prepays the entire $200,000 on May 1, 2012. Star then refuses to perform.
>
> Star's promise to perform is not within the one-year provision, because Producer has fully performed. That's true even though Producer's performance didn't occur until more than one year after the making of the contract.

F. Applies to all contracts: The rule that a contract incapable of performance within one year must satisfy the Statute applies to *all* contracts (including those that just miss falling within some other Statute of Frauds provision). For instance, even though the special UCC sale-of-goods statute (discussed below) requires a writing only where goods are to be sold for more than $500, a contract to sell goods for $300, to be delivered 8 months after the contract is made, must be in writing. [288]

VI. CONTRACTS FOR THE SALE OF GOODS

A. General rule: UCC § 2-201(1) says that "a contract for the sale of goods for the price of *$500 or more* is not enforceable...unless there is some writing sufficient to indicate that a contract for sale has been made...." So an oral contract for goods at a price of $500 or more is unenforceable under the UCC. [289-293]

B. Exceptions: Even if a sales contract is for more than $500, it is *exempted* from the Statute of Frauds requirement in three situations: [290-293]

1. Specially manufactured goods: No writing is required if the goods are to be *specially manufactured* for the buyer, are not suitable for sale to others, and the seller has made "either a substantial beginning of their manufacture or commitments for their procurement." § 2-201(3)(a).

2. Estoppel: A writing is also not required "if the party against whom enforcement is sought *admits* in his pleading, testimony or otherwise in court that a *contract for sale was made*, but the contract is not enforceable under this provision beyond the quantity of goods admitted." § 2-201(3)(b).

3. Goods accepted or paid for: Finally, no writing is required "with respect to goods for which *payment has been made* and accepted or which have been *received and accepted*." § 2-201(3)(c).

> **Example:** Buyer orally orders three pairs of shoes from Seller for a total of $600. Buyer then sends a check for this amount in advance payment. Once Seller takes the check and deposits it in the bank, Seller loses her Statute of Frauds defense.

VII. SATISFACTION BY A MEMORANDUM

A. General requirements for: Even if there is no signed "contract," a signed *"memorandum"* summarizing the agreement may be enough to meet the Statute of Frauds. A memorandum satisfies the Statute if it meets all of these requirements:

❏ it reasonably *identifies the subject* of the contract,

C
A
P
S
U
L
E

S
U
M
M
A
R
Y

❑ it indicates that a ***contract has been made*** between the parties,

❑ it states with reasonable certainty the ***essential terms*** of the contract, and

❑ it is ***signed*** "by or on behalf of ***the party to be charged.***" [293-297]

B. Signature: Because of the requirement of a signature "by the ***party to be charged,*"** some contracts will be enforceable against one party, but not against the other. [294]

> **Example:** Buyer orally agrees to buy Owner's house for $200,000. Buyer then sends a document marked "confirmation," which states, "This confirms our agreement whereby I will buy your house for $200,000. [signed, Buyer]" Owner can enforce the agreement against Buyer, but Buyer cannot enforce it against Owner, since only Buyer has signed the memorandum.

C. UCC: Under the UCC, a writing satisfies the Statute if it is "sufficient to indicate that a contract for sale has been made between the parties and [is] signed by the party against whom enforcement is sought...." § 2-201(2). [295-297]

1. Omissions: Even if the writing contains a ***mistake*** as to a term, there will often be enough to satisfy the Statute, under the UCC. For instance, a mistake on ***price*** or quantity, or even description of the item, will not be fatal (but plaintiff may only recover for the quantity actually stated in the memorandum). Contrast this with non-UCC cases, where a major mistake is likely to invalidate the memorandum.

2. Confirmation: Under the UCC, there is one situation in which a memorandum will be enforceable even against a party who does ***not*** sign it: if the deal is ***between merchants***, one merchant who receives a signed ***confirmation*** from the other party will generally be bound, unless the recipient ***objects*** within 10 days after receiving the confirmation.

> **Example**: Buyer and Seller are both merchants (i.e., they deal in goods of the kind in question). Buyer telephones Seller to order 1,000 widgets at $10 apiece. Immediately after receiving the order, Seller sends a written confirmation, correctly listing the quantity and price. Assume that this confirmation constitutes a memorandum which would be enforceable by Buyer against Seller. Unless Buyer objects in writing within 10 days after receiving the memo, he will be bound by it, just as if he had signed it.

VIII. ORAL RESCISSION AND MODIFICATION

A. Oral rescission: Where a contract is in writing, it can be ***orally rescinded*** (i.e., orally cancelled) even though the original was required to be in writing because of the Statute. That is, ***a rescission does not have to satisfy the Statute of Frauds.*** [298]

B. Modification: Application of the Statute of Frauds to oral ***modifications*** is trickier.

1. General rule: Generally, to determine whether an oral modification of an existing contract is effective, ***the contract as modified must be treated as if it were an original contract***. This is true whether the original contract is oral or written. [298]

    a. Consequence: If the modifications are unenforceable under this test, ***the original contract is left standing***. That is, the modification is treated as if it never occurred.

2. Reliance on oral modification: But if either party ***materially changes his position*** in ***reliance*** on an oral modification, the court may enforce the modification despite the Statute.

3. Modification of contracts under UCC : Contracts under the UCC work pretty much the same way: if the contract ***as modified*** would (if it were an original contract) have to meet the Statute of Frauds, any modification of a ***key term*** (e.g., price or quantity) must probably be in writing. [299]

C
A
P
S
U
L
E

S
U
M
M
A
R
Y

a. **Original left standing:** So if the modification of a key term is unenforceable under this rule, then the original contract is probably left standing (though this is not certain).

> **Example:** Seller agrees in writing to sell Buyer 100 widgets for a total of $1,000. The parties then orally agree to change the quantity to 150, for $1,500. The modification is not binding because not in writing. In that event, the original contract would probably be left in force.

  i. **Minor term:** But probably a *minor term may* be modified orally, as long as the major terms (description, price and quantity) remain unchanged. For instance, on the above example, suppose that the oral modification consists of a 2-week change in the delivery date. It's likely that a court would find that this change is effective even though oral, because it's on a minor point. (This is the "passing through" theory — the original writing "passes through" to the revised deal.) [299]

C. **No-oral-rescission-or-modification clauses:** The parties are always free to *agree*, in the original writing, that the contract may not be rescinded or modified except via a writing signed by both. Such a clause will be *enforced*. [299]

  1. **Sale of goods:** In the case of contracts for the sale of goods, the UCC expressly provides for the enforcement of such no-oral-rescission-or-modification clauses: "a signed agreement which *excludes modification or rescission* except by a signed writing *cannot be otherwise modified or rescinded*...." (§ 2-209(2).) [299]

   a. **Invalid change as waiver:** If an oral rescission or modification of a contract for the sale of goods is ineffective because it violates a no-oral-rescission-or-modification clause in the original contract, the rescission or modification may nonetheless "operate as a *waiver.*" (§ 2-209(4).) This means that if, following such an ineffective rescission or modification, one party *changes his position* (as by buying the contracted-for goods elsewhere), the other party will have waived his rights to insist upon enforcement of the original contract.

    i. **Retraction:** However, such a waiver may be *retracted* "unless the retraction would be unjust in view of a material *change of position* in reliance on the waiver." (§ 2-209(5).) [299]

> **Example:** Buyer and seller agree in writing that Seller will ship certain goods to Buyer to arrive by Dec. 1. The total contract price is $10,000 (bringing the contract within the Statute of Frauds). The contract says that no oral modifications will be effective. On Nov. 15, Seller phones Buyer and says, "Our shipping department is running a little behind; can we have until Dec. 10?" Buyer says, "Yes." One hour later, Buyer realizes that the later shipment will cause him problems, so he phones back and says to Seller, "I must now insist on the original Dec. 1 date."
>
> Assuming that during the intervening hour, Seller has not changed his position in reliance on the extra time, Buyer's retraction of the waiver will be effective, and the due date is now restored to the original Dec. 1 date.

IX. RESTITUTION, RELIANCE AND ESTOPPEL

A. **Quasi-contractual recovery:** A plaintiff who has rendered *part performance* under an oral agreement falling within the Statute of Frauds may recover in *quasi-contract* for the *value of benefits* he has conferred upon the defendant.

> **Example:** Landlord orally agrees to rent Blackacre to Tenant for two years, at a rent of $1,000 per month. After Tenant has occupied the premises for two months, Tenant moves out. Even

though the agreement is unenforceable because it is for an interest in land and must therefore be in writing, Landlord can recover the reasonable value of Tenant's two-month occupancy.

1. **Not limited by contract price:** The plaintiff's quasi-contract recovery is *not limited* to the *pro-rata contract price*, in most courts. (*Example*: On the facts of the above example, if Landlord can show that the fair market value of a lease for Blackacre is $2,000 a month, he may recover this amount times two months, even though the pro-rata lease amount is only $1,000 per month.)

B. **Promissory estoppel:** Instead of a quasi-contract suit (which will generally protect only the plaintiff's restitution or reliance interest), a plaintiff who has relied on a contract that is unenforceable due to non-compliance with the Statute of Frauds may instead use the doctrine of *promissory estoppel*. Where one party to an oral agreement foreseeably and reasonably *relies to his detriment* on the existence of the agreement, the court may enforce the agreement notwithstanding the Statute, if this is the only way to avoid injustice. [300-302]

   Example: P works for an established company, and has good job security. He orally accepts a two-year oral employment agreement with D, another company. By leaving his present employer, P loses valuable pension and other rights. Once P leaves the old employer to take the job with D, a court may well apply promissory estoppel to hold that the P-D agreement is enforceable notwithstanding non-compliance with the Statute of Frauds, since injustice cannot be otherwise prevented.

   1. **Misrepresentation regarding Statute:** Courts are especially likely to apply promissory estoppel where the defendant has intentionally and falsely told the plaintiff that the contract is *not* within the Statute, or that a writing will subsequently be executed, or that the defense of the Statute will not be used. [301-302]

   2. **UCC:** Courts are split about whether promissory estoppel may be a substitute for the Statute of Frauds in a *UCC context*. [302]

   3. **Degree of injury and unjust enrichment:** The more grievously the plaintiff is injured (or the more extensively the defendant is unjustly enriched) by application of the Statute, the more likely the court is to allow promissory estoppel to be a substitute for compliance with the Statute. [302]

CHAPTER 10

REMEDIES

I. INTRODUCTION

A. **Distinction:** Distinguish between a suit brought *on the contract*, and a suit brought off the contract, i.e., in *quasi-contract*. [310]

   1. **Suit on the contract:** Where the parties have formed a legally enforceable contract, and the defendant (but not the plaintiff) has breached the contract, the plaintiff will normally sue *"on the contract."* That is, he will bring a suit for breach of contract, and the court will look to the contract to determine whether there has indeed been a breach, and for help in calculating damages.

   2. **Quasi-contract:** But in other circumstances, the plaintiff will bring a suit in *"quasi-contract."* Here, the plaintiff is not really asking for enforcement of the contract; instead, she is usually asking for damages based on the actual value of his performance, irrespective of any price set out in the contract. Situations where a quasi-contract recovery may be available include:

      a. Where the contract is unenforceably *vague*;

      b. Where the contract is *illegal*;

      c. Where the parties are discharged because of *impossibility* or frustration of purpose;

d. Where plaintiff has herself *materially breached* the contract.

II. EQUITABLE REMEDIES

A. Two types: Sometimes the court will award *"equitable remedies"* instead of the usual remedy of money damages. There are two types of equitable relief relevant to contract cases: (1) *specific performance*; and (2) *injunctions*. [311-317]

  1. Specific performance: A decree for *specific performance* orders the promisor to *render the promised performance*. (*Example*: A contracts to sell Blackacre to B on a stated date for a stated price. A then wrongfully refuses to make the conveyance. A court will probably award specific performance. That is, it will order A to make the conveyance.)

  2. Injunction: An *injunction* directs a party to *refrain* from doing a particular act. It is especially common in cases where the defendant is sued by his former employer and charged with breaching an employment contract by working for a competitor.

  Example: D signs a contract with P, his employer, providing that D will not work for any competitor in the same city for one year after termination. D then quits and immediately goes to work for a competitor. If P sues on the non-compete, a court will probably enjoin D from working for the competitor for the year.

B. Limitations on equitable remedies: There are three important limits on the willingness of the court to issue either a decree of specific performance or an injunction: [312-314]

  1. Inadequacy of damages: Equitable relief for breach of contract will not be granted unless *damages are not adequate to protect the injured party*. Two reasons why damages might not be adequate in a contracts case are: (1) because the injury cannot be estimated with sufficient certainty; or (2) because money cannot purchase a substitute for the contracted-for performance. (*Example* of (2): Each piece of land is deemed "unique", so an award of damages for breach by the vendor in a land sale contract will not be adequate, and specific performance will be decreed.) [312-315]

  2. Definiteness: The court will not give equitable relief unless the contract's terms are *definite enough* to enable the court to frame an adequate order. [314]

  3. Difficulty of enforcement: Finally, the court will not grant equitable relief where there are likely to be significant difficulties in *enforcing* and *supervising* the order. (*Example*: Courts usually will not grant specific performance of a personal service contract, because the court thinks it will not be able to supervise defendant's performance to determine whether it satisfies the contract.) [314-314]

C. Land-sale contracts: The most common situation for specific performance is where defendant breaches a contract under which he is to convey a particular *piece of land* to the plaintiff. [314]

  1. Breach by buyer: Courts also often grant specific performance of a land-sale contract where the seller has not yet conveyed, and it is the *buyer who breaches*. (*Example*: A contracts to sell Blackacre to B. If A fails to convey, a court will order him to do so in return for the purchase price. If B fails to come up with the purchase price, the court will order him to pay that price and will then give him title.)

D. Personal services contracts: [315]

  1. No specific performance: Courts almost *never* order specific performance of a contract for *personal services*. This is true on both sides: the court will not order the employer to resume the employment, nor will it order the employee to perform the services.

2. **Injunction:**   But where the employee under an employment contract breaches, the court may be willing to grant an ***injunction*** preventing him from working for a competitor. The employer must show that: (1) the employee's services are ***unique*** or ***extraordinary***; and (2) the likely result will not be to leave the employee without other ***reasonable means of making a living***.

E. **Sale of goods:**   Specific performance will sometimes be granted in contracts involving the ***sale of goods***. This is especially likely in the case of ***output*** and ***requirements*** contracts, where the item is not in ready supply. [316]

> **Example:** P, a utility, contracts with D, a pipeline company, for D to supply all of P's requirements for natural gas for 10 years at a stated price. In a time of tight energy supplies, a court is likely to find that damages are not adequate to redress D's breach, because no other vendor will enter a similar fixed-price, long-term contract; therefore, the court will probably grant a decree of specific performance ordering D to continue with the contract.

III. VARIOUS DAMAGE MEASURES

A. **Three types:**   There are three distinct kinds of interests on the part of a disappointed contracting party which may be protected by courts: [318]

1. **Expectation:**   In most breach of contract cases, the plaintiff will seek, and receive, protection for her *"expectation interest."* Here, the court attempts to ***put the plaintiff in the position he would have been in had the contract been performed***. In other words, the plaintiff is given the *"benefit of her bargain,"* including any ***profits*** she would have made from the contract.

2. **Reliance:**   Sometimes the plaintiff receives protection for his ***reliance interest***. Here, the court puts the plaintiff in ***as good a position as he was in before the contract was made***. To do this, the court usually awards the plaintiff his ***out-of-pocket*** costs incurred in the performance he has already rendered (including preparation to perform). When reliance is protected, the plaintiff does not recover any part of the profits he would have made on the contract had it been completed.

   a. **When used:**   The reliance interest is used mainly: (1) when it is impossible to ***measure*** the plaintiff's expectation interest accurately (e.g., when profits from a new business which the plaintiff would have been able to operate cannot be computed accurately); and (2) when the plaintiff recovers on a ***promissory estoppel*** theory.

3. **Restitution:**   Finally, courts sometimes protect the plaintiff's *"restitution interest."* That is, the court forces the defendant to pay the plaintiff an amount equal to the ***benefit which the defendant has received*** from the plaintiff's performance. Restitution is designed to prevent unjust enrichment.

   a. **When used:**   The restitution measure is most commonly used where: (1) a non-breaching plaintiff has partly performed, and the restitution measure is greater than the contract price; and (2) a breaching plaintiff has not substantially performed, but is allowed to recover the benefit of what he has conferred on the defendant.

   Note: In contract actions, all three of these measures are used at least some of the time. In quasi-contract actions, expectation damages are almost never awarded, but reliance and restitution damages frequently are. (For instance, reliance damages are often used in promissory estoppel cases where the suit is really in quasi-contract, and restitution is used by materially-breaching plaintiffs who are in effect suing in quasi-contract.)

IV. EXPECTATION DAMAGES

A. Defined: Expectation damages are the usual measure of damages for breach of contract. The court tries to ***put the plaintiff in the position he would have been in had the contract been performed by the defendant***. The plaintiff should end up with a sum equal to the ***profit*** he would have made had the contract been completed. [318-319]

> **Example 1:** On March 1, D, the owner of Blackacre, contracts to sell it to P on July 1 for $500,000. Real estate prices rise, and D reneges. On July 1, D sells the property for $700,000 (which is the highest price any likely buyer would have paid). P will be permitted to recover $200,000 from D, the difference between the contract price and the market price at the time of breach, since that amount will put P in the position he would have been in (making a $200,000 profit) had the contract been performed.

B. Formula for calculating:

Here's a good general formula for computing a plantiff's expectation damages:

> [1] *the amount by which the value of the defendant's **actual performance** was less than the **value of the promised performance***
>
> minus
>
> [2] *whatever **benefits**, if any, the plaintiff received from **not having to complete his own performance**.*

Generally, the benefits in [2] are ***expenditures*** which the plaintiff would have had to make to complete his performance under the contract, but which he didn't have to make because the defendant breached first. [319-323]

> **Example of formula:** Contractor contracts with Owner to renovate an office building owned by Owner. The contract requires that the renovation be completed in time for Tenant, the sole tenant, to take possession by August 1. Tenant is scheduled to pay Owner August rent of $10,000. It would cost Owner $2,000 in utilities to operate the building for August if Tenant is there, but $0 if Tenant has not moved in yet. Contractor breaches by not completing the work until August 30, so that Tenant moves in on September 1. The only consequence to Owner from the delay is the loss of August's rent.
>
> Owner's expectation damages are: (1) the value to Owner of the August rent that he didn't receive because of the delay ($10,000) less (2) the $2,000 that Owner saved in utilities by virtue of the delay. So Owner can recover only $8,000.

C. Construction contracts: Many problems involving the computation of damages involve ***construction contracts***. We'll call the person doing the construction the "builder," and the person receiving the benefit of the work the "owner." [320]

1. Builder breaches: First, let's look at how the owner's damages are computed if the ***builder breaches***, and the owner has the work completed by a second builder. [320] A good formula for computing the owner's damages is:

> [1] The value the building ***would have had*** if it had been completed as agreed upon ...
>
> [2] Less the value of the building ***as completed*** by the second builder ...

> [3] Plus the amount by which (a) the ***totals paid*** by the owner to the first and second builders together ***exceed (b) the contract price*** ...
>
> [4] Plus any consequential damages from the ***delay***.

Example: Builder 1 contracts to build a house on Owner's land for $500,000. Builder 1 does the initial work defectively, then abandons the job in the middle of construction. At the time of abandonment, Owner has paid Builder 1 $200,000. If the house had been completed as contracted for, it would have been worth $600,000 (i.e., Owner made a favorable contract). Owner hires Builder 2 to complete the job for $400,000. Because the defective work done by Builder 1 before abandonment can't be readily remedied, the house as completed is worth only $550,000. Due to the delays caused by the breach, Owner loses $50,000 in rental income.

Owner can recover from Builder 1:

(1) $600,000 (value if completed as per the original contract) ....

(2) Less $550,000 (value as actually completed, due to Builder 1's poor work) ...

(3) Plus the difference between $600,000 (the sum of the $200,000 Owner paid to Builder 1 and the $400,000 he paid to Builder 2) and $500,000 (the contract price), or $100,000 ...

(4) Plus $50,000 lost rental as delay damages.

So Owner recovers:

$600,000 - $550,000 + 100,000 + $50,000, or

$200,000

2. **Owner breaches:** Now, let's look at how the ***builder's*** damages are computed if the ***owner breaches*** when the work has ***not yet been completed***.[1] [320] A good formula for computing the builder's damages is:

> [1] The money the builder has ***spent so far*** in fulfilling the contract (the builder's "***reliance***" cost; see *infra*, p. C-59, for more about reliance) ...
>
> [2] Less any ***salvage value*** to the builder from the partial performance, such as materials purchased that can be used on another project ("***loss avoided***") ...
>
> [3] Plus the ***profit*** the builder ***would have made*** had the contract been completed ...
>
> [4] Less any ***progress payments*** already made by the owner.

Example: Builder contracts to build a house on Owner's land for $500,000. At a time when Owner has paid Builder $60,000 and Builder has spent $200,000, Owner repudiates. Builder cancels and sues. The $200,000 spent by Builder includes $20,000 of lumber that he can use on another job. If the contract had been completed, Builder would have made a profit of $100,000. Builder can recover:

(1) The $200,000 he has spent in "reliance";

---

1. If the work has been completed, the builder will simply recover the contract price less any prior payments made by the owner.

(2) Less the $20,000 he can get for the lumber ("loss avoided");

(3) Plus the $100,000 profit he would have made had the project been completed on both sides;

(4) Less the $60,000 already paid by Owner.

So Builder recovers:

$200,000 - $20,000 + 100,000 - $60,000, or

$220,000

D. Overhead: The plaintiff's cost of completion (the amount he has saved by not having to finish) does *not* include any part of his *overhead*. [321]

E. Cost of completion or decrease in value: Where defendant has defectively performed, plaintiff normally can recover the *cost of remedying* defendant's defective performance. But if the cost of remedying defects is *clearly disproportionate* to the *loss in market value* from the defective performance, plaintiff will only recover the loss in market value. [321-322]

1. **Economic waste:** This principle is often applied where the defect is minor, and remedying it would involve *"economic waste,"* such as the *destruction of what has already been done*. [322-323]

   Example: Contractor contracts to build a house for Owner, with Reading pipe to be used. After the house is completely built, it is discovered that Contractor used Cohoes pipe rather than Reading pipe; the two are of virtually the same quality. Owner will be allowed to recover (or to subtract from the unpaid contract balance) only the difference in value between the two pipes (a negligible sum), not the much greater cost of ripping out the walls and all of the existing piping to make the replacement. [*Jacob & Youngs v. Kent*]

F. "Reasonable certainty": The plaintiff may only recover for losses which he establishes with *"reasonable certainty."* Mainly, this means that a plaintiff who claims that he would have *made profits* had the defendant not breached must show not only that there would have been profits, but also the likely *amount* of those profits. [323-325]

1. **Profits from a new business:** Courts are especially reluctant to award lost profits from a *new business*, that is, a business which at the time of breach was not yet in actual operation. [323-324]

2. **Cost of completion unknown:** Also, the "reasonable certainty" requirement may fail to be met where the plaintiff cannot show accurately enough what his *cost of completion* would have been. [324]

   Example: Contractor contracts to build a house for Owner for $100,000. After Contractor has done about half the work, Owner repudiates. If Contractor cannot demonstrate what his cost of completion would have been, he will be unable to recover expectation damages, and will have to be content with either reliance or restitution damages.

V. RELIANCE DAMAGES

A. Generally: *Reliance* damages are the damages needed to put the plaintiff in the *position he would have been in had the contract never been made*. Therefore, these damages usually equal the amount the plaintiff has *spent* in performing or in preparing to perform. They are used either where there is a contract but expectation damages cannot be accurately calculated, or where there is no contract but some relief is justifiable. The main situations where reliance damages are awarded are: [326-328]

1. **Profit too speculative:** Where expectation damages cannot be computed because plaintiff's *lost profits* are too speculative or uncertain. (For instance, where defendant's breach prevents plaintiff from developing a new business, profits are probably too speculative to be computed.) [327]

2. **Promissory estoppel:** Where plaintiff successfully brings an action based on *promissory estoppel*. Here, the suit is usually not truly on the contract, but is rather in quasi-contract. The court is trying to reduce injustice, so it gives plaintiff a "half-way" measure, less than expectation damages, but better than nothing. [327]

B. Limits on amount of reliance recovery: The plaintiff's reliance damages are sometimes *limited* to a sum smaller than the actual expenditures: [328]

1. **Contract price as limit:** Where D's only obligation under the contract is to pay a sum of money (the contract price), reliance damages will almost always be *limited to this contract price*. [328]

2. **Recovery limited to profits:** Also, most courts do *not* allow reliance damages to *exceed expectation damages*. However, the defendant has to bear the *burden of proving* what plaintiff's profit or loss would have been. [328]

   a. **Subtract amount of loss:** Another way to express this idea is that there will be *subtracted* from plaintiff's reliance recovery the amount of the *loss* which defendant shows plaintiff would have suffered had the contract been performed.

3. **Expenditures prior to signing:** The plaintiff will not normally be permitted to recover as reliance damages expenditures made *before the contract was signed*, since these expenditures were not made "in reliance on" the contract. [329]

C. Cost to plaintiff, not value to defendant: When reliance damages are awarded, they are usually calculated according to the *cost to the plaintiff* of his performance, not the value to the defendant. [329]

VI. RESTITUTION

A. Generally: The plaintiff's restitution interest is defined as the *value to the defendant of the plaintiff's performance*. Restitution's goal is to *prevent unjust enrichment*. [330]

1. **When used:** The main uses of the restitution measure are as follows: (1) a non-breaching plaintiff who has partly performed before the other party breached may bring suit on the contract, and not be limited by the contract price (as she would be for the expectation and reliance measures); and (2) a breaching plaintiff who has not substantially performed may bring a quasi-contract suit and recover the value that she has conferred upon the defendant. [330-331]

2. **Market value:** Restitution is based on the *value rendered to the defendant*, regardless of how much the conferring of that value costs the plaintiff and regardless of how much the plaintiff was injured by the defendant's breach. This value is usually the sum which the defendant would *have to pay to acquire the plaintiff's performance*, not the subjective value to the defendant.

B. Not limited to the contract price: The main use of the restitution measure is that, in most courts, *it is not limited by the contract price*. If the work done by P prior to D's breach has already enriched D in an amount greater than the contract price, this entire enrichment may be recovered by P. This makes restitution sometimes very attractive, compared with both reliance and expectation measures. [331]

> **Example:** Contractor agrees to build a house for Owner for $100,000. After Contractor has done 90% of the work, Owner repudiates. At trial, Contractor shows that Owner can now resell the mostly-built house for $120,000, not counting land. Contractor will be permitted to recover the whole $120,000 on a restitution theory, even though this sum is greater than the contract price (and thus greater than the expectation damages would be), and greater than the reliance measure (actual expenditures by Contractor).

1. **Not available where plaintiff has fully performed:**   If at the time of D's breach, P has *fully performed* the contract (and D only owes money, not some other kind of performance) most courts do *not allow P to recover restitution damages*. [331]

C. **Losing contract:**   Restitution may even be awarded where P has partly performed, and *would have lost money* had the contract been completed. [331] (*Example*: On the facts of the above example, assume that Contractor would have lost $10,000 had the contract been fulfilled. Contractor may use the restitution measure to collect $120,000, thus turning a $10,000 loss into a $10,000 profit.)

VII. SUBSTANTIAL PERFORMANCE AS A BASIS FOR SUIT ON THE CONTRACT

A. **Substantial performance generally:**   Where one party *substantially performs* (i.e., does not materially breach), the other is not relieved of his duties. If the latter refuses to perform, the substantially performing party has an action for breach of contract. [333]

1. **Expectation damages:**   Putting it more simply, *a party who substantially performs may sue for ordinary (expectation) damages for breach of contract, if the other party fails to perform*. The other party has a set-off or counterclaim for the damages he has suffered from the plaintiff's failure to completely perform. [333]

    Example: Contractor contracts to paint Owner's house for $10,000, with performance to be complete by April 1. There is no "time of the essence" clause, and no reason to believe that April 1 completion is especially important. Contractor finishes work on April 3. Owner refuses to pay. Contractor will be able to bring suit on the contract, and to recover expectation damages (the profit he would have made). Owner is not entitled to refuse to pay, and must simply be content with a counterclaim for damages (probably nominal ones) due to the late completion.

B. **Divisible contracts:**   If the contract is *divisible* into separate pairs of "agreed equivalents," a party who has substantially performed *one of the parts* may recover on the contract for that part. That's true even though he has materially breached with respect to the other portions. [335]

VIII. SUITS IN QUASI-CONTRACT

A. **Where allowed:**   There are a number of situations where recovery "on the contract" is not possible or allowed: (1) situations where there was no attempt even to form a contract, but the plaintiff deserves some measure of recovery anyway; (2) cases where there was an attempt to form a contract, but the contract is unenforceable because of Statute of Frauds, impossibility, illegality, etc.; (3) cases where there is an enforceable contract, but the plaintiff has materially breached, and therefore may not recover on the contract; and (4) cases where the defendant has breached but the plaintiff is not entitled to damages on the contract. In all of these situations, the plaintiff will often be allowed to recover in *"quasi-contract."* [335]

1. **Measure of damages:**   Courts almost never award expectation damages in quasi-contract suits. Both reliance damages and restitution damages are frequently awarded in quasi-contract suits (with courts deciding which of these two to use based on the equities of the particular case.). [335]

B. **No contract attempted:**   The courts sometimes award P a quasi-contractual recovery where *no contract was even attempted*.

1. **Rationale:** Courts do this on the theory that a person who has been **unjustly enriched** at the expense of another should be required to **make restitution**. [335] A person (P) may recover on such a theory if she meets the following requirements:

    [1] P **rendered a benefit** to another (D), who would be **unjustly enriched** if he were not required to pay for that benefit; and

    [2] P did **not** confer the benefit on D **"officiously,"** that is, she did not thrust the benefit upon D **against his will** or in circumstances where she should have known that D would not want the benefit; and

    [3] P did **not** confer the benefit on D **"gratuitously,"** i.e., **without expectation of compensation**.

2. **Emergency services:** The most common example is where P supplies **emergency services** to D, without first forming a contract to do so. [335]

    Example: P, a doctor, sees D lying unconscious in the street, and gives D CPR. The court will probably allow P to recover the fair market value of her services, in an action in quasi-contract.

C. **Unenforceable contracts:** The parties may attempt to form a binding contract which turns out to be **unenforceable** or avoidable. This may happen because of the Statute of Frauds, mistake, illegality, impossibility, or frustration of purpose. In any of these cases, the court will usually let P sue in quasi-contract, and recover either the value of the services performed (restitution) or P's reasonable expenditures (reliance). [336]

D. **Breaching plaintiff:** A plaintiff who has **materially breached** may normally bring a quasi-contract suit, and recover his **restitution interest**, less the defendant's damages for the breach. This is sometimes called a recovery in **"quantum meruit"** ("as much as he deserves"). [337]

    Example: P agrees to work for D for one year, payment of the $20,000 salary to be made at the end. P works for six months, then unjustifiably quits. P cannot recover "on the contract," because he has not substantially performed. But he will probably be allowed to recover in quasi-contract, for the fair value of the benefits he has conferred on D. The court will estimate these benefits (which will probably be one-half of the $20,000 annual salary), and will subtract the damage to D of P's not performing the second six months.

    1. **Construction cases:** Quasi-contract recovery by a breaching plaintiff is most often found in **construction** cases. Here, the builder gets to recover the **value to the owner of the work done**, even where the work does not constitute substantial performance of the contract. [337]

    2. **Limited to pro-rata contract price:** When a defaulting plaintiff sues in quasi-contract for his restitution interest, recovery is almost always limited to the **pro-rata contract price**, less the defendant's damages for breach. [339]

    3. **Willful default:** In many states, a defaulting plaintiff may not recover in quasi-contract if his breach is **"willful."** [340]

        Example: Contractor agrees to build a house for Owner for $100,000. The contract expressly provides that all walls will be insulated with non-asbestos-based insulation. Contractor instead knowingly installs asbestos-based insulation, in order to save $2,000 in material costs. Even though the resulting house has substantial value, many courts will not permit Contractor to recover anything at all, on the grounds that his breach was not only material but "willful," i.e., intentional and done for Contractor's financial advantage.

    4. **UCC gives partial restitution to breaching buyer:** The UCC gives a **breaching buyer** a right to partial restitution with respect to any **deposit** made to the seller before the buyer breached. Under

§ 2-718(2), the seller can only keep **20% of the total contract price** or **$500**, whichever amount is smaller — the balance must be refunded to the breaching buyer. [340]

> **Example:** Seller contracts to sell to Buyer 1,000 widgets at $2 each. The contract does not contain a liquidated damages clause. Buyer sends in a $700 deposit. Buyer cancels the order just before Seller is to ship. Seller suffers no damages, because he has a limited supply of the widgets, and sells the ones he had earmarked for Buyer to X instead, at the same price.
>
> Even though Buyer has breached, Seller may not keep the entire $700 deposit. Instead, Seller is entitled to keep only the lesser of: (i) 20% of the contract price ($400) and (ii) $500. Therefore, Seller may keep only $400, and must refund the other $300.

a. **Seller's counterclaim:** But where the buyer establishes such a right to restitution, the seller may **offset** the buyer's claim by any **actual damages** which he sustained as a result of the buyer's breach (computed by using Article 2's regular damages measures). § 2-718(3). So the seller owes the buyer a refund of the deposit in excess of the lesser of 20% of the contract price and $500, but can subtract from this refund seller's actual damages.

IX. FORESEEABILITY

A. **General rule:** The "rule of *Hadley v. Baxendale*" limits the damages which courts will award for breach of contract. The "rule" says that courts will not award consequential damages for breach unless the damages fall into one of two classes: [343-344]

1. **Arise naturally:** The damages were **foreseeable** by any reasonable person, regardless of whether the defendant actually foresaw them; or

2. **Remote or unusual consequences:** The damages were **remote or unusual**, but only if the defendant had **actual notice** of the possibility of these consequences.

> **Example:** P operates a mill, which has suspended operations because of a broken shaft. He brings the shaft to D, a carrier, to have it brought to another city for repairs. D knows that the item to be carried is a shaft of P's mill, but does not know that the mill is closed because of the broken shaft. D negligently delays delivery, causing the mill to stay closed for extra days. P sues for the profits lost during these extra days.
>
> *Held*, P cannot recover for these lost profits. The lost profits were not foreseeable to a reasonable person in D's position, nor was D on notice of the special fact that the mill was closed due to the broken shaft. [*Hadley v. Baxendale*]

B. **Parties may allocate risks themselves:** The rule of *Hadley* may always be **modified** by express agreement of the parties. For instance, if P puts D on notice of the special facts, this may cause damages to be awardable which would not otherwise be. Alternatively, the parties can simply agree that even unforeseen consequential damages shall be compensable. [344]

X. AVOIDABLE DAMAGES

A. **General rule:** Where P **might have avoided** a particular item of damage by reasonable effort, he **may not recover** for that item if he fails to make such an effort. This is sometimes called the **"duty to mitigate"** rule. (But it's a "duty" only in the sense that if P fails to do it, he'll lose the right to collect damages, not in the sense that P has breached some obligation.) [347]

> **Example:** P agrees to work as an employee of D for a two-year period, at an annual salary of $50,000. After two weeks on the job, P is wrongfully fired. P must make reasonable efforts to get another job. If he does not, the court will subtract from his recovery the amount which it

believes P could have earned at an alternative job with reasonable effort. Thus if the court believes that P could have lined up a $40,000-a-year job, P will only be allowed to recover at the rate of $10,000 per year for the remainder of the contract.

1. **Reasonableness:** The "duty to mitigate" only requires the plaintiff to make *reasonable efforts* to mitigate damages. For instance, P does not have to incur substantial expense or inconvenience, damage his reputation, or break any other contracts, in order to mitigate. [347-348]

B. **Sales contracts:** Here's what the UCC says about an aggrieved buyer or seller's obligation to mitigate: [350-351]

1. **Buyer:** If the seller either fails to deliver, or delivers defective goods which the buyer rejects, the *buyer* must *"cover"* for the goods if he can reasonably do so — he may not recover for those damages (e.g., lost profits) which could have been prevented had he covered. See UCC § 2-715(2)(a) (defining "consequential damages" to include only those losses "which could not reasonably be prevented by cover or otherwise…"). (If buyer does not cover when he could have done so, he will still be entitled to the difference between the market price at the time of the breach and the contract price, but he'll lose the ability to collect consequential damages that he might otherwise have gotten.) [350]

2. **Seller:** The *seller* has much less of a duty to mitigate, when it is the buyer who breaches by wrongfully rejecting the goods or repudiating before delivery. The seller can choose between reselling the goods (and collecting the difference between resale price and contract price), or not reselling them (and recovering the difference between market price and unpaid contract price); seller may also be able to recover lost profits. [350]

3. **Summary:** So in UCC cases, it is really only the buyer who has a practical duty to mitigate.

C. **Losses incurred in avoiding damages:** If the aggrieved party tries to mitigate his damages, and incurs *losses* or *expenses* in doing so, he may recover damages for these losses or expenses. As long as plaintiff acted *reasonably* in trying to mitigate, it does not matter whether his attempt was successful. [352]

XI. NOMINAL AND PUNITIVE DAMAGES

A. **Nominal damages:** Where a right of action for breach exists, but no harm has been done or is provable, P may get a judgment for *nominal damages*. That is, he may recover a small sum that is fixed without regard to the amount of harm he has suffered. [355]

B. **Punitive damages:** Punitive damages are rarely awarded in breach of contract cases. [355]

1. **Tort:** But if the breach of contract also *constitutes a tort*, punitive damages *are* recoverable. (*Example*: D, a car dealer, sets back the odometer on a used car before selling it to P. D then falsely claims that the car is "new." P will probably be able to recover punitive damages, because seller's act, although it was part of a contract, also constitutes the independent tort of fraud.) [355]

a. **Bad faith as tort:** Many courts now regard a party's *bad faith* conduct in connection with a contract as *being* itself a tort, for which punitive damages may be awarded. For instance, if a party breaches voluntarily, in order to make a better deal elsewhere, the court may find that this conduct constitutes bad faith punishable by punitive damages. [356]

i. **Insurance company refusal to settle:** If an *insurance company* refuses in bad faith to *settle a claim* that is covered by a policy it wrote, courts are quite likely to hold that the insured has suffered a tort, and can recover punitive damages against the insurer.

XII. LIQUIDATED DAMAGES

A. **Definition:** A *"liquidated damages clause"* is a provision, placed in the contract itself, specifying the **consequences of breach**. (*Example*: Contractor contracts to paint Owner's house for $10,000. In the basic contract, the parties agree that for every day after the deadline that Contractor finishes, the price charged by him will be reduced by $100. This provision is a liquidated damages clause.) [356]

B. **General rule:** Courts will enforce liquidated damages provisions, but only if the court is satisfied that the provision is not a *"penalty."* That is, the court wants to be satisfied that the clause really is an attempt to estimate actual damages, rather than to penalize the party for breach by awarding "damages" that are far in excess of the ones actually suffered. Therefore, in order to be enforceable, the liquidated damage clause must always meet one, and sometimes two, requirements: [356]

   1. **Reasonable forecast:** The amount fixed must be **reasonable** relative to the anticipated or actual loss for breach; and

   2. **Difficult calculation:** In some courts, the harm caused by the breach must be **uncertain or very difficult to calculate accurately**, even after the fact.

C. **Reasonableness of amount:** All courts refuse to enforce liquidated damages clauses that do not provide for a *"reasonable"* amount. [357-359]

   1. **Modern view:** Courts disagree about the **time** as of which the amount must appear to be reasonable. Most courts today will enforce the clause if **either**: (1) the clause is a reasonable forecast when viewed **as of the time of contracting**; or (2) the clause is reasonable in light of the **actual** damages which have occurred. [357]

      a. **Unexpectedly high damages:** This means that a clause which is an unreasonable forecast (viewed as of the time of contracting) can still be saved if it turns out that P's damages are unexpectedly high, and therefore in line with the clause.

   2. **No loss at all:** Courts are split about whether to enforce a liquidated damages clause where P has sustained **no actual losses at all**. The Restatement does **not** enforce the clause if it turns out that no actual damage has been sustained. [358]

   3. **Blunderbuss clause:** A *"blunderbuss"* clause stipulates the same sum of money as liquidated damages for breach of **any** covenant, whether trivial or important. Where the actual damage turns out to be **trivial**, most courts will **not enforce** a blunderbuss clause (or will interpret the clause as not applying to trivial breaches). [358]

      Example: Contractor contracts to renovate Owner's office building by June 1, to get it ready for occupancy by Tenant beginning on August 1. The contract provides that if Contractor is late in completing work, he will forfeit $100,000, whether the delay is one day or 90 days. In the actual event, Contractor is two days late, and Owner deducts the full $100,000.

      Since the clause produces the same damage amount regardless of how much actual damage is sustained by Owner (a one-day delay wouldn't prevent Tenant's on-time occupancy, but a 70-day delay would), and since the actual damage has turned out to be trivial, the clause will be struct down as a blunderbuss clause. [358]

      a. **Major loss:** But if the breach turns out to be a **major** one (so that the liquidated amount is reasonable in light of the actual loss), courts are split on whether the blunderbuss should be enforced. The modern view is to **enforce** the blunderbuss where the actual loss is roughly equal to the damages provided in the clause. [359]

D. UCC rules: The UCC basically follows the common-law rule on when a liquidated damages clause should be awarded. The UCC follows the modern view, by which the party seeking enforcement of the clause will succeed if the sum is reasonable viewed *either* as of the time the contract is made or viewed in light of the actual breach and actual damages. See UCC § 2-718(1) (clause enforceable if "reasonable in the light of the anticipated or actual harm caused by the breach…"). [360]

XIII. DAMAGES IN SALES CONTRACTS

A. Where goods not accepted: If the buyer has *not accepted* the goods (either because they weren't delivered, or were delivered defective, or because the buyer repudiated), the UCC gives well-defined rights to the injured party: [364-368]

1. Buyer's rights: If the seller fails to deliver at all, or delivers defective goods which the buyer rightfully rejects, the buyer has a choice of remedies. [365]

    a. Cover: The most important is her right to *"cover,"* i.e., to buy the goods from another seller, and to recover the *difference between the contract price and the cover price* from the seller. § 2-712(2). The buyer's purchase of substitute goods must be *"reasonable,"* and must be made "in good faith and *without unreasonable delay.*" § 2-712(1). [365]

    b. Contract/market differential: If the buyer does *not* cover (either because she can't, or decides she doesn't want to), she can instead recover the *contract/market differential*, i.e., the difference between the contract price and the market price "at the time when the buyer learned of the breach…." § 2-713(1). [365-366]

        i. Time of breach: Typically, the buyer "learns of the breach" (setting the time for measuring the market price) at the time the breach in fact occurs (either through non-delivery or through receipt of defective goods). But if the breach takes the form of a *repudiation* in advance of the time for performance, most courts hold that the market price is to be measured as of the time the buyer learns of the repudiation. (See p. C-47.)

        ii. Buyer contracts to resell at fixed margin: Notice that the contract/market differential may not correctly compensate the buyer where the market is rising and the buyer has *already made a fixed-price or fixed-margin contract to resell* the goods. If the market-price increase times the quantity is greater than the profit margin on the buyer's resale contract, giving the buyer the contract/market differential will put the buyer in a *better position* than she would have been in had the contract been fulfilled.

            [1] Minority view limits buyer to lost profits: Therefore, a few courts *limit the buyer to the profits the buyer would have* made under the resale arrangement.

            [2] Majority view doesn't limit buyer: But *most* courts hold that the buyer is *entitled to the full contract/market differential even where this would put her in a better position* than had the contract been fulfilled, because limiting damages to the buyer's lost profits would *incentivize the seller to breach.*

            Example: Seller contracts to sell to Buyer 10,000 widgets (not yet manufactured) at $1 per widget, delivery to occur 90 days later. Buyer immediately contracts to resell the widgets, when produced, to Thirdco, a third party, for $1.30. (Assume that the contract with Thirdco says that if Buyer's source of supply fails to deliver, Thirdco can't sue Buyer.) By the delivery date, the market price of widgets has soared to $2.

            If Buyer is given the contract/market differential, Buyer will collect damages of $10,000, even though had Seller delivered Buyer would have made only $3,000. Yet most courts will give Buyer the contract/market differential anyway, since limiting Buyer to the $3,000 "profits it would have made" would give Seller an incentive to breach: Seller pockets an extra $10,000, pays out $3,000 in damages, and is ahead of the game for having breached.

    iii. Probably not available to covering buyer: Probably the buyer may recover the contract/market differential *only where she did not cover*. This means that if the market price declines between the time the buyer learns of the breach and the time he covers by buying substitute goods, the buyer can't get a windfall — limiting him to the contract/market differential puts him in the same position he would have been in had the contract been fulfilled, not a better one.

  c. Consequential and incidental damages: The buyer, regardless of whether he covers, may recover for *"incidental"* and *"consequential"* damages. [366]

    i. Consequential: *Consequential* damages include the *profits* which the buyer could have made by reselling the contracted-for goods had they been delivered. But remember that these profits must be proved with appropriate certainty, and must be shown to have been reasonably foreseeable at the time of the contract. [366]

    ii. Incidental damages: *"Incidental"* damages include such items as transportation expenses, storage expenses, and other small but direct expenses associated with the breach and buyer's attempts to cover for it. [366]

  d. Rejection: All of the above are judicial remedies. But the buyer who receives non-conforming goods can also exercise the self-help remedy of *rejecting the goods*. The buyer thus throws the goods back on the seller and cancels the contract. (Observe that where the buyer has actually made a losing contract, rejection lets him escape his bad bargain.) [368]

2. Seller's damages for breach: Where it is the buyer who breaches, by wrongfully refusing to accept the goods (or by repudiating the contract before shipment is even made), the seller has several possible remedies: [368-373]

  a. Contract/resale differential: Normally, the seller will *resell the goods* to a third party. Assuming that the resale is made in good faith and in a "commercially reasonable" manner, seller may recover the difference between the *resale price* and the *contract price*, together with incidental damages. [368]

  b. Contract/market differential: If the seller does *not* resell the goods, he may recover from the breaching buyer the difference between the *market price* at the time and place for delivery, and the *unpaid contract price*, together with incidental damages. § 2-708(1). (Probably a seller who has resold the goods may *not* use this contract/market differential, but must use the contract/resale differential.) [369]

  c. Lost profits: The contract/resale differential (for a reselling seller) and the contract/market differential (for a non-reselling seller) may not make the seller whole. Where this is the case, § 2-708(2) lets the seller recover his *lost profits* instead of using either of these differentials. [369]

    i. "Lost volume" seller: Most importantly, this means that the *"lost volume"* seller may recover the profit he has lost by reason of the breach. In the usual case of a seller who has resold the item, a "lost volume" seller is one who (1) had a big enough supply that he could have made both the contracted-for sale and the resale; (2) probably would have made the resale anyway as well as the original sale had there been no breach; and (3) would have made a profit on both sales. [369]

    Example: Auto Dealer sells cars made by Smith Motors. Auto Dealer can get as much inventory from Smith as Auto Dealer can sell. Auto Dealer contracts to sell a particular 1999 Thunder Wagon to Consumer for $10,000. Consumer repudiates just before delivery. Auto Dealer resells the car for the same $10,000 price to X, a walk-in customer.

The traditional contract/resale differential (here, $0) would not make Auto Dealer whole, since he could have sold cars to both consumer and X and made a profit on each. Therefore, Auto Dealer can recover from Consumer the profit he would have made had the contract with Consumer been fulfilled. Auto Dealer is on these facts a "lost volume" seller.

d. Action for contract price: In a few situations, the UCC allows the seller to sue for the ***entire contract price***: [371]

i. Accepted goods: First, if the buyer has ***"accepted"*** the goods, the seller may sue for the entire contract price (though the buyer has a counterclaim for damages for non-conformity). (*Example*: Buyer orders 10 widgets at $50 each from Seller. Seller ships the goods late, but Buyer keeps the goods for 30 days without saying anything. Buyer will be held to have "accepted" the goods, and Seller can therefore sue for the entire contract price, $500. But Buyer may counterclaim for the damages he has actually suffered due to the late delivery.) [371]

ii. Risk of loss: Second, if the ***risk of loss*** has passed to the buyer, and the goods are lost in transit, the seller may sue for the entire contract price. (*Example*: As per the contract, Seller ships goods "F.O.B. Seller's plant." The goods are destroyed while on the trucking company's truck. Seller can sue for the whole price; Buyer's remedy is against the trucker.) [371]

iii. Unresaleable goods: Lastly, if the seller has already ***earmarked*** particular goods as being ones to be supplied under the contract, and the buyer rejects them or repudiates before delivery, seller may recover the entire contract price if he is ***unable to resell them*** on some reasonable basis. Most commonly, this applies to ***perishable*** goods and ***custom-made*** goods. [371]

e. Incidental damages: A seller who pursues and achieves one of the four above remedies (resale, contract/market differential, lost profits, action for price) may ***also*** recover ***"incidental damages."*** These include such items as transportation charges, storage charges, and other charges relating to the seller's attempt to deal with the goods after the buyer's breach. See § 2-710. [372]

f. Consequential damages: Nearly all courts hold that the seller may ***not*** recover ***"consequential damages."*** This is a big difference from how buyers are treated. [372]

B. Accepted goods: If the buyer has ***accepted*** the goods (and has not rightfully revoked this acceptance), then the remedies given to buyer and seller are different: [373]

1. Seller's action for price: If the buyer has accepted the goods, the seller may recover the ***full contract price***. (But if the goods are non-conforming, Buyer may counterclaim for breach of warranty.) [373]

2. Buyer's claim: If the buyer has accepted the goods, and they turn out to be defective, buyer's remedy is to sue for breach of contract. [373]

a. Breach of warranty: Most importantly, buyer may sue for ***breach of warranty***. These may be either express warranties or warranties implied by the UCC. The measure of damages for breach of warranty is "the difference at the time and place of acceptance between the value of the goods accepted and the value they would have had if they had been as warranted, unless special circumstances show proximate damages of a different amount." § 2-714(2). [373]

    b. Non-warranty damages: Buyer may also be able to recover for non-warranty damages. For instance, damages resulting from seller's *delay* in shipping the goods, or his breach of an express promise to *repair* defective goods, may be recovered on top of or instead of breach-of-warranty damages. [375]

CHAPTER 11

CONTRACTS INVOLVING MORE THAN TWO PARTIES

I. ASSIGNMENT AND DELEGATION GENERALLY

A. Assignment distinguished from delegation: Be sure to distinguish *assignment* from *delegation*: [386]

    1. Assignment: When a party to an existing contract transfers to a third person her *rights* under the contract, she has made an *assignment*.

    2. Delegation: When an existing party appoints a third person to perform her *duties* under the contract, she has made a *delegation*.

    3. Combination: Frequently, an existing party will both assign and delegate. That is, she will both transfer her rights to a third person, and appoint the latter to perform her duties. But don't presume that where there is an assignment, there is necessarily a delegation, or vice versa — there will often be just an assignment, or just a delegation.

II. ASSIGNMENT

A. Present transfer: An assignment is a *present* transfer of one's rights under a contract. Thus a *promise* to transfer one's rights in the future is not an assignment, even though it may be a contract. [386]

    1. No consideration: Because an assignment is a present transfer, *no consideration is required* for it (just as no consideration is required for a present gift).

B. Terminology: An assignment is a *three-part* transaction. The *"assignor"* assigns to the *"assignee"* the performance due the assignor from the *"obligor."* (*Example*: Contractor contracts to paint Owner's house for $10,000. Contractor then assigns to Bank Contractor's right to receive the $10,000 when due. Contractor is the assignor, Bank is the assignee, and Owner is the obligor.)

C. UCC rules: The *UCC* applies to many assignments, even ones not involving contracts for the sale of goods. In general, if a party assigns his *right to receive payment* under a contract as security *financing*, *Article 9* of the UCC applies to the terms of the assignment. [387-388]

    Example: Contractor contracts to paint Owner's house for $10,000. Contractor assigns his right to receive payment to Bank, in return for a present payment of $9,500. Even though there is no contract for the sale of goods, Article 9 of the UCC applies to this assignment, and governs such items as whether the assignment must be in writing, the rights of Bank against Owner if Owner does not pay, etc.

D. Writing: At common law, an assignment of contract rights does *not have to be in writing*. However, many states have statutes requiring certain types of assignments to be in writing. [388]

    1. Article 9: In particular, where a party assigns to a third person his *right to receive payment*, in a financing-type transaction covered by Article 9 of the UCC, the assignment is not enforceable against either the assignor or the obligor unless the assignor has signed a document called a *"security interest."* See § 9-203.

E. Gratuitous assignments: A *"gratuitous assignment"* is an assignment that is in the nature of a gift, i.e., one in which the assignor receives nothing of value in return. Gratuitous assignments are generally *enforceable*, just like ones given for value. [388]

   1. Revocability: But gratuitous assignments, unlike ones given for value, are automatically *revoked* if the assignor does any of the following three things:

   [1] The assignor *dies*;

   [2] The assignor makes a *subsequent assignment* of the same right to a different person; or

   [3] The assignor gives *notice* to *either the assignee or the obligor* that the assignment has been revoked. [388]

   a. Becomes irrevocable: But a gratuitous assignment may become *irrevocable* in some circumstances: [389]

   i. Delivery of symbolic document: This can happen if the contract right being assigned is evidenced by a *document* that commonly *symbolizes* the right, and that document is delivered to the assignee.

   Example: Insured, who owns an insurance policy on his own life, delivers the policy to Friend, with the words, "I am assigning you this policy." At that moment, the assignment becomes irrevocable, even though it was gratuitous.

   ii. Writing: If the assignor puts the assignment *in writing*, most courts treat it as irrevocable if the writing is delivered to the assignee.

   iii. Reliance: If the assignee *relies to his detriment* on the assignment, and the reliance is reasonably foreseeable by the assignor, the assignment is irrevocable.

   iv. Obligor's performance: If the obligor gives the assignee the *payment* or performance, the assignment becomes irrevocable.

F. What rights may be assigned: All contract rights are *assignable*, unless they fall within a small number of *exceptions*, most of which are noted below: [389-393]

   1. Materially alter the obligor's duty: If the obligor's duty would be *materially changed* by the assignment, the assignment will be disallowed. [390-391]

   a. Personal services contract: This happens most commonly in certain *personal services* contracts. If there is a special relationship of *trust* or *confidence* between the parties, for instance, assignment will usually not be allowed.

   Example: Star, a movie star, hires Secretary for a below-market wage, which Secretary agrees to take because she wants to work closely with Star. Star probably cannot assign the contract to Friend, thus requiring Secretary to work for Friend for the same wages, because the assignment would materially alter Secretary's duties.

   2. Materially vary the risk: Assignment will also not be allowed if it will materially *vary the risk* assumed by the obligor. This is most commonly true of *insurance* policies. [391]

   3. Impairment of obligor's chance to obtain return performance: An assignment may not be made if it would materially impair the obligor's chances of obtaining *return performance*. [391]

   Example: Brenda, a famous fashion designer, contracts to have Manco custom-manufacture certain dresses that Brenda says she will sell under her own name for $2,000 apiece. Brenda has agreed to pay Manco $500 each for the dresses. The contract is silent about assignability.

Manco has agreed to a relatively low price because it wants to be able to advertise in the trade that it makes dresses for the famous and prestigious Brenda. Brenda then assigns her rights under the contract to Schlock, a mass-market designer of goods that are widely regarded as of low quality.

A court might well hold that this assignment is void, on the grounds that it would materially impair Manco's chance of obtaining return performance. That's because, even though Brenda remains liable for payment, a meaningful part of the "return performance" anticipated by Manco — being able to say that Brenda sells clothes Manco makes — has been taken from it.

G. Contract terms prohibiting assignment: Normally, if the contract itself contains a ***clause prohibiting assignment***, the courts will ***enforce*** the clause. But there are a number of important exceptions. [393]

1. Restatement: Under the Restatement, an anti-assignment clause is generally enforceable, but subject to the following rules: [393-394]

    a. Fully performed: Assignment is allowed if the assignor has already ***fully performed***. (In other words, an assignor who has already earned the ***right to payment*** by doing the contracted-for work may always assign the payment right.)

    b. Total breach: The right to ***sue for damages*** for breach of contract may always be assigned.

    c. Ban on assigning "the contract": If the anti-assignment clause states that ***"the contract"*** may not be assigned (as opposed to stating that "rights under the contract may not be assigned"), the contract will be interpreted to bar only ***delegation***, not assignment.

    d. Damages: An assignment made in violation of an anti-assignment clause generally does ***not*** render the assignment ineffective. All it does is to give the obligor a right to ***damages*** against the assignor for breach.

    e. Rules of construction: In any event, these rules are merely ***rules of construction***. If the parties clearly manifest a different intent, that intent will be honored.

2. UCC: Where a party assigns his ***right to payment*** (or creates a ***"security interest"*** in his right to payment, as collateral for a loan), an anti-assignment clause is automatically ***invalid***. That's because the UCC has two special provisions (§§ 2-210(3) and 9-406) that have this effect, whether the underlying contract that gave rise to the right to payment was for the sale of goods or not. [394]

    Example: Painter agrees to paint Owner's house for $10,000. The contract says that Painter can't assign his right to payment. Before doing the work, Painter assigns his right to payment to Bank, to which he owes money. The anti-assignment clause won't be effective, because of the UCC provisions barring such clauses. Therefore (1) Owner can't cancel the contract if he finds out that Painter has assigned; and (2) Owner has to pay Bank, not Painter, once Owner gets notice of the assignment (under the rule explained in (H)(1) below).

H. Assignee vs. obligor: As a general rule, the assignee ***"stands in the shoes of his assignor."*** That is, with a few exceptions, he takes ***subject to all defenses, set-offs and counterclaims which the obligor could have asserted against the assignor***. This is the most important single rule to remember about assignment. [395-401]

    Example: Contractor contracts to paint Owner's house for $10,000. Contractor assigns his right to payment to Wife, to satisfy an alimony obligation. If Owner fails to make payment,

Owner may raise against Wife any defense, counterclaim or set-off that Owner could have raised against Contractor. Thus if the work was not done in a merchantable manner, Owner may raise this defense against Wife just as he could have raised it against Contractor.

1. **Effect if obligor gives performance to assignor:** Once the obligor has received **notice** of the assignment (from either the assignor or assignee), **she cannot thereafter pay** (or otherwise give her performance to) **the assignor**. If she does, she won't be able to use the defense of payment against the assignee. But if the obligor pays the assignor or otherwise gives him the required performance **before** she has received notice of the assignment, she may use this as a defense against the assignee. [396]

2. **Modification of contract:** The right of the obligor and assignor to **modify** the original contract depends mainly on whether the modification takes place before the obligor has notice of the assignment: [397]

   a. **Before notice:** **Before** the obligor has received notice of the assignment, he and the assignor are **completely free** to modify the contract. (See UCC § 9-318(2).) [397]

   Example: Contractor contracts to paint Owner's house for $10,000, does the work, then assigns his right to payment to Bank. Before Owner receives notice of the assignment, Owner and Contractor can together agree to modify the contract, and this will be binding on Bank. For instance, they may agree to reduce the contract price.

   b. **After notice of assignment:** But **after** notice of assignment has been given to the obligor, he and the assignor may modify the contract **only if the assignor has not yet fully performed**. [397]

   Example: Same facts as above example. Now, assume that Contractor has already finished painting the house, and that Bank has notified Owner of the assignment. At this juncture, any attempt by Owner and Contractor to lower the contract price will not be binding on Bank.

      i. **Assignee gets benefits under modified contract:** Where modification **is** allowed, the assignee gets the benefit of whatever new rights are given to the assignor by the modification.

3. **"Waiver of defenses" clause:** Many contracts contain **"waiver of defenses"** clauses, by which one party agrees that if the other assigns the contract, the former will not raise against the assignee defenses which he could have raised against the assignor. Most commonly, the buyer of goods on credit agrees that the seller may assign the installment contract, and that the buyer will not assert against the assignee (usually a bank or finance company) defenses which the buyer might have against the seller. The enforceability of such "waiver of defenses" clauses depends mostly on whether the transaction is a consumer one. [398-399]

   a. **"Real" defenses:** A waiver-of-defenses clause is **never** effective as to so-called **"real"** defenses. "Real" defenses include: (1) infancy, incapacity, or duress; (2) illegality of the original contract; and (3) misrepresentation that induced the buyer to sign the contract without knowledge of its essential terms ("fraud in the essence"). See UCC § 9-403(b). [398]

   b. **Consumer goods:** Very importantly, waiver-of-defenses clauses in **consumer transactions** are basically **unenforceable**. This stems mainly from an FTC regulation. [398]

      i. **Commercial contracts:** By contrast, the FTC regulation does **not** apply to **commercial** contracts. So a businessperson who, say, buys goods on installment may not raise defenses such as breach of the implied warranty of merchantability against the assignee, typically a financing institution. [399]

4. **Counterclaims, set-offs, and recoupment by the obligor:** Most states (and the UCC) follow these rules for determining when the obligor may assert a *counterclaim*, *set-off* or *recoupment* in a suit brought against him by the assignee: [399-401]

    a. **Claim relates to assigned contract:** If the obligor's claim against the assignor is related to the *same contract* that has been assigned to the assignee, the obligor may use this claim whether it arose *prior to* or *subsequent* to the obligor's receipt of notice of the assignment. See UCC §9-318(1). This is called a "recoupment." It may only be used to reduce the assignee's claim, *not to yield an affirmative recovery* for the obligor. [399]

    Example: Contractor agrees to paint Owner's house for $10,000. Contractor assigns to Bank on July 1, and Bank notifies Owner of the assignment on July 2. If Contractor has done the work in a slightly improper or late way (whether the defect occurred before or after the July 2 notice), Owner may assert this as a defense in any suit brought by Bank for the money, and Bank's recovery will be diminished by this amount. (But no affirmative recovery by Owner will be allowed even if the damages aggregate more than $10,000.)

    b. **Claim unrelated to assigned contract:** If the obligor's claim against the assignor is *not related to the contract* which has been assigned, the obligor may assert this claim against the assignee *only if the claim accrued before the obligor received notice of the assignment*. This is called a *"set-off."* Like recoupment, a set-off may not yield affirmative recovery. [400]

    c. **Counterclaims:** The obligor may obtain an *affirmative recovery* against the assignee only if the claim relates to a transaction *directly between the obligor and the assignee*. This is called a *counterclaim*. [400]

    Example: Same facts as above two examples. Assume that Owner also has a claim against Bank for lending him money at a rate in violation of state usury laws. Assuming that the claim is allowed to be part of the same suit under state practice rules, this claim can not only wipe out any recovery by Bank as assignee of the Contractor-Owner contract, but also may yield an affirmative recovery for Owner. But no claim by Owner relating to the Owner-Contractor contract may yield an affirmative recovery, since only dealings directly between the obligor (Owner) and the assignee/plaintiff (Bank) may yield such a recovery.

I. **Rights of successive assignees of the same claim:** Where there are *two assignees* of the same claim, and assuming that both assignees gave value and the later one did not know about the first, here is the way most states treat their relative rights: [401-402]

1. **Restatement rule:** In transactions not governed by Article 9 of the UCC, the Restatement *"four horsemen"* rule is applied by most states. The subsequent assignee loses to the earlier assignee, unless the subsequent one did one of four things: (1) he received *payment* or other satisfaction of the obligation; (2) he obtained a *judgment* against the obligor; (3) he obtained a *new contract* from the obligor by novation; or (4) he *possessed* a *writing* of a type customarily accepted as a symbol or evidence of the right assigned (e.g., a bank book or insurance policy). [401]

2. **UCC:** In transactions governed by Article 9 of the UCC (most assignments of the right to receive money in return for financing), rights of successive assignees are governed by a *filing system*. In general, the assignee who *files first* has priority, regardless of whether he received his assignment first, and regardless of whether he gave notice of the assignment to the obligor first. [401]

J. **Rights of assignee against assignor:** If the obligor is *unable to perform*, or in some other way the assignee doesn't obtain the value he expected from the contract, the *assignee* may be able to recover *against the assignor*. [402]

1. **Gratuitous assignments:** If the assignment was a *gratuitous* one, the assignee probably will *not* be able to recover against his assignor. Exceptions exist where the assignor interferes with the assignee's ability to collect the performance, or where the assignor makes a subsequent assignment. But in the more common case where the obligor simply *fails to perform*, the assignee has no *claim* against the assignor under a gratuitous assignment. [402]

2. **Assignments made for value:** But it is quite different if the assignment was made *for value*. Every assignor for value is held to have made a series of *implied warranties* to the assignee. If these warranties turn out not to be accurate, the assignee may sue the assignor for damages. These warranties are: [403]

   a. **No impairment:** That the assignor will do nothing which will *interfere* with the assignee's enforcement of the obligation. [403]

   Example: Assignor implicitly promises that he will not try to collect the obligation himself, and that he will not assign it to some third party.

   b. **Claim is valid and unencumbered:** That the assigned claim is a *valid* one, not subject to any *limitations or defenses* other than those that have been disclosed. [403]

   Example: Contractor agrees to paint Owner's house for $10,000. Contractor performs the work sloppily, giving Owner a partial defense. Contractor then assigns to Bank his right to be paid. Regardless of whether Contractor knows, at the time of assignment, that Owner has a defense, Contractor breaches his implied warranty to Bank if he does not disclose to Bank Owner's defense of non-performance.

   c. **Documents valid:** That any documents which are delivered to the assignee that purport to evidence the right are *genuine*. [403]

   d. **No warranty of solvency or willingness to perform:** But the assignor does *not* warrant that the obligor is *solvent*, or that he will be *willing or able to perform*. Thus if the obligor turns out to be unwilling or unable to perform, the assignee has *no recourse* against the assignor. [403]

   Example: Same facts as above example. If Contractor does the work properly, but Owner goes broke, or simply refuses to pay, Bank cannot sue Contractor.

      i. **Free to agree otherwise:** But the assignor may explicitly *agree* to guarantee the obligor's performance, in which case the assignee can sue if the obligor fails to perform.

   e. **Sub-assignees not covered:** Unless the assignor indicates otherwise, his warranties do not extend to any *sub-assignee*, i.e., one who receives the assignment from the assignee. [403]

   f. **Rules of construction:** All of the above rules on warranties are generally *common law*, rather than statutory. Most states treat them as *rules of construction*, which may be varied by showing that the parties intended a different result. [406]

III. DELEGATION OF DUTIES

A. Definition: Recall that "delegation" refers to *duties* under a contract, not to rights. If a party to a contract wishes to have another person perform his duties, he delegates them. [407]

B. Continued liability of delegator: When the performance of a duty is delegated, *the delegator remains liable*. [407]

Example: Owner contracts with Contractor for Contractor to paint Owner's house for $10,000. Contractor delegates his duties to Painter. If Painter fails to perform in the manner required by the original Owner-Contractor contract, Owner may sue Contractor for breach, just as if Contractor had improperly performed the work herself.

1. **Novation:** But the obligee may expressly agree to accept the delegate's performance in place of that of the delegator. If he does so, he has given what is called a *novation*.

C. **Non-delegable duties:** In general, a duty or performance is *delegable*, unless the obligee has a *substantial interest in having the delegator perform*. [408-410]

1. **Particular skills:** Contracts which call for the promisor's use of his *own particular skills* are normally *not* delegable. Thus contracts involving *artistic performances*, the *professional services* of a lawyer or doctor, etc., are not delegable. [408]

> **Example:** Client is charged with murder. He signs an engagement letter (a contract) with Lawyer, a solo practitioner who specializes in white-collar criminal defense work, under which Lawyer will represent him at the trial for a fixed fee of $30,000. The contract says nothing about assignment or delegation. One month before trial, Lawyer sends Client an e-mail that Lawyer is delegating his duties to his friend Barrister. Barrister is in fact much more suited than Lawyer to represent Client, because Barrister specializes in murder cases whereas Lawyer has never done one before.
>
> Client need not accept performance from Barrister — the contract calls for personal professional services, and Lawyer's duties under it were therefore not delegable without Client's consent. If Lawyer insists on making the delegation, Client can refuse and hire someone else (and sue Lawyer for breach). Alternatively, Client can accept the proposed delegation, in which case Lawyer will remain liable if Barrister fails to deliver a defense of the quality called for in the contract.

   a. **Close supervision:** Similarly, contracts in which one party has a duty of *close personal supervision* may not be delegated by that party. [408]

2. **Construction and repair contracts:** *Construction* contracts, and contracts for the repair of buildings or machinery, are normally delegable. [410]

3. **Agreement of parties:** The parties have complete freedom to determine whether duties may be delegated. This cuts both ways: they may agree that duties which would otherwise be delegable may not be delegated, or conversely that duties normally thought to be too personal may in fact be delegated. [410]

D. **Delegate's liability:** [410]

1. **Two forms:** A delegation agreement between delegator and delegate may be in one of two forms: (1) the delegator may simply give the delegate the *option* to perform, with the delegate making no promise that she will perform; or (2) the delegate may *promise* that she will perform. [410]

   a. **Option:** If the delegate is given the *option* to perform, the delegate is *not liable* to *either* the delegator or the obligee.

   b. **Promise:** If the delegate has promised to perform, the delegate may or may not be liable to the *obligee*. That is, the obligee may or may not be a *third party beneficiary* of the delegate's promise. This is normally a question of intent of the parties — if delegator and delegate intend that the obligee get the benefit of the delegate's promise, then the obligee may sue the delegate.

   > **Example:** Contractor promises Owner that Contractor will paint Owner's house for $10,000. Contractor gets too busy to perform, but wants to make sure that Owner is not inconvenienced by a bad or tardy performance. Contractor therefore delegates perfor-

mance to Painter, under terms that permit Painter to keep the $10,000 fee when earned. Painter expressly promises to perform the work. A court would probably hold that Owner was an intended third party beneficiary of Painter's promise, so that Owner may sue Painter (not just Contractor) if Painter fails to perform.

2. **"Assumption":** If a delegate is held to have undertaken liability to the obligee as well as to the delegator, he is said to have *assumed* the delegator's liability. [411]

3. **Assignment of "the contract":** If a party purports to "assign the contract" to a third person, this language will normally be interpreted to constitute a *promise* by the assignee to perform, and the obligee will normally be interpreted to be an *intended beneficiary* of this promise. [411-412]

   a. **Obligee can sue both:** In other words, the assignee/delegate under such a general assignment clause will normally be held *liable to both parties* to the original contract if she fails to perform. [411]

   Example: Owner contracts with Contractor for Contractor to paint Owner's house for $10,000. Contractor then signs a document saying he "assigns to Painter my contract to paint Owner's house." Painter accepts the assignment. Under the standard view, there are three consequences:

   (1) Contractor is deemed to have *delegated* his duties to Painter (not just assigned his rights, such as the right to payment);

   (2) Painter, by accepting the assignment, is deemed to have *promised* Contractor that Painter will perform the duties owed by Contractor; and

   (3) Owner is an *intended beneficiary* of this promise by Painter to Contractor, so if Painter doesn't perform, Owner can sue Painter (as well as Contractor).

   b. **Exception for land sales:** But an assignment of "the contract" made by a *vendee* under a *land contract* will *not* usually be found to follow this rule. That is, the assignee under a land sale contract usually does *not* incur liability to the original seller. [411]

   c. **UCC:** The UCC, in § 2-210(4), follows the common-law rule: "An assignment of 'the contract' or of 'all my rights under the contract'…is an assignment of rights and unless the languages or circumstances…indicate the contrary, it is a *delegation of performance* of the duties of the assignor and its acceptance by the assignee constitutes a *promise by him* to perform those duties. This promise is enforceable by *either* the assignor or the other party to the original contract." [412]

      i. **Security:** But if a general assignment is made for the purpose of giving *collateral* to the assignee in return for a *loan*, the lender will *not* normally be deemed to have undertaken to perform the assignor's duties. [412]

      Example: Owner contracts with Contractor for Contractor to paint Owner's house for $10,000. Contractor then assigns "the contract" to Bank as security for a loan of $9,000. Bank will not be deemed to have promised to paint the house, and may not be sued by Owner if the house does not get painted.

IV. THIRD PARTY BENEFICIARIES

A. **Introduction:** A *third party beneficiary* is a person whom the promisee in a contract intends to benefit. [415]

   Example: Contractor agrees to paint Owner's house for $10,000. Contractor wants to pay off a debt he owes Creditor, so he provides that upon completion, payment should be made not to Contractor but to Creditor. Creditor is a third party beneficiary of the Owner-Contractor contract.

B. When beneficiary may sue: The most important question about third party beneficiaries is: When may the third party beneficiary sue the promisor on the contract? The modern rule, exemplified by the Second Restatement, is that *"intended"* beneficiaries may sue, but *"incidental"* beneficiaries may not sue. [416]

1. Intended beneficiaries may sue: "Intended beneficiaries" fall into two categories: [417]

    a. Payment of money: First, a person is an intended beneficiary if the performance of the promise will satisfy an obligation of the promisee to *pay money* to the beneficiary. This is sometimes called a *"creditor beneficiary."* [417]

    Example: Contractor agrees to paint Owner's house for $10,000. The contract provides that payment should be made to Creditor, to satisfy a debt previously owed by Contractor to Creditor. Since Owner's fulfillment of his side of the contract will cause money to be paid to Creditor, Creditor is an intended beneficiary, of the "creditor beneficiary" variety.

    b. Intended beneficiary: Second, a person will be an intended beneficiary if the circumstances indicate that the promisee *intends to give the beneficiary the benefit* of the promised performance. A person may fall into this class even if the purpose of the promisee is to give a gift to the beneficiary (in which case the beneficiary is sometimes called a *"donee* beneficiary"). But intent to make a gift is not necessary — a beneficiary may fall into this "intended beneficiary" class even if the promisee's purpose is not to make a gift, but rather to fulfill some other business objective. [417]

    Example: Tycoon contracts with Painter for Painter to paint a portrait of Magnate, a businessman friend of Tycoon, and to deliver the portrait to Magnate. Since Tycoon intends for Magnate to get the benefit of Painter's performance, Magnate is an intended beneficiary who may sue Painter for non-performance; this is true even though Tycoon's motive is to butter up Magnate so that Magnate will do business with Tycoon.

        i. Promisee's intent versus promissor's intent: Most courts hold that a person will be an intended beneficiary if the promis*ee* (alone) intended to benefit the beneficiary. But a minority hold that the person is an intended beneficiary *only* if *both* promisee *and promisor* intend to benefit her. (So in such a court, Magnate couldn't sue Painter unless Magnate showed that Painter, as well as Tycoon, intended to benefit Magnate.) [418]

2. Incidental beneficiaries: A beneficiary who does not fall into the above two classes is called an *"incidental"* beneficiary. An incidental beneficiary may *not* sue the promisor. [417]

    Example: Developer contracts with Contractor to have Contractor put up an expensive building on developer's land. Neighbor, who owns the adjoining parcel, would benefit enormously because her land would increase in value if the building were built. However, since the parties don't intend to benefit Neighbor, and aren't paying money to her, Neighbor is an incidental beneficiary, not an intended one. Therefore, Neighbor cannot sue Contractor if Contractor fails to perform as agreed.

3. Public contracts: When *government* makes a contract with a private company for the performance of a service, a *member of the public* who is injured by the contractor's non-performance generally may *not* sue. [418]

    Example: City contracts with Water Co. to supply water for fire hydrants. P's house burns down when Water Co. does not give adequate hydrant pressure. *Held*, P is not an intended beneficiary of the City-Water Co. contract, and therefore may not recover. [*H.R. Moch & Co. v. Rensselaer*]

    a.   **Exceptions:**   But there are two exceptions — a member of the public may sue: (1) if the party contracting with the government has ***explicitly promised*** to undertake liability to members of the public for breach of the contract; or (2) if the government has a ***duty of its own*** to provide the service which it has contracted for. (*Example*: City contracts to have its street-repair duty picked up by Contractor. A member of the public who is injured when the street is improperly maintained may sue Contractor.)

    4.   **Mortgage assumptions:**   In a fact pattern involving one party taking over another's ***mortgage payments***, distinguish between two situations: (1) the mortgagor sells the property ***"subject to"*** the mortgage, in which case the purchaser does not promise to pay off the mortgage, though he bears the risk of losing the property if the mortgage payments are not made; and (2) the purchaser ***"assumes"*** the mortgage, in which case he makes himself personally liable for repayment (so that the mortgagee may not only foreclose but also obtain a deficiency judgment against the purchaser). These two scenarios have different third party beneficiary consequences: [419-420]

        a.   **Assumption:**   If the purchaser has ***assumed*** the mortgage, the mortgagee (i.e., the lender) is a ***creditor beneficiary*** of the assumption agreement between seller and buyer. The mortgagee may therefore sue the purchaser to compel him to make the mortgage payments. If the purchaser then sells to a sub-purchaser who also assumes, the lender may sue either the purchaser or the sub-purchaser if payments are not made. [420]

        b.   **Subject to:**   Where the mortgagor sells to a purchaser who takes ***"subject to"*** the mortgage, the mortgagee cannot sue that purchaser, since the purchaser has incurred no liability. But if this non-assuming purchaser sells to a sub-purchaser who ***does*** assume, courts are ***split*** on whether the mortgagee can recover personally against the assuming sub-purchaser. [420]

C.   **Discharge or modification by the original parties:**   The modern view is that the original parties' power to ***modify*** the contract ***terminates*** if the beneficiary, before he ***receives notification*** of the discharge or modification, does any of three things:

    [1] materially ***changes his position*** in justifiable ***reliance*** on the promise;

    [2] ***brings suit*** on it; or

    [3] ***manifests assent*** to it at the request of either of the original parties. [420]

    1.   **Original parties maintain right to modify or discharge:**   This rule means that until one of the three events listed above occurs, the original parties ***maintain the power to modify or discharge*** the beneficiary's rights. But if any of the three events occurs before the beneficiary gets notice of a modification or discharge, the beneficiary's rights ***"vest,"*** and can no longer be altered by the original parties. [420]

        Example: Uncle and Landowner, the owner of Blackacre, sign an agreement under which Uncle promises to deposit $100,000 in Landowner's bank account by April 1, and in return Landowner promises that on April 2, he will convey Blackacre to Uncle's nephew Nick. (Assume that Nick is an intended beneficiary of this agreement.) Uncle sends a copy of the agreement to Nick, and says, "Let me know whether you agree to receive title to Blackacre as provided in this document." On March 26, Nick responds, "That's great, yes, I agree. Thanks, Unc." On March 30, Uncle and Landowner sign an amendment to the agreement, purporting to discharge Uncle's obligation to pay the $100,000 and Landowner's obligation to transfer title to Nick.

        When Nick "manifested assent" to the agreement at the request of one of the original parties, this assent took away Uncle's and Landowner's power to modify the agreement as it concerned Nick. Therefore, Nick can sue both Uncle and Landowner for breach on account of their purported modification. The same would be true if Nick, instead of manifesting assent, had changed his position in reliance (e.g., by giving up the chance to buy some alternative property because he knew he could count on receiving Blackacre).

2. **Clause preventing modification:**   The original parties may themselves agree at the time of contracting that no subsequent modification may occur without the beneficiary's consent. Such a clause will be honored. [421]

D. **Defenses against the beneficiary:**   The promisor-defendant may assert against the beneficiary *any defenses which he could have asserted had he been sued by the promisee*. The beneficiary is said to *"step into the shoes of the promisee."* [421]

1. **Defense based on promisee's breach:**   Most importantly, this means that the promisor-defendant may defend on the ground that the promisee never rendered the performance which he promised under the contract, i.e., that the *promisee breached*. [421]

    Example: Contractor agrees to paint Owner's house for $10,000, with payment to be made to Friend, in repayment of a debt owed by Contractor to Friend. If Owner does not make payment and Friend sues Owner as a third party beneficiary, Owner may defend on the grounds that Contractor did not perform the painting work as promised.

2. **Set-offs not allowed:**   But this principle that the beneficiary "stands in the shoes" of the promisee is limited — only defenses *relating to the main contract* may be asserted by the promisor-defendant. The promisor-defendant may *not* assert against the beneficiary defenses or claims from *unrelated transactions* with the promisee. [422]

    Example: Same facts as above example. Contractor performs the painting work correctly. However, Contractor also owes Owner $2,000 in damages from work previously done incorrectly by Contractor for Owner on a different contract involving Owner's office. If Friend sues Owner for the $10,000 fee, Owner may not reduce the payment by the $2,000 owed on the office contract.

E. **Other suits in beneficiary contracts:**

1. **Beneficiary v. promisee:**   When the beneficiary sues the promisor, the beneficiary does *not* waive his right to later sue the promisee. [422]

    Example: Same facts as above example. Friend sues Owner, but recovers only $4,000 because Owner shows that Contractor did not perform the house-painting work correctly. Friend may now sue Contractor for the remaining $4,000 due.

2. **Promisee vs. promisor:**   Most courts allow the promisee to bring her own suit against the promisor, if the promisor breaches. [422]

    a. **Third party is creditor beneficiary:**   This is most important where the third party is a *creditor* beneficiary. Here, most courts let the promisee-debtor recover from the promisor the amount which the promisor promised that he would pay the creditor (at least where the promisee has already paid the debt to the creditor). [422]

    Example: Contractor agrees to paint Owner's house for $10,000, with payment to be made to Friend, in repayment of a $10,000 debt owed by Contractor to Friend. Contractor does the work correctly, but Owner does not make any payment to Friend. At least if Contractor pays his debt to Friend first, Contractor may sue Owner to recover the $10,000. (Some courts would let Contractor bring the suit even if he *hadn't* yet paid off Friend.)

CHAPTER 12

IMPOSSIBILITY, IMPRACTICABILITY, AND FRUSTRATION

I. INTRODUCTION

A. Nature of the problem: The parties may be *discharged* from performing the contract if: (1) performance is *impossible*; (2) because of new events, the fundamental *purpose* of one of the parties has been *frustrated*; or (3) performance is not impossible but is much more *burdensome* than was originally expected (*"impracticable"*). If a party is "discharged" from performing for such a reason, he is *not liable* for breach of contract. [431]

B. Risk allocation: The doctrines of impossibility, impracticability and frustration apply only where the parties themselves *did not allocate the risk* of the events which have rendered performance impossible, impracticable or frustrated. Thus the parties are always free to agree explicitly that certain contingencies will or will not render the contract impossible, etc., and these understandings will be honored by the courts. [432]

    1. Question to ask: Therefore, in evaluating a problem that seems to involve impossibility, frustration, etc., always ask, "Did the parties expressly allocate the risk?" If they did, this allocation controls regardless of the general doctrines discussed here.

II. IMPOSSIBILITY OF PERFORMANCE

A. Generally: If a court concludes that performance of the contract has been rendered *"impossible"* by events occurring after the contract was performed, the court will generally *discharge* both parties. [433]

> **Example:** Contractor agrees to paint Owner's house for $10,000. Just before painting starts, the house burns down. A court will almost certainly conclude that performance has become impossible, and will therefore discharge both parties. Contractor does not have to do the painting, and Owner does not have to pay anything.

B. Three classes: There are three main types of impossibility: (1) destruction of the subject matter; (2) failure of the agreed-upon means of performance; and (3) death or incapacity of a party. [433]

    1. Destruction of subject matter: If performance involves particular goods, a particular building, or some other tangible item, which through the fault of neither party is *destroyed* or otherwise made unavailable, the contract is discharged. The discharge will occur only where the particular subject matter is *essential* to the performance of the contract. [433-437]

        a. Specifically referred to: If property which the performing party expected to use is destroyed, that party is discharged only if the destroyed property was *specifically referred to* in the contract, or at least understood by *both* parties to be the property that would be used. It is not enough that the party who seeks discharge intended to use the destroyed property. [434]

        Example: Contractor agrees to paint Owner's house for $10,000. Unknown to Owner, Contractor intends to use 100 gallons of paint which Contractor has left over from another job. After the signing, this paint is destroyed in a fire. Contractor will not be discharged by impossibility, because the specific left-over paint is not referred to in the contract, and is not understood by both parties to be the particular paint to be used in the contract.

        b. Construction contracts: If a building contractor contracts to *construct* a building from scratch on particular land, and the building is destroyed by fire when it is partially completed, most courts hold that the contractor may *not* use the defense of impossibility. [434]

c. **Repair of buildings:** But when a party contracts to *repair* an *existing* building, she usually *will* be discharged if the building is destroyed. [435]

d. **Sale of goods:** Contracts for the sale of goods may or may not be discharged when there is destruction of the "subject matter" of the contract. [435-437]

    i. **General rule:** The general UCC section applicable here is § 2-615(a), which provides that unless otherwise agreed, "delay in delivery or non-delivery...is not a breach of [seller's] duty under a contract for sale if performance as agreed has been made impracticable by the occurrence of a contingency the non-occurrence of which was a *basic assumption on which the contract was made....*" [435]

    ii. **Destruction of identified goods:** If a contract calls for the delivery of a particular *identified* unique good, and that good is destroyed before the "risk of loss" has passed to the buyer, the contract will be discharged. (*Example*: A contracts to sell to B a painting hanging on A's wall. If the painting is destroyed before the delivery process starts, this will normally be before "risk of loss" has passed to B, and both parties will be discharged.) [436]

    iii. **Goods not identified at time of contracting:** Usually, sale contracts call for goods to be taken from the seller's *general inventory*, not for particular identified goods. Where such unidentified goods are to be *shipped* by seller, and are destroyed *in transit*, the result depends on whether the contract is a "shipment" contract or a "destination" contract. [437]

       [1] **"Shipment" contract:** In a "shipment" contract, where the seller's only obligation is to deliver the goods to the carrier (the contract usually says, "F.O.B. seller's plant" in this case), the *risk of loss passes to the buyer as soon as the seller delivers the goods to the carrier*. So if the carrier loses the goods, the buyer bears the loss and must pay the purchase price, and sue the carrier.

       [2] **"Destination" contract:** But if the contract is a *"destination"* contract ("F.O.B. buyer's place of business"), the risk of loss does not pass to the buyer until the carrier actually delivers. Here, the seller cannot use the impossibility defense if the goods are destroyed while in transit.

2. **Impossibility of intangible but essential mode of performance:** If an *essential* but *intangible* aspect of the contract becomes impossible, the contract may be discharged, just as where the "subject matter" is destroyed. [437-440]

    Example: Seller contracts to deliver 100 widgets to Buyer at a stated price; both parties understand that Seller will get the widgets from Widget Co., with whom Seller has a long-term supply contract. If Widget Co. breaches or goes bankrupt, a court might hold that an essential intangible aspect of Seller's ability to perform has been nullified, and might let Seller use the impossibility defense.

a. **Impossibility due to failure of third persons:** Where a *middleman* contracts to supply goods that he will be procuring from some third party, and the third party cannot or will not supply the goods to the middleman, the middleman's ability to use the impossibility defense depends on the precise situation: [438-440]

    i. **Source not specified in contact:** If the contract does *not specify* the source from which the seller is to obtain the goods, then the seller whose source does not pan out will almost surely *not* be allowed to use the impossibility defense. [439]

    ii. Seller unable to make contract: Similarly, if the seller-buyer contract contemplates that the seller will procure the goods from a given supplier, and that supplier is ***unwilling to contract*** to sell the items to the seller, the seller generally may ***not*** use impossibility. [439]

    iii. Where seller's supply contract is breached: But if the contract contemplates that seller will make a particular supply contract, and seller does make a contract with this supplier, many courts will allow the impossibility defense if the ***supplier breaches***. [439]

3. Non-essential mode of performance: If ***non-essential*** aspects of the contract — such as ones dealing with the ***means of delivery*** or the means of payment — become impossible, usually the contract will ***not*** be discharged. Instead, a ***commercially reasonable substitute*** must be used. (*Example*: If *A* agrees to ship goods by post office to *B*, and the post office goes on strike, *A* must use a truck, UPS, or other commercially reasonable substitute.)

4. Death or illness: If a contract specifically provides that performance shall be made by a ***particular person***, that person's ***death or incapacity*** will discharge both parties. [440]

    a. Death or illness of a third party: A contract may similarly be discharged by virtue of the death or illness of some ***third person***, who is necessary to performance of the contract even though he is not himself a party to it. (*Example*: Impresario contracts with Arena Co. to have Singer appear in a concert at Arena Co. If Singer develops laryngitis the day of the concert, the Arena-Impresario contract will be discharged by reason of impossibility, even though Singer is not directly a party.) [440]

    b. Temporary impossibility: If events render performance of the contract only ***temporarily*** impossible, this will normally merely ***suspend*** the duty of performing until the impossibility ends. But if after the temporary impossibility is over, performance would be much more burdensome, then suspension will turn into discharge. [442]

III. IMPRACTICABILITY

A. Modern view of impracticability: Modern courts generally equate ***"extreme impracticability"*** with "impossibility." In other words, if due to changed circumstances, performance would be ***infeasible*** from a commercial viewpoint, the promisor may be excused just as he would be if performance were literally impossible. [442-443]

1. UCC: The UCC deals with impracticability this way: § 2-615(a) provides that the seller's non-delivery is excuse "if performance as agreed has been made impracticable by the occurrence of a contingency the non-occurrence of which was a basic assumption on which the contract was made...." Complete cutoffs of supplies (e.g., because of war, crop failure due to drought, strike, etc.) will often be found to be covered by § 2-615, thus relieving the seller. [443]

2. Cost increases: Most impracticability cases relate to ***extreme cost increases*** suffered by sellers who have signed ***fixed-price contracts***. Here, while it is theoretically possible for the seller of goods or services to escape the contracts on the grounds of impracticability, sellers generally ***lose***. The reason is that such sellers are generally found to have implicitly ***assumed the risk*** of cost increases, when they signed a fixed-price contract. This is true both in services contracts and in sales contracts governed by the UCC. It is especially likely that the seller will lose where the cost increase was ***foreseeable***. [444]

    Example: Oil Co. contracts to sell to Utility oil for 10 years at a price of $10 per barrel. Due to increased price discipline by OPEC, Oil Co.'s cost per barrel jumps from $9 to $29. A court will probably hold that Oil Co. cannot escape the contract on grounds of impracticability, because: (1) Oil Co. implicitly assumed the risk of price increases by agreeing to a fixed-price contract; and (2) disturbances in the supply of oil, with consequent price increases, were reasonably foreseeable to Oil Co. at the time it signed.

3. **Allocation of risk by parties:** In both UCC and non-UCC cases, the parties are always free to *make their own allocation of the risk of impracticability,* and the courts will *enforce* that allocation. So, for instance, if the parties decide that the seller should not have the right to raise the impracticability defense in the event that all potential suppliers to the seller fail, the court will refuse to allow the defense in that scenario even though the requirements for impracticability might otherwise be met. [444]

   a. **Implicit allocation:** This type of re-allocation by the parties of the risk of impracticability can be either explicit or *implicit*. Thus the UCC commentary to § 2-615 says that the impracticability defense "[does] not apply when the contingency in question is *sufficiently foreshadowed* at the time of contracting to be *included among the business risks which are fairly to be regarded as part of the dickered terms,* either consciously or as a matter of *reasonable, commercial interpretation from the circumstances.*" [444]

      i. **Risk of technological breakthrough:** For instance, suppose that Seller and Buyer agree that Seller will develop a not-yet-existing product to meet certain specifications, and both parties are aware that a *technological breakthrough* will be required in order for Seller to perform. A court would probably conclude, as a matter of "reasonable, commercial interpretation from the circumstances," that the risk of non-occurrence of the breakthrough was to rest upon Seller (the party with greater insight into the looming obstacles), in which case Seller would *not* be excused by impracticability if the breakthrough did not develop despite Seller's best efforts.

IV. FRUSTRATION OF PURPOSE

A. **Frustration generally:** Where a party's *purpose* in entering into the contract is destroyed by supervening events, most courts will discharge him from performing. This is the doctrine of *"frustration of purpose."* [445]

   1. **Distinguish from impossibility:** Be sure to distinguish frustration of purpose from impossibility. In frustration cases, the person seeking discharge is not claiming that he "cannot" perform, in the sense of inability. Rather, she is claiming that it *makes no sense* for her to perform, because what she will get in return *does not have the value she expected* at the time she entered into the contract.

      Example: P rents his apartment to D for a two-day period, at a very high rate. As known to P, D's purpose is to view the coronation of the new king. The coronation is cancelled because of the king's illness. *Held,* D is discharged from performing because his purpose in entering the contract has been frustrated. [*Krell v. Henry*]

   2. **Usually used by buyers of goods and services:** You also need to understand the *difference* between the defenses of *impracticability* and *frustration*. The two defenses are similar, in that each gives a party a chance to escape from a bargain that has turned out to be unfavorable because an event occurred whose non-occurrence was a basic assumption on which the contract was made. The main practical difference between the two is that:

      [1] where it is the *seller or supplier* of goods, land or services who wishes to escape the bargain, that party typically claims *impracticability*; whereas

      [2] where it is a *buyer or recipient* of goods, land or services who wishes to escape the bargain, that party typically claims *frustration*. [446]

B. Factors to be considered: Here are the two main factors courts look to in deciding whether to apply the doctrine of frustration: [446]

    1. Foreseeability: The less *foreseeable* the event which thwarts the promisor's purpose, the more likely the court is to allow the frustration defense. (*Example*: In *Krell*, it was quite unlikely, at the time of the contract, that the king would be too sick to be crowned.)

    2. Totality: The more *totally* frustrated the party is in achieving the benefits he anticipated from the transaction, the more likely he is to be allowed to use the defense.

C. Extreme economic dislocation: Sometimes a party who has agreed to buy or pay for goods, land or services relies on *extreme economic dislocation* as the reason she should be allowed to escape from the bargain by use of the frustration defense. For instance, suppose that due to some macro-economic event, the good or service for which the plaintiff has agreed to pay a fixed price suddenly becomes *vastly less valuable* than indicated by the contract price. The plaintiff argues that requiring her to pay will *cause her serious economic loss* of a sort that neither party had reason to anticipate.

    1. Usually unsuccessful: Such claims by buyers based on a plunge in the market value of the contracted-for good or service typically *fail*. The court is likely to rule that in the circumstances, a market-price plunge — no matter how great — was *not the sort of event the non-occurrence of which was a basic assumption* on which the contract was based. In other words, the court is likely to take the position that where buyer and seller agree on a *fixed price* or fee for some good or service, allocating the *risk of a plunge* in market prices to the buyer (and the risk of a sharp *rise* in market prices to the *seller*) is the *very purpose* of the contract.

        Example: P takes out a home mortgage loan on her home from D, a bank. The Great Recession occurs, causing the market value of P's home to drop to less than 50% of the amount then owed by P on the mortgage. P falls behind in her payments, and D begins a foreclosure proceeding. P asserts that she should be permitted to use the frustration doctrine to be relieved from her loan obligations; she argues that the non-occurrence of an extreme real estate depression, and the consequent drastic loss of value of the property, were basic assumptions made by the parties under the loan contract.

        The court is highly unlikely to allow the frustration defense, probably on the grounds that the parties implicitly allocated the not-unforeseeable risk of a real estate crash on the borrower. [Cf. *Bean v. BAC Home Loans Servicing, L.P.*] [448]

V. RESTITUTION AND RELIANCE WHERE THE PARTIES ARE DISCHARGED

A. Generally: Where the contract is discharged because of impossibility, impracticability or frustration, the courts generally try to adjust the equities of the situation by allowing either party to *recover the value* he has rendered to the other, and sometimes even the expenditures made in preparation. [453]

B. Restitution: Courts generally allow one who has been discharged by impossibility or frustration to recover in quasi-contract for *restitution*, i.e., for the value of the *benefit* conferred on the other party. [453]

    1. Time for measuring benefit: Usually, the benefit is measured *just before the event* causing the discharge. (*Example*: Contractor contracts to paint Owner's house for $10,000. After half the work is done, the house burns down. A court will first discharge both parties from the contract. It will then probably measure the benefit conferred by Contractor on Owner as of the moment just before the fire; if it concludes that $5,000 "worth" of work had been done as of that moment, it will award this amount to Contractor.) [453]

2. **Pro-rata contract price:** Where the performance has been partly made, recovery will normally be limited to the ***pro-rata contract price***, if such a pro-rating can be sensibly done. But if the reasonable value to the other party is *less* than the pro-rata contract price, this lesser value will be awarded. [454]

3. **Down payment:** If one party has made a ***down payment*** to the other prior to discharge, he will generally be allowed to recover this down payment. [453]

C. **Reliance:** Occasionally, if restitution will not "avoid injustice," the court will protect the parties' *reliance* interests instead. This might allow a party to recover his ***expenditures*** made in ***preparation*** for performance. [454]

1. **Rare:** Courts only *rarely* give reliance damages — if the performance does not actually render a benefit to the other party before discharge, the partly performing plaintiff is usually out of luck.

CHAPTER 13

MISCELLANEOUS DEFENSES

I. ILLEGALITY

A. **Generally:** In general, if a contract is found to be *"illegal,"* the court will ***refuse to enforce it***. [460]

B. **Kinds of illegal contracts:** Here are some of the kinds of contracts frequently found to be illegal and thus unenforceable: (1) *"gambling"* or "wagering" contracts; (2) lending contracts that violate *usury* statutes; and (3) contracts to ***perform services*** where the provider lacks a required *license* or *permit*. [460]

1. **Non-compete covenants:** A very important type of possibly illegal contract is a ***covenant not to compete***. In general, if a non-compete agreement is ***unreasonably broad***, it will be held to be illegal and not enforced. [461]

   a. **Sale of business:** If the ***seller of a business*** is selling its "good will," his ancillary promise that he will not compete in the same business as the purchaser will be ***upheld***, provided that it is not unreasonably broad either *geographically*, in *duration*, or in the ***definition of the industry*** in which competition is prohibited. [461]

   b. **Employment contracts:** ***Employment agreements*** often include a clause by which the employee agrees not to compete with his employer if he leaves the latter's employ. Such covenants are closely scrutinized by courts, and will be enforced only if they are designed to safeguard either the employer's ***trade secrets*** or his ***customer list***. Even where these objectives are being pursued, the non-compete will be struck down if it is unreasonably broad as to either *geography* or *duration*. [461]

      i. **Divisibility and the "blue pencil" rule:** If a non-compete is overly broad, most courts today will enforce it ***up to reasonable limits***. Some courts apply the ***"blue pencil"*** rule, by which the clause will be enforced only if it can be narrowed by striking out certain portions (so that a ban on competing in "Ohio and Pennsylvania" could be modified by striking out "and Pennsylvania," but a ban lasting for "20 years" could not be modified by reducing it to "five years," since this would require redrafting, not merely striking). Most courts today, however, do *not* follow the blue pencil rule, and will "redraft" the non-compete to bring it back to within reasonable limits. [462]

2. **Agreements concerning family relations:** Questions often arise about the enforceability of contracts regarding *family relations*, such as pre-nuptial agreements and agreements regarding cohabitation.

    a. **Pre-nuptial agreements:** A *prenuptial agreement* is one in which the "non-moneyed" spouse, typically the wife, agrees that in the event of divorce or separation, that spouse will receive lesser alimony, or a smaller property division, than the standard legal rules of the jurisdiction would impose. [464-465]

        i. **Modern approach tends to enforce:** Most courts today are willing to *enforce* prenuptial agreements, especially where basic conditions of procedural fairness are observed before signing. For instance, about half the states have enacted the *Uniform Premarital Agreement Act*, under which voluntarily-signed prenuptial agreements are enforceable if *either*:

           [1] the agreement was *not unconscionable* when signed; or

           [2] even though the agreement *was* unconscionable when signed, the signer was either *provided a fair and reasonable disclosure* of the other party's financial condition, *knew or reasonably could have known* of that financial condition, or voluntarily and expressly *waived* in writing any right to such disclosure.

    b. **Cohabitation:** Many courts refuse to enforce *cohabitation* agreements, i.e., agreements regarding property division entered into by couples who are living together without marriage. But a growing minority of courts now enforce such living-together arrangements, at least where they do not explicitly trade sex for money. [465]

C. **Enforceability:** As a general rule, *neither party to an illegal contract may enforce it*. This is not an ironclad rule. In general, contracts that are still *wholly executory* are less likely to be enforced by the court than those that have been at least partly performed. [465]

1. **Wholly executory:** If the contract is *completely executory* (i.e., neither party has rendered any performance), there are only a few situations where the court will allow one party to recover damages for breach: [466]

    a. **Ignorance of facts:** Where one of the parties is justifiably *unaware* of the facts which make the contract illegal, and the other is not, the former may usually recover. (*Example*: Owner hires Electrician to perform electrical work; Owner does not know that Electrician is unlicensed. Owner may enforce the contract, even if he discovers the illegality before any work is done or payments made.) [466]

    b. **Wrongful purpose:** Where only one party has a *wrongful purpose*, the other may recover for breach, at least if the wrongful purpose does not involve a crime of serious moral turpitude. (*Example*: A sells diamonds to B knowing that B plans to smuggle them into an Eastern Bloc country, where such importation is not allowed. A may recover for breach before money or goods changes hands, even if A knew of the proposed smuggling at the time of signing.) [466]

    c. **Statute directed at one party:** If the statute is designed to *protect one party*, the person for whose protection the statute is designed may enforce the contract or sue for its breach. (*Example*: A agrees to sell stock to B, in violation of Blue Sky laws. B, as an investor whom the statute is designed to protect, may enforce the contract.) [466]

2. **Partly- or fully-performed illegal contracts:** Where one or both parties have *partly or fully performed*, the courts are more willing to enforce the contract or at least grant a quasi-contractual remedy. The three above situations will generally lead to enforcement as in the wholly-executory situation. Also:

a. **Malum prohibitum:** If the conduct is illegal even though it does *not involve moral turpitude* (a contract involving *"malum prohibitum"* rather than *"malum in se"*), the court may allow the partly-performing party to recover at least the restitutionary value of his services. [466]

Example: Where a contractor fails to obtain a permit or license, and the permit or license is merely a revenue-raising rather than public-protection mechanism, the contractor may be able to recover the value of the work he has done.

b. *Pari delicto:* If one party, although blameworthy, is *much less guilty* than the other party, he may use the doctrine of *"pari delicto"* to gain enforcement. This may only be used where the plaintiff is not guilty of serious moral turpitude (but may be used even by a plaintiff who knew of the illegality). [467]

Example: If Bank lends money to Contractor for Contractor to build a house, even though Bank knows that Contractor is not licenced, there is a good chance that Bank will be held not to be "in *pari delicto*," and will thus be permitted to recover on the loan. But if Bank financed a cocaine deal, Bank's conduct would be found to be of serious moral turpitude, so the *pari delicto* doctrine would not apply, and Bank could not recover.

c. **Divisibility:** Finally, if a *divisible part* of the contract can be performed on both sides without violating public policy, the court will enforce that divisible portion. [467]

Example: Owner contracts to have Plumber supply a bathtub, and to install the bathtub. Plumber does not have a license. A court might hold that Plumber cannot recover that portion of the contract attributable to services, but might still allow Plumber to recover for the value of the tub he supplied.

II. DURESS

A. **Generally:** The defense of *duress* is available if D can show that he was *unfairly coerced* into entering into the contract, or into modifying it. Duress consists of "any wrongful act or threat which *overcomes the free will* of a party." [469]

1. **Subjective standard:** A *subjective standard* is used to determine whether the party's free will has been overcome. Thus even though the will of a person of "ordinary firmness" might not have been overborne, if D can show that he was unusually timid, and was in fact coerced, he may use the defense.

B. **Ways of committing:** Here are some of the acts or threats that may constitute duress: (1) *violence* or threats of it; (2) *imprisonment* or threats of it; (3) wrongful *taking* or *keeping* of a party's *property*, or threats to do so; and (4) threats to *breach* a contract or commit other wrongful acts. [470]

1. **Abusive or oppressive acts:** If one party *threatens another* with a certain act, it is *irrelevant* that the former would have had the *legal right* to perform that act — if the threat, or the ensuing bargain, are *abusive* or *oppressive*, the contract will be void for duress.

Example: Client hires Lawyer to prepare Client's defense against criminal charges, for a flat $10,000 fee. The night before the trial is to begin, Lawyer tells Client, "Double the fee, or I'm resigning from the case." Client agrees. A court will probably hold that given the timing of Lawyer's threat, the threat and/or the ensuing bargain were abusive or oppressive, in which case the court will not enforce the modification.

C. **Threat to breach contract:** Most commonly, duress arises in contract cases because one party *threatens to breach the contract* unless it is *modified* in his favor; the other party reluctantly agrees, and the question is whether the modification is binding. In general, courts apply a *"good faith"* and *"fair dealing"* standard here: if the party seeking modification is using the other's vulnerability to extract an unfair advantage, the duress defense is likely to succeed. If, by contrast, the request for modification is due to unforeseen difficulties, the duress defense will probably fail. [470]

III. MISREPRESENTATION

A. Generally: If a party can show that the other made a *misrepresentation* to him prior to signing, he may be able to use this in either of two ways: (1) he may use this as a *defense* in a breach of contract action brought by the other; or (2) he may use it as the grounds for *rescission* or damages in a suit in which he is the plaintiff. [471]

B. Elements of proof: [471]

1. **Other party's state of mind:** P does *not* generally have to prove that the misrepresentation was *intentionally* made. A *negligent* or even *innocent* misrepresentation will usually be sufficient to avoid the contract, if it is made as to a *material fact*. [471]

2. **Justifiable reliance:** The party asserting misrepresentation must show that he *justifiably relied* on the misstatement. [471]

3. **Fact, not opinion:** The misrepresentation must be one of *fact*, rather than of *opinion*. [471]

   Examples: A salesman's statement, "This is a very reliable little car," is probably so clearly opinion, or "puffing," that the buyer cannot rescind for misrepresentation by showing that the car in fact breaks down a lot. But, "This car gets 30 miles per gallon in city driving," is an assertion of fact, so it can serve as the basis for a misrepresentation claim.

C. Non-disclosure: As a general rule, only *affirmative statements* can serve as the basis for a misrepresentation action. A party's *failure to disclose* will generally *not* justify the other party in obtaining rescission or damages for misrepresentation. But there are some exceptions, situations where non-disclosure *will* support an action: [472]

1. **Half truth:** If *part of the truth* is told, but another part is not, so as to create an overall misleading impression, this may constitute misrepresentation. [473]

2. **Positive concealment:** If a party takes *positive action* to *conceal* the truth, this will be actionable even though it is not verbal. (*Example*: To conceal termite damage, Seller plasters over wooden beams in the house he is selling.) [473]

3. **Failure to correct past statement:** If the party knows that disclosure of a fact is needed to prevent some *previous assertion* from being misleading, and doesn't disclose it, this will be actionable. [473]

4. **Fiduciary relationship:** If the parties have some kind of *fiduciary relationship*, so that one believes that the other is looking out for her interests, there will be a duty to disclose material facts. [473]

5. **Failure to correct mistake:** If one party knows that the other is *making a mistake* as to a *basic assumption*, the former's failure to correct that misunderstanding will be actionable if the non-disclosure amounts to a "failure to act in *good faith*." (*Example*: Jeweler lets Consumer buy a stone, knowing that Consumer falsely believes that the stone is an emerald when it is in fact a topaz worth much less. This would probably be such bad faith that it would constitute misrepresentation.) [473]

IV. UNCONSCIONABILITY AND ADHESION CONTRACTS

A. Adhesion contracts: *"Adhesion contract"* is an imprecise term used to describe a document containing non-bargained clauses that are in fine print, complicated, and/or exceptionally favorable to the drafter. Generally, adhesion contracts are found in situations where the non-drafter has very little bargaining power, because all potential parties on the other side have similar terms that they offer on a non-negotiable "take it or leave it" basis. [475]

   1. Steps for avoiding contract: A litigant who wants to avoid enforcement of a contractual term on the grounds that it is part of an adhesion contract usually has to make *two showings* [475-476]:

   [1] that the contract itself is an *adhesion contract*; and

   [2] that the contract (or the clause complained of) either (i) violates his *reasonable expectations* or (ii) is *unconscionable*.

   a. Reasonable expectations: When the court decides whether the plaintiff's *"reasonable expectations"* were thwarted, this determination is based mostly upon whether a *reasonable person in P's position* would have *expected* that the clause in question was *present in the contract*. So a very *unusual and burdensome clause* stuck into the *fine print* on the back of a standard form contract might flunk this "reasonable expectations" test, and entitle the plaintiff to avoid the contract. [476]

   Example: RentalCo, a car rental agency, sticks a clause in the fine print that says the renter is liable for four times the actual cost of any damage to the car, even if the renter is completely without fault. A court would probably say that this clause is so unusual and burdensome that its presence would thwart the renter's "reasonable expectations." In that event, the clause would probably be held unenforceable, even without the renter's having to show that it was "unconscionable."

   2. Tickets and other "pseudo contracts": Refusal to enforce what the court finds to be a "adhesion contract" is especially likely where the transaction is one in which the non-drafter does not even *realize that he is entering into a contract at all*. Parking-garage tickets, tickets for trains or planes, and tickets to sporting events, are examples: there is often contractual language in fine print on the back of the ticket, but the purchaser does not understand that by buying the ticket she is agreeing to the printed contractual terms. [477]

   a. Refusal to enforce: The language printed on the ticket will generally be enforced only if: (1) the purchaser signs or somehow *manifests assent* to the terms of the ticket; and (2) the purchaser has *reason to believe* that such tickets are regularly used to contain contractual terms like those in fact on the ticket. Even if the ticket is found to be generally enforceable, the court will strike *unreasonable terms*.

B. Unconscionability: If a court finds that a contract or clause is so unfair as to be *"unconscionable,"* the court may decline to enforce that contract or clause. See UCC § 2-302(1). [478]

   1. No definition: There is no accepted definition of unconscionability. The issue is whether the clause is so *one-sided*, so unfair, that a court should as a matter of judicial policy refuse to enforce it. [478]

   2. Consumers: Courts have very rarely allowed *businesspeople* to claim unconscionability; only *consumers* are generally successful with an unconscionability defense. [478]

   3. Varieties: Clauses can be divided into two categories for unconscionability analysis: (1) "procedural" unconscionability; and (2) "substantive" unconscionability. [479]

a. **Procedural:** The *"procedural"* sort occurs where one party is induced to enter the contract without having any **meaningful choice**. Here are some possible types: (1) burdensome clauses tucked away in the fine-print boilerplate; (2) high-pressure salespeople who mislead the uneducated consumer; and (3) industries with few players, all of whom offer the same unfair "adhesion contracts" to defeat bargaining (e.g., indoor parking lots in a downtown area, all disclaiming liability even for gross negligence). [479]

b. **Substantive:** The *"substantive"* sort of unconscionability occurs where the clause or contract itself (rather than the process used to arrive at the contract) is unduly unfair and one-sided. [479]

   i. **Excessive price:** An important example of substantive unconscionability is where the seller charges an **excessive price**. Usually, an excessive price clause only comes about when there is also some sort of procedural unconscionability (e.g., an uneducated consumer who doesn't understand what he is agreeing to), since otherwise the consumer will usually simply find a cheaper supplier. [479-480]

   ii. **Remedy-meddling:** Also, a term may be substantively unfair because it unfairly limits the buyer's **remedies** for breach by the seller. Types of remedy-meddling that might be found to be unconscionable in a particular case include: (1) disclaimer or limitation of **warranty**, especially prohibiting consequential damages for personal injury; (2) limiting the remedy to **repair or replacement**, where this would be a valueless remedy; (3) unfairly broad rights of **repossession** by the seller on credit; (4) waiver of defenses by the buyer as against the seller's **assignee**; and (5) a **cross-collateralization** clause by which a secured seller who has sold multiple items to a buyer on credit has the right to repossess all items until the last penny of total debt is paid. [480-485]

4. **Arbitration clauses:** A large number of unconscionability claims are attempts to strike down so-called *"mandatory arbitration"* clauses. By such a clause, both parties to the contract agree that any dispute between them **must be subject to arbitration** rather than resolved by a **lawsuit. Consumers** and **small businesses** that are required to sign such clauses as part of a large market-leading company's "take it or leave it" adhesion contract are usually the ones who, after signing, claim that the arbitration clause is unconscionable. [481]

   a. **Class-action waivers combined with arbitration clauses:** A claim that a mandatory-arbitration clause is unconscionable is especially powerful when the clause **combines** a mandatory arbitration provision and a **waiver** of the **right to bring a "class" arbitration.** [482]

      i. **Ban on class arbitration:** The issue arises because large corporations often specify, in the mandatory-arbitration clause, that any arbitration must be *"one on one" (or "bilateral")*, i.e., must involve **only a single plaintiff**. (The big company hopes that where each contract and claim tends to be for a small amount, no lawyer is likely to find it worthwhile to take a one-on-one arbitration case on contingent fee, since only a small recovery, and thus a small attorney fee award, is likely.) [482]

      ii. **Struck down by state courts:** State courts have often been **sympathetic** to the claims of plaintiffs — especially consumers — that a combined mandatory-arbitration and no-class-arbitrations clause is unconscionable because it tends to leave plaintiffs in small-dollar-amount contract cases **without an effective remedy.** [Cf. *Scott v. Cingular Wireless*] [482]

   b. **The U.S. Supreme Court steps in (the *AT&T Mobility* case):** But the U.S. Supreme Court **has taken away** a large portion of the right of courts to find that mandatory- arbitration clauses — including ones that prohibit class arbitrations — are unconscionable under state law. In *AT&T Mobility v. Concepcion* (2011), the Court held that a federal statute intended to encourage arbitration (the "FAA") will often **pre-empt** the right of state court to strike down on state-law unconscionability grounds a mandatory-arbitration clause that forbids class arbitrations and class actions. [483]

i.   **Effect of *Mobility* case:** At the least, *AT&T Mobility* seems to mean that state law is preempted if that law (whether judge-made or statutory) makes class litigation unconscionable merely because there is *no other effective remedy*. [484]

Example: Multiple Ps sign service contracts with D, a cellular telephone company. Each P's contract involves a small amount of money. The contracts state that each P waives the right to sue in court for breach; instead, each agrees that any dispute will be subject to mandatory arbitration, and that each arbitration will involve only one claimant. The Ps now want to bring a class action lawsuit against D claiming fraud in D's marketing; the Ps want the class to consist of the hundreds of thousands of customers who have signed identical contracts. The Ps argue that the arbitration clause, insofar as it bans any kind of collective proceeding, is unconscionable and thus unenforceable.

Before *AT&T Mobility*, the state court would have been free to rely heavily on the fact that the contracts' ban on class arbitrations and class action lawsuits would leave small-dollar plaintiffs liked the proposed class members without any effective remedy. The court could therefore hold (as one did on essentially these facts, in *Scott v. Cingular Wireless* [483]) that because of the "lack of effective remedy" problem alone, the individual-arbitrations-only clause is unconscionable and thus unenforceable under state law, so that the Ps can bring their class action lawsuit.

But *Mobility* seems to mean that such a state-law-based holding of unconscionability on these facts is now *pre-empted* by the federal FAA statute. The Supreme Court held in *Mobility* that Congress's purpose in enacting the FAA was to enforce arbitration clauses as written. Letting consumers use the state-law doctrine of unconscionability to force corporate defendants into class-based rather than individual arbitrations would (the Court said in *Mobility*) make arbitration so much less attractive to corporate defendants that it would defeat the pro-arbitration purposes of the FAA. Therefore, the FAA as interpreted in *Mobility* probably pre-empts state courts from making widespread use of unconscionability to block anti-class-arbitration clauses. There may be an exception if the particular arbitration clause is hugely unfair or one-sided (e.g., it provides that a consumer claimant must not only bring an individual arbitration, but must, if she loses, pay triple the corporate winner's actual attorneys fees); a holding that such a rare and patently one-sided clause is unconscionable might have such a small effect on the general attractiveness of arbitration as not to be pre-empted by the FAA. But if the state court merely wants to find a generic no-class-arbitrations clause unconscionable because small-dollar plaintiffs wouldn't be able to attract a lawyer to take the case, that's the sort of broad state-law holding about unconscionability that is probably no longer allowed post-*Mobility*. [484]

5.   **Remedies for unconscionability:** Here are some of the things a court might do to remedy a clause or contract which it finds to be unconscionable: [485]

a.   **Refusal to enforce clause:** Most likely, the court will simply *strike the offending clause*, but enforce the rest of the contract;

b.   **Reformation:** Alternatively, the court may *"reform"* the offending clause (e.g., by modifying an excessive price to make it a reasonable price);

c.   **Refusal to enforce whole contract:** Very occasionally, the court may simply refuse to enforce the *entire contract*, denying P any recovery at all.

V. CAPACITY

A. Generally: Certain classes of persons have only a limited power to contract. Most important are *infants* and the *mentally infirm*. For these people, any contract they enter into is *voidable* at their option — they can enforce the contract or escape from it. [486]

B. Infants: Until a person reaches majority, any contract which he enters into is *voidable* at his option. That is, the minor has the power to *"avoid"* or *"disaffirm"* the contract. The age of majority is a matter of statute, and in most states is now 18. [486-489]

> **Example:** *A*, a 16-year-old, agrees to sell Greenacre to *B*. Two weeks later, *A* later changes his mind and refuses to go through with the sale. *B* may not enforce the agreement against *A*. But *A*, if he wishes, may enforce it against *B*, e.g., by suing *B* for damages for failure to go through with the purchase.

1. Disaffirmance: In nearly every state, an infant may avoid the contract even *before* he reaches majority. He may do this orally, by his conduct (e.g., refusing to go through with the deal), or by a defense when sued for breach. [487]

   a. Land conveyances: But where the contract is for a conveyance of *land*, most states do not allow the infant to disaffirm the contract until he has reached majority.

2. Ratification: A contract made by an infant is not void, but merely voidable, so the infant can choose to *enforce it* if he wishes. If he does this, he is said to have *ratified* the contract. [487-487]

   a. Must reach adulthood: The most important thing to remember about ratification is that the minor *may not ratify until she has reached adulthood*. Ratification may occur in three ways:

      i. Failure to disaffirm: By *inaction* — if the infant does not disaffirm within a reasonable time after reaching majority, she will be held to have implicitly ratified.

      ii. Express: *Expressly* — the contract may be ratified by words, either written or (in most states) oral.

      iii. By conduct: By *conduct* — if the former infant actively induces the other party to perform, this conduct may constitute a ratification (e.g., both parties begin to exchange performances after the infant's majority). But mere part payment or part performance by the former infant is probably not by itself a ratification.

3. Economic adjustment: After disaffirmance, courts will try to make an *economic adjustment* to unwind the contract. [487]

   a. Where infant is defendant: If the infant is a *defendant* to a breach-of-contract suit brought by the non-infant, the latter will not be allowed to recover profits he would have made, or any other contract damages. But he will have a limited right of *restitution*, the right to require the defendant infant to *return the goods* or other value *if he still has them*. [487]

   b. Where infant is plaintiff: If the infant is a *plaintiff* who is suing to recover money already paid by him, the court will require the infant to return any value which he has, and will in fact subtract from the infant's recovery any value obtained and dissipated. [488]

   Example: Infant buys a car for $4,000 in cash from D. Infant then disaffirms and sues to recover his $4,000. To recover the $4,000, Infant will have to return the car. If Infant has wrecked the car, or sold it for money which he has then spent, the value of the car will be subtracted from any recovery by Infant. So if the car was in fact worth $4,000, Infant will recover nothing if he no longer has the car.

   c. Necessaries: Virtually all jurisdictions allow a person who supplies *"necessaries"* to an infant to recover in *quasi-contract* (not on the contract) for the *reasonable value* of those necessaries. The minor cannot avoid such a recovery by disaffirmance. What constitutes "necessaries" varies from state to state, but needed *food, clothing, shelter, medical care* and *legal services* are among the items that are likely to be covered. [487]

> **Example:** Minor shows up at the emergency room of Hospital with appendicitis. Minor agrees to pay the bill. Hospital treats him. Hospital will be entitled to recover the reasonable value of the services directly from Minor — since the services were "necessaries," Minor does not have the right to disaffirm.

4. **Lies about age:** If the infant *lies about his age*, all courts let the other party *avoid the contract* on grounds of fraud. In other words, the infant who falsely claims adulthood loses his power to ratify the contract. [488]

C. **Mental incompetents:** A *mental incompetent* is governed by the same basic rules as an infant — he may either disaffirm the contract or ratify it. A person lacks capacity to contract because of mental incompetence if either: (1) he doesn't understand the contract; or (2) he understands it, but acts irrationally, and the other person knows he is acting irrationally. [489-491]

D. **Intoxication:** *Intoxication* will give a party the power of avoidance only if: (1) he is so intoxicated that he cannot *understand* the nature of his transaction; *and* (2) the other party has a *reason to know* that this is the case. [490]

CHAPTER 14
WARRANTIES

I. WARRANTIES GENERALLY

A. **Types:** Under the UCC, a seller may make several warranties that are of importance: (1) an *express* warranty; (2) an implied warranty of *merchantability*; and (3) a warranty of *fitness for a particular purpose*. If the seller breaches any of these warranties, the buyer may bring a damage action for breach of warranty, which can be viewed as a special type of breach-of-contract action. [497]

II. EXPRESS WARRANTIES

A. **Definition:** An express warranty is an *explicit* (not just implied) promise or guarantee by the seller that the goods will have certain qualities. See UCC § 2-313(1)(a): "Any *affirmation of fact or promise* made by the seller to the buyer which relates to the goods and becomes part of the *basis of the bargain* creates an express warranty that the goods shall conform to the affirmation or promise." [498]

1. **Description:** A *description* of goods can be an express warranty. (*Example*: A bill of sale issued by Jeweler to Consumer recites, "Three carat flawless white diamond ring." This constitutes an express warranty that the ring is a diamond with those characteristics.) [498]

2. **Sample or model:** If the buyer is shown a *sample* or *model*, this will normally amount to an express warranty that the rest of the goods conform to the sample or model. [499]

3. **Puffing:** If the seller is clearly *"puffing,"* or expressing an *opinion*, he will not be held to have made a warranty. [498] (*Example*: A used-car salesperson's statement that, "This is a top-notch car," will probably be held to be mere puffing, not an express warranty of anything. But the statement, "This car will do 30 m.p.g. in city driving," is specific enough to amount to an express warranty.)

III. IMPLIED WARRANTY OF MERCHANTABILITY

A. Generally: The most important warranty given in the UCC is the implied warranty of *merchantability*. UCC § 2-314(1) provides: "Unless excluded or modified…a warranty that goods shall be merchantable is *implied* in a contract for their sale if the seller is a *merchant* with respect to goods of that kind." [499]

B. Meaning of "merchantable": There is no precise definition of "merchantable." The most important meaning is that the goods must be *"fit for the ordinary purposes for which such goods are used."* § 2-314(2)(c). (*Example*: Dealer sells a new car to Buyer. Due to a manufacturing defect, the car cannot go more than 25 m.p.h. Since cars are generally sold and used for high-speed highway driving, this would be a breach of the implied warranty of merchantability, even though Dealer never expressly promised any particular speed.) [499]

C. Always given unless disclaimed: The implied warranty of merchantability is *always* given by a merchant seller, unless it is expressly excluded by a *disclaimer* that meets stringent formal requirements imposed by the Code.

IV. WARRANTY OF FITNESS FOR PARTICULAR PURPOSE

A. Generally: Depending on the circumstances, a seller may be found to have impliedly warranted that the goods are *fit for a particular purpose*. UCC § 2-315 provides that "where the seller at the time of contracting has *reason to know* any particular purpose for which the goods are required and that the buyer is *relying on the seller's judgment* to select or furnish suitable goods, there is…an implied warranty that the goods shall be fit for such purpose." [500]

B. Elements: The buyer must prove three things to recover for breach of this implied warranty: (1) that the seller had reason to know the buyer's *purpose*; (2) that the seller had reason to know that the buyer was *relying* on the seller's skill or judgment to furnish suitable goods; and (3) that the buyer *did in fact rely* on the seller's skill or judgment. [500]

    1. Use of trade name: If the buyer insists on a particular *brand* of goods, he is not relying on the seller's skill or judgment, so no implied warranty of fitness for a particular purpose arises. [501]

V. PRIVITY

A. Definition: Two persons are *"in privity"* with each other if they contracted with each other. [501]

B. When privity is necessary: UCC § 2-318, stating when privity is necessary for a UCC breach-of-warranty action, actually has three separate alternatives. Each has been adopted in some states. [501]

    1. Alternative A: Alternative A extends the seller's warranty (express or implied) only to a member of the buyer's *family* or *household*, or a house guest, and only where it is foreseeable that the person may use and be injured by the goods. A person other than the buyer thus cannot recover in states adopting Alternative A unless he is *physically injured*, and is a *relative or house guest* of the buyer. [501]

    2. Alternative B: Alternative B covers any person, even if not a relative or house guest of the buyer, who may reasonably be expected to use or be affected by the goods. But, as with Alternative A, only *personal injury* is covered. [502]

    3. Alternative C: Alternative C is the broadest: it extends the warranty to all persons who may be expected to use or be affected by the goods. Most importantly, it covers *property* and *economic* damage as well as personal injury, and may even cover intangible economic loss. [502]

VI. DISCLAIMERS OF WARRANTY

A. Generally: The UCC limits the extent to which a seller may *disclaim* warranties. [502-504]

B. Express warranties: The seller is basically free to disclaim *express* warranties, as long as he does so in a clear and reasonable way. However, this rarely happens — since nothing forces the seller to make an express warranty in the first place, he will usually have no reason to disclaim it after making it. [502]

C. Implied warranties: Disclaimers of the two *implied* warranties (merchantability and fitness for particular purpose) are tightly limited by the Code: [503-504]

    1. Explicit disclaimers: The seller may make an *explicit disclaimer* of these warranties, but only by complying with strict procedural rules: [503]

        a. Merchantability: A disclaimer of the warranty of *merchantability* must *mention the word "merchantability."* § 2-316(2). The disclaimer does not have to be in writing, but *if it is in writing, it must be "conspicuous."* In other words, the disclaimer cannot be buried in the *fine print* of the contract. (Usually, capital letters, bold face type, bigger type, or a different color type are used to meet the "conspicuous" requirement where the disclaimer is written.) [503]

        b. Fitness for a particular purpose: A disclaimer of the warranty of fitness for a particular purpose *must be in writing*, and must also be *conspicuous*. (But it does not need to use any particular words, in contrast to a disclaimer of the warranty of merchantability.) (*Example*: The following language, if in writing and conspicuous, would suffice: "There are no warranties which extend beyond the description on the face hereof.") [503]

    2. Implied limitations and disclaimers: There are also several ways in which the implied warranties may be *implicitly* limited or disclaimed: [503]

        a. Language of sale: The *language of the sale* may implicitly disclaim the warranty. Most importantly, if the sale is made *"as is,"* this will implicitly exclude all implied warranties.

        b. Examination of sample or model: If the buyer is asked to *examine* a *sample* or *model*, or the *goods themselves*, there is no implied warranty with regard to defects which an examination ought to have revealed. UCC § 2-316(3)(b). (*Example*: Buyer buys a floor sample T.V. from Dealer. If inspection of the cabinetry would have shown a dent, Buyer cannot claim that the dent is a violation of the implied warranty of merchantability.)

        c. Course of dealing: An implied warranty can be excluded or modified by *course of dealing*, *course of performance*, and *usage of trade*. (*Example*: The dealings of the parties on prior contracts might create a "course of performance" to the effect that the goods are bought "as is" in return for a lower price.)

VII. MODIFYING CONTRACT REMEDIES

A. UCC limits: Instead of disclaiming warranties, the seller may try to *limit* the buyer's *remedies* for breaches of warranty or other contract breaches. (*Example*: Seller may insert a clause that Buyer's remedies are limited to repair or replacement of defective goods or parts, with no consequential damages.) But the UCC limits the seller's right to do this "remedy meddling" in two ways. [504-505]

    1. "Failure of essential purpose": First, if the remedy as limited by seller would *"fail of its essential purpose,"* the standard UCC remedies come back into the contract. [504]

Example: Seller sells yarn to Buyer, knowing that Buyer will dye the yarn and use it in products. Seller limits the warranty to repair or replacement of defective yarn. Buyer then spends a great deal of labor knitting the yarn into expensive sweaters, which fall apart due to poor quality yarn. A court might hold that here, repair or replacement of yarn that has already been expensively knitted into sweaters would be a useless remedy, in which case the basic Code remedy of money damages for breach of the implied warranty of merchantability would re-enter the contract.

2. **Unconscionability:** Second, the court will refuse to enforce a damage limitation if it finds that this is *unconscionable*. According to § 2-713(3): (1) barring consequential damages for *personal injury* will virtually always be unconscionable; but (2) limiting damages where the loss is *commercial* will generally not be unconscionable. [504-505]

CHAPTER 15

DISCHARGE OF CONTRACTS

I. RESCISSION

A. Mutual rescission: As long as a contract is *executory* on both sides (i.e., neither party has fully performed), the parties may agree to *cancel* the whole contract. This is a *"mutual rescission."* [509]

1. **No writing:** In most states, a mutual rescission does *not have to be in writing*. This is true even if the original contract fell within the Statute of Frauds. [510]

2. **Fully performed on one side:** If the contract has been *fully performed* on one side, a mutual rescission will *not be effective*, because there is no mutual consideration. [509]

B. Unilateral rescission: Where one of the parties to a contract has been the victim of fraud, duress, mistake, or breach by the other party, he will generally be allowed to cancel the contract, terminating his obligations under it. Some courts call this a *"unilateral rescission."* But it is better to say that the innocent party may *"cancel"* or "terminate." [510]

II. EXECUTORY ACCORDS, AND "ACCORD AND SATISFACTION"

A. Executory accord generally: An *executory accord* is an agreement by the parties to a contract under which one promises to render a *substitute performance* in the future, and the other promises to *accept that substitute* in discharge of the existing duty. [510]

Example: Debtor owes Creditor $1,000 due in 30 days. Creditor promises Debtor that if Debtor will pay $1,100 in 60 days, Creditor will accept this payment in discharge; Debtor promises to make the $1,100 payment in 60 days. The new agreement is an executory accord.

B. Consequences: Executory accords are enforceable. However, an accord does *not discharge* the previous contractual duty as soon as the accord is made; instead, no discharge occurs until the terms of the accord are *performed*. Once the terms of the accord are performed, there is said to have been an *"accord and satisfaction."* [510]

1. **Failure to perform accord:** If a party *fails to perform* under the terms of the executory accord, the other party may sue for breach of the *original agreement*, or breach of the accord, at her option. [511]

Example: On the facts of the above example, if Debtor fails to make the $1,100 payment, Creditor may sue for either $1,000 plus damages for failure to get the money in 30 days, or $1,100 plus damages for failure to get the money in 60 days.

III. SUBSTITUTED AGREEMENT

A. Nature of substituted agreement: A *"substituted agreement"* is similar but not identical to an executory accord. Under a substituted agreement, the previous contract is ***immediately discharged***, and replaced with a new agreement. [511-513]

> **Example:** On the facts of the above example, if the new agreement were be found to be a substituted agreement rather than an executory accord, and Debtor then failed to make the payment in 60 days, Creditor would only be able to sue on the new promise, not the old promise.

1. Distinguishing: In determining whether a given agreement is a substitute agreement or executory accord, an important factor is whether the claim is a disputed one as to liability or amount — if the debtor in good faith ***disputes*** either the existence of the debt or its amount, the presumption is that there is a substituted agreement. If the amount and obligation are undisputed, the presumption will be that there is an executory accord. [512]

a. Level of formality: Another important factor in distinguishing substituted agreements from executory accords is the ***level of formality:*** the more ***deliberate and formalized*** the agreement, the more likely it is to be a substituted agreement. For instance, an ***oral*** agreement is very likely to be an ***accord***, not a substituted agreement, because of its informality. [512]

B. Writing: If the substituted agreement would have to satisfy the Statute of Frauds were it an original contract, the substituted agreement must be in ***writing***. (Some states also require the substituted agreement to be in writing if the original is in writing, even where neither falls within the Statute of Frauds.) [513]

IV. NOVATION

A. Definition: A *"novation"* occurs where the obligee under an original contract (the person to whom the duty is owed) agrees to relieve the obligor of all liability after the duty is ***delegated*** to some third party. A novation thus substitutes for the original obligor a stranger to the original contract, the delegate. [513]

> **Example:** Contractor agrees to paint Owner's house for $10,000. Contractor does not have enough time to get the job done, so with Owner's consent he recruits Painter to do the job instead. If Owner agrees to release Contractor from liability, the result is a novation: Painter steps into the shoes of Contractor, and only Painter, not Contractor, owes a duty to Owner.

B. Consent: The obligee must ***consent*** to the novation. But the obligor, who is being discharged, need not consent. (*Example*: On the facts of the above example, Owner must consent to the novation, but Contractor need not consent, at least to the delegation/release aspect of it.) [513]

V. ACCOUNT STATED

A. Generally: Where a party who has sold goods or services to another sends a ***bill***, and the buyer holds the bill for an unreasonably long time ***without objecting*** to its contents, the seller will be able to use the bill as the basis for a suit on an *"account stated."* The invoice is not dispositive proof that that amount is owing, but the burden of proving that the invoice is wrong shifts to the buyer. [513]

VI. RELEASES

A. Generally: Where a contract is executory only on one side, the party who has fully performed may give up his rights by virtue of a ***release***, a document executed by him discharging the other party. [514]

B. Formal requirements: In most states, a release must either be supported by ***consideration***, or by a statutory substitute (e.g., a signed writing). [514]

   1. UCC view: Under the UCC, a signed writing can release a claim for breach of contract, even without consideration.

CHAPTER 1

INTRODUCTION

I. MEANING OF "CONTRACT"

A. **Definition:** A "contract" can be defined for most purposes as an *agreement* which the law will *enforce* in some way. See C&P, p. 1.

    1. **Containing at least one promise:** A contract must contain at least one *promise*, i.e., a commitment to do something in the *future*. A contract is thus said to be "executory," rather than "executed."

        Example: Suppose *A* transfers title to her car to *B*, and in return simultaneously receives $1,000 from *B*; this whole transaction is done on the spur of the moment. No contract has been created. Since the transaction contains no promise by either party of a *future* performance, it is completely executed, rather than executory. If, on the other hand, *A* had *promised* that she would transfer title to *B*, and *B* had promised to give *A* $1,000 (or had in fact given *A* the $1,000 immediately), there *would* be a contract, since *A*'s performance was to occur in the future.

    2. **Written vs. oral contracts:** The term "contract" is often used to refer to a written document which embodies an agreement. But for legal purposes, an agreement may be a binding and enforceable contract in most circumstances even though it is *oral*. The few kinds of contracts for which a written document is necessary are discussed in the chapter on the Statute of Frauds, *infra*, p. 275.

    3. **Contracts vs. quasi-contracts:** Contracts must be distinguished from what are sometimes called *"quasi-contracts."* A quasi-contract is not a contract at all, but is rather the term used by some courts to denote a recovery imposed by law where justice so requires, even though the parties have not made any agreement. Thus a physician who renders emergency services to an injured pedestrian he finds on the sidewalk might be allowed to recover in quasi-contract even though his services were not requested by the victim (or by anyone else). Quasi-contractual recovery is discussed more fully *infra*, p. 335.

        a. **Implied in law:** A quasi-contractual recovery is often called "implied in law" recovery. The term "implied in law" should not be confused with a contract that is "implied in fact." An "implied-in-fact" contract is a real contract, but one in which agreement is reached by the parties' actions, rather than their words. If a person visits a doctor to discuss an ailment, an agreement to pay a reasonable fee will be "implied in fact" even though neither party mentions payment. Implied-in-fact contracts are treated exactly like "express" contracts (i.e., contracts agreed upon by words) for almost all purposes, but are treated very differently from "implied-in-law" contracts (i.e., quasi-contracts).

II. VOID, VOIDABLE AND UNENFORCEABLE CONTRACTS

A. **Differing legal consequences:** The usual contract, which may be enforced by either party, is said to be "enforceable." There are, however, certain kinds of agreements which are not fully enforceable.

1. **Void contracts:** Some kinds of agreements are said to be *"void,"* although this is a contradiction in terms. What is meant is that these agreements have no legal effect. Thus a gambling contract might be said to be "void as against public policy."

2. **Voidable contracts:** A *"voidable"* contract is one which one party may at his option either enforce or not enforce. Thus a *minor* who has made what would otherwise be a binding agreement, or a person who has been induced to agree by *fraud*, has the choice of either "avoiding" the contract (i.e., acting as if no agreement had ever been made), or enforcing it.

3. **Unenforceable contracts:** An *"unenforceable"* contract is one which does not give an immediate right to judicial relief, but which nonetheless has some legal status. The most important difference between an "unenforceable" contract and a so-called "void" contract is that the unenforceable contract may be converted into a fully binding contract by the act of one of the parties, while a void contract may not.

    a. **Statute of Frauds:** A common example of an unenforceable contract is an oral agreement of a type for which a writing is necessitated by the Statute of Frauds (e.g., a contract for the sale of land). If, after such an oral agreement has been reached, one party produces a written statement of its terms, the agreement is rendered enforceable against him. (A "void" contract, on the other hand, can never be rendered enforceable by the act of just one party.)

III. ECONOMIC ANALYSIS OF CONTRACT LAW

A. **Generally:** An important development in the law of contracts over the last few decades has been the increasing use of *economic theory* to analyze contracts problems.

    1. **The "Chicago school" of legal analysis:** The use of economic analysis is closely associated with the University of Chicago Law School, so much so that the predominant wing of economics-and-law is known as the "Chicago school." That wing has been led by Richard Posner and Frank Easterbrook, both University of Chicago law professors who subsequently became judges on the U.S. Court of Appeals for the Seventh Circuit.

B. **Focus on efficiency:** The central tenet of economic analysis is that *"efficiency"* should be the major objective of contract law. Most scholars who promote efficiency as an objective have in mind two main sorts of goals:

    1. keeping *"transaction costs"* (e.g., litigation costs and legal fees) as *low as possible*;

    2. *allocating resources* to their *most highly valued uses*.

        K&C, p. 11.

C. **Various contexts:** We will be encountering a number of contexts in which economic analysis of particular contract-law rules seems especially useful. Most of these contexts involve "remedies," that is, the means by which courts attempt to protect a contracting party when the other party breaches the agreement.

    1. **Some examples:** It is hard, at this early point in your Contracts course, to give you good examples of how economic analysis may be used in contract law. However, here are a couple of illustrations, both connected with the problem of compensating a party who has been the victim of breach.

Example 1: Treadmill Co. manufactures electric treadmills, for which it needs many component parts. Treadmill Co. gets an order for 10,000 machines from Wal-Mart stores. Treadmill Co. contracts with Component Corp. to have Component Corp. custom manufacture 100,000 precisely machined gears, 10 of which are needed for each treadmill. Component Corp. custom manufactures the first 10,000 gears, delivers them to Treadmill Co., and is paid. Wal-Mart than cancels the remainder of its contract with Treadmill. Treadmill Co. immediately tells Component Corp. to stop making any more gears. The president of Component Corp. replies, "I've got a contract, and I'm going to make the remaining 90,000 gears and insist that you pay for them." Because these gears are to be custom machined, they will have no other use, and will only be saleable for their salvage value.

If the law of Contracts permits or encourages Component Corp. to insist on finishing the contract and recovering the full contract price, economic waste — inefficiency — will obviously result. (Time and materials will be spent making the 90,000 pieces, which will just end up being sold for scrap by either Component Corp. or Treadmill.) Therefore, a court will instead require that Component *"mitigate its damages."* (See *infra*, p. 347.) That is, Component will not be permitted to recover for any of its costs incurred after receiving the stop-manufacturing notice from Treadmill. Component will instead be allowed to recover the profits it would have made from the last 90,000 pieces, and no time and materials will be wasted. See K&C, p. 1010.

Example 2: Same initial facts as Example 1. Assume that the price under the contract with Treadmill is $1 per gear. Also, assume that after Component Corp. has custom manufactured the 100,000 gears, a new customer, Bicycle Co., says to Component Corp., "We need 100,000 gears [which coincidentally require the same specs as the ones made for Treadmill] by tomorrow, and we'll pay $3 per gear." There's no time for Component to make an additional 100,000 gears, so it will either have to forgo the Bicycle order or breach the Treadmill contract by giving Bicycle the gears made for Treadmill. Assume that the gears, if timely delivered, would be worth $1.50 per unit to Treadmill, so that Treadmill would suffer a "loss" of 50¢ by not getting the shipment on time.

Economic analysis says that the law of Contracts should impose a rule of damages such that the gears will end up going to Bicycle instead of to Treadmill. Indeed, that analysis says that the rules should be ones that encourage Component to **break its contract** with Treadmill and deliver to Bicycle. The standard "expectation" measure of damages — which gives Treadmill a damage award of 50¢ per gear, the difference between the contract price and the value of the gears to Treadmill — will do this: Component can charge Bicycle $3, pay 50¢ damages to Treadmill, and pocket the remaining $2.50 (which is $1.50 more than it would have gotten had it honored the contract). So each party is better off than it would have been under a system which compels or strongly encourages the parties not to breach (e.g., a scheme under which Component had to pay Treadmill 10 times its actual losses in the event of a breach).

Note: These two examples over-simplify many aspects of the analysis. For instance, Example 2 ignores transaction costs, such as Treadmill's legal fees in having to bring suit to collect the 50¢ per gear difference between the contract price and the value of the gears to it. Furthermore, our analysis ignores the fact that the parties always have the power to agree to a consensual "buy out" of the contract, so that a damages rule that facilitates breach is not the only way to bring about an efficient result. For instance, even if the rule was that the breaching seller (Component) had to pay 10 times the buyer's actual damages, Treadmill Co. could agree to surrender its contract rights for, say, $1 per gear, leaving all three parties better off.

Despite the oversimplification inherent in these two examples, they indicate that economic analysis can help:

(1) explain why the standard rules of contract law are what they are; and

(2) in a few instances, perhaps, show why the standard rules should be changed to produce more efficient outcomes.

IV. SOURCES OF CONTRACT LAW

A. The UCC: In most states, most aspects of contract law are governed by case law (i.e., "common law"), rather than by statutes. But in every state except Louisiana, *sales of goods* (i.e., sales of things other than land or services) are governed by a statute that is roughly the same in all states, called the *Uniform Commercial Code*. The UCC has a number of Articles, concerned with a variety of kinds of transactions; here, our principal interest will be in *Article 2*, which deals with *sales of goods*.

1. State enactments: The UCC is a "model statute," originally drafted by, and now periodically updated by, a group called the National Conference of Commissioners of Uniform State Laws ("NCCUSL"). Each state legislature makes its own decision about whether and when to adopt revisions of the various UCC articles proposed by the NCCUSL.

   a. 2003 Revision: The NCCUSL drafted a *revision* of Article 2 in *2003*. That revision made some significant changes, especially in the area of electronic commerce. However, this 2003 Revision failed spectacularly in the "marketplace" of state legislatures: *no state adopted it*. Therefore, the NCCUSL withdrew the 2003 revision in 2011. Consequently, the version of Article 2 in force virtually everywhere in the U.S. as of this writing (mid 2015) is the *1990 text*.

   b. Our text: Therefore, when this book refers to an Article 2 provision, the reference is to the *1990 version* of Article 2, which is essentially unchanged since the original promulgation of Article 2 in 1957.

2. Common-law residue: Even in a transaction involving the sale of goods, if the UCC is silent as to a particular question, the case law controls. Thus UCC § 1-103(b) provides that the "principles of law and equity" control "unless displaced by the particular provisions of [the UCC]."

B. The Restatements: In order to organize and summarize the American common law of contracts, the American Law Institute published the *Restatement of Contracts* in 1932. Since then, the Restatement has had enormous importance. A second edition of the Restatement, usually referred to as the *Second Restatement of Contracts*, was published in 1980 and is frequently cited here.

CHAPTER 2

OFFER AND ACCEPTANCE

ChapterScope

This chapter discusses the first major requirement for a valid contract: that the parties have reached "mutual assent" on the basic terms of the deal. Here are a few of the key principles covered in this chapter:

■ **Mutual assent:** For a contract to be formed, the parties must reach *"mutual assent."* That is, they must *both intend to contract*, and they must *agree* on at least the *main terms* of their deal.

■ **Objective theory of contracts:** In determining whether the parties have reached mutual assent, what matters is *not* what each party *subjectively intended*. Instead, a party's intentions are measured by what a *reasonable person in the position of the other party* would have thought the first party intended, based on the first party's actions and statements. This principle is known as the *"objective theory of contracts."*

■ **Offer and acceptance:** Normally, for a contract to come into existence, there must be an "offer" and an "acceptance."

❏ **Offer:** An *"offer"* is a statement or act that creates a "power of acceptance." When a person makes an offer, she is indicating that she is willing to be *immediately bound* by the other person's acceptance, *without further negotiation.*

❏ **Acceptance:** An *"acceptance"* is a statement or act that indicates the offeree's immediate intent to *enter into the deal* proposed by the offer. As long as the acceptance takes place while the offer is still outstanding, *a contract is formed as soon as the acceptance occurs.*

■ **Duration of the power of acceptance:** When you analyze facts to see whether a valid offer and acceptance occurred, one of your key jobs is to figure out whether the offer *ended* before the "acceptance" occurred (in which case there's no contract). The main ways in which an offer can end are:

❏ the offer is *rejected* by the offeree;

❏ the offeree makes a *counter-offer*;

❏ the offeror *revokes* the offer;

❏ the offer *lapses* by passage of time;

❏ either the offeror or the offeree *dies* or becomes incapacitated.

I. INTENT TO CONTRACT

A. Mutual assent: For a contract to be formed, the parties must reach an agreement to which they "mutually assent." This mutual assent is almost invariably reached through what are called "the offer" and "the acceptance" (see *infra*, p. 9).

1. **Not subjective agreement:** However, this requirement of "mutual assent" does not mean that the parties must have *subjectively* (i.e., in their minds) been in agreement. Rather, it means that each party must *act* in such a way as to lead the other to reasonably believe that an agreement has been reached. The doctrine that only the parties' acts, and not their subjective thoughts, are relevant in determining whether there has been mutual assent, stems from the *objective theory of contracts*, discussed below.

2. **Agreement required only as to major terms:** The requirement of mutual assent does not mean that the parties must agree (even by the objective standard) on *all* the terms of the contract. Instead, they must agree on the "major" or "essential" terms. If they disagree on minor terms, or if they have simply not provided for such minor terms, the court may conclude that one party's understanding controls, or may supply the missing terms. But the parties must, despite the minor gaps or minor disagreements, *intend* to have a contract. For a more full discussion of missing or misunderstood terms, see *infra*, p. 67 and p. 155.

B. Objective theory of contracts: Because neither contracting parties nor courts are mind-readers, it is important that the existence and terms of contracts be determined from the *manifestations* made by each of the parties, rather than by each party's subjective intention. Thus a party's intentions are to be gauged *objectively*, rather than subjectively.

1. **Test for intent:** The objective measure of a party's intention is, in most circumstances, *what a reasonable person in the position of the other party would conclude that his objective manifestations of intent meant*. C&P, p. 26.

> **Example:** *A* says to *B*, "I'll sell you my house for $1,000." *B* says, "OK, you've got a deal." *A*'s house is in fact worth considerably more than $1,000, and *A* refuses to consummate the deal. *B* sues. If *B* can demonstrate that *A*'s tone of voice or *A*'s known lack of business acumen led *B* to the reasonable conclusion that *A*'s offer was serious, the court will treat *A* as having intended to contract. This will be so even though *A* proves definitively that he intended a joke (e.g., by producing *X* to testify that *A* told *X* right after the offer that he intended a joke).
>
> If, on the other hand, a person in *B*'s position would reasonably have understood that *A* was joking (e.g., if *B* should have recognized the bantering tone in *A*'s voice, or should have known that *A*'s house was worth so much more than $1,000 that the offer could only have been made in jest), the court will treat *A* as not having intended to contract, and no contract will be found to have been formed.
>
> Similarly, if *A* can prove that *B* knew *A* was joking (e.g., *A* produces a witness who says that *B* told him, "I knew *A* was joking, but I'm going to try to force the sale anyway"), there is no mutual assent, even though it would not have been unreasonable for *B* to think *A* was serious. This is because *B* is charged with both knowledge that he actually had about *A*'s intent, and the knowledge that he should reasonably have had. If *B* either knew, or should have known, that *A* was joking, there is no mutual assent and no contract. C&P, p. 27.

   a. **Secret intent:** A corollary of the objective theory of contracts is that a party's *secret* intentions (that is, secret from the other party) are *irrelevant* in determining whether a contract exists, and what its terms are.

2. **Other uses for objective theory:** The objective theory of contracts will be used not only to determine whether the mutual assent necessary to form a contract has occurred, but also to determine the *meaning* of particular terms of the contract.

> **Example:** *A* and *B* sign a complex agreement for a sale of goods by *B* to *A*. The contract makes no mention of whether *B* is to insure the shipment. *B* has always done so in past deals with *A*, but this time he subjectively intends not to insure the goods, because insurance prices have gone up. He says to *A*, however, "This deal's just like the ones we've done before." A court would probably hold that *A* reasonably expected *B* to insure the shipment as he had always done, and *B* will be placed under a contractual obligation to do so, despite his subjective intent to the contrary.

C. **Intent to create legal relations:** What happens if the parties go through all of the motions of giving mutual assent to what appears to be a contractual agreement, but subjectively neither party expects the "contract" to be enforceable in court?

1. **Modern view:** Under modern case law, the importance of the parties' intention, or lack of intention, that the contract be legally enforceable, depends largely upon the *context* of the agreement.

2. **Business agreements:** Where the transaction is one which would normally be considered a *"business"* transaction, it will be *presumed* that the parties intended that the agreement be *legally enforceable.* Rest. 2d, § 21.

    a. **Contract made in jest:** Thus in a business context, even if one party makes an offer *in jest*, and the other party reasonably believes that she is serious, and seriously accepts the offer, the contract will be binding.

    > **Example:** P offers the Ds (husband and wife) $50,000 for their farm. The Ds write out a one-line statement — "We hereby agree to sell to [P] the Ferguson Farm complete for $50,000, title satisfactory to buyer" — and they sign it. When the Ds fail to go through with the sale, P sues. The Ds defend on the ground that they were drunk when they signed the document, and were only joking, and that they thought that P was also only joking. Also, they claim that they told P, even before he left the premises, that they didn't really intend to sell the farm.
    >
    > *Held*, the Ds are bound, even if they subjectively did not intend to sell, and were only joking. The evidence indicates that P took them completely seriously, and that he was not unreasonable in doing so. "A person cannot set up that he was merely jesting when his conduct and words would warrant a reasonable person in believing that he intended a real agreement." *Lucy v. Zehmer*, 84 S.E.2d 516 (Va. 1954).

    b. **Manifest intent not to have legal relations:** There is one exception to this general rule that what appears to be a business transaction shall be presumed to have been intended to be enforceable. The exception is that where *both* parties to a business arrangement *explicitly* manifest their understanding that the arrangement is not to be legally binding, it will not be enforced by a court. C&P, pp. 29-30; Rest. 2d, § 21.

3. **Domestic and social situations:** Where an agreement arises in a *social* or *domestic* situation, on the other hand, the presumption is that legal relations were *not* intended.

Example: Husband promises to pay a certain monthly allowance to Wife, with whom he is living amicably at the time of the promise. The couple later separate; Wife sues for the payments owing.

Held, the agreement is not enforceable, because agreements between family members living amicably together are presumed not to have been intended as legally enforceable. *Balfour v. Balfour*, 2 K.B. 571 (1919).

Note: Where an agreement is made between family members *not* living together amicably (e.g., a separation settlement), the agreement will usually be presumed to have been intended to be legally enforceable. Even in the *Balfour* situation, the contract will be enforced if the parties explicitly agree that it is to be enforceable. See Rest. 2d, § 21, Comment c.

D. **Intent to memorialize agreement in writing:** Suppose two parties negotiate with each other, reach a mutual assent on all the terms of the proposed agreement, and also decide that they will *subsequently put their entire agreement into a formal written document* which both will sign. Is there a contract as soon as the mutual assent is reached, or only when the formal document is written up and signed? The question can arise not only when the parties conduct their preliminary negotiations orally, but also when they exchange letters or documents.

1. **Where intent to be bound manifested:** If the parties' actions or words make it clear that they intend to be bound even before the legal document is drawn up, the courts will almost always find an enforceable contract, even if the document is never drawn up. Murray, p. 34. C&P, pp. 47-48.

2. **Where intent not to be bound manifested:** If the parties' actions or words make it clear that they intend *not* to be bound unless and until the document is drawn up, the courts will not find an enforceable contract until the document is drawn up. *Id*.

3. **Where no intent manifested:** Where the parties have not manifested any intent at all about whether they want to be bound before the document is drawn up, and have indicated only that they wish such a document to be produced, the courts are split as to whether there is a contract.

   a. **Majority view:** Most have held that in this situation a contract exists *as soon as the mutual assent is reached*, even if no formal document is ever drawn up. C&P, p. 48. Murray, p. 35.

4. **Letter of intent, contemplating more formal agreement:** A similar problem can arise where the parties sign a so-called *"letter of intent"* (or, as it is sometimes called, an "agreement in principle.") Such a document memorializes the basic terms on which the parties have agreed, but anticipates *further negotiations* on more minor issues. Often, the letter of intent indicates that a fuller and more formal agreement will be prepared later. If the parties are unable to settle the supposedly small issues, what happens if one party asserts that the letter of intent is binding, and the other disagrees?

   a. **Intent of parties, as shown by document:** All courts agree that the test is whether the parties *intended to be bound* by the letter of intent itself. Most courts further agree that the most important indication of the parties' intent is the terms of the letter agreement itself (since under the objective theory of contracts a party's subjective intentions are meaningless, and the best objective indication of intent is the written document).

   b. Clues in the document: The letter of intent may contain a number of clues about whether the parties intended to be immediately bound. Here are some examples:

❏ If the letter says that it is *"subject to"* a formal asset purchase agreement or the like, this is a strong clue that the letter itself was not intended to be binding.

❏ If the document discloses particular issues on which *further negotiation is necessary*, and these issues appear non-trivial, that militates against a finding that the letter was to be binding.

❏ Any reference to *procedural formalities* that one or both parties must go through before any closing (e.g., shareholder approval) cuts against enforceability.

❏ The *larger or more complex* the transaction, the less likely it is that the letter of intent was intended to be binding.

II. OFFER AND ACCEPTANCE GENERALLY

A. Requirement of offer and acceptance: The "mutual assent" necessary for the formation of a contract generally takes place through what are called an *"offer"* and an *"acceptance."* That is, one party proposes a bargain (this proposal is the offer) and the other party agrees to this proposed bargain (this agreement is the acceptance).

B. Restatement definition: The Second Restatement defines an offer to be "the manifestation of *willingness to enter into a bargain*, so made as to justify another person in understanding that his assent to that bargain is invited and will *conclude* [the bargain]." Rest. 2d, § 24.

C. Promise contained in offer: In most cases, the offer will contain a conditional promise, and will propose that the other party accept the proposal by making a promise in return.

    Example: *A* makes the following offer to *B*: "I offer to buy your 2010 Toyota for $10,000, delivery and payment to occur three months from now." What *A* has done through his offer is to make a promise to pay *B* $10,000, conditional on *B*'s making a promise to deliver the car to *A*. Thus *A* has proposed that the parties exchange *promises*.

   1. Unilateral contracts: In some instances, the offer will propose not an exchange of promises, but rather an exchange of the offeror's promise for the offeree's *act*. A contract in which only one party promises to do something, and the other party is free to act or not as she wishes, is called a *unilateral* contract.

    Example: *A* says to *B*, "If you walk across the Brooklyn Bridge, I promise to pay you $1,000." The bargain which *A* has proposed is not an exchange of promises, since *A* does not seek to have *B* promise to do anything. Instead, *A* has proposed that he exchange his promise (to pay $1,000) for *B*'s act of walking across the Bridge. Thus *A* has made an offer for a unilateral contract, since *B* is not bound to do anything, and the offer is accepted (if at all) by *B*'s act, rather than his promise. (For an explanation of what constitutes an acceptance of an offer for a unilateral contract, see *infra*, p. 20.)

2. **Bilateral contracts:** A contract which consists of an *exchange of promises*, on the other hand, is called a *bilateral* contract. Most contracts are bilateral, since usually both parties promise to do something. If, in the above example, *A* had said, "I promise to pay you $1,000 on April 15 if you promise to walk across the Brooklyn Bridge on April 1," *A*'s offer would have been for a bilateral contract, i.e., an exchange of promises.

3. **Distinction less significant:** The distinction between unilateral and bilateral contracts is probably less significant than it used to be. The Second Restatement, in fact, does not even use the "unilateral" and "bilateral" terminology. (But it does make what is in practice the same distinction, by referring in § 45(1) to an offer which "invites an offeree to accept by rendering a performance," in contrast to an offer which invites acceptance by promise.) The "unilateral"/"bilateral" language is also absent from the Uniform Commercial Code.

    a. **Still significant:** The distinction between the two types of contracts is, however, still significant in some contexts. For instance, somewhat different rules apply to the question of whether the offeror may *revoke* the offer once the offeree relies on the offer to his detriment; compare the rules for offers for unilateral contracts, *infra*, p. 55, offers whose unilateral/bilateral status is unclear, *infra*, p. 58, and offers (whether for bilateral or unilateral contracts) where there are pre-acceptance preparations (*infra*, p. 58).

D. **Offer creates power of acceptance:** The legal effect of an offer is to create a *power in the offeree to enter into a contract*. Murray, p. 36. The offeree enters the contract by making his *acceptance*.

1. **Options:** In most cases, the offer does not by itself bring a contract into being, and the contract is formed only when the offer is accepted. One kind of offer, however, the *option*, is not only an offer to contract, but is at the same time a contract in which the offeror promises that she will keep the offer open for a certain time. See Rest. 2d, § 25.

    Example: *A* grants *B* an option to buy Blackacre for $1,000 at any time during the next month. *B* pays $10 for this option. The option constitutes not only an offer of sale, but also a contract binding *A* to keep the offer open for 30 days. Cf. Rest. 2d, § 25, Illustr. 2.

III. VALIDITY OF PARTICULAR KINDS OF OFFERS

A. **Offer made in jest:** An offer which the offeree knows or should know is made *in jest* is not a valid offer, and even if it is purportedly "accepted," no contract is created. See the example on p. 6, *supra*; see also *Leonard v. Pepsico, Inc.*, *infra*, p. 13 (P should have known that D's TV ad purporting to offer a $23 million Harrier Jet for $700,000 worth of "Pepsi Points" was a joke, and thus not a valid offer).

B. **Offer distinguished from expression of opinion:** An offer must contain a *promise* or *commitment*, rather than merely an *opinion*. C&P, p. 32.

1. **Objective test:** The test for distinguishing a bona fide offer from an expression of opinion, like the test for distinguishing an offer from a jest, is the objective "reasonable person" test. That is, the question is whether a reasonable person in the position of the

"offeree" would have understood the "offeror" as having proposed a bargain, rather than as having merely stated an opinion.

C. Preliminary negotiations distinguished from offers: A party desiring to reach a contract may make a statement which is not an offer but rather a *solicitation* of an offer from or further discussions with the other party. Such statements cannot be "accepted," but instead merely serve as a basis for *preliminary negotiations*.

1. **Objective test:** Here, again, the test is whether a person in the "offeree's" shoes would reasonably have understood that the "offeror" was merely seeking to invite an offer or start preliminary negotiations. The subjective intent of the "offeror" is irrelevant. Rest. 2d, § 26.

   Example: Uncle mails a letter to Nephew that states: "I am thinking of selling my pickup truck, which you have seen and ridden in. I would consider taking $7,000 for it." A reasonable person in Nephew's position would understand that Uncle is making merely a solicitation of an offer, not an offer. Therefore, when Nephew writes back, "I will buy the truck for $7,000 cash," this is an offer, not an acceptance, and no contract has yet been formed. Cf. Rest. 2d, § 26, Illustr. 4.

2. **Statement of future intention:** An announcement by a person that he *intends to contract in the future* will not usually be considered an offer.

   Example: *A* says to *B*, "I am going to sell my car for $500." No offer has been made, since *A*'s statement should reasonably be understood by *B* to be merely an expression of *A*'s future intent to contract. C&P, p. 34.

3. **Offer must indicate that other party can seal the bargain:** For an expression to be an "offer," the other person must be justified in thinking that the would-be offeror has intended to give that other person the ability to *"seal the deal" immediately, without further assent from the offeror.* As the Restatement puts the idea, "A manifestation of willingness to enter into a bargain is *not an offer* if the person to whom it is addressed knows or has *reason to know* that the person making [the manifestation] *does not intend to conclude a bargain* until [the maker] has *made a further manifestation of intent.*" Rest. 2d, § 26.

   a. **More details to work out:** Therefore, if a statement by one party, call her *A*, to *B* indicates that *A* believes that *further details must be worked out* between *A* and *B* before a deal is completed — details that *A* must approve — *A*'s statement is almost certainly *not* an offer, but rather, merely an invitation to continue discussions or negotiations.

   b. **"Let's discuss":** Thus if *A* and *B* have had discussions about a deal, and *A* then makes a statement or proposal accompanied by words like *"Let's discuss,"* those words probably put *B* on notice that *A* has not just made an offer, but has merely invited continuing negotiations. In that event, there is nothing for *B* to "accept," and *B* cannot unilaterally bind *A* to a contract by *B*'s response.

   Example: The Ps bring a products liability suit against D, a large corporation. A jury awards the Ps a verdict for a particular amount. After the verdict, it is necessary for the parties to agree on additional numerical items like the pre-judgment interest that D owes on this verdict. Lawyers for the two sides (Brooks for D and Gray for the Ps) each propose figures, and realize that there is some sort of clerical discrepancy between the two sides' numbers.[1] Then, on Nov. 2, Brooks emails Gray a set of computations that Brooks says shows the amount that D "believes is appropriate." The email adds, "Please review these, then let's discuss." Gray makes no response, but his co-counsel, Maywhort, responds by writing to Brooks' co-counsel, Thomasch, "We accept Brooks' Nov. 2 offer." The two lawyers for D immediately respond that Brooks' Nov. 2 email was not an offer, and that there *was* no offer on the table for the Ps to accept. The Ps sue to obtain enforcement of a contract based on what they say was D's Nov. 2 emailed offer.

Held, for D. Brooks' Nov. 2 email used only "qualifying and indefinite language" (by describing the calculations as being what D "believes is appropriate"). Furthermore, the language of that email ("Please review [then] let's discuss") "did not solicit an acceptance but rather solicited a return call." Therefore, the email was merely a continuation of prior discussions about the discrepancies in computation; it did not do what an offer must do, which is to justify the recipient in understanding that he is being asked to give an assent that will ***"conclude a bargain."*** *Sumerel v. Goodyear Tire & Rubber Co.*, 232 P.3d 128 Col. Ct. of App. 2009) (also discussed *infra*, p. 165).

D. Price quotations distinguished from offers: It is a frequent business practice for one person to request a ***"quote"*** from another. In such a situation, is the person who makes the quote making an offer? Courts typically consider the following factors in deciding the answer:

1. **Quantity:**   The quote will only be an offer if it, or the request to which it is a response, makes clear the ***quantity*** in question. Thus a quotation consisting of merely a "per unit" price, with no reference to the number of units which the seller is willing to sell at that price, is not an offer (unless the quote is in response to a request for a per unit price for a particular quantity).

2. **Addressee:**   If the quote is not addressed to a particular person, but is merely part of a general price list, or is sent out pursuant to a large mailing, it is unlikely to constitute an offer.

3. **Use of term "quote" or "offer":**   The precise words used in the alleged "offer" are often relevant. For instance, if the proposal itself refers to the fact that it is a quotation (e.g., "We quote you apples at 40¢ per pound"), it is less likely to be an offer than if there were no such reference. Conversely, if the document says "I offer…," this will make it more likely that a formal offer will be found to have been made.

4. **Need for further expression of assent:**   Recall that an offer creates on the part of the offeree a "power of acceptance," i.e., the power to enter into a contract. (See *supra*, p. 10.) It follows from this that a proposal is not an offer if it ***reserves to the proposer*** the power to close the deal.

   Example: The local branch office of Seller sends to a prospective customer a solicitation. The solicitation contains enough specific price and quantity information to con-

---

1. For a more detailed discussion of the facts of the case, see *infra*, p. 165.

stitute an offer. However, it also contains the proviso that "No orders will be shipped until approved by the home office." This provision indicates that Seller is reserving to itself the power to consummate the deal; therefore, the proposal is not an offer, and an order sent in response is not an acceptance. See Farnsworth p. 136.

5. **Reluctance to find contract:** If the existence of an offer presents a close question, the court will generally find that there was ***not an offer***. Farnsworth, p. 134. Whereas once a contract has been found to exist, courts will be quite willing to supplement the actual terms with provisions on which the parties have not explicitly agreed (*infra*, p. 68), they are much less willing to take liberties with the language of what is asserted to be an offer. This reflects the general view that a person should not be found to have "taken the significant step of creating a power of acceptance unless he quite clearly made a commitment." C&P, p. 45.

E. **Advertisements as offers:** Most ***advertisements*** appearing in the mass media, in store windows, etc., are ***not*** offers to sell, because they do not contain sufficient words of commitment to sell. Rest. 2d, § 26, Comment b.

> **Example 1:** D, a clothing store, sends out a circular saying, "StormKing Extra Insulated wool coats, $100." This is not an offer, because of the absence of any further details about what D is actually committing to do (e.g., the number of coats being offered at that price). Cf. Rest. 2d, § 26, Illustr. 1.

> **Example 2:** D (Pepsico) runs a television ad for a "Pepsi Stuff" promotion, under which people who buy Pepsi get points that can be redeemed for merchandise. The end of the ad shows a teenager redeeming 7 million Pepsi Points for a Harrier Fighter Jet which he intends to use to commute to school. The ad mentions that the merchandise being offered is contained in a "Pepsi Stuff catalog." P, a consumer who sees the ad, consults the Pepsi catalog, and discovers that it does not list a Harrier Jet among the items that can be purchased with Pepsi points, but also sees that the catalog allows Pepsi Points to be purchased for 10 cents each. P sends D a check for $700,000 and orders a Harrier Jet (the real-world cost of which is $23 million), then sues to enforce the alleged contract.

> *Held*, for D. "The general rule is that an advertisement does not constitute an offer." It's true that an advertisement can be an offer if it is "clear, definite, and explicit, and leaves nothing open for negotiation." But that was not the case here — the TV ad was not sufficiently definite, since it reserved the details of the offer to a separate writing (the catalog). (Also, an obvious joke cannot be a valid offer — see *supra*, p. 10 — and the mention of the Harrier Jet here was an obvious joke.) *Leonard v. Pepsico, Inc.*, 88 F.Supp.2d 116 (S.D. N.Y. 1999).

1. **Specific terms or promises:** But if the advertisement contains words expressing the advertiser's commitment or promise to sell a ***particular number of units***, or to sell the items in a ***particular manner***, there may be an offer.

> **Example 3:** Same facts as Example 1 above. Now, however, suppose that the circular also contained this sentence: "15 coats available at this price, to be sold first-come first-served starting this Saturday at 9 AM." That sentence probably indicates sufficient commitment to sell 15 units under a particular procedure that it *would* amount to

an offer. Consequently, if P showed up with a check for $100 before anyone else at 9 AM Saturday, she would be able to accept the offer and have a contract. Cf. Rest. 2d, § 26, Illustr. 1.

Example 4: A manufacturer advertises that it will pay $100 to anyone who contracts influenza after using its anti-influenza medicinal smoke-balloon for two weeks. *Held*, the advertisement constitutes an offer, because its language contains an express commitment. *Carlill v. Carbolic Smoke Ball Co.*, Q.B. 256 (1893). Observe that the "acceptance" of this offer was not by a return promise to use the product, but by the purchaser's *act* of using the product. That is, the contract was unilateral.

F. Offers at auctions: When an auctioneer puts an item up for *auction*, has he made an offer? Under modern case law and the UCC, the auctioneer, by opening the bidding on an item, does *not* make an offer. Instead, he solicits offers (bids) from the audience. UCC § 2-328. See also Rest. 2d, § 28.

1. With reserve: Auction sales under the UCC are said to be *"with reserve"* unless the goods are explicitly put up "without reserve." The auctioning of goods "with reserve" means that even after the start of bidding, the auctioneer may withdraw the goods from the sale. That is, putting up goods "with reserve" *does not constitute an offer to sell them*. It is only when the auctioneer concludes the sale by letting the hammer fall that she is deemed to have "accepted" the last bid, and the contract of sale is complete. UCC § 2-328(3).

2. Without reserve: But if it is made clear to the public that the goods to be auctioned will be sold *"without reserve,"* the auctioneer is deemed to have made an *irrevocable offer to sell the goods to the highest bidder*. Once the bidding starts, the auctioneer cannot then withdraw the goods because the bids are too low. UCC § 2-328(3).

3. Withdrawal of bids: Whether or not an auction is with reserve, a bidder may withdraw his bid at any time prior to completion of the sale. If the most recent bid is withdrawn, earlier bids are not automatically reinstated. UCC § 2-328(3).

G. Invitations to bid: Where bids are solicited through the sending out of *invitations to submit bids*, the invitation is not an offer unless it contains language so indicating. In the usual case, the invitation is simply a solicitation of offers, the bids are offers, and it is up to the inviter to decide which, if any, of the bids to accept.

1. Language indicating offer: If the invitation to submit a bid contains language indicating a *commitment* on the part of the inviter to award the contract or sale to the highest bidder, the invitation may be held to constitute an offer, and the inviter will be bound to a contract with the highest bidder.

Example: *A* advertises, "I offer my farm Blackacre for sale to the highest cash bidder and undertake to make conveyance to the person submitting the highest bid received at the address below within the next thirty days." *A* has made an offer. Each bid operates as an acceptance, whose effectiveness is conditional on no higher bid being received within 30 days. Rest. 2d, § 28, Illustr. 3.

H. Seller's response to inquiry: Where a *seller responds* to an *inquiry* from a customer about whether the seller has available a particular quantity of items for delivery at a particular time, the seller's response with details of what she has for sale is likely to contain sufficient words of commitment to *constitute an offer*, even though the response does not contain the word "offer."

Example: Buyer emails Seller: "Do you have 100 widgets for immediate shipment?" Seller emails Buyer: "Yes, at a price of $2.37 per widget." Seller's response is an offer, because it implies that Seller is willing to let Buyer *immediately conclude* a contract for the items.

I. Indefinite offers: For a contract to be formed, the parties must reach mutual assent on *all of the essential terms of the agreement*. These essential terms are usually held to be:

- ❑ *parties*;
- ❑ *subject matter*;
- ❑ *time for performance*; and
- ❑ *price*

1. Vague offer: What purports to be an offer will in some cases not contain all of these essential elements. Can such an offer nonetheless give rise to a valid contract? If the acceptance does not supply the missing essential terms, there will be no contract because of *indefiniteness*.

Example: *A* says to *B*, "I'll sell you any quantity of widgets you want for $5 each." *B* says, "OK, I accept." Since the offer does not contain details as to the quantity to be contracted for, and since the acceptance does not fill in this missing term, there is no contract because of indefiniteness.

2. Ways of avoiding indefiniteness: Even though the offer and acceptance do not themselves contain all of the essential elements, the contract may be saved from fatal indefiniteness if the parties' later actions supply the missing terms by implication, or if the court is willing to supply the missing terms through what are sometimes called "gap fillers."

Note: Because the problem of indefiniteness is not purely a problem of inadequate *offer*, but rather a problem of an offer and acceptance which together are insufficiently definite, the full discussion of indefiniteness is given *infra*, p. 67.

J. Offers proposing a series of contracts: It may not be clear whether a particular offer looks to one acceptance, or to a series of acceptances from time to time, and therefore a series of contracts. The court will decide whether the offer contemplates one or several contracts by judging what a reasonable person in the position of the offeree would think. The distinction between a single contract with several installments, and a series of contracts, is important for purposes of revocation of the offer as well as for the consequences of a breach.

Example: *A* says to *B*, "I will sell you all of your requirements of coal during the next twelve months, not exceeding 100 tons in any month, provided you promise not to buy coal from anyone else during this period." This offer is for a single contract in which a series of orders are to be made. If the offer had said "I promise to sell you whatever quantities of coal you order at any time during the next twelve months, provided that I

Figure 2-1
Is the "Offer" Valid?

A valid offer is one that instills in the offeree the power to enter into a contract simply by saying "yes." (The chart uses the word "offer" to refer to expressions that may or may not be true offers. Where an expression is a true offer -- i.e. a statement that if accepted will automatically form a contract -- the chart calls that expression a "valid" offer.) This chart helps you determine whether a given communication really *is a*n offer.

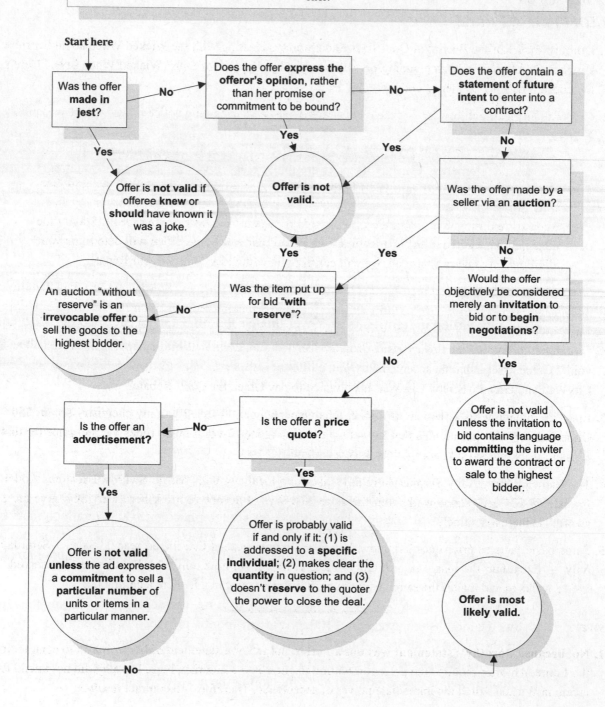

have that much in stock," the offer would probably give rise to a series of contracts, one for each order placed by *B*.

    The difference between the two is significant. *A* has the right to revoke his offer prospectively any time he wishes in the "series of contracts" case, even if *B* has already placed previous orders; he may not revoke in the "single contract, several installments" case once *B* has accepted initially. See Rest. 2d, § 31, Illustr. 1 and 3.

Quiz Yourself on
VALIDITY OF OFFERS

1. Dorothy, owner of the Wizard of Odd-Sizes Shoe Store, is chatting with the Wicked Witch about her ruby slippers. Dorothy says, "I'm planning on selling my ruby slippers for $50." Wicked Witch says, "Here's my check. I accept." Is there a contract?

2. CityWatt, an electric utility serving the city of Metro, posts the following notice on its website on January 1, 2015:

To All CityWatt Homeowner Customers — Solar Rebate Program

If you placed a Qualifying Solar Panel Installation ("QSPI") [a term carefully defined elsewhere in the website] in service at your home during calendar year 2014, under our Solar Rebate Program you are eligible for a 10% credit against the cost of your QSPI. Submit the information required in the application form below, and our home office will determine your eligibility; if you are approved, we will contact you with the amount of your Rebate.

Gary Green, a CityWatt customer who made what was in fact a Qualifying Solar Panel Installation during 2014, submits on Jan. 15, 2015 all information required by the online application form. However, before CityWatt makes any further contact with Green, the company on Jan. 17 posts this notice on its website: "We regret to say that the Solar Rebate Program has been canceled. All pending applications are null and void." Green asserts that he accepted CityWatt's offer of a rebate on Jan. 15. Is there a contract between CityWatt and Green whereby CityWatt is obligated to pay Green the QSPI Rebate?

3. Einstein, intending his statement as a joke, tells Oppenheimer, "I'll sell you my chemistry set for $50." Oppenheimer, who has no idea that the set's plutonium alone is worth many times the $50 price (or that Einstein is joking) says, "I accept." Is there a contract?

4. The Camelot Army/Navy Surplus Store advertises in a local circular, "Magic Swords, Excalibur model, for sale @ $24 ea." Lance walks into the store, and says "I accept your ad; here's my $24, give me 1 sword." Is there a contract?

5. Same basic facts as prior question. Now, however, assume instead that the ad reads: "Sale — Saturday only — Excalibur, the magic sword. Only one left. Was $500, now only $24. First come, first served." Lance walks in and makes the same response as in the prior question. Is there a contract?

Answers

1. No, because Dorothy's statement was not an offer, but rather a statement of her intention to contract in the future. An offer requires the present intention to enter into a contract; here, Dorothy did not intend to create in Wicked Witch the immediate power of acceptance. Therefore, no contract results.

2. No, because a reasonable person in Green's position would have understood that CityWatt did not intend to be bound until its home office determined an applicant's eligibility. Rest. 2d, § 26 says, "A manifestation of willingness to enter into a bargain is *not an offer* if the person to whom it is addressed knows or has *reason to know* that the person making [the manifestation] *does not intend to conclude a bargain* until [the maker] has *made a further manifestation of intent*." Here, the communication that Green asserts was an offer — the Jan. 1 website notice — tells customers to submit an "application form," and says that CityWatt's "home office will determine your eligibility." These references to an application and a determination of eligibility would give the customer reason to know that (in the Restatement's words), CityWatt did not intend for any "bargain" (agreement to award a rebate) to be concluded until CityWatt had made a "further manifestation of intent," namely at least a determination of eligibility, and probably also contact with the customer. In other words, the website made it clear to one in Green's position that the customer's application would be the *offer*, and that acceptance would not occur until the home office's determination of eligibility and notice of such to the customer. Cf. *McAtee v. City of Austin*, 2013 Tex. App. LEXIS 12518 (Ct. App. Tex. 2013) (same basic facts as this question).

3. Yes, probably. If a reasonable person in Oppenheimer's position would have no reason to know of the value of the plutonium (or any other reason for thinking that Einstein was joking), then under the *objective theory of contracts*, Einstein's offer would create an immediate power of acceptance in Oppenheimer. The fact that Einstein actually was joking is irrelevant; it's the *appearance* of a valid offer that counts. If, however, Oppenheimer *knew* that Einstein had a very dry sense of humor, and realized at the time that Einstein was joking, there'd be no valid offer and thus no contract. (An "offer" which the offeree *knows* is made in jest is not a valid offer, regardless of what any other "reasonable person" might think.)

4. No. Mass-market advertisements are generally construed as invitations for offers, not offers themselves, because they do not contain sufficient words of commitment to sell.

5. Yes, because under these facts, Camelot's offer was specific as to quantity ("one left"), price ($24), and the person to whom the offer was made ("first come"), and was, in general, worded as a *commitment* to enter into a deal on proposed terms. As such, it created an immediate power of acceptance in anyone who chose to purchase the sword under the terms advertised.

IV. THE ACCEPTANCE

A. Acceptance defined: For as long as an offer is in force, the person to whom it is addressed may conclude the bargain — cause a contract to come into existence — by *"accepting"* the offer. An "acceptance" is the offeree's manifestation of *assent to the terms of the offer*, made in a manner invited or required by the offer. Rest. 2d, § 50.

B. Who may accept the offer: An offer may be accepted *only* by a person *in whom the offeror intended to create a power of acceptance.* (Rest. 2d, §§ 29, 54).

> **Example:** *A* sends *B* an order for ice. *C*, from whom *A* previously has refused to buy such goods, has purchased *B*'s business. *C* ships ice to *A* without notifying him of the change in the ownership of *B*'s business. *Held*, *A* did not create a power of acceptance in *C*; therefore, *C*'s "acceptance" is ineffective, and there is no contract. *Boston Ice Co. v. Potter*, 123 Mass. 28 (1877).

Note: Of course, under the objective theory of contracts what counts is not whether *A* subjectively intended not to deal with *C*, but whether a reasonable person in *C*'s position should have realized that *A* would not want to deal with *C*. On these facts, *C* should have realized this, so he was not empowered to accept the offer.

C. Must be in response to an offer: An acceptance must be *in response to an offer,* not in response to something other than an offer such as a *solicitation* of offers.

> **Example:** Reconsider the Example on p. 11: An uncle mails a letter to his adult nephew that says: "I am thinking of selling my pickup truck. I would consider taking $7,000 for it." The nephew writes back, "I will buy the truck for $7,000 cash." Because the uncle's letter was a solicitation of offers, not an offer, the nephew's response "I will buy" was *not an acceptance* (but was instead itself an offer).

D. Offeree usually required to know of the offer: An acceptance is usually valid only if the offeree *knows of the offer* at the time of his alleged acceptance. C&P, p. 71; 1 Corbin § 59.

1. **Restatement formulation:** The Restatement expresses this idea by saying that "It is essential to a bargain that each party manifest assent *with reference to the manifestation of the other.*" Rest. 2d § 23.

2. **Rewards:** This rule means that where a *reward* is offered for a particular act, a person who does the act without *knowing* about the reward *cannot claim it.*

   a. **Exceptions:** However, a number of states have granted a *noncontractual* right to recover in the reward situation, if the reward is offered by a public agency. See C&P, p. 72, n. 8. Also, a *"standing offer"* by a governmental body (e.g., $1,000 to anyone furnishing information leading to the conviction of any person for arson) may be held to confer a contractual right on one who furnishes such information without knowing about the standing offer. See Rest. 2d, § 23, Illustr. 3.

3. **Cross offers:** The requirement that an accepting party know of the offer, and be responding to it, means that *"cross-offers,"* even if they match precisely, will not create a contract.

   > **Example:** *A* has on previous occasions discussed with *B* *A*'s possible interest in selling Blackacre to *B* for $100,000. (Assume, however, that the discussions between them never amounted to either an offer or a contract.) Some time thereafter, on Oct. 1, *A* sends *B* a letter saying, "I'll sell you Blackacre, as we discussed, for $100,000, if you reply promptly." Also on Oct. 1, *B*, without realizing that *A* has sent a letter, sends her own letter to *A* saying, "I hereby offer to buy Blackacre from you for $100,000." The two letters cross in the mail. There is no contract, because neither letter was with reference to the other, and therefore neither letter could serve as an acceptance. Cf. Rest. 2d § 23, Illustr. 4.

   a. **Subsequent performance as creating a contract:** However, in sale-of-goods cases governed by UCC Article 2, a contract may result even though the offers cross. This can happen if the *subsequent conduct* of both parties *"recognizes the existence of a contract."* UCC § 2-207(3). This provision is discussed *infra*, p. 36. Thus suppose the exchange of letters in the above example had involved, say, a rare book. Suppose further that after *A* got *B*'s letter, *A* wrote, "I'm glad that we've agreed; tell me where to send the book," and *B* responded by sending a mailing address. This later conduct by both parties, showing their belief that they had a deal, would be enough to create a contract under § 2-207(3) even though it's hard to say exactly what acts constituted the offer and the acceptance.

4. **Objective manifestation is what counts:**   Despite the general rule that the offeree must be aware of the offer in order to accept it, it is important to remember that the objective theory of contracts applies to the acceptance. That is, as long as the offeree's conduct leads the offeror to reasonably conclude that the offeree knew of the offer, it does not matter that subjectively the offeree was unaware of the offer. See C&P, p. 73.

   a. **Acceptance of unknown terms:**   Similarly, an offeree can by her actions bind herself to an offer even though she is ignorant of certain of its terms. Here, as in the case in which the offeree does not even know that there is an offer, the offeree will be bound if her conduct reasonably leads the offeror to conclude that the offer has been accepted.

   Example: *A* sends to *B* an offer to sell a particular lot for $5,000. The offer also states terms as to time of payment, mortgage, taxes and insurance. *B* is so anxious to buy the lot that without reading these additional terms, she sends an acceptance to *A* that does not list any conditions. Because *B*'s act has reasonably led *A* to conclude that his offer has been accepted, there is a contract on the terms stated in *A*'s offer. See Rest. 2d, § 23, Illustr. 7.

E. **Method of acceptance:**   The offeror is the *"master of his offer."* This means, in part, that he may prescribe the *method* by which it may be accepted. For instance, he may require that it be accepted by a telegram, letter, signature, etc.

   Example: *A* sends *B* a letter proposing to sell Blackacre for a stated price. The letter says, "You may accept this proposal only by signing this letter on the dotted line provided for your signature, and returning it to me by Sept. 1." *B* sends *A* a telegram on Aug. 31, saying "I hereby accept your offer." *B* has not accepted (and there is no contract), because *B* has not used the method of acceptance specified by *A*. See Rest. 2d, § 30, Illustr. 1.

1. **Can suspend mailbox rule:** The offeror's right to prescribe the method of acceptance means that the offeror can *suspend* the usual *"mailbox"* rule, under which an acceptance is effective upon dispatch. (See *infra*, p. 60). The offeror can do this by saying, "No acceptance shall be effective until received by offeror" — such a provision will be *enforced*.

2. **Mode of acceptance where not specified in offer:**   If the offer does *not specify* the mode of acceptance, the acceptance may be given *"in any manner and by any medium reasonable in the circumstances."* Rest. 2d, § 30(2).

3. **Acceptance of unilateral contract:**   Suppose that the offeror's offer proposes that the offeree accept by performing an act, rather than by making a promise. Such an offer looks to a *unilateral* contract.

   a. **Option contract arising on part performance:**   When an offer to a unilateral contract is made, it can be accepted only by *full* performance. But if the offeree begins to perform, most courts treat the offer as having become temporarily irrevocable; that is, the offeree receives an option contract. See Rest. 2d, § 45. This topic is discussed further *infra*, p. 55.

b. Intent to accept implied: If *A* makes *B* an offer for a unilateral contract, and *B* performs the requested act, it is of course possible that *B **did not intend*** by doing the act to make a contract. If it is clear from *B*'s words or conduct that he did not intend his act to constitute an acceptance, there will be no contract. But if there is no evidence, one way or the other, about whether *B* intended the act to constitute an acceptance, *B* will usually be treated as having intended to accept, and a contract will be found.

4. **Acceptance of bilateral contract:** If the offer looks to a ***bilateral*** contract (i.e., looks to an acceptance that is by promise rather than performance), the acceptance will usually be in words (e.g., a letter stating "I accept your offer of May 23"). But the acceptance may also be in the form of ***actions***, if these fairly indicate to the offeror that the offeree intends to enter into the contract.

     a. Assent must be implied: But, under the objective theory of contracts, the conduct will only be an acceptance if it reasonably appears to the offeror that this is what the offeree has intended.

     b. Account stated: One kind of acceptance by action rather than words is called an ***account stated***. An account stated comes into existence when a creditor sends a bill to his debtor, and the debtor accepts the bill as an accurate estimation of the charges (usually by simply failing to object to it within a reasonable period of time). See p. 513, *infra*.

     c. Notice of acceptance of bilateral contract: There are a few situations in which the offeree may accept merely by being ***silent***; these are discussed *infra*, p. 23. Generally, however, for the acceptance to be effective, the offeree must at least ***attempt*** to ***communicate it*** to the offeror, in a reasonably prompt manner. Rest. 2d, § 56.

     Example: *A* writes *B*, "I hereby offer to sell you Blackacre for $10,000." *B* composes a letter to *A* accepting the offer, but he doesn't mail it for several days, during which time *A* purports to revoke the offer. The acceptance never became effective, since *B* never made a reasonably prompt attempt to communicate it to *A*.

     Note: But if *B* had mailed the letter of acceptance, it would have become effective upon dispatch (not merely when *A* received it). This "acceptance effective upon dispatch" rule is discussed further *infra*, p. 60.

       i. Where offer indicates notification unnecessary for acceptance: However, if the ***offer itself*** indicates that an acceptance can become effective even before any attempt to communicate it is made, then the acceptance will indeed become immediately effective.

5. **Where offer invites either promise or performance:** It will often be the case that the offer does not make clear whether acceptance is to occur through a promise or through a performance. That is, it is unclear whether the offer seeks a unilateral or a bilateral contract. In this ambiguous situation, the offer "is interpreted as inviting the offeree to accept ***either*** by promising to perform what the offer requests or by rendering the performance, as the offeree chooses." Rest. 2d, § 32.

     a. Language of offer relevant to mode of acceptance: The language of the offer, and the circumstances under which it is made, must be scrutinized in order to determine whether the offeror is really indifferent as to whether the offer is accepted by promise or by performance.

Example: *A* writes to his nephew, *B*, aged 16, that if *B* will refrain from drinking, smoking and gambling until he is 21, *A* will pay him $5,000 at age 21. *B* writes to *A*, "I promise to refrain from doing these things." The circumstances and language of the offer indicate that *A* probably was not interested in having *B*'s *promise* to refrain, but was only interested in having *B actually* refrain. If so, *B*'s promise is not an acceptance. (But if *B* begins to refrain, *A*'s offer becomes irrevocable under Rest. 2d, § 45 for as long as *B* continues to refrain, and if he refrains until he is 21, there is a contract under which *A* must pay $5,000.) See *Hamer v. Sidway*, 124 N.Y. 538 (1891); see also Rest. 2d, § 32, Illustr. 4, drawn from *Hamer*.

b.   **Shipment of goods:**   One common situation in which the offer may not make it clear whether acceptance is to be through promise or performance is where the offer is a request that ***goods be shipped***. In this situation, the UCC follows the Restatement view that either shipment or a promise to ship constitutes acceptance: "…an order or other offer to buy goods for prompt or current shipment shall be construed as inviting acceptance either by a prompt promise to ship or by the prompt or current shipment of conforming or non-conforming goods.…" UCC § 2-206(1)(b).

    i.   **Acceptance by shipment of non-conforming goods:**   Sometimes the seller may ***accept and breach with the same act,*** by ***shipping non-conforming goods.*** Notice that § 2-206(1)(b), quoted above, says that an order can normally be accepted "by the prompt or current shipment of conforming or ***non-conforming goods***[.]" Ignoring for the moment the issue of an accommodation shipment (one in which the seller *knows* that she is shipping non-conforming goods and explains that she is doing so to help the buyer, as discussed in sub-Paragraph (ii) below), you can see from this language that a seller who in response to an order ***ships non-conforming goods without acknowledging that they are non-conforming both accepts and breaches at the same time.***

       Example: Retailer, an office supply store, orders 1,000 dozen "No. 2 pencils" from Manufacturer, for immediate shipment. Due to an error in the shipping department, Manufacturer ships 1,000 dozen "No. 3 pencils." By making the shipment, Manufacturer has accepted the order. Furthermore, since Manufacturer has shipped non-conforming goods (without qualifying for the "accommodation shipment" scenario), Manufacturer has breached the agreement. Therefore, Retailer will be entitled to reject the non-conforming shipment, and if any cure period (see *infra*, p. 233) expires without a cure, Retailer will be entitled to sue for breach.

    ii.   **Accommodation shipments:**   There is one important exception to the rule just summarized, that an order to buy goods for current shipment will ordinarily be deemed accepted if the seller ships conforming or non-conforming goods. This is the ***"accommodation shipment."*** The last sentence of UCC § 2-206(1)(b) (which comes after the clause quoted in Par. (b.) above) says, "Such a shipment of non-conforming goods does not constitute an acceptance if the seller seasonally notifies the buyer that the shipment is offered only as an ***accommodation*** to the buyer."

That is, the seller can ship what she knows to be non-conforming goods ***without risking being found in breach***, by accompanying the shipment with a message saying words to the effect, "I know I'm sending goods that don't match your order, and I'm doing this only to accommodate you. You may keep the goods and pay for them, or you may return them in which case there will be no contract between us."

(1) Buyer's choice: When the seller makes such an accommodation shipment, the shipment is generally treated not as an acceptance, but rather as a ***counter-offer*** of the goods that have been shipped as they are. Thus if the seller ships 50 widgets instead of the 100 that were ordered, the seller is making a counter-offer for a contract of 50 widgets. Similarly, if the buyer orders green widgets and the seller ships blue ones, the seller is making a counter-offer for a contract for blue widgets.

When the buyer receives the non-conforming goods shipped as an accommodation, he has a choice: (1) he can ***keep*** the non-conforming goods, in which case there is a ***contract for the goods as they are***, at the price the seller has indicated she will charge for them; or (2) the buyer can ***reject*** the shipment and thus prevent a contract from coming into existence at all (in which case ***neither party will be liable*** for breach of anything).

But what the buyer ***cannot*** do is to ***hold the seller in breach*** for having shipped non-conforming goods, or ***demand conforming goods*** — that's the whole point of the accommodation-shipment provision of § 2-206(1)(b).

Example: Buyer sends Seller an order for "100 red gizmos, at $5.75 each, for immediate shipment." Seller sends 100 blue gizmos, with a note reading "I'm all out of red gizmos. I've taken the liberty of shipping you 100 blue ones instead, at the same price, hoping that they'll do for you."

Seller's shipment of the blue gizmos is an accommodation shipment under § 2-206(1)(b). Therefore, Seller's shipment does not constitute an acceptance. Instead, it is a counter-offer of blue gizmos. Buyer can accept the counter-offer (by keeping them, in which case he owes the $5.75 for each with no discount for the non-conformity) or reject the counter-offer (by sending them back). If Buyer rejects the counter-offer by sending the blue gizmos back, Seller has not breached (because there was never any accepted order), so Seller does not owe Buyer any compensation.

6. **Acceptance by silence:** May the offeree accept by virtue of his *silence*? Although the common law never treated silence as acceptance, modern courts and authorities recognize that silence may sometimes manifest an intent to accept.

   a. **Common-law rule:** The common-law rule is expressed by the phrase "he who is silent does not give his consent." This rule often led to unfair results.

   Example: *A* has insured *B*'s house for years. *A* then notifies *B* that it will continue *B*'s policy in force, unless it hears from *B* to the contrary. Relying on this statement, *B* does not reply. *B*'s house burns down, and *A* claims that there was no contract. Under the common-law approach, *B* would have no contractual recourse against *A*. *Prescott v. Jones*, 69 N.H. 305 (1898).

b. **Modern view of implied-in-fact contracts:** Modern courts, and the Second Restatement, try to correct such injustices by *recognizing silence* as a mode of acceptance in several scenarios. These scenarios in which the parties do not expressly exchange an offer and acceptance, but in which they *indicate by their silence (or non-verbal conduct)* their understanding that a contract is being formed, are sometimes said to involve *"implied-in-fact"* contracts. Here are some of the scenarios where silence can give rise to an implied-in-fact contract, according to the Second Restatement:

     i. **Reason to understand that silence is consent:** Where the offeror has given the offeree *reason to understand that silence will constitute acceptance*, the silence or inaction of the offeree will operate as an acceptance *if* she subjectively intends to be bound. Rest. 2d, § 69(1)(b).

     Example: Suppose the facts are the same as in *Prescott v. Jones* (the previous example). The insurer has explicitly indicated to the offeree that the latter's silence will constitute acceptance. In this situation, the offeree's silence will constitute acceptance *if and only if* he subjectively intended to accept.

     ii. **Acceptance of services:** An offeree who *silently receives the benefit* of *services* (not goods) will be held to have accepted a contract for them if she (1) had a reasonable opportunity to *reject* them and (2) *knew or should have known* that the provider of the services *expected to be compensated* for them. Rest. 2d, § 69(1)(a).

     Example: *A*, a private music teacher, gives several piano lessons to *B*'s child. *A* tells *B* that the cost of a series of 20 lessons will be $100. *B* has never asked for the lessons, and remains silent when *A* tells him the cost of the course. *B* finally stops the lessons after 10 have been given. *B* has by his silence accepted *A*'s offer of a 20-lesson course, and must pay the contract price, not just the value of the lessons actually given.

        (1) **Distinguish from quasi-contract:** The implied-in-fact contract which exists in the above conscious-acceptance-of-benefits example must be distinguished from the *quasi-contractual* right of recovery of one who provides services in an emergency, without the consent of the recipient (e.g., emergency aid by a doctor to an unconscious patient; see *infra*, p. 336). In the quasi-contract situation, the provider of the services may recover only the *reasonable value* of his services. In the conscious-acceptance-of-a-contract-by-silence case discussed above, on the other hand, the service-provider receives the contract price, which will often, but not always, be more than the reasonable value of the services.

        (2) **Intra-familial transactions:** The requirement that the provider of services *"expected to be compensated"* means when one party performs small-scale services for another and the two are *close relatives*, if neither party expressly

explains to the other that payment is expected, the court is likely to conclude that the services were a *gift* rather than a commercial transaction.

Example: Dad, an 80-year-old living alone, breaks a hip in a fall. He says to his grown son Sam, "For the next month, please come over once a week to mow the lawn and rake the leaves." Sam does so, and each time Dad looks on, says "Thanks," and says nothing further.

If Sam sues Dad for the reasonable value of these yard services on an implied-in-fact contract theory, the court will almost certainly conclude that no such contract came into existence, because the intra-familial context should have led one in Dad's position to believe that Sam was rendering these services for free rather than in expectation of payment.

iii. **Prior conduct making acceptance by silence reasonable:** Even if the offeror has not indicated to the offeree that silence will constitute acceptance, the prior *course of dealing* of the parties may make it reasonable that the offeree's silence be construed as consent. This will be the case when the prior dealings make it "reasonable that the offeree should *notify* the offeror if he does not intend to accept." Rest. 2d, § 69(1)(c).

Example: *A* Corp., through its salespeople, has frequently solicited orders from *B*. These orders have always been subject to approval by the *A* home office, but in every case the goods have been promptly shipped to *B* with no notice to *B* except a bill on shipment. This time *B* gives an order to *A*'s salesperson, and *A* fails to ship or notify *B* that it will not ship. *B*, relying on his order, does not buy from anyone else. Because *B* reasonably assumed that had *A* rejected *B*'s order (i.e., *B*'s "offer"), *A* would have so notified him, *A* by its silence has accepted *B*'s order. Therefore, there is a contract. See Rest. 2d, § 69, Illustr. 5.

Note: Observe that in this situation, where the prior dealings of the parties lead the offeror to believe that if the offeree decides not to accept he will so notify the offeror, the objective theory of contracts applies. That is, the test is whether the offeree's conduct was such that a person in the offeror's position would reasonably expect to be notified of any rejection, not whether the offeror subjectively expected such notification. See C&P, p. 82.

iv. **Acceptance by dominion:** Where the offeree receives goods, he may be held to have accepted a contract for the goods even though he does not intend to do so. She may make such an unintentional acceptance by *exercising "dominion"* over the goods in a way inconsistent with the offeror's ownership of the goods. Rest. 2d, § 69(2). See also UCC § 2-606(1)(c).

Example: *A* sends *B* a letter saying "Would you like to become a member of the *A* Book Club? If so, just fill out the enclosed card and send it to us." *A* then starts sending books to *B*, even though *B* has not sent the card in. *B* takes the books and gives them away as gifts. *B*'s giving away of the books is inconsistent with *A*'s ownership of them, so *B* will be held to have accepted *A*'s offer, even though he did not intend to do so. If *B* had merely kept the books, waiting for *A* to ask for them back, there would be no contract since *B* would not have exercised dominion. See Rest. 2d, § 69, Illustr. 7 and 8.

Note: The above example indicates that silence coupled with the exercise of "dominion" over goods may constitute acceptance. Many states, however, have statutes changing this result where unsolicited goods are sent by mail. N.Y. Gen. Obl. L. 5-332, for instance, allows the recipient of unsolicited goods sent by mail to treat them as an "unconditional gift." This statute is sometimes called the "Book of the Month Club" statute.

7. **Notice of acceptance of unilateral contract:** Where an offer looks to a *unilateral contract*, most courts now hold that the offeree must give *reasonably prompt notice* of his acceptance after he has done the requested act (unless the offeror promptly learns of the acceptance in some other way). If the offeree does not do this (and the offeror doesn't otherwise learn of the acceptance or indicate that notice is unnecessary), the contract that was formed by the act is *discharged*. Rest. 2d, § 54(2).

> **Example:** On Feb. 1, Tycoon sends Artist, a painter, a color photo of himself, and says in the accompanying letter, "I'm interested in having you paint my portrait in oils, on a canvas of at least 24 x 36. Do not proceed unless you're willing to do the work for $10,000." Artist receives the letter on Feb. 3, says nothing to Tycoon, and immediately starts work. On Feb. 10, Artist finishes the work, but does not for months notify Tycoon either that he started the work or that he finished it. On July 1, Artist finally sends Tycoon the painting, together with a bill for $10,000. Does Tycoon have to take and pay for the painting?
>
> No. It's true that Artist's commencement of work constituted an acceptance of the offer, since the offer was reasonably interpreted to call for either acceptance by promise to paint or acceptance by the beginning of actual painting. But continuation of the contract was subject to Artist's giving Tycoon *reasonably prompt notice of acceptance* once Artist completed the work (assuming that Tycoon didn't learn about the completion by some other means, or indicate that no notice was necessary). Because Artist did not do this, the contract will be "*discharged*." So Tycoon will have no obligation to pay the contract price, unless he keeps the painting.

   a. **Suretyship contracts:** The principle that the offeree must give the offeror prompt notice of acceptance after the offeror has accepted by beginning performance is important in *suretyship cases.*

> **Example:** Own, a property owner, is having Con, a contractor, do work on Own's house. Own writes to Hardware, a hardware store, "if you extend credit to Con for materials that Con will use on my house, I will make good if Con defaults."
>
> Own would probably be held to have made an offer for a unilateral contract — Own is looking mainly for the actual extension of credit, not a promise to extend credit. The offer can therefore be accepted by Hardware's advancing credit. But Own's duty to guarantee payment by Con will be *discharged* if Hardware does not give Own *prompt notice* that Hardware extended the credit.

Quiz Yourself on
THE ACCEPTANCE

6. Jackson Pol-lick, an avant-garde artist who paints landscapes with his tongue, sends a letter to Artie Snob, an art dealer, offering to sell his painting "Sunset Over Breakfast" for $5,000. At the same time, Snob sends Pol-lick a letter offering to buy "Sunset Over Breakfast" for $5,000. The letters cross in the mail. Nothing further happens. Is there a contract?

7. As Elvira knows, Lilly Munster often gives ten-lesson private classes on the art of interior decorating for a total of $400. (The market price for such courses tends to be more like $300.) Lilly and Elvira meet at a party, and Lilly says, "I could come to your house and teach you." Elvira says nothing. Lilly then shows up at Elvira's house every Thursday evening for ten weeks, and teaches Elvira her decorating tricks. Elvira never says anything to indicate that she's expecting to pay for the lessons. At the end of the ten weeks, what, if anything, does Elivra owe Lilly, and on what basis?

8. Prince Charming finds a glass slipper on the sidewalk in front of his house. Unbeknownst to him, Cinderella has offered $1,000 as a reward for the slipper's return. Charming goes from house to house, looking for the slipper's owner. He finally finds Cinderella and returns the slipper to her. Is there a contract between Cinderella and Charming for payment of $1,000?

Answers

6. No. Under these facts we have two offers and no acceptance. Neither letter was sent with the expectation that it would create a binding contract, because neither was sent in response to what the sender knew to be an offer.

7. $400, on a contract. Elvira accepted the benefit of Lilly's services, having had the opportunity to reject them, when she knew or should have known that Lilly expected to be compensated for them at Lilly's standard rate. Therefore, she will be held to have impliedly agreed to a contract for those services, on what she knew to be Lilly's standard terms. The "market rate" or "market value" of such lessons is irrelevant, since the implied-in-fact contract was for Lilly's standard terms ($400), not for lessons at the prevailing market rate.

8. No. An offer can generally be accepted only by a person who knows of the offer and intends to accept. This rule applies to rewards. Charming didn't know about the reward, so his actions of returning the slipper did not constitute a valid acceptance.

V. ACCEPTANCE VARYING FROM OFFER

  A. Problem generally: In some situations, the acceptance will accept *all* of the terms of the offeror's offer. Often, however, the acceptance will be a qualified one, e.g., "I accept your offer if you will ship the goods by the middle of next week." When the terms of the acceptance diverge from those of the offer, either by conflicting with terms in the offer or adding terms not present in the offer, it is often difficult to tell whether a contract exists. If it is determined that a contract does exist, it is also frequently difficult to determine what the terms of that contract are.

B. Common-law view: Under the common law, the offeree's response operates as an acceptance only if it is a ***precise mirror image*** of the offer. If the response conflicts to the slightest extent with the terms of the offer, or if it adds new terms on issues not even discussed in the offer (except for terms which the offer explicitly left to the offeree's choice, e.g., quantity of goods in many contracts), the reported acceptance is in fact not an acceptance but a rejection and counter-offer.

  1. Injustice: This strict common-law interpretation frustrated many commercial transactions, and often led to unjust results. Most significantly, the "mirror image" rule often let one party ***slip out of the deal*** for reasons that had nothing to do with the variation between offer and acceptance.

   Example: On March 1, Buyer sends Seller a purchase order for 1,000 widgets at $20 each, shipment to occur June 1. The purchase order says, in boilerplate, that shipment will be "FOB Buyer's place of business." Seller promptly sends a form marked "Acknowledgment" that agrees with the quantity, price, time-of-delivery and all other terms in the purchase order, except that it says, in boilerplate, that shipment will be "FOB Seller's plant." (For what these two FOB terms mean, see *infra*, p. 437.) Neither party notices that the two forms disagree. 10 weeks go by. The price of widgets skyrockets, causing Seller to decide that it wants to get out of the contract prior to making shipment.

   Under the common-law mirror-image rule, Seller would be able to claim that because its acknowledgment (the purported "acceptance") deviated from the purchase order (the offer) in this small way, the acknowledgment was not an acceptance after all, so that there is no contract. This would be true even if Buyer could prove to the court that Seller's reliance on the minor inconsistency between the forms was just a pretext to let Seller get out of what it later decided was a bad bargain.

C. Liberal UCC view: The UCC attempts to ***prevent a party from slipping out of the contract,*** as she was frequently able to do under the common-law "acceptance must be a mirror image of offer" rule. Not only does the UCC provide that a contract may in some cases be created where the acceptance does not match the offer, but the Code also attempts to specify what the terms are of such a contract. Both of these things are done in UCC § 2-207, which we explore in detail because of its great importance.[2]

  1. "Battle of the forms": Before we examine the text of § 2-207 in detail, it will be useful to examine the factual context in which most § 2-207 cases arise. It is relatively rare that the offeror sends an offer that is completely handwritten or typewritten, and that consists of terms drafted especially for the particular deal at hand; similarly, it is rare that the acceptance is a completely custom-drafted document. Rather, both the offer and the acceptance are usually ***pre-printed forms***, with blanks left for the particular "negotiated" terms to be filled in.

   a. Purchase order: Thus the buyer's purchase order department typically sends a pre-printed ***"purchase order"*** form, filled with lots of fine-print clauses favoring the buyer

---

2. In non-UCC cases, most modern courts (and the Second Restatement) follow the general approach of § 2-207. See p. 44.

(e.g., extensive warranties). The buyer simply fills in the blanks for product description, quantity, shipment date and one or two other aspects that vary from deal to deal.

b. **Acknowledgment:** The seller's order department then typically responds with a pre-printed *"acknowledgment form,"* containing fine-print clauses that favor the seller (e.g., a complete disclaimer of all warranties); this form, too, has blanks, and the seller probably copies these terms from the corresponding entries on the purchase order.

c. **Performance:** Sometimes, a dispute will arise following this exchange of purchase order and acknowledgment forms, but prior to any shipment of goods. More typically, however, the seller goes ahead and ships the goods and, either before or after the buyer has paid for them, some dispute erupts concerning the adequacy of the seller's performance (e.g., a dispute about the quality of the goods). Only then do the parties consult the purchase order and acknowledgment, and discover that these forms are not in complete agreement on some or many of the "non-negotiated" terms.

2. **Role of § 2-207:** § 2-207 has two main jobs to perform in this *"battle of the forms"* situation: (1) to determine whether a contract has been formed at all by the exchange of documents; and (2) if a contract has been formed, to determine what the terms of that contract are.

3. **Text of § 2-207:** Because of § 2-207's extreme importance, it is worth reproducing that section here in its entirety before we dissect it:

§ 2-207 Additional Terms in Acceptance or Confirmation:

(1) A definite and seasonable expression of acceptance or a written confirmation which is sent within a reasonable time operates as an acceptance even though it states terms additional to or different from those offered or agreed upon, unless acceptance is expressly made conditional on assent to the additional or different terms.

(2) The additional terms are to be construed as proposals for addition to the contract. Between merchants such terms become part of the contract unless:

(a) the offer expressly limits acceptance to the terms of the offer;

(b) they materially alter it; or

(c) notification of objection to them has already been given or is given within a reasonable time after notice of them is received.

(3) Conduct by both parties which recognizes the existence of a contract is sufficient to establish a contract for sale although the writings of the parties do not otherwise establish a contract. In such case the terms of the particular contract consist of those terms on which the writings of the parties agree, together with any supplementary terms incorporated under any other provisions of this Act.

4. **Summary:** § 2-207 makes two major changes from the common-law approach:

❏ it provides, in § 2-207(1), that a document can constitute an acceptance "even though it states terms additional to or different from those offered or agreed upon," thus *abolishing the common-law "mirror image" rule*; and

❏ it provides, in § 2-207(2), that between merchants, the *additional terms* proposed in the acceptance can ***become part of the contract*** in certain circumstances if the other party (the offeror) merely ***remains silent***. § 2-207(2) thus effectively modifies the common-law rule that a proposal for a contract cannot be accepted by silence.

D. **Detailed discussion:** We now proceed to our detailed discussion of the various aspects of § 2-207. Rather than examining the section clause by clause, we will examine seven different types of factual situations, and analyze how the section governs each of these situations. In this, we follow more or less the approach used in W&S, pp. 6-24. The situations which we will examine are:

1. the purported "acceptance" is ***expressly made conditional*** on the ***offeror's assent*** to terms additional to or different from those contained in the offer;

2. the acceptance deals with a certain issue, on which the ***offer*** is ***silent*** (what § 2-207 calls an ***"additional"*** term);

3. the offer deals with a certain issue, on which the ***acceptance*** is ***silent***;

4. the acceptance and the offer deal with a particular issue in ***conflicting*** ways (making the acceptance's handling of the issue a ***"different"*** term in § 2-207's vernacular);

5. the purported "acceptance" recites terms which ***diverge*** so much from those contained in the offer that ***no contract is in fact formed*** by the exchange of documents;

6. the parties make an oral agreement, then one or both sends a ***confirming*** document which adds to, or conflicts with, the oral agreement; and

7. the parties do not use form documents at all, but rather, exchange documents that are completely ***custom-drafted***.

E. **Acceptance expressly conditional on assent to changes:** § 2-207(1) provides that any "expression of acceptance" or "written confirmation" acts as an acceptance even though it states terms that are "additional to or different from" those contained in the offer. (This is the general rule, which, as noted, overturns the common-law "mirror image" rule.) However, that subsection also contains one extremely important proviso: the "expression of acceptance" does ***not*** form a contract if it is ***"expressly made conditional on assent to the additional or different terms."***

1. **Significance of exception:** This exception means that if the purported "acceptance" contains additional or different terms from the offer, and also states something like "This acceptance of your offer is effective only if you agree to all of the terms listed on the reverse side of this acceptance form," ***there is no contract*** formed by the exchange of documents.

    Example: Buyer sends a purchase order for steel coils to Seller. Seller sends back an acknowledgment form. The acknowledgment form contains the following clause: "Seller's acceptance is, however, expressly conditional on Buyer's assent to the additional or different terms and conditions set forth below and printed on the reverse side. If these terms and conditions are not acceptable, Buyer should notify Seller at once."

    Held, no contract was formed by the exchange of purchase order and acknowledgment. The clause quoted above fell within § 2-207(1)'s "expressly conditional" exception, thus preventing what would otherwise have been an acceptance from being one (since Buyer never did assent to the additional or different terms). Thus even after sending the form, Seller would have been free to decide not to ship and could have walked away from the deal with no liability. (However, Seller did in fact ship, and Buyer paid for the goods. Therefore, a contract by performance, under § 2-207(3), came into existence; see *infra*, p. 36.) *C. Itoh (America), Inc. v. Jordan Int'l Co.*, 552 F.2d 1228 (7th Cir. 1977).

a. **Danger to offeror:** Observe that the possibility that the offeree may use a clause like the one in *C. Itoh* represents a significant risk to an offeror that sends out numerous purchase orders. If the buyer/offeror does not read the seller/offeree's acknowledgment form containing such an "expressly conditional" clause, and believes that a contract has been made, he will later discover to his chagrin that he has no contract claim if the seller then fails to ship the goods. Thus the moral of the story, at least for buyer/offerors, is: read the seller's fine print.

2. **Restrictive reading:** However, courts will not lightly presume that language in the "acceptance" insisting on the offeree's terms falls within the "expressly conditional" exception to § 2-207(1). In general, courts have taken the view that the exception will be triggered and a contract avoided *only if* the offeree makes it clear that he is **unwilling to close the deal** unless the offeror agrees to the additional or different terms.

a. **Must virtually track language of § 2-207(1):** Therefore, as a practical matter the offeree's response will be found to be "expressly conditional" only if the offeree's language *virtually tracks the phrasing* of § 2-207(1)'s expressly-conditional clause. F&E, p. 635.

3. **Offeror's assent to changes:** If the offeree uses an "expressly conditional" acceptance, the original offeror may, of course, *assent* to the changes; in that event, the changes become part of the contract.

F. **Additional term in acceptance:** We turn now to the situation in which the offeree's response contains an *"additional"* term, i.e., a clause taking a certain position on an issue with which the offer does not deal at all. (We assume that the offeree's response is not made expressly conditional on the offeror's assent to this additional term.) There are two issues: (1) Does the additional term prevent the offeree's response from being an acceptance?; and (2) If not, under what circumstances can the additional term become part of the contract?

1. **Contract formed:** Of key significance is the fact that the additional term *does not prevent the offeree's response from giving rise to a contract*. It is precisely in this situation that § 2-207 changes the common-law "mirror image" rule, by which the additional term would have been enough to make the offeree's response a counter-offer rather than an acceptance. Remember, § 2-207(1) says that "[a] definite and seasonable expression of acceptance or a written confirmation which is sent within a reasonable time *operates as an acceptance even though it states terms additional to or different from* those offered or agreed upon[.]"[3]

---

3. We are putting aside for the moment, until *infra*, p. 36, the situation in which the additional term so drastically changes the deal the offeror had in mind that it prevents the offeree's response from being a "definite and seasonable expression of acceptance" under § 2-207(1).

Example: Seller emails Buyer with an offer to sell Buyer green widgets. This offer says nothing about whether Seller is making any warranties. Buyer sends back a "purchase order" form that says, "Seller, by shipping, warrants that any goods will be fit for Buyer's particular purposes of re-selling the goods for use by children younger than 3."

Buyer's form *constitutes an acceptance* under § 2-207(1), even though the warranty term is an "additional" term. That is so because Buyer's form indicates an intent to enter into the proposed transaction, and does not make the deal expressly conditional on Seller's agreement to make the warranty. So regardless of whether the warranty term becomes part of the contract (we discuss this below), the important thing is that *the fact that the two forms did not agree did not prevent a contract from coming into existence.* (The same would be true if Buyer's form contained a "different" provision, i.e., one conflicting with a clause in Seller's offer.)

2. **Proposal for addition to the contract:**   Under § 2-207(2), whether the additional term becomes part of the contract depends, in the first instance, on whether both parties are *merchants*.

   a. **Who is a merchant:**   "Merchant" is defined in § 2-104(1) to mean "a person who deals in *goods of the kind* or otherwise by his occupation holds himself out as having *knowledge or skill peculiar to the practices or goods involved* in the transaction...." As Comment 2 to § 2-104 points out, in the offer-and-acceptance context the transactions at issue are "non-specialized business practices such as answering mail." Therefore, the Comment suggests, for purposes of § 2-207(2) *almost every person in business* will be considered a "merchant"; the Comment gives as examples *banks* and *universities*.

3. **At least one party not merchant:**   If at least one party is *not a merchant*, the only way the additional term can become part of the contract is if the offeror *explicitly assents* to it. That is, the additional term becomes a "proposal for addition to the contract" (§ 2-207(2)), and must be accepted as if it were a self-standing offer. In this situation, § 2-207(2) does not change the common-law rule requiring affirmative assent.

4. **Both parties merchants:**   But if *both parties* to the transaction *are merchants*, § 2-207(2) makes a dramatic exception to common-law practices. The additional term *automatically becomes part of the contract*, as a general rule. Only if one of three exceptions is triggered does the addition fail to become part of the contract. The three exceptions are recited in § 2-207(2)(a), (b) and (c); the additional terms become part of the contract unless

   > "(a) the offer *expressly limits* acceptance to the terms of the offer;
   >
   > (b) they *materially alter it*; or
   >
   > (c) notification of *objection* to them has already been given [by the offeror] or is given within a reasonable time after notice of them is received."

   a. **Objection:**   Subsections (a) and (c) are aspects of the same concept, namely, that the addition will not become part of the contract if the offeror affirmatively *indicates that he does not want it to*.

b. Materiality: The most important of the three exceptions is that given by (b), that the addition not be one which ***"materially alter[s]"*** the contract. No satisfactory definition of material alteration has emerged, and the issue is more or less faced anew in each case.

  i. Disclaimer of warranty: A ***disclaimer of warranty*** will almost always be considered a ***material alteration***. See § 2-207, Comment 4. Therefore, the disclaimer term will not become part of the contract.

  Example: P, a software reseller, orders 142 copies of a software package from D in a series of transactions. For each transaction, P sends a purchase order and D follows up with an invoice. Both documents contain essentially identical terms governing price, quantity, shipping and payment. No reference is made to any disclaimer of warranties or a limitation of remedies provision. However, when D ships the software, each package of software has printed on its box (as part of a "box-top license") a disclaimer of all express and implied warranties. P then sells the software to its customers, and almost immediately starts receiving complaints about it. P sues D for various breaches of warranties. D defends on the theory that the disclaimer-of-warranty clause became part of the contract.

  Held, for P. The warranty disclaimer in the box-top license should be treated as a proposed additional term to the contract. Because the proposed term would have materially altered the contract, it could not have become part of the contract unless P expressly agreed to it (which P never did). Therefore, the disclaimer did not become part of the contract, and P may maintain its suit for breach of warranty. *Step-Saver Data Systems, Inc. v. Wyse Technology,* 939 F.2d 91 (3d Cir. 1991).

  ii. Arbitration clause: A number of cases have focused on whether a clause calling for ***arbitration*** of disputes under the contract is a material alteration. The courts have been quite split on this issue. Some have said that the clause always constitutes a material alteration, some that it never does, and some that its materiality depends on case-by-case factors such as custom of the particular industry involved.

5. Recap of how additional terms are handled: To review § 2-207's treatment of an "additional" term in the acceptance, let's consider the following hypothetical:

  Hypothetical: Buyer sends a purchase order to Seller for 100 widgets at a particular price on a particular day. The purchase order says nothing about the forum in which disputes should be resolved. Seller sends back an acknowledgment form, repeating the same product, price and delivery terms, but also including a clause providing for arbitration in the event of any dispute relating to the contract. Assume that both parties are merchants, and that Buyer makes no response once it receives the acknowledgment form.

  Under § 2-207(1), Seller's acknowledgment was a "definite and seasonable expression of acceptance," and consequently operated as an acceptance, even though it contained the additional term (the arbitration clause). Therefore, a contract has been formed. The arbitration clause is an "additional" term, since it deals with an issue not covered in Buyer's purchase order. Therefore, it becomes a proposal for addition to the contract. Since both parties are merchants, it will automatically become part of the contract unless one of the subsections of § 2-207(2) is triggered. Here, we assume that the purchase order does not "expressly limit acceptance to the terms of the offer," and the facts tell us that Buyer makes no objection.

Therefore, the only event that could prevent the arbitration clause from becoming part of the contract would be if it "materially alters" the bargain. On this issue, as noted above, the courts are split. If the arbitration clause was found not to be a material alteration, that clause would become part of the contract. If the court *did* find it to be a material alteration, it would not become part of the contract, but the contract would continue without that clause (and ordinary judicial redress would be available to either party).

6. **Additional term in first document but not second:** As a brief aside, let's consider the much easier situation of an issue which is handled in the first document (the offer), but *not in the second* (the acceptance). For instance, suppose that the buyer's purchase order contains an arbitration clause, and the seller's acknowledgment form is silent on the issue of a forum for litigation. In this situation, § 2-207 says nothing specifically on point. However, it seems quite clear that, assuming that the seller's form was a "definite and seasonal expression of acceptance" (i.e., assuming that it did not so diverge from the offer on other terms that it was blocked from being an acceptance), it will be deemed to have accepted *all* terms of the offer, not just those on which the writings agree. Therefore, the arbitration clause becomes part of the contract. See W&S, p. 13.

G. **Different (conflicting) terms in documents:** We turn now to one of the most troublesome situations with which § 2-207 must deal: the situation in which an issue is covered one way in the offering document and another (*conflicting*) way in the acceptance. In the terminology of § 2-207(1), the acceptance's term is one which is *"different from"* (rather than "in addition to") the corresponding term in the offer.

1. **Two approaches:** Courts and commentators have evolved two dramatically different approaches to this situation.

   a. **"Knockout" rule:** A majority of courts, and most commentators, have subscribed to what is sometimes called the *"knockout"* rule. Under this approach, the conflicting clauses "knock each other out" of the contract, so that *neither enters the contract*. Instead, a UCC "gap-filler" provision is used if one is relevant; otherwise, the common law controls. See, e.g., *Northrop Corp. v. Litronic Industr.*, 29 F.3d 1173 (7th Cir. 1994) (stating that "the majority view is that the discrepant terms fall out and are replaced by a suitable UCC gap-filler").

   Example: Buyer and Seller are both merchants. Buyer sends a purchase order to Seller for 1,000 bicycles. The purchase order contains a clause in which Seller expressly warrants that the bicycles will not break for 1 year. Seller sends an acknowledgment form that matches the purchase order in all material respects, except that it contains a complete disclaimer of warranties. Buyer makes no response to the acknowledgment. Seller then ships the bicycles, some of which prove defective. Buyer wants to sue for breach of warranty. A court following the "knockout" rule will analyze the situation in the following steps:

[1] A contract was formed by the exchange of documents, since they matched well enough to indicate generally agreement about the terms of the deal.

[2] The disclaimer-of-warranties clause in the acknowledgment (the acceptance) materially altered the terms of the purchase order (the offer). Therefore, that clause did not become part of the contract, but was instead, under § 2-207(2)(b), merely a proposal for an addition to the contract. Buyer never accepted that proposal for addition.

[3] Buyer's warranty clause (bikes won't break for a year) and Seller's clause (complete disclaimer of warranty) squarely conflict, so these clauses "knock each other out," and each clause disappears.

[4] The contract then consists of the clauses on which the parties' forms agree (price, quantity, etc.), plus all relevant UCC gap-fillers. One of those gap fillers is an implied warranty of merchantability (§ 2-314), so the contract contains that implied warranty.

    i. **Rationale:** Nothing in the text of § 2-207 explicitly mandates the "knockout" rule. But the majority of courts and commentators supporting the knockout rule point to Comment 6 to § 2-207, which provides that "where clauses on confirming forms sent by both parties conflict each party must be assumed to object to a clause of the other conflicting with one on the confirmation sent by himself. As a result the requirement that there be notice of objection which is found in subsection (2) is satisfied and the conflicting terms do not become a part of the contract." (But opponents of the knockout theory argue that this language applies only to "confirming forms," not to a conflict between a form that is an offer and a form that is an acceptance. See W&S, p. 12.)

    b. **Alternative approach:** A few courts and commentators have proposed an alternative to the knockout theory. Under this approach, the clause proposed in the second form (i.e., the acceptance) simply *fails to have any effect*. The result is that the clause appearing in the offer enters the contract. This is the approach urged by Professor Summers; see W&S, p. 12.

  2. **Criticism:** One powerful criticism of the "knockout" theory is that it leads to the result that "An offeror has been defrocked of his prime common-law prerogative, that of ***determining the basis on which he is willing to contract....***" 34 Bus. Law. 477, 1484-86, quoted in Farns., p. 297.

    a. **Explanation:** As this criticism points out, the knockout doctrine is much more devastating to the offeror's ability to control his offer than is the "additional term" provision of § 2-207(2); the latter only applies where the variance is immaterial. With the knockout rule, by contrast, the offeror's term on a very major issue can be knocked out, and he can find himself being bound to a contract in which the UCC "gap-filler" becomes a term. For instance, an offeror/seller who is only willing to contract based on a complete disclaimer of warranties will, if the buyer's acceptance contains a conflicting warranty term, find himself bound to the § 2-314 implied warranty of merchantability.

H. Response diverges too much to be acceptance: Not every response which purports to "accept" an offer will in fact be regarded as an acceptance under §2-207(1). That section treats as an acceptance only a "definite and seasonable expression of acceptance." Thus a purported acceptance may in fact *diverge so materially* from the terms of the offer that it will *not serve as an acceptance at all.*

1. **Agreement on bargained terms:**   There is no hard-and-fast rule about what kinds of discrepancies between offer and "acceptance" will be great enough to prevent a contract from being formed. White and Summers (3rd Edition, p. 32) state the following general principle: "[I]n the usual purchase order-acknowledgment context the forms [do not fail to give rise to a contract] if [they] do not diverge as to price, quality, quantity, or delivery terms, but only as to the *usually unbargained terms on the reverse side* concerning remedies, arbitration, and the like."

I. Contract by parties' conduct: If the offer and "acceptance" diverge so much that there is no contract, and neither party begins to perform, that will be the end of the matter — neither party will have any liability to the other. But what often happens in this case of offer/acceptance divergence is that the parties go ahead and make full or partial *performance*. In that case, the parties' *conduct* implicitly creates a contract.

1. **Solution:**   The UCC recognizes that this can happen, by saying in § 2-207(3) that "Conduct by both parties which *recognizes the existence of a contract* is sufficient to *establish a contract* for sale although the writings of the parties do not otherwise establish a contract."

   a. **Two main scenarios:** There are two main scenarios of "contract by conduct." These are where:

   [1] **Too much divergence:**   The parties exchange documents (say a purchase order and an acknowledgment), and the *two documents diverge so much* that the second one does not constitute an acceptance, but the seller *ships goods* that the *buyer keeps*.

   Example: Buyer's purchase order is for 100 widgets at $5 each. Seller's acknowledgment form is for 200 widgets at $7 each. Buyer does not say anything in response to the acknowledgment form. Seller ships the 200 widgets, and Buyer keeps them. Even though the exchange of documents did not create a contract, the parties' conduct gave rise to a contract by performance, for 200 widgets (at a price to be supplied by the UCC's "gap filler" provision, discussed below, in this case, a "reasonable price").

   [2] **Buyer keeps goods:** There are *no writings*, or just *one writing* (e.g., a purchase order), but the seller *ships goods* that the *buyer keeps*.

   Example: Buyer sends a purchase order for 100 widgets at $5 each. Seller does not send any acknowledgment or other writing, but ships the 100 widgets and Buyer keeps them. Even though there was no exchange of documents, the parties' conduct gave rise to a contract by performance, for 100 widgets at $5 each.

   b. **Summary**:   The basic idea is that if the parties behave in a way indicating that they *think they have an agreement*, that agreement will be enforced even if there *never* *was a formal offer or acceptance*, or even a recognizable *attempt* at making an offer or acceptance.

c. **Terms:** Where such a contract-by-conduct is formed, the *terms* "consist of those terms in which the writings of the parties agree, together with any *supplementary terms* incorporated under any other provisions of this Act." § 2-207(3). (These "supplementary terms" are called *"gap fillers."*) For instance, the *price term* would be a "reasonable price at the time for delivery," as imposed by § 2-305's price "gap filler."

d. **"Acceptance by conduct" can occur in non-UCC contracts:** The principle that acceptance can occur by conduct applies also to *non-UCC cases.* Thus Rest. 2d, § 19 says that "the manifestation of assent may be made wholly or partly by written or spoken words or *by other acts* or by failure to act."

   i. **Acts during course of extended negotiations:** "Acceptance by conduct" often occurs during the course of *extended negotiations* that fail to culminate in words or documents that constitute acceptance. While the parties go back and forth on their attempts to form an explicit contract, one will start to perform, and this start of performance may justify the conclusion that that party was non-verbally accepting a then-outstanding offer.

   Example: Owner negotiates over a period of time with Contractor to have Contractor re-pave Owner's driveway. At one point, Contractor sends a proposal to Owner listing a proposed price of $5,000. Owner sends a response, "$5,000 won't work, but how about $4,000?" Contractor doesn't make a verbal response, but shows up and paves the driveway. A court is likely to conclude that Contractor's work of paving the driveway constituted his acceptance by conduct of Owner's offer of $4,000.

J. **Confirmation of oral agreement:** So far, we have generally discussed only those situations where no contract exists up until the time the parties exchange documents. Sometimes, however, the parties initially reach an *oral agreement*. Although in some cases this agreement may not be enforceable due to failure to comply with the Statute of Frauds (see *infra*, p. 275), it is nonetheless a contract. Therefore, a document subsequently sent by one party to the other cannot be viewed as an "acceptance." § 2-207 treats it as a separate category, the *confirmation.*

1. **Additional terms in confirmation:** A confirmation containing terms that are *additional* to the oral agreement is treated exactly the same as an acceptance containing terms additional to the offer. That is, the confirmation's additional terms become part of the contract unless one of the three subsections of § 2-207(2) is satisfied. Since subsection (a) (offer expressly limiting acceptance to terms of offer) will never be applicable in the confirmation case, the additional terms in the confirmation become part of the contract unless they *materially alter* the oral agreement, or the party receiving the confirmation *objects* to the additional terms.

2. **"Different" terms in confirmation:** Assume now that a clause contained in the confirmation is *"different"* from a term on the same issue reached in the oral agreement. In this situation, the court will almost certainly say that the different term in the confirmation does *not* enter the contract, even if the party receiving the confirmation fails to object. Furthermore, the "knockout" rule (which most courts apply in the case of a different term

in the exchange-of-documents context; see *supra*, pp. 34-35) will almost certainly not be applied, and the term in the oral agreement will remain in force, rather than being "knocked out." This result is easily justified on the theory that if the parties have indeed reached an oral agreement, one party should not be permitted to contradict that agreement by his unilateral act.

3. **Request that confirmation be signed:**   Suppose that, after an oral agreement, one party sends a confirmation, and *requests that the other party sign and return that confirmation.* In this kind of scenario, there will be *no consequence* if the recipient doesn't sign or return the confirmation — the deal is complete when the confirmation is received.

   Example: Buyer and Seller are both merchants. Buyer telephones Seller and says, "Send me 100 blue widgets, your Model 101, at $3, delivery to occur in 30 days." Seller says, "OK." Seller then faxes a confirmation, with a cover sheet that says, "Please sign and return this confirmation." Buyer doesn't sign the confirmation, but instead puts it in the file. The price of widgets rises, and Seller sends a notice (before 30 days have passed) saying "Because you didn't sign or return the confirmation, we have no deal and will not deliver."

   Seller has breached. The parties' deal was completed no later than the moment when Seller sent the confirmation (and probably was complete even earlier, at the moment of the oral agreement). Therefore, Buyer's failure to sign and return the confirmation had no effect, and Seller was obligated to fulfill the contract.

K. **"Terms to follow" contracts (a/k/a "rolling" contracts):**   Goods are sometimes sold under what is sometimes called a *"terms to follow"* or *"rolling" contract.* In such a contract, the buyer, usually a consumer, orders and pays for the goods *without seeing most of the contract terms.* The detailed terms are then contained *on or in the box* containing the goods. When the buyer receives the goods, she is told that if she does not agree with the detailed terms, she has a certain time within which to return the goods for a full credit.

There are two interesting questions raised by such rolling contracts: (1) when is the contract formed? and (2) what are its terms? A court's answer to the second of these questions tends to depend on its answer to the first. There are two main approaches to the first question.

1. **First approach: "Contract not formed until receipt":**   A number of courts have taken the approach that *no contract is formed until the buyer has received the goods and has kept them* for beyond the prescribed return period. This approach tends to yield a contract that includes *all of the seller's terms,* on the theory that the action of the buyer in keeping the goods rather than returning them should be interpreted as an *acceptance by performance,* an acceptance that includes the buyer's assent to all of the seller's proposed terms.

   a. **The *Hill v. Gateway 2000* case:**   Probably the best-known decision taking the "no contract formed until the buyer receives and keeps the goods" approach is *Hill v. Gateway 2000, Inc.*, 105 F.3d 1147 (7th Cir. 1997). The author of the opinion was Judge (and former University of Chicago law professor) Frank Easterbrook, known for his economics-oriented approach to law. *Hill* involved the issue of what terms were included when consumer ordered a computer by phone, and *first saw the detailed contract terms in a document contained in the box in which the computer was shipped.* Easterbrook decided that (1) *no contract was formed until the buyer received the*

TABLE 2-1
RECAP: UCC § 2-207 Battle of the Forms[a]

Situation	Example	Test/Outcome
[1] B's form is silent; S's form has "*additional*" term; both parties are "merchants"	B (retailer), orders widgets from S. Order silent about implied warranties. S's acknowledgment says, "All warranties are hereby disclaimed." B makes no response.	**Rule 1:** There is a contract if S's doc doesn't diverge so much that it fails to be a "definite expression of acceptance." Here, there is a contract. **Rule 2:** The disclaimer becomes part of the contract *unless* (a) offer says acceptance must be *limited* to the terms of the offer (not present here); (b) disclaimer "*materially alters*" the deal; or (c) B *objects* to the disclaimer within a reasonable time (not present here). **Outcome:** Disclaimer doesn't become part of contract, because warranty disclaimers are always held to be "material alterations."
[2] Same as [1], but at least one party is *not a merchant*	B (consumer), orders widgets from S. Order silent about implied warranties. S's acknowledgment says, "All warranties are hereby disclaimed." B makes no response.	**Rule 1:** There's a contract if S's doc doesn't diverge so much that it fails to be a "definite expression of acceptance." This didn't happen here, so there is a contract. **Rule 2:** Since at least one party (B) is not a merchant, S's warranty disclaimer becomes a "*proposal* for addition to the contract," and won't become part of it unless B *explicitly approves* (which B didn't). **Outcome:** Since B didn't approve, the contract includes the standard UCC warranties.
[3] B's form and A's form have "*different*" (i.e., *conflicting*) versions of same term	B (retailer), orders widgets from S. Order says, "B shall have 30 days to pay." S's acknowledgment says, "All sales are C.O.D." B makes no response.	**Rule 1:** There's a contract if S's doc doesn't diverge so much that it fails to be a "definite expression of acceptance." Here, there is a contract. **Rule 2 (Majority view):** The conflicting clauses (credit vs. C.O.D.) "*knock each other out.*" UCC gap-fillers, if any, apply. **Outcome:** The gap-filler on credit is that there is none, i.e., all sales are C.O.D. That's what applies.
[4] S's acceptance is made *expressly conditional* on B's assent to changes	B (retailer), orders widgets from S. S's acknowledgment says, "This acceptance is expressly conditional on your assent to all the terms on the rear of this form. If you object, notify us ASAP." One of the terms on the rear is a disclaimer of all warranties. B makes no response.	**Rule:** If "acceptance" containing changed terms is made "*expressly conditional on assent* to the additional or different terms," then *no contract is formed* by exchange of documents. **Outcome:** No contract formed by B's order and S's acknowledgment. Unless the parties then make a contract by performance (e.g., S ships anyway, and B keeps the goods), there's no contract.

a. This table assumes that Buyer ("B") sends in an "order" (which is an offer) for goods, and Seller ("S") responds with an "acknowledgment" (which may or may not be an acceptance). This chart tells you: (1) Is there a contract?; and (2) If so, what are its terms? We cover only the most important scenarios here.

*comp*uter together with enclosed detailed terms and kept the computer beyond the pre-scribed return period; and (2) *all of the detailed terms contained in the box became part of the contract.*

i. **Facts:**   In *Hill*, the Ps (the Hills) ordered a computer from Gateway (D) by phone, apparently without being told anything about the detailed terms that would govern the purchase. They paid by credit card before shipment. The computer arrived at their home, and inside the box was a contract document containing a variety of terms, *including a mandatory-arbitration clause*. The document recited that all terms in it would become the parties' contract unless the customer returned the computer for a full refund within 30 days. The Hills kept the computer, then were unhappy with the computer's performance. They brought a federal-court class action on behalf of themselves and similarly-situated Gateway owners, claiming that Gateway was a racketeer and seeking treble damages. Gateway sought to dis-miss the suit on the theory that the contract was not formed until the Hills kept the computer for 30 days, thereby agreeing to the terms-in-the-box, including the arbi-tration clause. The Hills seem to have argued, *inter alia*, that the contract was formed at the time they ordered, that the case was governed by UCC § 2-207, and that under that section the arbitration clause never became part of the contract.

ii. **Decision for Gateway:** Judge Easterbrook *found for Gateway*, accepting the argument that the contract was only formed when the Hills kept the computer for 30 days, thus making the arbitration clause part of the contract.

(1) **§ 2-207 argument rejected:**   Easterbrook rejected the Hills' argument that UCC § 2-207 should apply. The Hills had argued not only that § 2-207 should apply,[4] but that the way it should be applied was that the arbitration clause was an "additional term" to be construed as a "proposal for addition to the con-tract"; they further argued that because they were not "merchants," the pro-posal never became part of the contract (as it might have done had they been merchants, under the second sentence of § 2-207(2) — see *supra*, p. 32). But Easterbrook, describing § 2-207 as "the infamous battle-of-the-forms section," asserted that *"when there is only one form, 'section 2-207 is irrelevant'."*

Note: Judge Easterbrook's conclusion in *Hill* that § 2-207 does not apply to any case in which only one party uses a form is *clearly incorrect.* See, e.g., 71 Fordham L.Rev. 743 at 753: "Easterbrook was plainly wrong about section 2-207's applicability. Nothing in the text of the section limits it to transactions involving more than one form." Easterbrook's incorrectness is shown by Offi-cial Comment 1 to § 2-207, which says that the section applies "where an agreement has been reached ... orally ... and is followed by one or both of the parties sending formal memoranda embodying the terms so far as agreed upon and adding terms not discussed." (An oral agreement followed by one party's sending of a formal memorandum is obviously not a multi-form scenario, so Easterbrook's "only applies to multiple-form scenarios" rule cannot be cor-rect.)

---

4. You may want to review the text of § 2-207, and our discussion of the section, beginning on p. 29 *supra*.

2. **Second approach: "Contract is formed at time of order":** The other major approach to the rolling contract problem is to hold that § 2-207 *does* apply, and that its application means that *a contract is formed at the time of the order.* Under this approach, the *buyer* is usually considered to be the *offeror*, the *seller* is an **offeree** who is proposing additional or different terms, and at least where the buyer is a consumer those terms *never become part of the contract* unless the buyer expressly agrees to them (which she usually doesn't).

a. ***Klocek v. Gateway, Inc.:*** The leading case applying this § 2-207-based approach is probably another Gateway case, ***Klocek v. Gateway, Inc.***, 104 F.Supp. 1332 (D. Kan. 2000). The court there was a mere federal district court rather than the mighty Seventh Circuit that decided *Hill*, but the *Klocek* court seems to most observers to have gotten the better of the argument.

   i. **Facts:** The facts of *Klocek* were a virtual repeat of those of *Hill*. Plaintiff ordered a Gateway computer, Gateway shipped one to him, and the box arrived with a standard form contract inside containing an arbitration clause. P brought a class action for breach of warranty, and Gateway claimed, as it had in *Hill*, that the terms of the form contract, including the arbitration clause, became part of the contract when P kept the computer beyond the return period. The only difference in the factual settings was that this time, the return period was limited to five days instead of 30 days.

   ii. **Holding:** But this time, the court *found for P*, holding that the *arbitration clause never became part of the contract,* so that P's judicial suit could go forward. In reaching this conclusion, the court completely *rejected* the *Hill* decision. Instead, the *Klocek* court concluded that *§ 2-207 applied*, and produced the result that the arbitration clause never became part of the contract.

      (1) **§ 2-207 applies to a single-form case:** First, the court concluded that *Hill* was simply wrong when it concluded that § 2-207 could not apply to a case involving only one form. The court acknowledged that § 2-207 *often* involves "battle of the forms" cases, i.e., cases in which each party uses a preprinted form. But, the court said, § 2-207 by its terms "applies to an acceptance or written confirmation [and] states nothing which requires another form before the provision becomes effective." Therefore, § 2-207 applied to this fact pattern in which buyer places an order without using a form, and seller ships the product together with a form document (which in this case the court referred to as Gateway's "Standard Terms").

      (2) **Buyer is offeror:** The court next discussed who was the offeror and who the offeree. Here, as in the typical consumer transaction, the court said, *"the purchaser is the offeror, and the vendor is the offeree."* Whether the transaction took place by phone, mail order or in-store purchase,[5] Gateway accepted either by agreeing to ship, and/or actually shipping, the computer. (The court cited § 2-206(b) on this point: "An order or other offer to buy goods for

---

5. The record was unclear about whether the transaction was an in-person transaction at a retail store or a phone or mail order, and the court did not decide. However, the court's conclusion about whether the arbitration clause ever became part of the contract did not depend on the precise method by which a contract was reached.

prompt or current shipment shall be construed as inviting acceptance either by a prompt promise to ship or by the prompt or current shipment[.]")

    (3) Status of Standard Terms: Since Gateway accepted by shipping or agreeing to ship, the court next had to determine the status of Gateway's inclusion of its Standard Terms with the product. Under § 2-207, the court said, the Standard Terms constituted "either an expression of acceptance or [a] written confirmation." It didn't matter which; either way, the contents of the Standard Terms were ***proposals for "additional or different terms."*** Since there was nothing to indicate that Gateway had made its acceptance conditional upon the buyer's assent to Gateway's Standard Terms, and since buyer (P) was not a merchant, under § 2-207(2) "any additional or different terms ***did not become part of the parties' agreement unless [P] expressly agreed to them.*** There was no evidence that P had agreed to any of the additional or different terms, including the provision that by keeping the computer for five days P was agreeing to make all of the Standard Terms part of the contract. Therefore, P's act of keeping the computer had no legal effect, and none of the additional terms in the Standard Terms document (including the arbitration clause) ever became part of the contract. Consequently, P did not have to arbitrate, and could sue instead.

   3. Evaluation: As between the basic approach of *Hill* on the one hand (§ 2-207 does not apply to the rolling-contract scenario in which only seller uses a form, so no contract is deemed formed until buyer receives the goods and the seller's form), and *Klocek* on the other (§ 2-207 applies to the one-form situation, so a contract is formed at the time of the order, and if the buyer is a consumer any proposed additional terms don't become part of the contract unless agreed upon by the buyer), the *Klocek* view seems more in keeping with the intent of § 2-207.

L. Negotiations not involving standardized forms: In all of the categories considered above, we have assumed that one or both parties used standardized, non-negotiated forms. If the parties do not proceed via the standard form route, and instead send ***draft agreements*** back and forth between each other, together with letters proposing various changes, traditional offer and acceptance analysis must be used to determine what document contains enough information to be an offer, and what document constitutes the first bona fide "acceptance" under § 2-207(1).

In this actively-negotiated context, it may well be that there never do emerge both an offer and an acceptance, since deviations between one party's view and the other's are more likely to be considered significant (and thus fatal to the existence of a contract) than where standard form documents are exchanged. In this situation, there are two possible outcomes:

(1) the court will find that there simply was never any contract, and either party is free to walk away; or

(2) the court will find that ***by their conduct*** (e.g., by the seller's shipping the goods and the buyer's holding them or paying for them), the parties recognized the existence of an unwritten contract. In this latter situation, § 2-207(3) will be applied.

M. Electronic commerce, and its effect on contract formation: The rise of "electronic commerce" or ***"e-commerce"*** poses some special problems for determining whether a contract has been formed, and if so what its provisions are. In e-commerce, frequently one party (in a goods case, that party is usually the seller) is *not represented by a human being* who is consciously involved in making a decision to sell. Instead, the "I agree to sell" decision is essentially made by the computer, acting as what is sometimes called an *"electronic agent."*

1. **Contract formation:** Let's consider the first question formed by the use of an electronic agent representing (let's assume) the seller: *can a contract be formed* when a human buyer interacts with a computer program or website that "represents" the seller?

   a. **Existing law unclear:** Article 2 is *unclear* on this point — not surprisingly, the existing language (dating from the late 1950s) does not contemplate computer programs or other non-humans acting as contract-formers. There are few cases on point, perhaps because transactions large enough to be worth litigating over are not yet very often handled on even one side without human intervention. But it seems likely that, depending on how the order flow works, the computer can make an "offer," or can "accept" the buyer's "offer" (her order).

   Example: Let's take the garden-variety scenario in which Consumer orders a book from Amazon's website. Assume that at some point in the process, the website asks Consumer, "Do you confirm your order for *War and Peace*, price of $19.95 + $2 shipping and handling?" Consumer clicks the "yes" button (and leaves the "no" or "cancel" button unchecked). A court would likely conclude that Amazon has made an offer of *War and Peace*, and that Consumer has accepted that offer, even though no human acted from the Amazon side.

2. **Terms of the resulting contract:** If a contract is formed by such an interaction of a human and an electronic agent, *what are its terms?* Let's assume that what we are talking about is a purchase by buyer from seller's website.

   a. **Terms fully shown to human buyer:** If the seller's website *fully disclosed* the proposed terms to the buyer in a document that the buyer must have seen before the buyer indicated assent,[6] the odds are very good that a court interpreting Article 2 would conclude that *all of the terms* in the seller's set of proposed terms will *become part of the contract*. That's because, if the court is willing to treat the text of the seller's website as being a contract document at all, it will likely treat those terms as being equivalent to a document, and a buyer who signs the seller's proposed contract document will be deemed to have agreed to all non-unconscionable terms in it. That is, a party who receives the other party's contract form normally has a *"duty to read"* the form (i.e., is bound by its contents even if not read), and the computer version of a party's form would likely receive the same judicial treatment.

   b. **Terms not necessarily shown to human buyer:** But now, suppose that due to lax lawyering or lax programming, the seller's website is designed in such a way that the buyer does *not* necessarily see (or assent to) all of the proposed terms. Here, a court

---

6. By "must," I mean that the website was constructed in such a way that the terms scrolled onto the buyer's screen before she confirmed the order, and the buyer was asked to acknowledge that she saw these terms and knew that her order was contingent upon her acceptance of them. This is now the standard "clickwrap" format for order-entry screens.

may well find that terms that the buyer *could* have seen on the website but did not actually see or assent to *do not become part of the contract. Cf. Specht v. Netscape Communications Corp.*, 306 F.3d 17 (2d Cir. 2002), where the court reached this result, so that the seller's website's terms did not become part of the resulting contract.

N. Modern view of divergences in non-UCC cases: In contracts that are not for the sale of goods (i.e., service contracts, construction contracts, and other contracts not falling under the UCC), a modern court may well follow the Second Restatement approach to divergences between offer and acceptance, rather than the common-law rule (by which the acceptance must mirror the offer).

    1. Matches UCC: The Restatement's basic handling of such divergences *matches* the approach of UCC § 2-207(1):

        a. Acceptance forms a contract: Thus Restatement 2d, § 61, states that "An acceptance which requests a *change or addition* to the terms of the offer is *not thereby invalidated* unless the acceptance is made to *depend on assent* to the changed or added terms."

        b. Conditional on assent to new terms: § 59, in turn, states that where a reply to an offer purports to accept that offer, but *is* conditional on the offeror's assent to the new terms, the offeree's response is not an acceptance, but is a counter-offer.

    2. Does not specify what the terms are: But the Second Restatement does not attempt to specify *what the terms of the contract* are when the acceptance proposes new terms. So it's far less specific than the UCC in this regard.

Quiz Yourself on
ACCEPTANCE VARYING FROM OFFER

9. Fern owns an antique shop, Junk Is Us. She makes a written offer to buy Euphrates Antique Wholesalers' entire inventory of old string over a period of months. Fern's offer promises that she'll pay any invoice within 30 days, but says nothing about what happens if Fern doesn't pay on time. Nor does the offer says anything specific about what kind of response by Euphrates will constitute an acceptance. Euphrates immediately sends a written response that says, "We accept your offer." The response includes an extra clause providing for 8% interest (a rate typical in the industry) on overdue invoices. Fern makes no response to the overdue-invoices clause, receives the first shipment of string and places it into her inventory.

(A) Is there a contract?

(B) If your answer to (A) is yes, is the overdue-invoices clause part of that contract?

10. Wallflower Mart sends a purchase order to Harry's Wholesale Florist for 500 dried flower arrangements, style 402, for $3 each, to be paid in full 60 days after receipt of goods. Harry's sends back an acknowledgment form confirming that it will sell 500 dried flower arrangements, style 402, for $3 each, to be paid in full 10 days after receipt of goods. At the bottom of the acknowledgment form there is the following statement in bold type: "This acknowledgment shall operate as an acceptance if and only if you assent to any terms in it that may be different from terms in your order. If you do not so assent, you should notify us immediately."

(A) Assume that Wallflower receives the acknowledgment, reads it, and makes no response. Harry's has not yet made shipment. At this moment, is there a contract? If so, what are the contract's payment terms?

(B) Now, assume that Harry's, not having heard any response to its acknowledgment form 5 days after sending it, sends the flower arrangements. Wallflower Mart receives the flowers and immediately resells them. Is there a contract? If so, what are its payment terms?

11. Willie Wonka places an order with Nuts To You for 1,000 pounds of Grade A almonds at $1.25/pound, to be delivered in five days to his chocolate factory. A clause in the boilerplate of the order form states that Willie Wonka will be entitled to recover his reasonable attorney's fees should he have to sue over a problem with the contract.

(A) Nuts To You sends an acknowledgment form in which it states that it will sell Willie Wonka 1,000 pounds of Grade A almonds, to be delivered in five days to his chocolate factory. In the boilerplate language in the acknowledgment form, Nuts states that each party will be responsible for its own attorney's fees should a suit arise from the contract. Is there a contract? If so, what does the contract say about who will pay Willie's attorney's fees if he has to sue?

(B) Same as part (A), except now assume that the Nuts To You acknowledgment form, instead of mentioning attorney's fees, changes the grade of almonds to Grade B at a $1.25/pound price. (Grade B almonds are perceived in the marketplace as being significantly less good-tasting than Grade A ones, and typically sell for about 10% less.) Is there a contract? If so, what does the contract say about the Grade?

Answers

9. **(A) Yes.** This is a contract covered by Article 2 of the UCC (since it's for the sale of goods). Under § 2-207(1), the fact that an "expression of acceptance" "states terms additional to or different from those offered or agreed upon" does not prevent that expression from operating as an acceptance, unless the expression is "expressly made conditional on assent to the additional or different terms." Since Euphrates' response didn't indicate that Euphrates was unwilling to enter the deal if Fern wouldn't agree to the over-due-invoices clause, the response was not "expressly made conditional on [Fern's] assent" to the overdue-invoices clause, and that response therefore served as an acceptance.

(B) Yes. Unlike at common law, under the UCC terms in an acceptance that fail to match those in the offer can nonetheless become part of the contract in some circumstances. Under § 2-207(2), if both parties are merchants, an "additional" term in the acceptance will become part of the contract unless either: (a) the offer expressly limits acceptance to the terms of the offer; (b) the additional term "materially alters" the offer; or (c) the offeror gives notice of her objection to the additional term either before the acceptance, or within a reasonable time after the offeror receives notice of the additional term.

Here, Fern and Euphrates are both merchants. (Since we're told that Fern has an antique shop, we know she's in the business of dealing in the type of merchandise in question, i.e., antiques.) The facts make it clear that neither (a) nor (c) applies — Fern didn't indicate in advance that Euphrates had to accept exactly on the offer's terms, and she remained silent after she got notice of the new clause in the acceptance. As to (b), The overdue-invoices clause is probably not a material alteration to the contract, since: (i) it will apply only if Fern fails to do what she's already promised she'd do (pay on time), and (ii) a charge for overdueness that's of a size typical for the industry probably isn't a material change to the overall agreement. Therefore, § 2-207(2) says that the clause became part of the contract.

10. (A) No, there is no contract. Under § 2-207(1), an "expression of acceptance" acts as an acceptance even though it contains different or additional terms, "unless acceptance is expressly made conditional on assent to the additional or different terms." Harry's acknowledgment form was "expressly made conditional on assent," since the form made it clear that Harry's was only willing to enter into the transaction if Wallflower assented to all the terms in Harry's form, which Wallflower did not do. Wallflower's mere silence (and failure to comply with Harry's directive that Wallflower immediately indicate if it's unwilling to assent to all aspects of Harry's form) doesn't change the fact that Wallflower has failed to assent to Harry's form in its entirety. Therefore, Harry's acknowledgment form was a rejection and counter-offer, which Wallflower could either accept or reject. As of the moment of the question, Wallflower hadn't done either, so there's no contract.

(B) Yes; it's not clear whether payment will be due on receipt, or within 10 days. Even though no contract was formed by the exchange of documents (see (A)), the parties later created a contract by their *actions* (i.e. shipping and accepting the goods). See § 2-207(3), first sentence ("Conduct by both parties which recognizes the existence of a contract is sufficient to establish a contract for sale although the writings of the parties do not otherwise establish a contract.") The terms of the contract will be those "on which the writings of the parties agree" (*id.*, second sentence). The terms will also include any "supplementary terms incorporated under any other provisions" of the UCC (*id.*), so that the Code's "gap fillers" for the terms on which the parties did not agree also become part of the contract. In this case, payment on delivery would probably be such a gap-filler, since § 2-310(a) says that "Unless otherwise agreed, … payment is due at the time and place at which the buyer is to receive the goods." But a court might, instead, hold that the writings agreed on giving Wallflower at least 10 days (since even Harry's less-generous form gave Wallflower this much time). In that case, Wallflower would get the 10 days.

11. (A) Yes, there is a contract; Willie will have to pay his own fees. Under the UCC, the fact that documents purporting to be an offer and an acceptance deviate from each other does not prevent the two documents from forming a contract (assuming they agree on essential points). § 2-207(1) (see previous question, part (A), discussing this aspect.) When a term differs between the offer and acceptance, most courts apply the "knockout" rule. Under this approach, both conflicting terms are knocked out of the contract and replaced with a UCC gap filler, if one applies, or with a provision derived from the common law. Here, the parties have agreed on all major terms of the contract and disagree only as to who will be responsible for attorney's fees should a conflict arise. The conflicting terms will be knocked out and replaced with the common-law rule that each party to a commercial transaction is responsible for his own fees should a dispute arise.

(B) There is no contract. Under these facts, the parties significantly disagree over a material term of the contract: the Grade (quality) of product to be shipped. As a general rule, when the purchase order and acknowledgment forms differ significantly as to price, quality, quantity, or delivery terms, courts will hold that the acknowledgment diverges so materially from the offer that it is not an acceptance at all but rather a counter-offer. Therefore, no contract has been formed yet, and Willie Wonka can either choose to accept Nuts To You's counter-offer or reject it.

VI. DURATION OF THE POWER OF ACCEPTANCE

A. Determining whether the acceptance is timely: The material which follows sets forth the rules for determining whether a power of acceptance exists at a particular moment. After this discussion, the rules for determining when an acceptance becomes effective are set out. For an acceptance to be valid, it must become effective while the power of acceptance is still in effect. When there is any doubt as to whether the acceptance is timely, the student must therefore pinpoint *the moment at which the purported acceptance became effective*, and must then determine *whether the power of acceptance was in effect at that moment*.

B. "Continuing offers" implied: An offer gives to the offeree a *continuing power of acceptance* until this power has been terminated. This power of acceptance may be terminated in a variety of ways.

C. Four ways of terminating offer: There are *four main ways* in which the offeree's power of acceptance may be terminated. Rest. 2d, § 36(1). These methods of termination are:

(a) *rejection* or *counter-offer* by the offeree;

(b) *lapse of time*;

(c) *revocation* by the offeror; and

(d) *death* or *incapacity* of the offeror or the offeree.

We'll consider each of these methods separately.

By the way, these four ways in which the power of acceptance may be terminated apply only to what are called *"revocable"* offers, as opposed to irrevocable offers. The ordinary offer is revocable at the offeror's wish; an irrevocable offer is usually called an "option contract." Option contracts are treated *infra*, p. 52.

D. Offer terminated by offeree's rejection: If the offeree *rejects* the offer, her power of acceptance is terminated unless either:

[1] the *offeror* indicates that the offer *still stands* in spite of the rejection; or

[2] the *offeree* states that although she does not now intend to accept the offer, she wishes to *consider it further*.

See Rest. 2d, §§ 38(1) and (2).

> **Example:** *A* makes an offer to *B*, and adds, "I'll keep this offer open for a week." *B* rejects the offer the following day, but later in the week attempts to accept it. There is no contract, since *B*'s power of acceptance has terminated when he rejected the offer. But now, suppose that, instead of rejecting the offer outright, *B* had said to *A*, "I'm pretty sure I don't want to take your offer, but I'd still like to think about it." Here, the power of acceptance would *not* have been terminated.
>
> Similarly, if *B* had rejected the offer outright, but *A* had said, "Think about the offer some more," *B*'s power of acceptance would not have terminated. See Rest. 2d, § 38, Illustr. 1.

E. Counter-offer terminates power to accept: If the offeree makes a *counter-offer*, his power to accept the original offer is terminated just as if he had flatly rejected the offer.

> **Example:** *A* offers to sell *B* Blackacre for $5,000, stating that the offer will remain open for 30 days. B replies, "I'll give you $4,800 for the property." *A* rejects that proposal. *B* then says, "I accept at $5,000." Because *B*'s counter-offer terminated his power of acceptance, there is no contract. See Rest. 2d, § 38, Illustr. 1.

1. **Contrary statement of offeror or offeree:** But just as is the case with a rejection, a counter-offer does not terminate the power of acceptance if either the offeror or the offeree *indicates otherwise*.

> **Example:** Suppose that on the facts of the above example, *A* had said, "I'll shake hands on the deal right away at $4,800. But if you won't take $4,800, I'd like to think about your $5,000 price for the rest of the 30 days." This would not have been a rejection, and the power of acceptance would not have been terminated — although *A* would thereby have made a counter-offer, his indication that he wished to keep the original offer under advisement would have been sufficient to prevent his power of acceptance from being terminated.

> **Note:** Recall that an offeree's response may, under UCC § 2-207(1), be a valid acceptance, rather than a counter-offer, even if it contains some terms different from or in addition to those of the offer. See *supra*, p. 29. The offeree's power of acceptance is terminated only when his response is a true counter-offer, rather than a qualified acceptance of the sort referred to in § 2-207(1).

2. **Counter-offer when original offer is irrevocable:** If the offer is *irrevocable*, a counter-offer will not terminate the offeree's power of acceptance. This rule is discussed as part of the general treatment of irrevocable offers (principally "option contracts") *infra*, p. 52.

3. **Distinguish counter-offer from exploration:** Be careful to distinguish a counter-offer from a response by the offeree that is too *equivocal* or *uncertain* to be a counter-offer, and that instead merely *explores the possibility of some other arrangement* while keeping the original offer alive. Statements like *"Would you consider...?"* or "I might be interested instead in ..." will typically have this non-counter-offer effect.

> **Example:** On Feb. 1, Seller writes to Buyer, "I'll sell you 2,000 widgets @ $20; you must take all or none." On Feb. 5, Buyer faxes Seller, "Would you consider letting me buy 1,800 at the $20 price?" Seller makes no response. On Feb. 9, Buyer faxes an order for all 2,000 at $20.

> Buyer's order for all 2,000 is a valid acceptance. That's because Buyer's Feb. 5 fax, although it explored an alternative arrangement, was not so definitive that it should be considered a counter-offer (which would have had the effect of terminating Seller's offer). Instead, the Feb. 5 fax had no effect on the validity of the Feb. 1 offer, so that offer remained in place to be accepted by Buyer on Feb. 9.

F. **Lapse of time:** Because the offeror is "master of his offer," he can set a time limit for acceptance. At the end of this time limit, the offeree's power of acceptance automatically terminates by *"lapse."* See Rest. 2d, § 41(1).

1. **Expiration after reasonable time:** If the offer does not set a time limit for acceptance, the power of acceptance terminates "at the end of a *reasonable time period.*" Rest. 2d, § 41(1).

    a. **Question of fact:** The court must determine what a reasonable time for acceptance is as a question of fact, "depending on all the circumstances existing when the offer and attempted acceptance are made." Rest. 2d, § 41(2).

b. Offer made by mail: If the offer is made by mail, the Second Restatement takes the position that an acceptance is, as a general rule, timely if it is mailed the same day that the offer is received. Rest. 2d, § 40(3).

c. Speculative transactions: If the offer relates to the sale of an item that is subject to sharp fluctuations in value, a reasonable time for acceptance would probably be shorter than if the item has a relatively stable value. See Rest. 2d, § 40, Comment f.

d. Offeror's tacit approval of late acceptance: If the offeree does not accept until after the time for acceptance has lapsed, the acceptance is invalid, and the offeror is under no obligation to notify the offeree that his acceptance is invalid. However, the late acceptance acts as an *offer*, and may then be accepted by the original offeror. Furthermore, the silence of the original offeror may be the kind of manifestation of assent which would constitute tacit acceptance; see *supra*, p. 23, for a discussion of acceptance by silence. C&P, p. 89.

e. Direct negotiations: When parties are bargaining face-to-face or over the telephone, the power of acceptance continues *only during the conversation*, unless the parties' words or actions indicate that they intend the power of acceptance to continue. See Rest. 2d, § 41, Comment d.

G. Revocation: Except in the case of an option contract (see *infra*, p. 52) the offeror is free to *revoke* his offer at any time before it is accepted. The following rules determine when a revocation becomes effective:

1. Effective upon receipt: *A revocation by the offeror does not become effective until it is received by the offeree.* Rest. 2d, § 42.

> **Example:** *A* sends *B* an offer by mail to buy Blackacre. *A* then sends a letter revoking his offer, but before *B* receives the revocation, *B* dispatches his own acceptance. The offer is not revoked until *B* actually receives the letter of revocation. Since *B*'s acceptance was effective upon dispatch (see *infra*, p. 60), there is a contract.

a. Contrary state statutes: However, several states (e.g., California) have *statutes* making revocations effective upon *dispatch*.

2. Lost revocation: If the letter or telegram revoking the offer is *lost* through misdelivery, the revocation *never becomes effective*.

3. What constitutes receipt of revocation: The offeree is deemed to have received the revocation when it comes into his own possession, the possession of someone authorized to receive it for him, or when it is put into his mailbox.

> **Example:** *A* sends a letter of revocation to *B*. The letter is delivered to *B*'s house, where a servant takes it and misplaces it. *B* is deemed to have received the revocation when his servant received it, even though *B* never actually sees the letter. Had the letter been put in *B*'s mailbox, that would have constituted receipt, even if the letter had then been stolen from the mailbox.

a. UCC approach: The UCC applies virtually the same test for determining when a revocation (or any other notice) has been "received." See UCC § 1-202(e).

4. **Indirect communication of revocation:** If the offeror behaves in a way *inconsistent with an intention to enter the contract* she has proposed, and the offeree learns indirectly that the offeror has taken such an action, there is a revocation, even though the offeror never intended to communicate directly with the offeree.

> **Example:** *A* offers to sell Blackacre to *B* at a stated price, and gives *B* a week in which to respond. Within the week, *A* contracts to sell the land to *C*, and *B* learns of this through a tenant of Blackacre. *B* nonetheless sends a formal acceptance, which is received by *A* within the week. There is no contract between *A* and *B*, because *A*'s offer to *B* was revoked at the time that *B* learned that *A* had made the contract with *C*. See Rest. 2d, § 42, Illustr. 1.

   a. **Where offeree learns of offer made to third party:** As the above example indicates, there is an indirect revocation when the offeree learns that the offeror has taken a *definite step* inconsistent with the proposed contract, as by selling the land in question to another.

      i. **Negotiations or offer not enough:** But the mere fact that the offeror has entered into *negotiations* with a third person, or even that she has made an *offer* to a third person, is generally *not* sufficient to constitute a revocation when the original offeree learns of it.

      ii. **Mere rumor not sufficient:** Similarly, if the offeree merely hears *rumors* that the offeror has or will take action inconsistent with the offer, and she reasonably disbelieves the rumor, there is no revocation, even if the rumor turns out to have been true. Rest. 2d, § 43, Comment d.

      iii. **Act not learned of by offeree:** If the offeror takes an act inconsistent with the outstanding offer (as by selling land to a third person) but the offeree does *not* learn of the inconsistent act, his power of acceptance is *not revoked.* So the offeree can then accept the contract (assuming her power of acceptance hasn't terminated for some other reason, such as lapse of time), and if the offeror does not perform, sue him for breach.

      Note: Not all offers are revocable. A discussion of various kinds of irrevocable offers is given *infra*, p. 52.

5. **Revocation of general offer:** Suppose that an offer has been made by *newspaper* advertisement or other general *public notice*. If so, it may be revoked by a similar general notice (e.g., publication in the same newspaper as the original offer).

   a. **Offeree does not learn of revocation:** Such a revocation by general notice will be effective even if one of the potential offerees *does not learn about it* and acts in reliance on the offer (e.g., by capturing a criminal to get a reward.) Rest. 2d, § 46.

H. **Death or incapacity of offeror or offeree:** If either the offeree or the offeror *dies*, or if either loses the *legal capacity* to enter into the contract (e.g., she becomes insane; see the discussion of capacity, *infra*, p. 486) the power to accept is *terminated.* This is so even if the offeree does not learn of the offeror's death or incapacity until after he has dispatched what he intends as an acceptance. See Rest. 2d, § 48.

Table 2-2
RECAP: Ways a Revocable Offer Can Terminate

Method	Example	Notes/Variations
Rejection by offeree	On 1/1, A offers to sell Blackacre to B for $100K. On 2/1, B says, "No thanks." On 3/1, B says, "I accept." There's no contract, because B's power of acceptance ended when he rejected on 2/1.	But the rejection *won't* terminate the power of acceptance if *either*: • Offeror indicates the offer still stands (*Example:* At left, after B says "No thanks" on 2/1, A responds, "Why don't you think about it some more?" The offer remains open.) OR • Offeree states that she doesn't intend to accept now but wants to keep considering it.
Counter-offer by offeree	On 1/1, A offers to sell Blackacre to B for $100K. On 2/1, B says, "I'll pay you $75K." On 3/1, B says, "I changed my mind; I accept the $100K offer." There's no contract, because B's counter-offer on 2/1 terminated B's power of acceptance.	Same as above (for rejection). That is, the counter-offer won't terminate the power of acceptance if *either*: • Offeror indicates the offer still stands (see above *Example* in Rejection); OR • Offeree states that she doesn't intend to accept now but wants to keep considering it.
Revocation by offeror	On 1/1, A offers Blackacre to B for $100K. On 1/2, A sends telegram "Offer revoked" (which B gets that day). On 1/3, B sends acceptance. No contract, because A's revocation terminated the offer.	• Revocations (unlike properly-addressed acceptances) are not effective until *received*. • Revocation can be *indirect*. For instance, at left, suppose that on 1/2, B learns from a third party that A has sold to C. That's an indirect revocation, so B can't accept any longer.
Lapse of time	On 1/1, A offers publicly-traded stock to B. Offer will lapse when A's offer says it will lapse. If offer is silent, it will lapse "after a reasonable time."	What's a "reasonable time" depends on circumstances. Two rules of thumb: • In face-to-face or phone negotiations, offer usually lapses at end of conversation. • In fast-moving markets, offer lapses earlier than in slow-moving ones.
Death or incapacity of offeror or offeree	On 1/1, A offers Blackacre to B, saying, "Offer will remain open for one month." On 1/3, A dies. On 1/4, B "accepts" (not knowing of A's death). A's death made the offer terminate on 1/3, so the "acceptance" was not effective.	If it's an "option" contract (irrevocable because consideration was paid for it to remain open), death of offeror or offeree does *not* terminate the offer.

1. **Exception for objective theory:** Observe that the "revocation by death" rule, when it is applied to an offeror's death that is unknown to the offeree, is a sharp exception to the gen-

eral objective theory of contracts — under the objective theory, "a manifestation of assent is effective without regard to actual mental assent" (Rest. 2d, § 48, Comment a), so the offeror's unseen death should not terminate his assent. See Farnsworth, § 3.18.

2. **Option contracts:**   If the offer is an option contract (i.e., an irrevocable offer), the offeree's power to accept it is *not* terminated by the death or incapacity of either party. Thus if the offeror dies before acceptance, the offeree can by accepting bind the offeror's estate; similarly, if the offeree dies before accepting, his estate may choose to exercise the option. See Rest. 2d, § 37. Option contracts are discussed below.

3. **Impossibility of performing contract:**   Even in the option contract case, however, the death of one of the parties may, although not preventing the formation of a contract, render the performance of the contract impossible. For the consequences of impossibility of performance, see *infra*, p. 432.

I. **Supervening illegality:**   If a contract that would have been legal at the time the offeror proposed it becomes *illegal* through a new statute (e.g. a new usury law), the power of acceptance is terminated. (For the consequences of illegality occurring *before* the offer, see the section on Illegality, *infra*, p. 460.)

J. **Irrevocable offers:**   The ordinary offer is *revocable* at the will of the offeror. This is so even though the offer *states that it will remain open for some stated period of time*, and even though that statement is in writing.

> **Example:** *A* writes to *B*, "I hereby offer to sell you Blackacre for $100,000. This offer will remain open for 30 days. You must accept in writing." After 20 days, *A* dies, unbeknownst to *B*. On the 24th day, *B* sends a letter of acceptance. The letter of acceptance will be ineffective, because the offer lapsed when *A* died (see p. 50 *supra*); the fact that the offer said that it would remain open for 30 days is irrelevant.

1. **Exceptions:** There are, however, several *exceptions* to the general rule allowing revocation:

> [1] the standard "*option contract*";
>
> [2] "*firm offers*" under the UCC; and
>
> [3] temporary irrevocability as the result of the offeree's *part performance* or *detrimental reliance*.

We consider each of these exceptions in turn.

2. **The standard option contract:**   One way to make an offer irrevocable is for the offeror to grant the offeree an *"option"* to enter into the contract. The irrevocable offer so formed is usually called an "option contract."

   a. **Common-law requirement of consideration:**   At common law, the only way an option contract could be formed was if the offeree gave the offeror *consideration* — essentially, something of value — in return for the offer. (See the chapter on Consideration, p. 85, *infra*.) Otherwise the so-called "option" was revocable.

   b. **Recitals of consideration sufficient under Restatement:**   But the modern approach, exemplified by the Second Restatement, does *not* continue this common-law requirement that an option be supported by ***actual consideration***. Rest. 2d, § 87(1)(a), provides that a written and signed option contract can be formed without the actual giving of consideration as long as it ***"recites a purported consideration*** for the making of the [irrevocable] offer." Thus the option contract need merely say "Upon consideration of $1.00 rendered this day, I promise to keep this offer open for two weeks," and the option contract is enforceable. This is the case even though no dollar is ever paid.

i.   **Gratuitous options:**   Under the Restatement, even if the offeror *states that his offer is irrevocable* for a certain period, and even if he uses the word "option," the offer is nonetheless *revocable* unless there is a written recitation to the effect that consideration has been paid, *or* consideration has in fact been paid.

   Example: On Feb. 1, *A*, knowing that *B* desires to purchase Blackacre, sends a letter to *B* saying, "I hereby grant you an option to purchase Blackacre from me for $100,000 cash. This offer shall be irrevocable until March 1." *B* does not give *A* anything of value in return for this promise of irrevocability. On Feb. 27, *A* sends *B* a telegram, "Sorry, I have to revoke your option." On Feb. 28, *B* shows up at *A*'s premises with $100,000 cash, demanding to purchase the property.

   Even under the Restatement (and modern) view, *A* was entitled to revoke, and *B* therefore has no ability to accept and no claim for breach. (But the offer would be irrevocable until March 1 if *A*'s letter had also said that the option was granted "in consideration of your having paid me $1," even if no dollar was ever really paid. Also, if *B* relies to his detriment on the promise of irrevocability, such as by making preparations, B's reliance may cause the offer to become temporarily irrevocable; see *infra*, p. 58.)

c.   **Counter-offer does not terminate power of acceptance:**   If an irrevocable offer exists (whether because consideration was paid or because, under the Restatement, there was a recital of consideration), ***the usual rule that a counter-offer terminates the power of acceptance does not apply***.

   Example: In return for a payment of $50 by Buyer, Seller gives Buyer a two-month option to purchase a certain tract of land on certain terms. Before the option expires, Buyer sends Seller a letter stating that it will exercise the option if Seller will give better terms. Soon afterwards, Buyer attempts to exercise the option on the original (less favorable) terms. Seller claims that Buyer's attempt to get better terms constituted a counter offer which terminated the option contract.

   Held, Buyer's attempt to get better terms did not terminate the option contract. "If the original offer is an irrevocable offer [as in the case of an option contract] the rule that a counter-offer terminates the power of acceptance does not apply." *Humble Oil & Refining Co. v. Westside Investment Corp.*, 428 S.W.2d 92 (Tex. 1968).

3.   **"Firm offers" under the UCC:**   The UCC allows the formation of an irrevocable offer under certain circumstances even if no recitation of the payment of consideration is made. UCC § 2-205 creates so-called ***"firm offers."*** That section says that an offer to buy or sell goods is ***irrevocable*** (i.e., is a "firm offer") if the offer meets three conditions:

❏   it is by a ***merchant*** (defined in § 2-104 to mean a person who "deals in goods of the kind or otherwise by his occupation holds himself out as having knowledge or skill peculiar to the practices or goods involved in the transaction"); and

❏ it is in a *signed writing*; and

❏ it gives *explicit assurance* that the offer will be held open.

Such an offer is irrevocable even though there is *neither consideration nor a recital* that consideration has been paid.

a. **Reasonable time period:** If the UCC firm offer offer does not state for how long a time the offer will be held open, it is irrevocable *"for a reasonable time."* (§ 2-205).

b. **Stated time:** If the offer states a time period during which it is irrevocable, that time period controls.

c. **Three month limit:** Whether or not a time period is stated, an offer under §2-205 *cannot be made irrevocable for a longer period than three months*. (If the offeree gives consideration for the irrevocability, the offer will be irrevocable for whatever period is stated. § 2-205 deals only with firm offers for which no consideration is given.)

Example: On July 1, Dealer, a car dealer, sends a signed email to Consumer offering to sell Consumer a Model X car with certain specs for $20,000; the email says that the offer "will remain open until the end of the year." On Nov. 1, Dealer phones Consumer to say, "The offer is withdrawn." Consumer immediately purports to accept, citing the "open until the end of the year" language.

No matter what the offer said, it was not irrevocable under § 2-205 past September 30 (three months). Therefore, Dealer's revocation was effective, and Consumer's acceptance was not effective. (But if Dealer had purported to revoke on *August 1* and Consumer purported to accept on August 2, then the revocation would have been ineffective and the acceptance would have been effective.)

d. **Forms supplied by offeree:** If the firm offer is contained on a form drafted by the offer*ee*, the offer is irrevocable only if that particular "firm offer" clause is *separately signed by the offeror*. See Comment 4 to § 2-205.

e. **Effect if not by a merchant:** Be on the lookout for a purported firm offer that relates to a sales contract, but that is *made by a non-merchant* — such an offer is *not firm*, and will therefore be *revocable*.

Example: Consumer sends a letter to Furniture Co. offering to sell it some used office shelving presently on the walls of Consumer's house. The letter says that the offer "will remain open for the next 60 days." After 40 days, Consumer sends another letter, saying "I sold the shelving to someone else."

This revocation letter is effective, because Consumer is not a "merchant," and only "merchants" can make firm offers. (Remember that § 2-204 says that a merchant is one who "deals in goods of the kind or otherwise by his occupation holds himself out as having knowledge or skill peculiar to the practices or goods involved in the transaction.") For purposes of firm offers, virtually any person who is making an offer during the course of her business is a "merchant," but Consumer does not meet this definition. Consequently, the offer was revocable even though it recited that it wasn't.

f. Effect if not firm: Suppose a merchant makes an offer that almost, but not quite, satisfies the UCC firm-offer rules. When this happens, the offer *may still be a valid and open offer* — as long as the merchant offeror has not revoked the offer as of the moment in question (and it hasn't lapsed by the passage of more than a "reasonable time" under the circumstances), it's *still valid even though it's not "firm".*

Example: Merchant makes an offer of particular goods at a particular price to Customer "Good for the next 12 months." Five months go by, at which point Customer purports to accept. The acceptance will form a contract — even though the offer was not firm beyond three months (the limit on firm offers under § 2-205), it was still an ordinary offer, since it hasn't been revoked or lapsed for passage of time. Therefore, it was capable of being accepted.

    i. Same rule in non-UCC cases for option without consideration: By the way, a very similar principle applies in the non-UCC context: when an offer purports to be irrevocable (i.e., to be an option), but isn't because of lack of consideration or because of some other contract term, *the offer can still be accepted until it is revoked.*

4. Part performance or detrimental reliance: *Part performance* or *detrimental reliance* by the offeree may render the offer *temporarily irrevocable*. This exception is sufficiently complex and important that we consider it as a separate section, beginning in the next paragraph.

K. Temporary irrevocability caused by part performance or detrimental reliance: There are a number of situations in which an offeree might, before the formation of a formal contract, take action in *reliance* upon the offer. She might, for instance, *begin the performance* that is called for by an offer looking to a unilateral contract. Or, she might make costly *preparation* in anticipation of a contract before she in fact makes the promise necessary for acceptance.

Modern courts, and the Second Restatement, therefore recognize several situations in which an offeree's actions in reliance upon an offer may render that offer *temporarily irrevocable*. The three main situations in which this may occur, each of which is treated as a separate numbered section below, are:

❏ the offer is for a *unilateral* contract, and the offeree *begins to perform*;

❏ it is not *clear* whether the offer is for a unilateral or bilateral contract, and the offeree *begins to perform*; and

❏ the offeree makes *preparations* prior to acceptance (whether acceptance is to be by promise or by performance).

Although the offeree obtains protection in each of these situations, the degree to which s*he* is bound, and the extent of the protection given to her, are different in the three situations.

1. Offer for unilateral contract: If the offer makes it clear that acceptance can occur only through performance, and not through promise (i.e., the offer is for a unilateral contract), the *beginning of performance* by the offeree creates an *option contract*. That is, *once the offeree starts to perform, the offer becomes temporarily irrevocable*. Rest. 2d, § 45(1).

Example: D offers to sell a particular piece of property at a particular price to X, and also offers to pay P (a real estate broker) a commission if X buys the property. Both offers have a 6-day time limit. Shortly before expiration of the 6 days, D revokes both offers. Then (still before the end of the 6 days) X agrees to buy the property on the terms originally proposed by D, D refuses, and P sues D for the commission.

Held, for P. D's offer to P was for a unilateral contract (since P was to accept by performance, i.e., by finding a willing buyer). Assuming that P had begun to perform before he received notice of D's revocation (an issue to be left to the trial court), this beginning of performance made D's offer of a commission irrevocable. Since P later completed the desired performance (finding a willing buyer), he is entitled to the commission. *Marchiondo v. Scheck*, 432 P.2d 405 (N.M. 1967).

a. **Offeror's duty conditional upon complete performance by offeree:** Although in this unilateral contract situation, the beginning of performance by the offeree makes the offer irrevocable, the offeror's duty under the contract is conditional on the offeree's *completing* performance as specified in the offer. Rest. 2d, § 45(2). He must not only do whatever is specified in the offer, but he must do it within the time specified in the offer.

Example: Mrs. Hodgkin, a widow, writes to her daughter and son-in-law, the Brackenburys, who live in another state. The letter states that if the Brackenburys give up their home, and come to live with and care for Mrs. Hodgkin during her life, Mrs. Hodgkin will leave them her farm when she dies. The Brackenburys give up their home, move in with Mrs. Hodgkin, and begin caring for her.

No contract exists until the Brackenburys have completed the performance asked for in Mrs. Hodgkin's offer (i.e., until they have cared for her up to her death). However, because the Brackenburys have begun to perform, Mrs. Hodgkin is bound by an option contract, and her offer is irrevocable as long as the Brackenburys continue to perform. The Brackenburys are not bound by any contract, and may cease performance whenever they wish (thus declining to exercise their option). See *Brackenbury v. Hodgkin*, 116 Me. 399 (1917). See also Rest. 2d, § 45, Illustr. 6 (drawn from the *Brackenbury* case).

b. **Two limitations:** There are two important limitations to the types of situations with which Rest. 2d § 45 is designed to deal:

i. **Unilateral contract:** First, § 45 is limited to cases where the offer is for a *unilateral* contract, i.e., where the offer calls for acceptance by *performance*, rather than by promise. (If the offer does not make clear whether acceptance is to come by promise or performance, Rest. 2d, § 62, not § 45, applies; § 62 is discussed below.)

ii. **Preparations for performance:** Secondly, § 45 takes effect only when the offeree starts the *actual performance* requested by the offer. It does not take effect upon *preliminary preparations* that are not explicitly called for by the offer.

Example: D holds a mortgage on P's property. D offers to give P a $780 reduction in the amount of the principal if P will pay off the mortgage before the end of May. In late May, P goes to D's house and tells him "I have come to pay off the mortgage." D replies that he has sold the mortgage. P shows that he has enough cash to pay the principal less the $780 discount, but D refuses to take it. P (who has contracted to convey the property free and clear to someone else) is then required to pay the full principal amount of the mortgage to the person who bought it from D. P sues D, claiming that P accepted an open offer for the $780 reduction.

Held, for D. The only act requested by D's offer was the actual tender of payment. Until that tender, D was free to revoke his offer. Since D revoked before P made the actual tender, there was no contract. *Petterson v. Pattberg*, 161 N.E. 428 (N.Y. 1928).

Note: *Petterson* was decided before there was a Restatement. Nonetheless, it is probable that a court today would agree that no ordinary contract came into existence. P's act of contracting to sell the property free and clear to another, and his act of going to D's house with the cash, would probably be held to be merely **preparations** to perform, not the beginning of actual performance. Therefore, Rest. 2d, § 45 would not apply. However, P would today probably be able to recover "to the extent necessary to avoid injustice" under Rest. 2d, § 87(2), discussed *infra*, p. 59. (§ 45 and § 87(2) differ in that a plaintiff under § 45 gets the full "expectation" measure of damages under a contract, i.e., the lost profit, whereas a plaintiff under § 87(2) gets only his "reliance" damages, i.e., the amount by which he has suffered by relying on the offer. In the *Petterson* case, both measures seem to produce the same result, $780.)

(Incidentally, where the performance that is requested is payment, all the offeree need do to fully accept is to *"tender"* payment, that is, to show that he has payment on hand and that he is willing to transfer it. Thus in the *Petterson* situation, had P been able to whip out his money and say, "I'm here to pay off the mortgage" before D had been able to say "I revoke," there would have been a full acceptance, even had D refused to take the money. This result would be true even if § 45 did not exist.)

c. **Offer explicitly revocable:** Even if the offeree starts the actual performance requested by the offeror, the offer will not be irrevocable if the *offer itself* makes clear that a right of revocation is *reserved* to the offeror. See Rest. 2d, § 45, Comment b.

d. **Prior common-law view:** Prior to the 1932 adoption of the First Restatement, the common-law view was that the offeror could revoke an offer for a unilateral contract any time up until the *completion* of the requested performance. As many a law professor put it, if *A* were to offer B $100 for crossing the Brooklyn Bridge, *A* could wait until *B* had gotten halfway across the bridge and then say "I revoke."

e. **UCC view of partial performance:** The UCC does not deal with whether an offer may become temporarily irrevocable upon the beginning of performance by the offeree. This possibility is left to the common law (supposedly codified by § 45 of the Second Restatement); see Comment 3 to § 2-206. The UCC does specify, however, that where the beginning of performance would be a reasonable form of *acceptance*, it is effective as an acceptance only if the offeree seasonably notifies the offeror that he has accepted. § 2-206(2).

2. **Unclear whether offer is unilateral or bilateral:** Suppose that the offer does not make clear whether it is to be accepted by a promise or performance. (See the discussion of such ambiguous offers, *supra*, p. 21.) This will often be the case, for example, where one party sends the other a request for work that does not make it clear whether acceptance is to occur by the seller's promise to perform (i.e., his sending of an acknowledgment form), or by his actual performance. In this situation the offeree may accept *either* by promising to perform or by performing, at the offeree's option. Rest. 2d, § 32. Also in this situation, an acceptance occurs as soon as the offeree *begins to perform*. Rest. 2d, § 62.

> **Example:** Consumer ships a well-worn leather chair to Upholsterer, together with a note saying, "I'd like this chair re-upholstered to match the enclosed swatch, if you can do it for $100." It's not clear from the context whether Consumer expects Upholsterer to accept by promising to do the work, or by doing the work itself. Therefore, Upholsterer can accept by starting the work. The moment Upholsterer starts the job, Consumer can no longer revoke.

a. **Effect of beginning to perform:** So as the above Example shows, where the offeree has a choice between accepting by promise or accepting by performance, the offeree is protected against the offeror's revocation as soon as the offeree accepts by beginning performance. In this respect, he receives the same protection under Rest. 2d, § 62 as § 45 gives to the offeree who begins to perform under an explicitly unilateral contract. However, there is an important difference between the § 45 case (where acceptance must be by performance) and the § 62 case (where the offeree may choose between accepting by promise and accepting by performance) — in the § 62 case, once the offeree begins to perform, *he has accepted the contract, and is bound to complete performance*.

> **Example:** In the above Example, as soon as Upholsterer starts the job, he's bound, just as Consumer is bound. So Upholsterer can't do part of the work, change his mind, undo the work and send back the chair in its original condition.

b. **Preparations for a performance:** § 62 of the Second Restatement, like § 45, only takes effect when actual performance has begun, not when preparations for performance are made. Here, again, however, preparations may make the offer temporarily irrevocable under Restatement 2d, §87(2), discussed below.

c. **Notice of acceptance required under UCC:** UCC § 2-206(2), like Rest. 2d, § 62, contemplates that an offeree may bind both himself and the offeror (i.e., accept the offer) by beginning his requested performance. Under § 2-206(2), however, the beginning of performance operates as an acceptance only if the offeror is *notified of the acceptance within a reasonable time.*

3. **Offeree makes preparations prior to acceptance:** §§ 45 and 62 of the Second Restatement, discussed above, apply only in those situations where the offeree begins actual performance. What happens if the offeree makes *preparations* that are not explicitly required by the contract, but which are necessary before performance may begin? If the offeree makes such preparations prior to his acceptance, may he ever by his reliance turn the offer into an irrevocable one, or otherwise recover his expenses?

a. **Restatement view:** The answer is *"yes"* under § 87(2) of the Second Restatement. That section provides that "an offer which the offeror ***should reasonably expect to induce action or forbearance of substantial character*** on the part of the offeree before acceptance and which ***does induce such action or forbearance*** is ***binding*** as an option contract to the ***extent necessary to avoid injustice.***"

b. **§ 87(2) distinguished from §§ 45 and 62:** Rest. 2d, § 87(2) can apply not only to preparations made prior to an acceptance by *promise* (as in *Drennan v. Star Paving*, discussed shortly below), but also to preparations made prior to an acceptance by *performance*. Thus in situations where the actual beginning of true performance would fall under § 45 or § 62, preparations for performance may fall under § 87(2).

    i. **Enforceability limited:** However, the important difference between § 87(2) on the one hand, and §§ 45 and 62 on the other, is that under § 87(2), the offer is irrevocable only to the *"extent necessary to avoid injustice."* Thus in particular situations, a court may find that it is not necessary to hold the offeror to the proposed contract, as long as he is willing to reimburse the offeree for any damages he has suffered by ***reliance***. See the discussion of reliance damages *infra*, p. 326. See also Comment e to § 87(2).

c. **Offers by sub-contractors:** § 87(2) is most often often used in the case of offers by ***sub-contractors*** to general contractors. Where the sub-contractor submits a bid to the general contractor, who then ***relies upon it in figuring his own over-all bid,*** the sub-contractor's bid is usually held to be irrevocable for at least the time necessary for the general contractor to obtain the job and then accept the sub-contractor's bid.

Example: *S*, a sub-contractor, submits a written offer for paving to *G*, a general contractor. Since *S*'s bid is the lowest, *G* relies on it in preparing its own bid, and also submits *S*'s identity as required in the bidding procedure for the general contract. *S* then notifies *G* that its bid was too low because of an error. *G*'s bid on the general contract is accepted, and *S* refuses to perform.

Held, because *G* justifiably and substantially relied upon *S*'s offer (its bid), *S*'s offer was irrevocable until *G* had a reasonable chance to notify *S* of the award and of *G*'s acceptance of *S*'s bid. (But if *G* should have realized, from the low bid, that it was probably due to an error, *G*'s reliance would not have been "justifiable," and there would have been no recovery.) *Drennan v. Star Paving*, 51 Cal. 2d 409 (1958). See also Rest. 2d, § 87(2), Illustr. 6 (drawn from *Drennan*).

    i. **Change from prior law:** The *Drennan* opinion, written by Justice Traynor, represents a sharp departure from previous law. For instance, in the older, well-known, case of *James Baird Co. v. Gimbel Bros.*, 64 F.2d 344 (2d Cir. 1933), a sub-contractor's bid was relied upon in almost precisely the same circumstances as in *Drennan*. The court, in an opinion written by Judge Hand, held that promissory estoppel could not apply, because there was no binding promise of an irrevocable offer, and there was no consideration for such a promise. Nor was the court willing to treat the sub-contractor's bid as an option contract, because there was "not the least reason to suppose that the defendant meant to subject itself to such a one-sided obligation." (The obligation would have been one-sided for the reason described in the following paragraph.)

    ii. Binding the general contractor: Observe that the approach of Rest. 2d, § 87(2) and *Drennan* can be criticized as **unfair to the sub-contractor:** the sub-contractor is bound to do the work at the price quoted to the general contractor, but the general contractor is *not bound to award the job* to the sub-contractor even if the general gets the job.

VII. WHEN ACCEPTANCE BECOMES EFFECTIVE

   A. Introduction: So far, we have considered the rules governing the length of time during which a power of acceptance is effective. We turn now to the rules governing the time at which an acceptance becomes effective. The underlying question in this area is always the same: At the moment at which the acceptance became effective, was the power of acceptance (i.e. the offer) still in effect? If so, a contract has been formed.

   B. General "mailbox" rule: Most courts follow the general rule that the acceptance *is effective upon proper dispatch*. The rule is often called the *"mailbox"* rule (since deposit of a letter of acceptance into a mailbox will cause the acceptance to become effective). However, the rule also applies to acceptances dispatched by means other than letters (e.g., telegrams, emails).

     1. Restatement's language: As the Second Restatement puts it, "[A]n acceptance made in a manner and by a medium invited by an offer is operative and completes the manifestation of mutual assent *as soon as put out of the offeree's possession, without regard to whether it ever reaches the offeror....*" Rest. 2d, § 63(a).

        Example: *A* sends *B* a letter offering to sell him wool; the letter of offer is delayed in the mails. Upon receipt of the offer, *B* mails an acceptance. After *B* has mailed the acceptance, but before *A* receives it, *A* sells the wool to someone else. There is a binding contract between *A* and *B*. (The offer lasted for a "reasonable time," which presumably had not elapsed as of the moment *B* mailed his acceptance. Because *B*'s acceptance became effective when he mailed it, a contract was formed.) *Adams v. Lindsell*, 106 Eng. Rep. 250 (1818).

     2. Rationale: The mailbox rule was, during the nineteenth century, usually justified on the theory that an offeror who makes an offer by mail makes the Post Office his agent to receive the acceptance; thus under this theory, the offeror "constructively receives" the letter as soon as it is mailed.

       a. Criticism: However, this theory makes little sense, since under U.S. Postal Regulations, the sender of a letter has the power to stop delivery and reclaim the letter.

       b. Better explanation of rule: A better explanation of the mailbox rule is that "the offeree needs a dependable basis for his decision whether to accept." (Rest. 2d, § 63, Comment a.) In other words, it is useful to the offeree to know that if he accepts, the deal will be closed immediately, and that he will not have to run the risk that the offer will be revoked before the acceptance has been received.

i. Criticism: However, this argument does not seem very compelling, since the offeree can almost always accept by either telephoning or sending a telegram. The rule seems principally due to historical accident, in the form of some early-nineteenth-century cases, including *Adams v. Lindsell.* (See C&P, pp. 106-07.)

c. Applies only to acceptances by promise, not by performance: The mailbox rule applies only to acceptances by *promise*, *not acceptances by performance.* That is, all of this material relates to acceptances dispatched by mail, telegram, etc., not acceptances which occur through either part or full performance. As we said above, the commencement of performance may constitute an acceptance (in the case of so-called offers for unilateral contracts). Here, we are concerned with the time at which a *promissory* acceptance becomes effective.

d. Faxes and e-mails: In discussing the mailbox rule, we use examples of acceptances sent by mail, telegram and telegraph, since these were the methods of communication that gave rise to the doctrine. However, there is no reason to believe that the rules would be any different with respect to more modern methods of communication, such as *facsimiles* and *e-mail* messages. For example, an acceptance sent by e-mail presumably would be effective as soon as the offeree hits the "send" button on her computer, even if the offeror did not download the e-mail from his Internet provider until much later.

3. Acceptance followed by rejection: In *Adams v. Lindsell, supra,* the result of the court's adoption of the "mail box" rule was to bind the offeror. However, the mail box rule is also applied to *bind the offeree.* That is, once the offeree has placed his acceptance in the mail, he cannot thereafter change his mind and send a rejection, even if the rejection is received by the offeror before the acceptance is received. This issue is discussed more extensively *infra,* p. 62.

4. Exception where offer provides otherwise: The mailbox rule does not apply if the offer *provides otherwise.*

> **Example:** *A* sends *B* a letter containing an offer and stating "this offer will be accepted when and if your letter of acceptance is personally received by me." The acceptance is not effective until it is received by *A*.

C. Misdirection of acceptance: The "acceptance effective upon dispatch" rule always applies where the offeree has chosen a reasonable manner of sending his acceptance, and has not behaved negligently. But what if he has used a *slow means* of communication where the offer indicates the necessity for haste? Or what if he has carelessly *misaddressed* the envelope? Is the acceptance still effective upon dispatch?

1. General view: Most courts, and the Second Restatement, take the view that even if an unreasonable means of communicating the acceptance is used, or the acceptance is misaddressed, it is still effective when dispatched *if it is received within the time in which a properly dispatched acceptance would normally have arrived*. See Rest. 2d, §§ 67 and 68. See also UCC § 1-201(36). If it is not received within this time, it is effective only as of the time it is actually received.

Example: On July 1, *A* sends an offer letter to *B*, and says that *B* should "give me your answer in writing by July 10." On July 8, *B* mails an acceptance letter, but uses a slightly wrong address for *A*. Assume that a properly addressed letter would have been delivered on July 10. *B*'s letter arrives on July 11. Meanwhile, *A* revokes by phone on the evening of July 10.

B's letter is not effective upon dispatch, because it did not arrive within the same time in which a properly addressed letter would have arrived. (But if the misaddressed letter had arrived on July 10, at the same time as a properly-addressed letter, it would have been retroactively deemed to have been effective upon dispatch, and a revocation by *A* on July 9 would have been too late.)

D. Acceptance lost in transmission: If the acceptance is properly dispatched, the mailbox rule applies, and the acceptance is effective at the time of dispatch *even if it is lost and never received by the offeror at all*.

   1. Loss of acceptance may discharge offeror: Although the acceptance becomes effective upon a proper dispatch, even if it never reaches the offeror, courts will frequently *discharge* the latter from his contractual obligation if he never receives notice of the acceptance. As Comment b to Rest. 2d, § 63, puts it, "The language of the offer is often properly interpreted as making the offeror's duty of performance conditional on receipt of the acceptance. Indeed, where the receipt of notice is essential to enable the offeror to perform, such a condition is normally implied."

   Example: *A* has a limited supply of widgets in stock, and sends a letter to *B* offering to sell and ship them to *B*. The offer states that *A* will sell the widgets to someone else if he does not hear from *B* within a reasonable time. *B* promptly mails a properly-addressed acceptance, but the letter is delayed, and is not delivered to *A* until after an unreasonably long time, by which point *A* has sold the widgets to *C*.

   Although acceptance became effective upon dispatch, and there was a contract between *A* and *B*, *A* is *discharged* from the contract due to the failure to seasonably receive the notice he needed to perform (i.e., an order to ship). If by the time *A* finally received the acceptance, he had not already sold the widgets to someone else, but he wished to escape from the contract because their value had increased, he would be less likely to be discharged from the contract.

E. Where offeree sends both acceptance and rejection: Suppose the offeree sends an acceptance followed by a rejection, or vice versa. Since a rejection terminates the power of acceptance (see *supra*, p. 47) it is important to know at what time a rejection becomes effective.

   1. Rejection sent before acceptance: Initially, let's consider the scenario in which the offeree *first* dispatches a *rejection*, then dispatches an acceptance.

   a. Effectiveness of rejection: Here, the Second Restatement applies the following rule: a rejection does not terminate the offeree's power of acceptance until it is received, but any acceptance dispatched by the offeree after she has dispatched the rejection is *not effective unless the acceptance is received by the offeror before he receives the rejection*. Rest. 2d, § 40. In other words, the acceptance has no effect unless it *overtakes* the previously-dispatched rejection.

Example: *A* makes *B* an offer by mail. *B* mails a letter of rejection. Then, still within the period for acceptance, *B* changes his mind and telegraphs an acceptance. This acceptance creates a contract only if *A* receives it before he receives the rejection. See Rest. 2d, § 40, Illustr. 1.

b. Rationale: This rule is ***necessary to protect the offeror.*** If the acceptance was effective upon dispatch, and the rejection not effective until receipt, then the offeror might receive and ***rely*** upon the offeree's rejection, not knowing that the offeree had subsequently changed his mind and sent a binding acceptance before the offeror had received the rejection.

2. Acceptance dispatched before rejection: The rule stated above only applies if the rejection is dispatched ***before*** the acceptance is dispatched. What happens if the offeree ***first sends an acceptance***, and then sends a rejection?

a. Formally binding contract: In this situation, the contract is ***binding as soon as the acceptance is dispatched,*** and the subsequently-dispatched revocation of acceptance ***does not undo the acceptance***, whether it is received by the offeror before or after his receipt of the acceptance.

Example: Buyer signs a contract for the purchase of real estate. He mails the contract to Seller. Seller signs the contract, and puts it in the mail to Buyer. After Seller has mailed the contract, but before it has been received by Buyer, Seller calls Buyer's lawyer and repudiates the contract. Buyer attempts to enforce the contract.

Held, a contract came into existence as soon as Seller put the contract in the mail, and thus Seller's attempt to get out of the contract failed. Good arguments can be made either for or against the mailbox rule in this situation. However, since the rule has tradition behind it, and no compelling argument can be made against it, the court will apply it. *Morrison v. Thoelke*, 155 So. 2d 889 (Fla. App. 1963).

b. Estoppel: However, if the revocation-of-acceptance is received by the offeror before he receives the acceptance, and he ***relies*** upon the revocation, the offeree may be ***"estopped"*** from enforcing the contract. See Rest. 2d, § 64, Illustr. 7.

F. Acceptance of option contracts: The acceptance of an ***option contract*** (i.e., an irrevocable offer; see *supra*, p. 52) is effective ***not upon dispatch, but upon receipt by the offeror***. Rest. 2d, § 64(b).

Example: For consideration, Owner grants Buyer an option to acquire Blackacre for $100,000, the option to be valid "for 30 days." The document says that the option shall be exercised by "Buyer's payment of a non-refundable $2,000 deposit." The document does not say whether exercise will be deemed to have occurred when Buyer sends the $2,000 deposit or only when Owner receives it. On the 30th day, Buyer sends a letter with the check, but Owner doesn't receive it until the 34th day. A court would likely hold that the option was not timely exercised, because an acceptance of an option (i.e., exercise) is effective only upon receipt, not dispatch.

1. Rationale: The general rule that an acceptance is effective upon dispatch is designed to protect the offeree against revocation while his acceptance is in transit. (See Rest. 2d, § 63, Comment a.) Since an offer in an option contract is irrevocable, this protection is not

Figure 2-2

The Mailbox Rule: Determining When an Acceptance Becomes Effective

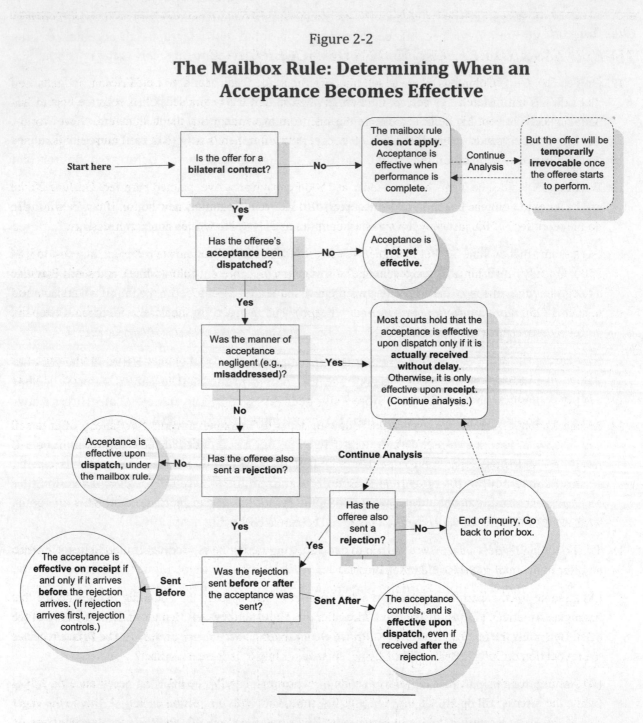

required. Furthermore, business custom dictates that unless otherwise specified, an option is exercised only upon notification to the offeror. See Rest. 2d, § 64, Comment f. See also C&P, p. 113.

G. Effective date of revocation of offer: By way of review, recall that a *revocation* by the offeror is treated essentially like a rejection: the revocation is *not effective until it is received* by the other party (the offeree). See *supra*, p. 49.

Quiz Yourself on

TIMELINESS AND EFFECTIVENESS OF ACCEPTANCE

12. On Feb. 10, Chris Columbus offers to sell his powerboat, the Santa Maria, to Leif Ericson, and tells Leif that Leif has until March 1 to decide. On Feb. 20, before Leif has responded, Chris sells the boat to Isabella instead. On Feb. 25, Leif overhears of the sale from two strangers at the local tavern, Newe Worlde. On Feb. 26, Leif sends an email to Chris, "I accept your offer, here's my credit card number." Is there a contract between Leif and Chris?

13. Washington decides he wants his new house at 1500 Pennsylvania Ave. painted barn red. On June 20, he send a letter to Potomac House Painters that says, "I'd like you to paint my new house. If you're willing to do the work for $1500, just show up and start painting by July 4. No written contract necessary."

(A) Assume that on June 30, Potomac buys (expressly for this job) the requisite red paint, at a cost to it of $500. On July 3, Washington decides he likes the mansion in its present color (white), and sends Potomac a telegram, "I revoke my offer." Potomac would have made a profit of $750 on the job (it would have had to spend $250 more in labor charges to finish the job). The red paint is valueless to Potomac if the paint won't be used on this job. Is there a contract in force, and if so, how much may Potomac recover?

(B) Same basic facts. Now however, assume that Washington waits until Potomac arrives at the house and spends one day sanding it (a necessary part of the painting job); Washington then says, "I revoke." Is there a contract in force, and if so, how much may Potomac recover?

14. Jessica Rabbit's Microbrewery sends the following letter to Toontown Tavern: "We hereby offer to sell you 50 kegs of beer at a price of $40 per keg. This offer shall remain open for 2 months from the date of receipt." Toontown does not give or promise anything of value in return for this offer. After six weeks, Jessica Rabbit's Microbrewery sends another letter that says, "As we have not heard from you in all this time, we revoke our offer." A week later, Toontown Tavern faxes a letter to the Microbrewery saying, "We accept your offer of 50 kegs at $40 per keg." Is there a contract?

15. The Founding Fathers select Ben Franklin to choose a king for the newly-formed United States. He sends an offer in the mail to Prince Henry of Prussia.

(A) Assume for this part that a few days after the offer is sent by Ben, the Founding Fathers decide that having an American king isn't such a hot idea after all. They therefore tell Ben to send a revocation of the offer. Ben mails the revocation on July 4. Prince Henry mails an acceptance on July 6. The Prince receives the revocation on July 7. Ben receives the acceptance on July 8. Is there a contract?

(B) Assume for this part that Ben never sends a revocation. The Prince mails an acceptance on July 4 (while the offer is still open). He then changes his mind, and mails a rejection on July 7. Due to the vagaries of the Pony Express, the rejection arrives at Ben's house on July 10, and the acceptance arrives on July 11. Is there a contract?

(C) Same basic facts as (B). Now, however, assume that the Prince mails a rejection on July 4, then changes his mind and mails an acceptance on July 6. The rejection arrives on July 8, and the acceptance arrives on July 10. Is there a contract?

16. Selznick, a film producer who is looking for a female lead in his new Civil War picture, mails an offer for the role to Esther Plotkin. Plotkin is overjoyed, and immediately mails back her acceptance, properly addressed. The postal service loses the letter, and, alas, Selznick never receives it. Is there a contract?

Answers

12. **No.** An offer is terminated when the offeree learns of an act by the offeror that is inconsistent with the offer. Selling the subject of the offer to someone else would certainly qualify as a revocation (though merely looking for other potential buyers would not). Consequently, Chris' offer was revoked at the moment Leif learned of the sale. Therefore, there was no live offer for Leif to accept as of the moment he sent his "acceptance" telegram, and that telegram had no effect.

13. **(A) No conventional contract is in force, but Potomac can recover its $500 reliance damages, since this sum will be needed to avoid injustice.** First, notice that the offer by Washington was for a *unilateral* contract (since it was to be accepted by Potomac's performance, not by its promising to perform.) Under Rest. § 45, once Potomac started to actually perform on a unilateral contract, it would have had a temporary option to enter into a fully-binding contract (see part (B) below). But the buying of the red paint would probably be held to be a mere *preparation* to perform, not the commencement of performance; in that case, § 45 wouldn't apply. However, under Rest. 2d § 87(2), "an offer which the offeror should reasonably expect to induce action … of substantial character on the part of the offeree before acceptance and which does induce such action … is binding as an option contract to the extent necessary to avoid injustice." This would apply here. Since giving Potomac the $500 it spent on paint would be enough to "avoid injustice," this is all the court will do — Potomac won't be entitled to true enforcement of the contract (i.e., to recover the $750 it profit it would have made on top of the $500 it spent).

(B) Yes; Potomac can recover $1250. Once the offeree under an offer for a unilateral contract commences *actual performance*, the offer gives rise to an option contract, i.e., it becomes *temporarily irrevocable* for the time needed for the offeree to promptly performance in accordance with the terms of the offer. Rest. 2d § 45. The sanding represented a true commencement of performance (not just preparations to perform), so the offer became temporarily irrevocable when the sanding was done. Consequently, Washington lost the ability to revoke. Potomac will be entitled to full contract damages of $1250, which is the sum needed to give it the profit it would have made had the job been completed (i.e., the $1500 contract price less the $250 cost saved by Potomac in not having to perform.)

The key point is that in part (A), Potomac didn't have a true contract, and gets only its reliance damages to avoid injustice; here, since performance began, Potomac gets true contract remedies.

14. **Yes.** At common law, there would be no contract, because the Tavern gave no consideration for the promise of irrevocability — at common law, offers are revocable even if they say otherwise, unless separate consideration has been given for an option. But the UCC provides for what it calls *"firm offers"*; under UCC § 2-205, a merchant will be held to have made an irrevocable offer — even though no consideration is given by the offeree — if the merchant makes the offer in writing and with explicit assurances that the offer will remain open for a specified period of time. That's what the Microbrewery did here. Therefore, the Microbrewery had no ability to revoke its offer before the two-month time period had lapsed, and the offer was still open when Tavern accepted.

15. **(A) Yes.** Under the mailbox rule, the acceptance was *effective upon dispatch* (July 6), provided that at the time it was dispatched, the offer was still open. A revocation does not become effective until it is received by the offeree; so the revocation could not have become effective until July 7. By then, the contract was already in force (it came into force on July 6), and the revocation was of no effect.

(B) Yes. Again by the mailbox rule, the acceptance became effective on dispatch, July 4. The subsequently-dispatched rejection did not change this, even though Ben received that rejection before he received the acceptance.

(C) No. Where a rejection is dispatched before an acceptance, there is an exception to the usual mailbox rule for acceptances: in this situation, the acceptance is effective if and only if it *overtakes the rejection*, which did not happen here. (This makes sense — once Ben got the rejection, he ought to have been entitled to assume that the deal was dead, and to make other arrangements.)

16. **Yes.** Under the mailbox rule, an acceptance is effective when it is sent. This is true even if the offeror never actually receives it, provided it was properly dispatched in the first place (i.e. correct address and amount of postage). However, Selznick would be entitled to be discharged (excused) from performance, if he reasonably believed that Plotkin wasn't interested, and made other arrangements before learning that Plotkin had accepted.

VIII. INDEFINITENESS

A. **Problem of indefiniteness generally:** Even though two parties who are negotiating with each other may intend to make a contract, and indeed think that they have made a contract, there is no contract if the terms of their "agreement" are unduly *indefinite*. A proposed agreement whose terms are too uncertain to form a contract is said to be *"void for indefiniteness."*

B. **Modern view more liberal:** Although older common-law cases tended to require a high degree of specificity in the terms of the contract, the Second Restatement and the UCC tolerate much more uncertainty before voiding a contract for indefiniteness.

  1. **Restatement test:** The Second Restatement states that the terms of a contract are sufficiently definite "if they *provide a basis for determining the existence of a breach* and for *giving an appropriate remedy.*" Rest. 2d, § 33(2). Thus as long as the agreement is definite enough to allow the court to determine whether one party has breached it, and to award some kind of reasonable damages to the wronged party, the contract is not void for indefiniteness.

  2. **UCC test:** The UCC applies a similar test: "Even though one or more terms are left open, a contract for sale does not fail for indefiniteness if the parties have *intended to make a contract*, and there is a *reasonably certain basis for giving an appropriate remedy.*" UCC § 2-204(3).

C. **Necessary terms:** There are four *essential elements* which an agreement must cover (either expressly or impliedly) in order for it to be enforceable:

  ❏ *parties* to the contract;

  ❏ *subject matter* of the contract;

  ❏ *time* for performance and

  ❏ *price*.

  1. **Court may supply missing term:** However, if the parties fail to make an explicit statement as to one or more of these essential elements, there are nonetheless several kinds of situations in which the court will attempt to *supply the missing term*. These situations include the following:

a. Where parties intend to leave term to reasonable implication: It may be the case that although the parties fail to state explicitly a term of their agreement, both parties manifest an *intent that a reasonable term will apply.*

Example: Consumer telephones Storekeeper, and orders 10 pounds of potatoes. Storekeeper agrees, and has them sent over. The absence of any discussion of price does not make the agreement void for indefiniteness. A court would probably hold that Consumer had impliedly agreed to pay whatever Storekeeper's current price for potatoes was.

b. Agreement to agree: The parties may have left certain terms (e.g., price or time for performance) to be determined by a *future mutual agreement.* In this situation, the UCC and the Second Restatement may authorize the court to supply the missing term, if the parties fail to reach agreement.

c. Indefiniteness cured by performance: An agreement which is too indefinite for enforcement at the outset may later *become sufficiently definite* through the *actions* of one or both parties. If so, the court may hold that such action filled the missing term.

Note: Before we examine each of the kinds of situations listed above, you should note that the question is always whether the *contract* is too indefinite, not whether the *offer* is too indefinite. An offer which does not by itself contain sufficient detail for enforceability may solicit the requisite details from the offeree. For instance, if *A* offers to sell *B* any quantity of widgets that *B* wishes, at $10 per widget, the offer itself does not contain all requisite details; obviously, a quantity term is needed. But if the quantity is supplied by the acceptance, the contract is sufficiently definite. Therefore, in all of the situations described below, the words and actions of *both* parties must be examined to determine whether all necessary terms have been expressed or may be implied.

2. **Implication of reasonable terms, generally:**   If the parties have omitted any attempt to express an intention regarding a particular term, the court will frequently fill the gap by supplying a *"reasonable"* term.

   a. UCC approach: The UCC has led the way for supplying "missing terms." Provided that the parties "have *intended to make a contract* and there is a *reasonably certain basis for giving an appropriate remedy,"* (§ 2-204(3)), the court is authorized to fill in a number of terms if the parties have omitted to specify these terms. The terms which may be filled in include *price, place for delivery, time for shipment or delivery, time for payment,* etc.

   i. Open price term: § 2-305(1) allows the parties to form a contract in some situations even though the *price term* is not decided on. For there to be a contract, the parties must *intend* that one be formed, and in addition one of the three following things must be so:

   ❏ *nothing is said* in the contract as to price; or

   ❏ the price is *left to be agreed upon* by the parties and they *fail to agree;* or

   ❏ the price is to be "fixed in terms of some agreed market or other *standard* as set or recorded by a third person or agency and it is not so set or recorded."

If the relevant conditions are met, the price is "a *reasonable price at the time for delivery.*"

As an example of the third category above, if the parties agree that a particular price will be adjusted to reflect changes in the federal government's **Consumer Price Index**, and the government stops publishing the *Consumer Price Index*, the court would supply a reasonable price or a reasonable substitute standard.

ii. **Absence of specified place for delivery:** If the contract does not specify *where the goods are to be delivered*, the place for delivery is the *seller's place of business* or, if he has none, her residence. (§ 2-308(a)). The only exception to this rule is that if at the time of contracting the goods are known by the parties to be somewhere other than at the seller's business or residence, that place is the place of delivery. (§ 2-308(b)). In other words, where the contract is silent, the court will construe the contract so as to require *the buyer to pick up the goods*.

iii. **Time for shipment or delivery:** If the contract is silent as to the *time* for shipment, for delivery, or for any other action under the contract, that time shall be "a *reasonable* time." (§ 2-309).

iv. **Time for payment:** If the contract does not specify whether the buyer is to have credit, payment is due at *the time and place at which the buyer is to receive the goods*, even if this place is the seller's place of business. In other words, the buyer is *not entitled to credit unless the contract says so.* (But he apparently does have the right to pay by check unless otherwise agreed.) (§ 2-310(a)).

Note: These UCC "gap filler" provisions only come into play when the parties' agreement (defined broadly to include "course of performance," "course of dealing" and "usage of trade") is silent in a particular term. These gap-fillers are based on the assumption that these are the terms that most parties would have agreed on if they had focused on the issues in advance.

3. **Implied obligation of good faith:** In both UCC and non-UCC contracts, courts find an implied obligation of *good faith* and *fair dealing*. Thus Rest. 2d § 205 says that "[e]very contract imposes upon each party a duty of good faith and fair dealing in its performance and its enforcement." Similarly, UCC § 1-304 says that "every contract or duty within this Act imposes an obligation of good faith in its performance or enforcement." (UCC § 1-201(19) then defines good faith as "*honesty* in fact and the observance of *reasonable commercial standards of fair dealing*.")

a. **Consistency with other party's expectations:** An important aspect of this duty of good faith is that a party is required to behave in a way that is consistent with the other party's *reasonable expectations* about how the contract will work. Thus the Restatement says that "good faith performance or enforcement of a contract emphasizes faithfulness to an agreed common purpose and *consistency with the justified expectations of the other party*[.]" Rest. 2d § 205, Comment a.

Example: Insurer writes a homeowner's policy on Owner's home. The policy says that in the event Owner suffers a loss, Owner must report the loss "in detail" and in writing to Insurer within 30 days. 28 days after Owner's home is burglarized, he submits a one-sentence description of the loss to Insurer. Insurer says merely, "Your description is not specific enough," but refuses to tell Owner what type of detail must be added. (Assume that Insurer's evasiveness is an intentional attempt to prevent Owner from submitting a claim meeting the requirements of the policy.) The deadline passes without Owner's rewriting the description, and Insurer refuses to pay to the claim.

A court would probably find that Insurer's intentionally evasive behavior violated the implied duty of good faith, because it was an attempt to deprive Owner of his reasonable expectation that his loss would be covered by the policy. Cf. Rest. 2d § 205, Illustr. 7.

b. **Interference with or refusal to cooperate in other party's performance:** A common type of bad-faith conduct consists of *A*'s *interference with*, or *refusal to cooperate with*, *B*'s performance. This is especially likely where *B* must perform an act in order to satisfy a "condition" to *A*'s duty. (Conditions are discussed *infra*, p. 203.) If *A*'s non-cooperation or interference with *B*'s attempt to satisfy a condition to *A*'s duty is in bad faith, then *A* will be found in breach. Thus on the above example, it was a condition of Insurer's duty to pay the claim that Owner have submitted a timely detailed notice of loss; Insurer's refusal to help Owner understand what was required — made with an intent to deprive Owner of the fruits of the contract — was a refusal to cooperate with Owner's performance, and thus a breach of Insurer's implied duty of good faith.

c. **Output and requirements contracts:** One situation in which the obligation of good faith becomes important is in so-called *"output"* and *"requirements"* contracts (discussed *infra*, p. 115). Such contracts (which call for the buyer to buy all of his needs from the seller, or provide that the buyer will buy the seller's entire output) were formerly sometimes held to be too indefinite for enforcement, since they did not specify quantity. Under UCC § 2-306(1), however, such output and requirements contracts are explicitly authorized, and are construed to involve "such actual output or requirements as may occur *in good faith*, except that no quantity unreasonably disproportionate to any stated estimate or in the absence of a stated estimate to any normal or otherwise comparable prior output or requirement may be tendered or demanded." (§ 2-306(1)).

d. **Good faith irrelevant where clause explicit:** But the obligation of good faith will generally *not* be employed to override a *specific contractual clause*.

Example: Suppose that P is a franchisor for D, a fast-food chain. The franchise agreement expressly says that the agreement may be terminated "at any time, for any reason, by either party upon 10 days written notice to the other." After P has successfully run his restaurant for 10 years, X is appointed president of D. X unreasonably dislikes P from prior business dealings they have had that are unrelated to the restaurant industry. X causes D to terminate the franchise agreement with P because "I don't believe you are the kind of operator we want."

Even though this termination might otherwise have constituted a violation of the duty of good faith and fair dealing, a court would probably not void the termination (or award damages for it), because the duty of good faith will generally not be found to override an express contractual provision, such as the termination provision here.

4. **Trade usage or other external evidence:** In attempting to make what appears to be indefinite sufficiently definite, the court will look to *"trade usage"* (i.e., industry custom), *"course of dealing"* between the parties to the contract, or other external evidence. Such evidence may be consulted either on the theory that it shows that the parties had already in fact reached an agreement on the term (but had simply neglected to make that agreement explicit in the contract), or on the theory that this evidence helps show what the parties would have agreed upon had they focused on the issue. (The former rationale really uses this evidence in order to "interpret" the contract; see *infra*, p. 192.)

> **Example:** P, a textile company, makes a "forward" contract to buy cotton from D, a cotton ginner. The contract fixes a price and delivery date, but does not specify the number of pounds to be sold; rather, it specifies a certain number of acres, and provides that all cotton produced on that acreage is to be sold under the contract. Between the signing of the contract and the time for delivery, the price of cotton more than doubles, and D attempts to escape from the contract by claiming that the quantity term is unenforceably vague. If P can show that it is common in the cotton trade to use acreage figures as a quantity term, the contract will be found to be sufficiently definite to be enforced.

5. **Need for an intent to contract:** The court will supply the missing terms *only if the parties have manifested an intention to create a binding contract*. Indeed, the fact that one or more terms are missing — especially if they are important ones — will often itself be *evidence* that the parties did not intend to bind themselves until later. Thus the Second Restatement cautions that "the fact that one or more terms of a proposed bargain are left open or uncertain may show that a manifestation of intention is not intended to be understood as an offer or as an acceptance." (Rest. 2d, § 33(3).) The more terms that are left unresolved, the more likely it is that the parties were only negotiating, and did not intend to be bound.

   a. **Duration of employment:** For instance, most courts have been unwilling to supply a term to set the *duration of an employment contract*. Courts generally hold that if an employment contract does not contain a length-of-employment term, the arrangement is merely a series of offers, each for one day's employment, and that it may be terminated, at any time, by either party, with no liability except for services that have already been performed. Murray, p. 51. But some courts have placed limits on when and how such an "at will" employment arrangement may be terminated (e.g., that it may not be terminated for a bad faith reason). See the fuller discussion of this topic *infra*, pp. 197-198.

6. **Agreement to agree:** The parties may form a contract with an essential term unfilled, intending to *agree upon that term in the future.*

   a. **Common-law view:** Until the enactment of the UCC, such "agreements to agree" were usually held to be fatally indefinite.

   > **Example:** Seller and Buyer agree that Buyer will sell a certain quantity of newsprint each month to Seller. Their agreement specifies the price per ton for the first four

months of the contract; it says that after this period, the price for each upcoming month's shipment shall be "as agreed upon by the parties in the last week of the prior month." Assume that there is evidence that the parties intended themselves to be legally bound by the agreement.

Under the pre-UCC approach, the parties' "agreement to agree" on the price would render their arrangement fatally indefinite, and thus unenforceable.

b. UCC approach: The UCC, however, provides that as long as the parties *intend* to make a binding contract, their "agreement to agree" does not make the contract fatally indefinite, at least if it is the price term that is left open. UCC § 2-305(1)(b) allows the court to supply a reasonable price term if "the price is left to be agreed by the parties and they fail to agree.…"

Example: Thus in the above Example of the contract for newsprint, the contract would probably be valid under UCC § 2-305(1)(b).

c. Unilateral concession: Also, if the term to be agreed upon is one which is subject to *complete concession* by the party seeking enforcement of the contract, he will usually be able to obtain enforcement by making this complete concession.

Example: D gives P an option to buy particular real estate at a particular price. The option contract provides that the "manner and form" of payment are to be left to later agreement. When P wishes to exercise the option, D refuses to negotiate with respect to how payment should be made (since he does not want to honor the option). If P shows that he is willing to make payment either in all cash (probably the most favorable to D) or on any other terms specified by D, the court will enforce the agreement. (It will probably make P's complete concession on the terms-of-payment issue part of the contract to be enforced.) See Farnsworth, pp. 219-220.

d. Non-UCC cases — court supplies a missing term: In non-UCC cases, modern courts have tended to follow the liberal approach suggested by UCC § 2-305(1), and have grown increasingly willing to *supply a reasonable term* for the issue on which the parties were unable to agree. (But courts in non-UCC situations have insisted, just as does UCC § 2-305(1)(b), that a court may supply the missing term only if there is evidence that the *parties themselves intended to make a binding contract*.)

i. Lease renewals: One situation, however, in which many courts have been reluctant to follow the UCC lead is that in which a tenant and landlord agree that the tenant shall, at the end of the lease term, have the option to *renew it* at a rental "to be agreed upon." Some courts have been willing to supply a "reasonable" rental figure, but many, perhaps most, have refused to do so. See, e.g., *Joseph Martin, Jr. Delicatessen v. Schumacher*, 417 N.E. 2d 541 (N.Y. 1981), where the court refused to supply a "reasonable rent," on the grounds that "[T]here is not so much as a hint at a commitment to be bound by the 'fair market rental value' … [N]owhere is there an inkling that either of the parties directly or indirectly assented … to subordinate the figure on which it ultimately would insist, to one fixed judicially.…" See Farnsworth, p. 217-218, n. 4 and 5, for cases on both sides.

e. Damages for failing to make good-faith efforts to agree: Instead of supplying a missing term, a court may hold a party liable for *failing to make good-faith efforts to reach agreement* about the missing term.

　　i. Agreement-to-agree contained in other agreement: For instance, suppose the parties execute one clearly-binding agreement, and in it they agree to negotiate a *second, related agreement* in the near future. The court may well hold that this *promise to negotiate* is binding, and imposes a *duty to bargain in good faith*.

7. Contracts where terms are left to one party's specifications: The parties may agree that *one* of them has the *right to determine a particular term of performance* at a subsequent date. While pre-UCC cases often found that this kind of "term to be specified later by one party" arrangement was fatally indefinite, the UCC takes a different approach.

　　a. UCC view: UCC § 2-311(1) provides that as long as the parties intend to make a contract, and there is a *reasonably certain basis for giving an appropriate remedy* (see § 2-204(3)), the contract "is not made invalid by the fact that it leaves particulars of performance to be specified by one of the parties. Any such specification must be made in *good faith* and within *limits set by commercial reasonableness*." (§ 2-311(1)). If the party who has the right to make such a specification fails to do so, the other party may treat this failure as a breach of contract.

　　　　i. Seller may perform: If it is the buyer who has the right and obligation to set the specification, and she does not do so, § 2-311(3)(b) gives the seller the right to "perform in *any reasonable manner.*"

　　　　Example: Buyer agrees to buy a certain tonnage of motor oils from Seller, with Buyer to select, prior to shipment, how many cans of oil in each of various weights it wishes to buy. Buyer then refuses to make the selection. Seller may make a reasonable selection of weights, deliver them to Buyer, and oblige him to accept them. Seller may then recover the full purchase price, rather than merely his lost profits (which is what he would recover if he merely declared a breach and made no shipment).

8. Indefiniteness cured by part performance: Even if an agreement is too indefinite for enforceability at the time it is made, the *subsequent performance* of the parties may cure this indefiniteness. See Rest. 2d, § 34(2).

　　Example: *A* promises to make a tailor-made suit for *B* for $500. The initial agreement does not specify the kind of material to be used. If *B* changes his mind before *A* has started to work, and indicates he does not wish to continue the agreement, it will probably be held void for indefiniteness. But if *A* begins making the suit with cotton cloth, and *B* knows this and raises no objection, the indefiniteness will be deemed cured by this part performance. See C&P, p. 52.

IX. MISUNDERSTANDING

A. Misunderstanding generally: For there to be a contract, there must of course be a "meeting of the minds." (See *supra*, p. 5.) That is, both parties must be agreeing to a deal. It may happen, however, that although both parties *think* that they are agreeing to the same terms, each has a different subjective belief about what the deal is. If this discrepancy in subjective belief (traditionally called *"misunderstanding"*) is sufficiently major, it may *prevent a contract from existing at all*.

1. **Material term, and no fault:** If the misunderstanding concerns a *material term*, and *neither party* knows or has reason to know of the misunderstanding, *there is no contract*. Rest. 2d, § 20(1).

B. Ambiguity: The most common cause of such a misunderstanding is that a term used in the agreement is *"ambiguous."* An ambiguous term is one which has two, inconsistent, meanings. If the ambiguous term is a major one, and the two parties do not attach the same subjective meaning to it, there will be *no meeting of the minds and thus no contract*.

> **Example:** *A* offers to sell *B* goods shipped from Bombay on the steamer *Peerless*. *B* accepts. There are in fact two steamers each named *Peerless* in Bombay at the time of contracting; one is scheduled to leave much later than the other. *A* subjectively intends to ship on the later *Peerless*; *B* subjectively intends to accept an offer of shipment on the earlier *Peerless*. *B* expects the earlier shipment, does not get it, and then refuses the later shipment.

> *Held*, there is no contract, because *A* and *B* were in subjective disagreement as to the meaning of the term "Peerless," and neither had reason to know of the disagreement. *Raffles v. Wichelhaus*, 2 H&C 906 (1864). Cf. Rest. 2d, § 20, Illustr. 2.

1. **Where both parties have identical subjective understanding:** Of course, the fact that a term used in the offer or acceptance is ambiguous does not matter as long as both parties have the same subjective understanding with respect to it. For instance, in the *Raffles* case, *supra*, the fact that there were two ships named *Peerless* would not have made any difference had both parties understood that shipment was to be made on the first Peerless. Thus in the context of "ambiguity," *the objective theory of contracts does not strictly apply*. In order to determine whether or not there is a contract, it is necessary to ascertain whether the subjective intent of both parties was the same. (Obviously, this subjective intent can only be gauged with respect to the parties' actions. But the point is that these actions may be taken as evidence of subjective intent even if they were never communicated to the other party.)

2. **Where one party knows or should know the meaning understood by the other:** If a term in the offer or acceptance is ambiguous, and one party *knows* that she has a different understanding as to the meaning of that term than does the other party, a contract will be formed *on the term as understood by the other (unknowing) party*.

> **Example:** Assume the same situation as in Example 1, *supra*, p. 74. *A* knows that there are two ships named *Peerless*, and he also knows that *B* thinks the contract is for shipment on the first *Peerless*. *A* subjectively intends to ship on the second *Peerless*. Because *A* knows that he and *B* subjectively disagree as to which *Peerless* shipment is to be made on, a contract is formed for shipment on the first *Peerless* (i.e., the *Peerless* understood by *B*, the "innocent" party). See Rest. 2d, § 20, Illustr. 3.

a. Where one party has reason to know of ambiguity but does not: Essentially the same rule applies if one party *should* know of the ambiguity, but does not, and the other party neither knows nor should know. As in the previous Example, the party who is "more at fault" is bound by a contract on the other party's terms.

b. Fault system: Thus in determining whether there is a contract in such cases of ambiguity, a *"comparative fault"* system applies. As Comment d to Rest. 2d, § 20, puts it, "no contract is formed if neither party is at fault or if both parties are equally at fault." If one party is more at fault than the other, she is bound by the other's understanding.

C. UCC approach: The UCC has no provisions dealing directly with the consequences of misunderstanding; this area is thus left to case law.

D. Misunderstanding as to minor term: The situations discussed thus far involve a misunderstanding which goes to an important, essential, term of the bargain. If the misunderstanding, however, involves only a *minor* aspect of the deal, the court will not usually conclude that no contract was formed, or that either party may avoid the contract. Instead, the court will usually attempt to choose the more reasonable, or fairer, of the meanings, and will enforce the contract on that basis.

E. One party's waiver of the misunderstanding: Even if there is the sort of misunderstanding that in a case like *Raffles v. Wichelhaus, supra,* p. 74, might constitute a failure of mutual assent and therefore a failure to contract, one party may *waive* the misunderstanding and enforce the contract in accordance with the understanding of the other party. See Rest. 2d, § 201, Comment d, last sentence.

> **Example:** In the *Raffles* situation, *B*, the buyer, could have learned of the mistake, then decided to wait for the second *Peerless* steamer and to accept the goods on it. If *A* (the seller) later discovered that *B* had originally expected shipment to take place on the first Peerless, *A* could not demand the goods back and escape from the contract on the grounds of a misunderstanding. Similarly, once *B* learned that the goods were coming on the wrong ship, if he did not seasonably object, he too would be held to have "waived the misunderstanding." See Rest. 2d, § 201, Comment d.

F. Other types of mistake: The topic of "misunderstanding," examined here, is related to the topic of "mistake." We discuss the general problem of "mistake" in a separate chapter devoted solely to the subject, beginning *infra*, p. 155. There is a key difference between the types of mistake covered in that chapter, and "misunderstandings," covered here. This difference is that a misunderstanding, if it is related to a material term, *prevents a contract from ever existing* at all. The consequence of other types of "mistake," by contrast, is that the contract exists, but may be *avoided* by the mistaken party.

Quiz Yourself on

INDEFINITENESS AND MISUNDERSTANDING

17. Samantha's House of Magic agrees to buy 50 silk top hats from Esmerelda's Supply.

(A) Assume that the parties never discuss the time for shipment. Is there a contract? If so, for what time of shipment?

(B) Assume instead that Samantha's order form says that shipment will be made in 5 days, and Esmerelda's acknowledgment form recites that shipment will be made in 90 days. Neither party notices the discrepancy until one month after Samantha receives Esmerelda's acknowledgment form, when Samantha wonders where the shipment is. Is there a contract? If so, for what time of shipment?

18. The Lucrezia Borgia Exterminating Company decides to buy rat poison from the Rodent-A-No Manufacturing Company. Rodent-A-No sends out its list of terms (price, shipping, etc.) and Borgia wires back, "We will order most of our rat poison from you for next year, at your stated price and shipping terms." Is there a contract?

19. Tweedle Dee enters into a contract with Mad Hatter Catering to purchase some pies for a party he is giving. The contract specifies that Mad Hatter will provide 10 "moon pies" for the occasion. Prior to the contract, Tweedle Dee was at a friend's house and was served an unusual pie made out of chocolate and green cheese, and the friend told him it was a moon pie — this is what Tweedle Dee meant to be ordering. Unbeknownst to Tweedle Dee, the pie Mad Hatter calls "moon pie" is made with ollaliberries and tang. The night of the party, Mad Hatter delivers his version of moon pies. Tweedle Dee is stunned when he sees the fruity concoction and refuses to accept them.

(A) Assume Mad Hatter had no reason to know that Tweedle Dee thought moon pies were made out of cocoa and green cheese, and Tweedle Dee had no reason to know that Mad Hatter thought moon pies were made with fruit. What result?

(B) Now assume that, just prior to their first meeting, Mad Hatter had heard Tweedle Dee tell Cheshire Kitty, Mad Hatter's receptionist, about the delicious chocolatey-cheesy moon pies he was hoping to serve at his party. What result?

Answers

17. **(A) Yes, for shipment at a "reasonable" time.** There is a contract because the UCC will provide a "gap filler" to complete a contract when it is otherwise clear that the parties intended to be bound. Here, the time for shipment will be a "reasonable time" (§ 2-309(1). What is a reasonable time will be determined based upon looking at the parties' prior course of dealing, if there is any, or by looking at trade usage (what is customary in the industry).

   (B) No, probably. The fact that the order and acceptance (or, more generally, the parties' beliefs about the deal) diverge somewhat does not prevent a contract from coming into existence. But if the parties are in substantial disagreement about an essential term of the contract, their expressions of intent to contract will be deemed to be so divergent that no contract was ever formed (i.e., there never was a "meeting of the minds.") A discrepancy between 5 days and 90 days on the shipment date would probably be found to be major enough to block formation of a contract.

18. **No, because there's no quantity term, making the contract too vague to enforce.** This is true even under the UCC rules for contracts between merchants, where "gap filling" occurs more readily. Note that the contract *looks* like a requirements contract — but it's not. That's because for a requirements contract to be valid, the buyer must agree to buy *all* of her requirements of a stated item from the seller, not *most*. Unless a buyer agrees to buy all of an item from the seller, her discretion hasn't been diminished at all, making her promise illusory and unsupported by consideration (as you'll see in the next chapter).

19. **(A) There is no contract, so Tweedle Dee can refuse to accept the pies.** When the parties to a contract have a misunderstanding about a material term in the contract and neither party knows or has reason to

know of the misunderstanding, there is no "meeting of the minds" and therefore no contract.

(B) There is a contract, on the terms as understood by Tweedle Dee, and Mad Hatter is liable for breach. Unlike the facts in (A), here Mad Hatter *did* know that the parties had different interpretations of the term "moon pie." Where one party knows that his interpretation of a term is different from that of the other party, he is considered to be more "at fault" for not clearing up the misunderstanding. In that event, a contract will be found to exist and it will be on the terms understood by the *other* party. So there was a contract for the chocolate-style pies, which Mad Hatter breached by preparing fruity ones. Mad Hatter not only can't get the contract price from Tweedle Dee, but he's liable to Tweedle Dee for consequential damages for the non-delivery (e.g., damage to the quality of the party, stemming from the lack of appropriate food).

Exam Tips *on* OFFER AND ACCEPTANCE

Offer

☛ **Identifying an offer:** Many essays require you to determine initially whether a valid offer has been made. Remember that this *question of fact* is analyzed from the viewpoint of a *reasonable offeree.* Ask yourself: Has the party *exhibited a willingness to be bound without further action on her own part*?

   ☞ Distinguish offers from mere *inquiries* or expressions of *interest*, which are not offers because they don't indicate a willingness to be immediately bound:

      Example: "Will $2,000 buy your piano?" is a mere inquiry, not an offer.

   ☞ *Trap:* Don't be misled by a party's own characterization of a statement as an "offer." Analyze the relevant statement yourself from the perspective of a "reasonable offeree" — something the speaker (or listener) refers to as an "offer" may not be one.

   ☞ Look out for circumstances and words indicating that the person speaking retains the right to give final approval to the deal — these indicate that the speaker is not making an offer, because the speaker doesn't intend to give the other person the power to seal the seal by "accepting."

      Example: After months of negotiation over a proposed contract, *A* sends *B* a draft, with a cover email saying, "I've put in the terms you wanted. Let's discuss this document." Since the email indicates that *A* believes a further discussion will be needed, the sending of the draft cannot be an offer, and *B* cannot cause the contract to be formed even if he emails back, "I accept the deal on exactly the terms proposed in your draft."

   ☞ Look out for the following special situations which frequently appear on exams:

      ☞ **Quotations**: A price quotation is usually construed as an invitation, but may be considered an offer if it's *specific enough* that the offeree is reasonable in perceiving it as an offer.

☞ **Advertisements**: These are usually considered invitations unless they include sufficient promissory language. (*Example:* "Ten pearl necklaces on sale for $300 to the first ten cash buyers" would qualify.) Language such as "while they last" probably does *not* indicate an intent to be bound.

☞ **Solicitations for bids**: These are usually mere invitations, with the responding bids considered offers.

> *Example:* X sends a letter to A, B, C and D which states: "I need to sell my heart-shaped diamond ring by January 15 for $1,500. If interested, please contact me before January 15." On January 14, X receives a letter from A agreeing to pay $1,500. X doesn't respond. On January 17, X receives a letter from B agreeing to pay $1,700. X responds to B: "I agree to the terms of your letter." A can't sue X for breach because X's letter was not an offer (just an invitation to make an offer), so A's letter was an offer that X never accepted.

> ❏ *Exception:* **Words of commitment**. Watch for a solicitation that includes words indicating a commitment to sell to the highest bidder by a certain date. In this case, the solicitation becomes an offer and the solicitor is bound to the person fulfilling the stated conditions.

☞ ***Exam-writing tip***: Remember that since questions involving offers should be viewed from the perspective of the reasonable offeree (an objective standard), most questions will present gray-area fact patterns. ***Don't forget to argue both sides***. (But be sure to point out the one you think would prevail.)

Acceptance

Here are things to look out for when you analyze something that might be an acceptance:

☞ Just as an offer must contain language of commitment, an acceptance must be ***unequivocal***.

   ☞ But keep in mind that acceptance may be ***implied through conduct***, such as shipment of the items, payment for the items, or the offeree's later statement (to the offeror or to a third party) that a contract exists.

☞ **Manner of acceptance**: Make sure that the ***manner*** of acceptance was one that the offer allowed (or that was reasonable if the offer didn't say what manner was acceptable).

   ☞ Remember that where the offeror is ***indifferent*** as to the ***manner*** of acceptance, the offer can be accepted ***by performance or promise.*** (*Example:* Under the UCC, the seller can usually accept *either* by shipping or promising to ship.)

   ☞ Also, remember that even without an explicit acceptance, the ***parties' conduct can give rise*** to an ***"implied-in-fact"*** contract. (*Example: A*, a professional music teacher, gives music lessons to *B*'s child, while *B* stands silently by, knowing that *A* expects payment. *B*'s silent acquiescence gives rise to an implied-in-fact contract to pay *A*'s standard rate.)

Unilateral Contracts

☛ Offers for unilateral contracts appear often on exams. Look for a situation where an offeror is requesting the performance of a particular action. Most common: offers of an *award* or *reward*.

  ☞ **Offeree aware:** Remember that *the offeree must know about the offer* in order to accept it. Common scenario: A reward is offered for a lost possession and somebody returns it without knowing that the owner has offered a reward — not an enforceable contract.

  ☞ *Trap:* Remember that *promises are irrelevant* if the offer is truly for a unilateral contract. Don't get sidetracked by a party who promises to perform the act requested. The promise doesn't transform the agreement into a bilateral contract. The offer may be revoked even after such a statement has been made.

    Example: H announces to a group in a bar: "I'll pay $1,000 to anyone who tells me the name of the thief that stole a hand-carved stool out of my garage last night." This is an offer for a unilateral contract, which can be accepted only by supplying the name, not by promising to tell the name.

  ☞ **Revocation:** It's important to note when performance has occurred, because the acceptance of the offer *prevents revocation* by the offeror.

  Example: P is about to enter law school and plans to marry during winter break. His father offers him $1,000 if he postpones his wedding plans until after he has completed his first year. P postpones the wedding as requested, and shortly thereafter his father dies. The father's death does not terminate the offer because P already accepted the offer prior to the father's death by postponing the wedding. P is therefore entitled to the $1,000.

    ☞ Also remember that under the Restatement, an offer for a unilateral contract becomes *temporarily irrevocable* if the offeree has *commenced but not yet completed performance* (recall the "Brooklyn Bridge" hypo — If P starts to cross the Bridge, D can't revoke).

      ☞ Make sure, however, that the party has already begun the actual *performance* requested, not just made mere *preparations* to perform.

Acceptance Varying from Offer

☛ **Battle of the forms:** Be prepared for "battle of the forms" problems, such as where buyer's purchase order and seller's acknowledgment contain different or conflicting terms.

☛ **No deal:** First, make sure that the two forms agree on the basic terms (price, quantity, delivery date) well enough that they form a contract. If they don't, then there's *no agreement* unless the subsequent actions of the parties (e.g., seller ships, buyer accepts the goods) is enough to form a contract.

☛ **Material alteration:** Remember the basic rule that an additional or different term in the second form is merely a *proposal for addition* to the contract.

☞ That term *doesn't* become part of the contract if:

    ☞ one or both parties is *not a merchant*; or

    ☞ the term *materially alters* the deal. *Example:* Arbitration clauses, and disclaimers of warranties, are usually held to be material alterations, so they don't become part of the contract unless the other party agrees to them.

☞ If the term in the second form *directly conflicts* with a term in the first form, probably the two *"knock each out."* Then, any relevant Code "gap filler" can be used.

Example: Buyer's p.o. says, "You warrant that the machine you're selling us is fit for use in our manufacturing operation, and that it will perform properly for 10 years." Seller's acknowledgment says, "No warranties, express or implied." Since the Seller's clause materially alters the deal, the two clauses cancel each other. But the Code's implied warranty of merchantability would "fill the gap."

Duration of the Power of Acceptance

☛ Make sure that the moment at which "acceptance" occurred was a moment at which the *offer was still open.*

☞ **Mailbox rule:** Remember that an acceptance is *effective upon dispatch*, provided it is communicated by a method specified in the offer (or by a reasonable method, if none is specified).

    ☞ **Offeror can suspend:** But also keep in mind that the offeror, as "master of the offer," can *suspend* the mailbox rule (e.g., by saying "I must receive your acceptance by 5 p.m. Tuesday").

☛ **Counter-offer**: Remember that a counter-offer effectively terminates the power to accept just as if there was an outright rejection of the offer.

☛ **Lapse of time:** Determine whether an acceptance has been communicated in time:

☞ If the offer specifies when an offer lapses, it lapses automatically on that date. *Tip:* Watch for an offer sent by mail. Unless otherwise specified, the time begins to run from the date the offer is *received*.

☞ If the offer doesn't specify when the offer lapses, it expires within a *reasonable amount of time*. Look at the nature of the contract to determine what would be considered a reasonable amount of time. In a land sale deal, for example, six days' time would probably not be considered an unreasonable amount of time in which to accept, but one month probably would.

☛ **Revocation**: Be sure that the offer wasn't revoked before it was accepted. Here are the two methods of rejection:

☞ An unequivocal statement of revocation (e.g., offeror says, "The deal is off").

☞ Revocation by an *indirect* communication. This is the most frequently tested mode of revocation. Look for an offeror who behaves in a way that is *inconsistent with the intention of entering into the proposed contract*, where the *offeree learns* of the inconsistency.

Example: X, who has offered to buy Y's garden tractor, learns from Z that Y has already sold the tractor to Y. Once X gets this knowledge, the revocation has occurred.

Firm Offers and Option Contracts

When you analyze an offeror's ***promise to hold an offer open***, it's key that you start with deciding whether the UCC applies:

☞ **UCC Transactions:** If the offer involves the sale of goods (i.e., it's a UCC Article 2 transaction), here's a recap of the main rules:

   ☞ An offeror who is a ***merchant*** — one who deals professionally in the kind of goods in question — may extend an irrevocable ***firm offer***, even without consideration, as long as the writing is ***signed***.

   ☞ A firm offer for which no consideration is given ***cannot be made irrevocable*** for a period ***longer than three months***.

      ☞ If the offer purports to be irrevocable for longer than three months, it ***becomes revocable*** after the passage of three months, but can then ***still be accepted*** if nothing has caused it to terminate.

   ☞ A ***non-merchant*** who gratuitously (i.e., without consideration) promises to hold an offer open is ***not*** held to that promise.

      Example: *A*, a non-merchant, posts a message on e-bay.com saying, "I offer to sell my 1953 Barbie & Ken set to highest bidder over $100. This offer is firm, and I won't revoke it before 11:59 p.m. March 17." *B* makes a $150 offer, which is the highest as of 11 p.m. on March 17. *A* revokes at 11:45. There's no contract, because *A* could revoke any time he wanted even though he said he wouldn't, since: (1) he's a non-merchant; and (2) offers by non-merchants aren't irrevocable without consideration.

☞ **Non-UCC transactions:** For non-UCC transactions (sales of realty and services), there's just one rule:

   ☞ An offer that purports to be irrevocable for a certain period is ***not irrevocable***, unless the offeree gives ***consideration*** for the irrevocability. This is true even if the offeror is a businessperson (i.e., would be a "merchant" if this were a sale of goods).

      Example: On the facts of the above e-bay example, suppose *A* were a professional developer who offered to sell Blackacre to the highest bidder, with a promise that the offer wouldn't be revoked before conclusion of the auction. *A* could revoke anyway, since no offeree is giving consideration for the promise of irrevocability.

   ☞ But remember that consideration can be ***non-monetary***.

      Example: *A* offers to sell Blackacre to *B* for $100,000. *B*, who lives 150 miles from the property, wants to inspect it but doesn't want to take the trip if *A* might sell to someone else in the interim. Therefore, *A* promises to hold the offer open for one week, in return for *B*'s promise to visit the property during that week. *A*'s offer is irrevocable for the week, because *B*'s return promise to travel is consideration.

☞ For both UCC and non-UCC contracts, remember that the acceptance of an option contract is effective not upon dispatch, but upon *receipt by the offeror*.

Temporary Irrevocability

☛ Look for instances where an offer is *temporarily irrevocable*, such as the following:

☞ Where a party has *commenced performance of a unilateral contract*.

☞ Where a *sub-contractor* submits a bid to a general contractor. If the sub-contractor's bid is relied upon by the general contractor when he submits his overall bid to the customer, it is irrevocable for the time necessary for the general contractor to receive the job and accept the sub-contractor's bid.

☞ However, in this sub-contractor-bid situation, what's being applied is in effect *promissory estoppel*, so the sub's offer is only irrevocable to the extent needed to *avoid injustice*. (*Example:* If the general contractor still has time to amend his own bid after receiving the news that the sub has revoked his sub-bid offer, enforcement of the sub's bid won't be necessary to avoid injustice.)

Indefiniteness

☛ Agreements with indefinite terms appear quite often in fact patterns. When analyzing an agreement, look for the *four essential elements:* Parties to the contract, subject matter, time for performance, and price. But don't automatically void an agreement for indefiniteness if one of these terms is missing.

☞ **UCC test:** Under the UCC, the agreement is not void if it expresses an intention by both parties to be bound and there is a *reasonably certain basis for giving an appropriate remedy*. (Most courts today apply pretty much the same approach in non-UCC cases.)

Example: If the items to be supplied (e.g., name of product) or the quantity are missing, and there's no way for a court to know reliably what was intended, the contract will be void for indefiniteness.

☞ **Missing terms:** Be sure to fill in any omitted terms. Most fact patterns will present a situation where the essential terms are specified, so then the court (i.e., you, the exam writer) may supply a reasonable term. Be on the lookout for these common contexts where terms are omitted:

☞ **Real estate transactions**. The same general rules apply, even in a non-UCC context. *Examples of terms whose omission would probably **not** be fatal:* Type of deed, type of title or type of warranty, dates of tendering of down payment and completion of transaction.

Example: X agrees in writing to sell to Y a property called Farmland for $8 an acre. X later claims that the agreement is void for indefiniteness. Several details are missing from this contract: the total price (because the aggregate number of acres is unknown), the time for performance, the type of deed and condition of title Y will receive. *Solution:* Aggregate acres could be ascertained by a survey, and the total price could then be calculated by multiplying the acres times $8. The other terms could be implied from what is customary in the area.

❑ ***Remember that price is an essential term in a realty contract and its absence violates the Statute of Frauds.***

☞ **Sale of goods.** The most commonly omitted terms in this type of transaction are the manner of payment (cash or credit), the place of delivery, total contract price and type of warranties. If the contract doesn't otherwise specify, delivery is at the seller's place of business, a cash payment is due at that time and the normal implied warranties will accompany the sale. If there's no price specified, the court can supply a "reasonable" one, provided that the parties intended to be bound even though no price was set.

☞ **Past performance:** Watch for a situation where the parties have already been conducting business under an agreement that one party is now claiming is void because it is "indefinite." The parties' *past performance* may show that there is mutual agreement regarding the supposedly indefinite term.

☞ **Open term:** Don't worry if the contract indicates that a term will be specified by one of the parties (or agreed on by both) in the future: the contract will still be enforceable if there is a reasonable way for a court to fill the gap and to determine damages.

Example: A purchase agreement reads in part: "*B* Aircraft Company agrees to sell and *A* agrees to buy 50 planes to be delivered as ordered within the next year at these prices: Gulls — $100,000 each; Terns — $200,000 each. *A* to specify shipping dates. Number of each type wanted on each shipment to be specified by *A* at least thirty days before each shipping date." After *A* places and receives an order of 10 planes, he refuses to place an order for any more. Although the quantity of each type of plane isn't specified, there is a reasonably certain basis for awarding damages by figuring that the least *A* would have bought prospectively was 40 Gulls (the least expensive plane).

Misunderstanding

☛ **Ambiguous term:** Where a contract term is ambiguous and one party should know the meaning understood by the other party, a contract is formed based on the other party's understanding.

Example: In October, *C*, an art collector, telephones *A*, an artist, and says, "In February I saw your painting of Sunflowers. Is it still available, and, if so, how much do you want for it?" The contract they later sign states: "*A* hereby sells to *C A*'s sunflower painting..." *C* was referring to a painting entitled "Sunflowers." In July *A* had painted another picture of sunflowers entitled "Sunflowers II," and *A* subjectively was referring to this painting in the contract. *C* had the first "Sunflowers" in mind. Since *C* mentioned that he had seen the painting in February, *A* should have known that *C* was referring to the first "Sunflowers." Therefore, a contract exists, and for the first Sunflowers.

On the other hand, if neither party was at fault in the misunderstanding, the lack of agreement on which painting was intended would be great enough to cause the contract to be void for misunderstanding.

CHAPTER 3

CONSIDERATION

ChapterScope

This chapter describes the next important element to look for after you have identified a valid offer and acceptance: consideration. In brief, consideration is a "bargained-for-exchange for something of legal value."

■ **Consideration is required:** If either party to a contract has not given consideration, the agreement is *unenforceable* unless it falls under one of the exceptions covered in the next chapter.

■ **Definition of consideration:** A promise is supported by consideration if *two* requirements are met:

  [1] The promis*ee* (the party who's receiving the promise being analyzed) *gave up something of value*, or *circumscribed her liberty* in some way. (This is called the *"legal detriment"* requirement.)

  [2] The promisor made his promise as part of a *"bargain"*; that is, he made his promise *in exchange* for the promisee's giving of value or circumscribing of liberty. (This is the *"bargain"* requirement.)

■ **Mutuality of consideration:** *Each party* is required to furnish consideration to the other. So if *A*'s promise is not supported by consideration from *B*, then not only is *A* not bound, *B* is not bound either. This is the called the requirement of *"mutuality of consideration."*

I. INTRODUCTION

A. **Consideration as a requirement for a contract:** It is often said that for there to be a binding contract, there must be not only "mutual assent" (i.e., the offer and acceptance, discussed previously), but also something known as "consideration." This chapter describes what "consideration" is. At the outset, however, you should be aware that consideration is *not* required in all contracts. Chapter 4, in fact, describes several sorts of contracts which are enforceable even though there is no consideration; these include contracts made under seal, promises which induce substantial reliance, and promises to pay for benefits received.

   1. **Look for consideration first:** You should, however, first determine whether the contract is supported by consideration. It is only if it is not so supported that the exceptions to the consideration requirement become relevant.

B. **Purpose of consideration doctrine:** Not all promises are legally enforceable. Promises to make gifts, for example, are not usually enforceable. The function of the consideration doctrine is to distinguish between those promises that are enforceable and those that are not. As a general rule, a court will not enforce a promise unless the promisee has given "consideration" for the promise.

1. **Functions of consideration doctrine:** The requirement that a promise, to be binding, must be supported by consideration serves two primary functions:

   a. **Evidentiary function:** The existence of consideration helps to provide *objective evidence* that the parties intended to make a binding agreement. It helps courts distinguish those agreements that were intended by the parties to be legally enforceable from promises which were intended merely as obligations of honor, promises of gifts which neither party expected to be enforceable in court, or any other arrangement as to which the parties did not contemplate legal consequences.

   b. **Cautionary function:** The requirement that promises be supported by consideration serves a *cautionary function* as well. If the parties are aware that the providing of consideration by one will make the other's promise enforceable, the parties may *act more carefully*, and will be less likely to make thoughtless or bad bargains or mistakes. Conversely, parties may take fewer precautions during negotiations because they know that their statements will not be not enforceable in the absence of consideration; fewer precautions during the initial stages of the bargaining process will in turn reduce transaction costs.

C. **Definition:** A promise is supported by consideration if two things are true:

   [1] The promisee *gives up something of value*, or circumscribes his liberty in some way. (If the promisee does either of these things, he's said to suffer a *"legal detriment."*)

   AND

   [2] The promisor makes his promise as part of a *"bargain"*; that is, he makes his promise *in exchange* for the promisee's legal detriment (i.e., in exchange for the promisee's giving of value or circumscription of liberty).

1. **More about "legal detriment":** What qualifies as the *"legal detriment"* (the "something of value or circumscription of liberty") that the promisee must exchange for the promisor's promise? The detriment can consist of *any of the following* kinds of things:

   ❏ an *act* by the promisee.

   Example: Promisor promises to pay $100 if Promisee actually walks across the Brooklyn Bridge. Promisee does the walk. The act of walking is consideration for Promisor's promise to pay $100.

   ❏ a *forbearance* by the promisee.

   Example: Promisor promises to pay $100 if Promisee refrains from smoking for the next month. Promisee in fact refrains. Promisee's forbearance from smoking is consideration for Promisor's promise to pay $100.

   ❏ a *return promise* by the promisee.

   Example: Promisor promises to pay $100 if Promisee promises now to walk across the Brooklyn Bridge next Saturday. Promisee makes this promise. Promisee's making of the promise to walk is consideration for Promisor's promise to pay $100.

   ❏ an act, forbearance or return promise by a *third person* (someone other than the promisee).

Example: Promisor promises Promisee that if Promisee's sister Sue paints Promisor's house, Promisor will pay Promisee $100. Even though Sue is not the promisee, her act of painting will be consideration for Promisor's promise to pay Promisee the $100.

❏ A promise or act by the promisee, delivered ***to a third person***, rather than to the promisor.

Example: Promisor promises $100 to Merchant, if Merchant delivers $100 in groceries to Son, Promisor's son. Merchant delivers. The fact that the bargained-for performance is rendered to one other than Promisor does *not* prevent Merchant's delivery to Son from being consideration for Promisor's promise to pay $100.

See generally Rest. 2d, § 71.

D. Two kinds of problems: The two aspects of the consideration definition (i.e., the "bargain" aspect and the "legal detriment" aspect) correspond to two very different kinds of cases in which consideration problems arise:

❏ The ***"bargain"*** aspect is mainly important in situations that ***do not involve business dealings***, such as a ***promise to make a gift***.

❏ The ***"legal detriment"*** aspect is mainly important in business-related contracts where it is not clear that one party has ***really given anything up.*** An example of this would be a deal between a debtor and creditor whereby the creditor promises more time to pay, but the debtor does not promise anything except that he will make the payment he was originally required to make.

We consider the scenarios raising the "bargain" issue first.

II. THE BARGAIN ELEMENT — GIFT PROMISES

A. The bargain element generally: For a promise to be supported by consideration, the promisee's "detriment" must have been ***bargained for*** by the promisor. One of the principal purposes of the "bargain" requirement is to ***prevent the enforcement of promises that are in reality promises to make gifts***.

1. **"Bargain" defined:** The Second Restatement defines "bargain" this way: "A performance or return promise is bargained for if it is ***sought*** by the promisor ***in exchange*** for his promise and is ***given*** by the promisee ***in exchange*** for that promise." Rest. 2d, § 71(2).

B. Ordinary gift cases: In the ordinary case of a promise to make a gift, the promise fails to be enforceable for lack of consideration not only because the promise is not part of a bargain, but also because no "legal detriment" is suffered by the promisee.

Example: *A* says to *B*, "I promise to pay you $1,000 next year." *A*'s promise fails to be supported by consideration (and is therefore unenforceable) in two respects. First, *A* did not make his promise as part of a bargain; that is, he was not attempting to obtain anything from *B*. Secondly, *B* suffered no "legal detriment."

1. **Bargains vs. conditional gifts:** In some cases involving promises of gifts, however, the promisee undergoes a detriment, and there is a lack of consideration for the promise only because of a lack of a bargain. These cases are typically ones in which the promisee must

meet certain **conditions** in order to receive the gift, but the meeting of these conditions is not really "bargained for" by the promisor, i.e., the meeting of the conditions is not the promisor's motive for making the promise.

Example: *A* promises his widowed sister-in-law *B* a place to live "if you will come down and see me." In response to this promise, *B* travels to see *A*, thereby incurring expenses. *A* then refuses to make good on his promise. *B* has suffered a "legal detriment" (the expenses) sufficient to meet the legal detriment requirement for consideration. But *A* did not promise *B* a place to live because he wanted to see her; that is, he was not "bargaining" for a visit from his sister-in-law by promising her a place to live. Instead, her coming to see him was simply a necessary pre-condition of her accepting the gift. Therefore, *A*'s promise is unenforceable. *Kirksey v. Kirksey*, 8 Ala. 131 (1845).

Note: In situations like that in *Kirksey*, where the promisee suffers substantial detriment preparing to accept a promise which turns out to be unenforceable for lack of consideration, the court may apply the doctrine of **promissory estoppel**. This doctrine (discussed *infra*, p. 136) provides, in brief, that where a promisor makes an unenforceable promise which induces substantial reliance by the promisee, the promisor may be required to reimburse the promisee's reliance expenses.

2. **Test for distinguishing bargains from pre-conditions:** To determine whether the condition for accepting a gift is bargained for or not, ask whether the occurrence of the condition is of **benefit to the promisor**. 1 Williston § 112. In the above example, for instance, you should ask whether the sister-in-law's visit to the promisor was something the promisor actively desired. If so, the promisee's action was probably "bargained for." If not, the promisee's action was merely a necessary pre-condition.

   a. **Question of fact:** This will, of course, often be a difficult question of fact. Thus in the "sister-in-law case" above, the court would have to look at whether the promisor really liked his sister-in-law and wanted her around, or was simply doing her a favor which would bring him no particular pleasure. Had he said to her "I'll give you a place to live if you will come see me and be my housekeeper," the result would obviously have been different, since there would be indications of a bargain. C&P, p. 176.

3. **Non-economic benefits:** A bargain may be present even though the promisor does not receive any **economic benefit** from the transaction.

   Example: A promises his nephew $5,000 if the latter will refrain from smoking, drinking and gambling until he reaches the age of 21. The nephew so abstains.

   Held, the uncle's promise was "bargained for," and therefore supported by consideration. While the uncle may have derived no actual economic benefit from his nephew's abstinence, he was clearly attempting to obtain something he regarded as desirable (his nephew's health, morality, etc.), and was therefore bargaining. See *Hamer v. Sidway*, 124 N.Y. 538 (1891). See also C&P, p. 176. Another aspect of this case, involving the "detriment" issue, is discussed *infra*, pp. 94.

a. **Altruistic pleasure not sufficient:**   But the fact that one who promises to make a gift expects to derive *altruistic pleasure*, or love and affection, from making the gift is *not* sufficient to constitute a "bargain."

Example: *A* promises *B* a gift of $1,000, saying to *B,* "I believe that it is more blessed to give than to receive, and it would give me great Christian happiness to have you accept my gift." Because *A*'s intent is clearly donative, the "bargain" element of consideration is lacking, and his promise is unenforceable. A court is highly unlikely to hold that the pleasure *A* receives out of gift-making is something that he is bargaining for.

i. **"Motive" not dispositive:**   However, if there are any substantial indications that some kind of bargaining took place, the bargain element is met even though other evidence indicates that the promisor had an overriding, altruistic, motive for doing the bargaining. That is, the court does not look to whether the promisor's deep and ultimate objective was charitable or otherwise, but simply checks to see whether there are *some aspects of a bargain.*

Example: Testator tells several witnesses that he wants his wife, P, to have the use of his house for the rest of her life; he then dies, and his will contains no such bequest. His executors, the Ds, sign an agreement with P whereby she is given a life estate in the house, in return for her promise that she will pay to the estate $100 per year in rent, and that she will keep the house in good repair. Courts will likely find the agreement is supported by consideration, even though the actual motive of the Ds may have been an altruistic desire to respect Testator's wishes.

ii. **Mixture of bargain and gift:**   The fact that only "some aspects of a bargain" are required means that where a transaction is a *mixture of a bargain and a gift,* the consideration requirement is *satisfied*. See Rest. 2d, § 71, Comment c. For instance, if one party promises to sell the other an item at a price that both parties recognize is a *large discount* to its market value, that promise is supported by consideration (in the form of the buyer's promise to pay, or actual payment of, the discounted price).

Example: *A* is a close friend of *B*. *B* has long admired *A*'s painting "Irises" by Picasso, which as both parties know has a market value of $200,000. *A* promises to sell "Irises" to *B* for $20,000, and *B* promises to buy it for that price. The contract is enforceable because each promise is supported by consideration, notwithstanding the presence of a significant "gift" element to the exchange. Cf. Rest. 2d, § 71, Illustr. 6.

4. **Business context does not negate donative intent:**   Even in a business context, a promise may occasionally be unenforceable because of lack of the requisite "bargaining."

Example: Landlord gives Tenant an "option" to renew tenant's lease. Relying on this promise to allow renewal, Tenant employs an architect to draw up plans to alter the premises, and pays the architect. Landlord's promise to allow renewal will be unenforceable for lack of consideration. Although Tenant has suffered a detriment (payment of the architect), Landlord did not "bargain" for this detriment. (Note, however, that a court might apply the doctrine of promissory estoppel [*infra*, p. 327] to allow Tenant to recover her expenditures.)

5.   **Absence of overt bargaining not fatal:**   Suppose the defendant can show that the plaintiff ***never overtly bargained*** for the defendant's promise to do something. Does that help the defendant establish that his performance was a gift, and was thus unsupported by consideration? The answer is ***"not necessarily,"*** especially in a business context. As long as the court concludes that D's promise ***induced*** P's promise or performance, the fact that D didn't expressly bargain in return for that promise won't matter.

> **Example:**   D gives P free recycled ash for use in a construction project. The ash turns out to be defective, so P sues D for breach of contract. D replies that it has no contractual obligations to P, because any promise it may have made (such as a warranty of non-defectiveness) was not supported by consideration from P. D says it merely made a gift of the ash on the condition that P come pick it up; D didn't explain why it wanted P to take away the ash, and didn't "bargain" for P's performance.
>
> *Held*, there *was* consideration if the reason D offered the ash for "free" was because it wanted someone else to come remove it, and thus save D the cost of disposing of the ash itself. The "bargain" theory of consideration does not mean the parties must *actually bargain* over the terms of the agreement—it just means the promise made by D and the detriment to P must *induce* each other. Here, P has alleged that D *wanted* P to come take the ash and benefited when P did so, and that that was why D made the offer. If P's allegation is true, consideration was present. *Pennsy Supply, Inc. v. American Ash Recycling Corp.*, 895 A.2d 595 (Pa. Sup. 2006).

C.   **Sham and nominal consideration:**   The parties to agreements that are essentially promises of gifts frequently recite that the agreement is made "in consideration of $1 paid," or some other small sum. While it is true that the law does not normally concern itself with the ***adequacy*** of consideration, provided that that consideration was truly bargained for (see *infra*, p. 95), the recital of purely nominal consideration is usually an ***indication that there was no bargain at all***, but rather, a gift.

> **Example:**   *A* says to *B*, "Because you are my friend, I promise to give you $1,000." *B*, aware that such promises are not binding without consideration, suggests to *A* that they draw up an agreement containing the promise, and also containing a statement that *B* has paid $1 "in consideration for *A*'s promise."
>
> Whether or not *B* has actually paid *A* the $1, it is clear from the facts that *A* did not really give his promise "in exchange" for *B*'s dollar. Therefore, *A*'s promise is unenforceable. It is unenforceable not because *B* has failed to suffer a detriment (even the payment of $1, or the promise to pay $1, could be sufficient detriment) but because the facts indicate that there was no bargain, just an attempt to make a gratuitous promise enforceable by cloaking it in the form of a bargain. Rest. 2d, § 71, Comment d and Illustr. 5.

D.   **Importance of whether recited consideration was actually paid:**   Where the agreement recites that a particular form of consideration has been given, that recital may of course be ***false***. Under what circumstances may the party resisting enforcement show the falsity of the consideration? And if she is permitted to make such a showing, what effect will the showing have? These issues usually arise in the context of a recital that a particular sum of money has been paid; it is on this typical fact setting that we focus.

1. **Right to make showing:** Most courts will *allow* the party resisting enforcement to show that the recited consideration was never paid. A few courts, however, hold that such a showing may not be made, either on the theory that the parties are "estopped from contradicting the writing" or on the theory that the recital of consideration gives rise to an implied promise by the promisee to pay it. See C&P, p. 177.

2. **Significance of showing:** But even in courts following the majority rule, and thus allowing a showing that the consideration was not paid, such a showing will *not necessarily mean that there is no consideration.* The underlying issue is always *was there a bargain*? — the truth or falsity of a recital that consideration was paid is merely *nondispositive evidence* on this issue. Thus if other evidence shows that there was in reality a bargain, the fact that the recited sum was never paid will not generally render the contract unenforceable.

   Example: D signs an agreement stating that P has lent D $2,000. But the actual loan is approximately $25. *Held*, P may recover the full $2,000, because there was in reality a bargain despite the falsity of the recital of consideration. *Batsakis v. Demotsis*, 226 S.W.2d 673 (Tex. Civ. App. 1949). (The case is discussed more extensively *infra*, p. 96.)

   a. **Close cases:** In close cases, the recital may make a difference. This is especially likely to happen where it is *unclear whether there was a bargain or not.* For instance, suppose that in *Kirksey v. Kirksey, supra*, p. 88, the brother-in-law had promised in writing, "In consideration of your coming down and seeing me, I will give you a place to live." This recital might well have been enough to induce the court to find that the brother-in-law was bargaining for the visit, rather than merely setting a condition whose fulfillment he did not actively desire. See Farnsworth, p. 89.

E. **Promisee must be aware of promise:** If the promisee is *not aware* of the promise, any act she performs is obviously not *bargained for*. For this reason, most courts hold that where a *reward* is promised for a certain act, and the act is performed without the actor being aware of the reward, she cannot recover.

   Example: D offers a reward of $500 to anyone who captures escaped prisoner. P captures the prisoner and returns him to jail, without having been aware of the existence of the reward.

   Held, D's promise of a reward was not supported by consideration. (Apparently this was because P and D could not be said to have "bargained" together.) *Broadnax v. Ledbetter*, 99 S.W. 1111 (Tex. 1907).

   Note: The holding in *Broadnax* was also based on the law of offer and acceptance, i.e., that since P never knew of the offer, he could not be said to have accepted it, and therefore no contract ever existed. See the discussion of the requirements for a valid acceptance, *supra*, p. 18.

F. Consideration doctrine not applicable to executed gifts: It is only the *promise* to make a gift, not the making of the gift, that is unenforceable for lack of consideration. That is, *once the promisor makes the gift*, she *cannot rescind it* for lack of consideration. Thus it is critical to distinguish between "executed" gifts (which cannot be undone, and as to which the consideration doctrine is irrelevant) and "executory" gifts (i.e., promises to make a gift), which are unenforceable for lack of consideration. See Emanuel on *Property* for the elements required to complete a gift.

III. THE BARGAIN ELEMENT — "PAST CONSIDERATION"

A. "Past consideration" not sufficient: Another kind of situation in which the "bargain" is missing (and where there is therefore no consideration) is that in which the promise is made in return for detriment *previously* suffered by the promisee. Where the detriment has been suffered before the promise is made, it is obviously not "bargained for" by the promisor.

1. "Past consideration" a misnomer: In such situations, the detriment occurring before the promise is frequently called *"past consideration,"* and the court then often makes a statement such as *" 'past consideration' is not valid consideration."* Such a statement is *true*. That is, the term "past consideration" is a misnomer, since it is not consideration at all.

> **Example:** P, a middle-age woman, has worked for D Corp. for 37 years. The corporation passes a resolution that P be given the right to retire at any time with a $200 per month lifetime pension. P continues to work for a few more years, then retires and receives the pension for a number of years. After the founder of D dies, the pension is cut off, and P sues.
>
> *Held*, the services performed by P prior to the awarding of the pension rights were not the consideration for those rights, since "past services are not a valid consideration for a promise." Furthermore, the fact that P worked for a couple of years between the time she had the right to receive the pension and the time she actually retired was not consideration for the pension rights; it was clear that she had had the right to retire and draw the pension as soon as the promise of it was made. (In other words, her additional years of work were not bargained for.)
>
> But because P *relied* to her detriment on the promise (by choosing to retire when she could have gone on working), the promise will be enforced under the doctrine of *promissory estoppel*. This doctrine, and a further discussion of this case, are presented *infra*, pp. 136 and 141. *Feinberg v. Pfeiffer Co.*, 322 S.W.2d 163 (St. L. Ct. App., Mo. 1959).

B. Pre-existing debt: A sub-category of the rule that "'past consideration' does not constitute consideration" relates to situations in which the promisor promises to pay a *pre-existing debt*. Suppose, for instance, that *A* once owed *B* $1,000, but the running of the statute of limitations now prevents *B* from collecting this debt. *A* then promises to pay the debt. Most courts hold that there is *no consideration* for *A*'s promise, since he has not bargained for anything (he obviously received the original loan before making the promise). Variations on this "promise to pay a pre-existing debt" problem are discussed as part of our treatment of the "pre-existing duty rule," *infra*, p. 101.

1. **Possibly binding without consideration:** By the way, many courts hold that this sort of "promise to pay a pre-existing debt" is enforceable *even without consideration*. See *infra*, p. 127.

C. **Promise to pay for past services received:** Similarly, a promise to pay for *services received in the past* is usually held not to be supported by consideration.

> **Example:** D's son, a 25-year-old, becomes ill while traveling, and is nursed by P. D writes to P, promising to pay P's expenses.
>
> *Held*, D's promise was not supported by consideration, since P's services were not given at D's request. (Also, since the son had long since left home, his own request for assistance should not be imputed to his father.) *Mills v. Wyman*, 3 Pick. 207 (Mass. 1825).

1. **Possibly binding without consideration:** Again, however, certain types of promises to pay for past services or benefits received may be binding without consideration. For instance, if the son in *Mills* had been a minor (for whom the father was still responsible), the court would probably have held the promise binding. Situations in which such promises to pay for past benefits are enforceable without consideration are discussed *infra*, p. 129. See particularly *Webb v. McGowin, infra*, p. 130 and Rest. 2d, § 86.

Quiz Yourself on
THE BARGAIN ELEMENT

20. George Washington's friend Benny Arnold tells him, "If you walk across the street with me now and go into the hardware store, I'll buy you an axe." Washington crosses the street and enters the store. Arnold reneges. Has Arnold breached a contract?

21. Lion Hart is walking through the woods when he steps on a thorn. He languishes in pain for hours, screaming. Furdley Naturelover walks by and sees Lion's predicament. Acting as a good samaritan, without any expectation of payment, Furdley removes the thorn. Lion, immensely relieved, says, "Boy, am I grateful. I'm going to send you $1,000 a month as long as I live." Is Lion's promise supported by consideration?

22. Alexander the Great throws a birthday party for his mom, Mrs. the Great. In between mouthfuls of cake and ice cream, washed down with cheap champagne, Alexander writes on a sheet of his stationery, "In consideration of today being Mom's birthday, I promise to give her Italy." Mrs. the Great's eyes light up. Is Alex's promise enforceable?

Answers

20. **No, because there was no consideration, and promises without consideration are generally unenforceable.** These facts highlight the difference between: (a) consideration, and (b) a condition on a gift. In these kinds of cases, you have to look at whether the detriment in question is something the promisor *bargained* for (a requirement for consideration). In other words, did the promisee's detriment *motivate* the promisor to make the promise? Here, Arnold wasn't really motivated by a desire to have Washington

cross the street and enter the store; instead, these acts were merely a condition to facilitate Arnold's making of the purchase. Since Arnold didn't bargain for Washington's crossing the street, there was no consideration for Arnold's promise. Therefore, that promise was an unenforceable promise to make a gift.

21. **No.** Consideration requires a bargained-for exchange. If the promisee's detriment occurred *before* the promise was made, then the promisor could not have bargained for that detriment. Here, Furdley has already performed by pulling out the thorn, so his performance wasn't bargained for in exchange for Lion's promise to pay him $1,000 a month. As such, Lion's promise is not supported by consideration. (But the promise might be enforceable without consideration, especially if Furdley somehow relied on the promise; see the next chapter.)

22. **No,** unfortunately for Mrs. the Great. Promises are generally not enforceable without consideration. In order for consideration to exist, the promisor, Alex, has to bargain for a benefit to him (or detriment to the promisee) in exchange for his promise. Although he uses the word "consideration" here, his words are a statement of sentiment, not a recital of legal consideration — he's not bargaining for anything from his mother in return for his promise. Since there's no bargain, there's no consideration to back up Alex's promise, and it's unenforceable.

IV. THE "DETRIMENT" ELEMENT GENERALLY

A. **The "detriment" aspect of consideration:** We turn now to the other aspect of the consideration requirement, i.e., that not only must there be a bargain, but that the promisee must undergo a "detriment" of a sort that the law recognizes as adequate. Some courts say that this detriment must be "legal detriment," but this label is merely conclusory; the courts have developed rules, outlined below, concerning what sort of value given by the promisee constitutes the requisite detriment.

B. **"Detriment" idea summarized:** The "detriment" idea is, broadly, that the promisee must *do something he does not have to do*, or *refrain from doing something that he had a right to do*.

1. **Non-economic "detriments":** A detriment may be sufficient to constitute consideration even though it involves no economic disadvantage to the person involved, and even if, indeed, it aids him morally, physically, or spiritually. *As long as the party has circumscribed his freedom of action*, she has incurred sufficient detriment, regardless of whether there is "harm" to him in the commonly-accepted sense.

    Example: Recall *Hamer v. Sidway, supra,* p. 88, in which Uncle promised Nephew $5,000 if the latter would refrain from drinking, gambling, etc. Nephew, by so refraining, did not suffer any economic harm, and probably even benefited morally and physically. However, because he circumscribed his freedom of action, his forbearance was the kind of "detriment" that was sufficient to constitute consideration for Uncle's promise. Therefore, Uncle's promise was enforceable. Another way of looking at it is that Uncle "benefited" by Nephew's forbearance, and this benefit was sufficient to satisfy the "detriment" requirement.

C. **Consideration may be either promise or performance:** The "detriment" given or suffered by the promisee may be either a promise or a performance. If the detriment is a performance, the contract is of the kind traditionally called "unilateral." If the detriment is a promise, the contract is "bilateral."

Example: *A* says to *B*, "I promise to pay you $10 if you'll sell me that book." By the language of his offer, *B* has a choice between accepting by a promise and accepting by performance. (See *supra*, p. 21; see also UCC § 2-206(1)(a).) If *B* says "All right, I promise to sell you the book," he has furnished consideration for *A*'s promise by his own promise to deliver the book. If, on the other hand, he simply takes the book and hands it to *A* saying "It's yours for $10," he has furnished consideration by performance.

> **Note:** As a general rule, a promise can be a sufficient detriment if and only if the performance that has been promised would be a sufficient detriment. See Rest. 2d, § 75.

D. Where issue arises: Among situations in which the adequacy of the detriment arises are the following, all of which are discussed in this chapter:

[1] Where the promisee *forbears from suing on a claim*, in return for the promisor's counter-promise to pay a *settlement*;

[2] Where a creditor promises to accept a *smaller sum than is actually owed*, in discharge of the debtor's debt;

[3] Where the promisee performs or promises to perform a thing which she was *already legally obligated to do*;

[4] Where the promisee reserves power to *determine the extent of his own performance* (as in requirements and output contracts); and

[5] Where the promisee makes a promise that is *conditional upon the happening of some future event.*

E. Court will not inquire into "adequacy" of the detriment: There are some situations in which the parties exchange things that do not have roughly equivalent value. This may be due to the donative intent of the parties, to the fact that one party is more ignorant than the other, to the fact that the parties are mistaken, etc. In such situations, as long as the promisee suffers *some detriment*, no matter how small, the court will not find consideration lacking merely because what the promisee gave up was of *much less value* than what he received. As Rest. 2d, § 79, puts it, "If the requirement of consideration is met, there is no additional requirement of…(b) equivalence in the values exchanged." Or as the idea is often stated, *"the court will not inquire into the adequacy of the consideration."*[1]

> **Example:** During World War II, P, a Greek resident, lends D, also a Greek resident, 500,000 drachmae, at the time worth $25. In return for the loan, P requires D to sign a promissory note for $2,000, payable at the end of the War. After the War, P sues to collect the $2,000; D defends on the grounds that there was a failure of consideration for the note.
>
> *Held*, P is entitled to recover the $2,000 recited in the note. The transaction amounted to a sale by P to D of the 500,000 drachmae in return for signing of the

---

1. Remember, we're talking here only about the "detriment" requirement; recall that extreme lack of equivalent value may indicate that the *bargain* element is not satisfied; see *supra*, p. 90.

instrument. D got exactly what she bargained for. "Mere inadequacy of consideration will not void a contract." *Batsakis v. Demotsis*, 226 S.W.2d 673 (Tex. Civ. App. 1949), *supra,* p. 91.

Note: The promissory note in *Batsakis* actually contained a recital that D had received from P the $2,000 which she was promising to repay. Observe that the *Batsakis* court followed the majority rule, allowing D to present evidence that she never in fact received the $2,000. That is, the court permitted demonstration of the falsity of the recital of consideration. But the court also followed the majority path in another respect, in that it found that despite the falsity of the recital of consideration, there was an actual bargain. See *supra*, p. 90, for a more complete discussion of the general rule that the falsity of a recital of consideration will not prevent consideration from being found as long as the bargain and detriment elements are satisfied by the actual (as opposed to the recited) deal.

1. **Minor effort or other thing of non-monetary value:**   The principle that courts will not acquire into the adequacy of the consideration means that consideration can consist of the promisee's doing something that requires *only a tiny bit of effort and has no financial value.* For instance, the promisee's effort in *clipping a coupon* or *filling out a contest entry form* — even though this effort is minimal and has no monetary value — will typically be *enough* to constitute consideration for the other side's promise.

   Example: Suppose D, an auto manufacturer, displays an online contest-entry form that says, "Fill out this form, and if your entry is drawn, you'll get a brand new D-mobile plug-in electric Model T worth $40,000." P sees the form, spends 30 seconds filling it out online, and is lucky enough to have his entry selected. D then refuses to deliver the car, defending on the grounds that its promise is not binding because P did not furnish consideration for that promise. P sues to enforce the award.

   P would almost certainly win. A court would almost certainly hold that P's act of spending even 30 seconds filling out the form — and identifying himself to D for, say, marketing purposes — constituted consideration sufficient to support D's promise of a car to the winner.

2. **Equity courts have different rule:**   Courts of *equity*, as opposed to courts of law, have traditionally been much more *willing to examine the adequacy of consideration* for a contract. Equity courts have traditionally been in charge of actions for *specific performance* (see *infra*, p. 311), *injunctions*, etc. Therefore, when the action is for equitable relief, the court will often deny relief to a party whom they believe to have *thrust an unfair bargain* on his adversary.

   Example: P is a wealthy and sophisticated land owner. He helps the Ds, a couple with limited financial means and business know-how, to buy 80 acres of resort land near P's property. P promises the Ds some help in getting business for the resort they plan to establish, and also makes them a loan of $5,000, which they use in buying the property. In return, the Ds promise that they will not cut down trees on the property, or build any new buildings closer to P's property than the present buildings. These restrictions are to last for 25 years. The resort is not successful, and the Ds wish to add a trailer park and tent camp; to do this, they invest $9,000 in putting in utilities and buying bulldozing equipment. P then sues to enjoin them from making these improvements, arguing that this would violate their promise.

Held, imposition of these restrictions would be extremely burdensome to the Ds, a burden which far outweighs the value of the $5,000 loan (which was repaid), and the small amount of business which P helped the Ds get. Furthermore, P would not be able to see the camp from his home. Therefore, the agreement is "unfair and based upon inadequate consideration," and the injunction will be denied. *McKinnon v. Benedict*, 157 N.W.2d 665 (Wis. 1968).

a. **Separate equity courts abolished:** The vast majority of states no longer maintain a separate system of equity courts apart from their law courts. Instead, a single trial system administers *both* legal claims (e.g., a claim for damages based on breach of contract) as well as equitable claims (specific performance, injunction, etc.) Nonetheless, courts are still somewhat more likely to inquire into the "adequacy" of the consideration where the claim is one that historically would have been considered equitable rather than legal.

3. **Inadequacy of consideration as evidence of fraud, duress, unconscionability, etc.:** While a law court will not take into account whether the things exchanged by the parties are roughly equivalent for purposes of determining whether consideration is present, a gross inequality between the two things exchanged may be evidence of *fraud, duress, unconscionability*, or *mistake*. See Rest. 2d, § 79, Comment c.

a. **Duress:** For instance, in *Batsakis v. Demotsis, supra*, p. 91, D might have made a quite plausible argument that whether or not there was consideration, her promise was void for *duress*. In support of this argument, she could have contended that there was widespread starvation and other suffering in Greece during the War (see Dawson and Harvey, pp. 167-68), and that P took unfair advantage of D's utter desperation.

   i. **Probably fails:** However, this argument probably would *fail* in today's courts, because P was not in any way responsible for D's predicament. As the Second Restatement's materials on duress put it, "Parties are generally held to the resulting agreement, even though one has taken advantage of the other's adversity, as long as the contract has been dictated by **general economic forces**." Rest. 2d, § 176, Comment f.

b. **Unconscionability:** Similarly, where the value of the things exchanged by the parties is grossly unequal, the court may, although it will not inquire into "the adequacy of the consideration," hold that the agreement is void because it is *"unconscionable."* The notion of unconscionability, which originated with the courts of equity, is now embodied in UCC § 2-302. § 2-302(1) provides that "if the court as a matter of law finds the contract or any clause of the contract to have been unconscionable at the time it was made the court may refuse to enforce the contract...." Unconscionability will be discussed in a subsequent chapter (see *infra*, p. 478). It is important to note, however, that the voiding of a contract for unconscionability has nothing to do with the consideration doctrine.

V. THE PRE-EXISTING DUTY RULE

A. The pre-existing duty rule generally: If a party does or promises to do what she is *already legally obligated* to do, or if she forbears or promises to forbear from doing something which she is not legally entitled to do, she has not incurred the kind of "detriment" necessary for her performance or forbearance to constitute consideration. This is the so-called *"pre-existing duty"* rule.

1. **Exceptions:** The courts have, however, shown much ingenuity in creating exceptions and limitations to the pre-existing duty rule, many of which we will be discussing below. The UCC has gone even further — it has essentially abolished the rule.

2. **Two party and three party cases:** The courts distinguish between those cases in which the promise to perform a pre-existing duty is made to the person to whom the duty is owed (the so-called *"two party"* cases) and those in which the promise to do the duty is made to some third person, not the person to whom the duty was owed (the *"three party"* cases). We shall first consider the "two party" cases. (The three party case are discussed *infra*, p. 105.)

B. General pre-existing duty rule in two party cases: Most courts hold that where one person promises another that he will do what he is *already legally obligated to do* for that other person, this promise is *not a "detriment" sufficient to satisfy the consideration requirement*.

1. **Promise to modify:** The pre-existing duty rule means that if parties to an existing contract agree to *modify* the contract *for the sole benefit for one of them,* the modification will usually be unenforceable at common law, for lack of consideration.

2. **Deterring hold-up behavior:** A key reason for the pre-existing duty rule as applied to contract modifications is that courts want to *deter "hold-up"* behavior, by which one party attempts to *take unfair advantage* of the other by threatening not to live up to his obligations.

> **Example:** The Ps, a group of workmen, sign contracts at a fixed rate to work on D's ship during the salmon canning season, as the ship goes from San Francisco to Alaska and back. When the ship arrives in Alaska, the men tell D that they will not do any more work unless D gives them a very substantial increase in salary. Since D has nowhere to get replacement men, it agrees; the Ps work on the way back to San Francisco. D then refuses to pay the extra money, and the Ps sue.
>
> *Held*, for D. The agreement to pay the extra money was without consideration, since by agreeing to work on the way back to San Francisco, the Ps were simply agreeing to do what they were already bound to do under the contract. Furthermore, the Ps' conduct was coercive. *Alaska Packers Ass'n v. Domenico*, 117 F. 99 (9th Cir. 1902).

3. **Construction contracts:** One situation in which the pre-existing duty rule often arises is the case of *construction contracts*.

> **Example:** Contractor agrees to pave Owner's driveway for $5,000, the job to be completed by May 1. Halfway through the project, Contractor tells Owner, "I've gotten very busy. Increase the price to $6,000, or I'll have to finish 6 weeks late." Owner

says, "OK, I agree to pay you $6,000, now just finish on time." Contractor finishes on time, but Owner refuses to pay more than $5,000. Contractor sues for the extra $1,000.

Owner's promise to pay the extra $1,000 (a modification of the contract) will ***not be enforceable*** — the contract was modified to the sole benefit of Contractor, who was merely promising to do what he was already legally obligated to do. Therefore, he did not furnish consideration to support Owner's promise of the extra $1,000.

4. **Restatement view:** The Second Restatement is in accord with the majority of courts, in holding that an agreement to do what one is already legally obligated to do is not consideration. ***"Performance of a legal duty owed to a promisor which is neither doubtful nor the subject of honest dispute is not consideration...."*** (Rest. 2d, § 73).

5. **The "unforeseen circumstances" exception:** Most courts, and the Second Restatement, recognize an important *exception* to the pre-existing duty rule as applied in cases of modification: the rule does not bar a modification that's *fair* in light of an *unexpected change in circumstances.* Thus Rest. 2d, § 89(a) *makes a modification binding* if it is "fair and equitable in view of circumstances *not anticipated* by the parties when the contract was made."

> **Example:** Maher contracts with the city of Newport to collect garbage. Although the contract entitles Maher to $137,000 per year for five years, Maher twice requests an additional $10,000 per year from the city council, because his operating costs have substantially increased due to an unanticipated spurt of new dwelling units. After the additional payments are made, a citizen sues to have the additional payments refunded to the city.
>
> *Held,* the modification is enforceable. The modification was fair and equitable, voluntarily entered into, and motivated by events which were not anticipated at the time the original contract was created. *Angel v. Murray,* 332 A.2d 630 (R.I. 1974).

6. **Promissory estoppel:** If the party who benefits from the modification *changes position in reliance* on it, then the doctrine of *promissory estoppel* may apply, to make the modification binding even if it was not motivated by a major change in circumstances.

a. **Restatement:** Thus Rest. 2d, § 89(c) allows the use of promissory estoppel to make a modification binding "to the extent that justice requires enforcement in view of *material change of position* in reliance on the [modification]."

> **Example:** An apartment lease calls for rent of $10,000 per year. Because of war conditions, many vacancies occur, and the landlord, L, agrees to reduce the rent of the tenant, T, to $5,000. This reduced rent is paid and accepted for five years. L then sues for back rent of $5,000 per year for the five years.
>
> A court will likely hold that T does not owe the back rent — by staying in the apartment for five years in reliance on the promise of lower rent (rather than moving out to cheaper premises), T has qualified for promissory estoppel: justice requires enforcement of the modification, even though T did nothing in return for it that he wasn't already required to do. Cf. Rest. § 89, Illustr. 7. (But if the lease had more time to run, L would have the right to *prospectively* raise the rent back up to $10,000 per year, i.e., to withdraw the modification.)

7. **Where extra duties assumed:**   Another very important exception to the pre-existing duty rule in modification cases is this: if the party who promises to do what she is already bound to do assumes the ***slightest additional duties*** (or even ***different*** duties, with the new duties substituted for the old), her undertaking of these new duties ***does*** constitute the required "detriment." This may be the case even though the new performance promised is less burdensome than the old one.

> **Example:** Contractor agrees to build a house for Owner for $30,000. Midway through the job, Contractor realizes he's losing money, and threatens to walk off the job if Owner does not increase the price to $40,000. In return for this price increase, Contractor is willing to change the kind of fittings in the windows, as requested by Owner; this change will actually save Contractor money. Most courts would probably hold that the change of specifications, even though actually less burdensome to Contractor, constituted consideration for Owner's promise to pay more for the house.

a. **Where change is mere pretense:**   The "additional" or "different" duties promised by the person already legally bound must not, however, be merely a ***pretense*** for avoiding the pre-existing duty rule. As the Restatement Second puts it, "A performance [similar to that previously due] is consideration if it differs from what was required by the duty in a way which reflects more than a pretense of bargain." Rest. 2d, § 73.

8. **Duty owed to third person rather than to promisor:**   Another exception recognized by most modern courts is that the pre-existing duty rule does not apply where the promisee owes the pre-existing contractual duty ***to a third person*** rather than to the promisor. Rest. 2d, § 73, Comment d.

> **Example:** Parent's daughter Dee attends School, a private school. Parent makes the following promise to Teacher, Dee's teacher at School: "If Dee gets a 4 or 5 on the AP calculus exam at the end of the year, I will interpret this as being due in major part to your fine teaching, and I will pay you $1,000." School's policy allows teachers to collect such rewards from parents. Dee gets a 4, and Parent refuses to pay. Teacher sues, and Parent defends on the grounds that all Teacher did was the teaching she was already contractually required to do, so that Parent's promise was not supported by consideration on account of the pre-existing duty rule.
>
> In a court applying the prevailing modern approach, Parent will lose with this argument — because Teacher's pre-existing duty was owed to a third person (School) rather than to the promisor (Parent), the pre-existing duty rule does not apply, and Teacher's doing the teaching that produced the 4 was therefore "fresh" consideration for Parent's promise. Consequently, the promise was binding.

9. **Some states have rejected rule:**   Some states have simply ***repudiated the pre-existing duty rule***, and allow promises to modify contracts without any consideration at all. See, e.g., N.Y.G.O.L. § 5-1103, making a modification enforceable if it is in writing and is signed by the party against whom enforcement is sought.

a. **UCC changes the rule:**   In the case of contracts to sell goods, the UCC has in effect ***abolished the pre-existing duty rule***. It has done so by § 2-209(1), which provides that "an agreement modifying a contract within this article needs no consideration to be binding." There are some qualifications to this rule, including a duty of good faith and a requirement that if there is a no-oral-modification clause in the original written agreement, the modification must also be written. The UCC approach to modification is discussed more extensively *infra*, p. 131-132.

10. Rewards and bonuses: Outside of the modification context, a promise to pay a ***reward*** or ***bonus*** will be unenforceable under the pre-existing duty rule, if the promisee is already under a legal obligation to perform the act being rewarded.

> **Example:** Officer, employed by City, has the duty to investigate crimes and arrest the guilty. He learns of a reward offered by City for "information leading to the arrest and conviction of..." the person responsible for a particular robbery. Officer arrests a suspect, who is convicted. Officer won't be entitled to the reward, because there is no consideration for his act of making the arrest — he was only doing what his job already required him to co.

C. Agreements to accept part payment of debt in satisfaction of whole: A common application of the pre-existing duty rule involves a creditor's agreement to accept a payment by his debtor of *a lesser sum in satisfaction of the full debt*. Since the debtor owes the full amount, he is not by paying a partial amount doing anything that he was not already legally obligated to do. Therefore, most courts hold that *the creditor's promise not to require payment of the full amount is not binding, for lack of consideration*.

1. Extra time to pay: These courts also hold that a creditor's promise to allow the debtor *extra time to pay* is, similarly, not binding for lack of consideration.

2. Rule of *Foakes v. Beer*: These two rules (barring the enforceability of promises to take a lesser sum, and of promises to give more time to pay) follow what is often called the "rule of *Foakes v. Beer*," after the case set forth in the following example.

> **Example:** P obtains a judgment for £2,000 against D. The parties agree that P will accept in full satisfaction of this judgment £500 in cash and the rest in installments. D fully complies with this agreement, and the amount of the judgment is eventually completely paid off. P then brings suit for interest on the part of the judgment that was paid off in installments. D claims that the "installment payment plan" agreed to by P constituted a discharge of any obligation by D to pay the interest.
>
> *Held*, such an extended payment plan cannot constitute consideration for a promise of discharge, since D only promised what he was already obligated to do. *Foakes v. Beer*, 9 App. Cas. 605 (Eng. 1884).

3. Inroads on the rule of *Foakes v. Beer*:   Most courts and commentators feel that the rule of *Foakes v. Beer* serves no useful function, since it discourages what is frequently a useful commercial transaction, and breeds litigation. Therefore, in most jurisdictions the rule of *Foakes v. Beer*, although still followed, has been stripped to its barest bone: it applies only when the debtor makes part payment of an amount that is indisputably due, and due on the date that the part payment is made. If, in addition to making part payment, the debtor does any of the following things, he **has given consideration** for the discharge of the larger amount:

[a] the debtor **gives security** in addition to the part payment;

[b] she **refrains from bankruptcy** or insolvency proceedings which she would otherwise employ;

[c] she arranges for a **"composition agreement"** in which several creditors agree to take less than the full amount due them;

[d] she pays part of a claim the full amount of which is in *bona fide* **dispute** (see *infra*).

See C&P, pp. 212-13.

4. **Overruling of the *Foakes v. Beer* rule:** A few jurisdictions have simply ceased to follow the rule of *Foakes v. Beer*, and allow a creditor's promise to forgive part of a debt to be enforced where the debtor makes payment of the remainder, even if the debtor suffers no other kind of detriment.

5. **UCC also overrules:** UCC § 2-209(1), providing that "an agreement modifying a contract within this article needs no consideration to be binding," essentially **overrules the *Foakes v. Beer* doctrine.** That is, when the creditor agrees to take a partial payment in discharge of the full debt, he presumably has "modified" the contract. However, there are some potential "strings attached" to the use of this UCC modification provision; see *infra*, p. 132.

6. **Unliquidated or disputed debts:** The rule of *Foakes v. Beer* applies only to those debts as to which the parties are in agreement as to amount and liability (often called *liquidated* debts). If the debtor in good faith and not unreasonably disputes his *liability* on the debt, or if he reasonably and in good faith disputes the *amount of the debt* (an *"unliquidated"* debt), then a settlement by which the creditor agrees to take less than *he* thinks is due is enforceable.

    Example: Creditor asserts that Debtor owes him $1,000. Debtor claims, reasonably and in good faith, that he owes Creditor only $500. Creditor agrees to accept a $750 check in settlement of the debt. Debtor's payment of the $750, since it is payment on a claim whose amount is legitimately in dispute (i.e., an "unliquidated" debt), is a "detriment," and is consideration for Creditor's promise to discharge any part of the debt which might still be remaining. Therefore, Creditor cannot later sue for what he asserts is the balance due on his claim.

    The same result would be reached if Debtor denied that he had any liability to Creditor at all, but agreed to pay a certain sum in settlement. See Rest. 2d, § 73, Comment c.

7. **Detrimental reliance:** If the debtor can show that he has clearly **relied to his detriment** on the creditor's promise to discharge part of the debt, the court may decide to dispense with the requirement of consideration.

8. **Cashing of check tendered as settlement:** The above example assumes that the creditor agrees to a settlement of the debt disputed in good faith by the debtor. What frequently happens, however, is that the debtor simply **sends the creditor a check** for an amount less

than the creditor believes is due, and marks it *"payment in full"* or similar words. If the creditor then cashes the check, has she in effect made a promise to discharge the debtor from any additional obligation? Can the creditor prevent such a discharge by crossing out the words "payment in full" and writing something like "under protest"?

a. Common-law view: The common-law view was that even if the creditor writes the words "under protest" or "reservation of rights" on the check, her act of cashing it constitutes an enforceable discharge of the debtor. However, this rule was subject to several important exceptions, which we will not go into.

b. UCC in accord: Under modern law, the check-cashing problem is dealt with in the UCC, even in non-goods cases. This is done by a detailed provision, § 3-311. (Article 3 is the article dealing with negotiable instruments.) Most of the time, the creditor who cashes a check marked "in full settlement" or the like *will lose* under § 3-311, no matter what the creditor writes on the check.

§ 3-311 provides that the claim will be *discharged* by the cashing of the check (i.e., the *debtor will win*), if these three conditions are met:

❏ the check or accompanying written communication contained a *"conspicuous statement* to the effect that the instrument was tendered as full satisfaction of the claim," and

❏ the claim was either *"unliquidated"* or was "subjected to a *bona fide dispute*," and

❏ the debtor acted in *good faith.*

i. Right to return payment: There's an important exception that can hurt the debtor, though: the creditor has the right, within 90 days after cashing the check, to reverse the transaction by *paying the debtor back* the amount of the check; the creditor is thereby restored to the rights it had before cashing the check. § 3-311(c)(2).

ii. If creditor is an "organization": If the creditor is an *"organization"* (as opposed to an individual), the debtor must make an additional showing before getting the benefit of the "cashing the check discharges the claim" rule of § 3-311: she must show that "an *agent* of the [creditor] having direct responsibility with respect to the disputed obligation *knew* that the instrument was tendered in full satisfaction of the claim, or received the instrument and any accompanying communication."

(1) Rationale: The basic idea behind this "organization" clause is to make sure that the creditor will be found to have waived its rights only when an employee of the creditor with knowledge of the underlying transaction *knew* that the debtor was proposing an accord and satisfaction. This rule ensures that the debtor can't slip a fast one past a large creditor by sending the check to the creditor's accounts receivable department, where the overworked clerks will not notice the "in full settlement" language.

iii. Summary: So in cases of unliquidated or disputed claims, as long as the debtor follows the above simple rules, he will be *discharged* when the check is cashed, *no matter what the creditor writes on the check.*

iv. **Check from insurance company:** By the way, there is one context in which § 3-311 will work in favor of the large organization at the expense of the consumer (in contrast to the usual situation where the new rule favors the consumer/debtor): when an ***insurance company*** sends a check to an insured in settlement of a claim, and the insured cashes the check after writing "under protest" on it, the insured will be found to have accepted an accord and satisfaction.

v. **Enacted nearly everywhere:** Virtually all states and the District of Columbia have adopted § 3-311.

D. Extension agreements: Suppose a creditor agrees to give his debtor ***extra time*** in which to pay off a debt which both agree the debtor owes. Is the creditor's promise to forbear from bringing immediate suit on the debt supported by consideration? *Foakes v. Beer, supra,* p. 101, implies that such an extension agreement is not supported by consideration. But as in the part-payment situation discussed above, most modern courts try to avoid this result.

1. **Promise to pay interest:** If the debtor promises to pay ***interest*** for the period of forbearance, most courts agree that the creditor's promise of extra time to pay is supported by consideration:

   ❏ If the debtor agrees not only to pay interest, but also agrees that he does not have the right to ***pay off the debt before the end of the extension period*** (and thus does not have the right to terminate the running of interest), *all* courts agree that the creditor's promise of an extension is binding. See Rest. 2d, § 73, Illustr. 8.

   ❏ If no interest is promised (a relatively rare situation), many courts would probably still follow *Foakes v. Beer* and hold the agreement unenforceable for lack of consideration.

   See C&P, p. 201, n. 6.

E. Settlement of other kinds of suits: As we saw earlier, if the existence or amount of a monetary claim is in reasonable and *bona fide* dispute, a settlement will not be invalid for lack of consideration. A similar rule is usually applied to the settlement of other kinds of potential or pending litigation, such as ***tort suits***.

1. **Valid claim surrendered:** If a plaintiff promises to waive a ***valid claim***, all courts are in agreement that this promise is "detriment" to the plaintiff, and constitutes consideration for the defendant's promise to pay a settlement. See C&P, p. 180.

2. **Surrender of invalid claim:** If, on the other hand, the claim that the plaintiff promises to forbear from suing on is ***invalid*** (or of uncertain validity), things are trickier. But most of the time, even here the promise to forbear will be consideration for the return promise to pay.

   a. **Modern/Restatement view:** The modern view (represented by the Second Restatement) is that the forbearing plaintiff gives consideration if ***either:***

      ❏ the plaintiff's forborne claim is one ***whose validity is uncertain***, *or*

      ❏ the plaintiff ***subjectively believes*** that the forborne claim has possible merit (even if it doesn't in fact have any possible merit).

      See Rest. 2d, §§ 74(1)(a) and (b).

Example: Mary becomes pregnant. She honestly believes that Dave is the father. Before the baby is born, she orally promises not to sue Dave for child support if Dave will promise to pay her pre-birth medical expenses. Dave orally so agrees. The child is born, and a DNA test shows that Dave is not the father. Dave refuses to pay the medical expenses.

A court applying the modern/Restatement view would find that Dave's promise to pay the expenses was supported by consideration, because the child support claim that Mary was promising not to assert was one that she honestly — even though incorrectly — thought was valid. Therefore, Mary's promise to forbear from bringing the invalid claim was consideration for Dave's return promise to pay the medical expenses, and Dave's promise will be enforceable.

i.   **Execution of release:** Even if the would-be plaintiff who is forbearing from asserting her claim *does not subjectively believe* that the claim is valid, if the plaintiff *executes a written instrument settling the claim,* and the prospective defendant *bargained* for that instrument, in most states the instrument itself will be sufficient consideration for the defendant's counter-promise. Rest. 2d, § 74(2).

Example: Same basic facts as above Example, except that Mary never believes that Dave is the father. Dave, worried about a possible bad-faith paternity suit down the road from Mary, says to her while she's still pregnant, "If you will sign a document agreeing that I am not the father and promising never to sue me for child support, I will agree to pay your medical maternity expenses." Mary signs the agreement, but after a post-birth test shows that Dave could not be the father, he refuses to pay the medical expenses.

Even though the child-support claim that Mary was agreeing not to assert was invalid, and even though she did not believe it was valid, her execution of a written settlement agreement was by itself enough to constitute consideration for Dave's promise to pay expenses, and his promise will therefore be enforceable.

F.   **The "three party" pre-existing duty cases:** The pre-existing duty cases discussed above involve promises made between the two parties to the original contract. Where the promise to do what one is already obligated to do is made to a *stranger to the original contract*, however, the courts have been *more willing* to hold that the promise constitutes consideration.

Example: Contractor contracts with Sub-contractor to have the latter install heating units in a house being built by Contractor for Owner. Contractor becomes insolvent and discontinues work. Owner promises to pay Sub-contractor the price Sub-contractor would have received from Contractor, if Sub-contractor will complete the units.

Sub-contractor's completion of the units (or his promise to complete the units) is consideration for Owner's promise to pay Sub-contractor. This is so even though Sub-contractor was already contractually obligated (albeit to a now-insolvent party) to complete the units. There is consideration regardless of whether Owner's promise is to pay the same amount, or an increased amount. See Rest. 2d, § 73, Illustr. 11.

1.   **Rationale:** The reason that some courts and the Second Restatement give for abandoning the pre-existing duty rule where the promise to do one's duty is made to a stranger to the

Figure 3-1

Contract Modifications and Settlements, and the Pre-Existing Duty Rule

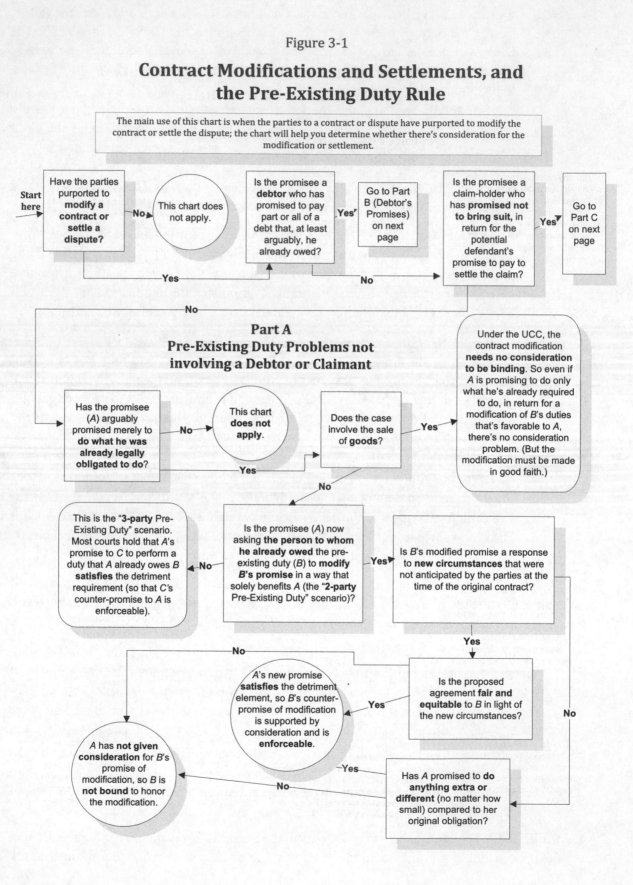

The main use of this chart is when the parties to a contract or dispute have purported to modify the contract or settle the dispute; the chart will help you determine whether there's consideration for the modification or settlement.

Start here → Have the parties purported to **modify a contract or settle a dispute?**

— No → This chart does not apply.

— Yes →

Is the promisee a **debtor** who has promised to pay part or all of a debt that, at least arguably, he already owed?

— Yes → Go to Part B (Debtor's Promises) on next page

— No →

Is the promisee a claim-holder who has **promised not to bring suit,** in return for the potential defendant's promise to pay to settle the claim?

— Yes → Go to Part C on next page

— No →

Part A
Pre-Existing Duty Problems not involving a Debtor or Claimant

Has the promisee (*A*) arguably promised merely to **do what he was already legally obligated to do?**

— No → This chart **does not apply**.

— Yes →

Does the case involve the sale of **goods**?

— Yes → Under the UCC, the contract modification **needs no consideration to be binding**. So even if *A* is promising to do only what he's already required to do, in return for a modification of *B*'s duties that's favorable to *A*, there's no consideration problem. (But the modification must be made in good faith.)

— No →

Is the promisee (*A*) now asking **the person to whom he already owed** the pre-existing duty (*B*) to **modify *B*'s promise** in a way that solely benefits *A* (the "2-party Pre-Existing Duty" scenario)?

— No → This is the "**3-party** Pre-Existing Duty" scenario. Most courts hold that *A*'s promise to *C* to perform a duty that *A* already owes *B* **satisfies** the detriment requirement (so that *C*'s counter-promise to *A* is enforceable).

— Yes →

Is *B*'s modified promise a response to **new circumstances** that were not anticipated by the parties at the time of the original contract?

— Yes →

Is the proposed agreement **fair and equitable** to *B* in light of the new circumstances?

— Yes →

A's new promise **satisfies** the detriment element, so *B*'s counter-promise of modification is supported by consideration and is **enforceable**.

— No →

Has *A* promised to **do anything extra or different** (no matter how small) compared to her original obligation?

— Yes → *A*'s new promise **satisfies** the detriment element...

— No → *A* has **not given consideration** for *B*'s promise of modification, so *B* is **not bound** to honor the modification.

Figure 3-1

Contract Modifications and Settlements, and the Pre-Existing Duty Rule (cont.)

Part B
Debtor's Promise of Payment in Return for Concession from Creditor

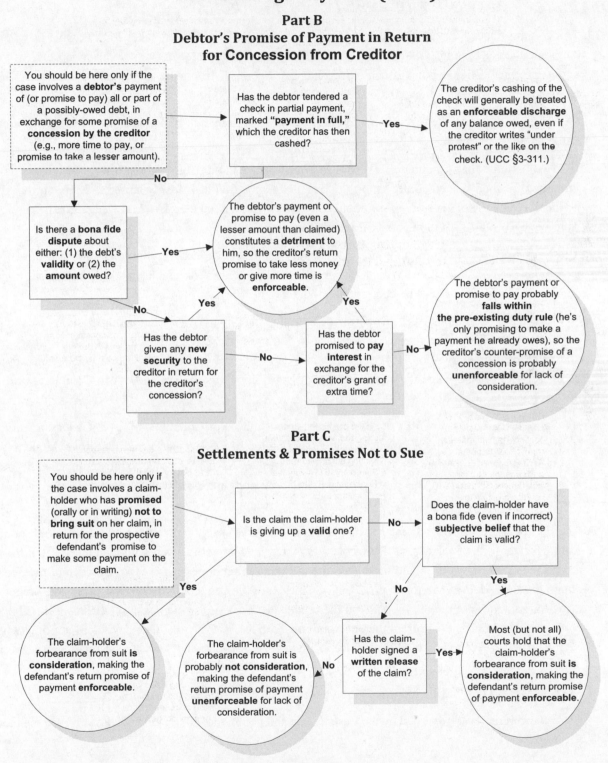

Part C
Settlements & Promises Not to Sue

original contract, is that "there is less likelihood of economic coercion or other unfair pressure than there is if the duty is owed to the promisee." (Rest. 2d, § 73, Comment d.)

Quiz Yourself on

DETRIMENT, AND THE PRE-EXISTING DUTY RULE

23. The Trianon Bakery has a contract with Marie Antoinette to deliver 1,000 cakes for a Bastille Day Party Antoinette is conducting. Trianon fails to deliver, and Antoinette threatens to sue. Trianon says, "If you agree not to sue, I'll give you a strand of priceless black pearls." Antoinette agrees, and accepts the pearls. Both parties reasonably believe that Antoinette's claim may be valid.

    (A) Assume that Antoinette's claim is in fact valid. Is Antoinette's promise not to pursue her claim enforceable?

    (B) Now assume that Antoinette's claim is invalid, because the jurisdiction just shortened the statute of limitation for food-related contracts to five days, and that period has already lapsed. Assume further that neither Antoinette nor Trianon knows about this change, and that their lack of knowledge is reasonable. Is Antoinette's promise not to pursue her claim enforceable?

24. The New World Cruise Company hires Christopher Columbus to perform a publicity stunt for them — Columbus promises to sail due West to discover America, in return for which New World promises to pay $5,000 on completion, plus a lifetime supply of dramamine.

    (A) Just before Columbus is set to sail, he decides that the payment isn't big enough, and refuses to go unless New World ups the ante. New World says, "OK, we'll also name the capital of Ohio after you if you're successful." Columbus agrees, sails, discovers America, and collects his $5,000 + dramamine. New World refuses to name the capital after him. Under common-law principles, can Columbus enforce this capital-naming promise?

    (B) Same facts, but assume that the original agreement called for Columbus to leave Genoa on April 1. Assume further that when Columbus balked at starting the trip, New World said that it would name the Ohio capital after Columbus if he left on March 30 instead of April 1, and successfully completed his mission. Columbus leaves on March 30, completes the mission, and now wants to compel New World to honor the capital-naming promise. Is that promise enforceable?

25. Charlie Tuna's Fish Shack contracts to buy 100 pounds of fresh salmon over the next month at $3 a pound from Chicken of the Sea, a fresh fish wholesaler. After the contract is entered into, an unexpected freeze affects the salmon migration and makes it more difficult (and more expensive) for Chicken of the Sea to obtain the fish. Melissa Mermaid, president of Chicken of the Sea, calls Charlie and says, "We've got to talk. I'm going to lose money if I sell you the salmon at $3 a pound. Let's make it $4 and we'll still both come out ahead under the present market conditions. Agreed?" "Agreed." One day later (at a time when Melissa hasn't yet relied on the higher price in any way), Charlie says, "Sorry, I won't pay the $4. We've got a contract at $3 a pound; I'll expect you to deliver."

    (A) Can Melissa enforce the modification to the contract?

    (B) If the contract was governed by the Restatement and not by the UCC, could Melissa enforce the modification?

26. E.T. signs up for a long distance calling service with MCI (Make Calls Intergalactically). The calling plan

says that calls made "between 7 and 11" will be 10 cents a minute, and calls made at all other times will be 15 cents a minute. E.T. gets a bill for $187 for one month's calls, properly computed based on MCI's assumption that "between 7 and 11" means between 7 and 11 p.m. E.T. thinks that "between 7 and 11" should also apply to the 7-11 a.m. period. (Assume that a court would probably find for MCI on this issue, but that E.T.'s reasoning is not crazy, and is done in good faith.) E.T. decides to pay only what he thinks he owes, and sends in a check for this lesser amount ($125). At the bottom of the check he writes, in neon green ink, "Paid in Full." He sends the check, along with a note explaining why he believes this is all he owes, to MCI. MCI cashes the check but writes next to its endorsement, "Under Protest, and With Reservation of Rights." MCI then sues E.T. for the $62 difference. Can MCI recover?

Answers

23. **(A) Yes.** The agreement is supported by consideration in the form of Antoinette's promise not to assert her claim. When a party promises to waive a valid claim, that is sufficient "detriment" to constitute consideration for the other party's promise to pay a settlement (here, the pearl necklace).

    (B) According to most courts, yes. Even though Antoinette's claim is not valid — and she is therefore actually giving up nothing (i.e. suffering no "detriment") — the majority rule is that her promise not to sue will be sufficient consideration if (1) she had a *bona fide* subjective belief that her claim was valid, and (2) that belief was reasonable. Both appear to be the case under these facts. (Some courts, and the Restatement, go further: they'll enforce the settlement if it's the case that *either* the promisor had a subjective believe that her claim was valid, *or* such a belief would have been reasonable.)

24. **(A) No, because New World's promise to do so was not supported by consideration.** Consideration requires a bargained-for exchange, and either detriment to the promisee or benefit to the promisor. At the moment New World made its capital-naming promise, Columbus was already obligated to sail West and discover America. Therefore, he was promising merely to do exactly what he was already obligated to do. A promise to perform a *pre-existing duty* does not involve a detriment to the promisor.

    (B) Yes, because he did something beyond what he was originally obligated to do. Even in courts following the majority/common-law rule that a promise to do what one is already obligated to do cannot be consideration, the promisor's promise to undertake different or additional duties (no matter how slight the difference) is consideration for the return promise. So Columbus' agreement to leave 2 days earlier was consideration for the capital-naming promise, making that promise enforceable.

25. **(A) Yes.** Under the common-law "pre-existing duty rule," contract modifications generally require independent consideration to be enforceable. However, the UCC abolishes this rule with respect to contracts for the sale of goods. Under § 2-209(1), sales contracts can be modified without any additional consideration, even if the other party merely promises to do exactly what it had previously promised to do. So even though Melissa is merely promising to supply the same quantity of fish she was already required to supply, Charlie's agreement to raise the price was binding. Once he made that agreement, he couldn't retract it, even though Melissa hadn't relied on the modification yet.

    (B) Yes. Under Rest. 2d § 89, a modification of a contract that has not yet been fully performed on either side is binding, if the modification is "fair and equitable in view of circumstances not anticipated by the parties when the contract was made." The freeze and consequent price run-up certainly qualify as such an unanticipated circumstance.

26. **No.** Under UCC § 3-311, a creditor who cashes a check thereby surrenders his underlying claim, provided that: (a) the check or accompanying written communication contains a "conspicuous statement" that the

check is being tendered in full satisfaction of the claim; (b) the claim is either unliquidated, or subjected to a bona fide dispute; and (c) the debtor acted in good faith. (a) is clearly satisfied by the "Paid in Full" notation and the accompanying letter. (b) is probably satisfied, since we're told that E.T.'s reasoning is plausible, though not necessarily likely to prevail. (c) is also satisfied, since we're told in the facts that E.T. is acting in good faith. So when MCI cashed the check, this act released E.T. (it acted as an accord and satisfaction), and nothing MCI wrote on the check could change this result.

VI. MUTUALITY OF CONSIDERATION

A. Requirement that each side furnish consideration: For a contract to be binding, there must be what is often called *"mutuality of consideration."* That is, *each party must furnish consideration to the other*, or the entire agreement fails to be enforceable by either. To put it another way, each of the contracting parties must undergo a "detriment" which was bargained for by the other.

1. Capsule summary of argument: As we'll see in much more detail below, the essence of a mutuality-of-consideration defense is that the defendant is saying, *"Because you never bound yourself to do anything, I shouldn't be bound, either."*

B. Consideration in bilateral contracts: The problem of mutuality really only arises with respect to *bilateral* contracts, i.e., contracts where each party makes a promise to the other.[2]

1. Determining when a promise is consideration: In the case of bilateral contracts, the mutuality problem consists of determining whether a given *promise* constitutes consideration for another promise. We start with a simple rule: A promise in a bilateral agreement is consideration *only if the performance which is promised would be sufficient consideration.*

2. How the problem arises: The mutuality problem arises because it is it is frequently more difficult to tell whether a promise constitutes consideration than it is to determine whether an act constitutes consideration. This is so because some promises don't really bind the promisor to do any act that would constitute consideration.

    a. Choice of acts: For instance, a promise may give the promisor a *choice* of acts, only one of which would be a sufficient "detriment."

    Example: Suppose *P* says to *D*, "In return for your promise not to sue me right now for the $100 I owe you, I promise either to buy your car or to pay you the $100 immediately." In this situation, *P* is not really bound, because she can elect the "branch" that does not constitute a legal detriment (here, paying money she already owes). Therefore, *D* can argue that she is not bound to forebear from suit — she can say, "You, *P*, did not bind yourself to do anything you weren't already obligated to do, so my return-promise can't be binding on me."

---

2. In a unilateral contract, the mutuality problem doesn't arise for the following reason: "Lack of consideration" only becomes an issue if raised by the defendant. The defendant in a unilateral contract situation is always the promisor (rather than the offeree, who accepted by performing the requested act.) The essence of any defendant's "no mutuality of consideration" argument is, "You weren't bound [i.e., you didn't give consideration], so I can't be bound." But in the unilateral situation, the defendant can't make this argument, because the offeree furnished consideration by performing the requested act.

b. Analyzing promises: Therefore, the remainder of this chapter addresses some of the problems encountered in determining whether particular kinds of promises constitute consideration for counter-promises.

C. "Mutuality of obligation": In the standard case of a bilateral contract, the requirement that both parties give consideration means that ***both parties must make promises that somehow bind them.*** This requirement that in bilateral contracts both parties be bound is usually called the requirement of ***"mutuality of obligation."***

1. **How the issue arises:** In these bilateral contract situations, it is obviously always the defendant who alleges that there was no consideration. Since there will rarely be any doubt as to whether the defendant's promise constituted "detriment" (the very fact that the plaintiff is asking her to do something she doesn't want to do virtually assures that the defendant's promise is a "detriment"), the defendant will typically assert that the *plaintiff's* promise was not a "detriment," and that it therefore did not constitute consideration for the defendant's counter-promise.

   In other words, the defendant says in effect: "It is true that my promise was consideration to support your promise, but ***your promise was not consideration for mine.*** Therefore, there is no mutuality of consideration, and no contract." (The P-D example earlier on this page is an illustration.) The rest of this chapter thus examines whether various ***promises made by plaintiffs*** constitute consideration for the defendant's counter-promise.

VII. ILLUSORY, ALTERNATIVE, AND IMPLIED PROMISES

A. Introduction: We now examine two situations in which the plaintiff's promise may fail to constitute consideration because the plaintiff is not really bound:

❑ promises that are ***"illusory,"*** which means that they appear to promise a performance that would constitute consideration, but don't really do so; and

❑ sets of ***alternative*** promised performances, where the plaintiff gets her choice of which performance to render, and one of those alternatives would not be consideration. An alternative that allows the plaintiff to ***terminate*** the contract may fall into this category, depending on its precise terms.

B. Illusory promises: One kind of "promise" that is not sufficient consideration to support a counter-promise is called an ***"illusory"*** promise. An illusory promise is a statement which appears to be promising something, but which in fact does not ***commit*** the promisor to anything at all.

> **Example:** *A* offers to deliver to *B* at $2 a bushel as many bushels of wheat as *B* may choose to order within the next thirty days. *B* replies, "OK, you've got a deal." *B* then gives *A* an order, and *A* refuses to sell at the $2 a bushel price (perhaps because the market price has gone up). *B* sues for breach of contract. *B*'s promise is illusory, since she has not clearly committed herself to do anything. All she has said to *A* is, in effect, "I promise to buy from you whatever I choose to buy from you." Therefore, her

"promise" does not constitute consideration for *A*'s counter-promise, and *A* is not bound to sell the wheat. See Rest. 2d, § 77, Illustr. 1.

Note: If, however, in the above example, *B* had promised that if she bought any wheat during the 30-day period, she would buy it from *A*, her promise *would* be consideration for *A*'s counter-promise to sell. See the discussion of requirements and output contracts *infra*, p.115.

1. **Reservation of right to change mind:** One common kind of "illusory" promise occurs when the promisor reserves the right to *change his mind*.

   Example: D's husband owes money to P, as evidenced by a promissory note. When the note becomes due, D signs the back of it, thereby agreeing to pay the note if her husband does not. She does this in return for P's promise that he will not put the note in his bank for immediate collection, but will instead "hold it until such time as I want my money." P refrains from collecting on the note for two years, and then sues D on her endorsement. D argues that since P did not really bind himself to refrain from collecting, there was no consideration for D's endorsement.

   Held, for D. P did not really promise to forbear, since he could have sued immediately, and this would have been evidence that he had decided that he wanted his money. Therefore, there was no consideration for D's endorsement. The fact that P actually refrained from suing for two years is irrelevant, since he did not promise to do so. (But if D or her husband had asked for forbearance, and P had said *nothing at all*, and had then refrained from suing, this would have been consideration. It was the fact that P explicitly denied that he was promising to forbear that prevented consideration from existing.) *Strong v. Sheffield*, 39 N.E. 330 (N.Y. 1895).

   a. **Promissory estoppel theory:** A promise to guarantee someone else's obligation might be binding, even without consideration, on a ***promissory estoppel*** theory. Under Rest. 2d, § 89, a guarantee is binding if "…(c) the promisor should reasonably expect the promise to induce action or forbearance of a substantial character on the part of the promisee or a third person, and the promise does induce such action or forbearance."

      i. ***Strong***: Thus on the facts of *Strong*, *supra*, a court today might find that D's guarantee of her husband's repayment should reasonably have been expected to induce P to refrain for a while from suing, that it did in fact have this effect, and that his forbearance was of a "substantial character." In that event, D would have been bound, even though there would have been no formal consideration. See the discussion of other aspects of promissory estoppel *infra*, pp. 136-149.

   b. **Objective standards:** Also, if the promisor's right to change her mind is *limited* by some *objective standard*, consideration is likely to be found present. For instance, if the promise of forbearance in *Strong* had provided some *objective standards* for determining when P could or could not ask for his money, rather than leaving this to P's uncontrolled discretion, P would probably have been found to have been sufficiently bound for his promise to be consideration for D's counter-promise. Thus had P promised that he would not ask for his money unless he had a "real financial need" for it, this modification would probably have been sufficient.

C. Alternative promises: A promise which reserves to the promisor several *alternative* performances is generally consideration only if *each of the alternative performances would have been consideration if it had been bargained for alone*. See Rest. 2d, § 77(a). (Alternatively, there is consideration if one of the alternative performances would be consideration and there is a "substantial possibility" that before the promisor makes his choice, events will eliminate the other alternatives. Rest. 2d, § 77(b).)

> **Example:** *A* offers to sell *B* a book if *B* will promise either to give *A* a different book, or to pay *A* $5 which *B* has previously owed *A*. *B* accepts. *B* decides he wants to make the exchange of books, but *A* changes his mind. Because one of the alternative performances open to *B* under the offer would not have constituted consideration (i.e., the paying of the $5 *B* already owed *A*; see *supra*, p. 93), *B*'s promise is not consideration for *A*'s counter-promise, even though *B* is willing to give the books.

> **Note:** If, in the above example, *B* had actually tendered to *A* the book that *A* wanted, and *A* had taken it, *A* would probably be bound to give the other book in exchange. A court would probably reach this result by treating *B*'s tender of the book, and *A*'s taking it, as having transformed the contract from a bilateral contract into a unilateral one. *B*'s tender was the act requested by *A*, and would be valid consideration for *A*'s counter-promise to give *B* the other book. The process of converting a bilateral contract invalid for lack of consideration into a valid unilateral contract is sometimes called "forging a good unilateral contract out of a bad bilateral contract." See C&P, p. 210.

D. Right to terminate agreement: Some contracts provide that one of the parties may *terminate* the agreement at his option. The courts are split as to whether and when a party has furnished consideration if he may escape the contract by exercising his power of termination.

1. **Where termination possible only after partial performance:** If one party to a contract has the right to terminate only *after he has done an act* which *by itself would constitute consideration,* his promise is *not illusory*, and constitutes consideration.

    > **Example:** *A* promises *B* that *A* will act as *B*'s agent for three years, starting immediately. *B* agrees that *A* may act as agent, but reserves the power to cancel the agreement on 30 days notice. *B*'s agreement is consideration for *A*'s promise, since *B* can exercise his cancellation right only after the agency relationship has run for 30 days. (The granting of a 30-day agency relationship would by itself be consideration.) See Rest. 2d, § 77, Illustr. 5.

    a. **Employer's give-up of right to immediately terminate employee:** This principle — that a party who gives up the right to terminate until after he's done some act that would itself be consideration — is sometimes applied to an employer who *agrees not to fire an "at will" employee* for at least a short period of time, in exchange for that employee's return promise of some sort (say, a non-compete). The employer's curtailment of what would otherwise be its right of immediate termination will be consideration for the employee's promise.

2. **Termination based upon party's inability to perform:** Similarly, if the contract provides that a party may terminate if he is *unable to perform* in a certain respect (as opposed

to merely unwilling), this right of termination will ***not*** render the contract void for lack of consideration.

3. **Unfettered right to terminate with notice:**   Where the agreement provides that one party may terminate simply by giving ***notice at any time***, the older cases hold that the party with the termination right has not furnished consideration. These courts reason that this party has not promised anything at all, since he has reserved an unfettered right to change his mind.

    a. **Modern view:**   The more modern cases, however, generally take the view that even where one party has the right to terminate an agreement by giving notice, that party's termination power does ***not*** prevent him from having given consideration. The rationale is that the ***duty to give reasonable notice*** of termination itself constitutes consideration. (Furthermore, if no notice requirement is expressly stated in the contract, some courts will imply it.)

    b. **Duty to notify under UCC:**   A court that wishes to uphold an agreement in which one party has what appears to be an unfettered right of cancellation can obtain assistance from the UCC in cases falling under the Code. UCC § 2-309(3) provides that "Termination of a contract by one party except on the happening of an agreed event requires that ***reasonable notification*** be received by the other party and an agreement dispensing with notification is invalid if its operation would be unconscionable." This section can enable a court to find an ***implied duty to give notice*** of cancellation even when the contract is silent as to any notification obligation. See C&P, p. 206.

    c. **Other statutory limits on termination:**   Other statutes, both state and federal, may similarly limit a party's right to terminate a contract. For instance, the Automobile Dealers Day in Court Act, 15 U.S.C.A. § 1221 *et seq.*, allows an automobile dealer to sue the manufacturer with whom he has a franchise agreement if the latter has failed to act in good faith in performing or terminating the franchise contract.

E. **Other kinds of implied promises:**   Just as an implied promise to give reasonable notice of cancellation is often implied by the courts, and constitutes consideration, so other sorts of promises have been implied. The most famous case finding consideration through an ***implied promise*** is ***Wood v. Lucy, Lady Duff Gordon***, a Cardozo opinion set forth in the following example.

> **Example:** Defendant, Lucy, Lady Duff Gordon, is a fashion designer. She makes an agreement with the plaintiff, a businessman, whereby the latter is to have the right to place the Lucy, Lady Duff Gordon endorsement on fashion designs. Lucy agrees that the plaintiff shall be the only person to have this right, and the plaintiff agrees to give Lucy one-half of any profits derived from the sales of such endorsed designs. Lucy then puts her endorsement on the designs of third persons (without sharing the profits with plaintiff) and plaintiff sues for breach of the agreement. Lucy asserts that the contract failed for lack of consideration, on the grounds that the plaintiff did not bind himself to do anything, since he was not obligated under the contract to sell any endorsed designs at all.
>
> *Held*, the plaintiff can be impliedly found to have promised to use "reasonable efforts" to market Lucy's designs. This implied promise is a sufficient "detriment" to

the plaintiff to constitute consideration for Lucy's counter-promise that she would not place her endorsement upon anyone else's designs. Therefore, the contract is binding, and Lucy has breached it. See *Wood v. Lucy, Lady Duff Gordon*, 222 N.Y. 88 (Ct. App. 1917).

VIII. REQUIREMENTS AND OUTPUT CONTRACTS

A. **Requirements and output contracts:** Suppose Buyer agrees with Seller that Buyer will buy all of his requirements for a particular good from Seller at an agreed-upon price. Has Buyer given consideration sufficient to support such a contract (called a *"requirements"* contract)? Similarly, if Seller agrees to sell all of his output of a particular product to Buyer, has Seller given sufficient consideration for this contract (called an *"output"* contract)?

1. **Earlier approach held no consideration to be present:** Earlier cases, especially ones decided before the advent of the UCC, frequently held that such output and requirements contracts were *invalid* for lack of consideration (as well as for indefiniteness).

2. **Contracts usually valid today:** But such requirements and output contracts are very likely to be *enforced* today, at least if it can be found that the buyer has *implicitly promised to use his best efforts to sell the goods* (or that the seller in an output contract has implicitly promised to attempt to maintain his production at a reasonable level), and the bargain is not otherwise unduly one-sided.

B. **UCC approach:** The *UCC explicitly validates requirements and output contracts.* UCC § 2-306(2) provides that

> "A term which measures the quantity by the output of the seller or the requirements of the buyer means such actual output or requirements as may occur in *good faith*, except that no quantity *unreasonably disproportionate* to any *stated estimate* or in the absence of a stated estimate to any *normal or otherwise comparable* prior output or requirements may be tendered or demanded."

1. **Rationale:** Comment 2 to § 2-306 explains that requirements and output contracts *do not "lack mutuality of obligation* since under this section, the party who will determine quantity is *required to operate his plant or conduct his business in good faith and according to commercial standards of fair dealing in the trade* so that his output or requirements will *approximate a reasonably foreseeable figure.*"

2. **Exclusivity implied in requirements contracts:** § 2-306 contemplates that the buyer in a requirements contract will deal *exclusively* with the seller with whom he has contracted. In other words, the buyer must promise that he will buy *all* of his requirements from that particular seller. This promise, coupled with the buyer's good faith obligation to order quantities that are not "unreasonably disproportionate to any stated estimate...or to any normal or otherwise comparable prior...requirements," *constitutes consideration* for the seller's counter-promise to meet the buyer's needs.

   Example: P (Eastern Airlines) agrees to buy all of its jet fuel requirements in specified cities from D, a jet-fuel supplier, and D commits to supply those requirements at a price pegged to the industry-wide posted price for crude oil. The price then increases dramatically due to actions by the OPEC cartel, and D reneges on the agreement.

When P sues, D asserts that the contract is void for lack of mutuality, since P wasn't bound to buy any specific quantities.

Held, for P. P bound itself to act reasonably and in good faith in estimating the quantities of fuel it required in each city. Since P was bound, D's return promise was not void for lack of mutuality of obligation. *Eastern Airlines Inc. v. Gulf Oil Corp.*, 415 F.Supp. 429 (S.D.Fla. 1975).

3. **Best efforts imposed on buyers and sellers:** There is a special type of good-faith obligation imposed by § 2-306 on buyers and sellers under requirements contracts. § 2-306(2) says that "A lawful agreement by either the seller or the buyer for exclusive dealing in the kind of goods concerned *imposes* unless otherwise agreed an obligation by the *seller to use best efforts to supply the goods* and by the *buyer to use best efforts to promote their sale.*"

   a. **Significance:** Therefore, under a requirements contract the buyer must make best efforts to promote the sale of the goods, and *cannot simply decide that the entire product line is not worth carrying*. Conversely, under an output contract the seller cannot simply decide to *stop selling or manufacturing* the item, and must instead make best efforts to supply the goods.

   Example: Donut Co. and Retailer agree that Retailer will buy all of Seller's output of honey-glazed donuts for the coming year, at a particular price. Both parties anticipate that Donut will produce 2,000 dozen such donuts over the course of the year, but the contract does not oblige Donut to produce any particular number. Shortly after the contract has started, and when Donut has supplied only 20 dozen donuts, Donut gets a new contract from Wal-Mart to supply hundreds of thousands of cinnamon donuts. Donut decides that it will not make any more honey-glazed donuts at all, and will instead shift the machine on which it had intended to make these donuts to making cinnamon donuts for Wal-Mart. Retailer sues for breach, and Donut responds, "It's not that we're selling our output of honey-glazed to someone other than you, we simply don't have any output of this product at all anymore, so we're not breaching."

   A court would probably conclude that Donut has breached the implied obligation that § 2-306(2), in all cases involving requirements or output contracts, places on the seller to "use best efforts to supply the goods."

4. **No speculation allowed under requirements contracts:** When a change in market conditions makes it highly advantageous for a requirements buyer to *increase his requirements sharply*, the UCC probably does not permit such abuse of the contract. This is especially true where the buyer uses the extra purchases to *speculate*, rather than using them in the ordinary course of his business.

   a. **Rationale:** Such sharply increased requirements should be invalid either under the buyer's duty to purchase in "good faith," or as being "*unreasonably disproportionate*...to any normal or otherwise comparable prior...requirements." § 2-306(1). (These code restrictions would also prevent the *seller* under a fixed-price output contract from taking advantage of a sharp *drop* in market price by greatly increasing his production.)

5. **Sale of the business:** What if the business that's subject to the requirements or output

contract is **sold** — can the contract be assigned as part of the sale? That's not clear — the assignment might be invalid on the grounds that it **materially increases the risk** on the other party, something that will be determined based on the non-UCC law of assignment (see *infra*, p. 391). But even if the assignment *is* valid, § 2-306 makes it clear that the benchmark for the requirements or output is the requirements or output of the **old** owner, not the new one. See Official Comment 4 to § 2-306: "Assuming that the contract continues, the output or requirements in the hands of the new owner continue to be measured by the **actual good faith output or requirements under the normal operation of the enterprise prior to sale.** The sale itself is not grounds for sudden expansion or decrease."

C. **Requirements and output contracts distinguished from continuing offers:** You must distinguish requirements and output contracts from **continuing offers**. If a seller says to a buyer, "I will sell you all the widgets you order at $2 per widget," and the buyer says "OK," there is no consideration for the seller's promise, since the buyer has not bound himself at all. If, however, a return promise by the buyer (such as a promise not to order from anyone else) can be implied, the contract is then enforceable. Otherwise, the seller must be treated as having made an **offer looking to a series of contracts;** this offer is **revocable at will,** and each order given by the buyer would constitute a separate contract.

Quiz Yourself on

MUTUALITY PROBLEMS: ILLUSORY, ALTERNATIVE AND IMPLIED PROMISES, AND REQUIREMENTS AND OUTPUT CONTRACTS

27. Princess promises to sell her golden ball to Frog for $200 "unless I change my mind." Can Frog enforce Princess's promise?

28. Medusa is a magician. Her best trick is to turn her assistant to stone. Medusa hires an agent, Farley Mythical. The contract between them provides that for one year, Medusa will use Farley and no one else as her agent, and that Farley will receive in return 10% of Medusa's earnings. The contract says nothing about how hard Farley must try to get engagements, and does not set any minimum number of engagements which, if Farley fails to procure them, will entitle Medusa to terminate. Before Farley has gotten Medusa any engagements, Medusa repudiates. Is there a binding contract on which Farley may recover?

29. Hercules Manufacturing agrees to buy "all the thing-a-ma-bobs we need to produce our what-cha-ma-callits for the next year" from Zeus Metalworks. Zeus declines to deliver.

    (A) Is Zeus bound?

    (B) Assume instead that the agreement was for Hercules to buy "all the thing-a-ma-bobs we order for the next year." Is Zeus bound?

Answers

27. **No, because Princess's promise is illusory.** An illusory promise is one unsupported by consideration due to one party's completely unrestricted right to renege on her promise. Here, there is no restriction whatsoever on Princess's freedom of action — she can change her mind at will. Therefore, her promise is illusory and unenforceable.

28. **Yes.** Medusa's argument would presumably be, "You weren't bound to do anything, so I'm not bound

either." (This is an argument based on the mutuality-of-consideration doctrine, which says that if one party has not furnished consideration, the other party is not bound.) However, in an exclusive-dealing contract such as this one (remember, Medusa's given up her right to use any other agent), a court would imply a duty on Farley's part to use his best reasonable efforts to get engagements for Medusa. By making this promise, he has restricted his freedom and thereby incurred a "detriment" sufficient to constitute consideration, and that detriment is sufficient to support Medusa's return promise.

29. **(A) Yes.** This is a typical "requirements" contract. Both requirements and output contracts are enforceable under the UCC, because they are deemed to be supported on both sides by consideration. This is so because the UCC imposes an implied obligation of good faith upon the parties, as well as one of exclusivity, in such output and requirements contracts. That is, Hercules has implicitly agreed to run his business in a good-faith way, so that he will continue to have a need for thing-a-ma-bobs. This (together with his agreement that he will not buy any thing-a-ma-bobs from anyone but Zeus), provides sufficient consideration to make the contract enforceable. Since Hercules has bound himself, Zeus' return promise is supported by consideration, making Zeus also bound.

(B) No. Under these facts, Hercules has not restricted his freedom in any way — he can choose to buy one unit, 100 or none. His promise is therefore illusory, and does not constitute consideration. Consequently, that promise cannot serve as consideration for Zeus' return promise, and Zeus is therefore not bound.

IX. MISCELLANEOUS CONSIDERATION PROBLEMS

A. **Conditional promises:** If the performance of a promise is made *conditional* upon the happening of some future event, is the promise "illusory," and thus not consideration for a counter-promise? In most cases, the existence of such a condition will *not* prevent the conditional promise from constituting consideration.

   1. **Conditions outside of the promisor's control:** If the condition is *outside of the promisor's control*, that condition will almost never prevent his promise from being consideration, even though it turns out that he does not have to perform.

> **Example:** *A* and *B* are brothers-in-law. They agree that regardless of what amount is left to each by their father-in-law, the two will share equally in the total bequest. *A* is left $10,000, and *B* is left nothing. *B* sues *A* for $5,000, and *A* defends on the ground that there was no consideration for his own promise; he argues that *B* has in fact not promised anything at all (since he has not received anything under the bequest to share). However, since the happening of the event upon which *B*'s promise is conditioned (i.e., the leaving to *B* of some money) was outside of *B*'s control, his promise constitutes consideration for *A*'s counter-promise, and the contract is enforceable. Murray, p. 148.

> **Note:** There would be consideration in the above example even though the father-in-law's will had already been drawn before the brothers-in-law made their agreement. In other words, as long as the brothers-in-law *thought* that there was a possibility that either would have to perform his promise (i.e., share some of the money left to him), their promises were consideration for each other, even though in reality, it was already the case that *B* would not have to perform anything. See Murray, p. 154.

a. **Conditions that cannot occur:** But even if the condition is outside of the promisor's control, a conditional promise is not consideration if the promisor *knows* at the time the promise is made that the condition *cannot occur*. See Rest. 2d, § 76(1). For instance, suppose that in the above example, *B* had *known* that his father-in-law had already drawn a will leaving *B* nothing, and that the father-in-law would not change his will. In that event, *B*'s promise would not be consideration for *A*'s, and *B* would not be able to recover.

2. **Where condition is within partial control of the promisor:** If the performance of a promise is contingent upon the occurrence of an event *within the control of the promisor*, or partially within his control, most modern decisions *imply* a promise to *attempt to make the condition occur*. This promise will therefore constitute consideration for a counter-promise.

> **Example:** Owner, who owns Blackacre, agrees to sell it to Buyer. The agreement is contingent upon Buyer's obtaining the necessary financing. Buyer obtains the financing, but Seller refuses to sell, claiming that Buyer's promise was illusory since it left to Buyer the option of not obtaining financing. Since, however, Buyer could be said to have impliedly promised to use "best efforts" to obtain the necessary financing, his promise was not illusory, even though conditional, and it constituted consideration for Seller's counter-promise to sell. See C&P, p. 208.

> **Note:** A similar result is usually reached where one party to a contract can make the contract conditional upon her obtaining a particular *license* necessary to conduct the business which she plans to conduct, or any other event which that party wishes to make a condition in order to protect herself. See C&P, p. 208.

3. **Promisee's discretion:** But if one party's performance is left completely to his *discretion*, so that he may choose not to perform at all, he *has not furnished consideration* for the other party's promise.

> **Example:** *A* offers to sell *B* as many widgets at $2.75 as *B* wishes to order. *B* says "OK, you've got a deal; I'll probably need some next week." *B* has not really promised anything, since his performance is solely within his discretion. Therefore, he has given no consideration, there is no contract, and if *B* sues *A* to get damages for *A*'s refusal to accept his order, *A* will win. See, e.g., *Strong v. Sheffield, supra*, p. 112.

B. **Voidable and unenforceable promises:** Suppose two parties exchange promises, but one party's promise is *voidable* at his option, or is *unenforceable*. This might, for example, be the case if that party is a minor, is senile, is the victim of fraud, or his promise is an oral one that violates the Statute of Frauds. Since the promisor with the option of avoiding the contract has not definitely bound himself, can the other party also avoid the contract, on the grounds that his own promise is not supported by consideration? This argument will *not succeed*. "The fact that a rule of law renders a promise voidable or unenforceable does not prevent it from being consideration." Rest. 2d, § 78.

1. **Rationale:** Some courts reach this result simply by saying that voidable promises are an exception to the requirement of "mutuality of obligation." Other courts reason that since the party who has the power to avoid the contract must act affirmatively to do so, he has incurred a detriment by putting himself in a position where he must either perform the contract or make an affirmative act of avoidance. See C&P, p. 202. In any case, all courts agree that a voidable promise may constitute consideration, and most agree that this is also true of an unenforceable one.

Example 1: Car Dealer makes a contract to sell a car to Minor. Minor, by virtue of his youth, is given the legal power to avoid the contract if he so wishes. Nonetheless, he decides he wants to buy the car, but Dealer refuses to sell. Minor sues, and Dealer defends on the grounds that because Minor had the power to avoid the contract, Minor never really bound himself, and thus furnished no consideration for Dealer's promise to sell the car.

Dealer's defense will be *unsuccessful*. A voidable or unenforceable promise constitutes consideration, if the promised performance meets all other requirements for consideration (e.g., it is not the performance of a pre-existing legal duty).

Example 2: *A* makes an oral promise in exchange for *B*'s return promise. Although *A*'s promise is unenforceable under the state's version of the Statute of Frauds, this fact does not prevent *A*'s promise from being consideration for *B*'s promise. Rest. 2d, § 78, Illustr. 2.

C. Forging a good unilateral contract out of a bad bilateral one: A bilateral agreement that is unenforceable for lack of mutuality of obligation may be transformed into an enforceable unilateral contract or series of contracts if one party *relies* on the bilateral agreement. You can think of this as *"forging a good unilateral contract out of a bad bilateral one."*

1. Non-competition clause: One situation in which courts will often forge a good unilateral contract from a bad bilateral one is one where an employee under an *at-will employment arrangement* signs a *non-competition* agreement. Even though the employer is not really promising to do anything (since he can fire the employee at any time, because of the at-will nature of the arrangement), the non-compete clause will *become* enforceable, according to many courts, if the employer does in fact keep the employee on the job for a substantial time. (Non-competition agreements are discussed in more detail *infra*, p. 461.)

Quiz Yourself on
MISCELLANEOUS CONSIDERATION PROBLEMS

30. Papa Bear agrees to sell, and Goldilocks to buy, four bushels of oats from the next season's harvest. The agreement further provides that Papa Bear's duty will be conditional on Papa's planting of one more acre of oats than he planted the prior season. (Papa's decision on whether to plant the extra acre will be based solely on his decision about how hard he wants to work.) Papa Bear in fact plants the extra acre, and tenders the resulting four bushels to Goldilocks. Is Goldilocks bound to accept and pay for them?

31. Nero is a big fan of gladiatorial bouts. His favorite gladiator is Spartacus. Nero finds out that his friend, Romulus, has title bout tickets; if Spartacus wins his next two bouts, he'll be in the title bout. Nero tells Romulus, "If Spartacus makes it to the final round, I'll buy your tickets for $50." Romulus accepts. Spartacus makes it to the finals. Nero wants the tickets for $50; Romulus refuses to sell them at that price. Is their oral agreement enforceable?

Answers

30. **No, because Goldilocks' promise was not supported by consideration, in that Papa Bear's return promise was illusory.** An illusory promise is one that does not constitute consideration because the promisor has an unrestricted right to renege on his promise. One type of illusory promise is a promise that is conditional upon an event, which event is solely within the promisor's control. That's what we have here: Papa's duty to sell was subject to a condition (his planting of the extra acre), but Papa was solely in control of whether that condition was satisfied. Now, the doctrine of "mutuality of consideration" says that one party's illusory promise (here, Papa Bear's) cannot serve as consideration for the other party's return promise (here, Goldilocks' promise to buy). So Goldilocks' promise was not supported by consideration, and she's therefore not bound.

31. **Yes.** As in the prior question, the issue here is conditional promises, and the circumstances under which they fail for lack of consideration. It's true that Nero would not have been bound to anything if Spartacus had not made it to the finals. But we judge consideration as of the moment of contract's making, and at that moment Nero was conditionally bound. If the satisfaction of the condition had been solely within Nero's control (see the prior question for an example of this), Nero would not have furnished consideration, and neither party would have been bound. But satisfaction of the condition here was not solely within Nero's control, so the fact that there was a condition did not prevent Nero's promise from constituting consideration. Since Nero gave consideration, Romulus' return promise did not fail for lack of consideration, and he's bound as well.

Exam Tips *on* CONSIDERATION

Consideration

☞ Always check whether or not a contract is supported by consideration. Consideration is a *legal detriment suffered by the promisee in exchange for the promisor's promise*.

Example where there is a legal detriment: X, the owner of a chain of dry cleaning stores, promises to give to Y, her cousin, a franchise if Y promises to move from a distant state to where X lives. Y promises to do so. It is irrelevant whether X gains any benefit from Y's move. What matters is that Y has promised to suffer a detriment in exchange for X's promise. Therefore, there's consideration for X's promise.

Example where there isn't a legal detriment: University receives a pledge from X, an alumnus, for a donation of $50,000. X later withdraws the pledge. The promise lacks consideration because University hasn't suffered a legal detriment. (But the promise may still be enforceable without consideration, through promissory estoppel.)

☞ Remember that something can be consideration even though it is done by (or for) a *third person*, one who is *not a party* to the contract.

Example 1: A promises B that A will pay B $100 if B's son drives A to the airport. Even though B's son is not the promisee (B is), the son's act of driving will be consideration for *A*'s promise to pay *B*.

Example 2: A promises B $100 if B promises to drive *A*'s daughter to the airport. The fact that the performance being given in exchange for *A*'s promise is to be rendered to someone other than *A* (the promisor) doesn't matter.

☛ Where the issue of consideration is prominent in an essay, it usually manifests itself in one of the following four situations:

(1) **Promises to make gift:** D promises to make a *gift*, usually to a relative or charity. There's no consideration supporting D's promise, so it's not enforceable (unless it falls under one of the exceptions to the consideration requirement, covered in the next chapter).

☞ **Mixture of bargain and gift:** But a transaction that's a *mixture of bargain and gift satisfies* the consideration requirement, making the generous party's promise enforceable.

Example: D promises to sell P D's antique car at a 90% discount to its market value, in return for P's promise to buy it at this low price. As long as there is some sort of a "bargain," the fact that there's a gift element doesn't prevent D's promise from being supported by consideration (P's promise of payment).

(2) **Promises to pay for past services:** D promises to pay for *past services* which P rendered to him. Most commonly, P is a *Good Samaritan* who saves D, an unconscious person, who later promises compensation and then reneges.

☞ **No compensation reasonably expected:** A promise to pay for past services isn't supported by consideration where the services were performed with *no reasonable expectation of compensation.* Fact patterns may trick you into thinking that under certain circumstances consideration has in fact been offered. Don't be fooled if:

❑ The unconscious person regains consciousness *immediately after* the rescue and then promises to pay the savior.

❑ The savior happens to be someone with medical expertise, such as a *retired doctor.*

❑ A *relative* of the party who was saved promises after the fact to pay the savior (still no "bargained for" exchange).

❑ The promise to pay is made *in writing* and/or is promised "in consideration" for services rendered.

In all four of the above scenarios, there is no consideration for the promise to pay for the past services. (But the promises might be binding without consideration, to the extent necessary to avoid injustice — see the next chapter.)

These examples should be distinguished from emergency medical services provided by parties who *would* reasonably expect compensation, such as an ambulance service or hospital emergency room. Here, there would be consideration for the patient's (or patient's relative's) subsequent promise to pay.

(3) Pre-existing duty. P promises to pay (or perform services) that P is already legally obligated to pay/perform — D's return promise is not supported by consideration.

☞ **Contract modifications:** The most common scenario is a *contract modification.* Here, you must distinguish between the UCC and non-UCC situation.

☞ **Non-UCC:** If P merely promises to do what P already promised to do under the contract, and there are no unanticipated circumstances, D's new promise (e.g., more money) given in return is not supported by consideration.

Example: D promises to pay $5,000 if P paints D's house by June 14. After the house is halfway painted, P threatens to walk off the job unless D raises the price to $7,500. D agrees. D's promise to pay the extra $2,500 is not supported by consideration, because P merely promised to do what he was already contractually required to do.

☞ **Substitute performance by P:** But if P *changes his own duty,* however slightly, in response to D's promised modification, then D's counter-promise *is* supported by consideration. (*Example:* In the above example, if P promised to finish the job one day earlier [or to use a different color of paint] than previously promised in return for the extra $2,500, D's counter-promise of the extra $2,500 would be supported by consideration.)

Common scenario: A party who is owed money due on a later date agrees to accept a lesser amount in exchange for a promise of immediate tender of payment. The creditor has received consideration for the promise to take less.

☞ **Unanticipated circumstances:** Also, if the modification is a response to *new circumstances unanticipated by the parties* when they made their original deal (e.g., a well-driller hits rock, and asks for a higher price to finish the job), remember that most modern courts will find that the modification is binding.

☞ **UCC:** Under the UCC, the pre-existing duty rule simply doesn't apply to the contract-modification scenario — under Article 2, "An agreement modifying a contract within [Article 2] needs no consideration to be binding."

Example: On the above house-painting example, if P had promised to sell paint to D rather than perform painting services, the lack of consideration for D's promise to pay more would not prevent D's new promise from being binding.

(4) Settlement of claim: Similarly, if a party who has a contractual claim for money agrees to take less in a *"settlement,"* the promise to take less is supported by consideration, so long as the other party *disputed* in good faith the *amount* or *validity* of the claim.

Example: P, a painting contractor, agrees to paint O's house for $5,000. The contract provides that P will deliver a satisfactory result. When the job is completed O tells P that he doesn't find the work satisfactory, but he's willing to call it "square" if P will accept $4,500. P agrees to take the less amount in payment. P's promise to take the lesser amount is supported by consideration (O's willingness not to dispute whether P performed), so that promise is binding, and P can't change his mind and demand full payment.

☞ **Invalid claims:** This is true *even if the claim is not valid,* so long as the holder of the claim *believes in good faith* that the claim is valid.

Example: *B,* acting as a Good Samaritan without expectation of payment, saves *A*'s life. *A* promises in writing to pay *B* $1,000. *B* honestly believes that *A*'s promise is binding. *A* then reneges. *B* threatens to sue, then agrees to forebear from suing if *A* will sign a new writing promising to pay $750. *A* signs the new writing. *A* will be bound — even though *A*'s original promise to pay was not binding (it was a promise to pay for past services, rendered without expectation of payment), the new promise is supported by consideration, since it was in settlement of *B*'s good-faith claim for breach of the prior promise.

Illusory Promises

☛ **Total discretion by one party:** When you spot a contract that gives one party *total discretion on whether to perform*, that party's promise is illusory, because the party hasn't committed to anything. Therefore, the other party isn't bound, either.

Example: Seller offers Buyer an annual contract for the sale of widgets at a stated price, with the quantity to be "whatever quantities you choose to order, up to a maximum of 10,000." Notice that Buyer isn't obligated to purchase *anything* under these terms. Therefore, Seller's promise isn't supported by consideration, and Buyer can't sue Seller for refusing to fill the orders Buyer places.

But keep in mind that contracts with apparently-illusory promises may nonetheless be wholly or partly enforceable. Some situations to watch for:

☞ **A divisible contract:** If there is a long-term agreement in which the seller's promise is illusory, but the buyer places individual orders, the seller's promise will be interpreted as an offer for a *series of unilateral contracts*, and each order will be an *acceptance of a unilateral contract* (which the seller is then bound to fill).

Example: Buyer requests an annual price quote for fuel oil from Seller. On Dec. 24, Seller writes to Buyer, "I offer to supply you with any no. 2 fuel oil ordered by you during the next year beginning January 1 under the following terms: 14 cents a gallon to be ordered only in 3,000 gallon tank cars." On Dec. 30, Buyer writes, "I accept your offer." Since there isn't any language indicating a quantity (e.g., Buyer's requirements) or exclusivity of source, the contract is illusory at this point (and either party could cancel it completely).

But now, suppose that on the following Jan. 20, Buyer writes, "My first order is for 6,000 gallons." This would probably be interpreted as an acceptance of Seller's outstanding offer to enter into a series of unilateral contracts. Therefore, Seller would have to fulfill the order. (But Seller could cancel at any time, and not have to fill any orders placed after the cancellation date.)

☞ **An implied promise by a party:** In certain circumstances a promise may be *implied*, thus making that party's duty not illusory.

☞ **Exclusive distributorships:** Where Buyer has exclusive rights to distribute (resell) Seller's product, Buyer has an implied duty to *use her reasonable efforts* to sell the product. This implied duty will furnish consideration for Seller's return duty to sell to Buyer.

☞ **Requirements contracts:** Similarly, in a *requirements* contract, Buyer's promise of exclusivity supplies consideration for Seller's return promise to supply Buyer.

☞ **Good-faith quantities:** Remember that the *quantity* in both requirements and output contracts is measured by the actual quantity that occurs *in good faith.* However, the quantity can't be an amount which is unreasonably disproportionate to any stated estimate or, in the absence of a stated estimate, to any normal or otherwise comparable prior output or requirements.

Example: *S* and *B* have an exclusive five-year contract whereby *S*, a chair manufacturer, supplies a certain type of chairs to *B*, a chair distributor. (*S* is to sell this type of chair only to *B*, and *B* is to buy this chair only from *S*.) Orders for the first three years are 330, 100 and 250 chairs, respectively. *B* orders 1,000 chairs in the fourth year and *S* cannot produce that amount. *S* will probably not be liable for breach, because the amount requested is disproportionate to the prior requirements.

☞ **Personal satisfaction of party.** Look for a contract where a party's duty to pay arises only if he's personally satisfied with the work done by the other party. His promise to pay isn't illusory because of the requirement that dissatisfaction, if it occurs, be in *good faith.*

☞ **Notice of cancellation:** Lastly, if a party can *cancel* the contract at any time, but only on some period of notice, the obligation to give the notice (and to perform or be bound til them) supplies consideration for the other party's promise.

☛ Two further points to remember:

☞ Courts seldom care about the *"adequacy"* of consideration. So a big imbalance between the "value" of what *A* got and what *B* got won't mean a lack of consideration.

☞ A promise to make a gift is unenforceable, as noted. However, a gift, *once it has been completed*, can't be rescinded by the donor.

CHAPTER 4

PROMISES BINDING WITHOUT CONSIDERATION

ChapterScope

This chapter covers the exceptions to the rule requiring consideration. Here are the key exceptions, situations in which a promise can be enforceable even though there is no consideration for it:

■ **Promises to pay past debt:** Most courts hold that a promise to pay a *past debt* that is no longer legally enforceable is binding without consideration, if it is *in writing*.

■ **Promise to pay for benefits received:** Similarly, a promise to *pay for services already received* is enforceable in many situations.

■ **Modification:** The UCC provides that a *modification* of a contract for the sale of goods does not have to be supported by consideration.

■ **Option contract:** An *option* contract (i.e., a promise to *hold an offer open* for a set amount of time) usually does not need consideration, if the option is in a writing signed by the offeror, and recites that consideration has been paid for the option.

■ **Guaranty contract:** A *guaranty* (i.e., a promise to pay the already-existing debt of another person) is usually enforceable if it is in a writing that (1) is signed by the guarantor, and (2) states that consideration has been paid for the guarantee.

■ **Promissory estoppel:** Under the "promissory estoppel" doctrine, a promise will be enforceable without consideration if: (1) the promisee *acts or forbears in reliance on the promise* and (2) this action or forbearance was *reasonably foreseeable* by the promisor. The doctrine is often applied in a situation where there has been a *promise to make a gift.*

I. INTRODUCTION

A. **Types of promises that may not need consideration:** This chapter covers the circumstances in which a contract may be enforceable even though it is not supported by consideration. It also discusses the situations in which the doctrine of promissory estoppel can serve as a substitute for consideration.

1. **Listing of situations:** The above ChapterScope lists the most important types of promises that may be enforceable without consideration.

II. PROMISES TO PAY PAST DEBTS

A. **Promises to pay past debts that are no longer legally enforceable:** Suppose the debt owed by a debtor to a creditor has been *legally discharged.* This discharge may have occurred, for instance, because the debtor became *bankrupt*, or because the *statute of limitations has run* on the creditor's claim. If the debtor then makes a gratuitous promise (i.e., a promise for which he receives nothing in return) to *pay the now-barred debt*, is this promise enforceable? Most courts agree that it is *enforceable*, *even though there is no consideration*.

B. "Moral consideration":   Some courts justify making such a promise enforceable by stating that there is *"moral consideration"* for the promise to pay the now-barred debt. But this "moral consideration" label is simply conclusory, since there is no "bargain" present, and therefore there is nothing resembling the traditional consideration idea. A better explanation is that courts simply feel that the enforcement of such promises to pay pre-existing obligations is socially beneficial.

1. **Restatement view:**   The Second Restatement takes the position that promises to pay debts that are barred by the *statute of limitations*, or that have been discharged in *bankruptcy*, are *binding without consideration*. See Rest. 2d, §§ 82 and 83.

2. **Requirement of a writing:**   Statutes in most states require that for a promise to pay a debt barred by the statute of limitations to be enforceable, it must be in a *signed writing*. A few states similarly require a signed writing where the debt has been discharged in bankruptcy. See C&P, p. 233; Rest. 2d, § 82, Comment a and § 83, Comment a.

3. **Promises to pay inferable from acts or statements:**   Sometimes the promise to pay the discharged debt will be explicit. In many situations, however, the debtor will take actions which the creditor claims constitute an *implied* promise to pay the now-discharged debt.

   a. **Bankruptcy discharges:**   Where the promise is to pay a debt that has been discharged in *bankruptcy*, most courts probably share the view of the Second Restatement (§ 83), which will enforce only an *express* promise and will not infer such a promise from the debtor's actions.

   b. **Statute of limitations:**   Where the debt has been discharged by the running of the *statute of limitations*, on the other hand, most courts (and the Second Restatement) recognize several situations in which a promise to pay the debt may be *implied* from the debtor's actions. The Second Restatement (§ 82) lists the following acts or statements as giving rise to a promise to pay a time-barred debt:

      i. "A voluntary *acknowledgment* to the obligee, *admitting the present existence* of the antecedent indebtedness";

      ii. "A voluntary *transfer* of money, a negotiable instrument, or other thing by the obligor to the obligee, made as *interest on or payment of or collateral security for* the antecedent indebtedness";

      iii. "A statement to the obligee that the statute of limitations *will not be pleaded as a defense*."

C. Scope of promisor's duty: If the promise to pay a previous debt is held enforceable, it is only enforceable *under the precise terms of the promise*, and the promisor *cannot be held for more than that*.

> **Examples:** If the debtor promises only to pay a portion of the pre-existing debt, only that portion may be collected. Similarly, if she promises to pay it "if I am able," the promise is only enforceable if the debtor does achieve an objective ability to make the payment. And if the debtor acknowledges that the debt still exists, but states that she

does *not* intend to pay it, her acknowledgment does not operate as a promise, in view of the opposite intention she has manifested.

III. PROMISE TO PAY FOR BENEFITS RECEIVED

A. Promise to pay for benefits received generally: Suppose *A* has rendered a service to *B*, without having come to an express contractual agreement for the service (e.g., *A* has saved *B*'s life in an emergency). If, after the service has been rendered, *B* promises to pay a specified amount for it, is that promise enforceable? It is clearly not supported by consideration, since it was not even made until the services had already been rendered, and cannot therefore be said to have been bargained for by *A*. The question is therefore whether such a *promise to pay for past service*s is enforceable without consideration. The enforceability of such a promise is likely to depend on several factors, including whether the recipient initially requested the services, and whether the donor rendered them in expectation that he would receive payment.

1. **Where services were requested, and rendered with an expectation of payment:** Where the services were initially *requested* by the recipient, the enforceability of the later promise to pay *doesn't matter* very much, because the initial request probably created an implied-in-fact contract to pay for them. (This assumes that the person who performed the services *expected to be paid for them*.)

   a. **Requested act performed as favor:** Now, suppose that the services were requested, but the person performing them intended that they be a *gift*. If the recipient later promises to pay for the services, most courts (and Rest. 2d, § 86(2)(a)) will *not* enforce the promise. See C&P, p. 227.

2. **Benefits previously received but not requested:** The most interesting case is where *A* renders services to *B* *without* *B*'s having expressly requested the services, and *B* then promises to pay. We assume that at the time A renders the services, he is *not intending a gift.*[1]

   a. **Split of authority:** Here, the cases are *split*. The older cases generally hold that *B*'s promise is *unenforceable*. But "the trend is clearly in favor of *increased enforceability*" of such promises. Farnsworth, § 2.8.

   Example: Recall the facts of *Mills v. Wyman* (*supra*, p. 93): D's son, a 25-year-old, becomes ill while traveling, and is nursed by P. D later writes to P, promising to pay P's expenses.

   The court hearing the case (in 1825) held that D's promise was not supported by consideration, since P's services were not given at D's request. But a modern court might well hold that such a promise made on account of "moral obligation" should be enforced.

   b. **Where benefit and cost are substantial:** Even in courts that would not automatically hold that a promise to pay for unrequested past services should be automatically enforced, the court may choose to enforce the promise where the benefit to the recipi-

---

1. If *A* intends a gift, then pretty much all courts agree that a later promise by *B* to pay for the services should not be enforced. See Rest. 2d § 86(2)(a) (denying enforcement for any benefit intended as a gift).

ent of the services (and/or the cost to the provider) was *substantial*. The case set forth in the following example is the classic illustration.

Example: *A* saves *B*'s life in an emergency, and is totally disabled in so doing. *B* then promises to pay *A* $15 every two weeks for the rest of *A*'s life, and makes these payments regularly for over eight years until he dies. The estate then refuses to continue the payments and *A* sues on the promise.

Held, *B*'s promise is enforceable, even without consideration, because *B* incurred a substantial material benefit from *A*'s act, even though *B* did not request the act. See *Webb v. McGowin*, 168 So. 196 (Ala. Ct. App. 1935). See also, Rest. 2d, § 86, Illustr. 7 (drawn from *Webb*).

   c. **Restatement view:** The Second Restatement more or less follows the more modern, liberal, view. Receipt of an unrequested material benefit, followed by the receiver's promise to pay for the benefit, is *enforceable without consideration*, but only *"to the extent necessary to prevent injustice."* Rest. 2d, § 86(1).

      i. **Intent to make gift of services:** The Restatement gives one illustration of a situation in which enforcement will definitely *not* be necessary to prevent injustice (and thus not enforceable): where the promisee "conferred the benefit as a *gift*." Rest. 2d, § 86(2)(a).

      ii. **Request irrelevant:** The Restatement does not distinguish at all between benefits that are *requested* by the promisor and those that are not. (In *both* situations, the promise is not binding if the promisee conferred the benefit as a gift; nor will the promise be enforced if its "value is disproportionate to the benefit." *Id.*)

   d. **State statutes:** Some states have enacted *statutes* to make enforceable promises to pay for services previously received. See, e.g., N.Y. Gen. Oblig. L. § 5-1105 and Cal. Civ. Code § 1606.

   e. **Restitution possibility:** Also, in certain situations (e.g., emergencies and mistakes), the law of *quasi-contract*, or "restitution," allows the person rendering the services to recover their reasonable value. See *infra*, p. 335. Where such a restitutionary recovery is possible, a subsequent promise by the recipient of the services to pay a particular sum for them may at least constitute *evidence* of the value of the services, even though the promise is not directly enforceable.

Quiz Yourself on

PROMISES TO PAY PAST DEBTS AND PROMISES TO PAY FOR BENEFITS RECEIVED

32. Donald owed Mickey $100 and gave him a promissory note to that effect. Mickey has never enforced the note and the statute of limitations has now passed. Donald now sends a letter to Mickey that says, "Dear Mickey, I know I still owe you some money under my promissory note. I'll pay you $75 next month." Donald does not pay the $75 the next month. How much, if anything, may Mickey collect?

33. Opie became extremely ill one day while visiting his Aunt Bee. Aunt Bee, a retired nurse, ended up nursing him back to health for several days and spent $200 on medications for him. When Opie recovered, he said, "Aunt Bee, I know you devoted several days of your time to caring for me, and I appreciate it greatly. I promise to repay you by giving you $500 for your services, plus an additional $200 to reimburse you for the medications." Opie never pays up. According to the modern view, can Aunt Bee enforce the promise? If so, to what extent?

Answers

32. **$75.** Under the Second Restatement (and according to most courts), a promise to pay a debt that is barred by the statute of limitations or that has been discharged in bankruptcy is binding *without consideration.* Most states require that the new promise be made in writing, but that requirement is satisfied here. However, states enforcing promises to pay limitations-barred debts almost always limit enforcement to the precise terms of the promise. Since Donald promised only $75, that's all Mickey can collect. (But if Donald, in addition to promising an immediate $75, had specifically acknowledged that the full $100 was presently owing, this acknowledgment of present-indebtedness would have been enough, at least under the Restatement's view, to bind Donald to pay that full $100, even though Donald didn't expressly promise to pay the entire $100.)

33. **Yes, but probably only for the $200 spent on drugs.** Under the modern and Restatement view, a promise to pay someone for benefits received is enforceable without consideration — but only to the extent necessary to **prevent injustice.** Here, Aunt Bee would likely be able to enforce the promise to reimburse her for the medicines, since it's probably unjust that she be left with this out-of-pocket expense after Opie promised otherwise. However, she would probably *not* be able to enforce the promise for the additional $500 for the value of her services: since Aunt Bee is not only a *retired* nurse but also a relative of the recipient, it's highly likely that a court would conclude that Bee intended the services as a gift, not as something for which she expected to be paid. If she intended a gift, prevention of injustice would not require that she be paid.

IV. OTHER CONTRACTS BINDING WITHOUT CONSIDERATION

A. **Promise to perform a voidable duty:**   Suppose that *A* owes a duty to *B*, but *A*'s duty is **voidable** at her option. This might, for example, be the case if *A* had been induced to make her promise through fraud or duress, or at a time when *A* was an infant. If, after *A* has discovered her option to avoid her promise, she reaffirms the promise, the **subsequent promise is enforceable,** even though made without consideration. See Rest. 2d, § 85.

> **Example:** *B*, in order to induce *A* to promise to lend her $10,000, misrepresents his ability to repay *A*. *A* agrees to make the loan. Before he actually makes the loan, *A* discovers *B*'s fraudulent representation of ability to repay, and has the right to avoid the loan on grounds of fraud. However, he says to *B*, "I'll lend you the money anyway." *A*'s second promise is enforceable, even without consideration. See C&P, p. 234.

B. **Modification of contracts:**   In the chapter on Consideration, we saw that most courts in a non-goods situation hold that a modification of a contract which benefits only one party is unenforceable for lack of consideration. (See *supra*, p. 98.) The **UCC**, however, explicitly **removes the consideration requirement for modifications of existing contracts:** "An agreement modifying a contract within this article needs no consideration to be binding." § 2-209(1).

Example: Seller sells an airplane to Buyer on credit, with Buyer to make payments of $10,000 per month over five years, at 0% interest. After one year, Buyer develops money problems, and tells Seller that he can no longer afford to pay more than $7,000 per month. Seller agrees to let Buyer pay this lesser monthly amount (still at 0% interest) until the plane is paid off. One year later, Seller becomes dissatisfied with the arrangement, and demands that Buyer start paying at the original $10,000 per month or the plane will be repossessed. When Buyer threatens to sue for breach of the modified agreement, Seller retorts that Buyer gave no consideration for the original modification, since Buyer was merely agreeing to do what he was already required to do.

Under the UCC, the modification is binding on Seller, even though Buyer gave no consideration for it.

1. **Contracts containing a "no oral modification" clause:**   However, UCC § 2-209 does have a limitation. § 2-209(2) provides that "a signed agreement which ***excludes modification or rescission except by a signed writing cannot be otherwise modified or rescinded***, but except as between merchants such a requirement on a form supplied by the merchant must be separately signed by the other party."

    a. **Meaning of § 2-209(2):**   § 2-209(2) thus provides that if the original written agreement states something to the effect of "this contract may not be subsequently modified except in writing," that clause will be ***enforced***, and any subsequent oral modification (even if proved beyond a doubt, and even if benefiting both sides) is not binding. A clause falling under § 2-209(2) is usually called a ***"no oral modification"*** clause.

    b. **"No oral modification" clause must be separately signed:**   However, such a "no oral modification" clause in the original agreement is ***ineffective*** if it is contained on a form supplied by a merchant (essentially, a business person — see § 2-104(1)) unless either (1) the other party is ***also a merchant***; *or* (2) the other party has ***separately signed*** the n.o.m. clause.

        Example: Consumer buys a washing machine from Dealer. The machine is to be paid for under the contract, at the rate of $20 a month for 36 months. The written contract states that "this contract may not be modified except in writing." The machine develops problems and to placate Consumer, Dealer says to Consumer "I'll let you reduce the payments from $20 a month to $15 a month." Consumer agrees with this reduction, then fails to make the payments. Dealer sues. He seeks the full $20 per month price, claiming that the "no oral modification" clause in the contract rendered the subsequent oral modification ineffective.

        Because of § 2-209(2), the "no oral modification" clause is ineffective to bar the subsequent modification unless it was separately signed by Consumer. Thus if Consumer merely signed the overall sales agreement, and did not place his signature next to the "no oral modification" clause, Dealer is bound by the subsequent oral modification.

    c. **May be overridden by waiver:**   Also, a no-oral-modification clause is not completely ironclad, because the party who later tries to enforce the clause may be found to have ***waived the benefit*** of the clause. For instance, UCC § 2-209(4) provides that "[a]lthough an attempt at modification … does not satisfy the requirements of [a valid no-oral-modification clause] it can operate as a *waiver*." (Courts in non-UCC cases similarly apply waiver principles.)

Example: Buyer and Seller sign a contract containing a no-oral-modification clause, and also setting a firm delivery date. Buyer later orally says to Seller, "I won't insist on firm adherence to the delivery date — you can take an extra three weeks." If Seller *relies* materially on this statement, Buyer will probably be held to have *waived* the benefit of the no-oral-modification clause, and will thus be held to have effectively modified the contract to provide for a later delivery date. See W&S, pp. 33-34.

2. **Good faith and unconscionability in modifications:** The traditional non-UCC requirement that there be consideration to support a modification was designed in part to prevent one party from extorting concessions from the other by threatening to breach. (See *supra*, p. 98.) The Code, although it removes the consideration requirement for modifications, nonetheless guards against such extortion. It does this through two provisions: (1) the requirement that "every contract or duty within this act imposes an obligation of *good faith* in its performance or enforcement" (§ 1-304); and (2) the court's right to refuse to enforce any contract which it finds to be "unconscionable" (§ 2-302).

C. **Option contracts:** Many courts do *not* require consideration for an *offer to be irrevocable*. That is, in many courts an *option contract* will sometimes be binding without consideration.

1. **Restatement:** Thus the Second Restatement states that an option contract is binding if it satisfies four requirements:

[1] it is *in writing;*

[2] it is *signed by the offeror;*

[3] it "*recites a purported consideration* for the making of the offer," and

[4] it proposes "an exchange on *fair terms within a reasonable time*...."

Rest. 2d § 87(1)(a).

a. **No consideration really required:** This Restatement provision, although it applies only where the offer "recites a purported consideration," does not require true consideration. As long as the terms of the proposed agreement are fair, it does not matter that the consideration recited in the document was *never in fact paid*, or that it was not bargained for. See Rest. 2d, § 87, Comment c.

b. **Fairness of exchange:** Notice requirement [4] above: Under the Restatement (and in many states), the court will inquire into the *fairness* of the proposed terms under the option, even though it will not inquire as to whether the recited consideration was actually paid. If these terms are unfair, the option will not be binding.

Example: In consideration of $1 paid by *B*, *A*, an ignorant widow, gives *B* a 10-year option to mine phosphate from her farm for a royalty of 25¢ per ton. As *B* knows, but *A* does not, the prevailing royalty for phosphate is more than $1 per ton. The option is unenforceable, not for lack of consideration, but because of the gross unfairness of the option price. See Rest. 2d, § 87, Illustr. 2.

2. **Offers which induce reliance:** An offer which induces foreseeable detrimental reliance by the offeree may be treated by the court as an option, pursuant to Rest. 2d, § 87(2). See *supra*, p. 53. In this sort of unintentional option, there is no consideration requirement; the offeree by hypothesis has undergone a "detriment," but usually not one which has been "bargained for" by the offeror.

3. **Firm offers under the UCC:** The UCC's *"firm offer"* provision (§ 2-205) similarly allows the creation of an option contract without consideration. That section (discussed *supra*, p. 53) provides that a written and signed offer by a merchant to buy or sell goods which states that the offer is irrevocable is indeed irrevocable, even though no consideration is given for it. The provision is limited, however, to a maximum of three months of irrevocability. (If consideration is given by the offeree, of course, the option can be indefinite.)

D. **Guaranties:** A *guaranty* is a promise by one person (the guarantor) to pay the debts incurred by another person (the debtor) owed to a third person (the creditor).

1. **Guaranty given simultaneously with creation of debt:** If the guarantor gives his guaranty *at the same time* that the debt he is guaranteeing is created, there is no problem of consideration, since the guarantor is bargaining for a detriment to be incurred by the creditor, i.e., the loan to the debtor. (The consideration doctrine does not require that any benefit flow directly to the person doing the bargaining; thus the fact that the loan proceeds go to the debtor, and not the guarantor, does not negate the existence of consideration.)

> **Example:** Son wants to buy a car from Dealer. Dealer will allow Son to buy the car on credit only if Son's Father will guarantee repayment. If Father makes such a guaranty as part of the sale of the car to Son, Father's guaranty is supported by consideration. This is so because Father's guaranty is given in exchange for (i.e., "bargained for") Dealer's agreement to sell the car to Son on credit.

2. **Guaranty given after underlying debt has arisen:** Where the guaranty is not given until *after* the underlying debt has been created, however, consideration will not necessarily be present for the promise of guaranty. In the above example, for instance, if Dealer went to Father after the sale to Son, and simply said "Would you guarantee your Son's repayment?", Father's guaranty would not be supported by consideration. (There might, of course, be new consideration given for the guaranty, such as a promise by Dealer not to repossess the car if Son falls behind on his payment, or any other meaningful change in the terms of the debt.)

   a. **Guaranty without consideration is invalid in some jurisdictions:** In many jurisdictions, a guaranty that is not supported by consideration is *unenforceable*.

   b. **Recitals of consideration under modern decisions:** Most modern decisions, however, take the view that if the guaranty is *in writing*, and *states* that a consideration (even a nominal one) has been paid by the creditor to the guarantor for his guaranty, the guaranty is *enforceable* even if the purported consideration was never in fact paid or is in fact merely a sham.

      i. **Restatement in accord:** This is also the view of the Second Restatement, which in § 88(a) provides that a guaranty is binding if "the promise is in *writing* and

signed by the promisor and recites a purported consideration...." The Restatement's treatment of guaranties is thus similar to its treatment of options (see *supra*, p. 133), in that both are binding without consideration as long as a signed document reciting the payment of consideration exists.

    ii. UCC view is similar: The UCC similarly takes the view that a written guaranty is not unenforceable for lack of consideration. § 3-408 states that "[N]o consideration is necessary for an instrument given in payment of or as security for an antecedent obligation of any kind." Comment 2 to § 3-408 explains that this rule is intended to make a written guaranty of another's obligation binding without consideration. Observe that this section goes even further than the Second Restatement, in that it does not even require the "recital" of a purported consideration.

    c. Promissory estoppel: Alternatively, the guaranty might be binding under the theory of *promissory estoppel*, if the guarantor should reasonably have expected the person to whom the guaranty is made to rely on him (e.g., by not suing on the underlying obligation that has been guaranteed), and this reliance actually occurs. See Rest. 2d, § 88(c).

E. Contracts under seal: Under the common law, an agreement made ***under seal*** was enforceable, even though not supported by consideration. The "seal" was a mark of wax, an impression, a notary's mark, or any other insignia denoting the fact that the parties intended their promise or agreement to be binding. See C&P, pp. 270-271.

    1. Rationale: The theory for making promises made under seal enforceable without consideration was that the seal made it clear that the parties intended to be bound, and thus served the same evidentiary and cautionary functions as the giving of consideration (see *supra*, p. 85).

    2. Statutory abolition of modification: Most states have enacted statutes which ***modify or abolish*** the effect of the seal. See Rest. 2d, Chap. 4, Topic 3, Statutory Note ("Rest. Note").

        a. Abolition: At least 34 states have enacted statutes that either explicitly abolish the seal or that give sealed and unsealed contracts the same effect. (Rest. Note.)

        b. UCC abolition of seal: Where an agreement involves sale of goods, the seal is ineffective in all jurisdictions which have enacted the UCC (i.e., all states except Louisiana). UCC § 2-203 states that "the law with respect to sealed instruments does not apply to...a contract [for goods]."

        c. Presumption of consideration: Even among states which have not completely abolished the seal, most have statutes providing that a seal imports only a ***rebuttable presumption*** of consideration. (Rest. Note.)

Quiz Yourself on

OTHER CONTRACTS BINDING WITHOUT CONSIDERATION

34. The Great Philosophers Mint offers to consumers a collection of commemorative plates, each with the likeness of a great philosopher on it. Plato, an amateur collector of plates, signs a contract with Great Philosophers to purchase the entire 12-plate set for $300, payment to be at the rate of $10 a month for 30 months, no interest. The contract contains a clause in the boilerplate (which Plato never noticed) saying that no modification will be effective unless it's in a writing signed by both parties. Plato gets the plates, makes the first 2 months' payments, then loses his job writing philosophy tracts. He and Great Philosophers orally agree that he can pay just $5/month til the debt is paid off, still no interest. After one month of this arrangement, Great Philosophers says, "We want the original $10/month." Is Plato obligated to resume paying $10/month?

35. Jerry Seinfeld is a part-owner of a soup store called The Soup Nazi. On Aug. 1, Jerry and his friend George Costanza sign an option agreement that reads as follows: "In consideration of $10 paid this day by Costanza to Seinfeld, Seinfeld hereby grants to Costanza an option to purchase Seinfeld's interest in The Soup Nazi for $10,000 cash, this option to be exercised no later than Sept. 1." ($10,000 would be a fair price for Jerry's interest.) George never in fact paid Jerry the $10 for the option, as Jerry knew when he signed the option agreement. On August 15, Jerry tells George that the option is terminated, because he has decided his interest is worth more than $10,000. Will a court enforce the option?

Answers

34. **No.** First, the fact that Plato is not giving consideration in return for Great Philosophers' concession is irrelevant: under UCC § 2-209(1), "an agreement modifying a contract within [Article 2] needs no consideration to be binding." Next, § 2-209(2) generally enforces No Oral Modification clauses, such as the one here. However, where the deal is between a merchant and a consumer, an N.O.M. clause on a form supplied by the merchant is not enforceable against the consumer unless the clause has been separately signed by the consumer. Since the facts tell us that Plato didn't even notice the clause, he clearly didn't "separately sign" it. Therefore, the clause isn't enforceable, and the modification was effective, under the general rule that oral modifications are enforceable.

35. **Yes.** Under the Restatement and prevailing modern view, an option does not need consideration to be binding, provided that the option is in writing, recites a purported consideration (whether actually paid or not), and proposes an exchange on fair terms within a reasonable time. Rest. 2d, § 87(1)(a). All of these conditions are satisfied here, so the option is enforceable. The significance of the option's enforceability, of course, is that Jerry cannot revoke the option (in contrast to the usual rule making offers that are not supported by consideration revocable even where the offer recites that it's irrevocable).

V. PROMISSORY ESTOPPEL

A. **Introduction:** The consideration doctrine is designed to enforce promises which are "bargained for." There are some promises which, although the promisor makes them without bargaining for anything in return, nonetheless induce the promisee to *rely to his detriment*. The doctrine of *"promissory estoppel"* is being used by an increasing number of courts to enforce such promises which, although not supported by consideration, induce detrimental reliance by the promisee. See C&P, p. 250.

1. **Other applications:** The promissory estoppel doctrine's scope has also been broadened by some courts to bind promisors even where the promisee has *not* relied detrimentally (e.g., promises to make charitable donations). The following material, after setting forth the Restatement definition of promissory estoppel, considers several of the contexts in which the doctrine is most frequently applied.

B. Restatement definition: The First and Second Restatements have been instrumental in shaping the doctrine of promissory estoppel. (In fact, § 90 of each Restatement, dealing with this subject, is probably the most important single section of each.) Rest. 2d, § 90(1) sets forth the doctrine of promissory estoppel as follows:

"A ***promise*** which the promisor ***should reasonably expect to induce action or forbearance*** on the part of the promisee or a third person and which does induce such action or forbearance ***is binding if injustice can be avoided only by enforcement of the promise***. The remedy granted for breach may be ***limited as justice requires***."

> **Example:** P owns a tract of land on which he desires to construct a commercial building or shopping center. P and D sign a document in which D promises to obtain a $70,000 construction loan for P, or to supply the loan himself if he cannot find anyone else to do so. The document does not specify the amount of monthly installments on the loan to be provided, the amount of interest to be charged, or when interest is to be paid. Following the signing, D urges P to demolish buildings presently on the tract (having a value of about $58,000), so that the new construction can take place quickly once the loan comes through. P does the demolition. D is unable to find a lender, and refuses to lend the money himself; P sues. D defends on the grounds that the document is not an enforceable contract, because it is indefinite with respect to basic terms.
>
> *Held*, P may recover on a promissory estoppel theory; he shall be compensated for his "foreseeable, definite and substantial reliance." However, he is entitled to recover only his reliance damages (i.e., the money required to "put [him] in the position he would have been in had he not acted in reliance upon the promise"), not his expectation damages (the profits he would have made had the loan been given). *Wheeler v. White*, 398 S.W.2d 93 (Tex. 1965).

C. Unbargained-for reliance: The essence of the promissory estoppel idea is that the maker of a promise may be bound by that promise, even though it is not supported by consideration, if the promisee ***relies upon the promise to her detriment***, and the promisor should have foreseen this reliance.

1. **Use:** The promissory estoppel doctrine was originally applied chiefly to ***gratuitous promises*** (i.e., promises to make gifts) which were relied on by the promisee, and then retracted by the promisor. But the doctrine has been expanded to cover certain commercial situations, such as where the parties engage in preliminary negotiations, one party gives assurance to the other that they will be able to reach a binding agreement, the other relies on this assurance to his detriment, and then the contract falls through. (See, e.g., *Hoffman v. Red Owl Stores, infra*, p. 144.)

2. **Not necessarily contractual:** There is a dispute about the precise function of the promissory estoppel doctrine.

   a. **Contract action:** Some courts (and the Second Restatement) view the doctrine as simply ***supplying consideration*** which would otherwise be lacking. If this is the theory, then an action based on promissory estoppel is an action ***on the contract*** (though courts following this approach will nonetheless often apply reliance damages rather than the usual contract "expectation" measure; see *infra*, p. 148).

b. Tort action: Other authorities, however, view promissory estoppel as having a large component of *tort law*. As the idea has been expressed, "One person has caused harm to another by making a promise that he should reasonably have expected would cause such harm, and he is therefore held liable for the harm caused." Farnsworth, p. 100. Under this view, the appropriate measure of damages will almost *always* be reliance, rather than expectation.

3. Actual reliance: The promisee must *actually rely* on the promise. So if the claimed reliance is an affirmative act, the promisee must show that he would not have taken the act except for the promise, i.e., that there was a cause and effect relationship between the promise and the act. And if the claimed reliance is a *forbearance* from doing something, the promisee must show that he could have and would have done the act but for the promise.

> **Example:** P, a travelling salesman, is 65 and has worked for D for 25 years. D suggests that P retire, and tells P that if P does so, D will pay P a $20,000 per-year pension for the rest of P's life. P retires. The day after he does so, for reasons having nothing to do with the retirement, P suffers a stroke that completely and permanently paralyzes him. D pays the pension for one year, then stops.
>
> On these facts, P will probably not be able to use the promissory estoppel doctrine to recover on the promise of the pension. The reason is that P *has not significantly relied on the promise* to his detriment — even without the promise, he still would have been forced to stop working.

4. Foreseeability of reliance: The promisee's reliance must also have been *reasonably foreseeable* to the promisor. This requirement probably means not only that it must have been reasonably foreseeable to the promisor that the promisee would rely, but also foreseeable that the promisee would rely *in the particular way* that he did in fact rely. Farnsworth, p. 96.

> **Example:** Suppose that the plaintiff in *Wheeler v. White, supra,* p. 137, had relied on the promise of a loan not by demolishing structures on the land, but by buying a new house in anticipation of the profits he would make from the forthcoming construction. A court would almost certainly say that this *type* of reliance was not reasonably foreseeable by the defendant. (Alternatively, promissory estoppel might fail in this situation because the plaintiff's reliance would probably be held to have been "unreasonable.")

D. Promises to make gifts: The promissory estoppel doctrine is often applied to enforce promises to *make gifts* that induce detrimental reliance.

1. Intra-family promises: Promissory estoppel may be used to enforce certain promises made by one member of a family to another, if the latter reasonably and detrimentally relies on the promise. See C&P, p. 251.

> **Example:** Grandfather, distressed because his Granddaughter has to work in a store, gives her a promissory note, telling her that he has done this so that she will not have to work anymore. She quits her job. He then dies, and his estate refuses to pay the note.

Held, Granddaughter justifiably and foreseeably relied on Grandfather's promise of payment, by giving up her job. This reliance made the note enforceable, and operated to "estop" the executor from denying that the note was given for valid consideration. See *Ricketts v. Scothorn*, 57 Neb. 51 (1898).

a. **Utility of doctrine:** Ordinarily, promises made by one family member to another are unenforceable, either because the parties lack an intent to contract (see *supra*, p. 7) and/or because there is no consideration since the promise is not bargained-for (see *supra*, p. 87). The promissory estoppel doctrine thus fills an important function in the intra-family promise situation, since it at least allows the promisee some legal remedy if he *relies* on the promise to his detriment. However, most courts do not give a full contractual measure of damages (i.e., "lost profits") in this situation, but merely recompense the promisee for his *out-of-pocket losses.*

2. **Oral promises to convey land:** A promise to make a gift of *land*, like any other gratuitous promise, is unenforceable for lack of consideration. If the recipient of such a promise, acting in reasonable reliance on the promise and with the continuing assent of the promisor, incurs detriment with respect to the land, the promise may be enforced under the promissory estoppel doctrine.

Example: *A* orally promises to make a gift of Blackacre to his son *B*, who takes possession of the land. *B* builds a house on the land and lives in it for twenty years until *A* dies. *B* may obtain, from *A*'s estate, a decree ordering specific performance of *A*'s promise to convey the land. See *Seavey v. Drake*, 62 N.H. 393 (1882). See also Rest. 2d, § 90, Illustr. 16 (using fairly similar facts).

Note: The Statute of Frauds requires that a contract to convey land, to be enforceable, must be in writing. If one party to an oral contract to convey land relies to her detriment on the contract, she may be able to use the promissory estoppel doctrine to recover her reliance interest. In other words, promissory estoppel may be used as a *substitute for compliance with the Statute of Frauds,* just as it may be used to substitute for consideration. See C&P, p. 252.

E. **Charitable subscriptions:** Suppose a person promises to give a specified sum of money to a particular *charity*. Such a promise would not ordinarily be enforceable, since a charitable donor usually does not "bargain for" anything in return for his promise, and therefore there is no consideration. The doctrine of promissory estoppel is being used with increasing frequency to *enforce such promises of charitable subscription.*

1. **Pre-promissory estoppel theories of consideration:** Before the use of the promissory estoppel doctrine became widespread, courts enforced such promises of charitable contributions by finding consideration to be present. Some courts found an *implied promise by the donee* to use the gift for charitable purposes. Other courts found that the promises of other prospective donors to make donations were consideration for the particular donor's promise. In any case, these "consideration" theories were tenuous at best, since the prospective donor almost never truly "bargained" for his promise. In a few cases, the finding of consideration for a promise of charitable contribution was reasonable, as in the following example.

Example: D promises to give $5,000 to P, a charitable organization. The parties agree that the $5,000 will be used to establish a scholarship fund to be named after D. D gives $1,000, which is put aside by P for the fund, and then D repudiates her promise. She dies, and P sues her estate for the remaining $4,000.

Held (by the New York Court of Appeals, in an opinion by Judge Cardozo), there was an enforceable bilateral contract. The consideration for D's promise was P's promise to name the scholarship fund after her. (The opinion also mentioned the possibility of using promissory estoppel to enforce the promise, although the case was in fact decided on a contractual basis.) See *Allegheny College v. National Chautauqua County Bank of Jamestown*, 246 N.Y. 369 (1927).

2. **No reliance necessary in charitable subscription case:** Although in most contexts promissory estoppel will apply only when the promisee relies to his detriment, the courts often do *not* impose such a detrimental reliance requirement where the promise is a *charitable subscription*, i.e., a *written promise* to make a charitable contribution. Thus § 90(2) of the Second Restatement states that "a charitable subscription ... is binding under subsection (1) [which sets forth the promissory estoppel doctrine] without proof that the promise induced action or forbearance."

   a. **Oral promises to charities not covered:** But observe that the phrase "charitable subscription" means a *written* promise to a charity, and the rule that no reliance needs to be shown for a charitable subscription is thus generally *not held* to apply to an *oral* promise to make a charitable gift.

F. **Gratuitous bailments and agencies:** Suppose that *A* promises, as a favor to *B*, to collect *B*'s mail while *B* is on vacation. Is this promise enforceable? If *A* fails to perform, and the mail is stolen from *B*'s mailbox, is *A* liable?

1. **Theories of liability:** The courts have traditionally found a *"gratuitous bailee"* (one who takes care of another's property for no consideration) liable if she actually begins to perform the bailment. But if she never starts to perform the bailment at all, most courts have traditionally denied liability for any harm suffered by the would-be bailor. Recently, however, courts have begun to make use of the doctrine of promissory estoppel where the bailee neglects to perform altogether, and the bailor suffers a loss.

2. **Gratuitous agents:** The same rules apply where a person gratuitously promises to act as another's *agent* for some purpose. Thus if *A* promises to *procure insurance* for *B*, and gets the wrong kind of policy, he may well be held liable for any loss suffered by *B*. If he never gets any insurance at all, older courts would not hold him liable. A modern court, however, might well apply promissory estoppel theory.

   a. **Reluctance in insurance cases:** But courts are more *hesitant* to use promissory estoppel in insurance-procurement cases than in other cases involving gratuitous promises to act as agent. This is so because the promisor would typically be *exposed to an enormous liability*, and the promisee's (i.e., the prospective insured's) reliance on the promise is often unreasonable. See Comment e to § 90 of the Second Restatement, urging "caution" in applying the doctrine of promissory estoppel in the context of promises to obtain insurance.

G. Promises to pay pensions: The doctrine of promissory estoppel has occasionally been applied to promises by employers to pay ***pensions*** and other fringe benefits. Many such promises, insofar as they represent an employer's attempt to ensure continued service by his employees, are supported by consideration, and are therefore enforceable as ordinary contracts. But where the promise of pension is made after the employee has retired, or made under terms allowing the employee to retire immediately, the bargain element necessary for consideration will usually not be present. It is in this kind of situation that the courts have used the promissory estoppel theory to bind the employer (see *supra*, pp. 136).

> **Example:** Employer promises Employee a pension when she retires. She retires shortly after this promise is made, apparently at least in part in reliance upon it. She does not seek other employment, and is eventually stricken with cancer, making further employment completely impossible.
>
> *Held*, the promise to pay the pension is binding under the promissory estoppel theory, since Employee has reasonably and detrimentally relied upon it. Her reliance came in choosing to retire, since she was already of such an age (57) that finding another job would have been impossible even had she not gotten sick. *Feinberg v. Pfeiffer Co.*, 322 S.W.2d 163 (Mo. App. 1959).

H. Offers by sub-contractors: Suppose a sub-contractor renders a ***bid*** to a general contractor, who relies upon that bid to figure out her own bid on a job which she obtains. Is the sub-contractor's bid binding? As we discussed above (*supra*, p. 59), many courts treat the sub-contractor's bid as temporarily irrevocable, for the period necessary to allow the contractor to obtain the job and accept the sub-contractor's bid. Such holdings in effect apply the doctrine of promissory estoppel, since they are based on the theory that the general contractor has ***reasonably relied upon the sub-contractor's bid***, and would suffer a loss (or at least a reduced profit) if the sub-contractor backed out and a new one had to be found. See Rest. 2d, § 87(2).

1. Reliance by general contractor: In the sub-contractor-bid scenario, be sure to ***check for reliance by the general contractor.*** If there is no real (and justifiable) reliance by the general contractor on the sub-contractor's bid, the general contractor will ***not be permitted to use promissory estoppel*** to make the sub-contractor's bid temporarily irrevocable.

> **Example:** Suppose the sub-contractor discovers its bid is too low and tells the general about this *before* the general's own bid has been opened by the owner. In this scenario, the general contractor might be able to avoid the problem by revising or withdrawing its master bid. If the general has this opportunity and doesn't use it, then the general has not reasonably relied, and will not qualify for promissory estoppel.

a. GC must post a bond: In the sub-contractor-bid situation, the general contractor (GC) is often ***forced to rely*** on the sub's bid by virtue of the fact that the owner (the one receiving bids for the overall job) requires each general contractor who bids to ***post a bond*** ensuring that the GC's bid will be honored. Such a bond prevents the GC from changing or withdrawing the bid based on the sub-contractor's withdrawing his own bid (the GC loses the bond amount if he does so), so the GC meets the requirement of reliance in this situation.

I. **Promise to perform business service:**   A person who promises to *perform some business service* for another may be liable under a promissory estoppel theory, if the other person relies on the promise by entering or failing to enter some other transaction.

    1. **Promise to obtain insurance:**   For instance, suppose an insurance agent or broker promises a business operator to *"bind" an insurance policy*, i.e., to cause an insurance company to cover a particular risk faced by the operator. If the operator relies on the promise by failing to get the insurance through some other mechanism, promissory estoppel may apply to turn the agent into, in effect, an insurer.

        Example: Biz, a business owner, wants fire insurance on his warehouse. He phones Agent to tell him this. Agent says, "I'll get you $200,000 of coverage from Allstate today. Consider it done." This is probably not a contract, since Biz has not given consideration (he has probably not taken an act or made a promise in return, and if he has done either, it has not been "bargained for" by Agent). But if Agent neither gets the insurance nor tells Biz that he hasn't done so, and the warehouse burns down, there is a good chance that Biz can recover his fire losses from Agent on a promissory estoppel theory: Biz has reasonably and foreseeably relied on the promise, by forbearing from getting insurance from some other source.

    2. **Promise to make a loan:** Similarly, a person who promises to *make a loan* may be liable to the would-be borrower, if the latter does something in reliance on the promise, and the promisor then refuses to make the loan.

        Example: Owner owns a house with a dilapidated but still functional garage in the back. After Owner applies for a loan to Lender, Lender makes a written and unconditional promise to Owner that Lender will lend Owner $20,000, secured by the real estate, to cover the costs of tearing down the old garage and building a new one. Owner, in reliance, tears down the old garage. Lender then refuses to make the loan, and Owner can't get a loan from anyone else because his credit has worsened.

        A court would likely hold that Owner can recover his reliance expenditures (at least the cost of tearing down the old garage, and probably the lessening of value between a dilapidated-but-functional garage to no garage at all) from Lender, on a promissory estoppel theory.[2]

J. **At-will jobs and other at-will relationships:**   Another important domain in which courts sometimes apply promissory estoppel is that of promises to enter or continue in *at-will relationships.* Typically, the promisor promises to enter into or continue in an at-will arrangement, and the promisee relies; the promisor then changes her mind. When the promisee sues for promissory estoppel, the promisor defends by saying, "Any relationship would have been at-will, so I was free to change my mind at any time. Therefore, you could not have reasonably relied on my promise."

---

    2. Note that on the facts as stated, Owner can't recover under standard contract principles, because he hasn't given any consideration in return for Lender's promise of a loan. If, however, Owner had promised that he would use Lender, rather than some other lender, if he decided to borrow (or if Owner had paid an application fee), that promise or fee *would* have constituted consideration for Lender's promise, and promissory estoppel would not be needed.

However, courts have often disagreed with the promisor's argument, concluding that the mere fact that the promise involved an at-will relationship does not mean that reliance upon that relationship's continuation for at least some additional period was *per se* unreasonable.

1. **Promise of at-will job:** Most commonly, this all arises in an employment context: an employer has promised an *at-will job* to an employee, and then revokes the promise before the employee shows up for work, or very soon thereafter. Meanwhile, the employee may have *quit his previous job*, *turned down other job offerings*, or otherwise relied on the job promise. In this scenario, a court may well hold that even though the employer could have fired the employee at any time after he started the job (in theory, even after a single day), the employer is *not free to withdraw the promised job* without giving the employee at least some chance to "show her stuff." Cf. *Grouse v. Group Health Plan, Inc.*, 306 N.W.2d 114 (Minn. 1981).

2. **Promise of continued at-will business relationship:** The "promise of an at-will relationship" scenario can also arise *outside of the employment context*. There are many at-will arrangements in business. For instance, "sales agency" arrangements are often made, in which one person resells another's goods or services, and either party is free to discontinue the arrangement on very short notice. If one party tells the other that he intends to continue in the arrangement for the time being, and the other relies somehow to her detriment, the court may well use promissory estoppel to allow the relier to recover at least her reliance damages.

   Example: P is a liquor distributor, and D is one of P's largest suppliers. P has recently lost some other large suppliers, and is financially weak. P is now negotiating to sell itself to N, another distributor. P tells D about these negotiations, and says to D that it has received an offer to be purchased by N, but that it will reject N's offer if D assures P that D has no present intention to terminate its supply arrangement with P. D repeatedly assures P that D has no intention of ending the relationship. In reliance, P turns down N's offer. Later that very day, D terminates the supply arrangement. This termination so weakens P that P is forced to go back to N, and to accept a new offer that is $550,000 lower. P sues D on a promissory estoppel theory for the $550,000 price reduction. D defends on the grounds that because the P-D contract was terminable at will, any reliance by P on D's promise was unreasonable as a matter of law.

   Held, for P. P's reliance on D's continuation (at least temporarily) of the contract was probably reasonable and foreseeable to D. Furthermore, the cancellation of the agreement predictably undermined P's bargaining power in the P-N negotiations, since once the cancellation was publicly announced N knew that P had no choice but to sell or liquidate. Therefore, the reduction in the purchase price was precise and calculable, making it a form of reliance damages (like the damages of an employee who incurs moving expenses to take an at-will job), not a form of non-recoverable expectation damages (like the reduction in P's future profits from the P-D contract.) Consequently, P may recover the price reduction to the extent it was caused by D's failure to keep its promise. *D & G Stout, Inc. v. Bacardi Imports, Inc.*, 923 F.2d 566 (7th Cir. 1991).

K. Duty to bargain in good faith: So far, we have seen the doctrine of promissory estoppel applied to fairly specific promises and offers, such as a promise to pay a pension. But the promissory estoppel doctrine, or something like it, has also been applied to a much more general type of promise: the promise to **bargain in good faith**. By entering into **negotiations** with another party, a person may be found to have **promised**, either explicitly or implicitly, that he **will make a good-faith effort to reach agreement with the other party**. If the court finds that this promise to bargain in good faith has been breached, it can either award contract damages, or damages based on promissory estoppel.

1. **Letter of intent:** For instance, if two negotiating parties sign a **letter of intent** in which they agree that they will attempt to reach a binding contract, the court may find that this letter of intent amounts to a promise to negotiate in good faith. The court can then enforce this "contract to negotiate" just as it would enforce any other contract — it can award contract-based damages, and need not expressly rely on promissory estoppel (though the effect is much the same as if promissory estoppel were used). See Farnsworth, p. 206.

2. **Promises of franchises:** Courts sometimes find that a party made an **implied** (but nonetheless **enforceable**) promise to negotiate in good faith. Courts seem most likely to find an implied promise of good faith where the negotiations relate to the award of a **franchise**.

   a. **The scenario:** Typically, what happens is that a large national corporation (the franchisor) indicates to a prospective franchisee (typically an individual) that the franchisee's application for a franchise will be accepted. The prospective franchisee then incurs expenses in reliance on this promise (e.g., she sells her existing business, or rents retail space). The deal then falls through, and the prospective franchisee sues to recover her losses and possibly the profits she would have made had the franchise been granted. Courts have frequently been sympathetic to the franchisee in this context, and have sometimes **awarded damages** based either on promissory estoppel or on breach of the implied promise to negotiate in good faith. See Farnsworth, pp. 202-03. For instance, they may award P reliance damages equal to sums he spent preparing to receive the franchise.

   b. **Contractual recovery irrelevant:** Liability in the franchise-negotiation situation may exist under a promissory estoppel theory **even though the contract contemplated by the parties** (but never entered into) **would not have been enforceable**. In other words, promissory estoppel is not always, strictly speaking, a substitute for consideration; it does not necessarily enable the court to find an enforceable contract. Instead, it is sometimes a **separate remedy** that contains elements of contract, quasi-contract, and tort. This is illustrated by *Hoffman v. Red Owl Stores*, a very significant case set forth in the following example.

   Example: P negotiates with D Corp. to become a supermarket franchisee of D Corp. D assures P that if he raises $18,000 worth of capital and does certain other things, he will be given the franchise. In order to conform with D's recommendations and conditions, P sells his bakery, purchases and then resells a small grocery store to gain experience, makes a payment on the site of the proposed store, moves his residence to a location near where the store is to be, and borrows the $18,000 from his father-in-law. D Corp. then decides that as long as the $18,000 is merely on loan to P, his credit standing is not good enough, and tells P that the deal is off unless P can procure from his father-in-law a statement that the $18,000 is a gift rather than a loan. P refuses and sues.

Held, P may recover for all of the out-of-pocket expenses and losses he suffered in reliance on D's promise of a franchise. The promissory estoppel doctrine applies even though at the time of suit the negotiations between the parties were highly indefinite; no agreement had been reached as to such items as "the size, cost, design and layout of the store building; and the terms of the lease with respect to rent, maintenance, renewal, and purchase options." Thus the parties had not finalized the details of their proposed bargain sufficiently enough even to constitute an offer, let alone a contract. Nonetheless, promissory estoppel recovery is awarded on the grounds that such recovery is not "the equivalent of a breach of contract action." See *Hoffman v. Red Owl Stores*, 26 Wisc.2d 683 (1965).

3. **Promises by lenders to renegotiate troubled mortgages:** Another context in which a promise to negotiate in good faith has occasionally been enforced via promissory estoppel is that of ***discussions between mortgage lenders and homeowner/borrowers*** regarding possible ***modification of a troubled mortgage***. During and after the Great Recession that began in 2008, millions of homeowners had trouble paying their mortgages, and lenders often conducted discussions with these owner/borrowers about possible modifications of the mortgage to avoid foreclosure.

In the typical fact pattern, the lender tells the borrower, "If you first follow certain procedures, we'll then work with you to try to modify your mortgage to help you avoid a foreclosure." The borrower follows those procedures — which may include ***letting the mortgage go into default*** — but the lender then refuses to even discuss a modification, and instead forecloses. A few of these disappointed borrowers have been found to ***state a valid claim*** for promissory estoppel, even where the lender didn't specifically promise to modify the mortgage, and merely promised to negotiate *towards* a possible modification.

a. **The *Dixon v. Wells Fargo* case:** Probably the leading case of this type is ***Dixon v. Wells Fargo, N.A.***, 798 F.Supp. 336 (D. Mass. 2011).

   i. **Facts:** Taking as true the facts recited in the plaintiffs' complaint, here's what happened in *Dixon*. The Ps, a married couple, owned a home with a mortgage held by D (Wells Fargo Bank). At a time when the Ps were apparently under financial distress but had not yet been late on any mortgage payments, they contacted the D to ask about the possibility that D would modify the mortgage to be more affordable to them. D's employee told the Ps that in order for them to be eligible to have the bank consider a modification, the Ps would have to stop making payments on their loan.[3] The employee also instructed the Ps to furnish certain financial information to the bank. Once the Ps stopped making mortgage payments and furnished the information, the employee said, a bank officer would then sit down with the Ps to see whether the loan could be restructured.

---

3. Although the opinion does not say so, apparently the loan-modification program being run by D applied only to borrowers who were no longer making timely mortgage payments. In other words, the employee of D who spoke to the Ps seems to have correctly described this "you must be in default" requirement of the modification program.

(1) Foreclosure: The Ps did as D's employee instructed: they stopped making payments, and they submitted the requested financial information. But six months or so after the conversation, without any negotiations to modify the mortgage having occurred, D started a foreclosure proceeding. The present lawsuit was an attempt by the Ps to get a state-court injunction against this foreclosure, and to have the bank be ordered to resume negotiations for a modification.[4] It fell to the federal judge hearing the suit to decide whether the Massachusetts courts would apply the promissory estoppel doctrine to these facts.

ii. **The holding:** The court concluded that the facts of the complaint, if proven, *would* justify application of the promissory estoppel doctrine, entitling the Ps to some sort of relief.

iii. **A reasonably definite "promise":** As the court noted at the outset, the promissory estoppel doctrine requires that the party against whom it is asserted have made a *"promise"* — a commitment to do something, or refrain from doing something. And, in fact, the promise must be (as the Massachusetts courts put it) sufficiently *"definite and certain in its terms"* to be enforceable.

(1) Bank opposes: This requirement that there be a reasonably definite promise was the heart of Wells Fargo's main defense. The bank noted, correctly, that it had never promised the Ps that it would *actually modify their mortgage.* At most, it had indicated that if certain conditions were met, the bank would *begin negotiations* with the Ps that might culminate in her modification. And the bank never indicated anything about what the contents or outcome of those negotiations would be if they occurred. Thus even if the bank was found to have "promised to negotiate," it argued, that promise was *fatally indefinite*.

(2) Argument taken seriously: The judge conceded that the Massachusetts courts had often rejected, on indefiniteness grounds, similar claims that a defendant's promises to negotiate or to try to reach agreement should trigger promissory estoppel liability.

(3) The "dangling on a string" scenario: But the judge identified one particular type of fact pattern in which, he said, the Massachusetts courts had been especially *willing* to apply promissory estoppel to enforce even a somewhat indefinite promise: "where there has been a pattern of conduct by one side which has *dangled the other side on a string,*" by repeatedly *misleading* that other side. These were cases involving *extended negotiations*, in which the *powerful defendant* appeared to have tried to *get the upper hand* over the *weaker plaintiff* by promising that the plaintiff would receive some desired benefit if he jumped through a series of hoops. In such cases the Massachusetts courts were quite likely to apply promissory estoppel, at least if they believed that the defendant had acted "in a manner *not consonant with fairness* and *designed*

---

4. The opinion is by a federal district judge in Massachusetts because the bank, as a non-Massachusetts citizen, exercised its right to remove the case from state to federal court.

to induce action by the plaintiff to his harm."[5]

(4) "Dangling" fits the facts here: The facts alleged here by the Ps, the *Dixon* court said, fell within this "unfair dangling" scenario. The bank hadn't just made a promise (to negotiate a modification) that it broke. Rather, the bank had induced the Ps to ***take an action that was foreseeably to their detriment*** (stopping payment and thus ***putting themselves in default),*** and did this for the bank's benefit. As the judge concluded, "where, like here, the promisor ***opportunistically has strung along*** the promisee, the imposition of liability despite the preliminary stage of the negotiations ***produces the most equitable result.***"

(5) Trial ordered: Therefore, the judge in *Dixon* ordered a ***full trial,*** in which the Ps would be given a chance to prove their factual allegations. If they could do so, the judge said, he would somehow "enforce" the bank's obligation to negotiate.

iv. Remedy: Suppose that at trial in *Dixon*, the Ps were able to prove all their allegations, and the judge applied promissory estoppel. What would be the appropriate ***remedy***? The judge indicated that the appropriate reliance-based measure would probably involve putting the Ps in the position they ***would have been in had they not detrimentally relied on the promise of negotiations by stopping payments on their mortgage.*** Thus the court indicated that reliance damages would consist of ***"returning [the] loan to non-default status,"*** so that if the Ps still couldn't make payments, they could again be foreclosed on. (For more about the reliance aspect of the case, see *infra*, p. 148.)

4. Summary: So cases like *Hoffman* and *Dixon* can be viewed as granting a party to ***unsuccessful negotiations*** recovery for the losses reasonably and foreseeably sustained by him as a result of the other party's ***negligence*** or ***lack of good faith*** during the bargaining process.

a. Alternative rationales: Sometimes the recovery is based upon violation of a "duty to bargain in good faith." At other times it is based explicitly on promissory estoppel — one party's otherwise-unenforceable promises to the other about the probable result of the negotiations is enforced to the limited extent of giving the latter his reliance damages.

b. Typical contexts: Use of promissory estoppel for unsuccessful contract negotiations is most likely to be applied in cases involving ***franchises, government contracts, and mortgage lending to consumers***, all contexts in which there is typically ***great inequality of bargaining power.*** But the doctrine is also sometimes used in other negotiating situations that don't culminate in contracts.

c. Tort law: It may be best to view this trend as bringing an element of ***tort law*** into contract law: the defendant is held blameworthy for intentionally or negligently induc-

---

5. Note that *Hoffman v. Red Owl Stores, supra*, p. 145, falls quite neatly into this "stringing along" fact pattern, so presumably the Massachusetts courts would agree with the application of promissory estoppel in *Hoffman*.

ing the other party to rely on the negotiations, and is thus held liable for something akin to misrepresentation. See generally Farnsworth, pp. 202-07.

L. Theories of recovery: Promissory estoppel is based essentially on the idea of reliance, that one who has relied on another party's promise, to his own detriment, is entitled to be made whole.

1. **Reliance as damage measure:** Therefore, the most common measure of damages in promissory estoppel actions is the *"reliance"* measure, by which the plaintiff is ***placed in the position he would have been in had the promise never been made***. Often, reliance damages consist of the plaintiff's *"out-of-pocket" expenses* incurred in reliance on the promise.

> **Example 1:** In *D & G Stout v. Bacardi Imports* (*supra*, p. 143), P was entitled to recover the difference between the purchase offer it turned down in reliance on D's assurances that the P-D contract would continue in force, and the lower offer that P was forced to accept once D reneged. This recovery was in the nature of reliance damages — P was entitled to recover the quite fixed, definite sum that it turned down, not the "profits" that it would have made from a continuation of the P-D relationship.

> **Example 2:** In *Dixon v. Wells Fargo*, *supra*, p. 145, recall that the Ps were a home-owning couple who let their mortgage go into default in reliance on the bank's promise to negotiate towards a modification of the mortgage if and only if the mortgage was in default. The judge indicated that a reliance-based verdict would involve putting the Ps into the position they would have been in had they not relied to their detriment, i.e., *"returning their loan to non-default status[.]"*

2. **Other theories of recovery:** Although reliance-based damages are the standard in promissory estoppel cases, there are ***other theories*** of recovery which will in some situations be appropriate.

   a. **Restitution:** The plaintiff may be able to argue that he has ***conferred something of value*** on the defendant, for which the latter should be required to pay. Recovery is thus based on ***restitution***, or prevention of ***unjust enrichment***.

   > **Example:** D, a property owner, asks P, a contractor, to help him plan for putting up a building on D's land. P makes trips to the property, does a survey, and gets data for an application to a government agency, all in the reasonable expectation of being awarded a contract for the work. D then gives the work to another contractor, and P sues for the reasonable value of the work he did. *Held*, P may recover the reasonable value of his services. *Hill v. Waxberg*, 237 F.2d 936 (9th Cir. 1956).

   b. **Expectation measure:** In some promissory estoppel cases, the traditional contract measure of damages, *expectation* damages, will be appropriate. The expectation measure places the plaintiff in the position he would have been in had the contract (or here, promise) been fulfilled. Typically, this means that the plaintiff is awarded the ***profits he would have made*** had the promise been kept. (See *infra*, p. 318.)

      i. **Limited view on lost profits:** However, as in the ordinary contract situation, courts will not award lost profits where these are too ***speculative*** or ***uncertain***. (See *infra*, p. 323.)

Example: In the franchise negotiation context discussed above, it will usually be the case that even had the promised franchise been awarded, it would have been terminable at some point by the franchisor; therefore, a court awarding damages for failure to grant a promised franchise may limit recovery for lost profits to the period up until the earliest time the franchisor could have terminated.

ii. **Lack of good faith:** If the promisor is shown to have acted in ***bad faith***, this fact will weigh in favor of an award of expectation rather than reliance damages. See Rest. 2d, § 90, Illustr. 9.

Example: In *Hoffman v. Red Owl, supra*, p. 145, suppose that D knew at the time it made the promise of a franchise to P that the franchise would never be awarded. This fact would have improved P's chances of recovering some profits he might have made from operating of the supermarket (in addition to or instead of the reliance expenditures that he in fact recovered).

M. Promissory estoppel under the UCC: The doctrine of promissory estoppel is not explicitly recognized in the UCC. However, most courts have held that a party to a contract for the sale of goods may nonetheless invoke the doctrine in appropriate circumstances. See W&S, p. 26. Furthermore, in one situation which is sometimes handled by promissory estoppel, the case of an offeror who revokes his offer after inducing the offeree to reasonably rely on it, the Code may supply its own solution: the offer may be irrevocable under § 2-205's "firm offer" provision (*supra*, p. 53).

Quiz Yourself on
PROMISORY ESTOPPEL

36. Mark Antony promises to buy a new barge for his girlfriend, Cleopatra, as a token of his love for her. He shows her the brochure of the model he has chosen and tells her the boat will arrive in five days. Cleo goes out and leases a berth on the Nile, hires a crew, purchases barge accessories, and, most importantly, buys a new sailing wardrobe. Antony changes his mind and never gives her the gift. Can Cleo enforce the promise? If so, what will the damages be?

37. Ali Baba is out hiking on his property one day and stumbles into a hidden cave that is stuffed with ancient treasure. He runs home and calls his girlfriend, Scheherezade. She is thrilled. Ali tells her, "Naturally, I'll split it with you." The value of Scheherezade's 1/2 of the treasure would be $1 million (in 1999 dollars).

(A) One hour after making the promise, before Scheherezade has even really started to think about what the treasure will mean to her life, Ali has a change of heart. He immediately calls Scheherezade back and reneges on his promise to split the treasure with her. Can Scheherezade recover anything from Ali, and if so, what amount?

(B) Assume that during his initial phone call with Scheherezade, Ali adds, "I know how much you have been wanting that 200-camel-power convertible Porsche. Now you will be able to buy it." As soon as she hangs up the phone, Scheherezade races over to the Porsche dealer and puts a down a $25,000 deposit on the car of her dreams, which has a market value of $250,000. Ali then decides to keep the treasure all for himself. The dealer refuses to refund any part of the deposit, and Scheherezade can't afford the car without the treasure. Can Scheherezade recovery anything from Ali, and if so, what amount?

Figure 4-1

Promises Binding Without Consideration

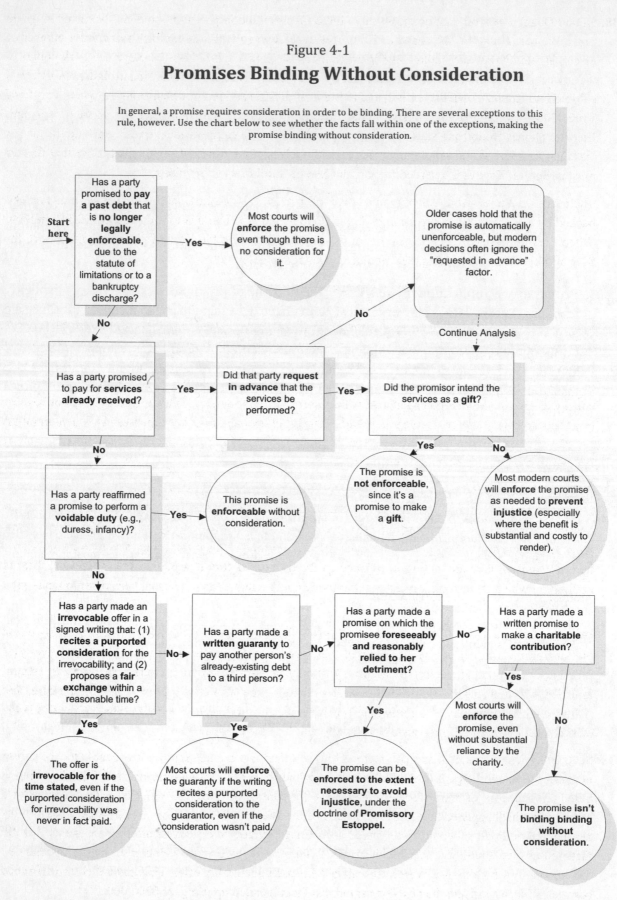

In general, a promise requires consideration in order to be binding. There are several exceptions to this rule, however. Use the chart below to see whether the facts fall within one of the exceptions, making the promise binding without consideration.

Start here → Has a party promised to **pay a past debt** that is **no longer legally enforceable**, due to the statute of limitations or to a bankruptcy discharge?

— Yes → Most courts will **enforce** the promise even though there is no consideration for it.

— No ↓

Older cases hold that the promise is automatically unenforceable, but modern decisions often ignore the "requested in advance" factor.

Continue Analysis ↓

Has a party promised to pay for **services already received**?

— Yes → Did that party **request in advance** that the services be performed?

— Yes → Did the promisor intend the services as a **gift**?

— Yes ↓ The promise is **not enforceable**, since it's a promise to make a **gift**.

— No ↓ Most modern courts will **enforce** the promise as needed to **prevent injustice** (especially where the benefit is substantial and costly to render).

— No ↓

Has a party reaffirmed a promise to perform a **voidable duty** (e.g., duress, infancy)?

— Yes → This promise is **enforceable** without consideration.

— No ↓

Has a party made an **irrevocable** offer in a signed writing that: (1) **recites a purported consideration** for the irrevocability; and (2) proposes a **fair exchange** within a reasonable time?

— No → Has a party made a **written guaranty** to pay another person's already-existing debt to a third person?

— No → Has a party made a promise on which the promisee **foreseeably and reasonably relied to her detriment**?

— No → Has a party made a written promise to make a **charitable contribution**?

— Yes ↓ The offer is **irrevocable for the time stated**, even if the purported consideration for irrevocability was never in fact paid.

— Yes ↓ Most courts will **enforce** the guaranty if the writing recites a purported consideration to the guarantor, even if the consideration wasn't paid.

— Yes ↓ The promise can be **enforced to the extent necessary to avoid injustice**, under the doctrine of **Promissory Estoppel**.

— Yes ↓ Most courts will **enforce** the promise, even without substantial reliance by the charity.

— No ↓ The promise **isn't binding binding without consideration**.

38. Hound Dogg, a general contractor, wants to bid on a construction project to be done for casino magnate Steve Winner: a hotel in the shape of Elvis Presley. Hound solicits sub-contract bids from a number of electrical sub-contractors, including Elektra Cution. Elecktra's sub-bid on the electrical work comes in the lowest, $1 million. (The next lowest bid, by Juice Corp., is $1.2 million.) Hound figures in Electra's sub-bid into Hound's own master bid, and bids a total of $10 million, on which Hound projects a profit of $300,000 (it's a low-margin industry, unlike operating casinos.) Two hours after Hound submits its bid, Elecktra phones Hound and says, "My bid was due to a terrible computational error. I can't do the job for less than $1.25 million. I revoke my offer to do the job for $1 million." Hound tells Elektra that Elektra must perform if Elektra is awarded the job, but Elektra still insists on revoking.

The terms of Winner's bid-solicitation say that all master bids are final, and that all such bids must be backed by a construction-completion bond (as Hound's bid is.) Hound is awarded the job at $10 million. When Elektra persists in refusing to honor its original $1 million bid, Hound gives the job to Juice for $1.2 million. What, if anything, can Hound recover against Elektra?

Answers

36. Yes, but she'll only recover for her reasonable expenditures. Despite the lack of consideration, Antony's promise is enforceable due to promissory estoppel — Cleo's reliance to her detriment on Antony's promise was both reasonable and foreseeable. Note, however, that a court will generally only enforce a promise under the p.e. doctrine to the extent *necessary to avoid injustice.* That generally means that a court will award *reliance* damages, rather than specific performance. So here, Antony will not have to buy Cleo a barge, but he will have to reimburse her for all her out-of-pocket expenses. Also, a court might find that although Cleo's basic reliance was reasonable, some of her particular expenditures were not; in that case she wouldn't recover for the unreasonable ones.

37. (A) No, because Scheherezade did not suffer a detriment in reliance on Ali's promise. First, remember that of course promises to make gifts are generally not enforceable, because they're not supported by consideration. Promissory estoppel can overcome this problem, but p.e. only protects against the promisee's reasonable and foreseeable detrimental reliance on the promise. Here, the facts tells us that Scheherezade did not take any action in reliance on the promise before it was retracted. Therefore, there is nothing on which the promissory estoppel doctrine could operate, and the usual "promises to make gifts are not enforceable" rule applies.

(B) Yes, but only $25,000. Here, unlike in part (A), Scheherezade has reasonably and foreseeably relied on Ali's promise to her detriment. She will therefore be able to enforce his promise under a theory of promissory estoppel. However, the promise will only be enforceable to the extent necessary to prevent injustice, which means that only Scheherezade's reliance expenditures will be protected. In this case, that will mean that Ali will have to reimburse Scheherezade for the forfeited deposit money, since this is the only respect in which Scheherezade has actually relied on the promise.

38. $200,000. Most courts treat sub-contractors' bids as offers that are temporarily irrevocable for the period necessary to allow the contractor to obtain the job and accept the sub-contractor's bid. The reasoning is based on the theory of promissory estoppel, since the contractor justifiably relies on the sub-contractor's bid. That's what happened here. (If Hound had had the chance to withdraw or amend his own bid to Winner, his failure to do so would have made his continued reliance on Electra's offer unreasonable; but the facts tell us that Hound was stuck with his bid.) The recovery will protect Hound's reliance interest, i.e., the amount by which he was worse off than had Elektra honored her offer. That amount is the difference between Elektra's bid and the next-lowest bid that Hound ended up using, or $200,000.

Exam Tips *on*
PROMISES BINDING WITHOUT CONSIDERATION

☛ *General Tip:* When a fact pattern contains a contract that you think is enforceable despite the fact that it's not supported by consideration, first discuss your conclusion that consideration is lacking, then discuss why the contract's enforceable regardless of this flaw.

Modification

☛ **UCC:** A modification of a contract for **goods** is enforceable even if it isn't supported by consideration.

☞ Look for a **one-sided change** in the terms of a sales agreement — even though the change is benefits only one party, it's still enforceable.

    ☞ *Example:* W, a wholesaler of office supplies, contracts with R, a retailer, for the sale of 50 printer cartridges for $450. Two weeks later, W calls R and says that due to a shortage of materials, his costs have increased drastically and that he has to raise the price to $650. R agrees in writing to the change in price. A few days later R purchases 50 cartridges from another supplier for $500 and later rejects delivery of the cartridges from W. The contract between W and R is enforceable at the $650 price.

☞ Watch for the following *traps:*

    ☞ A modification of an agreement for **services**. Such a modification must normally be supported by consideration (see prior chapter), and a modification in which only one party's duty changes (and there are no unanticipated circumstances) does not qualify.

    ☞ A modified agreement that violates the **Statute of Frauds** (i.e., the sales price is greater than $500 and the modification is not in writing). The modified contract will be unenforceable, not because of consideration problems but because of the lack of a writing reflecting the change. (See Ch. 9.)

    ☞ A **"no oral modification"** (N.O.M.) clause. In both UCC and non-UCC cases, a N.O.M. clause will be enforced (so even consideration won't save an oral modification that violates such a clause).

    ☞ But remember, an N.O.M. clause can be **waived**. So if one party foreseeably relies to her substantial detriment on the other party's oral promise to modify the agreement, despite an N.O.M. clause, you should argue that promissory estoppel dictates that the promise be enforced to the extent needed to protect the person who relies.

    Example: Contractor agrees to paint Owner's house for a stated price, work to be completed by August 15, with time of the essence. The contract says that there may be no oral modifications. Contractor's worker gets sick, so Contractor orally asks Owner to give him til Sept. 1. Owner says ok. Contractor relies on the extension, and finishes on Sept. 1. The N.O.M. clause will be deemed waived because a waiver is needed to protect Contractor's reliance interest.

Assignment

☞ If the fact pattern involves an assignment of rights or duties, remember that *consideration isn't required* because an assignment is a present transfer of rights, not a promise.

Guaranty

☞ When you have one person guaranteeing another's debt, look at the timing of the guaranty:

☞ If the guaranty is given *at the same time the debt is being created*, there is no problem of consideration because the guarantor is bargaining for the loan (even though the loan is given to someone else).

☞ When the guaranty is given *after the underlying debt has been created*, see if there is any independent consideration. If not, point out that most modern courts hold that the guaranty is enforceable if it's in writing and includes a *recital* of consideration — even if no consideration is actually paid.

Promissory Estoppel

☞ In the absence of consideration, a contract is enforceable if the promisee *foreseeably and reasonably relies* upon the promise to her detriment.

☞ Look for fact patterns in which a *powerful business* (call it *A*) *"strings along"* a less powerful business or consumer (*B*), by indicating over a period of time that if *B* takes various actions, *A* will consider forming some business relationship with *B* to *B*'s benefit. (*Example: A* is a bank, and promises *B*, a borrower with a cash shortage, that if *B* stops making payments, *A* will consider modifying the mortgage.) Courts are especially likely to order P.E. in this "stringing along" situation.

☞ Most tested issue: Has there been *actual reliance*? Look for these common scenarios where reliance has occurred:

☞ **Intra-family promises and oral promises to convey land.** The problems otherwise encountered in these two situations may be surmountable if you can show foreseeable detrimental reliance.

> **Example:** After being told of Daughter's engagement, Father promises her a new home as a wedding present. He shows her the plans and promises that he will build the house on a lot which he owns. Daughter is so pleased with the plans that she immediately cancels a contract which (as Father knows) she has already made for the purchase of a different home, forfeiting a $20,000 deposit. After Father has caused the home to be half-way built, he refuses to complete it or to convey the land to Daughter.
>
> Father's promise (to make a gift) is unenforceable as a contract, since it was given without consideration (Father didn't bargain for Daughter to cancel

her prior contract.) However, Daughter may be able to use promissory estoppel to argue that the agreement should be enforced, at least to the extent of reimbursing her for the lost $20,000 deposit, since her reliance on Father's promise seems to have been reasonable, and foreseeeable to him.

☞ **Sub-contractor's bid.** If the sub-contractor's bid is relied upon by the general contractor when he submits his overall bid to the customer, the sub-contractor is promissorily estopped from revoking the bid for the time necessary for the general contractor to receive the job and accept the sub-contractor's bid.

☞ *Exception 1:* There's probably no promissory estoppel if the general contractor would still have *time to revise its bid* to the potential customer.

Example: C, a general contractor, has a 3:00 pm deadline for submission of a bid to a potential customer and he solicits bids from sub-contractors for the job. S, a sub-contractor, submits his bid to C at 1:30 pm. C, relying on S's bid, immediately submits his overall bid to the potential customer. S, realizing he has made a mistake in calculating, calls C at 2:58 to withdraw the bid and revise it. S is promissorily estopped from revoking his bid because C reasonably relied on it in submitting his overall bid to the customer. However, if the revocation call from S had come in at 1:40, and there was time for C to revise his bid by taking the next-lowest sub-bid, then C's promissory estoppel argument would probably not work.

☞ *Exception 2:* The sub-bid (like any promise covered by promissory estoppel) is only enforceable "to the extent *necessary to avoid injustice.*" So if the next-lowest bidder is only $x more, the general contractor's recovery will presumably be limited to $x (and the general won't have the right to recover expectation damages as in the ordinary case of breach).

☞ In any p.e. fact pattern, after you have spotted reliance, make sure it's *justified,* i.e., *reasonable*. Confirm that there has been an *express or implied promise*.

Example: Sub, a sub-contractor, submits a bid to General, a general contractor on a project. General responds, "Right now you're the low bidder, so if nothing changes and I get the contract, you'll get the work." Sub then reads in the paper that General got the contract. Therefore, Sub buys $30,000 of materials for the job, which have only scrap value if not used on the job. General gives the job to X, a different sub-contractor who bid $1 more than Sub. Probably Sub's reliance on continuing to be the low bidder, and thus getting the job, wasn't reasonable. If so, she won't collect the $30,000 she spent (let alone the profits she would have made had she gotten the job and performed).

☞ Remember that a *promise to donate money to charity* is generally not supported by consideration. However, most courts will apply the doctrine of promissory estoppel — even if there *hasn't been detrimental reliance* — if the promise to donate is *made in writing*.

CHAPTER 5

MISTAKE

ChapterScope

This chapter deals with situations in which a contract exists and a party attempts to rescind it because one or both parties acted on a *mistaken belief about an existing fact.* The chapter discusses two categories of mistake: mutual (made by both parties) and unilateral (made by one party).

■ **Mutual mistake:** Where *both parties* have acted on the same mistaken belief (*"mutual mistake"*), the party seeking rescission must show three things:

❑ **Basic assumption:** that the mistake concerns a *"basic assumption"* on which the contract was made.

❑ **Material effect:** that the mistake had a *major effect* on the fairness of the deal.

❑ **Allocation of risk:** that the *risk* of this type of mistake was not *allocated* to the party who is trying to rescind. An allocation of risk can occur either by intent of the parties, or by the court's own decision about what is reasonable. (*Example:* The seller of a parcel of realty bears the risk that valuable minerals will later be discovered on it, because it's commonly understood that the seller bears this risk.)

■ **Unilateral mistake:** Where only *one party* has acted on the mistaken belief (*"unilateral mistake"*), it is harder for her to get rescission than in the mutual-mistake situation.

❑ **Additional requirement:** In addition to the three requirements discussed above for mutual mistake, the mistaken party must shown that either: (1) enforcement of the contract would be *unconscionable*; or (2) the other party had reason to *know* of the mistake or actually *caused* it.

I. NATURE OF MISTAKE GENERALLY

A. Difficulty of analysis: The Second Restatement defines "mistake" as "a *belief that is not in accord with the facts.*" Rest. 2d, § 151. "Mistakes," so defined, can crop up in numerous contexts during the formation and performance of a contract. This chapter attempts to analyze some of the situations in which one or both parties holds "a belief that is not in accord with the facts," and acts on that belief.

B. Confusion in case-law: The decisions in cases involving "mistake" are often confused, and many courts seem to make a visceral determination of what the just result is and then work backward, looking for a rationalization for this result.

1. Unilateral vs. mutual mistake: One distinction which courts frequently seize upon to justify their conclusion is that between *"unilateral"* and *"mutual"* mistake. Where the mistake is "unilateral" (i.e., made by only one party), courts often hold that no relief can be granted to that party. Where, on the other hand, the mistake is shared by both parties, it is often held that no contract was formed at all, or that the contract should be subject to either rescission (i.e., cancellation) or reformation (i.e., re-writing by the court).

2. **Distinction not always applied:**   However, there are numerous situations in which relief has been granted for what is apparently a "unilateral" mistake, and also many situations in which relief for supposedly "mutual" mistakes is denied. The distinction remains of significance, however, and we use the two terms here.

3. **Material not covered here:**   Not all types of "mistake" are covered in this chapter. Here, we deal only with those situations where a contract exists, and one party attempts to *avoid* the contract by claiming that she (or both parties) was mistaken on some essential aspect. We do not cover the type of mistake which occurs where the parties have a fundamental misunderstanding about the terms of their deal, such that there is no "meeting of the minds" and thus no contract. (This type of mistake is discussed under the heading "misunderstanding," in the chapter on offer and acceptance, *supra*, p. 73.) Nor do we cover here the situation in which a contract exists, the parties have differing understandings of what it means (but not so different as to prevent a "meeting of the minds"), neither party is trying to avoid the contract, and the dispute is simply about whose interpretation should prevail. (This topic is discussed generally in the materials on interpretation, beginning *infra*, p. 188.)

II.   GENERAL RULE ON MISTAKE

A. **Restatement position:**   The modern treatment of mistake is exemplified by the Second Restatement. Under the Restatement's approach, before one can determine whether a party may avoid the contract on the grounds of mistake, one must first determine whether the mistake was made by *both parties* (traditionally called "mutual mistake") or by only the one party seeking avoidance (traditionally called "unilateral" mistake). Traditionally, only mutual mistake could serve as grounds for avoidance. But the Restatement allows avoidance based on unilateral mistake as well; however, the conditions for such avoidance are significantly more stringent than in the mutual situation. We consider the mutual and unilateral contexts separately, below.

B. **Definition of "mistake":**   Before we begin, it is important to understand that not every erroneous idea is a "mistake" as we use the term here. A "mistake" refers only to a mistaken belief about an *existing* fact, *not* an erroneous belief about *what will happen in the future*. (Erroneous beliefs about the future are handled by the doctrines of impossibility, impracticability and frustration of purpose, discussed in Chap. 12.)

> **Example:** Seller agrees to sell to Buyer all Buyer's requirements for oil for the next five years. Their contract sets a price of $20 per barrel. Both parties believe (reasonably) that the price of oil will increase no more than 10% per year over the life of the contract. Instead, the market price of oil quadruples during the first four years of the contract. If Seller wants to avoid the contract because of this erroneous assumption regarding market prices, he will not be able to use the doctrine of "mistake" discussed in this chapter, since the parties were not mistaken about the facts as they existed at the

time the contract was made. Since the error was one concerning the future, Seller will have to rely upon the doctrine of impracticability (discussed *infra*, p. 442).

1. **Mistake of law:** One or both parties may be mistaken about a *legal principle*, as embodied in a statute, regulation, court decision, etc. The traditional rule was sometimes stated as being that such a "mistake of law" could *not* furnish grounds for avoidance of the contract; courts stating this rule analogized to the comparable principle in criminal law that "ignorance of the law is no excuse."

   a. **Modern view:** However, the modern view, as exemplified by the Second Restatement, *does* allow a mistake of law to serve as the basis for avoiding a contract, if the other requirements for the mistake doctrine are satisfied. That is, the modern approach "treat[s] the law in existence at the time of the making of the contract as part of the total state of facts at that time." Rest. 2d, § 151, Comment b.

III. MUTUAL MISTAKE

A. **Restatement position:** We now turn to detailed consideration of the circumstances under which a party may avoid the contract based upon a mistake by *both parties* (the "*mutual* mistake" situation).

B. **Restatement's three requirements:** The modern approach is illustrated by the Second Restatement. In § 152, the Restatement imposes *three requirements* which must be satisfied before the adversely-affected party may avoid the contract on account of mutual mistake:

   [1] The mistake must concern a *basic assumption* on which the contract was made;

   [2] The mistake must have a *material effect* on the "agreed exchange of performances"; and

   [3] The adversely-affected party (the one seeking avoidance) must *not bear the risk* of the mistake.

   Let's consider each requirement in turn.

C. **Meaning of "basic assumption":** The requirement that the mistake be as to a *"basic assumption"* on which the contract is founded is not simple to apply. The problem lies with the inescapable vagueness of the word "basic." The underlying concept is clear enough: If the assumption is a central part of the bargain, it is "basic," but if the assumption relates merely to a collateral or peripheral aspect of the contract, it is not.

1. **General test:** In determining whether an assumption is "basic" to the underlying bargain, a good method has been suggested: "[O]ne must search the facts for *unexpected, unbargained-for gain* on the one hand and unexpected, unbargained-for loss on the other." C&P, p. 350.

   Example: P is an elderly collector of (but not dealer in) rare violins. D is a famous violinist and violin collector. D buys two violins from P's collection. Both parties believe that one violin is a rare Stradivarius and the other a rare Guarnerius. The contract sets a price of $8,000 for the two violins. It turns out that both violins are mere imitations, not rare and valuable originals. D sues for rescission, and presents evidence that each violin is worth at most $300.

Held, D is excused from paying the $6,000 he still owes on the $8,000 contract price. (The court applied a warranty theory rather than mistake doctrine, but modern mistake analysis would support the same result.) *Smith v. Zimbalist*, 38 P.2d 170 (Cal. Dist. Ct. App. 1934).

2. **Market conditions and financial ability:**   Rest. 2d, § 152, Comment b mentions two types of assumptions which will generally *not* be "basic" ones: mistakes as to *market conditions* and ones concerning *financial ability*.

    a. **Market conditions:**   Thus if Seller agrees to sell Blackacre to Buyer, and both parties believe that comparable land is then worth $5,000 per acre, neither party will be able to avoid the contract if it turns out that comparable land is in fact worth much more, or much less, than this amount.

    b. **Financial ability:**   Similarly, if Seller sells land to Buyer on credit, Buyer's ability to pay the purchase price is a collateral, not basic matter, and Seller's later discovery that Buyer is insolvent will not allow him to avoid the contract for mistake. (But a showing that Buyer lied about his financial condition might support an action for fraud.)

3. **Existence of subject matter:**   The *existence* of the subject matter of the contract will usually be a "basic" assumption.

    Example 1: In a contract to sell land whose value depends mostly on how much timber is on it, a mistaken belief by both parties that the land is covered with timber will be grounds for the buyer to avoid the contract, if it turns out that at the time of the contract the timber had already been destroyed by fire. Rest. 2d, § 152, Illustr. 1.

    Example 2: If *A* buys from *B* an annuity on *C*'s life, it is a basic assumption of the contract that *C* is alive. Therefore, *A* may rescind the contract and obtain a refund if it turns out that *C* was already dead at the time the contract was signed. (But the fact that *C* was in bad health at the time the contract was signed, and died shortly thereafter, will *not* entitle *A* to rescind — a court would almost certainly find that the risk of an early demise should be allocated to *A*, just as the risk of a late demise is allocated to *B*, by the very nature of annuity contracts.)

4. **Quality of subject matter:**   A major mistake as to the *quality* of the contract's subject matter is often viewed as a mistake on a "basic assumption," allowing the disadvantaged party to avoid the contract. The origin (and therefore quality) of the violins in *Smith v. Zimbalist*, *supra*, p. 158, is one example of this principle. Another illustration occurs in one of the most famous mistake case in all of Contracts, *Sherwood v. Walker*, recounted in the following example.

    Example: Seller agrees to sell Buyer a cow (Rose 2d of Aberlone), which both parties believe to be barren. The contract price is approximately $80. Prior to delivery of the cow, Seller realizes that she is pregnant, and refuses to deliver her. Her value as a breeding cow is at least $750.

    Held, Seller may rescind the contract. A party may avoid a contract if "the thing actually delivered or received is different in substance from the thing bargained for, and intended to be sold...." Here, the mistake went "to the very nature of the thing. A barren cow is substantially a different creature than a breeding one." *Sherwood v. Walker*, 33 N.W. 919 (Mich. 1887).

a. Contrary view: But the cases involving mistake as to the quality or value of the contract's subject matter are not consistent. For instance, consider *Wood v. Boynton*, 25 N.W. 42 (Wis. 1885), a case universally contrasted to *Sherwood*. In *Wood*, Seller sold a small stone to Buyer for $1. Both parties believed the stone to be a topaz, though neither was sure. The stone turned out to be an uncut diamond worth about $700. The court denied rescission to Seller, reasoning that (at least in the absence of fraud), this was not a mistake as to the "identity" of the thing sold, and that mere "adequacy of price," no matter how extreme, could not by itself be grounds for rescission.

b. Difficulty of distinguishing: On their face, the *Wood* and *Sherwood* cases are extremely hard to distinguish. For instance, the *Sherwood* Court's statement that a barren cow is "substantially a different creature" than a breeding one could be made equally (or more) plausibly about the difference between a topaz and a diamond.

c. Restatement approach: The modern approach, embodied in the Restatement, at least has the merit of not involving vague, manipulable distinctions like that between an object's "mere quality" and its "very nature" (terms used by the *Sherwood* court). Under the Restatement approach, in both *Sherwood* and *Wood* the question would be whether the characteristic on which the parties were mistaken was a ***"basic assumption."*** Phrased in this way, both *Sherwood* and *Wood* seem to have involved such a mistaken "basic assumption." See Farnsworth, pp. 627-28.

    i. Risk of loss: However, a plausible argument can be made that the cases are distinguishable based on differences in the way they ***allocated the risk of mistake*** (a factor discussed *infra*, p. 160). Under the doctrine of "conscious ignorance" (see *infra*, p. 161), a party who ***knows*** that his knowledge of the facts is limited will be held to bear the risk of an unfavorable mistake. In *Sherwood*, both parties were quite confident that the cow was barren. In *Wood*, however, the parties both ***knew that they did not know*** the identity of the stone (though they suspected it to be a topaz).

        (1) Rightly decided: Therefore, the two cases can be distinguished on the grounds that only in one (*Wood*) did the adversely-affected party bear the risk of mistake. So under this view, each case was correctly decided on allocation-of-risk grounds. See C&P, pp. 350-51.

5. Releases: A party may agree to *release* another party from all claims arising out of a certain transaction; this usually occurs as part of a negotiated settlement. If the party doing the releasing is materially mistaken about the facts surrounding the transaction, may he rescind the release for mistake? As in other contexts, an important factor is whether the mistake involves a "basic assumption" of the parties. The courts are somewhat less inclined to set aside the release for mistake in commercial transactions than in those involving personal injuries.

a. Commercial setting: If the release occurs in a *commercial* setting, such as the termination of a contractual dispute, the court will generally be reluctant to set aside the settlement for mistake, in view of the strong policy in favor of encouraging settlement of claims.

   b. Personal injury claims: But if a release is signed by an individual who has suffered *personal injuries*, in favor of an insurance company or person who has allegedly caused the injuries, the courts are much more willing to void the release when the injuries turn out to be *different from*, or much more *serious than*, the releasor had suspected when he executed the release.

D. Material effect on agreed exchange: In addition to showing that the mistake was on a "basic assumption" shared by the parties, the person seeking to avoid the contract for mistake must also show that the mistake has a "*material effect* on the *agreed exchange of performances*." Rest. 2d, § 152(1). This showing is not made merely by proof that the party would not have made the contract had it not been for the mistake. The party must show "that the resulting imbalance in the agreed exchange is so *severe* that he *cannot fairly be required to carry it out*." Rest. 2d, § 152, Comment c.

   1. Advantage to other party: The courts are more likely to find this showing to have been made where the mistake not only disadvantages the party seeking avoidance but also *advantages* the other party, than where the other party's position is *not improved* by the mistake.

   Example: Observe that in *Sherwood v. Walker*, *supra*, p. 158 (the "Rose of Aberlone" case), the buyer was enriched by the mistake to precisely the same extent as the seller was disadvantaged. This fact, coupled with the large discrepancy between the sale price and the cow's value to the seller, satisfied the requirement that there be a "material effect on the agreed exchange of performances."

   2. Significance of other relief: In determining whether the mistake has a "material effect on the agreed exchange of performances," the fact that *other types of relief* apart from rescission are available will make it less likely that rescission will be allowed. For instance, the court's ability to *reform* the contract, or to order a restitutionary payment, may be enough to undo the effect of the mistake, thereby rendering avoidance unnecessary.

   Example: A land sale contract contains a price per acre, and also contains a mistake about the number of acres. The court will order a pro rata adjustment of the purchase price, rather than allowing the party who is disadvantaged by the mistake to escape the contract entirely. See Rest. 2d, § 152, Illustr. 11.

E. Allocation of risk: Even if the mistake is as to a "basic assumption," and the mistake "materially alters the agreed exchange of performances," the disadvantaged party will still not be able to avoid the contract if the risk of that mistake is *allocated to him*. Rest. 2d, § 154 lists three different ways in which the risk of loss will be allocated to a party:

[1] the risk is allocated to that party *by agreement of the parties*;

[2] he is "aware, at the time the contract is made, that he *has only limited knowledge* with respect to the facts to which the mistake relates but *treats his limited knowledge as sufficient*;" or

[3] the risk is allocated to him "*by the court* on the ground that it is *reasonable in the circumstances* to do so."

Let's consider each of these in turn.

1. **Agreement of the parties:** If the parties themselves allocate their risk of a mistake, this allocation will, not surprisingly, be binding. For instance, if a contract for sale of land calls for the seller to convey only such title as he possesses (i.e., a "quitclaim deed"), and the seller makes no representations as to his title, the buyer may not obtain relief even if it turns out that the seller has no title at all in the property. Rest. 2d, § 154, Illustr. 1.

2. **Conscious ignorance:** The situation described in Sub-paragraph [2] above is sometimes called that of *"conscious ignorance."* The basic idea is that a party who knows that his knowledge is incomplete, but who elects to proceed anyway, must bear the risk that "what he doesn't know will hurt him."

   > **Example:** Recall that in *Wood v. Boynton, supra*, p. 159, both the seller and buyer of the stone were unsure about what kind of stone it was (though both believed it to be a topaz). Since the seller proceeded in "conscious ignorance" of the nature of the stone, he was held to bear the risk of an unfavorable mistake stemming from that ignorance.

3. **Allocation by court:** Probably the most common way in which the risk will be allocated to a particular party is when the *court* makes the allocation, "on the ground that it is *reasonable* [under] the circumstances to do so." Rest. 2d, § 154. There is no more specific standard for deciding when risk-allocation is "reasonable." However, several fairly common situations in which the court will make such an allocation can give an idea of how courts proceed:

   a. **Minerals in land:** Suppose that Seller contracts to sell land to Buyer, with both parties assuming that the land is suitable only for farming. If before the closing, or shortly thereafter, *oil, gas* or other valuable minerals are found under the land, may Seller avoid the contract? The universal answer is *"no."* Under the Restatement scheme, the reason for this is that the court will allocate the risk of a mistake about minerals to the seller. See Rest. 2d, § 154, Comments a and d. This allocation is reasonable because a contrary rule would *disturb* the *valuable finality* of real estate transactions See Farnsworth, p. 629.

   b. **Building conditions:** Suppose Builder contracts to construct a building on land owned by Owner. Both parties assume that sub-soil conditions are normal. It turns out, however, that because the land contains large quantities of rock, or because of some other unexpected condition, *construction is much more expensive* than either had expected. A court will not relieve Builder of his construction obligation, since allocating the risk of this kind of mistake to Builder is reasonable, in view of Builder's actual or presumed greater expertise in judging sub-soil conditions. See *Watkins & Son v. Carrig*, 21 A.2d 591 (N.H. 1941); see also Rest. 2d, § 154, Illustr. 5, and Farnsworth, p. 629.

   c. **Used paintings and other collectibles:** Suppose the owner of a painting or other *used "collectible"* sells it in a private sale, and the object turns out to be of a fundamentally different — and more valuable — nature than either side believed. Courts generally have allocated this risk to the ***owner/seller***, on the theory that he had the opportunity to ascertain the true value and can't complain if he fails to learn what could have been learned.

Example: Appraiser is hired by Estate (a decedent's estate) to assess the value of various property in Estate. Appraiser disclaims any knowledge of fine art, and says that she sees none in Estate's collection. Acting on Appraiser's recommendations, Estate sells two oil paintings together for $60. Buyer assumes the paintings are not originals but likes their appearance. Buyer later learns that the paintings are indeed the original work of a well-known artist and are worth over a million dollars. Estate sues Buyer to rescind the contract of sale, claiming it was invalidated by mutual mistake: neither side thought the paintings were valuable. (Estate also sues Appraiser, but Appraiser has few assets and that case is settled for a small amount.)

Held, the contract cannot be rescinded. The parties may both have been mistaken about the value of the paintings, but the risk of that mistake is properly allocated to Estate. Estate had a full opportunity to research the paintings. It knowingly chose an appraiser who was not competent to identify and appraise fine art. Estate thus assumed the risk that such art might exist among its holdings without its value being noticed. *Nelson v. Rice,* 12 P.3d 238 (Ariz. App. 2000).

F. **Relation to breach of warranty:** Where a buyer and seller are both mistaken about the nature or quality of goods, in a way that makes the goods less valuable than expected, the buyer may also have a claim against the seller for ***breach of warranty.*** (See *infra,* p. 497). The two types of claims are not mutually exclusive — the fact that there is a breach of warranty claim does not mean that the buyer cannot instead decide to rely on a claim for rescission based on mutual mistake.

G. **Misunderstanding:** One topic closely related to "mistake" is handled in the chapter on offer and acceptance, *supra,* p. 73, rather than in the present chapter. This is the topic of ***"misunderstanding,"*** in which the parties have different subjective understandings about the meaning of a material term in the contract, usually because the term is ambiguous. The general rule is that if neither party knows or has reason to know of the misunderstanding, there is no meeting of the minds and therefore ***no contract*** at all (assuming that the term is a material one).

1. **Consequence:** Functionally, there will often not be much difference between a finding that there was no contract (the typical result in the "misunderstanding" situation) and a finding that a mistaken party may rescind, i.e., avoid the contract (the usual remedy for the types of mistakes discussed in this chapter).

Quiz Yourself on
MUTUAL MISTAKE

39. Jack agrees to sell Giant a goose for $20. Both parties think the goose is a regular goose, which Giant wants for breeding.

   (A) Before the goose is transferred or the $20 paid, the goose begins laying golden eggs, which makes her priceless. Jack refuses to uphold the agreement, and Giant sues to enforce the contract. Will a court force Jack to sell for $20?

(B) Assume instead that before the goose is transferred or the $20 paid, both Jack and Giant witness the goose laying eggs that are gold in color. Giant says, "Wow, that's bizarre. What do you suppose those eggs are made of?" Jack replies, "I don't know, but I think it's some alteration of the albumin content. Anyway, you can still have her for $20 if you want her." Giant, who believes Jack's assessment, agrees to go through with the deal. Shortly thereafter, Jack finds out the eggs are actually made of gold and refuses to consummate the sale. Will a court enforce the agreement?

40. After doing some spring cleaning in his wine cellar, Gatsby decides to sell several bottles of wine from the Magenta region of France. He enters into a contract with Daisy to sell the wine for $250. Both believe this to be the fair market value of the wine at the time. In actuality, wines from the Magenta region have gone up in value recently and the collection is really worth $500. Gatsby learns of this just before the sale is completed, and he seeks to avoid the sale. Can Daisy enforce the contract?

Answers

39. **(A) No, due to the parties' mutual mistake.** A mistake by both parties, which goes to a ***"basic assumption"*** on which the contract was made, will generally be grounds for avoidance. Here, this standard is satisfied: the parties thought they were bargaining for a regular goose when in fact they were bargaining for a vastly more-valuable goose that lays golden eggs. Were the court to enforce this contract, Giant would wind up with a tremendous windfall and Jack would suffer a significant loss. Although the court will not allow rescission if it's proper to allocate the risk of the mistake to the party seeking avoidance, nothing in these facts makes it appropriate to allocate the risk of this mistake to Jack. Therefore, the court will allow Jack to rescind.

(B) Yes, under these facts, the court *would* enforce the contract. Even where a mistake is mutual, a court will not allow a party to avoid the contract if the risk of the mistake is properly allocated to that party. One of the ways such allocation will occur is if a party is aware that he has only ***limited information*** regarding some aspect of the deal, but treats his limited information as sufficient. (This is sometimes called "conscious ignorance.") Here, Jack knew that there was an issue as to whether the eggs were different from the usual goose eggs, but chose to rely on what he knew was his own imperfect (and wrong, as it turned out) assessment. Having made that choice, he's stuck. (But the result would be otherwise if Giant *knew* that the eggs were gold; this would be a unilateral mistake, of which the non-mistaken party was aware — see the treatment of unilateral mistake later in this chapter.)

40. **Yes.** Even a mutual mistake will not be grounds for rescission if the mistake is one the risk of which is properly allocated to the party now seeking rescission. A mistake about the general state of market conditions will almost certainly fall into this category, since a contrary rule would give parties an incentive to remain ignorant of something they could easily check. Therefore, Daisy can enforce the contract as it is written.

IV. UNILATERAL MISTAKE

A. **The problem generally:** We turn now to the type of mistake traditionally called ***"unilateral."*** This is a mistake which is made by ***only one party***.

B. **Traditional rule:** Traditionally, courts have been ***much less willing to allow rescission*** for unilateral mistake than for mutual mistake. In the unilateral situation, "avoidance of the contract will more clearly disappoint the expectations of the other party than if he too was mistaken." Rest. 2d, § 153, Comment c. Therefore, the traditional rule has been that avoidance for unilateral mistake would be allowed only where the non-mistaken party knew or had reason to know of the mistake at the time the contract was made. C&P, p. 354.

C. Modern view: The modern view, exemplified by the Second Restatement, is more willing to allow rescission in unilateral mistake situations. But even the Restatement makes such rescission *more difficult to obtain* than in the mutual mistake context.

1. Requirements: Under Rest. 2d, § 153, the following requirements must be met in order for a party to avoid a contract based on a mistake by him alone:

   a. Three basic requirements: First, the same three basic requirements must be satisfied as in the bilateral situation (i.e., the mistake must be as to a "basic assumption" on which the contract was made, the mistake must have a "material effect on the agreed exchange of performances," and the party seeking relief must not "bear the risk of the mistake").

   b. Additional requirement: Additionally, *either* of two things must be the case:

   [1] the mistake is such that enforcement of the contract would be *"unconscionable"*; or

   [2] the other party had *reason to know of the mistake*, or his *fault caused* the mistake.

2. An offer "too good to be true": As we just indicated in Par. 1(b) above, a person who wants to avoid a contract on account of unilateral mistake will often try to show that the *other party had reason to know of the mistake.* In the case of a mistake reflected in an *offer* that the offeree accepted, and that the offeror now wants to rescind on grounds of offeror's mistake, the offeror will try to show that *offeree knew or should have known* that the offer (with the mistake embedded in it) was *"too good to be true."*

   a. "Snapping up" the offer: If the offeror can make this "too good to be true" showing, she will have a good chance of meeting all the elements for rescission on grounds of unilateral mistake. As the idea is usually put, "[a]n offeree *may not snap up an offer* that is on its face *manifestly too good to be true." Lange v. U.S.*, 120 F.2d 886 (4th Cir. 1941).

   b. Mechanical errors and "mental blunders": A common source of "offers too good to be true" is where the party now seeking avoidance for unilateral mistake made a written offer, and the offer was the product of a *"mechanical error"* or a *"mental blunder."* FSCB&G, p. 848. So, for instance, if an offeror makes a *clerical error* in *computing the price* at which he is proposing to buy or sell, and it should be evident to the offeree that this price is "too good" (from the offeree's perspective) to be anything but the result of a mistake, an offeree who tries to "snap up" the offer — i.e., to immediately accept it without further discussion — is likely to find that the court will permit the mistaken party to avoid the contract.

   Example: Several Ps bring a products liability action against D and X. At trial, the Ps are awarded a total of $1.3 million among them, a portion of which (36% as to some Ps, and 48% as to other Ps) is assessed against D, the rest against X. After trial, since the verdict is to be adjusted to account for pre-judgment interest and other factors, the two sets of lawyers (Maywhort and Gray for the Ps, and Thomasch and Brooks for

Ds), exchange various computations about the final amount D owes. During the course of this process, on Nov. 2 Brooks, on behalf of D, emails some further computations and back-up charts to Gray; the text of the email suggests that D owes the Ps $2.7 million, and says to Gray, "Let's discuss." This $2.7 million is in fact a clerical error — it reflects the overall amount that D and X would *together* owe the Ps, rather than the 36% and 48% share allocated by the jury to be paid by D alone.

Gray and/or Maywhort immediately recognize that this $2.7 million number is $500,000 higher than their own computations show to be due from D. But instead of either lawyer's calling Brooks to discuss the discrepancy, Maywhort phones and faxes Thomasch (without copying Brooks) saying that the Ps thereby "accept" D's "offer" of $2.7 million. D refuses to recognize a contract. It argues that even if the Nov. 2 email was an offer (which D disputes), under the rules for avoiding unilateral mistakes, D should be granted rescission and required to pay only the correctly-computed $2.2 million.

Held, for D. First, the Nov. 2 email was not even an offer, and therefore could not be accepted.[1] But even if a contract *did* come into force by Maywhort's phone call and fax, that contract is ***avoidable*** by D on grounds of unilateral mistake. On the key issue of whether the Ps "knew or had reason to know" that the "offer" by the Ds was "too good to be true," the answer is clearly *yes*: Ds' lawyers' prior statements during the negotiations show that they knew D was responsible for (depending on the P) only 36% and 48% of the total jury award, and intended to submit computations reflecting this fact. Therefore, when the Ps' lawyers received that email with the supposed "offer" of $2.7 million on behalf of D, that offer contained "obvious inconsistencies" that put the Ps on notice that the $2.7 million was probably a clerical mistake.

On the related issue of whether D's case for rescission satisfies the requirement that the party seeking avoidance ***must not "bear the risk of the mistake"*** (see *supra*, p. 160), Comment f to Rest. 2d § 153 states that "It is, of course, unusual for a party to ***bear the risk of a mistake that the other party had reason to know of[.]*** Since the Ps had reason to know of D's mistake, that fact alone demonstrates that the parties did not intend to place the risk of such a mistake on D. Therefore, the court grants D relief from the mistake, by denying the Ps the right to recover anything beyond the already-correctly-paid $2.2 million. *Sumerel v. Goodyear Tire & Rubber Co.*, 232 P.3d 128 (Col. Ct. of App. 2009).

3. **Construction bids:** The most common type of unilateral mistake occurs where a ***contractor*** or ***sub-contractor*** makes an error on a ***bid*** for a construction job.

   a. **Unconscionability:** Assuming that the party receiving the mistaken bid did not cause or have reason to know of the mistake, the bidder must show that enforcement of the contract would be ***unconscionable***. This will normally require her to show not only that she herself will be severely harmed if forced to perform, but also that the other party ***has not relied*** on the bid.

   Example: Contractor solicits sub-contracts for the electrical work on a project. Sub-contractor makes a bid of $50,000. Contractor relies on this bid in preparing his own

---

1. For the offer-and-acceptance aspect of the case, see *supra*, p. 12.

master bid for the entire project. Contractor is awarded the contract, and then enters into the sub-contract with Sub-contractor. Sub-contractor then discovers that its original bid was $25,000 lower than it should have been, due to a mistake in computation. Because Contractor has already relied on the sub-contract bid (by using that price in preparing his own master bid) Sub-contractor will not be able to make the requisite showing that enforcement of the contract would be "unconscionable." See Farnsworth, p. 633. Cf. *Drennan v. Star Paving Co.,* 333 P.2d 757 (Cal. 1958) (also discussed *supra,* pp. 59) and Rest. 2d, § 153, Illustr. 7 (based on *Drennan*).

    i.   **Relevance of profit:**   To make the requisite showing of unconscionability, the contractor will normally have to show that the mistake represents a ***significant portion*** of the overall bid. (He would have to make this showing anyway, in order to satisfy the basic requirement that the mistake have a "material effect on the agreed exchange.") He will also usually have to show that the mistake deprives him of all or most of his ***profit***.

b. **Clerical errors:** As in non-bid situations (such as *Sumerel, supra*), the most common kind of mistake in bidding (and the one for which courts are most likely to give relief) is a ***clerical error*** in ***computing the amount*** of the bid. Other types of clerical errors will also qualify for relief (e.g., the bidder's failure to read closely the job specifications).

    i.   **Judgment:**   Courts are much less willing to allow rescission where the error is a mistake in *"business judgment"* rather than a clerical error. For instance, if the bidder makes a mistake in estimating the ***amount of labor required to do the work***, he will not be entitled to avoid the contract; the court will hold that the risk of a mistake on this item should reasonably be allocated to him, rather than to the recipient of the bid. See Rest. 2d, § 154, Illustr. 6.

c. **"Snapping up" of offer:** Recall that if the other party ***knows*** or has ***reason to know*** of the error, the requirement of "unconscionability" will not apply (*supra*, p. 165). This means that the recipient of the bid cannot "snap up" a bid that he should know was too low to have been intended. This will be true even where the recipient of the bid has relied upon it (since reliance simply goes to whether enforcement would be unconscionable).

Quiz Yourself on
UNILATERAL MISTAKE

41. Mike Angelo, newly arrived in the United States from Italy, develops an immediate fascination with baseball. He visits "Leo's Locker," a baseball memorabilia store, to check out some baseball cards. The owner, Leo diVinci, has a slogan, "I love to dicker" — so he doesn't put a price tag on anything. Mike spots an old card with a famous name on it, and offers Leo $5,000 for it. Leo realizes that Mike has mistaken the player on the card — Babe Root, of the 1929 New York Spankies (an amateur team) — for Babe Ruth, whose card *would* be worth $5,000. Leo quickly accepts Mike's offer, knowing the card is worth about fifty cents. Leo writes up a contract that they both sign, and Mike goes to the bank to get the $5,000. When he tells the bank teller about his find, the teller laughs hysterically, telling him of his mistake. Mike reneges on the deal. Leo sues. Mike defends on grounds of mistake. Who wins?

42. Shah Jihan is building himself a monument and needs a rock-cutting machine. He sees Mimzeh's ad in the Bargain Trader Newspaper for a rock-cutting machine for $10,000. Shah goes to Mimzeh's house and inspects the machine. Mimzeh accurately answers all questions Shah asks. Shah offers Mimzeh $10,000 for the machine, which she accepts. Before the transaction takes place, Shah finds out the rock cutter will not cut marble, which, unbeknownst to Mimzeh, is the type of stone Shah uses. Can Shah avoid the contract due to his mistake?

43. James Beardless, Army chef, solicits bids for a custom-built food processor with a work bowl large enough to hold 500 lbs. of chipped beef.

(A) For this part, assume that Beardless receives bids on the project of $90, $600, $700, and $800. The $90 bid was from the Come-N-Get-It Food Supply House. Come-N-Get-It intended to bid $900, but made a careless clerical error in its bid. Beardless is impressed by Come-N-Get-It's very low bid. Beardless thinks that Come-N-Get-It must be a very efficient producer; he doesn't suspect that the bid's lowness may be due to clerical error, and he therefore doesn't re-confirm the price (though a reasonable person in Beardless' position would have done so). Soon after Beardless accepts, Come-N-Get-It tells Beardless that it made an error, and that its bid should have been for $900. Can Beardless enforce the $90 bid price?

(B) Say instead that the bids were for $500, $600, $700 and $800, with Come-N-Get-It's bid coming in at $500. Come-N-Get-It actually meant to bid $650, but made an error when adding up the figure for its estimate. Beard has no suspicion that there may have been an error (and a reasonable person would not have had such a suspicion). Beardless accepts the offer of $500 and now Come-N-Get-It wants out. Can Beardless enforce the $500 bid price?

Answers

41. **Mike.** The issue here is the effect of a unilateral mistake. In addition to the requirements necessary in a mutual mistake situation (mainly that the mistake must relate to a "basic assumption" and the risk must not be one properly allocated to the party seeking to avoid it), a party who wants to avoid a contract based on unilateral mistake must also prove that *either:* (1) enforcement of the contract would be unconscionable, *or* (2) the other party **knew** or **should have known** of the mistake or somehow was **at fault** for creating the mistake. Here, Leo was aware from the get-go that Mike was mistaken about the value of the card, but failed to correct Mike. Mike is therefore able to satisfy requirement (2), and can avoid the contract.

42. **No.** Again, the issue here is whether Shah's unilateral mistake is grounds for avoiding the contract. Remember that to avoid a contract based upon unilateral mistake, the rules for avoiding a contract based on mutual mistake must first be satisfied. That is not the case here: Shah knew that he needed a machine for cutting marble, yet he failed to adequately inspect and investigate to see if Mimzeh's machine was suitable for this purpose before entering into the contract. Shah's "conscious ignorance" of this fact will therefore bind him to the agreement as made.

43. **(A) No.** A person receiving bids may not "snap up" an unduly low bid — that is, if the recipient either knows or has reason to know that the bid is likely to be an error, the bidder will be able to use the unilateral-mistake doctrine (assuming the other requirements for the doctrine, such as a mistake as to a "basic assumption," are met). So neither the fact that the mistake in bid was due to Come-N-Get-It's own negligence, nor the fact that Beardless didn't actually suspect error, will block Come-N-Get-It from using the doctrine.

(B) Yes. Under these facts, the bid presented is not so out of whack with the others that it should have alerted Beardless to the problem. Therefore, Come-N-Get-It's only chance to avoid for mistake will be to show that enforcing the contract under the mistaken terms would be *unconscionable*. To do this, Come-N-Get-It would probably have to show that it would be severely harmed by enforcement of the contract; it's very unlikely that Come-N-Get-It will be able to do this.

V. DEFENSES AND REMEDIES

A. **Negligence usually not a defense:**   Where a party seeks to avoid the contract because of his own (or both parties') mistake, the fact that the mistake was due to his *negligence* will ordinarily *not prevent relief*. (If the rule were otherwise, the entire doctrine of relief for mistake, at least in unilateral-mistake cases, would be almost irrelevant.) See Rest. 2d, § 157.

> **Example:** Sub-contractor is solicited to prepare a bid for the electrical work on a building. He submits a bid of $100,000 to Contractor. After he is awarded the sub-contract, he discovers that his bid failed to include $50,000 for one part of the job, due to an error in addition. Even if the error is due to Sub-contractor's clear negligence in preparing the bid, he will not be precluded from obtaining rescission of the contract (assuming that the other requirements for relief from unilateral mistake are satisfied). See Rest. 2d, § 157, Illustr. 1.

1. **Failure to act in good faith:**   But the party's fault may be so great that it *does* preclude her from avoiding the contract. Traditionally, the type of negligence for which relief will be denied has been described a as *"gross"* or *"culpable."* But under the Restatement view, fault will not deprive a party of avoidance unless it "amounts to a failure to act in *good faith* and in accordance with reasonable standards of *fair dealing*." Rest. 2d, § 157.

> **Example:** Assume that on the facts of the above example, Contractor asks Sub-contractor to check his figures to make sure that there has been no mistake. If Sub-contractor says that he has done so, when in fact he has not (and when a check would have revealed the error), Sub-contractor's conduct will be held to show a lack of good faith and fair dealing, and he will be prevented from rescinding the contract. Rest. 2d, § 157, Illustr. 2.

2. **Failure to read writing:**   If the mistake for which rescission is sought stems from a party's *failure to read the contract*, he will *not* normally be entitled to rescind. "[O]ne who assents to a writing is presumed to know its contents and cannot escape being bound by its terms merely by contending that he did not read them; his assent is deemed to cover unknown as well as known terms." Rest. 2d, § 157, Comment b. (However, if there has been a prior oral agreement, which the written agreement does not match, the party who has failed to read the writing may be able to obtain reformation; see *infra*, p. 170.)

B. **Remedies:**   There are several distinct remedies which may be appropriate for mistake, depending on the situation.

1. **Avoidance:**   The most common remedy is that of *avoidance* of the contract. "Avoidance" is synonymous with *"rescission."* If this remedy is granted, the court will essentially treat

the contract *as if it had never been made*, and will attempt to *return each party to the position he was in* just prior to execution of the contract.

   a. **Restitution as element of avoidance:**   Often, returning each party to the position he was in prior to execution of the contract will mean that one party must pay *restitution* to the other. (Restitution is discussed more fully *infra*, p. 330.) In essence, the requirement of restitution means that *each party must return to the other benefits she has received from that other.* In the simple case of a contract for the sale of land or goods, restitution will mean that the seller must return any money she has received from the buyer, and the buyer must return the goods or re-convey the property.

   Example: Seller agrees to sell its interest in a particular parcel of vacant land to Buyer. The contract calls for a down payment plus annual installments. Buyer makes it clear to Seller that Buyer's only intended use for the property is to grow the shrub jojoba on it, something which requires adequate water supplies. After the purchase, wells drilled by Buyer show that there is no adequate water beneath the property. Buyer sues Seller for rescission on grounds of mutual mistake.

   Held, for Buyer. Buyer is entitled to return of its down payment. However, Buyer must pay Seller for the *fair rental value* of the property during the time Buyer had possession of it. Conversely, Seller must compensate Buyer for any increase in the value of the property brought about by Buyer's efforts. (But Buyer may not recover its reliance damages, i.e., the money it spent drilling test wells.) *Renner v. Kehl*, 722 P.2d 262 (Ariz. 1986).

2. **Reliance damages:**   Occasionally, restitution will not be adequate to place the parties in the position they were in prior to execution of the contract. In that event, the court may use other measures of damages; for instance, *reliance* damages may be awarded.

3. **Adjustment of contract as substitute for avoidance:**   The court may conclude that justice is best served by making an *adjustment to the contract* rather than by permitting either party to avoid it entirely on account of mistake. Under the Restatement approach, the availability of an adjustment to the contract is to be taken into account in determining whether the mistake has a "material effect on the agreed exchange of performances" (Rest. §§ 152(1) and (2)) — if such an adjustment would redress the unfairness, the requisite "material effect on the agreed exchange" will not be present.

   Example: Seller agrees to convey Blackacre to Buyer. The parties both believe that the tract has 100 acres, and the contract price is calculated based on a per-acre figure. The tract turns out to have only 90 acres. The court will probably order a 10% reduction in the purchase price, rather than allowing Buyer to avoid the contract entirely. Rest. 2d, § 158, Illustr. 1.

   Note: Observe that the availability of a court-ordered adjustment to the contract terms may prevent a party from weaseling out of the contract, i.e., seizing upon a mistake to avoid a bargain that is (for reasons entirely unrelated to the mistake) a bad one. For instance, on the facts of the above example, suppose that Buyer realized after making the contract that, apart from the acreage, the price per acre was far above market value. Avoidance would let Buyer escape the bad bargain entirely, whereas adjustment of the purchase price to reflect the missing acreage would keep the basic bargain intact, certainly the fairer result.

VI. REFORMATION AS REMEDY FOR ERROR IN EXPRESSION

A. Error in expression: A quite different kind of mistake is that in which the parties orally agree on a deal, but by mistake prepare and execute a ***document*** which ***incorrectly reflects the oral agreement***. In this situation, either party may obtain from the court a ***reformation*** (i.e., a re-writing) of the written document, so that it correctly reflects the prior agreement.

> **Example:** Seller orally agrees to sell Blackacre to Buyer for $100,000; their oral deal includes a provision that Buyer will also assume an existing mortgage of $50,000. Buyer's lawyer, in preparing the written agreement, neglects to include the assumption provision, and neither Buyer nor Seller notices the omission. At either party's request, the court will reform the document so that it includes the assumption provision. See Rest. 2d, § 155, Illustr. 1.

B. Failure to read: The party resisting reformation may generally ***not*** do so on the grounds that the party seeking reformation was ***negligent*** in not carefully reading the writing to see whether it conformed with the prior agreement. This rule may be viewed as an application of the more general rule that a party's negligence does not prevent him from obtaining relief for mistake (see *supra*, p. 168). See Rest. 2d, § 157, Comment b.

C. Not a remedy for underlying disagreement about deal: Note that reformation is a proper remedy only when the writing ***incorrectly summarizes*** the parties' joint understanding, ***not when the parties fundamentally disagree on what the deal is*** and the writing matches the understanding of one party. In the latter circumstance, typically a court will conclude that there is ***no contract at all*** on account of a ***mutual mistake*** that prevented a meeting of the minds.

> **Example:** Owner has two small structures at the back of his property, a tool shed and a storage shed. He stands with Contractor on the deck of the house overlooking the back yard, and says "Tear down that shed." First, suppose that both parties understand that Owner was referring to the tool shed, but that a writing prepared by Contractor's assistant mistakenly specified the storage shed, and both parties signed without noticing the problem. Here, reformation would an appropriate remedy — a court will order that the document be interpreted as if it called for demolition of the tool shed.
>
> But now, suppose that Owner intended to refer to the tool shed, but Contractor reasonably believed that Owner was referring to the storage shed. If Contractor's assistant drafts a writing calling for demolition of the storage shed, and both parties sign it without Owner's recognizing that it doesn't match his understanding, reformation will not be an appropriate remedy because the parties do not agree on what the underlying deal is. Instead, the correct remedy is to discharge the contract for mutual mistake about a basic aspect of the agreement (see *supra*, p. 157).

D. Relevance to parol evidence rule: The right to obtain reformation of a writing that does not correctly reflect a prior agreement may be viewed as an exception to the ***parol evidence rule***.

That rule (*infra*, p. 176) prevents a party to certain types of writings from showing that there were prior written or oral understandings that conflict with the writing.

Quiz Yourself on

DEFENSES, REMEDIES AND REFORMATION

44. Oliver Douglas enters into the following contract with Arnold Ziffel: "Douglas hereby agrees to sell and Ziffel hereby agrees to buy Green Acres, a 10-acre parcel, at the price of $600 per acre for a total of $6,000." Ziffel plans to use the property as a country home, as Douglas knows.

(A) Before the deal is completed, Lisa, a county surveyor, measures the property and informs the parties that it is only nine acres. Ziffel wants out of the contract. What relief, if any, would a court likely grant?

(B) Assume instead that the survey showed the property was really only five acres, and that this would be insufficient for Ziffel's stated purpose for the land. Before the parties learned of this mistake, Ziffel invested in farming equipment at a cost of $3,000. He bought the equipment used at an "As Is" sale, cannot return it, and is not likely to buy a comparable property any time soon at which he could use the equipment. What relief, if any, would a court likely grant?

45. Little Jack Horner enters into an oral agreement with Big Bad Wolf ("BBW") whereby, if BBW can obtain two blackberry pies baked by Little Red Riding Hood's mother within the next two weeks, Little Jack Horner will buy them for $3 a pie. BBW has his attorney draft up a written confirmation of the agreement. The attorney mistakenly writes up the contract as being for three pies at $2 each. No one notices the problem until after the contract is signed; both parties are equally at fault in this. A week later, BBW wants to enforce the terms of the agreement. Little Jack Horner reviews the contract and offers either to take the pies for $2 apiece or rescind the contract. BBW refuses to do either, and seeks the court's assistance to enforce the terms of the oral agreement ($3 price for 2 pies). What result?

Answers

44. (A) Adjustment of the price to $5,400. Although the parties were under a "mutual mistake" with respect to the size of the property, the court will probably not allow the contract to be rescinded, because: (1) the 10% deviation in the size of the property does not have a "material effect on the agreed exchange of performances" (a requirement for relief under the doctrines of both mutual and unilateral mistake); and (2) an adjustment to the contract could alleviate any unfairness created by the mistake. The court will therefore probably adjust the contract to reflect the actual size of the parcel: $600 per acre for *nine* acres, for a total of $5,400.

(B) Rescission, plus a splitting of Ziffel's out-of-pocket loss. In contrast to the facts in (A), here the mistake appears to go to the very purpose of the contract. Therefore, a court would likely grant rescission of the contract. Rescission, however, will not be sufficient to put the parties back in the positions they were in before the contract was made, since Ziffel has incurred $3,000 in reliance expenses which he cannot avoid by returning the equipment or using it somewhere else. A court will try to split the loss the best it can. Reliance damages may probably appropriate here, and would likely take the form of an order for Ziffel to sell the equipment and then, if there is a shortfall, recover half that shortfall from Douglas.

45. The court will reform the contract to reflect the intended price and quantity. When parties have reached an oral agreement and then the agreement is incorrectly reflected in a written document, the court will in essence re-write the agreement to make it conform to the original agreement. This is called a "reformation."

Exam Tips on *MISTAKE*

Mistakes as to Existing Fact

☛ Use the term "mistake," and the analysis in this chapter, only to cover those situations involving a mistake as to the facts *as they existed just prior to the contract.* Where the parties are operating under a mistaken assumption about *future* events (e.g., future market prices), use the Impossibility/Impracticability analysis given in Ch. 12.

Mutual Mistake

☛ The topic most frequently tested from this chapter concerns a mistaken assumption made by *both* parties to the contract (mutual mistake). Before concluding that there has been a mutual mistake — and that the contract can therefore be avoided by a party who is injured by the mistake — make sure that all 3 requirements are met:

(1)   **Mutuality.** Make sure that *both parties* made the same (ultimately wrong) assumption when entering into the agreement.

(2)   **Materiality.** Make sure the assumption was *"basic"* to the bargain, and that the mistake had a *material effect* on the agreed-upon exchanges. Watch for these situations:

☞ **Real estate transactions.** Look out for a sale where there has been a *mistaken acreage count* and the total acreage contained in the contract can't be conveyed by the seller.

☞ If the portion of land that cannot be conveyed is large or otherwise significant, then its inclusion was probably a basic assumption of the contract. Bit if the parcel that cannot be conveyed is insignificant (e.g., a 3-foot-wide strip along one end of a 50 acre parcel), then it probably would not be considered a basic assumption of the contract.

☞ **Purchase of a unique good.** Look for the purchase of a unique work of art where the parties are mistaken as to its origin or creator. These will probably be basic assumptions.

Example: D, an art dealer, receives from one of her purchasing agents a painting entitled "Sunset" which she is informed was painted by Van Goon. C, an art collector, sees the painting at D's gallery and says to D, "What an interesting Van Goon." D responds (honestly believing that he's telling the truth), "Yes, it is." C pays $50,000 for the painting, its worth had it been a genuine Van Goon. C later finds out that the painting is a forgery worth only a few hundred dollars and stops payment on her check. The assumption about authorship was almost certainly a basic assumption, so C's nonperformance is probably not a breach.

(3) Allocation of risk. Make sure the parties did not explicitly or implicitly *allocate the risk* of the mistake to the party who is now trying to avoid the contract. (If they did so allocate the risk, that party can't use the doctrine.) Also, remember that the court can allocate the risk of mistakes wherever it is "reasonable" to do so.

Examples of situations where courts usually find an implicit allocation of risk of mistake:

☞ **Minerals in the land:** The risk that there will turn out to be valuable mineral deposits is allocated to the *seller*. (*Example:* S and B enter into an agreement for the sale of Farmland for $8 an acre . Oil is then discovered under the land. S may not avoid the contract, because he'll be found to have implicitly borne this risk, assuming the contract is silent.)

☞ **Building conditions:** In a construction contract, the risk of undiscovered unfavorable building conditions (e.g., unexpected rock that makes excavation much more expensive) is normally allocated to the *contractor*.

However, always make sure that the contract language or surrounding circumstances don't effectively allocate the risk in a different way.

Unilateral Mistake

☛ Where only *one party* has made a mistake (unilateral mistake), he is excused from performance *only if the other party knew or should have known of the mistake.*

☞ If you don't know whether the other party knew or should have known of the mistake, argue the evidence in support of each view, and then state that the result depends on which way the "knew/should have known" issue is resolved.

☞ *Common fact pattern: A* makes *B* an *offer* that *B* realizes (or should realize) is *"too good to be true"* (e.g., because it looks like *A* made a computational error). If *B* tries to "snap up" the offer, *A* will likely to able to get the contract rescinded or reformed for unilateral mistake.

☞ **Distinction:** On the other hand, if the error in an offer or bid is *not obvious* to one in the offeree's position, then when the offeree accepts, unilateral mistake probably *won't* apply.

Example: C, a contractor, solicits bids from sub-contractors for a construction job to be performed for X. S, a sub-contractor, delivers a bid for the foundation work in the amount of $140,000. The next lowest bid that is submitted to C is $150,000. Relying on S's bid, C immediately submits its overall bid to X. Fifteen minutes later, S telephones C and says that there was a mistake in the calculation and revises its bid to $170,000. Since the next lowest bid was only $10,000 more than S's bid, C probably did *not* have reason to know that S's bid was a mistake, in which case S will be not be able to rescind based upon unilateral mistake.

Reformation

☛ If there is a clerical error and a written agreement *doesn't accurately reflect the parties' agreement,* the aggrieved party can have the contract *reformed* to reflect the prior agreement. This usually occurs regarding price: the contract states a different price than the one agreed upon, or leaves out the agreed-upon price altogether.

Chapter 6

PAROL EVIDENCE AND INTERPRETATION

ChapterScope

This chapter focuses on two areas dealing with the judicial construction of contracts: the parol evidence rule, and the interpretation of contract terms.

- ■ **Parol evidence rule:** The parol evidence rule governs the effect of a ***written agreement*** on ***any prior oral or written agreements*** between the parties. Simplifying somewhat, the rule provides that a writing intended by the parties to be a full and final expression of their agreement may not be ***supplemented or contradicted*** by any oral or written agreements made prior to the writing.

  - ❑ **Subsequent oral agreement:** The parol evidence rule does not bar admission of evidence of oral agreements made *after* the writing.

  - ❑ **Interpretation:** The parol evidence rule does ***not*** bar admission of evidence about the *meaning* the parties intended to give to particular contract terms.

- ■ **Rules of interpretation:** There are a number of general rules or "maxims" for interpreting the meaning of ambiguous contractual terms. For instance:

  - ❑ **Ambiguous terms:** Generally, an ambiguous term will be construed against the draftsman.

  - ❑ **Custom:** Evidence of "custom" may be admitted to show that the parties intended for a contract term to have a particular meaning. Sources of custom include ***"course of performance"*** (how the parties have interpreted the term during the life of the present contract), "course of dealing" (how the parties have interpreted the same term in prior contracts between them) and "trade usage" (the meaning attached to a term within a particular industry).

- ■ **Omitted terms:** The court may *supply* a reasonable term in a situation where the contract is silent. (*Example:* Courts in contract cases frequently supply a duty to act in good faith.)

I. THE PAROL EVIDENCE RULE GENERALLY

A. How the rule applies: Before signing a written agreement, the parties typically engage in preliminary oral negotiations. Furthermore, they may exchange pieces of paper (e.g., letters, lists of items for discussion, etc.) that are not intended to be contracts in themselves. When the written contract is finally signed, it may fail to include any treatment of some of the issues raised in these preliminary oral discussions or written documents, or it may deal with these issues in a way that is different from their treatment in the earlier discussions. When this occurs, to what extent may one party later try to prove in court that these earlier oral or written discussions are part of the contract, despite their absence from the writing?

1. **Effect of the rule:** The "parol evidence rule," whose precise formulation varies from one authority to another, attempts to answer this question. In its more strict forms, the parol evidence rule results in barring from the factfinder's consideration *all evidence of certain preliminary agreements that are not contained in the final writing*, even though this evidence might persuasively establish that the preliminary agreement did in fact take place and that the parties intended it to remain part of their deal despite its absence from the writing.

II.   TOTAL AND PARTIAL INTEGRATION

A. **The concept of "integration":** A written document does not always represent a deal that the parties consider final. The writing may, for instance, be intended only as a tentative draft of their agreement. But if the parties do intend a document to represent the *final expression of their agreement*, the document is said to be an *"integration"* of their agreement. The parol evidence rule applies, as we shall see, only to documents which are integrations, i.e., final expressions of agreement.

B. **"Partial" vs. "total" integrations:** Once it is determined that a document is an integration (i.e., a final expression of agreement), it must be determined whether the parties intended that integration to contain all of the details of their agreement, or only some of these details. If the document is intended only as a memorandum of the agreement, it may state only the most important details, and leave the others to the parties' recollection.

1. **Partial integration:** If the document is not intended by the parties to include all details of their agreement, it is said to be a *"partial"* integration.

2. **Total integration:** If, on the other hand, the document is intended by the parties to include all the details of their agreement, it is called a *"total"* integration.

C. **Statement of the parol evidence rule:** Having defined the concepts of "partial integration" and "total integration," we are now ready to state the parol evidence rule. The rule has, in effect, two parts, one dealing with partial integrations, and the other with total integrations. The rule provides as follows:

[1] **Partial integration:** When a writing is a *partial* integration, no evidence of prior or contemporaneous agreements or negotiations (oral or written) may be admitted if this evidence would *contradict* a term of the writing.

[2] **Total integration:** When a document is a *total* integration, no evidence of prior or contemporaneous agreements or negotiations (oral or written) may be admitted which would *either contradict or even add to* the writing.

1. **Summary of rule:** In summary, the parol evidence rule provides that evidence of prior agreement:

❏ may never be admitted to *contradict an integrated writing*, and

❏ may furthermore not even *supplement* an integration that is intended to be *complete*.

See Rest. 2d, § 213.

> **Example:** Seller and Buyer make an oral agreement for the sale of the Ardsley Acres Hotel, together with all the furniture in the hotel. They reach oral agreement as to the purchase price of the hotel, and also agree that Buyer shall have one year in which to complete payment of this price. The parties then employ a lawyer to prepare a written contract. He does so, and they sign it. It does not mention furniture, or make any reference to personal property. It also provides that Buyer shall only have six months in which to complete payment.
>
> If Seller can show that the written contract was intended as the final expression of the parties' agreement (i.e., that it is an *integration*), Buyer will not be allowed to show that the original oral agreement gave him a year, rather than six months, to pay. He would not be allowed to show this because of the rule that prior oral or written evidence may not be introduced to contradict an integrated writing.
>
> If Seller can also show that the written agreement was intended to be a *complete* or *total* integration (i.e., that it contained all the terms on which the parties were finally in agreement), Buyer would not be allowed to prove that hotel furniture was to be included in the deal. This is because the oral agreement as to furniture would be a consistent additional term, and may not be introduced to supplement a total integration. If, on the other hand, Seller is unable to show that there is a total integration (as might be the case if the writing contains a statement that it deals only with the hotel real estate, and leaves untouched any oral agreement as to personal property that the parties might have reached), Buyer will be able to introduce evidence that the parties agreed to include the furniture. See Rest. 2d, § 213, Illustration 4.
>
> **Note:** Observe that the parol evidence rule protects the sanctity of final written documents, even at the expense of fulfilling the parties' actual intentions. Thus in the above example, once Seller is able to show that the written document was intended to be a total integration, the court must ignore all evidence by Buyer that furniture was included in the deal, *even if this evidence would show absolutely conclusively that the parties did intend to include the furniture*. However, the force of this rule is somewhat dissipated by the fact that, as it is discussed below, the judge, in determining whether the writing is an integration, and whether it is partial or complete, may consider all evidence.

D. Contemporaneous and subsequent expressions: Thus far, we have spoken only of oral or written expressions that occur *prior to* a written integration. If an oral agreement occurs *at the same time as* the writing is signed, most courts treat it as they would treat a prior oral statement, i.e., precluding it from being introduced to contradict the writing, or to supplement the writing if it is a total integration.

1. **Contemporaneous writing:** If an *ancillary writing* is signed at the same time a formal document is signed, the ancillary document will usually be treated as *part of the writing*, and will thus not be subject to the parol evidence rule. In other words, the writings will be treated as if they formed one document, and everything in them will be considered by the court in construing the contract. C&P, p. 122.

2. **Subsequent agreements:** It is essential to remember that the parol evidence rule *never bars consideration of subsequent oral agreements*. That is, *a written contract may always be modified after its execution, by an oral agreement.* "The most ironclad written contract can always be cut in two by the acetylene torch of parol modification supported by adequate proof." *Wagner v. Graziano Constr. Co.*, 136 A.2d 82 (Pa. 1957).

   a. **No-oral-modification clauses:** Of course, the parties often put into their writing a *"no oral modification" (N.O.M.) clause.* As the name implies, an N.O.M. clause says that the writing cannot be modified except via an amendment signed by both parties.

      i. **Enforceability:** Courts typically *enforce* N.O.M. clauses, holding that where such a clause exists, a true "modification" or amendment to the writing cannot be made except by another signed writing.

      ii. **Subject to waiver:** However, the practical effect of N.O.M. clauses is frequently *weakened* by courts' use of the doctrine of *"waiver"* — the contract is not modified by a later oral agreement, but *A* is frequently held to have waived the benefit of the N.O.M. clause by inducing *B* to rely on *A*'s oral statements that some provision of the contract won't be insisted upon.

      iii. **Change orders in construction contracts:** The tendency of the waiver doctrine to weaken the effect of an N.O.M. clause is frequently illustrated in *construction contracts*. Such contracts generally contain a type of N.O.M. clause inserted for the owner's benefit, providing that *no request for extra work* will be effective unless it is made in a writing signed by the owner. Yet this kind of clause is often ineffective because of the waiver doctrine.

      Example: A construction contract between Own and Contractor has a clause saying that no request by the owner or architect for extra work will be effective unless in a writing signed by Own. Own requests that Contractor add one foot in length to the porch Contractor is building. Contractor says, "OK, but that'll cost you $1,000 extra; please sign the change order." Own says, "I don't want to be bothered with the paperwork, after all, we're good friends and we don't need the written contract to tell us what we've worked out, right? Just do the work, and I'll make sure you're paid." Contractor does the work, and Own refuses to pay.

      If the court believes that this conversation happened, the court is likely to hold that Own's oral statement constituted a waiver by him of the benefits of the N.O.M. clause, so that Own will have to pay the agreed-upon extra amount.

      iv. **Explicit modification required:** But for a "no-oral-modification" clause to be rendered ineffective, it is usually required that something more occur than a *mere oral agreement* to overlook the clause. For a waiver of the no-oral-modifications clause to be effective, the party trying to escape from the clause must generally show that she *relied*, i.e., that she *materially changed her position* in reliance upon the waiver.

      Example: On the facts of the above example, Contractor's doing the work clearly constitutes material reliance, so waiver would almost certainly be found. But suppose the "Just do the work" conversation occurred but that before Contractor began the work, Own changed his mind and said, "Don't do it." Here, the court would probably *not* find that a waiver of the N.O.M. clause had occurred, because Contractor didn't materially rely on the waiver before it was withdrawn.

v. UCC: When a "no oral modification" clause is present in a contract governed by the *UCC*, a similar rule regarding waiver applies. Recall that under UCC § 2-209(2), a no-oral-modification clause will generally be effective. (See *supra*, p. 132.) But even though this statutory provision seems to make no-oral-modification clauses more readily enforced than they are at common law, § 2-209(4) undercuts some of the practical impact of using such a clause: "Although an attempt at modification...does not satisfy the requirements of [a valid no-oral-modification clause] it can operate as a *waiver*."

So if the parties purport to make an oral modification of a sales contract containing a no-oral-modification clause, the attempted modification will probably be *effective as a waiver*, at least where the party claiming waiver has materially changed his position in reliance. See W&S, pp. 32-33.

E. The UCC's parol evidence rule: The parol evidence rule set forth in the UCC is basically the same as the common-law version of the rule, described above.

1. Text of rule: § 2-202 provides that:

"Terms with respect to which the confirmatory memoranda of the parties agree or which are otherwise set forth in a writing intended by the parties as a *final expression* of their agreement with respect to such terms as are included therein *may not be contradicted* by evidence of *any prior agreement or of a contemporaneous oral agreement* but may be *explained or supplemented*:

(a) by course of performance, course of dealing or usage of trade; and

(b) by evidence of *consistent additional terms* unless the court finds the writing to have been intended also as a *complete and exclusive statement* of the agreement."

2. Summary of Code provision: So to summarize the Code rule:

❏ If a writing is a *final* expression of the parties' agreement (i.e., an *"integration"*), it *may not be contradicted* by evidence of any prior agreement, whether written or oral, nor of any oral agreement that is contemporaneous with the writing.

❏ Even a final expression may, however, be *"explained or supplemented"* (as opposed to "contradicted") by:

❏ evidence of course of dealing, trade usage, and course of performance (all discussed *infra*, p. 193); and by

❏ evidence of *"consistent additional terms,"* unless the court concludes that the writing was intended not only as a final statement, but also as a "complete and exclusive statement" of the terms of the agreement (i.e., a *"complete"* or *"total"* integration).

3. Special terms: Under the UCC (and probably in most non-UCC cases as well), even a complete integration may be explained or interpreted by reference to "course of dealing," "usage of trade," and "course of performance," terms which are discussed in the later part of this chapter. (Evidence relating to these terms does not usually provide the substance of the agreement, but instead aids in the interpretation of the meaning of the parties' own words; for this reason, such evidence is not subject to the parol evidence rule, either under the UCC or under non-UCC common law.)

4. **Difference between Code and non-Code law:** The Code language quoted above sets forth almost precisely the same parol evidence rule as was summarized earlier in the non-Code context. The principal differences between the Code rule and non-Code common law relate to how the judge determines the existence of an integration, and how she determines whether an integration is "complete" or "partial." This topic is discussed immediately below.

Quiz Yourself on

THE PAROL EVIDENCE RULE, AND "TOTAL" VS. "PARTIAL" INTEGRATION

46. Washington and Adams agree for Adams to sell Washington 1000 Declaration of Independence Commemorative Placemats, which Washington intends to re-sell. They sign a written contract, which both parties intend to represent all aspects of their agreement, and which both parties intend to be final. One day after the writing is signed, the parties orally agree that the price to Washington will be adjusted from $ .40 per mat to $ .30. The writing says nothing about subsequent oral agreements. Adams ships the mats, and bills at the $ .40 price. If Washington refuses to pay more than $ .30 and Adams sues, may Washington prove in court that the oral modification occurred?

47. Cagney and Lacey enter into a written contract to open "Tried and True," a store specializing in used guns recovered from murder scenes. The writing is a 2-paragraph handwritten document, prepared during a 1-hour meeting. The writing states that each party will receive 50 percent of any net profits and that each will devote 30 hours a week to the venture. Both parties regard the writing as a final expression of their deal.

    (A) Subsequently, Cagney sues Lacey for breach because Lacey has been working only 20 hours per week over the last few months, which are summer months. In defense, Lacey attempts to testify that just prior to the parties' signing of the writing, Cagney orally agreed that for the approximately four months a year when Lacey's young children were on vacation from school, Lacey could work only 20 hours a week. Is Lacey's testimony admissible?

    (B) Assume that in the same lawsuit, Lacey counterclaims for lost profits due to certain small merchandise discounts that Cagney gave to her adult children. Cagney tries to testify that before the writing was signed, the parties orally agreed that each party could sell up to $500 per year in merchandise, at a 20% discount, to members of that party's immediate family. The writing says nothing about whether and when such merchandise discounts will be given. Is Cagney's testimony admissible?

Answers

46. **Yes.** The parol evidence rule would prevent Washington from showing an oral agreement that occurred prior to or contemporaneously with the writing, and that either contradicted or supplemented the writing. But the parol evidence rule doesn't prevent (or even deal with) *subsequent* oral modifications to contracts. Since the writing has no No Oral Modification clause, the oral modification may be proved (and will be enforced).

47. **(A) No.** The parol evidence rule bars any evidence of a prior or contemporaneous oral agreement where such evidence would ***contradict*** a term of a written contract that was intended as a "final" (even if not "total") integration, i.e., expression of the parties' agreement. The facts tell you that the writing is a final integration, so this rule applies here. The writing specifically requires both parties to work 30 hours a week, and an oral clause that would reduce Lacey's time by 1/3 for 1/3 of the year certainly seems to be a contradiction of the agreement, not a mere supplementation or interpretation of it.

(B) Yes, probably. The merchandise-discount clause merely supplements the writing, and doesn't contradict it, since the writing is silent on the subject. The parole evidence rule provides that a final integration may be supplemented (not contradicted) by prior oral agreement if and only if the integration is partial rather than total (that is, only if the writing was *not* regarded by the parties as covering all aspects of the deal). Here, the relatively short length of the writing, the fact that it was handwritten, and the fact that it was entirely drafted in one hour, all make it likely that the parties intended the integration to be merely partial. If so, the supplementary oral term will be admissible.

III. THE ROLES OF THE JUDGE AND JURY

A. **Preliminary determinations made by judge:** One of the principal reasons for the parol evidence rule was the fear that juries would not recognize the superior trustworthiness of a written document, as compared to oral testimony about alleged oral agreements. To make sure that this function of the rule is fulfilled, virtually all courts hold that a determination of whether a writing was intended as an integration, and if so, whether the integration is "partial" or "total," is to be made **by the judge**, not the jury. Furthermore, courts almost universally hold that it is the judge who decides whether particular evidence would supplement the terms of a complete integration. See Rest. 2d, §§ 209(2), 210(3).

   1. **Consequence:** Because the modern tendency is to allow the judge to consider almost all evidence in making these decisions, the parol evidence rule has much more bite in a jury trial (where operation of the rule may mean that the trier of fact is prevented from ever considering allegations of previous oral agreements) than where the case is tried to a judge.

B. **Conflicting views on how judges decide:** How is the trial judge to go about determining whether a writing is a partial integration, a total integration, or no integration at all? And how is she to decide whether particular evidence contradicts, supplements, or merely explains, the document? Should she answer these questions solely by examining the writing, or may he consider oral evidence about the alleged prior agreements? These questions relating to the trial judge's role in applying the parol evidence rule have given rise to one of the greatest disputes in the history of modern contract law, a dispute between Professors Williston and Corbin. In addition to the Williston and Corbin views, we shall summarize here a third, "middle" view, set forth in the UCC.

   1. **Williston's view:** Professor Williston believed that the judge should decide whether a writing was an integration, whether it was "partial" or "total," and whether a given piece of evidence about a prior agreement contradicted or supplemented the writing, by the following steps:

a. **Merger clause:** First, the trial judge should examine the writing itself. Many writings contain a *"merger" clause*, i.e., a clause indicating that the writing constitutes the sole agreement between the parties. Such a clause will *conclusively establish that the document is a total integration*, unless the document is obviously incomplete, or the merger clause was included as the result of fraud or mistake, or there is some other reason to set aside the contract. (Fraud, mistake, and other facts that show the contract to be void or voidable, are never barred by the parol evidence rule; see *infra*, p. 184-187.)

b. **Rest of writing:** If there is no merger clause, then, according to Williston, the writing as a whole should be examined. If the writing is obviously incomplete on its face (e.g., a lease with no mention of price), or if it expresses the duty of only one of the parties (as is the case with deeds, promissory notes, etc.), the writing will be treated as a partial integration. Therefore, consistent additional terms may be demonstrated through oral evidence. If, on the other hand, the writing appears on its face to be a complete expression of the rights and duties of both parties, it should be deemed a total integration unless the alleged oral additional terms were ones which might naturally have been made as a separate agreement by reasonable parties in the position of the actual parties to the contract. 4 Williston §§ 633-39. C&P, pp. 131-132.

c. **"Four corners" approach:** Williston would have the trial judge determine whether there is an integration, and whether it is total or partial, by looking *exclusively at the document.* This approach is sometimes called the *"four corners"* approach (because the judge does not look beyond the "four corners" of the document in making his decision). Williston thus adopts a "reasonable person" standard; he is interested in whether *reasonable people* in the position of the contracting parties would have naturally put the terms of the alleged oral agreement into the final writing, or would instead have left them out.

2. **The Corbin view:** Professor Corbin took a sharply different view from Professor Williston as to how the court should handle parol evidence questions, particularly how it should decide whether integration was partial or total. He believed that the *actual intention* of the parties should be looked to in disposing of this question. If all the evidence introduced by the parties shows that they in fact did not intend the written contract to contain all terms of their agreement, and that in fact other oral agreements were made and were intended to be binding, this evidence would then be given to the jury. Corbin thus places much less emphasis on the writing itself than did Williston, and looks much more to the *actual intent* of the parties. See Corbin, § 582; C&P, pp. 132-133.

a. **Effect of Corbin position:** The Corbin view comes close to *eviscerating* the parol evidence rule. Since the court uses all available evidence to determine whether the parties intended the writing to replace previous oral agreements, the court in effect follows the general rule that a later agreement supersedes an earlier one, if the parties intend that it do so. No parol evidence rule is necessary for this general rule to be followed. Corbin's view of the parol evidence rule strips the written document of the almost sacrosanct quality that Williston gave it. See Murray, pp. 231-32.

3. **The UCC approach:** The UCC, like both Corbin and Williston, entrusts to the trial judge the decision about whether a partial or total integration exists. In instructing the

judge on how to make this decision, the Code seems to take a middle view between Williston's and Corbin's (though probably closer to Corbin's).

> **a. Text of UCC:** In explaining § 2-202(b)'s statement that evidence of "consistent additional terms" may be given unless the court finds that the writing was intended as a "complete and exclusive statement of the agreement" (i.e., a total integration), Comment 3 states: "If the additional terms are such that, if agreed upon, they **would certainly** have been included in the document in the view of the court, then evidence of their alleged making must be kept from the trier of fact."

> **b. Effect:** Whereas Williston would not allow evidence of consistent terms if they "might naturally" have been included in the writing by reasonable people, the Code would bar these terms only if they "would certainly" have been included in the document. But the Code does not go as far in allowing the jury to consider additional terms as Corbin does; Corbin would look to the "actual intention" of the parties, not to whether reasonable people "would certainly" have included the terms in the document. See Murray, p. 235.

C. Deciding whether a writing is an integration, and whether particular terms contradict or supplement it: In the summary of the Corbin, Williston, and UCC views on how the judge applies the parol evidence rule, we have focused on the chief area of controversy, i.e., how the judge determines whether a writing which has already been decided to be an integration (i.e., a final expression of agreement) is "partial" or "total." This issue is most often the critical one in parol evidence disputes, since frequently the oral agreement sought to be shown does not contradict the writing, but supplements it. But the judge will also have to decide:

❏ whether the writing is in fact a *final expression* (i.e., an integration), and

❏ whether the oral terms sought to be introduced *contradict* or, rather, *supplement*, the writing.

All authorities agree that these decisions are to be made *exclusively by the judge.*

Quiz Yourself on
THE ROLES OF THE JUDGE AND JURY

48. Marshall and Blackstone have a written contract whereby Blackstone will sell Marshall 10,000 "Scales of Justice" candy dishes. Marshall subsequently sues Blackstone, alleging breach of what Marshall says was an express oral warranty by Blackstone that the dishes would appreciate in value by 30% in the first year, and that if they did not, Marshall could return them.

(A) Marshall wishes to demonstrate that both he and Blackstone regarded the written contract as covering only some aspects of their deal, and that warranties were not one of the aspects intended to be covered by the writing. May Marshall, consistent with the parol evidence rule, testify to this effect, for purposes of showing that the writing is not a total integration?

(B) Assume this is a jury trial. Further assume, for this part only, that the evidence in Part A is admissible. Who (judge or jury) will decide each of the following issues: (i) whether the writing is a "final" integration; (ii) whether the writing is a "total" integration (in which case it cannot even be supplemented by prior or contemporaneous oral agreements); and (iii) whether the oral warranty that Marshall is alleging supplements, or instead contradicts, the writing?

_____

Answer

48. A. Yes. The parol evidence rule only forbids introduction of prior agreements or contemporaneous oral agreements that vary, modify or contradict a "totally integrated" contract — one intended by the parties to be the final and complete expression of their agreement. Therefore, evidence that the writing was not intended to be a total integration is always admissible on this threshold issue that determines whether and how the parol evidence rule will apply.

B. The judge will decide all of these issues. All of these issues are viewed as being essentially procedural ones that involve primarily legal reasoning. Therefore, all are unsuitable for the jury. The jury will consequently be left with at most the job of determining whether Blackstone made the alleged oral warranty, and whether the goods breached that warranty. (The jury won't even get to decide these issues unless the judge first decides either that the integration was not total, or that it was total but that the alleged warranty only supplements the writing).

IV. SITUATIONS IN WHICH THE PAROL EVIDENCE RULE DOES NOT APPLY

A. **Rule does not bar a showing of fraud, mistake or other voidability:** Even if a writing is a complete integration, a party may always introduce evidence of earlier oral agreements to show *illegality, fraud, duress, mistake, lack of consideration*, or any other fact that would make the contract void or voidable. In other words, the parol evidence rule never prevents the introduction of evidence that would show that *no valid contract exists* or that the contract is *voidable.* C&P, p. 140; Farnsworth, p. 439.

> **Example:** After numerous meetings and discussions, Buyer buys an apartment building from Seller. The contract of sale contains a standard "merger" clause (see *supra*, p. 182) reciting that the contract constitutes the sole agreement between the parties. Buyer later discovers that Seller has lied about the profitability of the property, and sues to rescind the deal. The parol evidence rule will not prevent Buyer from showing that Seller made fraudulent misrepresentations to induce him to enter into the contract.

1. **Specific disclaimer of representations:** Where the contract contains only a general merger clause, as in the above example, all courts agree that the clause does not prevent a showing of fraud, mistake, or other act that would make the contract void or voidable. But suppose the contract instead contains a very specific statement that no representations of a *particular sort* have been made. For instance, suppose that the contract of sale in the above example provided that "Buyer has made his own inspection of the property, and no representations that may have been made by Seller concerning the condition or profitability of the premises have been relied upon by Buyer or are part of this agreement." Does such a clause change the outcome?

    a. Majority view: Even where this kind of specific disclaimer is present, most courts will allow a party to show that the other party intentionally and falsely made the claims or misrepresentations covered by the disclaimer. That is, even such a specific clause will not be enough to trigger the parol evidence rule.

B. Existence of a condition: The parties may orally agree that the contract shall not *come into existence* until a particular event occurs. Or, they may agree that *performance* by one or both of them will *not become due* until a particular event occurs. In either case, they have imposed a *condition*; in the first case, they have made the contract's very existence conditional, and in the second, they have made the duty of performance conditional. If the parties then sign a writing which does not include the condition that was orally agreed to, almost all courts *allow proof of this condition* despite the parol evidence rule.

    1. Justification: Many courts, and the Second Restatement, justify this position on the grounds that the very existence of the condition shows that the writing was not completely integrated, and the condition only supplements, rather than contradicts, the writing. See Rest. 2d, § 217. (These courts would presumably not allow oral evidence of a condition that was clearly inconsistent with the writing.) See C&P, p. 142.

        Example: *A* and *B* agree that *A* will sell a patent to *B* for $10,000 if *C*, an engineer advising *B*, approves. *A* and *B* sign a written agreement that appears to be complete, except that the contract does not mention *C*'s approval; as they sign the contract, *A* and *B* both agree orally that it will take effect only if *C* approves. Virtually all courts would *allow B to prove that the oral agreement was in fact made.* Some courts would hold that this proof demonstrated that *C*'s approval was a condition to the formation of the contract; others (and the Second Restatement) would hold that proof of the necessity of *C*'s approval would not prevent the contract from existing, but would make *B*'s duty to perform conditional on that approval. See Rest. 2d, § 217, Illustr. 1.

        If, however, the written contract contained a statement that "no approval of any third person shall be necessary for the activation of any duty under this contract," evidence of the oral agreement would probably not be admissible (except to show fraud or mistake).

C. Collateral agreement supported by separate consideration: An oral agreement that is *collateral* to the main agreement, and that is supported by *separate consideration,* may be demonstrated, even though it occurred prior to what seems to be a completely integrated writing.

        Example: *A* and *B*, in an integrated writing, promise that *A* will sell a specific automobile to *B*. As part of the transaction, the two orally agree that *B* may keep the car in *A*'s garage for the next year, at a rent of $50 per month. This oral agreement may be proved despite the parol evidence rule, since it was supported by separate consideration, the $50 per month charge, and since it's not inconsistent with the writing. Cf. Rest. 2d, § 216, Illustr. 3.

    1. Not inconsistent with total integration: However, if the writing is a total integration, the separate agreement must not be *directly inconsistent* with the writing.

Figure 6-1

The Parol Evidence Rule

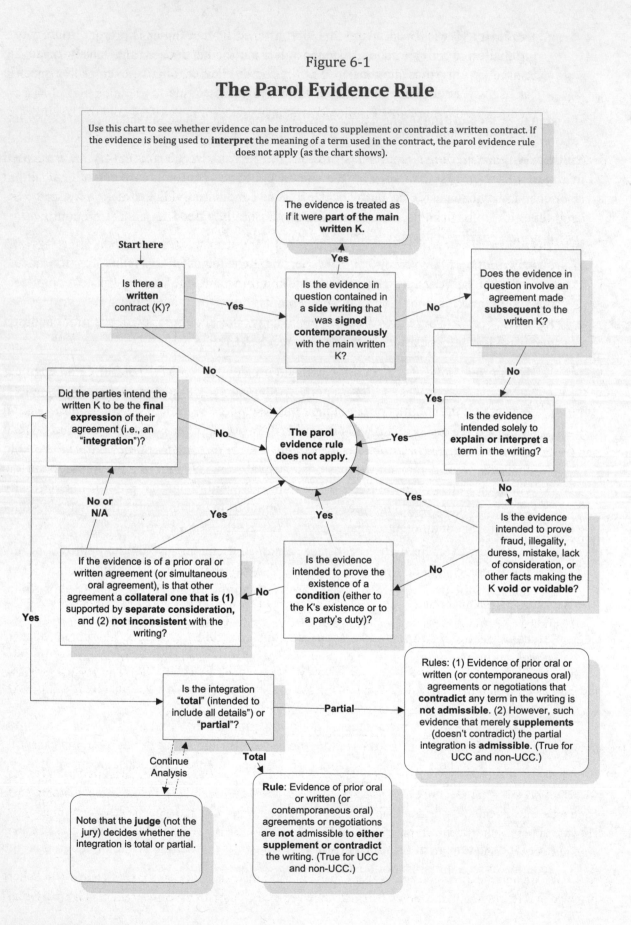

Example: Same facts as above example. Assume the writing has a merger clause, saying that there are no other agreements between the parties regarding the automobile transaction. Suppose further that the writing says, "*B* shall have no right to keep the car in *A*'s garage at any time." *B* will not be allowed to prove the alleged oral agreement, since that agreement is directly inconsistent with the writing, and the writing is a total integration.

D. Subsequent transactions: As we said earlier, the parol evidence rule never bars evidence that *after the signing of the writing*, the parties orally or in writing agreed to modify it or rescind it. In other words, the parol evidence rule bars only evidence of transactions that occurred prior to (or in some cases contemporaneously with — *supra*, p. 177), the writing.

E. Interpretation: The parol evidence rule does not bar extrinsic evidence when offered to aid in the *interpretation* to be given to an *ambiguous term* of the contract. This rule is discussed extensively in the next section, "Interpretation," beginning on p. 188 *infra*.

Quiz Yourself on

WHEN THE PAROL EVIDENCE RULE DOES NOT APPLY

49. Enrico Fermi patents a new invention: a solar-powered flashlight. He enters into a written agreement to sell the patent to Albert Einstein. The parties orally agree that the contract will not become effective until the patent is reviewed and approved by a patent expert, Moe Howard, of the patent law firm Larry, Moe, and Curly Joe, P.C. Howard reviews the patent and tells Einstein, "It's bogus. Only a stooge would buy this." Fermi sues Einstein, seeking to enforce the contract. Einstein wants to introduce evidence of the oral condition. Will the parol evidence rule prevent him from doing so?

50. Gary Gullible enters into a contract with Sam Slick, owner of the "Better than New" used car lot, for the purchase of a used car. While examining the car, Gary asks Sam if it had ever been in any accidents. Sam says, "Absolutely not. This car is in the same condition it was in the day it left the assembly line." On the sales contract, Gary is required to initial a clause stating as follows:

> "Buyer has had an opportunity to inspect this vehicle and to satisfy himself of its condition prior to the purchase. Buyer accepts this vehicle in its current condition. Buyer is not relying in any way on any oral representations concerning the vehicle's condition that may have been made by Seller."

A few months later, during a routine service, a mechanic points out some obvious repair work indicating the car has been in a major accident sometime in the past. Gary sues to have the contract rescinded. At trial, may Gary enter evidence that Sam knowingly lied about the accident issue?

Answers

49. No. The parol evidence rule only operates when a contract is *effective*. This means that anything showing it's *not* effective — fraud, a lack of consideration, duress, mistake, or, as here, failure of a condition to the contract's effectiveness — *is* admissible. Here, the allegation is that the agreement is only binding if Howard approves the patent. If true, this would be a condition to the contract's effectiveness, so Einstein *can* introduce evidence to prove the condition was agreed upon.

50. Yes. Even though the disclaimer states that Buyer assumed the risk of the car's condition and that Seller made no oral representations, Gary will be able to introduce evidence of his conversation with Sam during the negotiations for the sale. The parol evidence rule does not bar evidence designed to prove fraud, such as that the other party ***intentionally misrepresented*** an aspect of the deal otherwise covered by a disclaimer clause.

V. INTERPRETATION

A. Interpretation generally: The parol evidence rule deals with whether and when the parties to a written contract may use evidence of a prior oral or written agreement to add new, substantive terms that either contradict or supplement the writing. We turn now to a different, but related problem — how the parties may show the ***meaning*** of terms contained in a writing. This is a problem of interpretation. That is, the parties seek not to introduce new terms that are not contained in the writing, but to ***interpret the meaning of the terms*** which are contained in the writing.

1. **The problem generally:** When the parties are in dispute about what *meaning* is to be attached to terms used in the contract, problems relating to extrinsic evidence arise just as they do in the contexts dealt with by the parole evidence rule. That is, one party will frequently argue that the meaning of the term is perfectly apparent without resort to any evidence other than the document itself, whereas the other party will argue that the term is ambiguous, and can only be interpreted by resort to evidence beyond the document.

    Therefore, we need to understand the "rules of the road," that is, the procedures by which the court goes about deciding (1) whether to admit any extrinsic evidence concerning interpretation; (2) who should hear that extrinsic evidence if it is to be allowed; and (3) which types of extrinsic evidence should be allowed. As it turns out, courts are in nearly perfect agreement as to some of the relevant rules, but in sharp disagreement as to others.

2. **Extrinsic evidence in the case of ambiguous terms:** ***All courts agree*** that if a term is found by the trial court to be ***ambiguous*** — capable of more than one meaning — ***extrinsic evidence must be allowed***. Furthermore, courts are in near-universal agreement that this extrinsic evidence is to be ***evaluated by the jury***, not by the judge. Finally, courts are in unanimous agreement that the types of extrinsic evidence that are to be allowed to help resolve the meaning of the ambiguous term are ***extremely broad***. In particular, courts agree that evidence about what the parties' own ***pre-contract negotiations*** indicated to be the meaning of the ambiguous term is to be ***admitted***, and heard by the jury.

    Example: Suppose that Buyer contracts to buy a business from Seller, and that part of the purchase price is to be a particular percentage of the "Gross Profit" earned by the business in the year after acquisition. Assume further that within the document itself there is no attempt to define "Gross Profit," perhaps because the parties believe that this term is unambiguous. A dispute breaks out about how gross profit is to be measured, and Seller sues Buyer. Assume for the moment that the trial court determines that the term "Gross Profit" is ambiguous. (Let's not worry for now about how the trial court comes to this determination. As we'll see in a moment, this question "How does the trial court determine whether there is ambiguity?" is actually the most controversial question in this whole area.)

Virtually all courts agree that once the term is found by the trial judge to be ambiguous, *it is up to the jury*, not the judge, to decide on the meaning of this term. Virtually all courts further agree that a *wide range of extrinsic evidence* should be allowed to be presented to the jury on the meaning of the term "Gross Profits." Now, suppose that Seller wants to present the jury testimony by Seller that while the parties were negotiating the transaction, Buyer said to Seller, "We'll compute 'Gross Profits' the way your accountant has always done, in the financial statements that your accountant has prepared for the business in past years." Even though this type of extrinsic evidence — evidence about what the parties said during their negotiations — is the most troublesome kind of extrinsic evidence, virtually all courts will *allow* the jury to hear it, because the judge has already made the threshold determination that the term is ambiguous and its meaning is to be decided by the jury.

a. **Course of dealing and course of performance:** Where a term used in the writing is ambiguous, courts also allow evidence of *trade usage, course of dealing and course of performance* to show what the ambiguous term was intended to mean. This topic is explained in detail *infra*, p. 192.

3. **Unambiguous terms:** Now, let's suppose that the trial judge decides that the term in question is completely *unambiguous*. (Again, let's put aside the very controversial issue of how the judge is to make this determination.) Here, too, courts are in virtual unanimity about what happens next. Since the term is unambiguous, it is *for the judge*, not the jury, to *say what the term means*. Consequently, the jury will be instructed by the judge on the term's meaning, and the jury will never hear any sort of extrinsic evidence about what the term means.

4. **How judge determines existence of ambiguity:** The principal "fighting issue" — the issue on which courts disagree — is *how the judge should decide whether the term is ambiguous*. On this controversial issue, there are three main approaches, which we will term: (1) the *"four corners"* rule; (2) the *"plain meaning"* rule; and (3) the *"liberal"* rule.

a. **The "four corners" rule:** The *"four corners"* rule is the most stringent of the three. Under this approach, when the judge decides whether the term is ambiguous, the judge *may not consult any extrinsic evidence whatsoever.* That is, the existence of ambiguity is to be determined *solely by looking within the "four corners" of the contract itself.* Thus not only will the court not consider evidence about the parties' negotiations, it will not even consider evidence about the context surrounding the making of the agreement. This hyper-strict rule is followed by relatively few courts.

b. **The "plain meaning" rule:** The *"plain meaning"* rule or approach, as it is generally applied, is in the *middle* of the three approaches in terms of strictness. The most significant aspect of the plain meaning rule is that when the court goes to decide whether a term used in the agreement is ambiguous, the court *will not hear evidence about the parties' preliminary negotiations.* (However, the court *will* hear evidence about the circumstances, or *"context,"* surrounding the making of the agreement.) Farnsworth, § 7.12, pp. 477-478.

c. **The "liberal" rule:** Finally, what might be called the *"liberal"* rule rejects — or at least significantly weakens — the plain meaning approach. Under the liberal view, "*evidence of prior negotiations* is *admissible* ... for the limited purpose of enabling the trial judge to determine whether the language in dispute lacks the acquired degree of clarity." Farnsworth, § 7.12, pp. 479-80. The Second Restatement seems to take this view; the Comments say that "determination of meaning or ambiguity should only be made in light of the ... preliminary negotiations." Rest. 2d § 212, Comment b. The most famous case applying the liberal view — and thus allowing the judge to look to the parties' *pre-signing negotiations* to determine whether a contract term is ambiguous — is set forth in the following example.

Example: D contracts to do some repair work on P's steam turbine. In the contract, D promises to indemnify P "against all loss, damage, expense and liability resulting from…injury to property, arising out of or in any way connected with the performance of this contract." During the work, the turbine is damaged. D seeks to argue that by this clause, the parties meant for D to pay only for damage to the property of third persons, not for damage to P's own property.

Held, D has the right to attempt to prove, by oral testimony, that this was what the parties intended. The trial judge was incorrect in applying the plain-meaning rule, i.e., in looking solely at the document itself and in concluding that by its "plain language" the document required D to pay for injuries to P's property. "A rule that would limit the determination of the meaning of a written instrument to its four-corners merely because it seems to the court to be clear and unambiguous, would either deny the relevance of the intention of the parties or presuppose a degree of verbal precision and stability our language has not attained." Before allowing D to put on extensive testimony, however, the trial judge should first make a preliminary review to ascertain whether the contract was at least "fairly susceptible" of D's interpretation. *Pacific Gas & Electric Co. v. G. W. Thomas Drayage & Rigging Co.*, 442 P.2d 641 (Cal. 1968).

i.   **Limitations on liberal view:** The liberal view runs the risk of significantly *weakening the parole evidence rule*, by giving a litigant a chance to use the parties' pre-contract statements to prove that "The contract doesn't mean what it seems to mean." Courts following the liberal approach are aware of this danger. Consequently, they take pains to ensure that the evidence of prior negotiations is admissible only for the purpose of "interpreting," not "contradicting," the writing. Where, then, is the dividing line between interpretation and contradiction? "Interpretation ends with the resolution of problems that derive from the failure of language, that is to say, with the resolution of *ambiguity* and *vagueness*. Accordingly, even under the liberal view, extrinsic evidence is admissible [while the judge is deciding whether the document is ambiguous] only where it is relevant to ambiguity or vagueness *rather than inaccuracy or incompleteness*." Farnsworth, § 7.12, p. 480.

5.   **Burden of persuasion:**   A party who is allowed to give testimony about what the parties intended by a term will still have problems of proof. If he is the plaintiff, his burden of persuading the court that the meaning favorable to him was *in fact the one intended by the parties* may be substantial.

Example: D, an American corporation, agrees to export to P, a Swiss corporation, a certain quantity of eviscerated "chickens." D ships "stewing" chickens (older, heavier birds), which P rejects, claiming that the contract contemplated young "broilers" or "fryers." P argues that there is a trade usage by which "chicken" means "young chicken."

Held, P has failed to sustain its burden of showing that the stewing chickens are not "chicken." Trade usage is binding on D only if it had "actual knowledge" of the usage, or the usage is "so generally known in the community that [D's] actual individual knowledge of it may be inferred." Here, D was quite new to the poultry business, and P did not prove that the alleged trade usage was sufficiently well established; on the contrary, its witnesses testified that they were careful to say specifically "broilers," rather than merely "chicken," when they wanted young chickens. Furthermore, U.S. Department of Agriculture regulations in force at the time included "stewing chickens" among the various classes of "chickens." D was entitled to use the meaning included in these regulations, particularly since P's first inquiry referred to "grade A government-inspected" chickens, as did the contract.

Since D has proved that its subjective understanding of the word "chicken" (i.e., "stewing" chickens) coincided with at least one objective meaning of that word (as shown by the government regulations and by the realities of the marketplace, among other factors), P has not sustained the burden of showing that both parties intended only the narrower use of the word. *Frigaliment Importing Co. v. B.N.S. International Sales Corp.*, 190 F.Supp. 116 (S.D.N.Y. 1960).

B. Maxims of interpretation: There are a number of frequently cited "maxims" that courts make use of in deciding which of two conflicting interpretations of a term should be followed. Several of the best-known of these are as follows:

1. **Primary purpose rule:** If the *"primary purpose"* of the parties in making the contract can be ascertained, that purpose is given "great weight." Rest. 2d, § 202(1).

2. **All terms made reasonable, lawful and effective:** All terms will be interpreted, where possible, so that they will have a *reasonable, lawful and effective meaning*. Rest. 2d, § 203(a).

3. **Construction against the draftsman:** An ambiguous term will be *construed against the drafter*. Rest. 2d, § 206.

4. **Negotiated terms control standard terms:** A term that has been *negotiated* between the parties will control over a standardized portion of the agreement (i.e., the fine print "boilerplate") that is not separately negotiated. Rest. 2d, § 203(d).

   a. **Typewritten or handwritten words:** This will usually mean that a clause that has been *typewritten* in as a "rider" to a pre-printed form contract, or a clause that has been *handwritten* onto a typewritten agreement, will have *priority* in case of a conflict.

C. One party knows or should know of the other's meaning: Where the parties *attach different meanings to a particular term,* some special rules of interpretation apply:

❏ If one party *knows* (or has *reason to know*) that the two parties attach different meanings to the term, and the other *does not know or have reason to know* this, then the meaning given by the latter *("innocent") party controls*;

❏ If *neither* party *knows or should know* that the two parties attach different meanings to the term, then ***neither party is bound*** by the other's meaning. In that case, the court will ***supply a reasonable value*** for the unagreed-upon term.

See Rest. 2d, §§ 201(2) and (3).

Example: Contractor agrees to paint Owner's house for a fixed price. Owner specifies "Enamel" paint of a certain color. Contractor intends to use a relatively low-durability and inexpensive paint known as "Enamel" in the painting trade. Contractor has reason to know that Owner has in mind a higher-quality paint known among wealthy homeowners as "Enamel." Owner neither knows nor has reason to know that the two parties have different understandings of "Enamel." A contract exists for the type of "Enamel" as understood by Owner (the high-quality one).

On the other hand, if *neither* party knew or had reason to know of the misunderstanding, neither would be bound to the other's meaning. If the disagreement was so major (and on such an essential point) that it prevented there from being a meeting of the minds entirely, a court would probably find that no contract at all was formed. But if the disagreement was not so major, a court would supply a "reasonable" meaning for the disputed "Enamel" term.

VI. TRADE USAGE, COURSE OF PERFORMANCE, AND COURSE OF DEALING

A. Common-law use of "custom":   Words and phrases frequently have more than one meaning. The meaning of a particular word or phrase may vary from one region of the country to another, from one industry to another, etc. At common law, a party who argued that a particular meaning should be used could show that this meaning was in accord with a ***"custom,"*** or traditional usage. However, he was allowed to introduce evidence of a particular custom only if it met a stringent series of requirements, including that it be "lawful," "reasonable," "notorious," "universal," "ancient," etc. Murray, p. 255.

B. Modern tendency exemplified by UCC: The modern tendency is to allow a party ***much more leeway in showing*** that a particular meaning is in accord with custom or usage. Furthermore, the tendency is to distinguish between broad customs, such as customs existing throughout a particular industry, and narrower customs, such as those historically in existence between two particular contracting parties. We will focus here on the treatment of custom in the UCC.

1. **Three sources of meaning in the UCC:**   The UCC recognizes three different sources which may be used in interpreting the terms of a contract: ***course of performance, course of dealing***, and ***usage of trade***.

   a. **Course of performance:**   A "course of performance" refers to the way the parties have conducted themselves in performing ***the particular contract at hand***. If, for instance, the contract calls for repeated deliveries of "highest grade oil," evidence as to the quality of oil delivered and accepted in the first installments would be admissible as a course of performance to help determine whether oil delivered in a later installment met the contract's standards. The idea is that the parties' own actions in performing the contract supply evidence as to what they intended the contract terms to mean. UCC § 1-303(a).

b. Course of dealing: A "course of dealing" is also a pattern of performance between the two parties to the contract, but it refers to how they have acted with respect to *past contracts*, not with respect to the contract in question. Thus if a particular term had been used in previous contracts between the same parties, and had been interpreted by them in a certain manner, this interpretation would be admissible to show how the term should be interpreted in the current contract. § 1-303(b).

c. Usage of trade: The Code defines a *"usage of trade"* as "any practice or method of dealing having such *regularity of observance* in a *place, vocation or trade* as to justify an expectation that it will be observed with respect to the transaction in question." § 1-303(c). Thus the meaning attached to a particular term in a certain region, or in a certain industry, would be admissible.

> **Example:** Customer orders 1,000 letterheads from Printer. Assume that it is a custom in the printing industry that where a particular quantity is ordered, any variation by the printer from that quantity is acceptable as long as it is not greater than 5% above or below it. If Printer delivers 960 letterheads, she will normally be able to introduce this custom as a "trade usage." (However, Printer will have to show that the custom is so regularly observed in the industry as to *"justify an expectation that it will be observed* with respect to the transaction in question" — § 1-303(c). But Printer doesn't have to show that Customer *actually* knew of the trade usage, merely that Customer *should* have known of it, due to its regular observation in the industry.)

C. Effect on the parol evidence rule: The greatest significance of course of dealing, course of performance, and usage of trade, is that these customs may be introduced to help interpret the meaning of a writing *even if it is a complete integration*. § 2-202(a). These sources are thus not affected by the parol evidence rule, which as we have seen ordinarily bars even evidence of "consistent additional terms" where a complete integration exists. In other words, even though a writing is found to be the final and exclusive embodiment of the agreement, it may still be explained by evidence from these three sources.

1. Customs that are "carefully negated": The writing may, however, bar introduction even of course of dealing, course of performance and trade usage, if these sources are *"carefully negated"* during the negotiation. Comment 2 to § 2-202.

> **Example:** Same facts as above example (Customer orders 1,000 letterheads from Printer, and receives 960). Despite the existence of a "trade usage" permitting 5% variation either way, if Customer can show that either in his purchase order or orally he indicated to Printer that he needed precisely 1,000 to do a mailing to 1,000 people, the trade usage will not be binding on him.

D. Allowable to add or subtract from the agreement: Course of dealing and of performance and trade usage are admissible not only to help interpret a particular phrase, but also actually to *add or subtract terms* to or from the contract. Thus § 2-202, the basic parol evidence rule, states that these sources may not only explain but *"supplement"* a writing, even a complete integration. For instance, a particular warranty may be implied through course of dealing or usage of trade (§ 2-314(3)), and a requirement that one party notify the other in certain circumstances (e.g., the termination of an at-will contract) might also be supplied through these sources. See Murray, p. 253.

1. **Contradiction of express term under the UCC:**   The UCC states that course of dealing, course of performance and trade usage may not be used to *contradict* the express terms of a contract — § 1-303(e) provides that these items must be construed as consistent with the express terms wherever it is reasonable to do, and then goes on to say that "if such a construction is unreasonable, *express terms prevail over course of performance*" and "*course of performance prevails over course of dealing and usage of trade*[.]"

   a. **Consequence:** So if the court concludes that there is no way to harmonize, say, a trade usage asserted by one of the parties with an express provision of the contract, the court *must treat the express term as controlling.*

   b. **Chipping away at express term:** However, some courts have gone to great lengths in order to find that a particular custom or usage merely "*supplemented*," and did not "contradict," an express contractual term. One way courts do this to hold that the custom or usage merely removes *part* of the express term, rather than negating that express term completely. So long as the custom or usage does not wholly swallow up the express term, the court may find that the two can be reasonably construed to co-exist.

      Example: Seller contracts to sell asphalt to Buyer under a long-term supply contract. The written contract provides that the price will be "[Seller's] Posted Price at time of delivery." After the contract has been in force for several years, the market price of asphalt increases dramatically. On December 31, 1973, Seller raises its price by 75%, effective January 1, 1974. Seller refuses to give Buyer any "price protection;" that is, Seller refuses to keep the lower price even for quantities ordered by Buyer prior to December 31 but to be shipped after January 1. (Seller has granted Buyer several months of price protection on two prior occasions.) Buyer sues Seller for breach, arguing that the trade usage granting reasonable "price protection" should be deemed part of the contract, and thus breached by Seller.

      Held, for Buyer. The price increase asserted by Seller, effective on one day's notice, did indeed match the express price term in the written contract ("Posted Price at time of delivery"). But the custom of "price protection," adequately proven by Buyer to be a trade usage in the local asphalt industry, can be construed consistently with this express price term. This is because the price protection trade usage "forms a broad and important exception to the express term, but *does not swallow it entirely,*" and exceptions will be allowed if they don't totally negate the express term. Therefore, a reasonable jury could have found that the price protection, as a trade usage, was incorporated into the written agreement. (By contrast, a trade usage that Buyer was to set the price would be a "total negation" of the express term, and would therefore have to be rejected in favor of the express term.) *Nanakuli Paving & Rock Co. v. Shell Oil Co., Inc.*, 664 F.2d 772 (9th Cir. 1981).

E. **Priorities:**   In a particular case, it may happen that course of dealing, course of performance, and/or trade usage, are inconsistent with one another. As we noted above, the Code resolves this problem by stating that the *most specific pattern controls*. Thus an *express contractual*

provision controls over a ***course of performance***, which controls over a ***course of dealing***, which controls over a ***trade usage***. § 1-303(e).

VII. OMITTED TERMS SUPPLIED BY COURT

A. Court may supply term: In the discussion of "indefiniteness" of the contract (*supra*, p. 67), we saw that where the offer and acceptance together are not completely definite as to all essential terms, the modern tendency is for courts to ***supply the missing terms*** in many situations, at least if it is apparent that the parties wanted to bind themselves. For instance, the UCC allows the court to supply a reasonable price (§ 2-305(1)); a place for delivery (§ 2-308); a time for shipment or delivery (§ 2-309(1)); and a time for payment (§ 2-310(a)).

1. Relation to interpretation: This process of supplying missing terms is obviously related to the process of "interpretation," discussed previously. However, interpretation is merely the art of construing what the parties ***actually meant*** by the words they used; when the court supplies missing terms, it is almost always dealing with questions that the parties never even thought of, and consequently did not address in the contract. Since courts have traditionally not liked to admit that they are "making a contract for the parties," they often disguise this process by stating that they are merely interpreting the parties' intent.

B. Restatement rule: The increased willingness of modern courts to supply missing terms, and admit that they are doing so, can be seen by one of the relatively few sections in the Second Restatement that has no counterpart in the First Restatement; Rest. 2d, § 204 provides that: "When the parties to a bargain sufficiently defined to be a contract have not agreed with respect to a term which is ***essential*** to a determination of their rights and duties, ***a term which is reasonable in the circumstances is supplied by the court.***"

1. Duty of "good faith": One of the terms most frequently supplied by the courts is a ***"duty of good faith."*** For instance, in *Wood v. Lucy Lady Duff-Gordon, supra*, p. 114, the court supplied a requirement that the plaintiff make good-faith, reasonable, efforts to promote the defendant's fashion creations. Similarly, in requirements and output contracts, UCC § 2-306(1) expressly limits the contract to "such actual output or requirements as may occur in good faith...." See the more extensive discussion of the duty of good faith *supra*, pp. 69-70.

2. Duty to continue business: One common situation in which courts have occasion to supply an omitted duty arises where one party is to derive benefits from the other's conducting of a business. A requirements contract is one example of such a contract; agreements providing for payment of royalties based upon the number of units sold constitute another example. In this situation, may the one party defeat the other's economic expectations by ***going out of business*** (e.g., failing to have any further "requirements," or to pay any royalties because there are no more sales)? It is impossible to state a general rule applicable to these situations. However, we can say this:

a. Requirements and output contracts: Generally no obligation to continue in business will be found in ***requirement and output*** contracts. However, the previously-referred-to duty of ***good faith*** will prevent one party from sabotaging the other by changing the product required or produced just enough to escape from the contract, or by making decisions that appear to be based solely on the desire to get out of the contract, or doing anything else that strikes the court as being unfair. C&P, p. 215.

i.   **UCC view:**   The UCC deals explicitly with the going-out-of-business problem with respect to requirements contracts. Official Comment 2 to § 2-306 states: "Reasonable elasticity in the requirements is expressly envisaged by this Section and good-faith variation from prior requirements are permitted even when the variation may be such as to result in *discontinuance*. A shut-down by a requirements buyer for lack of orders might be permissible when a shut-down merely to curtail losses would not. The central test is whether the party is acting in good faith." (Apparently the same rule applies for output contracts, though the Comment does not explicitly so state.)

ii. **Severity of loss:**   One factor useful in distinguishing between a shutdown that is in "good faith" and one that is not is the *severity* of the financial hardship leading to the shut-down. The more severe the losses to the party from continuing in the business, the more likely it is that his shut-down will be found to be in good faith. A lack of profit, or even a small financial loss, will not usually be enough to entitle a party to a requirements or output contract to change his business in a way that eliminates the requirements or output.

3. **Limits on competing with other party:**   Where one party distributes a product on which the other is to receive *royalties*, at least some limits will be placed on the former's right to *carry competing products*. If at the time of the contract the parties contemplated that there would not be such competition, it will not later be allowed if the purpose or principal effect is to diminish the royalty payments.

a. **Effect of substantial minimum payment:**   If, in addition to a royalty or other profit-sharing arrangement, one party makes a *substantial minimum payment* to the other for use of a product or facility, the court is less likely to prevent the former from selling a competing product, going out of the business that is producing the royalties, or otherwise hurting the latter's financial interest.

4. **Termination of dealership or franchise:**   One situation in which the court is frequently asked to imply a term is where one party holds a *franchise* or *dealership* for another's products, and the latter exercises a right, recited in the contract, to *terminate* the arrangement without cause. When this happens, the dealer or franchisee commonly asserts the existence of an implied duty on the part of the franchisor/manufacturer not to terminate without cause, and to provide reasonable notice prior to termination.

a. **Implied term:**   Courts have become substantially more willing to find such an implied duty in recent years. See e.g., *Shell Oil Co. v. Marinello*, 307 A.2d 598 (N.J. 1973), enjoining Shell from cancelling a gas station dealership without cause, even though the contract explicitly allowed such termination. But many courts still refuse to override an express contractual provision allowing for termination without cause.

b. **Reasonable notice:**   Some courts have followed a "middle ground." They allow termination without cause, but they find an implied requirement of a *reasonable period of notice* prior to the termination.

5. **Termination of employment contract:** The court will sometimes have to supply a missing term in deciding whether and when an employer may ***terminate an employment agreement***. In many employment relationships, the parties do not expressly set the terms under which the agreement can be terminated. Therefore, two questions arise: (1) What termination provision should be implied? and (2) If the agreement is to be treated as "at will" (whether by implication or because it is expressly so made), should there be an exception implied to prevent the employer from a ***bad faith*** termination? We consider each of these questions in turn.

a. **At-will clause generally implied:** In a normal employment situation, especially one where the arrangement is not reduced to a writing, the parties often do not specify the term of the agreement, or the circumstances under which it could be terminated. Typically, the employer simply offers the applicant a job, and the employee accepts by coming to work. In this ambiguous situation, courts almost invariably supply an ***"at will"*** term. That is, courts almost always presume that the parties intended for either to be able to terminate the arrangement on no or virtually no notice.

i. **"Permanent" job:** This is true even where the job is described as a ***"permanent"*** one — the court will still presume (in the absence of proof to the contrary) that the parties intended that either party could terminate at will. See Farnsworth, p. 513.

b. **Traditional rule allows untrammeled termination:** Assume, now, that the arrangement is at-will (either because the parties have expressly defined their arrangement as being at-will, or because the court has implied an at will term from an arrangement that is silent on the issue of termination). In this common situation, courts have traditionally held that the at-will arrangement may be terminated by either party ***for no reason at all***, or even ***for a bad faith reason***. In other words, courts have traditionally interpreted the "at will" concept very literally.

c. **Emerging trend toward requiring good faith:** But a ***significant minority*** of courts has, in the last 30 or so years, ***modified*** this traditional rule. According to this emerging minority, even in an ostensibly at-will employment relationship, the employer is not permitted to ***terminate the arrangement in bad faith***. Some of the particular motives on the employer's part that may give rise to liability for bad-faith firing have been:

❑ intent to deprive the employee of a ***pension*** for which she will soon qualify;

❑ intent to retaliate because the employee ***refused to commit wrongdoing*** at the employer's urging, or because the employee ***refused to keep silent about wrongdoing committed by others*** (the so-called ***"whistle-blower"*** scenario); or

❑ intent to retaliate for the employee's filing of a worker's compensation, sex-discrimination or other ***statutory claim***.

See Farnsworth, pp. 514-15.

i. **Clause requiring good faith supplied as a matter of law:** Of the minority of courts imposing on the employer a duty to refrain from bad-faith firings, some impose this duty as a matter of ***law***, i.e., without regard to the actual intent of the parties.

ii. **Implied-in-fact clause requiring good faith:** Other courts rejecting the unrestricted at-will-employment theory review the particular contract to determine whether there is an *"implied-in-fact"* clause prohibiting bad faith terminations. According to this group of courts, even if the written employment contract appears to be at will, *oral statements* made by the employer, *personnel manuals*, company practices, or other dealings by the employer may *create a justified understanding on the part of the employee* that he will not be fired except for reasonable cause. In this situation, the court is (at least in theory) simply construing the contract, rather than imposing its own limitation on firing.

iii. **Tort cause of action:**   Of those courts that give the plaintiff a cause of action for bad-faith discharge, not all do so on the basis of contract law. Some courts have defined a *tort* of *wrongful discharge*. When courts have defined such a tort, they have generally done so in situations where the employee was fired for reasons that *violate public policy.*   Common examples are the retaliatory firings of employees who are *"whistle-blowers,"* or who *refuse to participate in illegal actions demanded by the employer.*

6. **Relation to parol evidence rule:**   The court is free to supply a "reasonable" omitted term *even if the contract is a completely integrated one* (i.e., one to which, under the parol evidence rule, not even consistent additional terms may be added). In this situation, evidence of the parties' prior negotiations or oral agreements may be given as evidence of what is "reasonable," but may *not* be given for the purpose of *supplying the omitted term itself.* In other words, it is the court's judgment as to reasonableness, not the parties' prior negotiations, that determines whether the missing term is to be added.

Quiz Yourself on

INTERPRETATION; TRADE USAGE, COURSE OF PERFORMANCE, AND COURSE OF DEALING; OMITTED TERMS SUPPLIED BY THE COURT

51. Wally, Eddie and Lumpy are members of a secret club. They use a secret code to help keep their communications private. As part of their code, "red" really means "blue," and "shirt" really means "sweater." Wally and Lumpy enter into a written contract whereby Wally is to sell to Lumpy his "red shirt" for $5. Wally tenders his red shirt and Lumpy sues for breach, claiming that he is supposed to get Wally's blue sweater for the $5. Under the modern view towards such matters, can Lumpy introduce evidence about the boys' secret code?

52. Shirley Dimple, child actress, enters into a deal with World Studios whereby she agrees to "dance and act" in three movies of World's choice over the next three years. Dimple makes the film, "The Good Ship Bubble Gum" in the first year, in which she not only dances and acts, but also sings. In the second year, World wants Dimple to be in "Tap Dancing Orphans," in which she is also expected to sing, dance and act. Dimple refuses, saying that her contract only obligates her to dance and act, and that she no longer wishes to sing on film. World sues for breach of contract.

(A) Dimple offers evidence that the custom in the film industry is to use the term "dance" in talent contracts only to refer to dancing, not singing and dancing. Is Dimple's evidence admissible?

(B) Assume that Dimple's evidence, offered in Part (A), is admitted. Assume further that World is permitted to show in rebuttal that in the first movie, Dimple raised no objection to singing, and did not indicate that she was being asked to do something that her contract did not require. How should the judge instruct the jury as to the relative weight to be given to Dimple's evidence and World's rebuttal evidence?

Answers

51. **Yes.** Under the *traditional* view to parol evidence and interpretation, the "plain meaning" rule (which says that terms and provisions that on their face are unambiguous may not be altered by parol evidence) would apply. In that event, Lumpy Lumpy would be out of luck, since there is nothing ambiguous on its face about the term "red shirt." The modern approach, however, is to reject the plain-meaning rule, and allow testimony about what the parties intended by any term or provision, even if that term or provision, viewed solely in the context of the document's "four corners," seems unambiguous. So under the modern approach, Lumpy will be entitled to testify that he and Wally were applying their secret-code meaning to the terms, not using these terms' ordinary-language meaning.

52. **(A) Yes, the evidence comes in.** Even in jurisdictions that follow the "plain meaning" rule (see prior question), evidence of "course of performance" (same contract), "course of dealing" (prior contracts between same parties), and "trade usage" (industry customs) can be introduced to help in interpreting the meaning of contract terms. The evidence Dimple seeks to introduce would be considered "trade usage" evidence, and it will be allowed.

(B) That precedence should be given to World's evidence. If evidence about course of performance, course of dealing and/or usage of trade is introduced and one type of evidence contradicts another, the court will give priority to the *most specific* pattern. In other words, course of performance controls over both course of dealing and usage of trade, and course of dealing controls over trade usage. Therefore, World's evidence (course of performance, since all the pictures are under a single contract) will be given priority over Dimple's evidence (trade usage).

Exam Tips *on*
PAROL EVIDENCE AND INTERPRETATION

☛ **Overall rule:** Remember the standard parol evidence rule:

> Evidence of a prior (oral or written) agreement may ***never*** be admitted to ***contradict*** any ***final writing*** (integration), and may not even ***supplement*** a final writing that was intended to constitute the ***complete*** agreement (total integration).

(For more about making the distinction between partial integrations and total ones, see the last three paragraphs of these tips, on p. 201.)

☛ **Focus on exceptions:** Most exam questions involve not the standard parol evidence rule (or at least not just that rule), but situations where the rule does not apply. Look for the three most-often-tested such situations:

  (1) **Clarification of ambiguity:** Evidence of prior or contemporaneous negotiations *is* admissible to properly ***define*** an ***ambiguous*** term, even one contained in a total inte-

gration. The ambiguity may either be apparent on the face of the contract or derive from the underlying circumstances.

> **Example:** A written contract between *C*, a building contractor, and *S*, a carpentry sub-contractor, states that *C* agrees to "reimburse *S* for all material purchased by *S* for the job." *S* purchases $5,000 worth of lumber and only uses $3,000 worth of it. (Assume that the writing is intended as the final and complete expression of the parties' agreement.) *C* refuses to reimburse *S* for more than $3,000 worth of lumber. *S* may testify to a conversation which took place prior to the signing of the contract in which *C* agreed that he would pay for materials purchased but not actually used — this evidence will not contradict or supplement (add a term to) the agreement, it will merely aid in the interpretation of the ambiguous phrase "purchased for the job."

> ☞ *Hint*: Some ambiguities will only become apparent after you analyze the unique circumstances surrounding the contract. The above example is an illustration.

> ☞ **Can't change the meaning:** Be sure that the extrinsic evidence is truly offered for the purpose of interpreting an ambiguous clause, *not adding or changing* an unambiguous one (in which case the standard parol evidence rule applies).

> **Example:** In a contract between a laboratory and a disposal company, the disposal company agrees that "the specified waste products are to be removed from the site within 48 hours of our being notified that the waste containment vessel is 80 percent filled." On one occasion, the waste container isn't emptied until 96 hours after notification because notice was given the day before a holiday weekend. The disposal company may not show that during contract negotiations, the parties agreed that the 48-hour deadline wouldn't apply to holiday weekends. This is so because the language isn't ambiguous ("48 hours" can only have one meaning) and the evidence the company seeks to introduce would *change* rather than *clarify* the terms of the writing.

> ☞ Remember that ambiguities are construed against the party who prepared the contract.

(2) Custom: There are several ways in which *"customs"* may be introduced to interpret the meaning of a contract. When one of these ways applies, there is no parol evidence problem, because the custom is being introduced for interpretation, not in order to vary the writing. The two most frequently tested types of custom:

☞ **"Course of dealing":** This is evidence about a *pattern of performance between the two parties under past contracts.* (Distinguish this from "course of performance," which is how the parties have behaved under the current contract — the same rule allowing proof applies to course of performance.) Evidence of how the parties acted with respect to the past contracts may be used to show how a term in the current contract should be interpreted.

> **Example:** *B*, a retail florist, has been ordering roses from *S*, a flower whole-

saler, for more than a year. The orders are for "roses," and have always been filled with roses of assorted colors. Evidence of these past transactions can be introduced by *B* to show that when she placed her present order for "roses," she did not want (and the "contract," — i.e., the present order — didn't call for) only red roses.

☞ **"Usage of trade":** This is evidence of a ***generally accepted practice*** or method of dealing in a ***given industry or field.*** This can be introduced to clarify an otherwise ambiguous term.

> **Example:** *S*, a wholesaler of widgets, signs a contract with *B*, a retailer of widgets, for a "gross" of widgets. *B* sends 144 widgets. *S* refuses delivery, stating that "gross" in the widget industry means 100 units, not 144. Even if the writing is a complete integration, *S* will be permitted to show that under a widget-industry trade usage, "gross" means 100 units.

(3) **Existence of a condition and/or formation defect.** Parol evidence can be introduced as proof of a ***condition*** not included in the writing, as well as proof that the contract ***never legally came into existence.***

Example of condition: Painter signs a contract in which she agrees to paint Dave's portrait. Painter finishes the work, and demands payment. Dave asserts that he and Painter orally agreed that Dave would not have to pay for the painting unless Dave's wife liked it (which she doesn't). Even if the contract is an integration (final expression of parties' intent), Dave will be permitted to show that the parties agreed to the wife's-satisfaction condition.

Example of non-formation of contract: X and Y enter into a written contract whereby X agrees to build a brick fireplace for Y, and Y agrees to pay the sum of $1,000 to X's daughter on her birthday, February 12. Before signing the writing, X and Y orally agree that Y will make a reasonable effort to obtain a loan to pay for the work, but that if she is unsuccessful by January 1, the agreement will be canceled. Y is unable to obtain the loan by January 1 and calls off the deal. Y may introduce the evidence of the prior oral agreement, because it was a condition precedent to the formation of the contract.

☛ **Two types of integration:** Where a writing (or group of writings) represents only the entire ***written*** contract of the parties, but not their ***complete*** agreement, it is merely a ***"partial integration,"*** and evidence of ***consistent*** verbal understandings is ordinarily admissible (though evidence of inconsistent ones is not). But if the agreement does represent the complete agreement (***"total integration"***), it can't even be ***supplemented*** by evidence of prior agreements.

☞ The more ***informal*** and ***shorter*** the writing is, the ***more likely*** it is to be found to be ***merely a partial integration*** (which can therefore be supplemented by proof of consistent additional terms).

Example: If the agreement is in the form of a one- or two-sentence letter, its brevity will usually indicate that it wasn't intended to be a total integration.

CHAPTER 7

CONDITIONS, BREACH, AND OTHER ASPECTS OF PERFORMANCE

ChapterScope

This chapter deals with the *performance* of contracts. In particular, it deals with when and how the parties owe each other performance under the contract, and with how the existence of a breach of contract is determined. Key principles and terms:

■ **Condition:** A *"condition"* is an event which must occur before a party's performance is due. Conditions can be either "express" or "constructive."

❏ **Express:** An *"express"* condition is a condition on which the parties have **agreed** (either explicitly or implicitly). When a party's duty is subject to an express condition, *strict compliance* with the condition is ordinarily required before the performance will be due.

❏ **Constructive:** A *"constructive"* condition is a condition that was not agreed upon by the parties, but that is *supplied by the court* to ensure fairness. Only *substantial* (not strict) compliance with constructive conditions is generally required.

❏ **Exchange of performances:** In most cases, each party's *substantial performance* of any promises that have come due is a constructive condition to the performance of any *subsequent* duties by the *other* party. (*Example:* If *A* hasn't substantially performed his duty to paint *B*'s house, *B*'s duty to pay for the painting doesn't come due.)

■ **Right to cancel for material breach:** When a party has *failed to "substantially perform"* her obligations under a contract, she is said to have committed a *"material"* breach. The other party is then entitled to *cancel the contract* (as well as to recover damages).

❏ **Factors for determining material breach:** Only "material" breaches, not lesser ones, allow the nonbreaching party to cancel. The more the breach defeats the entire purpose of the contract and the expectations of the nonbreaching party, the more likely it is to be considered "material."

■ **Anticipatory repudiation:** When a party indicates that she will certainly be *unable or unwilling to perform in the future*, this is called an *"anticipatory repudiation."* The other party may respond to an anticipatory repudiation by immediately cancelling the contract.

I. INTRODUCTION

A. Concept of "condition" generally: In a bilateral contract, each party has promised the other one or more performances. Generally speaking, some or all of these performances will be *conditional* on the happening of some event. An event which must occur before a particular performance is due is called a *"condition"* of that performance.

Example: Seller promises to ship Buyer 100 widgets; Buyer promises to pay for the widgets within 30 days of receipt. The parties agree that if the widgets do not meet Buyer's specifications, she may return them and will not have to pay for them. It is a condition of Buyer's duty of payment that the widgets be shipped, and that they meet her specifications. Or to put it another way, Buyer's duty to pay is conditional on the shipment of satisfactory widgets.

II.   CLASSIFICATION OF CONDITIONS

A.   Precedent/Subsequent distinction: Courts have traditionally distinguished between "conditions precedent" to a duty, and "conditions subsequent" to a duty. While the distinction is not of great substantive importance, it has great procedural implications, discussed below.

  1.   Condition precedent: A condition *precedent* is any event, other than a lapse of time, which must occur *before* performance under a contract is due. See Simpson, p. 300; C&P, p. 398.

  2.   Conditions subsequent: A condition *subsequent* is an event which operates by agreement of the parties to discharge a duty of performance *after* it has become absolute.

    a.   Insurance suits: True conditions subsequent are rare. One situation in which they occur is in insurance contracts stating that suit on a claim must be brought within a certain time, or the claim is discharged.

  3.   No substantive difference: It makes *no substantive difference* whether a condition is termed precedent or subsequent. The non-occurrence of a condition precedent (e.g., filing proof of insurance loss) or the occurrence of a condition subsequent (e.g., expiration of time to sue for loss) both operate to discharge a contractual duty. C&P, p. 400.

    a.   Procedural distinction crucial: Procedurally, however, it may make a great deal of difference whether a condition is deemed "precedent" or "subsequent." The choice of label will often determine which party bears the *burden of proof*.

      i.   Condition precedent: A party *to whom a duty is owed* must prove the occurrence of all conditions *precedent* to that duty in order to compel the party owing that duty to perform, or to show that the latter has breached by not performing. See C&P, p. 400; Simpson, p. 303-04.

      ii.   Condition subsequent: If the duty is deemed to be subject to a condition *subsequent*, on the other hand, it is the party *owing the duty* who must bear the burden of proving that the condition has occurred and discharged him.

  4.   Second Restatement eliminates terms: The Second Restatement abandons the terms "condition precedent" and "condition subsequent" entirely. What most courts would consider a "condition precedent" is called simply a "condition" in the Restatement. The true "condition subsequent" (i.e., an event discharging a duty of performance that has already become due) is not treated by the Restatement as a condition, but is instead treated as an event of discharge; see Rest. 2d, § 230.

a. **Restatement favors condition over discharge:** The Restatement also explicitly provides that where there is any doubt as to whether an event is a condition (i.e., in pre-Restatement Second language a "condition precedent") or an event of discharge (i.e., in older language a "condition subsequent"), it is to be treated as a condition. See Rest. 2d, § 227(3), and Comment e.

5. **Concurrent conditions:** A *concurrent* condition is a particular kind of condition precedent which exists only when the parties to a contract are to exchange performances at the *same time*. (Rest. 2d, § 234(1); C&P, p. 399).

> **Example:** *A* promises to deliver his car to *B* on a certain date, at which time *B* is to pay for the car. Delivery and payment are "concurrent conditions" in the sense that their performance is to be rendered simultaneously. However, each person's performance is, analytically, a condition precedent to the other person's duty to perform. That is, unless *A* shows up with the car (i.e., unless he "tenders" it — see UCC § 2-503), *B* does not have to pay. Conversely, unless *B* has the money on hand, *A* does not have to give up the car.

a. **Sales and land contracts:** Concurrent conditions are found most frequently in contracts for the sale of *goods* (as in the above example) and contracts for the *conveyance of land*. See C&P, p. 399.

B. **Express and constructive conditions:** An event may be made a condition either by agreement of the parties, in which case it is an *express* condition, or by a term supplied by the court, making it a *constructive* condition (or condition "implied-in-law"). (Rest. 2d, § 226; C&P, p. 402).

1. **Express conditions may be implied-in-fact:** The term "express condition" applies to any condition on which the parties agree, whether their agreement is stated explicitly, or merely implied from the parties' conduct. Thus an express condition may be "implied in fact," under the objective theory of contracts, just as an acceptance of an offer may be implied in fact. See Rest. 2d, § 226, Comment a; C&P, p. 402.

> **Example:** Contractor agrees to paint Owner's house. The contract says that Owner will pay Contractor the agreed-upon amount, $5,000, "within 10 days after satisfactory completion of the work." Satisfactory completion of the work by Contractor is an express condition to Owner's duty. This is true even though the agreement does not use the language of conditions. The express condition is "implied in fact"; that is, a court would reason that the parties intended to provide that Owner's payment duty would not fall due until 10 days after satisfactory completion.

2. **Constructive conditions:** A constructive condition is one not agreed on by the parties (even by implication), but which the court *imposes as a matter of law, in order to ensure fairness.*

> **Example:** *A* promises to perform certain services for *B*, for $1,000. When the parties make their agreement, neither has said anything about whether payment is to be made before or after *A* does the work. *A* then refuses to do the work unless *B* pays for it first, and sues *B* for the money. A court will probably hold that *A*'s performance of the work

is a constructive condition of *B*'s duty to pay, and therefore that *B* does not have to pay until the work is done.

The judge will make this holding not because the parties have either explicitly or impliedly agreed that the work must be done before payment (i.e., there is no express condition), but rather out of a sense of fairness, that *B* should not be required to pay for services he has not received. The judge may also base her holding on the judicial and business tradition that services must be performed before payment is rendered. See C&P, p. 412.

3. **Importance of distinction:**   The distinction between an express and a constructive condition is extremely important in relation to performance of the condition. ***Strict compliance*** with express conditions is ordinarily necessary before the other person's duty of performance arises. By contrast, ***substantial compliance*** is ordinarily adequate to satisfy constructive conditions. These requirements will be discussed *infra*.

> **Note:** The line of demarcation between conditions that are "implied in fact" (and hence "express") and those that are "implied in law," or constructive, is often indistinct. For instance, in the above example, if a judge were convinced that it was standard business practice for payment for services to be made after performance of the services he might hold that the parties' silence on the issue of time for payment constituted a tacit agreement that the usual practice would be followed. The performance of the services would in that event be an express, not constructive, condition.

III. DISTINCTION BETWEEN CONDITIONS AND PROMISES

A. **Importance of distinction:**   Suppose that *A* and *B* have a contract containing a reference to a particular act by *B*. If *B*'s act is a condition to *A*'s duty, then *B*'s non-performance will discharge *A*'s duty. If the contractual reference to *B*'s act constitutes a ***promise*** by him to do that act, then *B*'s non-performance will be a breach of contract, entitling *A* to damages. It may be the case that the act is both a condition and a promise. However, ***the fact that an act is a condition does not by itself make it also a promise***.

> **Example:** Landlord promises Tenant that Landlord will make any necessary repairs on the leased premises, providing that Tenant gives her notice of the need for such repairs. Landlord does not, however, retain any right to enter the premises. Tenant's giving notice of the needed repairs is an express condition to Landlord's duty to perform the repairs. Tenant has not promised to give such notice, however, and if he fails to do so, he has not breached the contract.
>
> If, on the other hand, Tenant had agreed to give Landlord notice of any needed repairs and gave Landlord the right to enter the premises to make such repairs, in return for Landlord's promise to make any needed repairs, Tenant's failure to give notice would be *both* the failure of a condition of Landlord's duty to repair and a breach by Tenant, for which Landlord could recover damages (if, for instance, the premises depreciated in value due to the undone repairs). See Rest. 2d, § 226, Illustr. 7.

1. **Rules for distinguishing promises from conditions:** The courts have laid down a number of "rules of thumb" for determining whether an event is a condition, a duty, or both:

   a. **Intent of parties:** The *intent of the parties* is of paramount importance. This intent may be indicated by their choice of words. Words such as *"if,"* "on condition that," *"provided that," "unless,"* etc., usually indicate that the parties intend a condition. See Simpson, p. 305. Words such as "I covenant that," "I stipulate that," or "I promise that," generally indicate an intent to make an event a duty rather than a condition.

      i. **Intent more important than words:** But the words chosen by the parties are only one indication of their intent. If the actions of the parties or the circumstances of the case make it clear that a promise was meant, contractual language using terms such as "conditional" will be ignored.

   b. **Interpretation as promise preferred:** An interpretation is preferred which makes a term a *promise* creating a duty on the obligee that an event occur rather than a condition of the obligor's own duty, if fulfillment of the term is *within the obligee's control.* Rest. 2d, § 227(1).

      i. **Unilateral contract:** In the case of notice provisions in *insurance policies*, for instance, the insured will generally be found to have made a promise to give prompt notice, not an agreement to treat the giving of notice as a condition of the insurer's duty to make payment.

      ii. **Rationale:** There are sound policy reasons for preferring an interpretation creating a duty on the obligee rather than a condition to the obligor's duty. If a party's performance of an act is treated as a condition to another's duty, a non-performance of that act *completely discharges* the latter from her obligation, even though the failure of the condition to occur has damaged her little or not at all. A party who breaches a promise, on the other hand, is liable only for whatever damage he causes by the breach.

      Thus if a party's performance *deviates only slightly* from that specified in the contract, the result to him is less harsh if his performance is treated as a promise which he has breached (in which case he is liable for only nominal damages) than if it is treated as a condition to the other party's performance (in which case the latter is discharged completely.) See Rest. 2d, § 227, Comment b.

      Example 1: Insurer covers Owner's house for fire. The policy says that in the event of a fire, "Owner shall give notice of the fire to Insurer within 3 days of the occurrence." This clause will probably be interpreted as being a promise by Owner to give 3-day notice, but not as a condition on Insurer's duty to pay. So if Owner gives notice in 4 days, Insurer will still have to pay (but it can recover damages for the late notice to the extent that it can prove them). Interpreting the duty to give prompt notice as a condition would greaten the risk that by being one day late, Owner would unfairly forfeit the entire insurance payment.

      Example 2: Contractor and Owner sign an agreement, by which Contractor is to build a residence for Owner. The contract specifies that "all wrought-iron pipe must be well galvanized … pipe … of Reading manufacture." Contractor instead inadvertently installs Cohoes pipe, of a grade approximately equal to that of the Reading pipe specified in the contract. After the pipe has been put in and enclosed, Owner discovers the discrepancy, and refuses to pay the remaining $3,500 owing on the contract unless Contractor will change the pipe. This change of pipe would be extremely expensive for Contractor, since the walls would have to be virtually torn down and rebuilt. He therefore refuses, and sues for the amount remaining owing under the contract. Defendant defends on the grounds that the installation of Reading pipe was an express condition of the contract, and that his duty to pay the remaining amount due under the contract is discharged by the non-occurrence of this condition.

Held (in an opinion by Judge Cardozo), the installation of Reading pipe was a *duty* of Contractor under the contract, and Owner may recover damages (in this case, nominal ones — see *infra*, p. 310, for the means of calculating damages in this case) for the breach of this duty. The installation of the correct pipe was not, however, a *condition* of the contract. To treat it as a condition would be extremely unjust to Contractor, since he will be penalized in an amount far beyond the amount by which Owner is damaged by the deviation from the contract's terms. In order to avoid this *forfeiture*, the court will therefore find only a promise, not a condition. See *Jacob & Youngs v. Kent*, 230 N.Y. 239 (1921) (also discussed *infra*, pp. 210, 228.)

Note: Observe that however defensible the result in *Jacob & Youngs* is from the perspective of fairness, it deprives one in Owner's position from getting what he bargained for. It thus represents a significant interference with the parties' right to insist that performance be on the terms agreed to. The rationale of *Jacob & Youngs* might lead a court to find a promise rather than a condition even where words such as "expressly conditional upon" are used.

2. **Express language of condition as implied promise:**   Express language of condition may, in addition to creating a condition, give rise to an *implied promise* relating to the occurrence of that condition. This is likely to be the case if the occurrence of the condition is within the *control* of the *promisor*. See Simpson, p. 306; C&P, p. 404.

Example: Defendant promises to purchase Plaintiff's laundry business; the sale is made conditional upon Defendant's obtaining a "satisfactory lease" from the owner of the building. Defendant fails to bargain at all with the landlord, and claims that the existing lease is unsatisfactory, thus discharging him from his duty of purchase. The conditioning of the contract on Defendant's securing a satisfactory lease put an implied obligation on him to use his "best efforts" to obtain a satisfactory lease. Failure to perform this implied duty constituted breach of the contract by defendant (as well as the non-occurrence of a condition of Plaintiff's duty to sell).

Quiz Yourself on

CLASSIFICATION OF CONDITIONS, AND THE DISTINCTION BETWEEN CONDITIONS AND PROMISES

53. Noah is to buy a boat from Acme Houseboats. Noah agrees to pay "40 days after the boat is delivered to me." Is Acme's delivering the boat an express condition or a constructive condition?

54. Santa and Rudolph agree that "If it snows before 9 am on Dec. 24, Rudolph will plow Santa's driveway by 5 pm, in which event Santa will pay Rudolph $25." Is Rudolph's plowing of the driveway by 5 pm a promise, a condition, both or neither?

55. Old Woman who lives in a Shoe offers to sell the Shoe to Mother Goose. Mother Goose agrees to buy, provided she can get a bank loan at no more than 8% to cover the purchase price. In addition to her promise to buy the Shoe, what other promise, if any, will Mother Goose be found to have made?

Answers

53. **It's an express condition, of the implied-in-fact variety.** Although the parties did not explicitly state that Acme's payment duty would not arise until 40 days after delivery, a court would probably find that the parties in fact intended the payment duty to be conditional upon delivery 40 days before. If so, this is an express condition, because it's one the parties actually intended (not one imposed by the court for fairness, which would make it a constructive condition). But this express condition is of the "implied in fact" variety, because we have to look at the surrounding circumstances, not just at the language, to know whether the parties intended a condition.

54. **It's both a condition and a promise.** It's a promise, since it's a commitment by Rudolph to perform (even though the promise is itself conditional on snow falling before 9 am); so if Rudolph doesn't perform, Santa can sue for breach. But it's also a condition on Santa's duty of payment: if Rudolph doesn't plow by 5 pm, Santa doesn't have to pay. In fact, the condition is probably an express (intended) one; if so, Rudolph will have to strictly comply with the deadline, and substantial performance (e.g., plowing, but doing it 3 hours late), won't suffice.

55. **Mother Goose has impliedly promised to use her best efforts to obtain a bank loan.** When a party makes a conditional promise and the occurrence of the condition is somewhat within that party's control, she'll usually be held to have made an implied promise to do what she can to make the condition occur.

IV. EXPRESS CONDITIONS

A. **Strict compliance:** *Strict compliance* with an express condition is ordinarily necessary. See Rest. 2d, § 225(1); C&P, p. 403.

> **Example 1:** A contract for the sale of residential real estate provides that the contract is "subject to and conditional upon the buyer's obtaining first mortgage financing … from a bank or other lending institution in an amount of $45,000 for a term of not less than twenty (20) years and at an interest rate which does not exceed 8 1/2 percent per annum." The only bank in the area that will lend as much as $45,000 charges a minimum of 8 3/4 percent.
>
> *Held*, strict compliance with the condition is required, and such compliance has not occurred. This is true even though the seller has offered to subsidize the interest payments so that the net cost to the buyer will be 8 1/2 percent. Therefore, buyer is discharged from his duty to close the sale. *Luttinger v. Rosen*, 316 A.2d 757 (Conn. 1972).

Example 2: P works for D under an employment contract. He is fired on March 24. He sues D on April 5 for breach of the contract, and service of the complaint is made on April 14. D defends on the grounds that the contract requires P to give written notice to D within 30 days of any claim, and that it bars P from suing sooner than six months after such notice is given; D points out that the contract expressly makes fulfillment of these requirements a "condition precedent to any recovery." P argues that the filing of the suit and service of the complaint constituted the requisite written notice to D.

Held, for D. Service of the complaint "probably gave [D] actual knowledge of the claim. But that does not serve as an excuse for not giving the kind of written notice called for by the contract." Since the contract barred suit until six months had passed from notice, this provision would be rendered meaningless if filing of the suit were itself treated as notice. Since adequate notice is no longer possible within 30 days of the firing, D's claim is dismissed. *Inman v. Clyde Hall Drilling Co.*, 369 P.2d 498 (Alaska 1962).

1. **Avoidance of forfeiture:** However, courts frequently *avoid* applying the "strict compliance" rule where a *forfeiture* would result. A "forfeiture" would occur when one party has *relied* on the bargain (either by *preparing to perform* or by actually making *part performance*), and insistence on strict compliance with the condition would cause him to *fail to receive the expected benefits* from the deal. See Rest. 2d, § 227(1) and Comment b.

   a. **Defective performance:** This will frequently be the case where one party's duty is made expressly conditional on the performance of some act by the other, and the latter's performance, while deviating slightly from the terms of the condition, nonetheless *renders a benefit* to the former. In this situation, the court will often simply refuse to strictly enforce the condition, and will hold that it is met by *"substantial performance"* of the condition. Otherwise, extreme hardship to the party who has defectively performed (forfeiture) will result. See, e.g., *Jacob & Youngs v. Kent, supra*, p. 208 (decided on the slightly different ground that no express condition was intended).

   b. **Excuse of condition:** Alternatively, rather than finding that an express condition has been fulfilled through "substantial performance," a court may instead find that the fulfillment of the condition is *"excused"* where extreme forfeiture would occur. See Rest. 2d, § 229.

      i. **Liability insurance cases:** Excuse is especially likely in cases involving *liability insurance*, where the policyholder fails to give prompt notice, which the policy says is a condition to the insurer's duty to defend and pay.

         Example: D, a ship owner, carries cargo belonging to P under a contract stating that it is an express condition of D's liability for any cargo damage that P give written notice of damage to D within 10 days after P receives the goods. On receipt of the goods, P discovers damage, and immediately gives D oral notice of the damage, while holding the goods for D to inspect. P does not give D written notice until 25 days after receipt.

         Since depriving P of his damage claim would cause a large forfeiture, and since the damage to D's interests from the lack of written notice is minor (because D has received actual notice, and has had the opportunity to inspect, the purpose for which the written notice requirement was imposed), the court will probably find that the express condition of written notice within 10 days was *excused*. See, e.g., Rest. 2d, § 229, Illustr. 2.

ii. **Prejudice must not result from excuse:** However, even if forfeiture would result from enforcement of the condition, the condition will generally be excused only if such excuse would *not cause material prejudice* to the interests of the party (the promisor) for whose benefit the condition existed. Or, as the Restatement puts it, the court will *not* excuse a condition if "its occurrence was a *material part of the agreed exchange*." Rest. 2d, § 229, Comment b.

Example: Same basic facts as in the above example. Now, however, assume that after P discovers the damage, it destroys the damaged goods, and waits 6 months to notify D of the claim. A court would probably find that the delayed notice (and the destruction) so interfered with D's ability to determine whether the claim was valid that excusing the notice would cause material prejudice to D's interests. In that event, the condition would not be excused, and D would have no duty to pay, even though this would impose on P a forfeiture (failure to get the expected benefits from the policy).

c. **Performance due "when" or "after" some event happens:** Sometimes a party is obligated to perform a duty *"when"* or *"after"* some event outside either party's control has happened. When the promise is structured this way, the court will favor an interpretation under which the triggering event is viewed as merely a means of *measuring the passage of time* (not as a formal express condition), and if the triggering event becomes impractical to use the court will employ an *alternative measurement of time* if necessary to *prevent forfeiture*. Rest. 2d, § 227, Comm. b and Illustr. 1.

Example: Lender, who is 20, lends $1,000 to Borrower, the loan to be repaid "within 30 days of Lender's 21st birthday." Two months before Lender's 21st birthday, Lender is killed in a car accident. Lender's estate will be permitted to recover 30 days after the date on which Lender would have turned 21 had he lived — the "within 30 days ..." language will be interpreted as a means of measuring time, and an alternative time measurement, keyed to calendar time, will be used by the court. That way, the court will avoid a forfeiture under which Lender's estate is deprived of the benefit of the bargain Lender struck.

d. **Anti-forfeiture statutes:** Some states have *statutorily* enacted the preference for avoiding forfeitures. See, e.g., Civil Code § 3275, which allows the court to relieve a party of a "forfeiture," if he makes "full compensation" to the other party, and has not been grossly negligent, willful or in fraudulent breach.

2. **Interpreted in light of parties' intentions:** In examining what seems to be an express condition, remember that language which appears to impose an express condition is always interpreted in light of the *parties' intentions*. If, because of the circumstances surrounding the case, parol evidence, industry custom, or anything else, it appears that the parties did not intend to impose a strict express condition, this will not be done despite contractual language that appears to contain such a condition.

    a. Contrary interpretation: But the use of industry custom, parol evidence, etc., can also cut the other way, and help the judge resolve the case in favor of a finding that language *is* an express condition.

B. Satisfaction of a party: A contract may make one party's duty to perform expressly conditional on that party's being ***satisfied*** with the other's performance. Such a "satisfaction" clause may refer either to the subjective satisfaction of the obligor or to an objective standard (i.e., the satisfaction of a reasonable person in the position of the obligor).

  1. Subjective vs. objective: When there is doubt as to which standard the clause implies, the court will usually presume that an ***objective*** standard of "***reasonable*** satisfaction" was meant. However, the court's choice between the objective and subjective standard will depend in part on the nature of the subject matter of the contract:

    a. Contracts as to which objective test used: Where the performance of the contract relates to ***mechanical fitness***, ***utility***, or marketability, as in a building contract or in sales of goods, the contract is usually construed to require the ***objective*** standard of satisfaction.

    b. Subjective test used: Where, however, the object of the contract is to ***please the tastes or convenience of a person***, on a matter for which there is no real objective standard, his subjective satisfaction is normally required. C&P, p. 453; Simpson, p. 310. Typical of the contracts in which the subjective standard will be followed are ones for portraits, clothing, artistic performance, special foods or drink, and interior decoration.

    Example: P is hired by D to paint a portrait of the latter's deceased daughter. The parties agree that if the portrait is not completely satisfactory to D, he does not have to take it or pay for it. P shows the finished portrait to D, who refuses to take it, but does not state his objections.

      Held, for D. D's own satisfaction was the only thing that mattered. "It may be that the picture was an excellent one and that [D] ought to have been satisfied with it and accepted it, but under the agreement [D] was the only person who had the right to decide this question." *Gibson v. Cranage*, 39 Mich. 49 (1878). See also Rest. 2d, § 228, Illustr. 4 (based on *Gibson*).

  2. Subjective satisfaction: If a condition ***clearly*** calls for the ***subjective*** satisfaction of a party, the condition does not occur if he is honestly, ***even though unreasonably***, dissatisfied. Thus in *Gibson*, the result would be unchanged even if several art experts testified that any reasonable art lover would love the portrait.

    a. Good-faith test: Even under this standard, however, the party's dissatisfaction must be in ***good faith***. (Rest. 2d, § 228, Comment a).

    Example: Seller and Buyer contract for the sale of 400 barrels of preserved cherries, "quality satisfactory." Delivery is to be made in installments. Seller delivers a total of 97 barrels, for which Buyer pays. Buyer then states that he is dissatisfied, and he refuses to accept any new deliveries.

      Held, seller must be given a chance to show that Buyer rejected for reasons other than lack of satisfaction. Seller might do this by showing that Buyer expressed satisfaction at the time of the first deliveries, or that Buyer had a motive for bad faith in that his potential for reselling the cherries had dropped sharply. *Devoine Co. v. International Co.*, 136 A. 37 (Md. 1927); see also Rest. 2d, § 228, Illustr. 2, based on *Devoine.*

    i. Evidence of unreasonableness: Where a subjective test of satisfaction is applied, some courts allow testimony as to the ***unreasonableness*** of the expressed dissatisfaction as supportive, though not conclusive, evidence of bad faith by the obligor. (C&P, pp. 453-54; Rest. 2d, § 228, Comment a.) Thus in the above example, Seller might be allowed to show that his cherries are always selected and preserved with great care, and that he never has complaints about them.

C. Satisfaction of a third person: The duty of performance of a party to a contract may be expressly conditioned on the satisfaction of some ***independent third party***, usually an architect or other professional. In this case, the third party's subjective judgment usually controls, largely because the courts are unwilling to substitute their judgment for that of a professional on whose abilities the parties have agreed to rely. See Rest. 2d, § 228, Comment b; § 227, Comment c; C&P, p. 454.

    1. Architect's certificates: The most common example of a third-party-satisfaction condition is a requirement in a construction contract that the builder obtain from the owner's architect a ***certificate*** stating that the specifications have been complied with; final payment by the owner is typically made conditional on the issuance of such a certificate. See Simpson, p. 312.

    2. Good faith required: Although the subjective standard is applied in most jurisdictions, proof of dishonesty, fraud, collusion with the obligor, or similar ***bad faith*** will excuse the condition.

        Example: D's architect refuses to issue a completion certificate to P, a contractor, because D wants to cut down the payment by several hundred dollars based on a claim that the architect himself does not agree with.

        Held, the architect's refusal in this situation bordered on the fraudulent, and D is entitled to payment even without the certificate. *Rizzolo v. Poysher*, 99 A. 390 (N.J. 1916).

        a. Lack of careful consideration: If there is an indication that the third party did not even ***give careful consideration*** to the issue requiring satisfaction, this will be powerful evidence that the third party did not act in good faith. In that case, the court will treat the satisfaction condition as being waived.

        Example: Owner's duty to make progress payments to Builder for construction of a house is made conditional upon approval of each phase of the work by Architect, Owner's architect, and the payments are due 5 days after such approval. Builder submits to Architect a description of the work done up to a particular point, and requests the progress payment. Architect goes out of town for two months, does not inspect the work, and sends an email from abroad saying "I don't approve the work." Builder waits one more month, then cancels the contract for non-payment. Owner sues him for breach.

Builder will almost certainly win — a court would almost certainly hold that Architect's failure to inspect the work means that his lack of satisfaction was not determined in good faith, and that the non-occurrence of the condition of satisfaction should therefore be deemed waived by Owner. Consequently, when Owner didn't pay, that non-payment was itself a breach justifying Builder in canceling the contract.

3. **Reasonableness:** An ***unreasonable***, but not bad-faith, refusal to express satisfaction by the outside third party is ***not*** an excuse for failure of the condition, according to most courts.

   a. **Quasi-contract recovery:** But even in states following the majority "unreasonableness is no excuse" rule, a person who has failed to obtain the requisite approval will often be able to recover the value of his performance in *quasi-contract*. See *infra*, p. 337; Simpson, p. 313.

Quiz Yourself on
EXPRESS CONDITIONS

56. Pope hires Michelangelo to paint the ceiling of the Sistine Chapel. Michelangelo is to be paid $100,000 upon completion, "provided that Pope is personally satisfied with the work." When Michelangelo is done, Pope comes to inspect, examines the ceiling for several minutes, and says, "Hmm, it's really not my style. Sorry, Pal." Michelangelo sues for the purchase price.

    (A) At trial on Michelangelo's contract action, Michelangelo offers testimony by 10 esteemed art experts that the Sistine ceiling is one of Europe's greatest works of art. Pope offers no rebuttal, except his own testimony that he prefers Abstract Expressionism. Assuming that the court believes that Pope's dislike is sincerely-felt but unreasonable, must Pope pay?

    (B) For this part only, assume that when Pope visited the chapel, he glanced only perfunctorily at the ceiling for 10 seconds, then made the "Hmm . . ." statement quoted above. Michelangelo wishes to offer evidence that prior to completion of the ceiling, Pope ran out of money and that that's his real reason for saying he doesn't like the ceiling. May Michelangelo offer this evidence, and if so, what result should it have if believed by the court?

57. Tuileries Construction Company agrees to build a house for Madame de Pompadour for $500,000. The contract states, "Owner's duty to pay anything under this contract shall be expressly conditional upon Contractor's strict compliance with the specifications for materials and workmanship in this contract." The house as built conforms strictly to specifications, except for the Maison de Whoopee mirror tiles on the bedroom ceiling — de Pompadour had specified Brand X mirror tiles, and Tuileries intentionally used Maison de Whoopee tiles because they were available with a shorter delivery time. Brand X and Maison de Whoopee tiles look nearly the same, are of the same general quality, and cost the same. It would cost over $100,000 now to rip out the Maison de Whoopee tiles and substitute Brand X ones.

    de Pompadour refuses to pay Tuileries anything due to the contract deviation. de Pompadour's anger over the deviation is genuine, although probably unreasonable. The contract as written contains a substantial profit margin for Tuileries ($100,000), in part because a comparable house would only have a market value of $450,000. If Tuileries sues de Pompadour for payment, may Tuileries recover under the contract?

Answers

56. (A) No. Where a condition clearly calls for the subjective satisfaction of a party, the condition will not be deemed to occur if the party is honestly, though unreasonably, dissatisfied.

(B) Michelangelo may offer the evidence, and if the court believes it, Pope will have to pay. Even a "subjective satisfaction" clause, like the one here, applies only to *honest* dissatisfaction. The provider of the goods or services always has the right to show that his opponent's professed lack of satisfaction is really a bad-faith manifestation of some other motive, such as the lack of financial resources being asserted here. If the court believes that lack of money was Pope's real reason, the court will deem the condition excused, and Pope will have to pay.

57. Yes. The condition here is obviously an express one. It's true that express conditions generally require "strict" compliance. However, courts will usually wriggle out of the strict-compliance requirement and settle for substantial compliance if enforcing the strict terms of the contract would result in a *forfeiture*. Here, the substitution of mirror tiles did not materially impair the overall purpose or value of the contract. If Tuileries were deprived of the right to recover under the contract, it would still be entitled to recover under quasi contract (discussed later in this chapter) for the fair value of the house, but it would lose much of the benefit of its bargain (its profit margin). This would amount to a forfeiture. Therefore, the court will enforce the contract. However, de Pompadour will be allowed to assert a counterclaim for any actual damage that the substitution of tile has cost her.

V. CONSTRUCTIVE CONDITIONS

A. Use of constructive conditions in bilateral contracts: Constructive conditions, as we have seen (*supra*, p. 206) are conditions which are not agreed on by the parties, but which are supplied by the court for fairness. The principal use of constructive conditions is in bilateral contracts (i.e., contracts in which each party makes one or more promises to the other).

    1. Each party's performance conditional on other's: Where each party makes one or more promises to the other, *each party's substantial performance of his promise is generally a constructive condition to the performance of any subsequent duties by the other party.*

        Example: Insurer issues a group health insurance policy covering Employer's employees for one year beginning January 1. Employer promises to pay the premium for the policy on February 15, but during the first six weeks of the coverage Insurer rejects 90% of the claims filed by Employer's employees without apparent justification. Employer refuses to pay the premium due on February 15. Insurer's fulfillment of its promise (i.e., to make payment on claims) is a *constructive condition* of Employer's duty to pay the premiums.

        This means that if Insurer has failed to substantially perform its promise (i.e., it has materially breached its promise), Employer's obligation to pay does not become due. Thus not only can Employer sue Insurer for damages (e.g., lost employee goodwill), but Insurer cannot sue for the premium, since the constructive condition to payment of the premium (performance by Insurer) has not occurred.

2. Historical development: It has not always been the case that each party's performance was a constructive condition of the other's duty to perform. Until the late 1700's, promises were assumed to be independent. Thus if the fact situation in the above examples had arisen in 1750, Employer would have been liable to pay the premium even though Insurer had already breached the contract. Employer would have been permitted to recover damages for breach, of course, but the breach would not have relieved him of the duty to fulfill his own promise (to pay the premium). Each party's promise was said to be "independent" from the other's, and breach by one did not excuse the other.

   a. Landmark case: The first important case holding that, in a bilateral contract situation, one party's performance was a constructive condition to the other party's subsequent duties, was ***Kingston v. Preston***, 99 Eng. Rep. 437 (K.B. 1773).

      i. Facts of *Kingston:*   In *Kingston*, defendant had agreed to sell his business to plaintiff, payment to be made in installments out of the proceeds of the business. Plaintiff promised to post a security bond (guaranteeing payment of the installments if the business did not generate enough proceeds) before the sale. Plaintiff did not do so, defendant refused to consummate the sale, and plaintiff sued for breach of contract. Plaintiff contended that defendant's obligation to convey the business was independent of plaintiff's obligation to post the bond, and that defendant's remedy for plaintiff's failure to post the bond was not to refuse to sell, but to sue for breach.

      ii. Constructive condition found: The court (per Lord Mansfield) held that the promises were ***not independent***, and that the giving of security by plaintiff was a condition to defendant's duty to convey the business. To compel the defendant to turn over his business to the plaintiff, without the security for which he had explicitly bargained, and to leave defendant only the remedy of an action for breach, by which time the business might be hopelessly ruined and the buyer judgment-proof, would be "the greatest injustice."

B. Order of performance: The parties to a bilateral contract do not always make clear the ***order*** in which performance is to occur. If they do, then that order applies, and substantial performance of the duty which is due first is a constructive condition of the other party's later duty.

   Example: *A* agrees to paint *B*'s house. The parties agree that *A* must complete the job before *B* pays the cost. *A*'s completion of the job is a constructive condition to *B*'s duty to pay. If *A* fails to substantially perform the job, *B*'s duty to pay never arises. (*A* may, however, have an action in quasi-contract for the value to *B* of his performance. See *infra*, p. 335.) If *A* substantially performs, but his performance deviates slightly from the agreement, the constructive condition to *B*'s duty of payment is satisfied. *B* would then have to pay, but he would have an action for breach with respect to the deviations. See the discussion of substantial performance, *infra*, p. 226.

1. Periodic payments or other alternating performance: The parties may agree that their performances shall ***alternate***. This will typically be the case, for instance, where payment on a contract is to be in installments, each installment to represent payment for work previously done. In such a situation, a ***series of alternating constructive conditions arises***;

each party's duty to perform his duty is constructively conditioned on the other's having performed the *prior* duty. In this kind of case, it becomes important to decide who was the *first* to fail to substantially perform, since that failure of substantial performance is the non-occurrence of a constructive condition of the other party's subsequent duty.

> **Example:** Contractor contracts to build a home for Owner. The job is to take 10 months. On the last day of each month, Owner is to pay Contractor 1/10 of the contract price, approximately representing the value of the work done by Contractor the previous month. The parties agree on a schedule for construction, by which the foundation is to be laid within a certain time period, the main wooden substructure of the building constructed within another period, etc. During the first month, Contractor does not complete as much work as the schedule says he should have. Owner refuses to pay the full 1/10 of the contract price, but gives Contractor what Owner estimates is the correct pro-ration of the contract price for the work done, 1/15 of the contract price. Contractor, infuriated, walks off the job, claiming that Owner has breached the contract by refusing to pay the agreed-upon amount. Owner then finds another contractor, but the job ends up costing 20% more than it would have under the original agreement. Owner and Contractor sue each other, each claiming that the other breached first, and that he himself was therefore excused from further performance.
>
> The court will hold that each party's substantial performance is a constructive condition to the other party's subsequent duties. Thus substantial performance by Contractor of his duties during the first month is a constructive condition of Owner's duty to pay the agreed-upon 1/10 sum. If the court determines that Contractor, although he was slightly behind schedule, had substantially performed (as where time is determined not to have been of the essence; see *infra*, p. 228), then Owner will be held to have had a duty to pay the 1/10 price.
>
> The court will then have to determine whether Owner's payment of 1/15 of the price was substantial performance of his own obligation to make progress payments. If so, then Contractor will not have been excused from further performance, and will be held to have breached the contract by the walk-off. If, on the other hand, Owner's 1/15 payment was not a substantial performance (as would be the case if Contractor was only one day behind on the schedule, and time was not of the essence), then a constructive condition of Contractor's further duty of performance (i.e., partial payment by Owner) will be held not to have occurred, and Contractor will be under no duty to continue to perform, and will not be liable for breach of contract.
>
> It is thus critical to determine who was the first to materially breach (i.e., to fail to substantially perform) his obligation; that party is not only liable for breach, but also loses his right to sue the other for damages, since that other is discharged by the non-occurrence of the constructive condition.

a. **Materiality difficult to determine:** Observe that a party frequently bears a very difficult burden of determining whether the other party's breach is *material* (i.e., whether the other party has failed to substantially perform). If she takes a position that there has been such a material breach, and she cancels his own performance, she runs the risk of later being held to have responded merely to a non-material breach, so that she is herself the first person to breach. On the other hand, if she is timid, and goes ahead with her own performance, this performance may turn out to have been unnecessary and costly.

Example: P leases a large neon sign to D. The lease agreement provides that P "agrees to maintain and service the sign [at its own expense].... This service is to include cleaning and repainting of sign in original color scheme as often as deemed necessary by [P] to keep sign in first class advertising condition and make all necessary repairs to sign and equipment...." Shortly after the sign is installed, someone hits it with a tomato. It also starts to rust slightly, and little "spider cobwebs" form in its corners. D calls P several times to ask for maintenance. After more than two months of no response, D sends a telegram, cancelling the contract and stating that no further payments will be made. A week or so later, P fixes the sign, but D still refuses to pay, and P sues.

Held, for P. P's failure to give maintenance may have been a breach of the contract, but it was not a material breach, which is what is needed to release D from the contract. (The cobwebs could have been cleaned off by D; there could not have been much rust so soon after the installation; the tomato stain was probably partly washed off by the rain.) Therefore, D, by not paying, was the first to breach. "[T]he injured party's determination that there has been a material breach, justifying his own repudiation, is *fraught with peril*, for should such [a] determination, as viewed by a later court in the calm of its contemplation, be unwarranted, the repudiator himself will have been guilty of [a] material breach and himself have become the aggressor...." *Walker & Co. v. Harrison*, 81 N.W.2d 352 (Mich. 1957).

2. **Where no order of performance agreed upon:** If the parties do not agree upon the order of performance, the courts apply several general rules to determine the order:

   a. **Where only one party's work requires period of time:** Where the performance of one party requires a *period of time*, and the other's does not, the *performance requiring time must ordinarily occur first*, and its performance is a constructive condition to the other party's performance. See Rest. 2d, § 234(2); Simpson, p. 322.

      i. **Services:** This principle is applicable to contracts for *services*. A party who is to perform work will be held obligated to *substantially complete that work* before he may receive payment. (This rule assumes, however, that the parties have not reached an express or *implied* agreement for periodic payment.)

      Example: P contracts to do certain construction work for D. The written contract contains no provision regarding when payment will be made. P works for a month, then submits a bill for that month's work; D refuses to pay, claiming that nothing is due until the entire job is completed. P walks off the job and sues.

      Held, if the parties reached an oral agreement regarding time of payment, or both understood that there was a certain custom regarding payment (e.g., 85% of each month's work paid at the end of the month, as P claims was the custom), this will be enforced. But if there was no such agreement or custom, P was not entitled to anything until he finished the job, and his walking off before that was a breach on his part. "Where a contract is made to perform work and no agreement is made as to payment, the work must be substantially performed before payment can be demanded." *Stewart v. Newbury*, 115 N.E. 984 (N.Y. 1917).

ii. Wage earners: Periodic payment will usually be *implied* in the case of *wage-earners*. Thus if Employer hires Employee on a one-year contract, and the parties do not specify when payment is to be made, the court will usually hold that Employee is entitled to payment by the week or month. Such a holding may be based upon a state statute entitling employees to periodic payment, or it may be based on the theory that custom requires such periodic payment, and that the parties impliedly agreed to such payment.

b. Simultaneous performances: If each party's promised performance can occur at the same time as the other's, the court will normally require that the two occur *simultaneously*. See Rest. 2d, § 234(1). In this situation, the two performances are "*concurrent conditions*." This means that each party's duty to perform is constructively conditioned upon the other's manifestation of an ability and willingness to perform. As the idea is often put, each party must *"tender"* (i.e., conditionally offer) performance to the other. The main use of concurrent conditions is in *sales of goods and land*.

i. Rationale: The presumption in favor of simultaneous performances gives each party maximum protection, since he avoids the risk of performing and then having the other party breach. Simultaneity of performance also avoids placing on either party the burden of financing the other party until performance.

ii. UCC rule: The UCC expressly provides for simultaneous performances for both buyers and sellers of goods. UCC § 2-507(1) provides: "Tender of delivery is a condition to the buyer's duty to accept the goods and, unless otherwise agreed, to his duty to pay for them." UCC § 2-511(1) provides: "Unless otherwise agreed tender of payment is a condition to the seller's duty to tender and complete any delivery."

iii. Meaning of "tender": A party "tenders" performance if he either performs or else *offers to perform* with a *present ability to do so.* (See Rest. 2d, § 238). A seller tenders delivery under the UCC, for instance, even if he does not actually hand over the goods to the buyer, as long as he "hold[s] [the] goods at the buyer's disposition and give[s] the buyer any notification reasonably necessary to enable him to take delivery." § 2-503(1).

Example: Seller and Buyer agree on the sale of a machine for $10,000, delivery to be made on July 1 at Buyer's place of business. The parties make no agreement as to the granting of credit to Buyer. Under the UCC, Buyer must pay at the time of delivery (§ 2-310(a)). Furthermore, Seller's duty to deliver is conditional on Buyer's ability and willingness to pay on delivery, and Buyer's duty to pay is conditional on Seller's ability and willingness to deliver on July 1. Thus if Seller's truck pulls up with the machine, and Buyer says "I'll give you a check tomorrow," Seller's duty to deliver is discharged by Buyer's failure to tender payment. Buyer therefore cannot sue Seller for breach. Furthermore, Seller has an action for breach for Buyer's failure to pay on delivery, since Seller tendered delivery (i.e., he put the machine at Buyer's disposal) and the condition of Buyer's duty to pay (i.e., tender of delivery) was thus met.

Conversely, if Buyer has the $10,000 waiting on July 1, and Seller comes to see Buyer, but without the machine, and says "Give me the money now and I'll deliver next week," Buyer does not have to pay, since tender of delivery by Seller is a condition to Buyer's duty of payment. (Buyer will also have a claim for breach of contract for the non-delivery, since Seller had a duty to deliver conditional upon Buyer's tender of payment.) If, however, Seller did not deliver on July 1 but Buyer did not have the money available that day anyway, neither party would be under an obligation to perform (since the other party did not tender performance) and thus *neither party breached*. See Rest. 2d, § 238, Illustr. 1.

C. Independent vs. dependent promises: In the normal bilateral contract, the court will *presume that the promises are in exchange for each other*. The court will therefore treat the promises as being *mutually dependent*, and will make each party's duty of performance constructively conditional upon *the other's substantial performance of all previous duties*. Rest. 2d, § 232.

> **Example:** D, a sub-contractor, contracts to do some construction work for P, the owner and general contractor on a project. The contract provides that "progress payments will be made each month during the performance of the work [based upon requisitions].... Contractor will pay these requisitions, less a retainer equal to ten per cent, by the tenth of the month...." The contract also provides that "all work shall be performed in a workmanlike manner...," and that D will carry liability insurance against damage to P's property. During the course of the work, D's bulldozer operator damages P's house. D submits various requisitions, which P refuses to pay, on account of the damage. D discontinues work because of non-payment, and P has someone else finish up the work at extra cost. P sues both for the damage and for the excess cost of completion.
>
> *Held*, for P. P's obligation to make the progress payments was dependent upon fulfillment of all D's prior promises, including that the work would be performed in a workmanlike manner. Therefore, when the house was damaged (assumed by the court to be a violation of the guarantee of workmanlike performance), a condition to P's duty to make progress payments failed to occur, and P did not have to make payment. "[T]here is a presumption that mutual promises in a contract are dependent and are to be so regarded, whenever possible." Since P was not in default in refusing to make payment, D breached the contract by walking off the job, and is liable for P's extra cost of completion. (The court rejected D's argument that P's only remedy was to attempt to collect on the insurance which D had furnished.) *K & G Construction Co. v. Harris*, 164 A.2d 451 (Ct. App. Md. 1960).

1. Independent promises: There are a few situations, however, in which the circumstances indicate that promises in a bilateral contract are *independent* of each other. In such situations, the court will *not* apply the theory of constructive conditions. The two most common such situations involve *insurance policies* and *real estate leases*.

   a. Insurance policies: In the normal *insurance* contract, the insurance company promises to pay a large sum upon the happening of a certain event (e.g., the death of the party covered by a life insurance policy). The policy holder in turn promises to pay the premium. Largely for reasons of fairness and compassion, the courts have **refused** to apply the theory of constructive conditions to this exchange of promises. That is, the **non-payment of the premium** by the policy holder does not act as the non-occurrence of a constructive condition so as to relieve the insurance company of the duty to pay off on the policy. See C&P, pp. 433-34; Simpson, p. 327.

    i.   **Express condition:**   The courts' refusal to find constructive conditions in the insurance policy case does not prevent the insurance company from making the policy *expressly* conditional on payment of the premiums. In fact, most insurance policies provide that the insurer's duty to pay the policy is expressly conditional on the insured's payment of all premiums. Such language of express condition will generally be respected by the court, so that the beneficiaries of the negligent policy holder are usually out of luck. But if the insurance company's drafters are careless, and do not insert language making payment of the premiums an express condition of the insurer's duty of payment under the policy, the court will not make the policy holder's payment a constructive condition of the insurer's duty to pay.

  b.   **Real estate leases:**   The courts have traditionally treated the promises contained in the typical **real estate lease** as being **independent** of each other. Thus a tenant's promise to pay rent, and a landlord's return-promise to make repairs, have been treated as independent, so that the performance of one is not a constructive condition of the duty to perform the other. Under this approach, if the landlord does not make the repairs, the tenant cannot refuse to pay the rent, but must instead bring an action for breach against the landlord.

    i.   **Law is changing:**   But the law regarding the independence of real estate covenants is changing. A growing number of courts — perhaps by now a majority — treat the landlord's and tenant's promises as being dependent on each other. Therefore, each is a constructive condition of the other, and the tenant whose landlord refuses to make repairs can refuse to pay rent without breaching the contract.

D. **Divisible contracts:**   In applying the doctrine of constructive conditions, courts frequently give special treatment to what are usually called "*divisible*" contracts. A divisible contract is one in which both parties have divided up their performances into **corresponding pairs of part performances**, so that the parts of each pair are regarded (by the parties) as **agreed-upon equivalents.** Rest. 2d, § 240.

  1.   **Payment for each part:** Typically, this means that one party promises to deliver a series of part performances (delivery of goods or services), and the other party promises to **pay a separately-quoted amount** for each of those part performances.

  2.   **Significance:**   If the contract is found to be divisible, here's the significance: if one party partly performs — that is, **performs the entirety of one unit or installment** — the other will have to make **full payment for that part**, regardless of whether the first party ever performs the **later unit(s).** By contrast, if the contract is not divisible, then the non-breaching party won't have to pay anything at all (at least under the contract).

    a.   **Series of contracts:**   So if a contract is found to be divisible, it will for purposes of constructive condition be treated as a **series of separate contracts**.

3. **Test for divisibility:** The test for the divisibility of a contract is "whether, had the parties thought about it, as fair and reasonable people, they would be *willing to exchange the part performances in question irrespective of what transpired subsequently* or whether the divisions made are merely for the purpose of requiring periodic payments as the work progresses." C&P, p. 432. Or as the Second Restatement puts it, a contract is divisible if it can be "apportioned into *corresponding pairs of part performances* so that the *parts of each pair* are properly regarded as *agreed equivalents….*" Rest. 2d, § 240.

    Example: P agrees to drive 10,000 logs down a river to D's logging boom. The contract sets a price of one cent per log mile. Because of a flood, P drives only 5,763 logs to D's boom (an average distance per log of 100 miles), and leaves the other logs on the river banks on the way to the boom. D expects to resell the logs and can resell the 5,763 at the same price per log as if he had received the whole 10,000.

    A court would likely hold that the driving of a log the entire way and the corresponding one cent per mile price are agreed equivalents; however, the driving of a log *part* of the way and the corresponding one cent per mile price are not. Therefore, P may recover the pro-rata contract price ($5,763) for the 5,763 logs he has driven all the way to D's boom. But he may not recover anything for the logs that he took only part of the way. (P's failure to drive the other logs all the way to the boom will, unless it is excused because of the flood, be a breach, for which D may separately recover damages.) Rest. 2d, § 240, Illustr. 8. See also *Gill v. Johnstown Lumber Co.*, 25 A. 120 (Pa. 1892) (on which Illustr. 8 is loosely based).

    a. **Construction contracts:** Often, the fact that there are "periodic" payments (i.e., payments payable at different times) will suggest that each payment is an agreed equivalent for some performance by the other party. But not all contracts in which there are periodic payments are "divisible." In most *construction* contracts, for instance, the owner is required to make "progress" payments, but this does *not* normally mean that the contract is divisible into a number of components.

        Example: P contracts to do construction work on D's house. The contract provides for four $1,000 payments to be made at various stages of the construction, plus a final $2,000 payment. The first installment comes due after ten days of work; D claims that P has done the work incorrectly, and pays only $800. D also prevents P from doing any further work.

        Held, the contract was not divisible. "The total consideration was to be paid for the total work specified in the contract. The fact that a schedule of payments was set up based on the progress of the work does not change the character of the agreement." Thus P was not entitled to the $1,000 progress payment (as he would have been had the contract been divisible into $1,000 portions, and had P completed that first portion.) However, P may recover in quasi-contract for the reasonable value of the work he did. (See *infra*, p. 337.) *Kirkland v. Archbold*, 113 N.E.2d 496 (Ct. App. Ohio 1953).

    b. **Service contracts:** Most *service* contracts, on the other hand, *are* looked on as being divisible. Usually, the contract will be divided into lengths of time equal to the *time between payments*. Thus if the employee is paid by the week, the contract will be divided into one-week "sub-contracts;" payment for a particular week will be constructively conditioned only on the employee's having worked that week, not on his having fulfilled the entire contract.

Example: Employee signs a one-year employment contract with Employer, for an annual salary of $52,000. The contract provides for Employee to be paid every two weeks. She works for several months, then unjustifiably quits. Employer has not yet paid her for the last two weeks he worked. A court would probably hold that Employee is entitled to her last two-week check, on the theory that each two-week period was a sub-contract in which the two weeks work and the $2,000 salary payment were agreed equivalents. (However, Employer would have the right to sue for damages based on the breach of contract.) Had Employee worked only one week of a two-week salary period, she would probably not have been entitled to one-half of the regular salary check, though this is not completely clear.

c. **Principle of fairness:** In deciding whether the contract should be regarded as divisible, the court will consider whether so treating it would be *fair to the party who has not breached*. Such a consideration will sometimes result in a finding that the contract is not divisible even though the contract states separate prices for the part performance.

    i. **Value to other party:** The "fairness" of treating a contract as divisible will be determined largely from the perspective of the party who has only received partial performance. "[F]airness requires that a party, having received only a fraction of the performance that he expected under a contract, not be asked to pay an identical fraction of the price that he originally promised on the expectation of full performance, unless it appears that the *performance that he actually received is worth to him roughly that same fraction* of what full performance would have been worth to him." Rest. 2d, § 240, Comment e.

    ii. **"Per unit" prices not dispositive:** Thus the mere fact that the contract assigns specific prices to each deliverable (i.e., unit) does *not* automatically mean that each deliverable, and the price listed in the contract for that deliverable, are agreed equivalents. For instance, the contract will not be treated as divisible (and the buyer will not be required to pay at the contract rate for partial performance) if he *cannot make full use* of one deliverable without the remainder of the performance. *Id.*

    Example: P agrees to custom-manufacture a type of weapon for D (a federal defense agency) according to specs set out by D. The contract provides that P will deliver a single "demonstration" sample (to prove that P can manufacture the item successfully) for what the contract lists as a $50,000 price, and then 10 additional working copies for $2,000 each, which will be actually used for combat. The full contract price ($70,000) is to be paid after all 11 units are delivered. P produces the sample as per the contract. P then, without excuse, fails to produce any of the 10 working copies. D buys 10 substitute weapons from X for $20,000.

        If P tries to recover $50,000 for the sample, on the theory that the contract was divisible and the sample was a designated portion valued at $50,000, P will lose.

That's because the court is unlikely to treat the contract as divisible into a $50,000 "demonstration sample" piece and a $20,000 "10 working copies" piece. The court would likely find that the sample piece was "incidental" to the working-copy piece, which is what D was really interested in obtaining. Therefore, the court would conclude that the parties did not intend each of the two contract portions to have independent values equal to the amounts listed in the contract for that portion. Cf. *Pennsylvania Exchange Bank v. U.S.*, 170 F. Supp. 29 (Ct. Cl. 1959).

4. **Clues as to divisibility:** In a class hypo or exam question, the professor will have to give you some pretty strong *clues* before a problem can turn on divisibility. Not only will the contract have to consist of separate (and separately-priced) pieces, but the question will have to somehow make it clear that each piece, and the price for it, form a separate *"agreed equivalent."* To do this, the prof will usually have to make it clear that there is *no "cross-subsidizing,"* i.e., that each separately-quoted price is *fair for the corresponding deliverable*. Therefore, if the fact pattern seems to be going out of its way to stress the close correspondence between each price and the value of the work for that price, the problem will probably turn on divisibility.

5. **Consequence of breach on later portion:** Keep in mind that when one party fully performs one installment of the divisible contract and then breaches a second installment, the innocent party still has the right to *deduct damages* attributable to the breach of the second installment. Therefore, the innocent party will owe the full contract amount for the first installment, offset by actual damages from the breach of the second one.

   Example: In a single document, Contractor agrees to build a deck for Owner and renovate Owner's kitchen. The contract lists a price of $30,000 for the kitchen renovation and $20,000 for the deck. Payment on the entire contract is due when all work is done. Contractor completes the deck but never even starts to do the kitchen, in breach of his obligations on that kitchen. Assume that the contract is found to be divisible into two parts (i.e., that the court decides that $30,000 for the kitchen, and $20,000 for the deck, were each "agreed equivalents").

   Owner will be required to pay $20,000 for the deck even though he never gets the kitchen. But the important point right now is that Owner will be able to *deduct his actual damages for the kitchen breach.* So if it costs Owner $40,000 ($10,000 beyond the contract price) to have someone else do the kitchen, then Owner can subtract his $10,000 of kitchen damages from the $20,000 contract price he owes for the deck.

6. **UCC approach:** The UCC *discourages* the treatment of contracts for the sale of goods as being "divisible." UCC § 2-307 provides that unless the parties have agreed to permit delivery in installments, "all goods called for by a contract for sale must be *tendered in a single delivery*...." Thus if no installment deliveries are agreed upon, but the seller delivers only a partial shipment, he has *breached the entire contract*, and may not recover on the contract for that installment, even though the price of that installment could be calculated by pro-rating the contract price.

   a. **Where installments permitted:** Even where the parties agree to allow installment deliveries, the Code frequently penalizes the seller who delivers a defective installment, or fails to deliver a particular installment at all. First of all, the buyer may reject a defective installment if the defect substantially impairs the value of that installment. (§ 2-612(2)). Furthermore, the buyer may treat a defective installment, or a default in making an installment, as a "***total breach***" if the defect or default "***substantially impairs the value of the whole contract.***" (§ 2-612(3)). See the further discussion of UCC installment contracts *infra*, p. 230.

Example: Seller contracts to sell Buyer 1000 bushels of corn, delivery to be made in 10 equal installments, but payment to be made after all 10 installments have been made. Seller makes satisfactory delivery of the first five installments, but then delivers a badly defective installment. Buyer has in turn contracted to sell each installment to X, and X cancels his contract with Buyer when he finds out about the defective installment.

Since the defective installment has "substantially impaired the value of the whole contract" for Buyer, he may treat the entire contract as being breached. This means that he does not have to accept any more installments, and that he does not have to make payment on the contract for any of the first five installments. (Seller may, however, be able to recover for these in quasi-contract.)

Quiz Yourself on
CONSTRUCTIVE CONDITIONS

58. Queequeg agrees to swab the decks on Ahab's boat once a month between the months of February and August for $10 a swab. Queequeg's fee is payable within 30 days of his performance. In June, Queequeeq swabs the deck, as required under the agreement. In July, Queequeeg does not swab the decks. On August 1, can Ahab withhold payment to Queequeg for the June swabbing on account of Queequeeq's failure to swab in July?

59. Mr. Peabody contracts with the Nutty Professor to have Nutty build a "Way Back Machine" to Mr. Peabody's specifications so that Peabody and his trusty sidekick, Sherman, can travel back in time. To save money, Nutty will send the component parts to Mr. Peabody as he creates them, and Mr. Peabody will put it all together himself. It will take 10 months to make all the parts. Nutty agrees to send the parts as they are ready on the first of each month for the next ten months. Mr. Peabody agrees to break up the $50,000 total cost into 10 monthly installments of $5,000 each, with each payment due upon receipt of that month's parts. After three months of exchanging parts for dollars, Nutty sends the April parts shipment three days late. Mr. Peabody, charging that Nutty has breached their agreement, cancels the agreement and refuses to pay for the April shipment. What are the rights of the parties?

60. The Grinch hires Pollyanna to undertake a broad public relations campaign to try to improve his public image. He agrees to pay her $3,000 for the work. Nothing is said in their contract about timing of payment. When Grinch calls for a progress report a few weeks later, Pollyanna tells him she hasn't begun work because she is waiting for the money. Grinch sues for breach. What result?

Answers

58. **No, because the contract is "divisible" into one-month sub-contracts.** Usually, each party's substantial performance of his promise is a constructive condition to any subsequent duty of the other party. However, this rule does not apply where a contract is "divisible," i.e., properly viewed as a series of ***agreed-***

upon pairs of part-performance. That's what happened here: the parties divided up their performances into one-month installments, with each monthly swabbing by Queequeg paired in value with Ahab's payment of $10. In this divisibility scenario, the court will treat the arrangement largely as if it were a series of individual contracts, each for one month. Queequeg did not breach the contract to swab in June, and his failure to swab in July won't prevent the June swabbing and the June payment from being agreed-upon equivalents.

Therefore, Ahab must pay for June, and his only recourse is to: (1) sue Queequeg for breach of the July installment, provided he can prove he suffered any damages; and (2) cancel the remainder of the contract, if the July failure substantially impaired the value to Ahab of the remaining monthly performance (e.g., Ahab had to hire a replacement because he couldn't safely rely on Queequeg anymore).

59. Nutty can recover for material breach, and may also cancel the whole contract if he wishes. Mr. Peabody has only the right to recover damages for non-material breach, not the right to cancel or withhold his own performance.

When parties have structured a contract to require periodic payments or alternating performances, a party's duty to perform a portion of the contract is constructively conditioned upon the other party's having substantially performed any prior corresponding duties. The issue under these facts is which party was the first to fail to *substantially* perform. It is true that Nutty was the first to deviate from the terms of the contract. However, his sending parts only three days late, when there was no evidence that time was of the essence under the contract, is unlikely to amount to a material breach. Therefore Mr. Peabody was the first to materially breach (i.e., fail to materially perform) when he refused to pay that month's installment. Consequently, Nutty can not only recover for the breach, but can also elect to cancel the contract if he wants. By contrast, all Mr. Peabody has is a claim for non-material breach, not the right to cancel or to withhold payment for April.

60. The Grinch wins. Where the performance of one party requires a period of time to complete and the performance of the other party does not, the court will hold that the performance requiring time must occur first and that its completion is a constructive condition to the other party's duty to perform. Here, performance of Pollyanna's duties will take time and Grinch's payment will not. Since the parties did not agree otherwise, Pollyanna has to perform her PR services before Grinch has to pay. Pollyanna's refusal to do so was therefore a breach, for which Grinch may recover.

VI. SUBSTANTIAL PERFORMANCE

A. **Doctrine of substantial performance:** As we stated earlier (*supra*, p. 215), it is a constructive condition to a party's duty of performance that the other party have made a *"substantial performance"* of the latter's previous obligations under the contract. That is, if one party fails to substantially perform, the other party's remaining duties do not fall due. We examine here the doctrine of substantial performance in more detail, including the factors which determine if a performance is substantial or not.

1. **Relation to material breach:** "Substantial performance" is the opposite of *"material breach."* If a party has "materially breached" her duty under a contract, he has not "substantially performed" her obligation, and the other party is discharged. Thus the question whether there has been a "material breach" is exactly the same as the question whether

there has been "substantial performance" — either a party has substantially performed, or he has materially breached. See Rest. 2d, § 237, Comment d.

2. **Consequences of non-material breach:**   Keep in mind that where a party breaches the contract by deviating from its terms, but nonetheless performs well enough that the breach is not material, the other party always has a claim for *damages* resulting from the breach. See *infra*, p. 333. The importance of determining whether the breach is material is that if it is, the non-breaching party may not only recover damages, but may also suspend, or be discharged from, his own obligations under the contract.

B. **Suspension followed by discharge:**   If a party fails to substantially perform, but the defects in the performance could be fairly easily cured, the other party's duty to give a return performance is merely *suspended*. The defaulting party then has a chance to *cure* his defective performance. If on the other hand, the defect is so substantial that it cannot be cured within a reasonable time, or if the defaulter fails to take advantage of a chance to cure it, the other party is then completely *discharged* from any duty to perform, and he may also sue for breach of contract. See Rest. 2d, § 237.

> **Example:** A contract provides that Housepainter will paint Owner's house for $1000. (As we have seen previously, *supra*, p. 218, in this sort of service contract, payment is not normally deemed due until after the services have been performed.) Housepainter paints the house, but does a shoddy job on part of the work; the problem could be remedied, but as it now stands it constitutes a lack of substantial performance. Housepainter's initial failure to substantially perform temporarily suspends Owner's duty to pay; that is, the lack of substantial performance is the non-occurrence of a constructive condition of Owner's duty to pay.
>
> At this point, although Owner's duty to pay is suspended, Housepainter has the right to *"cure"* his breach by remedying the defects, and Owner will then have to pay. In other words, Owner is not yet discharged. But if Owner requests that Housepainter make the repairs, and he refuses to do so, or remains silent and does nothing for a significant period, Owner will then be *discharged*. Housepainter will have lost the right to cure his performance, and Owner will never have to pay the contract price (although he may be liable in quasi-contract for the value to him of Housepainter's services). (See *infra*, p. 335.)

C. **Factors determining whether a breach is material:**   There are a number of factors which must be considered in determining whether a particular breach is material or not. The overall principle is that the more the breach defeats the entire purpose of the contract, and the expectations of the non-breaching party, the more likely it is to be considered material. The following factors are listed by the Second Restatement (§ 241, Comment a) as being important:

1. **Deprivation of expected benefit:**   The extent to which the non-breaching party is deprived of the *benefit which she reasonably expected* from the contract is a crucial factor. In determining how greatly the non-breaching party has been injured, the *"essence"* of the contract (i.e., the *principal reason* for which the parties made the contract) must be examined.

2. **Adequacy of compensation for loss:**   The extent to which the non-breaching party may be adequately compensated for his loss by the awarding of *damages* is another important

factor. The question usually relates to whether damages may be adequately calculated; if calculation of damages at the time of breach is impossible because the injury is too speculative, a court will be less willing to find that there has been substantial performance (and will thus let the non-breaching party be discharged from his obligations).

3. **Part performance:**   The *greater the part of the performance* which has been rendered by the breaching party, the less likely it is that a breach will be deemed material.

    a.   **Rationale:**   The more a breaching party has done on a contract, the greater will be the resultant *forfeiture* if recovery is denied because she has materially breached.

    b.   **Breach at the outset:**   A breach which occurs at the very beginning of the contract is highly likely to be deemed material, even though relatively trivial. This is because the breaching party will suffer no forfeiture in such a situation. In the case of the sale of goods (discussed *infra*, p. 229), a buyer has the right to reject a seller's goods for small defects, since because the seller can resell the goods, no forfeiture is usually involved.

4. **Likelihood of cure of breach:**   If the breaching party seems likely to be able to and willing to *cure* the breach, the breach is less likely to be deemed material.

5. **Willfulness of breach:**   A *willful* breach is more likely to be regarded as material than a breach caused by negligence or other factors. "Willful breach" usually is found in cases where the breaching party abandons the contract, deliberately substitutes inferior materials, or otherwise acts in bad faith.

    a.   **Trivial defects still allowed:**   Because truly trivial defects in performance are simply ignored by the courts, a party who has intentionally but trivially deviated from the contract will probably still be allowed to recover under the substantial performance doctrine.

        Example: A construction contract calls for the installation of "Reading" pipe. The contractor intentionally installs "Cohoes" pipe instead; this pipe is of the same grade as Reading. The contractor has substantially performed, even though the deviation might be said to be "intentional," because the deviation is extremely trivial. See *Jacob & Youngs v. Kent*, 30 N.Y.239 (1921) (also discussed *supra*, pp. 207-208).

6. **Delay in performance:**   A *delay* in performance will generally constitute a material breach only if it operates to *significantly deprive the other party of the benefit* of the contract.

    a.   **Time not necessarily of essence:**   At common law, there was a presumption that "time is of the essence" in any contract, so that any delay almost always constituted material breach. Today this is no longer the rule, and the presumption is that *time is not "of the essence"* unless the contract so states, or other circumstances make the need for promptness apparent.

    b.   **Express conditions:**   The parties to a contract are always free to make performance by a certain time an *express* condition of their agreement, in which case the rules requiring strict compliance with express conditions apply (see *supra*, p. 209). However, slight delay will *not* be considered a material breach solely on the grounds that the contract contains a *"time is of the essence"* clause. Either the parties must use expressly conditional language (e.g., "the buyer shall have no duty to pay for the goods unless seller delivers on or before March 4th"), or the *circumstances surrounding the bargain* must indicate that performance by the date mentioned in the contract is *vital* to the agreement. (Rest. 2d, § 242 Comment d).

c. **Suspension:** Keep in mind that, even where time is not of the essence, a delay in performance *suspends* the other party's duty under the contract. (See *supra*, p. 227.) But the breaching party usually has some time to cure his breach before discharge occurs. Even if he cures, however, he will still be liable for damages.

d. **Substitute arrangements:** If a delay is likely to hinder the non-breaching party from making *substitute arrangements*, the delay is more likely to be considered material.

Example: *A*, theater manager, contracts with *B*, an actress, for *B* to perform for three months in a play that *A* plans to present. *B* becomes ill during the third week of production, and is unable to perform. Afraid that his production may be ruined, A immediately hires another actress to take *B*'s place for the remainder of the three months. *B* recovers in a week and offers to perform for the last month of the play's run, but *A* refuses.

If *A* was reasonable in thinking that it was necessary to hire the second actress for the full balance of the run (rather than just for however long *B* turned out to be ill), *B*'s breach will be considered material, and *A* will be deemed to have been discharged from the contract. He would thus not have to pay anything to *B* for the time she missed (and might even be able to avoid paying *B* for the time she performed, although *B* would still be able to recover in quasi-contract for this time). See Rest. 2d, § 242, Illustr. 2.

D. **Material breach in contracts for the sale of goods:** The above rules for determining whether a breach is material generally apply only to non-UCC contracts. Where a contract involves the sale of goods, and the seller's performance is less than perfect, the UCC sets forth what might be called the *"perfect tender" rule*, but with numerous exceptions.

1. **UCC provision:** UCC § 2-601 provides that as long as a contract does not involve installments (i.e., multiple deliveries), "...unless otherwise agreed..., if the goods or the tender of delivery fail *in any respect* to conform to the contract, the buyer may (a) reject the whole; or (b) accept the whole; or (c) accept any commercial unit or units and reject the rest."

2. **The "perfect tender" rule:** UCC §2-601 appears to give the buyer the right to "reject" goods that are defective "in any respect," no matter how immaterial. The term "reject" is a term of art under the Code, and will be discussed further *infra*, p. 231; basically, when a buyer rejects, she gives the goods back to the seller, and is completely discharged from the contract. § 2-601 therefore *seems to resurrect the common law "perfect tender" rule*, by which the buyer has the right to cancel the contract, and refuse to pay, if the goods deviate from the contract terms in any respect, no matter how slight.

a. **Rule not strictly applied:** However, the courts have not interpreted this provision literally. In fact, the courts have generally allowed buyers to reject the seller's tender only if the defect was a ***substantial*** one. This has led White and Summers to state that the UCC ***virtually abolishes*** the perfect tender rule. See W&S, pp. 300-02.

b. Rationales used by courts: In order to prevent buyers from slipping out of bad bargains by seizing on trivial defects, the courts often use a number of ploys:

❏ First, the court may look to ***"trade usage,"*** "course of dealing," and "course of performance" (*supra*, p. 192; see § 1-303) in determining whether the tender was defective at all, and may well conclude that it wasn't.

   Example: Buyer contracts to buy "10 gross" (i.e., in ordinary usage, 10 times 12 dozen) of bricks from Wholesaler. Wholesaler delivers 1,400 bricks. Buyer rejects the entire shipment as non-conforming. If Wholesaler can prove (as it might well be able to do) that under construction-industry trade usage, a "gross" does not mean "144 exactly" but instead means "any number in the range of 140 to 155," then Wholesaler's tender will be found to have been completely conforming, and Buyer, not Wholesaler, will be found to be in breach.Cf. W&S, p. 301.

❏ Second, the court may find that the buyer failed to follow the Code ***procedures*** for ***"rejecting"*** a tender; there are, for instance, fairly stringent rules about timeliness of rejection (discussed below, in Par. 4, "The mechanics of rejection").

❏ Third, the seller generally has the right to ***"cure"*** the defect (a right which is discussed below), and the court may hold that the seller cured, or that she could have cured had buyer not wrongfully deprived her of the chance to do so.

3. Installment contracts: The Code is ***more lenient to sellers*** under ***installment*** contracts (i.e., contracts calling for several deliveries) than in single-delivery contracts. In the case of an installment contract, "the buyer may reject any installment which is non-conforming if the non-conformity ***substantially impairs the value*** of that installment and ***cannot be cured*....*" § 2-612(2). This rule has two major consequences:

[1] A ***slight non-conformity*** in one installment does ***not*** allow the buyer to reject that installment, as he could in a single-delivery contract.

   Example: Cotton, Inc. contracts to deliver 100 blue towels each month to Hotel for one calendar year. This monthly delivery is intended to replenish Hotel's existing stock of towels as they wear out. In July, Cotton delivers only 97 blue towels, and indicates that it will make up for this shortage by delivering 103 towels in August. Assume that there's no reason to believe that Hotel can't simply keep 3 of its pre-July towels in service for one extra month.

      The non-conformity (the 3-towel shortage) hasn't "substantially impaired the value" of the July installment. Therefore, Hotel can't reject the 97 towels (as it could in a one-shot deal for 100 towels, assuming that the shortage was not curable).

[2] Even where the non-conformity is major, the buyer can't reject the installment without giving the seller a ***chance to cure*** if circumstances permit. (This rule is the same as in the non-installment "one shot" scenario.)

a. Cancellation of whole contract for substantial impairment: In addition to the buyer's right to reject a defective *installment* given by § 2-612(2), the buyer may also sometimes have the right to cancel the *entire contract* if the defect in one installment is grave enough. UCC § 2-612(3) provides that non-conformity of one installment gives the buyer the right to reject subsequent installments and cancel the contract if the non-conformity of the one installment *"substantially impairs the value of the whole contract."*

    i. Later installment valueless: A defective installment might impair the value of the whole contract if the *later installments are valueless* without a cure of the defective installment, and the defective one cannot be cured.

    Example: Seller contracts to deliver a computer on May 1, as well as a printer on June 1 customized to work only with that computer. Buyer's application requires both parts to work successfully. Seller delivers a defective computer on May 1, fails in its first attempt to cure, and says that it won't make any further attempts to do so. Buyer can cancel the whole contract, since the defect in the computer substantially impairs the value to him of the whole contract, including the customized printer.

    ii. Reasonable fears of later non-conformities: Another way the defective installment might impair the value of the whole contract is if the defect in the early installment gives the buyer *reasonable fears* that the seller will not adequately perform on the later installments, and the seller fails to give satisfactory assurances that this will not be the case.

4. The mechanics of rejection: As we have seen, the buyer may in theory reject goods under a non-installment contract if they are slightly defective, and goods under an installment contract under somewhat more limited circumstances. The buyer's right to "reject" is, however, subject to some fairly strict procedural rules, mostly regarding the time within which rejection must be made.

a. Time for rejection: "Rejection of goods must be within a *reasonable time* after their delivery or tender. It is ineffective unless the buyer seasonably notifies the seller." (§ 2-602(1)).

b. Must not be preceded by acceptance: The buyer loses his right to reject if he *"accepts* the goods." "Acceptance," like "rejection," is a term of art under the Code. § 2-606(1) defines acceptance by listing several situations in which the buyer will be deemed to have "accepted" goods:

    (a) "After a *reasonable opportunity to inspect the goods* [the buyer] signifies to the seller that the goods *are conforming* or that he will take or retain them *in spite of* their non-conformity;" or

    (b) the buyer fails to make a timely rejection (as required by § 2-602(1), above), *"but such acceptance does not occur until the buyer has had a reasonable opportunity to inspect [the goods];"* or

    (c) the buyer "does any act *inconsistent with the seller's ownership*; but if such act is wrongful as against the seller it is an acceptance only if ratified by him."

Note: The language of subsections (a) and (b) above is fairly self-explanatory. (c), however, has caused problems. White & Summers conclude that the section should apply only where a buyer attempts to reject the goods (e.g., by sending a letter of "rejection" to the seller) but then continues to use the goods. W&S, pp. 295-96.

5. **Revocation of acceptance:**   If a buyer has not yet accepted goods, he may, as we have seen, "reject" them (i.e., cancel the contract and make the seller take back the goods) fairly easily. But if she has "accepted" the goods, and then discovers a defect, she may nonetheless be able to cancel the contract. She may do so by *revoking* his acceptance. If she revokes her acceptance, the result is the same as if she had never accepted, and had instead properly rejected the goods.

   a. **When revocation is allowed:**   A buyer may revoke his acceptance of non-conforming goods in two situations:

      i. If she accepted the goods "on the reasonable *assumption* that [their] *non-conformity would be cured* and it has *not* been seasonably cured;" or

      ii. If she accepted the goods "*without discovering* [their] non-conformity [and] if her acceptance was reasonably *induced* either by the difficulty of discovery before acceptance or by the seller's assurances."

      § 2-608(1).

   b. **Limitations:**   Even if the situation falls within one of the above two categories, the buyer may revoke his acceptance only if the non-conformity substantially impairs the value of the goods *"to him."* § 2-608(1). Thus, the buyer must show not only a defect, but that this defect is of significance to the particular use to which she wanted to put the goods.

   c. **Timeliness of revocation:**   The revocation must be made in a *timely manner.* § 2-608(2) provides that revocation must occur "within a *reasonable time* after the buyer *discovers* or *should have discovered* the ground for it and before any substantial change in condition of the goods which is not caused by their own defects. It is not effective until the buyer notifies the seller of it." However, at least some courts have indicated that where the buyer and seller are negotiating to cure the defect, and the seller repeatedly promises cure, this will extend the time during which revocation may be made; see W&S, p. 308.

   d. **Revocation vs. rejection:**   What's the practical difference between a rejection and a revocation of a previously-given acceptance?

      ❑ The principal difference is that the *period of time* within which a buyer who has not accepted the goods may reject is probably *longer* than that available to a buyer who has accepted and now wishes to revoke his acceptance.

      ❑ Also, the buyer who seeks to revoke must make a *stronger showing of non-conformity* than the buyer who seeks to reject. The former must show that the non-conformity "substantially impairs" the value of the contract to him; the latter must merely show that the goods failed to conform "in any respect." (However, as stated above, courts often ignore the UCC's language, and require significant non-conformity even in the rejection case.)

6. Cure: Both the buyer's right to reject and his right to revoke an acceptance are subject to an extremely important limitation: the seller's right to **cure** the non-conformity.

a. Statutory provision: UCC § 2-508(1) provides that "where any tender or delivery by the seller is rejected because non-conforming and the time for performance has not yet expired, the seller *may seasonably notify the buyer of his intention to cure* and may then within the contract time *make a conforming delivery.*"

b. Beyond contract period: By the language just quoted, a seller has a right to cure within the remaining time for performance, no matter how great the breach is. Even *after* the time for performance under the contract has passed, the seller may still have a limited right to cure. He has such a right as follows:

> "Where the buyer rejects a non-conforming tender which the seller had reasonable grounds to believe would be acceptable with or without money allowance the seller may if he seasonably notifies the buyer have a further reasonable time to substitute a conforming tender." (§ 2-508)(2))

That is, the seller gets additional time to cure *even after the time for delivery under the contract has passed if the seller reasonably thought that either:*

[1] the goods, though non-conforming, would be *acceptable* to the buyer; *or*

[2] the buyer would be satisfied with a *money allowance*.

Example: D contracts to purchase an Acousticon model A-660 hearing aid from P. P then supplies an Acousticon model A-665, which is a "modified and improved" version of the A-660. D returns the hearing aid after learning that it is not an A-660. Shortly thereafter, before D has bought any other hearing aid, P notifies D that it will get him either a model A-660 or an A-665, whichever D chooses. D refuses to accept either model, and P sues for the balance due on the contract.

Held, for P. The case is governed by UCC § 2-508(2). Even though D was entitled to receive the model that he ordered, P, at the time it delivered the model A-665, had reasonable grounds to believe that this newer model would be acceptable to D. When P told D that it would get him the originally-ordered model if he wished, D had not yet bought any other hearing aid; consequently, P's notice of intention to substitute a conforming tender was "seasonable." Therefore, even though P did not in fact tender the contracted-for model until after the time for performance, P remained in compliance with the contract, and it is D who breached. *Bartus v. Riccardi*, 284 N.Y.S.2d 222 (Utica City Ct. 1967).

c. Effectiveness of cure: If the seller substitutes goods that completely conform to the contract, she has obviously made an effective cure. It is less clear under the Code whether the granting of a *price allowance* to compensate the buyer for the lesser value, or the substitution of goods that are different from, but equal in quality to, the goods called for by the contract, are acceptable cures. The language of § 2-508, which refers to cure by "conforming delivery," indicates that such allowances and substitutions are not effective cures. White & Summers, however, argue that the Code should be interpreted to allow such allowances and substitutions, because these are the means by which businesspeople typically attempt to cure non-conformities. W&S, pp. 53-54.

7. **Buyer's obligation after rejection or revocation:** Once the buyer has validly rejected the goods, or revoked his acceptance, his only further obligation is normally to *"hold them* with reasonable care at the *seller's disposition* for a time sufficient to permit the seller to remove them." (§ 2-602(2)(b)). The buyer must, however, obey "any reasonable instructions received from the seller with respect to the goods and in the absence of such instructions … make reasonable efforts to sell them for the seller's account if they are perishable or threaten to decline in value speedily," if and only if all three of the following conditions are met:

❏ "The seller has no agent or place of business at the market of rejection;"

❏ The buyer is a "merchant" (i.e., one who deals in goods of that kind); and

❏ The goods are in the buyer's possession or control.

§ 2-603(1).

a. **Reimbursement of buyer:** If the case does meet all of these three requirements, and the buyer incurs expenses in selling the goods or returning them to the seller, the buyer may take his expenses out of any proceeds he receives. He may also use these proceeds to reimburse himself for any payment on the goods he has already made to the seller. § 2-603(2).

8. **Other remedies after rejection or revocation:** Once a buyer has properly rejected goods, or revoked his acceptance, other additional remedies are available to him. These will be discussed more fully in the chapter on remedies (*infra*, p. 309). Here, we shall summarize the three principal ones:

a. **Cover:** The buyer may *purchase conforming goods from a third party*, and recover from the seller the difference between the contract price and the price he has paid the third person; this is called the right of *"cover."* (§ 2-712).

b. **Contract-market differential:** If the buyer does not "cover," he may recover the difference between the *contract price* and "the *market price* at the time when the buyer learned of the breach." (§ 2-713(1)).

c. **Incidental and consequential damages:** The buyer may also recover any "incidental damages," principally those expenses involved in storing, selling, or returning the rejected goods, and in procuring substitute goods. More importantly, the buyer may also recover *"consequential damages,"* defined to include "any loss resulting from general or particular requirements and needs of which the seller at the time of contracting had reason to know and which could not reasonably be prevented by cover or otherwise"; and "injury to person or property proximately resulting from any breach of warranty." (§§ 2-715(2)(a) and (b)). This is roughly the rule of *Hadley v. Baxendale (infra*, p. 343).

Quiz Yourself on
SUBSTANTIAL PERFORMANCE

61. Sylvester Stallion, action flick icon, decides to leave the film industry and open up "Boys Will Be Boys," a toy store specializing in toys of mass destruction. He orders a gross of Mighty Might Super Hero action figures from Action Plastics. Stallion specifies that he wants red-caped figures. Action Plastics, however, sends a gross of blue-caped figures.

(A) Assume that color of the cape distinguishes the various super heroes' identities in the Mighty Might family; the one with the red cape is named "Destructo Man" and the one with the blue cape is named "Emotionally Sensitive Man." The figures are otherwise identical in looks, and identical in cost and in market value. May Stallion send the toys back and refuse to pay for them?

(B) Now assume that the figures come in a variety of colors, but that the color differences have no particular significance to most consumers. As before, Stallion specifies red-caped figures, but receives blue-caped ones. Assume further that in the action-toy industry, manufacturers frequently send whatever color toys they recently have produced to fulfill a purchase order, and that small deviations from buyer-specified colors are deemed insignificant. May Stallion send the blue-caped figures back and refuse to pay?

(C) Same basic facts as part (A). Now assume that the date for delivery is September 15 and that Stallion receives the blue figures on September 5. Assume further that Stallion rightfully considers the shipment to be defective, that he rejects the shipment that same day, and that he immediately notifies Action Plastics of the rejection immediately. That same day, may Stallion cancel the contract?

(D) Assume the same facts as in Part C above, except that the delivery of the original shipment takes place on September 15. Assume further that Action Plastics: (i) knew it was shipping goods that were non-conforming because blue; and (ii) believed, reasonably though erroneously, that Stallion would accept the blue figures. After Stallion rejects the goods on Sept. 15, may he immediately cancel the contract?

62. Humphrey Bogart's granddaughter, Helen, opens up a chain of kitchenware stores called "Here's Cooking At You, Kid." She orders 100 blenders from the Whirlie Bird Co., to be paid for two weeks after delivery. The blenders arrive in individual boxes. She takes one out, plugs it in and tries a few cycles. Everything seems just fine, so puts the shipment in inventory, and signs the delivery receipt "received, HB." Two weeks later, Helen uses one of the blenders in an in-store demonstration. When she pushes the button for frappé, the blade spins so fast that it flies out of the bowl and across the room, nearly injuring several patrons. Helen calls Whirlie Bird back, describes what just happened, and says, "I'm sending these goods back to you, and I won't pay a penny." Assume that the blenders in fact breached Whirlie Bird's implied warranty of merchantability. What are the rights of the parties under contract law? (Ignore tort issues).

Answers

61. **(A) Yes.** Under the UCC's "perfect tender" rule, a buyer has the right to reject goods if they fail to conform to the contract in any respect. Stallion has the right to reject the blue figures even though they are of equivalent value (and almost equivalent looks) to the red figures, especially since they represent a different character from the one Stallion wanted to sell at his store.

(B) No. Although the "perfect tender" rule states that a buyer can reject goods if the goods are defective in any way, the court will look to such things as course of performance, course of dealing and usage of trade to help define the term "defective." Here, usage-of-trade evidence will prove that the figures are fungible goods regardless of color. As such, Action Plastic's shipment will likely be considered substantial performance, despite the fact that the shipment deviates from the specific terms of the contract!

(C) No. A party who has received a defective shipment may reject the goods, and may suspend his own performance (here, payment). But if the time for performance has not yet expired, the seller has a statutory right to *cure* within the contract period, no matter how severe the breach, provided that he gives prompt notice of his intention to cure. UCC § 2-508(1). Therefore, Stallion must give Action a reasonable opportunity to say that it intends to cure by shipping conforming goods. If Action says it will do so, Stallion may not cancel until the delivery time expires without Action's having in fact shipped conforming goods. Until then, Stallion must simply wait, until such time as Action's failure to give reassurances of cure itself amounts to a new act of material breach (which would justify Stallion in cancelling immediately).

(D) No. Even if the time for performance under the contract is up, under § 2-508(2) a buyer has to give the seller a reasonable extension of time to cure a defective shipment if the seller shipped non-conforming goods that it thought were going to be acceptable to the buyer (called an "accommodation shipment"). That's the case here, so Stallion has to give Action Plastics one more shot. Once again, however, Stallion's duty to pay is suspended until he receives the right stuff. Note that there is no evidence that time is of the essence in this contract. If it were, then Stallion would not have to grant any extension.

62. **Helen has the right to do what she did; Whirlie won't be able to collect anything, and Helen can recover for material breach.**

    Helen's act of signing the delivery receipt and putting the goods in inventory constituted an *"acceptance"* of the goods, as that term is used in the UCC. Once a buyer has accepted, she normally loses her ability to reject the goods (i.e., her ability to throw them back on the seller), even if they're non-conforming. However, a buyer who has accepted may "revoke" the acceptance (and then reject the goods) if two things are true: (i) the buyer did not know of the non-conformity at the time of acceptance, and the acceptance was induced by the difficulty of discovering the defect or by the seller's assurances; and (ii) the non-conformity substantially impairs the value of the goods to the buyer. § 2-608(1). Since the problem couldn't easily have been discovered (and, indeed, wasn't discovered during Helen's brief initial test), (i) is satisfied. The physical dangers suggest that the goods' value to a professional merchant such as Helen has been substantially impaired, thus satisfying (ii). Therefore, Helen was entitled to revoke her acceptance and to send the goods back. She's also entitled to sue for breach, as anyone receiving (and even accepting) non-conforming goods may do.

VII. EXCUSE OF CONDITIONS

A. **Introduction:** Normally, if a party's duty under a contract is conditional, he does not have to perform that duty unless the condition occurs. But there are a number of situations in which even though the condition does not occur, the party must nonetheless perform the duty. In such situations, the condition (or its non-occurrence) is said to be "excused." This section summarizes some of the circumstances in which the non-occurrence of a condition is excused, and the party who benefitted from the condition is obliged to perform.

B. **Hindrance or wrongful prevention:** Suppose that a particular party's duty is conditional on an event, and that same party's wrongful conduct *prevents* the occurrence of the condition. In such a situation, the *non-occurrence of the condition is excused*, and the party must perform despite the non-occurrence. Rest. 2d, § 245.

Example: P agrees to live with D, his 75-year-old grand-uncle, and to care for him for the rest of his life, in return for the promise that he will inherit D's fortune on D's death. He lives with D for seven years, during which time D is constantly drunk and abusive to P, making it impossible for P to continue living with him.

P will be able to recover on the contract even though he did not care for D for the remainder of his life, because it was D's wrongful conduct, not any fault of P, that caused the condition to D's promise not to occur.

1. **Mortgage clause:** A common situation in which the party whose duty is conditional will be found to have wrongfully prevented the occurrence of the condition is that of *"mortgage contingency"* clauses in contracts for the sale of real estate. If the buyer's duty to close is conditional on her getting a mortgage meeting certain specifications, and she doesn't make good-faith efforts to get such a mortgage, she'll be held to have wrongfully interfered with the condition and the non-occurrence of the condition will be *excused*.

2. **Intent of parties controls:** In determining whether a party has wrongfully interfered with the occurrence of a condition of his duty, the ***intent of the parties*** controls. If the court finds that one party ***assumed the risk*** that the other might act in such a way as to make the occurrence of a condition more difficult or impossible, that condition will ***not*** be excused.

   a. **Risk that other party will buy up supplies:** One situation in which it is often held that one contracting party bears the risk that the other may hinder his performance occurs in contracts for the supply of limited commodities. A party who contracts to sell such commodities is usually held to bear the ***risk that the market price will go up***, including the risk that it will go up due to ***purchases made by the other party***. See C&P, pp. 439-440.

3. **Implied promise of cooperation:** The "prevention of occurrence of a condition" concept is often put slightly differently, by saying that one party makes the other an *"implied promise of cooperation."* Under this analysis, failure to cooperate is a breach, and if it is material, it relieves the other party from performing and entitles him to damages (as with breach of any other material promise).

   a. **Causality issue:** But whenever there's an issue about whether the beneficiary of a condition failed to use reasonable efforts to cause the condition to be satisfied, be alert to whether the beneficiary's failure to make reasonable efforts had a *causal connection* to the non-occurrence of the condition. The condition won't be deemed excused unless the beneficiary's failure to make reasonable efforts *substantially contributed* to the non-occurrence of the condition. That is, if the condition *wouldn't have been satisfied even if the beneficiary had made all reasonable efforts to make it be satisfied*, no constructive waiver will be found. Cf. Farnsworth, § 8.6.

   Example: Seller contracts to sell Blackacre to Buyer. Buyer's duty to close is made subject to Buyer's obtaining a mortgage of at least $200,000 at no more than 7% from First Bank. Buyer never submits any application to First Bank. However, in a breach action brought by Seller, Buyer shows that even if Buyer *had* submitted a complete and truthful application to First Bank, First Bank would not have given a loan of at least $200,000 at an interest rate of 7% or lower.

In this scenario, Buyer's failure to make the reasonable efforts to satisfy the condition (i.e., failure to make an application) did not change the outcome — the condition wouldn't have been satisfied anyway — so Buyer will be entitled to rely on the non-occurrence of the condition.

C. Intent to forego the benefit of the condition ("waiver"):   A party who owes a conditional duty may indicate that she will not insist upon the occurrence of the condition before performing. In some circumstances, her willingness to forego the benefit of a condition will excuse that condition. When this occurs, the promisor is often said to have *"waived"* the condition.

1. Waiver after contract: Sometimes a party's manifestation of willingness to forego the benefit of a condition occurs *after* the contract is formed, but *before* the condition fails to occur. Since the party by "waiving" the condition has in effect modified the contract, *consideration* for the waiver would normally be required. However, the courts have not required consideration in at least several situations:

   a. Condition not a material part of the bargain: If the condition was not an important part of the original bargain, the courts will usually find that a party's subsequent waiver of the condition is binding on him, even without consideration.

   b. Promissory estoppel: If the party's manifestation of waiver induces the other party to *change his position in reliance* on the waiver, the courts will also hold the waiver binding even without consideration. This is an application of the doctrine of *"promissory estoppel."* See *supra*, p. 136. See also Rest. 2d, § 230(3).

   Example: A law professor agrees to write a series of books. The contract provides that if the professor totally abstains from alcohol during the writing, he is to be paid $6 per page; otherwise he is to be paid at $2 per page. While he is in the process of writing the book, the publisher assures him that strict compliance with the condition on alcohol is not necessary. He finishes the books, drinking as he goes.

   Held, the publisher has waived the condition by inducing the professor to rely on its statement that strict compliance is not necessary. Therefore, the professor gets $6 per page. *Clark v. West*, 193 N.Y. 349 (1908).

   c. UCC: The need for consideration for the waiver does not arise in a contract for the sale of goods, since UCC § 2-209(1) provides that "an agreement modifying a contract ... *needs no consideration* to be binding."

      i. Statute of Frauds: A modification must, however, be *in writing* if the contract as modified would be within the Statute of Frauds (i.e., is for more than $500 — see § 2-201). However, even if the Statute of Frauds is not met (i.e., the modification excusing the condition is oral, and the contract is for more than $500), § 2-209(4) states that the "attempt at modification" may "operate as a waiver." But such a waiver may be *retracted*, "unless the retraction would be *unjust* in view of a *material change of position in reliance* on the waiver." (§ 2-209(5).) Thus the UCC applies virtually the same promissory estoppel theory as is generally applied in non-UCC cases.

2. Waiver after non-occurrence: *After* a condition has failed to occur, the party whom the condition was intended to benefit may choose to ignore the non-occurrence, and continue with his performance. Such a waiver after non-occurrence is not really a promise, and therefore *does not need consideration* or detrimental reliance to be binding.

a. **Implied waiver:** When the waiver is made by express language, it is of course binding. In addition to such an express waiver, there are two situations in which a waiver will usually be *implied*: **(1)** the continuation of performance by the person who would have been benefitted by the condition; and **(2)** the acceptance of benefits under the contract by that person.

b. **Continuation of performance:** If a promisor *continues his own performance* after learning that a condition of his duty has failed to occur, his conduct operates as a waiver of the condition.

Example: Plaintiff gives notice to defendant insurance company of a loss covered by his insurance policy. Plaintiff's notice is late, and therefore does not satisfy a condition in the policy requiring immediate notice. However, D collects information on the claim, attempts to make a settlement, and does other acts which lead P to believe that D is assuming liability for the loss. D's subsequent cancellation of the policy without settlement is not effective, since by its prior acts D has waived the condition as to notice. See Rest. 2d, § 84, Illustr. 5.

i. **Strictly construed:** But there will be held to have been a waiver only if the party voluntarily continues to perform, with knowledge that such performance is not required given the non-occurrence of the condition. The mere fact that the party has *refrained from cancelling* the contract, and is waiting for the other party to attempt to satisfy the condition, will *not* give rise to a waiver.

c. **Acceptance:** If a person *retains benefits* under a contract after learning that a condition of the contract has not been met, he will be held to have waived the condition. See Rest. 2d., § 246; see also UCC § 2-606(1).

i. **Clarification:** But this rule of waiver only applies where the benefits received by the promisor, and the performance that the promisor owes, are part of the same exchange. If the benefits received are not part of this exchange, but are merely payment for a performance that the promisor has *already* rendered, the condition is not excused. "In this case, the promisor is only getting what he is entitled to in any event, and his acceptance thereof has no effect on his right to refuse to perform further." Murray, p. 235.

Example: Contractor and Owner contract for the former to build a home on Blackacre, owned by Owner. The contract states that every Monday during the course of the contract, Owner will pay for the work done the previous week. Contractor performs the first week's work, and asks for a check the following Monday. Homeowner asks Contractor to wait until the following Monday, promising that he will pay then for the first two weeks' work. Contractor agrees, and does the second week's work. The next Monday, she asks for payment, and Homeowner gives her only one week's pay.

Contractor may accept the one week's pay and at the same time, refuse to perform further. The one week's pay was payment for performance already rendered by Contractor, not payment for the work Contractor was to do in the future. Therefore, payment in accord with the contract remains a constructive condition of Contractor's further duties under the contract, a condition which is not waived by acceptance of the part payment.

d. Election: When a condition fails to occur, the beneficiary of that condition may, as just stated, waive it impliedly or expressly. If she does so, the contract continues in force, but she will still be able to sue later for *damages* if the non-occurrence of the condition also constitutes a breach (see *supra*, p. 206). Alternatively, rather than waiving the condition, the party can terminate her performance (i.e., cancel the contract), and sue for total breach. The party obviously cannot follow both of these routes at once. Thus she is said to be faced with an *election* of one or the other. If she elects to continue the contract, she will *not subsequently be able to change her mind and cancel the contract*.

e. Waiver of subsequent conditions: If a contract contains a *series* of similar conditions, will waiver of one condition (e.g., by the acceptance of a defective performance) excuse the later conditions? Generally, the answer is "no." However, *if a party accepts several similarly defective performances without objecting, his conduct may lead the other party to justifiably conclude that all conditions were intended to be excused*. If so, these later conditions are *waived*.

Example: P contracts to build a movie theater for D. The contract price is to be paid in installments, and an architect's certificate is a condition to D's duty to make each installment. However, six or seven payments are made without such a certificate. When P does not receive the final portion of the contract price, he sues; D's architect testifies that there were no unauthorized deviations from the specifications. D defends on the grounds that no architect's certificate for the last payment was ever procured.

Held, for P. D, by his continued failure to enforce the requirement of a certificate, has waived his right to assert that condition as to the final payment. This is particularly true insofar as D constantly supervised the work, and made no complaints about it while it was being done. *McKenna v. Vernon*, 101 A. 919 (Pa. 1917).

f. Right to damages not lost: When a party retains the benefits of a defective performance, or continues his own performance after breach, or otherwise waives a condition, he has *not* necessarily lost his right to recover *damages for breach* of the condition.

Example: Landlord contracts to lease Blackacre to Tenant. The premises are to be available for occupancy by Tenant on March 1st. When March 1st arrives, the previous tenant has not yet left the premises, and Tenant is unable to move in. He suffers a loss of business, and is finally able to move in on April 1st. By moving in, Tenant will probably be held to have accepted benefits under the contract, and will be held to have waived the constructive condition that the premises be available on March 1st. He thus loses his right to cancel the contract and to refuse to pay the rent. But since no enforceable modification of the contract took place, Tenant still has the right to recover damages for Landlord's failure to have the premises habitable on time.

g. No duty to specify reason for rejection: In non-UCC cases, a party who receives a defective performance is *not ordinarily under an obligation to specify how the per-*

formance was defective. As long as the defective performance constituted the breach of an express condition, or the material breach of a constructive condition, the party receiving performance may simply refuse to perform, without giving any reason at all.

i. **Insufficient reason:** What if the recipient of performance *does* give a reason, but the reason is something other than the non-occurrence of the condition? Is the condition excused, or may the recipient rely on it in the subsequent law suit? The recipient may rely on the unstated failure of the condition *unless the breaching party would have been able to cure the failure had he been notified of it*, and the non-breaching party knew or should have known of the failure. Rest. 2d, § 248.

   Example: P, a general contractor on a construction project, sub-contracts with D for installation of a roof deck. The contract provides that P may cancel the contract on five days written notice if any one of a number of events should occur, including if D "persistently fails to supply enough properly skilled workmen." As D is doing the work, it receives a telegram from P cancelling the contract on five days notice; the only ground for termination stated in the telegram is D's failure to supply sufficient workmen. At trial, P tries to show that D breached the contract in a number of other respects as well. D argues that when P sent the telegram listing only one breach, it was thereafter prevented from asserting any other breach.

   Held, for P. P will be held to have waived its right to assert other breaches only if D can show that it relied to its detriment on the fact that only the one ground was listed. Such detrimental reliance would exist only if D would otherwise have been able to cure the non-listed defects. But the contract did not allow any right to cure defects; the five-day notice provision was intended only to allow the sub-contractor to remove his men from the job in an orderly fashion, not to give him time to cure. Therefore, D could not have cured these defects, so P is not barred from asserting them. *New England Structures, Inc. v. Loranger*, 234 N.E.2d 888 (Mass. 1968).

ii. **Insufficient reason in UCC case:** In the UCC context, a buyer's failure to state the correct reason for her cancellation of the contract is dealt with more harshly than in the non-Code situation described above. UCC § 2-605(1) provides that if a buyer fails to specify a particular defect which is "ascertainable by reasonable inspection," she will be unable to rely on that defect to justify her rejection of the goods, or to establish breach, in two different situations:

   (1) "where the seller *could have cured* [the defect] if stated reasonably;" or

   (2) "between merchants when the seller has after rejection *made a request in writing for a full and final written statement of all defects* on which the buyer proposes to rely."

   UCC § 2-605(1).

h. **Retraction of waiver:** If there has been no consideration given for the waiver, and the party receiving the benefit of the waiver *has not detrimentally relied* on it, the person who waived may at any time *retract* the waiver, thereby *reinstating* the condition. Rest. 2d, §§ 84(2), 230(3).

Example: On February 1, Sehl agrees to sell his house to Bye. Bye makes a $5,000 deposit. The contract provides that closing will occur on April 1, with time to be of the essence, so that if Bye is not ready to close by exactly April 1, Sehl may retain the deposit. On February 15, Sehl tells Bye that Sehl will not insist on the April 1 date, and that Sehl will convey as long as Bye is ready to close by May 1. On February 20 (before Bye has relied in any way on the later closing date), Sehl tells Bye, "I've changed my mind. I'm insisting that you close by April 1, or I'll keep your deposit."

Since Bye has not yet detrimentally relied on Sehl's waiver of the condition (that Bye be ready to close by April 1), Sehl's reinstatement of the condition was proper. Therefore, if Bye isn't ready to close on April 1, and tries to close on April 9, Sehl can refuse to do so, and can keep Bye's deposit. Cf. Rest. 2d, § 84, Illustr. 8.

But now suppose that Bye *relied* on the Feb. 15 waiver, by waiting until March 20 to apply for a mortgage (a date that would still have been enough in advance of the new May 1 closing date to allow Bye to get an appropriate mortgage). Suppose further that on March 28, Sehl attempted to reinstate the April 1 closing date. Bye's material change of position would make it unjust for Sehl to reinstate the condition, so Sehl will not be permitted to do so, and the waiver (postponement until May 1) will stand.

Quiz Yourself on
EXCUSE OF CONDITIONS

63. Michael Corleone contracts to buy a house from his brother Sonny for $2 million. The contract contains the following clause: "Provided, however, that Michael shall have no obligation to consummate the purchase unless he receives by Sept. 1 a commitment for mortgage loan, at a rate of no more than 8%, from the Cosa Nostra Savings & Loan." Michael applies for such a loan, but fails to comply with the bank's reasonable request for a certified copy of his most recent tax return. The bank refuses to issue the loan by Sept. 1, and Michael refuses to close on the purchase of the house. May Sonny recover against Michael for breach of contract?

64. On August 1, Marie Antoinette contracts in writing to buy a diamond necklace from Bohmer for $500,000, the closing to take place on Sept. 15. The market value for large diamond necklaces is changing rapidly, due to the unstable political climate. On Sept. 1, Antoinette calls Bohmer and says she's having trouble getting the money together. Bohmer orally promises not to insist on the Sept. 15 date, as long as Marie pays within 30 days thereafter.

(A) For this part only, assume that on Sept. 2, Bohmer phone Marie and says, "I've changed my mind. If you can't come up with the money by the original Sept. 15 date, I'm cancelling the contract." Marie can't get the money by then, and Bohmer cancels. (Assume that Marie would not have been able to raise the money by Sept. 15 even if Bohmer had never promised an extension.) Marie sues for breach, and shows that she would have been able to arrange to borrow the money by Sept. 30. Can Marie recover?

(B) Same basic facts. However, for purposes of this part, assume that: (1) Bohmer still phones Marie to retract his promise of an extra 30 days, but does this on Sept. 13, not Sept. 2; (2) Marie tries, but cannot arrange the loan by the Sept. 15 deadline; (3) if Bohmer had never promised the extra 30 days in the first place, there's a 40% chance that Marie could have and would have had time to arrange the loan so as to be able to close on Sept. 15. May Marie recover for breach?

65. Tweedle Dee and Tweedle Dum enter into the following agreement: If it rains for the next four days, Tweedle Dee will grocery shop and cook for Tweedle Dum for a week, and Tweedle Dum will pay Tweedle Dee $50 for his services. It rains for three days but is sunny and clear on the fourth. Nevertheless, after the fourth day Tweedle Dee heads off to the grocery store. He buys food and proceeds to cook for Tweedle Dum for three days. Then he stops. Tweedle Dum sues Tweedle Dee for breach of contract. Who wins?

Answers

63. Yes, because the condition will be excused. Where a party's duty is conditional on an event, and that same party's wrongful conduct prevents the occurrence of the condition, the non-occurrence of the condition will be excused. Michael will be held to have impliedly promised to use his reasonable efforts to ensure that the bank issues a loan on the stated terms. Since Michael did not make such efforts, his conduct will be deemed wrongful. Since that wrongful conduct prevented the condition from occurring, the condition will be excused.

64. (A) No, because Bohmer was permitted to retract his waiver. A party whose duty is subject to the occurrence of a condition can waive the benefit of the condition, by indicating that he won't insist on strict compliance with it. That's what Bohmer did here, by saying Marie could have the extra 30 days. However, if the condition is a meaningful part of the deal (as it probably was here, due to the fast-changing diamond market), and the other party has not yet materially relied on the promise not to insist on the condition, the waiving party can *retract* the waiver. Bohmer's Sept. 2 phone call was such a retraction. The facts tell us that Marie couldn't have materially relied on the waiver, because we're told that Marie wouldn't have been able to meet the Sept. 15 date anyway. So the retraction was effective.

(B) Yes, because Marie materially relied on the promise to waive the condition. As described in the answer to part (A), a party who has waived the benefit of a condition (here, Bohmer) may ordinarily retract that waiver. However, retraction is no longer possible once the other party has *materially and detrimentally relied* on the waiver. Here, the facts tell us that Marie would have had a 40% chance of meeting the original Sept. 15 date (the condition) if Bohmer had not promised the extra 30 days. Marie's giving up of this chance is probably enough to constitute "material" reliance, even though there was a less-than-even chance that the waiver changed the outcome. If so, this reliance prevented Bohmer from retracting.

Bohmer might argue that his original promise to waive the condition was void for lack of consideration, since Marie didn't give Bohmer anything of value (or suffer any legal detriment) in return for that promise. Under this view, the promise to waive was in effect a modification of the contract. However, Bohmer's argument will be unsuccessful, for at least one of these two reasons: (1) the UCC would regard the modification as binding without consideration, provided that the need for it was dictated by events unanticipated at the time the contract was formed (something that Marie may be able to establish); and (2) even if consideration were ordinarily required for such a modification, a court would almost certainly hold that Marie's justifiable reliance on the modification acted as a substitute for consideration, under the promissory estoppel doctrine.

65. Tweedle Dum. Even though Tweedle Dee's duty to perform was conditioned upon it raining for four days, Tweedle Dee waived this condition by beginning his performance with the knowledge that the condition was not satisfied. When a party continues his performance after learning that the condition of his duty has failed to occur, his conduct operates as an implied waiver of the condition.

VIII. REPUDIATION AND PROSPECTIVE INABILITY TO PERFORM AS FAILURES OF CONSTRUCTIVE CONDITIONS

A. **General effect of prospective breach:**   Where one party commits a material breach, the other party may, as we have seen, treat this breach as the failure of a constructive condition, and may refuse to perform. Sometimes, however, instead of committing an actual, present, breach, a party may indicate that he will *subsequently* be unable or unwilling to perform. Such an indication of *prospective non-performance* acts as the *non-occurrence of a constructive condition*, in the same way as a present material breach does — the other party has the right to *suspend his own performance*.

  1. **Anticipatory repudiation:**   Where a party indicates that he will later *refuse* to perform, he is said to have committed an *anticipatory repudiation* of the contract. If he indicates that he would like to perform, but will be *unable* to, he has not committed an anticipatory repudiation, according to most courts (see *infra*, p. 264), but the effect on the other party's duty of performance is the same — that other party can suspend his own performance.

     Note: Where the manifestation of prospective non-performance constitutes an anticipatory repudiation, the other party will have a right to bring an immediate suit for breach, even though the time for performance has not yet arrived — this is treated *infra*, p. 263. But here, we are concerned with the anticipatory repudiation, or other manifestation of prospective nonperformance, as a suspender of the other party's duty to perform.

  2. **Concept stated in condition language:**   To put the idea of prospective nonperformance in the formal language of conditions, it is a *constructive condition* of each party's duty of performance that the other party *not manifest a prospective inability or unwillingness to perform.*

     Example: Owner engages Contractor to build a house for him. The contract, signed on June 1st, provides that Owner shall make a down payment of $1,000 by July 1st, and that Contractor shall commence work after receipt of this down payment. On June 15, Contractor tells Owner that he will not perform the contract, because he has other, more lucrative, business.

       This anticipatory repudiation operates as the non-occurrence of a constructive condition of Owner's duty to make the payment (the condition that Contractor not manifest an unwillingness to perform), and Owner does not have to make the payment on July 1st. He will also be able to sue prior to July 1st for breach of contract, as described *infra*, p. 263.

B. **Insolvency or financial inability:**   One common example of prospective inability to perform is the *insolvency* or other financial incapacity of a party. When this occurs, the other party will be able to stop his own performance.

     Example: Artist is commissioned to paint Tycoon's portrait, payment to be made upon completion of the painting. As Artist is about to begin, he learns that Tycoon has gone broke, and is unlikely to be able to pay for the portrait. Artist may decline to perform, because of Tycoon's prospective inability to pay. If Artist were in the middle of the portrait, he would similarly have the right to stop work.

1. **Cancellation vs. suspension:** Where the prospective inability or unwillingness to perform is *certain* or almost certain, the party can not only suspend his performance, but can actually *cancel* the contract, and make alternate arrangements. But where it is not so clear that the first party will be unable or unwilling to perform (e.g., his financial condition is shaky but not hopeless), the other party may only *suspend* his performance, and must wait to see what happens before cancelling. (This distinction between suspension and cancellation is the same as that discussed *supra*, p. 227, in the context of a present breach.)

   a. **Anticipatory repudiation:** If a party anticipatorily repudiates, most courts hold that the other party is entitled to cancel, not merely suspend. If she does not cancel, the repudiator may have the right to retract his repudiation, in which case the other party must resume her performance — see *infra*, p. 266. See also UCC § 2-611(1), removing the repudiator's right of retraction as soon as the other party has "cancelled or materially changed his position or otherwise indicated that he considers the repudiation final."

C. **Right to adequate assurances of performance:** Often a party's conduct will not constitute an outright repudiation, but will instead be an ambiguous indication that that party may not perform. As was stated above, the other party may in this situation suspend, but not cancel, his performance. But he has another right as well — the right to *demand assurances* from the other party that the latter will perform. If the latter fails to provide these assurances, this failure will itself be considered a repudiation, entitling the other party to cancel the contract.

1. **UCC view:** The UCC has codified this right to demand assurances, but courts in non-Code cases follow basically the same rules. UCC § 2-609(1) provides: "A contract for sale imposes an obligation on each party that the other's expectation of receiving due performance will not be impaired. When reasonable grounds for insecurity arise with respect to the performance of either party the other may in writing demand adequate assurance of due performance and until he receives such assurance may, if commercially reasonable, suspend any performance for which he has not already received the agreed return." See also Rest.2d, § 251, which has the same effect for non-UCC cases.

2. **Situations where applicable:** The following situations are examples of actions which might give rise to "reasonable grounds for insecurity:"

   ❏ The buyer has *fallen behind in payment of her account* with the seller, even though the items for which she already owes are part of contracts completely separate from the one now in question.

   ❏ The seller under a contract for precision parts makes *defective deliveries* of the same kinds of parts to other customers, and the buyer finds out about these defective shipments.

   ❏ A manufacturer gives a dealer an exclusive franchise for the sale of his product, but *breaches by selling through other dealers* in several isolated situations, although there is no default in orders, deliveries or payments. See Comment 3 to § 2-609.

   ❏ The buyer under a contract for the sale of real estate learns that the *seller does not have present title* to the property, and there is no indication that she (the seller) has a reasonable prospect of gaining title by scheduled closing date. See Rest. 2d, § 251, Comment c.

3. **Must be based on new facts:** Observe that the text of UCC § 2-609(1) requires that the reasonable grounds for insecurity "*arise*." The idea seems to be that the reasonable grounds must be based on facts *not known* to the insecure party at the time of contracting. In other words, a party who has second thoughts about his deal, but not based on any new information or developments, may not use the demand for assurances as a means of rewriting the contract.

   a. **Worry about buyer's credit:** For instance, a seller who has second thoughts about the wisdom of agreeing to ship on open account will be permitted to use § 2-609 if he receives *new information* indicating the buyer's financial weakness. But the seller will not be permitted to use the provision if the buyer's condition remains the same as it was at the time of the contract (even if that condition is so weak that a reasonable person in seller's position would not have agreed to ship on open account in the first place). See § 2-609, Comment 1.

4. **Consequence of refusal to give assurances:** If such a request for assurance is given, the party receiving the request must either satisfy it or be held to have *repudiated* the contract. § 2-609(4) provides that "after receipt of a justified demand failure to provide *within a reasonable time not exceeding thirty days* such assurance of due performance as is adequate under the circumstances of the particular case is a *repudiation of the contract.*"

   a. **Application:** Thus in the four situations listed on p. 245 above, the seller, buyer, dealer and buyer, respectively, would have the right to demand reasonable assurances from the other party. If the other party did not respond with adequate assurances within at most thirty days (or, in a non-UCC situation, within "a reasonable time" — Rest. 2d, § 251(2)), she would be held to have repudiated the contract, and the aggrieved party would have the right to cancel the contract, refuse to perform, and sue for breach.

5. **What constitutes adequate assurance:** What constitutes "adequate assurance" of due performance is, according to § 2-609(2), to be determined "according to commercial standards," at least where the contract is between merchants.

   Example: Seller contracts to deliver certain precisely-machined parts to Buyer. Buyer then learns that Seller has made deliveries of comparable parts to other buyers recently, and those other deliveries have been defective. Buyer now demands reasonable assurances that Seller will deliver conforming parts. If Seller is a reputable merchant, and there is no evidence that he has frequently delivered defective goods in the past, his statement to Buyer that he is aware of the recent defects, and is sure that the Buyer's delivery will not be similarly defective, will be sufficient assurance. But if there is evidence that Seller is a known "corner cutter," verbal guarantees will not be enough, and Seller will probably have to post a performance bond. See Comment 4 to § 2-609.

Table 7-1
***ISSUES CHECKLIST:* Conditions and Breach**

Use this checklist to help you spot issues in analyzing the effects of (1) the non-occurrence of a condition, (2) a breach, and (3) a prospective inability to perform.

Issue	Rule or Recommendation	Examples
[1] Does the fact pattern involve a *condition* rather than (or in addition to) a *promise*?	In deciding, consider these rules: **Rule 1:** Intent of the parties controls. **Rule 2:** If fulfillment is within the obligee's control, an interpretation that makes the matter a *promise* by the obligee, *not a condition* on the obligor's duty, is preferred.	**Example of Rule 2:** Insurer writes fire coverage on Owner's house. Policy says that Owner "shall give notice of fire within 3 days." Court will probably say that this is a promise by Owner, but not a condition on Insurer's duty to pay. So if Owner gives notice on Day 5 after the fire, Insurer will still have to pay (but can recover any damages actually caused by the late notice).
[2] If there is a condition, is it *express* or *constructive*?	**Rule:** An express condition is one agreed to (perhaps implicitly) by the parties. A constructive condition is imposed by the court for fairness.	**Example of Constructive Condition:** B agrees to buy S's home. The contract says that (1) By April 1, S will present proof of marketable title; and (2) Closing will occur on April 15. Even if the parties don't say that S's proof of marketable title is a condition to B's duty to close, the court will impose a constructive condition making B's duty to close conditional on S's having presented proof of marketable title. (See Rule 3 in box [4].)
[3] If the condition is *express*, does its non-occurrence *relieve the obligor* of the duty to perform?	**Rule 1:** Yes, generally -- *strict compliance* with express conditions is ordinarily required. **Rule 2:** But courts look for reasons to "**excuse**" the non-occurrence of the condition, to avoid forfeiture.	**Example of Rule 1:** For $100, S gives B an option to buy S's house, option to be exercised by B's depositing the full contract price in escrow by April 15, "time being of the essence." Court will treat B's deposit by the April 15th date as an express condition on S's duty to convey; therefore, strict compliance is required, and if B is a day late, the condition will be deemed to have failed and S won't have to honor the option.
[4] If the condition is *constructive*, does its non-occurrence *relieve the obligor* of the duty to perform?	**Rule 1:** *Strict* compliance is *not* usually required. **Rule 2:** *Substantial performance* normally *is* required. **Rule 3:** In a bilateral contract, each party's substantial performance of his promise is generally a constructive condition of the other party's duty to perform a *subsequently-due* promise.	**Example of Rules 1 &2:** Same facts as [2] (S must give proof of marketable title by April 1). S presents proof of marketable title by April 3. Since timely proof is a constructive (not strict) condition on B's duty to close, S's substantial performance is enough to satisfy the condition, and B must close by the 15th.

Table 7-1 (cont.)

Issue	Rule or Recommendation	Examples
[5] If both parties owe future performances, what's the *order* in which the parties' performances are due?	**Rule 1:** Parties' intent counts. **Rule 2:** Where one party's performance requires **time**, and the other's doesn't, probably the performance requiring time must occur **first**. **Rule 3:** If performances *can occur simultaneously*, probably they *must* do so (i.e., they are *concurrent* conditions). So each party's duty of performance is conditioned on the other's tendering performance at the same time.	**Example of Rule 2:** Contractor contracts to paint O's house for $10K. Contract is silent about when payment is due. Contractor demands 1/2 payment when house is 1/2 painted. Since painting takes time, and paying doesn't, court will probably say that house must be fully painted before any payment is due. **Example of Rule 3:** B contracts to buy S's car on April 15 for $10K. The K says nothing about when payment is due. Payment and delivery of the car (and title to it) are concurrent conditions. If on the 15th S doesn't tender delivery (i.e., show himself presently able and willing to deliver immmediate title and possession), B doesn't have to pay the money. Conversely, if B doesn't tender the money (show it's available immediately), S won't be in breach for failing to tender delivery.
[6] Is the contract *divisible*?	**Rule:** If the contract can be divided up into corresponding pairs of part performances, such that one side of each pair is properly regarded as an agreed-upon equivalent of the other part, then the contract is divisible.	**Example:** Painter agrees to paint three identical statues on Owner's front lawn. Contract lists a price of $1,000 for each of the 3 paint jobs. Since each statute's painting and the payment of $1,000 are agreed equivalents, contract is divisible into 3 parts, one for each statue's painting. (See [7] for how this matters.)
[7] If the contract is divisible, did P *substantially perform* any part?	**Rule:** If yes, P can *recover at the contract rate* for that part, even if P materially breached all other parts.	**Example:** Same facts as Example in [6]. Painter paints the first statue, then abandons the job. Since the K was divisible (i.e., each statute's painting and the payment of $1,000 were agreed equivalents), Painter can recover $1,000 for the first statue, even though he didn't substantially perform the whole K. (But Owner can counterclaim for damages for the failure to paint the 2d and 3d statues.)
[8] Was the non-occurrence of the condition *excused*?	**Rule:** If obligor's *cooperation* is needed for the condition to occur, and obligor doesn't cooperate, condition's non-occurrence will be excused.	**Example:** B agrees to buy S's house, B's duty conditioned on B's getting a mortgage commitment on specified terms within 30 days of signing. B never even applies for a mortgage. Since B's cooperation was necessary for the condition to be satisfied, B's failure to cooperate excuses the non-occurrence of the condition, and B must close even without the mortgage commitment.

Table 7-1 (cont.)

Issue	Rule or Recommendation	Examples
[9] Did the beneficiary of the condition (the obligor) **waive** the benefit of that condition?	**Rule:** If obligor **waived** the benefit of the condition, the condition's failure to occur will be excused. (But obligor may **retract** the waiver if there's been no reliance by the obligee.)	**Example:** S contracts to ship 10 widgets to B, delivery to occur by May 1; payment due from B 30 days after delivery. On April 25, S asks for an extra 15 days to deliver. B agrees. S delivers on May 14. B must pay, because B waived the benefit of the condition (a constructive condition that delivery occur by May 1). (But if, after giving the 15 day extension, B called back within one hour to retract the extension, the retraction would be effective, if S hadn't yet relied on the extension.)
[10] Has a party (*A*) indicated that he will likely be **unable or unwilling** to perform a not-yet-due duty owed to *B* when the time comes?	**Rule 1:** *B* may request reasonable assurances of *A*'s performance, and may suspend his own performance until these are received. **Rule 2:** If *A* does not furnish the requested assurances within a reasonable time, *B* may treat the lack of assurances as a repudiation, and cancel the contract + sue for damages.	**Example of Rules 1 and 2:** Star agrees to perform 6 nights per week for 1 month in Producer's upcoming musical, performances to start May 1. Producer is to make an advance salary payment of $3K to Star on April 25. On April 20, Producer learns that Star has just signed with someone else to appear nightly beginning May 1. (1) Since Producer has reasonable grounds for insecurity about whether Star will perform, Producer can demand assurances, and suspend payment of the $3K advance until these are received. (2) If Star does not promptly (and reasonably) assure Producer that she can and will perform at the beginning of the May 1 run, Producer can cancel the agreement and sign someone else for the role (plus recover breach damages).

---

a. **Demand for more than contract allows:** A party who has grounds for insecurity must be careful lest his demand for assurances insists on *much more than the contract calls for*. Comment 2 to § 2-610 states that a demand "for more than the contract calls for in the way of counter-performance is not itself a repudiation.... However, when under a fair reading it amounts to a statement of intention not to perform except on conditions which go beyond the contract, it becomes a repudiation."

Example: Same facts as in the above Example on p. 246. If Buyer's request for assurance states, "We demand that you post a $100,000 performance bond indemnifying us against any future defective deliveries," this might well be held to be a "statement of intention not to perform except on conditions that go beyond the contract," and might therefore be a repudiation, entitling Seller to cancel his performance.

6. **Also applicable where performance has begun:** A party's "right to adequate assurance of performance" exists not only where performance on the contract has not yet begun, but

also where performance has ***already been partially***, and defectively, made. The mechanics of § 2-609 apply in exactly the same way as where performance is still entirely executory.

7. **Review case on assurances:** The facts of a 2010 case furnish a good chance to *review* the whole request-for-assurances mechanism. The case is ***Rocheux Int'l of N.J. v. U.S. Merchants Fin. Group***, 741 F.Supp. 2d 651 (2010). The opinion arose in the context of cross-motions for summary judgment, so it doesn't tell us who "won" on the merits. But reviewing the fact pattern, and the court's rulings on various issues of law, gives us a good chance to see how the pieces of a request-for-assurances dispute fit together. The back-and-forth exchange is lengthy, but be patient, because this kind of exchange is typical of escalating contract disputes, and you can't correctly determine "who wins" unless you calmly analyze each step of the dispute.

    a. **Facts:** Seller (Rocheux) was a plastics distributor, and Buyer (U.S. Merchants) bought plastics from it from time to time to use in producing packaging. In early 2006, Buyer ordered certain quantities of plastic to be delivered to its own facilities (goods which we'll call the "Direct Deliveries," and which we'll refer to as falling under "Contract 1"). At about the same time, Buyer ordered other quantities of plastic to be delivered to a warehouse designated by Buyer, as to which goods Seller would retain control until Buyer requested delivery to it and Seller authorized the warehouse to release them. (We'll call these the "Warehouse Goods," and refer to the contract for them as "Contract 2").

        i. **Seller's Sept. 21 demand:** By late September, 2006, D had not paid a very past-due bill for over $2 million for the Direct Deliveries under Contract 1, and had never asked for delivery of (or paid for) the approximately $1.5 million of Warehouse Goods covered by Contract 2. On Sept. 21, Seller wrote to Buyer asking for payment of the $2 million Contract 1, and threatened suit if this bill wasn't immediately paid. The Sept. 21 letter also said that if Buyer didn't take and pay for the Contract 2 Warehouse Goods by a much later deadline (Sept. 2009), Seller would sell them from the warehouse, and sue Buyer for any shortfall. (Buyer had previously indicated that the Direct Deliveries under Contract 1 were defective, an issue that was still under discussion between the parties by the time of Seller's Sept. 21 email.)

        ii. **"We'll pay C.O.D. or with letter of credit":** Buyer got Seller's Sept. 21 letter, and wrote back on Oct. 4. The response referred to certain of the not-yet-delivered Warehouse Goods, and said that if Seller promised by Oct. 5 to deliver these goods on a particular schedule, Buyer would then pay for them by either (at Buyer's option) giving the carrier at delivery a "C.O.D. ... company check," or by Buyer's opening up, pre-delivery, a letter of credit payable in 120 days after delivery.

        iii. **Seller says "no way":** Seller wasn't willing do as Buyer proposed, which would have allowed Buyer buy the new goods (from Contract 2) without first taking care of the past bill. Instead, on Oct. 6, Seller wrote back to say that Seller would ship the Warehouse Goods in question if and only if, prior to shipment, Buyer opened up an irrevocable letter of credit — effectively a form of cash in this situation —

to cover all sums previously due to Seller (presumably the $2 million). That was the last exchange between the parties before suit.

iv. **Seller sells the goods and sues for the balance:** When Buyer ignored the Oct. 6 letter and made no arrangements to take delivery of the Warehouse Goods, Seller eventually exercised its right to sell the Warehouse Goods to a third party at a loss (i.e., a sum less than the contract price Buyer had agreed to pay for these goods). Seller then sued Buyer for the "deficiency," the difference between the Seller-Buyer contract price for the Warehouse Goods, and the amounts received by Seller in the salvage sale to the third party.[1]

v. **Essence of suit:**   It was clear to all that Seller would be able to recover this deficiency if Buyer materially breached Contract 2, but not if Buyer didn't breach (or Seller breached first). So the case came down to, Who breached Contract 2 first? Each party moved for summary judgment, with each arguing that as a matter of law, the other had materially breached.

b. **No summary judgment:**   The court *denied both parties' motions* for summary judgment. Thus the court required a trial (we don't know from the public record whether one was held, let alone how it turned out). But the court's rulings on various legal arguments made by the parties are worth reviewing.

c. **Did Seller have grounds for insecurity:** The first issue was whether Seller, when it wrote the Sept. 21 letter, indeed had *"reasonable grounds for insecurity* aris[ing] with respect to the performance of [the other] party," as § 2-609 requires before a party is entitled to demand adequate assurances.

i. **Buyer's argument:**   Buyer argued that if it was in default at all, the default was *only as to Contract 1* (the Direct Deliveries contract), not Contract 2. Since the litigation was about whether Seller had correctly sold the *Contract 2* Warehouse Goods in a way that entitled Seller to recovery a deficiency judgment, Buyer could achieve what it really wanted — avoiding the deficiency judgment — if it could show that Seller did not have reasonable grounds for insecurity with respect to Buyer's performance *on Contract 2*. And, Buyer argued, a party's breach on one contract (here, Contract 1) "does not authorize the aggrieved party to *refuse performance under a separate and distinct contract"* (here, Contract 2).

ii. **Claim rejected:**   But the court *rejected* this argument, at least for purposes of Buyer's summary judgment motion. The court noted that under Comment 3 to § 2-609, "[A] ground for security *need not arise from* or be directly related to *the contract in question* ... Thus a buyer who *falls behind in 'his account'* with the seller, even though the items involved have to do with *separate and legally distinct contracts*, *impairs the seller's expectation* of due performance." Since Buyer was still in default as to $2 million on Contract 1, the court certainly could not say, as a matter of law, that this default did not give Seller grounds for insecurity as to Contract 2.

---

1. The opinion doesn't tell us what happened to the $2 million owed under Contract 1. By the time of the litigation, nothing about Contract 1 was part of the dispute.

(1) Likely outcome: If the case were tried, Seller would be highly likely to persuade the trier of fact that the very past-due status of Contract 1 was enough to give Seller reasonable grounds for insecurity about the relationship as a whole, and thus about whether Buyer would perform Contract 2. In that case, Seller would of course be entitled to demand reasonable assurances as to Contract 2.

d. **Was there a demand for assurances:** The next issue was whether, assuming Seller had reasonable grounds for insecurity, Seller in fact *made a valid demand* for assurances of performance. Seller claimed that its Sept. 21 letter, as well as a prior email it had sent, constituted valid demands for assurances of performance. Recall that in the Sept. 21 letter, Seller demanded immediate payment for the past-due Contract 1 Direct Deliveries; but Seller also said in that letter that if Buyer did *not* immediately make this payment, "This letter shall also constitute notice of [Seller's] intent ... to sell or otherwise dispose of the [Contract 2 Warehouse Goods] ... pursuant to UCC § 2-706 and recover any deficiency from you."

i. **Buyer says, "Not a demand":** Buyer pointed out (correctly) that the Sept. 21 letter *did not expressly demand assurances* of performance, or even use the term "assurance" — it merely threatened legal action if Buyer didn't do various things. Therefore, Buyer argued, the letter should, as a matter of law, *not* be considered to be a qualifying § 2-609 demand for assurances.

ii. **Court rejects argument:** But the court rejected this argument, too, at least for purposes of Buyer's summary judgment motion. "Although neither message [from Seller] included the exact term 'adequate assurance,' courts have generally *eschewed* applying *formalistic requirements* for the demand of adequate assurances, instead opting for a case-specific approach that considers a party's demands in the *context of its course of dealings* with the adverse party."

(1) Course-of-dealings history: Here, the parties had held multiple in-person meetings about Buyer's failure to pay on time for the Direct Deliveries. This course-of-dealings history meant that a reasonable jury could find that Seller's correspondence constituted a valid demand for adequate assurances.

e. **Did Buyer give adequate assurances:** The last major issue was whether Buyer had in fact *given Seller adequate assurances* of performance.

i. **Facts:** If you'll recall, the last thing Buyer said or wrote to Seller before the litigation was Buyer's Oct. 4 letter saying that if Seller would ship certain of the previously-specified Warehouse Goods to Buyer, Buyer would then pay for these new goods either by (at Buyer's choice) C.O.D. company check or letter of credit. Then, in the litigation, Buyer claimed that even assuming Seller had demanded adequate assurances of performance, Buyer's offer, "If you ship new goods, we'll pay for them either by C.O.D. company check or by letter of credit," itself *constituted the legally-required assurance as a matter of law*.

ii. **Court rejects:** But the court rejected this argument, as it had rejected all of Buyer's other arguments. If Buyer had actually *furnished* an irrevocable letter of credit for the full cost of the new merchandise, the court indicated, it was plausible that this act *would* have constituted reasonable assurance that Buyer would perform Contract 2. (Although the court didn't put it this way, an irrevocable letter of credit would have guaranteed Seller that it would be paid for the new goods under Contract 2, even if there were no progress on the old outstanding invoices from Contract 1; so with a letter of credit in hand Seller would at least be assured that it would not be worsening its position by shipping the Contract 2 goods without getting timely payment for them.)

(1) Distinction between promise and performance: But, the court noted, Buyer didn't actually *furnish* the letter of credit that Seller had requested — all Buyer did was to make a *promise* that it *would in the future* furnish the letter of credit (or else, at Buyer's option, make a commitment to pay by C.O.D. company check). And a mere promise of a future C.O.D. payment, rather than some sort of actual prepayment like an irrevocable letter of credit, was not — at least as a matter of law appropriate for summary judgment — an adequate assurance, especially given Buyer's long-standing delinquency in paying for Contract 1. "While some courts have recognized that an insecure party *may request* C.O.D. payments [emphasis added], ... the court is aware of no authority for the proposition that an insecure party *must accept* an assurance of C.O.D. [especially] where the delinquent party had fallen in arrears more than $2 million on goods delivered at the time that the insecure party sought assurances of performance."

(2) Context matters: The judge made it clear that when a court is deciding whether a given set of assurances by the possibly-breaching party is adequate, the **background** of the parties' prior dealings is critical. The court quoted Comment 4 to § 2-609, which gives an example where the buyer tells the seller that the buyer is worried that the seller has delivered some defective goods as part of an ongoing set of shipments. The Comment then says this about how the seller's past behavior and reputation will matter as to what assurances will suffice:

> [A] mere *promise* by a seller of *good repute* that he is *giving the matter his attention* and that the *defect will not be repeated,* is *normally sufficient.* Under the same circumstances, however, a *similar statement by a known corner-cutter* might well be considered *insufficient without the posting of a guaranty* or, if so demanded by the buyer, a speedy replacement of the delivery involved.

Here, the court concluded, Buyer's long delinquency in paying the $2 million due under Contract 1 was the sort of factual background that prevented Buyer's "trust me"-style promise of C.O.D. payment for the next delivery from automatically constituting reasonable assurance of performance.[2]

---

2. On this point, too, if the case were tried, it's highly likely that Seller would succeed in showing that the mere promise was *not* a reasonable assurance. For instance, even if Buyer kept its promise by furnishing the "company check" as C.O.D. at delivery, the check then could have bounced or been stopped, at which point Buyer would already be in possession of the goods.

Quiz Yourself on

REPUDIATION AND PROSPECTIVE INABILITY TO PERFORM AS FAILURES OF CONSTRUCTIVE CONDITIONS

66. Larry Flynt is holding a stag party for his buddy Hugh and on Sept. 1 hires Bunny, an exotic dancer, to perform at the bash. The party is set for October 15, with Bunny to be paid $250 after her performance. On Sept. 15, Flynt hears plausible-sounding rumors that Bunny has recently cancelled several other bookings at the last minute.

(A) You represent Flynt. Would you advise Flynt that he may immediately cancel the contract and hire someone else?

(B) Same facts as (A). Assume that you believe, or fear, that the answer to (A) is no. What would you advise Flynt to do?

(C) Assume the same facts as in Part (B), except that Flynt knew of Bunny's tendency to cancel at the last minute before they entered into their agreement, and has learned nothing new in this respect since the contract was made. Does this change your advice in part (B)?

Answers

66. (A) No. When a party makes an anticipatory repudiation — an advance, ***unequivocal*** refusal to (or manifestation of inability to) perform her contractual duties — the other party is permitted to cancel the contract immediately, without waiting for the time for performance to arrive. (He may also sue immediately for breach, as covered in the next chapter.) However, under these facts, Bunny's unreliability is not unequivocal, and Flynt cannot be certain or almost certain that Bunny will breach the agreement. Therefore, he cannot treat Bunny as having anticipatorily repudiated. Consequently, he has no immediate right to cancel the contract or sue.

(B) Advise Flynt to demand reasonable assurances of performance from Bunny. A party who after formation of a contract learns facts leading him to reasonably fear that the other party will be unable or unwilling to perform has the right to demand reasonable assurance of performances from that other party. If Bunny fails promptly to provide adequate assurances (probably either a demonstration that the reports of earlier cancellations are wrong, or an explanation of why it's unlikely to happen again), Flynt can treat this as an anticipatory repudiation. At that point, he would have the right to cancel the contract, sue her for any damages he may have suffered, and hire someone else.

(C) Yes. If a party already knew *at the time of entering into the contract* of facts indicating that the other party may be unwilling or unable to perform, he cannot rely on those facts as the basis for a demand for adequate assurances. Under this scenario, Flynt will just have to keep his fingers crossed and hope Bunny comes through as promised — he cannot cancel, and can't sue for breach unless and until she actually fails to perform on the scheduled date.

☞ *Exam Tips on*
CONDITIONS, BREACH, AND PERFORMANCE

Analyzing Conditions

☞ When a party's performance appears to be dependent upon the occurrence of a *condition* or event:

☞ First, **confirm that there is a condition**. A condition is an **event that must occur** (unless occurrence is excused) **before a party's performance is due.**

☞ Second, identify the **type of condition**: there are two types, **express** and **constructive**.

(1) Express condition: Express conditions are conditions that are **agreed to by the parties.**

☞ **Phrasing:** The parties' language can still constitute an express condition even though it doesn't use the phrase "conditional on" or "on condition that." Any phrasing that indicates that the parties have agreed that one party's performance **will not be due unless some event happens** is a condition.

Example: Painter and Owner agree that Painter will paint Owner's garage. The contract says that Owner will pay $3,000 for the work "when the work is completed to Owner's reasonable satisfaction." Since this language indicates the parties' explicit agreement that Owner will not have to pay until the work is completed to her reasonable satisfaction, such completion is an express condition to Owner's duty of payment.

☞ **Strict compliance:** The key thing to remember about express conditions is that **strict compliance** is usually required — "substantial" performance is usually not enough.

☞ **Satisfaction of a party:** A clause requiring a party to pay only upon his satisfaction is the most common type of express condition you'll encounter on exams. (The above example is typical.) A satisfaction clause will usually appear in contracts for the creation of an object or painting intended to please the taste of a particular person, so that subjective satisfaction is required.

☞ *Limitation:* A condition requiring subjective satisfaction is **valid** as long as the party's dissatisfaction with the object is in **good faith** (even if unreasonable).

(2) Constructive condition: Conditions that are not "express" are **"constructive"** or "implied in law." Here, the court is deducing that **had the parties thought about it,** they would have made one party's performance to be dependent on the happening of some event, typically the other party's prior or contemporaneous performance. The court reaches this conclusion to ensure fairness.

☞ Watch for a situation where, if a condition were not inferred, a party would end up with *so bad a deal* that it's fair to say that she never would have entered the arrangement.

Example: Inventor has invented a better mousetrap. Inventor and Manufacturer have discussions about the terms under which Manufacturer would produce the item and pay Inventor a royalty. Inventor then signs an agreement promising that in 6 months, Inventor will grant Manufacturer a 10-year exclusive license to make the product; in return, Manufacturer promises to tool up immediately to make the item. Manufacturer tools up, but due to technical difficulties in production, he is never in fact able to make any mousetraps.

Inventor will have a strong claim that her duty to issue the license was subject to a constructive condition that Manufacturer be capable of and willing to actually produce the item. (Inventor will be arguing that she never would have agreed to issue a license that would not be exploited.) If the court agrees, Inventor's duty to issue the license will be discharged for failure of the constructive condition.

☞ Third, after identifying the condition, ***confirm that the condition has been satisfied***.

☞ *Trap:* Be careful of fact patterns with multiple conditions. Be sure they have *all* been satisfied.

☞ Distinguish between express conditions, which must normally be strictly satisfied, and constructive conditions, as to which substantial performance is usually enough. (See the next section for more about the distinction.)

Strict Compliance and Substantial Performance

☛ **Express conditions:** Remember that if the condition is an "express" one (explicitly agreed to between the parties), ***strict*** compliance with it is normally required.

Example: Portraitist agrees to paint Sitter's portrait, with payment to be conditional on Sitter's actual good-faith satisfaction. Since this is an express condition, the court will strictly construe the condition — if Sitter is subjectively unsatisfied, the court will not deem the condition met merely because Portraitist "substantially" performed (e.g., painted a portrait that most people would say looked a lot like Sitter).

☞ **Forfeiture:** But the court can wriggle out of strict compliance if an ***excessive forfeiture*** would result.

Typical scenario for forfeiture doctrine: Owner takes out a property insurance policy with Insurer, requiring Owner to give notice within, say, 10 days of any loss. Owner is slightly late in giving notice of loss, but in a way that does not cause actual prejudice to Insurer's ability to investigate or defend. The court will hold that strict enforcement of the condition would cause a substantial forfeiture (a damage to Owner out of all proportion to the prejudice caused to Insurer by the lateness), and will excuse the condition.

☛ **Constructive conditions:** Where one party's duty is subject to a ***constructive*** condition, however, strict compliance with the condition will normally *not* be required.

☞ **Material breach / substantial performance:** Instead, the condition will be deemed satisfied if there was *"substantial performance"* by the party who had to satisfy the condition. Or, to put it conversely, the condition will only be deemed unsatisfied if there was a *material breach* on the part of the party who had to satisfy the condition.

☞ **Generic example:** So you're looking for fact patterns where *A* doesn't want to pay or perform because he says *B* breached first. You'll first have to check whether *A*'s duty of payment/performance was expressly conditioned on *B*'s performance. If not, you're dealing with a constructive condition. Then, you'll analyze the materiality of the breach: *A* won't be relieved of his own duty unless *B*'s breach was material (i.e., *A* won't be relieved if *B* substantially performed).

☞ **Factors making a breach material:** Here are the 3 *main factors* you should look at in deciding whether the breach was material:

❏ How completely was the party who benefits from the condition (*A* in the above generic example) *deprived of her expected benefit* in entering the contract? The more complete the deprivation, the more likely the breach is to be material.

❏ Can *A* be *adequately compensated* for the breach by *money damages*, instead of being relieved of performance? If damages will suffice, the breach is more likely to be non-material.

❏ Was the breach *willful* (intentional)? If so, it's more likely to be found material.

Example: P, an equipment company, promises to deliver and install 6 coolers for the grand opening of D, a meat market, on Sept. 1. The price is quoted on a per-cooler basis. P only gets 5 coolers installed by Sept. 1. On Sept. 3, D refuses to pay for any coolers, demanding that P remove the 5 since it breached. D offers to install the 6th cooler by Oct. 1, but P refuses. D sues for the pro-rata contract price. (Assume that because of the large amount of installation services required, this is not a UCC sale-of-goods contract.)

Unless there is a showing that the 5 coolers were rendered much less valuable by the temporary absence of the 6th, the court will hold that the breach was non-material (i.e., that P substantially performed). In that event, D will not be entitled to cancel the contract, and P will be entitled to collect the pro-rata contract price for the 5 coolers, less money damages for the delay on the 6th.

☞ **Divisibility:** Always be alert to the possibility that the contract is *"divisible"* into multiple pairs of corresponding part-performance (e.g., multiple services, each with its own price quoted in the contract). If the contract is truly "divisible," remember that a party who has *substantially performed one piece* is entitled to *recover the contract price* for that piece, even if that party materially breached as to all other pieces.

Example: In a single document, Paint agrees to paint Owner's kitchen for $1,000 and the master bedroom for $1500, both payments to be made at the end of the whole job. Paint paints the kitchen in substantial conformity with the specs, then unjustifiably walks off the job and never paints the bedroom. If the court is convinced that the two prices corresponded to the relative values the parties placed on each component, then Paint can recover at the contract price for the kitchen, even though he didn't substantially perform the overall contract. (But Owner can counterclaim for damages for the bedroom, if any.)

☞ **Clues to divisibility:** To set up a question that turns on divisibility, the prof will have to make it clear that each piece, and the price for it, forms a separate *"agreed equivalent."* To do this, the prof will usually have to make it clear that there is *no "cross-subsidizing,"* i.e., that each separately-quoted price is *fair for the corresponding deliverable*. (So in the above Example, the prof might tell you that the kitchen accounted for 40% of the total labor and materials cost, and the bedroom 60%. This would be a clue that each room, and its listed price, were "agreed equivalents," making the contract divisible.)

☞ **Sale of goods:** The issue of substantial performance/material breach most often arises in fact patterns involving the *sale of goods*.

"Perfect tender" rule: In theory, the UCC imposes the *"perfect tender"* rule: if the goods deviate from the contract even in just a *non-material* way, the buyer can *reject them*, i.e., send them back and refuse to pay.

☞ **Nonbreaching party has several options.** If a buyer receives a shipment made up of both *conforming and defective* goods he may: *reject the whole* shipment, reject *just the part* of the shipment that's defective, or *accept the entire shipment* and sue for damages.

☞ **Exceptions to perfect-tender rule:** But be on the lookout for the many *exceptions* to the UCC's perfect-tender rule. Most important:

☞ **Cure:** The seller usually has a right to try to *"cure"* the non-conformity after the rejection.

☞ **Revocation of acceptance:** If the buyer has *already "accepted"* the goods (e.g., paid for them, or inspected them and remained silent), the buyer may *revoke* the acceptance only if the non-performance is *substantial*.

☞ **Installment contracts:** If it's an installment contract, even if one installment is substantially non-conforming the buyer may not cancel the entire contract unless the problem with the one installment substantially impairs the value of the *entire* contract.

Excuse of Conditions

☛ **Hindrance:** A party can't *willfully prevent* the occurrence of a condition. If she does, the condition is *excused*.

☞ Look for a seller of real estate who purposely thwarts the sale of the property (e.g., by placing a mortgage on it after a contract of sale has been signed). This will result in her owing the real estate commission to the broker despite the fact that the sale doesn't go through — the seller's thwarting of the sale causes the condition to the commission (sale of the property) to be excused.

☛ **Waiver:** Where a party benefits from a condition (i.e., his duty is conditional on the condition's fulfillment), always be on the lookout for a waiver by him.

   ☞ For instance, if a party *begins performance after* learning that a condition to his performance has failed to occur, he may be held to have waived the benefit of the condition.

   ☞ However, don't find waivers to have occurred unless you're sure that the buyer *knowingly and intentionally* declined to take the benefit of the condition's non-occurrence.

   ☞ Also, keep in mind that a waiver can always be *retracted* if the other party hasn't yet *materially relied* on it.

   Example: In a house-sale contract, assume it's a condition of S's duty to convey that B be ready to close by April 1 (and time is made "of the essence.") On March 15, S tells B, "I won't insist on an April 1 closing, May 1 is good enough." S has waived the April 1 condition. But suppose on March 17, S says, "I've changed my mind — you must close by April 1." If B hasn't materially relied on the waiver, S has successfully retracted it, and has reinstated the original condition.

Requests for Assurances of Performance

☛ If a party has reason to worry that the other party won't perform, the insecure party may *demand assurances* that the other party will be able (and willing) to perform all its obligations. The demanding party may then suspend his own performance until he receives the assurances. A failure to provide assurances is a breach.

☛ **UCC:** Remember that the "demand for assurances" procedure is expressly codified in UCC § 2-609. You should try to remember, at least approximately, this part of the section's text:

> When *reasonable grounds for insecurity* arise with respect to the *performance of either party* the other *may in writing demand adequate assurance* of due performance and until he *receives* such assurance may, if commercially reasonable, *suspend any performance* for which he has not already received the agreed return.

☛ **Writing:** Note that under the UCC, the demand for assurances must be *in writing.*

☛ **Contents of demand:** The writing can probably qualify even though it does *not use* the precise words "demand" or "assurances." It's enough if the worried party (*A*) tells the other party (*B*), in effect, "Here's why I'm worried that you won't perform. [explanation of grounds for worry.] Be on notice that if you don't perform in a timely way, I will *exercise all my legal rights,* including canceling the contract."

☛ **Silence as repudiation:** Remember that, at least under the UCC, the party who receives a properly-issued demand for assurances *must* give those assurances within a reasonable time. if the recipient doesn't do this, the sender is likely to be justified in *treating the silence as a repudiation*, and therefore *canceling the contract* even *before it's time for the recipient to perform.*

☛ **Delegations and Assignments:** Demands for assurances often occur in situations where a contract has been delegated and/or assigned to another. An obligee party has a right to demand assurances from the delegate that the delegate is capable of performing under the contract, and the delegate will be deemed to have breached the contract if she does not provide such assurances.

Chapter 8

ANTICIPATORY REPUDIATION AND OTHER ASPECTS OF BREACH

ChapterScope

This chapter discusses the consequences of: (1) anticipatory repudiations (which are repudiations that occur before the repudiator's performance is due) and (2) repudiations that occur after the time for performance. Key concepts:

- **Anticipatory repudiation:** An anticipatory repudiation can occur where the promisor: (1) makes clear *statements* that he will not perform; (2) uses ambiguous language accompanied by *conduct* that evinces an unwillingness to perform; or (3) or commits a *voluntary act* that renders his performance impossible (e.g., a vendor conveys a parcel of land to a party other than the vendee).

  - ❑ **Immediate suit for breach:** When an anticipatory repudiation occurs, the repudiatee may generally *sue immediately* for breach, even though the repudiator's time for performance has not yet arrived.

  - ❑ **Retraction:** A repudiation may usually be *retracted,* if the retraction is communicated to the aggrieved party before he has changed his position materially in reliance on the repudiation.

- **Duty to mitigate:** A repudiatee may not ignore the repudiation and continue performing under the contract, if doing so would aggravate her damages. Instead, the repudiatee has a "duty to mitigate" — that is, she will barred from recovering for those damages which she could reasonably have avoided.

I. TOTAL AND PARTIAL BREACH

A. Total breach: When a party who owes a present duty under a contract fails to perform that duty, he has, of course, breached the contract. If this breach is relatively severe, it will, as we have seen (*supra*, p. 215) have the effect of suspending or discharging the other party's obligation to perform under the contract. Such a breach is sometimes called a *"total" breach*. A total breach also has the effect of allowing the wronged party to sue immediately for damages based on the entire contract. Usually, these damages will be such as would put the wronged party in the position he would have been in had the contract been completed; see *infra*, p. 318.

   1. Partial breach: If, on the other hand, the breach is not material, it does not relieve the aggrieved party from continuing to perform under the contract. Such a non-material breach is sometimes called a *"partial" breach*. Although the aggrieved party is not relieved from performing after a partial breach, he nonetheless has an immediate right to sue for damages stemming from the partial breach.

Example: Owen, the owner of Blackacre, contracts with Contractor for the latter to build a house on Blackacre. The contract provides that Owen is to make a progress payment every week for the previous week's work. Both parties perform as required during the first month of the contract. After the fifth week, however, Owen is three days late with the progress payment for that week. Assuming that this breach is not a material (or "total") one, Contractor is not discharged from the contract. She may, however, immediately sue for whatever damages she sustained as a result of the partial breach by Owen.

II. ANTICIPATORY REPUDIATION GENERALLY

A. **A recap:** A party may make it unmistakably clear, even before his performance under a contract is due, that he does not intend to perform. When he does so, he is said to have anticipatorily repudiated the contract. As we have seen in the treatment of conditions (*supra*, p. 244), such a repudiation allows the other party to suspend, and perhaps to cancel, his own performance. Here, a different aspect of anticipatory repudiation is treated — may the aggrieved party **institute a suit for breach even before the repudiator's time for performance has arrived?** As we shall see, the answer is generally **"yes."**

1. *Hochster v. De La Tour*: The foundation of the modern doctrine of anticipatory repudiation was laid in an English case called *Hochster v. De La Tour*, 118 Eng. Rep. 922 (Q.B. 1853).

   a. **Facts of *Hochster*:** *Hochster* involved a contract for services made between an employer and his employee. The contract was executed in April 1852, and provided that the employment was to begin on June 1, 1852. On May 11, the employer stated that he would not perform the contract. On May 22, the employee instituted an action for breach of contract. The employer asserted that as of the day suit was commenced, no breach had yet occurred.

   b. **Suit allowed:** The court held that the action was ***not premature.*** The court's reasoning, universally criticized today, was that if an immediate suit were not allowed, the plaintiff would either have to cancel the contract, giving up all his rights under it, or else ignore the repudiation completely, holding himself in readiness to perform until June 1 (and therefore not procuring another job). For some reason, the court did not recognize the possibility that the plaintiff could suspend his own performance (treating the repudiation as the non-occurrence of a constructive condition to the plaintiff's duty of performance), yet wait until an actual breach before suing. Had this possibility been recognized by the court, the reasoning behind its allowance of an immediate suit would have failed.

   c. **American view:** American courts now all permit a plaintiff this latter course of action, i.e., to suspend his own performance after the repudiation, but to wait until the time for the repudiator's performance before bringing suit. Nonetheless, the result in *Hochster* is followed by nearly all American courts.

B. *Hochster* **accepted:** All American jurisdictions except Massachusetts have concurred with the result (though not the reasoning) in *Hochster*, and allow the victim of an anticipatory repudiation to *sue before the repudiator's time for performance has arrived*.

> **Example:** Star promises Movie Co. that Star will act in Movie Co.'s movie, shooting for which is scheduled to commence in the U.S. on July 1. On June 1, Star announces to the press that he is going to live abroad for a year beginning the next day and will not do the movie. Under the rule of *Hochster v. De La Tour*, in force in nearly all states, Movie Co. can sue Star for breach as soon as he issues his press statement; Movie Co. need not wait until July 1, the time at which Star's performance is due.

C. What constitutes a repudiation: Sometimes a party will make it perfectly clear that he has no intention of performing the contract. Such a statement will, of course, undoubtedly constitute an anticipatory repudiation. But in other situations a party's statement regarding his intention or ability to perform will be more ambiguous.

1. **Traditional view:** Older cases often held that as long as the promisor left *any chance* open that she would perform, there was no repudiation.

2. **Modern view:** Modern courts, on the other hand, have generally held that a repudiation can be less clear than this. Thus one commentator defines a repudiation as being any "positive statement by the obligor to the obligee which is *reasonably interpreted* by the obligee to mean that the obligor *will not or cannot perform* his contractual duty…" Murray, p. 421. See Rest. 2d, § 250, Comment b. There are three categories of actions on the part of the promisor which may constitute repudiations:

   ❏ a *statement* by the promisor that he intends not to perform;

   ❏ an *action* by the promisor making his performance under the contract *impossible*; and

   ❏ an *indication* by the promisor or via some other means that the promisor will be *unable* to perform, although he desires to perform.

3. **Promisor's statement:** For a *statement* by the promisor to constitute a repudiation, it must appear to the promisee that the promisor is *quite unlikely* to perform, either because he does not wish to or because he will be unable to (a scenario discussed below).

   a. **Vague doubts:** It is *not enough* that the promisor states *vague doubts* about his willingness or ability to perform. Rest. 2d, § 250, Comment b. (But even the expression of such doubts may entitle the promisee to request *assurances of performance*, and the promisor's failure to give such assurances would be a repudiation. See *infra*, p. 271.)

   b. **Grudging willingness to perform:** Similarly, if the promisor merely indicates *unhappiness* about the deal, or a feeling that it is "unfair," or a wish to get out of it, this will not be a repudiation as long as the promisor either (1) indicates that if legally obligated to do so, he will perform or (2) refrains from any clear indication that he intends not to perform.

   c. **Made to promisee:** Most courts hold that the promisor's statement of unwillingness must, to be a repudiation, be made *to the promisee*, not to some third party. Rest. 2d, § 250, Comment b.

d. Proposals to modify the contract: Frequently the promisor will not flatly announce that she does not intend to perform, but will instead ask the promisee for *more favorable terms* (e.g., a better price), leaving an implication that if the new terms are not agreed to, the promisor will breach. Whether a particular request for more favorable terms constitutes a repudiation obviously depends on how clear the threat not to perform is; it is impossible to formulate a clear test. But the basic idea is that a request for greater performance than that provided for under the contract is repudiation "when under a fair reading it amounts to a statement of *intention not to perform except on conditions which go beyond the contract*." Comment 2 to UCC § 2-610.

4. **Voluntary acts rendering performance impossible:**   The promisor may commit an *act* which renders his performance impossible. The vendor under a land contract might, for instance, convey the land to some other person prior to the time for conveyance to the vendee. If he does so, the vendee may sue immediately for breach, without waiting for the date set in the contract for conveyance.

   a. Performance must be impossible: The act must (either actually or apparently) make the act *impossible*, not merely more difficult or less likely to occur. The act must also be *voluntary*. See Rest. 2d, § 250(b), and Comment c thereto.

5. **Prospective inability to perform:**   It may appear to the promisee that the promisor will be unable to perform, although he desires to do so. Where such *prospective inability to perform* is obvious, all courts agree that the promisee may *suspend his performance*; this was discussed *supra*, p. 244. Some courts further hold that the conventional doctrine of anticipatory repudiation applies, i.e., that the promisee may not only stop his own performance but *sue for breach*. Other courts, however, take the view that where the prospective inability to perform stems from factors beyond the promisor's control, the promisee should not be able to sue until the time for performance has arrived. See Murray, p. 423.

6. **Insolvency:**   A party's *bankruptcy* is generally considered to be an anticipatory repudiation, which has the effect of allowing the other party to make a claim in bankruptcy. On the other hand, a party's actual or apparent *insolvency* does not constitute an anticipatory repudiation, according to most courts.

   a. Grounds for insecurity: Under the UCC, the insolvency of a party is not in itself a repudiation. However, such insolvency would almost certainly give rise to "reasonable grounds for insecurity," (§ 2-609(1)), and would allow the other party to demand assurances of performance. Unless the insolvent party furnished such assurances (e.g., in the form of a bank statement) within thirty days, the contract would be deemed repudiated. § 2-609(4).

7. **Threatened breach must be material:**   Even where the statement of repudiation is unequivocal, or the act makes full compliance with the contract impossible, there will be an anticipatory repudiation only if the breach being threatened would itself be *material* or "total." Rest. 2d, § 250. That is, even the most bold-faced statement by a party that he will commit a "partial" breach does not constitute an anticipatory repudiation.

Quiz Yourself on

ANTICIPATORY REPUDIATION IN GENERAL

67. On Jan. 15, Dahlia and Agatha sign a written agreement wherein Dahlia promises to sell her estate, Totleigh Towers, to Agatha for $100,000. The property is to be conveyed on February 25. Agatha goes ahead and withdraws her bids on other pieces of property. On January 30, Dahlia sells Totleigh to Tom. May Agatha sue Dahlia for breach on Feb. 1?

68. Connie Tractor enters into an agreement to construct a custom home for Frank Lee Unreezonable. As part of the contract, Tractor is to use pale blue caulking around the master tub. Shortly after construction begins, Tractor says to Unreezonable, "I absolutely refuse to use pale blue caulking because I think it looks tacky and I don't want to blemish my reputation. I will use navy blue instead." (Assume that the difference in practical effect between pale blue caulking and navy blue caulking is minor.) Unreezonable is offended by Tractor's unwillingness to follow the terms of the contract, and wants to cancel the contract and sue immediately on an anticipatory repudiation theory. Can he do so?

69. Lady Godiva enters into a contract with Blacksmythe, her local blacksmith, for some designer shoes for her horse. The shoes, which will cost $200, will take several days to make. Shortly before Blacksmythe starts work on the shoes, he learns that Lady Godiva has debts substantially in excess of her assets, and that she has recently failed to pay some local tradespeople on time.

(A) May Blacksmythe cancel the contract and sue for breach?

(B) Putting aside cancellation of the contract, what other step(s) would you advise Blacksmythe to take immediately?

Answers

67. Yes. It is a constructive condition of each party's duty to perform that the other party not manifest an unwillingness or inability to perform. If a party does manifest such an unwillingness or inability, the other party can suspend her own performance and, under the doctrine of *Hochster v. De La Tour*, sue ***immediately*** for breach. Here, Dahlia's own conduct (selling Totleigh to Tom) has created her inability to perform under the contract. Therefore, Agatha's duty to perform is suspended and she can sue immediately, even though the time of performance is still several weeks away.

68. No. Even though Tractor has made is clear in advance that she intends to breach the caulking part of the contract, this would only amount to a minor ("partial") breach of contract, since the facts tell us that choice of the caulking color doesn't have much impact. In order for a party to sue prior to the date of performance based on anticipatory repudiation, the breach in question must be *material* — i.e., a total breach. Unreezonable will just have to wait to get his day in court on this one.

69. (A) No, probably. Blacksmythe cannot cancel the contract because "insolvency" (without bankruptcy) does not constitute anticipatory repudiation, according to most courts. For the same reason, Blacksmythe probably can't bring an immediate suit.

(B) He should suspend his own performance, and ask for reasonable assurances from Lady Godiva. Lady G's balance sheet and recent poor payment performance have given Blacksmythe reasonable grounds for feeling insecure about whether Lady G. will perform her end of the bargain (take the shoes and pay for them). Therefore, Blacksmythe's entitled to suspend performance and ask for assurance of performance. If Lady G. doesn't promptly provide adequate assurances, this failure *would* constitute an anticipatory repudiation, giving Blacksmythe the immediate right to cancel the contract and sue.

III. OTHER ASPECTS OF REPUDIATION

A. Repudiation after repudiator's performance has fallen due: We have spoken thus far of situations in which the repudiation is *anticipatory*, that is, where it comes before the repudiator's performance is due. Sometimes, however, a party will begin to perform as required by the contract, and will *then* announce that he does not intend to continue performance. Or, the time for performance arrives, and only then does the party announce that he will not perform. Although the repudiation in either case is not, strictly speaking, anticipatory, it is treated in the *same way* as a repudiation occurring before any performance is due. Thus it *discharges* the other party, and allows that other party to bring an *immediate action for total breach of contract*, i.e., for all the damages he has suffered and will suffer from the breach.

1. Same application: Most of the rules discussed in the remainder of this section (e.g., the rules on retracting a repudiation) apply in the *same way* to anticipatory repudiations as to repudiations occurring after performance has become due.

B. Retraction of repudiation: A repudiation may be *retracted* until the aggrieved party has either:

❏ *sued for breach,* or

❏ *changed his position materially in reliance on the repudiation*, or

❏ stated that he *regards the repudiation as final*.

Rest. 2d, § 256(1).

Example: D contracts to supply gas to P (the U.S.) for a certain period. Prior to the end of the period, D anticipatorily repudiates by stating that it will not continue to perform after a certain date. P advertises for new bidders, receives a bid from X Corp., and notifies D that unless D retracts its repudiation within three days, it will accept X Corp.'s bid. The three days pass, D does not retract, and P notifies X Corp. that it has accepted its bid. D then retracts, but P signs the contract with X Corp., and sues D.

Held, D's retraction came too late. P's statement to X Corp. that it had accepted its bid was a material change of position, even though the actual contract signing did not occur till later. (Also, P's letter to D giving it three days in which to retract amounted to a statement that the contract would be cancelled in three days if there were no retraction, and once the three days were up, this gave rise to cancellation.) *U.S. v. Seacoast Gas Co.*, 204 F.2d 709 (5th Cir. 1953).

1. Applies to both anticipatory and ordinary repudiation: The above rules on retraction apply both to anticipatory repudiations, and to repudiations that occur after the repudiator's performance has become due.

2. Means of retracting: Normally, a retraction will be written or verbal. If, however, the original repudiation was an act inconsistent with the contract (*supra*, p. 264), the retraction may consist of the repudiator's regaining an ability to perform. Whether the retraction is written, verbal, or by such an act, it is effective only if and when it is *communicated to the repudiatee*. See Rest. 2d, § 256(1).

3. **UCC view:** The UCC permits retraction of a repudiation in much the same way as the common law. § 2-611(1) states that "Until the repudiating party's *next performance is due* he can *retract* his repudiation unless the aggrieved party has since the repudiation *cancelled or materially changed his position* or otherwise indicated that he *considers the repudiation final*."

4. **Cancellation and new contract with someone else:** These retraction rules mean that if the repudiatee cancels the contract and *makes an alternative contract* with someone else, the repudiation can no longer be retracted.

   a. **UCC illustrations:** So, for instance, in a UCC context, the following events would *end* the repudiator's time to retract:

      ❏ The *buyer* repudiates, and the seller *sells the goods in question* to someone else;

      ❏ The *seller* repudiates, and the buyer instead *buys comparable goods* from someone else.

   b. **Real estate:** Similarly, in a *real estate* contract, if the buyer repudiates and the seller *sells the property* (or makes a *binding contract to sell the property*) to a *third party*, this sale or contract ends the buyer's time to retract, whether the buyer knows about it or not.

C. **The repudiatee's option to sue or continue the contract:** Where a repudiation (either anticipatory, or after the beginning of performance) occurs, the repudiatee may, as we have seen, sue immediately for total breach. But does she have the alternative of *ignoring* the repudiation, and continuing to perform and/or demanding performance from the repudiator? The answer is that the repudiatee may not ignore the repudiation and continue the contract if to do so would aggravate her damages; she is thus obligated to *mitigate damages*, or be disallowed from recovering for those damages which could have been avoided. C&P, p. 486; Rest. 2d, § 350, Comment f and Illustr. 17.

   > **Example:** Contractor contracts to build a house for Owner. Before Contractor starts to work, she repudiates the contract. Owner cannot ignore the repudiation, sitting by and waiting for damages to mount up. He must instead attempt to engage another contractor, or he will not be able to recover from Contractor the damages which could have been avoided. Similarly, if it was Owner who had anticipatorily repudiated the contract, Contractor would be under an obligation to find another project, to sell any materials she had bought for work on Owner's house, etc.

   1. **Same rule where performance already commenced:** The same rule requiring the repudiatee to mitigate damages applies where the contract has already begun, and the repudiation is thus not anticipatory. For instance, in the above example, had Contractor begun work on the house, and then repudiated, Owner would still have been under an obligation to procure a substitute contractor. C&P, p. 486.

   2. **UCC:** The UCC similarly requires the repudiatee to attempt to minimize his damages. § 2-610(a) states that the repudiatee may "for a commercially reasonable time await performance by the repudiating party...." Comment 1 states that if the repudiatee "awaits performance beyond a commercially reasonable time he cannot recover resulting damages

which he should have avoided." See the more detailed discussion of the measure of damages in UCC anticipatory repudiation cases, *infra*, p. 270.

3. **Where repudiation is ignored, then sued upon:** Suppose the repudiatee at first decides to ignore the repudiation, and demands that the repudiator perform. Assuming that by doing so he has not failed in his duty to mitigate damages, may she then change her mind and sue for breach of contract?

    a. **Traditional view:** The traditional view has been that once the repudiatee urges the repudiator to withdraw his repudiation, the former has *"reinstated" the contract* and loses her right to treat the repudiation as a breach. This rule makes life very difficult for the innocent repudiatee.

    b. **Modern view:** But most modern courts hold that the repudiatee does *not* lose any rights by insisting on performance, and that she may later change his mind and sue for breach. See Rest. 2d, § 257. (However, if, due to the repudiatee's urging, the repudiator retracts before the repudiatee materially changes her position, this retraction is effective; see *supra*, p. 266.)

    c. **UCC in accord:** The UCC similarly takes the view that the repudiatee's insistence on performance *does not constitute a waiver of his right to sue* for breach.

        i. **Party has choice of remedies:** Whether it is the buyer or seller who anticipatorily repudiates, § 2-610 sets out the repudiatee's options. This special provision applies only where a party "repudiates the contract with respect to a performance not yet due the loss of which will *substantially impair the value of the contract to the other."* If this "substantial impairment of value" standard is satisfied, § 2-610 gives the repudiatee the choice between:

            ❑ *"await[ing] performance* by the repudiating party" for a "commercially reasonable time"; or

            ❑ *"resort[ing] to any remedy for breach* ..., even though [the repudiatee] has notified the repudiating party that he would await the latter's performance and has urged retraction."

            Example: On Oct. 1, Buyer orders a new Vista automobile from Seller, delivery to occur Dec. 1. On Nov. 1, Seller repudiates by saying that he won't be able to ship the car for a full year. A full-year delay would certainly "substantially impair the value of the contract" to Buyer. (By contrast, Seller's announcement of a one-*week* delay in delivery probably *wouldn't* substantially impair the contract's value to Buyer, so Buyer would not have the second of the two options we're about to illustrate).

            Therefore, on Nov. 1, Buyer can choose: (1) he can wait to see whether Seller changes his mind and performs (and, if Buyer wishes, he can urge Seller to change his mind); or (2) he can immediately "resort to any remedy for breach." Choice (2) means that he can *cover* (i.e., buy the goods from a different seller) and immediately sue for the contract-cover differential under § 2-712, or alternatively *not cover* and sue for the contract-market differential under § 2-713. If Buyer elects course (1) (waiting and hoping), he can at any time switch to course (2).

D. Repudiatee's inability to perform: In the ordinary case of breach (failure to perform at the time performance is due), the non-breaching party must generally *tender* his performance (i.e., show an ability and willingness to perform) if he is to recover full damages for the breach. In the case of an anticipatory repudiation, a similar, though not identical, principle holds: the repudiatee (the injured party) may not recover if it is shown that he *would have been unable* or unwilling to perform his share of the bargain. Rest. 2d, § 254(1).

> **Example:** A corporation owns a particular apartment building. D, a bank which owns all of the stock in the corporation, gives P the right of first refusal to match any offer which D receives for the corporation's stock; the agreement requires D to notify P of any offer so that P can decide whether to match it (with P to have 60 days to come up with the money if he decides to match). D sells the stock to a third party without giving P the required notice. P sues D for breach. D argues that P, in order to recover, must show that P would have been willing and able to come up with the money to exercise his right of refusal.
>
> *Held* (on this point), for D. Even though D repudiated, D does not have to pay damages unless P shows that had he been given the required notice, he would have been willing and able to come up with the purchase price. In a concurrent contract, one party cannot put the other in default unless the former is ready, willing and *able* to perform. *Kanavos v. Hancock Bank & Trust Co.*, 479 N.E.2d 168 (Mass. 1985).

1. Impracticability or frustration: Similarly, the repudiator may be relieved from the duty to pay damages if the duty she has repudiated would have been discharged by *impossibility*, *impracticability*, or *frustration*. Rest. 2d, § 254(2).

E. Repudiatee owes no remaining duties: Recall that in *Hochster v. De La Tour (supra*, p. 262), the reason the court allowed immediate suit for the anticipatory repudiation was that it would be unfair to force the aggrieved party to continue his own preparations for performance before being allowed to sue. But where the aggrieved party *does not owe any further performance*, either because the contract was originally unilateral, or because he has already rendered all performance required of him under a bilateral contract, this rationale does not apply. For this reason, the courts have generally refused to allow an immediate suit for breach based on anticipatory repudiation where the plaintiff *owes no remaining duties under the contract*. Rest. 2d, § 253, Comment c.

1. Payment of money: The most common illustration of this principle is that *an anticipatory repudiation of an unconditional unilateral obligation to pay money at a fixed time does not give rise to a claim for breach until that time has arrived.*

> **Example:** On January 1, 2010, Buyer and Seller make a contract under which Seller promises to convey Blackacre to Buyer on February 1. In return, Buyer promises to pay $100,000 at that time, and the balance of $400,000 in four equal annual installments, each due on Feb. 1. On Feb. 1, 2010, as scheduled, Seller conveys to Buyer and Buyer pays the $100,000 initial payment. On April 1 of that year, Buyer announces that he will not make any further payments. Because Seller owes no further duties, he won't be permitted to sue Buyer now, and must wait until Buyer fails to make the Feb. 1, 2011 payment. Cf. Rest. 2d, § 253, Illustr. 6.

a. **Disability payments:** The same principle is also frequently applied where an insurance company cancels a ***disability policy***, and refuses to make payments under it. In this situation, even if disability appears to be permanent, the plaintiff may sue only for those payments already due as of the time of suit, not those which will come due subsequently. See *New York Life Insur. Co. v. Viglas*, 297 U.S. 672 (1936).

b. **Acceleration clauses:** For this reason, loans and mortgages usually contain an ***"acceleration clause,"*** under which the fact that a party misses one payment causes all future installments to become immediately due. That way, the creditor can sue immediately, and on a single occasion, for all outstanding principal.

F. Damages for repudiation under UCC: Most aspects of damages, including the rights upon breach of both sellers and buyers, are treated in the chapter on Remedies. Here, we consider one aspect of damages: the damages of a buyer under a goods contract whose seller has anticipatorily repudiated the contract.

UCC § 2-713(1) provides that "the measure of damages for … repudiation by the seller is the difference between the market price ***at the time when the buyer learned of the breach*** and the contract price, together with any incidental and consequential damages."

1. **When does buyer learn of breach:** The phrase "***at the time when the buyer learned of the breach***" is ambiguous in some cases. In a case where the seller does not repudiate the contract, and simply fails to deliver, the "time when the buyer learned of the breach" is not difficult to ascertain — it is the time when the goods should have been tendered and were not. But where the seller repudiates the contract *before* the time for delivery, how do we interpret the words "when the buyer learned of the breach"? Does this refer to (1) the time when the buyer "learned of the repudiation" or (2) the time at which performance is finally due?

   a. **Majority approach:** Most courts have followed the first of these approaches, and have held that the time for computing damages is the time when the buyer ***learns of the repudiation.*** See W&S, p. 223, n. 6.

      i. **Criticism:** But this interpretation has been *criticized* on the grounds that it thwarts the buyer's right to "for a commercially reasonable time ***await performance*** by the repudiating party," a right given him by § 2-610(a). For if the buyer's damages are the difference between the contract price and the market price at the time of repudiation, then the buyer (at least one who does not "cover," i.e., procure alternative goods) would have to suffer without recovery ***any further loss*** occurring if the market price continued to rise between the repudiation and the end of the "commercially reasonable" period.

   b. **Measurement at "time for performance":** An alternative is to measure the contract/market differential as of the ***time for performance***.

      i. **Argument in favor:** The biggest merit of this approach is that it does not deprive the buyer of his chance to wait a "commercially reasonable time" before covering. In fact, he can wait this time, then decide not to cover, and still recover the contract/market differential at the time for performance.

G. **Right to demand assurances of performance:** A party's speech or conduct will sometimes not constitute an unequivocal repudiation, but will give the other party reasonable grounds for *insecurity* about whether there will be performance. In this situation, the party who is insecure has the right to *demand assurances* from the other party that the latter will perform. If the latter fails to provide these assurances, this failure *will itself be considered a breach*, on which immediate suit can be brought (and the contract cancelled). See Rest. 2d, § 251, UCC § 2-609(1).

1. **Cross-reference:** The right to demand assurances is treated more extensively in the prior chapter, *supra*, at p. 245. (That discussion focuses on the relation between the right to make such a demand, and the right to suspend or cancel the contract. However, a party's failure to respond to a justified request for such assurances is also deemed a breach, entitling the injured party to bring immediate suit.)

Quiz Yourself on

OTHER ASPECTS OF REPUDIATION

70. Blanche agrees to buy Kowalski's bar, A Streetcar Named Desire, for $50,000. The transaction is to take place July 15. On June 10, Blanche calls and says she's changed her mind and that she intends to move away and get married. Kowalski says, "I hope you change your mind, and I'll have to sue you if you don't go through with the deal." Blanche says, "I have always depended on the kindness of strangers, and therefore I don't think that you'll sue me, stranger."

    (A) On June 20, Blanche calls Kowalski back and says the engagement is off, and that as far as she's concerned, the deal is still on. As of the 20th, Kowalski has re-listed the bar with a broker, but hasn't done anything else in response to Blanche's June 10 phone call. On the 21st, Kowalski gets an offer for $60,000. Can Kowalski take the higher offer, or must he sell to Blanche?

    (B) Same basic facts as (A). Now, however, assume that during the June 10th conversation, Kowalski says to Blanche, "OK, I'm interpreting this as a breach of contract. I have nothing further to say to you, and I'll see you in court." However, Kowalski has not yet sued Blanche (or listed the bar with a broker) when she calls back on June 20 to reinstate the contract. Can Kowalski take the $60,000 offer, or must he sell to Blanche?

71. Spock contracts to buy a tribble fur coat from the Klingon Fur Company. Spock prepays the $2,000 purchase price on March 1; Klingon is to deliver the coat April 1. On March 15, Klingon calls Spock and says it will not deliver the coat. Does Spock have an immediate cause of action on the basis of anticipatory repudiation?

Answers

70. **(A) Kowalski must sell to Blanche.** A repudiation may be *retracted* until the aggrieved party has done one of three things: (1) sued for breach; (2) changed his position materially in reliance on the repudiation; or (3) stated that he regards the repudiation as final. Rest. 2d, § 256(1). Kowalski has done none of these things by the time he gets Blanche's retraction call on the 20th. (His mere re-listing the bar with a broker isn't likely to be found to be a "material" change of position.) Therefore, Blanche is entitled to retract her repudiation, in which case the contract is reinstated as if there had been no repudiation.

    (B) He may take the $60,000 offer. As the answer to part (A) shows, one of the ways in which a repudiator loses the ability to retract the repudiation is if the aggrieved party states that that party regards the repudiation as final. Kowalski's statement to Blanche that he'd see her in court probably qualifies as such a statement, so at that point Blanche lost the ability to retract. Consequently, the breach was complete and final on June 10, making Kowalski free now to regard the contract as cancelled and to make other arrangements.

71. No. Ironically, when it comes to suing after an anticipatory repudiation, a party who has fully performed has lesser rights than a party whose performance has not yet come due: there is a special rule that says that when the party aggrieved by an anticipatory repudiation has already given all the performance he was required to give, that party may not sue immediately, and must instead wait for the time for performance before suing. So Spock may not sue until Klingon actually fails to deliver the coat on April 1.

Exam Tips *on* ANTICIPATORY REPUDIATION AND OTHER ASPECTS OF BREACH

☛ An anticipatory repudiation occurs when, *before performance is required,* a party to a contract says or does something which indicates that she *will not perform* as required. The other party's obligations are discharged, and that party may immediately sue for breach of contract.

   ☞ **Words or action:** Look for an indication by the promisor that she won't be able to perform her promise, either through a reasonably clear *statement,* or a voluntary *action* which renders performance impossible.

   Example: Sue owns a farm in County. She hires Driller to drill a well to supply her with better tasting drinking water than the County water she has been using. The contract provides for a guaranteed completion by June 1. Two hundred feet down Driller's drill strikes rock and breaks, plugging the hole. Driller tells Sue that he won't be able to complete a substitute well any earlier than August 1. Sue refuses to let Driller start the drilling of a new well, cancels the contract, and hires someone else. Sue's refusal/cancellation was not a breach of the agreement because Driller's acknowledgment that he couldn't complete the job except two months late was an anticipatory repudiation.

   ☞ Make sure that performance has been made *impossible* and/or that the statement of intention not to perform is *reasonably clear*. Remember, if the promisor takes an action which makes her only *temporarily* unable to perform, performance isn't *impossible*, just improbable. In that case, the other party's obligation is usually merely *suspended*, but not actually discharged.

   Example: On the facts of the above Example, suppose that after the first hole got plugged, Driller said, "I don't think I'll be able to finish by June 1." This statement is not a repudiation, so Sue can't cancel the contract. But she could *demand assurances of performance* — for instance, she could demand that Driller explain how he plans to overcome the problems. If Driller doesn't give the explanation, she can then cancel. Also, while she's waiting for the explanation, she can *suspend* her own performance (e.g., any progress payments that the contract said she must make while the work progressed).

☞ **Delegation:** Watch for a fact pattern where there is a delegation of a contract for *personal services* or one calling for *special, unusual skills*. These types of contracts usually cannot be delegated; doing so probably constitutes an anticipatory repudiation.

Example: Client hires Lawyer to handle a tort suit. It is clear that Client is relying on Lawyer's particular trial skills, which are well known. Lawyer sells his practice to Barrister, a much less well-known lawyer with lesser credentials, and tells Client that Barrister will handle the case. The delegation is probably an anticipatory repudiation; if so, Client may immediately cancel the contract.

☞ **Retraction:** Remember that a repudiation, an anticipatory repudiation, or an indication of prospective unwillingness/inability to perform can initially be *retracted* (*withdrawn*) by the repudiator, in which case the contract is restored.

Example: In the above example, suppose that after Client objects to the delegation, Lawyer says, "OK, I'll stay on to handle your case." At that moment, Client can no longer cancel the contract, because Lawyer has retracted the repudiation. (But see immediately below for how the repudiator may lose the right to retract.)

☞ **Loss of right to retract:** The repudiation *can no longer be retracted* if any of these things happens:

❏ The other party *materially (and reasonably) relies* on the repudiation (e.g., by procuring a substitute contract).

❏ The other party *sues for breach*.

❏ The other party says that she *regards the repudiation as final.*

Example: In August, Pete enters into a written contract with Resort, a corporation that owns and operates a summer resort, providing that Pete will work as the caretaker of the hotel from the following October through April. Two weeks later, Pete enlists in the U.S. Navy for a three-year period beginning in September. Resort's owner sees notice of Pete's enlistment in the local newspaper; Resort therefore enters into a substitute contract with Mark that is identical to the one previously entered into with Pete. In September, Pete fails the navy physical examination and is rejected for service. He then tells Resort he's still counting on showing up for work. Resort has justifiably relied on the repudiation (the enlistment), so Pete cannot retract it by saying he's available; therefore Pete can't sue for breach.

☛ **Immediate suit for breach:** Remember that when a party learns of a repudiation, she may *immediately sue for breach*, even if damages have not yet accrued.

Example: In January, Buyer and Seller enter into a contract whereby Seller is to deliver 10,000 bolts per month to Buyer for a ten-month period, beginning March 1, at a cost of 10 cents per bolt. On Feb. 1, Seller notifies Buyer that he will not be delivering the bolts to Buyer because he has just contracted with another buyer for the sale of his entire output of bolts at a higher price. On Feb.10, Buyer enters into a cover contract at a cost of 10.5 cents a bolt. Buyer may sue immediately for the cover/contract differential, even though the time for Seller's performance has not arrived, and even though Buyer has not yet laid out any money under the cover contract.

CHAPTER 9

STATUTE OF FRAUDS

ChapterScope

This chapter covers the "Statute of Frauds," which in every state provides that certain types of contracts must be *in writing* in order to be enforceable.

- **Five main types:** Here are the five important types of contracts that fall under the Statute of Frauds, and that must therefore ordinarily be in writing:

  - ❏ **Suretyship agreement.** A *guaranty*, i.e., a promise to pay the legally enforceable *debt of another*, is normally within the Statute of Frauds, and must therefore be in writing.

  - ❏ **Marriage provision.** A promise for which the consideration is *marriage* (or a promise of marriage) must be in writing.

  - ❏ **Land contract.** A promise to *transfer an interest in land* must be in writing. (Not just *sales*, but other transfers of an interest in land, such as *mortgages* and *leases*, are covered.)

  - ❏ **One-year provision.** A contract which *cannot possibly be fully performed within a year of its making* must be in writing.

    - ❏ **Mere possibility enough:** However, if there is *any* possibility, no matter how small, that the contract can be completed in a year, it need not be in writing. (*Example:* An employment contract that is to last for the rest of the employee's lifetime does not have to be in writing, because it is possible that the person will die within one year after the contract is made.)

  - ❏ **Sale of goods:** A contract for the *sale of goods for a price of $500* or more must normally be in writing.

- **Elements of the writing:** To satisfy the Statute of Frauds, there must be a signed writing. The writing must normally (1) reasonably *identify the subject* of the contract; (2) indicate that a contract has been made between the parties; (3) state with reasonable certainty the *essential terms* of the contract; and (4) be *signed* "by or on behalf of the *party to be charged*."

I. INTRODUCTION

A. **Some contracts require a writing:** Most contracts can be valid despite the fact that they are only oral. A few types of contracts, however, are *unenforceable*, in almost every American jurisdiction, unless they are *in writing*.

B. **English Statute of Frauds:** The rules requiring certain kinds of contracts to be in writing stem from an English statute known as the Statute of Frauds. This statute received this name because its primary purpose was to avoid fraudulent claims, by requiring the claimant to produce a writing that would prove the claim's existence.

C. Adoption in America: All American jurisdictions except Louisiana have adopted some form of the original English Statute of Frauds. In all of these states except Maryland and New Mexico, the adoption has been by statute; in these two states, it is by case law. There is some variation from state to state in the precise provisions, but as a general rule, the states have adhered quite closely to the original English formulation of the Statute.

D. Five categories of contract: There are five categories of contract which, in almost every state, fall within the Statute of Frauds and must therefore be in writing:

[1] **Executor-Administrator:** A contract of an *executor or administrator* to answer for a *duty of her decedent*;

[2] **Suretyship:** A contract to *answer for the debt or duty of another*;

[3] **Marriage:** A contract made upon *consideration of marriage*;

[4] **Land contract:** A contract for the *sale of an interest in land*;

[5] **One year:** A contract that is *not to be performed within one year* from its making.

> **Note:** In the following discussion of these categories, the first, the executor-administrator provision, is encompassed within the second, the suretyship provision, because of the similarity between the two.

1. UCC: In addition to the above five classes of contracts which must be in writing to be enforceable, the *UCC* requires a writing in the case of a contract for the *sale of goods* for the price of *$500 or more* (§ 2-201).

II. SURETYSHIP AGREEMENTS

A. General rule: A promise to *pay the debt* or default of *another* is within the Statute of Frauds, and is therefore unenforceable unless it is in writing. Rest. 2d, § 110(1)(b).

> **Example:** Son, who is 19, wants to lease a 2012 Ford Mustang from Dealer. Son's credit is not very good, so Dealer tells Son that he'll lease the car to Son only if some responsible adult with a good credit rating agrees to guarantee the lease payments. Son brings his father, Dad, to the dealership, and Dad says to Dealer, "I promise that any lease payment that Son doesn't make, I'll make."
>
> Dad's promise is a promise to pay the debt of another (Son); therefore, Dad's promise is unenforceable because not in writing. Nor does it matter that Son's own primary promise (to make the lease payments) is in writing — what's required is that the guarantor's promise be in writing.

1. Purpose of rule: Like the other Statute of Frauds provisions, the provision requiring that suretyship agreements be in writing serves principally an *evidentiary* function. That is, it is designed to make sure that this kind of contract is not enforced unless there is sufficient evidence of its existence. But the suretyship requirement also serves the *cautionary* function of "guarding the [surety] against ill-considered action." (Rest. 2d, Comment a to § 112.) In other words, by making a suretyship promise enforceable only if it is in writing, the Statute makes sure that the surety will take his time, and not make hasty oral promises which he may later regret.

2. **Applies to defaults as well as debts:** Frequently, the suretyship agreement will provide that the surety will pay the *debt* of the obligor, if the obligor does not pay it himself. But the agreement may also provide that the surety will perform *any other kind of contractual obligation* on the part of the obligor. Thus a surety's promise to *complete work* on a construction project should the obligor fail to do this work himself is the kind of agreement that falls within the suretyship provision of the Statute, and must therefore be in writing.

3. **Other person must be liable:** The suretyship provision applies only where there is a guarantee of *another person's* legally enforceable debt or obligation. If that other person does not legally owe the duty in question, the fact that the "surety" orally undertakes liability is not enough to bring the promise within the Statute of Frauds.

    Example: S calls up Retailer, and says to him "Deliver three pair of pants to D, and if D doesn't pay for them, I will." D is not liable for the goods, since she has not ordered them. Therefore, S is not a surety, and his promise does not fall within the suretyship provision of the Statute of Frauds. S's promise is thus enforceable, even though oral. See Rest. 2d, § 112, Illustr. 5.

4. **Promise must be made to creditor:** For a promise of suretyship to fall within the Statute of Frauds, it must be made *to the creditor*, not to the debtor. Thus the right of a creditor beneficiary to enforce a promise is not affected by the Statute of Frauds. Murray, p. 648.

    Example: Surety says to Debtor, "If you can't pay your debt to Creditor, I'll pay it." Because this promise has been made to Debtor, and not to Creditor, it does not fall within the suretyship provision of the Statute of Frauds, and is enforceable even though oral.

    a. **Promises of indemnity:** By this rule, the ordinary promise of *indemnity* is not within the suretyship provision, since it is a promise made to the indemnitee to hold her harmless against any obligation which she may incur to someone else. See Murray, p. 648. To put it another way, a promise of "indemnity" is *by definition* a promise made to the person whose debt is to be satisfied, and not to the creditor.

B. **The main purpose rule:** In the kinds of cases we have looked at so far, it is clear that the promisor's chief purpose in promising to answer for the debt of a third person is to benefit that third person, not the promisor. If, however, the facts are such that the promisor's chief purpose in making his promise of suretyship is to further *his own interests*, his promise does not fall within the Statute of Frauds. This rule, which has developed as a matter of case law, is often called the "*main purpose rule*." See Rest. 2d, § 116.

1. **Examine consideration:** To determine whether the promisor is primarily seeking to further his own interest by making the suretyship promise, *the consideration that is given in return for his promise* should be examined. If this consideration is of *direct benefit* (usually economic) *to the promisor*, this fact will be a strong indication that the case falls within the main purpose rule, and therefore not within the Statute. (For the suretyship promise to be enforceable, there must of course always be some sort of consideration. But as we have seen, *supra*, p. 105, this consideration may be entirely for the benefit of someone other than the promisor. The question here, therefore, is not whether there is valid con-

sideration for the promise of suretyship, but whether this consideration furnishes a direct benefit to the promisor.)

> **Example:** Contractor contracts to build a house for Owner. In order to obtain the necessary supplies, Contractor seeks to procure them on credit from Supplier. Supplier, however, is unwilling to look solely to Contractor's credit, and tells Owner that he will not give Contractor credit unless Owner agrees to guarantee payment. Owner, in order to get the house built, gives such an oral agreement guaranteeing payment.
>
> Because Owner's main purpose in giving the guaranty is to *further his own economic interest* (getting the house built), his promise does not fall within the suretyship provision, and is therefore not required to meet the Statute of Frauds.

C. **Memorandum requirement:** A document signed by the surety will meet the requirement of a writing even if it is ***not addressed to the obligee***, even if it is not created until ***long after the oral promise*** of guarantee, and even if it is ***never seen*** by the obligee. (See p. 293 for more about what type of document satisfies the memorandum requirement.)

> **Example:** *A* orally promises *B* that if *B* will extend credit to *C*, *A* will guarantee repayment. *B* extends credit to *C*. Two months later, *A* writes a letter to *C*, saying "I'm not sure you knew this, but I guaranteed *B* that I would repay your debt if you do not." The promise by *A* falls within the suretyship provision: *C* is the primary obligor, and *A* is the surety. However, the letter to *C* satisfies the writing requirement — even though this writing was not addressed to *B*, or ever sent to him, it is a sufficient memorandum. Therefore, *A*'s oral guarantee is enforceable against him.

Quiz Yourself on
SURETYSHIP AGREEMENTS

72. Medici calls the Florence Art Supply Store and says, "Send a box of scented magic markers to Botticelli at his studio, and I will pay for them." The markers cost $25. The Store does so, Botticelli doesn't pay for the markers, and the Store sends Medici a bill. Must Medici pay?

73. Same basic facts as prior question. Now, however, assume that Medici and Botticelli visit the Store together. Botticelli asks to be given the markers on credit. The Store refuses, because of Botticelli's past credit problems. Medici then says, "If he doesn't pay the bill within 30 days, I will." The Store agrees, and Botticelli doesn't pay the bill. Must Medici pay?

74. Marie Antoinette is having Tuileries Construction Co. build a new palace for her. The contract calls for a gold-plated mirror. The only place around that stocks such a mirror is the local No Value Hardware store, which sells it for $399. Tuileries hasn't been paying its bills to No Value recently, so No Value is unwilling to extend credit to Tuileries unless someone with good credit gives a guarantee. Marie therefore orally says to No Value, "Put the mirror on Tuileries' account. If they don't pay promptly, I will." No Value does so, and Tuileries doesn't pay promptly. Must Marie pay the bill?

Answers

72. Yes. The suretyship provision says that promises to "pay the debt of another" must be in writing. This means that the "other" must have the primary obligation to pay the debt, and the "surety" is merely a guarantor. Here, Botticelli never became liable (he didn't place the order), so Medici is primarily liable, not secondarily. Consequently, the suretyship provision never applied, so the promise didn't have to be in writing.

73. **No.** In contrast to the last question, here Botticelli is primarily liable, and Medici is a true guarantor. Therefore, his promise falls within the suretyship provision, and is unenforceable because not in writing.

74. **Yes.** Marie has agreed to pay the debt of another person, so ordinarily her promise would have to be in writing, under the suretyship provision. But the most important exception to the suretyship provision is the *"main purpose"* rule, which says that if the promisor's chief purpose in making his promise of suretyship is to further his own interests, his promise does not fall within the suretyship provision. That's the case here: Marie's main reason for guaranteeing Tuileries' debt is not to help Tuileries, but because she, Marie, wants the mirror installed. Therefore, Marie's promise is enforceable even though not in writing.

III. THE MARRIAGE PROVISION

A. **Contract made upon consideration of marriage:** A promise for which the *consideration* is *marriage* or a promise of marriage is within the Statute of Frauds. Rest. 2d, § 124.

> **Example:** Tycoon says to Starlet, his girlfriend, "If you will promise to marry me, I'll transfer to you title to my Malibu beach home even before our marriage." Starlet replies, "It's a deal." No document is signed. If Tycoon changes his mind, Starlet cannot sue to enforce either the promise of marriage or the promise to convey the beach house, since the consideration for both of these promises was her return promise to marry Tycoon. Conversely, if Starlet changes her mind, Tycoon cannot sue for breach either. See Rest. 2d, § 124, Illustr. 2.

B. **Exception for mutual promises to marry:** If an oral contract consists *solely of mutual promises to marry* (with no ancillary promises relating to property transfer), the contract is not within the Statute of Frauds, and is enforceable even though oral. Rest. 2d, § 124. In other words, an ordinary oral engagement is an *enforceable contract.*

1. **Damages:** No one would plausibly sue for *specific performance* of the contract, but the jilted party could sue for contract damages, especially *reliance damages* like money spent on wedding preparations. So such a suit would not be foreclosed merely because the contract was oral.

IV. THE LAND CONTRACT PROVISION

A. **Contracts to transfer and buy land:** A promise to transfer or buy *any interest in land* is within the Statute of Frauds. Rest. 2d, § 125. The Statute does not apply to the conveyance itself (which is governed by separate statutes in most states), but rather to a *contract providing for* the subsequent conveyance of land. C&P, p. 732.

1. **Promise to pay:** Keep in mind that not only a promise to transfer an interest in land, but also the promise to *pay* for such an interest, falls within the Statute. However, we shall see later that if the vendor makes a conveyance under an oral contract, the promise to pay will be removed from the Statute of Frauds.

Example: Ohn, the owner of Blackacre, says to Bhuy, "I'll sell Blackacre to you for $100,000, to be paid in cash 30 days from today." Bhuy responds, "OK, we've got a deal." They shake hands on it.

Neither party is bound, because the agreement is for the conveyance of an interest in land, yet neither party's promise was in writing. Thus Bhuy can't sue Ohn for refusing to convey, and Ohn can't sue Bhuy for refusing to tender the purchase price.

B. Interests in land: In addition to the transfer of a fee simple interest in land, there are a number of other kinds of interests in land which fall within the Statute. The following are (unless we explain otherwise) interests in land a contract for the transfer of which falls within the Statute:

1. Leases: *Leases* are generally held to be interests in land. However, statutes in most states make an oral lease *enforceable* if its *duration is one year or less*. (What must be one year or less is generally the lease term itself, not the time between the execution of the lease and the end of the lease term). A lease for more than one year falls within the "one year" provision of the Statute in any case (see *infra*, p. 285), so the applicability of the land contract portion of the Statute does not arise.

2. Mortgages: A promise to give a *mortgage* on real property as security for a loan is usually held to be within the Statute. C&P, pp. 733-734.

3. Easements: A promise to grant an *easement* over land falls within the land-contract provision, and must therefore be in writing.

4. Crops: Crops, even though they are attached to the soil, are *not* considered to be interests in land. A contract for the sale of growing timber is an interest in land if and only if the contract contemplates that title will pass before the timber is cut. See UCC § 2-107(2). A contract for the sale of minerals, including oil and gas, involves an interest in land only if they are to be removed from the ground by the buyer. UCC § 2-107(1).

5. Contracts only incidentally related to land: It is irrelevant that the performance of the contract is closely related to an interest in land, if the subject matter of the contract itself is not the transfer of such an interest. Thus a contract to *build a building* is not within the statute, nor is a promise to *lend money* with which to buy land, or a contract between *partners* to *buy or sell real estate* and divide the profits. C&P, p. 735.

Example: Ohn, the owner of Blackacre, orally contracts with Contractor for Contractor to build a house on the property at a cost to Ohn of $100,000. The contract does not fall within the land-contract provision of the Statute, because it is not a contract to transfer an interest in land, even though it is a contract that "involves" land.

C. Effect of vendor's performance or vendee's reliance: Even if an oral contract for the transfer of an interest in land is not enforceable at the time it is made, *subsequent acts* by the parties may render it enforceable. There are two important ways in which such a contract can become enforceable: (1) by virtue of full performance on the part of the vendor; and (2) by virtue of significant reliance by the vendee.

1. Conveyance by vendor: If the vendor under an oral land contract makes the contracted-for *conveyance*, she may *recover the contract price*. In other words, although the promise to pay for the land is initially within the Statute of Frauds, it is removed from the Statute by the vendor's conveyance of the land to the vendee. Rest. 2d, § 125(3).

2. **Vendee's detrimental reliance:** The vendee under an oral land contract may, in reliance on the contract, take actions which both furnish evidence that the oral contract was in fact made, and also create a *reliance interest* on the part of the vendee in having the contract enforced. If the vendee performs such acts, he may be able to have the contract enforced through *specific performance* (i.e., a judicial decree ordering the vendor to convey the land) notwithstanding the fact that the contract was originally unenforceable due to the Statute of Frauds.

   a. **Payment of money alone not sufficient:** The fact that the vendee has paid the vendor the *purchase price* under the oral contract is *not by itself* sufficient for the vendee to obtain specific performance. The reason for this is that an action in quasi-contract to recover the purchase price will adequately protect the vendee's restitution interest. Specific performance, which is an equitable remedy, will only be ordered when the remedy at law (here, quasi-contract) is inadequate.

   b. **Part performance of the alleged contract:** But the court will often grant specific performance of an oral land contract if the vendee has *committed acts* (apart from payment to the vendor) that seem to have been made in reliance on the alleged contract, and that are of a sort that the vendee is *very unlikely to have committed* had the alleged oral contract not existed. Usually, the acts that the vendee claims to have made in reliance on the contract consist of his *making improvements on the property.*

      i. **Rationale based on reliable evidence:** Why does this acts-in-reliance exception exist? Well, one of the key functions of the Statute of Frauds in land-sale cases is to combat plaintiffs' incentive to give *perjured testimony* to the effect that the defendant orally agreed to make the sale. But if the vendee seems to have taken *real-world actions* in reliance on the asserted oral agreement — acts like improving the property — the risk that the vendee is falsely claiming that an oral agreement was made is reduced.

      ii. **The "unequivocally referable to the contract" standard:** Even if the would-be vendee has taken actions that she asserts were made in reliance on the vendor's oral agreement to sell her the property, how does the court *know* that these actions were indeed taken on account of such an oral agreement of sale, rather than for *some other agreement* relating to the land (e.g., an oral lease)? To guard against *false claims* of reliance, many courts apply a tough standard: the would-be purchaser has to show that her actions were *"unequivocally referable"* to the asserted oral agreement of sale, and not explainable by some other motive that's plausible under the known circumstances.

         (1) **Payments might be on account of lease:** For example, suppose the only acts that the plaintiff / vendee claims she committed in reliance on an oral promise of sale are the making of several small payments, one per month, that the plaintiff says were *partial payments* towards an oral installment-sale agreement. A court applying the tough "unequivocally referable" standard is likely to say that this standard is *not* met here, because the small, periodic pay-

ments might really have been intended to be *lease payments*, not installment-purchase payments.

(2) Strict interpretation of unequivocal-referable test: Some courts that apply the "unequivocally referable" standard do so in an especially *strict way*, by saying that the standard is satisfied only if the court, while considering *solely* the *acts* of alleged part performance — and *not* considering at all the words of the *asserted oral promise* — can conclude that the performance almost certainly can be explained only by the defendant's promise to transfer title. As the opinion that originated the "unequivocally referable" test put it, there must be "performance which *alone* and *without aid of words of promise* is *unintelligible* or at least *extraordinary* unless as an incident of [intended] ownership[.] ... [W]hat is *done must itself supply the key* to what is promised." *Burns v. McCormick*, 233 N.Y. 230 (1922) (Cardozo, J.).

(3) Looser interpretation of unequivocally-referable: But other courts, even while purporting to apply the unequivocally-referable standard, make the standard considerably *easier* than the *Burns* court did for the plaintiff / vendee to satisfy. These courts typically do so by tweaking the *Burns* approach in two ways:

[1] They consider *all of the surrounding circumstances,* and the alleged words of oral promise (not *just* the *actions* alleged to constitute part performance); and

[2] They require merely that an outsider would *"naturally and reasonably"* conclude (essentially a preponderance-of-the-evidence standard) from these circumstances that the alleged oral contract was really made, rather than requiring as the court did in *Burns* that there be *no other intelligible explanation* for the part performance aside from the alleged oral contract (essentially a beyond-a-reasonable-doubt standard).

The case in the following example illustrates this easier-to-satisfy version of the unequivocally-referable standard.

Example: Michael and Karen Brumlow are the would-be vendees (we'll call them the "Buyers") of a parcel of real estate from Warren Beaver ("Seller"). Michael has worked for Seller in Seller's business for a number of years. In 2000, Seller purchases 24 acres, and in 2001, the Buyers ask Seller whether Seller will sell some of this land to them so that they can put a home on it. Seller orally agrees to do so (or so the Buyers later claim), and the parties walk the specific boundaries of the land that Seller will sell. Karen Brumlow, acting in reliance (as Seller knows) on Seller's promise to convey, cashes in several retirement accounts in order to pay for a mobile home and various improvements to the land, and pays a substantial penalty for doing so. The Buyers take possession of the land, purchase a double-wide mobile home that they move onto the land, construct a skirt around the home, pour concrete footers and a concrete foundation, build a deck, and make other improvements to the site. In all, the Buyers spend $85,000 in reliance on Seller's promise to convey. In

2004, after the Buyers have been in possession for three years, but without the parties' having agreed on a date for the sale or on a specific price, Michael quits his job with Seller and starts working for a competitor. Seller, apparently in retaliation, refuses to enter into a written contract of sale, and instead requires the Buyers to sign a document that is in fact a monthly-rental agreement (which they don't read, and assume is an installment-sale contract). Seller refuses to consummate the sale, claims that the Buyers are in violation of the lease, and sues to have them ejected. The Buyers counterclaim, alleging that Seller is bound by his 2001 oral agreement to convey the property (for what Buyers say should be a fair-market price as determined by the court).

Held, for the Buyers. An agreement can be taken out of the Statute of Frauds by a part performance that is ***"unequivocally referable"*** to the alleged oral agreement. Seller claims that this standard is not met here, because the Buyers' actions are also consistent with ones "taken by a person who needs a place to live and who is given an opportunity to reside on another person's property." But the "unequivocally referable" concept does *not* require, as Seller contends, that outside of the alleged oral agreement there can be ***"no other plausible explanation"*** for the part performance. "Unequivocally referable" means *merely* that "an outsider, knowing all of the circumstances of the case except for the claimed oral agreement, would ***naturally and reasonably conclude*** that a contract existed regarding the [sale of] the land[.]" Here, where the Buyers took possession of the property and made valuable, permanent, and substantial improvements to it, all with the knowledge and consent of the Seller over a multi-year period, an observer could indeed "naturally and reasonably conclude" that the Buyers took these actions solely because Seller had promised to sell them the land for its fair-market value. *Beaver v. Brumlow*, 231 P.3d 628 (New Mex. Ct. of App. 2010).

iii. **Restatement goes beyond unequivocally-referable standard:** Some courts, and the Restatement, *skip* the above *"unequivocally referable"* rule *completely*, making it much *easier* for the vendee to demonstrate enough reliance on the oral agreement sufficient to remove the agreement from the Statute of Frauds.

(1) **Text of Restatement:** Here's how the Restatement phrases its reliance-based exception to the land-transfer provision:

> A contract for the transfer of an interest in land ***may be specifically enforced*** notwithstanding failure to comply with the Statute of Frauds if it is established that the party seeking enforcement, in ***reasonable reliance on the contract*** and on the ***continuing assent*** of the party against whom enforcement is sought, has ***so changed his position that injustice can be avoided only by specific enforcement.***

> Rest. 2d, § 129.

(2) **Abandons "unequivocally referable" requirement:** As noted, the Restatement explicitly ***abandons*** the "unequivocally referable" requirement, as long as *either* the overall circumstances furnish ***clear evidence*** of reliance by the vendee on the oral agreement, or the defendant/vendor ***admits*** the agreement's existence. See § 129, Comment d, stating that the unequivocal-referable

requirement "is not insisted on if the making of the promise is **admitted** or is **clearly proved**."

    iv. Must be action for specific performance: Most courts, and the Restatement, hold that for the part-performance doctrine to take a land-sale contract out of the Statute of Frauds, the would-be buyer must be **seeking specific performance of the contract**, not an award of damages.

Quiz Yourself on

THE LAND CONTRACT PROVISION

75. Witch orally agrees to sell her home, Gingerbread House, to Hansel, for $10,000. An hour later Gretel comes along and makes Witch a better offer — $15,000. Witch calls Hansel and tells him the deal is off. Can Hansel enforce the $10,000 deal?

76. Mayor of Munchkinland owns property next door to property owned by Dorothy. Mayor says to Dorothy, "Anytime you or your successors in interest to your property want to use the yellow brick road across my property, you're free to do so. This easement will be permanent." The next day, Mayor changes his mind, before Dorothy has ever used the road. May Dorothy have the easement enforced?

77. Pope orally agrees to sell his country place, Santa Maria del Grazie, to da Vinci. da Vinci gives Pope a down payment and Pope conveys the property to da Vinci. da Vinci moves in and begins to paint a giant mural, "The Last Supper," on one of the walls. da Vinci subsequently decides he doesn't like the décor of the place and moves out without paying another lira. Can Pope enforce the agreement?

78. Same basic facts as prior question. Now, however, assume that the parties orally agree on a purchase price and terms, and further agree that da Vinci will move onto the property and perhaps "do some painting and decorating there" in advance of the conveyance." (Pope knows that da Vinci paints great murals and ceilings.) No money changes hands, and da Vinci moves in and paints the mural. He then demands the conveyance, and Pope refuses to make it (though he's willing to pay da Vinci the fair market value of the mural). Will a court order Pope to make the conveyance?

Answers

75. No, because it violates the Statute of Frauds. Contracts for the sale of "an interest in land" require a writing to be enforceable.

76. No. An easement is considered an "interest in land." Therefore, a promise to convey it falls within the general rule that a promise to convey an "interest in land" must be in writing.

77. Yes. It's true that contracts for the sale of land normally require a writing. But where the seller has made the contracted-for conveyance, he can recover the contract price even though the original agreement was not in writing.

78. Probably not. The land-sale provision applies here, unless some exception to it applies. The only exception that might apply is the doctrine that where the vendee relies to his detriment, this may entitle him to specific enforcement. However, this exception applies only where the vendee's conduct is **"unequivocally referable"** to the alleged oral contract of conveyance (i.e., the vendee's conduct would never have occurred unless the alleged contract of conveyance actually occurred). Here, da Vinci, given his profession, might have moved temporarily onto the property just to paint the mural as a contract painting job for

Pope, so it probably can't be said that da Vinci's acts of moving in and painting the mural are "unequivocally referable" to the alleged contract of conveyance. Therefore, the detrimental-reliance exception probably doesn't apply, and the oral contract is unenforceable.

V. THE ONE-YEAR PROVISION

A. General rule: If a promise contained in a contract is *incapable of being fully performed within one year* after the making of the contract, the contract must be in writing. Rest. 2d, § 130(1).

> **Example:** Boss and Emp orally agree that Emp will work for Boss for a 2-year period commencing that day, the contract terminable on either side only for cause. Because this is an agreement that cannot be fully performed within one year from its making, the agreement is not binding on either side since it is not in writing — thus Boss can't sue Emp if Emp quits without cause, and Emp can't sue Boss if Boss fires him without cause.

1. Time runs from making of the contract: The one year period is measured from the *time of execution of the contract,* not the time it will take the parties to perform.

> **Example:** Network and Star agree on Jan. 20, 2012 that Star will appear in a one-hour live program to be broadcast on Feb. 15, 2013. This agreement will not be enforceable by either if not in writing, because the contract cannot be performed within one year of the date it was made. The fact that performance will only take one hour is irrelevant — what counts is whether more than one year will necessarily elapse between the making of the agreement and the end of performance, and that is so here. See C&P, p. 743.

B. Performance must be impossible within the one-year period: The one-year provision applies only if complete performance is *impossible* within one year after the making of the contract. The fact that performance within one year is *highly unlikely*, or that the parties fully expect that it will take more than one year, is *not* enough to make the contract fall within the Statute.

> **Example:** D, an insurance company, orally promises to insure P's house against fire for five years. P in turn promises to pay the premium within a week. The contract does not fall within the one-year provision, since it is possible (however unlikely) that the house might burn, and that D might pay up on the policy, within one year. See Rest. 2d, § 130, Illustr. 1.

1. Contingency judged from time of contract's execution: The possibility of performing the contract within one year must be *judged as of the time the contract is made,* not by benefit of hindsight. Thus if an insurance company orally agrees to pay a policy holder $10,000 on his death, the contract is not covered by the one-year provision (because the insured might die within one year of the contract's making), even if it turns out in fact that the insured does not die until 15 years after the contract was made. C&P, p. 745.

a. Contracts to leave bequest: Similarly, an oral promise to leave a bequest in one's will, or to pay a sum at the death of some other named person, is not within the Statute, since the death may occur within a year of the making of the contract. Many states, however, have statutes that extend the Statute of Frauds to contracts which are not per-formable before the end of a named person's lifetime, and to contracts to make a bequest. See C&P, p. 745.

2. **Impossibility or other excuse for non-performance:** But if the contract provides that performance is to continue for more than a year, the fact that the contract might be *discharged* by *impossibility, frustration*, or some other excuse for non-performance, will *not* take the contract out of the Statute of Frauds. Murray, p. 660. That's because it is only the possibility of "*performance,*" not the possibility of "*discharge*" that takes a contract out of the one-year provision.

   a. **Personal service contracts:** For instance, all personal services contracts automati-cally terminate at the death of the party who is to perform the services. Yet, according to most courts, the *possibility* that that party might *die within one year* is *not* enough to prevent the Statute of Frauds from applying. If the party dies, according to this majority view, the contract has merely been *discharged*, not *performed*. Rest. 2d, § 198, Comment b and Illustr. 5, 7.

   b. **Difficult line to draw:** It will often be difficult to tell whether a certain kind of pos-sible termination is by performance or by discharge. The test is whether, if the termi-nation in question occurs, the contract has *fulfilled its principal purpose*; if so, there has been performance. This test produces the following results:

      i. **Lifetime employment:** A promise to employ someone for his *lifetime* is proba-bly *not* within the one-year provision, since if that person dies, the essential pur-pose of guaranteeing him a job forever has been satisfied. See Rest. 2d, § 130, Illustr. 2.

      ii. **Employment contract for fixed term:** By contrast, a promise to *employ* some-one for a *fixed term* of more than one year *is* within the one-year provision, even though the employee might end the contract by dying or becoming permanently disabled — here, the employee's death or disability is usually considered to have prevented the contract from fulfilling its principal purpose (employment for the stated term). In other words, death or discharge is an event of discharge, not per-formance. So the contract falls within the one-year provision.

      Example: Boss and Worker orally agree that Worker will work for Boss for 5 years. Even though the contract would end at the moment of Worker's death or disability (which might happen in the first year), that possibility doesn't prevent the one-year provision of the Statute from applying. (Such an event would be a discharge, not a "full performance.") Therefore, the agreement is unenforceable against either party, because it's not in writing.

      iii. **Covenant not to compete:** On the other hand, a promise by a seller of a business *not to compete* with the buyer for, say, five years is *not* within the one-year provi-sion, since if the seller dies within a year, the buyer has received the equivalent of full performance. (He knows the seller will not be competing with him, which is the purpose of the contract.) See Rest. 2d, § 130, Illustr. 9.

C. Alternative performances: If the contract gives one or both parties the choice between two or more performances, the contract is not within the one-year provision if *any* of the alternatives can be performed within one year from the time of the making of the contract. C&P, p. 747.

1. Termination clauses: This rule has sometimes, but not always, been applied to a contract in which one or both parties has the choice between performing fully, or *terminating* the contract by giving notice. If the full performance must necessarily take more than one year, but the notice of termination may be given within one year of contracting, is the contract within the Statute? The courts are deeply *split*, and it is hard to say which view is followed by a majority of courts.

    a. Notice as discharge: The traditional view is that a contract that has a stated duration of more than one year, but that gives a party the right to terminate by giving notice within one year, is not *performable* within one year. Instead, the giving of notice simply *excuses* the contract, in the same way that impossibility would excuse it. Thus this view holds that the contract *must be in writing.*

    b. Other view: The alternative (and perhaps more modern) view is that such a contract does *not* fall within the one-year provision. Adherents of this position take the view that the giving of notice to terminate is a form of *performance*. In other words, the party with the right to terminate has a choice between performing for the more-than-one-year duration of the contract, or of performing for less than one year by terminating. This view would thus apply the ordinary rule relating to alternative promises, discussed above, and would *exempt* such contracts from the Statute.

        i. Second Restatement views intention of the parties: The Second Restatement does not make a clear choice between one position or the other, but simply requires the court to distinguish between a termination right that the parties intended as a *means of performance*, and a termination right that the parties intended as a kind of *discharge*. Thus Illustr. 6 to § 130, involving a five-year employment contract providing that either party may terminate by giving 30 days notice, is said to be "one of uncertain duration" and therefore not within the one-year provision of the Statute. Illustr. 7, on the other hand, sets forth the same contract but with a provision allowing the employee to "quit at any time." This contract, the Restatement says, is within the Statute.

        In other words a clause calling for a full 30 days notice is apparently to be viewed as manifesting the parties' intention that notice be a substitute form of performance; but a clause allowing the employee to simply quit is to be viewed as showing the parties' intention to allow one party to be discharged. See Murray, p. 661-62.

D. Full performance on one side: Suppose that a given oral contract is, at the time of its making, not capable of being fully performed on both sides within one year. If one party to the contract *fully performs*, does this full performance take the contract out of the Statute?

1. Full performance: Most courts, and the Second Restatement (§ 130), say yes: full performance by one party *removes the contract* from the one-year provision. And that's true even though it actually took (or would necessarily take) that party more than one year to perform. C&P, p. 812.

> **Example:** On Jan. 1, 2011, Producer and Star orally agree that Star will perform in Producer's Broadway show 6 nights a week for 18 months, beginning on July 1, 2012. Star's fee for the entire run is set at a total of $200,000. Because Star develops cash needs, Producer prepays the entire $200,000 on May 1, 2012. Star then refuses to perform. Star's promise to perform is not within the one-year provision, because Producer has fully performed. That's true even though Producer's performance didn't occur until more than one year after the making of the contract. Cf. Rest. 2d § 130, Illustr. 14.

2. **Part performance:** But *part* performance by one party does *not* remove the contract from the one-year provision, and thus neither side may sue to enforce it. Rest. 2d § 130, Comment e. However, in some cases this part performance may *estop* one or both parties from claiming the Statute of Frauds. See *infra*, p. 301.

E. **One-year provision applies to all contracts:** The rule that a contract that is incapable of performance within one year after its making must satisfy the Statute, applies to *all* contracts. For instance, even though a mutual exchange of promises to marry does not fall within the "marriage" provision of the Statute (see *supra*, p. 279), the engagement would have to be in writing if by its terms it was not to be fully performed (through marriage) within one year. Similarly, a *contract for the sale of goods* for, say, $400 that is incapable of being performed within a one-year period (as where delivery is specified for 18 months after signing of the contract) must meet the Statute even though under the UCC rules regarding sales contracts, only contracts for more than $500 are covered. C&P, pp. 751-52.

Quiz Yourself on
THE ONE-YEAR PROVISION

79. The Ramm Beau Weaponry Company hires Einstein as its research director. The term of the employment contract is five years. As Ramm Beau knows at the moment of signing, Einstein is terminally ill when the contract is created, and is not expected to live more than nine months.

   (A) Must the contract be in writing to be enforceable?

   (B) Assume instead that Ramm Beau hired Einstein as an employee for the rest of his life. Must the contract be in writing to be enforceable?

80. Lear agrees to lease his Castle to Cordelia for nine months, with the lease to begin six months from the signing of the contract.

   (A) Must the lease be in writing under the Statute of Frauds?

   (B) Say instead that the lease is to begin immediately, and to last for nine months. Must the lease be in writing?

81. Charlie Tuna orally agrees to supply Chicken of the Sea with all the fish bait she requires over the next 18 months. Charlie fully performs his end of the agreement, but Chicken of the Sea fails to pay up. Charlie sues. Chicken of the Sea defends by arguing that the contract is unenforceable because it falls within the one-year provision of the Statute of Frauds. (Ignore the UCC's Statute of Frauds provision, governing

goods sales for more than $500; just concentrate on the one-year provision). Who wins?

Answers

79. **(A) Yes, because by its terms, the contract cannot be fully performed within one year, and so falls within the Statute of Frauds.** Any contract that by its terms cannot be "fully performed" within one year from its making must be in writing. Ramm Beau's principal purpose in making the contract is to have a research director for five years; therefore, if (as seems almost inevitable), Einstein dies before the end of the five years, the contract will have been "discharged," not "fully performed."

Note, by the way, that it doesn't matter what *actually* happens (i.e., whether Einstein in fact lives and works for the five years). What counts is the terms of the contract, and whether, analyzed as of the moment the contract is made, there is any possible way that the contract could be fully performed within one year. Since the answer is "no" even to this easier-to-satisfy question, the contract falls within the Statute and must be in writing.

(B) No. Now the contract is removed from the Statute of Frauds and does not have to be in writing, because it is capable of being "fully performed" in less than one year. That's because the contract is, by its terms, for Einstein's "life" — if Einstein dies in less than a year, the contract will nonetheless have been fully performed.

80. **(A) Yes.** What counts is not the length of the lease once it begins, but the time from the making of the lease until its full performance (its expiration). Although the lease itself is only for nine months, the contract cannot be performed within one year from the execution of the contract, so a writing is required.

(B) No. Now no writing is required because the contract can be fully performed within one year of its making. (Remember that leases for one year or less in duration do not constitute an "interest in land," so the "Land Contract" provision of the Statute of Frauds would not come into play here, either.)

81. **Charlie, according to most courts.** Most courts (and the Second Restatement) now hold that *full performance* by one party removes the contract from the one-year provision of the Statute of Frauds — even though the contract could not have been (and was not) fully performed within one year of its making.

VI. CONTRACT FOR THE SALE OF GOODS

A. **Goods versus other property under the UCC:** The UCC imposes several different Statute of Frauds requirements, depending on the kind of personal property involved. We shall be concerned here primarily with the rules regarding contracts for the sale of *goods*, covered by Article 2.

B. **General rule as to goods:** UCC § 2-201(1) provides that "a contract for the sale of goods for the price of *$500 or more* is not enforceable by way of action or defense unless there is *some writing sufficient to indicate that a contract for sale has been made*...." That section goes on to state fairly lenient rules as to what this writing must contain; these are discussed *infra*, p. 295. Here, we are concerned only with the rules for determining when the writing requirement applies.

   1. **Contracts combining services and goods:** Keep in mind that the Article 2 Statute of Frauds applies only where the contract itself falls within Article 2. Thus where the contract is *primarily for the provision of services*, but also includes the provision of goods,

the contract is *not* within Article 2, and it is only the provisions of the common-law Statute of Frauds (e.g., contracts not performable within one year) that may apply.

> **Example:** A construction contract that requires the contractor to supply goods (e.g., lumber, plumbing supplies, etc.) as part of the job will not be covered by the sale-of-goods provision, if the services account for the bulk of the contract's value. This will be true even if the goods have a value (to be paid by the customer) of more than $500.

2. **Exceptions to the UCC Statute:** Even if a sales contract is for more than $500, it is *exempted* from the Statute of Frauds requirement in three situations, by § 2-201(3):

   a. **Goods specially manufactured:** No writing is required "if the goods are to be *specially manufactured* for the buyer and are *not suitable for sale to others* in the ordinary course of the seller's business and the seller, before notice of repudiation is received and under circumstances which reasonably indicate that the goods are for the buyer, has made either a *substantial beginning* of their manufacture or *commitments* for their procurement." (§ 2-201(3)(a)). The reason for this exception is that the seller is highly unlikely to start producing custom-made goods for the buyer unless there has in fact been an oral contract.

> **Example:** Seller, a manufacturer of customized shopping bags, begins to manufacture 100,000 bags with Buyer's corporate name and logo on them. While the bags are in the process of being printed, Seller learns that Buyer doesn't plan to pay for the bags. There is no writing, but Seller asserts that Buyer orally ordered the bags and agreed to pay $3,000 for them.
>
> A court will hold the contract enforceable, because: (1) the customization of the bags constituted a "special manufacture" of goods that are "not suitable for sale to others in the ordinary course of the seller's business," and (2) Seller "made a substantial beginning of [the goods'] manufacture."

   b. **Estoppel by pleading or testimony:** Nor is a writing required "if the party against whom enforcement is sought *admits* in his pleading, testimony or otherwise in court that a *contract for sale was made*, but the contract is not enforceable under this provision beyond the quantity of goods admitted." (§ 2-201(3)(b)).

      i. **Important change:** This provision marks a change from the common-law rule, which permitted the defendant to admit that an oral agreement had been made and at the same time to use the Statute of Frauds as a defense. The sales contract defendant who wishes to assert the Statute must therefore be excessively careful in his pleading and in his testimony not to concede that some oral agreement was made.

   c. **Goods accepted or paid for:** A writing is not required "with respect to goods for which *payment has been made* and accepted or which have been *received and accepted.*" (§ 2-201(3)(c).) This is a sort of "part performance" doctrine, by which if the contract is partly performed on either side, it is enforceable as to the part which is performed. The court will presumably attempt to apportion the contract price, so that if a sale of 100 units for $1,000 is agreed upon, and the buyer accepts 10 units, he will have to pay $100 regardless of the market price of the units accepted.

Figure 9-1

The Statute of Frauds (S/F)

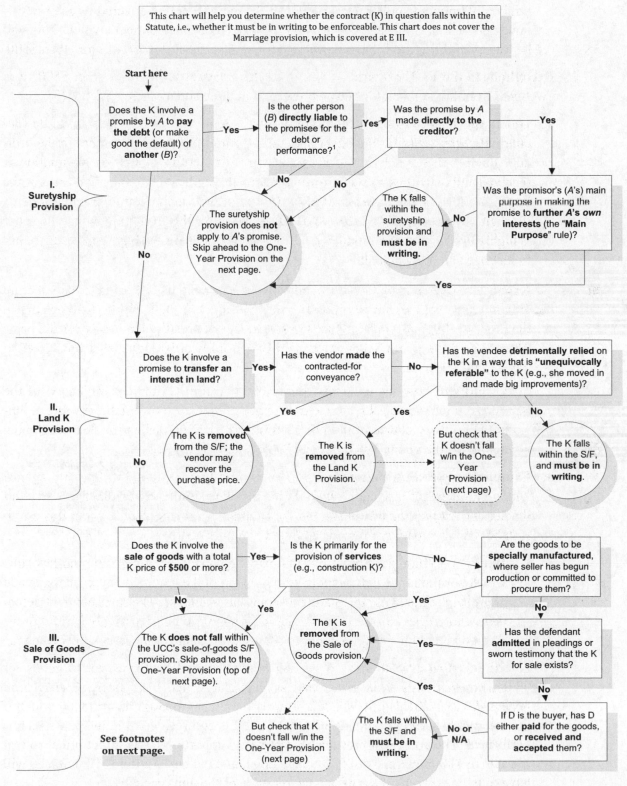

This chart will help you determine whether the contract (K) in question falls within the Statute, i.e., whether it must be in writing to be enforceable. This chart does not cover the Marriage provision, which is covered at E III.

Start here

I. Suretyship Provision

Does the K involve a promise by A to **pay the debt** (or make good the default) of **another** (B)?

— Yes → Is the other person (B) **directly liable** to the promisee for the debt or performance?[1]

— Yes → Was the promise by A made **directly to the creditor**?

— Yes → Was the promisor's (A's) main purpose in making the promise to **further A's own interests** (the "**Main Purpose**" rule)?

— No → The K falls within the suretyship provision and **must be in writing.**

— Yes → The suretyship provision does **not** apply to A's promise. Skip ahead to the One-Year Provision on the next page.

No / No → The suretyship provision does **not** apply to A's promise. Skip ahead to the One-Year Provision on the next page.

II. Land K Provision

Does the K involve a promise to **transfer an interest in land**?

— Yes → Has the vendor **made** the contracted-for conveyance?

— No → Has the vendee **detrimentally relied** on the K in a way that is "**unequivocally referable**" to the K (e.g., she moved in and made big improvements)?

— Yes → The K is **removed** from the S/F; the vendor may recover the purchase price.

— Yes → The K is **removed** from the Land K Provision.

— No → The K falls within the S/F, and **must be in writing**.

But check that K doesn't fall w/in the One-Year Provision (next page)

III. Sale of Goods Provision

Does the K involve the **sale of goods** with a total K price of **$500 or more**?

— Yes → Is the K primarily for the provision of **services** (e.g., construction K)?

— No → Are the goods to be **specially manufactured**, where seller has begun production or committed to procure them?

— No → The K **does not fall** within the UCC's sale-of-goods S/F provision. Skip ahead to the One-Year Provision (top of next page).

— Yes → The K is **removed** from the Sale of Goods provision.

— No → Has the defendant **admitted** in pleadings or sworn testimony that the K for sale exists?

— Yes → The K is **removed** from the Sale of Goods provision.

— No → If D is the buyer, has D either **paid** for the goods, or **received and accepted** them?

— No or N/A → The K falls within the S/F and **must be in writing**.

— Yes → The K is **removed** from the Sale of Goods provision.

But check that K doesn't fall w/in the One-Year Provision (next page)

See footnotes on next page.

Figure 9-1

The Statute of Frauds (cont.)

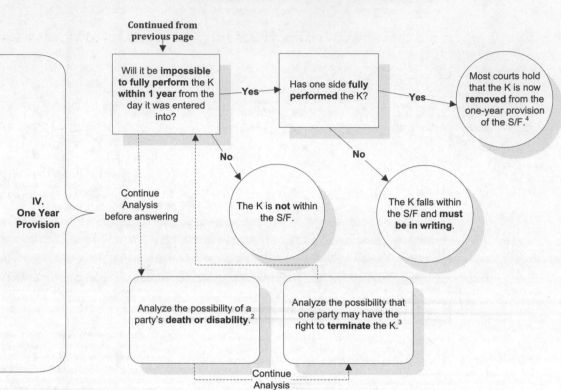

Notes to Figure 9-1

[1] The answer will be "no" where it's only the "surety" who's liable. <u>Example</u>: *A* telephones *B*, and says, "Send merchandise to *C*; I'll pay." Since *C* never ordered the merchandise, *C* isn't liable to *B*. Therefore, *A*'s promise isn't a true promise of surety, and isn't within the Suretyship provision.

[2] Depending on interpretation, a party's death or disability would either make performance "<u>complete</u>" within one year (in which case the contract would not be within the Statute) or would simply "<u>discharge</u>" the contract (in which case the contract would still be within the Statute). To decide which interpretation is correct, ask whether the <u>principal purpose</u> of the contract would be fulfilled even if a party died or became disabled within the year. If so, complete performance is possible within one year. See E V(B)(2).

<u>Examples where death/disability means full performance</u> (so the contract is not within the S/F): (1) *A* promises to employ *B* for *B*'s lifetime (if *B* dies, contract is fulfilled); (2) *A* sells her business to *B*, and promises not to compete for 5 years (if *A* dies, she won't be competing).

<u>Example where death means discharge</u> (so the promise is within the S/F and must be in writing): *A* employs *B* for a term of 4 years.

[3] Whether a party's exercise of the right to terminate the contract within the first year should be viewed as a form of "performance" (in which case the contract is not within the 1-year provision and need not be in writing) or as a form of "discharge" (with the opposite result) is determined by looking to whether the contract has fulfilled its principal purpose. See E V(B)(2)(b).

<u>Example</u>: A 5-year contract lets either party terminate by giving 30 days prior notice at any time. This would likely be found **not** within the Statute: the giving of notice in order to terminate would be a form of "performance" (the contract would have fulfilled its main purpose of lasting until proper termination), and that notice could happen within the first year.

[4] Therefore, the party who hasn't fully performed yet must <u>carry out the performance</u> that she orally agreed to make. That's true even if the fully-performing party's performance was not complete until more than one year after the contract was made.

d. **Non-statutory exceptions:**   In addition to these three statutory exceptions, case-law exceptions to the Code Statute of Frauds may also exist. For instance, an estoppel theory (*infra*, p. 300) might be used to protect the prospective buyer of a piece of machinery who had leased premises to house the machinery before the seller's repudiation of the oral agreement for the machine. See W&S, pp. 60-61.

Quiz Yourself on

CONTRACT FOR THE SALE OF GOODS

82. Kamp E-Kwipment Inc. agrees to sell fifteen pairs of hip boots to the Our Lady of 115th Street Convent for its annual retreat. The contract price is $700, although the merchandise has a wholesale price of $120. Must the contract be in writing to be enforceable?

83. Rosebud General Contractor agrees to build a fabulous home, Xanadu, for Charles Foster Kane in return for $750,000. The contract price includes all materials, which will have an aggregate value of $200,000. Must the contract comply with the Statute of Frauds?

84. Minnie and Mickey decide to get married. The Etty-Kette Paper Goods Company orally agrees to custom-make 350 party hats with Minnie and Mickey's names printed on them for the wedding for $675. After Etty-Kette begins to manufacture the hats, Minnie decides Mickey is a rat, and cancels the wedding. She also tries to cancel the hat contract. Can Etty-Kette enforce the oral agreement?

Answers

82. Yes. According to UCC § 2-201, a contract for the sale of goods priced at $500 or more must be in writing. The wholesale cost of the goods is irrelevant — what matters is the contract price.

83. No. Where, as here, the contract is primarily for the provision of services, the contract is not within Article 2 of the UCC, even though it also involves the sale of goods worth more than $500. Services contracts — no matter how large — need not be in writing (unless they cannot be completed in less than one year).

84. Yes. There is an exception to the "sale of goods" provision of the Statute of Frauds for goods that are "specially manufactured." § 2-201(3)(a). As long as the seller has made a "substantial beginning" on their manufacture, or has made "commitments for their procurement," the oral agreement will be enforceable. Since the facts tell us that Etty-Kette has begun manufacture, this condition is satisfied.

VII. SATISFACTION OF THE STATUTE BY A MEMORANDUM

A. **Requirement:**   In some cases, "the contract," in the sense of the entire agreement of the parties, will be in writing. If so, the Statute of Frauds is obviously satisfied. But the Statute may also be satisfied by something less than the complete written agreement of the parties; this something less is usually called a ***memorandum*** of the agreement.

B. **What memorandum must contain:**   A memorandum satisfies the Statute of Frauds if it meets all of these requirements:

❑ it reasonably ***identifies the subject*** of the contract,

❑ it indicates that a ***contract has been made*** between the parties,

❏   it states with reasonable certainty the ***essential terms*** of the contract; and

❏   it is ***signed*** "by or on behalf of ***the party to be charged.***" Rest. 2d, § 131.

1. **"Essential terms":**   There is no standard formula for determining what the "essential terms" are that must be listed in the memorandum. Many courts require only that the terms of the ***defendant's*** promise must be spelled out, and that the consideration he is to receive for his promise (i.e., in a bilateral contract, the plaintiff's promise) does not have to be contained in the memorandum. But other courts hold that since the defendant's obligation to perform is constructively conditional on the plaintiff's substantial performance (see *supra*, p. 215), the plaintiff's promise must be included in the memorandum. See Murray, p. 671.

2. **Oral evidence to supplement or interpret memorandum:**   The plaintiff may introduce ***oral*** evidence to aid in the interpretation of the memorandum, if it is ambiguous. But he may probably not introduce oral evidence to ***supplement*** the memorandum, if an essential term is simply missing rather than ambiguously recorded. C&P, p. 752-53.

3. **Item not intended as memorandum:**   A writing may suffice as a memorandum for Statute of Frauds purposes even though it was intended for a completely different purpose. Thus even a memorandum repudiating an oral agreement may suffice.

    Example: *A* and *B* make an oral contract in which *A* promises to sell Blackacre to *B* for $5,000. *A* writes and signs a letter to *B* in which he accurately summarizes the terms of the bargain, but adds "our agreement was oral. It is therefore not binding upon me, and I won't carry it out." The letter is a sufficient memorandum to bind *A*. Rest. 2d, § 133, Illustr. 4.

4. **Need not be addressed to or sent to other party:** The   memorandum   need   ***not***   be ***addressed to the other party*** to the agreement. Nor need it be ***sent*** to the other party, so a writing sent to some ***third party*** (or even one that ***never leaves the possession of the writer*** until the litigation) can suffice.

    Example: *A* orally promises *B* that if *B* will extend credit to *C*, *A* will guarantee repayment. *A* then writes a letter to *C*, saying "I have guaranteed *B* that I will repay your debt if you do not." Even though this writing was not addressed to *B*, or ever sent to him, it's a memorandum that satisfies the statute, making *A*'s guarantee enforceable against him.

5. **Can be created after the fact:**   A writing will satisfy the memorandum requirement even if it is created ***after*** the oral promise (even, according to most courts, after the suit has begun). See Rest. 2d, § 136, Comment b. Thus in the above example, even if *A* didn't write the letter to *C* until weeks after the oral promise, the letter would still satisfy the memorandum requirement.

C. **Signature:**   A memorandum must be ***signed by or on behalf of "the party to be charged,"*** i.e., the party against whom enforcement of the contract is sought. In the ordinary case this will be the defendant, but in the case of a counterclaim, it may be the plaintiff.

1. **Definition of signature:**   "Signature" is loosely defined. A party's initials will suffice, as will the typewriting of his name, if done under his direction.

a. **"Digital" signatures:** In fact, under a 2000 federal statute, the Electronic Signatures in Global and National Commerce Act (colloquially known as "E-Sign"), *"electronic" signatures must be recognized* for statute-of-frauds purposes. See 15 U.S.C. §§ 7001(a)(1) and (2). For instance, suppose a consumer sends a merchant an e-mail ("Send me 5 widgets at $149 apiece"), and the e-mail contains the consumer's name in the "Sender" field. Because of E-sign, the UCC's version of the statute of frauds will be deemed satisfied. The same is apparently true if the consumer enters into a merchant's web site information indicating an intent to buy goods.

2. **UCC exception:** Under UCC § 2-201(2), a memorandum sent by one merchant to another may under certain circumstances be enforceable against the recipient, even though the latter did not sign it. See *infra*, p. 296.

3. **Enforceable against only one party:** Observe that the requirement of a signature by the party to be charged means that some contracts will be enforceable against one party, but not against the other.

> **Example:** Buyer orally agrees to buy Owner's house for $200,000. Owner prepares two copies of a purchase-and-sale agreement that correctly matches the oral understanding, signs both, and sends them to Buyer. While the copies are in transit, Owner dies, and his estate asserts that there was no agreement.
>
> The court will conclude that the signed copies are sufficient as a memorandum binding against the estate. But notice that if the estate wanted to enforce the contract and it was *Buyer* that wanted to escape, Buyer would be able to do so — the signed copies would be a memorandum effective only against the estate (whose principal signed them), not against Buyer.

4. **Agent's signature:** If the memo is signed by a party's authorized agent, it will normally be enforceable against that party, even if the agent's authority is not itself in writing. Many states, however, have separate statutes providing that if a contract entered into by an agent on behalf of his principal must be in writing, the agent's authority must also be in writing. See C&P, pp. 757-58.

D. **UCC memorandum requirements:** The UCC imposes a somewhat more *lenient* memorandum requirement than is imposed by the non-UCC statutory and case law of most states. § 2-201(1) provides that where the Statute of Frauds applies, it must be satisfied by:

> "some writing *sufficient to indicate that a contract for sale has been made between the parties and signed by the party against whom enforcement is sought* or by his authorized agent or broker. A writing is not insufficient because it limits or incorrectly states a term agreed upon but the contract is not enforceable under this paragraph beyond the quantity of goods shown in such writing."

1. **Error or omission:** In non-Code cases, the omission of a material term, or an error as to such a term, renders the memorandum ineffective. But by the Code language quoted above, the memorandum is effective provided solely that it indicates "that a contract for sale has been made between the parties...." Comment 1 to the Section states that the memorandum "need not indicate which party is the buyer and which the seller.... The price, time and place of payment or delivery, the general quality of the goods, or any particular warranties may be omitted."

a. **Quantity term:** Notice carefully the last sentence of § 2-201(1): "the contract is *not* enforceable ... *beyond the quantity* of goods *shown in such writing*." So the plaintiff may recover only for the *quantity actually stated in the memorandum*, even if he can prove by convincing collateral evidence that the parties orally agreed on a larger quantity.

b. **Price term:** Since the memorandum may be sufficient even if the price term is not present, the plaintiff may introduce *collateral evidence* showing that a particular price was agreed upon. He might do this by showing that both parties intended to rely on a particular price list or catalog, or he might simply show that they intended the current "market" price. Recall that under § 2-305(1) the court may fix "a reasonable price at the time of delivery" if the parties have left the price term open. Thus not only does the plaintiff not have to produce a memorandum containing the price, but he does not necessarily even have to show that there was oral agreement as to price.

2. **Confirmation from one merchant to another:** In the non-UCC cases, the memorandum must be signed by the party against whom enforcement is sought. This is generally true under the Code, with one important exception:

> "Between merchants if within a reasonable time a writing *in confirmation* of the contract and sufficient against the sender is received and the party receiving it has reason to know its contents, it satisfies the requirements [of a writing] against such party unless written notice of objection to its contents is given within 10 days after it is received."

§ 2-201(2).

a. **Rule summarized:** In other words, a *merchant* who receives a *signed confirmation* from the other party will be *bound* by it just as if he had signed it, unless he promptly objects. The operation of this provision, and the reasons for it, are illustrated by the following example.

Example: Buyer and Seller are both merchants. Buyer telephones Seller to order 1,000 widgets, at $10 apiece. Immediately after receiving the order, Seller sends a written confirmation to the contract, correctly listing the quantity and price. This confirmation constitutes a memorandum which would be enforceable by Buyer against Seller.

In the absence of the provision quoted above, Buyer would be able to "play the market." That is, he could wait between the time of the contract and the time for delivery to see what happened to the market price of widgets; if the price went above $10, he could enforce the contract against the Seller by virtue of the confirmation; if the price fell below $10, he could refuse delivery, and be immune from suit because of the Statute. But by § 2-201(2), Buyer will be prevented from playing the market in this way. Unless he objects in writing within 10 days after receiving the memo, he will be bound by it, just as if he had signed it. (Of course, he still gets 10 days in which to play the market, but in the case of a contract contemplating delivery several months after contracting, his time for risk-free speculation has been considerably diminished.) See W&S, pp. 44-45.

Note: But remember once again the last sentence of § 2-201(1): "the contract is not enforceable ... ***beyond the quantity*** of goods ***shown in such writing.***" This rule applies to ***confirmations*** used against the non-signing merchant, too (not just to ordinary contract documents signed by both parties). So if, in the above example, Seller's confirmation erroneously contained the quantity "500" (instead of the orally-agreed-upon 1,000), that's all Seller could recover for.

VIII. EFFECT OF NON-COMPLIANCE

A. Effect where only part of the contract is within the Statute: Suppose that some of the promises contained in a contract are within the Statute of Frauds, but that other promises are not. As a general rule, ***no part of the contract is enforceable*** if ***any part*** of it fails to satisfy the Statute. The reason for this is that otherwise, the party whose promise did not fall within the Statute would be forced to perform it, while the other party would not have to perform his promise, obviously an unfair result.

1. **Exceptions:** However, there are a number of exceptions, in which part of a contract will be enforced even though other parts are within the Statute:

   a. **All promises within Statute already performed:** If ***all*** the promises that are within the Statute have ***already been performed***, the ***remaining promises are enforceable***. This rule is a fair one because it guarantees that the party who has performed will receive the agreed-for exchange, yet does not judicially force a party to perform a promise that is within the Statute. See C&P, pp. 765-66.

   b. **Partial enforcement:** If the ***plaintiff*** has ***fully performed his part*** of the agreement, and the defendant's performance consists of a part that falls within the Statute, and a part that does not, the court will order the defendant to ***perform that part which does not fall within the Statute***, if the plaintiff is willing to abandon his right to the part that does.

   Example: Plaintiff, a movie producer, orally agrees to pay D, an actor, $100,000 for two film appearances. The first, and most important, appearance is to occur four months after the oral agreement; the second is to occur two years after the agreement. If P makes the $100,000 payment, the court will order D to make the first appearance (which is not subject to the Statute) or pay damages, even though it will not order him to make the second one (since it falls within the one-year provision).

   c. **Full and part performance:** We have already seen that with respect to ***certain sections*** of the Statute, ***full*** or ***part*** performance on one side may render the contract enforceable.

      i. **Land contracts:** Thus full performance by the vendor under a land contract, or part performance plus detrimental reliance by the vendee, may render the contract enforceable. See *supra*, p. 280.

      ii. **One-year provision:** Similarly, full performance on one side takes a contract out of the one-year provision, in most jurisdictions. See *supra*, p. 287. Part performance, however, does not.

> **iii. Sales of goods:** A contract for a sale of goods is enforceable to the extent that the goods have been accepted, or paid for. See *supra*, p. 290.

IX. ORAL RESCISSION AND MODIFICATION

A. Oral rescission: Suppose that a particular agreement is reduced to writing, and that had this agreement not been in writing, it would have been unenforceable under the Statute of Frauds. Is a subsequent *oral rescission* (i.e., cancellation) of this contract effective? Generally, the answer is *yes*. See Rest. 2d, § 148. In other words, the *rescission does not have to satisfy the Statute of Frauds.*

B. Modification: Where a contract undergoes an oral *modification*, rather than a rescission, the applicability and effect of the Statute of Frauds depends largely on whether the contract, as modified, falls within the Statute.

   1. **Modified contract viewed as if it were original contract:** To determine whether an oral modification of an existing contract is effective (whether the existing contract is oral or written), *the contract as modified must be treated as if it were an original contract*. That is, both the terms contained in the original contract that are left unmodified, plus the newly-modified terms, must be examined to see whether anything is within the Statute of Frauds. Rest. 2d, § 149(1).

      a. **UCC:** The UCC explicitly imposes this result for contracts for the sale of goods. See § 2-209(3): "The requirements of the statute of frauds … must be *satisfied if the contract as modified is within its provisions*."

      Example: Seller orally agrees to sell Buyer goods worth $400. Two days later the parties modify the contract, so that it now calls for goods worth $600. The contract as modified must meet the Statute of Frauds, so an oral modification would be of no effect.

   2. **Effect of unenforceability:** Viewing the contract as described in Par. (1) above, if it is unenforceable because of the Statute of Frauds, under the majority approach *the original contract is left standing,* at least in non-UCC cases. In other words, the modification is treated as if it never occurred. Rest. 2d, § 149(2).

      Example: Seller promises to sell Buyer a particular house for $40,000, title closing to occur in 30 days. Both parties sign a sufficient memorandum, which does not contain any requirement that subsequent modifications be in writing. The next day, the parties orally agree for the closing to be postponed until 60 days. The oral modification is not enforceable, because the contract as modified must be viewed as a whole (i.e., as a contract for the sale of land, plus a closing date). As such, it is within the Statute of Frauds. Under the Restatement (and majority) view, because the modification is not enforceable the original contract remains enforceable as if the modification had not occurred. Cf. Rest. 2d, § 149, Illustr. 5.

      a. **UCC:** The UCC doesn't say whether the same result occurs when a contract for the sale of goods is modified by an oral agreement and the contract as modified would fall within the Statute.

    i.   **Supported by original documentation:** Some authorities suggest that in this situation, as long as the *original writing was sufficient* to make the original deal enforceable, the deal *as modified* will *also be enforceable* as long as its *basic terms* are the same. For instance, suppose that price and quantity are unchanged (and are reflected in the original memorandum); an oral change in some non-essential term like delivery date or warranty information might well be enforceable. This approach is sometimes called the *"passing through"* theory. FY&S p. 280.

  3.   **Reliance on oral modification:** Suppose that an oral modification is made, but turns out not to be enforceable because the contract as modified is within the Statute of Frauds. As we have seen above, the modification will not normally be enforced. But if either party has *materially changed his position in reliance on the modification*, the court may enforce the modification notwithstanding the Statute. Rest. 2d, § 150.

      Example: Suppose that in the above example, Buyer had extended his present apartment lease in reliance on the oral 30-day extension. Buyer's action in reliance on the modification will render the modification enforceable, even though strictly speaking the modification does not satisfy the Statute of Frauds.

C. **No-oral-rescission-or-modification clauses:** The parties are always free to *agree*, in the original writing, that the contract may not be rescinded or modified except via a writing signed by both. Such a clause will be *enforced*.

  1.   **Sale of goods:** In the case of contracts for the sale of goods, the UCC expressly provides for the enforcement of such no-oral-rescission-or-modification clauses: "a signed agreement which *excludes modification or rescission* except by a signed writing *cannot be otherwise modified or rescinded....*" (§ 2-209(2).) But, if such a written contract is between a merchant and a non-merchant, and the contract form is supplied by the merchant, the clause must be separately signed by the non-merchant. (§ 2-209(2).)

    a.   **Invalid rescission as waiver:** If an oral rescission or modification of a contract for the sale of goods is ineffective because it violates a no-oral-rescission-or-modification clause in the original contract, the rescission or modification may nonetheless "operate as a *waiver.*" (§ 2-209(4).) This means that if, following such an ineffective rescission or modification, one party *changes his position* (as by buying the contracted-for goods elsewhere), the other party will have waived his rights to insist upon enforcement of the original contract.

      i.   **Retraction:** However, such a waiver may be *retracted* "unless the retraction would be unjust in view of a material change of position in reliance on the waiver." (§ 2-209(5).)

      Example: Buyer and Seller agree in writing that Seller will ship certain goods to Buyer to arrive by Dec. 1. The total contract price is $10,000 (bringing the contract within the Statute of Frauds). The contract says that no oral modification will be effective. On Nov. 15, Seller phones Buyer and says, "Our shipping department is running a little behind; can we have until Dec. 10?" Buyer says, "Yes." One hour later, Buyer realizes that the later shipment will cause him problems, so he phones back and says to Seller, "I must now insist on the original Dec. 1 date."

Assuming that during the intervening hour, Seller has not changed his position in reliance on the extra time, Buyer's retraction of the waiver is effective, and the due date is now restored to the original Dec. 1 date.

X. RESTITUTION, RELIANCE AND ESTOPPEL

A. Remedies generally: We have seen a number of instances in which, although a contract is within the Statute of Frauds, actions by the parties remove it from the Statute. These rules, such as the rule regarding full performance by the vendor in a land contract, allow actual enforcement *of the contract* despite the Statute in order to prevent injustice.

Here, we'll examine the awarding of damages in *quasi-contract* to prevent injustice in Statute of Frauds cases; two distinct measures of damages, restitution and reliance, may be awarded in this context. Finally, we'll examine the use of *promissory estoppel* to prevent unjust use of the Statute of Frauds; under the promissory estoppel doctrine, the court may award either contract-based damages, or damages that are more typical of quasi-contract suits (i.e., restitution and reliance damages).

B. Quasi-contractual recovery: A plaintiff who has rendered part performance under an oral agreement that is within the Statute of Frauds may recover in quasi-contract for the *value of the benefits* she has conferred upon the defendant. These benefits may be in the form of a cash payment (as by the vendee under a land contract), or by the performance of services.

> **Example:** Gardener orally contracts to maintain the lawns at Homeowner's home for a 2-year term, at $100 per month. After he has worked for 4 months, Homeowner repudiates the contract. Gardener may sue in quasi-contract and recover the reasonable value to Homeowner of his services during the 4-month period.

1. Not limited by contract price: The plaintiff's quasi-contractual recovery is *not limited*, according to most courts, to the *pro-rata contract price.* See C&P, p. 771. Thus in the above example, if Gardener could show that the market value of his services was $700, he might be able to recover the sum, rather than $400 (which would be the pro-rata contract price).

2. Plaintiff must not be in material default: In order to recover in quasi-contract for part performance, the plaintiff must in most states show that he was *not materially in default* under the terms of the oral agreement. C&P, p. 769. In other words, even if the plaintiff has partly performed, he may not recover the value of his performance if it materially deviated from the terms of the (unenforceable) oral agreement.

3. Reliance damages: Usually, the measure of damages for a part-performing plaintiff whose contract is unenforceable because of the Statute is his restitutionary interest, i.e., the extent to which his performance has benefited the defendant. Increasingly, however, the courts have been willing to protect a plaintiff's *reliance* interest, i.e., the expenditures he has made in preparing to perform, even where these expenditures have not directly benefitted the defendant.

C. Promissory estoppel: When the plaintiff recovers in quasi-contract, she generally loses the "benefit of her bargain," since she is awarded only her restitution or reliance interests, and not her expectation interest (see *infra*, p. 335). But where the defendant's conduct foreseeably induces the plaintiff to change her position in reliance on the oral agreement, courts sometimes invoke the doctrine of *promissory estoppel*, and in some cases award *expectation damages*. In other words, the promissory estoppel doctrine is sometimes used to remove a contract completely from the Statute of Frauds, just as in some circumstances performance on one side removes it from the Statute.

1. **Traditional estoppel grounds:** Courts have always been willing to recognize one particular kind of estoppel to plead the Statute of Frauds: where the defendant has intentionally and falsely told the plaintiff that the contract is *not within* the Statute, or that a writing will *subsequently be executed*, or that the defense will not be used.

2. **Grounds broadened:** Most modern courts have extended the estoppel concept to include not only these cases, but also cases where the defendant's promise has *induced detrimental reliance* by the plaintiff, even where neither party ever referred to the need for or lack of a writing.

   Example: Natale and Carmela Castiglia orally promise D, Carmela's son by a previous marriage, that if he will abandon his plans to leave home and will devote himself to helping run the family farm, they will leave it to him when they die. D works for twenty years under this arrangement, and the value of the farm increases tremendously. Natale, shortly before he dies, secretly changes his will to leave his interest in the farm to his grandson, P. After Natale's death, P sues, asking to have the property partitioned; he asserts that the contract falls within the Statute of Frauds, since it is one "not to be performed during the lifetime of the promisor" (a special addition, in effect in California, to the one-year provision).

   Held, D has obviously relied to his detriment by staying on the farm for twenty years, giving up his chance at getting property of his own. Furthermore, Natale and his heirs would be unjustly enriched if they were allowed to escape enforcement of Natale's promise by use of the Statute. The principles of estoppel should not be limited to cases where the promisor has stated that no writing is necessary, since here, as in those cases, the underlying reliance is the same: that the oral agreement will be kept. Also, a quasi-contractual remedy for the value of services performed by D would not be adequate to compensate him. *Monarco v. Lo Greco*, 220 P.2d 737 (Cal. 1950).

   a. **Restatement view:** The Second Restatement agrees that plaintiff's detrimental reliance on defendant's promise can sometimes substitute for a writing. Rest. 2d., § 139(1) provides a special "Statute of Frauds version" of the general § 90 promissory estoppel doctrine. § 139(1) reads:

      "A *promise* which the promisor *should reasonably expect to induce action or forbearance* on the part of the promisee or a third person and which *does induce the action or forbearance* is *enforceable notwithstanding the Statute of Frauds* if injustice can be *avoided only by enforcement* of the promise. The *remedy* granted for breach is to be *limited as justice requires*."

      i. **Damage measures:** By this formulation, the court may enforce the contract by its terms, or may instead merely award restitution or reliance damages. To aid the court in determining whether a contract should be enforced according to its terms,

§ 139(2) lists five factors, among which are the availability of other remedies including "restitution," the extent to which there is other clear and convincing evidence that a contract was in fact formed, and the reasonableness and foreseeability of the reliance.

b. Some courts disagree: Not all courts agree with the Second Restatement's view (expressed in § 139(1) above) that the plaintiff's garden-variety reliance on the defendant's oral promise should be enough to avoid the Statute of Frauds. Where there is no showing that the defendant committed *fraud* (that is, knew at the time of the oral agreement that he would not fulfill its terms), these courts decline to find the Statute of Frauds inapplicable.

  i. Long-term employment contracts: Courts are especially likely to refuse to use promissory estoppel where the contract is an oral one for *employment* for more than one year, and plaintiff's claimed reliance is that she sacrificed *other employment opportunities.* In this context, many courts worry that detrimental reliance will be too easy for the plaintiff to claim, and too hard for the defendant to disprove, leading to an unjustified erosion in the "employment at will" doctrine (which provides that an employment arrangement is usually terminable by either party at any time).

c. Use under UCC: Some courts have permitted promissory estoppel to be a substitute for the Statute of Frauds in a *UCC context.* This is one of those situations in which a common-law doctrine gets applied in a UCC case, through UCC § 1-103(b)'s provision that "Unless displaced by the particular provisions of this Act, the principles of law and equity … shall supplement these provisions." See W&S, pp. 42-43.

  i. Use not allowed under UCC: But other courts have concluded that promissory estoppel may *never* be a substitute for the Statute of Frauds in a case governed by the UCC. See, e.g., *Lige Dickson Co. v. Union Oil Co. of Cal.*, 635 P.2d 103 (Wash. 1981) ("Promissory estoppel cannot be used to overcome the Statute of Frauds in a case which involves the sale of goods…." Therefore, even though seller made an oral "guaranty" to buyer that any increase in seller's price for asphalt would only apply to jobs booked thereafter, and even though buyer relied to his detriment on this guarantee, seller could escape the guaranty by pleading Statute of Frauds.)

3. Limit still imposed on doctrine: Even those courts that do allow reliance and estoppel as a means of avoiding the Statute of Frauds have been careful not to allow these doctrines to swallow up the entire Statute. One way some courts have done this is by allowing reliance to overcome the Statute, but *only* where it is the case that either:

❏ defendant *misrepresented* to plaintiff that the Statute's requirements had been complied with; or

❏ allowing the Statute of Frauds defense would impose *great injury* on the plaintiff, or would *unjustly enrich* the defendant.

If, for instance, there is no misrepresentation and plaintiff's reliance is such that his only loss will be *loss of a profit on resale*, there is a good chance that the court will reject the estoppel argument and enforce the Statute of Frauds.

Quiz Yourself on

SATISFACTION BY MEMORANDUM; EFFECT OF NON-COMPLIANCE; ORAL RESCISSION AND MODIFICATION; AND RESTITUTION, RELIANCE AND ESTOPPEL

85. Flybye Nite Co. orally agrees to sell the Fix-M-Up Hardware Store 500 electric-powered generators at $100 each. In a subsequent confirmation sent by Flybye Nite to Fix-M-Up, the deal is correctly recited, except that the quantity term is erroneously typed as "50." Fix-M-Up makes no response during the next two weeks, and at the end of those 2 weeks Flybye Nite ships 500 generators. Fix-M-Up returns all 500, and refuses to pay anything. How many generators, if any, was Fix-M-Up contractually obligated to take?

86. Louis owns Versailles. He makes an oral agreement with Robespierre in which he promises: (1) to sell Robespierre a cottage on part of the grounds for $100,000; and (2) to give Robespierre the right to use Louis' horse-drawn carriage 10 weekends per year, at $100/weekend.

(A) For this part, assume that one day after making the agreement, Louis changes his mind, and refuses to perform either part of the deal. Which part(s) of the agreement, if any, may be enforced by Robespierre?

(B) Now, assume that Louis tenders the cottage and Robespierre pays up. Louis then decides he wants to have his carriage available at all times, so he tells Robespierre that the carriage-use part of the deal is off. Can Robespierre enforce that part of the agreement?

87. On January 20, 2009, Miss Piggy enters into a written contract with the producers of The Nighty Night Show, a late-night talk show, to appear as a guest host on February 15, 2010. The show's standard contract includes a clause that gives the producers the right to select the other guests who will appear on the show. The document does not include a "no oral modifications" clause. Several days later after the document is signed, the parties orally agree that Miss Piggy will be given a veto power over which guests will appear the night of her performance. The following month, the producers sign a contract with Jessica Rabbit, Miss Piggy's arch rival, to be a guest on the show Miss Piggy will be hosting. Miss Piggy is furious and sues to enforce the oral modification. What result?

Answers

85. First, the fact that Fix-M-Up never signed any document doesn't matter: when a deal is between merchants, UCC § 2-201(2) says that if one sends the other a confirmation that is "sufficient against the sender" (i.e., signed by the sender, and containing the essential terms), and the recipient fails to make written objection within 10 days, the recipient is bound as if she had signed that confirmation. So Fix-M-Up is bound the same way Flybye Nite is bound, whatever that is.

Next, a separate provision of the UCC, § 2-201(1), says that in a deal for more than $500, the Statute of Frauds must be satisfied by "some writing sufficient to indicate that a contract for sale has been made between the parties." The section also says that "A writing is not insufficient because it omits or incorrectly states a term agreed upon but the contract is not enforceable under this paragraph beyond the quantity of goods shown in such writing." So the error doesn't prevent the confirmation from being a writing that satisfies the memorandum requirement, but Flybye Nite can't enforce the deal beyond the quantity shown on the confirmation, 50.

86. (A) Neither. As a general rule, if one part of an agreement is unenforceable because of the Statute of Frauds, no part of the agreement will be enforced (since enforcing part would be likely to distort the parties' total bargain). There are some exceptions, but none applies here. Since part (1) is unenforceable (it's a contract to convey an interest in land), part (2) will also be unenforceable even though it would not pose a Statute of Frauds problem if it stood separately.

(B) Yes. Once all the promises that fall within the Statute have been fully performed, the remaining promises will be enforced. Here, the provisions dealing with the sale of land have been fully performed, so Robespierre can enforce his right to take the carriage out for a spin.

87. Miss Piggy loses this round. When a contract undergoes an oral modification, courts will look to see if the new contract, as modified, falls within the Statute of Frauds. If it does, the modification will be ineffective, and the original contract will be left standing. Here, even with the additional term, the contract falls within the Statute because it is a contract incapable of being performed in less than a year from its making. Therefore, the court will enforce the original contract, the one with no veto clause.

Exam Tips on
STATUTE OF FRAUDS

☛ When you come across an *oral agreement*, always ask yourself whether the agreement should be in writing. The possible violation of the *Statute of Frauds* is frequently tested and can be easily overlooked by students preoccupied with more obvious issues. Look for the following types of contracts:

Guaranty or Surety Agreement

☛ Look for a party's agreement to *pay the debt of another party* ("answer for the debt of another") in case that party defaults. *Confirm that the guaranty is in writing*.

☞ **"Main purpose" exception:** The most frequently tested aspect of the guaranty/surety provision is the *"main purpose"* rule: Where the guarantor's *main purpose* for entering into the guaranty agreement is to benefit *herself*, the guaranty *doesn't* have to be in writing.

Example: Manco, a chair manufacturer, and Distribco, a company that distributes chairs, have a five-year written contract whereby Manco furnishes Distribco with chairs on credit. Distribco orders 150 chairs to be delivered by Manco directly to Cust, Distribco's customer. However, Distribco is already in arrears for 30 chairs, so Manco calls Cust and explains to Cust that, due to Distribco's outstanding bills, Manco won't provide the chairs to Cust unless Cust guarantees payment for them. Cust responds, "OK, I'll pay promises you directly for the chairs if Distribco doesn't pay." Since Cust's main purpose in making the guaranty was to ensure that he got the chairs, his guaranty promise is enforceable even though it wasn't in writing.

Land Contract Provision

☛ Remember that the Statute of Frauds applies not only to the sale of realty, but also to the transfer of *any interest in land*, such as *leasehold* interests.

   ☞ In a fact pattern involving a written land contract, be sure that the document includes the *price*. This is an *essential term* in a land contract and its omission will violate the Statute of Frauds.

   ☞ **Exception for part performance and detrimental reliance:** Remember that there's an exception where one party (usually the buyer) *detrimentally relies* on the oral agreement in a way that is *"unequivocally referable to the agreement"* — i.e., conduct that *would not have been undertaken had the oral contract not existed.* Most commonly on exams, this takes the form of moving on to the property and *making improvements.*

     Example: At *X* and *Y*'s wedding, *X*'s father, *F*, tells them that if they agree to live with him and take care of him for the rest of his life, he will deliver the deed to his home to them within a year. *X* and *Y* accept the offer, move into *F*'s home, and beginning caring for him. They use their own money to add a new wing to the house, to pay off the mortgage and to pay the outstanding property taxes. After a year, *F* refuses to deliver the deed and asks *X* and *Y* to leave his home.

     X and *Y* should be able to enforce the oral agreement because their actions of adding a new wing, paying off the mortgage and paying the property taxes are actions which are "unequivocally referable" to the oral agreement — that is, there's no other logical explanation for why *X* and *Y* took these actions than that the alleged oral agreement really existed.

One Year Provision

☛ Look to see if it would be *impossible* for the contract to be *"fully performed" within a year of the time it was made.* If so, the contract has to be in writing.

     Example of a promise that can't be fulfilled within a year: On August 1, 1999, Mom orally promises Daughter that if Daughter gets an average of better than 3.5 in her first year in college, Mom will pay for Daughter's second year of school. Grades for the first year won't be reported until late August of the following year. Mom's promise falls under the one-year provision (and is therefore unenforceable since not in writing), because it can't possibly be fully performed within a year of August 1, 1999.

   ☞ **Lifetime employment and other indefinite promises:** Don't be fooled by a party's promise to do something for an *indefinite* period of time — if he could die within the year yet still fully perform his promise, the contract doesn't fall within the one-year provision. For this reason, a contract for *"lifetime employment"* is *not* within the statute — the employee might die within the year, and courts look on this as being "full performance."

     Example: Son, S, asks his mother, M, to lend him $10,000 with which to pay past due bar bills. On September 1, M orally agrees that if S promises to go to law school and to stop drinking for the rest of his life, she will give him $10,000 on July 1 of the following year. Because it's possible that S could die within the year and still fulfill both promises, the contract is enforceable.

☞ **Discharge:** But if a contract can only be *"discharged,"* rather than "fully performed," within a year, it *does* fall within the statute.

Example: Boss hires Worker on a 5-year oral contract. This contract is invalid because it can't be "fully performed" within one year of its making — it's true that if Worker dies, the contract will be discharged, but a discharge is not deemed to be a full performance.

Sale of Goods or Personal Property

☛ This is the most frequently tested application of the rule. Several pointers:

☞ **$500:** The Statute of Frauds comes into play — thereby requiring a *written* contract — when the agreement is for the *sale of goods for the price of $500 or more*.

☞ **Personal property:** A contract for the sale of *personal property* that is not goods (e.g., assignment of the right to receive payment under a contract) must be in writing if it's for a price of *$5,000* or more.

☞ **Goods, not services:** Make sure the contract at issue is one for goods and *not services*.

☞ A contract that's *primarily* for the provision of services doesn't fall under the sale-of-goods S/F even if goods are, as an incidental matter, to be provided by the person performing services.

☞ **Modifications:** If a fact pattern involves an oral modification of a written contract, *calculate the total value of the contract as modified,* to see whether the $500-threshold is met. If it is, the modification won't be enforceable.

Example: A written contract for the sale of 2,000 widgets at $1 per widget is orally modified for the sale of 1,000 widgets at the same price. The modified contract amount is $1,000 and must be in writing. Probably the pre-modification contract remains in force.

Trap: Watch for an initial oral contract that doesn't fall under the Statute of Frauds (because it's for less than $500), followed by an oral modification that raises the total price beyond $500. The modification won't be enforceable (and probably the original oral deal remains in force).

☞ Three important *exceptions* applicable only to UCC cases:

☞ **Acceptance or payment:** Remember that if the buyer *"accepts"* the goods (e.g., receives them and keeps them without complaint for a significant time) or *pays* for them, the buyer can't assert the Statute as to the accepted or paid-for goods.

Example: Over the telephone, *B* agrees to buy from *S* 1,000 widgets at $2 per widget. Several days later *S* sends an initial installment of 200 widgets to *B*. *B* inspects the goods and puts them in his warehouse. One week later, *B* calls *S* and says that he never had a firm contract with *S* and that he is going to ship the 200 widgets back to *S*; he also warns *S* not to ship the 800 remaining.

B accepted the 200 widgets (by inspecting them and not complaining), so he's bound to keep and pay for them notwithstanding the S/F. But *B* is not obligated to accept or pay for the other 800.

☞ **Admission:** Also, look for a statement under oath (i.e. in a pleading, during a deposition or in court testimony) in which a party ***admits*** that a contract was made. In UCC cases, the Statute of Frauds doesn't apply to the extent of such an admission (but *does* apply notwithstanding the admission in *non-UCC* cases).

☞ **Written confirmation between merchants.** Pay attention when one merchant has sent a ***written confirmation*** of the oral agreement to the other merchant. This ***memorandum*** can of course satisfy the Statute of Frauds to enforce the contract against the party who sent it, if the document contains the essential terms of the agreement. More important, it can also be used to enforce the oral agreement against the party ***receiving*** the memorandum if that party ***does not object*** to its terms within 10 days of receipt.

The Memorandum Requirement

☞ Watch out for the following testable issues regarding the ***signature requirement*** in order for a writing (a "memorandum" of the agreement) to satisfy the Statute:

☞ Look for a ***stamped*** signature. A handwritten signature isn't necessary and a stamp (or typewritten signature) is sufficient as long as it was stamped *after* the document was written. All that's needed is an "***an intent to authenticate*** the document," and a stamped or typewritten signature will do that, as long as it's affixed after the document was written.

☞ The absence of a signature isn't necessarily fatal. Look for other signed documents to which the ***unsigned document relates.*** A majority of courts hold that when it's apparent that two or more documents refer to the same transaction, one that's unsigned may be considered part of the memorandum if there is external evidence demonstrating that the parties assented to the unsigned document.

> **Example:** *O* contracts in a signed writing to sell Greenacre to *B*. *B* doesn't sign this writing. *B* and *X* later enter into a written agreement where *B* assigns to *X* all his rights under the contract with *O* and *X* agrees to pay the contract price for Greenacre to *O*. *B*'s signature on the assignment to *X* probably satisfies the Statute of Frauds in the *B-O* contract, and *B* is therefore bound under that contract.

Reliance as Nullifying the Statute

☞ **Estoppel:** Watch for a party who has ***relied*** on the oral agreement to his detriment. Some courts allow for an ***estoppel*** that blocks application of the Statute, where there would be great injury to the plaintiff or unjust enrichment of the defendant.

☞ **Trap:** But make sure the reliance is more than just *de minimis,* or estoppel won't apply.

> **Example:** Over the telephone, *B* agrees to buy from *S* 1,000 widgets at $2 per widget. *S* then orders 1,000 clips from *X,* which are to be incorporated into the widgets he

agreed to sell to *B*. The clips cost S $.04 a piece. *B* later cancels the contract.

    S will not likely be successful if he claims detrimental reliance as a way around the Statute of Frauds problem. Although *S* relied on the contract with *B* when he ordered the 1,000 clips, his injury is not significant because the total cost of the clips was only $40. (*Note*: But this argument, though weak, is still worth making on an essay exam — you'd be showing that you are able to spot an issue and discuss its pros and cons.)

CHAPTER 10

REMEDIES

This chapter deals with the different remedies that are available to the nonbreaching and breaching parties to a contract. Key concepts:

- **Equitable relief:** The equitable remedies of *specific performance* (an order to render a promised performance) or an *injunction* (an order to refrain from doing something) will be directed by the court where certain requirements are fulfilled. Most importantly, it must be the case that *money damages* would be an *inadequate remedy*.

- **Remedies at law (money damages):** Ordinarily, however, in contracts cases the remedy will not be equitable. Instead, the remedy will consist of *money damages*. There are three main measures of money damages in contracts cases:

  - ❏ **Expectation damages:** "Expectation" damages are the *most common* remedy. They attempt to put the plaintiff in the *position she would have been had the defendant performed.* The plaintiff is awarded: (1) the out-of-pocket costs she has incurred; plus (2) the profit which she would have made had the contract been completed.

    - ❏ **Reasonable certainty:** Expectation damages may only be recovered if the plaintiff proves them with *"reasonable certainty."* When the plaintiff can't do so, one of the two other measures (reliance and restitution) will be used instead.

  - ❏ **Reliance damages:** "Reliance" damages attempt to put the plaintiff in *as good a position as she was in prior to the making of the contract.* This is done by allowing the plaintiff to recover her *out-of-pocket expenditures* incurred in performing the contract.

    - ❏ **When used:** Reliance damages are most commonly awarded when expectation damages are *too speculative* to be proved with reasonable certainty. (*Example:* The contract relates to a newly-formed business, and because of the newness we cannot say how much the business would have earned had D not breached.)

  - ❏ **Restitution:** "Restitution" damages attempt to prevent the *unjust enrichment* of the defendant by returning to a plaintiff who has partially performed *the value of the performance he has rendered to the defendant.*

    - ❏ **When used:** Restitution damages are sometimes awarded when a contract is *discharged* for various reasons (e.g., impossibility). They are also suitable where expectation damages are too uncertain to be awarded and reliance damages would not adequately compensate the plaintiff.

- **Substantial performance:** A plaintiff who has *"substantially performed"* (but not fully performed) may sue for expectation damages arising from the defendant's breach of contract. However, the defendant may counterclaim for damages arising from the plaintiff's incomplete performance.

- **Suits in quasi-contract:** Restitution and reliance damages are frequently awarded in so-called *"quasi contract"* suits. These are suits where recovery "on the contract" is unavailable. Two common quasi-contract scenarios:

❑ **Contract is unenforceable.** Quasi-contract is available where a contract is (or later becomes) *unenforceable* or *voidable*. (*Examples:* (1) A contract that violates the *Statute of Frauds*, but that is partly performed; (2) a contract that is discharged for *impossibility*.)

❑ **Recovery by breaching plaintiff.** Quasi-contract is available where a *plaintiff who has committed a "material" breach* (i.e., a plaintiff who has *not substantially performed*), has nonetheless performed enough to render some value to the defendant. The suit is sometimes said to be in "quantum meruit." (*Example:* A contractor who only partially completes work on the construction of a building may recover for the value of the partial construction.)

■ **"Duty to mitigate":** A plaintiff loses his ability to recover if he has not made *reasonable efforts to avoid damages*. (*Examples:* An employee must try to find another job; an aggrieved buyer must attempt to "cover" by purchasing substitute goods.)

■ **Liquidated damages:** A provision in a contract setting the amount of damages in case of a breach by one of the parties is called a *"liquidated damages"* clause. Such clauses are usually enforceable if they are a *reasonable estimate* of damages, viewed as of either the time of the contract or in hindsight when the actual loss is known.

I.   INTRODUCTION

A.   Recovery on and off the contract: In analyzing the remedies available to a party, one crucial distinction must be kept in mind: that between a suit brought *on the contract*, and a suit brought off the contract, i.e., in *quasi-contract*.

1.   Suit "on the contract": Where the parties have formed a legally enforceable contract, and the defendant (but not the plaintiff) has breached the contract, the plaintiff will normally sue *"on the contract."* That is, he will bring a suit for damages for breach of contract, and the terms of the contract will control for purposes of judging the defendant's wrongful conduct, and calculating damages.

2.   Suit in "quasi-contract": But in other circumstances, the plaintiff will bring a suit in what is called *"quasi-contract."* His damages will normally be based upon the actual value of the performance he has rendered, irrespective of any price set out in the contract. Situations in which a quasi-contractual recovery may be available include those in which:

❑ the contract is *unenforceably vague*;

❑ the contract is *illegal*;

❑ the parties are *discharged* from the contract because of *impossibility*, *impracticability* or *frustration of purpose*; and, most important,

❑ the plaintiff has *himself materially breached* the contract.

A fuller discussion of quasi-contractual recovery appears later in this chapter (see p. 335). The material prior to that deals exclusively with recovery on the contract, a fact which you must constantly keep in mind.

a. **"Restitution" distinguished:** Many writers refer to a quasi-contractual recovery as *"restitution."* The term "restitution," however, is also used to denote a certain measure of damages that may be awarded in suits on a contract, namely, the award to the plaintiff of the amount by which his performance under the contract benefited the defendant. In order to avoid confusing these two very distinct uses of "restitution," the term "restitution" will be used here only to refer to this measure of damages in contract actions. "Quasi-contract" will be the term used to refer to recovery off the contract. "Restitution" is discussed *infra*, p. 330.

B. **Law/equity distinction:** Another crucial distinction to keep in mind is that between remedies at *law* and remedies in *equity*. Equitable remedies for contract breach, and how they differ from legal remedies, are discussed in a separate major section beginning immediately below.

II. EQUITABLE REMEDIES

A. **Equitable relief generally:** The usual remedy for breach of contract is *money damages* awarded by a court to the aggrieved party. However, there are some situations in which money damages cannot adequately compensate the aggrieved party. This may be the case where the damages are *too speculative* or uncertain to be calculated, where damages are simply *not a substitute* for the defendant's performance of the contract (as where the defendant breaches a contract to sell a particular piece of land to the plaintiff), or where it is likely that a damage award could not be collected. In these situations, it may be appropriate for the court to grant *equitable relief*.

1. **Unified system:** Historically, equitable relief was granted by an entirely different system of courts (the courts of equity) than was the granting of money damages (which was done by the common-law courts). In America today, however, nearly all states have *unified* the common-law and equity courts, so that the same court may award either damages or equitable relief.

2. **Types of equitable relief:** There are two types of equitable relief that are relevant to contract cases. These are *specific performance* and *injunctions*. A decree for specific performance orders the promisor to *render the promised performance*. An injunction directs a party to *refrain* from doing a particular act.

   a. **Illustration of specific performance decree:** The classic illustration of a specific performance decree in a contract case is where the promisor has promised to *convey a piece of real estate*, and without justification refuses to make the conveyance. The court will *order her to make the conveyance*. If she persists in her refusal, the court will order the recording office to record the conveyance even without the promisor's participation.

   b. **Illustration of injunction:** The classic illustration of the use of an *injunction* in a contracts case involves the employee who has *breached an employment contract*. In this situation, the court will rarely award specific performance, since, among other difficulties, ordering the employee to perform smacks of involuntary servitude. What the court will often do, however, is to *prevent* the employee from *working for a competitor*.

Example: D, an opera singer, is under a contract to sing for the City Opera company (located in New York City) during the 1999-2000 season. The contract provides that D will not perform for any other opera company in New York City that season. D then announces that she will not perform at the City Opera, and that she will instead perform at the Metropolitan Opera (also in New York City).

City Opera will not be able to get specific performance, i.e., an order compelling D to do the scheduled performances with City Opera. But it *will* probably be able to get an injunction prohibiting D from singing for the Met or any other New York opera company during the season covered by the contract.

    i.   Limits: But there are significant *limits* on the injunctive relief likely to be awarded by a court in a personal services case; see *infra*, p. 315.

B. Limitations on the use of equity: Historically, equitable relief in contract cases (as in other cases) was only given where the common-law remedy was not adequate. Courts today impose fewer restrictions on the granting of equitable relief than they did in earlier centuries. Nonetheless, it remains the case that the standard, and preferred, remedy for breach of contract is the common-law award of damages, and that equitable relief will be given only where the common-law remedy is not adequate. There are three principal pre-conditions to the granting of equitable relief in contract actions:

❏ *Money damages* must be *inadequate* to protect the injured party;

❏ The contract's terms must be *definite* enough to allow the court to frame an adequate order; and

❏ The court's task of *enforcing and supervising* the relief must not be unduly difficult.

We discuss each of these pre-conditions below.

1. Inadequacy of damages: Most importantly, equitable relief for breach of contract will not be granted unless *damages are not adequate to protect the injured party*. Farnsworth, p. 773. There are a number of reasons for which damages may in a particular case be an inadequate remedy, two of which are as follows:

    a. Speculative or hard-to-calculate damages: It may be the case that the injury suffered from a breach of contract *cannot be estimated with sufficient certainty*. Farnsworth, p. 774.

        i. Matters of taste: For instance, the contract may involve matters of *taste or sentiment*, which make damages hard to fix with any accuracy (e.g., a contract to sell a work of art which has particular sentimental value to the purchaser).

        ii. Based on unknown future events: Or, the required performance may *vary according to not-yet-knowable future events*, perhaps ones many years in the future, in a way that makes computing a single estimate today of future damages very speculative.

        Example: Insurer promises to pay an annuity of $2,000 per month to Insured during Insured's life. Insurer repudiates the contract. Insured will be entitled to an order compelling Insured to keep making the monthly payments for the rest of Insured's life. That's because money damages are not an adequate remedy: it's unknown how long Insured will live, so a one-time award of a single sum cannot accurately estimate Insured's actual damages from the breach.

b. Purchase of substitute: It may be the case that money ***cannot purchase a substitute*** for the contracted-for performance.

    i. No other available counter-parties: This can happen, for instance, because no substitute counter-party is available to take the risk that the breaching party was willing to take, such as in a long-term supply contract.

    Example: P and D enter into a contract whereby D is to supply propane gas to P for various residential subdivisions. Although the contract gives P liberal cancellation rights, D is not permitted to cancel the contract unless the subdivisions convert to natural gas. After performing for some time, D refuses to supply any more gas, and purports to terminate the contract. P sues for specific performance, i.e., a decree ordering D to continue supplying the propane.

    Held, P is entitled to the decree. Money damages would not be adequate relief. Although propane is currently available from a number of other sources, there is no guarantee that P will be able to find the propane in future years, because of the uncertainty of world-wide energy supplies. Furthermore, evidence shows that P cannot find another propane supplier willing to enter into a long-term supply contract like the contract here. *Laclede Gas Co. v. Amoco Oil Co.*, 522 F.2d 33 (8th Cir. 1975).

    ii. Item is unique: It may be the case that the ***item*** being sold is ***unique***, so it's not available elsewhere.

        (1) Goods: In the area of sale-of-goods, for instance, the item might be one-of-a-kind, such as an ***antique***. See *infra*, p. 316, for more about unique goods under the UCC.

        (2) Uniqueness of land: Similarly, every parcel of ***land*** has traditionally been deemed to be "unique." Consequently, courts have traditionally held (and most still do) that money cannot purchase a "substitute" parcel, and that therefore a contract for the sale of land will be specifically enforced. This subject is discussed further *infra*, p. 314.

c. Other illustrations: Some other situations in which an award of damages is likely not to be adequate include the following:

    i. Forbearance: If performance consists of ***forbearance***, damages will generally be found to be inadequate. For instance, if the promise is that the promisor will ***not compete*** with the promisee, damages will not be an adequate substitute, and an injunction will often be granted. (See the discussion of injunctions in personal service cases, *infra*, p. 315.)

    ii. Sale of a business: A contract for the ***sale of a business*** may well fall within the damages-not-adequate category, if it shown that there is no closely comparable business available for sale. Similarly, ***shares of stock*** that would give ***control*** of a business will often fall within this class.

iii. Patents and copyrights: *Patents* and *copyrights* are unique, so that damages concerning these items of intellectual property will not normally be adequate relief. Rest. 2d, § 360, Comment c.

2. **Definiteness:** The court will not give equitable relief (whether a decree of specific performance or an injunction) unless the contract's terms are *definite enough* to enable the court to frame an adequate order. Farnsworth, p. 778. The stakes are especially high where an equitable order is involved, because a party who does not follow the order is subject to the punishment of *contempt of court* (which is not the case where a party fails to pay a damage award). Therefore, courts require that the rights and obligations of the parties be specified with *greater definiteness* if there is to be equitable relief than in the money-damages situation. *Id.*

3. **Difficulty of enforcement or supervision:** The court will not grant equitable relief where there are likely to be significant difficulties in *enforcing* and *supervising* the order. Farnsworth, pp. 781-82.

   a. **Construction contracts:** The most significant impact of this arises in connection with *construction contracts*. The difficulties of supervising the performance of highly complex work, and of judging the results, are often greater than the benefits to be gained.

   Example: D contracts to expand and modernize a steel fabricating plant owned by P. Work is not progressing as rapidly as the contract contemplates, and P seeks an order requiring D to put 300 more workers on the night shift, so that there will be a full crew on this shift. (The contract does not explicitly require that D supply a full second shift, nor does it mention the number of people to be put on the job.)

   Held, for D. The court will not order specific performance where it would be impractical to carry out the order. Granting P the order it seeks would commit the court to "supervising the carrying out of a massive, complex, and unfinished construction contract...." If D's delays constitute a breach of contract and damage P, P's appropriate remedy is a common-law action for damages brought after the fact. *Northern Delaware Industrial Development Corp. v. E.W. Bliss Co.*, 245 A.2d 431 (Del. Ch. 1968).

   b. **Personal service contracts:** Judicial reluctance to become enmeshed in complex supervision of performance also partly explains courts' unwillingness to order specific performance of *personal service contracts*. The subject of personal service contracts is discussed further *infra*, p. 315.

C. **Land-sale contracts:** The most common situation in which specific performance is decreed is that in which the defendant breaches a contract under which he is to *convey* a particular *piece of land* to the plaintiff. Because a particular parcel of land has no exact counterpart elsewhere, money damages will not adequately compensate the plaintiff. Furthermore, a decree of specific performance does not pose difficulties of *supervision*, since it is easy for the court to verify whether the defendant has made a conveyance, and even to order that the conveyance be recorded without the seller's participation. See Rest. 2d, § 360, Comment e.

1. **Buyer has contracted to resell:** Specific performance will be ordered even where the plaintiff buyer has *already contracted to resell* the property. In this situation, the courts generally accept the buyer's argument that if he is unable to make the reconveyance, he himself will be liable for damages in an amount which cannot accurately be determined without litigation. *Id.*

2. **Breach by buyer:** Courts are also generally willing to order specific performance of a land-sale contract where the seller has not yet conveyed, and it is the *buyer who breaches*. In this situation, the courts reason that the value of land is somewhat speculative, and that it will therefore be difficult for the seller to establish the difference between the contract price and the market price. *Id.*

   a. **Seller has already conveyed:** But if the seller has *already conveyed*, damages will be an adequate remedy if the buyer refuses to pay the purchase price; therefore, specific performance will not be ordered in this situation. *Id.* Instead, the seller must litigate a conventional action to receive the contract amount (plus any consequently damages) as money damages.

D. **Contracts involving personal services:** Equitable relief in connection with *contracts for personal services* is subjected to some especially severe limitations.

1. **No specific performance:** Courts will almost *never* order *specific performance* of a contract for personal services. Rest. 2d, § 367(1). This is true on *both sides*. That is, the court will not order the employer to resume the employment, nor will it order the employee to perform the services.

   a. **Rationale:** The policy against specific performance of such contracts "is based in part upon the undesirability of compelling the continuance of personal association after disputes have arisen and *confidence and loyalty are gone*...." *Id.*, Comment a. Also, in the case of an order against the employee, courts do not wish to impose "what might seem like *involuntary servitude*." *Id.*

   Example 1: *A*, a famous opera star, contracts to sing exclusively in *B*'s London opera house for the coming season. Before the first scheduled performance, *A* repudiates, in order to sing at *C*'s competing London opera house. *B* will not be entitled to a decree of specific performance ordering *A* to perform, even if *B* will suffer great loss which cannot be accurately estimated. Rest. 2d, § 367, Illustr. 1.

   Example 2: Same facts as the above example, except that it is *B*, the owner of the opera house, who repudiates the contract before the first performance. Even if *A* will suffer, in addition to lost earnings, a loss of prestige whose dollar value cannot be accurately ascertained, *A* will not be entitled to an order directing *B* to resume the engagement. *Id.*, Illustr. 2.

2. **Injunction:** Because specific performance will almost never be granted in connection with personal service contracts, the rules concerning the availability of *injunctive* relief are especially important in this context. Since a promise to render personal services is usually exclusive (i.e., it implies a duty not to render the promised services to anyone else), courts will often enjoin the breaching employee from working for a *competitor*. Generally, the employer seeking an injunction must overcome three hurdles:

a. **Unique skills:**   The employer must show that the employee's services are ***unique or extraordinary***, either because she has some ***special skill*** or because she has acquired ***special knowledge*** of the ***employer's business***. (The "special skill" criterion is often found to be satisfied in contracts involving ***professional athletes*** or ***entertainment*** stars.) This requirement stems from the requirement that damages not be an adequate remedy; if the employee's services are not "unique or extraordinary," damages will normally adequately protect the employer's interest.

b. **Other way to make living:**   The injunction will not be granted if its likely result will be to leave the employee ***without other reasonable means of making a living***. This requirement will not be satisfied if the ***only alternative*** which would be left open to the employee is to perform the contract. That is, the injunction will not be used as a direct substitute for specific performance.

c. **Employer's willingness to perform:**   Furthermore, even if there are other ways for the employee to make a living, if the ***probable*** result of the injunction will be that the employee performs the contract, "it should appear that the employer is prepared to continue the employment in good faith so that performance will not involve personal relations the enforced continuance of which is undesirable." Rest. 2d, § 367, Comment c.

E. **Sale of goods:**   Traditionally, it has been extremely difficult for a buyer to obtain specific performance of a contract to sell ***goods***. Generally, unless the buyer could show that the goods in question were ***unique***, and could not be obtained elsewhere in the market, he could not obtain an order that the seller deliver them.

1. **More liberal UCC rule:**   But the modern tendency, exemplified by the UCC, is to permit ***much more liberal use*** of specific performance in sales cases. § 2-716(1) makes the general statement that "Specific performance may be decreed where the goods are unique ***or in other proper circumstances.***" § 2-716(1).

   a. **Uniqueness:**   If the goods *are* "unique," money damages will probably be inadequate. ***Rare*** objects, and objects of ***sentimental value,*** tend to be "unique," such as a one-of-a-kind ***work of art*** or a ***family heirloom***.

      Example: Dealer contracts to sell Collector a painting, Cezanne's "The Card Players," for $10 million. Dealer then gets a higher offer from Tycoon, and contracts to sell the painting to him. Since there is only one "The Card Players," a court will likely conclude that money damages are inadequate, and will grant an order of specific peformance requiring Dealer to convey to Collector.

   b. **"Other proper circumstances":**   Even if the goods are *not* "unique," § 2-716(1) recognizes that there may be ***"other proper circumstances"*** for specific performance.

      i. **Inability to cover:**   Most importantly, the fact that the buyer has ***tried to cover*** and failed will be evidence of such circumstances. Comment 2 to § 2-716(1) states that "***[i]nability to cover*** is ***strong evidence*** of 'other proper circumstances.'" Thus a buyer who is ***unable to procure substitute goods*** within a reasonable time after the breach is likely to be awarded specific performance, even if the seller shows that the goods were not, strictly speaking, "unique."

ii. **Rise in market price not usually sufficient:** On the other hand, if there are other comparable items available in the market, the fact that the *market price* of those items (and of the item under contract) has *risen* will generally *not* by itself be enough to justify specific performance. See, e.g., *Klein v. Pepsico*, 845 F.2d 76 (4th Cir. 1988) (where three similar G-II corporate jets were available on the market, the fact that the price had risen was not enough to justify specific performance, since the price rise could be handled by money damages).

Quiz Yourself on
EQUITABLE REMEDIES

88. Acme An-teeks offers to sell Marge Scavenger the squirting rose boutonniere that George Washington wore to his Inaugural Ball for $5,000, and Marge agrees. Before the transaction takes place, Acme gets another offer for $7,000, which it accepts, thereby breaching the contract with Marge. Marge really wants the boutonniere itself (not just damages), because she's a collector of boutonnieres. Is there any remedy available to her?

89. Sisyphus is a well-known expert on hauling rocks. He enters into an employment contract with the Rocco Rock Hauling Co., in which he agrees to work for three years as Chief Operations Officer. His relationship with Rocco brings great prestige to the company; however, after six months Sisyphus finds the work unbearable and quits.

(A) When Rocco sues Sisyphus for breach of contract, will it be entitled to an order compelling him to come back to work and finish the contract?

(B) Assume for this part only that your answer to (A) is no. What other equitable remedy might be available to Rocco, and on what showing?

(C) Assume for this part that after six months, it's Rocco who's unsatisfied, and Rocco gives Sisyphus the heave-ho. Can Sisyphus obtain an ordering compelling Rocco to reinstate him?

Answers

88. Yes, an order for specific performance (i.e., a court order compelling Acme to honor the original deal with Marge). Where the subject matter of the contract is unique, as here, the court will likely grant specific performance, since damages will not be adequate to compensate Marge for the breach.

89. (A) No. Because of the personal relationship involved and the constitutional prohibition of involuntary servitude, courts will generally deny specific performance as a remedy for breach by an employee of an employment contract.

(B) An injunction against worker for a competitor of Rocco, for the remaining length of the contract. Rocco can receive an order enjoining Sisyphus from working for a competitor for the remaining 2.5 years, if it can prove the following: (1) that Sisyphus has a special skill (which he does, since we know he is an expert on hauling rocks); (2) that Sisyphus will not be left without any other reasonable means of earning a living (the injunction would most likely be limited in geographic scope so that he can get a job *somewhere* in his field); and (3) that if the probable result of the injunction would be that Sisyphus would just decide to come back to work for Rocco, Rocco would be ready, willing and able to take him back.

(C) No. The general rule against orders of specific performance in personal-services (i.e., employment) contracts applies to both employers and employees. Therefore, Sisyphus will not be able to require Rocco to take him back — his only recourse is to sue for damages for the breach.

III. KINDS OF DAMAGE MEASURES

A. **Three kinds of interest:**   Once it is established that a particular plaintiff may recover damages for breach of contract, there remains the often difficult question of how these damages should be calculated. Should the court attempt to put the plaintiff in the position he would have been in had the contract been fully performed? Should it try to put him in the position that he would have been in had the contract never been made? Should it make the defendant give back everything of value that the plaintiff has given him? American contract law recognizes three distinct kinds of interests on the part of a disappointed party which may be worthy of judicial protection:

1. **Expectation interest:**   The plaintiff's *"expectation"* interest is her interest in having the contract performed. In protecting the expectation interest, the court attempts to *put the plaintiff in the position she would have been in had the contract been performed*. Usually, this means that the plaintiff recovers the *profits she would have made* had the contract been fulfilled.

2. **Reliance interest:**   In a particular case, it may be impossible to measure the expectation interest of a plaintiff accurately. In such a situation, the plaintiff may instead recover her *"reliance" interest*. That is, the court will attempt to *put the plaintiff in as good a position as she was in before the contract was made*. To do this, the court will normally award the plaintiff his *out-of-pocket costs* incurred in the performance he has already rendered.

3. **Restitution interest:**   In a few instances, neither expectation nor reliance damages will be appropriate. If so, the court may protect what is called the plaintiff's *"restitution interest."* That is, the court will force the defendant to pay the plaintiff an amount equal to the *benefit which the defendant has received* from the plaintiff's performance.

We consider each of these interests in turn in its own major section. (For reliance, see p. 326; for restitution, see p. 330.)

IV. EXPECTATION DAMAGES

A. **Expectation interest:**   Expectation damages are the usual, and in some situations the only, measure of damages for breach of contract. In awarding expectation damages, the court attempts to *put the plaintiff in the position she would have been in had the contract been performed by the defendant*. Normally, this means that the plaintiff is awarded the *profit* which she would have made had the contract been performed.

> **Example 1:** On March 1, D, the owner of Blackacre, contracts to sell it to P on July 1 for $500,000. Real estate prices rise, and D reneges. On July 1, D sells the property for $700,000 (which is the highest price any likely buyer would have paid). P will be permitted to recover $200,000 from D, the difference between the contract price and the

market price at the time of breach, since that amount will put P in the position he would have been in (making a $200,000 profit) had the contract been performed.

Example 2: Plaintiff's hand is scarred from a severe burn. Plaintiff contracts with defendant surgeon for a skin graft operation which, the defendant promises, will make plaintiff's hand completely normal. Not only does the operation fail to correct the scar, but it also causes plaintiff's hand to become covered with hair.

Held, plaintiff may recover the difference between the value of a perfect hand and the value of the scarred and hairy hand. That is, plaintiff is awarded expectation damages, i.e., the difference between what he would have received had the contract been performed (a perfect hand) and the position he was left in after defendant's breach (a scarred and hairy hand). *Hawkins v. McGee*, 84 N.H. 114 (1929).

Note: Observe that the award of expectation damages in *Hawkins* produced quite a different result from that which would have been produced had reliance damages been awarded. Plaintiff's reliance damages would have been the difference between the value of the scarred (but not hairy) hand and the value of the scarred and hairy hand. That is, by reliance damages, plaintiff would have been restored to the position he was in before the contract was agreed upon.

1. **"Benefit of the bargain":** The idea behind expectation damages is often described as giving the plaintiff the *"benefit of her bargain."*

B. **Usual formula for calculating expectation damages:** A plaintiff's expectation damages can be expressed by this formula:

---

[1] *the amount by which the value of the defendant's **actual performance** was less than the **value of the promised performance***

minus

[2] *whatever **benefits**, if any, the plaintiff received from **not having to complete his own performance**.*

Generally, the benefits in [2] are *expenditures* which the plaintiff would have had to make to complete his performance under the contract, but which he didn't have to make because the defendant breached first. See Rest. 2d, § 347.

Example of formula: Contractor contracts to build a house for Owner for $300,000. The contract provides that after Contractor has done half the work, he is to receive $150,000. Contractor does half the work, and demands payment. Owner refuses, and announces that he does not wish Contractor to continue the building. At this point, it would cost Contractor (taking into account materials, but also payments to Contractor's employees) $100,000 to complete the house, a sum which Contractor has saved by virtue of Owner's breach. Contractor's expectation damages are equal to: (1) the difference between the value of Owner's promised performance ($300,000) and the value of Owner's actual performance ($0); minus (2) the benefit to Contractor of not having to complete ($100,000), or $200,000.

C. Construction contracts: Many problems involving the computation of damages involve *construction contracts*, so we'll look at these in some detail. We'll call the person doing the construction the "builder," and the person receiving the benefit of the work the "owner."

1. **Builder breaches:** First, let's look at how the owner's damages are computed if the *builder breaches*, and the owner has the work completed by a second builder. A good formula for computing the owner's damages is:

> [1] The value the building *would have had* if it had been completed as agreed upon ...
>
> [2] Less the value of the building *as completed* by the second builder ...
>
> [3] Plus the amount by which (a) the *totals paid* by the owner to the first and second builders together *exceed (b) the contract price*...
>
> [4] Plus any consequential damages from the *delay*.

Farnsworth §12.11 at 775-776.

Example: Builder 1 contracts to build a house on Owner's land for $500,000. Builder 1 does the initial work defectively, then abandons the job in the middle of construction. At the time of abandonment, Owner has paid Builder 1 $200,000. If the house had been completed as contracted for, it would have been worth $600,000 (i.e., Owner made a favorable contract). Owner hires Builder 2 to complete the job for $400,000. Because the defective work done by Builder 1 before abandonment can't be readily remedied, the house as completed is worth only $550,000. Due to the delays caused by the breach, Owner loses $50,000 in rental income.

Owner can recover from Builder 1:

(1) $600,000 (value if completed as per the original contract) ....

(2) Less $550,000 (value as actually completed, due to Builder 1's poor work) ...

(3) Plus the difference between $600,000 (the sum of the $200,000 Owner paid to Builder 1 and the $400,000 he paid to Builder 2) and $500,000 (the contract price), or $100,000 ...

(4) Plus $50,000 lost rental as delay damages.

So Owner recovers:

$600,000 - $550,000 + 100,000 + $50,000, or

$200,000

2. **Owner breaches:** Now, let's look at how the *builder's* damages are computed if the *owner breaches* when the work has *not yet been completed.*[1] A good formula for computing the builder's damages (using somewhat different components than the usual expectation formula on p. 319) is:

---

1. If the work has been completed, the builder will simply recover the contract price less any prior payments made by the owner.

> [1] The money the builder has ***spent so far*** in fulfilling the contract (the builder's "***reliance***" cost; see *infra*, p. 326, for more about reliance) ...
>
> [2] Less any ***salvage value*** to the builder from the partial performance, such as materials purchased that can be used on another project ("***loss avoided***") ...
>
> [3] Plus the ***profit*** the builder ***would have made*** had the contract been completed ...
>
> [4] Less any ***progress payments*** already made by the owner.

Farnsworth §12.10 at 770.

Example: Builder contracts to build a house on Owner's land for $500,000. At a time when Owner has paid Builder $60,000 and Builder has spent $200,000, Owner repudiates. Builder cancels and sues. The $200,000 spent by Builder includes $20,000 of lumber that he can use on another job. If the contract had been completed, Builder would have made a profit of $100,000. Builder can recover:

(1) The $200,000 he has spent in "reliance";

(2) Less the $20,000 he can get for the lumber ("loss avoided");

(3) Plus the $100,000 profit he would have made had the project been completed on both sides;

(4) Less the $60,000 already paid by Owner.

So Builder recovers:

$200,000 - $20,000 + 100,000 - $60,000, or

$220,000

D. Allocation of overhead: Where the plaintiff has not finished his performance at the time of the defendant's breach, should the plaintiff's cost of completion (the amount he has saved by not having to finish) include a portion of his ***overhead***? The answer given by most courts is "no" — since overhead is by definition fixed, there is no saving of any of it as a result of P's not having to finish the contract; this conclusion is to the plaintiff's advantage, of course. See, e.g., *Vitex Manufacturing Corp. v. Caribtex Corp.*, 377 F.2d 795 (3d Cir. 1967).

E. Cost of completion vs. decrease in value: The general principle in awarding expectation damages is, as we have seen, that the plaintiff should be put in the same position he would have been in had the contract been performed. This formula leads to difficulty, however, in those situations where the difference between the economic value of a complete performance under the contract and the value of the defendant's defective performance is ***less than the cost of remedying*** defendant's defective performance. In such a case, should the plaintiff be awarded the net economic loss he has sustained by virtue of the defendant's breach (the lesser sum) or the cost of remedying defendant's defective performance (the greater sum)? The problem is illustrated by the following example.

> **Example:** Plaintiffs own a farm containing coal deposits. They lease the premises to Defendant for a five-year term, for the purpose of allowing Defendant to strip-mine on the property. Because of the unsightliness of a strip-mining operation, Plaintiffs insist

that the lease contain a clause requiring Defendant to perform various work to restore the beauty of the property at the end of the lease term. Plaintiffs are unwilling to sign the lease without these terms, and they are included. At the end of the lease, Defendant fails to perform this restoration work. Evidence shows that it would cost Defendant about $29,000 to perform the work, because of the great quantities of dirt which would have to be moved. However, the value of the farm is only about $300 less than it would have been had Defendants performed this work. In fact, the total value of the farm is less than $5,000. In the Plaintiff's suit for damages for breach, should they be awarded $300 or $29,000?

Held, only the diminution in value, $300, should be awarded. This is true for two reasons: (1) the provision of the contract requiring the remedial work is only incidental to the main purpose of the contract; (2) the economic benefit which the Plaintiffs would receive from full performance of the work is grossly disproportionate to the cost of performing the work. Thus *"economic waste"* would be involved. *Peevyhouse v. Garland Coal & Mining Co.*, 382 P.2d 109 (Okla. 1962).

1. **"Clearly disproportionate" standard:**   Most modern courts would probably agree with the *Peevyhouse* court's approach. The Second Restatement provides that the court should not grant the cost of remedying defects "if the cost is … *clearly disproportionate* to the probable loss in value" to the plaintiff. Rest. 2d, § 348(2)(b). Since an expenditure of $29,000 is clearly disproportionate to the $300 by which P's property would have increased in value, the Restatement test would produce the same result as the court reached in *Peevyhouse*. (But under the Restatement approach, an expenditure of $30,000 to fix a defect which, if fixed, will increase the value of the property by $20,000, is *not* clearly disproportionate, so the $30,000 may be awarded. See Rest. 2d, § 348, Illustr. 3.)

2. **Economic waste:**   A court is particularly unlikely to award the cost of completion where the defect is minor, and its completion would involve what is sometimes called *"economic waste."*

   a. **Destruction of work already done:** Thus the court will often rely on economic waste to decline to award cost-of-completion where the situation involves a *building contract* and remedying the defect would require the *destruction of what has already been done*. *Peevyhouse* is an illustration. Another is given in the following example.

   Example: Contractor contracts to build a house for Owner. The contract specifies that Reading pipe must be used. Contractor inadvertently substitutes Cohoes pipe, which is of virtually the same quality as the Reading. Owner objects, and refuses to pay the remaining contract amount. In a suit by Contractor for the remaining contract amount, should Owner be entitled to subtract from the contract price the full cost of changing the pipe (a large sum, since all of the existing plumbing would have to be torn out), or merely the amount by which the house is diminished in value because of the substitution of pipe (a negligible sum)?

   Held: (1) Contractor may recover on the contract, since he substantially performed (see *infra*, p. 333). (2) The correct measure of damages is "not the cost of replacement, which would be great, but the difference in value, which would be either nominal or nothing." To hold otherwise would cause Contractor to suffer a forfeiture, without any correspondingly great benefit to Owner; the cost of completion is "grossly and unfairly out of proportion to the good to be attained." *Jacob & Youngs v. Kent*, 230 N.Y. 239 (1921). See also Rest. 2d, § 348, Illustr. 4 (based on *Jacob & Youngs*).

A dissent contended that this was not a case in which there was an "unsubstantial omission." Owner "contracted for pipes made by the Reading Manufacturing Company. What his reason was for requiring this kind of pipe is of no importance. He wanted that and was entitled to it...."

b.   Economic analysis: The situation of "waste" is a good example of how *economic analysis* (see *supra*, p. 2) can help explain some of the principles of contract law. Requiring the Contractor in *Jacob & Youngs v. Kent* to tear out the existing plumbing (or to pay for someone else to do it) is clearly economically inefficient, since the total "market value" of the remedy is far less than the cost of that remedy. Proponents of the law-and-economic school therefore typically approve of the result in a case like *Jacob & Youngs*.

   i.   Right to get what one bargained for: But critics of the law-and-economics school point out that the "waste" analysis deprives Owner of the ability to *get what he bargained for.* As one such critic has written, "It is simply right that one get what he was promised." 81 Colum. L. Rev. 111, 138, quoted in K&C, p. 1016. Furthermore, the law-and-economics approach often encourages promisors to *behave unethically*, especially since transaction costs (e.g., legal fees) will usually discourage the victim from suing.

c.   Willfulness: Perhaps out of fear of inducing breach, an important factor that tends to lead the court to award cost-of-completion, rather than diminution-in-value, is that the defendant's breach was *"willful"* and also intentional, in the sense that he knew all along that he was not complying with the contract. For instance, had the contractor in *Jacob & Youngs* known that he was substituting one pipe for another, and done so to save money, the court is far less likely to have docked him only for the lessening of value.

d.   Non-construction contracts: Practically all the cases where the cost-of-completion method rather than the diminution-in-value method is used involve *construction* contracts. Outside of the construction context, use of the cost-of-completion method will probably produce illogical results, since there is likely to be confusion about what the "thing" is that the plaintiff is entitled to complete.

F.   Requirement of reasonable certainty: The plaintiff may only recover for losses which he establishes with *"reasonable certainty."* Rest. 2d, § 352. That is, the plaintiff must not only show that he has had losses, but must also show the *amount* of these losses with reasonable certainty. The main application of this rule is that a plaintiff who claims that he would have *made profits* had the defendant not breached must show not only that there would have been profits, but also the likely amount of those profits.

1.   Profits from a new business: Where the plaintiff claims profits from a business or venture which at the time of breach was *not yet in actual operation*, the courts are reluctant to award such lost profits, due to their speculative nature.

a. **Old business used for estimation:**   However, modern courts may be willing to allow recovery of prospective profits from a new venture if the plaintiff can show that he ran a *previous operation* of a similar nature, or had experience in that particular industry.

Example: D breaches a contract to rent certain retail space to the Ps for a "book and bottle" shop (i.e., a combination liquor and book store).

Held, the Ps may recover the profits that would have been made. Profits from a new business are often not recoverable, but that this is only because such profits are usually uncertain. Given that the Ps had prior experience in both the book and liquor store industries, and presented detailed testimony concerning the profits typically made in these industries, there was enough evidence from which the jury could award lost profits. *Fera v. Village Plaza, Inc.*, 242 N.W.2d 372 (Mich. 1976).

b. **Doubts resolved against defendant:**   Another limitation on the principle that the plaintiff must show lost profits with reasonable certainty is that where the defendant's breach is the very thing that makes it difficult for the plaintiff to establish lost profits with certainty, the court will try to resolve the matter in a way that *punishes the defendant, not the plaintiff,* for the resulting uncertainty.

Example: P owns the hardcover publishing rights to the novel "Hunt for Red October." P licenses to D the rights to publish a paperback edition of the book, with D agreeing not to ship the paperback to stores earlier than October 1985. D jumps the gun, and makes shipments in September. P asserts that this breach has caused it to sell fewer hardcover books in September than P would otherwise have sold. However, P is unable to show precisely how many copies it would have sold in September absent the breach. The trial judge therefore assumes that P's sales for September would have been the same as those for August (even though sales were apparently trending downwards even before the breach).

Held (on appeal), the trial judge did not commit error: "Though the [trial] court accurately described its selection of August 1985 sales as its benchmark as 'generous[],' it was not improper, given the inherent uncertainty, to exercise generosity in favor of the injured party rather than in favor of the breaching party." *U.S. Naval Institute v. Charter Communications, Inc.*, 936 F.2d 692 (2d Cir. 1991).

2. **Public whim:**   Courts are especially unlikely to find that lost profits have been demonstrated with the requisite certainty where the venture is of a sort that *depends on the public whim*. Farnsworth, p. 832-33. This is true, for instance, of many *entertainment and sporting events* (e.g., a contract to stage a boxing match.)

a. **Evidence of comparable enterprises:**   Again, however, modern courts are more willing to allow evidence of profits made from closely comparable ventures. For instance, a modern court might well accept evidence of the profits earned by other title fights by the same champion, and perhaps even other fights of comparable stature put on by the same promoter. See Farnsworth, pp. 833-34.

3. **Cost of completion unknown:**   Expectation damages may be too uncertain to be awarded even where the only duty breached by the defendant was a duty to pay a price for the plaintiff's performance. This situation is illustrated most frequently by the case of a

plaintiff contractor, who sues for lost profits on a job that was terminated before its completion by the defendant owner's breach. Unless the contractor in this situation can show with some specificity what it would have *cost him to complete the job,* he will not be able to recover his expectation damages.

> **Example:** Contractor contracts to build a house for Owner for $30,000. After he has done roughly half the work, and expended $10,000, Owner repudiates the contract. Contractor's normal expectation measure of damages would be the contract price less his cost of completion. But if Contractor cannot demonstrate this cost of completion with adequate specificity, he will be unable to recover expectation damages at all. He may, however, be able to recover either reliance or restitution damages, as discussed below.

4. **Alternative damage measure chosen:** If lost profits are found to be too speculative, the courts will frequently adopt some alternative measure of damages. In many instances, this alternative measure will be the plaintiff's *reliance* damages (discussed in the next section). In cases involving equipment and farm land, the courts have often used the property's *rental value* as a substitute for the profits that could have been made from it.

5. **UCC has liberal certainty requirement:** The UCC takes a somewhat liberal view of the requirement that damages be proved with appropriate certainty. Comment 4 to § 2-715 (allowing the buyer to recover "consequential" damages) states that "the burden of proving the extent of loss incurred by way of consequential damages is on the buyer, but the section on liberal administration of remedies [§ 1-305] *rejects* any doctrine of certainty which requires *almost mathematical precision* in the proof of loss. Loss may be determined *in any manner which is reasonable* under the circumstances."

G. **UCC follows expectation rule:** As a general rule, the UCC awards both an aggrieved buyer and an aggrieved seller expectation damages. UCC § 1-305(a) provides that all Code remedies "shall be liberally administered to the end that the aggrieved party may be *put in as good a position as if the other party had fully performed*." However, the Code sets forth a number of specific rules for calculating damages both in the breaching-buyer and breaching-seller situations. These rules are discussed extensively in a special section devoted to UCC damages, *infra*, p. 364.

Quiz Yourself on
EXPECTATION DAMAGES

90. Drew Idd hires the Landmark Construction Co. to build the Stonehenge Resort on Idd's property. The contract price is $500,000. When the frame is complete, Idd commands Landmark to stop work, and he refuses to pay for the building. Up to that point, Landmark has spent $100,000, and would have needed to spend another $200,000 to complete the job. Idd paid $250,000 up front.

    (A) How much will Landmark be able to recover if it sues on the contract?

    (B) Assume that Landmark is unable to determine what its cost of completion would have been. Can it still recover its expectation damages?

91. Bo Peep decides to get out of the sheep business and open up a business selling household cleaners door-

to-door. She enters into a contract with Mr. Clean in which he agrees to supply her with household cleaners at wholesale cost for the next 12 months. Before Bo Peep gets her first shipment, Mr. Clean breaches the agreement. Bo Peep figures that with her pretty face and smooth-talking style, she could have made $1,000 a month in profits from her new venture.

(A) When Bo sues for breach, can she recover the $1,000/mo. she believes she would have made, for the 12 months covered by the contract?

(B) Now assume that Bo Peep had been in her new business for three years before she entered into her agreement with Mr. Clean, during which she had purchased comparable supplies at similar pricing from a different supplier. She can show that she made a profit of $1,000/mo. in the last year of that arrangement, and that she cancelled that arrangement to make the new one with Mr. Clean. She can further show that when Mr. Clean cancelled, any other then-available arrangement would have been so much more expensive (due to changing industry conditions) that she would have made no profit. May Bo recover the $1,000/mo. she believes she would have made from the contract with Mr. Clean, for the 12 months covered by the contract?

Answers

90. (A) $50,000 — that is, the balance of the contract price ($250,000) less Landmark's remaining cost to complete ($200,000).

(B) No. If a contractor cannot show with some specificity what it would have cost him to complete the job, he will not be able to recover his expectation damages. Under these facts, Landmark will likely only be able to recover the value of the benefit it has conferred upon Idd (restitution damages).

91. (A) No. A plaintiff can only recover damages that she can prove with reasonable certainty. Lost profits on a brand new business venture are normally too speculative.

(B) Yes. The fact that Bo has previously made $1,000/mo. under a similar arrangement means that there is a "reasonable certainty" that she would have made this amount in the new venture. Therefore, unless Mr. Clean can show some reason why past conditions would not have applied to the new contract, Bo will be able to recover, as expectation damages, $1,000 x 12 months, or $12,000.

V. RELIANCE DAMAGES

A. **General function of reliance damages:** In most contract situations, the award of expectation damages will adequately compensate the plaintiff. But in some contract situations, and several non-contractual situations, expectation damages are not suitable, and *reliance* damages may therefore be appropriate. These situations include those in which:

❑ plaintiff cannot show his *lost profits with sufficient certainty*, but can nonetheless show items of expenditure;

❑ plaintiff is a *vendee under a land contract* who sues the vendor for the latter's refusal to convey the property to him, and the jurisdiction is one in which expectation damages are not awardable in this situation; and

❑ there is *no legally enforceable contract* but the plaintiff is entitled to some protection (a situation typified by cases invoking the doctrine of *promissory estoppel*).

1. **Reliance damages as a component of expectation damages:** Before we look at the situations in which reliance is the total measure of damages, note that reliance damages are also a built-in ***component*** of the usual ***expectation*** damages award. Normally, reliance damages are hidden within the usual expectation formula: contract price minus cost of completion. Other formulas for calculating the expectation interest, however, make the reliance component more evident. Sometimes, for example, a plaintiff will calculate his expectation interest by the following formula:

> [1] *cost to P of work already performed +*
>
> [2] *the total profit P would have made on the contract,*
>
> where "total profit" is defined as:
>
> [3] *contract price – P's total cost of performing.*

The "cost to P of work already performed" is, of course, essentially a reliance measure.

> **Example:** P, a roofer, contracts to place 500 square feet of roofing on O's house. He is to be paid $4 per square foot. After he has put up 100 square feet, O repudiates the contract. At trial, P proves that: (1) he expended $300 for materials and wages for the work already done; (2) $4 per square foot is his standard price for roofing, and this was a standard job; and (3) from long experience with this kind of standard job, P knows that his profit is 25% of the contract price.
>
> Based on this proof, P will probably be entitled to recover the $300 already expended, plus the anticipated profit on the whole job (25% of the overall contract price, or $500). In other words, P's $800 total expectation interest award can be viewed as being composed of a reliance component (the $300 expended) and a net profit component (the $500).

B. **Reliance damages where profits too speculative:** As we have seen (*supra*, p. 323), lost profits may not be awarded where they are too ***speculative*** or ***uncertain***. Where proof of lost profits fails for uncertainty, the court may award the plaintiff compensation for expenditures he made in ***preparing to perform the contract***, and those he made in ***actually making part performance***. Reimbursement for these out-of-pocket expenditures thus protects the plaintiff's reliance interest. The "speculative lost profits" situation is the principal kind of suit ***on the contract*** in which reliance damages are awarded. See Rest. 2d, § 349, Comment a.

C. **Promissory estoppel:** Where the plaintiff brings an action based on ***promissory estoppel*** (*supra*, p. 136), the courts often refuse to grant the plaintiff the profits he would have made had the promise been kept, but instead grant the plaintiff his reliance damages. In so doing, the courts use reliance damages as a means of "avoiding injustice," the goal of promissory estoppel. That is, the court reasons that although the plaintiff should not be entirely barred from recovery, he should not have the full benefits of the usual contractual measure of recovery, since there was no traditionally-enforceable contract.

> **Example:** Plaintiff applies to Defendant, a radio distributor, for a franchise to sell Emerson radios. Defendant erroneously tells Plaintiff that the franchise has been approved, that Plaintiff can proceed to employ salespeople and solicit orders, and that

an initial shipment of thirty radios will be made. Plaintiff spends $1,150 in making preparations to do business, but does not receive either the franchise or the radios. Since no legally enforceable contract was ever formed, Plaintiff brings a suit based on promissory estoppel.

Held, plaintiff may not recover the profits he would have made had the thirty radios been received and sold. However, he may recover reliance damages, i.e., his expenditures in preparing to do business (the hiring of salesmen and the solicitation of orders). *Goodman v. Dicker*, 169 F.2d 684 (D.C. Cir. 1948).

D. Doctor-patient contracts: A few courts have awarded reliance damages in suits brought by *medical patients* against doctors (usually surgeons), where the plaintiff shows that the doctor affirmatively ***promised to achieve a particular result.*** (*Hawkins v. McGee, supra*, p. 319, was such a contract case, though expectation damages rather than reliance damages were awarded.)

Example: D, a plastic surgeon, promises P, a professional entertainer, that two operations which D will perform on P's nose will improve her appearance. D performs the two operations, but P's condition is worsened; a third operation fails to restore it to its original state. There is no evidence that D acted negligently. P sues on the contract.

Held, P may recover reliance damages. Restitution damages (see *infra*, p. 330) would be too meager a recovery, since these would be limited to the fee paid to D. Yet expectation damages (the difference between the value of the nose as it was before the operation and the value of the nose as D promised to make it) might be excessive, and would frighten doctors into practicing "defensive medicine." Therefore, reliance damages are an appropriate measure.

Consequently, P is entitled to: (1) the amount of the fee which she paid to D; (2) the difference in value between her nose as it was before the operation and her nose as it was thereafter; and (3) her pain and suffering and mental distress to the extent that these exceeded what would have been involved in a successful performance by D (i.e., at least the pain and suffering and mental distress involved in the third operation, attempted solely for restorative purposes). The court declines to determine whether the pain and suffering that would have been involved even in a successful operation may be recovered under the reliance theory (though such recovery is arguably required, since the suffering has been "wasted"). *Sullivan v. O'Connor*, 296 N.E.2d 183 (Mass. 1973).

E. Limitations on amount of reliance recovery: The plaintiff's reliance damages are sometimes *limited* to a sum *smaller than his actual expenditures*.

1. Contract price as limit: Where the defendant's only obligation under the contract is to pay a sum of money (the contract price), reliance damages will almost always be ***limited to this contract price***. The reason for this is that courts do not want to give the plaintiff a windfall in the form of reliance damages greater than his expectation damages would have been, and expectation damages will seldom be greater than the contract price.

2. Recovery limited to profits: As just stated, the plaintiff will almost never be allowed to recover reliance damages in excess of the contract price. A more difficult question, however, is whether the plaintiff's reliance damages are also limited to the contract price *minus* the cost of completion, where the plaintiff has not completed his performance. That is, *may the plaintiff's reliance damages exceed his expectation damages*? (Expenditures can exceed expectation damages only if the contract would have, if completed, resulted in a *loss* for the plaintiff.) Most courts *refuse to allow reliance damages to exceed expectation damages*, but place the *burden of proof on the defendant* to show what the plaintiff's loss would have been. This is the approach of the Second Restatement; see Rest. 2d, § 349.

    a. **Where no evidence of cost of completion:** If the defendant's breach has prevented the plaintiff from completing his performance, and neither the plaintiff nor the defendant brings forward satisfactory evidence of how much it would have cost plaintiff to complete the contract (and thus it is uncertain what plaintiff's net profit would have been), the plaintiff may normally *recover his entire reliance damages*, limited only by the contract price. Thus the plaintiff is not required to rebut the defendant's allegation that the plaintiff would have lost money on the contract, unless the defendant comes forth with actual satisfactory evidence of this allegation.

    b. **Where defendant proves that plaintiff would have lost money:** If, on the other hand, the defendant is able to *prove* that the plaintiff *would have suffered a net loss* on the contract had it been completed, the plaintiff's reliance recovery will be *limited to what his expectation damages would have been on completion.*

    Example: P enters into a contract with D to build a bridge for $150,000. After P is part way through the construction, D repudiates the contract and does not pay P anything. P has spent $100,000 in reliance expenditures. D proves at trial that P would have needed to spend an additional $110,000 to complete the project, resulting in an overall $60,000 loss for P had the contract been performed.

    There will be subtracted from P's reliance damages the amount of the loss which D shows that P would have suffered had the contract been performed. So P's recovery would be computed as follows: $100,000 in reliance damages less $60,000 loss to him if there had been completion, or a net recovery of $40,000.

  3. **Expenditures prior to signing of contract:** The plaintiff will normally not be permitted to recover as reliance damages expenditures made *before the contract was signed*, since these expenditures cannot be said to have been made "in reliance on" the contract.

F. **Cost to plaintiff, not value to defendant:** When reliance damages are awarded, they are usually calculated according to the *cost to the plaintiff* of his performance, *not* the *value to the defendant.* Thus even if the plaintiff's expenditures were all incurred in preliminary preparations to perform, and the defendant breached before plaintiff even began actual performance, plaintiff will be able to recover his cost of preparation. (In the case of *restitution* damages, discussed below, this will not always be the case; in restitution, the benefit to the defendant, not the cost to the plaintiff, is the usual measure.)

G. **Reliance damages under the UCC:** The UCC does not explicitly deal with the issue of reliance damages. However, it is clear that in cases brought on the contract, where the plaintiff cannot show lost profits with sufficient certainty he may recover his reasonable expenditures made in connection with the contract.

1. **Incidental damages:**   This is most clearly indicated by UCC § 2-715(1), which allows an aggrieved buyer to recover *"incidental damages,"* defined to include "expenses reasonably incurred in inspection, receipt, transportation and care and custody of goods rightfully rejected, any commercially reasonable charges, expenses or commissions in connection with effecting cover and *any other reasonable expense incident to the delay or other breach.*"

VI. RESTITUTION

A. **Restitution generally:**   Just as a court may award the plaintiff her expectation interest (her expenditures plus the profit she would have made on the contract) or her reliance interest (her expenditures), so the court may decide to protect the plaintiff's *restitution interest*. The plaintiff's restitution interest is defined as the *value to the defendant of the plaintiff's performance*. Restitution damages may be awarded to the plaintiff both in a suit on the contract (discussed here) and in a suit brought in quasi-contract (discussed on p. 335). The goal of restitution is the *prevention of unjust enrichment*.

1. **Calculation of value:**   The distinguishing quality of the restitution interest is that it is *value rendered to the defendant*, regardless of how much the conferring of that value cost the plaintiff, and regardless of how much the plaintiff was injured by the defendant's breach. If the performance has no value to the defendant, there can be no restitution damages, regardless of how much it may have cost the plaintiff to perform.

   a. **Market value is the standard:**   However, although it is the value to the defendant that is determinative, this value is usually the sum which the defendant would *have to pay to acquire the plaintiff's performance*, *not* the *subjective value* to the defendant, nor the amount for which the defendant could *resell* the plaintiff's performance. Rest. 2d, § 371(a).

   Example: Contractor contracts to build a grotesque outhouse on Owner's property. After Contractor has completed three-fourths of the work, Owner repudiates the contract. At trial, Contractor shows that he spent $15,000 out-of-pocket to do the three-quarters of the job which he did. Owner shows that contractor was highly inefficient, and that he (Owner) could have hired X to do the three-quarters of the work actually done for $10,000. Owner also shows that the three-quarters of an outhouse actually diminished the value of his property, and that even if the outhouse were completed, the value of the property would still be less than before the contract.

   In this situation, Contractor's restitution interest would probably be held to be $10,000, the amount which it would cost Owner to duplicate Contractor's work on the open market. The amount expended by Contractor in performing (i.e., his reliance damages) is irrelevant to this calculation; the diminution in value of Owner's property would also probably be irrelevant. See Murray, p. 482.

B. **Restitution as a remedy for breach of contract:**   When a party is in the process of performing a contract, and the other party commits a material breach of the contract, the aggrieved party has the right to *rescind the contract*, and recover restitutionary damages for the breach. Even though this rescission purports to dissolve the contract, plaintiff's suit is really on the contract (not in quasi-contract), and restitution damages are merely one option available to him, as are expectation and reliance damages.

1. **Where expectation damages can't be estimated:** The most common situation in which restitution damages are awarded in on-the-contract actions is where the plaintiff's expectation damages *cannot be estimated with sufficient certainty.*

   Example: Where a construction contractor does part of the work, and the owner breaches, the contractor may be unable to show what his cost of completion would have been. In that event, the contractor will normally be permitted to recover restitution damages, calculated as the market value of the partially-completed performance.

C. **Restitution not limited to the contract price:** The most significant utility of the restitution measure of recovery is that, according to most courts, *it is not limited by the contract price*. If the work done by the plaintiff prior to the defendant's breach has already enriched defendant in an amount greater than the contract price, this entire enrichment may be recovered by the plaintiff. The restitution measure is thus completely different from the reliance measure, which, as we have seen (*supra*, p. 328), is normally limited to the contract price.

1. **Rationale:** One rationale for allowing a plaintiff's restitution recovery to exceed the contract price (i.e., to allow restitution to exceed expectation damages) has been expressed as follows: "to permit [the defendant] to use his breached contract to limit a recovery against him would be to *pay him a premium for his own wrong*." *Johnston v. Star Bucket Pump Co.*, 274 Mo. 414 (1918).

   a. **Other reasons:** Also, where the contract price is expressed as a unit price (e.g., $23 per cubic foot excavated), the plaintiff may have named a lower unit price for a large volume of work than he would have had the work been limited to the amount he actually ended up performing. See F&Y, p. 504, Note 2. Furthermore, there may have been other anticipated benefits, external to the contract, which the plaintiff contemplated receiving and which he has lost through not being able to finish. For instance, a contractor might be eager to perform the entire job, so that he can show it to prospective customers as an example of his work.

2. **Restitution not available where plaintiff has fully performed:** If at the time of the defendant's breach, the plaintiff has *fully* performed the contract (and the defendant owes only money, not some other kind of performance), most courts do *not allow the plaintiff to recover restitutionary damages*. The plaintiff is then relegated to his expectation measure (usually the contract price, since by hypothesis there is no remaining cost of completion). Rest. 2d, § 373(2).

   a. **Anomalous result:** Limiting the fully-performing plaintiff to the contract price, but not so limiting the partly-performing plaintiff, can produce the anomalous result that the plaintiff is *penalized for finishing off his performance.*

D. **Restitution in losing contract:** Not only may the restitution award exceed what the plaintiff's expectation damages would have been, full restitution may even be awarded where the plaintiff has partly performed, and *would have lost money* had the contract been completed. Rest. 2d, § 373, Comment d; Farnsworth, p. 856-57.

Example: P contracts to perform sub-contract work for D, a general contractor. After only part of the work has been done, D unjustifiably fails to make certain payments, and P terminates work. At this time, P is already owed $37,000. D shows that had P completed the contract, P would have had an overall loss of more than $37,000; D thus argues that it should not owe any money (since P is already in a better position than it would have been in had it finished the contract).

Held, for P. Even though the normal expectation measure of damages will produce no recovery for P, P is entitled to recover in *quantum meruit*. P's measure of recovery will be "the *reasonable value* of [its] performance," i.e., "the amount for which such services *could have been purchased* from one in [P's] position at the time and place the services were rendered." The contract price may be evidence of this amount, but will not be dispositive on the question. Remanded for further calculation of the correct damage amount. *U.S. v. Algernon Blair, Inc.*, 479 F.2d 638 (4th Cir. 1973).

E. **Restitution for the breaching plaintiff:** The cases discussed so far in this chapter have involved plaintiffs who, at the time of the defendant's breach, were not themselves materially in default. If the plaintiff materially breaches the contract, he may be entitled to recover the amount by which the defendant has been enriched (whether or not the defendant was also in breach). However, the defaulting plaintiff's suit must be brought in quasi-contract, not on the contract. Discussion of the rights of the breaching plaintiff is therefore treated in the material on quasi-contract, *infra*, p. 337.

Quiz Yourself on
RELIANCE AND RESTITUTION DAMAGES

92. Maria von Trapp has never been in business before. She enters into a contract with Yoddle-Ey-Hee-Hoo, a chain of Bavarian clothing stores, to open a franchise. In anticipation of her store's opening, she spends $150 on printing for price tags, puts a $2,000 nonrefundable deposit down on a space for the store, and purchases $500 worth of mannequins. Yoddle-Ey-Hee-Hoo then pulls the rug out. Maria sues for breach. She estimates that her lost profits would have been $2,000 per month for the first year. None of the purchased items have any salvage value. Assuming that Yoddle is found to have breached, what are Maria's damages, and on what theory?

93. Neulla Rich enters into a contract with the Rococo House of Design to redecorate her New York penthouse. Rococo designers set to work immediately. They install new wallpaper and lighting in Neulla's house, and paint a mural of little cherubs on her dining room ceiling. Shortly thereafter, Neulla breaches the agreement by refusing to pay for anything. Rococo has spent $10,000 (including labor) on the installation of the wallpaper, lighting and mural, and the market value of these items is $15,000. The total redecorating contract was for $50,000.

    (A) Assume that Rococo cannot estimate with specificity what its cost of completion would have been. If Rococo sues, what damages can it collect?

    (B) Now assume that the total contract price was $12,000. How much may Rococo recover?

    (C) Now assume that Rococo has fully performed under the contract, and Neulla has refused to pay anything. Rococo spent $25,000 to perform. The market value of the new décor (what a reasonable home owner would expect to pay for it) is $60,000. The total contract price was $50,000. What damages can

Rococo recover?

Answers

92. **$2,650, on a reliance damages theory.** Maria will not be entitled to collect lost profits because she will be unable prove them with any certainty, since this is a new venture for her and she has never operated a comparable venture. However, Maria will be entitled to be reimbursed for the expenditures she made in preparing to perform under the contract. Her reliance damages will be $2,650, or the total of all she reasonably shelled out (and cannot salvage) in anticipation of the store's opening.

93. **(A) $15,000.** Where, as here, a party can't estimate her expectation damages with sufficient certainty, the party may recover restitution damages. Therefore, Rococo can collect restitution damages to compensate it for the benefit it has conferred upon Neulla. These damages will be $15,000, or the market value of the work it has done.

(B) $15,000. With restitution damages, a party who has not yet fully performed can collect an amount *in excess of* the total contract price. (Yes, this is paradoxical, but the law is pretty clear on this point.) So Rococo will be entitled to its $15,000 even though the contract price was only $12,000.

(C) $50,000. Ironically (in light of the answer to (B)), when a party has *fully performed* under a contract and the other party's breach amounts to a failure to pay money, most courts will *limit* the plaintiff's recovery to her expectation damages, even where the restitution damages would have been greater. So here, Rococo will be entitled to collect only the $50,000 contract price, not the $60,000 market value.

VII. SUBSTANTIAL PERFORMANCE AS A BASIS FOR SUIT ON THE CONTRACT

A. **Substantial performance generally:** As we said in the chapter on conditions (*supra*, p. 215), if one party fails to substantially perform his obligations, the other party is discharged from performing his duties. The corollary to this rule is that where one party does substantially perform (i.e., does not materially breach), the other party is not relieved of his duties. If that other party refuses to perform, *the substantially performing party has an action for breach of contract*.

1. **Rule:** To put the rule more simply, *a party who substantially performs may sue for ordinary (expectation) damages for breach of contract if the other party fails to perform*. The other party has a set off, or counterclaim, for the damages she has suffered from the plaintiff's failure to completely perform the contract.

   a. **What constitutes substantial performance:** The factors that are considered in determining whether the plaintiff has substantially performed are discussed in detail *supra*, p. 227. The general principle is that the contract has been substantially performed where its *"essential purpose"* has been met.

   Example: P contracts to build a house for the Ds for $26,765. After most of the work has been done, the parties get into a dispute about the quality of the work, the Ds refuse to continue payment, and P doesn't finish the house. P sues for the balance of the contract price, and the Ds defend on the grounds that there has been no substantial performance. The Ds rely particularly on the argument that to redo and complete the work so that the contract specifications are matched would cost 25% to 30% of the contract price; they claim, for instance, that a wall has been placed so as to make the living room one foot narrower than it would have been, and that this would cost $4,000 to correct.

Held, for P. "Substantial performance as applied to construction of a house does not mean that every detail must be in strict compliance with the specifications and the plans." The test is "whether the performance meets the essential purpose of the contract." Here, the house was built from stock floor plans, not plans specially prepared by the owner. Accordingly, deviations from the plans were not of great significance. The mis-locating of the wall by one foot did not affect the market price of the house, according to experts. Accordingly, there was substantial performance and P may recover on the contract (but D will have a counterclaim for damages). *Plante v. Jacobs*, 103 N.W.2d 296 (Wis. 1960). (For a discussion of the measure of damages applied in this case, see *infra*, 334.)

B. Calculation of defendant's damages: Where the plaintiff performs substantially but not completely, the *defendant* will always have a *counterclaim* for the *damages she has suffered by virtue of the plaintiff's deviations.* However, the calculation of these damages will vary from case to case; sometimes they will be pegged to the cost of remedying the defects, while at other times, they will be pegged to the diminution in value resulting from the deviations.

1. **Cost of remedying defect:** As long as the defects can be remedied without unreasonable economic waste, the defendant's damages are the *cost of such remedial work.*

2. **Where waste involved:** If, on the other hand, the defects are so hard to correct that the cost of correction would be much greater than the increase in value resulting from the correction (i.e., the correction would involve unreasonable *economic waste*), the defendant's damages are the difference between the *value* of the product which defendant *would have received* had the contract been completely performed, and the value of the product as *actually rendered* by the plaintiff. That is, the damages are equal to the *diminution in value resulting from the deviations.* (For more about courts' reluctance to award cost-of-correction where this would involve economic waste, see *supra*, p. 322.)

   Example: Assume the facts are those of *Plante v. Jacobs, supra,* p. 333. Since P has substantially performed, he is entitled to the contract price less the damages he has caused. D's damages should be measured *not* by the cost of *making the house comply* with the contract (i.e., cost-of-completion), but rather, the *diminution in market value* resulting from the breach. Particularly as to the wall built one foot in the wrong direction, tearing it down and rebuilding it would be "economic waste [that] is unreasonable and unjustified"; therefore, the cost of doing such repairs should not be awarded. As to the more trivial defects, such as plaster cracks in the ceilings, the cost of repair may be used by the court as an indication of the diminution in market value. *Plante v. Jacobs, supra.*

   Note: The means of calculating a defendant owner's counterclaim damages, discussed immediately above, are also the means by which the damages of an owner who is suing as plaintiff for a return of money he has paid to a defaulting contractor are calculated. Thus the measure of damages for the aggrieved owner is the same regardless of whether the owner is a plaintiff, or a defendant asserting a counterclaim.

C. Divisible contracts: If the contract is *divisible* into separate pairs of "agreed equivalents," a party who has substantially performed *one of the parts* may recover on the contract for that part. This is true even though he has materially (or even willfully) breached with respect to the other portions. For a more extensive discussion of the concept of divisibility, see *supra*, p. 221.

VIII. SUITS IN QUASI-CONTRACT

A. Situations where quasi-contract may be used: Thus far, we have treated cases in which the plaintiff sues "on the contract." There are a number of situations, however, where recovery on the contract is either impossible or as a matter of judicial policy not allowable. These situations may be grouped into four general classes:

[1] situations where there was *never even an attempt to form a contract*, but the plaintiff nonetheless deserves some measure of recovery;

[2] cases where there was an attempt to form a contract, but the contract is *unenforceable* due to *impossibility*, *illegality*, *Statute of Frauds*, etc.;

[3] cases in which there is an enforceable contract, but the plaintiff has *materially breached*, and therefore may not recover on the contract; and

[4] cases in which the defendant has breached but for some reason the plaintiff is *not entitled to damages on the contract.*

In each of these situations, the plaintiff will often be allowed to recover in what is called *"quasi-contract."*

B. Measure of damages: Any of the three measures of damages is theoretically awardable in a quasi-contract suit. However, courts will almost never award expectation damages (except as a limit on a breaching plaintiff's restitution or reliance damages — see *infra*, p. 339). Both *reliance* damages and *restitution* damages are frequently awarded in quasi-contract suits; courts determine which measure to apply by looking at the facts of the particular case, and guessing which measure will better serve the "equities" of that case.

C. Quasi-contract where no contract attempted: The courts may as a matter of judicial policy award plaintiff a quasi-contractual recovery in some situations where *no contract was even attempted*.

1. Rationale: Courts do this on the theory that "a person who has been *unjustly enriched* at the expense of another is required to *make restitution*." Rest. (Restitution) § 1. A person (P) may recover on such a theory if she meets the following requirements:

[1] P *rendered a benefit* to another (D), who would be *unjustly enriched* if he were not required to pay for that benefit; and

[2] P did *not* confer the benefit on D *"officiously,"* that is, she did not thrust the benefit upon D *against his will* or in circumstances where she should have known that D would not want the benefit; and

[3] P did *not* confer the benefit on D *"gratuitously,"* i.e., *without expectation of compensation*.

Farnsworth, § 2.20.

2. **Emergency services supplied:** The most common example of recovery in quasi-contract where there has not even been an attempt at contract formation is the situation in which the plaintiff supplies *emergency services* to the defendant, without first forming a contract to do so.

> **Example:** D is injured in a streetcar accident, and is unconscious. A bystander summons P, a doctor, to give D emergency medical aid. P performs a difficult operation and D dies.

> *Held*, P may recover, in quasi-contract, the reasonable value of his services, even though there was never any attempt to negotiate a contract. In determining the reasonable value of these services, the fact that D died, and thus did not receive any real benefit, is irrelevant. Nor may the jury consider D's financial condition in determining the value of the services; this value should be determined by expert testimony as to the usual charge for such services. *Cotnam v. Wisdom*, 83 Ark. 601 (1907).

   a. **Terminology:** Where no contract exists between the plaintiff and the defendant, plaintiff's recovery is sometimes called recovery on a *"contract implied-in-law."* This terminology is confusing, however, so we'll say, instead, that the plaintiff is permitted to recover *"in quasi-contract."* Keep in mind that a "quasi-contract" is *not a contract at all* — it is an obligation *imposed by law* in order to bring about justice and equity.

   b. **No recovery where contract with another exists:** A plaintiff will not usually be allowed to recover in quasi-contract for benefits conferred on the defendant if a *third person* was under contractual obligation to pay for those benefits.

      i. **Sub-contractors:** The rule that there can be no quasi-contract recovery against the defendant where the services were contracted for by a third person means that a *sub-contractor* on a building job (i.e., someone hired by the general contractor to do a particular piece of the work) *cannot sue the owner* of the building for the reasonable value of the work done, even if the general contractor is unable to pay. (But statutes in most states give a *mechanic's lien* to the sub-contractor, so that she can force a judicial sale of the property, and recover the value of her services from the sale proceeds. See F&Y, p. 83, Note 3.

   c. **No recovery if intended as a gift:** Also, there will usually be no recovery if the facts indicate that the service-provider *did not expect to receive payment*, and intended instead to *make a gift* of the services. (This is requirement [3] on p. 335 *supra*, the requirement that P not have conferred the benefit "gratuitously.")

> **Example:** Aunt and Nephew go on a picnic lunch together. Nephew takes a swim in a lake, and starts to drown. Aunt jumps in, rescues Nephew, and in so doing ruins her valuable watch. Aunt will probably not be able to recover from Nephew in quasi-contract for the value of the watch, because the Aunt-Nephew familial relationship indicates that Aunt did not expect to be paid for her emergency services.

D. **Unenforceable contracts:** The parties may attempt to form a binding contract which turns out to be *unenforceable* or voidable because of the *Statute of Frauds, mistake, illegality, impossibility,* or *frustration of purpose.* In such a situation, the court will normally allow the plaintiff to sue in quasi-contract, and recover either the ***value of the services performed*** (restitution) or the plaintiff's ***reasonable expenditures*** (reliance). Restitutionary damages are probably the more common measure.

> **Example:** P, a contractor, contracts to remove a wooden floor from defendant's warehouse, and to install a reinforced concrete floor in its stead. He removes the old floor, installs reinforced steel rods to support the concrete, and places temporary wooden forms that are to hold the concrete until it has dried. Before the contract is completed, fire destroys the warehouse, without either P's or D's fault.
>
> *Held*, P is discharged from completing the contract by the doctrine of impossibility. P may, furthermore, recover in quasi-contract for those expenditures which benefited D (i.e., removal of the wooden floor, and installation of the steel rods). P may not recover for the temporary wooden forms, since these were merely incidental preparations for P's performance, and did not directly benefit D. Thus P's quasi-contractual recovery here includes restitution, but not reliance, damages. *Carroll v. Bowersock*, 100 Kan. 270 (1917).

E. Quasi-contractual recovery by a breaching plaintiff: Where a plaintiff has substantially, but not completely, performed, he may, as we have seen (*supra*, p. 333) recover on the contract, with an allowance to the defendant for damages for the non-material breach. But what if the plaintiff's performance is ***not substantial***, but the defendant has nonetheless been benefited by the plaintiff's performance? Does the plaintiff forfeit everything he has done? At least where the plaintiff's breach was not "willful," the answer is "no" — the plaintiff may recover his ***restitution interest***, less the defendant's damages for the breach. Such recovery is sometimes said to be in ***"quantum meruit"*** ("as much as he deserves").

> **Example:** P agrees to work for one year for D, for $120, to be paid at the end of the year. P works for 9 1/2 months and then quits without justification.
>
> *Held*, P may recover the reasonable value of the services he performed. (This was found by the jury to be equal to the pro-rata contract price). If P were not allowed to recover anything, D would end up having gotten almost five-sixths of the value of the whole year's labor for free; this would be much more than D could possibly have sustained in the way of damage from the breach. It is true that in an employment contract, the employer has no ability to return the part performance once it has been rendered, as a seller of goods, say, could reject a smaller shipment than ordered or a defective shipment; in this sense, it is not quite as fair to require the employer to pay for the defective performance as it is to require the buyer to pay the reasonable value of a defective tender which he has nonetheless kept. But in the labor case, the employer may be said to have accepted ***in advance*** the possibility that there would be only part performance, so the cases are not really distinguishable. (However, P may recover only the benefit conferred upon D; this cannot exceed the pro-rata contract price, less the damages from the breach.) *Britton v. Turner*, 6 N.H. 481 (1834).

1. **Use in construction cases:** One frequent application of the doctrine allowing quasi-contractual recovery by a defaulting plaintiff occurs in ***construction*** cases, in which the builder has constructed something that fails to constitute substantial performance but which is nonetheless of value to the owner.

a. **Right to recover value to owner:** In this situation, the builder gets to recover the *value to the owner* of the work done, even where the work does not constitute substantial performance of the contract.

   i. **Lesser of "cost to owner" and "change in value to owner":** When the court measures the "value to the owner" of the builder's work, courts want to avoid unduly rewarding the breaching builder. Therefore, the court will typically award the breaching builder the *lesser* of:

   ❏ the amount by which the *value of the owner's property has been increased* due to the work; and

   ❏ the reasonable *cost to the owner* if the owner had had that work done by someone other than the breaching builder.

   See Rest. 2d, §§ 371, 374(1).

   Example: Ohn, a homeowner, contracts with Builder 1 to have Builder 1 renovate Ohn's kitchen. The contract price is $100,000, to be paid at the end of the job. Builder walks off the job without justification when the work is half done. Ohn gets the job completed for $50,000 by Builder 2. It would have cost Ohn $50,000 to have had Builder 2, or anyone else, do the first 50% of the job (the work done by Builder 1 before he walked off the job). But the completed renovation increases the value of Ohn's home by $150,000 (and even the first 50% of the job increased the value of the home by $75,000).

   Even though Builder 1 did not "substantially perform" (doing half the job is not substantial performance), Builder 1 can recover in quasi-contract from Ohn for the reasonable value to Ohn of the work Builder 1 did. But in measuring the "reasonable value to Ohn," the court will take the lesser of (1) the increase in value of the home due to Builder 1's work ($75,000) and (2) the reasonable cost that Ohn would have incurred had he had someone other than Builder 1 do the first 50% of the job ($50,000). So Builder 1 will recover only the $50,000, and Ohn in a sense gets a windfall.

2. **Payments made by party in breach:** Quasi-contractual recovery may also be allowed where the benefit conferred by the breaching party consists of *money paid* by him. While the courts have been slower to allow recovery in this situation than in the context of furnishing of services (exemplified by *Britton v. Turner, supra,* p. 337), the modern tendency is clearly to *allow* such recovery.

   a. **Land-sale contracts:** The most common illustration of a breaching plaintiff's quasi-contractual right to recover money payments is the *installment land-sale contract*.

   Example: P contracts to buy a tract of land from D for a price of $1,500, payable in installments. The contract contemplates that the land will not be conveyed by D to P until the last payment has been made. Ten months after all payments should have been made, P has paid only $1,070 of the purchase price. D then conveys the property to a third person for $1,300, but refuses to refund any of the money paid by P. P brings an action in quasi-contract.

Held, P may recover $870 in quasi-contract. Payments of this amount by D will put D in the position he would have been in had the contract been fulfilled (since he will have received a total of $1,500 in return for the land). That is, P is entitled to recover the benefits he has conferred on D ($1,070 of payments) less the damages D has suffered by the breach (i.e., resale for $1,300 rather than the $1,500 contract price). Adherence to the traditional rule denying recovery to one in P's position would produce the "surprising result … that a purchaser who pays a substantial portion of the purchase price before defaulting is in a much worse position than the purchaser who pays nothing.…" *DeLeon v. Aldrete*, 398 S.W.2d 160 (Tex. Civ. App. 1965).

b. **Retention of money as liquidated damages:** There is an important exception to the general right of a breaching plaintiff to recover payments he has made: where the contract *explicitly provides* that these payments are to be *retained by the other party* in case of breach, the court will *honor* this agreement, if the sum is a "reasonable one that would be sustained as liquidated damages had the parties stipulated it." Farnsworth, p. 877. The "reasonableness" of the sum is measured "in the light of the anticipated or actual loss caused by the breach and the difficulties of proof of loss." Rest. 2d, § 374(2). (See also the discussion of liquidated damages clauses *infra*, p. 356.)

Example: On the facts of *DeLeon v. Aldrete, supra*, assume that the contract explicitly provided that any payments made by P would be retained by D in the event of P's breach. Had P only paid, say, 20% of the $1,500 contract price by the time of breach, a court might well find that this amount constituted reasonable liquidated damages in view of possible difficulties of proof of loss; if so, it would allow D to keep the $300, even though D's actual loss turned out to be only $200. But it is highly unlikely that the court would find that the sum of $1,070 (the amount actually paid by P in the case, equalling more than two-thirds of the contract price) was a reasonable liquidated damages amount; therefore, the court would strike the entire retention-of-payments provision, and would require D to return all but his actual damages.

3. **Limited to pro-rata contract price:** Where the plaintiff is not in default, he may, as we have seen (*supra*, p. 331) sue on the contract to recover his restitutionary interest; as long as the plaintiff has not fully performed, his recovery is not limited to the pro-rata contract price, or even to the total contract price. Where the plaintiff is in default, however, the courts have been very strict in limiting the plaintiff's quasi-contract restitution-interest recovery to the *pro-rata contract price*, less the defendant's damages for breach. The reason for this limitation is that otherwise, the plaintiff would be able to *"profit by his own wrong."*

Example: P, a contractor, agrees to build a house for O for $200,000. P performs 70% of the work, and expends $160,000 in doing so; he then becomes insolvent. The partially completed house is worth $180,000 on the open market. P finds another contractor, X, to complete the work for $60,000, but O suffers a $10,000 loss due to rental payments which he has to make, because P's breach has delayed his being able to occupy the house. P, although he is in material breach of the contract, may recover in quasi-contract.

However, his recovery, though it is based on restitution (the $180,000 benefit conferred on O), is limited to the pro-rata contract price ($140,000) less O's damages from the breach ($10,000), or $130,000. If the partially completed house had had a market value of $120,000, rather than $180,000, P's recovery would have been $120,000 minus $10,000, or $110,000. That is, the benefit conferred on the defendant, or the pro-rata contract price, whichever is less, serves as the basis for the damage award; from this is subtracted the defendant's counterclaim for damages due to the breach. (Note that P's reliance interest, the $160,000 spent in performing, is irrelevant.)

4. **"Willful" default:**   In many jurisdictions, the defaulting plaintiff will be allowed to recover in quasi-contract *only if her breach is not "willful."* If the plaintiff's breach is willful, in these jurisdictions *she cannot recover anything at all*. A willful breach is one which is intentional, rather than accidental or negligent. See Farnsworth, p. 577.

   a. **Second Restatement view:**   The Second Restatement (in contrast to the First) does not explicitly bar quasi-contract recovery if the breach is "willful." Rest. 2d, § 374. However, Comment b to § 374 seems to accomplish the same result as a ban on recovery by willfully breaching plaintiffs, when it says that "a party who intentionally furnishes services or builds a building that is materially different from what he promised is properly regarded as having *acted officiously* and *not in part performance* of his promise and will be denied recovery on that ground even if his performance was of some benefit to the other party."

   b. **Convenience or financial advantage:**   Courts are especially likely to deny recovery if the breach is not only intentional, but made in *bad faith*. For instance, a *contractor* who *uses cheaper materials* in order to make an already profitable contract more profitable is less likely to be granted quasi-contractual recovery than a contractor who uses cheaper materials because he has underbid the job and will incur grievous losses on it if he does not make the change.

   c. **Employment contracts:**   Courts are less likely to treat "willfulness" as a bar to recovery in the context of *employment contracts* than in connection with most other types of contracts. For instance, *Britton v. Turner, supra*, p. 337, was such a case, since the plaintiff's decision to quit was clearly "intentional."

      i. **Statutory modifications:**   Even where there is no judge-made rule allowing willfully-breaching employees to recover, recovery may be facilitated by *statute*. Many states today have statutes which require that an employee be paid wages at specified intervals, and which allow the employee to recover for those periods which have already expired, when he wrongfully quits. (Also, the doctrine of *divisibility* may produce a comparable result; see *supra*, p. 221.) Even where a statute allows partial recovery, however, the employer has a *counterclaim for damages* which he sustained by reason of the employee's breach.

5. **UCC allows partial restitution to breaching buyer:**   The UCC gives a *breaching buyer* a right to *partial restitution* with respect to *payments he made to the seller* before he (the buyer) breached. UCC § 2-718(2) provides that:

   "where the seller justifiably withholds delivery of goods because of the buyer's breach, the buyer is entitled to *restitution* of any amount by which the sum of his payments *exceeds (a)* the amount to which the seller is entitled by virtue of [an enforceable *liqui-*

dated damages provision] or *(b)* in the absence of such [a provision], *twenty percent* of the value of the total performance for which the buyer is obligated under the contract or *$500*, whichever is *smaller.*"

Example: Seller contracts to sell to Buyer 1,000 widgets at $2 each. The contract does not contain a liquidated damages clause. Buyer sends in a $700 deposit. Buyer cancels the order just before Seller is to ship. Seller suffers no damages, because he has a limited supply of the widgets, and sells the ones he had earmarked for Buyer to X instead, at the same price.

Even though Buyer has breached, Seller may not keep the entire $700 deposit. Instead, Seller is entitled to keep only the lesser of: (i) 20% of the contract price ($400) and (ii) $500. Therefore, Seller may keep only $400, and must refund the other $300.

a. **Seller's counterclaim:** But where the buyer establishes such a right to restitution, the seller may *offset* the buyer's claim by any *actual damages* which he sustained as a result of the buyer's breach (computed by using Article 2's regular damages measures). § 2-718(3). So the seller owes the buyer a refund of the deposit in excess of the lesser of 20% of the contract price and $500, but can subtract from this refund seller's actual damages.

Example: Buyer agrees to buy a $10,000 widget from Seller, and gives Seller a $4,000 deposit. The contract does not contain any liquid damages provision. Before the date for delivery, Buyer says, "I don't want the widget — cancel my order." Let's assume that Seller cannot show actual damages, because he resells the widget to someone else for the same price, and that was the only widget Seller had or could get. In this situation, § 2-718(2) requires Seller to return the deposit minus the lesser of 20% of the contract price (i.e., $2,000) or $500; therefore, Seller must refund $3,500 to Buyer.

But now, assume that Seller is a "lost volume" dealer, i.e., he can get as many widgets as he has orders for. Assume also that Seller's cost per widget is $7,000. On these facts, Seller will be able to show that under the UCC's regular computation-of-damages measures, he has suffered actual damages of $3,000 by virtue of Buyer's cancellation, since even if Seller sells the particular widget earmarked for Buyer to someone else for the same $10,000, Seller will end up with $3,000 in overall lost profits by virtue of having done one less transaction. (See § 2-708(2), discussed *infra*, p. 369, dealing with "lost volume" sellers.) Therefore, under § 2-718(3)(a) Seller must refund only $1,000 to Buyer, and can keep the remaining $3,000 as actual damages.

F. **Plaintiff not entitled to contract damages:** In some cases, a contract exists and the defendant has breached, but the standard expectation measure damages produces no recovery for the plaintiff. In such instances, if the plaintiff has *conferred a benefit* on the breaching party, many courts will allow the plaintiff to recover the *fair value* of any goods or services he has conferred upon the defendant, even though such a recovery puts the plaintiff in a better position than the expectation measure would have. Farnsworth, p. 856-57. This topic is discussed more fully above. See, e.g., *U.S. v. Algernon Blair, Inc.*, discussed *supra*, p. 332.

Quiz Yourself on

SUITS IN QUASI-CONTRACT

94. Plato agrees to build a gazebo on Agamemnon's property in Pompeii, in return for $25,000. Plato spends $10,000 on materials and labor before Agamemnon's property is buried in lava from the Mount Vesuvius eruption. At the moment of the eruption, the partly-completed gazebo had a market value of $15,000. Will Plato be entitled to anything? If so, on what theory, and in what amount?

95. Dr. Welby is walking down the street when he sees a car hit Old Man River. Old Man River is lying unconscious in the street. Dr. Welby runs over and immediately begins CPR. He then pulls out his Swiss Army Knife, sterilizes it with a match and performs emergency surgery, saving Old Man River's life. Dr. Welby is a high-class Beverly Hills doctor who would normally charge $4,000 for the type of work he performed on Old Man River. The reasonable (market) value for this type of services, however, is $2,000. Dr. Welby sends Old Man River a $4,000 bill. Old Man River refuses to pay, arguing he never consented to have the work done and would not have done so had he been conscious at the time. Dr. Welby sues. How much, if anything, can Dr. Welby recover?

96. Scarlett O'Hara contracts to have Wilkes Construction to build a dream home for her, for a total cost of $1 million. The specifications include clay bricks and leaded glass windows. Wilkes decides to increase his profit margin a little by using plastic bricks and plain window panes; he figures Scarlett won't notice. When the work is about one-eighth done (and Wilkes has made outlays of $75,000), Scarlett notices the sub-standard work, and cancels the contract. It is not feasible to restore the house to the contracted-for specifications, since the bricks cannot be replaced without essentially demolishing what has already been built. The market value of the partly-completed house is $100,000. Scarlett has not paid anything yet on the contract price. If Wilkes sues Scarlett for the partly-done work, what (if anything) can he recover, and on what theory?

Answers

94. Yes, in quasi-contract, probably for $15,000. Where impossibility prevents the fulfillment of a partially-performed contract, the court will normally allow the party who has performed work to recover in quasi-contract. The court will choose between reliance damages (here, $10,000) and restitution damages (here, $15,000). Probably the court will allow restitution, even though Agamemnon got no *lasting* benefit from the gazebo — the court will likely reason that Agamemnon received a temporary benefit worth $15,000, and that he could have (and should have) carried insurance to cover the value to him of partly-completed construction work.

95. $2,000. Dr. Welby cannot recover his expectation damages ($4,000) because no contract was ever attempted under these facts. He can, however, recover the reasonable value of his services ($2,000) in quasi-contract. It is irrelevant that Old Man River claims after-the-fact that he didn't want the services performed — in emergency situations, the person who provides the services with a reasonable expectation of being compensated for them will be able to recover the reasonable value of the services.

96. Probably nothing. A plaintiff who materially defaults is not by that fact alone prevented from recovering; he will usually be permitted to recover in quasi-contract for the market value of the partial performance. But in most jurisdictions there is an exception: if the plaintiff willfully (i.e., intentionally) breaches, courts will often deny *all* recovery, especially where the breach was done to save money, and done in a deceptive manner. Wilkes' motive to save money by substituting inferior materials would fall into this category, so Wilkes will probably be denied all recovery. This is especially likely since there is no way for Scarlett to pay a reasonable amount to have the work transformed to something that meets her specifications.

IX. FORESEEABILITY

A. General limits on consequential damages: In the ordinary breach of contract situation, the court will attempt to protect the plaintiff's expectation interest; that is, the court will try to put the plaintiff in the position she would have been in had the contract been performed. In some situations, however, the plaintiff may sustain *unusual and great losses* as the result of a breach of contract. The sender of a telegram, for example, may lose a million dollar deal if the telegraph company mistransmits her bid. The courts have for a long time realized that to award the plaintiff full compensation for all of her losses due to the breach, no matter how bizarre or unforeseeable these losses are, would simply be unfair to the defendant, and possibly paralyzing to commerce as well. Therefore, the courts have developed certain limits on the kinds of damages which the plaintiff may recover.

B. *Hadley v. Baxendale:* The rules limiting the kinds of damages for which the plaintiff may recover are derived from the famous English case of *Hadley v. Baxendale*, 156 Eng. Rep. 145 (1854).

1. **Facts of *Hadley*:** Plaintiffs operated a mill which was forced to suspend operations because of a broken shaft. An employee of the plaintiffs took the shaft to the defendant carrier for shipment to another city for repairs. The carrier knew that the item to be carried was a shaft for the plaintiff's mill, but was not told that the mill was closed because the shaft was broken. The carrier negligently delayed delivery of the shaft, with the result that the mill was closed for several more days than it would have been had the carrier adequately performed the contract. Plaintiffs sued for the profits they lost during these extra days.

2. **Holding:** The court held that plaintiff could not recover for the lost profits. The loss of profits was not a consequence which "in the usual course of things" flows from a delay in the shipment of a shaft.

3. **The two rules of *Hadley*:** The court in deciding *Hadley* stated that a plaintiff suing for breach of contract may recover only damages which fall into one of two classes. These two classes are known today as the two "rules" of *Hadley v. Baxendale*. The damages must either:

   a. arise "*naturally,* i.e., according to the *usual course of things*, from [the] breach of contract itself...." or

   b. arise from "the *special circumstances* under which the contract was actually made" if and only if these special circumstances "were *communicated* by the plaintiff to the defendants...."

4. **Reformulation of rule:** Another way to express the two classes of damages allowed in *Hadley* is as follows:

    a. The court will *"impute" foreseeability* to the defendant as to those damages which any *reasonable person should have foreseen*, whether or not the defendant actually foresaw them; and

    b. The court will also award damages as to *remote or unusual consequences*, but only if the defendant had *actual* notice of the possibility of these consequences.

5. Application of facts of *Hadley*: The lost profit sought by the plaintiffs in *Hadley* did not fall into either of these two categories. That an enterprise might be shut down for lack of a shaft would not normally be foreseen by one in the position of the defendant carrier; therefore, the damages did not fall in the first class of "general" or "ordinary" damages. Nor did the plaintiffs give the defendant notice of the possibility of the shutdown of the mill; therefore, the damages did not fall in the second class. (The official head-notes to the case state that the defendant was told that the mill was shut down, but the opinion itself assumes that such notice was not given).

C. Universally followed: The rule of *Hadley v. Baxendale* is *followed* almost *universally* by American courts. See Rest. 2d, § 351.

1. Nomenclature used by courts: The courts have often called damages falling under the "first" rule of *Hadley v. Baxendale* *"direct"* or *"general"* damages. Damages falling under the second rule are usually called *"special"* or *"consequential."*

2. Factors bearing on unforeseeability: In determining whether particular damages are "reasonably foreseeable," and therefore fall under the first rule of *Hadley v. Baxendale*, the courts consider such factors as the separation in time and space between the breach and the consequences, customs in the plaintiff's and defendant's trades, etc.

3. Parties may allocate risks themselves: The parties are, of course, free to *allocate the risks* by express agreement in a way different from that prescribed by *Hadley v. Baxendale*. One way they can do this, of course, is for the plaintiff to give notice to the defendant of special circumstances, thus bringing the situation within the second rule of *Hadley*. Alternatively, the parties may agree that the defendant will not be liable for certain "reasonably foreseeable" consequences which would otherwise fall within the first rule of *Hadley*.

> **Example:** Telegraph Company makes every sender of a telegram sign a contract which provides that any remedy for mis-transmission of the message shall be limited to refund of the price of the telegram. This allocation of risk will probably be enforced by a court, even though in particular cases it will be obvious to Telegraph Company from the content of the message that substantial loss would result from mis-transmission.

4. Knowledge of consequential damages necessary: Under the second rule of *Hadley v. Baxendale*, damages other than those arising "naturally" are recoverable only if the defendant had *reason to know the special circumstances* which would give rise to these consequential damages. (See Rest. 2d, § 351(2)(b).) Two special situations are worth considering in detail:

    a. Contract to lend money: Where the contract calls for the defendant to *lend money* to the plaintiff, courts will usually presume that money is an "available commodity" which can be obtained from another source at the market rate of interest. Therefore, ordinarily, the injured borrower will only be able to recover the difference between the market rate of interest and the rate called for in the contract (if the latter is lower) even if the borrower can't in fact borrow elsewhere. But if the borrower can show that the lender was *aware* that the borrower would likely have a hard time borrowing from other sources, then more extensive damages may be recovered (e.g., profits that the borrower would have made with the borrowed money, if the lender is shown to have been on notice of the use to which the funds would be put). Farnsworth, pp. 827-28.

b. Liability to third party: A breach of contract may sometimes cause the injured party to become *liable to a third party*. If this third-party liability was foreseeable to the breaching party at the time the contract was made, the injured party may recover for this liability. For instance, if a seller of goods knows that the buyer has a contract to resell the goods, the seller will be liable for damages which the buyer is forced to pay to his own purchaser. Furthermore, the seller will be liable for the buyer's reasonable *litigation expenses*, and for the amount of any reasonable and foreseeable *settlement* which the buyer makes in order to avoid litigation. Farnsworth, p. 828.

5. Foreseeability distinguished from certainty: It is important to distinguish between the question whether particular damages were *foreseeable* (which is the *Hadley v. Baxendale* problem) and the question whether particular damages can be proved with adequate *certainty* (a question which is discussed *supra*, p. 323). Foreseeability relates to whether the possibility of the damages was sufficiently likely at the time the contract was made. Certainty, on the other hand, relates to how clear it is *at the time of suit* that the alleged losses in fact occurred, and that they were caused by the defendant's breach.

6. Time for measuring foreseeability: Whether particular consequences were sufficiently foreseeable must be determined *as of the time the contract is made*. If the defendant acquires knowledge of possible consequences after the contract is formed, but before the defendant breaches, this knowledge is *irrelevant*. Farnsworth, § 12.14; Rest. 2d, § 351.

7. UCC rule is liberal: The UCC applies a fairly liberal (from the plaintiff's perspective) view of *Hadley v. Baxendale*. § 2-715(2) allows a buyer to recover "*consequential damages* resulting from the seller's breach," defined to include "any loss resulting from *general or particular requirements* and needs of which the seller at the time of contracting *had reason to know* and which *could not reasonably be prevented by cover or otherwise,*" as well as "injury to person or property proximately resulting from any breach of warranty." Comment 3 notes that "particular needs of the buyer must be generally made known to the seller while general needs must rarely be known to charge the seller with knowledge." Thus both rules of *Hadley v. Baxendale* are in effect applied.

a. Failure to deliver: If the seller fails to deliver the goods at all, the buyer who *"covers"* (i.e., procures substitute goods; see *infra*, p. 365) may recover the amount by which the cost of cover exceeds the contract price, plus any costs of arranging the covering transaction. These losses are viewed by the Code as being "ordinary course" losses, and the seller must pay them even though he had no special knowledge. (This rule applies even where the spread between cost of cover and contract price is large, due to a sudden and extreme increase in market prices.)

b. Inability to cover: Problems of foreseeability arise only where the buyer is *unable to cover*. The Code assumes that in our market-based system the buyer will normally be able to procure substitute goods. Therefore, damages from inability to cover will be deemed foreseeable only if the seller was "aware of facts making the buyer's inability to cover itself foreseeable." Farnsworth, p. 827.

   i. Goods for resale: Consider the special case where the buyer is a *middleman*, i.e., one who intends to resell the goods for a profit. If the buyer is unable to cover, and assuming that this inability to cover was itself foreseeable to the seller (see the preceding paragraph), the seller will be held to have foreseen the possibility of lost profit as long as he knew that the buyer intended to resell. Farnsworth, p. 827-28. However, the seller will not be liable to the extent that the profits lost by the buyer are *extraordinarily large*. *Id.*

   ii. Buyer is manufacturer: If the buyer is not a middleman, but rather a *manufacturer* who is buying the item in order to use it to produce goods or services which will be resold for profit, a similar analysis applies. That is, in order to recover his lost profits, the manufacturer/buyer must first show that his inability to cover was foreseeable to the seller, and must then show that the *seller had reason to know that the buyer would be using the item to produce goods and services.* Even after all this is shown, recovery will not be allowed for lost profits that are *larger than the seller had reason to anticipate.* Farnsworth, p. 828.

c. Breach of warranty: Where an action is based upon breach of *warranty* (as opposed to the seller's failure to deliver the goods at all), the foreseeability rule is even more lax. Any injury to person or property may be recovered for, as long as it was *"proximately" caused* by the breach of warranty. (A breach of warranty action may in some jurisdictions be brought not only by the buyer, but by any person injured by the breach of warranty. Privity requirements for breach of warranty actions are discussed in the chapter on Warranties, *infra*, p. 501.)

   i. Lost profits: Many courts have allowed *lost profits* due to defective goods.

d. Limitation of damages by parties: Under the UCC (as under the non-Code law of most states), the parties are given substantial latitude to *modify* their liability for consequential damages. § 2-719(3) provides that "consequential damages may be limited or excluded unless the limitation or exclusion is *unconscionable.*"

   i. General rule on unconscionability: The section goes on to state that limitation of consequential damages for *injury to the person* in cases of consumer goods is "prima facie *unconscionable*," and that limitation of damages where "the loss is *commercial*" is *not* prima facie unconscionable. The section does not state anything about unconscionability where injury to the person resulting from commercial goods is involved, nor where economic loss to a consumer is involved. See the discussion of damages for breach of warranty, *infra*, p. 373.

8. Buyer who has to pay liquidated damages to third party: Suppose the plaintiff and defendant contract for the defendant to supply the plaintiff with some good or service needed for the plaintiff's business, and the plaintiff in reliance *makes a separate contract with a third party that contains a liquidated damages provision.* Let's assume the defendant's breach causes the plaintiff to be *unable to perform the other contract,* so that the plaintiff has to pay off on the other contract's liquidated damages clause. The question then becomes, do the plaintiff's damages include the cost of this liquidated-damages payment to the third party?

   a. Probably no liability: The answer will usually be *"no."* Unless the defendant had specific knowledge of the plaintiff's liquidated-damages deal on the third-party contract, the defendant will get the benefit of *Hadley v. Baxendale.* In other words, such a liquidated-damages clause does not come within the category of "general" or "ordinary" damages that would be reasonably foreseeable to a breaching seller who didn't have specific knowledge of the clause.

X. AVOIDABLE DAMAGES

A. General rule: All courts agree that where a plaintiff *might have avoided* a particular item of damage by reasonable effort, without undue risk, expense, or humiliation, *he may not recover for that item if he fails to make such an effort.* Rest. 2d, § 350. This rule arises from courts' desire to treat the breaching party fairly, and the desire to avoid economic waste.

   1. "Duty to mitigate": The rule preventing recovery for avoidable damages is often called the *"duty to mitigate"* rule. However, the plaintiff does not have any "duty" in the sense of an obligation for noncompliance with which judicial sanctions may be issued. If the plaintiff does not avoid his avoidable damages, he simply loses his ability to recover for them and nothing further happens. Rest. 2d, § 350, Comment b.

   Example: P contracts to have D build a bridge. Midway through construction, D tells P that it does not regard the contract as valid, and that P should not proceed any further. P nonetheless completes the bridge, and sues for the contract price.

   Held, P may not recover for any damages incurred after the stop-work order. "A plaintiff cannot hold a defendant liable for damages which need not have been incurred…." *Rockingham County v. Luten Bridge Co.,* 35 F.2d 301 (4th Cir. 1929).

B. Standard of reasonableness: The avoidable damages doctrine merely requires the plaintiff to make *reasonable efforts* to mitigate damages. The plaintiff is not expected to enter into dubious contracts, incur considerable expense or inconvenience, disorganize his business, damage his reputation or honor, or break any other contracts, in order to mitigate the damages done by the defendant's breach. Rest. 2d, § 350, Comment g.

   Example: Inventor contracts to invent, design, and produce a machine to be used by D in the latter's business. Inventor makes contracts with several suppliers for the parts which she will need to design and produce the machine. Before delivery of these parts, D repudiates the contract. Inventor may accept delivery of the parts, and recover the contract price less any costs saved by not having to perform (e.g., any resale value of the parts). She is not required to break her contracts with the suppliers, in order to mitigate her damages.

   1. Personal service contract: Where the contract is for *personal services*, courts are especially lenient toward the plaintiff, and do not require him to accept any position that is *substantially different from*, or inferior to, the one contracted for.

> **Example:** P (Actress Shirley MacLaine) contracts to perform in a movie musical to be made by D, called "Bloomer Girl." She is to be paid a salary of $750,000, and her contract provides that she has approval rights over the director and the screenplay. D then cancels the contract, but offers to pay P the same salary for a different movie, "Big Man." In this movie, she would not have approval over director or screenplay; also, the movie is a "Western Type" rather than a musical, and will not show P's dancing talents as the other one would have.
>
> *Held*, the second movie constituted a "different and inferior" employment from the first, and P was not required to accept it in order to mitigate damages. It was different in that it was a western rather than a musical, and did not involve P's dancing and singing talent. It was inferior in that it lacked director and screenplay approvals. Furthermore, the court will not inquire whether P acted reasonably in rejecting the second offer; the sole question is whether she made reasonable *efforts* to procure employment that was substantially the same as the canceled work. *Parker v. Twentieth Century Film Corp.*, 474 P.2d 689 (Cal. 1970).
>
> (A dissent argues that the two employments did not have to be identical for P to be required to accept the second one; it should be enough if they were of substantially the same kind, and there was no showing here that this was not so. Otherwise, a dismissed employee would never be forced to mitigate unless he were offered precisely his old job back by his old boss.)

    a. Offer of re-employment by D: Suppose an offer of "substitute employment" *comes from the defendant itself.* That is, suppose that after the defendant wrongfully fires the plaintiff, the defendant offers either to *reinstate* the plaintiff in her old job, or to employ her in a *new, substantially equivalent, position*. (Observe that this is what D claimed happened in *Parker, supra.*) In deciding whether the plaintiff's rejection of this offer of re-employment constitutes a failure to mitigate, is there anything legally significant about the fact that the offer is *coming from the same (breaching) employer?* The answer will depend on the circumstances, but is usually "yes": as a general rule, courts are sympathetic to the plaintiff if she declines the offer in the belief that there will *inevitably be ill-will between the parties stemming from the prior breach.*

        i. Rationale: As one court put it, the employee's rejection of an offer of re-employment will not diminish the employee's recovery for breach "if [the] circumstances are such as to *render further association between the parties offensive or degrading to the employee,*" which the court found to be likely in that particular breaching-employer situation. *Voorhees v. Guyan Machiney Co.*, 446 S.E.2d 672 (W.Va. 1994).

C. Burden of proof on defendant: Who should *bear the burden of proof* on the factual issue of whether the plaintiff made the required reasonable efforts to mitigate her damages? In both employment and non-employment scenarios, most courts *place the burden on the defendant.* That is, courts generally view the so-called duty to mitigate as an *affirmative defense*, and therefore impose on the breaching party the obligation to produce evidence that the non-breaching party / plaintiff failed to mitigate.

1. **Employment cases:** In employment cases where the plaintiff is an employee whose contract the employer has wrongfully breached, courts' tendency to place the burden of proof on the defendant employer is often of critical importance. In such cases, the employer is usually required to make an affirmative showing of both of the following propositions:

> [1] That the employee *failed to act reasonably in seeking substitute employment*; and

> [2] That there was at least *one comparable position* that the employee would likely have *obtained* had she made reasonable efforts to do so.

See K,C&P, p. 906.

   a. **No effort to find alternatives:** Notice that if the court follows the usual approach and places on the defendant employer the burden of proof as to both of the above propositions, the employer cannot succeed with the mitigation defense unless the employer proves step [2], that a *suitable replacement position existed* that the employee would likely have found and obtained.

   i. **D must show alternative jobs and their compensation:** In fact, even if the employer shows that the employee *made absolutely no effort to find another comparable position*, in most courts the employer will *lose* on the mitigation defense unless the employer *also*, with some specificity:

   ❏ *identifies one or more positions* that the employee would likely have succeeded in obtaining, *and*

   ❏ shows *how much the employee would have earned* had she been offered and taken one of these suitable replacement positions.

   It is often quite difficult for the employer to make both of these detailed showings, especially the second one — that's why, at least in employment cases, the breaching employer tend not to fare very well with the duty-to-mitigate defense.

   Example: P owns and runs a woodworking business. He sells the business to the Ds. As part of the sale transaction, he signs a three-year employment contract with the Ds by which he will continue to work in the business. Six months into the employment contract, the Ds fire P in what the court later finds to have been a breach of contract. P does not look for substitute employment, and sues the Ds for the entire salary that he would have earned between the firing date and the end of the three-year term. D demonstrates that P never made any efforts to find substitute employment. But D does not produce any evidence of what specific suitable alternative jobs would have been available to P, and thus shows no evidence as to how much any such substitute job would have paid P. The trial court finds that, although the Ds breached the contract by firing P, P's failure to make any effort to find substitute employment automatically means that P failed to mitigate damages, and is not entitled to any compensation.

   Held (on appeal), for P. In Tennessee, the failure to mitigate damages is an affirmative defense. Therefore, the employer must prove both the availability of suitable and comparable substitute employment and a lack of reasonable diligence on the part of the employee to find such employment. Furthermore, ***"only the amount that the plaintiff would have earned*** in the exercise of reasonable due diligence is applied to reduce his contractual damages." Therefore, the trial judge would have been correct in ruling, as he did, that P's recovery was completely eliminated (rather than merely reduced) "only if the proof show[ed] that the amount [P] would have earned in the exercise of reasonable diligence ***equaled or exceeded*** the amount he would have earned under the original employment agreement." Since the Ds presented no proof about the availability of comparable suitable substitute employment, the Ds were not entitled to *any reduction at all* under the duty-to-mitigate doctrine. *Maness v. Collins*, 2010 WL 4629614 (Tenn. Ct. App. 2010).

D. Sales contracts: The UCC sets forth certain rules regarding what an aggrieved buyer or seller must do to mitigate his damages.

   1. Obligation of aggrieved buyer: If the seller delivers defective goods, or does not deliver at all, the buyer will probably be obligated to minimize his damages by taking the following actions:

   a. Duty to "cover": If the seller either fails to deliver, or delivers defective goods which the buyer rejects, the buyer must usually attempt to ***"cover"*** for the goods if he wants to be eligible for consequential damages. That is, he must attempt to ***purchase substitute goods from another supplier***.

   i. How Code imposes this duty: § 2-712(1) merely ***permits*** the buyer to cover; if he does so, § 2-712(2) gives him as a measure of damages the difference between the cost of cover and the contract price, as well as any consequential damages (see *infra*, p. 365). But § 2-715(2)(a), in defining "consequential damages" to include only those losses "which ***could not reasonably be prevented by cover*** or otherwise" in effect provides that the buyer ***must*** cover where he can reasonably do so, and may not recover for those damages (e.g., lost profits) which could have been prevented had he covered.

   2. Seller's duty to mitigate: The ***seller*** of goods also has a *de facto* duty to mitigate damages. Where the buyer has wrongfully rejected goods, or has repudiated the contract before delivery, the seller has a choice of remedies. The Code does not expressly say that the seller has a duty to mitigate. However, the way the Code structures the seller's remedies means that a seller who does not attempt to mitigate may well bear the adverse consequences of not doing so.

   a. Choice of remedies: The seller has the following choice of remedies in the repudiation or non-acceptance scenario:

   i. Resale: The seller may choose to ***resell*** the goods (assuming that it's possible to identify which goods were the contracted-for ones), in which case the seller can recover the ***contract/resale differential.*** § 2-706(1). Resale is, of course, the conventional method of mitigating damages.

    ii. Contract/market differential: The seller may choose *not* to resell the goods. In that event, the seller normally recovers the difference between the *contract price* and the *market price* "at the *time and place for tender.*" § 2-708(1). The problem for the seller is that if she doesn't resell, and the *market price falls* after the time when delivery was called for in the contract, the seller, not the buyer, will bear this loss. So in that sense, the *seller will bear the risk of failing to mitigate* by a resale.

    iii. Contract price, where resale not feasible: In some instances, the seller can hold onto the goods and sue for the *contract price*. But the Code allows this only where "the seller is *unable after reasonable effort to resell* [the goods] at a reasonable price or the circumstances reasonably indicate that such effort will be unavailing." § 2-709(1)(b). This might be the case, for instance, if the goods were so highly customized (e.g., with the buyer's logo on them) that no other buyer would want them.

        (1) Can't sue for contract price: So in the usual situation of resaleable goods, the seller is *not* free just to sit on the goods and sue for the purchase price. He must normally resell them, or else be content with the difference between the contract price and the market price at the time for delivery.

    iv. Lost profits: If none of the above measures would protect the seller's expectation interest, he may recover *lost profits* from the transaction; see *infra*, p. 369.

  b. Procedures for sale: If the buyer does plan to resell the goods he may do so either at a *public sale* (typically, an auction) or a *private* sale. § 2-706(2). But if the resale is to be private, the seller must give the buyer reasonable *advance notice* of the seller's intent to resell. § 2-706(3).

E. Affirmative conduct by plaintiff which increases loss: The situations which we have discussed so far are those in which the plaintiff has failed to make reasonable affirmative efforts to decrease the loss. In other cases, however, the plaintiff may increase his loss not by failing to act, but by *acting affirmatively*. The rule here is the same: the aggrieved party may not recover for any damages which were caused by his own actions, and which he could have avoided by *reasonably* refraining from acting.

    Example: Farmer buys seed from D Manufacturing Company, which Farmer discovers to be defective before he plants it. He nonetheless makes an unreasonable judgment that things might turn out all right anyway, and goes ahead and plants it. If Farmer's crop fails, he cannot recover from D the value of a normal crop. His recovery will be limited to the price paid for the worthless seed.

F. Non-exclusive contracts: In the ordinary master-servant relationship, an employee who is wrongfully discharged is expected to seek other employment to mitigate damages. But if the employee (or independent contractor) had a *non-exclusive* relationship with the breaching party, so that the former was free to contract and work for others at the same time as for the breaching party, the gains which the aggrieved party made, or could have made, on other contracts after the breach are *not subtracted* from the plaintiff's recovery. The plaintiff would have been able to obtain these gains even if the defendant had not breached; they are therefore treated as independent of the breach, and do not affect the plaintiff's recovery.

Example: P contracts to do computer programming for D. The contract contemplates that P will work as an independent contractor, and that the work will take approximately 100 hours, spread over a period of several months. The contract does not place any limits on P's right to do programming for other clients. Assume that even with the P-D contracts, P has more work-hours available than she is able to sell to clients. D breaches, and P sues for the profits which she would have made had D carried out the contract.

Since P had both the right and the ability to contract with others in addition to D, D will not be able to claim that P could have mitigated damages by contracting with some other party for the services which she was going to provide for D. P may therefore recover full expectation damages.

1. **Sale of goods:** The "non-exclusive contracts" exception to the duty-to-mitigate rule is often applicable in sales of goods, particularly by a ***middleman***. The middleman can resell the goods that the defendant contracted for to someone else; however, if the middleman has a ***greater supply*** of them than his customers demand, he has not been made whole when he resells, since he will end up with ***one lost sale*** anyway. Such sellers, often called "lost volume" sellers, are discussed more fully *infra*, p. 369. See Rest. 2d, § 347, Comment f.

G. **Losses incurred in avoiding damages:** If the aggrieved party tries to mitigate his damages, and ***incurs losses or expenses in doing so***, he may ***recover*** damages for these losses. The expenditures must, however, have been reasonably incurred, and the damages which plaintiff is trying to mitigate must be the foreseeable result of the defendant's breach. It ***does not matter*** whether the plaintiff's attempt to mitigate damages is ***successful*** or not.

Example: *A*, a shipping company, contracts with *B* for *A* to deliver goods to New York in time to comply with the terms of a contract between *B* and *C*. The terms of this contract are known to *A* when he agrees to make the shipment, but he delays delivery past the contract deadline. In a reasonable effort to save the contract, *B* travels to New York to meet with *C*. *C* refuses to extend the deadline and *B* loses the contract. *B* may recover, in addition to the lost profits, the costs of the trip. See Rest. 1st, § 336, Illustr. 14.

Quiz Yourself on

FORESEEABILITY AND AVOIDABLE DAMAGES

97. The Three Little Pigs Cement Co. ("TLP") needs its main cement mixer to be taken back to the manufacturer for repairs. TLP calls the B. B. Wolf Transport Co. ("Wolf") and says, "How much would you charge to send a pair of drivers to drive our cement mixer to the manufacturer?" Wolf quotes a price of $500. TLP agrees, and says nothing else to Wolf. Wolf delivers the mixer to the wrong address, and it takes five days for the mistake to be tracked down. As a result, TLP must close down for those days, resulting in TLP's having $100,000 less of profits than had the delivery been done properly.

(A) Can TLP recover the $100,000 losses from Wolf?

(B) Now, assume that the day after the parties entered into the shipping deal and before the mixer was delivered anywhere, TLP called Wolf and said, "By the way, be extra careful to get the mixer to the right place at the right time, because we can't operate without it and every day until it's fixed, we lose about $20,000." Wolf mis-delivers the mixer anyway, with the same results as in part (A). May TLP recover its $100,000 losses from Wolf?

98. Anna Passemova is a prima ballerina for the 2 Left Feet Dance Company, a major company located in (and performing exclusively in) New York City. She has a three-year employment contract at $100,000 per year. Two years into the contract she is wrongfully dismissed.

(A) For this part only, assume that Passemova sits at home for the remaining year, eating cheese puffs and watching soap operas. If Passemova had notified her agent that she was again available to dance, there is a better-than-50% chance that Passemova would have secured comparable roles paying her at least $40,000 during the remaining year of the contract. At the end of the year, Passemova sues 2 Left Feet for $100,000, the amount she would have earned had 2 Left Feet honored the contract. Will Passemova's recovery be reduced by $40,000?

(B) For this part only, assume that Passemova, acting promptly after the firing, notifies her agent that she is again available. The only offer that comes in is from a major San Francisco opera company, offering a two-month guest engagement paying $15,000. Passemova declines the offer, preferring to stay in New York City where she can be near her two small children. Will the $15,000 that Passemova could have earned from San Francisco be deducted from her recovery against 2 Left Feet?

99. The puppetmaker Geppetto hires Jiminy Cricket to be a full-time tutor to teach Geppetto's puppet, five-year-old Pinocchio, how to speak and write English. The contract is for one year, at $3,000 per month, and may not be terminated by Geppetto except for cause. After Cricket has been on the job for five months with adequate performance, Geppetto, acting without cause, fires him in a drunken rage. At the end of what would have been the year of employment, Cricket sues Geppetto for breach, seeking $3,000 times the seven months post-firing. At the ensuing bench trial, Geppetto offers testimony that English teachers qualified to teach five-year-old puppets usually earn about $2,000 per month in that locality. Geppetto also shows, without contradiction from Cricket, that following the firing Cricket sat at home all day for the next seven months singing songs, made no effort to find replacement employment, and earned no income. Neither side offers any evidence about whether any particular jobs teaching English to five-year-old puppets were available locally during the seven-month period at issue, or about whether Cricket's credentials would have been sufficient to obtain any such job if there one had been open. How much, if anything, should the judge award Cricket in damages?

100. Scarlett owns a saw mill. Cal Carpetbagger contracts to deliver 40 tons of pine logs to the saw mill, at a total cost of $20,000, payable cash on delivery.

(A) For this part, assume that Carpetbagger fails to deliver the logs as promised. Scarlett could procure comparable logs on short notice from an alternative source for $30,000, in which case she could keep the mill running without interruption. However, the other supplier would require that the logs be paid for in cash. Because Scarlett's business has been poor, and because she was budgeting just the $20,000 that was to be charged by Cal, Scarlett does not want to (though she could) lay out the $30,000 the new supplier demands. Scarlett therefore instead closes down the mill for a week, until she can procure supplies priced at the same $20,000 as in the deal with Cal. Closing down the mill for the week results in $15,000 of losses to Scarlett. How much, if anything, may Scarlett recover from Cal?

(B) For this part, assume that Cal is willing and able to deliver, but that before he can do so, Scarlett wrongfully repudiates. On the day for delivery, the 40 tons have a market value of $20,000. These logs, like all the logs that Cal sells, come from his own land (he sells all the logs from his land as they mature).

Cal could sell the 40 tons earmarked for Scarlett on the day she repudiates, but Cal holds on to them, thinking the market price will rise. Instead, the price falls, and Cal continues to refuse to sell. He still owns the logs when he sues Scarlett for breach. At the time of trial, the logs are worth $9,000. How much may Cal recover from Scarlett? (Ignore storage and other incidental costs caused by the breach.)

Answers

97. **(A) No, because the lost profits were not reasonably foreseeable.** In order to recover consequential damages (i.e., damages resulting as a consequence of the breach), the plaintiff has to show either that a *reasonable person* in the defendant's position would have foreseen the damages as a *logical and ordinary result* of a breach, or that the defendant had *actual notice* that this type of damage could occur. (This is the rule of *Hadley v. Baxendale*.)

Here, there's nothing to suggest that Wolf should have known that Three Little Pigs would have to shut down if the mixer was misdelivered: Temporary unavailability of a mixer wouldn't ordinarily cause this magnitude of losses (especially since a business that was so dependent on such machinery would ordinarily have a spare), so the loss wasn't reasonably foreseeable to one in Wolf's position. And the facts, by saying that TLP said nothing to Wolf except a description of the job and a request for a quote, show us that TLP didn't give Wolf actual notice of the danger of loss. As a result, the lost profits will be considered unforeseeable, and Wolf won't be liable for them.

(B) No. Foreseeability will be measured as of the time the contract was made. It is irrelevant that Wolf *subsequently* learned about the danger of extensive damages, even though it got this knowledge before it breached. (This makes sense, since Wolf had already quoted a price calculated based on the absence of any exposure to large business-interruption losses.)

98. **(A) Yes.** A party who suffers a breach of contract must make reasonable efforts to mitigate her damages. The duty to mitigate extends to employment contracts: wrongfully dismissed employees must look for comparable work (just as employers whose employees have wrongfully quit must look for comparable replacements).

(B) Probably not. It's true that a party must make reasonable efforts to mitigate damages. However, where the contract is for personal services, courts are quite lenient towards the plaintiff, and do not require her to accept any position that is substantially different from (even if not necessarily inferior to) the one contracted for. Here, the San Francisco position was much shorter than, and more importantly, 3,000 miles away from, the one Passemova had with 2 Left Feet. Especially considering Passemova's family reasons for not leaving New York for extended periods, it is very likely that a court would conclude that the San Francisco position was substantially different from the contracted-for one.

99. **$21,000, i.e., no deduction for failure to mitigate damages.** Courts generally view the so-called duty to mitigate as an affirmative defense, and therefore impose on the breaching party the *burden of producing evidence* that the non-breaching party / plaintiff failed to mitigate. In an employment case, this placement of the burden of proof usually means that it's not enough for the employer to show that the employee failed to act reasonably in seeking substitute employment. Instead, the employer must also: (1) *identify one or more positions* that the employee would likely have succeeded in obtaining, and (2) show *how much* the employee would likely have earned had she been offered and taken one of these suitable replacement positions. Here, Geppetto has made showing (2) (that a comparable position, if available, would have paid about $2,000 per month); but he has not satisfied (1) (i.e., he has not identified any particular comparable position that Cricket would likely have been able to obtain during the relevant time-

frame). Therefore, the court will likely hold that Geppetto has failed to bear the burden of proving his fail-ure-to-mitigate defense, and is not entitled to any reduction at all in damages. See *Maness v. Collins*, 2010 WL 4629614 (Tenn. Ct. App. 2010).

100. **(A) $10,000, probably.** A buyer of goods must make reasonable attempts to mitigate damages, just as most other types of victims of breach must do. It is likely that a court would conclude that Scarlett's unwillingness to come up with an extra $10,000 to avoid $15,000 in losses was unreasonable. If so, the court will limit her to the amount she would have lost had she reasonably mitigated (i.e., the $10,000 dif-ferential between Cal's price and the new supplier's price), not the $15,000 she actually lost.

(B) Nothing. When goods are resaleable and the seller does not choose to resell, his recovery is normally limited to the difference between the contract price and the market price on the day for delivery. § 2-708(1). (A "lost volume" seller can recover his lost profits under § 2-708(2) even if there is no contract-market differential, but the facts tell us that Cal is not a lost-volume seller, since he's already selling all the mature logs on his own land.) That differential is $0, which is all Cal can recover. The fact that the contract-market differential widened after the delivery date (to $11,000 by the time of trial) is irrelevant — Cal bears the risk of such a widening, giving him in effect a "duty to mitigate."

XI. NOMINAL AND PUNITIVE DAMAGES

A. **Non-compensatory damages:**   The purpose of awarding damages in contract cases is nor-mally to **compensate** the aggrieved party for economic losses caused and gains prevented by the breach. In some cases, however, compensation may not be appropriate because the plain-tiff has not suffered any loss, cannot adequately prove any loss, or has suffered non-economic injury. An award of damages for something other than economic injury may be appropriate in such cases. Kinds of non-compensatory damages considered below are nominal damages, punitive damages, and damages for mental suffering.

B. **Nominal damages:**   Where a right of action for breach exists, but no harm has been done or is provable, the plaintiff may get a judgment for **nominal damages**. That is, he may recover a small sum that is fixed without regard to the amount of harm. See Rest. 2d, § 346(2).

C. **Punitive damages:**   Punitive damages (sometimes called "exemplary" damages) are fre-quently awarded in **tort** cases, but rarely in the usual breach of contract case. Such damages, whose purpose is to punish and deter a wrongdoer, are considered inappropriate in contract cases, where breach is not viewed as a moral wrong.

1. **Also a tort:**   Where, however, the breach of contract also **constitutes a tort**, punitive damages *are* recoverable. Rest. 2d, § 355; C&P, p. 542.

   a. **Fraud:** For instance, if the defendant commits **fraud** in inducing the plaintiff to enter the contract, punitive damages may be available.

      Example: D, a car dealer, sells a used car to P. D states that the car is "nearly new," with only 3,000 miles on it. In reality, however, D has set back the odometer from 3,000 miles, and has steam-cleaned the engine to make it look new. P discovers D's misconduct a few months after the purchase, and sues. P will be entitled to punitive damages, since D's conduct — fraud — constitutes a tort as well as a breach of con-tract.

2. **Bad faith as tort:** Also, an increasing number of courts now regard a party's ***bad faith*** conduct in connection with a contract as *being* itself a tort, for which punitive damages may be awarded. In fact, if the court believes that the party ***breached voluntarily*** rather than involuntarily, and did so in an effort to ***make a better deal elsewhere***, the voluntary nature of the breach may by itself be enough to constitute bad faith punishable by punitive damages.

   a. **Insurance company bad faith refusal to settle:** A very important aspect of bad faith breach involves ***insurance*** companies: if an insurer refuses in bad faith to ***settle a claim*** that is covered by a policy that it wrote, courts are especially likely to find that this refusal constitutes a tort punishable by the award of punitive damages. See Farnsworth, p. 789.

D. **Damages for mental suffering:** Damages for ***emotional disturbance*** as a result of breach of contract are recoverable only where the breach has also caused ***bodily harm***, or the contract or breach is "of such a kind that ***serious emotional disturbance*** is a ***particularly likely result***." Rest. 2d, § 353.

> **Example:** *A*, a burial home, contracts to conduct a funeral service for *B*'s husband, and to supply a suitable casket and vault. Shortly after the husband is buried, *B* discovers that, because *A* has knowingly failed to provide a sufficiently water-tight vault, water has entered the vault and reinterment is necessary. *B* suffers mental anguish and illness as a result. If *B* sues for breach of contract, her damages will include compensation for her suffering, because contracts for burial services are of a sort which are particularly likely to result in emotional disturbance if there is a breach. Rest. 2d, § 353, Illustr. 3.

XII. LIQUIDATED DAMAGES

A. **Reason for liquidated damages clauses:** Parties negotiating a contract often make an explicit agreement as to what each party's remedy for breach of the contract shall be. The parties to a sales contract may, for instance, agree that if the seller breaches by failing to deliver, the seller shall pay the buyer damages of $100, and that if the buyer fails to make all payments, the seller may repossess the goods and keep whatever payments the buyer has already made. Such an agreement as to the consequences of breach, placed in the contract itself, is called a ***liquidated damages provision***.

B. **Rules of enforceability:** Such liquidated damages clauses, where enforced by the court, determine the measure of damages which the court will award. In order to be enforceable, however, the liquidated damage clause must always meet ***one*** (and in some courts, ***both***) of these two requirements:

[1] **Reasonable forecast:** The amount fixed must be ***reasonable*** relative to the anticipated or actual loss from breach (all courts require this); and

[2] **Difficult calculation:** In some courts, the harm caused by the breach must be ***uncertain or very difficult to calculate accurately***, even after the fact.

See Rest. 2d, § 356(1); C&P, p. 589.

C. Policy against penalties: These two requirements reflect a long-standing judicial policy against the enforcement of *penalties* for breach of contract. The purpose of damages is to put the plaintiff in the same position he would have been in had the contract been fulfilled, not a better one. Where a provision that is labeled a "liquidated damages" clause really serves to penalize a party for breach in an amount far beyond the loss suffered by the plaintiff, the courts simply refuse to enforce the provision, and award ordinary damages.

1. **Intent irrelevant:** If the amount stipulated in the liquidated damages clause is unreasonable, it is irrelevant that the parties subjectively attempted to provide for liquidated damages rather than a penalty. Nor does the fact that the contract refers to the clause as "liquidated damages" rather than as a "penalty" save the clause in this situation.

D. Reasonableness of amount: All courts agree that a liquidated damages clause will be upheld, rather than being struck down as a penalty, only if it provides for a *"reasonable"* amount.

1. **Time for measuring reasonableness:** There is dispute as to the *time* for ascertaining the reasonableness of the amount: is the issue whether the amount was a reasonable one *as of the time of contracting* (i.e., a reasonable forecast of likely damages from breach)?, or is it whether the amount is reasonable when viewed *as of the time of breach or trial* (i.e., reasonable compared with the *actual* damages)?

   a. **Traditional view:** The traditional view has been that the reasonableness of the clause is to be viewed *solely as of the time of contracting*. This traditional view has two consequences:

   ❏ First, if the clause is a *reasonable forecast* viewed as of this time, the clause will be *enforceable* even though it turns out that the plaintiff has actually suffered much less damage than the liquidated amount.

   ❏ Secondly, if the clause sets an amount which is, viewed as of the time of contracting, unreasonably large, the clause *will not be saved* by the fact that plaintiff's actual damages have fortuitously turned out to be extraordinarily large.

   b. **The modern view:** The *modern* view, as exemplified by both the Second Restatement and the UCC, is that the clause should be enforced if it is the case that *either:*

   [1] the clause is a *reasonable forecast* when viewed as of the time of contracting *or*

   [2] the clause is reasonable in light of the *actual* damages which have occurred.

   See Rest. 2d, § 356(1). This modern view has two main consequences:

   i. **Damages smaller than expected:** First, if the forecast is reasonable (viewed as of the time of contracting), the clause will be enforced *even though it turns out that the plaintiff's damages are actually much less than might have been expected.* (This result is the same as would be reached under the traditional rule.)

   ii. **Unexpectedly high damages:** Secondly, a clause which is an *unreasonable forecast* (viewed as of the time of contracting) can nonetheless be *saved* if it turns out that the plaintiff's damages are unexpectedly high, and therefore in line with the clause. (This result is *contrary* to what would happen under the traditional rule.)

2. **No loss at all:** Suppose that the contract contains a liquidated damages clause, but the plaintiff sustains *no actual loss at all*. Assuming that the clause is a reasonable estimate viewed as of the time of contracting, both the traditional and modern rules would, if followed with strict logic, result in the *enforcement* of the clause in this situation. Some courts have indeed enforced the clause in this context.

   a. **Restatement view:** However, many other courts, and the Second Restatement, deviate from strict logic when it comes to this situation of no actual loss. These authorities will *not enforce* the liquidated damages clause if it turns out that *no actual damage* has been sustained. See Rest. 2d, § 356, Comment b and Illustr. 4. This approach has been criticized as resulting in a "somewhat arbitrary distinction between situations in which there is no loss at all and those in which there is only a little loss." Farnsworth, p. 845.

3. **Damage computation keyed to gross revenues or the like:** Where the damages clause is keyed to the plaintiff's lost *gross revenues*, lost *gross profit*s, or other financial figure that is *not necessarily tied to actual lost profits*, the court is likely to view the clause skeptically as being a *poor estimate* of actual losses, and thus unenforceable if it deviates materially from the actual losses.

   Example: P, who operates a retail store, rents the store's premises from D, a municipality, under a 30-year lease. The lease provides that if D cancels the lease, D will pay P as damages an amount equal to 25% of P's average annual gross receipts for the three years preceding the breach. D cancels the lease after 17 years. P sues for enforcement of the liquidated damages provision, which would produce a recovery of $290,000.

   Held, the case must be remanded for a factual determination of the reasonableness of the clause. "[D]amages based on gross receipts run the risk of being found unreasonable. Generally speaking, gross receipts do not reflect actual losses incurred because of the cancellation." Here, for instance, P's tax returns for the prior three years showed that the business never had a taxable profit of greater than $3,700, a far cry from the $290,000 amount the clause would generate. *Wasserman's Inc. v. Township of Middletown*, 645 A.2d 100 (N.J. 1994).

4. **Single damage amount regardless of severity of breach ("blunderbuss"):** Some liquidated damages clauses stipulate a *single sum of money*, regardless of the extent to which the breach damages the plaintiff. For instance, the clause might contain a single damage formula for the breach of any covenant, whether a trivial or important one; such a clause is sometimes called a *"shotgun"* or *"blunderbuss"* clause. See Farnsworth, p. 943. Courts tend to be very skeptical of damage formulas that are *"invariant to the gravity of the breach."* *Lake River Corp. v. Carborundum Co.*, 769 F.2d 1284 (7th Cir. 1985).

   a. **Actual damage is trivial:** Where the actual damage turns out to be *trivial*, most courts will not enforce a blunderbuss clause (or will interpret the clause as not applying to trivial breaches).

   Example: Contractor contracts to renovate Owner's office building by June 1, to get it ready for occupancy by Tenant beginning on August 1. The contract provides that if Contractor is late in completing work, he will forfeit $100,000, whether the delay is one day or 90 days. In the actual event, Contractor is two days late, and Owner deducts the full $100,000.

Since the clause produces the same damage amount regardless of how much actual damage is sustained by Owner (a one-day delay wouldn't prevent Tenant's on-time occupancy, but a 70-day delay would), and since the actual damage has turned out to be trivial, the clause will be struck down as a blunderbuss clause.

b. **Non-compete covenants:** This "no enforcement of blunderbuss clauses" rule is often applied to *non-compete* clauses. If the non-compete calls for the *same fixed amount* of damages *regardless of the severity* of the violation, that fixed amount will *not* be recoverable, and instead the plaintiff will be limited to those damages she can actually prove.

Example: A group of four pediatricians located in midtown Manhattan stipulates in their partnership agreement that if any one of them leaves the practice, he will not render care in Manhattan to an existing patient of the group for a period of one year following his departure. The agreement also states that "Because of the difficulty of proving damages from breach" of the one-year provision, a flat $50,000 in damages will be recoverable by the group for any breach. Each of the pediatricians earns about $90,000 annually. D then leaves the group, and 11 months later, furnishes services worth $50 to a teenager who is a patient of the group. The partnership sues D for $50,000.

The partnership will *not* be entitled to recover the liquidated damage amount of $50,000 from D. That's because the clause purports to impose the same recovery regardless of the severity of the breach — a former member who treats one patient one time one month before the non-compete is to expire is handled the same way as one who "steals" half the group's practice over the full twelve months. Since the blunderbuss clause is unenforceable, only the actual damages the group has suffered from the one patient treated by D (probably $50) can be recovered.

5. **Major loss:** But if the breach turns out to be a *major* one (so that the liquidated amount is reasonable in light of the actual loss), courts are split on whether the blunderbuss should be enforced. The prevailing modern approach is to *enforce* the blunderbuss where the actual loss is roughly equal to the damages provided in the clause.

E. **Difficulty of fixing damages:** In addition to the "reasonableness" of the amount (discussed above), most courts also take into account the *difficulty* in *estimating* or *proving* actual damages. Some cases, especially older ones, claim that it is an absolute prerequisite to the enforceability of a liquidated damages clause that it be difficult to prove that loss has occurred or to show its amount with the requisite certainty (see *supra*, p. 323).

1. **Modern view:** But the modern view, illustrated by the Second Restatement, is that the difficulty of proving loss is merely a *factor*, along with reasonableness. As Rest. 2d, § 356, Comment b puts it, "If the *difficulty of proof of loss is great, considerable latitude* is allowed in the *approximation* of anticipated or actual harm. If, on the other hand, the difficulty of proof of loss is slight, less latitude is allowed in that approximation."

F. **Damage clause limiting probable recovery:** The discussion above has focused on those liquidated damages clauses which threaten to be penalties, i.e., which provide for sums *greater* than the actual loss caused by the breach. In some situations, however, the liquidated damages clause may operate to the *defendant's* benefit, as a *limitation on liability.* The courts are in disagreement about when such a contractual limitation of liability is effective. But such liability limitations are rarely struck down on liquidated-damages principles.

> **Example:** Suppose that D, a security company, agrees to install a system on P's premises that will detect fires and burglaries, and report these by telephone to the police. The contract provides that if D shall be found liable for breach of the contract, D's liability "shall be limited to a sum equal to 10% of the annual service charge or $250, whichever is the greater." The system fails to operate properly, and P's premises burn down, at a cost to him of $50,000. P sues for breach of contract, and D asserts that the contractual limitation should be enforced.
>
> On these facts, courts are split both as to analysis and result. Some courts would treat this as a liquidated damages provision, in which case they might either enforce it as a reasonable estimate of damages, or refuse to enforce it on the grounds that it is not a reasonable estimate. Other courts reason that such a clause is not really a liquidated damages provision at all, but rather, an attempt to limit liability; they then tend to uphold it unless they find it unconscionable (see *infra*, p. 361), which they usually do not find it to be. Probably most courts, regardless of which theory they use, will enforce such a liability in the alarm context.

1. **Chance to buy extra coverage:** Whenever the validity of a provision limiting liability to a stated amount (less than the likely actual damages) is at issue, courts tend to give great weight to whether the defendant offered the plaintiff *extra coverage* for an extra price: if the defendant did so, it has a much better chance of having the provision enforced.

   a. **Common carrier:** For instance, UCC § 7-309(2) allows a *common carrier* to contractually limit its liability if it makes additional liability available to the shipper for an additional charge. Thus the typical overnight-delivery-service contract, which limits damages to, say, $100, but sells "insurance" for several dollars per hundred dollars of extra coverage, would be enforced by almost every court, whether on a liquidated-damages theory or not.

G. **UCC rules on liquidated damages:** The UCC takes a more friendly view of liquidated damages clauses than do the traditional common-law rules. § 2-718(1) provides that "damages for breach by either party *may be liquidated* in the agreement but only at an amount which is *reasonable* in the light of the *anticipated or actual harm* caused by the breach, the *difficulties of proof of loss*, and inconvenience or nonfeasibility of otherwise obtaining an adequate remedy. A term fixing *unreasonably large* liquidated damages is *void as a penalty.*"

1. **Alternative test:** This language gives the party seeking to enforce a liquidated damages clause *two chances* to prove that the stipulated sum is reasonable: the reasonableness of the sum may be measured:

   [1] as of the time the *contract is made or*

   [2] *after the breach*.

(See the phrase, "reasonable in the light of the *anticipated or actual harm* caused by the breach…"). In this respect, the Code matches the Second Restatement, and makes liquidated damage provisions more easily enforceable than the common-law rule, which requires reasonableness as of the time of contracting.

2. **Unconscionability:** Even if a liquidated damages clause meets the standard of § 2-718(1), however, it may still be declared ***unconscionable*** under the general unconscionability provision of § 2-302 (*infra*, p. 478).

3. **Code's own liquidated damages provision:** Where the parties do not agree on a liquidated damages provision, the Code in effect supplies one with respect to a seller who justifiably withholds delivery of goods because of the buyer's breach. In such a situation, the seller may keep all payments made by the buyer up to $500 or 20% of the full contract price, whichever is less. (§ 2-718(2)(b) — see *supra*, p. 340.) In addition to this, the seller may recover actual damages for the breach beyond the amount that he is able to keep. If the contract contains a valid liquidated damages clause, the seller may keep the buyer's payments up to the amount of this clause.

4. **Limitation on consequential damages:** Particularly in cases of sales contracts drafted by merchant-sellers, the contract may contain a provision ***limiting the seller's liability***. § 2-719(3) provides that "consequential damages ***may be limited or excluded*** unless the limitation or exclusion is ***unconscionable***." Most litigation involving this provision has arisen in the context of limitation of liability for breach of warranty, a subject which is discussed *infra*, p. 504.

H. **Consequence of unenforceability:** If the liquidated damages clause is struck down as a penalty, the plaintiff is not left without remedy. Instead, he merely reverts to his ***common-law damages***, usually expectation damages.

Quiz Yourself on
NOMINAL AND PUNITIVE DAMAGES; LIQUIDATED DAMAGES

101. Acme Generators has a contract with Sonja's Ice Sculptures, whereby Acme is to install a generator to ensure continuous operation of Sonja's freezers. It turns out that Acme's owner, Frosty Snowman, has a brother in the ice sculpture business. To help his brother, Frosty installs a faulty generator at Sonja's. The power to Sonja's freezers fails during a storm, the generator does not kick on, and her inventory of valuable ice sculptures melts. In her breach of contract suit against Acme, might she be awarded punitive damages?

102. The Bride of Frankenstein contracts with Miss Havisham to buy her used wedding gown for $150. Shortly before Bride's wedding date, Miss Havisham calls and says that she cannot part with her gown and that she refuses to go through with the contract. Bride immediately starts looking for a replacement dress. While out shopping, she runs into her friend Liz, who has been married eight times. Liz offers to sell Bride one of her used gowns for $150. Bride accepts with pleasure, knowing what impeccable taste Liz has. Bride then sues Miss Havisham for breach of contract. What damages will she be entitled to?

103. Ben Hur contracts with Athena contractors to construct a shopping mall, the Parthenon, on his property. To take advantage of the Christmas shopping season, the contract stipulates that the mall must be completed by November 1.

(A) For this part only, assume that the contract provides that if the mall is not done by November 1, Ath-

Table 10-1

ISSUES CHECKLIST: **Main Issues in Remedies**

Note: This Table does not deal specifically with Remedies in Sales Contracts.

Issue	Rule or Recommendation	Examples / Notes
[1] Is *legal* relief *inadequate*?	If yes, award *equitable relief* (*injunction* or order of *specific performance*).	**Example 1 (specific performance):** D contracts to sell P a parcel of land. D refuses to convey. P can get order of specific performance, since each parcel is deemed unique. **Example 2 (injunction):** D sells a business to P and agrees not to compete within 1 mile for 1 year. In 6 months, D starts competing. P can get injunction prohibiting D from competing for the rest of the year.
[2] Has P proved expectation damages with *reasonable certainty*?	If no, award *restitution* or *reliance*.	**Example:** D (a bank) contracts to lend P (a builder) $400K to build a house, which P hopes to sell for a $100K profit. After P has spent $20,000 preparing to build the house, D breaches. If P can't show with reasonable certainty what his profit would have been, the court should award $20,000 (his reliance damages).
[3] Has P breached, but *substantially performed* (i.e., any breach was not "material")?	If yes, award P *expectation* damages, subject to *counterclaim* for D's damages from the non-material breach.	**Example:** P (a builder) contracts to build a house for D on D's land, for $300K. The contract specifies a 15x25 ft. master bedroom. Inadvertently, P builds the house so that the master is 6 inches too narrow. The fair value of the house as built is $250K; if it had been built exactly to spec, its value would have been $255K. Since P has substantially performed, P can recover $300K (the contract price) less $5K (the lost value from the breach). P is not limited to the fair value of his work (the $250K figure). E VII(B). (But see item [4] below for the "willful breach" problem.)
[4] If this is a construction contract where D (contractor) has breached, will giving P (owner) cost-of-repair damages *encourage waste?*	If yes, award *change-in-value* damages instead of cost-of-repair.	**Example:** Same facts as Example in [3]. Assume it would cost $100K to rebuild the master bedroom to add the 6 inches. The court will deduct the loss in value ($5K), not the cost of repair ($100K), to avoid economic waste. (However, if D's breach was "willful," i.e., intentional, the court might award the $100K.)
[5] Has P breached and not "substantially performed," but done *some meaningful work* on the contract?	If yes, award P *restitution* damages, limited by the *pro-rata contract price*. *Note:* However, in some jurisdictions, if P's default was "*willful*" (e.g., he walked off the job to take a higher-paying contract), P may not be allowed to recover even restitution.	**Example:** P contracts to build a house for D for $300K. When the work is 1/2 done, P walks off the job without cause. The value of the uncompleted house is $100K. Since P has not substantially performed, he cannot recover "on the contract" (even with a deduction for D's damages from non-completion. However, P can recover the *value to D* of the work done ($100K), but only to the extent that this does not exceed the pro-rata contract price ($150K). (But see Note at left about "willful" breach.)

Continued on next page

Table 10-1 (cont.)

***ISSUES CHECKLIST:* Main Issues in Remedies**

Issue	Rule or Recommendation	Examples / Notes
[6] Assuming D breached, is some portion of P's damages due to a loss item that was neither ***"naturally occuring"*** nor due to special circumstances of which D was ***aware***?	If yes, D cannot recover these special damages, under the rule of *Hadley v. Baxendale*.	**Example**: D contracts to fix P's broken drill-press for $1K, the work to be finished in 7 days. D breaches by taking 20 days. P's entire factory is out of business for the extra 13 days, costing P $100K in lost profits. Unless D knew that the delay would cause the factory to shut at enormous loss, P can't recover the $100K.
[7] Assuming D breached, is P seeking items of loss that P could reasonably have ***avoided*** (e.g., by finding an alternative supplier)?	If yes, P cannot recover these "avoidable damages." P is said to have failed in his ***"duty to mitigate."***	**Example**: D contracts to sell P 1,000 widgets at $2 apiece, delivery due 6/1. D fails to deliver on 6/1. P could procure the items from an alternative supplier for $3. P unreasonably delays in doing so until 9/1, when the price is now $5, at which point P covers. P can recover $1 per item, but not $3 (since the final $2 was due to P's unreasonable delay in covering).
[8] Does the contract include a formula or fixed sum as agreed-upon damages if D breaches (***"liquidated damages"***)?	If yes, P cannot recover the agreed-upon sum unless it was either: (1) a ***reasonable forecast*** of the loss, as of the time of the contract; or (2) reasonably close to the damages ***actually suffered*** by P. A clause that doesn't meet either of these tests is an unenforceable ***"penalty."*** *Note:* A penalty is likely to be found where the same amount is assessed regardless of the severity of the breach (as in the Example at right).	**Example**: In a construction contract with Owner, Builder agrees to have deducted from the $300K contract price $75K for a delay, whether the delay is 1 day or 30 days. At the time of the contract, it's clear that Owner will suffer no damages from a delay of less than 10 days, but large damages for any delay longer than that. Builder is 2 days late. The court will not allow Owner to deduct the $75K, because this figure was neither a reasonable estimate of loss as of the time of contract, nor reasonably close to Owner's actual damages ($0). (This type of clause, assessing the same amount of liquidated damages regardless of the severity of the breach, is called a ***"blunderbuss"*** clause, and will rarely be enforceable unless it happens to produce an estimate that turns out to be close to the actual damage.)

---

ena will be liable for a flat-fee liquidated damages amount of $100,000. (The amount does not change with the length of the delay.) Viewed as of the moment of contracting, the $100,000 is a good estimate of the damages likely to be caused by a delay of between 1-2 weeks, but is not a good estimate of damages from a delay of less than 1 week, or more than 2 weeks. In reality, the mall opens on November 8. If Ben Hur presents evidence that his actual damages from the delay are $80,000, how much will the court award?

(B) For this part, assume the same facts, except that the delay is 2 days, and Athena shows at trial that Ben's damages are only $20,000. How much will the court award?

(C) Assume instead that the contract states as follows: For every calendar day completion is delayed by Athena, Athena will pay $10,000 in liquidated damages, which is what Ben reasonably anticipates earning in gross profit on a daily basis. Athena slips behind schedule and the mall is not complete until

November 15. Ben's actual damages turn out to be $75,000. How much may Ben recover?

Answers

101. **Yes.** Frosty clearly acted in bad faith here by purposely installing a faulty generator. Although punitive damages are not normally granted in contract actions, an increasing number of courts now regard a party's extreme bad faith conduct in connection with a contract as being itself a tort, for which punitive damages may be awarded. Conduct that occurs within the context of a contractual relationship, but that is motivated by the defendant's improper desire to harm the plaintiff, is the sort of extreme bad faith that can properly be punished by a punitive-damage award.

102. **Nominal damages only.** Since Bride was able to mitigate her actual damages completely through her cover contract with Liz, she has no economic harm that requires redress. Nonetheless, the court will award Bride nominal damages (probably $100 or less) as a way of acknowledging that she was wronged when Miss Havisham breached their contract.

103. **(A) Probably $100,000.** A liquidated damages clause will be struck down (under the modern approach) unless it meets either of two tests: (1) it is a reasonable forecast viewed as of the time of contracting; or (2) it is a reasonable estimate, viewed after-the-fact. Here, the clause amount satisfies (2), since it is reasonably close to the actual loss. Therefore, the court will probably uphold the award.

(B) Probably $20,000. As we explain in the answer to part (A), a liquidated damages clause will be valid if it's a reasonable estimate of likely damages, viewed as of the moment of the contract, even if the estimate turns out to be quite badly off. However, a *"blunderbuss"* clause that assigns the same damage award regardless of the severity of the default will generally not be considered a reasonable advance estimate, considering the variation in scenarios (and damage amounts) that the clause will cover. The clause here, which is invariant to the length of delay, would probably be considered a blunderbuss clause. Even a blunderbuss clause will be saved if it turns out to be reasonably accurate. But the estimate of $100,000 is not reasonably close to the $20,000 actual delay, so there is no after-the-fact accuracy to save the clause. Consequently, the court will probably strike it down, and award just the actual damages suffered by Ben.

(C) $150,000, i.e., the amount called for by the clause. As noted in the prior parts, a damages clause will be valid if it's a reasonable forecast viewed as of the moment of contracting, even if the estimate turns out to be quite inaccurate. That's what happened here: keying damages to the number of days of delay, multiplied by a reasonable estimate of each day's damages, is certainly a reasonable method of forecasting loss. Therefore, the clause won't be rendered invalid by the fact that the actual damages turned out to be much less than the forecasted ones. (Note that the per-day calculation method is what prevents this from being a "blunderbuss" clause like the one in parts (A) and (B).)

XIII.   DAMAGES IN SALES CONTRACTS

A. **Distinction between acceptance and rejection:** The UCC gives a variety of remedies to the seller or buyer who is injured by a breach of contract. In analyzing these remedies, it is important to distinguish between those situations in which the buyer has *accepted* defective goods (and never revoked his acceptance) and those in which the buyer has either rejected the goods (rightfully or wrongfully) or revoked his acceptance of them, or failed to receive delivery from the seller at all. We shall first consider the latter group of situations (rejection, revocation, or failure to deliver) in which the buyer does not end up with the goods on hand.

B. Buyer's damages generally, where goods have not been accepted: If the seller *fails to deliver* the goods at all, or delivers *defective goods* which the buyer rightfully *rejects* (or accepts but then revokes his acceptance), the buyer has a *choice* of remedies:

❏ The most important of these is his right to *"cover,"* i.e., to buy the goods from another seller, and to recover the *difference between the contract price and the cover price* .

❏ If he decides not to purchase the goods elsewhere, he can recover the traditional contract measure of damages, i.e., *the difference between the contract price and the market price at the time of breach*.

❏ Thirdly, in a few situations he may obtain a decree ordering *specific performance* of the contract.

No matter which of these three remedies he obtains, the buyer may also recover *"incidental" and "consequential" damages* stemming from the breach.

> **Note:** For our discussion of buyer's damages where the buyer *accepts* the goods (and never revokes the acceptance), see *infra*, p. 373.

1. Right of cover: Where the seller does not deliver, or delivers defective goods which the buyer rejects, the buyer will normally want to *purchase substitute goods, or "cover."* If she does so, she can recover her extra costs.

    a. Code rule: This is accomplished by § 2-712(2): "The buyer may recover from the seller as damages *the difference between the cost of cover and the contract price* together with any incidental or consequential damages … but less expenses saved in consequence of the seller's breach."

    b. Reasonableness of cover: The buyer's purchase of substitute goods must be "reasonable," and must be made "in good faith and without unreasonable delay." § 2-712(1).

2. Contract/market differential: In most instances, the buyer will cover. Occasionally, however, he may decide that he does not need the contracted-for goods after all, or is unable to find a reasonable substitute. Where the buyer *does not cover,* the Code gives him the traditional pre-Code measure of damages for sales contracts: the *difference between the contract price and the market price* "at the time when the buyer learned of the breach…" (§ 2-713(1)). In addition to this contract/market differential, the buyer may also recover any incidental and consequential damages arising from the breach, but expenses saved by virtue of the seller's breach are deducted from his recovery.

    a. Expectation interest not protected: Observe that awarding the buyer the difference between the contract price and the market price at the time of breach does *not* necessarily protect his *expectation interest*. The recovery awarded by the contract/market differential may be either greater or less than the expectation measure, and will equal it only by coincidence.

        i. Buyer who has fixed resale contract: The problem that the contract/market differential may not correctly compensate the buyer is especially acute where the market is rising and the buyer has *already made a fixed-price or fixed-margin contract to resell* the goods. If the market-price increase times the quantity is greater than the profit margin on the buyer's resale contract, giving the buyer the contract/market differential will put the buyer in a ***better position*** than she would have been in had the contract been fulfilled.

> **(1) Minority view:** A *minority* of courts has therefore concluded that the contract/market differential in this buyer-has-already-contracted-to-resell situation should be ***limited to the profit that the buyer would have made*** on the completed transaction had there been no breach, at least where the resale contract is written in such a way that the buyer's buyer can't sue the buyer for similar contract/market damages.

> **(2) Majority view:** But *most* courts hold that the buyer is ***entitled to the full contract/market differential even where this would put her in a better position*** than had the contract been fulfilled, because limiting damages to the buyer's lost profits would ***incentivize the seller to breach.*** See, e.g., *Tongish v. Thomas*, 840 P.2d 471 (1992).

> **b. Contract/market differential not available to covering buyer:** The buyer may recover the contract/market differential ***only where he did not cover.*** See Comment 5 to § 2-713.

3. **Consequential and incidental damages:** Just as a buyer who covers may, in addition to the contract/cover differential, recover for "incidental" and "consequential" damages, so may the ***non-covering*** buyer recover incidental and consequential damages in addition to the contract/market differential.

> **a. Consequential damages:** "Consequential" damages (defined in § 2-715(2)) include the ***profits which the buyer could have made by reselling*** the contracted-for goods, had they been delivered. For a more complete discussion of consequential damages, including the requirements that they be proved with appropriate certainty and that they be reasonably foreseeable, see *supra*, p. 343.

> **b. Incidental damages:** Incidental damages are defined in § 2-715(1) to include expenses "reasonably incurred in ***inspection***, receipt, ***transportation and care*** and custody of goods rightfully rejected, any commercially reasonable charges, expenses or commissions in connection with ***effecting cover*** and any other reasonable expense incident to the delay or other breach."

> **Example:** Buyer rightfully revokes his acceptance of an airplane which Seller has misrepresented to be airworthy.

> *Held*, Buyer may recover, among other damages, "incidental damages" for the expenses of storing the plane, oiling it, and insuring it. *Lanners v. Whitney*, 247 Ore. 223 (1969).

4. **Specific performance:** In a few situations, the buyer may obtain an order of specific performance, i.e., a court decree ordering the seller to supply the goods provided for in the contract. § 2-716(1) provides that specific performance may be decreed "where the goods are unique or in other proper circumstances." Specific performance in UCC cases is discussed more extensively *supra*, p. 316.

Figure 10-1

Buyer's Remedies under Sales Contract (UCC)

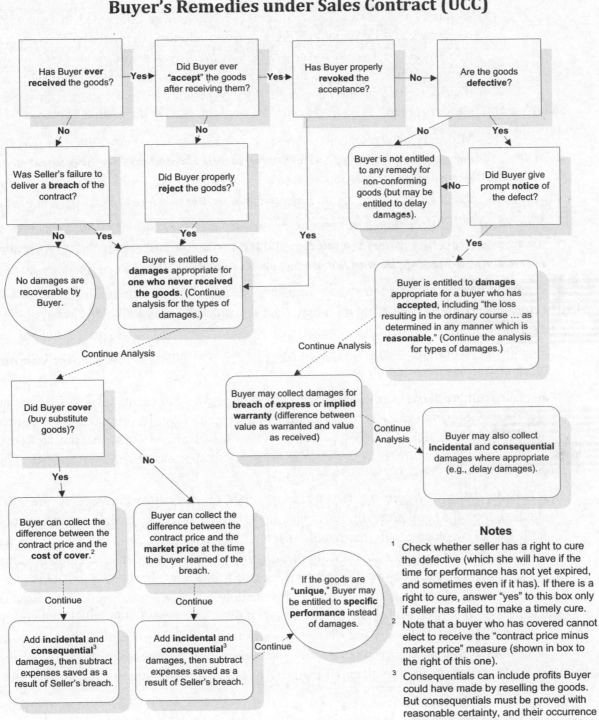

Notes

[1] Check whether seller has a right to cure the defective (which she will have if the time for performance has not yet expired, and sometimes even if it has). If there is a right to cure, answer "yes" to this box only if seller has failed to make a timely cure.

[2] Note that a buyer who has covered cannot elect to receive the "contract price minus market price" measure (shown in box to the right of this one).

[3] Consequentials can include profits Buyer could have made by reselling the goods. But consequentials must be proved with reasonable certainty, and their occurrence must have been reasonably foreseeable to one in Seller's position.

5. **Rejection as a remedy:**   In addition to the above judicial remedies, the buyer to whom the seller delivers non-conforming goods has a crucial self-effectuating remedy, the right to *reject the goods*. By exercising his right of rejection, the buyer can throw the goods back on the seller, thus cancelling the contract. See the discussion of rejection, *supra*, p. 231. In the usual case where the buyer, after rejecting the defective tender, covers (and possibly recovers the contract/cover differential), the right of rejection has simply enabled her to protect her expectation interests by approximating the position she would have been in had the contract been completed.

C. **Seller's damages for breach:**   The Code provides an aggrieved *seller* with a choice of several damage measures:

❏ If the seller has *resold* the goods, he may recover the ***difference between the contract price and the resale price***. (See p. 368.)

❏ If the buyer wrongfully *refuses to accept* the goods (i.e., wrongfully *rejects* them), wrongfully *revokes his acceptance* of them, or *repudiates* the contract before shipment is even made (and the seller *doesn't resell* the goods), the seller may recover the ***difference between the contract price and the market price***. (See p. 365.)

❏ If neither of the above two just-listed measures (contract-market differential and contract-resale differential) is adequate to compensate the seller, he may be able to recover *"lost profits."* (See p. 369.)

❏ Where the goods have been *accepted* by the buyer, the seller may recover the ***contract price***. (See p. 371.)

❏ Lastly, even if the buyer never formally accepted the goods, the seller may in some situations (e.g., where the goods are unresaleable because custom-made) be able to recover the ***entire contract price***. (See p. 371.)

We consider each of these measures separately.

1. **Resale by seller:**   Where the buyer rejects goods or repudiates before they are even shipped, the seller will normally *resell them* to a third party. If the resale is "made in good faith and in a commercially reasonable manner," the seller may recover "the *difference* between the *resale price* and the *contract price* together with any incidental damages…but less expenses saved in consequence of the buyer's breach." § 2-706(1). This measure will put the reselling seller in approximately the position he would have been in had the contract been performed by the buyer. (If the resale price is *higher* than the original contract price, the seller may keep the extra profit rather than turning it over to the original buyer.)

    Example: Seller contracts to sell Buyer 100 "truth rings," which will allegedly change color if the wearer lies. The total contract price is $200. Before shipment, Buyer wrongfully repudiates the contract. Seller resells the lot of 100 rings to X, who pays $100 for them. Assuming that the resale was made "in good faith" and "in a commercially reasonable manner," Seller may recover damages of $100 (the contract price minus the resale price) from Buyer. (If X pays $300, Seller may keep the $100 profit over the original contract price.)

a. **Public versus private sale:** The resale may be at either a *public* sale (i.e., an auction) or at a *private* one. Whether the sale was made publicly or privately, it must be made "in a commercially reasonable manner" and "in good faith." § 2-706(1)). The treatment of the two kinds of sale differs principally concerning the kind of notice that must be given to the breaching buyer:

   i. **Notice in private sale:** Where the seller plans to resell *privately*, he is required only to give reasonable notice to the buyer that he intends to resell, and need not specify the time at which resale is to occur or anything else.

   ii. **Notice of public sale:** If the resale is to be *public*, the seller must give the buyer "reasonable notice of the time and place of the resale," (§ 2-706(4)(b)), unless the goods are "perishable or threaten to decline in value speedily." The public sale must take place at a "usual place or market for public sale" if one is available. The seller may purchase at the public sale.

2. **Contract/market differential:** If the seller does *not resell* the goods, he may recover from the non-accepting or repudiating buyer "the *difference* between the *market price* at the time and place for tender and the *unpaid contract price* together with any incidental damages … but less expenses saved in consequence of the buyer's breach." § 2-708(1). Thus the seller who does not resell receives the traditional contract/market differential, just as does the buyer who does not cover.

   a. **Use by seller who has resold:** May a seller who has *resold* the goods recover the *contract/market differential* rather than the contract/resale differential? It's not clear. White & Summers conclude that the question is a close one, but recommend that the seller who has resold *not* be allowed to obtain the contract/market differential, since to allow him to do so would put him in a better position than he would have been in had the contract been fulfilled. (Obviously, the seller who has resold will only try to use the contract/market differential if it is greater than the contract/resale differential.) W&S, p. 261.

3. **Lost profits:** A seller who has resold may in some cases not be adequately compensated by the contract/resale differential. Similarly, the seller who has not resold may sometimes not be fully compensated by the contract/market differential. Another Code provision, § 2-708(2), lends relief to such sellers:

   > "If the measure of damages provided in subsection (1) [the contract/market differential] is *inadequate* to *put the seller in as good a position as performance would have done* then the measure of damages is the *profit* (including *reasonable overhead*) which the seller *would have made from full performance* by the buyer, together with any *incidental* damages…, due allowance for costs reasonably incurred and *due credit for payments or proceeds* of resale."

   a. **Situations where this applies:** This *"lost profits"* section thus explicitly allows the court to grant the aggrieved seller expectation damages. There are two common kinds of situations in which the section will be applied:

      i. **The "lost volume" seller:** Many sellers can make or acquire *enough units* of the item in question to sell to meet all foreseeable demand. Therefore, when the buyer from such a seller breaches his contract, and the seller resells the item to the substitute customer at the same price, the seller will end up making *one fewer sale* because of the breach. This is because the new customer would have bought a unit of the item anyway, regardless of whether the first customer had breached. The seller in this situation, frequently called a *"lost volume"* seller, will be able to use § 2-708(2) to recover the profit he has lost by reason of the breach.

Example: P, a manufacturer of medical X-ray machines, contracts to sell one of its RayGun 2000 machines to D, a hospital, for $300,000. D refuses to take delivery or to pay the balance due under the contract. P resells that particular machine to X for the same price at which it was to be sold to D. P then sues D, asserting that it is entitled to recover its "lost profits," the difference between the $300,000 contract price and P's marginal costs in producing the machine. D argues that P sold the machine to X for the contract price, so P has not suffered any loss.

If P can show that it had enough manufacturing capacity that it could have timely and profitably fulfilled the contract with X (and any other outstanding contracts it had for the RayGun 2000) while *also* fulfilling the one with P, P will win. If P makes such a showing, it will be treated as a "lost volume" seller — it made one fewer sale because of D's breach. As a lost volume seller, P would not be adequately compensated by recovering merely the contract/resale differential (which, here, is $0). Therefore, P will be entitled to "the profit (including reasonable overhead) which the seller would have made from full performance by the buyer" (§ 2-708(2)).

(1) **Overhead as profit:**   § 2-708(2) provides that the lost profits recovered by a seller suing under that section may include *"reasonable overhead."* What this means is that the seller's recovery is the contract price minus any *variable* costs associated with the particular item, but not minus the overhead costs (i.e., the fixed costs) which the seller would have incurred whether or not he had ever sold the item in question.

Thus in the above example, the profit which D has "lost" will be computed by taking the contract price, and subtracting D's direct costs in producing the machine (e.g., cost of parts, cost of labor to assemble the parts, cost of testing, etc.), since those costs were incurred by D only in connection with the particular machine in question. But a pro rata amount for D's rent, electricity, administrative expenses, etc., does *not* have to be subtracted, since these are items of overhead and D would have incurred those costs even if it had never sold the machine in question to anyone.

(2) **Available only where seller was not limited in supply:**   The seller is a "lost volume" seller, and thus entitled to recover lost profits, only where he had *as many units of the item available for sale as he could plausibly sell.* If the demand for his product was greater than his supply, he has not lost anything by virtue of the breach, since with or without the breach he will end up selling the same number. (Also, some courts require the seller to show that he could have made a sale both to the buyer and to the resale buyer at a *profit.*)

  ii. **"Jobbers":** Another group of sellers who will benefit from the "lost profits" remedy given by § 2-708(2) are usually called ***"jobbers."*** A jobber is a ***middleman*** who as a matter of course does not purchase goods until he has already made a contract for their sale. Where a jobber finds a buyer for goods, who then repudiates the contract, the jobber never acquires the goods at all, and obviously does not resell them. The contract/market differential will not compensate an aggrieved jobber as long as the market price is close to the contract price. Yet such a jobber has, by virtue of his buyer's breach, lost the chance to make a profit on the goods which he never acquired. Therefore, he will be able to obtain the profits he would have made by resorting to § 2-708(2).

4. **Seller's action for the price:** Where one of the three seller's remedies discussed above (contract/resale differential, contract/market differential, lost profits) is applied, the seller's recovery will almost always be something less than the contract price. Either the seller will have resold the goods for some amount, or the goods will still have some market value at the time of breach, or under the "lost profits" formula the seller will be saved some direct costs because he does not have to perform. But in a few circumstances, the Code allows an aggrieved seller to sue for ***the entire contract price***. § 2-709 gives the seller such a right in three different circumstances:

 ❑ Where the goods have been ***"accepted"*** by the buyer;

 ❑ Where the goods have been ***lost or damaged*** within a reasonable time after the ***risk*** of their loss ***passed to the buyer***; or

 ❑ Where goods have been ***"identified to the contract,"*** and the seller is ***unable to resell them*** at a reasonable price.

Let's take a look at each scenario.

  a. **Accepted goods:** If the buyer has ***"accepted"*** the goods (acceptance is discussed *supra*, p. 231), it is reasonable to allow the seller to sue for the full contract price. § 2-709(1) does this: "When the buyer fails to pay the price as it becomes due the seller may recover, together with any incidental damages ... the ***price (a) of goods accepted[.]"***

  The buyer may, however, have a counterclaim for damages if the goods didn't conform to the contract specs. (This right is discussed further below, in the discussion of buyer's and seller's remedies with respect to accepted goods; see *infra*, p. 373.)

  b. **Risk of loss has passed:** The Code lays down several rules for determining when the ***risk of loss*** or damage to the goods passes from the seller to the buyer. These rules are discussed in the chapter on Impossibility, *infra*, p. 436. Once the risk of loss has passed to the buyer, the Code takes the position that the obligation to use or dispose of the goods is placed upon the buyer, and the seller should be able to recover the full contract price. § 2-709(1)(a).

  c. **Unresaleable goods:** Where the seller has already ***earmarked*** particular goods as being the goods he will supply under the contract, and the buyer either rejects them or repudiates before delivery, the seller may recover the contract price if he is "unable after a reasonable effort to sell them at a reasonable price or the circumstances reasonably indicate that such effort will be unavailing." § 2-709(1)(b). This section deals with those situations in which the market price of the contract goods has dropped so sharply that there is virtually no market left, or where the goods are *custom-made* and therefore unresaleable.

Example: Seller contracts to custom-manufacture for Buyer, for a total price of $100,000, 10,000 book bags with Buyer's name and logo on them. After seller has sewn the 10,000 bags and has put Buyer's name and logo on 8,000 of them, Buyer wrongfully cancels the contract. Assume that there is no reasonable resale market for the bags (even the 2,000 that don't yet have a name/logo), because of their unusual design.

Seller will be entitled to recover the entire $100,000 contract price from Buyer, because "the circumstances reasonably indicate that [an] effort [to resell] will be unavailing."

5. **Incidental damages:** No matter which of the above remedies the seller pursues, he has a right to recover *"incidental damages"* suffered in connection with the breach. Under § 2-710, these incidental damages include "any commercially reasonable charges, expenses, or commissions incurred in stopping delivery, in the transportation, care and custody of goods after the buyer's breach, in connection with return or resale of the goods or otherwise resulting from the breach."

6. **No consequential damages:** Nearly all courts hold that the seller may *not*, however, recover *"consequential damages"* from the breach. Such consequential damages are, as we have seen, always available to an aggrieved buyer; *supra*, p. 366. But nowhere in Article 2 is the seller explicitly given the right to receive consequential damages. The seller will seldom have any consequential damages from the breach anyway; since the only thing he was entitled to under the contract was the contract price, an award of this price, or some portion thereof, will normally fully compensate him. But examples can be imagined where the seller does suffer consequential losses (e.g., the breaching buyer is a "reference account" that the seller was counting on being able to point to with other prospective customers), and if he does, the general rule seems to be that he cannot recover them.

   a. **Contrary view:** But a few commentators and courts believe that a seller should be able to recover consequential damages even though the UCC nowhere explicitly awards them. Section 1-305(a) provides that consequential damages are not available unless they are expressly called for in the UCC "or by other rule of law." This minority believes that *general common-law* principles can and should be construed to make consequential damages available to all contracting parties, and that these common-law principles are "other rules of law," to be imported into the Code via § 1-103(b). See W&S, pp. 287-290.

7. **Liquidated damages:** The seller may also recover *liquidated damages* in some circumstances. If the contract has a valid liquidated damages clause, the seller may recover under that clause. See *supra*, p. 360. Even if the contract is silent about liquidated damages, the seller may be able to keep all or part of any *deposit* paid in advance by the buyer, as a kind of liquidated damages clause supplied by the UCC. (More precisely, the seller may keep

$500 or 20% of the contract price, whichever is less, and must return the rest; see § 2-718(2), discussed further *supra*, p. 340.)

D. Damages where the goods are accepted: All of the remedies discussed above apply only where the buyer has never accepted the goods (or has revoked his acceptance). His non-acceptance may result from the seller's failure to deliver at all, the seller's delivery of a defective tender which the buyer rightfully rejects, the buyer's repudiation and the seller's consequent non-delivery, the buyer's wrongful rejection of the seller's conforming tender, etc. But if the buyer does accept the goods (and does not rightfully revoke his acceptance), a different set of Code remedies comes into play. In the seller's case, the action is one for the ***contract price***. In the buyer's case, the action is for ***breach of warranty***.

1. **Seller's action for price:** When the buyer accepts the goods, the seller may recover the ***full contract price*** under § 2-709(1)(a). This is so whether the buyer keeps the goods, resells them or otherwise disposes of them. However, if the goods are defective, the seller's action for the contract price will be subject to the buyer's right to counterclaim for breach of warranty, discussed immediately below.

2. **Claim of buyer who has accepted:** A buyer who has accepted goods which turn out to be defective may sue (or counterclaim) for breach of contract. In order to preserve his right to sue for breach, "the buyer must ***within a reasonable time*** after he ***discovers or should have discovered*** any breach ***notify*** the seller of breach or be ***barred*** from any remedy." (§ 2-607(3)(a).)

   a. **General measure of damages:** If the buyer has accepted goods and given the appropriate notification, "he may recover as damages for any non-conformity of tender the loss resulting in the ordinary course of events from the seller's breach as determined in ***any manner which is reasonable***." (§ 2-714(1).) Thus the court is given great discretion in calculating the measure of damages.

   b. **Incidental and consequential damages:** In addition to awarding direct damages, the court may award "any ***incidental and consequential damages***...." These damages (discussed further *supra*, page 366) are awardable to the buyer on the same basis where he has accepted as where he has rejected or has never received delivery.

   c. **Breach of warranty:** A merchant-seller gives, according to the Code, a number of ***implied warranties***, of which the most important is the warranty of merchantability (§ 2-314). Also, any seller, whether a merchant or not, may give ***express*** warranties. Warranties, both express and implied, are discussed in the chapter on Warranties, *infra*, p. 497. If the buyer, after accepting the goods, discovers that any applicable warranty has been breached, § 2-714(2) gives him the right to recover for that breach of warranty. That section provides that the measure of damages for breach of warranty is "the ***difference*** at the time and place of acceptance between the ***value of the goods accepted*** and the ***value they would have had if they had been as warranted***, unless special circumstances show proximate damages of a different amount."

      i. **Measure of value:** In computing the difference between the value as warranted and the value as delivered, the court will generally consider the contract price as ***conclusive evidence*** of the value the goods would have had had they been as warranted. The value of the goods as delivered, however, poses more difficult mea-

Figure 10-2

Seller's Remedies under Sales Contract (UCC)

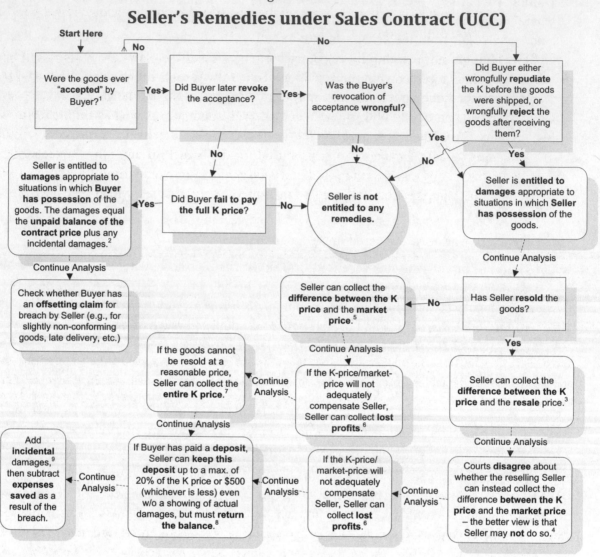

Notes

[1] See E VI(D)(4)(b) (of this chapter) for a discussion of when a buyer is deemed to have "accepted" goods.

[2] Note that a buyer who has covered cannot elect to receive the "contract price minus market price" measure (shown in box to the right of this one).

[3] See UCC §2-709(1)(a). For a discussion of incidental damages, see §2-714(1) and E XII(B)(3)(b).

[4] See E XII(C)(2)(a).

[5] See UCC §2-708(1). Marke price is determined as of the time and place for tender.

[6] See UCC §2-708(2) and E XIII(C)(3). This "lost profits" measure of damages will apply most

often in these 2 situations: (1) Seller is a "lost volume" seller (i.e., one who has more supply than customers, so the breach costs Seller one net sale); and (2) Seller is a middleman (and can get as much supply as needed).

[7] See UCC §2-709(1)(b). This remedy will apply where the goods were custom-made for Buyer, or where the market for such goods has disappeared for some reason.

[8] See UCC §2-718(2)(b). However, the amount kept by Seller may be greater or lesser than this, if there is a valid liquidated-damages clause. Id. See E XIII(C)(7).

[9] See UCC §2-710; E XII(C)(5).

surement problems. If the defect can be repaired, the court will probably take the *cost of repair* as an objective measurement of the difference between the value as is and the value as warranted. If the goods are so defective that repair is impossible, the courts will usually award the cost of *replacing* the goods, less the *salvage value* of the goods.

d. **Damages not relating to warranty:** In most cases the claim of an aggrieved buyer who has accepted the goods will be based on breach of warranty. But §2-714(1) (quoted above) allows the buyer to base a damage claim on the seller's failure to perform the particular obligations specified in the contract, as well as for breach of warranty. Thus, the buyer may sue for the seller's *delay* in delivery, the seller's refusal to *repair* defective machinery as promised, or the breach of any other covenant in the contract. Any loss resulting in the ordinary course of events from the seller's breach may be compensated, and may be measured in any manner which is reasonable. §2-714(1).

Quiz Yourself on
DAMAGES IN SALES CONTRACTS

104. Batman thinks the Batmobile is a little too ostentatious for everyday use, and contracts to buy a new car from the Superhero Car Dealership. He chooses a Penguin Swinger, a popular sub-compact. The cost to the dealer is $9,500, and the sticker price is $10,500, which Batman has agreed to pay. Superhero orders the Swinger from the factory, but when it arrives, Batman repudiates the contract. Superhero sells many Swingers, and it has no trouble selling the one Batman ordered to Spiderman. (Supplies of this model are freely available, and Superhero can get as many as it can find buyers for.)

(A) Under the UCC, is Superhero entitled to damages from Batman? (Ignore incidentals, reasonable overheads and saved expenses from breach.)

(B) Assume instead that Batman had custom-ordered a car with a turbo-charged ejection button and hot pink leather seats. The contract price is $20,000 and the cost to the dealer is $19,000. After Batman repudiates the contract, Superhero decides to place the vehicle up for auction and gives Batman notice of the sale. The car goes for $19,500. The auction costs Superhero $250. What damages can Superhero collect from Batman now?

105. The DiCaprio Boat Supply Wholesaler contracts to deliver 500 lifeboats from its inventory to the Titanic Boat Company for $10,000. (These models are in short supply, and DiCaprio can sell all it can obtain.) However, when DiCaprio tries to deliver the lifeboats to Titanic, Titanic wrongfully refuses to accept the shipment. DiCaprio places an ad for the lifeboats, and sells them to the I-Can Canoe Co., for $10,000. Under the UCC, will DiCaprio be able to recover the cost of the ad from Titanic?

106. Orville Wright orders 1,000 giant rubber bands to power his airplane from Da Vinci Aircraft Supplies, for a contract price of $1,000. When the rubber bands arrive, Wright notes that they are seriously defective (they are frayed). However, he doesn't send them back, but instead begins using them, because he doesn't want to wait for replacements.

(A) For this part, assume that Wright notifies Da Vinci of the fraying as soon as he spots it, but says that he'll keep the bands anyway. Wright uses the bands successfully in his flight, and then retires them. Wright then refuses to pay Da Vinci's bill, and Da Vinci sues for the $1,000 contract amount. Wright counterclaims for damages for breach of warranty, and alternatively, asks the court to rescind the contract (in which case Wright is happy to return the used rubber bands and pay nothing). The frayed rubber bands (if their fraying were recognized) would have a market value of $200. The bands were actually worth $900 to Wright at the moment he received them, because he didn't have time to procure substitutes, and if he delayed he might not have become the first person to fly. How will the court resolve the parties' claims?

(B) For this part only, assume that all facts are the same as in part (A), except that Wright's plane crashes because the defective rubber bands break. The plane, which had a value of $2,000, is completely destroyed. Assume that Da Vinci, being in the aircraft-supplies business, knew that a foreseeable (though not highly probable) result of using frayed aircraft rubber bands would be a crash such as that suffered by Da Vinci. Assume further that because of the extreme time pressure on Wright to be the first to fly, his decision to use the bands was not unreasonable. If Da Vinci sues for the $1,000 contract price, and Wright counterclaims for breach of warranty, what outcome?

(C) For this part only, assume that Wright receives the rubber bands, notices the fraying, realizes the danger of breakage, but says nothing to Da Vinci. He uses the rubber bands, and they break as in Part (B). Wright continues to say nothing to Da Vinci because he's busy doing other things. Finally, two months after shipment, Da Vinci sues for the $1,000 contract price, and at this point Wright first asserts (as a defense in the litigation) that the bands were frayed and caused a crash. All other facts are as in Part (B). What outcome?

107. Princess Mary is about to get married, and orders her wedding dress from the tailor who clothes her entire family, Savvy Row. The dress is to cost $3,000. When the dress is delivered, two weeks before the wedding, Mary is horrified to find that Savvy Row has cut the dress to the measurements of her grotesquely fat father, King Henry VIII, by mistake. She immediately ships the dress back (at a cost of $20) and orders the same type of dress from another tailor, Saville-Bassoon (who does not charge for shipping). Because of the short amount of time available, the replacement dress costs her $5,000.

Assuming Mary didn't pay Savvy Row anything up front, how much, if anything, will she be able to recover from them in damages?

Answers

104. **(A) Yes.** Superhero is a "lost volume" seller — a seller whose supply is greater than the demand. That's because Superhero will likely be able to prove that it would have made the sale to Spiderman regardless of Batman's breach: had Batman not breached, Superhero would have made *two* sales. Under § 2-708(2), a seller who would not be made whole by the contract/resale differential may recover his lost profits; lost-volume sellers are prime examples of persons entitled to use 2-708(2). Therefore, Superhero is entitled to collect its lost profits from Batman's breach. Those profits equal $1,000 (the list price less the wholesale price).

(B) $750. Under these facts, the car in question is a unique item. Therefore, Superhero is no longer a "lost volume" seller — he could sell the custom car only once. Consequently, Superhero is no longer entitled to collect its lost profit. Superhero is now limited to more traditional seller's remedy: the difference between the contract price and the resale price, plus incidentals. Here, that is ($20,000 - $19,500) + $250 in auction costs, for a total of $750.

105. **Yes.** The cost of the ad (like the cost of attempting delivery to Titanic) is recoverable as "incidental damages." Note that DiCaprio is not entitled to any compensatory damages, since a seller who resells the mer-

chandise (and who is not a lost-volume seller) receives only the difference between the contract and resale price, which here is $0 (DiCaprio got the same price from I-Can as it was expecting to get from Titanic). So incidentals will be DiCaprio's *sole* item of damages.

106. **(A) It will order Wright to pay $200.** First, a buyer who accepts the goods must normally pay the contract price; Wright could have rejected the shipment had he acted promptly, but by using them he lost the right to do so, and is liable for the contract price. However, Wright has a counterclaim for breach of the implied warranty of merchantability (since frayed rubber bands are not merchantable). The usual measure of damages for breach of warranty is the difference between the value the goods would have had had they been as warranted, and their actual value. The contract price ($1,000) will be highly persuasive evidence of the goods' value had they been as warranted. The "actual" value will probably be deemed to be the market value of the goods as they were, not their special value to Wright. Since that market value is $200, Wright will have a counterclaim for $800. He will have to pay the difference between the two amounts, $200 (which, not coincidentally, was the goods' market value in their defective condition).

(B) Probably a net $1,800 recovery for Wright. Da Vinci will still be entitled to the $1,000 contract price — nothing we've added to the facts of part (B) changes this. However, Wright will have a larger counterclaim for breach of warranty. He'll still be entitled to the difference between the contract price and the value of the goods as warranted (an $800 difference). But he'll *also* be entitled to the $2,000 in consequential damages (loss of the plane), an item of damages the facts tell us was reasonably foreseeable to one in Da Vinci's position. (In other words, the $2,000 is covered by the "ordinarily foreseeable" branch of *Hadley v. Baxendale*.) So Wright has a total claim of $2,800, which will produce a net judgment in his favor of $1,800 after being offset against the $1,000 contract price.

(C) Probably, judgment for $1,000 to Da Vinci. UCC § 2-607(3)(a) says that when a "tender has been accepted," the buyer "must, within a reasonable time after he discovers or should have discovered any breach *notify* the seller of breach or be barred from any remedy." So given that Wright remained silent about the breach for two months, right up until the lawsuit, a court would almost certainly conclude that Wright had failed to give notice of breach within a reasonable time after he discovered the breach. Consequently, Wright will lose his right to counterclaim for breach of warranty (see § 2-714(1), noting that the accepting buyer's right to recover damages for breach of warranty is subject to his having "given notification" under 2-607(3)). This will leave the $1,000 contract price, awarded to Da Vinci, as the sole award to either side.

107. **$2,020.** A buyer has the right to cover by procuring substitute merchandise. In that event, buyer's damages equal the different between the contract price and the cover price, plus any incidentals. So Mary will recover the $2,000 contract-cover differential, plus the $20 shipping expenses as incidental damages.

 Exam Tips on
REMEDIES

The three most frequently tested subjects from this chapter are the equitable remedy of ***specific performance***, suits in ***quasi-contract***, and damages in ***sales contracts***. Be sure to bone up on these important topics.

Specific Performance

☞ Specific performance is the most important *equitable* remedy for test purposes. When reading a fact pattern, remember that the most important issue is *whether money damages would be adequate to protect the injured party* — if they would, that party can't get specific performance.

   ☞ **Unique good:** Look for a *rare or unusual object* that's the subject of the contract — money damages are less likely to be adequate, because exact substitutes can't be found. (*Examples:* An antique car; a highly unusual ring; a work of art.)

   ☞ **Speculative damages:** Look for cases where *damages* would be *hard to measure*. This is especially likely where the contract involves a *new business or new product*.

      Example: *S* agrees to sell *B* the rights to make commercial use of a new secret-formula sauce for hamburgers. If *S* reneges and *B* sues for specific performance, *B* will have a good chance of prevailing. This is so because, due to the formula's newness, it will be hard to predict what *B*'s profits or losses would have been for the formula, making it hard for *B* to recover money damages.

   ☞ **Land contract:** In a straight contract for the sale of land in return for money, specific performance will normally be granted *to the buyer*, because courts consider each piece of land to be unique, so that the buyer can't adequately be compensated by a money-damage award.

      ☞ If the suit is brought by the *seller* (i.e., it's the buyer who refuses to close), note in your answer the possibility of several outcomes:

        ❏ Some states *allow specific performance* to be ordered on behalf of the seller.

        ❏ Of those who don't, some permit the seller to collect only the out-of-pocket costs incurred in making the agreement. Others permit the seller to recover only the difference between the contract price and the market price, which is often zero.

   ☞ **Employment contract:** An *employment contract* is *not* usually enforceable (on either side) by specific performance. This is so because employment contracts are a form of personal service contract, and enforcement would violate the public policy against involuntary servitude (if the employee is the defendant) or against forcing an employer to accept services of an unwanted worker (if the employee is the plaintiff).

☞ **Liquidated damages available:** Remember the majority rule that the existence of a *liquidated damages* award does not bar the remedy of specific performance.

   Example: Buyer, a corporate transferee from out of town, contracts with Seller for the purchase of Seller's house. Because Buyer plans to move her family on April 20, the contract provides that the house is to be vacant and ready for occupancy by that date. The contract also contains a liquidated damages clause and provides for payment to Buyer of $75 for each day after April 20 that the house isn't ready for occupancy. On

April 20, Buyer moves her family into town and the house isn't vacant, so they stay at a motel. On May 1, Seller informs her that he doesn't intend to go through with the contract. Buyer may sue *both* for specific performance of the land contract and for liquidated damages — since specific performance would be otherwise appropriate (it's a contract for the sale of land), the court won't deny that remedy merely because Seller is also subject to a liquidated damages clause.

Expectation Damages

☛ This is the *standard measure of damages* for breach of contract. Expectation damages are awarded to *put the plaintiff in the position she would have been in had the contract been performed.*

   ☞ **Formula:** Expectation damages are usually calculated as:

      the *value of defendant's promised performance* (generally the contract price) *less*

      the *benefits to plaintiff* (i.e., money saved) from *not having to perform* her end of the contract.

    Hint: You should always discuss expectation damages in any fact pattern where the contract was valid and one party materially breached.

   ☞ *Common scenario*: A contractor *partially performs,* and either the hiring party obtains a substitute performance, or the contractor wants to be reimbursed for his partial work.

    Substitute performance example: Owner owns a farm in County. She hires Driller to drill a water well. The contract provides for a guaranteed completion by June 1. The contract price is $10 a foot and Driller is to be paid $3,500 in advance, with any refund or additional payment to be made on completion. Two hundred feet down, Driller's drill strikes rock and breaks, plugging the hole. Driller refuses to start a new hole. Owner hires Dan to drill the well for $4,500. Dan strikes water at 300 feet.

      Because of Driller's repudiation of the contract, Owner may recover the $3,500 advanced to Driller (since she got no value for that advance) *and* the $1,500 difference between the price for the substitute performance and the contract price (which would have been $3,000 for a 300-foot well).

    Reimbursement example: Contractor, a building contractor, enters into a contract with Manco, a manufacturer, for the construction of a two-story factory on Manco's parcel of realty for $250,000, to be paid upon completion. When the factory is partially completed, Manco decides to retire from the manufacturing business, and tells Contractor to stop work. Contractor has already spent $180,000 on the construction and would need to spend another $35,000 to complete the building.

      Contractor can collect expectation damages of $215,000, calculated as the contract price ($250,000) minus the cost to him of completion ($35,000).

Reliance Damages

☛ Reliance damages come into play when expectation damages would not adequately compensate the plaintiff, or where there is no enforceable contract, but plaintiff is entitled to some protection anyway. Most commonly, reliance damages generally appear on exams in questions involving **promissory estoppel.**

☞   **Example:** Buyer and Seller orally agree that Seller will sell Blackacre to Buyer for $200,000, with Seller to deliver the property with a presently-existing unsightly shed at the back removed. Seller spends $5,000 to remove the shed. At the time for closing, Buyer fails to tender the purchase price. Seller won't be able to recover contract damages, since the contract is for the sale of an interest in land, and thus was required to be in writing. However, Seller will probably be able to recover on a promissory estoppel theory, in which case he'll recover the $5,000 spend on shed-removal, since that cost was incurred in direct and reasonable reliance on the oral agreement.

Restitution Damages

☛ Restitution damages are defined as the value **to the defendant** of the **plaintiff's performance**. (Think **unjust enrichment**.) Restitution damages can be awarded in a suit **on the contract,** or in a suit brought in **quasi-contract.**

> **Example (suit on the contract):** Duster, the owner of crop-dusting planes, enters into a contract with Farmer, a farmer, for the dusting of Farmer's crop four times a year for four years for a total of $10,000, which is paid upon the signing of the contract. After two years, Duster sells her business to Newco, assigning the contract with Farmer to Newco.
>
> If Newco fails to perform, Farmer may collect as damages from Duster the $5,000 unearned portion of the money paid to Duster, since Duster has been enriched by not performing the final two years. (Alternatively, Farmer could try to recover the "benefit of her bargain" — the amount, if any, by which the $10,000 contract price was less than Farmer's total payments would be by the time she procured a substitute duster for the last 2 years. But the point is that even without proof of cost-of-substitution, Farmer can recover the unpaid deposit on a restitution-damages theory.)

Quasi-contract

☛ Quasi-contract recovery is an important possibility to keep in mind whenever you are discussing the possible remedies available. Always consider relief based on quasi-contract when the **aggrieved party is not entitled to damages for breach of contract.** Remember that recovery will be the **reasonable value of the services rendered.** Watch for these situations:

☞   **Contract never formed:** Look for a fact pattern where an enforceable contract was never formed. The party providing the services may be entitled to recover in quasi-contract if he had a **reasonable expectation of payment** for those services (i.e., he did not intend them as a gift).

☞   **Common trick scenario:** A party performs **emergency services** for a person in peril. *Usual conclusion:* The savior has performed **without an expectation of payment** for services or for losses incurred as a result, and therefore **may not recover** in quasi-contract.

☞   **Contract rendered unenforceable:** Look for an originally-enforceable contract that only later **becomes** unenforceable, i.e., where a party is **excused** from performing for some reason. Although the performing party isn't entitled to contract damages, he may still be able to recover in quasi-contract. This is most likely in cases of ***impossibility/ impracticability*** and ***frustration of purpose***.

Example: Owner owns a piece of undeveloped land adjacent to City Airport. On January 2, Owner enters into a contract with Architect, an architect, whereby Architect agrees to produce and deliver by May 1 a design of a ten-story hotel which Owner wishes to build on that land. On March 31, it's announced that City Airport flight operations will cease at the end of the year, making it pointless for Owner to build the hotel. Owner refuses to accept the completed hotel design from Architect on May 1.

If Owner is excused from performing because of frustration of purpose, Architect will still be able recover the reasonable value of services rendered up until March 31, when the event excusing Owner's performance occurred.

☞ **Building destroyed before completion:** Look for a fact pattern where, through no fault of either party, the structure that is being built is ***destroyed*** and the contractor refuses to begin work again:

❏ If the construction is of a ***new*** structure, the contractor is usually allocated the risk, so he isn't excused from performing, and therefore ***may not collect damages in quasi-contract*** for the value of the services performed through the time of destruction.

❏ If the construction involves a repair of an ***existing*** structure, then the contractor will probably be ***excused*** from performing because of frustration of purpose and/or impossibility, since the continued existence of the building is a basic assumption upon which the contract is based. The contractor may, in that case, recover in quasi-contract for the value of the work performed up until the time of the destruction.

☞ **Partial performance, then breach:** Quasi-contract remedies are frequently used by the party who has ***partially performed*** but then breaches a contract, as a way to set-off the damages it owes to the nonbreaching party. Look for a ***breaching contractor*** who ***hasn't substantially performed*** but has nonetheless provided the owner with something of value.

Example: O contracts to have *C*, a contractor, build *O* a house on *O*'s land. The contract price is $300,000. *C* does about half the work, then defaults. The reasonable value to *O* of the work done is $125,000. *C* has received a $60,000 deposit. It will cost *O* $225,000 to get another contractor to finish the job (meaning that if *O* has to pay the full value of *C*'s work less the deposit, *O* will be $50,000 worse off than had *C* fully performed). *C* can recover $15,000, calculated as follows:

Reasonable value of work done, less *deposit received* and less *O's damages for the breach,* or

$125,000 minus ($60,000 + $50,000) = $15,000

Consequential Damages

☛ **Extra damages:** If the standard expectation measure doesn't fully compensate a party for her losses, remember that the additional damages can also be recovered. These are often called *"consequential"* damages.

Example: C agrees to renovate O's house for $50,000, by March 1. C gets a $25,000 deposit, does half the work, then defaults. O hires a replacement, X, who finishes the job for $25,000. The standard expectation "benefit of the bargain" measure would give O $0 recovery, because there is no difference between the contract and market price. But if X can't finish the job until April 30, and O can't move in during the month of April, O will probably be able to recover the cost of procuring substitute lodging for that month — the lodging costs will be "consequential" damages, and will be on top of the contract/market differential.

☞   **Foreseeability:** But remember that consequential damages are subject to an important limitation: the requirement of *foreseeability*. Determine whether the additional losses were either: (1) *reasonably foreseeable* to an objective observer in D's shoes, based on general principles; or (2) foreseeable based on the plaintiff's *special requirements,* of which D had *notice*. (Remember that this is basically the rule of *Hadley v. Baxendale*.) If the losses don't fall into either category, they're not recoverable.

Example: Seller and Buyer enter into a contract for the sale of 10,000 pounds of specifically described bolts each month for a period of ten months beginning March 1; the contract has a total value of $40,000. On March 1, Seller informs Buyer that he will not deliver any bolts to Buyer because he has just contracted to sell his entire output to another buyer for a higher price. It takes Buyer 61 days to find a new supplier; the new supplier charges the same price. Because of the delay in finding a new supplier, Buyer is late in delivering motors to End User, a company with which Buyer has a contract containing a valid liquidated damages clause providing for damages of $10,000 a day for delays in delivery of motors. Although Seller knew that Buyer sold motors, Seller didn't know about Buyer's specific contract with End User. May Buyer recover from Seller the $610,000 he is required to pay End User under the liquidated damages clause?

Probably not, because it probably wasn't foreseeable to Seller that a 2-month delay in delivery on a $40,000 contract would bring about $610,000 in losses. Buyer's needs — in particular his need to avoid heavy liquidated damages — were probably "special requirements" that cannot be the basis for recovery unless Seller knew about them at the time of contracting.

Mitigation

☛ Be sure to discuss whether the nonbreaching party has attempted to *mitigate damages* in a situation where the loss was partially or totally avoidable — if she didn't, any damages that would probably have been avoided by such an attempt are non-recoverable.

☞   Look for a *terminated employee,* who fails to make reasonable efforts to find a suitable *replacement job*.

☞   Look for a *disappointed buyer or recipient of services.*

Example: B, the owner of a furnace-repair company, maintains a fleet of personal trucks for his employees' use and drives his personal station wagon when visiting customers' homes. On February 15, *B* orders a new station wagon from *S*, a car dealer, to be delivered by March 5. On March 4, *B* sells his old station wagon because of the expected delivery of the new car the following day. However, the new car isn't delivered to *S* until March 30. *B* sues *S* for lost profits because of his inability to travel to customers. *B* won't recover for this: although business losses were foreseeable at the time of contracting, *B* could have mitigated his damages by renting a car or using one of the company's trucks.

Liquidated Damages

☞ **Reasonableness:** Remember that the liquidated damages amount will be deemed (in most courts) reasonable if it is a reasonable estimate as of *either* the *time of contracting* or the *time of the actual loss.* Normally, you should try to analyze the reasonableness as of *each* time frame.

☞ Other points to watch for:

☞ Pay attention to what the clause remedies. Even where the clause is enforceable, other types of damages can still be awarded to address problems not covered by the clause.

Example: *O* and *C*, a contractor, enter into an agreement for various repairs to be made to *O*'s home. The contract provides that the repairs are to be completed within sixty days, and that if *C* fails to complete the job on time, *C* will pay *O* $50 per day as liquidated damages. After the repairs are finished, *O* discovers that *C* did a faulty job on one aspect, the roof; she has another contractor redo the repair for $1,000. Since the liquidated damages clause only redresses *late* performance, it doesn't eliminate the possibility of *O*'s collecting damages for *defective* performance in the amount of $1,000.

☞ Be on the lookout for *"blunderbuss"* clauses, where the clause gives the *same damage award regardless of the severity* of the breach. Such a clause is likely to be a penalty, at least where it ends up costing D much more than the *actual* damages she's caused.

Example: Boss is a CPA and Emp is his employee (also a CPA) under a 2-year contract. As part of the contract, Emp agrees to a non-compete, under which if Emp leaves and does work for any client of Boss during the 2 years, Emp owes Boss damages equal to three months' salary ($30,000). Emp quits and, with 1 week left in the 2 years, does $100 of work for one client of Boss. This "blunderbuss" clause (same $30,000 of damages assessed regardless of how much the competition cost Boss in lost revenues) will be found to be an unenforceable penalty.

Damages in Sales Contracts

☞ **Buyer's damages:** This area is more heavily tested than that of seller's damages. Several reminders:

☞ **Standard "contract/market" differential:** If a buyer returns defective goods (or fails to receive any shipment of goods from the seller) and doesn't purchase replacement goods elsewhere, she is entitled to the difference between the *contract price* and the *market price* at the time of breach.

☞ **Cover:** If a buyer returns defective goods (or fails to receive any shipment of goods from the seller) and *purchases them elsewhere*, she is entitled to the difference between the *contract* price and the *cover* price.

  ☞ The buyer's *cover price paid by the buyer must be reasonable in the circumstances*. Look the buyer's attempts to find a good price (or at least to verify the true "market" price) — if these are absent, discuss the possibility that the buyer may have behaved unreasonably and should be denied the full contract/cover differential.

☞ Remember that if the market price (or the cover price) and the contract price are the *same, there are no damages to collect*, except consequential or incidental ones.

  ☞ *Note:* Where the market price or cover price is *less* than the contract price, the buyer gets the benefit of the difference with no off-setting to what the seller owes for consequential or incidental damages.

☞ **Breach of warranty:** If a buyer accepts defective goods the damages are calculated as the difference between the value which the delivered goods had at the time of acceptance and the value which conforming goods would have had at the time.

☞ **Specific Performance:** The buyer can only get specific performance if the goods are *unique*.

☞ **Seller's damages:** The most testable issue in this area is whether a seller can be compensated for *lost profits*. *Trick:* The seller appears to have suffered no damage because he resold the item or items for the contract price or for an amount in excess of the contract price. Your inquiry should not end there, however.

☞ Look for a seller who has a *supply of goods in excess of the level of demand* (the *"lost volume"* seller). He has lost a sale and is entitled to his lost profits — even if he resold the goods in question — because he could have had *both* sales but for the breach.

  ☞ But if the seller resells *all* the available goods of the type that is the subject of the contract, then he is not a lost-volume seller and cannot collect lost profits for the breach.

☞ Remember to deduct from all recoveries the *costs* that the aggrieved buyer or seller *didn't incur* as a result of not having to complete his performance.

Punitive Damages

☞ Remember that punitive damages are ordinarily *not recoverable* in breach-of-contract actions. (However, if the breach was also independently a tort — as in fraud — punitives may be recoverable.)

CHAPTER 11

CONTRACTS INVOLVING MORE THAN TWO PARTIES

ChapterScope

This chapter considers contracts in which more than two parties are involved. The discussion focuses on multiple parties in two different kinds of contracts: (1) contracts in which a party seeks to *assign* his rights to a third person, or to *delegate* his duties to a third person; and (2) contracts in which a person who is not an actual party is a *beneficiary* of the contract. Key concepts:

- ■ **Assignment:** An *assignment* is a *present transfer* of a party's already-existing *rights under a contract.*

  - ❏ **Assignable rights:** The general rule (but subject to important exceptions) is that *contract rights are assignable*.

  - ❏ **Rights against obligor:** Generally, the *assignee takes subject to any defenses* which could have been asserted by the obligor against the assignor.

- ■ **Delegation:** A *delegation* is a present transfer of a party's already existing *duties* under a contract.

  - ❏ **Delegable duties:** The general rule is that *contract duties are delegable.* The exception is that a duty will be non-delegable if the non-delegating party has a substantial interest in having the delegator perform.

  - ❏ **Delegator remains liable:** After the delegation, the *delegator remains liable* to the obligee.

- ■ **Third party beneficiary:** A person who is not a party to a contract becomes a *third party beneficiary* at the time the contract is formed, if the parties to the contract *intend to confer a benefit* on that person.

  - ❏ **Right to sue:** A third party beneficiary has the *right to bring suit* against one of the original parties if the latter does not perform.

  - ❏ **Contrast with incidental beneficiary:** By contrast, an *"incidental"* beneficiary — one who would be benefited by performance, but upon whom the original parties did not intend to confer a benefit — may *not* sue.

  - ❏ **Vesting of rights:** The contracting parties' power to *modify or discharge* the contract *terminates* when the third party beneficiary's rights have *"vested."* Vesting occurs when, before the beneficiary receives notice of the modification, the beneficiary either: (1) *changes her position* in justifiable reliance on the contract, (2) *brings suit* on the contract, or (3) *manifests assent* to it.

I. ASSIGNMENT AND DELEGATION GENERALLY

A. Introduction: The following material deals with attempts by a party to an existing contract to *substitute another* in her stead. She may wish to do this by transferring to another her own rights in the contract, by appointing another to perform her duties under the contract, or both. The following pages discuss when such a substitution may be made, and what its effects are.

B. Assignment distinguished from delegation: When a party to an existing contract transfers to a third person his *rights* under the contract, he has made an *assignment*. If the existing party appoints a third person to perform his *duties* under the contract, he has made a *delegation.*

   1. Distinguished from other kinds of third-party relationships: Assignments and delegations are attempts to create rights or duties in a third person *after* the contract has been executed. They should therefore be distinguished from *third party beneficiary* contracts (discussed *infra*, p. 415), in which the rights of a third party are contemplated at the time the contract is made.

     a. Distinguished from novation: Assignment and delegation should also be distinguished from a *novation*, by which *both* the existing parties agree that a third party shall take the place of one of them. Assignment and/or delegation can generally occur at the will of one party, whereas a novation requires the consent of both original parties. Also, whereas one who delegates his duties *remains liable* if the delegate does not perform, a party who is released by a novation is *completely discharged* from all liability. (See the discussion of novation, *infra*, p. 408.)

II. ASSIGNMENT

A. Present transfer: An assignment is a *present* transfer of one's rights under a contract. That is, it is a completely executed transfer, in the same way that a gift is an executed transfer. Therefore, a promise to transfer one's rights in the future is not an assignment, although it may be a contract.

   1. Significance of distinction: The chief significance of the fact that an assignment is a present transfer is that *no consideration is required* for it. For instance, a party who is owed money under an existing contract may assign it to a third person gratuitously, and neither the assignor nor the original obligor will be able to avoid the assignment on the grounds that there was no consideration for it.

B. Assignor's right extinguished: When a valid assignment occurs, the assignor's rights under the contract are *extinguished* and may thereafter be exercised only by the assignee. There are some instances, however, in which a valid assignment may be *revoked* by the assignor; these instances are discussed *infra*, p. 388. But if the assignment is irrevocable, the *assignee, not the assignor*, is the *only one who can enforce the contract rights involved.*

   Example: Seller has contracted to supply 1,000 widgets to Buyer for a fixed price. X, sensing that the price of widgets will increase, pays Buyer $100, for which Buyer assigns to X all of his rights under the contract with Seller. This assignment extinguishes Buyer's rights under the contract. If Seller fails to deliver the widgets, only X, and not Buyer, can sue.

C. UCC rules on assignment: Thus far in this book the only part of the UCC which we have encountered is Article 2, dealing with sales of goods. In the case of assignments, however, another part of the UCC is of great importance: Article 9. Even more significantly, Article 9 applies to certain assignments *even in some situations not involving goods*. Article 9 lays down rules concerning such matters as whether an assignment must be in writing; when a clause in the contract prohibiting assignment is effective; whether the original obligor may assert against the assignee a defense which he could have asserted against the assignor; and perhaps most importantly, how the rights of multiple assignees under the same contract are to be determined.

1. **What assignments are covered by Article 9:** Article 9 does not cover every kind of assignment. The basic purpose of Article 9 is to regulate various aspects of *commercial financing*, including the giving of personal property as collateral to secure indebtedness. Because businesspeople who need to obtain working capital often put up as collateral their right to receive payment in the future from contracts which they have or will perform, most assignments of the right to receive payment under a contract (whether the contract is for goods or services) are covered by Article 9. Such an assignment is called a *"security interest."* A complete discussion of what kinds of assignments fall within Article 9 is beyond the scope of this outline; however, here are some of the key points:

   a. **Assignment of the right to receive payment only:** Article 9 only applies to assignments of the *right to receive payment*, not the right to receive some other kind of performance. Thus if an inventor has contracted to produce a machine for a corporation, and the corporation assigns its rights to the machine to a third person, the assignment is not covered by Article 9, since it is not the assignment of the right to receive payment.

   b. **Wage assignments exempted:** Article 9 does not apply to an employee's assignment of his right to receive *future wages*.

   c. **Sale of a business:** If an assignment is made in connection with the *sale of a business* from which the rights assigned arose, Article 9 does not apply.

   d. **Where assignee is also delegate:** If the assignee is also to *perform* under the contract (i.e., be both assignee and delegate), Article 9 does not apply. See § 9-109(d) for all of the above exceptions and others.

2. **Where Article 9 does apply:** Here is an illustration of the most common kind of situation in which an assignment is governed by Article 9.

   Example: Cleaning Co. runs a cleaning service for numerous industrial clients. It has a contract with each of its customers for a one-year period, January-December, 2011. Payment is to be made quarterly. Cleaning Co. is short on cash, so it assigns its rights to payment under each of these contracts to Bank, in return for a cash advance of 90% of the value of the payment rights. This assignment, whether it covers sums that have already been earned by Cleaning Co., sums that it will earn during the rest of the contract, or both, is covered by Article 9 of the UCC. Article 9 imposes the requirement that the assignment be in *writing*, negates any provision in the original contract which *purports to prohibit assignment*, and defines Bank's rights against Cleaning Co.'s creditors.

Note: Where an assignment is made of rights under a contract for a sale of goods, Article 2 of the Code is also relevant. Article 2's provisions on assignment, most of which relate to what kinds of contracts are assignable, include not only the assignment of the right to payment of money (which is the only kind of assignment that Article 9 covers), but also the assignment of rights to performance. A buyer who assigned his right to purchase goods under a sales contract would, for instance, be covered by the relevant provisions of Article 2, which are discussed below.

D. No writing required absent statute: Except in those kinds of assignments that are governed by statutes, an assignment of contract rights does *not have to be in writing*. See Rest. 2d, § 324.

   1. Assignment of real estate contracts: Most states have statutes providing that the assignment of a contract interest in *real estate* is not effective either against the assignor or the obligor unless there has been a writing.

   2. Assignments covered by Article 9: Recall that certain assignments of contract rights are governed by Article 9 of the UCC. If a particular assignment is covered by Article 9, it is generally *not enforceable* against either the assignor or the original obligor unless the assignor has signed a document called a *"security interest."* See § 9-203(b)(3)(A).

E. Gratuitous assignments: A party to a contract may wish to assign his rights under it to some third party without receiving anything in return. Such an assignment, which is in the nature of a gift, is generally called a *gratuitous assignment*. A gratuitous assignment is generally enforceable, but may under certain circumstances, discussed below, be revoked.

   1. Obligor has no defense: The obligor who must make the performance may *not* refuse to perform on the ground that the assignee *did not give consideration* for the assignment.

      Example: *A* owes *B* $1,000. *B* gratuitously assigns his right to this $1,000 to *C*. *A* must make the payment to *C*, and cannot assert as a defense that *C* did not give *B* any consideration.

   2. Revocation: Although a gratuitous assignment is effective, it will be automatically *revoked* if the assignor does any of the following three things:

      [1] The assignor *dies*;

      [2] The assignor makes a *subsequent assignment* of the same right to a different person; or

      [3] The assignor gives *notice* to *either the assignee or the obligor* that the assignment has been revoked.

   See Rest. 2d, § 332(2).

      a. Notice to the obligor: Option (3) above — *notice of revocation* given by the assignor either to the assignee or the obligor — means that a revocation of the gratuitous assignment can occur *without the assignee's even knowing about it.* So if the assignor tells the obligor to render performance to the assignor rather than to the assignee, this will act as a revocation, and the obligor must do what the assignor says.

Example: On April 1, Uncle orally says to Niece, "Debtor owes me $1,000, due next Jan. 1. I'll instruct Debtor to pay you instead of me." Uncle then so instructs Debtor. On Dec. 1, Uncle says to Debtor, "I've changed my mind because I'm angry at Niece. Pay me instead of Niece." This statement acts to revoke the assignment to Niece (since the assignment was gratuitous). Therefore, if Debtor obeys the instruction and pays Uncle, Niece has no claim against either Uncle or Debtor. That's true even though neither Debtor nor Uncle gave notice to Niece of the revocation.

Furthermore, if Debtor disobeys the instruction and pays Niece, Uncle can sue Debtor for the $1,000 — Debtor's payment to Niece won't serve as a valid defense.

3. **How gratuitous assignments may become irrevocable:** There are some situations in which a gratuitous assignment is, or becomes, *irrevocable*. The most important of these are as follows:

    a. **Delivery of symbolic document:** If the contract right being assigned is evidenced by a document that commonly *symbolizes* the right, delivery of the document to the assignee makes the assignment irrevocable. See Rest. 2d, § 332(1)(b). Thus if the owner of an *insurance policy* delivers it to a third person with appropriate words of assignment, the right to the proceeds becomes irrevocable; the same would be true of delivery of a *savings bank book* or of *shares of stock*.

    Example: Insured, who owns an insurance policy on his own life, delivers the policy to Friend, with the words, "I am assigning you this policy." At that moment, the assignment becomes irrevocable, even though it was gratuitous.

    b. **Writing by assignor:** If the assignor himself puts the assignment *in writing*, most courts (and the Second Restatement — see § 332(1)(a)) hold that the assignment is irrevocable if the *writing is delivered* to the assignee. Thus a buyer under a sales contract who delivers a signed writing to a third person assigning his rights under the sales contract has made an irrevocable assignment.

    c. **Reliance:** If the assignee *relies to his detriment* on the assignment, and this reliance is reasonably foreseeable by the assignor, the assignment becomes irrevocable. See Rest. 2d, § 332(4).

    d. **Obligor's performance:** If the obligor *gives the assignee the payment* or other performance the right to which has been assigned, the assignment becomes irrevocable. Rest. 2d, § 332(3)(a).

    Example: Assume the basic facts of the Uncle/Niece example above. Suppose Debtor pays the $1,000 to Niece early, on November 15, before Uncle tells him to pay Uncle instead of Niece. That payment will cause the assignment to become irrevocable, so that Uncle no longer has the power to revoke the assignment by instructing Debtor to pay him directly.

F. **What rights are assignable:** *All* contract rights are by default *assignable*. That is, an assignment is automatically valid unless it falls within a small number of exceptions, which we discuss below.

1. **Rationale:** The assignability of contract rights facilitates the financing of businesses, and makes commerce efficient in other ways as well.

2. **Exceptions:** However, there are a few *exceptions* to this general rule of assignability. the Second Restatement (§ 317(2)) lists three kinds of situations in which the general policy favoring assignability is outweighed by considerations of fairness to the parties, or other specific factors:

   [1] **Damage to obligor's interests:** The substitution of the assignee for the assignor "would *materially change the duty of the obligor*, or materially *increase the burden or risk imposed on him* by his contract, or materially *impair his chances of obtaining return performance*, or materially *reduce its value* to him." (See Pars. 3-5 below.) (See also UCC § 2-210(2), containing similar language.)

   [2] **Forbidden by statute:** The assignment is *forbidden by statute* or is "otherwise against public policy." (See Par. 8 on p. 393.)

   [3] **Anti-assignment clause:** The assignment is precluded by a valid and enforceable *anti-assignment clause* in the contract. (See Par. G on p. 393.)

3. **Assignments that would materially alter the obligor's duty:**   Since an assignment requires the obligor to render his performance to the assignee rather than to the assignor, the obligor's duty is always changed somewhat by the assignment. But it is only where the obligor's duty would be changed *materially* that assignment will be disallowed by the court.

   a. **Personal service contracts:**   If the contract requires a party to perform *personal services* for a particular employer, the employer may assign his right to receive those services if (and only if) there is *no special relationship* of *trust* or *confidence* between the parties, or any other factor which would render an assignment a *materially greater burden* to the party performing the services.

      Example 1 (not assignable): Star, a movie star, hires Secretary for a below-market wage, which Secretary agrees to take because she wants to work closely with Star. Star cannot unilaterally assign the contract to Friend, thus requiring Secretary to work for Friend for the same wages, because the assignment would materially alter Secretary's duties. (It would also materially reduce the contract's value to Secretary, a factor that by itself will prevent assignability.)

      Example 2 (assignable): D is a newscaster-anchorman for D.C. Channel Nine, owned by Post-Newsweek. After he has worked for one year of a three-year contract, the station is sold to P, and D's contract is assigned to P. A year after the sale, D goes to work for a competing station. P sues for an injunction. D defends on the grounds that the assignment was void because D had had a close, "almost family" relationship with the Post-Newsweek executives, who no longer work for the station following the sale.

      Held, for P. The services required of D following the sale were substantially the same as prior to it (e.g., he anchored the same news programs, was given the same number of special assignments, etc.) Nor did the contract guarantee D that he would work under the supervision of particular employees; rather, the corporation's duty under the contract was essentially to compensate D. Therefore, the contract was assignable, and P is entitled to the injunction. *Evening News Ass'n v. Peterson*, 477 F. Supp. 77 (D.D.C. 1979).

Caveat: Keep in mind that in a personal services contract, the restrictions mentioned above apply only where it is the person who is to *receive* the personal services who tries to assign his rights. The person who is to render the services, in return for money, *may normally assign his right to payment* (unless prevented by an anti-wage-assignment statute).

b. **"Requirements" and "output" contracts:** Before the UCC was adopted, it was generally held that *"requirements"* and *"output"* contracts (explained *supra*, p. 115) could *not be assigned* since the assignee's needs, or his output, would be different from those of the assignor.

   i. **UCC may allow assignment:** But the UCC appears to permit assignments of requirements and output contracts, at least if the assignee's output or requirements are *not "unreasonably disproportionate"* to the assignor's estimated output or requirements. See § 2-306(1) (imposing a general rule of good faith and reasonable quantity in such contracts) and Comment 4 to § 2-210 (stating that the "unreasonably disproportionate" test removes the "personal discretion" element, thus making assignments possible).

4. **Assignments that would materially vary the risk:** Just as an assignment will not be allowed if it will materially change the obligor's duty, assignment will not be allowed if it will materially *vary the risk* assumed by the obligor. This is the case even though the risk is merely different, not necessarily increased. C&P, pp. 681-82. The most common example of an assignment which would run afoul of this rule is an *insurance policy*.

   Example: Driver takes out a collision insurance policy on his 2012 Mustang. He then sells the car to Buyer, and attempts to assign the collision policy to him. The assignment is ineffective, since it materially varies the risk assumed by the insurance company. Although the property still has approximately the same value, the premium was presumably pegged in part to the past driving record of Driver, and Buyer's driving record is not necessarily the same.

5. **Assignments that would materially impair the obligor's chance to obtain return performance:** Both the Second Restatement (§ 317(2)(a)), and the UCC (§ 2-210(2)), prohibit an assignment which would *"impair materially [the obligor's] chances of obtaining return performance."*

   a. **How impairment might happen:** Since an assignment is the transfer of the assignor's *rights*, not his duties, an assignment by itself (i.e., not accompanied by a delegation of the assignor's duties) will usually not impair the obligor's chance to get return performance. But such a situation can still arise, as in the following example.

   Example: Brenda, a famous fashion designer, contracts to have Manco custom-manufacture certain dresses that Brenda says she will sell under her own name for $2,000 apiece. Brenda has agreed to pay Manco $500 each for the dresses. Payment is due 60 days after delivery. The contract is silent about assignability. Manco has agreed to a relatively low price (given the work involved) because it wants to be able to advertise in the trade that it makes dresses for the famous and prestigious Brenda. Before Manco starts work, Brenda assigns her rights under the contract to Schlock, a mass-market designer of goods that are widely regarded as of low quality.

A court might well hold that this assignment is void, on the grounds that it would "increase materially the burden or risk imposed on [Manco] by his contract, or impair materially his chance of obtaining return performance" (the standard for non-assignability under UCC § 2-210(2)). That's because, even though Brenda remains liable for payment, a meaningful part of the "return performance" anticipated by Manco — being able to say that Brenda sells clothes he makes — has been taken from him.

6. **Assignment by seller of right to payment:**   On the other hand, there's one big area in which assignment is *automatically allowed*. That's the assignment by a seller of her *right to payment.* Remember that UCC § 2-210(2) says that assignment is not allowed where it would "materially change the duty of the other party, or increase materially the burden or risk imposed on him by his contract, or impair materially his chance of obtaining return performance." But the phrase leading in to this clause says that it applies "except as otherwise provided in Section 9-406." § 9-406 in turn says, in sub-section (d), that a seller or other person who is owed money is normally (i.e., with some exceptions not relevant here) *permitted to assign that right to payment* even if the contract between seller and buyer says that assignment is *prohibited*. And that's true even if, on the facts, the buyer has reasonable concerns that her chances of getting return performance will be impaired by the assignment.

   Example: Same basic fact pattern as the Brenda-Manco example above. Now, assume that: (1) the contract says that Manco may not assign its right to payment for the dresses to anyone, and that any such assignment will be void; (2) Brenda doesn't assign her right to the dresses, furnishes the specs for them herself, and plans to take delivery herself; (3) Manco is in debt, so in advance of making the dresses he assigns his future right to payment for them to Factor, a creditor. Even before Manco starts production, Brenda discovers that Manco has assigned payment. Brenda (reasonably) fears that Manco now won't have an incentive to do good and timely manufacturing, because he won't get any fresh money for completing the contract. Brenda would therefore like to declare Manco in breach of contract because of the assignment, cancel the contract, and give it to someone else. But § 9-406(d) prevents her from doing this. Brenda is what § 9-406(d) calls an "account debtor," and § 9-406(d) says that the assignment of the "account" (the right to receive payment from Brenda) by Manco to Factor is *effective* even though prohibited in the contract between the assignor (Manco) and the account debtor (Brenda).

   The purpose of § 9-406(d) is to permit sellers to make untrammelled use of the modern technique of "factoring" (the sale of receivables) and other financing techniques (e.g., creation of security interests in receivables).

   a. **Creation of security interest can't be prohibited:**   As you probably would expect, since § 9-406(d) prevents the parties from agreeing to prohibit the seller from assigning his right to payment, that section also prevents the parties from agreeing that the seller won't take the less-drastic step of creating a *security interest* in the receivable. (See *supra*, p. 387 for a definition of "security interest.") See § 2-210(3), which says that "The creation, attachment, perfection, or enforcement of a *security interest* in the seller's interest under a contract is *not a transfer that materially changes the duty of or increases materially the burden or risk* imposed on the buyer or impairs materially the buyer's chance of obtaining return performance within the purview of subsection (2)" (unless actual foreclosure of the security interest occurs, and even then the security interest will still be enforceable).

Example: So on the above example, if Manco, instead of "selling" the receivable to Factor, gave Factor a security interest in the receivable to ensure repayment, this security interest, too, would be enforceable under §§ 9-406(d) and 2-210(3), notwithstanding the attempt in the Brenda-Manco contract to prohibit it.

7. **Assignment coupled with delegation:** In many instances, an assignment of rights is coupled with a *delegation* of duties. When this occurs, the assignment will not be valid if the delegation is not also valid. (The validity of delegations is discussed *infra*, p. 407.)

    a. **UCC allows demand for assurances:** Where an assignment is coupled with a delegation, and the underlying contract is one for the sale of goods, the UCC permits the obligor to "treat any assignment which delegates performance as creating reasonable grounds for insecurity" and allows him to "demand assurances from the assignee." (§ 2-210(5)). The assignee must render such assurances, or be held to have repudiated the contract. (§ 2-609.) The obligor may make such a demand for assurances even where the delegation would itself be permissible.

8. **Assignments forbidden by statute and "public policy":** Statutes in many states forbid the assignment of certain kinds of contract rights. The most common example is statutes prohibiting the assignment of *wages*. "Public policy" is also interpreted in many states to prohibit many kinds of assignments; the assignment of the right to *alimony payments which have not yet become due*, and the assignment of *tort claims to lawyers* for purposes of litigating them, are examples. C&P, pp. 683-84.

G. **Contract terms prohibiting assignment:** Parties to a contract often stipulate in the document itself that rights under the contract may not be assigned. The stipulation may say something like "No rights under this contract may be assigned," or a clumsier formulation may be used, e.g., "This contract may not be assigned." Courts have become increasingly less willing to honor such non-assignment provisions. Here, we'll discuss how the Second Restatement and the UCC handle such anti-assignment clauses.

1. **Second Restatement view:** The Second Restatement starts with the general rule that *a clause in the contract prohibiting the assignment of rights under it will be effective*. Rest. 2d, § 322. It then carves out a series of exceptions to and rules of construction for such anti-assignment clauses. Here are some:

    a. **Where assignor has fully performed:** If the assignor has already *fully performed* all of his obligations under the contract, she may assign her rights under that contract despite an anti-assignment clause. This rule has its most frequent application where the assignor has earned the *right to payment* for work which she has already completed under the contract.

b. Violation gives right to damages for breach: An assignment made in violation of an applicable anti-assignment clause does ***not render the assignment ineffective***, but does give the obligor a right to ***damages*** against the assignor for breach of the clause. Thus ***the assignee may compel the obligor to perform***, but any losses the obligor suffers from the assignment he may recover from the assignor.

c. For benefit of obligor: An anti-assignment clause is *for the obligor's benefit*; if she wishes, she can ***waive*** the clause's benefit and render the performance to the assignee as if there were no anti-assignment clause. Furthermore, if the obligor refuses to render performance to the assignee, the assignee may ***sue the assignor as if there were no anti-assignment clause***. (The rights of an assignee against her assignor are discussed *infra*, p. 402.)

d. Prohibition on assignment of "the contract": If the anti-assignment clause states that *"the contract"* may not be assigned (as opposed to stating that "rights under the contract may not be assigned"), the clause will be interpreted to bar only the ***delegation*** of the assignor's duties, ***not the assignment of his rights.***

e. All these are rules of construction: All the above rules laid down by the Restatement are merely ***rules of construction***. That is, the parties are free to change any of these rules if they make their intention to do so perfectly clear. Thus the parties might explicitly agree that the anti-assignment clause forbids even the assignment of the right to damages for total breach, or that any assignment shall be void as against the obligor.

2. UCC view: Article 2 of the UCC treats anti-assignment clauses in contracts for the sale of goods in much the same way as the Restatement handles these matters. The parties are given freedom to prohibit assignment, with the following exceptions and qualifications:

a. Damages for breach: As does the Restatement, the UCC (§ 2-210(2)) permits a party who has a claim for total breach (i.e., ***material breach***) to assign his claim even if the contract prohibits such assignment.

b. Assignor has completely performed: Again like the Restatement, the UCC permits a buyer or seller who has ***already completely performed*** to assign his rights under the contract even if the contract purports to prohibit such assignment. (§ 2-210(2); § 9-318(4)).

c. Assignment of "the contract": Unless the parties otherwise agree, "a prohibition of assignment of 'the contract' is to be construed as barring only the ***delegation*** to the assignee of the assignor's performance." (§ 2-210(3)).

Note: The first two of the above rules are ***firm statutory commandments***, not rules of construction as they are under the Restatement. Thus no matter how clear a sales contract makes it that the buyer is not to have the right to assign a claim for total breach, or a claim for performance once she has rendered her own performance, she may make such an assignment. The rule construing language prohibiting assignment of "the contract," on the other hand, is a rule of construction, and applies only where the parties have not manifested a contrary understanding of the meaning of the clause.

3. **Article 9's prohibition of anti-assignment clauses:** Recall that Article 9 of the UCC applies to the assignment of rights under certain contracts. See *supra*, p. 387. When a particular assignment falls within Article 9's coverage, the above provisions of Article 2 do not apply, even if the original contract was for the sale of goods. Instead, Article 9 itself provides, in § 9-406(d), that any anti-assignment term in a contract covered by Article 9 is *ineffective*. For a discussion of how this works, see Par. 4 *supra*, p. 392, and the Brenda-Manco Example following it.

4. **Provision prohibiting assignment without consent:** So far, we have assumed that the contract completely prohibits assignment. Usually, however, the contract says merely that the contract may not be assigned *"without the consent"* of the other party. Such clauses are generally *not construed strictly*:

   a. **Consent not to be unreasonably withheld:** Many modern courts hold that such a clause should normally be interpreted as if it contained a further provision that the other party *will not withhold its consent unreasonably.* In other words, a "no assignment without consent clause" will be enforced if the assignor fails to seek the other party's approval, or if the other party reasonably objects to the assignment, but will *not* be enforced if the other party's refusal to consent is unreasonable or capricious. Farnsworth, p. 718.

   b. **Prohibited assignment yields damages but is effective:** Furthermore, many courts hold that a no-assignment-of-the-contract clause should be "read as imposing a *duty* on the assignor not to assign, but [*not* as] making an assignment *invalid*." Farnsworth p. 717. In other words, the non-assigning party may sue the assignor for damages for breach, but the assignment is nonetheless *effective* to transfer to the assignee the assignor's rights. See Rest. 2d, § 222: "[A] contract term prohibiting assignment of rights under the contract, unless a different intention is manifested ... (b) gives the obligor a right to damages for breach of the terms forbidding assignment *but does not render the assignment ineffective*."

      i. **Parties can say otherwise:** But the preference for an interpretation that imposes a duty not to assign, but that does not prevent the assignment from being effective, can be foreclosed by the parties' own *explicit language to the contrary.* That is, the parties are always free to say something like, "Any assignment made without the express written consent of the non-assigning party shall be *null and void*," and if they do say that, any purported assignment will be ineffective, not just a breach of a promise.

H. **Rights of the assignee against the obligor:** As a general rule, the assignee *"stands in the shoes of his assignor."* That is, with the exceptions noted below, the assignee takes *subject to all defenses, set-offs, and counterclaims which the obligor could have asserted against the assignor*.

   1. **Significance:** This is the single *most important rule to remember* about assignment.

      Example: Dealer, a used-car dealer, leases a used 2010 Corvette to Speedster. Shortly after the lease, Dealer assigns to Bank all of Dealer's interest in the lease contract, including of course the right to receive the lease payments from Speedster. The car turns out to have twice as many miles on it as Dealer represented it to have.

If Bank sues Speedster for payment, Speedster will be entitled to assert against Bank any defenses or claims that he could have asserted against Dealer. This includes a counterclaim for breach of express warranty (i.e., that the mileage stated on the odometer was accurate). As we will see below (see p. 399), this defense cannot yield an affirmative recovery for Speedster. But it will serve as a "set off," and, if it's large enough, completely wipe out any lease payments that would otherwise be owed by Speedster.

2. **Effect of obligor's giving performance to assignor:**   However, in one extremely important respect, the assignee's rights can be ***better*** than the rights of his assignor. Once the obligor has received ***notice*** of the assignment (from either the assignor or the assignee), ***he cannot thereafter pay*** (or otherwise give his performance to) the assignor, and use this defense against the assignee, whereas he could use the payment defense against the assignor. See Rest. 2d, § 336(2). But if the obligor pays the assignor or otherwise gives him the required performance ***before*** he has received notice of the assignment, he ***may*** use this as a defense against the assignee. Cf. *Herzog v. Irace*, 594 A.2d 1106 (Me. 1991).

a. **UCC provision:** This result has long been part of the common law. But it's also now embedded in the UCC, by means of a provision in Article 9, which applies even in cases ***not involving the sale of goods.*** UCC § 9-406(a) refers to the obligor (the person who owns the money) as being an "account debtor," and says that (subject to a few minor exceptions):

> "[A]n account debtor ... may discharge its obligation by paying the assignor ***until, but not after,*** the account debtor receives a ***notification*** [signed by] the ***assignor or the assignee,*** that the amount due or to become due has been assigned and that payment is to be made to the assignee. After receipt of the notification, the account debtor ***may*** discharge its obligation by paying the ***assignee*** and may ***not*** discharge the obligation by paying the ***assignor.***"

Example: Painter agrees to paint Owner's house for $10,000. The contract says that Painter can't assign his right to payment. Before doing the work, Painter assigns his right to payment to Bank, to which he owes money. On Feb. 1, Bank notifies Owner of the assignment, and that when the job is complete, Owner is to pay Bank, not Owner. Owner receives this letter, reads it, and then forgets about it. Painter completes the job according to the contract, and sends Owner a bill on March 1. Owner pays the $10,000 to Painter, who does not pass the money on to Bank. Bank sues Owner for the $10,000.

Bank will win. First, as we saw *supra*, p. 392, the contract language forbidding assignment is ineffective because of the special UCC provision nullifying clauses that forbid assignment of a right to payment. Second, once Owner (the account debtor) received a notification from either the assignor (Painter) or the assignee (Bank), Owner was ***no longer allowed*** to render payment to Painter. When he did so anyway, he was not entitled to claim that payment as a defense in the suit by Bank.

i. **Limitation:** Keep in mind that the giving of notice of the assignment cuts off only defenses based on the *obligor's* payment (or his rendering of any required non-payment performance) to the assignor. If the *assignor fails to perform his duties* under the contract, the obligor may still use this breach as a defense in a suit by the assignee, even if, as will usually be the case, he received notice of the assignment. See Rest. 2d, § 336.

3. **Modification of the contract by obligor and assignor:** Frequently the obligor and the assignor will attempt, after an assignment has been made, to *modify* the original contract. Their ability to do so, and by so doing to change the rights of the assignee, depends on whether the modification occurs *before* the *obligor has notice of the assignment,* and on whether the contract is still at least partly *executory* (not yet fully performed) on both sides at the time of assignment.

   a. **Modification made before notice of assignment:** *Before the obligor has received notice* of the assignment, he and the assignor are *completely free to modify the contract.* However, both the Second Restatement (§ 338(1)) and the UCC (§ 9-405(a)) allow such a modification to affect the assignee's rights only if it is *"made in good faith."* (The Restatement adds that the modification must be "in accordance with *reasonable commercial standards.*")

      Example: Owner signs a contract with Contractor under which Contractor will build an office building on Owner's property, for $1 million. Contractor assigns the right to payment which he will have under the contract to Bank, to obtain financing. Neither Bank nor Contractor notifies Owner at this time about the assignment. Contractor completes the work. Owner has some financial problems, and begs Contractor to lower the contract price to $900,000. Contractor does so, in return for Owner's promise to pay within 30 days. Only after this modification does Bank finally notify Owner of the assignment.

      Assuming that the modification was made "in good faith" and "in accordance with reasonable commercial standards" (which it appears to have been — for instance, Contractor doesn't seem to have been trying to injure Bank for his own gain), the modification will be binding on Bank. This is true even though the modification occurred after Contractor had fully performed. Therefore, Bank can only collect $900,000.

   b. **Modification after notice of assignment has been given:** If notice of assignment has *already been given* to the obligor, then he and the assignor may modify the contract *only if the assignor has not yet fully performed*. (Again, the modification must be "made in good faith"; UCC §§ 9-405(a), (b).) If the assignor *has already fully performed* (and notice of assignment has been given), *no modification may affect the assignee's rights without his approval.* Rest. 2d, § 338(2); UCC § 9-405(b).

      Example: Same basic facts as the previous example. Now, however, assume that Bank (acting sensibly, this time) gave Owner notice of the assignment as soon as the assignment occurred. Again, assume that Contractor finished the work, and Owner and Contractor then secretly agreed to a 10% price reduction.

      This time, the modification (the price reduction) is *not binding* on Bank, because: (i) it occurred after Contractor (the assignor) had fully performed; and (ii) it was made without Bank's consent. So Bank's prompt giving of notice of assignment made the difference.

4. Waiver of defenses by obligor: Many sale and lease contracts which contemplate the extension of credit to the buyer or lessee contain a *"waiver of defenses"* clause. This clause typically provides that the seller or lessor may assign the contract, and that the buyer/lessee *agrees not to assert any defenses* against the assignee.

   a. UCC view: The UCC generally *enforces* waiver-of-defense clauses. § 9-403(b) sets forth the general rule that:

   > "an *agreement* between an account debtor and an assignor *not to assert against an assignee any claim or defense* that the account debtor may have against the assignor is *enforceable by an assignee that takes an assignment:* (1) for value; *(2) in good faith;* [and] (4) *without notice of [the] defense or claim[.]"*

   However, § 9-403 also sets out two very important *exceptions* to this general rule:

   i. "Real" defenses: First, a waiver-of-defenses clause is *not effective* as to "defenses of a type that may be asserted against a holder in due course of a negotiable instrument[.]" § 9-403(c). Some of the more important defenses (called *"real"* defenses) that, under this definition, are never waived by the obligor (as opposed to the so-called "personal" defenses which can be waived) are:

   (1) Infancy, incapacity, or duress;

   (2) Illegality of the original contract;

   (3) The obligor's discharge in bankruptcy; and

   (4) *"Fraud* that induced the obligor to sign the [contract] with neither knowledge nor reasonable opportunity to learn of its *character or its essential terms."*

   See UCC § 3-305(a)(2) for a list of these "real" defenses.

   Note: The kind of "fraud" defense that is not waived is that usually called *"fraud in the essence."* The common illustration of this is where a person is tricked into signing a piece of paper in the belief that it is merely a receipt or some other document, not a contract. If, on the other hand, the signer knows that he is signing a contract, but has been induced to sign it because of the other party's misrepresentations about the product's quality, the misrepresentation is said to be "fraud in the inducement" and is *not* covered by the language quoted above. Such a misrepresentation defense *is waived* by a valid "waiver-of-defenses" clause.

   ii. Statutes or decisions involving consumer goods: Secondly, the rule allowing such a waiver of defenses by a buyer or lessee is expressly made "subject to law other than this article which establishes a different rule for an account debtor who is an *individual* and who incurred the obligation primarily for *personal, family, or household purposes."* § 9-403(e). Many states have retail installment statutes which make such "waiver-of-defenses" clauses *unenforceable.* Even more important, a *Federal Trade Commission Rule* prohibits *any retail installment or credit contract from containing a waiver-of-defenses clause.* See 16 C.F.R. 433.2.

Example: Auto Dealer sells a car to Consumer on credit. Dealer then assigns the contract to Bank. The automobile turns out to be a lemon that breaches the implied warranty of merchantability. As a matter of federal law, Consumer must be permitted to assert against Bank any defenses Consumer could raise against Dealer. This means that Consumer may withhold payments from Bank in an amount equal to the damages suffered by Consumer from the breach of the merchantability warranty.

iii. **Commercial context:** In a *commercial* context, waiver-of-defenses clauses are almost always *enforceable* under the UCC. See the language of § 9-403(b), quoted *supra*, p. 398. Thus if a business person buys, say, equipment under a contract in which the seller grants him credit, and the seller then assigns the contract to a bank or finance company, the buyer *will not be able to withhold payments even if the equipment is in breach of warranty.* See, e.g., *Chemical Bank v. Rinden Professional Association*, 498 A.2d 706 (N.H. 1985).

5. **Counterclaims, set-offs and recoupment by the obligor:** Suppose the obligor has a claim that is valid against the assignor. May he *assert this claim* in a suit by the assignee, in order to diminish the assignee's recovery? In non-UCC cases, state statutes vary. Many states have adopted for non-UCC cases the same rules as those furnished by the UCC, which are as follows:

a. **Where obligor's claim relates to assigned contract:** If the obligor's claim against the assignor is *related to the same contract* that has been assigned to the assignee, the obligor may use this claim *whether it arose prior to or subsequent to the obligor's receipt of notice of the assignment.* § 9-404(a)(1). The obligor's claim in this situation, traditionally called a *"recoupment,"* may only be used to *diminish* the assignee's claim, and *may not yield an affirmative recovery* for the obligor.

Example: Assembler, which is in the business of assembling electronics for customers, agrees to take memory chips and circuit boards owned by Computer Corp. and insert the chips into the boards. The contract calls for assembly of 10,000 boards at $10 apiece. Computer Corp. supplies enough chips to assemble 15,000 boards, in case some of the chips are bad. After the contract is signed, Assembler assigns all of its contract rights (including the right to be paid by Computer Corp.) to Bank, in return for financing. Assembler does the work properly, delivers the completed boards to Computer Corp. and bills Computer Corp. the contracted-for $100,000. However, Assembler does not return the 5,000 extra chips, and instead sells them to a third party. Bank, as assignee of Assembler, demands payment of $100,000, and sues when Computer Corp. does not pay. Assume that the value of the missing chips is $60,000. Is Computer Corp. entitled to set off the $60,000 against the $100,000 owed to Bank, so that any recovery by Bank will be limited to $40,000?

The answer is "yes." UCC § 9-404(a)(1) incorporates the common-law rule that an assignee of contract rights (Bank) "stands in the shoes of the assignor," and has no greater rights against the obligor (Computer Corp.) than the assignor (Assembler) had. Since Computer Corp. (obligor) would have been able to assert the missing-chip claim against Assembler (assignor), it may assert that claim as a recoupment against Bank (assignee). This right is dependent upon the fact that Computer Corp.'s claim arises out of the *same contract* as the contract right which Assembler has assigned to Bank. (For how such a case would come out if the claims related to different contracts, see the discussion in Par. (b) below.)

Note: Keep in mind that the obligor's claim may only be used as a *"recoupment,"* (i.e., a defense), not as a true counterclaim. That is, the obligor's claim *may not yield an affirmative recovery* (see Par. (c) below). Therefore, if the value of the missing chips was $150,000, Computer Corp. could reduce Bank's recovery to $0, but could not obtain an affirmative judgment against Bank for the remaining $50,000 — instead, it would have to sue Assembler for that $50,000.

b. **Obligor's claim unrelated to assigned contract:** If the obligor's claim against the assignor *does not arise out of the contract* which has been assigned, the obligor may assert this claim against the assignee *only if the claim accrued before the obligor received notice of the assignment.* Such a claim is traditionally called a *"set-off,"* and, like the recoupment, *may not yield an affirmative recovery.* § 9-404(a)(2).

Example: Builder makes a contract with Owner (call it "Contract 1") in July, 2010 to renovate Owner's kitchen for $100,000. In August, 2010, Builder and Owner make a separate agreement (call it "Contract 2") for Builder to add a bedroom to Owner's house. In November, 2010, Builder assigns its right to receive payment under Contract 1 to Bank in return for a loan, and that same month notifies Owner of the assignment. In December, 2010, Builder properly completes performance of Contract 1. In January, 2011, Builder breaches Contract 2 by doing the bedroom work in a non-conforming way. In June, 2011, at a time when Owner has never paid Bank (or anyone) anything on Contract 1, Bank sues Owner for the $100,000 due under that contract. The issue is, can Owner raise against Bank the defense that Builder breached Contract 2?

The answer is "no," because Owner's claim under Contract 2 did not accrue until January, 2011, which was *after* the November 2010 date on which Owner received notice of the assignment of Builder's Contract 1 rights to Bank. (If Owner's Contract 2 claim had accrued *prior* to Owner's notice of the Contract 1 assignment, then Owner would have a "set off" against Bank based on Owner's Contract 2 claim, but that claim could only reduce the amount Owner owed to Bank, not yield an affirmative recovery.)

c. **Counterclaims:** The obligor may generally assert a *counterclaim* (i.e., a claim which can yield an *affirmative* recovery) against the assignee only if the claim relates to a *transaction directly between the obligor and the assignee*, not a transaction between the obligor and the assignor.

i. **Affirmative recovery where consumer has been totally defrauded:** However, there is a significant though narrow exception to the principle that the obligor may not obtain an affirmative recovery against the assignee if the claim relates to a transaction between the obligor and the assignor: if the obligor/buyer is a *consumer*, and the assignor/seller has so totally breached that the obligor/buyer would be entitled to *rescind* and get restitution of any payments had payments been made to the assignor/seller rather than to the assignee, most courts seem to agree that the buyer may recover from the assignee payments already made by the obligor/buyer.

Example: Suppose Consumer contracts to buy a car from Dealer, and signs a financing agreement which Dealer assigns to Bank. Consumer writes out a check to Bank for the first two months' payments, then never receives the delivery of the car. Probably Consumer can sue Bank for return of the two months' payments, since Dealer has so totally breached as to justify Consumer in rescinding the contract. The same result might be true if the car was such a total lemon that, under state law, Consumer would be able to rescind.

I. Rights of successive assignees of the same claim: A party who has rights under a contract may try to *assign* those rights to *two different persons.* Deciding which one of the asssignees owns the rights can be complex.

1. 1st assignment was revocable: If the first assignment was *revocable* at the time of the second assignment (which could only be the case if the first assignment was *gratuitous* — see *supra*, p. 388), the *second assignee has priority*, according to virtually all jurisdictions.

2. 1st assignment was irrevocable; 2d knew about first or didn't give value: Now, suppose the first assignment was *irrevocable* when made (e.g., because the assignee gave consideration for it), and the second assignee either *knew* about the first assignment or didn't give value. Here, the *first assignee takes priority*, again according to virtually all jurisdictions.

3. Both gave value; 2d did not know of 1st: The most common situation, however, is that in which *both assignees gave value*, and the subsequent one did not know about the first. Here, most courts follow the Second Restatement's approach.

    a. Restatement "four horsemen" rule: The Second Restatement (§ 342(b)) gives a *subsequent assignee* who receives his assignment in *good faith*, without knowledge or reason to know of the earlier assignment, and who has *given value* for it, *priority* over an earlier assignee for value, in four situations. For this reason, the Restatement rule is often called the *"four horsemen"* rule. The subsequent assignee must have done one of the following *four things* in order to take priority over the first:

        [1] He must have *received payment* or other satisfaction of the obligation; or

        [2] He must have *obtained a judgment* against the obligor; or

        [3] He must have *obtained a new contract* from the obligor by novation (defined *infra*, p. 408); or

        [4] He must *possess* *"a writing* of a type customarily accepted as a *symbol or as evidence of the right assigned"* (e.g., a bank book or insurance policy).

    If the second assignee does not do any of these four things, the first assignee takes priority.

    b. UCC rules: As we have frequently pointed out, *Article 9* of the UCC treats certain assignments as being *"security interests"* (see *supra*, p. 387). Where an assignment is treated as such a security interest, the Code allows the assignee to make a ***public filing*** of his interest. This filing system is used to resolve priorities between assignees of the same claim; the assignee who ***files first*** normally has priority, regardless of whether he received his assignment first, or gave notice of assignment to the obligor first.[1] § 9-322(a).

> **Example:** Contractor will soon be owed money by Owner from a large construction project that Contractor is working on. Contractor assigns his interest in the contract (i.e., his right to receive payment) to Bro, Contractor's brother, in return for a tide-me-over loan. Bro does not file a security interest, even though he could. Two months later, Contractor assigns the same contract rights to Bank in return for another loan. Bank files an Article 9 security interest in the appropriate public records. One day later, Bro files.
>
> Bank will win, because with respect to assignments that are for the purpose of financing (i.e., security interests), first-to-file normally wins under UCC Article 9, regardless of other factors.

J. Rights of assignee against assignor: An assignee may find himself frustrated in his attempt to realize on the rights that have been assigned to him. It may turn out that the obligor is unable to perform, or it may turn out that the assignment was of a right which is not assignable, or the assignor may subsequently assign the same right to someone else, in circumstances which give the subsequent assignee priority (*supra*, p. 401). In some, but not all, of these situations, the assignee will be able to recover damages against the ***assignor***.

1. Gratuitous assignments: If the assignment was a *gratuitous* one, the assignee will find it difficult to recover against his assignor.

    a. Later voluntary acts of interference by assignor: If the assignor intentionally ***interferes*** with the assignee's ability to realize the right (as where the assignor himself ***collects*** from the obligor money the right to which was assigned), the assignee may be able to recover damages if he can show that he ***relied to his detriment*** on the assignment. See Rest. 2d, § 332(4). Similarly, if the assignor made a ***subsequent assignment*** in circumstances that gave the later assignee superior rights, the first assignee might also recover damages based on detrimental reliance. In either case, the claim would probably be based on a ***promissory estoppel*** theory.

    b. No implied warranties: But the maker of a gratuitous assignment does ***not*** make the ***implied warranties*** that an assignor for value makes (e.g., that the claim is valid and unencumbered, as discussed below). Rest. 2d, § 333(1). So if the assigned claim simply turns out to be invalid, the assignee is out of luck, at least where the assignor did not know or have reason to know of the invalidity.

---

1. We say "normally," because there are some kinds of assignments that are covered by Article 9 but do not have to be filed. In particular, an assignment of an "account" (the right to payment under a contract) does not have to be filed if it "does not by itself or in conjunction with other assignments to the same assignee transfer a significant part of the assignor's outstanding accounts[.]" § 9-309(2). Where both the first and second assignments fall within this exception to the filing requirement, the first assignee wins.

2. **Assignments made for value:** If the assignment was made for value, the assignor will be held to have made a series of *implied warranties* to the assignee. If these warranties turn out not to be accurate, the assignee may sue the assignor for damages for breach of warranty.

    a. **List of warranties:** The warranties which the assignor is held to make are:

        [1] **No impairment:** That the *assignor* will do nothing which will *interfere* with the enforcement of the obligation by the assignee.

        Example: Assignor implicitly promises that he will *not assign the claim to someone else* and that he will *not attempt to collect the obligation himself* from the obligor.

        [2] **Claim is valid and unencumbered:** That the assigned claim is a *valid* one, and that it is not subject to any *limitations or defenses* other than those that have been disclosed to the assignee at the time of assignment.

        Example: As security for a bank loan from Bank, Contractor assigns to Bank the right to receive payment of $10,000 under a completed construction contract with Owner. Contractor impliedly warrants that he knows of no defenses that Owner can plausibly raise that would be good against Bank. But in fact, Contractor knows that Owner is claiming that the work was not done properly, and demanding a $3,000 discount from the $10,000 contract price. By not disclosing this claim to Bank at the time of assignment, Contractor is breaching his implied warranty that the claim is valid and unencumbered.

        [3] **Documents are genuine:** That any *documents* which are delivered to the assignee that purport to evidence the right are *genuine*.

        Rest. 2d, § 333(1).

    b. **No warranty of obligor's solvency or willingness to perform:** But the assignor does *not*, however, warrant that the obligor is *solvent*, or that he will be *willing or able to perform*. Rest. 2d, § 333(2). Therefore, if the obligor turns out to be unwilling or unable to perform, the assignee has *no recourse* against the assignor.

        Example: Same basic facts as above example. This time, however, assume that Owner has no complaint about the quality of the work. However, Owner goes broke, and doesn't pay Bank the $10,000. Contractor, by assigning to Bank the right to be paid $10,000, is not deemed to warrant that Owner will actually pay the $10,000. Therefore, Bank has no claim against Contractor when Owner doesn't pay.

        i. **Free to agree otherwise:** The assignor may, however, explicitly *agree* to guarantee the obligor's performance, in which case the assignee *can* sue her if the obligor fails to perform.

3. **Sub-assignees not covered:** Unless the assignor indicates otherwise, his warranties do *not* extend to any *sub-assignee*, i.e., one who receives the assignment from the assignee. The assignee does, however, make implied warranties to his own sub-assignee along the same lines, and the sub-assignee may sue him for breach of these warranties. Rest. 2d, § 333(4).

Figure 11-1

Analyzing Assignments

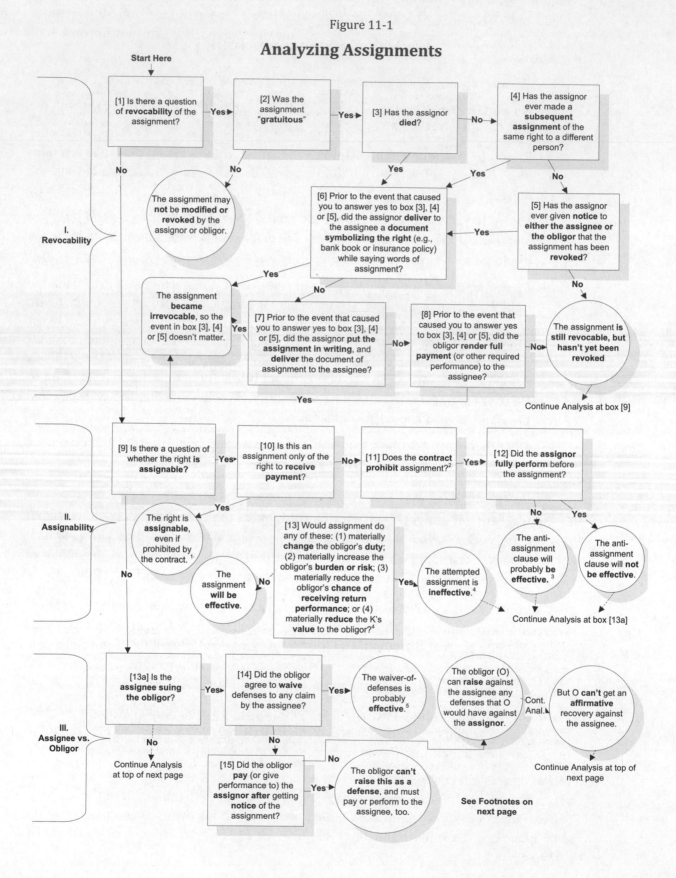

Figure 11-1

Analyzing Assignments (cont.)

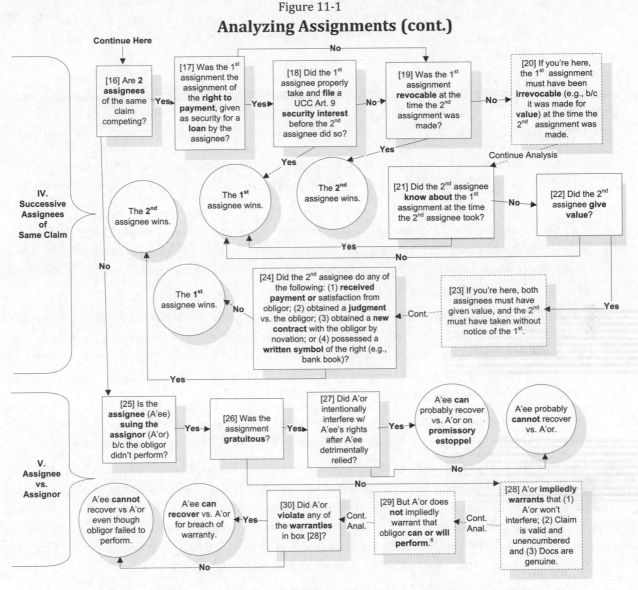

Notes

1. UCC §9-406(d) makes any contractual prohibition on the assignment of an "account" (the right to be paid) ineffective. See E II(F)(4).

2. If the anti-assignment clause says merely that "the contract" may not be assigned, this will normally be interpreted as barring only delegation, not assignment. See E II(G)(1)(d) and (2)(c).

3. But remember that if all that was assigned was the assignor's right to payment, the anti-assignment clause won't be effective.

4. Example: A agrees to paint B's house for $1K. B purports to assign to C this right to receive painting, so that A will have to paint C's house (which is

bigger). Since A's duty would be materially changed, the assignment is ineffective, and C can't sue A for refusing to paint C's house.

5. But a waiver-of-defenses is, by federal law, not valid in a consumer credit or installment agreement. See E II(H)(4)(a)(2).

6. Example: Paint contracts to paint O's house for $10K. Paint assigns the payment right to Cred for a $8K payment. The assignment is silent about what happens if O doesn't pay. If Paint does the work and O doesn't pay Cred, Cred can't recover against Paint.

4. **Rules of construction, not fixed principles:**   All of the above rules on warranties are generally common law, rather than statutory. The Second Restatement, § 333, treats them as rules of construction which may be varied by showing a "contrary intention." The UCC does not treat the issue of assignor's warranties, and therefore leaves this area to the common-law rules.

Quiz Yourself on
ASSIGNMENT

108. Noah Webster sells the movie rights for his dictionary to Sammy Goldfish for $2,000. Webster assigns his right to payment under the contract to his nephew, Spyder, without receiving any compensation from Spyder.

(A) After assigning his payment rights to Spyder, Webster assigns those rights to Webb Foote, a friend, before Spyder has collected anything. Webb Foote knows nothing of the prior assignment to Spyder. Webb Foote does not given any consideration to Webster for the assignment. As between Spyder and Webb, who has superior right to the $2,000?

(B) Same basic facts. Now, however, assume that Webster made the original assignment to Spyder in return for a cash advance of $1,000. He makes a subsequent assignment of the same right (fraudulently) to Webb Foote, in return for another advance, of $500. Webb did not know of the prior assignment to Spyder. Webster is not owed money by anyone else. The $2,000 has not been paid by Goldfish. As between Spyder and Webb, who has priority?

(C) Same facts as part (B). Now, however, assume that at the time of the second assignment (Webster to Webb), Webb knew of the prior assignment to Spyder. Who has priority, Spyder or Webb?

109. Euphrates Faceless claims to have Napoleon's diary in his possession. He sells it to the Liberté Publishing Company in return for royalties, on Euphrates' promise that the diary is genuine. The publishing contract calls for Liberté to make an advance of $50,000 against royalties one month after signing. Euphrates assigns this right to an advance to his nephew, Irving. Euphrates does this as a gift. Before Liberté pays the advance, the company learns that the diary is forged — for one thing, it's written in felt-tip pen — and Euphrates admits to the forgery. Liberté refuses to honor the contract.

(A) Does Irving have a valid contract claim against Liberté?

(B) Does Irving have a valid contract claim against Euphrates?

110. Alcazaba hires Granada to build a house on his estate, Alhambra. Alcazaba agrees to pay $100,000, of which Alcazaba advances Granada $15,000. Granada subsequently assigns its right to payment of the $100,000 under the contract to Moor, and Moor notifies Alcazaba of this assignment. Alcazaba thereafter pays the remaining $85,000 to Granada rather than to Moor. May Moor recover $85,000 from Alcazaba?

Answers

108. (A) Webb Foote. The assignment to Spyder was gratuitous (not made for consideration). A gratuitous assignment is automatically revoked by, inter alia, the assignor's subsequent assignment of the same right to someone else (even if the second assignment is also gratuitous). That second assignment therefore left Webb Foote with the only remaining rights to the assigned money.

(B) Insufficient facts, because we don't know who filed first under Article 9. This is something of a trick question. Where both assignees of the same claim took for value, and the assignment was a financing device, Article 9 normally governs. Therefore, whichever party first files an Article 9 security interest in the public records will win, and the facts don't tell us who did this first. (Normally, before a litigated controversy between the two, at least one would have filed.)

(C) Spyder. Where the first assignee gives value, and the second one knows of the prior assignment, the first assignee has priority. Many courts base this result on an estoppel theory: the second assignee is "estopped" from taking ahead of the first one, because his own knowledge of the prior right would make it unfair for him to have priority.

109. (A) No. The assignee stands in the shoes of his assignor. This means that Irving takes subject to all the defenses, set-offs, and counterclaims which Liberté could have asserted against Euphrates. Here, Euphrates guaranteed that the diary was genuine and then later admitted it was forged. Euphrates' breach of the contract nullifies Liberté's obligation to pay.

(B) Probably not, because the assignment was gratuitous. The maker of a gratuitous assignment does not make an implied warranty of the assigned claim's validity, as the maker of an assignment-for-value does. Therefore, the mere fact that the claim turns out to be invalid won't be enough to allow Irving to recover against Euphrates. However, if Irving can prove that he relied to his detriment on the assignment (e.g., that he charged an expensive vacation in reliance on it), it is conceivable that Irving may be able to recover under a kind of promissory estoppel theory against Euphrates; that is, Irving would claim that the assignment was an implicit promise by Euphrates that Irving would in fact collect the money, and that Irving's reliance was foreseeable and reasonable.

110. Yes. Once an obligor receives notice of an assignment, he pays the assignor at his own risk, since he (the obligor) won't be able to use this payment as a defense in a suit by the assignee. So Alcazaba was very stupid to ignore the notice of assignment and pay Granada, the assignor. (But any payments that Alcazaba made to Granada *before* Alcazaba received notice of the assignment are a defense vis à vis Moor, even if payment occurred after the assignment.)

III. DELEGATION OF DUTIES

A. Delegation generally: Recall that "delegation" refers to *duties* under a contract, not to rights. Thus if a party to a contract wishes to have another person perform his duties under that contract, he delegates them.

B. Continued liability of delegator: When a right is assigned, the assignor's interest in that right is normally extinguished. But when the performance of a duty is delegated, *the delegator remains liable.* Rest. 2d, § 318(3).

> **Example:** Owner contracts with Contractor for Contractor to paint Owner's house for $10,000. Contractor delegates his duties to Painter. If Painter fails to perform in the manner required by the original Owner-Contractor contract, Owner may sue Contractor for breach, just as if Contractor had improperly performed the work herself.

> **1. Rationale:** As Calamari & Perillo explain the reason for this rule, "[i]f this were not so, every solvent person could obtain freedom from his debts by delegating them to an insolvent." C&P, p. 698.

2. Novation: Of course, the obligee may explicitly agree to accept the delegate's performance in *substitution* for that of the delegator. If he does so, he has given what is called a "*novation*." The novation *does* release the delegator from all liability. In order for there to be a novation, the obligee must expressly agree to *accept the delegate's performance* in lieu of that of the delegator, and to *release* the delegator; the obligee's mere consent to the delegation is not enough.

C. Non-delegable duties: There are certain kinds of duties which are *not delegable*, just as certain kinds of rights are not assignable. In general, a duty or performance is delegable unless the obligee has a *substantial interest in having the delegator perform*. See Rest. 2d, § 318(2).

1. UCC: This principle is codified in UCC § 2-210(1): "A party may perform his duty through a delegate unless otherwise agreed or unless the other party has a *substantial interest in having his original promisor perform or control the acts required by the contract.*" Courts apply this same basic rule in non-UCC cases, too.

2. Contracts involving particular skills: Contracts which call for the promisor's use of his *own particular skills* are normally *not delegable,* on the theory that the other party has a substantial interest in having the promisor perform. Thus contracts involving *artistic performances*, and contracts involving the *professional services* of a lawyer or doctor, etc., are not delegable. (See Rest. 2d, § 318, Illustr. 6.)

> **Example:** Client is charged with murder. He signs an engagement letter (a contract) with Lawyer, a solo practitioner who specializes in white-collar criminal defense work, under which Lawyer will represent him at the trial for a fixed fee of $30,000. The contract says nothing about assignment or delegation. One month before trial, Lawyer sends Client an e-mail, "I have decided that you would be better represented by Barrister, my good friend, who is eager to represent you, and I hereby delegate him to do so." Barrister is in fact much more suited than Lawyer to represent Client, because Barrister specializes in murder cases whereas Lawyer has never done one before (as Client knew when he hired Lawyer).
>
> Client need not accept performance from Barrister — the contract calls for personal professional services, and Lawyer's duties under it were therefore not delegable without Client's consent. If Lawyer insists on making the delegation, Client can refuse and hire someone else (and sue Lawyer for breach). Alternatively, Client can accept the proposed delegation, in which case Lawyer will remain liable if Barrister fails to deliver a defense of the quality called for in the contract.

a. Duties of personal supervision: Similarly, contracts in which there are *duties of personal supervision* may not be delegated. Thus an employer may not delegate his duty to supervise his employee, where the employer-employee contract contemplates close personal supervision. C&P, p. 700.

b. Delegation by corporations: In many situations, a corporation will be allowed to delegate its duties to another corporation. But if the original contract was premised on the assumption that *particular employees* of the promisor corporation would perform the work, delegation to another corporation with other employees would not be permitted.

> **i. Hiring of agent:** But even if the contract contemplates that a corporation who is a party to it will not delegate the work, the corporation may be allowed to engage another corporation as **_its agent_**, provided that some supervision is maintained. Alternatively, a promisor corporation might avoid the difficulties of delegating personal services by agreeing to let its employees help the delegate perform.

3. **Delegate is a competitor of the obligee:** Another situation in which the delegation may be found to be invalid because it conflicts with the obligee's substantial interests is where the proposed delegate is a **_competitor of the obligee_**. For instance, suppose that *A* is the exclusive distributor of *B*'s products, and that *A* agrees to use best efforts to distribute the products as widely as possible. If *A* then proposes to delegate its distribution duties to *C*, a direct competitor of *B*, a court might well hold that *B* has a substantial interest in not having its products distributed by its competitor, and that *B* can therefore block the delegation.

> **Example:** Nexxus enters into a contract with Best under which Best becomes the exclusive distributor of Nexxus' hair care products for the state of Texas. Best implicitly (by operation of the UCC's provisions on exclusive distributorships) agrees to use its "best efforts" to distribute the Nexxus products as widely as possible in Texas. Best is later acquired by and merged into Sally Beauty, a wholly-owned subsidiary of one of Nexxus' biggest competitors, Alberto-Culver. Nexxus, upset at having its exclusive distributorship in effect fall into the hands of a competitor, refuses to continue the distributorship, on the grounds that the merger was an impermissible delegation. Sally sues Nexxus for breach.
>
> *Held*, for Nexxus. "[T]he duty of performance under an exclusive distributorship may not be delegated to a competitor in the market place — or the wholly-owned subsidiary of a competitor — without the obligee's consent." Nexxus was entitled to Best's "best efforts," and it was reasonable for Nexxus to think that having those efforts rendered by Nexxus' direct competitor was "a different thing than what it had bargained for." Therefore, the delegation ran afoul of UCC § 2-210(1), under which an unconsented-to delegation is not allowed if the other party has "a substantial interest in having his original promisor perform or control the acts required by the contract."
>
> (A dissenter, Judge Posner, criticized the majority's holding. He argued that Sally [and its parent, Alberto Culver] would have no incentive to lessen its efforts on behalf on Nexxus' products, because the likely damage to Sally's value as a distributorship would outweigh any possible advantage from increased sales of Alberto Culver products. Therefore, the possibility of damage to Nexxus, he said, was too speculative to render the delegation an impermissible interference with Nexxus' interests.) *Sally Beauty Co., Inc. v. Nexxus Products Co.*, 801 F.2d 1001 (7th Cir. 1986).

> **Note:** Judge Posner's dissent in *Sally Beauty* is a good example of the approach of the law-and-economics school's (*supra*, p. 2) approach to Contracts. Law-and-economics proponents often analyze the parties' own economic interests to see how they are likely to behave — that's what Judge Posner did here, leading him to conclude that the assignee (Alberto Culver), even though it was a competitor of the plaintiff, probably wouldn't have induced its subsidiary (Sally) to slack off in distributing P's products.

4. **Preference of other party:**   If the performance does *not* require a large degree of taste, discretion, or other particularized skill, it *will be* delegable even though the other party has a *personal preference* for performance by the named party to the contract.

5. **Delegation of duty of payment:** Since the delegator remains liable after delegation, she may normally delegate the *duty of payment,* even if the delegate's credit is not as sound as the delegator's. But if the original contract requires the promisor to execute a promissory note, the promisee will not be required to accept the delegate's promissory note, since such a note would not have the same market value. C&P, p. 761.

6. **Construction and repair contracts:**   *Construction contracts*, and contracts for the *repair* of buildings or machinery, *are* normally delegable.

   a. **Different intent by parties:**   But the rule allowing delegation of such repair or construction contracts is always subject to the understanding of the parties; if the original contract is based on the assumption that the promisor himself will do the constructing or repairing, delegation will not be allowed.

7. **Agreement of the parties as to delegability:**   The parties have almost completely unfettered freedom to decide whether duties under the contract may be delegated. They may agree that *duties which would otherwise be delegable may not be delegated*, or they may conversely agree to *allow* delegation of duties that would normally be thought to be too personal for delegation. This freedom of contract with respect to delegation should be contrasted with the rules on assignment, in which the parties are given less opportunity to make their own rules (*supra*, p. 393).

   a. **UCC rule of construction:**   As a rule of *construction*, the UCC provides that "Unless the circumstances indicate the contrary a prohibition of *assignment of 'the contract'* is to be construed as barring only the *delegation* to the assignee of the assignor's performance." § 2-210(3). Rest. 2d, § 322(1) is in accord.

D. **The delegate's liability:**   A delegation agreement between delegator and delegate may be in one of two forms:

   [1] the delegator may simply give the delegate the *option* to perform, with the delegate making no promise that he will do so;

   [2] the delegate may *promise* that he will perform.

In situation [1], the delegate will not have any liability either to the delegator or the obligee if he does not perform. But in situation [2], not only will the delegate be liable to the delegator, he may also be *liable to the obligee*, who may be a *third party beneficiary* of the delegate's promise. Rest. 2d, § 318, Comment b. (For a discussion of third party beneficiaries, see *infra*, p. 415.)

1. **Promise made solely for delegator's benefit:**   Sometimes in situation [2], the delegate's language or the surrounding facts will indicate that the delegate intended his promise to be *only* for the delegator's, and not the obligee's, benefit. If this is the case, the obligee will not be able to sue the delegate for non-performance. For instance, if the delegate is an *employee* of the delegator, or his *sub-contractor*, courts will normally hold that the delegate's liability runs only to the delegator, and the obligee is nothing more than an "incidental beneficiary of the delegation." C&P, p. 699.

2. **"Assumption":** If a delegate is held to have undertaken liability to the obligee as well as to the delegator, she is said to have **assumed** the delegator's liability.

3. **General "assignment" of the "contract":** A party to a contract sometimes makes an agreement with a third person under which he purports to **"assign the contract,"** or uses other such broad general language. By signing such a document, is the assignee held to have promised to perform, thus making him liable to the obligee? Normally, the answer is **yes**.

That's the approach of the Restatement. Rest. 2d, § 328(1), starts by saying that an assignment of "the contract" or of "all my rights under the contract," or any other similarly general assignment, operates as "an **assignment** of the assignor's rights <u>and</u> a **delegation** of his unperformed duties under the contract."

§ 328(2) then says that unless the circumstances indicate otherwise, "The acceptance by an assignee of such an assignment operates as a **promise** to the assignor to perform the assignor's unperformed duties, and the obligor of the assigned rights is an **intended beneficiary** of the promise."

a. **Obligee can sue both:** In other words, the assignee/delegate under such a general assignment clause will normally be held **liable to both parties** to the original contract if she fails to perform.

Example: Owner contracts with Contractor for Contractor to paint Owner's house for $10,000. Contractor then signs a document saying he "assigns to Painter my contract to paint Owner's house." Painter accepts the assignment. Under the standard (and Restatement) view, there are three consequences:

(1) Contractor is deemed to have **delegated** his duties to Painter (not just assigned his rights, such as the right to payment);

(2) Painter, by accepting the assignment, is deemed to have **promised** Contractor that Painter will perform the duties owed by Contractor; and

(3) Owner is an **intended beneficiary** of this promise by Painter to Contractor, so if Painter doesn't perform, Owner can sue Painter (as well as Contractor).

Note: Never forget that when a delegation occurs, **the delegator remains liable to the obligee,** unless the obligee **expressly agrees to a novation**, i.e., to release the delegator from its contractual obligation in return for having the delegate on the hook. So in the common fact pattern in which the obligor/assignor merely assigns "the contract" to the delegate, even if the obligee consents to the assignment/delegation the obligor remains liable unless the obligee expressly agrees to look only to the delegate for performance and liability. Thus in the above example, where Owner didn't agree to a novation, if Painter doesn't perform, Owner can sue Contractor as well as Painter.

b. **Sales of land:** However, if such a general assignment of "the contract" is made by one who has purchased **land** on which he still owes money, or by the holder of a contract to purchase land, the courts frequently hold that the assignee does **not** incur liability to the seller of the land. There is no good reason why the rule in land sale contracts should be different from that in other kinds of contracts, except that the land rule may have grown out of the principle that one who purchases land subject to a mortgage is not liable on the mortgage unless he expressly assumes it.

c. UCC view: In contracts for the sale of *goods*, the UCC applies a rule very similar to the general Restatement rule quoted above. § 2-210(4) states that "An assignment of 'the contract' or of 'all my rights under the contract' or an assignment in similar general terms is an assignment of rights and unless the language or circumstances (as in an assignment for security) indicate the contrary, it is a *delegation of performance* of the duties of the assignor and its acceptance by the assignee constitutes a *promise by him* to perform those duties. This promise is enforceable by either the assignor or the other party to the original contract."

    i. Assignment for security: The reference in the quoted UCC language to an *"assignment for security"* refers to the fact that where a general assignment is made for purpose of *giving collateral*, the lender will *not* normally be deemed to have undertaken to perform the assignor's duties. Thus if a seller who has signed a contract under which he is to deliver goods for a price assigns his contract rights to a bank to secure a loan, the bank will not be presumed to have undertaken to deliver the goods.

d. Sale of business: This problem of whether an assignment of "the contract" includes a delegation of duties as well as assignment also arises in the context of the *sale of a business*. Seller typically not only sells the company's assets to Buyer, but also usually assigns any contracts to which Seller is a party.

    i. Assignment of contracts: If the sale contract provides that Seller "assigns to Buyer all contracts to which Seller is a party," usually Buyer will be found to have *assumed the obligation to perform* under those contracts as well, if the sale of the contract does not explicitly deal with this issue. See Rest.2d, § 328(2), discussed further *supra*, p. 411.

    ii. "Continuation of business" theory: Even if the buyer of the business does not expressly undertake the liabilities, other rules of law (independent of assignment/delegation theory) may make the buyer liable on those obligations. For instance, if the transfer of assets from the selling corporation to the buying corporation is designed to *defraud* the seller's creditors, or if the selling and buying corporations are essentially the same corporation with a mere change of name, a court may well find that the buying corporation should be treated as if it had assumed the seller's liabilities. But courts will impose this kind of liability on a buyer who does not expressly assume the seller's debts only in narrow circumstances.

    iii. Summary: So in general, even where the owner of a business sells all of the assets of the business to a buyer, and the buyer continues the business, the buyer does not have to perform the seller's contractual obligations unless there is found to be an express or implied delegation (as discussed in paragraph (i) above), or one of a number of very narrow special circumstances exists (e.g., fraud on the seller's creditors). On the other hand, if the buyer *is* found to have expressly or implicitly promised the seller that the buyer will perform the seller's obligations, then the other party on those obligations (e.g., a customer who has a contract with the seller) will be treated as an ***intended beneficiary*** who can sue the buyer if the buyer fails to perform. See Farnsworth, pp. 749-750.

E. Delegation of non-delegable duties: If a party to a contract purports to delegate duties which are in fact too personal to be delegated, the promisee has the right to ***refuse to accept performance from the delegate***, and to hold the delegator liable.

    1. Promisee remains silent But if the promisee ***remains silent*** when he learns of the delegation, he will probably be held to have assented to this substituted performance, and to have lost his right to demand that the delegator perform.

        a. Delegator remains liable: However, the promisee ***will usually not by his silence be held to have consented to a novation.*** That is, although he will lose the right to insist that the delegator rather than the delegate perform, if the delegate performs defectively, the promisee may ***sue the delegator for breach***. See Murray, p. 620. In other words, the delegator ***continues to be liable*** if the promisee merely remains silent in the face of the delegation.

Quiz Yourself on
DELEGATION OF DUTIES

111. Madame Gioconda contracts to pay Leonardo da Vinci $10,000 to paint her portrait. Da Vinci delegates his duties under the contract to Picasso. Gioconda shows up at da Vinci's studio for her first sitting for the portrait, and is shocked to find Picasso instead of da Vinci waiting for her. She's familiar with Picasso's work, which is very different from da Vinci's.

(A) Suppose that Madame Gioconda immediately objects to the switch, and insists that da Vinci do the portrait. da Vinci refuses, claiming that Picasso's work is at least as good. Will Madame G. be in breach if she refuses to let Picasso do the work?

(B) For this part only, suppose that Madame Gioconda, though upset at the switch, nonetheless sits for her portrait, while Picasso paints it. May Madame G. recover against da Vinci for breach of contract?

112. Robert E. Lee agrees to lend Abe Lincoln $1,000. The loan agreement contemplates that in return for the money, Lincoln will execute a promissory note. Before Lee makes the actual loan or Lincoln signs the note, Lincoln signs a document that says, "I hereby assign to Jefferson Davis my loan agreement with Robert E. Lee, with the intent that Davis be substituted for me as borrower in said loan agreement." Lincoln hands this assignment document to Davis, who indicates his approval by signing his initials. Davis presents the assignment document, together with Davis' own promissory note, to Lee, and demands the $1,000.

(A) Assume that Lee does not want to go along with the assignment of the contract. Must Lee make the loan to Davis?

(B) For this part only, assume that the original Lee-Lincoln loan agreement does not call on Lincoln to execute a future promissory note. Instead, the loan agreement recites that Lincoln "shall be liable for any advances made by Lee to Lincoln pursuant to this agreement," and provides that Lee will make advances of up to $1,000. Before Lee has made any advances, Lincoln says to Lee, "I've assigned to Davis my right to receive the $1,000, so pay that sum to him." Lee does so. Davis does not sign any agreement with Lee. He does, however (just before receiving the $1,000) receive from Lincoln a document that says, "Lincoln hereby assigns to Davis Lincoln's loan agreement with Lee." Davis initials this document. If Davis does not repay the $1,000 to Lee, may Lee recover this sum from Davis?

(C) Same facts as part (B). Now, assume that Lee makes the loan to Davis, and Davis defaults, because he's broke after the Civil War. May Lee recover the $1,000 from Lincoln?

113. Khufu has Valley King Architects design a pyramid for him. Khufu takes the plans to Cheops General Contractor, and contracts to have Cheops build the pyramid for him. The contract says nothing about whether delegation by Cheops is permitted. Cheops delegates its duties under the contract to Tut General Contractors, a reputable contractor with reasonable experience in projects of this kind.

(A) Suppose Khufu objects to the delegation as soon as he learns of it. Cheops insists that it is permitted to make the delegation, and that Khufu must accept performance from Tut or be in breach. Khufu remains firm. Which, if either, original party (Khufu or Cheops) is in breach?

(B) For purposes of this part only, assume that the original Khufu-Cheops contract contains the following language: "Cheops hereby agrees to personally perform its duties under this agreement, and not to delegate or attempt to delegate those duties." As soon as Khufu learns of the attempted delegation, he objects. Assume that in the absence of the just-quoted clause, the attempted delegation would be invalid. Cheops refuses to do the work, and insists that its delegation is valid. Which, if either, original party is now in breach?

(C) Same basic facts as (B). Now, however, assume that the Khufu-Cheops contract's only provision relating to assignment or delegation says, "This contract may not be assigned." If Cheops insists on delegating its performance to Tut, and Khufu objects, who is breach, Cheops or Khufu?

Answers

111. **(A) No.** Duties to be performed under a contract are generally delegable. But where a contract calls for the performance of personal services by a person with particular personal skills, those services normally may not be delegated. Since portrait-painting involves personal skills that vary significantly from one person to another, such services may not be delegated without the consent of the person who is to receive the services. Therefore, Madame Gioconda can refuse to let Picasso paint her portrait and can insist that da Vinci do it. If she refuses to accept Picasso and da Vinci refuses to paint her portrait, he's breached the contract by repudiating it, and she can recover damages from him.

(B) No. If she sits for the portrait, she will be held to have implicitly assented to the delegation. She will thereby have waived her right to complain about the delegation, and must pay the contract price.

112. **(A) No.** To begin with, a document that purports to assign "the contract" will generally be interpreted as being an attempt at *both* an assignment of rights *and* a delegation of duties. Therefore, Lincoln's execution of the assignment document, and Davis' initialling of it, will constitute both: (1) an assignment by Lincoln to Davis of Lincoln's right to receive the money; and (2) an attempted delegation to Davis of Lincoln's obligation to tender a promissory note in return for the money.

The attempted delegation will be invalid, if Lee objects to it. That's because a duty as to which the promisee has a substantial interest in having only the original promisor perform is non-delegable. A promise that calls for the promisor's use of his own particular, unusual skills generally falls into this category. This principle is commonly applied to promissory notes: the promisee is not required to accept a promissory note from a different person than the original promisor, because the delegate's creditworthiness will not be the same as the promisor's. Therefore, if Lee objects, he need not accept Davis' promissory note as a substitute for Lincoln's, and he may refuse to lend the money to Davis.

(B) Yes, probably. As noted in the answer to part (A), a document that purports to assign "the contract" will generally be interpreted as being an attempt at both an assignment of rights and a delegation of duties. So Lincoln has, as in part (A), assigned his rights to the loan, and has attempted to delegate his duty (of repayment). Davis, by initialing the assignment document and receiving the money, has implicitly promised Lincoln that Davis will repay Lee. The more interesting question is whether Lee may sue on this promise, since Davis didn't make the promise to Lee, just to Lincoln. The answer is that Lee may sue if he was a ***third party beneficiary*** (a concept discussed later in this chapter) of Davis' promise to Lincoln. A court will probably hold that Lee was an "intended" beneficiary of Davis' promise (since Lincoln wanted Lincoln's repayment obligation to Lee to be discharged); in that case, Lee may sue Davis.

(C) Yes. Unless the promisee expressly indicates his consent to a ***novation*** (a complete substitution of one promisor for another), the mere fact that the promisee consents to an assignment and delegation does not discharge the assignor/delegator from liability. So here, the fact that Lee allowed the "assignment" of the contract (and made the loan to Davis) will not be interpreted as Lee's consent to substituting Davis for Lincoln. Therefore, Lincoln will remain liable, and may be sued if Davis defaults.

113. **(A) Khufu, probably.** Where the contract is silent, delegation is normally permissible unless either: (1) the promisee has a ***substantial interest*** in having the delegator perform (usually due to the delegator's unusual personal skills); or (2) the surrounding circumstances indicate that the parties both intended that the duty in question not be delegated. The facts indicate that (1) is not satisfied, since we're told that Tut is competent at work of this type, and the promisee's mere preference that the work be done by the promisor is not enough to constitute a substantial interest in having the work done by the promisor. As to (2), there's nothing in the surrounding facts to indicate that the parties ever thought about delegability, let alone implicitly agreed to forbid it. Therefore, as in most construction contracts, the duty of performance here will probably be found delegable.

(B) Cheops. A contract provision stating that the duties are not delegable will be enforced, even if the duties are ones that would, in the absence of the provision, be delegable. Therefore, Cheops is insisting on doing something that it has no right to do, and that insistence would be a breach (a repudiation).

(C) Cheops. A contract provision that prohibits "assignment of the contract" will, unless the circumstances indicate otherwise, be prohibited as barring the delegation of duties, but not the assignment of rights. (See UCC § 2-210(3), so stating, for sales-of-goods cases.) Here, there are no circumstances indicating otherwise. Therefore, Cheops' attempted delegation will be a breach of the "anti-assignment" clause (but Cheops' assignment of, say, its right to be paid for its work would not be.)

IV. THIRD PARTY BENEFICIARIES

A. **Introduction:** A party may form a contract the main purpose of which is to benefit not himself, but a third person. Thus *A* and *B* may make a contract in which *B* makes a promise that will benefit *A*, in return for *A*'s promise to give a performance that will benefit *C*, rather than *B*. The contract might provide that *A* will give *C* a sum of money that *B* intends as a gift for *C*. Or, it might provide that *A* will pay a sum to *C* that will satisfy a debt that *B* owes to *C*. In either case, *C* is said to be a ***third party beneficiary*** of the contract between *A* and *B*.

1. **Issue is who may sue:** If, in the above situation, *A* fails to perform, *B* may of course sue for damages, since he is a party to the contract. The "fighting issue," however, is ***whether***

C, the third party beneficiary, may sue. It is with this question that the rest of this chapter will be concerned.

B. Older cases and the First Restatement: Most older cases, and the first Restatement (§ 133(1)), allowed a third party beneficiary to sue only if he was either: (1) a ***"creditor beneficiary"***; or (2) a ***"donee beneficiary."***

    a.   Creditor beneficiary: If performance of a promise would satisfy ***an actual or supposed or asserted duty of the promisee to a third party***, and it does not appear that the promisee intended to make a gift to the third party, then the third party is called a ***"creditor beneficiary."*** (That is, the third party is a "creditor" of the promisee.) The practical reason for allowing such a creditor beneficiary to sue is that multiple law suits are prevented. That is, there is no danger that the law suit by the third party creditor against the promisee on the original obligation will be followed by a suit by the promisee against the promisor. Instead, the third party can sue the promisor directly.

    Example: X owes $300 to P. X then loans $300 to D, in return for D's promise to pay X's debt to P the next day. D fails to pay P, and P sues him.

    Held, for P. P may recover as a third party beneficiary of the contract between X and D. This is true even though D was not a "trustee" of the money paid by X. "Manifest justice" requires this result. *Lawrence v. Fox*, 20 N.Y. 268 (N.Y. 1869).

    b.   Donee beneficiary: If the promisee entered the contract for the purpose of conferring a ***gift*** on a third party, the third party is said to be a ***"donee beneficiary,"*** and is given the right to sue the promisor. The principal reason for allowing the donee beneficiary to sue is that if he can't, no one else as a practical matter can — the promisee's own damages will ordinarily be nominal. The promisor would thus be let off the hook, and might be unjustly enriched.

    Example: X, who is dying, wants to leave her house to her niece, P. X's present will leaves the house to X's husband, D. Because X will probably not live long enough for a new will to be drafted, D promises X that if she keeps her will the same, D will leave P enough money in his will to make up to P for not getting the house. After X's death, D fails to keep his promise in his own will, and after his death P sues his estate for the value of the house.

    Held, P may recover as a donee beneficiary of the agreement between X and D. P is the only one damaged by D's breach of promise. Furthermore, the cases have for a long time enforced promises to take care of the promisee's spouse or child; this same principle should be applied where, as here, the beneficiary is the promisee's beloved niece. *Seaver v. Ransom*, 120 N.E. 639 (N.Y. 1918).

C. Second Restatement's abandonment of the two category structure: Until recently, many courts refused to permit a third party beneficiary to recover unless she fell into either the creditor beneficiary or the donee beneficiary class. The Second Restatement ***eliminates*** the use of "donee beneficiary" and "creditor beneficiary," because of their "overtones of obsolete doctrinal difficulties..." (Rest. 2d, Introductory Note to Chapter 4.) Many modern courts have followed suit.

1. **"Intended" beneficiaries may recover:** Under this modern/Restatement approach, the third party may recover if she falls into the unified class of *"intended beneficiaries."* Otherwise, she is said to be an *"incidental beneficiary,"* and may not sue.

2. **Definition of "intended beneficiary":** For a third party to be an "intended beneficiary," it must first of all be the case that giving him the right to sue would be "appropriate to effectuate the *intentions of the parties*…"(Rest. § 302(1)). If he meets this test, he must furthermore fit into *one of the two following categories:*

   a. **Payment of money:** Either "the performance of the promise will satisfy an obligation of the promisee to *pay money* to the beneficiary;" or

   b. **Intended benefit:** "The circumstances indicate that the promisee *intends to give the beneficiary the benefit* of the promised performance." (§ 302(1)(a) and (b)).

   Note: These two kinds of "intended beneficiaries" sound a lot like the old "creditor" and "donee" beneficiaries. But Comment d to Rest. § 302 lists several situations in which a beneficiary will be "intended," although he would *not* have been either a "donee" or a "creditor" beneficiary. For instance, if the promisee *believes he owes* the third party a duty but he in fact does not, many older cases would have held that the third person was not a true "creditor beneficiary," and would not have allowed recovery, whereas the Second Restatement would allow such recovery.

3. **Incidental beneficiaries:** Even though the Second Restatement has broadened the class of third parties who may sue, it by no means gives such a right to all persons who would be benefited by the performance of a contract. The Restatement gives the following illustration of a contract in which the third person is merely an *"incidental"* beneficiary, rather than an "intended" one, and therefore *may not sue.*

   Example: "*B* contracts with *A* to buy a new car manufactured by *C*. *C* is an incidental beneficiary, even though the promise can only be performed if money is paid to *C*." Rest. 2d, § 302, Illustr. 17.

4. **Factors to determine who is "intended" beneficiary:** In determining who is an "intended beneficiary," the primary question is whether the *promisee* intended that the third party have the benefit of the contract. But where the promisee's intention is not clear from his language, several other factors may be considered.

   a. **Reliance:** If the beneficiary would be reasonable in *relying* on the contract as having been intended to confer a right on her, she is an "intended" beneficiary. That is, the purpose of the contract may be looked at from the beneficiary's point of view. See Comment d to Rest. 2d, § 302.

   b. **To whom performance runs:** If the performance is to *run directly* from the promisor *to the third party*, the third party is usually an intended beneficiary. On the other hand, if the performance is to run from the promisor to the promisee, and the third party's benefit will only be indirect, he is probably just an incidental beneficiary. C&P, p. 645.

   Example: Bank promises to give Borrower a loan, so that he can pay his creditor *C*. Since Bank's performance is to be made directly to Borrower, and *C* would benefit only indirectly, he would probably not be an intended beneficiary. If, on the other hand, the contract between Bank and Borrower provided that Bank was to pay *C* directly, C would be an intended beneficiary, and could sue Bank for breach of the contract. See C&P, p. 645. (Bank would also fall within the "payment of money" category of Rest. 2d, § 302(1)(a)).

Caveat: This "to whom performance runs" test will not always be dispositive, however — it's just one factor in the analysis. Thus in one well-known case, X, a testator, hired D, a lawyer, to write a will for him. The will was to make the Ps beneficiaries of a trust set up by D. However, it turned out that the trust was invalid, and the Ps ended up getting $75,000 less than they would have had the trust been valid. The court held that the Ps could theoretically recover from D on a third party beneficiary theory; their being benefited was the "main purpose" of the hiring of D to write the will, and it was irrelevant that in this case performance was not to be rendered to them. (However, the court found that there was no actual liability, since the rules on perpetuities and alienation, which caused the trust to be invalid, were so confusing that D's error was excusable.) *Lucas v. Hamm*, 364 P.2d 685 (Cal. 1961).

   c. Carrying out of parties' intentions: A beneficiary may be an "intended" one even though helping the beneficiary was not the ***"primary"*** intent of the parties, as long as giving him these benefits was ***part of the parties' overall object***.

   i.   Promisor's intent: Most courts seem to agree that the promis*ee*'s intent is the one of primary interest. Some courts seem to say that this is the *only* intent that matters, i.e., that if the promisee intends to benefit the third party, that third party is an ***intended*** beneficiary even if the promisor has no such intention. But other courts — though probably a minority — hold that ***both*** the promisor and the promisee must have intended to benefit the third party.

   5. Beneficiary's assent or knowledge unnecessary: The intended beneficiary has a right to sue despite the fact that at the time the contract was made, he didn't ***know about it***, or, if he did know about it, ***did not assent*** to it.

D. Some frequently arising situations: We examine now several frequently arising situations in which the right of a third party to sue is in question.

   1. Public contracts: *Governments*, whether federal, state or municipal, frequently make contracts with private companies under which the private company will perform services that will benefit the public. In all such cases, the contract is presumably for the benefit of the public. Yet as a general rule, ***a member of the public who is injured*** by the fact that the contractor does not perform may ***not*** sue.

   Example: Water Company enters into a contract with the city of Rensselaer, in which it promises to supply water for fire hydrants. A building in the city belonging to P burns down, due in part to the fact that Water Co. did not maintain adequate pressure in the hydrants.

   Held, P may not sue Water Co. The parties to the contract showed no intent to give each individual citizen the right to sue. (Furthermore, to allow each citizen to sue would make Water Co. an insurer against fire loss, with consequent prohibitive boosts in water rates.) *H.R. Moch Co., Inc. v. Rensselaer Water Co.*, 159 N.E. 896 (N.Y. 1928).

a. Exceptions: In several kinds of situations, however, members of the public will be allowed to recover against a contractor who breaches his contract with the government. The Second Restatement specifies two particular situations in which a member of the public *will be allowed to sue:*

i. Expressly provided: A member of the public may sue if the party contracting with the government has ***explicitly promised to undertake liability*** to members of the public for breach. Rest. 2d, § 313(2)(a).

ii. Government has own liability: If the government has a ***duty of its own*** to provide the service which it has contracted for, a citizen may sue the party who contracted to perform those services. Rest. 2d, § 313(2)(b).

Example: "*A*, a municipality, owes a duty to the public to keep its streets in repair. *B*, a street railway company, contracts to keep a portion of these streets in repair but fails to do so. *C*, a member of the public, is injured thereby. He may bring an action against *A* and *B* and can recover judgment against each of them." Rest. 2d, § 313, Illustr. 5.

2. Real estate neighbors: A party who owns ***real estate*** the value of which would be enhanced by construction on a ***nearby parcel*** is an ***incidental*** beneficiary, with respect to the parties who contract to perform or facilitate the construction. So the real estate owner can't sue either of the original contracting parties if one of them breaches.

Example: Ohn owns a vacant parcel of land adjacent to a parcel owned by Neigh. Bank contracts to lend Ohn enough money to build an office building on Ohn's parcel. If the building were built, Neigh's parcel would immediately become much more valuable. However, since there's no sign that Ohn (or Bank) is motivated by a desire to confer a benefit on Neigh, Neigh is just an incidental beneficiary of the Ohn-Bank contract. Therefore, if Bank fails to fund the promised loan, Neigh can't recover against Bank. Cf. Rest. 2d, § 302, Illustr. 16.

3. Mortgage assumptions: The transfer of ***mortgaged real estate*** gives rise to third party beneficiary problems in several different contexts. Before examining these problems, it is necessary to understand exactly what a mortgage is. It consists of two parts: (1) a promise by the mortgagor to pay back a loan made to him by the mortgagee; this promise is evidenced by a promissory note or bond; and (2) a security interest, which gives the mortgagee the right to foreclose upon the property if the mortgagor does not pay back the debt.

a. Two ways to transfer mortgaged property: When the mortgagor wishes to sell the mortgaged property, he can do so in one of two principal ways:

❏ First, he can sell the property ***"subject to"*** the mortgage. This means that the purchaser does not undertake to pay off the mortgage (i.e., he does not make himself personally liable for the amount of the mortgage debt). However, if he does not see that the mortgage payments are made, the mortgagee will be able to repossess anyway (but will not be able to get a deficiency judgment against the purchaser for the difference between the foreclosure price and the unpaid debt).

❑ Alternatively, the purchaser may *"assume"* the mortgage. If he assumes the mortgage, he makes himself personally liable for its repayment; if he falls behind, the mortgagee may not only foreclose, but may also obtain a deficiency judgment against the purchaser.

Let's consider each scenario, with the assumption one first.

b. **Mortgagee's rights where assumption has occurred:**   If the purchaser has *assumed* the mortgage, all courts agree that the *mortgagee* (i.e., the lender) is a *creditor beneficiary* of the assumption agreement between seller and buyer. The mortgagee may therefore *sue the purchaser to compel him to make the mortgage payments.* If this purchaser in turn sells to another purchaser (whom we shall call a "sub-purchaser"), who also assumes the mortgage, the mortgagee will be able to recover against the sub-purchaser as a third party beneficiary in the same way that he could against the original purchaser.

c. **Mortagee has no right where property is taken "subject to":**   If the purchaser merely takes *"subject to"* the mortgage, there is no promise by the purchaser to *anyone* that the purchaser will pay the mortgage. Therefore, there is *no promise* on which the mortgagee could possibly be a third party beneficiary, and his only remedy is to repossess, not to recover a deficiency judgment.

d. **Where first purchaser takes "subject to" the mortgage and second one assumes it:**   Now, suppose that in an initial transaction, the original mortgagor sells to a purchaser who takes subject to the mortgage rather than assuming it. As we've just seen, the mortgagee obviously cannot sue that purchaser, since he has never promised to pay. But then suppose that this non-assuming purchaser *sells to a sub-purchaser who does assume the mortgage.* May the mortgagee sue this assuming sub-purchaser? Courts are *split* on this issue.

E. **Discharge or modification by the original parties:**   Suppose that a contract has been created which creates enforceable rights in a third party. After these rights have been created, may the original parties then agree to *discharge or modify the contract*, changing or eliminating the third parties' rights?

1. **Second Restatement uses unified test:** Modern courts generally follow the Second Restatement's rule. Under that rule, the original parties' power to modify the contract *terminates* when the beneficiary, before he receives notification of the discharge or modification, does any of the following:

❑ materially *changes his position in justifiable reliance* on the promise; or

❑ *brings suit* on the promise; or

❑ *manifests assent* to it at the request of the promisor or promisee.

Rest. 2d, § 311(3).

a. **Original parties maintain right to modify or discharge:**   This rule means that until one of the three events listed above occurs, the original parties *maintain the power to modify or discharge* the beneficiary's rights. But if any of the three events occurs before the beneficiary gets notice of a modification or discharge, the beneficiary's rights *"vest,"* and can no longer be altered by the original parties.

Example: Uncle and Landowner, the owner of Blackacre, sign an agreement under which Uncle promises to deposit $100,000 in Landowner's bank account by April 1, and in return Landowner promises that on April 2, he will convey Blackacre to Uncle's nephew Nick. (Assume that Nick is an intended beneficiary of this agreement.) Uncle sends a copy of the agreement to Nick, and says, "Let me know whether you agree to receive title to Blackacre as provided in this document." On March 26, Nick responds, "That's great, yes, I agree. Thanks, Unc." On March 30, Uncle and Landowner sign an amendment to the agreement, purporting to discharge Uncle's obligation to pay the $100,000 and Landowner's obligation to transfer title to Nick.

When Nick "manifested assent" to the agreement at the request of one of the original parties, this assent took away Uncle's and Landowner's power to modify the agreement as it concerned Nick. Therefore, Nick can sue both Uncle and Landowner for breach on account of their purported modification. The same would be true if Nick, instead of manifesting assent, had changed his position in reliance (e.g., by giving up the chance to buy some alternative property because he knew he could count on receiving Blackacre).

    b. Clause preventing subsequent modification: The original parties may, however, themselves *agree* at the time of contracting that no subsequent modification may occur without the beneficiary's consent. Such a clause will be *honored*. Rest. 2d, § 311(1).

2. Life insurance policies: Most *life insurance* policies contain a clause reserving to the owner of the policy the right to change the beneficiary at will. Such a clause will almost always be *enforced*, and if the original beneficiary is dropped from the policy, he will not be able to sue the insurer. Conversely, if the policy states that power to change the beneficiary is not reserved, that clause will also be honored, and the original beneficiary can sue for the proceeds despite a purported change.

F. Defenses against the beneficiary: If a third party beneficiary leaps over all the hurdles which we have discussed thus far, he will be able to sue the promisor to compel him to perform. But as a general rule, the promisor-defendant will be able to assert against the beneficiary *any defenses which he could have asserted had he been sued by the promisee*. The beneficiary is said to *"step into the shoes of the promisee."* Thus the defendant may show that there was no mutual assent between the promisee and himself, that there was a mutual mistake, that the promisee gave no consideration, etc.

1. Defense that promisee breached: Most important, this principle means that if the promisee never rendered the performance which he promised under the contract (i.e., the promisee *breached*), the promisor may *assert this lack of performance* in defense to the beneficiary's suit. See Rest. 2d, § 309(2).

Example: Seller contracts to deliver goods to Buyer, who promises that upon delivery, he will pay $1,000 to Supplier, Seller's creditor. Seller delivers defective goods and fails to cure the non-conformity. Buyer refuses to pay the $1,000, and is sued by Supplier. Buyer may assert as a defense the fact that Seller breached the contract.

2. Exception for defense of modification or rescission: An exception to the general rule that the promisor may use against the beneficiary any defense which she could have used against the promisee, is that the promisor may not always assert the defense that the promisee has *discharged* her from the contract, or otherwise modified it. As was developed above, the beneficiary's right in some circumstances becomes "vested," and any subsequent modification or release granted by the promisee will not be valid as against the beneficiary. *Supra*, p. 420.

G. Beneficiary versus promisee: When the promisor promises to pay the promisee's debt to a creditor beneficiary, the latter may, as we have seen, sue the promisor directly. If the creditor does so, does she forfeit her right to sue the promisee?

1. Creditor may sue: Most courts, and the Second Restatement (§ 310(1)), hold that the answer is "no" — the creditor beneficiary, by bringing suit against the promisor, does not release the promisee, so the creditor *may later sue the promisee*. (She is, however, entitled to only one satisfaction.)

> **Example:** Contractor agrees to paint Owner's house for $10,000, with payment to be made to Friend, in repayment of a $10,000 debt owed by Contractor to Friend. Owner does not make payment, and Friend sues Owner as a third party beneficiary. Owner defends with partial success on the grounds that Contractor did not perform the painting work to the contract specifications. Therefore, Friend recovers only $6,000 from Owner (because the court gives Owner a set-off for $4,000 in damages for breach). Now, Friend may sue Contractor for the remaining $4,000 due on the original Contractor-Friend debt — Friend will not be deemed to have given up the right to sue Contractor by virtue of having sued Owner.

a. Suit by promisee: If the promisee ends up paying all or part of the claim to the creditor beneficiary, the promisee may recover *reimbursement* from the promisor. Rest. 2d, § 310(2).

2. Promisee's right against the promisor: Most courts allow the promisee to bring his own suit against the promisor for the benefit of the third party beneficiary, if the promisor breaches.

a. Third party is creditor beneficiary: This is most important where the third party is a *creditor* beneficiary. Here, most courts let the promisee-debtor recover from the promisor the amount which the promisor promised that he would pay the creditor (at least where the promisee has already paid the debt to the creditor).

> **Example:** Same facts as above Example. Now, however, assume that Contractor does the work correctly, but Owner doesn't pay any of the $10,000 due. At least if Contractor (the promisee/debtor) pays his debt to Friend first, Contractor gets to sue Owner (the promisor) to recover the $10,000. (Some courts would let Contractor bring the suit even if he hadn't yet paid off Friend.)

H. The UCC and third party beneficiaries: The UCC has no general provisions dealing with third party beneficiaries. It does, however, provide that in a sales contract, certain persons who are not parties to the contract may sue for breach of *warranties* that the seller has made. Two separate questions are involved: (1) May the buyer sue not only his immediate seller, but the person who sold the goods to the seller, or who manufactured them?; and (2) May anyone other than the buyer (e.g., a member of the buyer's household, a bystander, etc.), if he is harmed by a breach of warranty, sue either the buyer's immediate seller or the remote seller or manufacturer? These questions are discussed in the chapter on Warranties, *infra*, p. 497.

1. **Common law fills gap:** Other third party beneficiary problems that may arise in a sale-of-goods case are not disposed of by the Code. For instance, a buyer might contract for goods to be delivered to some third party to satisfy a business obligation; if the goods are never delivered (as opposed to being delivered in a defective state, breaching warranties), the Code provides no clue as to whether the beneficiary may sue. But remember that the Code, like any statute, is ***supplemented by the common law*** where the Code is silent. UCC § 1-103(b).

Quiz Yourself on
THIRD PARTY BENEFICIARIES

114. O'Hara owns Tara, a plantation. She hires Selznick to build a movie set in the backyard, which will enhance the value of the property next door, Twelve Oaks, owned by Wilkes. When Wilkes learns of the pending set project, Wilkes adds a souvenir hut to his front yard. Selznick breaches the contract with O'Hara and the set is never built. May Wilkes sue Selznick as a third party beneficiary to the O'Hara-Wilkes contract?

115. Gretel eats $500 worth of gingerbread from the walls of Witch's home, and Witch demands $500 from her. Shortly thereafter, Hansel, Gretel's brother, enters into a contract with Mother Goose Publishing to write his autobiography. In the publishing contract, at Hansel's request, Mother Goose agrees to pay part of the royalties to Witch to pay for the damage caused by Gretel. (Hansel doesn't like to see his sister burdened down by debt.) If Mother Goose doesn't pay the royalties to Witch, can Gretel sue Mother Goose?

116. Dorothy contracts to appear in Wizard's play. The agreement provides that Wizard will also tender a standard Actors Equity acting contract to Dorothy's friends Scarecrow, Lion and Tin Man, for co-leading roles in the production. Dorothy shows her friends her contract with Wizard. They express to her their delight that they'll be getting roles, and they all buy new wardrobes to be worn in the show. Subsequently, Wizard decides not to produce the play, and he and Dorothy agree to rescind the agreement.

    (A) Assume that the contract says nothing about whether or when the parties may modify or rescind the agreement. May Dorothy's friends recover against Wizard for failing to tender them contracts?

    (B) Assume, for this part only, that the Dorothy-Wizard contract contained the following provision: "The parties may at any time, by mutual agreement, modify or rescind this agreement without consideration." If all other facts are the same, may Dorothy's friends recover against Wizard for failing to tender them contracts?

117. Betsy Ross contracts to deliver 50 hand-sewn Stars and Stripes flags to Washington. Washington promises Betsy in return that once he receives the flags, he will pay off Betsy's $500 debt to Singer. Betsy tells Singer about the agreement. Betsy delivers the flags, but unfortunately the flags are red, white, and chartreuse instead of the contracted-for red, white and blue. Betsy refuses to correct the defect, and Washington refuses to pay Singer. Singer sues Washington for the $500. Does Washington have a valid defense?

Answers

114. No. A beneficiary may sue the promisor only if the beneficiary was an "intended" beneficiary. A beneficiary is "intended" if the circumstances indicate that the promisee intended to give the beneficiary the benefit of the promised performance. Here, there is no evidence that O'Hara (the promisee) intended to give Wilkes the benefit of the promised set — Wilkes was essentially a bystander whose very existence was probably not even considered by O'Hara when O'Hara made the set deal. Therefore, Wilkes was an "incidental" (not "intended") beneficiary, and as such, has no right to sue on the promise.

115. Yes. A non-party who would benefit by performance of a contractual promise may sue if the non-party is found to be an "intended" beneficiary. Where the promisee's purpose in bargaining for the promise is, at least in part, to confer a benefit on the beneficiary, the beneficiary is "intended." Here, although Hansel doesn't personally owe money to Witch, he clearly has a desire to see his sister's debt repaid. Therefore, he's intentionally attempting to confer a benefit on her by extracting the promise from Mother Goose that she'll part off the debt. Consequently, Hansel is an intended beneficiary, and may sue.

Note that these facts present an exception to the general rule-of-thumb that when performance does not run directly to the beneficiary, the beneficiary is probably not "intended" — here, the payment will go to Witch, not Gretel, but Gretel is still an intended beneficiary since Hansel intends that Gretel benefit by having her debt be extinguished.

116. (A) Yes, probably. The rule is that a beneficiary's rights "vest," making his rights irrevocable, when one of three events occurs: (1) the beneficiary materially changes his position in justifiable reliance on the promise; (2) he brings suit on it; or (3) he manifests his assent to the contract at the request of one of the parties. Here, the third party beneficiaries have materially relied on the contract to their detriment, by buying expensive wardrobes. Assuming that their reliance was reasonable, they will be able to recover in their suit. (An alternative rationale is that when the friends were shown the agreement by Dorothy and expressed their delight, this constituted their "assent" to the contract at Dorothy's request, making their rights irrevocable.)

(B) No, probably. Although a beneficiary's rights normally vest upon any of the three types of events described in the answer to Part (A), the original parties are always free to retain the right to vary this rule. Here, Dorothy and Wizard's retention of the right to modify or rescind the contract (even though they don't mention the effect this will have on the three friends) will probably be interpreted as an implicit variation of these normal vesting rules. If so, the fact that the friends materially relied on (or manifested their assent to) the promise will be irrelevant.

117. Yes. When an intended beneficiary (Singer) sues the promisor (Washington) under a contract, the promisor has the same defenses as he would have against the promisee (Betsy Ross). Thus, breach of contract (as here), lack of mutuality or consideration, fraud, duress, or mutual mistake will all be valid defenses against the beneficiary.

Exam Tips on
CONTRACTS INVOLVING MORE THAN TWO PARTIES

Material from this chapter is heavily tested. Look for a fact pattern where rights or duties are created in a third person either when or after the contract has been executed.

Assignment and Delegation

☛ Remember that an *assignment* is a transfer of contract *rights,* and a *delegation* is a transfer of contract *duties*.

☛ Be sure to check whether the contract may be assigned, and/or delegated:

When assignment is allowed:

☞ **Consideration:** Don't worry if the assignment isn't supported by *consideration*. Consideration is unnecessary where there's a present transfer of rights.

☞ **Generally permissible:** Where the contract is *silent* on whether assignment is allowed, the contract is *assignable,* even without the obligor's consent.

☞ **Anti-assignment clause:** If a contract contains an anti-assignment clause, an act of assignment gives the obligor a right to *damages* against the assignor for breach, but *does not render the assignment ineffective* (unless the assignment imposes an material additional burden on the obligor, or would be void for some other reason independent of the anti-assignment clause).

When delegation is allowed:

☞ **Nondelegable duties:** In delegation cases, check that the duties are in fact delegable. Remember that the main rule is that delegation is permitted unless the obligee (the one to whom the delegated performance is due) has a *"substantial interest in having the delegator perform."*

☞ **Personal services:** Contracts for performance of *personal services* are generally *not delegable* by the person who would do the work.

Example 1: Contracts of *employment*, which are not be delegable by the employ*ee*.

Example 2: Contracts with *independent contractors possessing special personal skills*, such as musical performers, architects, computer programmers, etc.

Note: In these personal-service circumstances, the delegation may be deemed an *anticipatory repudiation,* in which case the obligee can immediately cancel the contract and sue the delegator for breach.

☞ **Construction contracts:** Generally, an obligation under a *construction contract* is ***not*** considered a personal service and may be assigned.

☞ *Important distinction:* A **delegation** of the duty to perform personal services is more likely prohibited than an **assignment** of the right to receive the services (which is prohibited only if it materially alters the duty of the obligor).

> **Example 1:** The rights to receive the benefits of a one-year contract for gardening services performed for an owner of a condominium may probably be transferred to the party to whom he sells the condominium. (The duty to make payment may also be assigned, though the assignor remains liable as guarantor.)

> **Example 2:** The rights to a musical performance at one party's wedding may be transferred to another party having a wedding, if all the contract terms (place, time, date, contract price) are the same.

☞ **Waiver:** Remember that even if the contract is nondelegable, the right to object may be *waived*.

Example: Ohn, the owner of a piece of undeveloped land, enters into a contract with Arch, an architect, whereby Arch agrees to produce and deliver by May 1 a design of a ten-story hotel to be built on the land. On January 15, because of health problems, Arch is ordered to take a six-month break from work by his physician. Arch signs a documents "assigning" to Bench — a well-known architect with whom Arch has sometimes collaborated — all Arch's rights and duties under the contract with Ohn. One week later, Bench meets with Ohn to discuss preliminary plans with him. Thereafter, he communicates with Ohn by phone. When Bench submits the completed design on May 1, Ohn refuses to accept it.

Ohn, by failing to object to the assignment during his initial encounters with Bench, has probably waived his right to object.

☞ **Demand for assurances:** When the party who is owed the performance receives notice of a delegation of duties, she may demand **assurances of performance** from the delegate, and may suspend her own performance until assurances are furnished.

☛ **Rights and obligations on assignor/delegator side:** Remember to evaluate the ***rights*** and ***obligations*** of the ***assignor or delegator.***

<u>**Assignor's right to revoke:**</u>

☞ **Assignor relinquishes rights:** In an assignment, an assignor's rights are ***extinguished*** once there has been an effective assignment. Therefore, don't make the mistake of allowing the assignor to sue to enforce rights previously held by her.

☞ **Assignments for consideration are irrevocable:** Also, watch for an assignment that is supported by ***consideration*** — such an assignment is ***irrevocable***, so the assignor can't change her mind and cancel the assignment.

☞ **Gratuitous assignment:** By contrast, a ***gratuitous*** assignment is ***revocable*** by the assignor, unless one of the following happens:

❑ the assignor ***delivers a symbolic document*** evidencing the rights (e.g., hands over a bankbook, which would make assignment of the bank account irrevocable);

❑ the assignor puts the assignment in *writing*;

❑ the assignee *foreseeably relies* to his detriment on the assignment or

❑ the obligor *gives performance* to the assignee.

Delegator's ongoing liability:

☞ A delegation of contract duties doesn't divest the *delegator* of her obligations to the obligor. Thus, ***the delegator can be sued if the delegate breaches.***

> **Example:** Store, a retailer of home gardening supplies, enters into a one-year contract with Seedco, a wholesaler of seeds, whereby Seedco will supply Store with all of its requirements for rye grass seeds on a monthly basis. After delivering one delivery of rye grass seeds to Store, Seedco sells its business to Byer, who fulfills Store's next month's requirement of seeds. Store pays Byer for the seeds, but also demands that Byer assure it that it will be able to meet Store's future rye grass seed needs. Five weeks later Store has still not heard from Byer and notifies Seedco and Byer that it's canceling the contract.
>
> Store may successfully sue *Seedco* for breach of contract — the delegation by Seedco to Byer did not relieve Seedco of liability if Byer should not perform.
>
> ☞ *Trap:* A fact pattern may indicate that an obligee has *consented* to the delegation. This consent does *not* relieve the delegator of liability, unless the obligee *explicitly agrees* to release the delegator (in which case there is said to be a "novation.")

☛ **Rights and obligations of assignee:** Also, analyze the *rights* of the *assignee*.

☞ **Assignee steps into assignor's shoes:** The assignee is entitled to *enforce the contract rights* to the same extent that the assignor could have — the assignee *"steps in to the assignor's shoes."*

> ☞ **Subject to defenses:** However, the assignee's right to enforce the contract is *subject to any defenses* which could have been asserted against the assignor, such as *breach* of the assignor's return promise, *lack of consideration*, or occurrence of a *condition* to the defendant's duty.
>
> **Example:** Pawn, a pawnbroker, sells to Jewel, owner of a jewelry store, a ring for $2,500, representing it to contain a diamond. The following month, Pawn sells Jewel a pearl necklace for $2,200, to be paid for within thirty days. Before Jewel pays for the necklace, he learns that the ring he previously purchased contains a cubic zirconia and is worth only $300. A day later, Pawn assigns his rights to payment for the necklace to Art. Since Art steps into Pawn's shoes, if Art sues Jewel for payment on the necklace, Jewel can successfully assert against Art (at least as a set-off to reduce Art's recovery) the breach-of-contract claim regarding the ring.
>
> ☞ **Warranty of no defenses:** An assignor (at least one who assigns for value, rather than as a gift) makes an *implied warranty* that at the time of the assign-

ment, the obligor has *no defenses.*

> **Example:** Thus in the above example, if Pawn assigns to Art for value his right to payment from Jewel, Pawn has impliedly warranted to Art that Jewel has no defenses. Since Jewel has a defense against Pawn, Pawn has breached the implied warranty and is liable to Art for any amount by which Art's claim against Jewel is reduced.

☞ **Modification of assignee's rights by original parties:** In assignment scenarios, profs love to test whether/when the two original parties (the obligor [who owes the duty] and the assignor) may *modify the assignee's rights.* Remember that the assignee's rights depend on whether the modification took place *before or after* the assignee got notice of the assignment:

☞ **Modification before notice:** If the modification takes place *before* the assignee gets *notice of the assignment* (not the scenario that's usually tested), the modification is *binding* no matter what.

☞ **Modification after notice:** But if the modification occurs *after* the assignee has received notice of the assignment, the modification is binding *only if the assignor has not yet fully performed.*

> **Example:** Conti, a contractor, agrees to build a house for Owen, at a price of $300,000. Since Conti owes $400,000 to Bert, Conti's brother, Conti assigns to Bert Conti's right to receive payment from Owen, and immediately notifies Bert of the assignment. Then, Owen and Conti agree to a price reduction to $250,000. If the price reduction occurred before Conti finished the work, Bert is bound. But if the reduction occurred after Conti finished, the reduction is not binding on Bert, and Bert can sue for the whole $300,000.

☞ **Multiple assignments:** Also, look for a fact pattern where there have been *two assignments* of the same right. If the first assignment is irrevocable, then, generally, that first assignee has priority.

☞ **Prior payment as defense:** Remember that timing also counts where the obligor pays (or gives performance to) the assignor instead of the assignee. If the obligor pays the assignor (in part or in full) or gives the required performance *before he has received notice of the assignment*, he may *use this as a defense* against the assignee. But if the obligor renders payment/performance to the assignor *after* learning of the assignment, she may *not* use this as a defense vis a vis the assignee.

> **Example:** In the above example, suppose Owen paid $200,000 to Conti (rather than to Bert) after Owen got notice of the assignment. Owen would not be able to use this payment as a set-off in an action for the $300,000 brought against him by Bert.

Third Party Beneficiaries

☛ This topic is always a favorite on exams. The two most important issues to concentrate on are the distinction between intended and incidental beneficiaries, and the analysis of whether an intended beneficiary's rights have vested.

☞ **Intended vs. incidental:** You must distinguish between these two types of beneficiaries, because the *intended* beneficiary may *enforce* the contract whereas the *incidental beneficiary cannot.*

   ☞ **Creditor:** If the agreement is to *pay money* that one of the original parties owes to a third party, that third party is an intended beneficiary, and may sue. (This is the classic "creditor beneficiary" situation).

      Example: Own hires Gard to landscape Own's property for $90,000. The contract provides that Own is to pay $80,000 to Gard and the balance is to paid to Cred, to whom Gard owes money. Cred is an intended beneficiary of the contract between Own and Gard. Therefore, Cred may sue if Own doesn't pay.

   ☞ **To whom performance runs:** Look at whether the performance *runs directly* from the promisor to the third party. If it does, the beneficiary is probably "intended." If not, the beneficiary is probably incidental.

      Example: Whole, a wholesaler, agrees to supply to Ret, a retailer, 100 bicycles made by Manco. Ret is to pay Whole, who will then order from, and pay, Manco. Because Ret's performance (payment) is to run to Whole, not to Manco, Manco is not an intended beneficiary, and may not sue Ret if Ret cancels the contract.

   ☞ **Promisee's intent:** Pay the closest attention to the intent of the *promisee*, not the promisor — if the promisee didn't intend to benefit the third party, the latter is not an intended beneficiary.

      ☞ *Trap:* The mere fact that a third party is *mentioned* in a contract doesn't automatically mean that he's an intended beneficiary. Analyze whether the promisee really intended to benefit the third party.

      Example: Cli owes Lawr money for legal services. Lawr suggests to Cli, "I'd like you to pay me off by buying my nephew Neff a Goldray Special from the Zebra Car Agency — they've got good prices there." Cli responds, "If that's what you want, I'll be glad to do it." Neff is an intended beneficiary, because it's clear that Lawr (the promisee, to whom Cli owes money) intends to benefit Neff. (The fact that Cli has no particular desire to benefit Neff is irrelevant). On the other hand, there's no indication that Lawr intended to benefit Zebra — Lawr seems to have suggested Zebra by name merely because she wanted a good price, not because she had an affirmative desire to benefit Zebra. Therefore, Zebra is merely an incidental beneficiary.

☞ **Vesting as a bar to modification or discharge:** In exam fact patterns the two original parties often try to *modify or discharge* the obligation after it comes into existence. The general rule is that they may do this, but only until the beneficiary's rights have *"vested."* Vesting occurs when the beneficiary does one of these 3 things:

❑ she *manifests assent* to the promise,

❑ she *brings suit* on the promise, or

❏   she ***materially changes her position in justifiable reliance*** on the promise.

Examples of justifiable reliance: (1) A freelance book illustrator who is the beneficiary of full-time employment for a year notifies her other clients that she can't work for them. (2) A person who is the beneficiary of a promise to convey land cancels a contract for the purchase of a different parcel.

☞   **Beneficiary doesn't know of contract:** A common exam situation is that the beneficiary ***doesn't know of the contract*** prior to the time it's discharged or modified. In this situation, the beneficiary obviously can't do any of the 3 vesting events (manifest assent to the promise, bring suit on it, or materially change her position). Therefore, the original parties can modify or discharge the contract with impunity.

> **Example:** Frank, owner of a house, hires Paynt, a painting contractor, to paint Frank's residence. The contract price is $5,000, provided that Paynt delivers a "satisfactory result." A provision in the contract directs that payment be made to Paynt's daughter, Dot (intended as a wedding gift). When the job is completed, Frank says he doesn't find it "satisfactory." Paynt agrees to settle for a lower price of $4,500, provided the money's paid directly to him. Paynt doesn't give any of the money to Dot. Shortly thereafter, Dot finds out about the promise, and sues both Paynt and Frank for breach of the agreement. Dot will lose, because prior to the settlement (a modification), Dot didn't manifest assent to receiving the money, didn't bring suit on the agreement, and didn't materially change her position in reliance. Therefore, Dot's rights never vested.

CHAPTER 12

IMPOSSIBILITY, IMPRACTICABILITY, AND FRUSTRATION

ChapterScope

This chapter covers situations where, after the formation of a contract, unexpected events occur which affect the feasibility or possibility of a party's performance and cause the parties to be *excused from continued performance* under the contract. Key concepts:

■ **Impossibility:** If performance by a party has been made literally *impossible* by the occurrence of *unexpected events*, then the contract may be discharged. Common situations where a party's performance is rendered impossible include:

❑ *Destruction or unavailability of the subject matter* of the contract;

❑ *Death or incapacitating illness* of a party;

❑ *Supervening illegality* (where a contract is legal when it is entered into, but a subsequent change in the law renders its performance illegal).

■ **Impracticability:** If performance by a party has been made highly *impractical* by the occurrence of unexpected events, then the contract may be discharged.

■ **Frustration of purpose:** When unexpected events completely or almost completely *destroy a party's purpose* in entering into the contract, the parties may be excused from performing.

■ **Remedies:** When a contract has been discharged because of one of the above reasons, most courts allow parties to *recover in quasi-contract.* The measure of damages will be either *restitution* damages (the value of the benefit conferred by the plaintiff on the defendant) or *reliance* damages (expenditures the plaintiff made in partly performing or preparing to perform).

I. INTRODUCTION

A. **Nature of the problem:** During the performance of a contract, events may occur which were unexpected by either of the parties at the time of contracting, and which affect the feasibility or even the possibility of performing the contract. To deal with these kinds of unexpected events, the law provides that the parties may be *discharged* from performing the contract if:

[1] performance is *impossible* (the doctrine of *"impossibility"*);

[2] performance is not impossible but is much more *burdensome* or difficult than was originally expected (the closely-related doctrine of *"impracticability"*); or

[3] because of new events, the fundamental *purpose* of one of the parties has been *frustrated* (the doctrine of *"frustration"*).

If a party is "discharged" from performing for such a reason, he is *not liable* for breach of contract. See Rest. 2d, Ch. 11.

B. Risk allocation: The doctrines of impossibility, impracticability and frustration, discussed in this chapter, are essentially *gap fillers*. That is, these doctrines will be applied to discharge a party from performing only when *the parties themselves did not allocate the risk* of the events which have rendered performance impossible or impracticable, or which have frustrated the purpose of the contract.

  1. Parties' right to agree otherwise: Thus the parties are always free to agree that various contingencies which would render the contract impossible, etc., under the usual rules will *not* discharge the contract. Similarly, they are free to agree that certain contingencies *will* discharge the contract, even though these contingencies would not be sufficient, in the absence of an agreement, to fall within the doctrine of impossibility, etc.

C. Supervening impossibility: This chapter deals with *supervening* impossibility, i.e., impossibility which results from events occurring after the formation of the contract. Impossibility due to facts existing at the time of contracting (but unknown to one or both parties) is usually treated as mistake or fraud; see *supra*, p. 156.

D. Subjective vs. objective impossibility: Courts sometimes say that for impossibility to discharge a party, the impossibility must be *"objective"* rather than *"subjective."* As the Second Restatement puts it, "It is the difference between 'the thing cannot be done' and 'I cannot do it'." Rest. 2d, § 261, Comment e. It is often hard to tell whether a particular event renders performance "subjectively" or "objectively" impossible. The question arises most frequently in the following kinds of situations:

  1. Financial inability: If a party's ability to perform is destroyed by his own *insolvency* or lack of the necessary capital, he may *not* use the impossibility defense. The impossibility is "subjective," in this situation, since it is only from the viewpoint of the party who is financially incapacitated that performance appears impossible. C&P, p. 520.

  2. Strikes: If a *party's own employees* go on strike, most courts do not allow that party to use the impossibility defense. Some courts reach this result by saying that the struck party's inability to perform is "subjective," and that therefore she is not excused. Others hold that the inability is the struck party's "fault," thus denying her use of the doctrine. C&P, p. 507.

  3. Death or illness: When a party who has contracted to give personal services dies or becomes *too ill to perform*, it might be thought that her impossibility would be "subjective," and that therefore she would not be excused. However, the courts have taken the view that there *should* be a discharge in this situation, as long as it is clear that the contract was one for personal, non-delegable services. This subject is discussed further *infra*, p. 440.

  Note: Many modern courts, instead of trying to determine whether a particular event rendered performance "subjectively impossible" or "objectively impossible," simply try to determine whether the parties in fact allocated the risk of the event, and, if they did not, which party they would have cast the risk upon had they thought about it. In a case involving the insolvency of one party, for instance, a modern court might take the view that each contracting party impliedly bears the risk that it will be financially unable to perform, and would thus refuse to allow the impossibility defense. C&P, p. 520.

II. IMPOSSIBILITY OF PERFORMANCE

A. Supervening impossibility generally: Of the various kinds of events which can take the parties to a contract by surprise, the sort that present the clearest case for discharging the contract are those which render its performance *literally impossible*. The most common categories in which the court is likely to find literal impossibility are:

[1] *destruction* or other unavailability of the subject matter of the contract;

[2] failure of the agreed-upon *means of performance*;

[3] *death or incapacity* of a party; and

[4] *supervening illegality*.

B. Restatement approach: The Second Restatement illustrates the modern view of impossibility. (The Restatement doesn't use the term "impossibility" at all; it speaks only in terms of "impracticability," but uses this term to include cases that have traditionally been thought of as involving impossibility.) Here's what the Restatement says, in § 261:

"Where, after a contract is made, a party's performance is made *impracticable without his fault* by the occurrence of *an event the non-occurrence of which* was a *basic assumption* on which the contract was made, his duty to render that performance is *discharged*, unless the *language or the circumstances* indicate the contrary."

1. **Summary of Restatement approach:** So a party who wishes to be discharged on the grounds of impossibility/impracticability must show the following things:

   ❏ that the event occurred *after the contract was made*;

   ❏ that the event was one whose non-occurrence was a *"basic assumption"* on which the contract was made;

   ❏ that the event was not the *fault* of the party seeking the discharge; and

   ❏ that the *language or circumstances* don't dictate that discharge should be denied (e.g., because the parties *allocated the risk* of the event to the party now seeking to use the impossibility doctrine).

C. Destruction or unavailability of the subject matter: If performance of the contract involves particular goods, a particular building, or some other tangible item, which through the fault of neither party is *destroyed*, or otherwise made unavailable, the contract is *discharged*. The discharge of the contract will occur only where the particular subject matter is *essential* to the performance of the contract. If the subject matter is of collateral importance, the contract will be only partially discharged, as explained below.

1. *Taylor v. Caldwell:* The doctrine of impossibility through destruction of the subject matter was laid down in *Taylor v. Caldwell*, 122 Eng. Rep. 309 (K.B. 1863), discussed in the following example.

   Example: P contracts to hire D's music hall for a series of concerts. After the contract is signed, but before the first of the concerts, the hall is destroyed by fire. *Held*, D is discharged from performing, and his failure to perform is therefore not a breach of contract. The parties regarded the continued existence of the hall as the "foundation" of the contract, and the contract contained an "implied condition" that both parties would be excused if the hall ceased to exist. *Taylor v. Caldwell, supra.*

2. **Determining subject matter of the contract:** The most difficult issue in the destruction-of-essential-subject-matter cases is that of determining whether the contract calls for a particular subject matter, or merely a *kind* of subject matter, of which the destroyed items are one example. The difficulty is illustrated by the following example.

> **Example:** Brick Co. is a manufacturer of standard size bricks used for ordinary construction work. The company contracts to sell 1 million bricks to Contractor, to be delivered on June 1. Brick Co. expects to supply the bricks from its own production, and Contractor assumes that this is how Brick Co. will obtain the bricks. But Contractor does not care whether the bricks are Brick Co.'s own product, or are bought by Brick Co. from some other source. The contract does not specify where Brick Co. is to procure the bricks. Just as Brick Co. is preparing to manufacture the bricks which it expects to supply to Contractor, its plant is burned down. Brick Co. could buy the bricks from some other source, but the market price is at this point higher than the price which is set by the contract. Does the destruction of Brick Co.'s plant discharge Brick Co. from performing the contract under the impossibility doctrine?
>
> Most courts would probably hold that since the contract does not specifically require Brick Co. to produce the bricks itself, and since it could perform by buying them elsewhere (albeit at a loss), Brick Co. is *not* discharged. These courts would in effect be holding that the subject matter of the contract was any standard bricks, not just bricks produced by Brick Co.'s own plant. If, on the other hand, the contract explicitly required production of bricks by Brick Co., in its own plant, the contract probably would be discharged. See C&P, pp. 499-500. Also, even if the contract said nothing about where the bricks were to be produced, Brick Co. might obtain a discharge under the doctrine of *impracticability*, discussed below.

Note: UCC § 2-615(a), discussed below, would discharge Brick Co. only if the continued existence of its plant was a "basic assumption on which the contract was made." This test in effect lumps the defenses of impossibility and impracticability together.

3. **General rule:** If property which the performing party expected to use is destroyed, that party is discharged only if the destroyed property was *specifically referred to* in the contract, or at least understood by *both* parties to be the property that would be used. It is not enough that the party who seeks discharge by impossibility intended to use the destroyed property. This rule is applied in construction cases, building repair cases, and contracts for the sale of goods.

4. **Contract to build a structure from scratch:** Suppose that a building contractor contracts to construct a building *from scratch* on particular land. (Distinguish this from renovating an existing building, discussed in Par. (5) below.) If the building is *destroyed by fire* when the contractor has almost finished, may he claim impossibility, so as to be discharged from the contract? Or must he start all over again?

   a. **Majority rule:** Most courts hold that the contractor in this situation may *not* use the defense of impossibility, on the theory that the contract did not provide for the building of the particular structure that was destroyed, but simply for the building of *some* structure. Under this view, the builder can and must begin anew.

b. **Recovery where impossibility defense allowed:** Even in those courts which *would* allow the contractor to use the impossibility defense where her partially completed building is destroyed, the contractor will probably not come out whole. The impossibility defense *merely permits her to avoid having to rebuild, and to avoid liability for damages for breach.* It will not help her to *recover on the contract for the work she did before the destruction.* However, it is possible that the contractor will be able to recover in quasi-contract for the value of the partially-built structure as it existed just before the destruction.

c. **Destruction due to soil conditions:** Suppose the structure being built is destroyed not by fire but as the result of *poor soil conditions* (e.g., the building is built on quicksand, which caves in before completion). Here, the contractor is even less likely to be discharged than in the destruction-by-fire scenario. Courts typically hold that the contractor implicitly *assumed the risk* that the soil conditions would not be appropriate. See, e.g., *Stees v. Leonard,* 20 Minn. 494 (Minn. 1874).

5. **Building renovation:** Where a party contracts to *renovate or repair* an *existing* building, on the other hand, he will usually be *discharged* if the building is destroyed. As some courts would put it, the building to be renovated or repaired was the specific subject matter of the contract, and its destruction discharges the parties' obligations. Or as a modern court might reason, the continued existence of the building was a basic assumption upon which the contract was based.

a. **Quasi-contractual recovery:** The owner of the destroyed premises is also discharged from making payment on the contract, since his duty of payment was constructively conditional upon the contractor's performance — see *supra*, p. 215. However, the contractor will be *entitled to recover in quasi-contract*, at least for the value of the work which he did before the premises were destroyed (i.e., his restitutionary interest measured as of the time immediately before the destruction.) Some courts permit the contractor to recover not only his restitutionary interest, but also his reliance damages, including materials that were destroyed at the jobsite, and other expenses incurred in preparation (e.g., tests, drawings, etc.). See C&P, p. 503.

6. **Contracts for the sale of goods:** Where a contract is for the sale of goods, the "subject matter" of the contract may be destroyed in any of several ways. First, the seller's means of obtaining or producing the goods may be destroyed or otherwise rendered unavailable. Secondly, the contract may call for the sale of particular identifiable goods, which are destroyed after the contract is made. Thirdly, the contract may not refer to specific, unique goods, but instead call for any conforming goods that the seller wishes to take out of his inventory. In this last situation, the destruction or loss of the goods may occur before they are shipped, during shipment, or after delivery.

a. **Destruction of source of supply or means of production:** The contract may contemplate that the seller is to procure the goods from a particular source, or that he is to produce them himself. If the source becomes unavailable, or the seller's own means of production is rendered unusable, the seller will frequently try to obtain a discharge from the contract by using the doctrine of impossibility.

The relevant UCC section in this situation is § 2-615(a), which provides that unless otherwise agreed, "delay in delivery or non-delivery … is not a breach of [seller's] duty under a contract for sale if performance as agreed has been made impracticable by the occurrence of a contingency the non-occurrence of which was a ***basic assumption on which the contract was made.…***" This test is a non-mechanical one, and is designed to allow the court to "allocate the risk" between the parties, based on what it thinks the parties would have done if they had thought about the question.

i.   **Failure of source of supply:**   If the contract makes it clear that the parties agreed that the goods would be procured by the seller from a ***given source***, failure of production by that source "should, if possible, be ***excused*** since production by an agreed source is without a more basic assumption of the contract." (Comment 5 to § 2-615.) But if the seller is excused because of the failure of his source of supply, he may be required to turn over to the buyer his own right to sue his supplier for breach. *Id.*

ii. **Failure of production:**   If the parties contemplate that the seller will ***produce the goods herself***, and her means of doing so is destroyed by factors beyond her control, she will be discharged from performing, on the grounds that the destruction of facilities was a "contingency the non-occurrence of which was a basic assumption of which the contract was made.…"

iii. **Partial failure:**   If the failure of the seller's source of supply or means of production affects only ***a part*** of his capacity to perform, "he must ***allocate*** production and deliveries among his customers but ***may at his option include regular customers not then under contract*** as well as his own requirements for further manufacture. He may so allocate in ***any manner which is fair and reasonable***." (§ 2-615(b)).

   (1) **Reasonable allocation:** In other words, the seller may give the buyer under the contract only a portion of the goods called for under the contract, as long as he is ***allocating the goods among his various customers in a reasonable manner***.

b. **Destruction of identified goods:**   Some contracts call for the delivery of particular, *identified*, unique goods. A contract for the sale of a particular painting is an obvious example of such a contract. A contract for the sale of a piece of machinery, prior to the signing of which the buyer tests and selects a particular machine in seller's inventory, is another. If after the signing of the contract the goods are destroyed, lost, or otherwise harmed by the negligence of one party, that party must of course bear the loss. But if casualty to the goods occurs without fault of either party, § 2-613 sets up special rules for allocating the loss.

i.   **Where risk of loss has not passed:**   If the casualty occurs "before the risk of loss passes to the buyer," the contract is "avoided" if the loss is total. (§ 2-613(a)). (The time at which the risk of loss passes to the buyer is determined by a series of rules which are discussed below.) "Avoidance" of the contract where the risk is still on the seller at the time of casualty means that the seller in effect receives the benefit of the impossibility defense — she is discharged from the contract, and is not liable for breach. The buyer is also discharged.

ii. **Where risk of loss has passed to buyer:** If the "risk of loss" has already passed to the buyer before the casualty (as it might in an "FOB Seller's Plant" contract — see *infra*), the buyer must suffer the full effect of the loss. That is, he is liable to the seller for the full contract price even if he never gets any value from the goods.

iii. **Partial loss:** If the goods are only *partially lost*, or have *deteriorated* in such a way that they do not conform to the contract, and the risk of loss has not yet passed to the buyer, the buyer can inspect the goods and has a choice between either cancelling the contract (in which case neither party is liable), or accepting the goods with an allowance for the non-conformity (but with no right to sue for breach). (§ 2-613(b).)

c. **Goods not identified at the time of contracting:** In the most common case, the contract will call for goods to be taken from the seller's *general inventory*, not for particular identified goods. In this situation, the UCC provides precise rules for determining who bears the loss when casualty occurs at various stages. See § 2-509.

i. **Destruction of inventory or source of supply:** If the seller's whole inventory is destroyed, or his source of supply becomes unavailable, the question is resolved, as stated above, by determining whether the continued inventory or source of supply was a "basic assumption" when the contract was made.

ii. **Contracts requiring shipment:** Once the seller selects particular goods from his inventory or acquires particular goods from another source, the passage of the risk of loss will depend mostly on how the goods are to be delivered. In the usual case where the contract requires the seller to ship the goods by a carrier (e.g., a truck or plane, but not one belonging to the seller herself), the risk of loss will depend on whether the contract is a "shipment" contract or a "destination" contract.

(1) **FOB Seller's plant:** If the contract states that the seller's only obligation is to deliver the goods to the carrier (this is a "shipment" contract and is usually indicated by the words *"FOB Seller's plant"*), the *risk of loss passes to the buyer as soon as the seller delivers the goods to the carrier.* If the carrier loses the goods, the buyer bears the loss, and must pay the purchase price.

(2) **FOB Buyer's place of business:** If, on the other hand, the contract obligates the seller to see that the carrier delivers the goods to the buyer (a "destination" contract, usually indicated by the words *"FOB Buyer's place of business"*), the risk of loss does not pass to the buyer until the carrier actually delivers. In such a contract, if the *carrier loses the goods*, the *seller bears the risk* of loss. She is liable for breach of contract, just as if she had never delivered the goods to the carrier.

D. **Impossibility of intangible but essential mode of performance:** Just as a tangible object needed for performance may be destroyed or rendered unavailable (see above), so an *intangi-*

ble aspect of a performance may be rendered impossible. If this intangible aspect of the contract is an ***essential and critical*** part of the contract, the entire contract may be discharged.

1. **Defective or unrealistic specifications:** Contracts, particularly ones made with the government, often require a party to conform to particular ***specifications*** furnished by the other party. Not infrequently, these specifications turn out to be either defective (in the sense that they will not produce the desired result if followed) or unrealistic (in the sense that they are difficult or impossible to meet, although if met they would produce the desired result.) The party who is obligated to meet the specifications generally seeks to escape the contract by a claim of impossibility, and also frequently seeks to recover expenses which she has incurred in trying to meet the impossible requirements. The success of her impossibility claim usually turns on whether the party furnishing the specifications is held to have impliedly warranted that they would be feasible and produce the desired result.

   a. **Warranty of specifications:** When one party unilaterally prepares the specifications, most courts hold that it ***impliedly warrants*** that satisfactory performance will result if the specifications are followed. This is particularly likely to be held to be the case where the specifications are prepared by the ***government***. If the specifications are defective in that they do not produce the result required under the contract, the performing party is often ***discharged*** from the contract, and is also awarded the expenses he incurred in trying to perform. Alternatively, the party who prepared the specifications may be held to have breached an implied warranty (that the plans were adequate) and the other party may recover damages for the breach. See, e.g., *U.S. v. Spearin*, 248 U.S. 132 (1918).

   b. **State of the art not sufficient to meet specifications:** If, on the other hand, the difficulty is that current technology is not sufficient to meet the specifications themselves (rather than that meeting the specifications does not produce the contracted-for result), the supplier will often be held to have assumed the risk that she would not be able to develop the necessary "break through," and she will not be discharged or awarded costs of attempting to perform.

      i. **Mutual mistake analysis:** But where both parties believe, at the time of contracting, that the state of the art is sufficient to allow the specifications to be met, courts sometimes discharge both parties on the grounds that a "mutual mistake" has been made.

      ii. **Specifications drawn by vendor:** If the specifications are drawn up by the ***vendor***, rather than the purchaser, and it turns out that the state of the art is not sufficient to enable the vendor to meet the specifications, he is unlikely to be excused from performing. In this situation, he will almost inevitably be held to have ***implicitly borne the risk*** of not being able to make the necessary breakthrough.

2. **Impossibility due to failure of third person:** A promisor may be unable to perform because of a third person's failure to cooperate with him. The most common example of this is where a ***middleman*** contracts to supply goods that he and his buyer both expect him to procure from a given source, and the source cannot or will not supply the goods to the

seller. In this situation, the courts have in some cases allowed the seller to use the defense of impossibility.

a. **Source not specified in contract:** If the contract *does not specify the source* from which the seller is to obtain the goods, then the seller whose source does not pan out is almost always *out of luck.* This is so not only where the supplier simply refuses to deal with the seller, but also where the supplier breaches a contract that she has with the seller to supply the goods.

b. **Where seller is unable to make contract with supplier:** If the contract between the seller and buyer contemplates that the seller will procure the goods from a *given supplier*, and that supplier is *unwilling to contract* to sell the items to the seller, the seller may generally *not* assert an impossibility claim. The seller will normally be held to have *impliedly borne the risk that she would be unable to make the necessary contract* to procure the goods.

c. **Where seller's supply contract is breached:** But if the contract contemplates that seller will arrange to get the goods from a particular supplier, seller does make a contract with this supplier, and the supplier *breaches*, most courts *will* discharge the seller from his contract with the buyer, on the grounds of impossibility (or, in the jargon of UCC § 2-615, "impracticability").

Example: Selland contracts to buy four school bus bodies from King. (Selland plans to put each body on top of a chassis that it will buy from another source, GM.) The written agreement states that the bodies will be supplied by Superior Manufacturing. After the contract is signed, Superior goes out of business without ever delivering the bodies to King. Meanwhile, Selland has purchased the chassis from GM, and has to sell them at a loss when it can't get the bodies. Selland sues King for its losses on the chassis.

Held, for King (D). Supply of the bus bodies made by Superior was a basic assumption on which the contract was made, especially since Superior was specified in the contract as the source of the bodies. Neither party had any reason to anticipate the financial weakness of Superior, or that it would go out of business. Therefore, King cannot be said to have assumed the risk of Superior's insolvency. Consequently, the case is covered by UCC § 2-615, and King is not liable for breach. *Selland Pontiac-GMC, Inc. v. King*, 384 N.W.2d 490 (Minn. Ct. App. 1986).

Note: In the above example, the court was clearly justified in discharging King on the grounds that the Selland-King contract was expressly made conditional on Superior's performance of his contract with Seller. In other words, the parties can be said to have expressly allocated the risk of Superior's non-performance to Selland. In other situations, however, the court may conclude that the middleman seller and his buyer implicitly agreed that the risk of default by the seller's supplier would be borne by the seller. In determining whether to allow the impossibility defense in this middleman situation, the question to ask is "How did the parties allocate the risk?" If the answer is unclear, the question is then "How would the parties have allocated the risk had they thought about it?"

d. Breach by third persons in non-goods contracts: In non-goods cases, the same considerations generally apply to a party whose performance is rendered impossible by a third person's breach. If the contract is held to be conditional on that third person's performance, there will be a discharge. If the party whose performance requires a third person's performance can be said to have impliedly borne the risk of that third person's breach, she will not be discharged.

E. Death or illness: The *death or illness* of someone connected with a contract may prompt an attempt by either party to have the contract discharged for impossibility. The result depends in large part on whether the contract called for (or contemplated) performance by the particular person.

1. Death or illness of a party: First, let's look at the death or illness of a *party to the contract.*

a. No personal services by that party: If a contract does *not* call for significant personal services by a party, that party's *death* or *incapacity* generally does *not* terminate or discharge the contract. The reason for this is that the ill or dead person's duties can be *delegated* to some other person, and the contract continued. For instance, if a party is merely to pay money, or do some other duty that could easily be done by another, there will be no discharge.

Example: Boss hires Guy to run Boss' candy store, which Boss owns as a sole proprietorship. The contract is for two years. Boss is an absentee owner, who checks the books once a month and pays the bills. One year into the agreement, Boss dies.

Boss' estate will not be entitled to have the contract discharged, because the Boss-Guy agreement does not contemplate that material personal services will be performed by Boss, and whatever administrative tasks Boss used to do can be performed by someone else. Therefore, Guy can demand that Boss' estate fulfill the agreement.

b. Personal services by that party: But if the contract provides that performance shall be made by a *particular individual* who is a party, that person's death or incapacity will *discharge both parties* from the contract. This is true not only where the contract explicitly requires performance by the particular party, but also where the surrounding circumstances indicate that a personal relationship was intended.

Example: Same initial facts as the previous example. Now, 10 months into the contract, assume that Guy becomes permanently disabled, so he can't run the store anymore. Since the contract manifests an intention that Guy be the one who does the actual task of running the store, both parties will be discharged on account of Guy's disability — Guy can't sue Boss for breach, but neither can Boss sue Guy.

2. Death or illness of a third person: A contract may similarly be discharged by virtue of the death or illness of some *third person*, who is necessary to performance of the contract but who is not himself a party to it. Again, the issue is whether that the contract language or the surrounding circumstances indicate that the third person's participation was a basic assumption on which the parties both relied, and the risk of which was not allocated by the contract to the party now seeking a discharge.

Example: P, a theater owner, contracts with D, the manager of Great Lungs Opera Co., an opera company, whereby D promises to supply Great Lungs for a three week engagement. Maria Callous, the principal diva of Great Lungs, without whom the company cannot reasonably perform, becomes ill. D will be discharged from the contract as a result of Callous' illness, unless there is some indication that the parties intended to place the risk of such illness on D.

3. **Threat of illness or death:** A personal service contract may be discharged because a person necessary for its performance reasonably *fears* that he will suffer serious illness or death if he performs.

   Example: D, an impresario, contracts to present a play starring Walter Huston in P's theater. Prior to performance, Huston reasonably becomes concerned that he is getting throat cancer, and on the advice of his doctor cancels and undergoes medical treatment. It turns out that Huston is not getting cancer after all. P sues D for breach.

   Held, for D. Huston's fears were reasonable, and his cancellation discharged D from the contract. See *Wasserman Theatrical Enterprise, Inc. v. Harris*, 137 Conn. 371 (1950).

4. **Must not be a contrary allocation of risk:** Again, you must always keep in mind that the general principle stated here — that the death or illness of one who was to perform significant services under the contract will lead to discharge of the contract — applies only if the parties *have not allocated the risk otherwise* (to the person now seeking discharge).

   Example: Same facts as the prior example (the impresario presenting Walter Huston). Now, assume that Huston's stated fears of illness were completely unreasonable, and that he was really just trying to weasel out of his deal with D, the impresario. Here, even though D would not be at fault vis a vis P (the theater owner), a court would probably hold that in a contract between a theater owner and an impresario, the impresario normally bears the risk that the "talent" will break his contract with the impresario. If so, D would not have been discharged under the impossibility doctrine.

F. **Supervening illegality:** If performance of a contract would, at the time of contracting, be prohibited by law, the contract itself is called "illegal," and neither party is required to perform it. This kind of contract is dealt with in the chapter on illegality, *infra,* p. 460. But it may happen that a contract is legal at the time it is entered into, but its performance is prevented by a subsequent change in the law. In this situation, the *"supervening illegality"* is treated as a kind of impossibility, and the contract is discharged.

   Example: Contractor contracts to renovate a building owned by Owner in a coastal city, the work to be performed during October. A hurricane strikes the city in September, and the city forbids any new construction projects during the month of October because of the ensuing chaos. Performance is impossible, and both parties will be discharged from the contract.

1. **UCC:** The UCC makes the "supervening illegality" defense available to a *seller.* § 2-615(a) provides that "delay in delivery or non-delivery in whole or in part by a seller ... is not breach of his duty ... if performance as agreed has been made impracticable ... by

compliance in good faith with any ***applicable foreign or domestic governmental regulation or order*** whether or not it later proves to be invalid."

> **Note:** The UCC does *not* make the "supervening illegality" defense available to a *buyer*. Nor does it explicitly give the buyer a general impossibility defense analogous to that given to seller where a contract has been made "impracticable by the occurrence of a contingency the non-occurrence of which was a basic assumption on which the contract was made...." (§ 2-615(a)). See the discussion of this provision *supra*, p. 435.

G. Temporary impossibility: Events may render performance of the contract only ***temporarily*** impossible. The illness of a party who is to perform personal services, for instance, may merely prevent him from performing on time, not forever. "Temporary impossibility" ***suspends the duty of performing*** until the impossibility ends. See Rest. 2d, § 269. If, however, after the temporary impossibility ceases, performance would be much more burdensome on either party than had it occurred on time, the contract may be completely discharged. Hardships on both the party whose performance is temporarily prevented, and on the other party who is awaiting performance, are weighed in determining when the contract should be discharged rather than merely suspended.

> **Example:** Seller contracts to custom-manufacture and supply certain widgets to Buyer, delivery to occur no later than August 1 (90 days away). It is important to Buyer's business that she have the goods on time. Shortly after execution of the contract, Seller's workers go on strike.
>
> While the strike is going on, Seller's duty of performance will be temporarily suspended. If, during the course of the strike, it becomes clear that the strike is likely to prevent Seller from timely fulfilling the contract, Buyer will be entitled to cancel the contract (discharging both parties from liability for non-performance), so that she can procure a substitute supply. For instance, if the strike had still not been settled by July 1, and it would take Seller or any substitute at least three weeks to manufacture the goods, Buyer would clearly be entitled to cancel at that point, because the burden on Buyer of continuing to be locked into the contract with Seller would be unfairly great.

III. IMPRACTICABILITY

A. Impracticability as a kind of impossibility: In the situations considered previously, performance of the contract was a literal impossibility. In some cases, however, performance is extremely costly, time-consuming, or otherwise ***impracticable***, though not literally impossible. Many modern courts ***equate "extreme impracticability" with "impossibility."***

According to these courts, if, due to changed circumstances, performance would be infeasible from a commercial viewpoint (because of an extreme increase in cost, a tremendous increase in the time needed for performance, etc.), the promisor is excused just as she would be if performance were literally impossible. Rest. 2d, § 261. See also Rest. 2d. Ch. 11, Introductory Note and Reporter's Note.

> **Example:** D, who is building a bridge, contracts to procure all his requirements for gravel for the project from P's land, and to pay for it at a fixed rate per yard. D is able

to supply over half his needs by excavating the gravel above the water level on P's property. He refuses to excavate the gravel from below water level, however, on the grounds that such excavation would be at least ten times as costly as above-ground excavation.

Held, D is excused from excavating below the water level. The fact that performance would have been somewhat more expensive than anticipated by D would not have been enough to excuse him. "But where the difference in cost is so great [as to have] the effect…of making performance impracticable, the situation is not different from that of a total absence of earth and gravel." *Mineral Park Land Co. v. Howard*, 172 Cal. 289 (1916).

1. **Cost increase must be extreme:** If the defense of commercial impracticability is to be based upon an *increase in the cost of performance*, the increase must be *extreme*. Also, it must be shown that the contract itself has not explicitly or implicitly *cast the risk of impracticability* upon the party seeking to assert that defense. See Rest. 2d, § 261, and Comment d and Illustr. 9 thereto.

   a. **Foreseeability:** One factor in whether the parties cast the risk of impracticability on the supplier (the party seeking discharge) is how *foreseeable* the increase in costs was — the more foreseeable, the less likely it is that the parties intended that the buyer of the goods or services would bear the risk of a large cost increase.

      i. **Fixed price contracts:** Thus if the parties agree on a *fixed price* for a good or service, and the risk of a rise in the market price was foreseeable, the court will almost certainly hold that the parties *implicitly allocated the risk* of the price rise on the party agreeing to supply the good or service for the fixed price. Cases involving extreme run-ups in the cost of *energy*, for instance, have generally been resolved in favor of the buyer, and against the seller's claim of impracticability.

      Example: Gulf Oil Co. agrees to supply jet fuel to Eastern Airlines on a long-term basis. Because Gulf has agreed to be bound by so-called "posted prices" which fail to keep up with price increases, Gulf finds itself obligated to supply Eastern with jet fuel priced on the basis of $5 per barrel at a time when the free-market price is $11 per barrel (due to the run-up in OPEC prices in 1973-74). Gulf tries to escape the contract on grounds of commercial impracticability.

      Held, for Eastern. Even if this run-up in prices constituted a great hardship for Gulf (which the court finds not to be the case), Gulf cannot prevail with its impracticability defense because the events associated with the so-called energy crises were *reasonably foreseeable* at the time the contract was executed. At the time the parties signed, they were aware of the volatile Middle East situation, repeated interruptions to normal oil trade, and the arbitrary power of governments who controlled oil deposits. Since Gulf was aware of the possibility of sharp price rises at the time it signed, it must bear the risk of those rises. *Eastern Airlines, Inc. v. Gulf Oil Corp.*, 415 F.Supp. 429 (S.D.Fla. 1975).

B. **UCC in accord with modern view:** The UCC is in accord with the modern view that extreme impracticability will excuse performance, at least on the *seller's* part. § 2-615(a) provides that the seller's non-delivery, or a delay in delivery, is excused "if performance as agreed has been made ***impracticable*** by the ***occurrence of a contingency*** the ***non-occurrence of which was a basic assumption*** on which the contract was made...."

1. **What is impracticable under the Code:**   Comment 4 to § 2-615 elaborates on the kinds of things that may be considered impracticable:

   > ***"Increased cost alone does not excuse performance*** unless the rise in cost is due to some ***unforeseen contingency which alters the essential nature*** of the performance. Neither is a rise or collapse in the market in itself a justification, for that is exactly the type of business risk which business contracts made at fixed prices are intended to cover. But a ***severe shortage*** of raw materials or of supplies due to a contingency such as ***war***, embargo, ***local crop failure***, unforeseen s***hutdown of major sources of supply***, or the like, which either causes a ***marked increase in cost*** or altogether ***prevents the seller from securing supplies*** necessary to his performance, is within the contemplation of this section."

   a. **Price rises:**   Sellers have been almost completely ***unsuccessful*** in arguing that ***extreme cost increases*** should relieve them from having to perform. The *Eastern Airlines* case, *supra*, is an illustration of the tendency of sellers to lose under UCC § 2-615. White and Summers (p. 130) concur with this trend, saying, "In our judgment an increase in price, even a radical increase in price, is the thing that contracts are designed to protect against."

2. **Use by buyer:**   UCC § 2-615 on its face seems to allows only sellers to escape a contract on grounds of impracticability. But Comment 9 to § 2-615 seems to contemplate giving the ***buyer*** the exemption in certain circumstances (e.g., the buyer holds a defense contract and is buying under a sub-contract; if the main contract is cancelled, the buyer may be able to escape the sub-contract). Also, common-law principles might be used to give the buyer the impracticability defense, even if one interprets the UCC as not giving the buyer a statutory defense.

   a. **Frustration of purpose:**   Observe that when the buyer is given the impracticability defense, the result is very similar to that given under the doctrine of ***frustration of purpose***, discussed *infra*, p. 445. That is, the buyer is generally not unable to pay — rather, she finds it not worthwhile to trade the contract price in return for the thing that was contracted for.

3. **Allocation of risk by parties:**   In both UCC and non-UCC cases, the parties are always free to ***make their own allocation of the risk of impracticability,*** and the courts will ***enforce*** that allocation. So, for instance, if the parties decide that the seller should not have the right to raise the impracticability defense in the event that all potential suppliers to the seller fail, the court will refuse to allow the defense in that scenario even though the requirements for impracticability might otherwise be met.

   a. **Implicit allocation:**   This type of re-allocation by the parties of the risk of impracticability can be either explicit or ***implicit***. Thus the UCC commentary to § 2-615 says that the impracticability defense "[does] not apply when the contingency in question is ***sufficiently foreshadowed*** at the time of contracting to be ***included among the business risks which are fairly to be regarded as part of the dickered terms,*** either consciously or as a matter of ***reasonable, commercial interpretation from the circumstances.***"

   i. **Risk of technological breakthrough:** For instance, suppose that Seller and Buyer agree that Seller will develop a not-yet-existing product to meet certain specifications, and both parties are aware that a ***technological breakthrough*** will be required in order for Seller to perform. A court would probably conclude, as a matter of "reasonable, commercial interpretation from the circumstances," that the risk of non-occurrence of the breakthrough was to rest upon Seller, in which case Seller would ***not*** be excused by impracticability if the breakthrough did not develop despite Seller's best efforts.

   ii. **Foreseeability and relative expertise:** When a court has to decide whether the party whose performance is arguably made impractical by a particular event implicitly bore the risk of that event, two important factors are:

❏ the ***foreseeability*** of the risk (the more foreseeable it was, the more likely it is that the performing party will be found to have borne the risk of it); and

❏ the degree to which the performing party has ***greater expertise*** in evaluating the risk than the other (the greater the performing party's relative expertise, the more likely that party is to be found to have assumed the risk).

Example: Contractor contracts to build a house for Owner, which both parties know will require excavation of a 10-foot-deep basement. The contract calls for a fixed price, and makes no mention of the risk that when Contractor excavates for the basement, Contractor may find large boulders that are unusually expensive to excavate.

Given the high foreseeability of unusually-difficult excavation conditions, and the greater familiarity with excavation issues that a contractor has, compared with a homeowner, the court will likely conclude that Contractor bore the risk that excavation would be much more expensive than usual. In that event, Contractor will not be excused even if the excavation turns out to be so expensive that the contract will end up being a loss for him.

IV. FRUSTRATION OF PURPOSE

  A. **Frustration of purpose distinguished from impossibility:** Events may occur which destroy one party's ***purpose*** in entering into the contract, even though performance of the contract itself is not rendered impossible. Such events are said to constitute ***"frustration of purpose,"*** or "frustration of the venture." Where one party's purpose is completely or almost completely frustrated by such supervening events, most courts will discharge him from performing. See Rest. 2d, § 265.

    1. **The Coronation cases:** The doctrine of "frustration of purpose" had its origin in what are usually called the "Coronation cases." The example which follows is based on one of these cases.

Example: P rents his apartment to D for a two-day period. D's purpose in making this contract is to view the coronation of King Edward VII; D agrees to pay a price far beyond the ordinary rental value of the apartment for this privilege. The coronation is canceled because the King is taken ill. D does not use the premises, refuses to make the payment, and is sued by P.

Held, D is excused from performing because his essential purpose in entering the contract has been frustrated; the taking place of the Coronation "was regarded by both contracting parties as the foundation of the contract." Performance is not, strictly speaking, impossible, since D could stay in the apartment for two days and watch the sights. But because he would not derive any benefit from doing so, he must be excused from performing. *Krell v. Henry*, 2 K.B. 740 (1903).

2. **Restatement formulation:** The Restatement gives a useful formulation for the frustration doctrine: "Where, after a contract is made, a party's ***principal purpose*** is ***substantially frustrated without his fault*** by the occurrence of ***an event the non-occurrence of which was a basic assumption on which the contract was made,*** his remaining duties to render performance are ***discharged***, unless the ***language or the circumstances indicate the contrary.***" Rest. 2d § 265.

3. **Usually used by buyers of goods and services:** What is the ***difference*** between the defenses of ***impracticability*** and ***frustration***? After all, the two defenses are similar in that each gives a party a chance to escape from a bargain that has turned out to be unfavorable on account of the occurrence of an event the non-occurrence of which was a basic assumption on which the contract was made. The main practical difference between the two is that:

   [1] where it is the ***seller or supplier*** of goods, land or services who wishes to escape the bargain, that party typically claims impracticability; whereas

   [2] where it is a ***buyer or recipient*** of goods, land or services who wishes to escape the bargain, that party typically claims frustration.

   C&P Hnbk (6th), § 13.12.

B. **Factors to be considered:** In determining whether the defense of frustration of purpose should be allowed, the courts consider ***several factors***:

   ❏ the extent to which the event that thwarted the promisor's object was ***foreseeable*** (and foreseen) by the parties when the contract was made — the less foreseeable the event, the more likely the court is to excuse performance under the frustration doctrine;

   ❏ the extent to which the parties did or did not explicitly or implicitly ***allocate the risk*** of the event to the promisor — if the parties allocated the risk to the promisor, the court will not excuse performance;

   ❏ the extent to which the event deprived the promise of ***all*** (as opposed to just some) of his anticipated benefit from the contract — the more ***complete*** the thwarting of benefit, the more likely the court is to excuse performance.

   ❏ whether the party seeking discharge was ***at fault*** in bringing about (or failing to guard against) the event — major fault on that party's part will normally block use of the defense.

Example: In August, 1941, D leases property from P, for purposes of running a new-car dealership and a gas station. Shortly thereafter, the United States enters Would War II, and the Government sharply restricts the sales of new cars. P waives a lease restriction, thereby allowing D to use the premises for purposes other than the dealership and gas station. But D declines to make alternative use of the property, and vacates, claiming that he is released from the lease because of frustration.

Held, D is not entitled to the defense of frustration. First, it was quite foreseeable to the parties at the time the lease was negotiated that the U.S. might enter the War, and might restrict new-car sales. Secondly, D's primary business of selling new cars was not entirely nullified, but merely curtailed (albeit substantially) by the regulations; therefore, his ability to obtain benefits from the lease was not entirely frustrated. (Also, his degree of frustration was eased by the fact that he could have used the premises for any other reasonable purpose.) *Lloyd v. Murphy,* 153 P.2d 47 (Cal. 1944).

1. **Foreseeability and the allocation of risk:** The first two factors listed above — foreseeability and allocation of risk — are really different aspects of the same issue.

    a. **Easy to foresee:** If the parties *foresaw* the possibility of the event (or at least the possibility of the general category of events of which the particular event was an instance) in question, the contract's failure to explicitly excuse the promisor if the event should occur probably indicates that the parties ***intended that the promisor bear the risk of that event.***

        Example: Elder, aged 90, buys a lifetime annuity from Insurer for $100,000, under which Elder will receive $2,000 per month for the rest of his life. Two weeks later (before the first monthly payment is even made), Elder dies of a heart attack.

        If Elder's estate tries to recoup the $100,000 on the grounds that Elder's purpose in entering the contract has been frustrated, the court is likely to hold that it is quite foreseeable that a 90-year-old might die soon after the making of such a contract, and that the agreement implicitly allocated this risk to Elder (in return for Insurer's bearing the risk that it would have to pay Elder far more than $100,000 if he lived to be, say, 100).

        i. **Hard to foresee:** Conversely, if the event was one that was ***hard to foresee*** (so that the parties probably did not in fact foresee it), then the contract's failure to excuse the promisor in such an event does ***not*** justify the inference that the parties intended to allocate the risk of the event to the promisor.

2. **Extreme economic dislocation:** Often, a party who has agreed to buy or pay for goods, land or services relies on ***extreme economic dislocation*** as the reason she should be allowed to escape from the bargain by use of the frustration defense. For instance, due to some macro-economic event, the good or service for which the plaintiff has agreed to pay a fixed price suddenly becomes ***vastly less valuable*** than indicated by the contract price. In such cases, the argument is typically not that the party seeking avoidance (usually a buyer) cannot physically pay for her side of the bargain, but rather, that requiring her to pay will ***cause her serious economic loss*** of a sort that neither party had reason to anticipate.

a. **Usually unsuccessful:** Such claims by buyers based on a plunge in the market value of the contracted-for good or service typically *fail*. There are several reasons courts look with disfavor on this type of claim. But the most common is probably that in the circumstances, a market-price plunge — no matter how great — was *not the sort of event the non-occurrence of which was a basic assumption* on which the contract was based. In other words, the court is likely to take the position that where buyer and seller agree on a *fixed price* or fee for some good or service, allocating the *risk of a plunge* in market prices to the buyer (and the risk of a sharp *rise* in market prices to the *seller*) is the *very purpose* of the contract.

   i. **Great Recession and the plunge in house prices:** Consider, for instance, the *"Great Recession"* of 2008-09, in which residential real estate prices dropped precipitously, by percentages that had not been seen since the Great Depression of the 1930s. A number of homeowners who took out mortgages argued that they should be at least temporarily spared from foreclosure by use of the doctrine of frustration of purpose, given that the price drop left them *"under water,"* i.e., with a property worth less than the balance of the outstanding mortgage. These claims have virtually all *failed*.

   Example: P takes out a $267,000 home mortgage loan on her Arizona home from X, a bank, which eventually assigns its rights to D, a mortgage servicer. The Great Recession occurs, causing the market value of P's home to drop to less than 50% of the amount then owed by P on the mortgage. P falls behind in her payments, and D begins a foreclosure proceeding. P brings a separate suit to enjoin D from continuing the foreclosure. Among various arguments, P asserts that she should be permitted to use the frustration doctrine to be relieved from her loan obligations. More precisely, she contends that "[t]he non-occurrence of extreme real estate depression . . . and the non-occurrence of a drastic loss of value in the Property, were basic assumptions made by the parties under the loan contract," and that "[n]either Plaintiff nor [X] foresaw the market downturn." P alleges, in essence, that since the property is now worth less than half of the outstanding mortgage amount, her purpose of taking out an economically sensible mortgage has been frustrated by the price collapse.

   Held (at least on this point), for D. In Arizona, "[u]nder the frustration of purpose doctrine ... *'mere economic impracticality is no defense* to performance of a contract.'" Therefore, even though the "sudden depreciation" in the value of P's property may have rendered her loan agreement uneconomical, she is not entitled to avoid that agreement by use of the frustration doctrine. *Bean v. BAC Home Loans Servicing, L.P.,* 2012 WL 10349 (D. Ariz. 2012).

   Note: Although the court in *Bean* did not say so, the result there is consistent with the requirement that the party seeking to use frustration (or impracticability) must show that the contract did not explicitly or implicitly *assign to that party the risk of the type of unlikely event in question.* (See p. 444.) If the lender and borrower in *Bean* had thought about the risk of a "sharp decline in home values" at the time they entered into the loan, both would almost certainly have understood that the owner/borrower, not the lender, assumed the risk that the house would decline in value so much that it would be worth less than the outstanding mortgage principal.

The very reason lenders insist on minimum down-payments, maximum loan-to-value ratios, and personal guaranties is to minimize the lender's likely loss if the "value of the collateral" (the mortgaged home) suddenly declines; so the risk of such a decline is virtually never the sort of risk the parties intend to allocate to the lender.

C. UCC view: In sale-of-goods case, the *UCC* does *not* expressly grant the frustration of purpose defense either to sellers or to buyers. However, both sides in sales cases may nonetheless be able to use the doctrine.

1. **Use by buyers:** It's more likely that a *buyer* of goods would qualify for the doctrine. However, there's no specific language in Article 2 that a buyer can point to that directly suggests the availability of the frustration doctrine to buyers.

   a. **Common law fills in the gaps:** But remember that the UCC, like any statute, can and must be supplemented by the *common law*, which in this case is the common-law doctrine of frustration of purpose. See § 1-103(b), making the common law applicable "unless displaced by the particular provisions of this act...." So the common-law frustration doctrine is probably available to a buyer, if the buyer can convince the court that the Code's failure to give him any express impracticability defense does not mean that the drafters intended to preclude all common-law relief.

   Example: Suppose Buyer is a defense contractor who has a U.S. government contract to build a new generation of Stealth aircraft for the Air Force. Buyer contracts with Seller to buy from Seller 200 units of a particular radar detector, one unit to be installed in each of the 200 planes that Buyer is to build under the master government contract. The Buyer-Seller contract says nothing about the chance that Buyer's government contract might be cancelled. After Seller delivers the first 2 units, the U.S. government exercises a rarely-used right to cancel the entire Stealth contract for national budget reasons. Buyer now wants to cancel the remainder of the order with Seller.

   On these facts, a court would probably allow Buyer to make use of the common-law frustration doctrine, and to cancel. Buyer's primary (indeed only) purpose in making the contract with Seller was to use the radar detector in planes it was to build under the U.S. contract; that purpose has been entirely thwarted by the relatively unforeseen cancellation on the part of the U.S.

2. **Use by sellers:** It will be rare that the facts would lead a *seller* to try to use the frustration doctrine: the doctrine by its nature applies better to buyers of goods and services than to suppliers of goods or services. But in an appropriate case, a seller might be able to use § 2-615(a)'s general impracticability language to support a frustration defense. That is, the seller might be able to avoid the contract if performance has become impracticable "by the occurrence of a contingency the non-occurrence of which was a basic assumption upon which the contract was made." *Id.*

   Example: Suppose that Seller says to Buyer, a celebrity, "I'll sell 10 of my new super-deluxe widgets to you at 30% below my cost, if you'll agree to endorse the product in advertisements that I'll take out." Suppose further that, before delivery, Buyer is indicted and convicted of a widely-publicized white collar crime. Seller could probably successfully argue that his purpose in making this loss-leader contract (to procure a valuable endorsement) has been totally thwarted by Buyer's conviction and subsequent lack of value as an endorser, and that he (Seller) would not have made the contract had he foreseen this possibility.

Quiz Yourself on

IMPOSSIBILITY, IMPRACTICABILITY, AND FRUSTRATION OF PURPOSE

118. Whinney sells Hoof Hearted, her prizewinning horse, to Grunt for $50,000. Before Hoof Hearted changes hands, it dies from eating a bad batch of Purella Horsey Chow. Grunt tenders the $50,000 and then sues Whinney for breach. Will Grunt recover?

119. Polly Plastiskin contracts to buy 50 gallons of mineral water from the Pisarro Water Supply Co. The contract merely specifies that the water will be "pure mineral water." Pisarro gets its mineral water from several sources, but it primarily relies on the Fountain of Youth, and plans to fill Polly's order with Fountain of Youth water. (Polly doesn't know this — she's never heard of the Fountain of Youth.) Before Pisarro fills Polly's order, the Fountain of Youth is destroyed in an earthquake.

(A) May Polly recover damages from Pisarro for breach of contract?

(B) Same basic facts. Now, however, assume that the contract provides that Pisarro will deliver "pure mineral water from the Fountain of Youth." May Polly recover damages from Pisarro for breach of contract?

120. Michelangelo contracts to create and sell a statue of David to Allota Piazza. The statute is to be delivered on March 21.

(A) For this part, assume that on March 15, several days after Michelangelo finishes the sculpture, he dies. Is the contract discharged due to Michelangelo's death?

(B) For this part, assume that Michelangelo dies one month before he is due to finish the sculpture. At the moment of his death, 1/4 of the work (including the carving of a lot of details of David's lower anatomy) remains to be done. Is the contract discharged due to Michelangelo's death?

121. The Colossus Construction Company contracts to build a palace in Rome, on land owned by Emperor Nero. The job is to be paid for in full at the end of construction. Six months into the construction, during a terrible lightning storm, the building catches fire and is destroyed.

(A) Suppose that Colossus is now unwilling to start the work from scratch, unless Nero pays extra. Nero refuses, and tells Colossus that he expects it to do the work for the original contract amount, which Nero promises to pay on completion. May Nero recover against Colossus for breach?

(B) Assume instead that the palace was already in existence at the time of the Colossus-Nero contract. Assume further that Colossus had contracted to do an extensive remodeling job. The half-renovated palace is destroyed by a fire caused by lightning. Colossus has been paid the pro-rata contract amount for all work completed as of the moment of the fire, on which it earned half the total profit it would have made had the contract been completed. Nero rebuilds the palace from scratch, but has a different contractor (one specializing in palaces-from-scratch) do the rebuilding. Colossus therefore loses the chance to do the second half of the renovation project, and loses the profit it would have made ($100,000) on that second half.

May Colossus recover any damages from Nero, and if so, what amount?

122. Gilda contracts to buy a hot foreign sports car, the Pronto Lescargo, from Duke's, a local dealership. Delivery is to take place in six weeks, and the price is fixed in the contract. The newspapers have been filled with speculation (of which both Gilda and Duke's are aware) that the government might place an annual cap on the number of foreign cars that may be imported into the U.S., but nothing has yet happened at the time of the contract. The week after the contract is signed, the government imposes such a cap. The cap has the effect of reducing the annual U.S. imports of the Pronto by 40%. Duke's own allocation of cars from the manufacturer is reduced by the same 40%. The shortfall means that Duke's has more signed contracts for cars than it can fulfill under the delivery times listed in the contracts. Duke's tells Gilda that she can either cancel, or else delay by up to 4 months, her receipt of the car (her choice). Duke's plans to make delivery to Gilda and its other contract customers in first-signed/first-delivered order. (Duke's could deliver on time to Gilda, but only by breaching a contract with at least one other customer.) If Duke's offers Gilda this choice, will Duke's be in breach?

123. Superbowl XXXIX is to be held in New Orleans on January 20, 2002. In April, 2001, Rabb Id Fann signs a contract for 3 large suites at the Swank Hotel, for the week that ends on Superbowl day. The price is twice as high as the hotel usually charges for those suites for that week in a non-Superbowl year. At the time of booking, there has been labor peace in pro football for several years, and few observers expect that to change. In December, 2001, the NFL Players Association goes on strike, and the 2002 Superbowl is cancelled. The Hotel demands that Fann pay for the suites anyway.

(A) If you represent Fann, what doctrine will you assert in his behalf?

(B) If you assert the doctrine listed in your answer to (A), will Fann be required to pay for the suites?

Answers

118. **No.** The contract will be discharged due to the doctrine of impossibility. Here, the essential subject matter of the contract, Hoof Hearted, was destroyed through no fault of either party. Therefore, the contract cannot possibly be performed, and both parties are discharged from their obligation to perform.

119. **(A) Yes.** In impossibility and impracticability cases, discharge will occur only when three main conditions are satisfied: (1) the event relied on was one whose non-occurrence was a "basic assumption" on which the contract was made; (2) the event was not the fault of the party seeking discharge; and (3) the language or circumstances don't indicate that the parties allocated the risk to the party now seeking discharge. On these facts, test (1) is not satisfied — since Polly didn't know that Pisarro was contemplating using Fountain of Youth water, and since Pisarro could fill the order with other water, it's very unlikely that the unavailability of Fountain of Youth water would be held to be an event the non-occurrence of which was a basic assumption on which the contract was based.

(B) No. The fact that the contract specifically mentions Fountain of Youth as the source of supply indicates that the unavailability of Fountain water was an event the non-occurrence of which was a basic assumption on which the parties based their deal. Thus condition (1) listed in Part (A) is satisfied. Since the earthquake was not Pisarro's fault (condition (2) from Part (A)), and since there's no evidence that the parties intended Pisarro to bear the risk of such an event (condition (3)), Pisarro will be discharged.

120. **(A) No, because Michelangelo's estate can carry out the sale** — his personal contribution is not necessary to fulfilling the contract at this point.

(B) Yes, probably. If no truly equivalent sculptor is available to finish the work, Michelangelo's unavailability would be found to be an event the non-occurrence of which was a basic assumption on which the contract was made. If so, then since Michelangelo's death was not his "fault" (see the conditions for discharge, described in Part (A) to the prior question), and since there is no indication that the parties intended to allocate the risk of Michelangelo's death to him rather than to the buyer, the death would discharge Michelangelo and his estate.

121. **(A) Yes, probably.** The majority view is that when a contractor is to build a structure from the ground up, the contractor will normally *not* be excused from performing even if the partially completed building is destroyed by no fault of the contractor. Therefore, Colossus must start over for no additional compensation, or be declared in breach.

(B) No, Colossus may not recover anything. Where a party contracts to repair or remodel an existing building owned by another, *each party* will normally be discharged from its duty to perform by the doctrine of impossibility if the building is destroyed throughout fault of either. That is, in a repair or renovation contract, the destruction of the structure is normally deemed to be an event the non-occurrence of which is a basic assumption on which the contract was based. Since there's nothing to indicate that Nero and Colossus bargained for a different allocation of the usual allocation of risks (discharge for both in the event of destruction), they'll both be discharged. Discharge here means that Nero doesn't have to put Colossus in a position to finish the contract, or to pay Colossus what it would have earned from full performance.

122. **No.** It's true that the possibility of a cap was well-known to the parties at the time the contract was signed, so it's hard to say that the cap was a "contingency the non-occurrence of which was a basic assumption on which the contract was made" (quoting from § 2-615(a)'s general language giving sellers the impracticability defense). But there's another clause in § 2-615(a): sellers also get to delay or cancel delivery if the agreed-upon performance is caused by "compliance in good faith with any applicable *foreign or domestic governmental regulation or order*[.]" That right is *not* dependent on the regulation or order being an event the non-occurrence of which was a "basic assumption" in the contract. So the fact that both parties may have foreseen the cap won't block Duke's from using § 2-615(a).

§ 2-615(b) says that if the contingency "affect[s] only a part of the seller's capacity to perform," he must "allocate production and deliveries among his customers," but he may do this allocation "in any manner which is fair and reasonable." Duke's allocation of deliveries in contract-signing order is certainly "fair and reasonable," so he won't be in breach by making Gilda choose between cancellation and keeping her spot in the queue for late delivery.

123. **(A) The doctrine of frustration of purpose.**

(B) No. The frustration-of-purpose defense allows a party (usually a buyer of goods or services) to cancel the contract if: (1) the buyer's primary purpose in making the agreement has been completely or almost-completely thwarted by an event the non-occurrence of which was a basic assumption of both parties to the contract; (2) the parties did not allocate the risk of that event to the party seeking discharge; and (3) the party seeking discharge wasn't at fault for causing (or failing to guard against) the event.

Here, these conditions are satisfied. As to (1), the Hotel obviously knew that Fann was probably planning on attending the Superbowl (the Hotel's double room rates show it knew that that was the purpose of most guests booking for that week), so both parties knew that the playing of the game was a "basic assumption" behind the contract. As to (2), there is no evidence that the parties intended Fann, as opposed to the Hotel, to bear the risk that something would happen to prevent the game. Also, the relative unforeseeability of the event (continued labor peace was expected at the time the contract was signed) makes it even more likely that a strike was not an event the risk of which the parties thought about imposing on the party whose purpose would be thwarted by that event. As to (3), Fann hasn't been at fault in failing to guard against the strike, since there's little he could have done to protect himself against the strike's occurrence.

V. RESTITUTION AND RELIANCE WHERE THE PARTIES' OBLIGATIONS HAVE BEEN DISCHARGED

A. Shifting the losses: Before a party is discharged from performing by virtue of impossibility, impracticability, or frustration, he or the other party may have rendered a ***part performance*** or may have incurred expenses in preparing to perform. When this happens, should the court refuse to make one party pay anything to the other, thus "letting the chips fall where they may," as of the time the contract was discharged? Or should it award reliance and restitution recovery on a quasi-contract basis? Most courts attempt to adjust the equities of the situation by allowing either party to ***recover the value he has rendered to the other***, and sometimes even the expenditures he has made in preparing to perform. See Rest. 2d, §§ 272 and 377.

B. Return of down payment: If one party has made a ***down payment*** to the other prior to discharge of the contract for impossibility, he will generally be allowed to recover this down payment.

> **Example:** Seller, in England, contracts to sell and deliver a machine to Buyer, in Poland. Buyer makes a down payment of 1,000 pounds in advance on a total price of 4,800 pounds. World War II begins, and renders shipment impossible. Buyer sues to recover his down payment.
>
> *Held*, Buyer may recover the entire down payment, since otherwise Seller would be unjustly enriched. See *Fibrosa Spolka Akcyjne v. Fairbairn Lawson Combe Barbour, Ltd.*, A.C. 32 (1943).

C. Restitution: American courts generally agree that one who has been discharged by impossibility or frustration may recover in quasi-contract for ***restitution***, i.e., for the value of the ***benefit*** he has conferred on the other party.

1. Time for measuring benefit: As of what moment should the "benefit conferred" be measured? Where a party who has partly performed is then discharged for impossibility or impracticability, the event causing that discharge may also dramatically affect the value of the performance to the other party. For instance, if Contractor is in the process of making home improvements for Owner, and the home is destroyed by fire (through no fault of Contractor) halfway through the work, there is a sense in which Owner has derived no long-term benefit from Contractor's work. Nonetheless, the general rule seems to be that the benefit should be measured ***just before the event*** causing the discharge for impossibility or frustration. See Rest. 2d, § 377, Comment b.

a. Cheapest cost avoider: This result is based mostly on economic analysis: insurance markets are set up in such a way that the property owner will find it easier to ***buy insurance*** to cover the loss of the partly-done work than the contractor will. Therefore, it's more economically efficient to place the risk of loss on him. In economic jargon, the owner is the ***"cheapest cost avoider."***

2. **Pro-rata contract price:** Where the performance has been partly made, recovery will normally be limited to the ***pro-rata contract price***, if such a pro-rating can be sensibly done. See Rest. 2d, § 377, Comment b. (But conversely, if the reasonable value to the other party is *less* than the pro-rata price, only the reasonable value may be recovered.)

> **Example:** Plumber agrees to install 200 feet of iron pipe in an existing building. The contract price is $1,000. After Plumber has installed 100 feet, the building is destroyed through no fault of either Plumber or Owner. Plumber is excused from performing because of the destruction of the subject matter (see *supra*, p. 433). If the market value of the work done by Plumber is $600, he can recover in quasi-contract only $500 (the pro-rata portion of the contract price). If the market value of the work he did is $400, he is limited to this amount. The fact that Owner received no ultimate "benefit" from the performance, since the building was destroyed, does not relieve him of the obligation to recompense Plumber for the value of his performance — the existence of benefit is measured as of the moment before destruction occurred.

3. **Reliance:** Where a party has conferred a benefit on the other, all courts, as noted, agree that she can recover in quasi-contract once the contract is discharged for impossibility, impracticability or frustration. But the courts do not agree on whether he should be allowed to recover the expenditures she had made in ***preparation*** for performance (i.e., her ***reliance*** damages; see *supra*, p. 460), when these expenditures did not benefit the other party. The First Restatement, § 468, and most older cases take the view that such reliance expenses may not be recovered. But the Second Restatement, in § 272(2), provides that if restitution will "not avoid injustice," the court may "grant relief on such terms as justice requires including ***protection of the parties' reliance interests.***

   a. **Courts rarely give:** But courts have rarely followed the Restatement's lead by awarding reliance damages.

4. **Contrary intent shown by parties:** Just as the parties are free to specify that a discharge will not take place because of impossibility (*supra*, p. 432), they are free to make an explicit provision that a discharged party will not be entitled to recover anything for his part performance.

Quiz Yourself on

RESTITUTION AND RELIANCE WHERE THE PARTIES ARE DISCHARGED

124. Bay Area Design ("BAD") contracts with Rich N. Tasteless to redecorate his San Francisco home. The contract is for $50,000, to be paid upon completion of the project. After BAD has finished about one-third of the project, a terrible earthquake destroys the home. At the moment of the earthquake, BAD has spent $12,000 on labor and materials. The market value of the work done to that point is $18,000. The contract is discharged due to impossibility. However, BAD wants some compensation anyway. Is it entitled to any recovery, and if so, how much?

Answer

124. Yes, $18,000. Where a contract is discharged under impossibility, impracticability or frustration, a party who has already rendered a benefit to the other will normally be entitled to restitution damages. Restitution will usually be computed based on the market value of the benefit rendered (not the cost to the discharged party of rendering the benefit, which would be a reliance measure.) Therefore, BAD will receive the market value of the work done to that point, $18,000. Notice that it's irrelevant that Tasteless did not receive any long-term benefit from the partly-done work — courts figure that Tasteless could *buy insurance* to cover loss of partly-done renovation more easily than BAD could, so it's economically efficient to impose the burden of the loss on him.

Exam Tips on
IMPOSSIBILITY, IMPRACTICABILITY, AND FRUSTRATION

☛ Exams often hint at the possibility of a defense based on Impossibility/Impracticability/ Frustration (we'll call this "I/I/F" for short). Usually, your fact pattern won't mention any of these defenses — it'll be up to you to spot the issue, based on the fact that some unlikely event has occurred that makes it difficulty or senseless for one party to perform.

Issues Common to Impossibility/Impracticability and to Frustration

☛ **Failure of basic assumption:** Remember the basic standard for when I/I/F applies: it applies only when the parties made the contract on the *basic assumption* that the contingency in question *would not occur.* When you try to decide whether this test is met, focus on three sub-issues:

(1) **Assumptions shared by both parties:** Look first to see if *both* parties made this underlying basic assumption — if the party who's trying to avoid a discharge (i.e., who's trying to enforce the contract) *didn't know* that the contract was predicated on that assumption, I/I/F won't apply.

Example 1: Stu, a high school senior, interviews with Count, an accountant, for a position in his firm in January. Count then writes to Stu: "I offer you employment with my firm, beginning August 1, at $25,000 a year." Stu accepts the offer several days later. In March, Count sends Stu a letter stating: "It was my intention in hiring you to have you work with my International Union account. However, the Union no longer retains my firm. Therefore, I lack the funds and will not hire you. Good luck in securing other employment."

If Count asserts the defense of frustration, Stu can successfully contend that he wasn't apprised of the special reason for hiring him. Therefore, the keeping of the account wasn't a "basic assumption" of the contract, and Count can't be excused on grounds of frustration.

Example 2: In January, *O* and *A* enter into a contract under which A will design a ten-story hotel to be built on a piece of land owned by *O* adjacent to City Airport. The design is to be delivered on or before May 1. *A* is aware that *O*'s interest in building a hotel is on account of the business that will come from travellers using the airport. In March, the government announces that the airport will shut down at the end of the year.

O will probably be able to argue successfully that the continuation of the airport's operation was a basic assumption under both parties made the design contract. If he can show this, he'll probably be able to have the contract excused for frustration.

(2) Foreseeability: Remember that the more *foreseeable* the contingency was, the *less like* it is that the contingency represents the failure of a basic assumption.

☞ Circumstances which *are* usually foreseeable, and that therefore probably won't lead to discharge:

☞ **Increase in costs.** Look for a sudden large increase in the *cost* of labor or materials which the seller of goods or services claims makes it impossible to perform. Usually, such difficulties were relatively foreseeable when the contract was made, in which case they probably *won't* excuse performance. (But this won't always be true: if the cost increase is due to a truly unforeseen type of event — a sudden industry-wide strike, outbreak of war, etc. — impossibility will generally apply.)

☞ Circumstance which *may or may not* be deemed foreseeable:

☞ **Weather conditions.** Look for bad storms that either push off the date of completion of performance or destroy a crop. Note in your answer that foreseeability probably depends upon whether that type of weather was usual for that time of year in that region.

(3) Risk allocation: The last step in determining whether a party's obligations have been discharged because of I/I/F is to make sure that the *risk* of one of these outcomes wasn't implicitly *allocated to that party* by the contract.

☞ **F.O.B. contracts:** Watch for "F.O.B." and the name of a location in an agreement for the sale of goods. The phrase means that the parties agreed that the risk of loss would not pass to the buyer until the goods were delivered to a carrier at the location specified. Thus if the location specified is the *buyer's* factory ("F.O.B. buyer's plant"), the buyer does not assume the risk until the goods arrive at her factory.

Example: *B* agrees to purchase fifty gallons of chemicals from *S* at $5 a gallon "F.O.B. *B*'s factory." *S* delivers the chemicals to *T*, a trucking company, which loads it onto its truck. While en route to the city where *B*'s factory is located, the truck is hijacked by thieves. *B* doesn't have to pay for the chemicals (she's discharged from the contract), because the risk of loss didn't yet pass to her.

☞ **Fixed-price contracts:** When *S* agrees to sell goods to *B* at a *fixed price,* the existence of the fixed price usually means that the parties have agreed to allocate the risk of an *increase* in market prices to the *buyer*, and of a *decrease* in market prices to the *seller*. However, a truly unforeseen many-fold market-price increase (e.g., 10x) might be sufficient.

☞ **Supervening illegality:** When you find a fact pattern where parties have entered into an *illegal contract,* pay attention to *when* it became illegal. If it became illegal because of a change in law that took effect after the formation of the contract, then the frustration or impossibility defenses may apply. But if the illegality existed before the contract was signed, and one or both parties were unaware, analyze the problem under illegality (next chapter), not I/I/F.

Example: In February, *L*, a landlord, and *T*, a tenant, enter into a written lease agreement for two years beginning April 1 whereby *T* is to rent a building for use as a "sports book," an establishment where bets are made on horse races and other sporting events. The rent is $1,000 per month and 20 percent of *T*'s gross profits. *T* gives *L* a $2,000 deposit. Between the time of the signing of the lease and April 1, a law is passed which makes the operation of sports books illegal.

T may sue for the refund of his deposit and the parties will be excused from performing. This is so because *T*'s purpose, of which *L* was aware, has been frustrated by the supervening illegality.

Distinguishing between Impracticability and Frustration

☛ Both impracticability and frustration involve a significant event whose ***non-occurrence*** was a ***basic assumption*** on which the parties based the agreement. So it can be confusing to know which one to apply on given facts. Here's an easy way to tell which doctrine probably applies:

❑ where it is the ***seller or supplier*** of goods, land or services who wishes to escape the bargain, that party typically claims ***impracticability***; whereas

❑ where it is a ***buyer or recipient*** of goods, land or services who wishes to escape the bargain, that party typically claims ***frustration***.

Frustration of Purpose — Special Issues

☛ **Total frustration required:** When dealing with a fact pattern where one party claims frustration of purpose, make sure the purpose is ***totally*** (not just partially) ***frustrated***.

   ☞ **Illness:** For instance, in cases not involving personal services, a party's ***serious illness*** may not lead to total frustration, in which case it probably won't lead to excuse for frustration.

      Example: Sol, a homeowner, enters into a written contract with Byer for the sale of Sol's house in Illinois. Three months later Byer informs Sol that he's retiring down South because he has suffered a heart attack, and that he therefore won't be going through with the deal. If Sol sues Byer for breach of contract, Byer won't be excused from performing because of frustration — Byer could still buy the house and re-sell it, so his illness and retirement probably haven't *totally* deprived him of all possible benefits from the transaction.

☛ **Extreme drop in market value:** Look for situations in which a buyer who has agreed to pay a ***fixed price*** for goods, land or services relies on ***an extreme drop in the market value of the contracted-for item*** as the reason she should be allowed to escape the contract by use of frustration.

   ☞ **Claim usually fails:** In such a situation, you should probably say that the buyer's claim of frustration will ***fail***. Point out that where buyer and seller agree on a ***fixed price*** or fee for a good or service, allocating the ***risk of a plunge*** in market prices to the buyer is probably the ***very purpose*** of the contract.

Impossibility — Special Issues

☛ When you're dealing with a fact pattern where one party claims impossibility, make sure performance is ***totally impossible***, and that the event creating the impossibility was ***unforeseeable*** at the time of formation.

   ☞ **Destruction of subject matter:** Destruction isn't always an excuse.

      ❑ First, determine whether the parties ***allocated*** the risk to the party seeking to be excused — if it was, then impossibility/impracticability won't apply.

      Example: Where a builder agrees to build a new structure, most courts say that the builder implicitly assumes the risk of total destruction of the structure during construction (unless the contract expressly says otherwise).

      ❑ Next, if the risk remained with the party claiming impossibility, determine whether the subject matter is ***replaceable*** on a commercially sensible basis — if so, impossibility won't apply.

      Example: *B* enters into a written agreement to purchase 100 standard air conditioning units from *S*, F.O.B. *B*'s warehouse. While the truck carrying the units is en route to *B*'s warehouse, it overturns and the shipment is destroyed. Because *S* could readily obtain replacement units, *S* won't be excused on account of the destruction. (But *S would* be excused if what was being delivered was, say, a one-of-a-kind painting.)

   ☞ Also, make sure that the impossibility isn't due to the ***fault*** of the party claiming impossibility.

Impracticability — Special Issues

☛ **Increased expense:** Although an increased expense generally doesn't rise to the level of fulfilling the requirements for an impossibility defense, some jurisdictions sometimes allow a party to use the increased costs as an ***impracticability defense***.

   ☞ **Extreme increase:** In addition to ensuring that the parties didn't allocate the risk (e.g., an explicitly fixed-price sales contract), make sure that the impracticality is ***extreme***. Probably the cost of performance should be a minimum of five times the anticipated cost.

      ☞ **Slight reduction in profitability:** Also, make sure that the increase wouldn't just make performing ***slightly*** unprofitable. (For instance, even a 10x increase in the cost of one component wouldn't suffice, if the component was only a very small percentage of the seller's overall costs.)

Consequence of Excuse

☛ Remember that ***if parties are excused from performing, contract damages aren't awarded, because there hasn't been a breach***.

   ☞ However, ***quasi-contractual remedies*** for the value of ***work performed*** (or benefits rendered) may be appropriate. (See the chapter on Remedies.)

CHAPTER 13

MISCELLANEOUS DEFENSES: ILLEGALITY, DURESS, MISREPRESENTATION, UNCONSCIONABILITY, AND LACK OF CAPACITY

ChapterScope

This chapter discusses miscellaneous defenses that may be asserted by a party being sued for breach of contract. Key defenses:

- **Illegality:** A contract is *illegal* if the subject matter is unlawful, whether it is barred by statute or found to be against public policy. (*Examples:* gambling contracts, usurious contracts, unreasonably broad covenants to compete.)

  - ❏ **Neither party may enforce:** As a general rule, neither party to an illegal contract may enforce it — the court will leave the parties to the contract where it finds them.

- **Duress:** A party may assert the defense of *"duress,"* i.e., that he entered into or modified a contract because of unfair coercion arising from the other party's wrongful act or threat. The act or threat must be great enough to overcome the free will of the party asserting the defense.

- **Misrepresentation:** An aggrieved party may sue for rescission or breach or defend in a suit when the other party to the contract makes an intentional or even innocent *misrepresentation.* The aggrieved party must have *justifiably relied* on a misrepresentation of *fact* (not opinion).

  - ❏ **Concealment and disclosure:** There are some instances in which a party may rescind or recover on account of the other party's mere *failure to disclose* information (as opposed to that other party's making of an affirmative misrepresentation).

- **Unconscionability:** The *unconscionability* defense is available to consumers who enter into contracts that are so one-sided that they are considered *shockingly unfair.*

- **Capacity:** A party who does not possess the *capacity to contract* may generally avoid the contact. (The option to avoid the contract belongs solely to the party lacking capacity, not to the other party.)

  - ❏ **Infants.** Until a person has reached his *majority* (usually age 18), most contracts which he enters into are voidable at his option.

  - ❏ **Mental incompetents.** Persons who are *mentally incompetent* (the insane, mentally ill, retarded and intoxicated) may sometimes avoid contracts they sign.

I.   ILLEGALITY

A. **Kinds of illegal contracts:**   There are many kinds of illegal contracts, ranging from those that are explicitly barred by statute, to those that are rendered illegal only by judicial decisions that they are "against public policy." See Rest. 2d, § 178. (The Restatement does not use the term "illegal," but refers to such contracts as unenforceable on grounds of public policy. See Ch. 8, Topic 1, Introductory Note.) Because the *effects* of illegality on contractual recovery are more important to the contracts student than a cataloging of the various kinds of illegal contracts, we summarize here only a few classes of illegal contracts:

1. **Gambling contracts:**   Contracts involving *wagering* are generally held illegal, and thus unenforceable. The most common types of unenforceable gambling contracts are: (1) a *bet* between the plaintiff and the defendant (that is, the court will not allow the winner to sue the loser to collect on the bet); and (2) contracts involving the *lending of money* which the lender knows will be used for gambling (e.g., a casino that gives credit to one of its customers may ordinarily not recover against the customer, absent special legislation allowing casinos to do so — but such legislation exists in the few states that have legalized casino gambling).

    a. **Legality of underlying wager:**   The legality of a particular wagering contract will generally depend on whether the underlying wager is made a *crime*. For example, in a state where lotteries are run by the government, an agreement between two people that they will share ownership of what turns out to be a winning ticket will normally be enforced, whereas an agreement by two people to share ownership of an entry in an illegal numbers game would presumably not be upheld because the underlying wager itself is illegal.

2. **Contract to buy an illegal business:** Contracts relating to the ownership or operations of a *business* that both parties know or should know is principally engaged in *illegal operations* generally will not be enforced. For instance, a contract to purchase a business which the buyer knows to be a *criminal enterprise* typically will not be enforced against either party.

    Example: D agrees to purchase from P a corporation that is mainly in the business of manufacturing drug paraphernalia, such as bongs and roach clips. D signs promissory notes as part of the purchase price, then fails to pay on them. P bring suit on the notes.

    Held, for D, on grounds of illegality. There is a strong public policy against manufacturing paraphernalia that facilitates the use of an illegal drug. "Refusal to enforce the instant contract will further that public policy not only in the present circumstances but by serving notice on manufacturers of drug paraphernalia that they may not resort to the judicial system to protect or advance their business interests." *Bovard v. Amer. Horse Enterprises, Inc.*, 247 Cal.Rptr. 340 (Cal. App. 1988).

3. **Usurious contracts:**   Every state has its own *usury* statute, under which the legal rate of interest for particular kinds of loans is limited to a specified figure. A contract calling for interest to be paid above the legal rate is generally unenforceable (and the creditor cannot recover even a lower, legal, interest rate).

a. **Limits:** But the usury laws of most states apply only to loans made to *individuals*, not to those made to *corporations*. Furthermore, most statutes do not apply to *purchase money mortgages*, whereby the seller of real property gives the buyer credit, and retains a security interest in the property. In many but not all states, the usury statutes apply to retail installment credit sales, i.e., purchases made "on time."

4. **Covenants not to compete:** There are two main situations in which a person can promise *not to compete* with another person: as part of a *sale of his business* to that other person, and as part of his *employment* by that person. Since our economy is supposedly based on free competition, such covenants not to compete are carefully scrutinized; if they are *unreasonably broad*, they will be held to be illegal and not enforced. See Rest. 2d, § 188.

   a. **Sale of business:** If the seller of a business is selling its "good will" as well as its physical assets, her ancillary promise that she will not compete in the same business as the purchaser will be upheld, provided that it is *not unreasonably broad either geographically or in duration.*

      i. **Geographical overbreadth:** If the geographical area specified is substantially greater than that within which the seller and the buyer are now doing business, and even beyond the buyer's area of probable expansion, the covenant will probably be held to be unduly far-reaching.

         Example: D sells P a liquor store, whose customers almost all come from no more than 3 miles away. D has no plans to open new stores. As part of the sale, D agrees that for 3 years, D won't operate or work in any liquor store within a 200-mile radius of the store that's being sold. One year later, D opens a store 190 miles away. P seeks an injunction. A court is likely to hold that the restriction is unreasonably broad, geographically, in which case the court will deny the injunction.

      ii. **Length of time:** Similarly, if the non-compete is for a length of time longer than the seller's goodwill is likely to continue, it will also be invalid. See C&P, p. 634.

         Example: Same facts as above Example, except the non-compete is drafted to last for 15 years. Fourteen years later, D opens a competing store near the original store. A court is likely to hold that all the goodwill that D had at the time of sale has long-since been either lost, or transferred to P. Therefore, the court will probably deny the injunction.

   b. **As part of employment contract:** An employee will often be required, as part of his employment contract, to sign an agreement in which he promises not to compete with his employer if he leaves the latter's employ. Such covenants are usually more closely scrutinized than those mentioned above regarding sales of businesses. Courts will generally permit the employment covenant to stand only if it is designed to accomplish one of the following two purposes:

      [1] **Trade secrets:** To prevent the employee from *disclosing or using confidential information* or *trade secrets* gained from the employer; or

      [2] **Taking of good will:** To prevent the employee from taking advantage of his contacts with the employer's *customers* by approaching them and trying to *steal them* from the employer.

i. **Standards:** Even where an employee non-compete *does* merely prevent the employee from disclosing confidential information or soliciting the employer's customers, the non-compete will not necessarily be found "reasonable," and thus not necessarily enforced by the court. A good summary of most courts' approach is that "a restraint is reasonable only if it (1) is *no greater than is required* for the protection of the employer, (2) does not impose *undue hardship* on the employee, and (3) is *not injurious to the public*." (73 Harv. L. Rev. 648-49, quoted approvingly in *Hopper v. All Pet Animal Clinic, infra.*) Courts pay close attention to whether the non-compete is reasonable as to the *type of conduct* proscribed, the *geographical reach* of the prohibition, and the *length of time* for which it applies.

Example: D, who has recently completed her education as a veterinarian, goes to work for P, a pet clinic in Laramie, Wyoming. A few months after D starts to work for P, D and P sign an employment/non-compete agreement that provides that: (1) either party may terminate the employment on 30 days notice to the other; and (2) upon termination, D "will not practice small animal medicine for a period of three years from the date of termination within 5 miles of the corporate limits of the City of Laramie." Two years later, D begins negotiating to buy a competing practice, P fires her because of this, D buys the practice and starts competing, and P sues on the non-compete.

Held, the non-compete here is partially enforceable. When D first moved to Laramie and began work for P, D had no significant professional contact with the Laramie community. The introduction that P gave to D of P's "clients, client files, pricing policies, and practice development techniques provided information which exceeded the skills [D] brought to her employment." This exposure to clients and knowledge "had a monetary value for which [P is] entitled to reasonable protection from irreparable harm." The fact that P proved at trial that D successfully recruited 187 of P's clients to D's new practice shows that P suffered actual harm from D's unfair competition.

The subject-matter scope of the non-compete here was reasonable: the limitation of the non-compete to "small animal medicine" meant that while D could not care for domesticated dogs and cats and other household pets, she could still care for large animals, a significant area of practice in Wyoming. Nor was the five-mile radius unreasonable, since it allowed D to set up a practice in other parts of the county. However, the three-year duration was unreasonable as a matter of law, and should be replaced by a one-year limit. *Hopper v. All Pet Animal Clinic*, 861 P.2d 531 (Wy. 1993).

c. **Divisibility:** If the covenant not to compete, as written, is overly broad, most modern courts will enforce it up to reasonable limits. See Rest. 2d, § 183, Comment a and § 184, Comment b.

i. **Traditional rule:** Some courts still follow the more traditional rule that an unreasonably broad contract should not be enforced at all.

ii. **"Blue pencil" rule:** Other courts follow the *"blue pencil"* rule. Under this rule, the unreasonably broad contract will be enforced only if a hypothetical "blue pencil" could be ***drawn through certain portions*** of the agreement, leaving other portions intact to be enforced.

Example: To see how this blue-pencil rule would work, suppose the covenant in *Hopper, supra,* had said that D would not care for "cats, dogs, horses or cows." If the court decided that the limitation as to cats and dogs was reasonable but that the limit as to horses and cows was not, under the blue-pencil rule the court would be permitted to draw a metaphorical line through the words "horses or cows," leaving the prohibition in place as to cats and dogs. On the other hand, the court would not have been permitted to change the three-year duration to one year, because this would require replacement of words, not mere deletion of them.

    (1) Pros and cons: As you can see from the above Example, the blue-pencil rule is quite stilted and artificial. However, it does have the virtue of ***discouraging*** the draftsman of the contract from writing the most ***overreaching*** contract he can conceive of. See C&P, pp. 639-40.

  iii. Modern "reasonable" rule: Most courts today do not follow the blue-pencil rule. Instead, they tend to enforce an overly-broad noncompete ***up to reasonable limits***, even if those limits cannot be spelled out by use of the "blue pencil." This is the approach of the Second Restatement; see Rest. 2d, § 184(2), Comment b and Illustr. 2 thereto.

    Example: At the time the Ds come to work for P (a collection agency), they sign non-competes prohibiting them, for a two-year period after they leave P's employ, from maintaining any relationship with any past customer of P anywhere in the United States. Under substantive state law, a non-compete must involve time and territorial limits no greater than is necessary to protect the business interests of the employer.

    Held, this non-compete is overly broad, but the court will grant it limited enforcement. The court will do so by means of the "rule of reasonableness" rather than the "blue pencil" rule. That is, the court will enforce a one-year limitation rather than the stated two-year limit, will enforce it only as to customers who were clients of P at approximately the time the Ds left P's employ, and will enforce it only in the narrow geographical area where the Ds worked while they were in P's employ. *Central Adjustment Bureau, Inc. v. Ingram*, 678 S.W.2d 8 (Tenn. 1984). (But a dissent argued that the majority's approach "will permit an employer to insert oppressive and unnecessary restrictions into [non-compete] covenants, knowing that the courts will modify and enforce the covenants on reasonable terms.")

5. Commercial bribery: Nearly all states have statutes preventing the ***bribery of an employee*** to induce her to give the briber the employer's business, or to take other official action. See, e.g., N.Y. Penal Law § 180.00. Where a supplier procures a contract with a business by bribing the latter's employee, he will almost certainly not be able to recover on the contract, even if he has delivered the goods.

a. Bribe paid to third party: If the plaintiff has paid a bribe not to the defendant's agent, but to some ***third party***, the court is less likely to refuse to enforce the transaction than if payment had been made to the defendant's employee. But such a refusal to enforce may nonetheless occur if the court finds that the public policy behind the bribery statute is sufficiently compelling. See, e.g., *McConnell v. Commonwealth Pictures Corp.*, 166 N.E.2d 94 (N.Y. 1960).

6. **Exculpatory contracts:** There are a number of situations in which one party may contract to *indemnify* or hold harmless another from tort or contract liability. The legality of such contracts depends upon who the victim is, and on the kind of tort or contractual liability involved. See Rest. 2d, § 195.

   a. **Release by potential defendant:** If *A* promises *B* that *A* will not hold *B* liable for any *torts* which *B* may in the future commit against *A*, the agreement will be held to be *illegal* with respect to intentional torts. Such an agreement will normally be allowed, however, insofar as it applies to negligent torts.

   b. **Indemnification for torts and crime:** If *A* promises to indemnify *B* from any consequences that may occur in performing a *crime,* the contract will be unenforceable unless *B* acts in good faith and without knowledge of the illegality. But a contract by *A* to indemnify *B* against the consequences of *B*'s own negligence, where a third person is the victim, is normally not illegal.

7. **Licensing requirements:** Where a statute prohibits a person from engaging in a specified business or occupation without a *license* or *permit*, a contract for the performance of such services by an unlicensed person will be illegal "if the [statute] has a *regulatory purpose* and the interest in the enforcement of the promise is clearly *outweighed by the public policy* behind the [statute]." Rest. 2d, § 181.

   Example: A person who performs highly-regulated services such as those provided by stockbrokers, doctors, lawyers, etc., without having the necessary license or permit, will not be allowed to recover for those services, either on the contract or in quasi-contract.

8. **Impairment of family relations:** One area in which the courts have traditionally struck down parties' attempts to contract is the area of *family relations*, especially marriage. When parties attempt by contract to vary the legal treatment of such relationships as marriage, cohabitation, reproduction, and the like, courts often refuse to enforce the contract on grounds of public policy.

   a. **Prenuptial agreements:** The *"prenuptial agreement"* is a dramatic example of courts' historical hesitation to enforce agreements that modify the rules governing family relationships. (A prenuptial agreement is one in which the "non-moneyed" spouse, typically the wife, agrees that in the event of divorce or separation, that spouse will receive lesser alimony, or a smaller property-division, than the standard legal rules of the jurisdiction would impose.)

      i. **Traditional view:** Traditionally, courts have either entirely refused to enforce such agreements, or subjected them to much tighter scrutiny than other types of contracts, on the grounds that society has a strong interest in ensuring that men support their ex-wives. For instance, many courts traditionally declined to enforce a prenuptial agreement if the court concluded that the agreement did not make "reasonable provision" for the wife's financial needs. And frequently, the court phrased the issue as being whether the agreement was reasonable as viewed *as of the time of the divorce*, not merely reasonable as of the time it was signed. Therefore, in cases where the man was merely affluent at the time the agreement was signed and then became wealthy, there was a good chance that the court would conclude that the husband's increased fortune made the agreement no longer reasonable, and thus one which ought not to be enforced.

ii. **Modern approach:** But more and more courts are willing to *enforce* prenuptial agreements now, especially where basic conditions of procedural fairness are observed before signing. For instance, about half the states have enacted the *Uniform Premarital Agreement Act*, under which voluntarily-signed prenuptial agreements are enforceable if *either*: (1) the agreement was *not unconscionable* when signed; or (2) even though the agreement *was* unconscionable when signed, the signer was either *provided a fair and reasonable disclosure* of the other party's financial condition, *knew or reasonably could have known* of that financial condition, or voluntarily and expressly *waived* in writing any right to such disclosure.

So in a state that has adopted the UPAA, if the wife receives fair disclosure of the husband's financial condition before signing, or voluntarily signs an agreement in which she waives the right to get that information, the court will enforce the agreement *without ever even entertaining the question of whether the agreement was "fair" or "conscionable"* at the time it was made (and will certainly not look at whether *post-signing events* have made the agreement unfair). See UPAA § 6.

b. **Agreements regarding cohabitation:** Suppose two unrelated adults *cohabit* without getting married. Suppose further that one of them alleges (probably after the relationship breaks up), that both orally agreed early in the relationship on some *financial arrangement*, such as a sharing of assets obtained during the relationship. In theory, such an agreement regarding finances should be enforceable like any other oral agreement — it seems not to fall within any Statute of Frauds provision (see *supra*, p. 276), and should be enforced if the court is convinced that the alleged oral meeting of the minds in fact occurred.

i. **Traditional view:** But courts traditionally have *refused to enforce* such *"living together"* agreements, on the grounds that they amount to payment for sex, and are thus illegal. See, e.g., *Hewitt v. Hewitt*, 394 N.E.2d 1204 (Ill. 1979) ("enhancing the attractiveness of a private arrangement over marriage…contravenes the…policy of strengthening and preserving the integrity of marriage").

ii. **Emerging trend to enforcing:** But a strong emerging minority of courts is now willing to *enforce* such living together arrangements, at least where they do not explicitly trade sex for money. See, e.g., *Marvin v. Marvin*, 557 P.2d 106 (Cal. 1976).

B. **Effects of illegality on contractual recovery:** As a general rule, *neither party to an illegal contract may enforce it*. This is the case even where only one party's performance is illegal. Thus if *X* promises to do something legal in return for *Y*'s promise to do something illegal, neither *X* nor *Y* can sue for either specific performance or damages. C&P, p. 820. However, there are some exceptions to this general rule, which are explored below.

1. **Enforceability of contracts that are wholly executory:** If neither party to an illegal contract has rendered any performance, there are only a few situations in which the court will allow one party to recover damages for breach:

   a. **Ignorance of facts:** If one of the parties to an illegal bargain is justifiably unaware of the facts which make the contract illegal, and the other is not, the former will usually be allowed to recover damages for breach. Rest. 2d, § 180.

      Example: Contractor hires Electrician to perform the electrical work on a project being built by Contractor. Contractor does not find out that Electrician lacks the required license until after the contract is formed, but before Electrician has done the work. Contractor may cancel the contract, and sue Electrician for damages for breach, if Contractor had no reason to know of Electrician's lack of a license.

   b. **One party has wrongful purpose:** Some contracts are illegal solely because one of the parties has a *wrongful purpose*. For instance, a contract to sell goods to one who plans to smuggle them into another country is illegal, but if the person without the illegal purpose *does not facilitate the crime*, and the crime is not one involving "serious moral turpitude," the innocent party may recover for breach even though at the time of contracting he knew of the unlawful purpose. Rest. 2d, § 182.

      Example: *A* agrees to sell goods to *B*, knowing that *B* plans to smuggle them into the country. Since the crime is not one involving serious moral turpitude, A can recover for breach of contract. But if he *facilitates* the smuggling (as by packing the goods in such a way as to conceal them from customs inspectors), he will *not* be able to recover for breach. C&P, p. 823.

   c. **Statute directed at one party:** Some statutes are designed to *protect one party,* and make only the other one's conduct criminal. "Blue sky" laws, designed to protect investors from unscrupulous promoters, are an example. Where such a statute is involved, *the person for whose protection the statute is designed may enforce the contract,* or sue for its breach. Thus a person who agrees to buy stock in a transaction that would be prohibited by a blue sky law may nonetheless obtain specific performance of the contract, or sue for its breach. C&P, p. 824.

2. **Partially or fully performed illegal contracts:** If one or both parties have *partially or fully performed* an illegal contract, the courts are somewhat more willing to partially enforce it, or at least grant a quasi-contractual remedy. While the general rule is still that the court will leave the parties to the illegal contract where it finds them, there are a number of situations in which some remedy will be afforded. In addition to the circumstances described above, in which even before partial performance a party may have a remedy, courts will grant relief in the following contexts:

   a. *Malum prohibitum:* There are many statutes which render illegal conduct which cannot be said to involve moral turpitude. The illegal act in such a case is sometimes said to be *"malum prohibitum"* rather than *"malum in se."* Where the illegality is of this non-serious sort, the courts will sometimes allow the party who has partially performed to recover at least the ***restitutionary value*** of his services.

Example: Bank loans Borrower money at 10% interest, in a jurisdiction where the legal limit on interest is 8%. Because violation of the usury laws is usually held to be *malum prohibitum* rather than *malum in se*, Bank will probably be able to recover the principal, and perhaps the legal interest. It will not be able to recover the excess interest, and might be subject to either a penalty or to forfeiture of the entire interest.

    i. Licensing statutes: Thus many ***licensing statutes*** are held to be mere revenue-raising laws, and their violation is *malum prohibitum*. One who performs services without having the necessary license is allowed to recover the value of his services. This might be the case for a person who lacks a building contractor's license, where it is clear that the licensing fee is a disguised occupancy tax. But where the license is required to ***protect the public,*** such as a license to practice law, lack of it is usually deemed so serious that a person performing services is generally denied all recovery. C&P, pp. 826-27.

  b. *Pari delicto:* In addition to the *"malum prohibitum"* situation just discussed, a party who has performed an illegal contract may recover the value of his performance if he meets two requirements: (1) he was not guilty of serious moral turpitude; and (2) although he knew of the illegality and was blameworthy, he was ***less guilty*** than the other party. If these two requirements are met, the partially performing plaintiff is said not to be in ***"pari delicto"*** (i.e., not equally culpable).

Example: P, a Jew who is desperate to escape from Hitler-occupied France, gives $28,000 worth of jewelry to D, in return for D's promise to use the jewelry to bribe the Portuguese consul in France so that a visa will be issued to P. Instead of using the jewelry for this purpose, D absconds with it. P escapes by some other means, and happens across D in New York City. P sues for return of the jewelry.

Held, P is not in *pari delicto*, since he is less blameworthy than D, and since his offense (attempted bribery) is not, considering the circumstances, morally repugnant. Therefore, he may obtain restitution of the jewelry or its value. *Liebman v. Rosenthal*, 57 N.Y.S.2d 875 (N.Y. Sup. Ct. 1945).

    i. Deterrent effect: In deciding whether to apply the *pari delicto* doctrine, the court will mainly consider whether barring the plaintiff from recovery will ***encourage***, rather than deter, the illegal conduct in the future. If the court thinks that barring the plaintiff will encourage the wrongdoer to engage in the same kind of wrongdoing in the future, it will stretch towards a finding that the parties are ***not*** in pari delicto.

3. Divisibility: A key way in which courts avoid the unfairness that may result from total refusal to enforce an illegal contract, is by use of the doctrine of ***divisibility***. Recall that a party in breach may nonetheless recover on a portion of the contract if that portion was "divisible" and he substantially performed his side of that portion. (See *supra*, p. 221.) A similar doctrine is often applied in the case of an illegal contract: if a divisible part of the contract could be performed on both sides without violating public policy, the court will ***enforce that divisible portion.*** Rest. 2d, § 183.

Example: P, an unlicensed plumber, makes an agreement with D to do certain plumbing work for D for an agreed price. P completes the work by supplying both labor and materials. A local ordinance requires a plumber to be licensed in order to furnish plumbing services. P will be able to recover that portion of the contract price fairly representing the charge for materials, even though he may not recover the portion representing services.

a. Three requirements: There are three requirements which must be satisfied before the doctrine of divisibility will be applied in the illegal contract situation:

i. Divisibility: First, the contract itself must indeed be *divisible*, just as in other situations where divisibility is to be applied. That is, it must be possible to apportion the parties' performances into "*corresponding pairs* of part performances." Farnsworth, p. 354. Also, it must be fair to "regard the parts of each pair as *agreed equivalents*." *Id.*

ii. Not affect entire agreement: A second requirement is that the illegality *must not affect the entire agreement*. Farnsworth, p. 355. "If the entire agreement is part of an integrated scheme to contravene public policy, none of it will be enforced." Rest. 2d, § 183, Comment b.

iii. Serious misconduct: Finally, the party seeking performance "must not have engaged in *serious misconduct*." *Id.* For instance, suppose that P, a lawyer, promises to pay certain sums to D, a private investigator; some of the money is for D's services in finding a missing witness, W, and the rest is for D's persuading W to give false testimony. If D fully "performed," a court would probably deny him any recovery, even for his services in locating the witness, since his subornation of perjury was a serious offense.

Note: In all of the situations which have been treated thus far, the illegality existed both at the time the contract was made, and at the time it was to be performed. If a contract is legal at the time it is entered into, but due to subsequent legislative action *becomes* illegal before its performance, the problem is treated as one involving impossibility. See *supra*, p. 441. In such a situation, both parties are generally discharged, with restitution awarded to return them as nearly as possible to the positions they occupied prior to contracting. See *supra*, p. 453.

Quiz Yourself on
ILLEGALITY

125. Hy Nickin sells Bud Wizer his small beverage store in New York City for $25,000. As part of the deal, Hy promises that for the rest of his life (he's 32), he will never compete in the retail beverage business anywhere within 20 miles of the shop being sold. Eight years later, Nickin opens a beverage store of his own, six miles from Wizer's. Can Wizer enforce the covenant not to compete?

126. The U.S. has a ban on trade with Iraq. The Snakeoil Pharmaceuticals Company gets an unsolicited order for $100,000 worth of medicine from Abdul Hussein. It ships the medicine on credit to Hussein in New Jersey, knowing Hussein intends to smuggle it into Iraq. Hussein doesn't pay. Can Snakeoil recover the $100,000 due under the contract?

Answers

125. **Probably not, but it depends on the court's precise approach to non-competes that are unduly broad as drafted.** A person's promise not to compete, entered into as part of that person's sale of a business, will be enforceable if (but only if) the non-compete is *not unreasonably broad* as to either: (1) the type of activity constrained, (2) the non-compete's duration, and (3) the non-compete's geographic reach. Here, requirement (1) is no problem: the business being sold and the activity proscribed are in the same industry (retail beverage sales). But requirement (2) is probably a problem: Hy has an estimated remaining working life of over 30 years, which is longer than Bud's store's goodwill is likely to last, so a court will probably conclude that the lifetime duration is unreasonable. Requirement (3) is probably also a problem: it's unlikely that a small beverage store in a populous place like N.Y.C. has a 20-mile radius within which it competes with other similar stores; therefore, the 20-mile radius provision is probably unduly broad.

However, a court might enforce the non-compete up to reasonable limits. That is, if the court believes that an 8-year non-compete, applicable to, say, a 6-mile radius, would have been reasonable (which the court might well conclude), the court might choose to bar Hy even though the non-compete as written is way too broad. But not all courts will perform this task of "editing the contract down to reasonable limits." Some won't enforce an unduly-broad-as-written non-compete *at all*. Others will do so only if a hypothetical "blue pencil" could remove the offending provision and leave something left to enforce; since no amount of excision — as opposed to rewriting — can turn a lifetime limit into an 8-year limit, or a 20-mile radius into a 6-mile radius, a court following the blue-pencil rule would refuse to enforce this agreement no matter how reasonable it thought an 8-year or 6-mile-radius limit would be.

126. **Yes, probably.** Normally, neither party to an illegal contract may recover. But where only one of the parties has an illegal purpose, the other party may be able to enforce the contract, under the "pari delicto" doctrine. Under that doctrine, the "innocent" party can recover, even if it knew about the other party's illegal purpose, as long as: (1) the innocent party is not guilty of moral turpitude; and (2) the innocent party is less blameworthy than the party with the illegal purpose. That's probably the case here: Snakeoil's behavior probably isn't deeply blameworthy (since it involves medicine), and Snakeoil is clearly less blameworthy than Hussein, who's the one who's doing the smuggling.

II. DURESS

A. **Duress generally:** The defense of duress is available if the defendant can show that he was *unfairly coerced* into entering into the contract, or into modifying it. It is much more broadly available today than prior to this century, when it could be used only if a party's person or property was put in actual danger. Today, the essential rule is that duress consists of "any wrongful act or threat which *overcomes the free will* of a party." C&P, p. 309. See also Rest. 2d, § 175.

1. **Subjective standard:** A *subjective standard* is used to determine whether the party's free will has been overcome. That is, regardless of whether the will of a person of "ordinary firmness" would have been overborne, if the party can show that he was unusually timid, and was in fact coerced, he may use the defense. But the fact that the hypothetical "person of ordinary firmness" would or would not have been overborne has evidentiary value in ascertaining whether the party's own decision was coerced. C&P, p. 309.

B. Ways of committing duress: Facts which constitute duress seem to fall mostly into four categories: (1) *Violence* or threats of it; (2) *Imprisonment* or threats of it; (3) Wrongful *taking* or *keeping* of a party's property, or threats to do so; and (4) Threats to *breach* a contract or to commit other wrongful acts (e.g., threats to exercise legal rights in oppressive ways). See C&P, p. 311-12.

1. **General rule:** A detailed examination of these various categories is outside the scope of this outline, except for threats to breach a contract, discussed below. However, one important general principle may be stated: If one party threatens another with a certain act, it is *irrelevant* that he would have the *legal right* to perform that act, if the threat, or the ensuing bargain, are *abusive or oppressive.*

    Example: P works for D under an at-will arrangement, by which the employment may be terminated at any time at the option of either party. D threatens to fire P unless he agrees to sell shares of stock in D back to the company. This would probably be found to constitute duress, even though D theoretically has the right to fire P for no reason. Therefore, if P sold (or agreed to sell) the shares to D under these circumstances, a court would probably void the transaction.

C. Threat to breach contract: Perhaps the most frequently alleged form of duress in contract litigation occurs where one party *threatens to breach the contract* unless it is modified in his favor, or a new one drawn up. The modern rule seems to be that there will be duress in this situation if the threatened breach would, if it were carried out, result in *irreparable injury* that could not be avoided by a lawsuit or other means, and the threat is made in "breach of the duty of good faith and fair dealing." See Rest. 2d, § 176; see also C&P, p. 318.

    Example: D has a government contract to produce $6 million worth of radar sets for the navy. D sub-contracts with P for production of certain components of the sets. After P has begun delivery of these parts, D gets a second contract for more sets. P tells D that unless it receives a sub-contract for an even greater portion of this new work than it had under the first contract, and an increased price under the first contract, P will stop making deliveries under that contract. It then does indeed stop deliveries. D checks with all the sub-contractors on its approved list, but none can make deliveries under the first contract in time to meet the requirements of D's contract with the Navy. In desperation, therefore, D agrees to P's demands. After the last of the deliveries under both contracts, D stops making any more payments, and says that it will sue to get back the excess amounts paid. P sues first (for the balance due), and D counter-claims for these excesses.

    Held, D agreed to the modification and the second contract only under "economic duress," and is therefore entitled to damages. To prove such duress, D needed to show that it could not have gotten the goods elsewhere, but this showing was made here. *Austin Instrument, Inc. v. Loral Corp.*, 272 N.E.2d 533 (N.Y. 1971).

1. **Remedy:** Usually, the remedy for duress is *restitutionary* in nature. That is, the party claiming it is allowed to recover an amount sufficient to undo the *unjust enrichment* that the other party has obtained. Thus in *Austin Instrument*, D might have been able to recover the increased price in the first contract, and everything beyond a fair and reasonable price on the second contract (less, of course, the amount owed on that contract).

III. MISREPRESENTATION

A. Misrepresentation generally: A claim of *misrepresentation* can be used either as a defense against enforcement in a suit brought by the misrepresenting party, or as a grounds for rescission or damages by the misrepresented-to party suing as plaintiff. The contract law of misrepresentation is somewhat similar to misrepresentation in tort law; for a full discussion of the latter, see Emanuel on *Torts*. However, courts have generally made misrepresentation claims easier to establish in contract cases (particularly suits for rescission of contracts) than in tort cases. See Rest. 2d, Ch. 7, Topic 1, Introductory Note.

B. Elements of proof required: In order for a person to rely on misrepresentation for purposes of rescinding a contract, defending against a claim of breach of contract, or suing for breach, the person claiming misrepresentation (we'll call her "P") must show the following elements:

- ❑ D *misstated* a *material fact* (though the misstatement does *not* have to have been *intentional* or even *negligent*);

- ❑ P *in fact relied* on the misstatement;

- ❑ P's reliance was *justifiable*; and

- ❑ P was damaged in a *pecuniary way* from the misstatement.

1. Other party's state of mind: It is *not* usually necessary for the claimant to prove that the misrepresentation was *intentionally* made; a *negligent*, or even *innocent, misrepresentation* is generally sufficient to avoid the contract if it goes to a material fact. See Rest. 2d, § 164. (This is an important respect in which the contract law of misrepresentation is more liberal than the usually-applied tort principles.)

2. Justifiable reliance: The party asserting misrepresentation must show that he *justifiably relied* on the misstatement. This requires him to show not only that he *in fact* relied, but also that his reliance was *justifiable.*

a. Gullible people sometimes protected: However, the latter requirement, that the reliance be justifiable, has not been rigorously enforced in recent years. This is particularly true where the misrepresentation is *intentional*.

Example: P buys a house from D, in reliance on D's assurance that the house is suitable for multi-family rental use. D knows that his representation is misleading in that such a use would violate local zoning laws. P believes the misrepresentation without checking the public records, which would have disclosed the zoning problem.

Held, P may recover for misrepresentation despite his failure to exercise due diligence in checking the zoning laws. This is so in part because D knew that it was making misleading statements. *Kannavos v. Annino*, 247 N.E.2d 708 (Mass. 1969).

3. Must be misrepresentation of fact: The misrepresentation must be one of *fact*, rather than of *opinion*. If a new car dealer tells a potential customer, "This is a great little car," the buyer probably can't sue on a misrepresentation theory, even if he can prove that not only is the car not "great," but that the dealer had reason to know that it wasn't. This expression of opinion is likely to be termed "mere puffing" or "trade talk," and thus not actionable. See Rest. 2d, §§ 168 and 169.

a. **Thin line between opinion and fact:** But courts are increasingly willing to find that a statement has crossed over the thin line between opinion and fact. For instance, if a used car is represented to be "mechanically perfect," this may constitute a statement of fact. See C&P, p. 330.

b. **Special circumstances making opinion actionable:** Furthermore, the relationship between the parties may be such that even what is obviously an opinion is actionable. For instance, if there is a *fiduciary relationship* between the parties (e.g., a corporation and its shareholders), or the person making the statement *holds himself out as an expert* (e.g., a jeweler stating that his stone is, in his opinion, worth at least $1,000), the other party may claim that the opinion was a misrepresentation.

Example: P, a 51-year-old widow, becomes a student at D's dance school (an Arthur Murray franchise). During the space of 16 months, she is sold 14 "dance courses," totaling 2300 hours of dance lessons, for a total of cash price of over $31,000 (in 1968 dollars!). P does so in part because D repeatedly assures her that in D's opinion P has "excellent potential" for dance, and that she is developing into a "beautiful dancer." In reality, P has no dance aptitude whatsoever, and can barely hear the musical beat. P sues to have the contracts rescinded for fraudulent misrepresentation. D moves to dismiss on the grounds that he merely expressed his opinion about P's abilities, and that statements of opinion cannot be the basis for a misrepresentation suit.

Held, for P. It's true that as a general rule, a misrepresentation is actionable only if it is one of fact rather than opinion. But there are important exceptions, such as "where there is a fiduciary relationship between the parties, ... or where the representee does not have equal opportunity to become apprised of the truth or falsity of the fact represented." Here, D had *"superior knowledge"* about whether P had dance potential, so P's complaint falls within the exception, and states a cause of action. *Vokes v. Arthur Murray, Inc.*, 212 So.2d 906 (Fla. Dist. Ct. App. 1968).

c. **Statement of law:** It used to be generally held that a *"statement of law"* could not constitute a misrepresentation. Some courts said that this was because a statement about law was necessarily merely an opinion; others said that it was because "[e]veryone is presumed to know the law." C&P, p. 333.

   i. **More liberal modern rule:** But today, this rule is breaking down. Some courts have simply abolished the rule, and hold that a statement as to law may be the basis for a misrepresentation claim under the same circumstances as an opinion could be (e.g., when made by a person presumed to be an expert, such as a lawyer). Others hold that where a statement involving the law is really a statement about facts (e.g., "this house conforms to all building and zoning requirements"), it is actionable the same way any other statement of fact is actionable.

C. **Concealment and nondisclosure:** Most misrepresentations are affirmative statements (e.g., "This car has less than 50,000 miles on it."). If, however, a party has simply *failed to disclose* information, it has traditionally been much harder to make a case for misrepresentation. See Rest. 2d, § 161.

Example: P buys a house from D. At the time of sale, D knows that the house is infested with termites, but says nothing to P. After discovering the termites, P sues to recover the money he spent on repairs.

Held, P has no cause of action. There is no liability for "bare nondisclosure." "If this defendant is liable on this declaration every seller is liable who fails to disclose any nonapparent defect known to him in the subject of the sale which materially reduces its value and which the buyer fails to discover." The law has not reached the stage of imposing such a requirement. *Swinton v. Whitinsville Sav. Bank*, 42 N.E.2d 808 (Mass. 1942).

1. **More liberal present rule:** Today, courts are substantially more willing to allow a recovery based on a failure to give information. While it is still true that in a bargaining situation, there is *no general duty* to disclose information to the other party, there are a number of *special situations* in which this rule does not prevail:

   a. **Half truths:** If *part of the truth* is told, but another portion is not, so as to create an overall misleading impression, this may constitute misrepresentation. See Rest. 2d, § 159, Comment b.

   b. **Positive concealment:** If the party has taken *positive action* to conceal the truth, this will be actionable even though it is not verbal. See Rest. 2d, § 160. Thus if the defendant in *Swinton* had carefully swept up the evidence of termites and repainted the affected area just before the sale, this would probably be held to be actionable.

   c. **Failure to correct past statement:** If the party knows that disclosure of a fact is needed to prevent some *previous assertion* from being *misleading*, and doesn't disclose it, this will be actionable. See Rest. 2d, § 161(a), Comment c.

   Example: At the start of negotiations on January 1 for a house sale, Seller truthfully states, in response to a question by Buyer, that his house has no termites. But by the time the contract for sale is about to be signed in April, Seller knows that he now has termites. Seller's failure to disclose that fact will constitute a misrepresentation. (And that's true even if Buyer doesn't repeat the question — Seller has an affirmative duty to step forward and volunteer any information needed to prevent his previous statement from being misleading.)

   d. **Fiduciary relationship:** If the parties have some kind of *fiduciary relationship*, so that one believes the other is looking out for his interests, there will be a duty to disclose material facts. See Rest. 2d, § 303(d).

   e. **Failure to correct a mistake:** If one party knows that the other is *making a mistake* as to a *basic assumption*, the former's failure to correct that misunderstanding will constitute a misrepresentation if the non-disclosure amounts to a "failure to act in *good faith*" or to act "in accordance with reasonable standards of *fair dealing*." Rest. 2d, § 161(b).

   Example: Jeweler offers a stone for sale without stating what kind of stone it is. Consumer looks at it and says, "Oh, what a beautiful emerald." Probably Jeweler's failure to correct this basic misunderstanding would constitute bad faith, especially in view of

Jeweler's superior knowledge. If so, Jeweler's silence would constitute misrepresentation.

f. **Easier standard for rescission:** Finally, some courts have held that even where one party's silence does not justify the other in suing for damages, the court may grant the *equitable* relief of *rescinding* the contract.

Quiz Yourself on

DURESS AND MISREPRESENTATION

127. Wicked Witch corners Dorothy and her little dog, Toto, behind the stacks in the public library. Witch snatches Toto and says to Dorothy, "Sign this contract promising to sell me the ruby slippers for $100, or you'll never see Toto alive again." Witch's fingers close ominously around Toto's throat as she says this. Toto whimpers. Dorothy signs.

(A) Dorothy reneges, and Witch sues to enforce the contract. What result?

(B) Before Dorothy hands over the slippers, Witch changes her mind, says, "Forget it," and hands Toto back to Dorothy. Dorothy would actually rather have the $100 than the slippers. Will a court enforce the contract on her behalf? (Ignore the issue of whether the appropriate remedy is an order of specific performance or a damages award.)

128. Kermit takes his livestock to the county fair in hopes of selling it. Fozzie Bear shows a particular interest in one of Kermit's sows, "Miss Piggy." Kermit says the pig will cost Fozzie $10,000 because it is a special dancing pig. Fozzie asks for a demonstration, and he sees what he thinks is Miss Piggy dancing. In fact, Kermit has her pen electrified, and a few well-timed shocks are what create the appearance of "dancing." Fozzie buys Miss Piggy, and subsequently finds out she can't dance. He seeks his money back on grounds of misrepresentation. Assume that a person of ordinary credulity attending the fair would not have believed that Miss Piggy was dancing, but that Fozzie did believe that she was. May Kermit have the contract rescinded?

129. Gail Ible meets with her long-time stockbroker, Bully Bear, for some investment advice. Bully advises Gail to invest $2,000 in a local biotechnology company. Bully knows, but carelessly fails to mention, that the president of the company was just indicted on fraud charges and that no successor has yet been picked. (The news is not yet public — Bully knows the info through his contacts at the company.) Gail signs a contract to buy the stock through Bully's firm. After the news becomes public, the stock price falls by 50%. Gail sues Bully for contract damages based on misrepresentation.

(A) Will the fact that Bully's misstatement was negligent rather than intentional make a difference in the outcome?

(B) If you're representing Bully's firm, what defense will represent your best shot at getting him off?

(C) Will the defense you asserted in part (B) work?

Answers

127. (A) Dorothy can avoid the contract due to duress. The defense of duress is available whenever the other party makes a threat or wrongful act that overcomes the free will of the defendant. When the defense is available, the party asserting it is discharged from the contract.

(B) Yes. A contract entered into under duress is voidable only at the option of the *wronged* party, not at the option of the wrongdoer.

128. **Yes, probably.** Courts have traditionally said that a party may recover for contractual misrepresentation only if the party's reliance on the misrepresentation was "reasonable." However, the modern trend is to hold that if the misrepresentation was intentional, and the party asserting misrepresentation honestly believed the misrepresentation, the fact that the reliance was "unreasonable" will not bar recovery. Therefore, a court following the majority approach will find in favor of Fozzie, and allow rescission.

129. **(A) No** A contract action for misrepresentation can be based on a negligent (or even non-negligent but incorrect) misrepresentation of a matter of material fact — unlike a tort action for fraud or deceit, there is no particular mental-state element in a contract misrepresentation action.

(B) That Bully never made any affirmative misrepresentation; he merely failed to make a disclosure.

(C) Probably not. It's true that as a *general* rule, a party's failure to make a disclosure won't be treated as equivalent of an affirmative misstatement, and therefore won't serve as the basis for a misrepresentation action. But there are a number of exceptions to this general rule. On of those exceptions is that if there is a relation of ***"trust and confidence"*** between the plaintiff and the defendant, the defendant's failure to make disclosure will be treated as the equivalent of an assertion. Since the facts tell us that Gail has used Bully for a long time, and has come to him for advice, a court would probably hold that the requisite relation of trust and confidence existed between them.

IV. UNCONSCIONABILITY AND ADHESION CONTRACTS

A. **Weapons against unfair contracts:** A party is normally bound to the terms of a contract which he signs. The parol evidence rule, discussed in a previous chapter, is one indication of courts' unwillingness to tamper with the terms of a writing. But if the provisions of a contract are so grossly unfair as to shock the conscience of the court, the judge may decline to enforce the offending terms, or the entire contract. The two principal tools at his disposal for doing this are the special rules on adhesion contracts, and the related doctrine of unconscionability.

B. **Adhesion contracts:** Most business contracts in use today are probably "***standardized***"; that is, they consist of a large number of non-negotiated pre-drafted terms put together by one party, with room for negotiation as to only a few aspects of the deal (e.g., price and quantity). It is often the case that the party for whom the standard contract was drafted has substantially greater bargaining power than the other party to the transaction. It is also frequently the case that the standardized terms are complicated, unclear, exceptionally favorable to the drafter, and printed in small type. Such contracts are commonly called "***adhesion contracts***."

1. **Refusal to enforce:** Courts have always been reluctant to enforce such adhesion contracts; despite the objective theory of contracts (see *supra*, p. 6) they have generally relied on the theory that the non-drafter has ***not really assented*** to the bargain. This has led a number of courts to refuse to give effect to all or part of such contracts.

2. **Steps for avoiding contract:** A litigant who wants to avoid enforcement of a contractual term on the grounds that it is part of an adhesion contract usually has to make two showings:

[1] that the contract itself is an *adhesion contract*; and

[2] that the contract (or the clause complained of) either (i) violates his *reasonable expectations* or (ii) is *unconscionable*.

a. What is an adhesion contract: In determining whether a contract is an "adhesion contract," courts look at several factors. The most important two factors (both of which must usually be satisfied) seem to be:

i. Standardized form: That the contract was a *standardized form* (as opposed to one whose terms were individually negotiated). Thus an adhesion contract is generally offered to the other party on a *"take it or leave it"* basis — the offering party refuses to modify any terms.

ii. Gross disparity in bargaining power: That the complaining party had *grossly less bargaining power* than the party who drafted the standardized agreement. Thus if market conditions or the special circumstances of the case meant that the plaintiff had no other suppliers to choose from (or all the other available suppliers imposed the same terms), the requisite "gross disparity in bargaining power" is likely to be met. In general, *consumers* (especially ones who are poor and/or uneducated) are much more likely to be found to have been at a gross bargaining disadvantage than are *businesses*.

b. Proof as to reasonable expectations or unconscionability: Once the plaintiff has shown that the contract was a contract of adhesion, she must still show that her *reasonable expectations were thwarted* by the actual provisions of the contract, or that the contract is *unconscionable*:

i. Reasonable expectations: When the court decides whether the plaintiff's *"reasonable expectations"* were thwarted, this determination is based mostly upon whether a *reasonable person in P's position* would have *expected* that the clause in question was *present in the contract*. So a very *unusual and burdensome clause* stuck into the *fine print* on the back of a standard form contract might flunk this "reasonable expectations" test, and entitle the plaintiff to avoid the contract.

Example: Suppose P (a consumer) rents a car from D (a rental agency). D's standard form contract contains, buried in the fine print on the back of the form, a clause stating that "If the car is damaged in any way, whether due to the renter's negligence or not, the renter agrees to pay an additional rental fee equal to five times the actual out-of-pocket cost to the agency of repairing the damage." A reasonable renter in P's position would be unlikely to expect to find this kind of punitive no-fault provision in a car-rental contract. Therefore, a court would probably conclude not only that this agreement was an adhesion contract, but also that the clause in question fails the "reasonable expectations" test. If so, a court would decline to enforce the clause without ever reaching the issue of whether the clause was unconscionable.

ii. Unconscionable: Even if the contract or a disputed clause is not at variance with the plaintiff's "reasonable expectations" (e.g., the plaintiff knew exactly what the contract said), plaintiff can still get the contract or clause knocked out on the grounds that it is *"unconscionable."* Essentially, a contract or clause will be found unconscionable when it is so *shockingly unfair* that the court decides that it should not be enforced. The issue of unconscionability is discussed extensively beginning *infra*, p. 478.

3. **Tickets stubs and other "pseudo-contracts":** Most adhesion-contract cases involve plaintiffs who knew that they were entering a contract, and the only question was whether the court should decline to enforce the contract or a particular clause because it is unfair or because the plaintiff didn't understand its details. A related but different question arises where the non-draftsman does not even necessarily *realize that he is entering a contract at all*. For instance, when a person parks his car, and is handed a *ticket stub* with a number on it, he is likely to assume that this stub is merely a kind of receipt, to identify his car and enable him to get it back. If the stub includes a lot of fine print on it, in which the parking lot owner disclaims all liability for negligence, intentional torts, etc., the court is likely to hold that the customer had no idea he was making a contract at all, and that all the fine print is completely ineffective.

   a. **Restatement view:** The Second Restatement attempts to deal with this problem of the contract that does not necessarily appear to be a contract. Under Rest. 2d, § 211, a document binds a party only if she "signs or otherwise *manifests assent*" to it, and furthermore "*has reason to believe that like writings are regularly used to embody terms of agreements of the same type*...." Thus the parking lot owner would have to prove that the customer first of all gave some sign of being aware that there were contractual provisions on the ticket (e.g., testimony that the customer read the ticket), and further that an ordinary person in the customer's position would *expect to find terms similar to those which the ticket actually contained*. These would probably be difficult things for the parking lot to establish.

      i. **Which terms apply:** Once the party who drafted the document proves these things, the document is to be interpreted, if possible, by "treating alike all those similarly situated, without regard to their knowledge or understanding of the ... terms...." (§ 211(2)). This seems to apply a sort of "common denominator" standard, by which even if the customer were a lawyer who read the ticket in full, he would only be held to an interpretation which the average layman would make of the document.

      ii. **Terms that eliminate the transaction's purpose:** As a corollary, Rest. 2d, § 211(3), provides that if the drafting party has "reason to believe that the party manifesting ... assent would not do so if he knew that the writing contained a particular term, *the term is not part of the agreement*." Comment f to that section explains that the drafting party might have reason to believe that the term would not be assented to if "it *eviscerates the non-standard terms* explicitly agreed to, or ... it *eliminates the dominant purpose* of the transaction."

      Example: Suppose D sells P a generator under a contract that lists "1136 kilowatts" as part of the typewritten specifications, but that also includes a printed disclaimer of warranty. The disclaimer will not prevent D from being held to warrant that the generator will produce 1136 kilowatts. Otherwise, the non-standard term, 1136 kilowatts, would be "eviscerated." See Rest. 2d, § 237, Illustr. 8.

C. Unconscionability generally: The other principal judicial weapon against unfair contracts is the doctrine of ***unconscionability***. The idea that a contract may be unenforceable because it is shockingly unfair dates back hundreds of years. See W&S, pp. 83-84. Today, courts tend to turn away from time-honored methods of avoiding enforcement of unfair contracts (e.g., by holding that even completely clear, but unfair, language is ambiguous and therefore to be construed against the draftsman) and towards flat holdings that a contract, or part of it, is shocking and unconscionable.

1. **Restatement treatment:**   Thus Rest. 2d, § 208, allows a court to decline to enforce all or part of an unconscionable contract. That provision is almost word for word the same as UCC § 2-302(1), discussed below.

2. **Dependence on UCC cases:**   Most of the important unconscionability cases in recent years have involved sales of goods, and have therefore involved the UCC. Accordingly, non-sales cases (e.g., contracts to provide services) have generally looked to the Code, and to cases decided under it. Our discussion of unconscionability will therefore focus on the Code.

D. The Code view generally: UCC § 2-302(1) provides that "If the court as a matter of law finds the contract or any clause of the contract to have been unconscionable at the time it was made, the court may ***refuse to enforce the contract***, or it may ***enforce the remainder of the contract*** without the unconscionable clause, or it may so limit the application of any unconscionable clause as to avoid any unconscionable result."

1. **No definition of unconscionability:**   The statutory language of the Code itself does not define the word "unconscionable." Comment 1 to § 2-302 attempts to do so; it states that the test for unconscionability is "whether, in the light of the general commercial background and the commercial needs of the particular trade or case, the clauses involved are so ***one-sided*** as to be unconscionable under the circumstances existing at the time of the making of the contract." The Comment goes on to say that "the principle is one of the ***prevention of oppression*** and ***unfair surprise*** … and ***not of disturbance of allocation of risks because of superior bargaining power.***"

   a. **Look at contract as of signing:**   The contract must be judged ***as of the facts existing at the time of signing it***. The fact that one of the parties (usually the seller) acted in bad faith after the contract was signed (e.g., by delivering shoddy merchandise) has no effect on whether the contract itself was unconscionable. (But these post-contract actions may constitute a violation of the party's duty to perform in good faith, imposed by § 1-203.)

2. **Used mostly by consumers:**   Virtually the only successful use of unconscionability under the Code has been made by ***consumers***. See W&S, pp. 138-39. The courts usually presume that where a contract is between two ***businesspeople***, each is capable of protecting his own interests, and should not receive the benefit of judicial assistance via the unconscionability doctrine.

3. **Decision made by judge:**   Observe that by the language of § 2-302(1), the decision as to whether a contract is unconscionable is to be made by the ***judge***, not the jury.

E. Varieties of unconscionability: Elements which render a clause or entire contract unconscionable may be divided (as do W&S, pp. 135-149) into two main categories: (1) *"procedural* unconscionability" and (2) *"substantive* unconscionability." In those contracts found to be unconscionable, often there will be elements of *both* categories present.

1. **Procedural unconscionability:** *"Procedural* unconscionability" refers to the fact that one party was induced to enter the contract without having any *meaningful choice*. Thus oppressive clauses tucked away in the *boilerplate*, *high-pressure salespeople* misleading *illiterate consumers*, *oligopolistic industries* in which all sellers offer the same unfair "adhesion contracts" so that no bargaining is possible, are all indications of a lack of real assent.

   Example: P sells a freezer to D on credit. D speaks very little English, and the provisions of the installment contract which he signs are written in English. P's salesman neither translates nor explains the contract, and also tells D that the freezer will cost him nothing, because he will be paid a bonus of $25 for each sale which he later makes to his friends.

   Held, the contract is unconscionable, and P may not recover the contract price. (In addition to the misleading sales practice, the court was influenced by the fact that the total time-price was over $1,100, in contrast to a wholesale cost to P of $348 and a cash sales price of $900.) See *Frostifresh Corp. v. Reynoso*, 274 N.Y.S.2d 757 (1966), rev'd in part 281 N.Y.S.2d 964 (so that P could recover a reasonable profit, service and finance charges in addition to its own cost of $348).

   a. **Clues to procedural unconscionability:** Rest. 2d, § 208, Comment d, lists several factors indicating that the bargaining process was unconscionable. These include:

   [1] "belief by the stronger party that there is *no reasonable probability* that the weaker party will *fully perform* the contract";

   [2] "knowledge of the stronger party that the weaker will be *unable to receive substantial benefits* from the contract"; and

   [3] "knowledge of the stronger party that the weaker party is *unable reasonably to protect his interests* by reason of *physical or mental infirmities, ignorance, illiteracy* or *inability to understand the language of the agreement....*"

   The facts of *Frostifresh, supra*, are given as Illustr. 3 to § 208.

2. **Substantive unconscionability:** A clause is *"substantively unconscionable"* if it is unduly unfair and one-sided. Most of the cases involving substantive unconscionability involve either an *excessive price*, or an unfair *modification of either the seller's or buyer's remedies*. W&S, p. 140.

F. Excessive price: An important type of substantively-unconscionable provision is one where the *price is excessive*. For instance, *credit installment sales* in which the total price over the length of the contract is two or three times the standard cash market price of the item are often held unconscionable. The *Frostifresh* case, cited in the above example, is one such case. Another is described in the following example.

Example: The Ps, who are on welfare, contract to buy a home freezer for $900 from D, through its door-to-door salesperson. The various credit-related charges (interest, credit life insurance, etc.) add another several hundred dollars to the price. The Ps pay over $600 toward the purchase price, yet the evidence indicates that the freezer had a maximum retail value of about $300.

Held, the contract is unconscionable. This is principally due to the disparity between the $300 reasonable retail value and the $900 (before credit charges) price. Another factor is the "very limited financial resources of the purchaser, known to [D] at the time of sale...." Therefore, since the Ps have already paid more than $600, they may keep the freezer without further charge. *Jones v. Star Credit Corp.*, 198 N.Y.S.2d 264 Sup. Ct. Nassau Co. 1969).

1. **What constitutes excessive price:** The courts have not agreed on any well-defined test for determining whether a particular price is so excessive as to be unconscionable. However, almost all of the cases that have held a price to be unconscionably excessive involved prices that were *two to three times* the approximate "market price" at which similar goods were sold in the same areas. W&S, p. 143.

G. **Remedy-meddling:** The other main category of substantively unfair terms that has been recognized in courts is what has been called *"remedy-meddling."* W&S, pp. 144-45. The term refers to a variety of tactics by which creditor-sellers try to enlarge their rights upon default by the buyer, and to diminish their own liability for breach if sued by the buyer.

1. **Varieties of remedy-meddling:** There are a whole host of terms which a creditor-seller might insert into his form contract which under certain circumstances may be unconscionable remedy-meddlers. These might include a liquidated damages clause for when the buyer refuses to accept the goods, a clause limiting the seller's liability for consequential damages, a limitation of the seller's warranty liability, a clause allowing a secured creditor-seller to repossess the goods when he "deems" himself "insecure," etc. Some of these clauses are discussed explicitly or implicitly at various places in the Code:

    a. **Liquidated damages:** UCC § 2-718(1) provides that "a term fixing unreasonably large liquidated damages is void as a penalty." Presumably the same considerations used in unconscionability cases would be used in determining whether liquidated damages were "unreasonably large."

        i. **Sum set too low:** A liquidated damages clause setting an unreasonably *low* amount might also be held to be unconscionable, either on general principles governing liquidated damage clauses (see *supra*, p. 357) or on grounds of unconscionability.

    b. **Warranty disclaimer:** § 2-719(3) provides that "consequential damages may be limited or excluded unless the limitation or exclusion is unconscionable. Limitation of consequential damages for *injury to the person* in the case of *consumer goods* is *prima facie unconscionable* but limitation of damages where the *loss is commercial* is *not*." Disclaimers of liability are discussed in greater detail in the chapter on Warranties.

    c. **Limitation on remedies:** A seller may, rather than disclaiming warranties, try to *limit* the buyer's *remedies* for breaches of warranty that do occur. He might do this, for instance, by limiting the remedy to **repair or replacement** of the defective part or item. UCC § 2-719(2) provides that "where circumstances cause an exclusive or limited remedy to **fail of its essential purpose**," the other Code-provided remedies (e.g., suit for damages) may be used. Comment 1 to this section indicates that the section applies where the modification or limitation of remedy operates "in an unconscionable manner."

Example: Consumer buys a new car from Dealer. The purchase contract does not disclaim any warranties (such as the implied warranty of merchantability). But the contract does say that Consumer's sole remedy for any breach of any warranty, express or implied, shall be the right to have Dealer attempt to repair any defect, but only if the defect is called to Dealer's attention during the first 30 days of ownership. Three months after purchase, the transmission entirely breaks, due to a fundamental fault in it that Consumer could not reasonably have discovered by inspection during his first 30 days of ownership.

It is quite likely that a court would conclude that enforcement of the clause limiting remedies to attempted repair of defects discovered within 30 days would cause all of Consumer's remedies here to "fail of their essential purpose," since the defect couldn't have been caught earlier. If so, the court would find that the limitation of remedy was unconscionable and should be discarded. In that event, Consumer would be allowed to recover damages for the car's failure to be merchantable.

2. **Arbitration clauses:** The remedy-meddling clauses that have triggered the largest number of unconscionability claims are so-called **"mandatory arbitration"** clauses. By such a clause, both parties to the contract agree that any dispute between them **must be subject to arbitration rather than resolved by a lawsuit.**

   a. **Nature of arbitration:** In an arbitration, a private person (usually a lawyer) is appointed to hear and decide the dispute. Arbitration is sometimes thought of as "litigation lite" — it usually includes **limited discovery**, **abbreviated presentation** of **evidence**, and a written decision by the arbitrator that frequently does not include any **statement of reasoning**. Typically, the arbitration agreement prevents either party from **appealing** either the legal or factual conclusions made by the arbitrator.

   b. **Arbitration in employment contracts:** Arbitration clauses in **employment agreements** — in which the **employee agrees to mandatory arbitration for any claim against the employer** — have sometimes been found to be unconscionable. The California courts have been the leader in this area. While the California courts have not broadly found mandatory-arbitration clauses in employment contracts to be unconscionable, they have found such clauses unconscionable if the clause's design **is procedurally one-sided.**

      i. **"Modicum of bilaterality" required:** For instance, the California Supreme Court has held that arbitration agreements must have a **"modicum of bilaterality,"** and that a clause providing that **only claims by employees,** not those by employers, must be arbitrated is unconscionable for lack of bilaterality. *Armendariz v. Foundation Health Psychcare Services, Inc.*, 6 P.3d 669 (Cal. 2000).

c. Class-action waivers combined with arbitration clauses: A claim that a manda-tory-arbitration clause is unconscionable is especially powerful when the clause ***combines*** a mandatory arbitration provision and a ***waiver*** of the ***right to bring a "class" arbitration.***

   i. Rationale: A large corporation typically wants to be able to adjudicate each dis-pute separately. That's because the corporation typically wants to ***avoid*** in advance the possibility that the corporation's counter-parties in the contract (e.g., individ-ual consumers or employees) will ***join together*** somehow, and make the corpora-tion take the risk of being hit with a single large "bet the company" verdict. Putting a mandatory arbitration provision into each contract partially achieves this goal, because it ***prevents the filing of a class action lawsuit*** by hundreds or thou-sands of similarly-situated plaintiffs.

   ii. "Class arbitration" would defeat: But if all the large corporation does is to insert a generic mandatory-arbitration clause — without specifying ***the proce-dures*** to be used in the arbitration — a lawyer specializing in bringing plaintiffs' class actions will typically be free to bring a "class arbitration." That is, hundreds or thousands of plaintiffs who signed the same contract could band together in a single class-based arbitration proceeding, in which the same type of cripplingly-large money judgment and attorney award might result as in a class-action lawsuit.

   iii. Ban on class arbitration: Therefore, in recent years large corporations have tended to specify, in the mandatory-arbitration clause, that any arbitration must be ***"one on one" (or "bilateral")***, i.e., must involve ***only a single plaintiff***. That way, at least where each contract tends to be for a small amount, no lawyer is likely to find it worthwhile to take the case on contingent fee, since only a small recovery, and thus a small attorney fee award, is likely.

   iv. Struck down by state courts: State courts have often been ***sympathetic*** to the claims of plaintiffs — especially consumers — that a combined mandatory-arbi-tration and no-class-arbitrations clause is unconscionable because it tends to leave plaintiffs in small-dollar-amount contract cases ***without an effective remedy.*** The case in the following example is a good illustration of a successful unconsciona-bility claim.

   Example: The Ps sign service contracts with D, a cellular telephone company. The contracts state that each P waives the right to sue in court for breach; instead, each agrees that any dispute under the contract shall be subject to mandatory arbi-tration, and that the arbitration shall involve only one claimant. The Ps later con-clude that D is overcharging each of its customers about $40 each month. The Ps bring a class action lawsuit against D on behalf of all customers who were over-charged. D argues that the arbitration clause should be enforced as written, thereby requiring each individual plaintiff to bring a separate arbitration. The Ps argue that the arbitration provision, insofar as it bans any kind of collective proceeding, is unconscionable and thus unenforceable.

   Held, for the Ps: the combined arbitration / class action waiver provision here is substantively unconscionable. First, forbidding class actions and class arbitrations would reduce the public's ability to enforce the state's consumer protection laws.

Second, forbidding these class-oriented procedures would, as a practical matter, exculpate D from any liability for small harms it inflicts on customers, because in cases like those it will never make economic sense for the Ps to arbitrate with D individually; the stakes for each P are too small. Only a class action lawsuit makes it feasible to press small claims. *Scott v. Cingular Wireless*, 161 P.3d 1000 (Wash. 2007).

d. **The U.S. Supreme Court steps in (the *AT&T Mobility* case):** But in a dramatic 2011 development, the U.S. Supreme Court *took away* a large portion of the right of courts to find that mandatory-arbitration clauses — including ones that prohibit class arbitrations — are unconscionable under state law. In *AT&T Mobility v. Concepcion*, 131 S.Ct. 1740 (2011), the Court held that a federal statute intended to encourage arbitration pre-empted the right of the trial court to strike down on state-law unconscionability grounds a mandatory-arbitration clause that forbade class arbitrations and class actions.

   i. **The FAA statute:** The federal statute at issue in AT&T Mobility, the *Federal Arbitration Act (FAA)*, essentially *compels* both state and federal courts to *enforce as drafted any arbitration* clause that is part of any transaction "involving commerce," which today includes virtually all arbitration clauses.

      (1) **The "savings clause":** However, the FAA contains a so-called *"savings"* clause. That savings clause says that the FAA does *not* prevent either party to an arbitration clause from asserting any general state-law grounds allowing "for the *revocation* of any contract." Thus any general *defense* that state law would recognize as sufficient to allow a party to *avoid a "contract"* — defenses like lack of consideration, mistake, duress, fraud, and (of particular importance) *"unconscionability"* — may in theory be used by the plaintiff to avoid a bilateral-arbitration clause that would otherwise be enforceable under the FAA's main provision.

      (2) **Narrow view:** But as we'll see shortly below, the Supreme Court in *AT&T Mobility* took a *narrow view* of when the state-law defense of unconscionability may be used by a plaintiff to avoid an agreement to arbitrate.

   ii. **Facts:** In *Concepcion*, the Ps (a couple named Concepcion) purchased a cellphone service plan from D (AT&T), which advertised free phones as part of the plan. The Ps were not charged for the phones, but were charged $30.22 in sales tax based on the phones' retail value. Although the cellphone plan contained a mandatory bilateral-arbitration clause, the Ps nonetheless brought a conventional suit against D in federal district court for the Southern District of California. Their suit was later consolidated into a putative class action alleging various acts of fraud by D in cellphone marketing. D then moved to have the Concepcions' part of the case dismissed, and replaced by one-on-one arbitration as required under the Concepcions' original contract with D.

   iii. **D's motion for arbitration denied below:** But the federal district court *denied* D's motion, on the grounds that: (1) the California courts would regard this particular mandatory-bilateral-arbitration clause as being unconscionable; and therefore

(2) the FAA's "savings" clause applied, in a way that prevented the FAA from preempting the states' use of unconscionability doctrine to strike the arbitration clause.

iv. **FAA pre-empts state doctrine of unconscionability:** But by a 5-4 vote, the Supreme Court decided that Congress, in enacting the FAA, had never intended to allow the use of state-law doctrines treating bilateral arbitration as unconscionable.

(1) **Rationale:** The majority in *Concepcion* reasoned that Congress' "principal purpose" in enacting the FAA was to "***ensur[e]*** that ***private arbitration agreements are enforced according to their terms.***" California was subjecting class arbitration to a stricter unconscionability review than that to which it subjected individual arbitration. By so doing, the state's use of unconscionability was fundamentally altering the parties' agreement about arbitration, by ***letting consumers force corporate defendants into the much-less attractive (for the defendant) format of class arbitration.*** And because forcing defendants to use the class- rather than individual-arbitration format rendered arbitration less attractive, California's approach was pre-empted by the pro-arbitration purposes of the FAA.

(2) **Status:** It's not yet clear just how far state courts' powers to strike arbitration clauses for unconscionability are impeded by *Concepcion*. "Most courts apply *Concepcion* more or less mechanically, typically finding that state law is pre-empted if it makes class litigation unconscionable [merely because] there is ***no other effective remedy***." FSCB&G, p. 548.

Example based on *Scott*: For instance, it seems pretty clear that *Scott, supra,* p. 483, would have to be decided differently after *Concepcion*. The court in *Scott* concluded that a clause banning both class actions and class arbitrations was automatically unconscionable merely by virtue of the fact that it would leave any consumer who had only a small-dollar claim with no effective remedy. *Concepcion* almost certainly means that it takes ***more*** than a showing of "lack of effective remedy" to avoid pre-emption by the FAA of the court's power to strike that individual-arbitration clause as unconscionable under state law.

(3) **So one-sided as to still be unconscionable:** On the other hand, a defendant might come up with an arbitration clause that was ***so one-sided and unfair*** that even under *Concepcion*, a state court's use of unconscionability to strike the clause down would not be found to be pre-empted by the FAA.

Example: Suppose D, a powerful corporation with a near-monopoly over a particular consumer market, inserts into each consumer contract a clause providing that (1) not only must all disputes be subjected to individual (not class) arbitration, but (2) unless the consumer completely prevails in the arbitration, the arbitrator must make the consumer reimburse D for its actual legal fees, with no cap, and (3) even if the consumer *does* completely prevail, he may not recover *any* attorneys fees from D. It's doubtful that *Concepcion* would be interpreted to mean that the FAA preempts the state's ability to strike such a one-sided and substantively unfair clause as unconscionable.

3. **Other examples:** Two last types of remedy-meddling that courts have sometimes held unconscionable involve: (1) a clause whereby the buyer *waives all defenses* in a suit against him by the seller's assignee; and (2) a *"cross-collateralization"* clause by which a secured seller who has sold multiple items to a buyer on credit has the right to repossess all items until the last penny on the total debt to the seller has been paid.

> **Example 1 (waiver of defenses):** Buyer signs a contract to buy 140 record albums and a stereo from Seller, the price to be paid over a period of several years. Buyer also signs a separate promissory note for the purchase price. The contract contains a clause in which Buyer agrees that if he is sued for the contract price by any assignee of Seller, Buyer will not raise any defense related to Seller's defective performance. Immediately after the signing, Seller assigns the contract and the note to Finance Co., a company formed exclusively for the purpose of financing Seller's retail sales contracts. Seller delivers a few of the albums, but then fails to deliver the rest. Finance Co. sues Buyer for the contract price, and argues that the waiver-of-defense clause prevents Buyer from asserting Seller's default as a defense.

> *Held*, the waiver-of-defense clause is unconscionable, particularly since the beneficiary of the clause, Finance Co., is closely associated with the seller. *Unico v. Owen*, 232 A. 2d 405 (N.J. 1967).

> **Note:** After *Unico* was decided, *federal law* was changed to make such waiver-of-defenses clauses in consumer credit agreements illegal. See 16 CFR 433.2. So today, the buyer in *Unico* would be permitted by federal law to defend by showing Seller didn't deliver.

> **Example 2 (cross-collateralization):** D, a welfare mother with seven children, has made a number of purchases from P on credit. Each purchase was made under an installment contract containing a complicated cross-collateral agreement, by which any payment made by D is credited pro-rata against all purchases ever made by D. The effect of this is to give P a continuing right to repossess all the purchases until D has reduced her total balance to $0. D's last purchase is a stereo set for $515, bringing her total purchase from P to $1,800. After paying back over $1,400 of this amount, D falls into default, and P seeks to repossess not only the stereo but all other goods that she has bought from him.

> *Held* (by the Court of Appeals), the case must be remanded to the trial court, because the cross-collateral clause may well be unconscionable. "Unconscionability has generally been recognized to include an absence of meaningful choice on the part of one of the parties together with contract terms which are unreasonably favorable to the other party.... In many cases the meaningfulness of the choice is negated by a gross inequality of bargaining power." *Williams v. Walker-Thomas Furniture Co.*, 350 F.2d 445 (D.C. Cir. 1965).

H. Remedies for unconscionability: Once the court has found a particular clause or contract to be unconscionable, it has a number of options. It may merely *excise* the unconscionable clause, and then proceed to enforce the contract in the normal manner. Or, it may *"reform"* the contract by ***modifying*** the offending term, particularly where an excessively high price is involved. Finally, it may simply refuse to allow the plaintiff to ***recover at all*** on the contract. See § 2-302(1).

V. CAPACITY

A. Capacity generally: Certain classes of persons have only a limited power to contract. The most important of these classes are ***infants*** and the ***mentally infirm***. In most instances, these persons can in effect "have their cake and eat it, too." That is, if they enter a contract they can enforce it against the other party. But if they wish to escape from the contract, they may do so. In other words, the contact is voidable at their option (but not at the option of the other party).

B. Infants: Until a person reaches her majority, any contract which he enters into is ***voidable*** at her option. That is, the minor has the power to ***"avoid"*** or ***"disaffirm"*** the contract before, or soon after, reaching majority. The age of majority is a matter of statute, and in most states is now 18. See Rest. 2d, § 14.

> **Example:** *A*, a minor, agrees to sell Greenacre to *B*. *A* later changes his mind and refuses to go through with the sale. *B* may not enforce the agreement against *A*. But *A*, if he wishes, may enforce it against *B* (e.g., sue *B* for damages for failure to make the purchase).

1. Effect on third person: A minor's right to avoid, or disaffirm, a contract is sometimes effective even against ***third persons***. Thus if, in the above example, *A* had gone ahead with the conveyance to *B*, and *B* had conveyed to *C*, A could still disaffirm the contract, and in effect regain title from *C*. This would be so even if *C* had no knowledge of A's infancy.

    a. But UCC has different view: But under the UCC, the rights of a third person cannot be disturbed by the infant's disaffirmance. UCC § 2-403 provides that "a person with voidable title has ***power to transfer a good title*** to a ***good faith purchaser for value***." Thus if *A* had sold goods to *B*, who had then sold them to *C*, and *C* did not know of *A*'s infancy, *A* would not be able to avoid the contract and recover the goods from *C*. (But *A* would probably still be able to demand return of the goods from *B*, and recover damages from *B* if *B* could not return them.)

2. Unavoidable transactions: Statutes or case law may prevent an infant from avoiding certain kinds of contractual obligations. Obligations that are held to be unavoidable in many jurisdictions include an agreement by the infant to support his illegitimate child, a bail bond taken out to secure his bail, and a promise by a minor employee not to use his employer's secret customer lists. C&P, pp. 282-83. See Rest. 2d, § 14, Comment b.

3. Sales by guardian: Since people who know of a minor's right to disaffirm contracts will generally be reluctant to deal with him, statutes often allow the infant's ***guardian*** to contract on his behalf. Such sales must often be made with court approval, but have the advantage (from the other party's viewpoint) of not being disaffirmable. The Uniform Gifts to Minors Act, for instance, allows the guardian of an infant to whom securities have been given to sell the securities and to reinvest the proceeds for the infant's benefit. C&P, p. 283.

4. Disaffirmance: In every state except Michigan, an infant may avoid (or disaffirm), the contract *even before he reaches majority*. C&P, p. 283. He may do so orally, by his conduct (e.g., a manifest unwillingness to go through with the deal), by the entry of a defense of infancy when sued by the other party on the contract, or in any other way that brings home the fact that the infant does not wish to proceed.

    a. Conveyances of land: Where the contract is for a conveyance of land, however, most states do not allow the infant to disaffirm the contract until he has reached majority. This rule seems to be part of the general traditional judicial policy of treating land contracts more seriously; the theory seems to be that the infant is not mature enough to know whether the contract is in his interest or not until he has reached adulthood. C&P, p. 284.

    b. "Necessaries": Where the contract is for the provision of *"necessaries"* to the infant, (e.g., food, clothing or shelter), the contract may not be disaffirmed if the services have been rendered. See *infra*, p. 488.

5. Ratification: Because a contract made by an infant is not void, but merely voidable at his option, he can choose to enforce it if he wishes. If he so chooses, he is said to have *ratified* the contract. *He may not ratify it until he has reached adulthood*, since otherwise the whole purpose of the rule allowing disaffirmance would be thwarted. Ratification may occur in three separate ways:

    [1] **Failure to make a timely disaffirmance:** The infant may be held to have ratified the contract by inaction, if she *fails to disaffirm it within a reasonable time* after reaching her majority. There is no definitive test for determining what is a reasonable time; if the infant has received benefits under the contract both before and after she has attained her majority, a "reasonable period" will be shorter than if the contract remains completely executory. C&P, p. 284.

    [2] **Express ratification:** The contract may be ratified by *words*, either written or (in most states) oral. The more fully the contract has been performed, the less specific the words of ratification must be.

    [3] **Ratification by conduct:** If the former infant *actively induces the other party to perform*, this conduct may constitute a ratification. This will be the case, for instance, if both parties begin to exchange performances under the contract at a time after the infant's majority. But part payment or performance by the former infant, without express words or benefits received from the other party, is probably not a ratification. C&P, p. 287.

6. Economic adjustment after disaffirmance: When an infant disaffirms, courts have to deal with whether and how an *economic adjustment* should be made after disaffirmance. Because many courts have treated cases in which the infant is a plaintiff differently from that in which he is a defendant, we consider these two situations separately.

    a. Where infant is defendant: Frequently the issue of infancy and disaffirmance arises only when a suit is brought *against* the infant (or disaffirming ex-infant) because he has not gone through with the contract. In this situation, the non-infant will not be allowed to recover the profits he would have made under the contract, or any other kind of contract damages. But he will have a *limited right of restitution*, i.e., the right to require the defendant infant to *return the goods* or other value *if he still has them*. But if the infant has *disposed* of the goods or destroyed them, he has *no obligation* to pay for their reasonable value, although some courts may require him to return any goods which he received in exchange for them.

Example: Infant buys a car from P on credit. The contract price is $4,000. If P sues and Infant disaffirms the contract, P will not be able to recover any contract damages (e.g., the profits he would have made on the deal). But if Infant still has the car, he will have to return it to P. If Infant has wrecked the car, or sold it for cash which he has then spent, he will not have to make any kind of restitution. If he has traded it for another car, or received money for it which he still has on hand, he will probably be required to give the new car or the proceeds to P (but only up to the value of the original car). C&P, p. 288.

b. **Where infant is plaintiff:** If it is the *infant* who is suing to recover money already paid by her, most courts treat her less leniently than where she is the defendant. Not only must she return whatever consideration she received from the sale that she still has on hand, but any other value which she received and has *dissipated* will be *subtracted from her recovery.* In other words, the court will attempt to prevent the infant plaintiff from becoming unjustly enriched.

Example: P, an infant, buys a car from D, a dealer. Three months later (two months after she reaches majority), she returns the car to D, and sues to get her money back. P may get her money back, but D may recover on a counterclaim for the difference between the value of the car when it was bought and the value when it was returned.

c. **Necessaries:** Virtually all jurisdictions allow a person who supplies *"necessaries"* to an infant to recover in *quasi-contract* (not on the contract) for the *reasonable value* of those necessaries. The minor cannot use disaffirmance to avoid such a recovery. What constitutes "necessaries" varies from state to state, but needed *food, clothing, shelter, medical care* and *legal services* are among the items that are likely to be covered. Farnsworth, § 4.5.

Example: Minor shows up at the emergency room of Hospital with appendicitis. Minor agrees to pay the bill. Hospital treats him. Hospital will be entitled to recover the reasonable value of the services directly from Minor — since the services were "necessaries," Minor does not have the right to disaffirm the contract.

7. **False representations as to age:** If the infant willfully lies about his age, to induce the other party to contract with him, courts differ as to the effect of such misrepresentation.

a. **Greater restitution required:** Some courts place a greater burden of restitution on the infant than if he had not made the misrepresentation. Thus an infant defendant who had procured goods on credit by lying about his age might be required to pay the reasonable value of the goods, even if he no longer possessed them. But most courts nonetheless give the lying infant the right to disaffirm the contract, so that he can at least escape its executory portions and avoid having to pay expectation damages. C&P, p. 291.

b. Court action: Some states allow the party who has been lied to to bring an independent action in tort for misrepresentation against the infant, even though the contract itself may still be disaffirmed by the latter. Other courts, however, view such a tort action as merely a contractual action in disguise, and do not allow it. C&P, p. 291.

c. Avoidance by other party: Virtually all jurisdictions allow the party who has been lied to by the infant to *avoid the contract* on the grounds of fraud. This is in distinction to the usual rule, which is that the infant may, if she chooses, enforce the contract even if the other party is unwilling. C&P, p. 292.

C. Mental incompetents: Mental incompetents, like infants, are treated as having limited contractual capacity. This category includes not only the insane, but also those who are mentally ill, senile, mentally retarded, or drunk. In general, the rules applied to the mentally incompetent are similar to those that apply to infants.

1. Definition of mental incompetence: A broader class of persons would probably be found to be incompetent to contract today than several decades ago, where something bordering on lunacy was usually required. Rest. 2d, § 15(1), provides that a person lacks capacity because of mental illness or defect if either: (1) "He is unable to *understand* in a reasonable manner the nature and consequences of the transaction"; or (2) "He is unable to *act in a reasonable manner* in relation to the transaction and the other party has reason to *know* of his condition." That is, he lacks capacity if he doesn't understand the contract, or if he understands it, but acts irrationally, and the other person knows he is acting irrationally.

a. Total lack of understanding: Where the first branch of the Restatement test applies — the person is completely unable to *understand* the contract — the contract is voidable even where its substantive terms are *completely fair*, and even where the other party has *no reason to know* of the mental impairment.

b. Understands, but cannot act reasonably: Where the second branch of the Restatement test is relied on — that the person has some understanding of the transaction, but is *"unable to act* in a *reasonable manner* in relation to the transaction" — the transaction is less likely to be set aside. Here, the transaction will be set aside only if the person opposing it shows that: (1) the other person *knew* of the mental condition; and (2) the transaction is *not one which a reasonably competent person might have made*. See Rest. Rest. 2d, § 15, Comment b.

Example: P, a teacher in the D school system, has during her forty years of work built up a $70,000 credit in the system's retirement plan. She leaves work due to "involutional psychosis." (She has also been diagnosed as having cerebral arteriosclerosis, a life-threatening condition.) P has previously elected to receive a lower monthly retirement benefit so that her husband will receive benefits if she dies first. But after the onset of her psychosis, she revokes this election, borrows money from the plan, and elects to receive an extra $75 per month, in exchange for which her husband loses his right to benefits if she dies first. Two months after this change of election, she dies of cerebral arteriosclerosis. Her husband sues to avoid her change of election.

Held, P's husband should get a chance to prove that she was psychotic at the time of election; if he can do so, the election can be voided. D knew, or should have known, of P's mental illness, since she was on leave because of it. In view of P's arteriosclerosis and thus her reduced life expectancy at the moment she made her decision, that decision was foolhardy, and can only be explained on the theory that when P made the decision, she was unable to contemplate the possibility that she would die before her husband. Furthermore, while substantial performance, or reliance, by the other party (here, the retirement plan) might sometimes make it unfair to allow avoidance, in this case there were "no significant changes of position by the [retirement plan] other than those that flow from the barest actuarial consequences of benefit selection." *Ortelere v. Teachers' Retirement Board*, 250 N.E.2d 460 (N.Y. 1969). (See also Rest. 2d, § 15, Illustr. 1, based on *Ortelere*.)

    c. Right of avoidance terminates: Assuming that the right of avoidance exists because of a party's mental incompetence, ***how long*** into the contract does that right of avoidance last? Where the contract is not on fair terms, or the other party has knowledge of the mental illness or defect, the rule seems to be that the contract can be disaffirmed ***at any time*** until it is completed. But where the contract is made on fair terms *and* the other party has no knowledge of the mental illness or defect, then the power of avoidance "***terminates*** to the extent that the contract has been ***so performed in whole or in part*** or the circumstances have so ***changed*** that avoidance would be ***unjust***. In such a case, a court may grant relief as justice requires." Rest. 2d, § 15(2).

2. Intoxication: Intoxication will give a party the power of avoidance only if: (1) she is so intoxicated that she can't ***understand*** the nature of her transaction; and (2) the other party has ***reason to know*** that this is the case. Rest. 2d, § 16. Most (but not all) states agree with this Restatement approach. (A few states don't recognize the intoxication defense at all.)

    Example 1: Steve and Bill go out drinking. After Steve has had so many drinks that Bill knows (or should know) that Steve is very intoxicated, Steve says to Bill, "I'll sell my house to you for $100,000." Bill accepts. The fair market value of Steve's house is in fact $100,000. Steve will be able to avoid the transaction, because it was or should have been apparent to Bill that Steve did not truly understand the consequences of what he was saying, due to his extreme intoxication.

    Example 2: Steve writes a letter to Bill one day saying, "I will sell you my house for $100,000." Completely unbeknownst to Bill, at the time Steve wrote the letter he was utterly intoxicated. The fair market value of the house is $100,000. Steve will not be able to avoid the contract, even though he was so intoxicated as to not understand the nature or consequences of the proposed deal. This is because Bill had no way of knowing that Steve was intoxicated, and the objective theory of contracts (*supra*, p. 6) applies.

3. Voidability: Contracts made by an incompetent, like those made by an infant, are voidable, not void. Thus if the maker regains his mental capacity, or has a guardian appointed for him, the contract may be ratified. The other party never has the power of avoidance.

4. Restitution: No clear rule exists to determine what obligation of restitution a mental incompetent has to the other party to the contract. The general considerations are similar to those applied in the case of infants. Thus if the contract is wholly executory, the incompetent will have no obligation of restitution. Another factor considered by the courts is the *apparent mental state* of the incompetent at the time of contracting, if the incompetent seemed to be capable of intelligently contracting, the other party is more likely to be able to obtain restitution than if it should have been obvious that the incompetent was not in his right mind. C&P, p. 299.

5. **Exploitation:**   In many situations, a party's mental state may be less than alert, yet not so diminished as to allow him to avoid the contract under the above incompetency rules. The contracting party may, for instance, be slightly intoxicated, dull-but-not-retarded, slightly senile, etc. In such a situation, if the other party *took advantage* of the slight infirmity, the court may allow avoidance either on grounds of infirmity or fraud.

    Example: P is injured by D's railway train. He is in the hospital suffering from great pain and is under some anesthesia, but is not so narcotized that he is unaware of what he is doing. One of D's claims adjusters, knowing that P is in pain, procures a release from him in return for a $500 check. P's out-of-pocket expenses are much more than $500, as the adjuster knows. A court would probably void the release because of D's exploitation of P. See C&P, p. 303, n. 5.

Quiz Yourself on

UNCONSCIONABILITY AND ADHESION CONTRACTS; CAPACITY

130. The Krullen Heartless Appliance Store is located in a poor neighborhood. Sam Shyster is the sales manager. He puts a sign in the window reading, "New Dishwashers — only $19." Fred Farkus, fourth-grade dropout, sees the sign and asks, "Is it really $19?" Sam says, "Yeah — take a look at this contract. See? $19!" What Sam doesn't point out is that it's $19 <u>a month</u> for ten years, chargeable to a credit card. This is in small print buried toward the bottom of a 10-page contract. Sam tells Fred to sign, and he does, although he doesn't really understand the contract since it's all words and no pictures. The actual cost of the dishwasher under the contract, expressed as a present value, is $1,900; the same model is on sale nearby at an all-cash price of $600. Fred soon goes into default, and Sam not only seeks to repossess the dishwasher but also to collect the balance owed.

      (A) If you represent Fred, what defense should you assert on his behalf?

      (B) Will the defense you assert in (A) be successful.

131. Krullen Heartless, the same appliance store featured in the prior question, offers the same "$19/month for 10 years" deal, on the same dishwasher, to Pete, owner of Pete's Tavern. (Pete's tired of having to wash glasses in his bar by hand all night.) Sam Shyster, Krullen's sales manager, doesn't make any factual statements about the provisions of the contract — he just hands it to Pete and says, "Look, you can buy for no money down." Pete glances at the contract, doesn't realize that he'll be paying triple the cash price, signs, and then soon goes into default. Krullen sues on the contract. If Pete defends on grounds of unconscionability, what result?

132. Roger Thornhill, teetotaler, is at a party one night. He's delighted that there's a big punch bowl full of fruit punch. He drinks a lot of it, not realizing that it's *Electric Kool Aid*, a very potent brew indeed. He gets completely intoxicated, and in a drunken state calls Windshear Airlines and puts a plane ticket to South Dakota on a credit card. (The ticket agent thinks Roger sounds a bit weird, but doesn't realize he's dead drunk.) The ticket is not refundable. Before Roger's due to leave, he sobers up and wants to get out of the

purchase. Can he disaffirm the purchase?

133. Zeus, an adult, sells his chariot to Apollo, aged 17, for $50 down and $50 a month until the $2,000 purchase price is paid off. Apollo, while still 17, rides the chariot much too fast one day, and crashes it into a wall. It bursts into flames and is destroyed; Apollo jumps free, unhurt. He then disaffirms the contract with Zeus, and returns the remnants of the chariot in a shoebox.

(A) Can Zeus recover the remainder of the purchase price?

(B) Say instead that Apollo immediately sells the chariot to an acquaintance, Mars, for $1,000. (Mars thinks Apollo's 18, which is the age of majority in the jurisdiction.) Apollo then disaffirms the contract with Zeus, at a time when he still owes Zeus $1,950. Can Zeus recover any of the unpaid balance from (i) Apollo or (ii) Mars? If recovery from either is possible, how much will Zeus recover?

(C) Now assume that Apollo pays $2,000 cash for the chariot, and totally wrecks it so that it has no value. He then disaffirms the contract, and sues Zeus to get back the $2,000. How much, if anything, may Apollo recover?

(D) Now assume that, after the agreement for an all-cash sale is signed, but before Apollo has received possession or title to the car, Zeus realizes he can get more for it by selling it to someone else and tries to get out of the contract. Assume that Zeus realized, at the time of the agreement, that Apollo was a minor. Can Zeus escape the contract?

(E) Same facts as Part D, except now assume that before the contract is signed, Zeus is worried that Apollo may be underage. He asks Apollo his age, and Apollo falsely replies, "18." After the contract is signed, and before delivery, Zeus learns that Apollo has lied about his age; Zeus also realizes that he can get more money for the chariot from someone else. He therefore purports to rescind the contract on account of Apollo's underage status. If Apollo sues to have the contract enforced, will he prevail?

134. Lizzie Borden axe murders her parents when she is sixteen years old. She is acquitted of the crime on a technicality. While still a minor, she contracts with Shyster & Shyster Publishers to write her memoirs for $500,000. When she turns eighteen, she writes to Shyster & Shyster, reaffirming her acceptance of the contract terms. Shortly thereafter, Lizzie gets religious and decides she doesn't want to relive the horror of her past. Can she avoid the contract on the grounds that she was a minor when she made it?

Answers

130. (A) That the contract is unconscionable.

(B) Yes. A consumer contract will be held void for unconscionability under UCC § 2-302 if it is unduly one-sided under the circumstances existing at the time of signing. The fact that the party opposing a finding of unconscionability concealed the true nature of the contract from the other party will strongly militate towards a finding of unconscionability. So will the weaker party's lack of sophistication or education, as will the extreme substantive unfairness of the terms. Here, all of these factors work in favor of a finding of unconscionability, so that's what the court will probably do. As a remedy, the court will then probably either order the contract rescinded (in which case Fred would give back the used dishwasher and be relieved of the need to make further payments), or will "rewrite" the contract so that the payments due will approximate the dishwasher's fair value.

131. Pete will probably lose. Where the buyer is a business or a businessperson, it's exceptionally rare for the court to find the contract unconscionable. Here, where there's been no affirmative misstatement of the contract's terms — and the only unfairness is the substantive one of an excessive price — the court is unlikely to depart from this general refusal to use unconscionablity in commercial disputes.

132. **No.** A party seeking to avoid a contract that he entered into when drunk must show *both* (1) that he was so intoxicated that he couldn't understand the nature of his transaction, and (2) that the other party knew, or had reason to know, that this was the case. Here, the airline had no reason to know that Roger was drunk, so the second requirement isn't met.

133. **(A) No.** Apollo, as a minor, has a right to disaffirm the contract. An infant who disaffirms a contract and still has the consideration in his possession must return it. If the goods have been disposed of or destroyed, the infant has no obligation to pay for them. Since Apollo destroyed the chariot, he doesn't owe Zeus anything.

   (B) Probably, but just the $1,000, and just from Apollo. When a minor doesn't have the item in question anymore because he *sold* it, the UCC doesn't let the original seller recover from the good-faith third-party purchaser for value; UCC § 2-403. However, a court will probably require the minor in such a situation to return to the original seller whatever the minor received (and still has) for selling the item. So here, Apollo will probably have to fork over the $1,000 in sale proceeds, if he still has it.

   (C) Nothing. When the disaffirming infant is the plaintiff, most modern courts will cut his recovery by the diminution in value of the item. Since the chariot is worthless, what would otherwise be a $2,000 recovery will be reduced by the full $2,000 in diminished value, leaving Apollo with a $0 recovery.

   (D) No. Contracts that infants enter into are voidable at *their* option *only* — the other party does not have the option of voiding the contract.

   (E) No. Virtually all jurisdictions hold that where the infant lies about his age to induce the transaction, the other party may avoid the transaction. So the usual rule — that only the infant may disaffirm — does not apply to the fraud-by-the-infant scenario.

134. **No.** Lizzie's initial promise was voidable at her option due to her infant status. However, once she reached the age of majority, she had the right to reaffirm the contract. Once she exercised that right of reaffirmation, the contract became fully enforceable as if she had been an adult at the time the contract was made.

Exam Tips on
MISCELLANEOUS DEFENSES: ILLEGALITY, DURESS, MISREPRESENTATION, UNCONSCIONABILITY AND LACK OF CAPACITY

☛ The defenses in this chapter don't appear as frequently on exams as do those that are covered in the previous chapter. Basically focus your efforts on capacity, illegality and unconscionability.

Capacity

☛ **Who may disaffirm:** Pay attention to who's attempting to disaffirm. ***Only the minor may disaffirm***, not the other party.

   Example: Myner, a minor, and Deal, a motorcycle dealer, enter into a written agreement for the sale of a new motorcycle to Myner for $1,000, to be paid on delivery within two weeks. One week later, Deal notifies Myner that the motorcycle is ready for delivery, but that Deal will not deliver it unless Myner shows proof of majority or brings an adult as a co-purchaser. If Myner sues Deal for breach of contract, Myner will be successful because Deal is obligated to perform — only Myner can disaffirm the contract.

☛ **Offset:** If the minor is suing for rescission or restitution, her recovery is *offset by the reasonable value of the benefit* which she has received.

> **Example:** Mine, a minor, purchases a used car from Carman for $3,000. After two months, the steering fails, and Mine decides that the car is unsafe to drive. Therefore, she returns it to Carman and demands her money back. If the reasonable rental value of the car is $300 a month, Mine is entitled to $2,400 (purchase price less 2 months' rental value) when she returns the car.

Illegality

☛ Make sure *both parties are aware of the purpose* of the contract (though not necessarily aware of the illegality of that purpose). If only one party is aware, that party won't be able to claim illegality.

> **Example:** Tenn enters into a 2-year lease for premises from Land. Tenn intends to use the premises for an illegal bookmaking operation. At the time of the lease, Land has no idea that this is Tenn's purpose. Tenn will not be able to have the agreement declared void for illegality, because Land did not know of the illegal purpose; however, Land will probably be able to void the agreement.

☞ **Severable:** Look for a contract whose primary purpose isn't illegal, but which contains an illegal provision. Argue that the illegal provision should be *severed* and the remaining provisions enforced if these condition are all met:

❑ the contract is *divisible* (i.e. there are corresponding pairs of part performances),

❑ the illegality doesn't affect the *entire agreement*, and

❑ the party seeking performance *hasn't engaged in serious misconduct*.

> **Example:** A premarital agreement is signed by Wilma, a pregnant woman, and Alan, the man with whom she lives. The agreement provides, among other things, that in case of divorce, Alan will not be responsible for payment of child support for the unborn child, in return for the Alan's advance relinquishment of custody and visitation rights. A state statute says that mothers may not agree to waive the right to child support.
>
> The "no child support" provision is arguably severable, since: (1) the child support and custody provision are arguably a "corresponding pair of part performances; (2) other aspects of the agreement (e.g., division of property) are not affected by the illegal provision; and (3) signing the clause does not constitute serious misconduct by either party. If the court agrees, either Wilma or Alan may enforce the contract, except that the court will not enforce the child-support provision (or, probably, the custody/visitation waiver, since that was part of the illegal

trade).

Unconscionability

☛ Look for a contract involving a *consumer*. The unconscionability defense is rarely applied to a contract between businesspeople.

    ☞   Consider applying the doctrine in any non-UCC context involving a consumer contract, where the party seeking to use the doctrine has *substantially weaker bargaining power* and the contract or clause seems substantively or procedurally "unfair" to you.

    Example: Same facts as the above example (the premarital agreement between Wilma and Alan). Now, assume that Wilma has been living with Alan for 15 years, and that in the agreement she has agreed to waive not only her rights to child support but also her rights to alimony and to her share of any earnings by Alan during the forthcoming marriage. Alan is a wealthy businessman, and Wilma is unemployed as well as pregnant. Assume further than Alan told Wilma that if she didn't sign the agreement as drafted, he wouldn't marry her.

    On these facts, you should argue that Wilma should be given the benefit of the unconscionability doctrine as to the entire agreement, since it is substantively unfair, and the product of the parties' very unequal bargaining positions.

☛ Gauge for unconscionability *at the time the contract was made,* not later on.

☛ In order for a *price* to be unconscionable, it must be very excessive (e.g., two to three times the market price), not just substantially higher than the prevailing market price.

Capacity

☛ Where one party was under 18 at the time of the contract, remember that the minor has the power to "*disaffirm*" (avoid) the contract, whether before or shortly after reaching 18.

    ☞   But if the non-minor supplied "*necessaries*" to the minor (e.g., badly-needed food, shelter or medical care), then the supplier can recover in *quasi-contract* for the fair value of the supplies, even if the minor disaffirms the actual contract.

CHAPTER 14

WARRANTIES

ChapterScope

This chapter covers provisions of the UCC that govern certain express and implied guarantees made by a seller of goods to a buyer, called "warranties." Key concepts:

■ **Express warranties:** A seller will be found to make an *express warranty* if she makes an *explicit promise* that the goods will have certain qualities. Such a warranty can take the form of: (1) an *affirmation of fact* or promise; (2) a *description* of the goods; or (3) a *sample or model* upon which the buyer relies.

■ **Implied warranty of merchantability:** A merchant is normally held to make an *implied warranty of merchantability* as to the goods she sells, that is, an implied promise that the goods are "*fit for the ordinary purposes* for which such goods are used."

❏ **Disclaimer:** This warranty may be *disclaimed*. However, the disclaimer must mention the word "merchantability." Also, if the disclaimer is in writing, the disclaimer must be conspicuous.

■ **Implied warranty of fitness for a particular purpose:** A merchant may be held to have made an *implied warranty* that the goods she sells are *fit for a particular purpose.* This will happen where these conditions are all met:

[1] the merchant has *reason to know of the buyer's purpose* for purchasing the goods,

[2] the merchant has reason to know that the buyer was *relying on the seller's skill* or judgment to furnish suitable goods; and

[3] the buyer *did rely* on the seller's skill or judgment.

❏ **Disclaimer:** An express *disclaimer* of this warranty must be *in writing and conspicuous*.

■ **Implied limitations on implied warranties:** Implied warranties may be excluded or disclaimed by the seller's use of expressions like *"as is."* Implied warranties will not be held to exist with regard to defects which should have been *revealed upon examination* by the buyer.

I. WARRANTIES GENERALLY

A. **Nature of warranty:** A "warranty," as the term is used in the UCC, is a kind of guaranty or promise by a seller of goods that they will have certain characteristics. The warranties recognized by the Code are: the *express* warranty (§ 2-313), the implied warranty of *merchantability* (§ 2-314), the warranty of *fitness for a particular purpose* (§ 2-315), and the warranty of *title and against infringement* (§ 2-312).

B. **Proving breach of warranty:** The seller of goods is not an absolute insurer of their quality. In order to recover for breach of warranty, a buyer must prove several things, among which are:

[1] that the defendant *made a warranty*, express or implied, under one of the applicable Code sections;

[2] that the goods were *defective* at the time of sale (i.e., that they did not comply with the warranty);

[3] that the buyer's loss or injury was *proximately and actually caused by the defect* (and not by the buyer's negligent or inappropriate use of the goods); and

[4] that *any affirmative defense* raised by the defense, including disclaimer, statute of limitations, lack of privity, lack of notice, and assumption of the risk, is invalid.

II. EXPRESS WARRANTIES

  A. **Express warranty defined:**   An express warranty is an explicit (as opposed to implied) promise or guaranty by the seller that the goods will have certain qualities. § 2-313, the express warranty section of the Code, sets forth three ways by which an express warranty can come into being. The most important of these is § 2-313(1)(a)'s provision that "Any *affirmation of fact or promise* made by the seller to the buyer which relates to the goods and becomes part of the basis of the bargain creates an express warranty that the goods shall conform to the affirmation or promise."

  1. **Basis of the bargain:**   The requirement that the warranty be "part of the basis of the bargain" is a kind of watered-down requirement that the buyer *rely* on the seller's warranty.

      Example: Car Dealer tells Buyer that a particular car will go up to 150 mph, and Buyer says "Oh, I'm never going to take it above 55." Buyer will probably not be able to claim breach of warranty if the car won't go above 70 mph.

      a. **Fine print:**   But a representation contained in the fine print of the sales contract will almost always be found to be part of the "basis of the bargain," even if there is no indication that the buyer actually read and relied upon that language before signing.

  2. **Puffing:**   § 2-313(2) provides that "It is not necessary to the creation of an express warranty that the seller use formal words such as 'warrant' or 'guarantee' or that he has a specific intention to make a warranty, but an affirmation merely of the value of the goods or a statement purporting to be merely the seller's opinion or commendation of the goods does not create a warranty." In other words, a seller can be held to have made an express warranty even though he never uses the word warranty, but if he is merely *"puffing,"* or clearly expressing an opinion, he will not be held to have made a warranty.

      Examples: A used-car salesperson's statement that "This is a top-notch car" will probably be held to be mere puffing, not an express warranty of anything. But the statement that "This car will do 30 m.p.g. in city driving" is specific enough to amount to an express warranty.

  3. **Descriptions:**   A *description* of goods can be an express warranty. § 2-313(1)(b) provides that "Any description of the goods which is made part of the basis of the bargain creates an express warranty that the goods shall conform to the description." Thus if a box of screws

contains the label "7/8" screws," the manufacturer will be held to have warranted that the screws are in fact 7/8".

4. **Sample or model:** If the seller shows the buyer a *sample* or *model*, this will normally amount to an express warranty by the seller that the rest of the goods conform to the sample or model. See UCC § 2-313(1)(c): *"Any sample or model which is made part of the basis of the bargain creates an express warranty that the whole of the goods shall conform to the sample or model."*

> **Example:** Chef phones Rest, a restaurant supply company, and says he wants to order "light-blue dinner plates." Rest sends a sample plate, which is light blue and 10 inches in diameter, and which sells for $3 each. Chef, after looking at the sample, faxes back, "Send me 100 dinner plates at $3." Rest sends light-blue plates made of the same material as the sample, but 11 inches in diameter. Chef rejects the shipment, complaining that the plates are 1 inch too big. Rest responds, "By an industry-standard trade usage, a "dinner plate" is any plate having a diameter of 10 inches to 11 inches inclusive, so the ones I sent you qualify." (Assume that Rest is correct that this is a trade usage.)
>
> In a suit by Rest, Rest will lose. When Rest sent the sample and Chef ordered from it, Rest was making an express warranty that the goods he delivered would match the sample. His failure to send matching goods thus constituted a breach of this express warranty, entitling Chef to reject the goods for failing to conform to the warranty. (Remember that under the UCC's "perfect tender" rule, p. 229 *supra*, even a *slight* failure to conform to the contract will entitle the buyer to reject the goods, so Chef won't even have to establish that the difference in diameter mattered to him.)

III. IMPLIED WARRANTY OF MERCHANTABILITY

A. **The warranty of merchantability generally:** The implied warranty of *merchantability*, imposed by UCC § 2-314, is the most important warranty in the Code. § 2-314(1) provides: "Unless excluded or modified…, a warranty that goods shall be merchantable is implied in a contract for their sale if the seller is a merchant with respect to goods of that kind. Under this section the serving for value of food or drink to be consumed either on the premises or elsewhere is a sale."

B. **Meaning of "merchantable":** All definitions of "merchantable" are somewhat vague. § 2-314(2) lists six criteria which goods must meet in order to be merchantable.

1. **Fit for ordinary purposes:** The most important of these six criteria is given in § 2-314(2)(c), by which goods must be *"fit for the ordinary purposes for which such goods are used."*

   a. **Objective standard:** The "fit for the ordinary purposes" test is *objective*: it depends on what a *reasonable consumer* would expect, not on what the plaintiff happened to expect.

   > **Example:** P buys a fire blanket to protect part of a construction site where a blowtorch is being used. Drippings from the torch melt the blanket and start a fire. P sues

D, the maker of the blanket, for breaching its implied warranty of merchantability. P's welder testifies that he expected the blanket to be able to stop the fire.

Held, D is entitled to summary judgment, because P submitted no evidence, from experts or otherwise, showing that ordinary users of the blanket would expect it to stand up to the conditions in which P used it. The subjective views of a single user are not enough to support a claim for breach of warranty. *Koken v. Black & Veatch Construction, Inc.,* 426 F.3d 39 (1st Cir. 2005).

2. **Other criteria:** To be merchantable, goods must also "pass without objection in the trade under the contract description" (§ 2-314(2)(b)). Furthermore they must "run, within the variations permitted by the agreement, of even kind, quality and quantity within each unit and among all units involved" (§ 2-314(2)(d)), be "adequately contained, packaged, and labeled as the agreement may require" (§ 2-314(2)(e)), and "conform to the promises or affirmations of fact made on the container or label if any" ((§ 2-314(2)(f)).

C. **Cigarettes and alcohol:** Is a product which is no worse than that manufactured by the maker's competitors, but which nonetheless has dangerous features, merchantable? For instance, is a cigarette which causes cancer, but which is no more carcinogenic than other tobacco companies' cigarettes, merchantable? At least where the dangerous properties of the class of items (e.g., cigarettes) is widely known before the sale in question, a successful claim based on breach of warranty is unlikely. (A claim based on strict liability or fraud is much more likely to be successful.)

IV. WARRANTY OF FITNESS FOR A PARTICULAR PURPOSE

A. **Warranty of fitness generally:** The last of the UCC warranties relating to the quality of goods is the warranty of *fitness for a particular purpose*. This warranty is imposed by § 2-315, which provides that "Where the seller at the time of contracting has reason to know any particular purpose for which the goods are required and that the buyer is relying on the seller's judgment to select or furnish suitable goods, there is…an implied warranty that the goods shall be fit for such purpose."

B. **Conditions:** The buyer must therefore prove three things if he is to recover for breach of the implied warranty of fitness for a particular purpose:

[1] that the seller had *reason to know the buyer's purpose*;

[2] that the seller had reason to know that the buyer was *relying on the seller's skill or judgment* to furnish suitable goods; and

[3] that the buyer *did in fact rely* on the seller's skill or judgment.

Example: Printer tells Manufacturer that she wants to buy a press which will be suitable for printing high-quality work for advertising agency customers. Manufacturer recommends and sells a particular model press to Printer, without making any express warranties that the press will turn out the particularly high-quality work that Printer needs. Printer will probably be able to recover for breach of an implied warranty of fitness for a particular purpose if the machine does not turn out the needed high-quality work, even though no recovery under the implied warranty of merchantability or the express warranty sections of the Code is possible.

1.   **Use of trade name:**   If the buyer *insists* upon a particular *brand* of goods, he is not relying on the seller's skill or judgment, and no implied warranty of fitness for a particular purpose arises. (Comment 5 to § 2-315.) But the mere fact that the buyer uses a brand name will not by itself be sufficient to show that the buyer was not relying on the seller's judgment, as long as the buyer does not insist on the particular brand and merely uses it as a designation.

V.   THE WARRANTY OF TITLE AND AGAINST INFRINGEMENT

A.   **Definitions:**   § 2-312 imposes, in any sale of goods, an implied warranty that the seller has *full title* (free of any security interest) to the goods, and that the goods do not infringe upon any patent or trademark.

B.   **Colorable claims:**   The warranty of title is obviously breached if it turns out that the goods were stolen from some third person, or that there is a valid security interest in the goods of which the buyer was unaware at the time of purchase. If, however, some third person *unsuccessfully* asserts a claim (e.g., a security interest), it is less clear whether the warranty of title or infringement has been breached. If the third person's claim, though invalid, was "colorable," some courts will hold the warranty of title to have been breached, and will award the purchaser any expenses he incurred in defending against the third party claim. See W&S, p. 361.

VI.   PRIVITY

A.   **Definition of privity:**   Two persons are in privity with each other if they contracted with each other. Thus a consumer is in privity with the supermarket where she makes her purchases but not with the producers of the products which she buys there. And the consumer's child, even though she eats the food so bought, is not in privity with either the supermarket or the producers. (The child would be termed by some courts to lack "horizontal" privity with the supermarket, and the consumer would be said to lack "vertical" privity with the producer.)

B.   **When privity is necessary:**   It is impossible to generalize about when privity will be required for a UCC warranty action. The official version of the Code sets forth *three alternative privity sections* in § 2-318, each of which has been enacted by at least some states.

1.   **Alternative A:**   Alternative A, which contains the most strict privity requirement of the three, extends a seller's warranty (whether express or implied) to "any natural person who is in the *family or household* of his buyer or who is a *guest in his home* if it is reasonable to expect that such person may use, consume or be affected by the goods and who is injured in person by a breach of the warranty." Thus this alternative applies *only to personal injury*, and protects only the *relative or house guest* of a buyer.

   a.   **Silent on "vertical" privity:**   This Alternative does not speak to the question of whether a seller may be liable to the ultimate purchaser of a product which is sold by the seller to a middleman; Comment 3 to § 2-318 states that the Alternative "is not intended to enlarge or restrict the developing case law on whether the seller's warranties, given to his buyer who resells, extend to other persons in the distributive chain."

2. **Alternative B:**   Alternative B extends the warranty to *all cases of personal injury* involving any person "who *may reasonably be expected to use, consume* or *be affected by* the goods...." So people who are foreseeable users are covered even if they are not relatives or house guests of the buyer. But this alternative covers only personal injury, not property damage or economic loss (unless personal injury is also present).

3. **Alternative C:**   Alternative C, which has been enacted in New York, among other jurisdictions, is the broadest of all. It extends the warranty to *all* persons (and corporations) "who may reasonably be expected to use, consume or be affected by the goods." (So far, this is the same as Alternative B.) But unlike Alternative B, Alternative C also covers *property* damage not just personal injury, and may cover intangible *economic* loss (e.g., the difference between the value of the product as is and its value if it had been as warranted).

C. **Disclaimers:**   Alternatives A and B each contain a provision that "a seller *may not exclude or limit the operation of this section."* Alternative C provides that no disclaimer or limitation may be made with respect to personal injury, but does not prevent a disclaimer as to economic injury. Other aspects of disclaimers are discussed immediately below.

VII. DISCLAIMERS OF WARRANTY

A. **Disclaimers generally:**   The seller of goods will often attempt to escape warranty liability which he might otherwise incur, by *disclaiming* it. He is particularly likely to attempt to disclaim the implied warranty of merchantability, since that warranty is perhaps the most pervasive, and the one whose making he can least control. The Code drafters, recognizing that sellers would attempt to disclaim warranty liability to the greatest extent possible, have provided a number of limitations on the seller's right to disclaim such liability.

B. **Disclaimers of express warranty:**   It might seem hard to understand why a seller (at least an honest one) would ever try to disclaim an *express* warranty. There are, however, at least a couple of common situations in which the seller may give an express warranty, then attempt to disclaim it. To deal with these situations, § 2-316(1) provides that:

> "Words or conduct relevant to the *creation* of an express warranty and words or conduct tending to *negate or limit warranty* shall be construed whenever reasonable as *consistent with each other*; but subject to the provisions of this article on parol or extrinsic evidence (§ 2-202), *negation or limitation* is *inoperative* to the extent that such construction is *unreasonable*."

In other words, if the scope of the disclaimer is clear, and the scope of the alleged express warranty is not as clear, the court should construe the warranty narrowly, so that it will not conflict with this disclaimer. But if there is no reasonable way to construe the two as consistent with each other, the disclaimer is *ineffective* (provided that proof of the warranty does not run afoul of the parol evidence rule).

1. **Description amounting to a warranty:**   One situation in which an express warranty may conflict with a disclaimer is where the seller gives a *description* of the article which

amounts to a warranty (see § 2-313(1)(b)), and then attempts to disclaim all express warranties. "Thus a seller who explicitly 'warrants' or 'guarantees' that a car is without defects may not set up a disclaimer of express warranties when sued for the cost of repairing the clutch." W&S, p. 416.

2. **Oral warranties prior to written contract:** Another common way in which a conflict between express warranty and disclaimer might arise is if *an oral warranty is made*, and then a *written document* containing a *disclaimer* is signed. This might, for instance, occur if the oral express warranty is made by a salesman who is attempting to be persuasive, and who is unaware of the fact that the standard form contract contains disclaimers.

   a. **Parol evidence:** In this situation, the same rule applies — if the oral express warranty and the disclaimer *cannot be interpreted consistently with each other, the disclaimer is ineffective.* But, as § 2-316(1) reminds us, any proof of the oral warranty is "subject to the provisions of this article on parol or extrinsic evidence (§ 2-202)...." § 2-202 is discussed at greater length *supra*, pp. 179-180. For present purposes, it's enough to keep in mind that if the seller can show that the document was intended by the parties to be the *final and complete embodiment* of their agreement, the buyer will not be able to introduce proof that the alleged oral warranty was ever given.

C. **Disclaimers of implied warranty:** The two important implied warranties given by the Code (the warranty of merchantability and the warranty of fitness for a particular purpose) may be disclaimed or eliminated in several ways.

   1. **Explicit disclaimers:** If the seller wishes to make an explicit disclaimer of these implied warranties, he must follow some quite specific rules set forth in § 2-316(2).

      a. **Merchantability:** A disclaimer of the warranty of merchantability must *mention the word "merchantability."* The disclaimer does not have to be in writing, but if it is in writing, it must be *"conspicuous."*

         i. **Definition of "conspicuous":** "Conspicuous" is defined in § 1-201(10) as "so written ... that a reasonable person against which it is to operate ought to have noticed it." In other words, the disclaimer *cannot be buried in the fine print* of the contract.

      b. **Fitness for a particular purpose:** A disclaimer of the warranty of fitness for a particular purpose *must be in writing*, and must also be *conspicuous*. It need not, however, use any particular words (in contrast to a disclaimer of the warranty of merchantability). § 2-316(2) itself provides a sample clause which suffices to exclude all implied warranties of fitness: "There are no warranties which extend beyond the description on the face hereof."

   2. **Implied limitations:** While an express disclaimer of implied warranty must meet the conditions described above, there are several ways in which these implied warranties may be *impliedly* excluded or limited.

      a. **Language of sale:** § 2-316(3)(a) provides that "Unless the circumstances indicate otherwise, all implied warranties are excluded by expressions like *'as is', 'with all faults'* or other language which in common understanding calls the buyer's attention to the exclusion of warranties and makes plain that there is no implied warranty...."

b. Examination of sample or model: According to § 2-316(3)(b), "When the buyer before entering into the contract has *examined the goods or the sample or model* as fully as he desires or has refused to examine the goods there is no implied warranty with regard to defects which an examination *ought in the circumstances to have revealed to him*...." But Comment 8 to § 2-316 indicates that a buyer will be held to have "refused to examine the goods" only when the seller makes a "demand" that the buyer examine the goods fully, and not simply where the goods were made available for inspection.

    i. Express warranties not subject to waiver: Also, keep in mind that the seller may make statements about the goods' merchantability, their fitness for a particular purpose, etc., and that these statements are *express* warranties, not implied ones; they are therefore not waived because inspection would have disclosed defects.

c. Course of dealing: Lastly, § 2-316(3)(c) states that "An implied warranty can also be excluded or modified by course of dealing or course of performance or usage of trade." For instance, it has been held that when a cattle buyer inspects cattle and rejects those that he doesn't want there is a usage of trade that the ones he does take he takes irrevocably and without warranties. See W&S, p. 434, n. 28. For a discussion of the meaning of the terms "course of dealing," "course of performance," and "usage of trade" see *supra*, p. 192.

VIII. MODIFYING CONTRACT REMEDIES

A. Modification of remedies distinguished from disclaimers: Thus far, we have examined disclaimers of liability, i.e., ways of preventing certain warranty liability from ever coming into existence. There is, however, another way in which a seller may try to protect himself from lawsuits: she may try to limit the buyer's *remedies* for what are concededly breaches of the contract. For instance, she may insert a provision that the buyer's remedies are limited to *replacement of defective goods or parts*, and that no refund of consequential damages may be obtained.

B. Code limitations: As in the case of disclaimers, the Code declines to give the seller an untrammeled right to exclude or limit the buyer's remedies. The seller starts with a general right to limit the buyer's remedies (§ 2-719(a)), including the right of "limiting the buyer's remedies to return of the goods and repayment of the price or to repair and replacement of non-conforming goods or parts...." *(Id.)* But there are two important *limitations* on the seller's right to alter the buyer's remedies:

1. "Failure of essential purpose": Under § 2-719(2), "Where circumstances cause an exclusive or limited remedy to *fail of its essential purpose*, remedy may be had as provided in this Act."

    Example: P buys a new car, which is accompanied by an express warranty limited to repair or replacement of defective parts, and an explicit statement from the manufacturer that it will not be liable for any consequential damages. During the first several weeks of ownership, P uncovers 14 defects in the car, several major ones of which neither the dealer nor the manufacturer is able to repair.

The court will probably use § 2-719(2) to invalidate the disclaimer of liability for consequential damages. Because the car has so many defects, enforcing the warranty-limitation would deprive P of the substantial value of her bargain, which was to have an essentially defect-free new car, not a car with many unfixable defects.

2. **Unconscionability:**   A limitation of damages may be *unconscionable*. § 2-719(3) sets forth two guidelines for determining when a remedy limitation is unconscionable:

    (1) "Limitation of consequential damages for *injury* to the person in the case of *consumer goods* is *prima facie unconscionable*..."; but

    (2) "limitation of damages where the loss is *commercial* is *not* [prima facie unconscionable.]"

In other words, where a consumer has been physically injured the burden will be on the seller to show that a clause limiting or eliminating consequential damages is not unconscionable. But where the losses are ones suffered by a business person, she will have the burden of showing the unconscionability of a clause limiting damages in any way. The Code says nothing about the presumption of unconscionability in the case of a consumer who has suffered property damage, or a business user who has suffered personal injury.

a. **Unconscionable disclaimers:**   Keep in mind that the unconscionability guidelines quoted above from § 2-719(3) apply only to *limitations on remedy*, not to *disclaimers* of warranty liability. Thus where a seller disclaims, for instance, all express and implied warranties, the possible unconscionability of the disclaimer must be measured by the general Code unconscionability provision, § 2-302(1).

Quiz Yourself on

WARRANTIES (Entire Chapter)

135. Delilah wants to cut Samson's hair. She goes to Medusa's Beauty Supply Store to buy some shears. Medusa shows her a sample of the Exacto-Chop, manufactured by Exacto Corp. Exacto-Chop is a newly-invented hair-cutting machine that attaches to a vacuum cleaner hose; the device cuts the hair and sucks up the trimmings at the same time. Medusa tells Delilah, "This machine is foolproof: You just program in the style you want and it does all the work for you, with extreme accuracy." Delilah decides to buy one.

(A) Delilah takes home the box containing the Exacto-Chop, opens it, and finds an owner's manual. The manual contains the following statement (which Delilah reads before she uses the device): "Exacto-Chop cannot guarantee satisfactory results. Use at your own risk. ALL WARRANTIES ARE HEREBY DISCLAIMED." (Assume that the outside of the box contains no relevant information.) Delilah tries the machine on Samson, using it according to the instructions, and with the intent of giving Samson a regular crew-cut. Instead, Samson ends up looking like a cross between a bald eagle and a mangy sheep. If you represent Delilah, what type(s) of warranty action would you advise, and against whom?

(B) Will Delilah succeed in the action(s) you recommended in (A)?

(C) Now assume that Medusa does not make any express statement about the device, but that she simply shows the box to Delilah as something she might be interested in. The advertising copy on the outside of the box says, "Precise and Automated Hair Cutter!" Delilah buys one. (Assume that there's no disclaimer in or on the box.) When Delilah tries the machine on Samson, it has the same bad results as in Parts (A) and (B). What successful warranty claim(s), if any, can Delilah bring against Exacto Corp?

136. Saul Practitioner is an attorney in practice for himself. He decides it is time to update his computer system, but he knows very little about the latest technological options. He goes to a local computer dealer and consults with Tammy Techno, the owner. Saul explains that he needs a computer to keep track of his billable time, to generate his invoices, to do his accounting work and to do his word processing. Tammy shows him a computer that is "on special." Saul buys it, but when he gets it back to the office and sets it up, he discovers that the computer is completely inadequate for his needs. There is nothing inherently wrong with it, however — it is a perfectly fine computer for most kinds of tasks for which people customarily use a PC.

(A) Assuming the sale price meant he could not return the PC, can Saul recover for some kind of breach of warranty? If so, what kind, and what will he have to prove?

(B) Now assume that when Saul signed the sales slip, it contained the following language: "There are no warranties which extend beyond the product descriptions on the packaging of the items you are purchasing." This statement was printed in red ink (the rest of the sales slip was in black). Assume that in the absence of this statement, Saul would have a valid claim for breach of some sort of warranty. How does the clause affect Saul's rights?

Answers

135. **(A) An express-warranty action against Medusa, and a claim for breach of the implied warranty of merchantability against Exacto Corp.**

(B) Probably yes, as to both defendants. First, Medusa, by telling Delilah that the machine is "foolproof" and cuts with "extreme accuracy," has made an *express warranty* as to these performance attributes. And Exacto Corp., by manufacturing and selling the machine at all, has made an ***impliedly warranted*** the machine's "merchantability," which means that Exacto has implicitly said that the goods are, among other things, "fit for the ordinary purposes for which such goods are used." (§ 2-314(2)(c).) It seems highly likely that the machine doesn't in fact satisfy either of these warranties, so unless there has been an effective disclaimer, both defendants will lose.

The question, then, is whether the disclaimer statement in the owner's manual will be effective. The answer is that it will probably not be. The problem for both defendants is that the only disclaimer was contained in the owner's manual, which was inside the box. Since Delilah was not given an opportunity to read the manual before she made the purpose (and was not, so far as the facts tell us, otherwise aware of the disclaimer), a court will probably hold that the disclaimer was a post-contract fact, which had no impact on the parties' bargain.

(C) Breach of both an express warranty and the implied warranty of merchantability. The description on the outside of the box would constitute an express warranty that the machine will indeed precisely and automatically cut hair. Since it doesn't, that's grounds for recovery. And any good is impliedly warranted by its seller (Exacto is a "seller" for this purpose, even though it didn't sell directly to Delilah) to be "merchantable," which under UCC § 2-314(2)(f) includes conforming to promises or affirmations of fact made on the container or label.

136. (A) Yes, for breach of the implied warranty of "fitness for a particular purpose." In order to succeed, Saul will have to prove three things: (1) that Tammy knew what he needed the computer to be able to do, (2) that Tammy knew Saul was relying on Tammy's skill and judgment to recommend a suitable computer, and (3) that Saul did in fact rely on Tammy's advice.

(B) This statement will work as an effective *disclaimer* of the implied warranty of fitness for a particular purpose. UCC § 2-316(2) allows a merchant to disclaim implied warranties, provided that the merchant follows some specific rules. In the case of a warranty of fitness for a particular purpose, the rules are that the disclaimer must be: (1) in writing, and (2) "conspicuous." The statement on the sales slip will likely pass the test, because it is in writing and is conspicuous (due to the contrasting ink color).

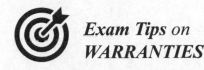

Exam Tips on
WARRANTIES

☛ **Express warranty:** Be on the lookout for descriptions of goods or services to be furnished, since such descriptions are usually express warranties. For instance, a *description of goods in a sales contract is an express warranty that the goods will have those qualities.*

Example: B agrees to purchase 250 2" x 4" "construction grade" wooden studs from S by a written contract in which she agrees to tender payment on delivery prior to inspection. After paying for the studs, B inspects them and discovers that they're utility grade instead of construction grade. B sends a letter notifying S that the studs are defective, but keeps them and uses them anyway. B is entitled to damages for breach of express warranty, since the description of the goods as "construction grade" amounted to an express warranty that the goods would have this feature, and B's use of the goods after inspection did not serve as a waiver of the warranty.

☛ **Implied warranty:** Remember that a contract providing that goods are to be sold *"as is"* serves to impliedly disclaim all implied warranties (including the warranty of merchantability and the warranty of fitness for a particular purpose). But such language does not exclude express warranties.

> **Example:** Seller offers, on e-bay.com, a "1951 Barbie & Ken matching 'Beach Party' doll set, sold as is." The words "as is" would prevent the buyer from suing on account of the poor condition of the set, even if a sale of dolls on e-bay would normally include an implied warranty that the goods were in good enough condition to be worth collecting. However, the words would not prevent the buyer from suing if the dolls turned out to be a 1980 set, because the description "1950" constituted an express warranty that the dolls were from that year, and the words "as is" do not modify or disclaim express warranties, only implied ones.

CHAPTER 15

DISCHARGE OF CONTRACTS

ChapterScope

This chapter focuses on various ways the parties to a contract can, by mutual consent, discharge one or both of them from their obligations under the contract. Key concepts:

- **Rescission:** If neither party has fully performed, the parties may agree to *rescind*, i.e., cancel, the contract. Each party gives up his rights under the contract in consideration for freedom from completing performance.

- **Accord and satisfaction:** An *"accord"* is an agreement in which one party to a contract promises to render a *substitute performance,* and the other party promises to accept that substitute performance in discharge of the existing duty.

   - **Satisfaction:** The discharge of the existing duty does not occur until the substitute performance is completed. The completion of the substitute performance is called a *"satisfaction"* of the accord. Therefore, if the substitute performance does not occur, the party who agreed to receive it has a *choice* of suing either for breach of the original contract or for breach of the accord.

- **Substituted agreement:** In a *"substituted agreement,"* the parties discharge the existing agreement by replacing it.

   - **Why it matters:** If a party agrees to a substituted agreement, she *loses the right to sue on the original agreement* if the other party breaches the substituted agreement. That's why it's important to distinguish between a substituted agreement and an accord.

- **Novation:** After a party delegates his duties to a third party, if the obligee agrees to *relieve the original obligor/delegator of all liability* and to hold *only* the substituted obligor/delegate liable, a *"novation"* has taken place.

I. RESCISSION

A. **Mutual rescission:** As long as a contract is executory on both sides (i.e., neither party has fully performed), the parties may agree to cancel the whole contract. Such an agreement is called a *mutual rescission*. It is enforceable because it is supported by consideration on both sides: each party is receiving freedom from his remaining obligations under the contract, in return for giving up his rights under the contract. See Rest. 2d, § 283.

   Example: *A* and *B* make a contract, by which *A* promises to paint *B*'s house and *B* promises to pay *A* $5,000. After beginning the work, *A* realizes that he will lose more money by completing the work than by giving up at once. Therefore, he makes *B* an offer to rescind the contract, and *B* accepts. There has been a mutual rescission, and the duties of both *A* and *B* are discharged. Rest. 2d, § 283, Illustr. 1.

B. **Where fully performed on one side:** If the contract has been *fully performed* on one side (either because it was originally a unilateral contract or because it was a bilateral contract that has subsequently been performed fully by one party), a mutual rescission will *not be effective*. The reason for this is that there is no mutual consideration; the party who has fully performed is giving up his rights to the other party's performance, and is not getting anything in return. However, he may give up his rights through what is called a *release*, *infra*, p. 514. But unlike a mutual rescission, a release must normally be supported by separate consideration (i.e., a payment), or must meet some statutory substitute for separate consideration (e.g., be in writing).

C. **Writing not necessary:**   A mutual rescission does *not normally have to be in writing*. Although older cases held that if the original contract was within the Statute of Frauds, a rescission of it had to be in writing, the modern view is that an oral rescission of the unperformed duties under a contract is always valid, notwithstanding the Statute. Rest. 2d, § 148.

D. **Duty to pay for benefits received:**   Often a mutual rescission will occur after one of the parties has partly performed. Is a party who has received the benefit of the other's part performance obligated to pay for it?

   1. **General view:**   Most courts take the view that neither party to a mutual rescission is obligated to pay for benefits she has already received, unless there is some affirmative evidence that the parties intended her to be so obligated. In other words, the question is what the parties intended, but the presumption is that they intended no obligation to pay. See Murray, p. 511. See also C&P, p. 796.

E. **Unilateral rescission:**   Where one of the parties to a contract has been the victim of fraud, duress, mistake, or breach by the other party, he will often be allowed to cancel the contract, terminating his obligations under it. If he does so, some courts say that he has *"unilaterally rescinded"* the contract. Because the term "rescission" is usually used to mean a mutual agreement to discharge an executory bilateral contract, it is probably a good idea to avoid the term "unilateral rescission" and instead to say that the victim of fraud, mistake, etc. may *"cancel"* or "terminate" the contract.

II. EXECUTORY ACCORDS AND "ACCORD AND SATISFACTION"

A. **Executory accord:**   An *executory accord* is an agreement by the parties to a contract by which one promises to render a *substitute performance* in the future, and the other promises to *accept that substitute performance* in discharge of the *existing duty*. See Rest. 2d, § 281(1).

> **Example:** Debtor has a contractual duty to pay Creditor $1,000 in 30 days. Creditor promises Debtor that if Debtor will pay $1,100 in 60 days, Creditor will accept this payment in discharge; Debtor promises to make the $1,100 payment in 60 days. The new agreement is an executory accord.

B. **Consequence of accord:**   Executory accords are enforceable. However, an accord does *not discharge the previous contractual duty as soon as the accord is made*; instead, no discharge occurs until the terms of the accord are *performed*. Rest. 2d, § 281(2). The possible effects of an accord may be illustrated by reference to the above example.

1. **Accord and satisfaction:** Suppose that, in the above example, Debtor pays the $1,100 in 60 days. His payment, pursuant to the terms of the accord, acts as a *satisfaction*. That is, it discharges his original obligation to pay $1,000, and Creditor will not be able to sue for any damages which he may have sustained as a result of the later payment. The combination of the original executory accord and the later satisfaction of it are referred to as an *"accord and satisfaction."*

2. **Failure to perform accord agreement:** But now suppose that Debtor does not pay the $1,100 in 60 days. Here, Creditor has an option. He may if he wishes sue for breach of the original contact to pay $1,000, or, he may sue for breach of the accord agreement. Thus he has the alternative of either recovering $1,000 plus damages for failure to get his money in 30 days, or $1,100 plus damages for his failure to get his money in 60 days. Rest. 2d, § 281(3).

3. **Breach by Creditor:** By making the accord agreement, Creditor impliedly promises that he will give Debtor 60 days in which to raise the money. If Creditor breaches this implied promise by suing for the $1,000 after 30 days, Debtor will have two choices. He can obtain specific performance of the accord agreement (i.e., obtain an order preventing Creditor from suing until the 60 days are up), or he can pay the $1,000 and recover damages for Creditor's failure to wait the full 60 days.

C. **Check cashing as an accord and satisfaction:** Suppose that Debtor owes a sum to Creditor but that the parties are in dispute as to the proper amount of the debt; Debtor claims that he owes $100, but Creditor claims that the debt is $200. Suppose further that Debtor sends Creditor a check for $150, marked "payment in full." If Creditor cashes the check, can he be said to have impliedly accepted an offer of accord and satisfaction, thus discharging Debtor? The brief answer is yes, in most cases. The subject is discussed more extensively *supra*, p. 102.

III. SUBSTITUTED AGREEMENT

A. **Substituted agreement distinguished from executory accord:** An accord agreement, as we have noted, does not discharge the debtor until he has performed according to its terms. Therefore, if she breaches the accord agreement, the creditor has the option of suing for breach of the *original contract*, or for breach of the accord. But rather than making an accord agreement, the parties may make a *substituted agreement*, by which the previous contract is *immediately discharged*, and replaced with a new agreement. See Rest. 2d, § 279(1).

> **Example:** Debtor owes Creditor $1,000, payable in 30 days. Creditor says to Debtor, "If you promise to pay me $1,100 in 60 days, I will immediately cancel the $1,000 debt that is payable in 30 days." Debtor promises to do so. The parties have made a substituted agreement, immediately discharging the original debt.

B. **Consequences of substituted agreement:** The substituted agreement, unlike the executory accord, *immediately discharges the original contract.* Thus if, in the above example, Debtor fails to pay the $1,100 in 60 days, Creditor has no option as to remedies. He must sue for breach of the *new agreement*, and *cannot recover for breach of the original one.* See Rest. 2d, § 279(2).

C. Distinguishing between an executory accord and a substituted agreement: It is important to distinguish between the substituted agreement and the executory accord, since under the former, the creditor immediately loses his right to enforce the original contract, whereas under the latter he does not. But it is frequently extremely difficult to tell whether a particular real-life transaction was one or the other. The answer, of course, depends on what the "intent of the parties" was, but this is often difficult to ascertain. Here are some presumptions that courts use:

1. **Disputed or unliquidated claim:** If, under the original contract, the debtor *disputed* either the existence of his debt, or its amount, the presumption is that there is a *substituted agreement* rather than an executory accord. "This is because it is assumed that the creditor enters into the new agreement to obtain the certainty of a promise rather than the uncertainty of an unliquidated claim." C&P, p. 804.

   a. **Liquidated claims:** Conversely, if the obligation under the original contract was *undisputed* and *certain as to amount*, "it will generally be presumed that the creditor *did not intend to surrender his prior rights* unless and until the new agreement is actually performed." C&P, p. 804. Therefore, an executory accord, rather than a substituted agreement, will be presumed.

2. **Formalized agreement:** The more *deliberate* and *formalized* the agreement is, the more likely it is that the parties intended to *substitute* the new agreement for prior claims. *Id.*

   a. **Informal agreement:** So a very *informal* (perhaps oral) modification of a formal agreement is probably an *executory accord*, not a substituted agreement; if so, the obligee can sue on the original contract.

D. Formal requirements for substituted agreement: A substituted agreement is often called a *"modification."* Depending on whether the contract falls under the UCC or not, a modification of it may have to satisfy a requirement of consideration, a requirement of a writing, or both.

1. **Consideration requirement:** Some states hold that where a modification operates solely to the benefit of one party, it is ineffective because it is not supported by consideration. (The party receiving the benefit of the modification has not given up anything in return.) Other states hold that even where the modification is completely one-sided, it is enforceable if it was made after *unforeseen difficulties* arose in performing the original agreement. And a few states have simply held that no consideration is necessary for a modification. C&P, pp. 184-85.

   a. **Some new obligation sufficient:** Even those states requiring consideration for a modification hold that a very small change in each party's duties is sufficient. Thus where a building contractor threatens to cease work unless the price is raised, a modification whereby he agrees to perform slightly different (even if not necessarily more burdensome) duties in return for a higher price will be upheld. See *supra*, p. 100.

   b. **UCC:** The UCC explicitly does away with the requirement of consideration for modifications of sales contracts. § 2-209(1) provides that "An agreement modifying a contract within this article needs no consideration to be binding."

2. **Requirement of a writing:** Virtually all states, and the UCC (§ 2-209(3)), agree that if a contract as modified must satisfy the Statute of Frauds, the modification must be *in writing.* The topic is discussed further *supra*, p. 298.

IV. NOVATION

A. **Definition of novation:** In the treatment of delegation of duties (*supra*, p. 407), we said that a party to a contract who delegates his duties under that contract to a third person remains liable. If, however, the obligee under the original contract (i.e., the person to whom the duty is owed) agrees to relieve the obligor of all liability after delegation, a *novation* is said to have occurred. The effect of the novation is to **substitute for the original obligor a stranger to the original contract**, the delegate. Thus the novation is a kind of substituted agreement, one involving a third person. See Rest. 2d, § 280, Comment b.

B. **Consent:** The *obligee* must obviously *consent* to the novation, since its effect is to take away his right to hold the obligor liable if the delegate fails to perform. Also, the delegate must obviously consent, since he is being charged with liability for performing. Most courts hold that the original obligor, who is being discharged from liability via the novation, need not consent. Rest. 2d, § 280, Comment c.

> **Example:** Bank holds a mortgage on Homeowner's house. Homeowner sells the house to X. If X agrees to be personally liable for payment of the mortgage, and Bank agrees to discharge Homeowner from liability on the mortgage, a novation has occurred. Most courts would not require Homeowner's consent, although in this situation he would obviously have an incentive to consent. (Recall that in this kind of mortgage situation, X is said to have "assumed" the mortgage — see *supra*, p. 419).

V. ACCOUNT STATED

A. **Discharge by account stated:** Suppose Debtor and Creditor have had several transactions, and Creditor sends Debtor a bill summarizing these transactions and attaching a price to each. If Debtor holds the bill for an unreasonably long time without objecting to its contents, Creditor will be able to use the bill as the basis for a suit on an "account stated." See Rest. 2d, § 282(1).

1. **Effect of account stated:** The advantage to Creditor of being able to sue on an "account stated" is that his burden of pleading and proof is simplified. He is not obligated to plead and prove the making and performance of each of the underlying contracts, but must merely show that he sent the account, and that it was not objected to. See Rest. 2d, § 282(2).

2. **Rebuttal by debtor:** Debtor is still free to show that the bill is not an accurate reflection of the contract which it purports to summarize. But the burden of making such a demonstration is upon him, whereas in the absence of an account, the burden of proving a contract would be on the plaintiff-creditor.

VI. RELEASE AND COVENANT NOT TO SUE

A. Release: Where a contract is at least partly executory on both sides, the parties may agree to call it off. Such an agreement, is, as we have seen, called a rescission and needs neither a writing nor consideration to be binding. But where a contract is executory only on one side, rescission is not available, because the person who has already fully performed would not be receiving any consideration for giving up his rights under the contract. He may, however, give up his rights by virtue of a ***release***, i.e., a document executed by him discharging the other party. See Rest. 2d, § 284(1).

B. Formal requirements: In most jurisdictions, a release must either be supported by ***consideration*** (e.g., a payment of a dollar amount), or by a statutory substitute for consideration. Some states, for instance, have statutes providing that a ***signed writing is a substitute for consideration***. See, e.g., N.Y. Gen. Oblig. L. § 15-503, which states that "a written instrument which purports to be a total or partial release of all claims...shall not be invalid because of the absence of consideration or of a seal."

    1. UCC view: The UCC similarly takes the view that a signed writing may sometimes constitute a valid release, even though it is not supported by consideration: "any claim or right arising out of an alleged breach can be discharged in whole or in part without consideration by a written waiver or renunciation signed and delivered by the aggrieved party." § 1-306. Note, however, that this UCC provision applies only to claims relating to an actual breach of contract, whereas the New York statute quoted above applies to any release, even of rights not yet due under the contract.

C. Covenant not to sue: A release is an executed transaction, i.e., one which takes effect immediately. Sometimes, however, a party who has a contract claim makes a ***promise not to sue*** on this claim, rather than releasing it immediately. Such a promise is commonly called a "covenant not to sue;" its effect is virtually the same as that of a release. See Rest. 2d, § 285.

Quiz Yourself on
DISCHARGE OF CONTRACTS (Entire Chapter)

137. Calvin hires Hobbes to build a treehouse out of cherry wood for him for $1,000. Hobbes builds the treehouse, but uses particle board instead. Calvin refuses to pay, despite Hobbes' frequent entreaties. Calvin finally says, "I'll give you $750 next Tuesday, and that's it. Do you accept?" Hobbes says, "Yes." On Tuesday, Calvin tenders the $750. Hobbs, however, says, "I've changed my mind, I want the full $1,000," and refuses to take the $750. If Hobbes sues for the full $1,000, can he recover this sum?

138. Mrs. O'Leary buys a cow from the Here-A-Moo Cow Farm on February 25 for $100, payable March 25. On March 10, she writes and says she is having a hard time coming up with the money. Here-A-Moo writes back a one-line letter: "We'll take a goat from your farm, instead of $100, if you deliver by April 15." Mrs. O'Leary writes back a 2-word response: "I agree."

(A) For this part only, assume that on April 1, Here-A-Moo announces to Mrs. O'Leary that it has changed its mind, and will require cash. On April 15, Mrs. O'Leary tenders a goat. May Here-A-Moo reject the goat and successfully sue for $100?

(B) For this part only, assume that Here-A-Moo never announces any change of mind. April 15 comes and goes, but Mrs. O'Leary never tenders her goat. What remedies can Here-A-Moo seek?

139. Stanley and Ollie enter into an agreement whereby Ollie will detail Stanley's car for $150. Ollie gets started, but doesn't do more than spit-shine the chrome around the headlights (a service worth about $10 on the open market) when he realizes this is not his cup of tea. He tells Stanley he wants out of the agreement. Stanley decides he should probably trust his car to a professional anyway, and agrees. Can Ollie sue to recover the $10 value of the partial performance he has rendered?

Answers

137. No. In answering this question, you should first try to figure out whether the parties intended to make a "substituted agreement" (in which the new deal, as soon as it's agreed to, completely extinguishes the old deal) or instead an "executory accord" (in which the new deal does not extinguish the old deal until the terms of the new deal are fully performed.) The most important single factor in distinguishing between the two types of deals is the level of formality: the more *in*formal, the more likely it is that the parties intended an accord. So here, the fact that the deal is oral suggests that it's an accord.

Therefore, if Calvin had not tendered the $750, Hobbes would have been able to sue for the full, original $1,000. But when Calvin tendered the $750, he was fulfilling the terms of the accord. Once performance (called "satisfaction") under the terms of the accord was tendered, this was enough to extinguish Hobbes' right to sue for the original amount.

138. (A) No. As in the prior question, the new deal here was probably an accord, not a substituted agreement. (That's because it was relatively informal, as manifested by the extreme brevity of the writings, and the fact that there's no indication of any intent by the parties to replace the prior agreement.) However, although an accord does not immediately extinguish the prior agreement, the accord is still a binding contract: each party has the right to tender performance in exchange for extinguishment of the original deal. So Mrs. O'Leary had a contractual right to tender a goat in full performance by April 15, and Here-A-Moo's announcement of a change of mind could not and did not remove that right.

(B) Here-A-Moo has a choice: it can sue on *either* promise — the original promise for $100, or the substituted one for the goat. As we indicated in Part (A), the agreement here was probably an accord, not a substituted agreement. Therefore, the mere making of the new deal did not extinguish Here-A-Moo's rights under the original deal (that extinguishment would have occurred only if Mrs. O'Leary tendered a goat by April 15.) Once Mrs. O'Leary breached her promise under the accord, Here-A-Moo got the right to sue under either the old deal or the new deal.

139. Probably not. What has happened here is that the parties entered into a "mutual rescission" — an agreement to cancel the whole contract. When this happens, most courts hold that neither party is obligated to pay for any benefits already received under the contract, unless there is some affirmative evidence that the parties intended otherwise. There is nothing under these facts to indicate that the parties intended to compensate Ollie for his spit shine, so he's out of luck.

Exam Tips on
DISCHARGE OF CONTRACTS

Discharge of Obligations Through Accord and Novation

☞ Watch for a fact situation in which both parties agree to perform *differently* than originally agreed, or agree to the substitution of a party to the contract.

☞ **Accord.** This is an agreement to accept a lesser obligation than the one which existed under the original contract. Watch for a *substituted performance* by both parties.

☞ **Consideration:** Be sure to identify the *consideration* given by both parties for the change in obligations. If there is no consideration, the new agreement is not binding and either party can try to enforce the original contract terms.

☞ **Satisfaction:** Look for a situation where there hasn't been "satisfaction" (performance) of the new obligation. If the accord has been breached by one of the parties, the other party can sue on the *original obligation.*

Example: *S* and *B* sign a contract for the sale of 500 bicycles to *B* for $50,000. The contract requires delivery prior to June 1 and payment within 30 days after delivery. *S* delivers the bicycles on May 15 and asks if *B* can pay immediately. *B* promises to pay within five days if *S* will accept $45,000 as payment in full. *S* agrees. By June 20, *B* has made no payment at all. *S* sues *B* for $50,000. Since there was no satisfaction of the accord by payment of $45,000, *B* is obligated to pay the original contractual amount, $50,000.

Caution: Be sure to distinguish between an accord and a substituted agreement: In an accord, *A* can still sue on the original deal if *B* breaches the accord. In a substituted contract, *A* can only sue on the substituted deal, not the original one, if *B* breaches the substituted deal. The more informal the new deal (e.g., it's oral), the more likely it is to be an accord, not a substituted agreement.

☞ **Check cashing:** Look for a fact pattern where a debtor sends to a creditor a check for a lesser amount than the creditor thinks is due him and it's clearly marked *"payment in full."* Even if the creditor marks the check "under protest," the recently-revised UCC rule (§ 3-311) is that the creditor's act of cashing it constitutes an enforceable *discharge* of the debtor as long as:

❏ the amount of the debt was *unliquidated* (not fixed) or subject to a *bona fide dispute*; and

❏ the debtor acted in *good faith*.

☞ **Novation.** Look for a *delegation of duties* where the obligee under the original contract agrees to *relieve the obligor of liability* and to hold *only* the delegate liable. This is a "novation."

☞ Make sure there has been consent by all parties. Although a novation can be implied, this will happen only if the facts indicate that the obligee has intended to *release the delegator from his obligations*. The mere fact that the obligee *remains silent* when told of the delegation and/or assignment (or even the fact that the obligee *consents to the delegation*) is *not enough* to constitute a novation.

ESSAY EXAM
QUESTIONS AND ANSWERS

The following questions were adapted from various Harvard Law School First-Year Contracts examinations of the past. The questions are reproduced almost exactly as they actually appeared, with only slight changes to the facts. The sample answers are not "official" and represent merely one approach to handling the questions.

QUESTION 1: David Dole, owner of 75,000 acres of forest land in Dover County, Maine, had attempted for several years without success to persuade state and local authorities to purchase the tract as a wildlife refuge. He was approached by Paul Pinsky, a prominent producer of motion pictures and creator of an entertainment park in California known as Pinsky Land. Pinsky said that he saw great possibilities in Dole's tract of land as a ski area if properly developed with access roads, motels and a summer resort, and if several hundred cottages were built for rental. However, extensive surveys would be needed before he would want to buy. Dole explained that the taxes assessed against the property were delinquent, and that the 2014 tax would be payable Dec. 11, 2014. Dole added: "I simply have to bail out by then." Dole then prepared and gave Pinsky the following document:

Oct. 9, 2014

I hereby give Paul Pinsky the privilege of entering my land in Dover County, Maine to survey and map it as a recreation area. I will sell him the whole tract of 75,000 acres for $7.5 million, provided he accepts this offer by giving me a certified check for $750,000 on or before Dec. 4, 2014.

/s/ Paul Dole

Pinsky sent a crew of surveyors and architects to the Dover County tract, where they worked for four weeks, at a cost to Pinsky of $100,000. Their activities became widely known and on Nov. 12, a group of five wealthy owners of land in Maine approached Dole, who informed them of his offer to Pinsky. They persuaded Dole that the land should be preserved unspoiled if possible. During the next two weeks the five secured pledges totaling $10 million from 500 persons, and on Nov. 30 the five gave Dole a check for $1 million and jointly signed a promissory note for the remaining $9 million. Dole then executed a conveyance of the 75,000 acre tract to the Wilderness Society, a non-profit corporation whose charter authorizes it "to receive and hold land that is still preserved in or can revert to its natural state and to dispose of such holdings only on such terms as will insure that its natural state is preserved so far as possible."

On Dec. 1, 2014, Pinsky called from California to Dole's home in Webster, Mass., gave his name, and said, "I have a $750,000 check for Mr. Dole. Where shall I mail it?" Acting on instruction from Dole, his wife replied, "He has moved. I don't know where he is." Pinsky arrived in Webster on Dec. 2 with a $750,000 check in his pocket. He inquired around the city and was told that Dole was last seen leaving town by bus with a lot of camping gear. Pinsky, in hot and continuous pursuit, proceeded to the Dover County tract and after searching through the forest finally found Dole in a secluded cabin on Dec. 6. Pinsky said: "Mr. Dole, I believe. Here is your check, well within your Dec. 11 tax deadline." Pinsky tendered a $750,000 certified check but Dole refused to accept it. Pinsky now consults your law firm. The senior partner instructs you to "prepare a memorandum discussing the legal and equitable remedies Pinsky may have against Dole and the Wilderness Society, and stating your best judgment of the likelihood of success concerning each possible remedy." Write the memorandum.

SAMPLE ANSWER TO QUESTION 1: *Was there an acceptance while the offer was still in force?* I am putting aside until later whether Dole's offer was an *irrevocable* one. Assuming that the offer was not irrevocable, the question is whether Pinsky accepted while the offer was still in force.

As a preliminary matter, it is not clear that Dole's offer of October 9th is sufficiently definite to give rise to an enforceable contract upon Pinsky's tender of a check (p. 67). The offer contemplates that Dole will give Pinsky $6.75 million worth of credit, but does not specify when this large sum must be paid, nor how it is to be secured. Nor does the offer specify a conveyance date. Thus a court might hold that even if we show that Pinsky did accept before Dole revoked or the offer lapsed, there is no enforceable contract for lack of definiteness. But I think we have a fair chance of showing that as of October 9th, the parties fully intended to reach sufficiently definite terms upon Pinsky's tender of a check. The court might therefore be induced to supply the missing terms with respect to time for full payment, conveyance date, security, etc. (p. 68).

Turning now to whether Pinsky did anything to accept while there was still a valid power of acceptance, the general rule is that the offeror has the right to set the time as of which his offer expires (p. 48). Thus, Dole's October 9th offer created a power of acceptance which lasted no later than December 4th. It is possible that we will be able to show that Pinsky's call to Dole's wife, in which he said that he had the check ready for mailing, constituted an acceptance. However, in all probability Dole will successfully contend that only receipt by him of the check, not a statement of Pinsky's readiness to send it, constituted an acceptance. Dole could point to the general rule that gives the offeror the right to prescribe the exact means by which his offer may be accepted (p. 20).

It is also possible that Pinsky's act of showing up in Webster with the check constituted a sort of "constructive" acceptance, in that he did everything in his power to give Dole a check at the place where Dole was supposed to be. Again, however, I would imagine that a court would hold that no acceptance could take place until Dole was actually given the check. We could argue that Dole's act of disappearing constituted an intentional interference with Pinsky's right of acceptance, and that therefore Dole has no right to insist upon the precise conditions of his offer (i.e., that the check actually be given to him in person.) However, since I am now assuming that Dole's offer was revocable at any time, presumably Dole had the right to thwart Pinsky by moving, just as he had the right to revoke the offer outright. This would be an indirect communication of revocation (p. 50).

We might try the argument that Dole in fact made two offers to Pinsky: one was the written offer, which terminated on December 4th, and the other was an oral offer which by its terms was to last until December 11th (Dole's tax deadline). Therefore, we would contend, the oral offer remained in force until expressly revoked, and Pinsky's December 6th tender of a check was a valid acceptance of this offer. (Dole's refusal to accept this check on the 6th probably would not be a revocation of the offer, since I think a court would hold that the tender of the check was sufficient to accept.)

I think, however, that this "two offers" theory is unlikely to prevail. Even if we convince the court that there were two offers, Dole will have a good chance of showing that the oral offer was revoked. An offeror can revoke his offer by indirect as well as direct means (p. 50). Restatement 2d, § 43, states that "An offeree's power of acceptance is terminated when the offeror takes definite action inconsistent with an intention to enter into the proposed contract and the offeree acquires reliable information to that effect." Dole could argue that when he went off into the wilderness without telling anyone of his whereabouts, and Pinsky learned of his having done so, it should have been clear to Pinsky that Dole meant not to accept the offer.

In summary, unless we can show that Dole's offer was irrevocable, I think we will have a very hard time showing that Pinsky accepted it while he still had a valid power of acceptance. I turn now to the irrevocability question.

Irrevocability of the offer: There are a number of theories which we might advance to establish that Dole's October 9th offer was *irrevocable* until December 4th. If we can succeed with any of these arguments, I think we will then be able to convince the court that Dole's running off into the wilderness was an interference with Pinsky's right to exercise his option, and that Pinsky should be regarded as having validly exercised the option by arriving in Webster with the check. (If the offer was irrevocable, Dole should not have the right to get around its irrevocability by making it impossible for Pinsky to accept.)

One theory is that the October 9th offer was a validly binding **option contract.** Restatement 2d, § 87(1)(a), makes an offer irrevocable as an option contract if it "is in writing and signed by the offeror, recites a purported consideration for the making of the offer, and proposes an exchange on fair terms within a reasonable time." (p. 133.) The difficulty with this provision is that Dole's October 9th document does not recite a purported consideration. Therefore, unless the jurisdiction in which Pinsky sues has a statute or case law analogous to the UCC "firm offer" provision, § 2-205 (by which a merchant's signed offer to sell that states that it will be kept open for a certain time is irrevocable, even without consideration — p. 53), I don't think a conventional option contract theory will work. We might conceivably be able to show that Pinsky's act of surveying was of benefit to Dole, and bargained for by him, and was therefore consideration for the option. But since there's a good chance that the court will find that Dole didn't care whether Pinsky surveyed or not, and that there was therefore no consideration for the option, I think this whole "binding option" contract theory will probably go down the drain.

A more promising theory is that Dole's offer was for a **unilateral contract,** and that when Pinsky began to perform the requisite act of acceptance (i.e., the tender of a check), the offer became temporarily irrevocable (p. 55). See Restatement 2d, § 45. To win with this theory, we would have to convince the court that from the time Pinsky got to Webster, he was engaged in the act of tendering the check (and not merely *preparing* to tender the check.) If we can establish this, we have a good chance of getting the court to follow Restatement § 45, and Pinsky will be able to get the full expectation measure of damages.

Promissory Estoppel: If all of the above theories fail, I think we can at least let Pinsky get his $100,000 in surveyors' fees, by use of the doctrine of **promissory estoppel.** Restatement 2d, § 87(2) provides that "An offer which the offeror should reasonably expect to induce action or forbearance of a substantial character on the part of the offeree before acceptance and which does induce such action or forbearance is binding as an option contract to the extent necessary to avoid injustice" (p. 59). This provision does not require that the offer have been supported by consideration, and seems to fit Pinsky's situation to a "T." Dole certainly knew that Pinsky planned to spend money on surveyors' fees.

The reason that this promissory estoppel theory is less than completely satisfactory is that, as the Restatement puts it, enforcement will be given only "to the extent necessary to avoid injustice." I'm afraid that the court is likely to award Pinsky only his $100,000 in fees, and not to give him the "benefit of his bargain" (i.e., the profits he could have made from Pinsky World, or even the $2.5 million profit he could have made by reselling the land to the wilderness group.) It's possible that we can convince the court that "justice" requires giving Pinsky at least this $2.5 million turnaround profit, but I wouldn't count on it.

Specific Performance Against Wilderness Society: If we can establish, by one of the above theories, that there is a valid contract between Pinsky and Dole, we might be able to get the court to order **specific performance,** in the form of a decree ordering Wilderness Society to convey the land to Pinsky (and a collateral decree ordering Dole to return the money raised to purchase the land for donation to the Society) (p. 314). In support of this request for specific performance, we can point out that the Wilderness Society people are not *bona fide* purchasers, but in fact had knowledge of the offer to Pinsky. But as a practical matter, I don't think we're likely to find a judge who would be willing to turn this land over to a developer like Pinsky, rather than keeping it in its natural state. Specific performance is a remedy very much left to the trial court's discretion, and I wouldn't get our hopes up about it. I think the best we can hope for is a breach of contract verdict against Dole, with damages of the $2.5 million profit that Pinsky could have made by selling the land to the Wilderness people. If we can come up with some very specific figures showing how profitable Pinsky World would have been, maybe we can get some damages for these lost profits as well, but I'm afraid they will be held to be too speculative unless Pinsky has previously operated a similar business. (p. 323).

QUESTION 2: The General Construction Co. of Memphis, Tennessee decided to build for itself a new headquarters building of an original and striking design. It secured much publicity in journals read by architects and builders by printing artists' sketches of the building, located at a dramatic site at a bend in the Mississippi river. In the publicity was included the announcement of a self-imposed deadline for completion, a deadline that was very short by usual standards of the construction industry for a building of that size.

The Frank Corporation is a steel fabricator that buys steel ingots and transforms them into structural steel. On September 1, 2013, the General Construction Co. and the Frank Corporation executed a written contract under which Frank undertook to fabricate and deliver the structural steel called for by General's specifications, which were made part of the contract. The contract provided a delivery schedule with five lots to be delivered as follows:

Lot I	March 6, 2014
Lot II	March 27, 2014
Lot III	April 10, 2014
Lot IV	April 24, 2014
Lot V	May 1, 2014

The contract also provided that although the tonnage and value of the lots would differ somewhat, the total contract price of $10 million would be divided into five installments of $2 million each, and that General would pay Frank $1.75 million "within five days after the timely and satisfactory delivery of each lot. The $250,000 withheld from each payment will be paid by General Co. after complete performance, satisfactory to the General Co., of all Frank Co.'s obligations." The contract also stated: "Because of the importance to the General Co. of completing its own building by the published completion date, time is declared to be of the very essence of this contract and for each day's delay in delivery of any lot General may retain $5,000 as damages."

Lot I was delivered on March 12 (6 days late) and on March 14 General mailed a check for $1.75 million to Frank. Lot II was delivered April 6 (10 days late). On April 9 General's President telephoned Frank's President to express her concern about the timeliness of future deliveries.

> "I know your reputation is on the line, but supplies of steel are getting short. My usual suppliers have failed me and I expect there will be some longer delays. But aren't you worried about the recent river floods?"

General President replied:

> "Don't you worry about us. You go ahead and deliver or I'm going to saw you off."

By the date of this conversation, April 9, the steel contained in Lot I had been all attached to the foundations of the structure and a few beams from Lot II had been attached (the rest was lying on the ground at the site) when, on the morning of April 11, the levee protecting the area burst and the flood waters of the Mississippi, which were then reaching their greatest height in 100 years, covered the building site to a depth of 15 feet. The Army Corps of Engineers estimates that the water will not subside at the site before the middle of June. Past experience makes it clear that lying under water for two months will make the steel at the site unusable unless cleaned of muck and rust and covered with a special rust inhibitor. The cost of this operation will be at least $1.2 million.

On April 12, Frank faxed General:

> "Have not yet obtained steel for Lot III. Best promise from any supplier is delivery to us on May 25. We can complete fabrication of Lot III and deliver it to you by June 15. After that I will do my best to obtain supplies."

General faxed in reply:

"You have been late with every delivery. We cannot accept any promises from you. We cancel."

After canvassing all steel fabricators with substantial supplies of steel, General now finds that the best delivery terms are offered by States Steel Corp., which will charge $7.5 million for the balance of the steel due under the Frank contract. States Steel Corp. will promise to begin deliveries July 1 and complete them by August 1. The architects' journals have published pictures of the original model of the General headquarters building and beside it some steel beams projecting from the river, with such captions as

"Old Man River Rolls Over General And Just Keeps Rolling Along."

The President of General expresses to you her dismay over the effects of these events on General's reputation, and her uncertainty as to whether to complete the submerged structure. She wants to know General's rights against and liabilities to Frank if the building is completed by contracting with the States Steel Corp. for the steel required. What would you advise? Why?

She also asks whether General's rights or liabilities would be altered if the whole building project is abandoned? What is your answer? Why?

SAMPLE ANSWER TO QUESTION 2: I will examine first whether General's cancellation of the contract constituted a breach, and will then discuss the question of damages.

The cancellation: I think General can make a fairly strong case that it was entitled to cancel the contract when it did. For a definite answer, a number of UCC sections, particularly those dealing with installment contracts, must be examined.

The contract was clearly an "installment contract," since it authorized in "separate lots," and since each lot would obviously be "separately accepted" (or rejected), due to the relatively long time periods between them. § 2-612(1)). The real crux of the breach issue is presented by § 2-612(3): "Whenever nonconformity or default with respect to one or more installments substantially impairs the value of the whole contract there is a breach of the whole...." (pp. 224, 230).

Frank will undoubtedly argue that the delay with respect to Lot III did not "substantially impair the value of the whole contract," and that General therefore had no right to cancel. Frank will base this argument on the evidence that General could not have used the steel had it been delivered on time, since it would have been submerged by the flood and would have cost a significant amount to clean. Thus, Frank will argue, the delay did not substantially impair the value of the contract, since it didn't make things any worse for General than they otherwise would have been.

I think General can make a fairly convincing response to this, to the effect that not only the delay on Lot III, but also the ***uncertainty*** about whether Frank could make a timely delivery (or any delivery at all) on Lots IV and V, must be considered in determining whether there was a "substantial impairment" of the whole contract (p. 231).

Frank in turn can respond that if it was anxiety about Lots IV and V that induced General to cancel, General's proper remedy was to "demand assurances" pursuant to § 2-609, and not to cancel (pp. 245-249.) However, I think that General can reply, successfully, that Frank's April 12th fax was itself a failure to furnish reasonable assurances in response to General's request for assurances on April 9th. In that event, General had the right to treat the lack of assurances as a repudiation (§ 2-609(4)), thus allowing it to cancel § 2-711(1)). Alternatively, General can contend that Frank's April 12th fax was an ***anticipatory repudiation*** (§ 2-610), giving General a right to cancel. However, this is not as powerful an argument, in my opinion, as the "failure to give assurances" argument previously stated.

Frank might attempt to avoid liability for breach by asserting the doctrine of ***impracticability*** or ***impossibility***. He could say that his source of supply dried up unforeseeably, making performance by him "... impracticable [because of] the occurrence of a contingency the non-occurrence of which was a basic assumption on which the contract was made...." § 2-615(a) (p. 436). But assuming that the Frank-General contract had not specified a particular source from which Frank was to obtain the deal, and assuming that a shortage of steel ingots is reasonably foreseeable in the industry, it is unlikely that he would prevail with this defense (p. 439).

In summary, I am fairly confident that: (1) General can establish that it had the right to cancel the entire contract on grounds of Frank's breach; and (2) Frank should not escape liability by virtue of any "impossibility" or "impracticability" defense.

Damages: Under § 2-607(1), "[t]he buyer must pay at the contract rate for any goods accepted." Thus General will be liable to Frank for the two lots of steel it accepted, although determination of the "contract rate," and the possibility of a countervailing damage claim by General against Frank, complicate the damage issue.

I suppose that General could argue that the "contract rate" is $1.75 million per lot, and the $250,000 per lot retainage is a separate sum which serves as compensation for completion of the whole project, not as part of the payment for the lot in question. But I don't think we will get far with this argument, since it seems to me that the retainage scheme really relates to the *time for payment*, not the items for which payment is to be made. In any event, I think the question is academic. If the "contract rate" is held to include the $250,000 retainage, we will recover this $250,000 in the form of the contract/cover differential, which is discussed in the next paragraph.

Assuming that General's deal with States Steel is "in good faith" and "reasonable" (§ 2-712(1)), General can recover from Frank the difference between the cost of the cover contract with States, and the cost of the original contract (p. 365). Assuming that the court treats the first two installments as having cost a total of $4 million, the difference between the cost of cover and the cost of completion under the original contract is $1.5 million ($7.5 million - $6 million). This recovery must be offset against the remaining $2.25 million which General would owe Frank on the first two lots. If the "contract rate" on the first two lots is held to be $1.75 million, not $2 million, the net result is still the same: General would owe Frank $750,000.

However, General has a right to ***"consequential damages"*** in addition to this cover/contract differential (§ 2-715(2)); (p. 274). Consequential damages would probably include any *delay* damages suffered by General, as General's need for prompt delivery was a "particular requirement of which the seller at the time of contracting had reason to know." (§ 2-715(2)). The contract fixes delay damages at $5,000 per day. However, since this contract clause fixes damages at $5,000 for each day *delivery* is delayed, and not every day completion of the building is delayed, it is not clear whether a court would enforce this clause, or would attempt to make its own estimate of damages. Frank will have a good chance of arguing that the damages clause applies only to a slightly delayed delivery, not to breach or other cancellation of the contract, and that ordinary damage rules should apply in the latter event.

Frank will also have a good contention that its non-delivery of Lot III saved General upwards of $1 million, since the steel would have been covered by the flood, and would have cost that much to clean off. Frank could point to § 2-715(2), which allows subtraction from the cover/contract differential of any "expenses saved in consequence of the seller's breach."

In summary, I would say that General will owe Frank $750,000, plus any consequential delay damages (probably measured by usual standards, not by the $5,000 per day clause), but that the consequential damages may be reduced by the amount which de-rusting the additional lots would have cost.

If General elects to abandon the building, and not make the deal with States, the only part of the analysis which would be different is that General would use the difference between the contract price and the "market price at the time when [General] learned of the breach," not the contract/cover differential. (§ 2-713(1)). I have no idea what this market price is. Nor do I know whether the "time when [General] learned of the breach" will be held to be April 10th (when delivery was due), April 12 (when the "repudiation" took place), or whatever the date was on which General cancelled the contract; a good argument can be made that it should be this last date, since that would best protect General's right to have "for a commercially reasonable time await[ed] performance by the repudiating party." (§ 2-610(a)) (p. 271).

QUESTION 3: The Alumalloy Co., manufacturer of metal sidings for home exteriors, has divided Brighton, a city of 800,000 population, into four districts for assignment of distributorships. The standard form of agreement used with its distributors contains an undertaking by Alumalloy to fill orders secured from customers at prices to be charged to the distributors according to a schedule attached to the agreement. Further, it appoints the distributor for a four year period, "provided, however, and on express condition that Alumalloy may terminate at any time the right of Distributor to sell Alumalloy products." The agreement also provides that the distributor will have the exclusive right for the duration of his appointment to sell Alumalloy products in the geographical district of Brighton to which he is assigned. Moreover, the distributor will purchase at his own expense all equipment required for the installation of Alumalloy products and for their refabrication where this is needed, and "Distributor undertakes for the duration of this agreement not to sell or solicit sales of Alumalloy products outside the area assigned to him by this agreement." [Assume that this territorial confinement clause is consistent with public policy and the antitrust laws.]

On Sept. 10, 2012, Alumalloy and Donald Dirk signed a copy of the Alumalloy standard agreement, assigning to Dirk District II in Brighton, as defined on a map prepared by Alumalloy and attached to the agreement. On Nov. 2, 2012, Alumalloy and Peter Pigeon signed a similar agreement assigning to Pigeon District III, as defined on a map that was similarly attached. Dirk and Pigeon each purchased installation and refabrication equipment at the cost to each of approximately $200,000. During the period prior to May 1, 2014, Dirk prospered while Pigeon suffered a net operating loss of $50,000. The losses by Pigeon were due to sales resistance that he met in District III, which was for the most part a blighted area, and to the high cost of refabricating sidings to fit the old-style houses located in most of the area. During early April, 2014, Pigeon's salespeople solicited orders in a 12-square-block area within District III but near its outer edge which adjoins District II. They discovered that Dirk had already invaded this area and sold and installed Alumalloy sidings in 25 relatively new houses in the area. The profit to Dirk on these installations averaged $3,000 per house.

(A) Pigeon inquires of you whether, if Alumalloy cancels his distributorship, he can recover any damages by suing either Alumalloy or Dirk. On the basis of the facts so far stated, what would you advise? Why?

(B) Pigeon then complained to the Alumalloy home office concerning Dirk's invasion of his territory and received the following reply on May 1, 2014: "We do not care that much who sells our products. We are completely satisfied with Dirk, to whom we are sending a copy of this letter. We are notifying him at the same time that, for the remaining period of the contract, we waive the termination condition that we originally reserved in his agreement. We will carry you along and won't cancel you out until you have got back your investment but you will have to work out with Dirk any problems you have with him." Since receiving this letter, Pigeon continued to purchase materials from Alumalloy as he pondered upon his course of action and noted that Dirk continued to purchase and install Alumalloy sidings in ever-increasing quantities. Pigeon now asks you whether this letter improves his chances of securing damages from Dirk for the latter's past invasions of Pigeon's territory. He also asks you whether, in light of all the facts, he would be able to enjoin Dirk from future invasions. What answers would you give, and why?

SAMPLE ANSWER TO QUESTION 3:

Part (A): Pigeon has a possibility of recovering damages against either Alumalloy or Dirk.

Pigeon vs. Alumalloy: Pigeon will only have a right of action against Alumalloy if he can show that the latter breached the contract. This will in turn depend principally upon whether the termination clause of the contract ("provided, however, and on express condition that Alumalloy may terminate at any time the right of Distributor to sell Alumalloy products") is to be literally enforced. There are several indications that the parties did not intend (or at least that Pigeon did not intend) that Alumalloy would have the right to terminate the distributorship for no reason at all.

First, the contract clearly contemplated the expenditure of large sums by Pigeon for installation and refabrication. It is unlikely that Pigeon would have agreed to this requirement, and would have in fact spent $200,000, if the understanding was that he could be terminated for no reason at all.

Second, the common practice of businesspeople in distributorship arrangements like this is to make the right of termination available only where the distributor does not perform satisfactorily. Pigeon could probably introduce evidence of this common business practice (a "trade usage" — see UCC § 1-205(2)) to show that this is how the termination clause should be interpreted. Such evidence would not run afoul of the parol evidence rule, since Pigeon would be seeking not to contradict the writing, but to "interpret" it (p. 193).

The termination clause is stated to be an "express" condition of the contract as to which strict compliance would ordinarily be necessary (p. 209). However, the court has the power to require merely substantial compliance, particularly where, as here, Alumalloy has received benefits under the contract (p. 210). Thus, the court could hold that the right of termination would be exercisable only if Pigeon did not perform satisfactorily.

Alternatively, the court might hold that the termination clause was *unconscionable*, allowing the court to refuse to enforce it. In support of this contention, Pigeon could point out that the clause was buried in a standard form contract, rather than being included upon the special attached sheets which contain the most important aspects of the deal. Also, Pigeon could obviously point to the extremely one-sided and unfair effect that literal enforcement of the clause would have. Alumalloy, on the other hand, could point to the fact that both parties are businesspeople, and that the unconscionability doctrine has been used relatively rarely in such business contracts (p. 478).

Assuming that the clause is interpreted to allow a right of termination only if Pigeon performs unsatisfactorily, the satisfactoriness of his performance would be in issue. Since the contract contains no requirement that Pigeon sell a certain number of units, there is no objective standard by which to measure his performance. In view of the fact that the district assigned to Pigeon was an unpromising one, and also considering Dirk's incursion into Pigeon's territory, Pigeon's performance would probably be held to have been adequate. In that event, Alumalloy would be held to have breached by terminating the contract.

Alumalloy might attempt to argue that the entire contract is invalid for *lack of consideration.* In support of this argument, it could point to the fact that Pigeon is not required to make a certain number of sales in the district, and has therefore not really promised to do anything. However, Pigeon could answer by citing *Wood v. Lady Duff Gordon*, and by saying that he had an implied obligation to make a good-faith effort to sell the Alumalloy products (p. 114). In all probability, Pigeon would succeed with this argument.

Damages against Alumalloy: If Pigeon establishes that Alumalloy breached, he could try to obtain either expectation or reliance damages. He will have difficulty establishing with sufficient certainty that he would have made any profits from the enterprise, and even more difficulty establishing a particular dollar amount. Most courts do not permit the plaintiff to prove lost profits from a new business (p. 323), and where the new business is losing money, the task is even more difficult.

Therefore, Pigeon will be better off trying to get reliance damages. Where expectation damages are difficult to measure, courts often use reliance as a measure of damages (p. 327). However, if the defendant can prove that the plaintiff was in a "losing contract," the court will not allow a full measure of reliance damages, as this might put the plaintiff in a better position than he would have been in had the contract been performed (p. 329). However, Alumalloy will bear the burden of proving that the contract would have been a losing one for Pigeon even if no breach by Alumalloy had occurred (*id*). Even if Alumalloy does prove that Pigeon would have lost, say, $75,000 over the four-year life of the contract, Pigeon still has a good chance of recovering his $200,000 gross reliance damages minus the $75,000 he would have lost anyway, or $125,000.

Pigeon vs. Dirk: In order for Pigeon to obtain damages from Dirk, he'll have to show that Dirk's promise not to infringe on any other distributor's district created enforceable rights in Pigeon. He can do this only by showing that he was a ***third party beneficiary*** of the Alumalloy-Dirk contract.

Dirk's promise to Alumalloy created rights in Pigeon only if Alumalloy *intended* to benefit Pigeon by inducing Dirk to make the promise (p. 417). Pigeon can make a powerful argument that Alumalloy's motive in inducing such a promise of non-infringement from each of its distributors was to be able to offer each distributor an exclusive area — without Dirk's promise of non-infringement, Pigeon might have been unwilling to make his contract with Alumalloy. Therefore, Pigeon can say he was an intended beneficiary.

Dirk can counter this argument by contending that Alumalloy's motive in making him promise non-infringement was to maximize its own sales by making sure that every territory was adequately staffed. But in all probability, Pigeon will succeed in showing that the primary motive of the non-infringement provisions, from Alumalloy's point of view, was to enable it to promise each of the other dealers, including Pigeon, an exclusivity. Pigeon would therefore be able to sue Dirk as a third party beneficiary of Dirk's promise of non-infringement.

Pigeon's damages against Dirk: Pigeon has a fairly good chance of recovering from Dirk the $75,000 in profits which Dirk made by virtue of his infringement. By the expectation measure, Pigeon's damages should be enough to put him in the position he would have been in had Dirk not infringed (p. 318). Dirk will undoubtedly argue that Pigeon was not as good a salesperson as he, and that Pigeon would therefore have made far less than $75,000 out of the neighborhood where infringement took place. This issue will turn on the facts as they develop at trial, but in view of Dirk's wrongful conduct, Pigeon will have a good chance of recovering the full $75,000.

Part (B): The letter is significant in two respects: (1) It sheds some light on whether Alumalloy originally intended Dirk's promise to benefit Pigeon or not; and (2) If Pigeon did have a right to sue Dirk as third party beneficiary, the letter may constitute a *modification* of Pigeon's rights.

(1) It is hard to say whether the letter makes it more or less ambiguous that the company intended to benefit Pigeon by extracting the non-infringement promise from Dirk. Pigeon can claim that the company's statement that it doesn't care who sells its products shows that its motive, when it made Dirk promise not to infringe, was to be able to offer an exclusive deal to Pigeon and the other potential distributors near Dirk, and not to maximize the company's sales. However, Dirk can just as easily argue that this statement of indifference shows that the company is not out to protect its other distributors (i.e., Pigeon), and that it did not therefore intend to benefit these other distributors by extracting such non-infringement promises.

Conflicting interpretations can also be advanced as to Alumalloy's statement that "You will have to work out with Dirk any problems you have with him." Pigeon can claim that this shows that the company contemplated a potential right of action by Pigeon against Dirk; Dirk can claim that this shows that the company just didn't care.

However, the question is what Alumalloy intended at the time it extracted the promise from Dirk, not what its intentions are currently. Therefore, Pigeon will still probably be able to show that he was (originally at least) a third party beneficiary of Dirk's promise.

(2) Dirk can argue that even if Pigeon originally had a third party beneficiary's rights, these rights have been *altered* (and destroyed) by Alumalloy's letter. He can make a perfectly reasonable argument that Alumalloy's refusal to enforce the non-infringement promise, and its communication of that refusal to Dirk, was an enforceable modification of any third party beneficiary rights Pigeon may have had. The modern view, however, is that once the third party beneficiary *changes his position in reliance on the promise,* his rights are vested, and cannot be altered (p. 420). Pigeon's signing of the contract, and his making of expenditures, could probably be shown to have been in reliance on the guaranty of exclusivity. Dirk can come back with the contention that Pigeon, by continuing to deal with Alumalloy after the letter, implicitly *assented* to the proposed modification.

Pigeon's right to injunction: If Pigeon can make his way through this thicket of argument and counter argument, and can establish his third party rights, he has a good chance of getting an *injunction*. Because his lost profits are hard to calculate, his legal remedy (i.e., his right to recover damages) is probably not adequate. Furthermore, the injunction sought here is a negative one, and can be much more easily policed by the court than an injunction requiring the defendant to do something affirmatively (p. 314).

In summary, if Pigeon can prove breach, he can probably get an injunction, to last for the remainder of Dirk's four-year contract, or until Pigeon's own contract is rightfully terminated, whichever happens first.

TABLE OF CASES

TABLE OF UCC REFERENCES

TABLE OF RESTATEMENT REFERENCES

SUBJECT MATTER INDEX